D0547226

NORTHERN CALIFORNIA HIKING

TOM STIENSTRA • ANN MARIE BROWN

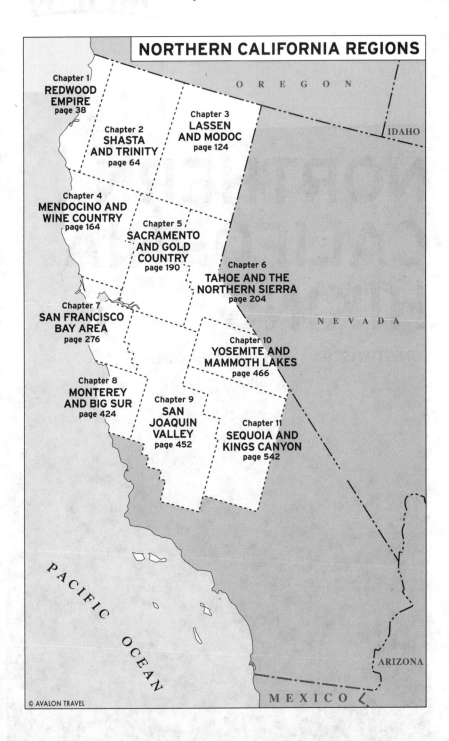

NORTHERN CALIFORNIA REGIONS

O R E G O N

IDAHO

Chapter 1
REDWOOD EMPIRE
page 38

Chapter 2
SHASTA AND TRINITY
page 64

Chapter 3
LASSEN AND MODOC
page 124

Chapter 4
MENDOCINO AND WINE COUNTRY
page 164

Chapter 5
SACRAMENTO AND GOLD COUNTRY
page 190

Chapter 6
TAHOE AND THE NORTHERN SIERRA
page 204

Chapter 7
SAN FRANCISCO BAY AREA
page 276

N E V A D A

Chapter 10
YOSEMITE AND MAMMOTH LAKES
page 466

Chapter 8
MONTEREY AND BIG SUR
page 424

Chapter 9
SAN JOAQUIN VALLEY
page 452

Chapter 11
SEQUOIA AND KINGS CANYON
page 542

P A C I F I C

O C E A N

ARIZONA

M E X I C O

© AVALON TRAVEL

Contents

Introduction 11

Author's Note 12

Best Hikes 14

BEST(Beach and Coastal Walks

BEST(Bird-Watching

BEST(Butt-Kickers

BEST(Fall Colors

BEST(Hikes with a View

BEST(Kids

BEST(Meadow Hikes

BEST(Redwoods

BEST(Self-Guided Nature Walks

BEST(Short Backpack Trips

BEST(Summit Hikes

BEST(Swimming Holes

BEST(Waterfalls

BEST(Wheelchair-Accessible Trails

BEST(Wildflowers

BEST(Wildlife

Hiking Tips 20

Hiking Essentials 20

Hiking Gear 22

Safety in the Outdoors 26

Hiking Ethics 33

Chapter 1
Redwood Empire..................................... 37

Chapter 2
Shasta and Trinity................................. 63

Chapter 3
Lassen and Modoc 123

Chapter 4
Mendocino and Wine Country.................... 163

Chapter 5
Sacramento and Gold Country 189

Chapter 6
Tahoe and Northern Sierra...................... 203

Chapter 7
San Francisco Bay Area......................... 275

Chapter 8
Monterey and Big Sur 423

Chapter 9
San Joaquin Valley 451

Chapter 10
Yosemite and Mammoth Lakes 465

Chapter 11
Sequoia and Kings Canyon 541

Resources 623

Index 631

How to Use This Book

ABOUT THE TRAIL PROFILES

Each hike in this book is listed in a consistent, easy-to-read format to help you choose the ideal hike. From a general overview of the setting to detailed driving directions, the profile will provide all the information you need. Here is a sample profile:

Map number and hike number →

1 SOMEWHERE USA HIKE

Round-trip mileage → **9.0 mi/5.0 hrs**

Difficulty and quality ratings ← 🏃3 ⛰8

(unless otherwise noted) and the approximate amount of time needed to complete the hike (actual times can vary widely, especially on longer hikes)

at the mouth of the Somewhere River ←

General location of the trail, named by its proximity to the nearest major town or landmark

Map on which the trailhead can be found and page number on which the map can be found →

Map 1.2, page 24 **BEST (**

Each hike in this book begins with a brief overview of its setting. The description typically covers what kind of terrain to expect, what might be seen, and any conditions that may make the hike difficult to navigate. Side trips, such as to waterfalls or panoramic vistas, in addition to ways to combine the trail with others nearby for a longer outing, are also noted here. In many cases, mile-by-mile trail directions are included.

Symbol indicating that the hike is listed among the author's top picks

User Groups: This section notes the types of users that are permitted on the trail, including hikers, mountain bikers, horseback riders, and dogs. Wheelchair access is also noted here.

Permits: This section notes whether a permit is required for hiking, or, if the hike spans more than one day, whether one is required for camping. Any fees, such as for parking, day use, or entrance, are also noted here.

Maps: This section provides information on how to obtain detailed trail maps of the hike and its environs. Whenever applicable, names of U.S. Geologic Survey (USGS) topographic maps and national forest maps are also included; contact information for these and other map sources are noted in the Resources section at the back of this book.

Directions: This section provides mile-by-mile driving directions to the trail head from the nearest major town.

Contact: This section provides an address and phone number for each hike. The contact is usually the agency maintaining the trail but may also be a trail club or other organization.

ABOUT THE ICONS

The icons in this book are designed to provide at-a-glance information on the difficulty and quality of each hike.

The difficulty rating (rated **1–5** with **1** being the lowest and **5** the highest) is based on the steepness of the trail and how difficult it is to traverse

The quality rating (rated **1–10** with **1** being the lowest and **10** the highest) is based largely on scenic beauty, but also takes into account how crowded the trail is and whether noise of nearby civilization is audible

ABOUT THE DIFFICULTY RATINGS

Trails rated **1** are very easy and suitable for hikers of all abilities, including young children.

Trails rated **2** are easy-to-moderate and suitable for most hikers, including families with active children 6 and older.

Trails rated **3** are moderately challenging and suitable for reasonably fit adults and older children who are very active.

Trails rated **4** are very challenging and suitable for physically fit hikers who are seeking a workout.

Trails rated **5** are extremely challenging and suitable only for experienced hikers who are in top physical condition.

MAP SYMBOLS

▨▨▨▨	Expressway	⑧⓿	Interstate Freeway	✗	Airfield
▨▨▨▨	Primary Road	⑩①①	U.S. Highway	✈	Airport
▨▨▨▨	Secondary Road	㉑	State Highway	○	City/Town
░░░░	Unpaved Road	㉖⑥	County Highway	▲	Mountain
··········	Ferry	◗ Lake	↟	Park
— ·· — ·	National Border	◌ Dry Lake	/ʃ	Pass
— ·· —	State Border	◌ Seasonal Lake	◉	State Capital

ABOUT THE MAPS

This book is divided into chapters based on major regions in the state; an overview map of these regions precedes the table of contents. Each chapter begins with a map of the region, which is further broken down into detail maps. Trailheads are noted on the detail maps by number.

Reference to adjacent region

Detail map number and page number

Grid line divides region into detail maps

Region border

REGION/CHAPTER MAP EXAMPLE

Locates region within state

Detail map 11.4 shown on next page

Indicates adjacent detail maps within region

Locates detail map within region

Map number → **Map 11.4**

Sites shown on detail map and the page range where those sites are listed →

Sites 105-117
Pages 564-570

DETAIL MAP EXAMPLE

Hike number

Region border

Reference to adjacent region

INTRODUCTION

Author's Note

If the great outdoors is so great, then why don't people enjoy it more? The answer is because of the time trap, and I will tell you exactly how to beat it.

For many, the biggest problem is finding the time to go, whether it is hiking, backpacking, camping, fishing, boating, biking, or even just for a good drive in the country. The solution? Believe it or not, the answer is to treat your fun just as you treat your work, and I'll tell you how.

Consider how you treat your job: Always on time? Go there every day you are scheduled? Do whatever it takes to get there and get it done? Right? No foolin' that's right. Now imagine if you took the same approach to the outdoors. Suddenly your life would be a heck of a lot better.

The secret is to schedule all of your outdoor activities. For instance, I go fishing every Thursday evening, hiking every Sunday morning, and on an overnight trip every new moon (when stargazing is best). No matter what, I'm going. Just like going to work, I've scheduled it. The same approach works with longer adventures. The only reason I have been able to complete hikes ranging from 200 to 300 miles was that I scheduled the time to do it. The reason I spend 125 to 150 days a year in the field is that I schedule them. In my top year, I had nearly 200 days where at least part of the day was enjoyed taking part in outdoor recreation.

If you get out your calendar and write in the exact dates you are going, then you'll go. If you don't, you won't. Suddenly, with only a minor change in your life plan, you can be living the life you were previously dreaming about.

—Tom Stienstra

Dipsea Trail

Author's Note

A wise person once said that a culture can be measured by the resources it chooses to preserve. If that's true, then the state of California is an immense credit to our culture. The Golden State is blessed with an abundance of parks and preserves, including more than 25 units of the National Park System, 19 national forests, 137 federally designated wilderness areas, 279 state parks, and thousands of county and regional parks.

This huge mosaic of parklands celebrates California's diverse landscape, which includes the highest peak in the contiguous United States (Mount Whitney at 14,495 feet or 14,505 feet, depending on which measurement is currently in vogue) and the lowest point in the western hemisphere (Badwater in Death Valley at 282 feet below sea level). Our state contains 20,000 square miles of desert, nearly 700 miles of Pacific coastline, an unaccountable wealth of snow-capped peaks and alpine lakes, a smattering of islands, and even a handful of volcanoes.

California also boasts its share of the world's tallest living things, the towering coast redwoods. And we are the only state that is home to the world's largest living trees (by volume), the giant sequoias. Also within California's borders are groves of the planet's oldest living things, the ancient bristlecone pines.

Quite simply, we live in a land of superlatives. California's public lands are some of my favorite places on earth, and I believe that everyone should have the chance to see them, and be awed and humbled by their wonders. But this wish comes with a caveat attached: We must tread lightly and gently on our parks, with great respect and care for the land. And we must do whatever is required to ensure the protection of these beautiful places for future generations.

I wish you many inspiring days on the trail.

—Ann Marie Brown

Best Hikes

Can't decide where to hike this weekend? Here are our picks for the best hikes in Northern California in several different categories, listed from north to south:

BEST(Beach and Coastal Walks

Rim Loop Trail, Patrick's Point State Park, Redwood Empire, page 53.

Lost Coast Trail/Mattole Trailhead, King Range National Conservation Area, Redwood Empire, page 58.

Lost Coast Trail/Sinkyone Trailhead, Sinkyone Wilderness State Park, Mendocino and Wine Country, page 169.

Coast Trail, Point Reyes National Seashore, San Francisco Bay Area, page 290.

Old Landing Cove Trail, Wilder Ranch State Park, Monterey and Big Sur, page 426.

Point Lobos Perimeter, Point Lobos State Reserve, Monterey and Big Sur, page 433.

BEST(Bird-Watching

Arcata Marsh Trail, Arcata Marsh and Wildlife Sanctuary, Redwood Empire, page 54.

Abbotts Lagoon Trail, Point Reyes National Seashore, San Francisco Bay Area, page 282.

Martin Griffin Preserve/Audubon Canyon Ranch Trail, Marsh Griffin Preserve, San Francisco Bay Area, page 303.

Arrowhead Marsh, Martin Luther King Regional Shoreline, San Francisco Bay Area, page 367.

Elkhorn Slough South Marsh Loop, Moss Landing, Monterey and Big Sur, page 429.

Chester, Sousa, and Winton Marsh Trails, San Luis National Wildlife Refuge, San Joaquin Valley, page 459.

Carrizo Plain and Painted Rock, Carrizo Plains National Monument, San Joaquin Valley, page 463.

Mono Lake South Tufa Trail, Mono Lake Tufa State Reserve, Yosemite and Mammoth Lakes, page 501.

BEST(Butt-Kickers

Devils Punchbowl (via Doe Flat Trail/Buck Lake Trail), Siskiyou Wilderness, Shasta and Trinity, page 71.

Shasta Summit Trail, Shasta-Trinity National Forest, Shasta and Trinity, page 88.

Rooster Comb Loop (Long Version), Henry W. Coe State Park, San Francisco Bay Area, page 418.

Half Dome, Yosemite Valley, Yosemite and Mammoth Lakes, page 520.

Don Cecil Trail to Lookout Peak, Kings Canyon National Park, Sequoia and Kings Canyon, page 567.

Alta Peak, Sequoia National Park, Sequoia and Kings Canyon, page 577.

Mount Whitney Trail, John Muir Wilderness, Sequoia and Kings Canyon, page 607.

BEST(Fall Colors

Whiskeytown Falls, Whiskeytown Lake National Recreation Area, Shasta and Trinity, page 120.

Mount Eddy Trail

American River Parkway, Sacramento and Gold Country, page 199.
Fallen Leaf Lake Trail, South Lake Tahoe, Tahoe and Northern Sierra, page 243.
Parker Lake Trail, Ansel Adams Wilderness, Yosemite and Mammoth Lakes, page 503.
Convict Canyon to Lake Dorothy, John Muir Wilderness, Yosemite and Mammoth Lakes, page 533.
McGee Creek to Steelhead Lake, John Muir Wilderness, Yosemite and Mammoth Lakes, page 534.
Blue Lake, John Muir Wilderness, Sequoia and Kings Canyon, page 553.
Tyee Lakes, John Muir Wilderness, Sequoia and Kings Canyon, page 555.
Farewell Gap Trail to Aspen Flat, Sequoia National Park, Sequoia and Kings Canyon, page 589.

BEST(Hikes with a View

Mount Eddy Trail, Shasta-Trinity National Forest, Shasta and Trinity, page 99.
Lassen Peak Trail, Lassen Volcanic National Park, Lassen and Modoc, page 150.
Rubicon Trail, D. L. Bliss State Park, Tahoe and Northern Sierra, page 235.
Perimeter Trail, Angel Island State Park, San Francisco Bay Area, page 320.
Clouds Rest, Yosemite National Park, Yosemite and Mammoth Lakes, page 484.
Sentinel Dome, Yosemite National Park, Yosemite and Mammoth Lakes, page 525.
Panorama Trail, Yosemite National Park, Yosemite and Mammoth Lakes, page 527.
Moro Rock, Sequoia National Park, Sequoia and Kings Canyon, page 584.
The Needles Spires, Giant Sequoia National Monument, Sequoia and Kings Canyon, page 602.

BEST(Kids

Rainbow and Lake of the Sky Trails, Tahoe National Forest, Tahoe and Northern Sierra, page 240.

Angora Lakes Trail, Tahoe National Forest, Tahoe and Northern Sierra, page 244.

Tomales Point Trail, Point Reyes National Seashore, San Francisco Bay Area, page 281.

Fitzgerald Marine Reserve, Moss Beach, San Francisco Bay Area, page 337.

Año Nuevo Trail, Año Nuevo State Reserve, San Francisco Bay Area, page 396.

Pinecrest Lake National Recreation Trail, Stanislaus National Forest, Yosemite and Mammoth Lakes, page 469.

Devils Postpile and Rainbow Falls, Devils Postpile National Monument, Yosemite and Mammoth Lakes, page 509.

Tokopah Falls, Sequoia National Park, Sequoia and Kings Canyon, page 578.

BEST(Meadow Hikes

Haypress Meadows Trailhead, Marble Mountain Wilderness, Shasta and Trinity, page 74.

Gray Butte, Mount Shasta Wilderness, Shasta and Trinity, page 91.

Carson Pass to Echo Lakes Resort (PCT), Tahoe and Northern Sierra, page 258.

Grass Valley Loop, Anthony Chabot Regional Park, San Francisco Bay Area, page 369.

McGurk Meadow and Dewey Point, Yosemite National Park, Yosemite and Mammoth Lakes, page 523.

Zumwalt Meadow Loop, Kings Canyon National Park, Sequoia and Kings Canyon, page 568.

Casa Vieja Meadow, Golden Trout Wilderness, Sequoia and Kings Canyon, page 613.

Manter Meadow Loop, Dome Land Wilderness, Sequoia and Kings Canyon, page 620.

BEST(Redwoods

Boy Scout Tree Trail, Jedediah Smith Redwoods State Park, Redwood Empire, page 42.

Tall Trees Trail, Redwood National Park, Redwood Empire, page 49.

Redwood Creek Trail, Redwood National Park, Redwood Empire, page 51.

Bull Creek Trail North, Humboldt Redwoods State Park, Redwood Empire, page 57.

Redwood Creek Trail, Muir Woods National Monument, San Francisco Bay Area, page 313.

Shadow of the Giants, Sierra National Forest, Yosemite and Mammoth Lakes, page 531.

General Grant Tree Trail, Kings Canyon National Park, Sequoia and Kings Canyon, page 561.

Redwood Canyon, Kings Canyon National Park, Sequoia and Kings Canyon, page 570.

Congress Trail Loop, Sequoia National Park, Sequoia and Kings Canyon, page 580.

Trail of 100 Giants, Giant Sequoia National Monument, Sequoia and Kings Canyon, page 603.

BEST(Self-Guided Nature Walks

McCloud Nature Trail, Shasta-Trinity National Forest, Shasta and Trinity, page 110.
Rainbow and Lake of the Sky Trails, Tahoe National Forest, Tahoe and Northern Sierra, page 240.
Trail of the Gargoyles, Stanislaus National Forest, Tahoe and Northern Sierra, page 270.
Shadow of the Giants, Sierra National Forest, Yosemite and Mammoth Lakes, page 531.
Methuselah Trail, Inyo National Forest, Yosemite and Mammoth Lakes, page 538.
Unal Trail, Sequoia National Forest, Sequoia and Kings Canyon, page 618.

BEST(Short Backpack Trips

Taylor Lake Trail, Russian Wilderness, Shasta and Trinity, page 95.
Toad Lake Trail, Shasta-Trinity National Forest, Shasta and Trinity, page 101.
Echo and Twin Lakes, Lassen Volcanic National Park, Lassen and Modoc, page 148.
Woods Lake to Winnemucca Lake, Mokelumne Wilderness, Tahoe and Northern Sierra, page 260.
Coast Trail, Point Reyes National Seashore, San Francisco Bay Area, page 290.
Black Mountain, Monte Bello Open Space Preserve, San Francisco Bay Area, page 349.
May Lake and Mount Hoffman, Yosemite National Park, Yosemite and Mammoth Lakes, page 483.
Glen Aulin and Tuolumne Falls, Yosemite National Park, Yosemite and Mammoth Lakes, page 491.
Ladybug Trail, Sequoia National Park, Sequoia and Kings Canyon, page 596.

BEST(Summit Hikes

Preston Peak, Siskiyou Wilderness, Shasta and Trinity, page 69.
Grizzly Lake, Trinity Alps Wilderness, Shasta and Trinity, page 83.
Shasta Summit Trail, Shasta-Trinity National Forest, Shasta and Trinity, page 88.
Lassen Peak Trail, Lassen Volcanic National Park, Lassen and Modoc, page 150.
East Peak Mount Tamalpais, Mount Tamalpais State Park, San Francisco Bay Area, page 307.
Mount Dana, Yosemite National Park, Yosemite and Mammoth Lakes, page 497.
White Mountain Peak Trail, Inyo National Forest, Yosemite and Mammoth Lakes, page 538.
Mount Whitney Trail, John Muir Wilderness, Sequoia and Kings Canyon, page 607.

BEST(Swimming Holes

McClendon Ford Trail, Smith River National Recreation Area, Redwood Empire, page 45.
Deer Creek Trail, Lassen National Forest, Lassen and Modoc, page 157.
Paradise Creek Trail, Sequoia National Park, Sequoia and Kings Canyon, page 585.
Alder Creek Trail, Giant Sequoia National Monument, Sequoia and Kings Canyon, page 604.

Burney Falls Loop Trail

BEST(Waterfalls

Burney Falls Loop Trail, McArthur-Burney Falls Memorial State Park, Lassen and
Modoc, page 134.

Feather Falls Loop, Plumas National Forest, Sacramento and Gold Country, page
194.

Grouse Falls, Tahoe National Forest, Tahoe and Northern Sierra, page 227.

McWay Falls Overlook, Julia Pfeiffer Burns State Park, Monterey and Big Sur, page
447.

Waterwheel Falls, Yosemite National Park, Yosemite and Mammoth Lakes, page 490.

Devils Postpile and Rainbow Falls, Devils Postpile National Monument, Yosemite
and Mammoth Lakes, page 509.

Upper Yosemite Fall, Yosemite Valley, Yosemite and Mammoth Lakes, page 514.

Mist Trail and John Muir Loop to Nevada Fall, Yosemite Valley, Yosemite and
Mammoth Lakes, page 518.

Bridalveil Fall, Yosemite Valley, Yosemite and Mammoth Lakes, page 522.

Tokopah Falls, Sequoia National Park, Sequoia and Kings Canyon, page 578.

BEST(Wheelchair-Accessible Trails

Taylor Lake Trail, Russian Wilderness, Shasta and Trinity, page 95.

Cory Peak/Kangaroo Lake Trailhead, Klamath National Forest, Shasta and Trinity,
page 98.

Lake Cleone Trail, MacKerricher State Park, Mendocino and Wine Country, page
171.

South Yuba Independence Trail, Nevada City, Sacramento and Gold Country, page
196.

Sierra Discovery Trail, PG&E Bear Valley Recreation Area, Tahoe and Northern Sierra, page 220.

Abbotts Lagoon Trail, Point Reyes National Seashore, San Francisco Bay Area, page 282.

McWay Falls Overlook, Julia Pfeiffer Burns State Park, Monterey and Big Sur, page 447.

Lower Yosemite Fall, Yosemite Valley, Yosemite and Mammoth Lakes, page 516.

Roaring River Falls, Kings Canyon National Park, Sequoia and Kings Canyon, page 567.

BEST❰ Wildflowers

Lake Margaret, Eldorado National Forest, Tahoe and Northern Sierra, page 253.

Chimney Rock Trail, Point Reyes National Seashore, San Francisco Bay Area, page 286.

Grass Valley Loop, Anthony Chabot Regional Park, San Francisco Bay Area, page 369.

Rocky Ridge and Soberanes Canyon Loop, Garrapata State Park, Monterey and Big Sur, page 434.

Path of the Padres, San Luis Reservoir State Recreation Area, San Joaquin Valley, page 461.

Lundy Canyon Trail, Hoover Wilderness, Yosemite and Mammoth Lakes, page 474.

Hite Cove Trail, Sierra National Forest, Yosemite and Mammoth Lakes, page 514.

Whitney Portal to Lake Thomas Edison (JMT/PCT), Sequoia and Kings Canyon, page 609.

BEST❰ Wildlife

Coastal Trail (Fern Canyon/Ossagon Section), Prairie Creek Redwoods State Park, Redwood Empire, page 50.

Spirit Lake Trail, Marble Mountain Wilderness, Shasta and Trinity, page 75.

Captain Jack's Stronghold, Lava Beds National Monument, Lassen and Modoc, page 129.

Tomales Point Trail, Point Reyes National Seashore, San Francisco Bay Area, page 281.

Pescadero Marsh, San Francisco Bay Area, page 352.

Año Nuevo Trail, Año Nuevo State Reserve, San Francisco Bay Area, page 396.

Tule Elk State Natural Reserve, San Joaquin Valley, page 464.

Hiking Tips

HIKING ESSENTIALS

Aside from the shoes on your feet, it doesn't take much equipment to go day hiking. Whereas backpackers must concern themselves with tents, sleeping pads, pots and pans, and the like, day hikers have an easier time of it. Still, too many day hikers set out carrying too little and get into trouble as a result. Here's our list of essentials:

Food and Water

Water is even more important than food, although it's unwise to get caught without a picnic, or at least some edible supplies for emergencies. If you don't want to carry the weight of a couple water bottles, at least carry a purifier or filtering device so you can get water from streams, rivers, or lakes. It should go without saying, but never, ever drink water from a natural source without purifying it. The microscopic organisms *Giardia lamblia* and *Cryptosporidium* are found in backcountry water sources and can cause a litany of terrible gastrointestinal problems. Only purifying or boiling water from natural sources will eliminate giardiasis.

There are plenty of tools available to make backcountry water safe to drink. One of the most popular for day hikers and backpackers is a purifier called SteriPEN, which uses ultraviolet light rays instead of chemicals to purify water. It's small, light, runs on batteries, and purifies 32 ounces of water in about 90 seconds.

Water bottle-style purifiers, such as those made by Bota, Sawyer, or Katadyn Exstream, are as light as an empty plastic bottle and eliminate the need to carry both a filter and a bottle. You simply dip the bottle in the stream, screw on the top (which has a filter inside it), and squeeze the bottle to drink. The water is filtered on its way out of the squeeze top.

There's even a straw that purifies water so you can drink right out of creeks and lakes, as long as you don't mind having to lie down next to the water to do it. It sounds a bit silly, but the LifeStraw Personal Water Filter could be a

© ANN MARIE BROWN

A brief stop along the trail to examine a map can save you time and frustration.

lifesaver in a survival situation. It costs about 20 bucks, fits in your pocket, and weighs almost nothing.

Of course, in many areas, you won't find a natural water source to filter from, so carrying water is still necessary. Remember that trails that cross running streams in the winter and spring months may cross dry streams in the summer and autumn months.

What you carry for food is up to you. Some people go gourmet and carry the complete inventory of a fancy grocery store. If you don't want to bother with much weight, stick with high-energy snacks like nutrition bars, nuts, dried fruit, turkey or beef jerky, and crackers. Our rule is always to bring more than you think you can eat. You can always carry it back out with you, or give it to somebody else on the trail who needs it.

If you're hiking in a group, each of you should carry your own food and water just in case someone gets too far ahead or behind.

Trail Maps

A map of the park or public land you're visiting is essential. Never count on trail signs to get you where you want to go. Signs get knocked down or disappear with alarming frequency due to rain, wind, or park visitors looking for souvenirs. Many hikers think that carrying a GPS device eliminates the need for a map, but this isn't always true. If you get lost, a map can show you where you are (via landmarks such as peaks, lakes, ridges, etc.) and can show you where the nearest trail is located. It can also show alternate routes if you decide not to go the way you originally planned.

Always obtain a map from the managing agency of the place you're visiting. Their names and phone numbers are listed in the Resource guide in the back of this book.

Extra Clothing

On the trail, conditions can change at any time. Not only can the weather suddenly turn windy, foggy, or rainy, but your own body conditions also change: You'll perspire as you hike up a sunny hill and then get chilled at the top of a windy ridge or when you head into shade. Because of this, cotton fabrics don't function well in the outdoors. Once cotton gets wet, it stays wet. Generally, polyester-blend fabrics dry faster. Some high-tech fabrics will actually wick moisture away from your skin. Invest in a few items of clothing made from these fabrics and you'll be more comfortable when you hike.

Always carry a lightweight jacket with you, preferably one that is waterproof and also wind-resistant. If your jacket isn't waterproof, pack along one of the $3, single-use rain ponchos that come in a package the size of a deck of cards. They're available at outdoors stores, hardware stores, and drugstores. If you can't part with three bucks, carry an extra-large garbage bag, which can be converted into a waterproof vest. In cooler temperatures, or when heading to a mountain summit (even on a hot day), carry gloves and a hat as well.

Flashlight

Just in case your hike takes a little longer than you planned, bring at least one flashlight and preferably two or three. Mini flashlights are available everywhere, weigh almost nothing, and can save the day—or night. We especially like the tiny squeeze flashlights, about the size and shape of a quarter, which you can clip on to any key ring. Make sure you buy the kind with an LED bulb, which lasts a long time, and with an on/off switch. Whatever kind of flashlight you carry, make sure it works before you set out on the trail. Always take along an extra set of batteries and an extra bulb, or simply an extra flashlight or two. You never know when the darn things will run out of juice.

Sunglasses and Sunscreen

You know the dangers of the sun. Wear sunglasses to protect your eyes and sunscreen with a high SPF rating on any exposed skin. Put on your sunscreen 30 minutes before you go outdoors so it has time to take effect. Reapply your sunscreen every two hours. In addition, protect the skin on your face with a good wide-brimmed hat, and don't forget about your lips, which burn easily. Wear lip balm that has a high SPF rating.

Insect Repellent

Several kinds of insect repellent now come with sunscreen, so you can put on one lotion instead of two. Many types of insect repellent have an ingredient called DEET, which is extremely effective but also quite toxic. Children should not use repellent with high levels of DEET, although it seems to be safe for adults. Don't leave it sitting on your dashboard, though. It can damage plastic, rubber, and vinyl. Other types of repellent are made of natural substances, such as lemon eucalyptus oil. What works best? Every hiker has his or her opinion. If you visit the High Sierra in the middle of a major mosquito hatch, it often seems like nothing works except covering your entire body in mosquito netting. For typical summer days outside of a hatch period, find a repellent you like and carry it with you. Currently, we're fond of a brand called Natrapel, which is DEET-free and available in various-sized spray bottles. It contains a 20 percent picaridin formula, which is recommended by the Centers for Disease Control and World Health Organization for insect bite protection.

First-Aid Kit

Nothing major is required here unless you're fully trained in first aid, but a few supplies for treating blisters, an antibiotic ointment, and an anti-inflammatory medicine (such as ibuprofen) can serve as valuable tools in minor and major emergencies. (For details on taking care of and preventing blisters, see *Shoes and Socks.*) If anyone in your party is allergic to bee stings or anything else in the outdoors, carry their medication.

Swiss Army-Style Pocket Knife

Be sure to carry one with several blades, a can opener, scissors, and tweezers. The latter is useful for removing slivers or ticks.

Compass

A compass can be a real lifesaver. Just be sure that you know how to use it.

Emergency Supplies

Ask yourself this question: "What would I need to have if I had to spend the night out here?" Aside from food, water, and other items previously listed, here are some basic emergency supplies that will get you through an unplanned night in the wilderness:

HIKING GEAR
Shoes and Socks

Every hiker eventually conducts a search for the perfect boot. This means looking for something that will provide ideal foot and ankle support and won't cause blisters. Although there are dozens of possibilities—in fact so many that it can be confusing—you *can* find the perfect boot.

For advice on selecting boots, two of the nation's preeminent long-distance hikers, Brian Robinson of Mountain View (7,200 miles in 2001) and Ray Jardine of Oregon (2,700 miles of Pacific Crest Trail in three months), weighed in on the discussion. Both believe that the weight of a boot is the defining factor when selecting hiking footwear. They both go as light as possible, believing that heavy boots will eventually tire you out. Arch support is also vital, especially to people who hike less frequently and thus have not developed great foot strength.

To stay blister-free, the most important factors are clean feet, good socks, and the flexibility of a boot. If there is any foot slippage from a too-thin or compressed sock, accumulated dirt, or a stiff boot, you can rub up a blister in minutes. Wearing two pairs of socks can sometimes do the trick—try two fresh sets of SmartWool socks ($15 a pop), or try one pair over the top of a lightweight wicking liner sock. If you still get a blister or two, know how to treat them fast so they don't turn your walk into a sore-footed endurance test.

THE JOHN MUIR TRAIL AND THE PACIFIC CREST TRAIL

You can have a foothold in the sky with every step on the John Muir Trail (JMT). The trail starts at practically the tip-top of North America—Mount Whitney—and takes you northward across a land of 12,000-foot passes and Ansel Adams-style vistas, then eventually pours you into nature's showpiece of the world, Yosemite Valley.

How could you top that? There is only one way: to hike the Pacific Crest Trail (PCT), which the JMT partially overlaps. The PCT extends from the Mexico border for 1,700 miles north to Oregon, and then beyond all the way to its end, at the Canadian border—a total distance of 2,650 miles.

The JMT and the PCT are the two premier expeditions in North America. The JMT usually takes about three weeks to complete, covering about 250 miles, including side trips for food drops and other forays. Some swear that the trip should be hiked from north to south, but most prefer south to north, starting with the awesome climb from Whitney Portal to the Whitney Summit, a climb of more than 5,000 feet. Three weeks later, the trip ends with a spectacular descent into Yosemite Valley, past hundreds of gawking tourists on the final three miles on the Mist Trail. Some cheat by starting at Tuolumne Meadows, thus avoiding a 4,000-foot climb out of Yosemite Valley, then heading south, but that is a hollow victory, having technically not completed the trip.

John Muir called the Sierra Nevada the "Range of Light." The trail that traverses it has become America's greatest hike—officially 211 miles from the Whitney Summit to Happy Isles in Yosemite Valley. It is a land spiked by 13,000-foot granite spires, untouched sapphire lakes loaded with trout, and canyons that drop as if they were the edge of the earth. There are many highlights, including the Mount Whitney Wilderness, John Muir Wilderness, Kings Canyon National Park, crossing the ice cut at Forester Pass, topping Muir Pass at Muir Hut, the incredible pyramidlike ridgeline near Selden Pass, catching golden trout where a cast can be like tossing a dog a bone, crossing the headwaters of Rush Creek, and finally dropping over Donohue Pass down to Lyell Fork and Tuolumne Meadows.

Yet the PCT goes far beyond this scope. It crosses through 37 wilderness areas, 20 national forests, and seven national parks, topping out at 13,180 feet at Forester Pass in the south Sierra. It also features the worst parts of the entire 2,700-mile route, the Hat Creek Rim (30 miles without water) and across the Mojave, where a siege of hot weather can have you praying for a sip of water out of a cow's hoof print.

All of the JMT and many of the PCT routes are detailed in this book, including how to get wilderness permits, directions to trailheads, maps, contacts, and trail highlights. Many hikers choose not to hike the entire JMT or PCT in one shot. Rather, they use a PCT trailhead, then head up to the crest, taking off on side trips as they choose.

SELECTING THE RIGHT BOOTS

In addition to finding boots with the proper flexibility, comfort, and arch support, you'll need to consider the types of terrain you'll be covering and the number of miles (or number of days) you'll be hiking. Investing in the correct shoes will take some time and research, but your feet will thank you for it.

There are three basic kinds of hiking footwear, ranging from lightweight to midweight to heavyweight. Select the right one for you or pay the consequences. One great trick when on a hiking vacation is to bring a couple different pairs, and then for each hike, wear different footwear. By changing boots, you change the points of stress on your feet and legs, greatly reducing soreness and the chance of creating a hot spot on a foot. This also allows you to go lightweight on flat trails with a hard surface, and heavyweight on steep trails with loose footing, where additional boot weight can help traction in downhill stretches.

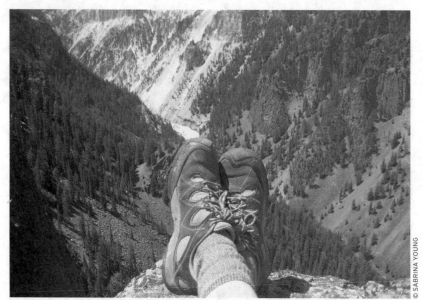

Lightweight hiking shoes are perfect for short treks and day-long trips.

LIGHTWEIGHT HIKING BOOTS

In the first category, lightweight hiking boots or trail-running shoes are designed for day-hiking and short and easy backpacking trips. For those with strong feet and arches, they are popular even on multiday trips. Some of the newer models are like rugged athletic shoes, designed with a Gore-Tex top for lightness and a Vibram sole for traction. These are perfect for people who like to hike fast and cover a lot of ground. Because these boots are flexible, they are easy to break in, and with fresh socks they rarely cause blister problems. Because they are lightweight and usually made of a breathable fabric, hiking fatigue is greatly reduced. For day-hiking, they are the footwear of choice for most. Many long-distance hikers are starting to choose these as well.

On the negative side, because these boots are so light, traction is not always good on steep, slippery surfaces. In addition, lightweight boots provide less than ideal ankle and arch support, which can be a problem on rocky or steep trails. Turn your ankle and your trip can be ruined. Lightweight hiking boots often are not very durable, either. If you hike a lot, you may wear a pair out in one summer.

MIDWEIGHT HIKING BOOTS OR BACKPACKING BOOTS

These boots are designed for both on- and off-trail hiking, and are constructed to meet the demands of carrying a light to moderately heavy pack. They usually feature high ankle support, a deep Vibram lug sole, built-in orthotics, arch support, and often a waterproof exterior. They can stand up to hundreds of miles of wilderness use, even if they are banged against rocks and walked through streams.

On the negative side, midweight or backpacking boots can be quite hot, as they are often made of leather and are not breathable. If the boots get wet, they can take days to dry. They weigh a fair amount and can tire you out, especially if you are not accustomed to having weight on your feet. This may reduce the number of miles you are capable of hiking in a day.

MOUNTAINEERING BOOTS OR HEAVYWEIGHT BACKPACKING BOOTS

Like midweight boots, these shoes are designed

ADDING TO THE PACK

If you're setting out on a long-distance adventure, it pays to add these two lightweight items to your backpack: an Ace elastic bandage and a pair of gaiters.

For sprained ankles and twisted knees, an Ace bandage can be like an insurance policy to get you back on the trail and out of trouble. There have been many cases where hikers with a twisted ankle or a sprained knee have relied on a good wrap with a four-inch bandage for the added support to get them home. Always buy the Ace bandage that comes with the clips permanently attached, so you don't have to worry about losing them.

Gaiters are leggings made of water-repellent fabric (Gore-Tex is a popular brand) that fit from just below your knees, over your calves, and attach under your boots. They are of particular help when walking in damp areas or in places where rain is common. As your legs brush against ferns or low-lying plants, gaiters will deflect the moisture. Without them, your pants will be soaking wet in short order.

Should your boots become wet, never try to force them to dry. Some well-meaning folks will try to dry them quickly at the edge of a campfire or actually put the boots in an oven. Although this may dry the boots, it can also loosen the glue that holds them together, ultimately weakening them until one day they fall apart in a heap. A better bet is to treat the leather so the boots become water repellent. Silicone-based liquids are the easiest to use and the least greasy of the treatments available.

A final tip is to have another pair of lightweight shoes or moccasins that you can wear around after a trip. This will give your feet the rest they deserve.

---

for both on- and off-trail hiking, but they can stand up to the rigors of carrying a much heavier load. They are designed to be worn on multiday backpacking trips (four days or more with substantial miles hiked each day). Mountaineering boots are identified by mid-range tops, laces that extend almost as far as the toes, and ankle areas that are as stiff as a board. The lack of "give" is what endears them to some mountaineers. Their stiffness is preferred when rock climbing, walking off-trail on craggy surfaces, or hiking down the edge of streambeds. Because these boots don't yield on rugged terrain, they can reduce ankle and foot injuries and provide better traction. Some are made so that they can accept crampons for travel on snow and ice.

The drawback to stiff boots is that if you don't have the proper socks and your foot starts slipping around in the boot, you will get a set of blisters that require so much tape and moleskin you will end up looking like a mummy. Also, heavyweight boots must be broken in for weeks or even months before taking them out on the trail.

At the Store

Hiking shoes come in a wide range of styles, brands, and prices. If you wander about comparing all their many features, you will get as confused as a kid in a toy store. Instead, go into the store with your mind clear about what you want. For the best quality, expect to spend $80-120 for lightweight hiking boots, $100-200 for midweight boots, and $150-250 for mountaineering boots. If you go much cheaper, the quality of the boot—and the health of your feet—will likely suffer. This is one area where you don't want to scrimp.

If you plan on using the advice of a shoe salesperson, first look at what kind of boots he or she is wearing. If the salesperson isn't even wearing boots, then take whatever he or she says with a grain of salt. Most people who own quality boots, including salespeople, will wear them almost daily if their job allows, since boots are the best footwear available.

Enter the store with a precise use and style in mind. Rather than fish for suggestions, tell the salesperson exactly what type of hiking you plan to do. Try two or three brands of the same category of shoe (lightweight, mid-weight, or heavyweight/mountaineering). Try on both boots in a pair simultaneously so you know exactly how they'll feel. Always try them on over a good pair of hiking socks (see *Socks*), not regular everyday socks. If possible, walk up and down a set of stairs, or up and down an incline, while wearing the boots. Your feet should not slide forward easily, and your heel should not move from side to side. Also, your heel should not lift more than one-quarter inch when you walk around. Are the boots too stiff? Are your feet snug yet comfortable, or do they slip? Do they feel supportive on the inside of your foot? Is there enough room in the toe box so that your toes can spread or wiggle slightly? If your toes touch the front of your boot, count on blisters.

Socks

People can spend so much energy selecting the right kind of boot that they virtually overlook wearing the right kind of socks. One goes with the other.

Your socks should be thick enough to cushion your feet and should fit snugly. Without good socks you might fasten the bootlaces too tight, and that's like putting a tourniquet on your feet. On long trips of a week or more, you should have plenty of clean socks on hand, or plan on washing what you have during your trip. As socks become worn, they also become compressed, dirty, and damp. If they fold over, you'll get a blister.

Do not wear cotton socks. Your foot can get damp and mix with dirt, which can cause a hot spot to start on your foot. Instead, start with a sock made of a synthetic composite, such as those made by SmartWool. These will partially wick moisture away from the skin.

If you choose to wear two pairs, or a pair of socks over a sock liner, the exterior sock should be wool or its synthetic equivalent. This will cushion your feet, create a snug fit in your boot, and provide some additional warmth and insulation in cold weather. It is critical to keep socks clean. If you wear multiple socks, you may need

to go up a boot size to accommodate the extra layers around your feet.

Blisters

In almost all cases, blisters are caused by the simple rubbing of skin against the rugged interior of a boot. It can be worsened by several factors:

The key to treating blisters is to work fast at the first sign of a hot spot. If you feel a hot spot, never keep walking, figuring the problem will go away. Stop immediately and remedy the situation. Before you remove your socks, check to see if the sock is wrinkled—a likely cause of the problem. If so, either change socks or pull them tight, removing the tiny folds, after taking care of the blister.

To take care of the blister, cut a piece of moleskin to cover the offending spot, securing the moleskin with white medical tape. Even better than moleskin is a product called Spenco Second Skin, which helps to heal the blister as well as protect it, and will stick to your skin without tape.

SAFETY IN THE OUTDOORS
Insects and Plants

Ticks, poison oak, and stinging nettles can be far worse than a whole convention of snakes, mountain lions, and bears. But you can avoid them with a little common sense, and here's how:

Ticks

The easiest way to stay clear of ticks is to wear long pants and long sleeves when you hike, and tuck your pant legs into your socks. But this system isn't fail-proof. The darn things sometimes find their way on to your skin no matter what you do. Always check yourself thoroughly when you leave the trail, looking carefully for anything that's crawling on you. Check your clothes, and also your skin underneath. A good friend can be a useful assistant in this endeavor.

Remember that if you find a tick on your skin, the larger brown ones are harmless.

Of the nearly 50 varieties of ticks present in California, only the tiny brown-black ones, called the western black-legged tick, can carry Lyme disease.

Most tick bites cause a sharp sting that will get your attention. But rarely, ticks will bite you without you noticing. If you've been in the outdoors, and then a few days or a week later start to experience flu-like symptoms like headaches, fever, muscle soreness, neck stiffness, or nausea, see a doctor immediately. Tell the doctor you are concerned about possible exposure to ticks and Lyme disease. Another early tell-tale symptom is a slowly expanding red rash near the tick bite, which appears a week to a month after the bite. Caught in its early stages, Lyme disease is easily treated with antibiotics, but left untreated, it can be severely debilitating.

The best way to remove a tick is by grasping it as close to your skin as possible, then pulling it gently and slowly straight out, without twisting or jerking it. Tweezers work well for the job, and many Swiss Army knives include tweezers.

POISON OAK

That old Boy Scout motto holds true: Leaves of three, let them be. Learn to recognize and avoid *Toxicodendron diversilobum,* which produces an itching rash that can last for weeks. The shiny-leaved shrub grows with maddening exuberance in California coastal and mountain canyons below 5,000 feet. If you can't readily identify poison oak, stay away from vinelike plants that have three leaves. Remember that in spring and summer, poison oak looks a little like wild blackberry bushes and often has red colors in its leaves, as well as green. In late fall and winter, poison oak goes dormant and loses its leaves, but it's still potent.

Avoid poison oak by staying on the trail and wearing long pants and long sleeves in areas that are encroached by it. If you prefer to wear shorts when you hike, try a pair of the convertible pants that are found at most outdoor stores. These are lightweight pants with legs that zip off to convert to shorts. Put the pant legs on when you come to an area that is rife with poison oak. If you accidentally touch the plant with your bare skin, wash off the area as

© ANN MARIE BROWN

poison oak

soon as possible. Waiting until you get home five hours later may be too late, so wash as best as you can, using stream water or whatever is available. Hikers who are highly allergic to poison oak should consider carrying packages of Tecnu, a poison oak wash-off treatment that is sold in bottles or individual foil packs. Carrying one little package could save you weeks of scratching.

Remember that if poison oak touches your clothes, your pack, or even your dog, and then you handle any of those items, the oils can rub off onto your skin. Wash everything thoroughly as soon as you get home.

If you do develop poison oak rash, a few relatively new products on the market can help you get rid of it. One product is called Zanfel, and although it costs a small fortune (about $30-40 a bottle), it is available at pharmacies without a prescription. You simply pour it on the rash and the rash vanishes, or at least greatly diminishes. Some hikers also swear by a product called Mean Green Power Hand Scrub, which costs about half what Zanfel does. No matter what you use, if you get a severe enough case of poison oak, the only recourse is a trip to the doctor for prednisone pills.

STINGING NETTLES

Ouch! This member of the nettle family is bright green, can grow to six feet tall, and is covered with tiny stinging hairs. When you brush against one, it zaps you with its poison, which feels like a mild bee sting. The sting can last for up to 24 hours. Stinging nettles grow near creeks or streams, and they're usually found in tandem with deer ferns and sword ferns. If the nettles zing you, grab a nearby fern leaf and rub the underside of it against the stinging area. It sounds odd, but it sometimes helps to take the sting out. If it doesn't help, you're out of luck, and you just have to wait for the sting to go away.

Wildlife

Snakes, mountain lions, and bears—these creatures deserve your respect, and you should understand a little bit about them.

RATTLESNAKES

Eight rattlesnake species are found in California. These members of the pit viper family have wide triangular heads, narrow necks, and rattles on their tales. Rattlesnakes live where it's warm, usually at elevations below 6,000 feet. Most snakes will slither off at the sound of your footsteps; if you encounter one, freeze or move back slowly so that it can get away without feeling threatened. They will almost always shake their tails and produce a rattling or buzzing noise to warn you off. The sound is unmistakable, even if you've never heard it before.

If you're hiking on a nice day, when rattlesnakes are often out sunning themselves on trails and rocks, keep your eyes open for them so you don't step on one or place your hand on one. Be especially on the lookout for rattlesnakes in the spring, when they leave their winter burrows and come out in the sun. Morning is the most common time to see them, as the midday sun is usually too hot for them.

Although rattlesnake bites are painful, they are very rarely fatal. More than 100 people in California are bitten by rattlesnakes each year, resulting in only one or two fatalities on average. About 25 percent of rattlesnake bites are dry, with no venom injected. Symptoms of bites that do contain venom usually include tingling around the mouth, nausea and vomiting, dizziness, weakness, sweating, and/or chills. If you should get bitten by a rattlesnake, your car key—and the nearest telephone—are your best first aid. Call 911 as soon as you can, or have someone drive you to the nearest hospital. Don't panic or run, which can speed the circulation of venom through your system.

Except for a handful of rattlesnake species, all other California snakes are not poisonous. Just give them room to slither by.

MOUNTAIN LIONS

The mountain lion (also called cougar or puma)

FACTS ABOUT MOUNTAIN LIONS

Mountain lion expert Steve Torres of the Department of Fish and Game (DFG) provided the following list of truths regarding mountain lions:

- Mountain lions are very shy and wary of humans. Attacks on people are extremely rare, which is why any threatening encounter can make the news—it is an anomaly.
- Mountain lions are rarely seen; they are masters of stealth. That is why repeat sightings are alarming and should be reported to the DFG headquarters in Sacramento (916/445-0411).
- Mountain lions are known for their silence and are rarely vocal. If you hear the cry or roar of a lion, your experience is likely a once-in-a-lifetime event.
- Mountain lions are not threatened or endangered in any way. Populations are stable to increasing. The biggest threat to mountain lions is loss of habitat to development.
- Mountain lions are not afraid of dogs. Whereas packs of trained hounds are capable of putting a lion in a tree, solitary pets of all kinds, including dogs, are fair game for mountain lions. In areas with documented mountain lion habitat, dogs should be kept inside at night.

lives in almost every region of California but is rarely seen. Most habitats that are wild enough to support deer will support mountain lions, which typically eat about one deer per week. When the magnificent cats do show themselves, they receive a lot of media attention. The few mountain lion attacks on California hikers have been widely publicized. Still, the vast majority of hikers never see a mountain lion, and those who do usually report that the cat vanished into the brush at the first sign of nearby humans.

If you're hiking in an area where mountain lions or their tracks have been spotted, remember to keep children close to you on the trail, and your dog leashed. If you see a mountain lion and it doesn't run away immediately, make yourself appear as large as possible (raise your arms, open your jacket, wave a big stick) and speak loudly and firmly or shout. If you have children with you, pick them up off the ground, but try to do it without crouching down or leaning over. (Crouching makes you appear smaller and less aggressive, more like prey.) Don't turn your back on the cat or run from it, but rather back away slowly and deliberately, always retaining your aggressive pose and continuing to speak loudly. Mountain lions are far more likely to attack a fleeing mammal than one that stands its ground. Even after attacking, lions have been successfully fought off by adult hikers and even children who used rocks and sticks to defend themselves.

BEARS

The only bears found in California are black bears (even though they are usually brown in color). A century ago, our state bear, the grizzly, roamed here as well, but the last one was shot and killed in the 1930s. Black bears almost never harm human beings—although you should never approach or feed a bear, or get between a bear and its cubs or its food. Black bears weigh between 250 and 400 pounds, can run up to 30 miles per hour, and are powerful swimmers and climbers. When they bound, the muscles on their shoulders roll like ocean breakers. If provoked, a bear could cause serious injury.

There's only one important fact to remember about bears: They love snacks. The average black bear has to eat as much as 30,000 calories a day, and since their natural diet is made up of berries, fruits, plants, fish, insects, and the like, the high-calorie food of human beings is very appealing to them. Unfortunately, too many California campers have trained our state's bears to crave the taste of corn chips, hot dogs, and soda pop.

Any time you see a bear, it's almost a given that it is looking for food, preferably something sweet. Bears have become specialists in the food-raiding business. As a result, you must be absolutely certain that you keep your food away from them. This is best accomplished with a bear-proof food canister, required equipment when backpacking in parts of Yosemite National Park, Sequoia and Kings Canyon National Parks, and much of the rest of the Sierra Nevada. At car campgrounds at these areas, metal bear-proof food storage lockers must be used. Never leave your food unattended or in your vehicle. Tickets are commonly issued for either of these violations. In addition, get an update from the rangers in your park about suitable bear precautions.

Bears are sometimes encountered on trails, although not as frequently as in campgrounds. If you're hiking, bears will most likely hear you coming and avoid you. If one approaches you, either on the trail or in camp, yell loudly, throw small rocks or pine cones in the vicinity, and try to frighten the bear away. A bear that is afraid of humans is a bear that will stay wild and stay alive.

Backpackers should always use bear-proof canisters to store their food for overnight trips. Hanging food from a tree is largely ineffective when done improperly, and the practice is now banned in much of the Sierra Nevada where bear-proof food canisters are required by law. You can rent or buy a bear canister from most outdoor stores, or from many ranger stations in national parks and national forests. For more information, or to rent a canister, contact Yosemite National Park at 209/372-0200, Sequoia and Kings Canyon National Parks at 559/565-3341, or Inyo National Forest at 760/873-2400.

If you are backpacking in an area where bear canisters are not required, or where bears aren't as bold as they are in the heavily visited areas of the Sierra Nevada, you can substitute a food hang for a bear canister. This is where you place your food in a plastic or canvas garbage bag (always double bag your food), then suspend it from a rope in midair, 10 feet from the trunk of a tree and 20 feet off the ground. Counterbalancing two bags with a rope thrown over a tree limb is very effective, but finding an appropriate limb can be difficult.

This is most easily accomplished by tying a rock to a rope, then throwing it over a high but sturdy tree limb. Next, tie your food bag to the rope and hoist it in the air. When you are satisfied with the position of the food bag, tie off the end of the rope to another tree.

Once a bear gets his mitts on your food, he considers it his. There is nothing you can do. If this happens to you once, you will learn never to let food sit unattended.

First Aid

HYPOTHERMIA

A leading cause of death in the outdoors is hypothermia, which occurs when your body's core temperature drops low enough that your vital organs can no longer function. Most cases of hypothermia occur at temperatures in the 50s, not below freezing, as you might expect. Often the victim has gotten wet, and/or is fatigued from physical exertion.

Initial symptoms of hypothermia include uncontrollable shivering, often followed by a complete stop in shivering, extreme lethargy, and an inability to reason. A hypothermic person will often want to lie down and rest or sleep. His or her hiking partners must jump into action to get the victim warm and dry immediately. Remove all wet clothes and put on dry ones. Cover his or her head with a warm hat. If someone in the group has an emergency space blanket (see *Hiking Gear Checklist*), wrap it around the victim. Get the hypothermic person to eat some quick-energy food, even candy, and drink warm beverages—this helps the body produce heat. Do not give the person alcohol, as this encourages heat loss.

HEAT STROKE

Usually the result of overexposure to the sun

and dehydration, symptoms of heat stroke include headache, mental confusion, and cramps throughout the body. Immediate action must be taken to reduce the body's core temperature. Pour water on the victim's head. Have him or her sit in a cool stream if possible. Make the person drink as much liquid as possible. Heat stroke is easily avoided by staying adequately hydrated and wearing a large-brimmed hat for protection from the sun.

ALTITUDE SICKNESS AND ADJUSTMENT

Many hikers experience a shortness of breath when hiking only a few thousand feet higher than the elevation where they live. If you live on the California coast, you may notice slightly labored breathing while hiking at an elevation as low as 5,000 feet. As you go higher, it gets worse, sometimes leading to headaches and nausea. It takes a full 72 hours to acclimate to major elevation changes, although most people acclimatize after only 24 to 48 hours. The best preparation for hiking at a high elevation is to sleep at that elevation, or as close to it as possible, the night before. If you are planning a strenuous hike at 7,000 feet or above, spend a day or two before doing easier hikes at the same elevation. Also, get plenty of rest and drink plenty of fluids. Lack of sleep, and alcohol, can contribute to your susceptibility to "feeling the altitude."

Serious altitude sickness typically occurs above 10,000 feet. It is generally preventable by simply allowing enough time for acclimation. But how do you acclimate for a climb to the top of Mount Whitney or Shasta, at more than 14,000 feet? The answer is you can't, at least not completely. Spending a few days beforehand hiking at 10,000 feet and above will help tremendously. Staying fueled with food and fully hydrated will also help. But if you've never hiked above a certain elevation—say 13,000 feet—you don't know how you are going to feel until you get there. If you start to feel ill (nausea, vomiting, severe headache), you are experiencing altitude sickness. Some people can get by with taking aspirin and trudging

onward, but if you are seriously ill, the only cure is to descend as soon as possible. If the altitude has gotten to you badly enough, you may need someone to help you walk. Fatigue and elevation sickness can cloud your judgment in the same manner that hypothermia does, so take action before your symptoms become too severe.

Safety on the Trail
NAVIGATIONAL TOOLS

For some hikers, it is quite easy to become lost. If you don't get your bearings, getting found is the difficult part. If you're hiking with a family or group, make sure everybody stays together. If anyone decides to split off from the group for any reason, make sure they have a trail map with them and that they know how to read it. Also, ensure that everyone in your group knows the rules regarding what to do if they get lost:

In areas above tree line or where the trail becomes faint, some hikers will mark the route with piles of small rocks to act as directional signs for the return trip. But if an unexpected

Rock cairns act as directional aids on the trail.

snow buries these piles of rocks, or if you get well off the track, all you are left with is a moonscape. That is why every hiker should understand the concept of orienteering. In the process, you become a mountaineer.

When lost, the first step is to secure your present situation—that is, to make sure it does not get any worse. Take stock of your food, foul-weather gear, camp fuel, clothes, and your readiness to spend the night. Keep in mind that this is an adventure, not a crisis.

Then take out your topographic map, compass, and altimeter. What? Right: Never go into the unknown without them. Place the map on the ground, then set the compass atop the map and orient it north. In most cases, you will easily be able to spot landmarks, such as prominent mountaintops. In cases with a low overcast, where mountains are obscured in clouds, you can take this adventure one step further by checking your altimeter. By scanning the elevation lines on the map, you will be able to trace your near-exact position.

Always be prepared to rely on yourself, but also file a trip plan with the local ranger station, especially if hiking in remote wilderness areas. Carry plenty of food, fuel, and a camp stove. Make sure your clothes, weather gear, sleeping bag, and tent will keep you dry and warm. Always carry a compass, altimeter, and map with elevation lines, and know how to use them, practicing in good weather to get the feel of it.

With enough experience, you will discover that you can "read" the land so well that you will hardly even need to reference a map to find your way.

Lightning

If you see or hear a thunderstorm approaching, avoid exposed ridges and peaks. This is disheartening advice when you're only a mile from the summit of Half Dome, but follow it anyway. If you're already on a mountain top, stay out of enclosed places, such as rock caves or recesses. Confined areas are deadly in lightning storms; hikers seeking refuge from lightning have been killed inside the stone hut on top of Mount Whitney. Do not lean against rock slopes or trees; try to keep a few feet of air space around you. Squat low on your boot soles, or sit on your day pack, jacket, or anything that will insulate you in case lightning strikes the ground.

Survival in the Outdoors

When facing hardship in the outdoors, there are three critical rules of survival:

Stop and stay put: People often tend to meander around, trying to find a familiar road or rock; they don't want to deal with the thought that they are lost. The first step in a survival scenario is to stop and stay where you are. This is important because when the search-and-rescue team comes looking for you, they're going to be looking at your last known location. The more you wander around, the farther you get away from them.

Identify survival needs: People get confused sometimes, but survival needs don't change, no matter where you are. You have to identify your survival needs and prioritize them:

Personal protection: clothing (dry clothes, protective layers, water-repellent shell, hat or ski cap), shelter (sleeping bag or space blanket), fire (lighter, matches, tinder), and meet them in that order. Stay warm, dry, and hydrated.

Signaling: It can be a flasher you purchase in a store or you can improvise (cell phone, whistle, signal mirror, flares, smoke devices, fresh batteries).

Sustenance: Water (or water purification tablets) and food (nutrition bars or equivalent). Water is extremely important; food not so important. (Everybody talks about food, but that is the least important of the survival essentials—you can live longer without food than without water.)

Travel: Only leave if the area you're in isn't meeting your needs or a rescue does not appear imminent. Ensure that you have maps, a compass, and a watch.

Health: Mental, psychological, and environmental—these are a constant. The only thing that changes might be how you improvise to meet them. In addition to a first-aid kit, consider including a family photo, spiritual material, or a book.

Improvise: You have to know how to improvise because it's doubtful everything will be at your disposal to meet your needs. Use manufactured materials as well as what nature provides—a car offers tons of improvising equipment: a mirror can be ripped off as a signaling device; seat cushions can be cut up for insulation; a spare tire can be burned as a smoke signal—but only if you know the search-and-rescue teams are close.

HIKING ETHICS

HIKING WITH DOGS

Dogs are wonderful friends and great companions. But dogs and nature do not mix well. Bless their furry little hearts, most dogs can't help but disturb wildlife, given half a chance. Even if they don't chase or bark at wildlife, dogs leave droppings that may intimidate other mammals into changing their normal routine. But kept on a leash, a dog can be the best hiking companion you could ask for.

Dogs are allowed on some trails in California and not on others. For many dog owners, it's confusing. When using this book, check the *User Groups* listing under each trail listing to see whether or not dogs are permitted. Always call the park or public land in advance if you are traveling some distance with your dog.

Here's a general guideline to park rules about dogs:

If you are visiting a national or state park, 99 percent of the time, your dog will not be allowed to hike with you. There are only a few exceptions to this rule within the national and state park systems. Dogs are usually allowed in campgrounds or picnic areas, but they are not allowed on trails in these parks. If you are planning to visit a national or state park, consider leaving your dog at home.

At other types of parks (county parks, regional parks, and so on), dogs may or may not be allowed on trails. Always follow and obey a park's specific rules about dogs. Oftentimes, if dogs are allowed, they must be on a six-foot or shorter leash. Don't try to get away with carrying the leash in your hand while your dog runs free; rangers may give you a ticket.

In national forest or wilderness lands, dogs are usually permitted off leash, except in special wildlife management areas or other special-use areas. Understand that your dog should still be under voice control—for his or her safety more than anything. The outdoors presents many hazards for dogs, including mountain lions, porcupines, black bears, ticks, rattlesnakes, and a host of other potential problems. Dogs are frequently lost in national forest areas. Keeping your dog close to your side or on a leash in the national forests will help you both have a worry-free trip and a great time.

Avoiding the Crowds

Although many regions of California exist where you can hike without seeing another soul, even on holiday weekends, some of our better-known parks and public lands are

© ANN MARIE BROWN

Check to make sure your dog is allowed on a trail.

TRAIL ETIQUETTE

© TOM STIENSTRA

Hiking is a great way to get out of the concrete jungle and into the woods and the wild, to places of natural beauty. Unfortunately, this manner of thinking is shared by millions of people. Following some basic rules of etiquette will ensure that we all get along and keep the outdoors a place we can enjoy... together.

- **Enjoy the silence and let nature's sounds prevail.** Keep your voice low and avoid making loud noises. You will increase your chances of encountering wildlife, plus help others enjoy their quiet time in the outdoors.

- **Be aware of other trail users and yield appropriately.** If you hear someone coming up behind you who is clearly traveling faster than you, stand aside and let them pass. On narrow trails, hikers going downhill should always yield to hikers going uphill. Get out of the way so uphill hikers can keep their momentum as they climb. Also, large groups of hikers should always yield to smaller groups or solo travelers.

- **Be friendly and polite to other trail users.** A smile or a "hello" as you pass others on the trail is always a good idea. And it may seem obvious, but if someone steps aside to allow you to pass, say "thank you."

- **Obey all posted signs and trail closures.** Only hike where it's legal. Do not invent "shortcuts" or hike across private property without the express permission of the owner.

- **Hike only on established trails.** As soon as you walk off a trail, you trample vegetation. Never cut switchbacks; hillside trails are built with switchbacks to keep the slope from eroding. Just a few people cutting the switchbacks can destroy a hillside.

- **Yield to equestrians.** Horses can be badly spooked by just about anything. Always give them plenty of room. If horses are approaching you, stop alongside the trail until they pass. If horses are traveling in your direction and you need to pass them, call out politely to the rider and ask permission. If the horse and rider moves off the trail and the rider tells you it's okay, then pass.

notorious for crowds. No matter where in California you want to hike, there's no reason to subject yourself to packed parking lots, long lines of people snaking up and down switchbacks, and trail destinations that look like Times Square on New Year's Eve. If you take a few simple steps, you can avoid the crowds almost anywhere, even in well-traveled parks near urban areas and in our famous national parks.

Hike in the off-season. For most public lands, the off-season is any time other than summer, or any time when school is in session. Late September through mid-May is an excellent period of time for hiking trips (except during the week between Christmas and New Year's and Easter week). Try to avoid periods near holidays; many people try to beat the crowds by traveling right before or after a holiday, and the result is more crowds.

Time your trip for midweek. Tuesday, Wednesday, and Thursday are always the quietest days of the week in any park or public land.

Get up early. Even Yosemite Valley is serene and peaceful until 8 or 9am. In most parks, if you arrive at the trailhead before 9am, you'll have the first few hours on the trail all to yourself. As an insurance policy, get to the trailhead even earlier.

If you can't get up early, stay out late. When the days are long in summer, you can hike shorter trails from 4pm to 7:30pm or even later. You may see other hikers in the first hour or so, but they'll soon disperse. Trailhead parking lots are often packed at 1pm, then nearly empty at 5pm. Note that if you hike in the late afternoon or evening, you should always carry a flashlight with you (at least one per person), just in case it gets dark sooner than you planned.

Get out and hike in foul weather. Don your favorite impermeable layer, and go where fair-weather hikers dare not go. Some of the best memories are made on rainy days, cloudy days, foggy days, and days when the wind blows at gale force. The fact is, the vast majority of hikers only hike when the sun is out. Witness nature in all its varied moods, and you may be surprised at how much fun you have.

Tips for Getting Along

When hiking with others, and especially over several days, it pays to do a little planning and a lot of communicating. Here are some tips to having a successful trip:

The destination and activities must be agreed upon. A meeting of the minds gives everybody an equal stake in the trip.

If backpacking, guarantee yourself refreshing sleep. Make certain that your sleeping bag, pillow, pad, and tent are clean, dry, warm, and comfortable.

Develop technical expertise. Test all gear at home before putting it to use on the trail.

Guarantee yourself action. Pick a destination with your favorite activity: adventuring, wildlife watching, swimming, fishing...

Guarantee yourself quiet time. Savor the views and the sound of a stream running free, and reserve time with people you care for, and your soul will be recharged.

Accordance on food. Always have complete agreement on the selections for each meal, and check for allergies.

Agree on a wake-up time. Then when morning comes, you will be on course from the start.

Equal chances at the fun stuff. Many duties can be shared over the course of a trip, such as navigating and preparing meals.

Be aware, not self-absorbed. Live so there can be magic in every moment, with an awareness of the senses: sight, sound, smell, touch, taste, and how you feel inside. Have an outlook that alone can promote great satisfaction.

No whining. You can't always control your surroundings, only your state of mind.

Wilderness Ethics

Take good care of this beautiful land you're hiking on. The basics are simple: Leave no trace of your visit. Pack out all your trash. Do your best not to disturb animal or plant life. Don't collect specimens of plants, wildlife, or even

HIKING GEAR CHECKLIST

BACKPACK

- Cell phone
- Compass or navigational device
- Extra clothing (lightweight jacket, rain poncho, gloves, hat)
- First-aid kit
- Flashlight or head lamp
- Food (energy bars, nuts, dried fruit, jerky)
- Insect repellent
- Pocket knife
- Sunglasses
- Sunscreen
- Trail map
- Watch
- Water or water filter

EMERGENCY SUPPLIES

- Extra shoelaces
- Matches in a waterproof container
- Mylar blanket
- Signal mirror
- Whistle

LONG DISTANCE TRAILS

- Ace bandage
- Bandana
- Bear canister
- Extra pair of socks
- Eyeglass cleaner or saline solution (for contacts)
- Gaiters
- Lightweight shoes or moccasins
- Toilet paper and zippered plastic bags
- Trekking poles

FUN STUFF

- Binoculars
- Book, including wildflower or bird identification guides
- Camera (with extra battery and memory card)
- Deck of cards
- Fishing license and equipment
- Picnic gear

pine cones. Never, ever carve anything into the trunks of trees. If you're following a trail, don't cut the switchbacks. Leave everything in nature exactly as you found it, because each tiny piece has its place in the great scheme of things.

You can go the extra mile, too. Pick up any litter that you see on the trail. Teach your children to do this as well. Carry an extra bag to hold picked-up litter until you get to a trash receptacle, or just keep an empty pocket for that purpose in your day pack or fanny sack.

If you have the extra time or energy, join a trail organization in your area or spend some time volunteering in your local park. Anything you do to help this beautiful planet will be repaid to you, many times over.

REDWOOD EMPIRE

Visitors come to the Redwood Empire for one reason: to see groves of giant redwoods, the tallest trees in the world. But the redwoods are only one of the attractions in this area. The Smith River canyon, Del Norte and Humboldt Coasts, and the remote edge of the Siskiyou Wilderness in Six Rivers National Forest all make this region like none other in the world. Three stellar areas should be on your must-see list for outstanding days of adventure: the redwood parks from Trinidad to Klamath River, the Smith River Recreation Area, and the Lost Coast. Redwood campgrounds are in high demand, and reservations are necessary in the peak vacation season. On the opposite end of the spectrum are primitive and remote settings in Six Rivers National Forest, the Lost Coast, and even a few surprise nuggets in Redwood National Park.

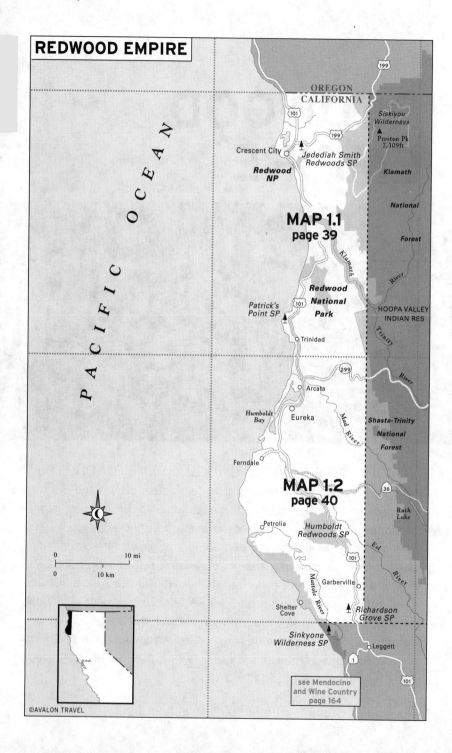

Map 1.1

Sites 1-22
Pages 41-53

1.2

©AVALON TRAVEL

Map 1.2

Sites 23-36
Pages 54-62

McKinleyville

Willow Creek

Blue Lake

Arcata

23 **24**

255

Arcata Bay

Six Rivers National Forest

Eureka

Humboldt Bay

Humboldt Bay NWR

see Shasta and Trinity page 64

Eel River Fortuna

25

Ferndale

Rio Dell **26** Bridgeville

Capetown

Bear River

Cape Mendocino

Cape Ridge

Rainbow Ridge

Pepperwood **27**

28-29
30

Humboldt Redwoods State Park

Petrolia

Mattole **31**

Punta Gorda

Honeydew

South Fork Eel River Weott

Myers Flat

AVENUE OF THE GIANTS

Phillipsville

King Range **32**

Conservation Area **33**

Lost Coast

Horse Mtn 1,920ft

Shelter Cove
Point Delgada

Briceland Redway

Garberville

Richardson Grove State Park

Benbow

34-35 **36**

0   5 mi
0   5 km

©AVALON TRAVEL

1 TOLOWA DUNES
2.5 mi/1.0 hr 🏃1 ⛰7

Tolowa Dunes State Park north of Crescent City

Map 1.1, page 39

This ancient sand dune complex seems to sweep on forever. It spans more than 10 miles from the mouth of the Smith River south along the Pacific Ocean, nearly reaching Crescent City, and is located adjacent to Lake Earl to the east. After parking at Kellogg Beach, walk north or south for five minutes or five hours—take your pick. Either way, you will feel like a solitary speck against the enormous backdrop of untouched sand dunes and ocean. Only rarely will you see other people. The area is known by several names, including Fort Dick Beach, Kellogg Beach, and Pelican Bay Sand Dunes, but by any name, it's a good place to escape to nothing but wide-open beach for miles.

User Groups: Hikers, dogs, and horses. Mountain bikes permitted but not recommended. No wheelchair facilities.

Permits: No permits are required. Parking and access are free.

Maps: For a free brochure and map, contact Tolowa Dunes State Park. For topographic maps, ask the USGS for Crescent City and Smith River.

Directions: Take U.S. 101 to Crescent City and Northcrest Drive. Turn northwest on Northcrest Drive and drive 1.5 miles to Old Mill Road. Turn left on Old Mill Road and drive 1.25 miles to the end of Old Mill Road and the junction with Sand Hill Road. Turn left on Sand Hill Road (at the Department of Fish and Game office) and drive 0.25 mile to the parking lot and the trailhead.

For trail and walk-in beach access: Take U.S. 101 to Crescent City and Northcrest Drive. Turn northwest on Northcrest Drive and drive six miles (it becomes Lake Earl Drive) to Lower Lake Road. Turn left on Lower Lake Road and drive 2.5 miles to Kellogg Road. Turn left and drive 0.5 mile to the trailhead.

Alternative access: Follow the above access directions, but after turning left on Lower Lake Road, drive five miles to Pala Road. Turn left and drive 0.5 mile to the trailhead.

Contact: Tolowa Dunes State Park, 707/465-7335, www.parks.ca.gov.

2 MYRTLE CREEK TRAIL
2.0 mi/0.75 hr 🏃1 ⛰7

in the Smith River National Recreation Area

Map 1.1, page 39

This interpretive trail follows year-round Myrtle Creek. The stream drainage runs along a geological boundary between typical local soils (which support redwood and Douglas fir forests) and dry, reddish, iron- and magnesium-rich serpentine soil (where rarer native species grow, such as Bolander's and Vollmer's lilies). It's an easy hike with a lot to look at and learn about, including the remains of an extensive hydraulic mining operation, dating back to 1853, when gold was discovered here; 15 interpretive stops are linked to a numbered brochure. Keep to the trail. Collecting artifacts or plants is prohibited.

User Groups: Hikers and dogs. No horses or mountain bikes.

Permits: Campfire permits (free) are required for overnight use. Parking and access are free.

Maps: For a free brochure and hiking guide, contact Smith River National Recreation Area. For a topographic map, ask the USGS for Hiouchi.

Directions: From Crescent City, drive north on U.S. 101 for three miles to U.S. 199. Bear right (east) on U.S. 199 and drive seven miles to the parking area and trailhead. Note: Park on the south side of U.S. 199 and cross the road to access the trailhead.

Contact: Smith River National Recreation Area, Gasquet, 707/457-3131, www.fs.usda.gov/srnf.

❸ BOY SCOUT TREE TRAIL
7.0 mi/3.5 hr   🥾2 ⛰10

in Jedediah Smith Redwoods State Park
northeast of Crescent City

Map 1.1, page 39   **BEST (**

This is the kind of place where a nature lover can find religion; where the beauty is pure and untouched. The trail is a soft dirt path—often sprinkled with redwood needles—that allows hikers to penetrate deep into an old-growth redwood forest, complete with a giant fern understory and high-limbed canopy. The trail leads 2.8 miles to Fern Falls, which makes this one of the area's better hikes in winter. The centerpiece is supposed to be the Boy Scout Tree, named after a scoutmaster, a double redwood that is located 2.5 miles in. Most people look for it and never see it. Look for a spur trail, unmarked—that's right, no sign—that leads to it.

This is an easy hike, nearly flat and with only small hills—yet it's extremely rewarding. Just walk into the forest, and a few hours later, walk out. Those few hours can change how you feel about the world. A bonus known to relatively few is Fern Falls, a 40-foot waterfall that flows in the rainy season. Reaching it requires a 3.5-mile hike one-way, making it a 7-mile round-trip hike.

User Groups: Hikers only. No dogs, horses, or mountain bikes. No wheelchair facilities.

Permits: No permits are required. The park entry fee is $8 at the main entrance.

Maps: A trail map is available for a fee from Jedediah Smith Redwoods State Park. For a topographic map, ask the USGS for Hiouchi.

Directions: From U.S. 101 in Crescent City, turn east on Elk Valley Road and drive one mile to Howland Hill Road. Turn right and drive 3.5 miles to the trailhead, on the left. The last two miles are unpaved.

Note: If you plan to camp at Jedediah Smith Redwoods State Park, use these directions: From Crescent City, drive north on U.S. 101 for three miles to U.S. 199. Bear right (east) on U.S. 199 and drive east (past the main entrance to Jedediah Smith Redwoods State Park) and continue just past Hiouchi to South Fork Road. Turn right on South Fork Road (County Road 427) and cross two bridges (stay right at the fork). At the junction, turn right on Howland Hill Road and drive about five miles to a small parking area and the signed trailhead, on the right side of the road.

Contact: Jedediah Smith Redwoods State Park, Crescent City, 707/465-7335, www.parks.ca.gov.

❹ STOUT GROVE TRAIL
0.7 mi/0.75 hr   🥾1 ⛰8

in Jedediah Smith Redwoods State Park
northeast of Crescent City

Map 1.1, page 39

The Stout Tree, a mammoth coastal redwood, used to be signed and ringed by a short fence, with a short trail directly from the parking lot to the tree. The sign and fence are gone. What you'll find now is a newer trail that is routed through the Stout Grove and beyond along the Smith River. You have to figure out on your own which tree is the Stout Tree, but most don't find that too difficult. The trail is a 10- to 15-minute walk that takes an easy course to the Stout Grove, on to the Stout Tree (off the trail to your right as you walk in) and beyond to the Smith River. Most people take their time, absorbing the surroundings. Most everybody makes the mandatory stroll to the nearby Smith River, located a few minutes' walk beyond the Stout Tree.

User Groups: Hikers and wheelchairs. No dogs, horses, or mountain bikes.

Permits: No permits are required. The park entry fee is $8 at the main entrance.

Maps: A trail map is available for a fee from Jedediah Smith Redwoods State Park. For a topographic map, ask the USGS for Hiouchi.

Directions: From Crescent City, drive north on U.S. 101 for three miles to U.S. 199. Bear right (east) on U.S. 199 and drive east past the main entrance to Jedediah Smith Redwoods State Park and continue just past Hiouchi to South Fork Road. Turn right on South Fork

Road (County Road 427) and cross two bridges. At the junction, turn right on Howland Hill Road and drive about two miles to a small parking area (on the right) and the signed trailhead. **Contact:** Jedediah Smith Redwoods State Park, Crescent City, 707/465-7335, www.parks.ca.gov.

5 CRAIG'S CREEK TRAIL
7.4 mi/4.25 hr   🏃3 ⛰8

in Smith River National Recreation Area
northeast of Crescent City

Map 1.1, page 39

This is an old miners' pack route, vintage 1800s, that has been converted into this hiking trail, an obscure path that is overlooked by most visitors. It starts along the South Fork Smith River, loops up the slopes of Craig's Creek Mountain and back down to the river, and ends where Craig's Creek enters the South Fork. In the process, it rises above the river and passes through forest, including old-growth redwoods and Douglas fir. You get several lookout points across the South Fork Smith canyon. Because of the contour of the mountain, the hike includes a good climb. The starting and ending elevations are the same (200 feet). Most of the time, you can have the entire trail to yourself. The South Fork Smith is very pretty here—a clear, free-flowing stream that drains a huge expanse of the Siskiyou Wilderness.

User Groups: Hikers, dogs, horses, and mountain bikes. No wheelchair facilities.

Permits: For overnight use, a campfire permit (free) is required. Parking and access are free.

Maps: For a free brochure and hiking guide, contact Smith River National Recreation Area. For a map, ask the U.S. Forest Service for Six Rivers National Forest. For a topographic map, ask the USGS for Hiouchi.

Directions: From Crescent City, drive north on U.S. 101 for three miles to U.S. 199. Bear right (east) on U.S. 199 and drive east past the main entrance to Jedediah Smith Redwoods State Park and continue just past Hiouchi to South Fork Road. Turn right on South Fork

Road (County Road 427) and drive approximately one-third mile and park in the signed area for river access. After parking, walk a short distance across South Fork Road to the north side of the second bridge. The trailhead is on the north side of the second bridge (called the Tryon Bridge).

Contact: Smith River National Recreation Area, Gasquet, 707/457-3131, www.fs.usda.gov/srnf.

6 STONY CREEK TRAIL
1.0 mi/0.5 hr   🏃1 ⛰8

in Smith River National Recreation Area
northeast of Crescent City

Map 1.1, page 39

This easy walk in an unblemished river setting will take hikers to the mouth of Stony Creek, right where it pours into the North Fork Smith River. It's the kind of special place where you just sit and listen to the flow of moving water as it gurgles and pops its way over stones smoothed by years of river flows. The hike is easy, with a few ups and downs as it follows a bluff adjacent to the North Fork Smith (a designated Wild and Scenic River), then is routed right out to the mouth of Stony Creek. You're surrounded by woods, water, and in the spring, wildflowers.

Note: For years, there has been an ongoing disagreement on how to spell it, either Stony or Stoney. The creek itself is spelled "Stony," so it only makes sense to spell it the same.

User Groups: Hikers and dogs. No horses or mountain bikes. No wheelchair facilities.

Permits: Campfire permits (free) are required. Parking and access are free, but parking space is very limited.

Maps: For a free brochure and hiking guide, contact Smith River National Recreation Area. For a map, ask the U.S. Forest Service for Six Rivers National Forest. For a topographic map, ask the USGS for Gasquet.

Directions: From Crescent City, drive north on U.S. 101 for three miles to U.S. 199. Bear right (east) on U.S. 199 and drive 14 miles to Gasquet and continue a short distance to Middle Fork Road. Turn left on Middle Fork, continue a short distance and bear right on Gasquet Flat Road. Cross the bridge and stay left at the intersection of Gasquet Toll Road and continue 0.8 mile to Stony Creek Road (signed). Turn right and drive a short distance to the trailhead.

Contact: Smith River National Recreation Area, Gasquet, 707/457-3131, www.fs.usda.gov/srnf.

7 ELK CAMP RIDGE TRAIL
7.5-16.4 mi/3.5 hr-2 days 🏃3 ⛰8

in Smith River National Recreation Area northeast of Crescent City

Map 1.1, page 39

This trail is like a walk through history. It was originally part of a pack trail between Crescent City and the gold mines in southern Oregon, and the memories of the old days can shadow your hike much of the way. The trailhead is at 1,200 feet, but the route climbs right up to the ridge, reaching more than 3,000 feet. Once you reach the ridge, you have excellent views of surrounding peaks (Preston Peak is the big one) and the Smith River Canyon. Hikers may also notice that much of the vegetation along the trail is stunted, a result of the high mineral content in the serpentine rocks. The trail keeps climbing and ends at 3,400 feet. From start to finish, the trail covers 8.2 miles, although most hikers only make it halfway before they return.

Note: This trail is closed in the rainy season to stop the transfer of Port Orford Cedar Root Disease.

User Groups: Hikers, dogs, horses, and mountain bikes. No wheelchair facilities.

Permits: Campfire permits (free) are required. Parking and access are free.

Maps: For a free brochure and hiking guide, contact Smith River National Recreation Area. For a map, ask the U.S. Forest Service for Six Rivers National Forest. For topographic maps, ask the USGS for Gasquet and High Plateau Mountain.

Directions: From Crescent City, drive north on U.S. 101 for three miles to U.S. 199. Bear right (east) on U.S. 199 and drive east past the main entrance to Jedediah Smith Redwoods State Park and continue just past Hiouchi to South Fork Road. Turn right on South Fork Road (County Road 427) and drive over the two bridges to a fork. Turn left on South Fork Road and drive 7.9 miles to Rock Creek Bridge and Forest Road 16N23. Turn right on Forest Road 16N23 and drive 0.9 mile (rough road, high-clearance advised). The trail begins at the creek.

This hike can also be done as a one-way trip with a shuttle. Leave second car on Howland Hill Road at a trailhead inside the park boundary for Jedediah Smith State Park.

Contact: Smith River National Recreation Area, Gasquet, 707/457-3131, www.fs.usda.gov/srnf.

8 CALIFORNIA COASTAL TRAIL/NICKEL CREEK CAMP
3-15.0 mi one-way/1 day 🏃3 ⛰8

in Del Norte Redwoods State Park south of Crescent City

Map 1.1, page 39

You get a little bit of heaven on this hike. It's one of the feature trips on the Del Norte coast, coursing through virgin forest and meadows (with beautiful wildflowers in the spring) and granting great coastal views in several spots. Most will camp at the Nickel Creek Campground, then launch off from there. The trail starts along the coast, veers up sharply into coastal spruce and fir, and then dips into dense, old-growth forest. That's the heaven. You will cross Damnation Creek, and then walk roughly parallel to U.S. 101. Most turn around at that point. You can extend the walk to make a one-way trip, with a car shuttle at your end point, with two crossings of U.S. 101 as you venture south; it's 15 miles to the second crossing of U.S 101. Note that the cut-off trail, the Damnation Trail, is closed to the beach due to erosion and slides. Note that when you cross meadows here, ticks can be a common problem.

User Groups: Hikers and mountain bikes (restricted to first six miles only). No dogs or horses. No wheelchair facilities.

Permits: No permits are required. The park entry fee is $8 at the main entrance.

Maps: A trail guide is available for a fee from Redwood National and State Parks (707/464-6101). For a topographic map, ask the USGS for Sister Rocks.

Directions: From Crescent City, drive south on U.S. 101 for about 2.5 miles to Milepost 23.03 and Enderts Beach Road. Turn right (west) onto Enderts Beach Road and drive for 2.5 miles to the trailhead at the end of the road.

Contact: Del Norte Redwoods State Park, Crescent City, 707/467-7335 or 707/465-5128, www.nps.gov/redw or www.parks.ca.gov.

9 MCCLENDON FORD TRAIL
3.0 mi/1.5 hr

in Smith River National Recreation Area east of Crescent City

Map 1.1, page 39   **BEST (**

This is a perfect trail for a hot summer day, complete with a swimming hole. Hike 0.5 mile on the South Kelsey Trail, then one mile on the McClendon Ford Trail to the river. It's an easy hike through a large forest of Douglas fir. The trail crosses Horse Creek, a small tributary, and then leads to a pretty beach on the South Fork Smith River. The starting elevation is 1,000 feet, and the ending elevation is 200 feet. Get the idea? Right, this trail follows an easy descent to the river, taking about 45 minutes to get there. The swimming hole on the river is secluded and out of the way of most vacationers, so most often, you have the place completely to yourself. You end up at a bouldered beach and a beautiful pool. It's called the McClendon Ford

because this is a historic river crossing, or ford, of the South Fork Smith.

Note: This is also the trailhead for South Kelsey Trail. If you are unfamiliar with the area, be sure to have a map of Six Rivers National Forest to reach the trailhead.

User Groups: Hikers, dogs, horses, and mountain bikes. No wheelchair facilities.

Permits: No permits are required. Parking and access are free.

Maps: For a free brochure and hiking guide, contact Smith River National Recreation Area. For a map, ask the U.S. Forest Service for Six Rivers National Forest. For a topographic map, ask the USGS for Ship Mountain.

Directions: From Crescent City, drive north on U.S. 101 for three miles to U.S. 199. Bear right (east) on U.S. 199 and drive east past the main entrance to Jedediah Smith Redwoods State Park and continue just past Hiouchi to South Fork Road. Turn right on South Fork Road (County Road 427), cross two bridges and bear left on South Fork Road and drive 13.7 miles (one mile past Steven Bridge) to Forest Road 15 (locals call it the "GO Road"). Turn right on Forest Road 15 and drive 3.5 miles to Forest Road FS15N39 (signed for Kelsey Trail; road turns to gravel here). Turn left and drive two miles to trailhead. Hike on South Kelsey Trail for 0.5 mile before connecting with McClendon Ford Trail.

Contact: Smith River National Recreation Area, Gasquet, 707/457-3131, www.fs.usda. gov/srnf.

10 SOUTH KELSEY TRAIL
3-9.0 mi/1.5 hr-2 days

in Smith River National Recreation Area east of Crescent City

Map 1.1, page 39

Back before cars, trains, and planes, Kelsey Trail spanned 200 miles from Crescent City eastward to Fort Jones near Yreka. It was built in the mid-19th century by Chinese laborers as a mule-train route. The trail is in good shape for about 4.5 miles then occasionally deteriorates in quality. The maintained section is on a beautiful piece of the South Fork Smith River. The trailhead is near Horse Creek, on the South Fork Smith River, at a 1,200-foot elevation. The trail initially drops down along the South Fork and continues south for 4.5 miles. A few camps are here along the river, including the Buck Creek shelter, which is heaven during a heavy rainstorm. The route then rises above the river, and at this point, seems to degenerate into oblivion if you try to follow it out of the canyon. Maps show the route extending to Baldy Peak and Harrington Lake.

User Groups: Hikers, dogs, and horses. Mountain bikes are permitted only to the wilderness boundary. No wheelchair facilities.

Permits: A campfire permit (free) is required. Parking and access are free.

Maps: For a free brochure and hiking guide, contact Smith River National Recreation Area. For a map, ask the U.S. Forest Service for Six Rivers National Forest. For a topographic map, ask the USGS for Summit Valley.

Directions: From Crescent City, drive north on U.S. 101 for three miles to U.S. 199. Bear right (east) on U.S. 199 and drive east past the main entrance to Jedediah Smith Redwoods State Park and continue just past Hiouchi to South Fork Road. Turn right on South Fork Road (County Road 427), cross two bridges and bear left on South Fork Road and drive 13.7 miles (one mile past Steven Bridge) to Forest Road 15 (locals call it the "GO Road"). Turn right on Forest Road 15 and drive 3.5 miles to Forest Road FS15N39 (signed for Kelsey Trail; road turns to gravel here). Turn left and drive two miles to trailhead.

Contact: Smith River National Recreation Area, Gasquet, 707/457-3131, www.fs.usda. gov/srnf.

11 SUMMIT VALLEY TRAIL
8.1 mi one-way/1 day   🏃4 ⛺8

in Smith River National Recreation Area east of Crescent City

Map 1.1, page 39

The pay-off here is the site of the old Summit

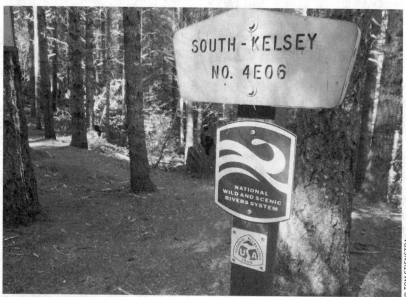

South Kelsey Trail

Valley Lookout, a quarter-mile side trip from the main trail after you climb out of the valley. You get views across to the Siskiyous on one side and to the coast on the other, with a chance on stellar days to even see distant Mount Shasta. It's best done as a one-way trip with a shuttle to avoid a return climb of 3,500 feet.

The trailhead is set on a ridge at 4,600 feet, and the first mile of the hike is on an old jeep road. It then becomes a hiking path as it travels through meadows, where the wildflowers are spectacular in early summer. The trail then drops, plunging into a canyon and landing hikers along the South Fork Smith River at Elkhorn Bar, a beautiful spot at an elevation of 1,160 feet. Here it junctions with South Kelsey Trail, where you'll find a few primitive campsites along the river. You then reach your other shuttle car for the trailhead for the Kelsey Trail.

This hike is best taken in the early summer when the wildflowers are blooming; the Smith River is running with a fresh, ample flow; and the temperature is not too warm. Nobody does this trip down and back; that would be a death march.

User Groups: Hikers, dogs, and horses. Mountain bikes are permitted only to the wilderness boundary. No wheelchair facilities.

Permits: A campfire permit (free) is required. Parking and access are free.

Maps: Write to Smith River National Recreation Area for a free brochure and hiking guide. For a map, ask the U.S. Forest Service for Six Rivers National Forest. For a topographic map, ask the USGS for Summit Valley.

Directions to start of trail: From Crescent City, drive north on U.S. 101 for three miles to U.S. 199. Bear right (east) on U.S. 199 and drive east past the main entrance to Jedediah Smith Redwoods State Park and continue just past Hiouchi to South Fork Road. Turn right on South Fork Road (County Road 427), cross two bridges and bear left on South Fork Road and drive 13.7 miles (one mile past Steven Bridge) to Forest Road 15. Turn right on Forest Road 15 and drive 15 miles to the trailhead, on the left. Park on the side of the road.

Directions to end of trail for shuttle car: From Crescent City, drive north on U.S. 101 for three miles to U.S. 199. Bear right (east) on U.S. 199 and drive east past the main entrance to Jedediah Smith Redwoods State Park and continue just past Hiouchi to South Fork Road. Turn right on South Fork Road (County Road 427), cross two bridges and bear left on South Fork Road and drive 13.7 miles (one mile past Steven Bridge) to Forest Road 15 (locals call it the "GO Road"). Turn right on Forest Road 15 and drive 3.5 miles to Forest Road FS15N39 (signed for Kelsey Trail; road turns to gravel here). Turn left and drive two miles to trailhead.

Contact: Smith River National Recreation Area, Gasquet, 707/457-3131, www.fs.usda.gov/srnf.

🔢 YUROK LOOP
1.0 mi/0.5 hr   👣1   ⛺8

in Redwood National and State Parks south of Crescent City

Map 1.1, page 39

The Yurok Loop is a great short loop hike that starts right next to pretty Lagoon Creek Pond in Redwood National and State Parks. Here's the deal: From the trailhead, it's a 10-minute walk above a beautiful beach with lots of driftwood, and a gentle climb to a great coastal overlook. From here you can scan miles of ocean and many rocky stacks. The prettiest view spans across False Klamath Cove. After enjoying the view, head south, and when you reach a junction, turn left and enter a forest where the trail burrows almost like a tunnel, heading gently downhill. It then emerges from the forest and leads back to the parking lot, making it a delightful and easy walk that is a perfect break for highway drivers.

Note: The Hidden Beach section of Coastal Trail (see listing in this chapter) junctions with this trail.

User Groups: Hikers only. No dogs, horses, or mountain bikes.

Permits: No permits are required. Parking and access are free.

Maps: A trail guide is available for a fee from Redwood National and State Parks Headquarters. For a topographic map, ask the USGS for Requa.

Directions: From Crescent City, drive south on U.S. 101 for approximately 14 miles. Turn right at the sign for the Lagoon Creek Parking Area. The trailhead is adjacent to the parking lot (on the ocean/north side).

Contact: Redwood National Park and California State Parks, Crescent City, 707/467-7335 or 707/465-5128, www.nps.gov/redw or www.parks.ca.gov.

13 COASTAL TRAIL (HIDDEN BEACH SECTION)
6.4 mi/3.0 hr

🏃2 ⛰8

in Redwood National Park south of Crescent City

Map 1.1, page 39

This trek starts at one of the greatest coastal views, at the Klamath Overlook, on California's north coast. You can scan the vast ocean-blue horizon, where it seems you can see the curvature of the earth. After parking, enjoy the view and then head off. It's a 3.2-mile trip, one-way, to Hidden Beach. Locals with two cars can set up a shuttle. Leave a vehicle at the parking area for the Yurok Loop. It's a 7.8-mile trip, one-way, with a climb of roughly 1,400 feet, excellent with a shuttle car. The trail runs along coastal bluffs and rocky cliffs, with sweeping views of the ocean. Pray for a clear day.

User Groups: Hikers only. No dogs, horses, or mountain bikes.

Permits: No permits are required. Parking and access are free.

Maps: A trail guide is available for a fee from Redwood National and State Parks Headquarters. For a topographic map, ask the USGS for Requa.

Directions: From Eureka, drive north on U.S. 101 for about 60 miles to the Klamath River.

Continue two miles north of the Klamath River Bridge to Requa Road. Turn west on Requa Road and drive 2.5 miles to the Klamath Overlook, at the end of the road. The trailhead is at the south end of the parking area. Head north on Coastal Trail.

Contact: Redwood National Park and California State Parks, Crescent City, 707/467-7335 or 707/465-5128, www.nps.gov/redw or www.parks.ca.gov.

14 LOST MAN CREEK TRAIL
2.0 mi/1.0 hr

🏃1 ⛰7

in Redwood National Park south of Klamath

Map 1.1, page 39

Lost Man Creek is very pretty, with many rock pools and lots of lush vegetation. It's also a destination that is easy to reach. The trail heads southeast, the first 1.5 miles nearly flat, then starts to climb moderately, and then nearly levels out along the creek. Bring your camera, because it is rare to reach such a pristine setting with such a short walk. The trail is actually an old logging road that the park service plans on reclaiming and turning into a more low-key setting. On-the-spot note: The two-mile round-trip is as far as virtually all hikers take it; the trail actually continues for 10 miles, all the way back down to Bald Hills Road, so steep that you'll be howling at the moon like a lone wolf.

User Groups: Hikers only. No dogs, horses, or mountain bikes.

Permits: No permits are required. Parking and access are free.

Maps: A trail guide is available for a fee from Redwood National and State Parks Headquarters. For a topographic map, ask the USGS for Orick.

Directions: From Eureka, drive north on U.S. 101 for 41 miles to Orick. Continue north for 3.5 miles just past Davison Road to Lost Man Creek Road. Turn right and drive 0.75 mile to the parking area and trailhead. Trailers and

RVs are not permitted on Lost Man Creek Road.

Contact: Redwood National Park and California State Parks, Crescent City, 707/467-7335 or 707/465-5128, www.nps.gov/redw or www.parks.ca.gov.

15 TALL TREES TRAIL
4.0 mi/2.25 hr   👣2 ⛰10

in Redwood National Park south of Klamath

Map 1.1, page 39   **BEST (**

This trail is the paradox of the Redwood Empire. The pay-off is an easy walk into a grove of tall and ancient redwoods of cathedral-like beauty, with the trail shaded and surrounded by a lush fern understory. Your mission here is to reach Tall Trees Grove, home of the Libby Tree (more about this to come). Problem is, the access road is unpaved and narrow, with no place to turn around, and the parking lot is small. So you need a permit and gate code to get past the gate; it's free at a visitors center. You provide your vehicle make and license plate, and the number of people with you. The hike in is an easy walk in the forest that leads to the Tall Trees Grove along Redwood Creek. In the 1960s, the Libby Tree was believed to be the tallest tree in the world and helped lead to the creation of Redwood National Park. The top of the tree, about 10 feet, broke off, and with la-ser-guided measuring techniques, the tree now rates 34th. Regardless, if you love big trees, this is a must-do.

User Groups: Hikers only. No dogs, horses, or mountain bikes. No wheelchair facilities.

Permits: A permit is required if you want to drive to the trailhead, with only a limited number of cars allowed per day. Permits are free and can be obtained at the Redwood Information Center starting at 9am. Just pick it up, get the gate combination, and then enjoy your trip.

Maps: A trail guide is available for a fee from Redwood National and State Parks Headquarters. For a topographic map, ask the USGS for Orick.

Directions: From Eureka, drive north on U.S. 101 for 40 miles. About a mile before reaching Orick, stop at the Redwood Information Center, at the west side of the highway. Here you secure a permit number, which is actually a gate combination number you'll need. Drive north on U.S. 101 through Orick and continue 0.25 mile to Bald Hills Road. Turn right on Bald Hills Road. Look for the Tall Tree Access sign and drive seven miles to a locked gate, on the right. Open the gate using your permit/combi-nation number, drive through, close and lock the gate, and then drive six miles down the gravel road (C-Line Road) to the trailhead. No RVs or trailers are permitted.

Contact: Redwood National Park and California State Parks, Crescent City, 707/467-7335 or 707/465-5128, www.nps.gov/redw or www.parks.ca.gov.

16 JAMES IRVINE TRAIL
7.5 mi/3.0 hr   👣2 ⛰10

in Prairie Creek Redwoods State Park

Map 1.1, page 39

This is one of the best hikes in the Redwood Empire: You pass world-class redwoods, Douglas fir, western hemlock and Sitka spruce, all in the 300-foot range. We advise a loop hike (and then doing Fern Canyon as a separate loop hike with the Coastal Trail), but the trail can be extended to Fern Canyon and beyond to the Coastal Trail and huge expanses of wilder-ness beachfront. The trailhead is located at the far end of the small parking lot for the Prairie Creek Visitors Center. From the trailhead, it's a 0.6-mile hike to the junction with the James Irvine Trail. Within a few steps, you'll know you're walking in history. The James Irvine Trail contours in and out of lush ravines filled with big trees for 2.6 miles. In one ravine, old-growth 300-foot mammoths rise up with a can-opy that blots out the sky, while a sloping wall of ferns and sorrel create an understory that extends 150 yards to the canyon bottom.

To complete the loop, turn left on the

© TOM STIENSTRA

Coastal Trail

Clintonia Trail and hike 1.4 miles past two more groves to the Miners Ridge Trail. Follow the Miners Ridge Trail 2.7 miles back to the visitors center and enjoy the good, clean feeling that comes with hiking a few hours in a pristine landscape. The James Irvine Trail is easy enough that anyone can get a feel for ancient forest within a mile or so, yet long enough that the entire loop delivers a sense of discovery and awe with each grove.

Permits: No permits are required. There is a state park day-use fee of $8 per vehicle.

Maps: Trail maps are available at the park visitors center for a fee. For a topographic map, ask the USGS for Fern Canyon.

Directions: From Eureka, drive north on U.S. 101 for 41 miles to Orick. Continue north for five miles past Orick and exit at Newton B. Drury Scenic Parkway. Travel west on the parkway for one mile to the park entrance on left. Turn left and drive a short distance to the visitors center and trailhead on right.

Contact: Prairie Creek Redwoods State Park, Orick, 707/488-2039, www.parks.ca.gov.

17 COASTAL TRAIL LOOP (FERN CANYON/ OSSAGON SECTION)
8.0 mi/3.5 hr   🏃🏃2   ⛰10

in Prairie Creek Redwoods State Park south of Klamath

Map 1.1, page 39   BEST (

This is a great hike, once one of the best coastal hikes anywhere. There is a good chance of seeing Roosevelt elk (about a dozen roam at Prairie Creek Redwoods State Park at the meadow and often along Davison Road), Fern Canyon (see listing in this chapter), a dense forest (quiet and pretty), and a series of hidden waterfalls. In addition, there is a huge beach that's spotless—that's right, not even a single piece of litter.

From the parking area, start the trip by crossing a shallow stream; most of the year, the crossing consists of a few rock hops. If it's higher, that's good news, because it means the narrow waterfalls are running along the trail up ahead. Small temporary bridges are often provided from June through September.

Once you cross Home Creek, this trips starts off as a near-level walk. On the Coastal Trail, you walk roughly 2.5 miles north (waterfalls, wilderness beach, ocean views, coastal forest) to the West Ridge Trail. Then turn right and climb 1.8 miles (towering Sitka spruce, Douglas fir) to Friendship Ridge. Turn right again, where the trail contours south for three miles (old-growth redwoods) and then descend one mile into Fern Canyon (vertical fern walls, waterfall, stream) and then back to parking.

We often see elk on this hike. The ones to be wary of are not the big bulls with the giant racks, but the smaller females guarding their yearlings. On the Friendship Ridge Trail, on the last leg of a loop hike at dusk, we found ourselves staring into the bugged-out eyes of what appeared to be a 175-pound juvenile female, about 40 feet away. It then ran straight at us. To avoid it, we barreled over a fallen log on the right side of the trail and down about 10 feet into a fern-covered gulch, and then laughed like hell over what seemed a bizarre experience.

Turns out 10 other hikers had been driven off the trail that day by female elk with young. Rangers say late fall is the most common time when the females' protective maternal instincts give rise to hiker encounters.

User Groups: Hikers and mountain bikes. No dogs or horses. No wheelchair facilities.

Permits: No permits are required. There is a state park day-use fee of $8 per vehicle. Overnight parking is not permitted.

Maps: Trail maps are available at the park visitors center for a fee. For a topographic map, ask the USGS for Fern Canyon.

Directions: From Eureka, drive north on U.S. 101 for 41 miles to Orick. Continue north for 2.5 miles to Davison Road. Turn west on Davison Road and drive eight miles to Fern Canyon Trailhead. No trailers or RVs are permitted.

Contact: Prairie Creek Redwoods State Park, Orick, 707/465-7347, www.parks.ca.gov.

18 FERN CANYON LOOP TRAIL

0.8 mi/0.5 hr

in Prairie Creek Redwoods State Park south of Klamath

Map 1.1, page 39

The Fern Canyon Loop is one of the most inspiring short hikes in California. When you walk along the bottom of Fern Canyon, you'll be at the base of 50-foot-high walls covered with giant ferns. It's unique, dramatic, beautiful, and romantic. A small waterfall, which pours in through a chasm in the canyon wall and gushes into Home Creek, adds to the beauty. It is Home Creek, which runs through the bottom of the canyon, which can cause the one serious problem here for some day hikers. In winter this creek can flood, making the trail impassable. Although bridges are provided from June through September, hikers often have to hop back and forth across the stream in order to reach the back of the canyon. Wear waterproof footwear. At the end of the canyon, turn left and climb the trail to the canyon rim, and then continue through the forest back to the trailhead. A bonus is the adjacent beach to the north, which is wide open and spans for miles. It is also common to see Roosevelt elk on the drive in. This trail is well known by many, so it can get a lot of use during the summer months. Yet it is the rainy months, winter through early spring, when it glows and people are few.

User Groups: Hikers only. No dogs, horses, or mountain bikes. No wheelchair facilities.

Permits: No permits are required. There is a state park day-use fee of $8 per vehicle.

Maps: Trail maps are available at the park visitors center for a fee. For a topographic map, ask the USGS for Fern Canyon.

Directions: From Eureka, drive north on U.S. 101 for 41 miles to Orick. Continue north for 2.5 miles to Davison Road. Turn west on Davison Road and drive eight miles to Fern Canyon Trail. No trailers or RVs are permitted.

Contact: Prairie Creek Redwoods State Park, Orick, 707/465-7347, www.parks.ca.gov.

19 REDWOOD CREEK TRAIL

3.0 mi/1.25 hr

in Redwood National Park south of Klamath

Map 1.1, page 39 **BEST (**

With easy access, a flat trail, and a great name, this has become an extremely popular trail, with high numbers of tourists in summer.

The trail is routed along Redwood Creek, a pretty stream that flows out to sea near Orick. In the first mile, there are no giant redwoods, and tourists wonder what's wrong. The enlightened few will instead notice the diversity of the forest, with spruce, alder, and maples, and a few redwoods, as well as lush blackberries and fern beds in some areas. The appeal is the riparian watershed, rather than old-growth, along the stream. In summer, for hikers, there are two temporary bridges put in over Redwood Creek. The first is about 1.5 miles in. Some big redwoods are on the far side of the creek, though it is mission accomplished for most tourists at that point, and they turn around and head back.

There's a chance to see elk near the parking area. Stinging nettles are also abundant here, so stay on the trail. The stream attracts a diversity of wildlife, with ducks, herons, and hawks the most common sightings, and ruffed grouse and eagles are occasionally seen. Note that during the winter, the creek can flood the trail in some areas, making it impassable.

User Groups: Hikers only. No dogs, horses, or mountain bikes. No wheelchair facilities.

Permits: No permits are required. Parking and access are free.

Maps: A trail guide is available for a fee from Redwood National and State Parks Headquarters. For a topographic map, ask the USGS for Orick.

Directions: From Eureka, drive north on U.S. 101 for approximately 41 miles to Orick and then about 0.25 mile north of Orick to Bald Hills Road. Turn right on Bald Hills Road and drive 0.25 mile to the access road. Turn right and drive 0.5 mile to the parking area and trailhead.

Contact: Redwood National Park and California State Parks, Crescent City, 707/467-7335 or 707/465-5128, www.nps.gov/redw or www.parks.ca.gov.

20 SKUNK CABBAGE TRAIL
5.6 mi/3.0 hr   🏃2 ⛰9

in Redwood National Park south of Klamath

Map 1.1, page 39

Like love, it's all about timing on this trail. In the spring, when the skunk cabbage, fern, and redwood understory reaches peak growth, this trail is a sensational 10. In the fall and early winter, when the vegetation gets knocked down, well, more like a 7. Since you now know this, we rated it a 9, assuming you will go in peak season. That done, few places anywhere cast an aura such as that found here on the Skunk Cabbage Trail in Redwood National

Park. Every step is filled with the sense that this is an ancient place for old souls and youthful spirits. The trail is routed 2.8 miles amid a stunning forest understory out to a coastal bluff that towers over the Pacific Ocean. Hidden in the Redwood Empire, this rainforest looks like a jungle right out of *Jurassic Park,* or at least interior Kauai. You might even swear that a T. rex must be lurking amid the massive vegetation, spruces, and redwoods. Instead of dinosaurs, you might see black bears, endangered northern spotted owls, or marbled murrelets. We've seen spots where bears have chewed the bark on trees here, too.

From the parking area, the trail quickly enters a dense redwood and spruce forest, where the canopy is often completely enclosed by towering tree limbs. The trail meanders along a small watershed, Skunk Cabbage Creek; set beneath is a luxuriant forest floor filled with huge sword ferns, sorrel, and the giant skunk cabbage. Since you probably wondered, skunk cabbage is an herbaceous plant with massive stalks, a perennial that reaches its full growth from May through June. It is called skunk cabbage because of its strong scent when taken in, up close and personal; it's even considered by some to be rank. But the smell isn't a factor on this trip; rather, it's about how the lavish growth of the plant adds a sense of age-old mystery to this quiet jungle. The trail eventually winds its way through redwoods as you near the coastal bluffs. That's the spot for your trail lunch and turnaround.

User Groups: Hikers only. No mountain bikes, dogs, or horses. No wheelchair facilities.

Permits: Parking and access are free.

Maps: Trail maps are available at the park visitors center for a fee. For a topographic map, ask the USGS for Fern Canyon.

Directions: From Eureka, take U.S. 101 north for 41 miles to the signed exit for Redwood Information Center (if you reach Orick, you have gone one mile too far) and get in the left turn lane. Turn left and go 150 yards to the parking area. After obtaining trail and park materials at the center, turn left (north) on U.S.

101 and drive two miles (through Orick) to the trailhead entrance road on the left (comes up suddenly), signed Skunk Cabbage Trail. Turn left and drive 0.25 mile to a parking area.

Contact: Redwood National Park and California State Parks, Crescent City, 707/467-7335 or 707/465-5128, www.nps.gov/redw or www.parks.ca.gov.

21 RIM LOOP TRAIL
5.0 mi/2.5 hr 🚶1 ⛰8

at Patrick's Point State Park north of Eureka

Map 1.1, page 39   **BEST (**

For visitors to Patrick's Point State Park, this trail is the rite of passage. Problem is, there has been erosion on the trail section located between Agate Beach and Mussel Rock, and the rate of trail repair in 2015 was like the pace of a Caltrans project. When it's completed, well, great (!), one of the best easy hikes is yours. If not, the trail is blocked off at the closed section.

Patrick's Point is set on a coastal headland that is lush with ferns, spruce, and wildflowers. It's bordered by the Pacific, which means visitors can go tidepooling or whale-watching. That means with this trail, you can get the best of these two worlds. At times, the trail tunnels through thick vegetation, and at other times it opens up to sweeping ocean views. Along the way, several spur trails provide access to many features, including Mussel Rock, Wedding Rock, Agate Beach, Rocky Point, Patrick's Point, Abalone Point, and Palmer's Point. The views are sensational at every one of these spots. The elevation of the trail is 200 feet and is nearly level its entire length. Each of the spur trails thus drops 200 feet to the beach. The spur trails, while short (they add just 1.5 miles to the hike), will make this a two- to three-hour trip, since you won't want to just rush through it. In addition, Octopus Tree Trail offers a short hike that starts just across from the northern end of Rim Loop Trail. This bonus trail provides a chance to see many spruce trees with roots that have straddled downed logs, hence the name "Octopus Trees."

User Groups: Hikers only. No dogs, horses, or mountain bikes. The best wheelchair-accessible hiking trail in this park is from the visitors center to the Sumeg Village.

Permits: No permits are required. A state park day-use fee of $8 per vehicle is charged.

Maps: A park map and brochure are available for a fee from Patrick's Point State Park. For a topographic map, ask the USGS for Trinidad.

Directions: From Eureka, drive north on U.S. 101 for 22 miles to Trinidad and continue north for 5.5 miles to Patrick's Point Drive exit. Take that exit and at the stop sign, turn left, and drive 0.5 mile to the entrance station. Continue to the Agate Beach parking area.

Contact: Patrick's Point State Park, Trinidad, 707/677-3570, www.parks.ca.gov.

22 TSURAI LOOP
1.5 mi/1.0 hr 🚶2 ⛰9

on Trinidad Head on the Humboldt coast north of Eureka

Map 1.1, page 39

The Tsurai Loop is a great, easy walk with coastal vistas, unique terrain, and a nearby restaurant. The terrain includes the 300-foot miniature mountain at Trinidad Head, the pretty beachfront to the north of the Trinidad Head area, and the Trinidad Pier. The trip is best done in a counterclockwise loop. It starts by hiking up for beautiful views to the north, eventually reaching this perfectly situated rock lookout of the ocean. On clear days in spring and early summer it can be an ideal spot to watch for the puff-of-smoke spouts on the ocean surface made by migrating whales. The trail circles the mountain and then climbs to the top, a flat summit, where the views are only fair. The views are actually a lot better just 50 yards to the south, looking south toward Eureka and Humboldt Bay. As you head back down, you get more views of the rocky Trinidad Harbor and coast. The restaurant? It's called

Seascape, and you can get a crab or shrimp omelet (always fresh crab, in season) for breakfast that'll have your mouth watering every time you start driving north of Eureka on U.S. 101. If there's a wait at the restaurant, don't hesitate to line up anyway.

User Groups: Hikers and dogs. Mountain bikes permitted but not recommended. No horses. No wheelchair facilities.

Permits: No permits are required. Parking and access are free.

Maps: For a topographic map, ask the USGS for Trinidad.

Directions: From Eureka, drive north on U.S. 101 for 28 miles to Trinidad. Take the Trinidad exit, turn left at the stop sign, and drive under the U.S. 101 overpass to Main Street. Continue on Main Street to Trinity Street. Turn left and drive a short distance to Edwards Street. Turn right on Edwards Street and drive to the parking area at the foot of the harbor.

Contact: Seascape Restaurant, Trinidad Pier, 707/677-3762, www.seascape-trinidad.com.

23 ARCATA MARSH TRAIL
2-4.5 mi/1-2.0 hr   🏃1 ⛰8

in Arcata Marsh and Wildlife Sanctuary on the northern edge of Humboldt Bay

Map 1.2, page 40   **BEST (**

The 307-acre Arcata Marsh is a great birdwatching area, a mosaic of ponds, marshes, and wetlands that border Arcata Bay. It's best explored by walking the loop. It is set on a levee above the marsh; the trail is short, flat, and routed in a loop for the best viewing possibilities. The loop is two miles, but it can be extended on other trails on levees for a longer trip. Several wooden photography blinds are available on the route, where you can hide yourself to view the ponds up close and take pictures of the birds. The setting is unique, with the coast, saltwater bay, brackish-water marsh, pond, foothills, and streams all nearby. This diversity means that an outstanding variety of species—more than 250 have been

verified—are attracted to the area. Sightings can include belted kingfishers, ospreys, peregrine falcons, black phoebes, and song and savannah sparrows. In other words, birds from nearly all habitats are represented. Guided bird walks are common on Saturday mornings. One side note is that many locals eat lunch at the parking area, and just like Pavlov's dog, tons of birds show up in the parking lot daily at noon for handouts. The rangers request that you don't feed the birds (but everybody does). The Arcata Marsh Interpretive Center is open daily and has free maps, literature, and a posted list of recent bird sightings.

User Groups: Hikers, dogs, and mountain bikes. No horses.

Permits: No permits are required. Parking and access are free.

Maps: For a free, detailed trail map, contact the City of Arcata and ask for the Marsh and Wildlife Trail map. For a topographic map, ask the USGS for Arcata South.

Directions: From Eureka, drive north on U.S. 101 for five miles to Arcata and the Samoa Boulevard exit. Take that exit and turn west onto Samoa Boulevard; drive to I Street. Turn left (south) on I Street and continue to G Street, then continue straight on South I Street to a sharp right turn. Turn right and continue (around Hauser Marsh to your left) to parking and a trailhead (Arcata Bay to the west, Klopp Lake to your east).

Contact: Arcata Marsh Interpretive Center, Friends of Arcata Marsh, 707/826-2359, www.arcatamarshfriends.org.

24 NATURE TRAIL
2.0 mi/1.0 hr   🏃1 ⛰8

in Arcata Community Forest in the Arcata foothills

Map 1.2, page 40

Arcata Community Forest provides a respite for students at nearby Humboldt State and for locals who want to wander amid a beautiful second-growth forest. A network of 18 trails covers about 10 miles and the Redwood Loop connects several of them. For newcomers a map is an absolute necessity. Mountain bikes are prohibited at about 50 percent of the trails in the forest, although these rules are occasionally broken. (On weekends, kamikaze mountain bikers tearing downhill can turn this hike into an extremely unpleasant experience.)

Start this trip at Redwood Lodge (mountain bikes not allowed) and take the Nature Trail. The trail will take you by many huge stumps, a small creek, and a forest of redwoods and spruce. At one point, you will see the awesome Octopus Tree, where the roots of a Sitka spruce have grown over the top and sides of a giant stump. At the junction of two trails, turn left twice for an easy and pretty trip. Trips in the Arcata forest can be expanded to include elevation gains and losses of 1,200 feet.

User Groups: Hikers, dogs, and horses. No mountain bikes. Certain sections of the trail are off-limits to horses and mountain bikes; check the trail map for details. No wheelchair facilities.

Permits: No permits are required. Parking and access are free.

Maps: For a free, detailed trail map, contact the City of Arcata and ask for the Community Forest Trail map. A free mountain bike trail map is also available. For topographic maps, ask the USGS for Arcata North and Arcata South.

Directions: From Eureka, drive north on U.S. 101 to Arcata and the 14th Street/Humboldt University exit. Take that exit to 14th Street. Turn right on 14th and drive a short distance to Union Street. Turn right on Union and drive a short distance to 11th Street. Turn left on 11th and drive a short distance to Bayview. Turn left on Bayview and drive (road curves to the right, becomes East Peak Road) to Redwood Lodge and trailhead.

Note: No mountain bikes are permitted. Bikers and equestrians should use the Meadow trailhead, located where 14th Street enters the park.

Contact: City of Arcata, Department of Parks, 707/822-7091, www.cityofarcata.org/rec.

25 LYTEL RIDGE/ EUCALYPTUS TRAIL

1.5 mi/1.0 hr

in Russ City Park in Ferndale south of Eureka

Map 1.2, page 40

Russ City Park is like an island wilderness. It is located at the southern edge of Ferndale, covers just 105 acres, and yet retains its primitive state for wildlife, birds, and hikers. The best trip is the short 350-foot climb up Lytel Ridge. You climb up Lytel Ridge, where you pass Francis Creek, with sections routed through heavy fern beds and large firs, and offering views of a small pond and the Eel River watershed and floodplain. The trip is relatively short and easy enough, yet the terrain is steep in spots, and heavy fog or rain can make it slippery. It feels quiet and secluded, and gets overlooked by out-of-towners.

User Groups: Hikers and dogs. No horses or mountain bikes. No wheelchair facilities.

Permits: No permits are required. Parking and access are free.

Maps: A free map and brochure can be obtained by contacting the City of Ferndale. For a topographic map, ask the USGS for Ferndale.

Directions: From U.S. 101, drive to the exit for Ferndale/Highway 211 (13 miles south of Eureka). Take that exit and continue to Highway 211, turn right and drive (over the Eel River Bridge) four miles to Ferndale and Main Street. Continue on Main Street to Ocean Street. Turn left on Ocean Street and drive 0.75 mile to a gravel parking area and trailhead on the right (where Ocean Street turns into Bluff Street).

Contact: Ferndale Chamber of Commerce, 707/786-4477, www.victorianferndale.com.

26 RATHERT GROVE/ MEMORIAL TRAIL LOOP

1.8 mi/1.0 hr   🚶1 ⛰10

at Grizzly Creek Redwoods State Park near Bridgeville

Map 1.2, page 40

This pretty hike is an easy walk through the redwoods, located on the southern side of the Van Duzen River. Most visitors instead walk to two redwood groves from a trailhead at the visitors center. On the north side of the Van Duzen, you have a chance to have the world to yourself in Rathert Grove. The trailhead is at the bridge at the Van Duzen River, just upstream from where Grizzly Creek enters the Van Duzen. The trail then is routed, about a 10-minute walk, to a junction with the Memorial Trail Loop. Turn right. The trail then circles the beautiful Rathert Grove, and then reaches a junction on the right with the Loop Trail; this is a short spur/circle at the Harriet Hunt Bard Grove. It then loops back to the Memorial Trail Loop, and you walk a short distance back to the bridge.

The Rathert Grove is one of seven relatively small yet pristine old-growth redwood groves protected in this park. There is nothing difficult about this or the other hikes in the park. In fact, stairs are provided in many of the few short, steeper spots. What makes this hike special is that on a weekday, you can have an entire old-growth redwood grove all to yourself. Where else can you do that? Grizzly Creek Redwoods State Park is one of the most overlooked redwood state parks in California, receiving fewer than 25,000 visitors per year—and most of those in July and August. It is often overlooked because it is not located on U.S. 101, but rather Highway 36, a curvy two-laner that provides access to some of the state's most remote areas. Many discover the park by accident, usually heading up to fish, canoe, or kayak the Van Duzen River; the state park provides an excellent river access point, as well as a campground.

User Groups: Hikers only. No dogs, horses, or mountain bikes are permitted. Some facilities are wheelchair-accessible, but there is no trail access for wheelchairs.

Permits: No permits are required. A fee of $8 per vehicle is charged for parking.

Maps: For a free brochure and map, contact Grizzly Creek Redwoods. For a topographic map, ask the USGS for Redcrest Quad.

Directions: From Eureka, drive south on U.S. 101 to the junction of Highway 36 at Alton. Turn east on Highway 36 and drive 17.2 miles to the park entrance, on the right.

Contact: Grizzly Creek Redwoods State Park, 707/777-3683, www.parks.ca.gov.

27 FIVE ALLENS TRAIL

2.2 mi/1.5 hr   🚶3 ⛰8

in Humboldt Redwoods State Park south of Eureka

Map 1.2, page 40

Most of the trails into beautiful redwood groves are on flats near watersheds. The Five Allens Trail is just the opposite: up, up, and up it goes, where you climb 800 feet in 1.2 miles. The payoff is a pretty redwood grove, the Allens Grove, gorgeous and quiet, just the reason most visitors venture to the Redwood Empire. You'll see a sign at the grove that says "The Five Allens," and it refers to five redwood trees. From the trailhead near the Eel River, walk under the highway and then start the climb. As it rises up, the trail passes through a forest of mixed conifers; the tree canopy provides needed shade in the summer. A bridged creek can be very pretty. After a good climb, you'll reach a fork. Bear left for the Allens Grove. You won't see the huge mammoth-sized redwoods here, but it is a quiet, peaceful spot that most tourists from out of state never see. That's why it's in the book.

User Groups: Hikers only. No dogs, horses, or mountain bikes. No wheelchair facilities.

Permits: No permits are required. The park entry fee is $8 at the main entrance.

Maps: A map can be obtained for a fee from

Humboldt Redwoods State Park. For a topographic map, ask the USGS for Weott.

Directions: From Eureka, drive south on U.S. 101 to the Redcrest exit. Take that exit and turn left, drive under the overpass, and continue a short distance to Avenue of the Giants. Turn right on Avenue of the Giants and drive south three miles (past High Rock Conservation Camp) to the Maria McKean Allen marker at pullout for trailhead parking. Cross through the pedestrian tunnel for U.S. 101.

For an alternate route from Garberville, drive north on U.S. 101 to the Founders Tree/Rockefeller Forest exit. Take that exit (north), turn right, and drive about 200 yards to Avenue of the Giants. Turn left on Avenue of the Giants, cross over the South Fork Eel River, and then bear right at the intersection in order to stay on Avenue of the Giants. Drive a short distance to the Five Allens trailhead parking.

Contact: Humboldt Redwoods State Park, Weott, 707/946-2409, www.parks.ca.gov.

28 FOUNDERS GROVE NATURE TRAIL

0.4 mi/0.3 hr 🥾1 ⛰8

in Humboldt Redwoods State Park south of Eureka

Map 1.2, page 40

The paradox of the tourist public makes this one of the highest visited trails in the Redwood Empire. As the tourists drive U.S. 101, they'll see the off-ramp for the Avenue of the Giants, and then, in the desire for a short walk among the giant redwoods, see the parking lot and trailhead, like, right there, 100 yards away. What you get is an old-growth grove with the classic sword fern-based understory on a flat route that makes for a short, easy walk. At the far end of the loop, you can extend the walk on a 0.2-mile link to the 0.5-mile Mahan Loop Trail. It's very beautiful and the photos are classics. Problem is, you see, it's too close to the highway. You can often hear traffic. We've been here in the winter, though, and it's like a

different planet: fewer people, little noise, moist and pristine. Truth is, if you want big trees—without the tourists—go instead to the next hike, just a few minutes away, the Bull Creek Trail North.

User Groups: Hikers only. There is wheelchair access, although the trail is a bit uneven. No dogs, horses, or mountain bikes.

Permits: No permits are required. There is a fee of $8 per vehicle.

Maps: A map is available for a fee from Humboldt Redwoods State Park. For a topographic map, ask the USGS for Weott.

Directions: From Garberville, drive north on U.S. 101 about 20 miles to the Founder Tree/Rockefeller Forest exit. Take that exit and drive a short distance to Avenue of the Giants. Drive 100 yards (cross Avenue of the Giants) to the Founders Grove Parking Area/Trailhead (well signed).

Contact: Humboldt Redwoods State Park, Weott, 707/946-2409, www.parks.ca.gov.

29 BULL CREEK TRAIL NORTH

7.4 mi/4.0 hr 🥾2 ⛰10

in Humboldt Redwoods State Park south of Eureka

Map 1.2, page 40 **BEST (**

This trail provides a walk amid the largest grove of old-growth redwood trees in the world. It's easy walking, with maybe a 200-foot rise, that's all. You are amid sorrel, sword ferns, and the redwoods with massive bases that rise up and seem to poke holes in the sky. Start at the trailhead at Bull Creek Flats (signed Lower Bull Creek Flats Trail), a short walk to the Federation Grove). The trail ventures west along Bull Creek, an easy grade as you hike upstream. All the while you're surrounded by forest, both redwoods and firs in a variety of mixes. In summer, there is a seasonal bridge at the Big Tree Area. A little over 3.5 miles in, you'll arrive at the Big Tree Area. There are many redwoods here that range from 5 to 10 feet in diameter and 30 to 40 feet around.

On-the-spot notes: The park installs summer bridges across Bull Creek in the Big Trees Area, mid-May to early October. Also: For years, a big attraction was the Flat Iron Tree, a huge leaning redwood that grew in strange dimensions in order to support itself. Well, it's not leaning anymore, because it fell down and went boom. On the broad side, the Flat Iron Tree measures more than 15 feet. An option: After the trail passes the Big Tree Area, it's routed to the mouth of Albee Creek and ends at Mattole Road. The trailhead here (at Mattole Road) provides a shorter hike of about a mile to the seasonal bridge at the Big Tree Area.

User Groups: Hikers only. No dogs, horses, or mountain bikes. No wheelchair facilities.

Permits: No permits are required. The park entry fee is $8 at the main entrance.

Maps: A map is available for a fee from Humboldt Redwoods State Park. For a topographic map, ask the USGS for Weott.

Directions: From Garberville, drive north on U.S. 101 about 20 miles to the Founder Tree/Rockefeller Forest exit. Take that exit and turn left and drive a short distance to Avenue of the Giants. Turn left and drive a short distance to Mattole Road (the sign will say Rockefeller Forest/Honeydew, not Mattole Road). Turn left and drive 1.3 miles to the Lower Bull Creek Flats trailhead.

Contact: Humboldt Redwoods State Park, Weott, 707/946-2409, www.parks.ca.gov.

30 WILLIAMS GROVE TRAIL
0.5 mi/20.5 hr   🏃1 ⛰️8

in Humboldt Redwoods State Park south of Eureka

Map 1.2, page 40

The Williams Grove is one of Humboldt's protected groves of old-growth redwoods. The launch point to enjoy this is the Williams Grove Day Use Area, which has a picnic area with barbecue grills along with restrooms. (It used

to be free, but easy access and the new mission of California's Department of Parks and Recreation means there is now an $8 fee.) We've always liked to start instead at the trailhead at the Hidden Springs Campground, an easy 1.75-mile walk (one-way). The camp is set in forest just above a big bend in the South Fork Eel River. The trailhead is located on the southwest side of the camp. The trail starts out nearly flat, then turns right and parallels the highway. It's easy walking all the way, amid redwoods both young and old. Then the trail crosses under the highway and down the hill to Williams Grove. If you camp at Hidden Springs, a short trail is also available that is routed a short distance to the Eel River and Hidden Springs Beach.

User Groups: Hikers only. No dogs, horses, or mountain bikes. No wheelchair facilities.

Permits: No permits are required. The park entry fee is $8 at the main entrance.

Maps: A map is available for a fee from Humboldt Redwoods State Park. For topographic maps, ask the USGS for Weott and Myers Flat.

Directions: From Garberville on U.S. 101, drive north for 16.4 miles to the exit for Myers Flat. Take that exit 0.2 mile to Avenue of the Giants. Turn right and drive 1.2 miles to Williams Grove parking area on the left. Note: For Hidden Springs Campground (open only during the summer), take the same exit. At Avenue of the Giants, instead turn left and drive 0.8 mile the campground and trailhead.

Contact: Humboldt Redwoods State Park, Weott, 707/946-2409, www.parks.ca.gov.

31 LOST COAST TRAIL/ MATTOLE TRAILHEAD
24.6 mi one-way/3 days   🏃2 ⛰️10

on the Humboldt coast south of Eureka in King Range National Conservation Area

Map 1.2, page 40   BEST (

For many, this is considered one of the greatest treks on the Pacific Coast. It spans 25 miles on some of the coast's most remote and beautiful landscapes and beaches. Always do the trip one-way, with a second shuttle car, north-to-south.

It's called the Lost Coast because of the isolation of the area, which is shielded on all sides by natural boundaries. The route is set on bluffs and beaches from the mouth of the Mattole River south to Shelter Cove. With two vehicles, one parked at each end of the trail, or a shuttle service, hikers can then hike the trail one-way. This hike is best done from north to south. That way the winds out of the north will be at your back, not in your face. Firm-fitting waterproof boots with good, gripping soles are a necessity. They should be firm fitting because some of the walking is in soft sand, waterproof because there are several small creek crossings, and good gripping because some scrambling over wet boulders is required. The trail surface, well, it often isn't much of a trail at all.

Bring a tide book. At several spots, you can only pass during low tides. In wet weather, landslides often cover the beach between Shipman and Buck Creeks. At times they are minor, but at other times, the slides can be significant. High tides and/or large swells wash against the base of these slides. During high tides and/or large swells, to pass through this landslide zone may be hazardous. Consult your tide book, keep an eye on ocean conditions, and plan to pass through this area at as low a tide as possible, particularly if ocean swells are large. Be cautious: This is an extremely isolated area. In many parts, there is no trail, and there is a lot of boulder hopping, where it is possible to twist an ankle. In winter after heavy rain, several streams can be impassable.

For a first visit and a great day hike, take the abandoned jeep trail from the campground at Lighthouse Road and head south three miles to the Punta Gorda Lighthouse. You'll get a glimpse of the greatness here, and you'll probably get the inspiration to continue on Lost Coast Trail, one of California's greatest weekend trips.

User Groups: Hikers, dogs, horses, and mountain bikes. No wheelchair facilities.

Permits: Day-use permits are required for organized groups only. A campfire permit (free) is required for overnight use. Parking and access are free.

Maps: A detailed trail map is available for a fee, and a free map and brochure can be obtained from the Bureau of Land Management. Specify the King Range Conservation Area map. For topographic maps, ask the USGS for Petrolia, Cooskie Creek, Shubrick Peak, and Shelter Cove.

Directions: From U.S. 101 in Garberville, drive north to the South Fork-Honeydew exit. Take that exit, drive west on Bull Creek Road, and continue 23 miles to Honeydew and Mattole Road. Turn right on Mattole Road and drive 14 miles (toward Petrolia). At the second bridge over the Mattole Road (one mile before Petrolia), turn left on Lighthouse Road. Drive west on Lighthouse Road to its end. The trailhead is just past Mattole Campground.

Shuttle: Lost Coast Trail Transport Service, 707/986-9909, www.lostcoasttrail.com; Lost Coast Shuttle, (707) 986-7437, www.lostcoastshuttle.com.

Contact: King Range National Conservation Area, 707/986-5400; Bureau of Land Management, Arcata Field Office, Arcata, 707/825-2300, www.ca.blm.gov; Sinkyone Wilderness State Park, 707/986-7711, www.parks.ca.gov.

32 KING CREST TRAIL
11.6 mi/1 day 　　　　🏃3 10

in King Range National Conservation Area south of Eureka

Map 1.2, page 40

King's Peak is one of the most prized destinations in the King Range. At 4,087 feet it's the highest point on the Northern California coast, and from it you get a view that can make you feel that you're perched on top of the world. The ocean seems to stretch on forever to the west, and on a perfect day you can make out the top of Mount Lassen behind the ridgeline of the Yolla Bolly Wilderness, to the east.

Reaching King's Peak requires a 5.8-mile hike from the Northside Peak trailhead on Smith-Etter Road. In the process, you climb about 800 feet. Making the trip on a clear day is an absolute necessity, since the climb through the fire zone is buffered by the reward of the sweeping views. Trail signs are very poor, and water supplies at trail camps are from dubious sources, so it's also essential to have a good map and a double-canteen water supply.

The entire King Crest Trail extends 10 miles one-way, starting from the trailhead listed in this hike to Saddle Mountain trailhead; then it descends four miles to the beach. That provides the alternative of a one-way overnight trip with a shuttle vehicle at the end of the trail. Note that the portion that heads down to the beach is called Buck Creek Trail and that it is very steep, one the steepest trails in California, with portions difficult to follow—this is considered an advanced hike; for some hikers, orienteering with a map and compass may be required.

User Groups: Hikers, dogs, horses, and mountain bikes. No wheelchair facilities.

Permits: A campfire permit (free) is required for overnight use. Parking and access are free.

Maps: A detailed trail map is available for a fee, and a free map and brochure can be obtained from the Bureau of Land Management; ask for the King Range Conservation Area map. For a topographic map, ask the USGS for Shubrick Peak.

Directions: On U.S. 101, drive to the South Fork-Honeydew exit (just north of Garberville). Take that exit to Wilder Ridge Road and turn southwest. Drive one mile to Smith-Etter Road and turn west. Drive six miles to the trailhead (this is a primitive, four-wheel-drive road and is closed from November 1 to March 31).

Contact: King Range National Conservation Area, 707/986-5400; Bureau of Land Management, Arcata Field Office, Arcata, 707/825-2300, www.ca.blm.gov.

33 SPANISH RIDGE TRAIL
9.6 mi/1 day   🏃3 ⛺8

in King Range National Conservation Area south of Eureka

Map 1.2, page 40

In just a few miles, you can gain access to some of the most remote sections of the California coast. But there's a price (and we'll get to that). The pay-offs are excellent views, a descent along a grassy ridge, and then down to a remote beach you'll have all to yourself. One big problem: You descend 2,400 feet to the beach. That means you have to climb 2,400 feet to get back to your car.

From the Spanish Ridge trailhead, hike 1.8 miles along Cooskie Creek Trail and climb an easy 300 feet before reaching the junction with Spanish Ridge Trail. You then descend 2,400 feet in three miles en route to the coast. Know what that means? Right. Unless you can get a helicopter ride back, you're looking at some serious grunt work.

The King Range is very rugged, primitive, and isolated. Thanks to that bumpy access road and the climb on the return trip, it's rare to see other people here. And because there are no water sources along this trail, each hiker should carry two canteens of water. This trail is for experienced hikers only, and as with several of the hikes in the King Range, you should bring a map and a compass.

User Groups: Hikers, dogs, mountain bikes, and horses. No wheelchair facilities.

Permits: A campfire permit (free) is required for overnight use. Parking and access are free.

Maps: A detailed trail map is available for a fee, and a free map and brochure can be obtained from the Bureau of Land Management; ask for the King Range Conservation Area map. For topographic maps, ask the USGS for Cooskie Creek and Shubrick Peak.

Directions: On U.S. 101, drive to the South Fork-Honeydew exit (just north of Garberville). Take that exit to Wilder Ridge Road and turn southwest. Drive one mile to Smith-Etter Road and turn west. Drive 10 miles (this is a primitive, four-wheel-drive road and is closed from November 1 to March 31) to Telegraph Ridge Road. Turn northwest on Telegraph Ridge Road and drive eight miles to the trailhead gate. In summer, continue driving two miles to the trailhead. When the gate is locked, the trailhead is accessible only by a two-mile walk.

Contact: King Range National Conservation Area, 707/986-5400; Bureau of Land Management, Arcata Field Office, Arcata, 707/825-2300, www.ca.blm.gov.

34 LOOKOUT POINT LOOP TRAIL
2.6 mi/1.5 hr

in Richardson Grove State Park south of Garberville

Map 1.2, page 40

Big woods. Big water. That's what Lookout Point Loop Trail supplies, with a tour through giant redwoods culminating at the canyon rim over the South Fork Eel River. Giant redwoods approaching 300 feet tall and estimated to be 1,000 years old are the highlight of Richardson Grove, while younger redwoods, firs, and tanoaks fill out the forest. Park at the visitors center. Start by walking through the old-growth redwoods for the first half mile. The trail crosses the road at the Madrone Campground Loop. Near the restroom, there is a signed trailhead for Lookpoint. The trail then rises through hardwoods (hence the name Madrone) about 300 feet over 0.4 mile to a 0.1-mile spur for Lookout Point. You get an excellent view of the South Fork. You can also see across the river to the Oak Flat Campground. To return, the trail loops back in a short circle over 0.3 mile to the trailhead sign.

As a free-flowing river, the South Fork Eel River can seem like a small trickle in late summer or a howling torrent during peak flows in winter. When looking down from Lookout Point during summer, it may seem hard to imagine how high the Eel has risen in high-water years. In 1955, 1963, 1986, 1997, and 1998, the river actually flooded its banks and wiped out several campgrounds in the state park. This is an easy and popular hike, both for daytime park visitors and for overnighters at Madrone Campground.

User Groups: Hikers only. No dogs, horses, or mountain bikes. No wheelchair facilities.

Permits: No permits are required. A state park entrance fee of $8 is charged per vehicle.

Maps: For a trail guide and brochure (free), write Richardson Grove State Park. For a topographic map, ask the USGS for Garberville.

Directions: From Santa Rosa, drive north on U.S. 101 to Leggett. Continue north on U.S. 101 about 17 miles to the park entrance, on the west side of the highway. Park at the visitors center (for campers, Madrone Campground; trailhead near restroom).

Contact: Richardson Grove State Park, Garberville, 707/247-3318, www.parks.ca.gov.

35 WOODLANDS LOOP TRAIL
1.6 mi/1.0 hr

in Richardson Grove State Park south of Garberville

Map 1.2, page 40

You want easy? You get easy. You want forest? You get forest. You want a campground trailhead? You get a campground trailhead. The Woodlands Loop, an easy, pretty trail that starts at the Huckleberry Campground, does all that and more. At the campground, the trailhead is near the ranger station. The trail crosses North Creek and then goes through both redwoods and tanoaks that are dense at times. It also includes a gentle uphill portion, rising about 250 feet. At the visitors center, get the brochure for the self-guided Quest Guide, which explains the flora you'll see along the way.

Note that this trail and camp are set on the west side of U.S. 101, and that the South Fork Eel River is on the east side of the highway.

There's no direct river access from this trail or the nearby campground.

User Groups: Hikers only. No dogs, horses, or mountain bikes. No wheelchair facilities.

Permits: No permits are required. A fee of $6 per vehicle is charged for parking.

Maps: For a trail guide and brochure (free), contact Richardson Grove State Park. For a topographic map, ask the USGS for Garberville.

Directions: From Santa Rosa, drive north on U.S. 101 to Leggett. Continue north on U.S. 101 about 17 miles to the park entrance, on the west side of the highway. The trailhead is accessible from the parking lot just inside the entrance.

Contact: Richardson Grove State Park, Garberville, 707/247-3318, www.parks.ca.gov.

36 TOUMEY GROVE TRAIL
3.8 mi/2.75 hr

in Richardson Grove State Park south of Garberville

Map 1.2, page 40

The Toumey Trail is one of Richardson Grove State Park's feature summer hikes. The hits just keep on coming. The trailhead is located between campsite Nos. 123 and 126 at Oak Flat Campground. The trail crosses the South Fork Eel River, where you cross on a summer bridge, and then enters the redwoods; take your time and enjoy the surroundings. You are routed through the redwoods. The trail climbs 300 feet, rising quickly to Panorama Point, with excellent views of the Eel River Canyon and Richardson Grove redwoods. It then is routed down, via a few switchbacks, to Kauffman Springs, and then ventures to a swimming hole on the South Fork Eel.

Note: This trail can be accessed only in the summer months.

User Groups: Hikers only. No dogs, horses, or mountain bikes. No wheelchair facilities.

Permits: No permits are required. A fee of $8 per vehicle is charged for parking.

Maps: For a trail guide and brochure (free), contact Richardson Grove State Park. For a topographic map, ask the USGS for Garberville.

Directions: From Santa Rosa, drive north on U.S. 101 to Leggett. Continue north on U.S. 101 about 17 miles to the park entrance, on the west side of the highway. Follow the signs to Oak Flat Campground. The trailhead is located between sites 123 and 126.

Contact: Richardson Grove State Park, Garberville, 707/247-3318, www.parks.ca.gov.

SHASTA AND TRINITY

At 14,179 feet, Mount Shasta rises like a diamond in a field of coal. Its sphere of influence spans a radius of 125 miles, and its shadow is felt everywhere in the region. This area has much to offer with giant Shasta Lake, the Sacramento River above and below the lake, the McCloud River, and the wonderful Trinity Divide with its dozens of pretty backcountry lakes and several wilderness areas. This is one of the best regions anywhere for outdoor adventures set near quiet wilderness. The most popular destinations are Shasta Lake, the Trinity Alps and their surrounding lakes and streams, Marble Mountain Wilderness, and the Klamath Mountains.

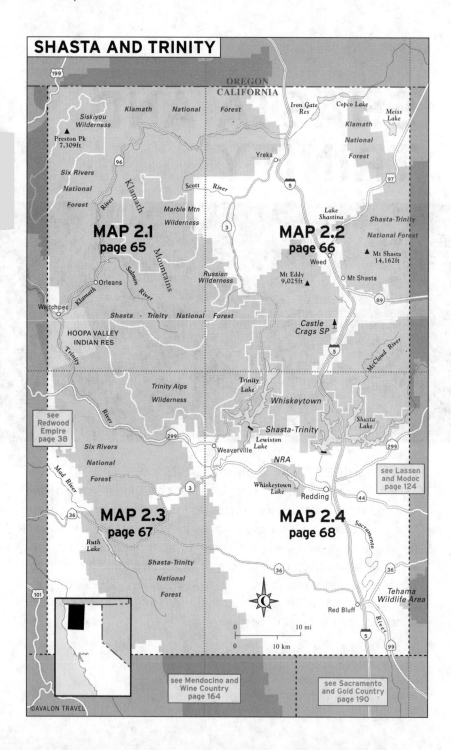

SHASTA AND TRINITY

OREGON
CALIFORNIA

Klamath National Forest

Siskiyou Wilderness

▲ Preston Pk 7,309ft

Iron Gate Res

Copco Lake

Meiss Lake

Klamath National Forest

Six Rivers National Forest

Scott River

Yreka

Marble Mtn Wilderness

Lake Shastina

Shasta-Trinity National Forest

MAP 2.1
page 65

Orleans

Salmon River

Russian Wilderness

Weed

Mt Eddy 9,025ft ▲

▲ Mt Shasta 14,162ft

○ Mt Shasta

MAP 2.2
page 66

Wejtchpec

Shasta - Trinity National Forest

HOOPA VALLEY INDIAN RES

Castle Crags SP

McCloud River

Trinity

Trinity Alps Wilderness

Trinity Lake

Whiskeytown

Shasta Lake

see Redwood Empire page 38

Mad River

Six Rivers National Forest

River

Shasta-Trinity

Lewiston Lake

Weaverville

NRA

see Lassen and Modoc page 124

MAP 2.3
page 67

Ruth Lake

Whiskeytown Lake

Redding

Sacramento

MAP 2.4
page 68

Shasta-Trinity National Forest

Tehama Wildlife Area

Red Bluff

0   10 mi

0   10 km

©AVALON TRAVEL

see Mendocino and Wine Country page 164

see Sacramento and Gold Country page 190

Map 2.1

Sites 1-21
Pages 69-83

Map 2.2

Sites 22-57
Pages 84-110

Map 2.3

Sites 58-64
Pages 111-115

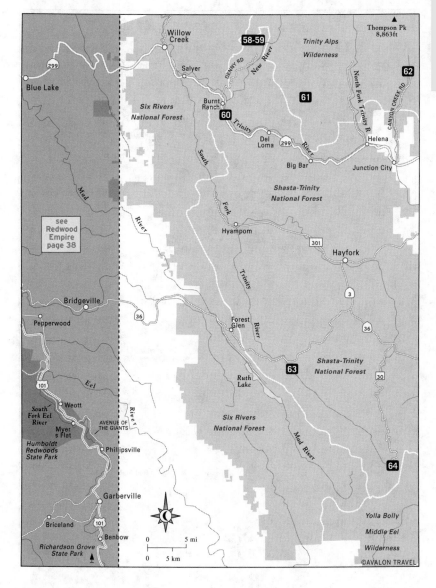

Map 2.4

Sites 65-76
Pages 115-122

1 YOUNGS VALLEY TRAIL
6.0 mi/1 day   🥾2 ⛰8

in the Siskiyou Wilderness east of Crescent City

Map 2.1, page 65

The 6.5-mile trip from Youngs Valley down Clear Creek to Youngs Meadow is a beautiful and rewarding trip. Youngs Meadow, set at an elevation of 4,500 feet on the western slope of Preston Peak, is very pretty and makes an excellent picnic area and campsite.

The drive to the trailhead is long and circuitous. It's long just to get to U.S. 199, and from there, you face more than an hour on forest roads. The trailhead is located near Sanger Lake, and some camp there the first night in. You start the trip by hiking on a decommissioned Forest Service road; it climbs 0.8 mile to a ridge and the boundary for the Siskiyou Wilderness. It turns to trail, then you descend 600 feet over two miles into Youngs Valley and to Clear Creek. Most continue along Clear Creek until they find a site for a trail lunch, and then head back. But listen up, because from here, the ambitious can take this trip farther—much farther. The Youngs Valley Trail is a great first leg of a multiday trip, ultimately where you head either down Clear Creek to Wilderness Falls, which is a very pretty setting (see the listing in this chapter), or to Rattlesnake Meadows on the slopes of Preston Peak, which requires a short but rugged climb.

User Groups: Hikers, dogs, and horses. No mountain bikes. No wheelchair facilities.

Permits: No permits are required. A campfire permit (free) is required for overnight use. Parking and access are free.

Maps: For a map, ask the U.S. Forest Service for Klamath National Forest. For a topographic map, ask the USGS for Devils Punchbowl.

Directions: From Crescent City, drive north on U.S. 101 for three miles to U.S. 199. Bear right (east) on U.S. 199 and drive 32 miles to Forest Road 18N07. Turn right and drive five miles to a signed junction for Forest Road 18N07. Continue on Forest Road 18N07 for 10 miles (slow, twisty) toward Sanger Lake. Just before Sanger Lake, bear right on Forest Road 4803 (signed Youngs Valley Trail) and drive one mile to the end of the road and the trailhead.

Contact: Smith River National Recreation Area, Gasquet, 707/457-3131, www.fs.usda.gov/srnf; Klamath National Forest, Happy Camp-Oak Knoll Ranger District, Happy Camp, 530/493-2243, www.fs.usda.gov/klamath.

2 PRESTON PEAK
19.0 mi/2 days   🥾5 ⛰10

in the Siskiyou Wilderness east of Crescent City

Map 2.1, page 65

Preston Peak is the awesome 7,309-foot monolith that rises above forest for miles in all directions. It has the qualities of a much larger mountain, and at the peak, it feels like you're on top of the world. But a word of caution: Only mountaineers need sign up for this trip. The last mile to reach the summit of Preston Peak is steep, rough, and primitive; it can be scary and dangerous for newcomers to mountaineering. With no marked trail on top, hikers must have the ability to scramble cross-country and recognize any dangerous spots—and then avoid them. That done, you'll gain the top. It's by far the highest spot in the region, with fantastic surrounding views. Even Mount Shasta, way off to the southeast, comes clearly into view, along with the famous peaks in the Trinity Alps and Marble Mountain Wilderness.

The best route to climb Preston Peak is to hike Youngs Valley Trail (see details about Youngs Valley Trail in this chapter) to Youngs Meadow (an easy five miles). Then head down the Clear Creek Trail (another easy mile) to a somewhat faint junction with the Rattlesnake Meadow Trail. Turn left on Rattlesnake Meadow Trail, where you start to climb, including two very steep, rough, and primitive miles to the flank of Preston Peak. At the end of Rattlesnake Meadow Trail, hikers must go cross-country for another mile or so to the

Preston Peak Summit. The last mile is a scramble. Pick your route very carefully and make no climbing mistakes. Although this is a nontechnical climb, there is one difficult spot that can be dangerous. You will see it: a mix of shale, loose gravel, and boulders, with no discernible route. Take your time and pick your way up one step at a time.

Special note: Always stay off this mountain in wet weather, because the route near the top is very slippery. Always avoid routes that cross through loose shale, which can be extremely dangerous. A fall here can kill you.

The cultlike group who climb Preston Peak often prefer the Doe Flat/Buck Lake Trailhead. We've tried this as well, and in the spring found the ford of Clear Creek to be wet, often deep and always cold. You have to spend a fair amount of time to remove your socks and then cross the river (with your boots on; your feet will go numb otherwise), and then have to dry your feet and re-boot before venturing on.

User Groups: Hikers only. Dogs are permitted but are strongly not recommended above tree line at Preston Peak. No horses or mountain bikes. No wheelchair facilities.

Permits: A campfire permit is required for overnight use. Parking and access are free.

Maps: For maps, ask the U.S. Forest Service for Six Rivers and Klamath National Forest. For a topographic map, ask the USGS for Devils Punchbowl.

Directions: From Crescent City, drive north on U.S. 101 for three miles to U.S. 199. Bear right (east) on U.S. 199 and drive 32 miles to Forest Road 18N07. Turn right and drive five miles to Forest Road 18N07. Continue on Forest Road 18N07 for 10 miles (twisty) toward Sanger Lake. Just before Sanger Lake, bear right on Forest Road 4803 (signed Youngs Valley Trail) and drive one mile to the trailhead, at the end of the road.

Contact: Klamath National Forest, Happy Camp-Oak Knoll Ranger District, Happy Camp, 530/493-2243, www.fs.usda.gov/klamath; Smith River National Recreation Area, Gasquet, 707/457-3131, www.fs.usda.gov/srnf.

3 DOE FLAT/BUCK LAKE TRAILHEAD

3.4 mi/2.0 hr   🏃2 ⛰8

in the Siskiyou Wilderness east of Crescent City

Map 2.1, page 65

Buck Lake is a little emerald jewel surrounded by old-growth firs. It's set in the heart of a wilderness forest at an elevation of 4,300 feet, a destination that makes for an excellent picnic, trail-style. After parking, the first 0.75 mile of this easy hike is on a closed Forest Service road. After that, a trail is routed through forest and then intersects with Buck Lake Trail. Turn right on Buck Lake Trail and hike 0.1 mile to the lake. We found three primitive campsites near the shore. There are plenty of deer and bears in the area, and the brook trout at the lake are abundant, though small. The area has beautiful meadows and forest, including Douglas, white, and red firs, along with some maples. In the fall, the changing colors of the maples add a pretty touch to the trip. The first time we saw Buck Lake was a Memorial Day weekend, the opening day of trout season here, and there were so many rising brook trout that all the dimples on the lake surface looked like rain drops.

Note: Long-time trail users will remember the days when you would drive to Doe Flat and from there, hike a half mile to Buck Lake, or venture down the canyon and take a cut-off trail up to Devils Punchbowl, or even continue down the ravine to Clear Creek and Trout Camp. Those days are long gone. Though most people still refer to this trailhead as the Doe Flat Trailhead, the closed road and new trail route you a half mile away from Doe Flat, and the trail now has a different route to the connection with the trail to Devils Punchbowl.

User Groups: Hikers, dogs, and horses. No mountain bikes. No wheelchair facilities.

Permits: No permits are required. A campfire permit (free) is required for overnight use. Parking and access are free.

Maps: For a free brochure and hiking guide,

write to Smith River National Recreation Area. For a map, ask the U.S. Forest Service for Six Rivers and Klamath National Forest. For a topographic map, ask the USGS for Devils Punchbowl.

Directions: From Crescent City, drive north on U.S. 101 for three miles to U.S. 199. Bear right (east) on U.S. 199 and drive 25 miles to Little Jones Creek Road/Jawbone Road (Forest Road 16). Turn right on Little Jones Creek Road/Jawbone Road (Forest Road 16) and drive south 9.6 miles to a fork with Forest Road 16N02. When the road forks, turn sharply left on Forest Road 16N02 and drive four miles to the trailhead at the end of the road. Take Doe Flat trailhead.

Contact: Smith River National Recreation Area, Gasquet, 707/457-3131, www.fs.usda. gov/srnf.

4 DEVILS PUNCHBOWL (VIA DOE FLAT/ BUCK LAKE TRAIL)
12.2 mi/1.5 days   🥾5 ⛺10

in the Siskiyou Wilderness east of Crescent City

Map 2.1, page 65   BEST (

The Punchbowl is a drop-dead beautiful lake, nestled in a glacial cirque with high granite walls towering overhead. The hike includes a steep climb with switchbacks of roughly 1,500 feet over the course of two miles. That aside, this one is paradise found. From the Doe Flat/ Buck Lake Trailhead, elevation 3,400 feet, the trip starts with a downhill glide of 0.75 mile on a closed Forest Service road. The trail is routed through forest and then intersects with Buck Lake Trail at 1.4 miles (Buck Lake is only 0.1 mile off to the right). Continue ahead and the trail descends gently through forest for another 1.8 miles to the junction with the Devils Punchbowl Trail. Turn right, and the trail climbs, steeply at times, for 1.2 miles to the lake. When you top the ridge, the route crosses Devils Creek and leaves the forest behind,

crossing bare granite domes. The trail is marked by cairns. You pass a smaller lake, cross a rise, and then the beautiful, gemlike Devils Punchbowl awaits. The elevation is 4,700 feet. This place is something of a legend. It's small but pristine, set in a mountain granite bowl, framed by an imposing back wall—a shrine.

Special note: The entire region surrounding Devils Punchbowl consists of sheets of bare granite. The few campsites here are merely small, flat sleeping spaces on rock. There is no firewood available, so bring a backpacking stove for cooking. Bring sealable plastic bags to carry out waste. With fresh snow, the trail cairns will be buried and low overcast will cover up landmarks; you need to be an expert with an altimeter, map, and compass to find your way back to the main trail. Guess how we know?

User Groups: Hikers and dogs. No horses or mountain bikes. No wheelchair facilities.

Permits: No permits are required. A campfire permit (free) is required for overnight use. Parking and access are free.

Maps: For a free brochure and hiking guide, write to Smith River National Recreation Area. For a map, ask the U.S. Forest Service for Six Rivers and Klamath National Forest. For a topographic map, ask the USGS for Devils Punchbowl.

Directions: From Crescent City, drive north on U.S. 101 for three miles to U.S. 199. Bear right (east) on U.S. 199 and drive 25 miles to Little Jones Creek Road/Jawbone Road (Forest Road 16). Turn right on Little Jones Creek Road (Forest Road 16) and drive south 9.6 miles. When the road forks, turn sharply left on Forest Road 16N02 and drive five miles to the trailhead, at the end of the road.

Contact: Smith River National Recreation Area, Gasquet, 707/457-3131, www.fs.usda.gov/ srnf; Klamath National Forest, Happy Camp-Oak Knoll Ranger District, Happy Camp, 530/493-2243, www.fs.usda.gov/klamath.

5 WILDERNESS FALLS
16.0 mi/2 days 🥾3 ⛰10

in the Siskiyou Wilderness east of Crescent
City

Map 2.1, page 65

Wilderness Falls is a bubbling torrent of
water created by Clear Creek. It crashes down
through a narrow cascading chute about 35 feet
into a boulder, and then pounds its way down
into a foaming pool that's 100 feet across. If you
can handle the cold water, it's a great swimming
hole. Wilderness Falls is one of the great secrets
of northwestern California. It's a true hidden
jewel, dramatic and pure, untouched and wild.

The recommended route is to start on Clear
Creek National Recreation Trail out of Youngs
Valley (see *Youngs Valley Trail* in this chapter).
You start the trip by hiking on a decommissioned Forest Service road; it climbs 0.8 mile
to a ridge and the boundary for the Siskiyou
Wilderness. It turns to trail, then descends 600
feet over two miles into Youngs Valley and to
Clear Creek. From here, you continue another
five miles with a gentle descent the rest of the
way. There is an excellent campsite about a
quarter of a mile upstream from the falls. It's
an easy hike to the waterfall, but the trip back
is up all the way and is best started very early in
the morning, when the temperature is the coolest. There is also a campsite called Trout Camp
near the confluence of Doe Creek.

Wilderness Falls can also be accessed out of
Doe Flat/Buck Lake Trailhead (see *Doe Flat/
Buck Lake Trailhead* in this chapter), and
we've also tried it that way. You descend to
Trout Camp, ford the river, then head down
to Wilderness Falls. In late May and June, this
route includes a wet, cold, and slippery ford
of Clear Creek. In summer, it is a much easier
river crossing.

User Groups: Hikers, dogs, and horses. No
mountain bikes. No wheelchair facilities.

Permits: A campfire permit (free) is required
for overnight use. Parking and access are free.

Maps: For a map, ask the U.S. Forest Service
for Six Rivers and Klamath National Forest.

For a topographic map, ask the USGS for Devils
Punchbowl.

Directions: From Crescent City, drive north
on U.S. 101 for three miles to U.S. 199. Bear
right (east) on U.S. 199 and drive 32 miles to
Forest Road 18N07. Turn right and drive five
miles to Forest Road 18N07. Continue on Forest
Road 18N07 for 10 miles (twisty) toward Sanger
Lake. Just before Sanger Lake, bear right on
Forest Road 4803 (signed Youngs Valley Trail)
and drive one mile to the trailhead, at the end
of the road.

Contact: Klamath National Forest, Happy
Camp-Oak Knoll Ranger District, Happy
Camp, 530/493-2243, www.fs.usda.gov/klam-
ath; Smith River National Recreation Area,
Gasquet, 707/457-3131, www.fs.usda.gov/srnf.

6 ISLAND LAKE TRAIL
13.0 mi/2 days 🥾4 ⛰8

in Siskiyou Wilderness east of Crescent City

Map 2.1, page 65

Island Lake is a mountain bowl framed by the
back wall of Jedediah Mountain, a wild, primitive area where threatened spotted owls are
more common than hikers. The trailhead is off
Doe Flat Road at the Bear Basin area. The hike
starts with a walk on a portion of trail (a former road) that is routed down to the South Fork
Smith River, where you'll enter the untouched
Siskiyou Wilderness. Enjoy the stream; the
hike that follows can have some begging for the
memory. The trail intersects with the old route
and then rises along a mountain spine, climbing up, up, and up for what seems like an endless three miles. It finally tops a ridge and turns
around a bend, where little Island Lake comes
into view. A great sense of relief will wash over
you. It is a long, tough climb.

There are two excellent camps at the lake,
set in trees near the lake's shore. The trout are
eager to bite, but most are very small, dinker-
sized brook trout. A great afternoon side trip is
to hike the rim around the lake, which is most
easily done in a counterclockwise direction to

the top of Jedediah Mountain—a perfect picnic site and a great lookout.

If you hiked to Island Lake back in the day, you will note that the trailhead has been moved a few miles, lengthening the distance to the lake from 4 miles to 6.5 miles. The purpose of this trailhead change is to keep vehicles away from the wilderness, because a fungus that is most commonly introduced from tires on vehicles threatens Port Orford cedars.

User Groups: Hikers, dogs, and horses. No mountain bikes. No wheelchair facilities.

Permits: A campfire permit is required. Parking and access are free.

Maps: For a free brochure and hiking guide, write to Smith River National Recreation Area. For a map, ask the U.S. Forest Service for Six Rivers and Klamath National Forest. For a topographic map, ask the USGS for Devils Punchbowl.

Directions: From Crescent City, drive north on U.S. 101 for three miles to U.S. 199. Bear right (east) on U.S. 199 and drive 25 miles to Little Jones Creek Road/Jawbone Road (Forest Road 16). Turn right and drive eight miles to Forest Road 16N02. Turn left and drive 2.5 miles to Forest Road 16N10. Turn right. The trailhead is located on your immediate right.

Contact: Smith River National Recreation Area, Gasquet, 707/457-3131, www.fs.usda.gov/srnf; Klamath National Forest, Happy Camp-Oak Knoll Ranger District, Happy Camp, 530/493-2243, www.fs.usda.gov/klamath.

⁊ SEIAD VALLEY TO OREGON BORDER (PCT)

36.0 mi one-way/3 days

in Klamath National Forest from Seiad Valley to the Siskiyou Mountains

Map 2.1, page 65

The few people you see on this section of the Pacific Crest Trail (PCT) are thru-hikers heading to Canada. It is the northernmost segment of the PCT in California. But it's a memorable chunk of trail, whether for a day hike or for the whole duration, all the way to Wards Fork Gap, on the edge of the Rogue Wilderness in southern Oregon. The ambitious few will head up from the trailhead to the junction of the Boundary National Recreation Trail, a seven-mile trip one-way. From Seiad Valley, elevation 1,443 feet, the first five miles are a steep climb out of the Klamath River Valley. You climb 4,600 feet to Upper Devils Peak at an elevation of 6,040 feet. This features sensational views to the south of 14,179-foot Mount Shasta.

This hike marks the final steps of the 1,700-mile Pacific Crest Trail in California, an epic journey for all, but always classic, even if only sections are enjoyed. If you decide to attempt the south-to-north route, see the *Grider Creek to Seiad Valley (PCT)* hike in this chapter.

User Groups: Hikers, dogs, and horses. No mountain bikes. No wheelchair facilities.

Permits: No permits are required. Parking and access are free.

Maps: A trail information sheet can be obtained by contacting the Happy Camp-Oak Knoll Ranger District. For a map, ask the U.S. Forest Service for Klamath National Forest. For a topographic map, ask the USGS for Seiad Valley.

Directions: From Yreka, take I-5 north to Highway 96. Turn west on Highway 96 and drive approximately 50 miles to Seiad Valley. Continue another mile west on Highway 96 to the trailhead, on the north (right) side. Parking is minimal; park across the highway.

Contact: Klamath National Forest, Headquarters, Yreka, 530/842-6131, www.fs.usda.gov/klamath.

⁕ GRIDER CREEK TO SEIAD VALLEY (PCT)

7.0 mi one-way/1 day

in Klamath National Forest, southeast of Happy Camp to the Grider Creek Trailhead

Map 2.1, page 65

Most hikers use this trailhead to head south into the Marble Mountain Wilderness, not north. For PCT hikers heading south to north, the trail is seven miles one-way, with an additional five miles of road to Seiad Valley on Highway 96. This is an excellent place for PCT hikers to pick up a food stash and dump garbage. You could walk the road, but most try to hitch a ride. The trail here follows Grider Creek, an easy descent northward as the stream pours toward the Klamath River. The only downer is that the last three miles are on a dirt Forest Service road, but for PCT hikers, it's a sign that the next restaurant is not far off. The area features magnificent stands of virgin timber—a mixed conifer forest of cedar, pine, and fir. A good Forest Service campground (Grider Creek Camp) is available about three miles before reaching Seiad Valley.

To pick up the next trail heading for the Oregon border, see the *Seiad Valley to Oregon Border (PCT)* hike in this chapter. If you are hiking this trail in reverse, see the *Etna Summit to Grider Creek (PCT)* hike in this chapter to continue south.

User Groups: Hikers, dogs, and horses. No mountain bikes. No wheelchair facilities.

Permits: A campfire permit (free) is required. Parking and access are free.

Maps: A trail information sheet can be obtained by contacting the Happy Camp-Oak Knoll Ranger District. For a map, ask the U.S. Forest Service for Klamath National Forest. For a topographic map, ask the USGS for Seiad Valley.

Directions: From Yreka, take I-5 north to Highway 96. Turn west on Highway 96 and drive approximately 40 miles to Walker Creek/Grider Creek Road (Forest Road 46N64), located one mile before Seiad Valley. Turn left on Walker Creek Road and drive about 50 feet (staying to the left as it runs adjacent to the Klamath River) to Grider Creek Road. Turn right and drive two miles to the trailhead.

Contact: Klamath National Forest, Headquarters, Yreka, 530/842-6131, www.fs.usda.gov/klamath.

9 HAYPRESS MEADOWS TRAILHEAD
29.0 mi/3 days   🥾3   ⛰9

in the Marble Mountain Wilderness near Somes Bar

Map 2.1, page 65   **BEST (**

The Cuddihy Lakes basin is one of the prettiest sections of the Marble Mountain Wilderness. It also is home to one of the largest concentrations of bears anywhere in California. This is a great trip, leading out to One Mile Lake and the Cuddihy Lakes. This area is perfect for backpacking, with beauty, lookouts, and good trail access. You'll see some remnants of past forest fires, but much of the area is a mix of high-country granite and sparse conifers that burned in a mosaic, so the impact is often fleeting and passing.

Park at the trailhead (at 4,500 feet), then begin the first two miles of trail, up and across a fir-covered slope of a small peak (a little butt-kicker of a climb). Then the trail descends into Haypress Meadows, a major junction. Turn right and head up Sandy Ridge, which is a long, steady climb. Plan to top the ridge and then camp at Monument Lake, Meteor Lake, One Mile Lake, or Cuddihy Lakes. The view from Sandy Ridge is a sweeping lookout of the Marble Mountains to the east and the Siskiyous to the west, with mountaintop glimpses of Mount Shasta and the Marble Rim. You can often see elk at Monument Lake and the meadow just beyond the lake.

User Groups: Hikers, dogs, and horses. No mountain bikes. No wheelchair facilities.

Permits: A campfire permit (free) is required for overnight use. Parking and access are free.

Maps: A trail information sheet can be obtained by contacting the Ukonom Ranger District. For a map, ask the U.S. Forest Service for Klamath National Forest or Marble Mountain Wilderness. For a topographic map, ask the USGS for Somes Bar.

Directions: From Willow Creek, at the junction of Highways 299 and 96, take Highway 96 north (twisty at first) for 42 miles to Orleans.

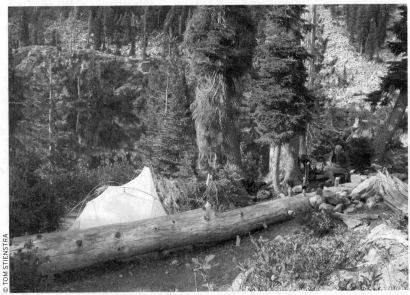

Monument Lake out of Haypress Meadows trailhead

Continue eight miles to Somes Bar and Salmon River Road. Turn right on Salmon River Road (Highway 93) and drive 100 feet to a sign that says Camp 3/Haypress Trailhead and Forest Road 15N17 (Offield Mountain Road). Turn left and drive 14.6 miles to Forest Road 15N17E. Turn left and drive 1.5 miles to the access road for Haypress trailhead. Turn left and drive one mile to the trailhead.

Contact: Six Rivers National Forest, Orleans Ranger District, Orleans, 530/627-3291, www.fs.usda.gov/srnf.

10 SPIRIT LAKE TRAIL
34.0 mi/4 days 　　🥾3 　⛰️10

in the Marble Mountain Wilderness near Somes Bar

Map 2.1, page 65 　　**BEST (**

We've hiked to hundreds and hundreds of mountain lakes, and Spirit Lake is one of the prettiest we've ever seen. It sits at the bottom of a mountain bowl encircled by old-growth trees, with a few campsites set at the side of the lake. Spirit Lake can be the feature destination for a week-long backpack loop. Start your trek at the Haypress Meadows Trailhead, which is routed up to Sandy Ridge. Most hikers will stop for the night at One Mile or the Cuddihy Lakes on the way out, and that is why those two areas get so much use. On the second or third day, continue to Spirit Lake, about 17 miles one-way. Spirit Lake is best visited during the first week of June, when the nights are still cold, the people are few, and the area abounds with fish and deer.

The Karuk tribe considers this a sacred place. The abundance of wildlife can be remarkable. The far side of the lake is a major deer migration route, ospreys make regular trips to pluck trout out of the lake for dinner, and the fishing is quite good, especially early in the summer.

User Groups: Hikers, dogs, and horses. No mountain bikes. No wheelchair facilities.

Permits: A campfire permit (free) is required for overnight use. Parking and access are free.

Maps: A trail information sheet can be obtained by contacting the Ukonom Ranger

District. For a map, ask the U.S. Forest Service for Klamath National Forest or Marble Mountain Wilderness. For a topographic map, ask the USGS for Somes Bar.

Directions: From Willow Creek, at the junction of Highways 299 and 96, take Highway 96 north (twisty at first) for 42 miles to Orleans. Continue eight miles to Somes Bar and Salmon River Road. Turn right on Salmon River Road (Highway 93) and drive 100 feet to a sign that says Camp 3/Haypress Trailhead and Forest Road 15N17 (Offield Mountain Road). Turn left and drive 14.6 miles to Forest Road 15N17E. Turn left and drive 1.5 miles to the access road for Haypress trailhead. Turn left and drive one mile to the trailhead.

Contact: Six Rivers National Forest, Orleans Ranger District, Orleans, 530/627-3291, www.fs.usda.gov/srnf.

11 KELSEY CREEK TRAIL
18.0 mi/2 days   🥾3 ⛰9

in the Marble Mountain Wilderness west of Yreka

Map 2.1, page 65

This section of the Kelsey Creek Trail offers many miles of beautiful streamside travel. For most hikers on the "Old Kelsey Trail," as we call it, the Paradise Lake basin is the intended destination. The trailhead for this section is set near the confluence of Kelsey Creek and the Scott River, and from there, the trail follows Kelsey Creek upstream. Wildflowers are abundant in the meadows. After four miles and two creek crossings, you'll reach Maple Falls, one of the few waterfalls in the region. The trail continues up the canyon, finally rising to intersect with the Pacific Crest Trail, just below Red Rock. From this junction, hikers have many options. The closest lake is secluded Bear Lake, a pretty spot with a nice campsite, but, alas, with some tules and mosquitoes; to reach it from the junction requires a short but steep drop into the basin to the immediate west. For Paradise Lake,

actually a small, shallow lake that is meadowing out, turn left on the PCT.

User Groups: Hikers, dogs, and horses. No mountain bikes. No wheelchair facilities.

Permits: A campfire permit (free) is required for overnight use. Parking and access are free.

Maps: A trail information sheet can be obtained by contacting the Scott River Ranger District. For a map, ask the U.S. Forest Service for Klamath National Forest or Marble Mountain Wilderness. For topographic maps, ask the USGS for Scott Bar and Grider Valley.

Directions: From Redding, take I-5 to Yreka and the exit for Highway 3/Fort Jones. Take that exit to the stop sign, turn left, and drive a short distance to the lighted intersection. Turn left on Highway 3 and drive 16.5 miles to Fort Jones and Scott River Road. Turn right on Scott River Road and drive 16.8 miles to the Scott River Bridge. Cross it and then turn left immediately, following the road for 0.3 mile. Bear right on another dirt road (do not continue to a second bridge) and drive 0.25 mile to the trailhead.

Contact: Klamath National Forest, Salmon/Scott River Ranger District, Fort Jones, 530/468-5351, www.fs.usda.gov/klamath.

12 PARADISE LAKE TRAIL
4.0 mi/2.75 hr   🥾3 ⛰8

in the Marble Mountain Wilderness west of Yreka

Map 2.1, page 65

Unlike the high-country trailheads of the Sierra, the trail takes you through extended deep forest. The first two miles climb 1,300 feet, with only occasional switchbacks to ease the gradient. The shade is a relief, even on a cool mountain morning, and you pass a mixed forest with hardwoods that transitions into conifers as you rise up, with occasional lush beds of bracken ferns. You then emerge from forest and hit the Pacific Crest Trail. It feels like you are walking through a door into a special world. You turn right for a break at Paradise

Lake, a small shallow lake, just five acres, that is meadowing out. Kings Castle, a massive outcrop with a vertical face, looms directly above. A small spring, a steady trickle of cold, clean water, is located just above the head of the lake in a tiny ravine, a must-know for PCT hikers and as sweet-tasting as anywhere in the world. The lake has a few shaded campsites. This is the shortest hike to a lakeside campsite in the Marble Mountain Wilderness, with many excellent side trips, including climbing Kings Castle (see the following hike).

User Groups: Hikers, dogs, and horses. No mountain bikes. No wheelchair facilities.

Permits: No permits are required. A campfire permit (free) is required for overnight use. Parking and access are free.

Maps: A trail information sheet can be obtained by contacting the Scott River Ranger District. For a map, ask the U.S. Forest Service for Klamath National Forest or Marble Mountain Wilderness. For topographic maps, ask the USGS for Scott Bar and Marble Mountain.

Directions: From Redding, take I-5 north for 95 miles to Yreka and the exit for Highway 3/ Fort Jones-Etna. At the stop sign, turn left and drive 0.1 mile (beneath underpass) to the intersection at Highway 3. Turn left and drive 15.4 miles to Fort Jones and Scott River Road. At Scott River Road, turn right and drive 14 miles to Indian Scotty Campground Road/ Forest Road 44N45. Turn left to drive over the Scott River bridge, and continue on Forest Road 44N45 for about five miles to a signed turn for Paradise Lake Trailhead. Bear right, and follow the dirt road for six miles to the parking area.

Contact: Klamath National Forest, Salmon/ Scott River Ranger District, Fort Jones, 530/468-5351, www.fs.usda.gov/klamath.

🔢13 KINGS CASTLE TRAIL
7.0 mi/1 day 🏃5 ⛰10

in the Marble Mountain Wilderness west of Yreka

Map 2.1, page 65

Kings Castle is the awesome crag that towers over Paradise Lake. To claim it, your mission is to climb 2,500 feet over 3.5 miles, with the last mile or so a faint route, steep and rocky, not marked on maps. Your reward is a world-class view: To the south, you can see 6,990-foot Marble Mountain, a megalith of white, marbleized limestone. Nearby is Black Marble. In the distance is Boulder Peak, 8,220 feet, the highest point in the Marbles. It can feel like a kill-me, eat-me trek, but is short enough to do round-trip in a day. The first section is from the trailhead to Paradise Lake (the previous hike, this chapter). At the Pacific Crest Trail, turn right for a short distance to a spur for adjacent Paradise Lake on your left. From the campground, walk toward the head of the lake and you'll find a spring with sweet, cold, pure water. Tank up. The route to Kings Castle is right there, and starts on a well-walked trail through vegetation. It emerges in rock, where a faint route arcs around the southern side of the lake and then up a steep canyon. Every step of the way, Kings Castle looms ahead. At times, the trail disappears in rock and the hike becomes an act of faith. Then you'll see a trail cairn and realize you're on course after all. A towering escarpment rises up to your left. As you emerge from the canyon, you'll arrive at a saddle below the final ridge. The final push is up the backside of the Castle. En route, you pass the blackened remains of a pine turned into charcoal from a lightning strike. From the top, you can see across the interior of the Marble Mountain Wilderness and to a half dozen significant mountain peaks. Below, Paradise Lake looks like an emerald pond. The trip passed our test: more bears than people.

User Groups: Hikers only. No dogs, horses, or mountain bikes. No wheelchair facilities.

Permits: No permits are required. A campfire

permit (free) is required for overnight use. Parking and access are free.

Maps: A trail information sheet can be obtained by contacting the Scott River Ranger District. For a map, ask the U.S. Forest Service for Klamath National Forest or Marble Mountain Wilderness. For topographic maps, ask the USGS for Scott Bar and Marble Mountain.

Directions: From Redding, take I-5 north for 95 miles to Yreka and the exit for Highway 3/Fort Jones-Etna. At the stop sign, turn left and drive 0.1 mile (beneath underpass) to the intersection at Highway 3. Turn left and drive 15.4 miles to Fort Jones and Scott River Road. At Scott River Road, turn right and drive 14 miles to Indian Scotty Campground Road/Forest Road 44N45. Turn left to drive over the Scott River bridge, and continue on Forest Road 44N45 for about five miles to a signed turn for Paradise Lake Trailhead. Bear right, and follow the dirt road for six miles to the parking area.

Contact: Klamath National Forest, Salmon/Scott River Ranger District, Fort Jones, 530/468-5351, www.fs.usda.gov/klamath.

🔢 MARBLE MOUNTAIN RIM
14.0 mi/2 days   🥾3 ⛰10

in the Marble Mountain Wilderness west of Yreka

Map 2.1, page 65

Marble isn't usually thought of as a precious stone, but it's gemlike for hikers on this trail. The trek to the Marble Mountain Rim is an off-trail side-trip from the Pacific Crest Trail. You end up walking along the top of this wide-topped megalith of white, marbleized limestone, with black marble at the summit. It tops out at 6,990 feet. The trailhead at Lovers Camp is one of the most popular in the wilderness, with the road paved, ideal for packers going by horse into Marble Mountain Wilderness (corrals and a campground are available near the trailhead). The route heads up Canyon Creek, a moderate climb of 1,200 over four miles, past

several creeks and a waterfall, and continue on to the junction with the Pacific Crest Trail. Turn north on the PCT for a short distance, about 10 minutes, and look for a route on the left. This spur climbs steeply up to Marble Gap, and mountaineers can trek to the Marble Rim. (The late, great Foonsky led our trip here to the Rim.) With a topo map, it is not difficult to figure your route along the Rim. The views are stunning, sweeping in both directions, with steep drop-offs adding to the quiet drama. The rock itself is unlike anything else in Northern California—a mix of white, black, red, and tan marble, something you'll never forget. To extend your trip by several days, venture to the Sky High Lakes, Little Elk Lake, Deep Lake, or Rainy Lake.

User Groups: Hikers only. No dogs, horses, or mountain bikes. No wheelchair facilities.

Permits: A campfire permit (free) is required for overnight use. Parking and access are free.

Maps: A trail information sheet can be obtained by contacting the Scott River Ranger District. For a map, ask the U.S. Forest Service for Klamath National Forest or Marble Mountain Wilderness. For topographic maps, ask the USGS for Scott Bar and Marble Mountain.

Directions: From Redding, take I-5 north for 95 miles to Yreka and the exit for Highway 3/Fort Jones-Etna. At the stop sign, turn left and drive 0.1 mile (beneath underpass) to the intersection at Highway 3. Turn left and drive 15.4 miles to Fort Jones and Scott River Road. At Scott River Road, turn right and drive 14 miles to Indian Scotty Campground Road/Forest Road 44N45 for eight miles to the campground spur on left. Continue a short distance to the end of the road, signed Lovers Camp Trailhead.

Contact: Klamath National Forest, Salmon/Scott River Ranger District, Fort Jones, 530/468-5351, www.fs.usda.gov/klamath.

15 SKY HIGH LAKES
11.4 mi/2 days 🥾3 ⛺10

in the Marble Mountain Wilderness west of Yreka

Map 2.1, page 65

The Sky High Lakes make for a great overnighter, a 6.5-mile hike each day, or an inspired one-day in-and-outer. From the Lovers Camp Trailhead, you take the Canyon Creek Trail (the creek is far below you on the left) for four miles with a 550-foot climb to a junction (a short distance past a small waterfall). Turn left (if you instead turn right, you will be routed past the Marble Valley and up to the east foot of Marble Mountain) and the trail is routed through forest and climbs over a sub-ridge, and then descends to beautiful Lower Sky High Lake. Just above is Upper Sky High Lake, connected by a small stream, and nearby is little Frying Pan Lake. Just to the south, a massive rock wall and outcrop provides a gorgeous backdrop. This is one of the prettiest settings in the Marbles.

User Groups: Hikers, dogs, and horses. No mountain bikes. No wheelchair facilities.

Permits: A campfire permit is required only for hikers planning to camp in the wilderness. Parking and access are free.

Maps: A trail information sheet can be obtained by contacting the Scott River Ranger District. For a map, ask the U.S. Forest Service for Klamath National Forest or Marble Mountain Wilderness. For a topographic map, ask the USGS for Marble Mountain.

Directions: From Redding, take I-5 north for 95 miles to Yreka and the exit for Highway 3/Fort Jones-Etna. At the stop sign, turn left and drive 0.1 mile (beneath underpass) to the intersection at Highway 3. Turn left and drive 15.4 miles to Fort Jones and Scott River Road. At Scott River Road, turn right and drive 14 miles to Indian Scotty Campground Road/Forest Road 44N45 for eight miles to the campground spur on left. Continue a short distance to the end of the road, signed Lovers Camp Trailhead.

Contact: Klamath National Forest, Salmon/Scott River Ranger District, Fort Jones, 530/468-5351, www.fs.usda.gov/klamath.

16 SHACKLEFORD CREEK TRAIL
13.0 mi/2 days 🥾4 ⛺8

in the Marble Mountain Wilderness west of Yreka

Map 2.1, page 65

Campbell, Cliff, and Summit Lakes are three pretty lakes in the Marble Mountain Wilderness. It is 5.5 miles to Campbell Lake, which you reach via the Shackleford Trail. That makes this a popular destination all summer long for those who know about it. The trail is routed up Shackleford Creek to a basin set just below the Pacific Crest Trail. Here you'll find the series of small mountain lakes.

Note that ambitious trekkers traveling off-trail, cross-country style, can create routes to little Gem, Jewel, and Angel Lakes. Trekking is not for everybody, however, which is why this trip rates a 4. If you want to extend the trip into a loop, you can hike up to the rim of the Pacific Crest Trail, then turn right and go three miles to the Sky High Lakes.

User Groups: Hikers, dogs, and horses. No mountain bikes. No wheelchair facilities.

Permits: A campfire permit is required only for hikers planning to camp in the wilderness. Parking and access are free.

Maps: A trail information sheet can be obtained by contacting the Scott River Ranger District. For a map, ask the U.S. Forest Service for Klamath National Forest or Marble Mountain Wilderness. For a topographic map, ask the USGS for Boulder Peak.

Directions: From Redding, take I-5 to Yreka and the exit for Highway 3/Fort Jones. Take that exit to the stop sign, turn left, and drive a short distance to the lighted intersection. Turn left on Highway 3 and drive 16.5 miles to Fort Jones and Scott River Road. Turn right on Scott River Road and drive seven miles to Quartz Valley Road. Turn left on Quartz Valley

Road and drive about four miles to the sign for Shackleford trailhead and Forest Road 43N21. Turn right and drive 6.5 miles to the trailhead, at the end of the road.

Contact: Klamath National Forest, Salmon/ Scott River Ranger District, Fort Jones, 530/468-5351, www.fs.usda.gov/klamath.

17 MULE BRIDGE TRAILHEAD
28.0 mi/4 days   🥾5 ⛺8

in the Marble Mountain Wilderness west of Etna

Map 2.1, page 65

The trailhead at Mule Bridge is set alongside the Salmon River; once you've tightened your backpack, get ready for a long climb up the river drainage. The trail follows the Salmon River all the way up to its headwaters, and in the process, you gain nearly 3,500 feet. Plan on climbing for 14 or 15 miles along the river until you reach the higher country where there are many lakeside camps. The trail forks eight miles from the trailhead. The right-hand fork leads to Shelly Meadows and the Pacific Crest Trail.

The main trail continues north for access to Upper Abbotts Camp and many lakes in the upper drainage. This trail ties in with Little North Fork Trail near Hancock Lake. The prettiest glacial-formed lakes in this region are Lake of the Island (12-mile hike), Abbott Lake (13-mile hike), and Lake Ethel (14-mile hike). Even more remote lakes are Wooley Lake, Milne Lake, and Osprey Lake. All of these are hard to reach and require cross-country travel. Several other lakes are in the region, allowing this trek to be extended by several days. The long, hot climb out of Quartz Valley, compared to the steady and shorter climbs from Lovers Camp and Paradise Lake Trailhead, is why few use this trailhead.

User Groups: Hikers, dogs, and horses. No mountain bikes. No wheelchair facilities.

Permits: A campfire permit (free) is required for campfires and stoves. Parking and access are free.

Maps: A trail information sheet can be obtained by contacting the Salmon Ranger District. For a map, ask the U.S. Forest Service for Klamath National Forest or Marble Mountain Wilderness. For a topographic map, ask the USGS for Sawyers Bar.

Directions: From Redding, take I-5 to Yreka and the exit for Highway 3/Fort Jones. Take that exit to the stop sign, turn left, and drive a short distance to the lighted intersection. Turn left on Highway 3 and drive southwest 28 miles to Etna. Turn west on Etna-Somes Bar Road (which is Main Street in town) and drive 21 miles to Idlewild Campground. As you enter the campground, take the left fork in the road and continue two miles to the trailhead.

Contact: Klamath National Forest, Salmon/ Scott River Ranger District, Fort Jones, 530/468-5351, www.fs.usda.gov/klamath.

18 LITTLE NORTH FORK TRAILHEAD
16.0 mi/2-3 days   🥾5 ⛺7

in the Marble Mountain Wilderness near Sawyers Bar

Map 2.1, page 65

Your destination options from this trailhead? There are many: Chimney Rock, Clear Lake, Lily Lake, and Chimney Rock Lake. Take your pick. Or devise a route where you hop from one to another. This trail provides an excellent trip, as long as you don't mind the long grind of a climb to reach the lakes. Like a lot of trails on the edge of the wilderness, this one starts with a long haul out of a river canyon. From the Little North Fork trailhead, start by climbing out toward Chimney Rock, grunting out a rise of about 4,000 feet as you leave the river lowlands and reach the Marble Mountain Wilderness. It's about an eight-mile trip to Clear Lake, a good first day's destination. Although you can simply return the next day, most people will take several days to venture deeper into the wilderness, with 13 lakes and 20 miles of stream in the Upper Abbotts Camp and English Peak areas.

User Groups: Hikers, dogs, and horses. No mountain bikes. No wheelchair facilities.

Permits: A campfire permit (free) is required for campfires and stoves. Parking and access are free.

Maps: A trail information sheet can be obtained by contacting the Salmon Ranger District. For a map, ask the U.S. Forest Service for Klamath National Forest or Marble Mountain Wilderness. For a topographic map, ask the USGS for Sawyers Bar.

Directions: From Redding, take I-5 to Yreka and the exit for Highway 3/Fort Jones. Take that exit to the stop sign, turn left, and drive a short distance to the lighted intersection. Turn left on Highway 3 and drive southwest 28 miles to Etna at Sawyers Bar Road. Turn right on Sawyers Bar Road and drive about 25 miles to Sawyers Bar. Continue west on the same road for four miles to Little North Fork Road (Forest Road 40N51). Turn right (north) and drive two miles to the trailhead at the end of the road.

Contact: Klamath National Forest, Salmon/Scott River Ranger District, Fort Jones, 530/468-5351, www.fs.usda.gov/klamath.

19 HORSE TRAIL RIDGE NATIONAL RECREATION TRAIL
13.0 mi one-way/2 days

in Six Rivers National Forest east of Hoopa

Map 2.1, page 65

This is one of the lesser-known national recreation trails in the western United States, but it has many excellent features, and, alas, a few negative ones as well. The six-mile trip to Mill Creek Lakes is set in the least-explored western sector of the Trinity Alps. Although some of the region has been burned severely by wildfire, the Mill Creek Lakes area remains untouched by fire, like an island of green, and makes for a good overnighter.

From the trailhead (at 4,800 feet), the grades are gradual, with relatively easy elevation climbs and descents. A majority of the forest

along the trail was burned in forest fires. While there are many continuous stretches of burned areas, there are also pockets of greenery that the fire missed and ground-level vegetation is making a good comeback. In all, the fire affects 10 miles of this route.

Special note: Do not drink the water available here without first treating it with the best filtration system you can afford.

User Groups: Hikers, dogs, and horses. No mountain bikes. No wheelchair facilities.

Permits: A wilderness permit is required for hikers planning on camping. Parking and access are free.

Maps: For a map, ask the U.S. Forest Service for Six Rivers National Forest. For topographic maps, ask the USGS for Tish Tang Point and Trinity Mountain.

Directions: From the Arcata area, take Highway 299 east to Willow Creek and Highway 96. Turn north on Highway 96 and drive about 12 miles into Hoopa Valley to Big Hill Road. Turn right (east) on Big Hill Road and drive 11 miles to the Six Rivers National Forest border (the road becomes Forest Road 8N01). Continue for 4.5 miles (the road becomes Forest Road 10N02) to the Redcap Trailhead (once off Hoopa reservation land, stay on the chip-seal road).

Contact: Six Rivers National Forest, Lower Trinity Ranger District, Willow Creek, 530/629-2118, www.fs.usda.gov/srnf.

20 LITTLE SOUTH FORK LAKE TRAIL
13.0 mi/2 days

in the Trinity Alps Wilderness near Cecilville

Map 2.1, page 65

You have to be a little bit crazy to try this trip, and that's why we signed up. This is one of the most difficult lakes to reach in California. Yet Little South Fork Lake has two idyllic campsites, excellent swimming, and large trout. This route is largely off trail and requires skirting around a big waterfall, but there's no better way in—we've tried all three different routes. If you want an easy, clearly marked trail, this is not the hike for you. If you want a challenge with a pay-off, this is it.

From the South Fork trailhead, the trip starts out easy enough. Start by hiking four miles along the Salmon River until reaching the Little South Fork Creek. Turn up the trail upstream along Little South Fork Creek. The trail quickly becomes faint and starts to resemble a game trail, and this is where so many people give up. The route eventually dead-ends into Little South Fork Creek. (A faint route on the other side of the creek, the north side, climbs through brush and up the canyon, and we came in that way once from the Caribou Lakes; it is like trying to make your way through a spider web of brush, and should be avoided.) From here, with no apparent route in Little South Fork Creek or out of the canyon, the best route, though still steep and very difficult, is to lateral across the slope on the right side of the stream. It is 1.25 miles upstream to a beautiful, pristine waterfall. Michael Furniss, the renowned hydrologist, named it Crystal Falls.

To get around the waterfall, loop back until you can project a safe route up the slope to the right, and trek with no trail in an arc around and above the waterfall; if you go to the left (which we've tried), you'll add several dreadful hours to the trip scrambling on all fours straight up the slope (plus we got stung by bees in a ground nest we accidentally disturbed). Remember that there is no trail and no marked route; this is a cross-country scramble and very slow going. It's another 1.5 miles to the lake, which can take hours of scrambling up and across the wooded slope until you emerge from the forest onto granite plates. Ahead is the lake, beautifully set in a rock bowl framed by a high back wall. There are excellent campsites at each end of the lake. When you arrive, you will collapse, believe me, or jump in the lake for a swim.

We hiked into this lake once from Caribou Lakes by climbing the Sawtooth Ridge and dropping down into the basin—the entire route, also off trail, but that creates a potentially hazardous proposition, with some rock climbing and descents with packs. On another trip from Caribou Lakes, we dropped down into Little South Fork Canyon, losing thousands of feet in altitude and in the process getting caught in a brush field like bugs in a spider web. Neither of these other two routes is recommended. In fact, the suggested route we detailed is not recommended either. During the review of the book, a local ranger said we were crazy to include it in the book and he would never recommend such a thing or ever do it himself. He was right, of course. You need to be a little crazy to get membership to the Little South Fork Club.

User Groups: Hikers only. Dogs are permitted but are strongly advised against. No horses or mountain bikes. No wheelchair facilities.

Permits: A free wilderness permit is required for hikers planning to camp.

Maps: For a map, ask the U.S. Forest Service for Klamath National Forest or Trinity Alps Wilderness. For a topographic map, ask the USGS for Thompson Peak.

Directions: From Redding, drive north on I-5 for 70 miles past Weed to the exit for Edgewood. At the stop sign, turn left and drive through the underpass to another stop sign to Old Highway 99. Turn right on Old Highway 99 and drive about six miles to Gazelle. Turn left on Gazelle-Callahan Road and drive 27 miles (twisty) to Callahan and continue a short distance to Cecilville Road. Turn left (west or right if coming from Yreka) on Cecilville Road and drive 28 miles to Caribou Road/County Road 1E003 (across from East Fork Campground). Turn left (south) on Caribou Road and drive 3.5 miles to a fork. Bear left at the fork and drive 2.5 miles to the South Fork trailhead. Bring detailed maps, not a GPS.

Contact: Klamath National Forest, Salmon/Scott River Ranger District, Fort Jones, 530/468-5351, www.fs.usda.gov/klamath.

21 GRIZZLY LAKE
12.0 mi/2 days or 38.0 mi/5 days

🚶5 ⛰10

in the Trinity Alps Wilderness north of
Junction City

Map 2.1, page 65   BEST (

This is a butt-kicker climb to Grizzly Lake, the
signature lake in the Trinity Alps. Problem is,
you might say, "Kill me, eat me," to your hiking partners by the time you get here. The lake
is gorgeous (and we'll get to that), the trek is
just plain hard (we'll get to that, too), but the
surprise is that despite the extreme difficulty
there always seem to be folks here in the summer. You only seem to get it to yourself in the
fall, when the nights are cold.

Grizzly Lake is set below awesome
Thompson Peak (8,863 feet), with one of the
most beautiful wilderness waterfalls anywhere,
80-foot Grizzly Falls, set at the lake's cliff out-
fall. The lake is so pristine that you can spend
hours just looking at it.

There are two ways to get in. Take your pick:
From the China Creek trailhead, a butt-kicking
six-mile climb with a 5,000-foot elevation gain
(with a 1,500-foot canyon descent included on
the way); or from the Hobo Gulch trailhead, a
moderate grade over the course of 19 miles to
make the lake.

Given a choice, most people take the short,
butt-kicker route, then cuss at themselves the
whole way in for doing so. There is almost
nothing rewarding about it, and most complete
the trip with head down, trying to think about
something else. Before you race off to this destination, think long and hard about whether
you are ready to pay a terrible physical toll to
get there. Surprisingly, many do this regardless of the price, and the place gets fairly heavy
use. It's one of the marquee destinations in the
north state.

Or, on the other hand, you could take the
longer but more gradual climb from the Hobo
Gulch trailhead, set deep in the national forest
along Backbone Ridge. On this route, Grizzly
Lake is 19 miles away. There's also a fair
amount of forest fire damage along the route.
So instead of camping along lakes, hikers camp
along pretty streams and flats, taking days
to reach the promised land at Grizzly Lake.
The trail from Hobo Gulch starts by heading
straight north about five miles along the North
Fork Trinity River to Rattlesnake Camp, climb-
ing very gently. Cross Rattlesnake Creek, and
continue another three miles past the Morrison
Cabin (from the mining days) and on to Pfeiffer
Flat. Here the North Fork Trinity is joined by
Grizzly Creek, an attractive backpacking destination. From Pfeiffer Flat, the trail follows
Grizzly Creek, rising high toward the Trinity
Sawtooth Ridge and requiring an uphill pull to
beautiful Grizzly Meadows and then to Grizzly
Lake; the final mile is a scramble over a clear
hiking route amid rock.

For rock climbers, climbing the lake bowl
in a clockwise direction makes for an exciting
scramble to Thompson Peak and a perch just
below the rock summit; to reach the tip-top of
the mountain requires a technical climb, dangerous for most.

User Groups: Hikers, dogs, and horses. No
mountain bikes. No wheelchair facilities.

Permits: A wilderness permit is required for
hikers planning to camp.

Maps: For a map, ask the U.S. Forest Service
for Shasta-Trinity National Forest or Trinity
Alps Wilderness. For a topographic map, ask
the USGS for Thurston Peaks.

Directions: To reach the China Creek trailhead from Redding, drive north on I-5 for 70
miles. Just past Weed, take the Edgewood exit.
At the stop sign, turn left and drive through
the underpass to another stop sign. Turn right
on Old Highway 99 and drive about six miles
to Gazelle. Turn left on Gazelle-Callahan Road
and drive 27 miles to Callahan and Cecilville
Road. Turn west on Cecilville Road and drive
27 miles to Forest Road 37N24. Turn south
and drive 3.8 miles to Forest Road 37N07 (well
signed). Take Forest 37N07 and drive six miles
to the trailhead.

To reach the Hobo Gulch trailhead from
Weaverville, drive 13 miles west on Highway

299 to Helena and East Fork Road. Turn north on East Fork Road (County Road 421) and drive 3.9 miles to Hobo Gulch Road. Turn left on Hobo Gulch Road (Forest Road 34N07Y) and drive 12 miles to the Hobo Gulch trailhead, located at Hobo Gulch Campground at the end of the road.

Contact: Shasta-Trinity National Forest, Weaverville Ranger Station, Weaverville, 530/623-2121, www.fs.usda.gov/stnf.

22 TREE OF HEAVEN TRAIL
0.5 mi/0.5 hr

on the Klamath River in Klamath National Forest northwest of Yreka

Map 2.2, page 66

The trail out of the Tree of Heaven Campground provides one of the few streamside trails anywhere along the Klamath River. This is a level, wheelchair-accessible trail that heads downstream along the Klamath, and is also an interpretive trail on neo-tropical bird migrations. Visit in fall for berry picking. The Tree of Heaven River access is also a good takeout point for drift boaters and rafters who make the all-day run down from Iron Canyon Dam. Note that this trail once extended 2.5 miles to a good fishing spot at the west end of the campground, but the trail is largely overgrown, with poor access; fishermen should instead wear waders to get out in the stream a bit and clear the shoreline brush.

User Groups: Hikers, dogs, horses, and mountain bikes. No wheelchair facilities.

Permits: No permits are required. Parking and access are free.

Maps: For a map, ask the U.S. Forest Service for Klamath National Forest. For a topographic map, ask the USGS for Badger Mountain.

Directions: From Yreka, drive north on I-5 for 10 miles to the Highway 96 exit. Turn west on Highway 96 and drive about five miles. Look for the Tree of Heaven Campground, on the left. The trailhead is located at the west end of the campground.

Contact: Klamath National Forest, Headquarters, Yreka, 530/842-6131, www.fs.usda.gov/klamath.

23 JUANITA LAKE TRAIL
1.75 mi/1.0 hr

in Klamath National Forest east of Yreka

Map 2.2, page 66

Not many people know about Juanita Lake, including many Siskiyou County residents. Once they find it, most will take this easy loop trail around the lake to get a feel for the place. The lake is set in a mixed conifer forest, though few trees here are large. Wildlife in the area includes osprey and bald eagles. In the last hour of light during summer, both osprey and eagles occasionally make a fishing trip to the lake. Juanita Lake is a small lake that provides lakeside camping and fishing for brook trout. The small fishing piers are wheelchair-accessible.

A good side trip is driving on the forest road up to Ball Mountain, about two miles southwest of the lake, for great views of Mount Shasta from the 7,786-foot summit.

User Groups: Hikers and leashed dogs. No mountain bikes or horses. The fishing piers are wheelchair-accessible.

Permits: No permits are required. Parking and access are free.

Maps: For a map, ask the U.S. Forest Service for Klamath National Forest. For a topographic map, ask the USGS for Panther Rock.

Directions: From Redding, take I-5 north for 68 miles to the exit for Central Weed/Klamath Falls (Highway 97). Take that exit to the stop sign, turn right and drive 0.5 mile (through town) to the lighted intersection with Highway 97. Bear right (north) on Highway 97 and drive 35 miles to Ball Mountain Road/Little Shasta Road. Turn left and drive two miles to a signed turnoff for Juanita Lake. Turn right and drive 2.7 miles to Forest Road 46N04. Bear right and drive 3.2 miles to the lake and campground. Start near the boat dock.

Contact: Klamath National Forest, Goosenest

Ranger District, Macdoel, 530/398-4391, www.fs.usda.gov/klamath.

24 DEER MOUNTAIN
4.0 mi/2.25 hr 🥾3 ⛰7

in Klamath National Forest north of Mount Shasta

Map 2.2, page 66

Deer Mountain is the second in a line of small peaks set on the north side of Mount Shasta that extend all the way to the Medicine Lake wildlands. North from Shasta, the first peak is the Whaleback, at an elevation of 8,528 feet, and the second is Deer Mountain, at 7,006 feet. Starting elevation at the parking area is 6,200 feet, and from here you climb 800 feet through forest consisting of various pines and firs to gain the summit. This route gets very little use, even though it's easy to reach and the destination is a mountaintop. Most out-of-towners visiting this area are attracted to the trails on Mount Shasta instead, and most locals just plain overlook it. These slopes get heavy use by hunters, usually from late September through late October.

User Groups: Hikers, dogs, horses, and mountain bikes. No wheelchair facilities.

Permits: No permits are required. Parking and access are free.

Maps: For a map, ask the U.S. Forest Service for Klamath National Forest. For a topographic map, ask the USGS for Whaleback.

Directions: From Redding, take I-5 north for 68 miles to the exit for Central Weed/Klamath Falls (Highway 97). Take that exit to the stop sign, turn right and drive 0.5 mile (through town) to the lighted intersection with Highway 97. Bear right (north) on Highway 97 and drive 16.8 miles to Deer Mountain Road/Forest Road 19 (Forest Road 42N12). Turn right and drive 3.8 miles to Deer Mountain Snowmobile Park and Forest Road 44N23. Turn left on Forest Road 44N23 and drive 2.3 miles. There is no designated trailhead; park off road and hike cross-country to the top of the mountain.

Note that Forest Road 43N69 loops around the base of the mountain; you may also hike from anywhere along that road. The road continues through remote forest to Highway 89.

Contact: Klamath National Forest, Goosenest Ranger District, Macdoel, 530/398-4391, www.fs.usda.gov/klamath.

25 THE WHALEBACK
3.0 mi/2.5 hr 🥾3 ⛰8

in Klamath National Forest north of Mount Shasta

Map 2.2, page 66

After you pass Mount Shasta on I-5, driving north, look off to your right and you'll see a large, humplike mountain that sits directly north of Shasta. It looks like a huge volcanic bump that was born when Shasta was active. That's because it is. This is the Whaleback, 8,528 feet high. It provides a hike with a payoff view at the top, and a surprise: a large crater. The Whaleback Summit is actually a volcanic cinder cone with a collapsed center. This interesting geology, along with the unsurpassed view of Mount Shasta to the south, makes this a first-rate hike. Yet almost nobody tries it, most likely because they don't realize how near you can drive to the top, or because there is no formal trail. After parking at the gate, you just hike cross-country style up to the rim; it's steep all the way. The 1.5-mile hike is a scramble only in a few places. In the process, you'll climb 1,100 feet, from a starting elevation of 7,400 feet, to Whaleback Rim.

User Groups: Hikers, dogs, horses, and mountain bikes. No wheelchair facilities.

Permits: No permits are required. Parking and access are free.

Maps: For a map, ask the U.S. Forest Service for Klamath National Forest. For a topographic map, ask the USGS for Whaleback.

Directions: From Redding, take I-5 north for 68 miles to the exit for Central Weed/Klamath Falls (Highway 97). Take that exit to the stop sign, turn right and drive 0.5 mile (through town) to the lighted intersection with Highway 97. Bear right (north) on Highway 97 and drive 15 miles to Deer Mountain Road. Turn right on Deer Mountain Road and drive four miles to Deer Mountain Snowmobile Park. Drive east on Deer Mountain Road/Forest Road 19 (Forest Road 42N12) for three miles to Forest Road 42N24. Turn right on Forest Road 42N24 and drive three miles to a gate. Park and hike in. There is no designated trail; you must hike cross-country from the road. The peak is about 1.5 miles from the gate.

Contact: Klamath National Forest, Goosenest Ranger District, Macdoel, 530/398-4391, www.fs.usda.gov/klamath.

26 WHITNEY FALLS TRAILHEAD

3.4 mi/2.5 hr   🏃4 ⛰️8

on the northwest slope of Mount Shasta

Map 2.2, page 66

This used to be a great, easy hike. No more. A flash flood, released upslope from the Whitney Glacier, buried the first mile of this trail under a flow of mud and debris. Although interesting to geologists, it requires hikers to negotiate rocks, boulders, logs, and deep erosion channels. It takes more than a mile of scrambling to intersect the former trail. It's difficult to find if you look close, near your feet. Instead, get higher, on one of the volcanic crags, and look ahead for the faint trail on the right side of the flow and a small gorge. That scramble is what makes this trek difficult.

The Whitney Falls trail then rises from about 5,600 feet uphill out of the drainage. The trail spans 1.6 miles to an unsigned fork at 6,400 feet. Take the right fork, a spur trail to an overlook at a deep gorge. On the far uphill side is hidden Whitney Falls, a 250-foot waterfall, with its thin, silvery wisp tumbling through a narrow chute in a dramatic ashen gorge. It takes perfect timing to see this waterfall at anything more than a trickle. The view to the north of Shasta Valley is outstanding, highlighted by the series of hummocks, which are actually chunks of Shasta's former summit that were carried here like miniature hilltops in a massive lava flow after Shasta's last eruption, 600 years ago.

Special notes: If you turn left at the fork instead, you'll venture through forest, then up through another gutted stream drainage. The trail ends, and mountaineers will have to pass Coquette Falls, and then near the peak at the Bolam Glacier, in order to make the summit. Safety gear and expert climbing skills are required. Stay off the Whitney Glacier. It has a crevasse that can be camouflaged with snow in spring and early summer; it is possible to plunge through the snowbridge and fall deep into the crevasse—it is the Venus flytrap of Mount Shasta.

User Groups: Hikers only. No dogs, horses, or mountain bikes. No wheelchair facilities.

Permits: Parking and access are free. A free wilderness permit is required for both day use and overnight use; $30 summit permit required for hikers climbing over 10,000 feet in elevation. All climbers are required to pack out waste and must bring a pack-out bag.

Maps: For a map, ask the U.S. Forest Service for Shasta-Trinity National Forest or Mount Shasta Wilderness. For a topographic map, ask the USGS for Mount Shasta.

Directions: From Redding, take I-5 north for 68 miles to the exit for Central Weed/Klamath Falls (Highway 97). Take that exit to the stop sign, turn right and drive 0.5 mile (through town) to the lighted intersection with Highway 97. Bear right (north) on Highway 97 and drive 12 miles to Bolam Road (Forest Road 43N21), which is usually unsigned. (If you reach County Road A12 on the left, you have gone 0.25 mile too far.) Turn right on Bolam Road for four miles (you'll cross railroad tracks) to the end of the road. A high-clearance vehicle is required.

Contact: Shasta-Trinity National Forest, Mount Shasta Ranger District, Mount Shasta, 530/926-4511, www.fs.usda.gov/stnf; Fifth Season Climbing Report, 530/926-5555; Shasta Mountain Guides, 530/926-3117 or www.shastaguides.com.

27 BLACK BUTTE TRAIL
5.0 mi/3.5 hr   🏃5 ⛺8

in Shasta-Trinity National Forest between I-5 and Mount Shasta

Map 2.2, page 66

Anybody who has cruised I-5 north to Oregon and gawked in astonishment at Mount Shasta has inevitably seen Black Butte right alongside the highway. That's right, it's that barren cinder cone set between the highway and Mount Shasta, and it can pique a traveler's curiosity. The trail is routed right to the top and can answer all of your questions. But you may not like all of the answers. Over the course of 2.5 miles, you'll climb 1,845 feet—much of it steep, most of it rocky, and in the summer, all of it hot and dry. Shade is nonexistent. There are only two rewards. One is claiming the summit, at 6,325 feet, where you'll find the foundation of an old U.S. Forest Service lookout and great 360-degree views; the other is that the hike is an excellent warm-up for people who are planning to climb Mount Shasta. (That is, providing you don't need a week to recover.) This trip is actually best done on a warm summer night under a full moon.

User Groups: Hikers and dogs. No horses or mountain bikes. No wheelchair facilities.

Permits: No permits are required.

Maps: A trail information sheet is available by contacting the Mount Shasta Ranger District. For a map, ask the U.S. Forest Service for Shasta-Trinity National Forest. For a topographic map, ask the USGS for Mount Shasta city.

Directions: From Redding, take I-5 north to the exit for Central Mount Shasta. Take that exit to the stop sign at Lake Street. Turn right and drive one mile east (through town) on Lake Street, and then bear left as it merges with Washington Drive (and becomes Everitt Memorial Highway). Continue on Washington/Everitt Memorial Highway (past the high school on the right) for about two miles, and look for the sign for Spring Hill Plantation (on the right) and Forest Road 41N18 (on the left). Turn left on Forest Road 41N18/Ash Flat (a gravel road), drive about 200 yards, and bear right, continuing on Forest Road 41N18 for 2.5 miles. After the road crosses under the overhead power line, turn left on Forest Road 41N18A (Black Butte Road) and drive 0.75 mile to the trailhead. Parking is limited; be sure to park off the road.

Contact: Shasta-Trinity National Forest, Mount Shasta Ranger District, Mount Shasta, 530/926-4511, www.fs.usda.gov/stnf.

28 SAND FLAT TRAILHEAD
3.4 mi/2.75 hr   🏃3 ⛺8

on the southern slope of Mount Shasta

Map 2.2, page 66

The hike from Sand Flat to Horse Camp, a distance of 1.7 miles with a climb of 1,000 feet, will give you a good taste of the Mount Shasta experience, and you're likely to savor the flavors. Many who make this day hike are compelled to return to climb all the way to the top.

Sand Flat provides a shaded parking area to start from, away from all the people in summer at Bunny Flat. The elevation is 6,800 feet. The trail immediately takes off uphill. The climb is gradual at first, but then it becomes quite steep. At 7,360 feet, it intersects with Bunny Flat Trail and then continues to rise through the forest. Along the way are amazing examples of how avalanches and windstorms have knocked down entire sections of forest. When you reach Horse Camp, at 7,800 feet, nearing timberline, you'll find many rewards. The first is spring water flowing continuously out of a piped fountain near the Sierra Hut; it's perhaps the best-tasting water in the world. The second is the foreboding view of Red Bank, which forms the mountain rim above Horse Camp. The third is the opportunity to hike up a short way above tree line for the sweeping views to the south of Castle Crags and Lake Siskiyou. After taking the first steps on Summit Trail, you'll likely yearn to keep going all the way to the very top of this magic mountain. If you wish to hike Summit Trail, see the following hike out of Bunny Flat trailhead.

User Groups: Hikers only. No dogs, horses, or mountain bikes. No wheelchair facilities.

Permits: Parking and access are free. A free wilderness permit is required for both day use and overnight use. A $25 Summit Permit, good for three days, is required for hikers climbing over 10,000 feet in elevation. An annual Summit Pass is available for $30. All climbers are required to pack out waste and must bring a pack-out bag.

Maps: For a map, ask the U.S. Forest Service for Shasta-Trinity National Forest or Mount Shasta Wilderness. For a topographic map, ask the USGS for Mount Shasta.

Directions: From Redding, take I-5 north to the exit for Central Mount Shasta. Take that exit to the stop sign. Turn right and drive one mile east on Lake Street, and then bear left on Washington Drive (it merges, and then Washington Drive becomes Everitt Memorial Highway). Continue on Washington/Everitt Memorial Highway (past the high school) for 9.7 miles to Sand Flat Road. Turn left and drive 0.4 mile to parking and the trailhead.

Contact: Shasta-Trinity National Forest, Mount Shasta Ranger District, Mount Shasta, 530/926-4511, www.fs.usda.gov/stnf; Fifth Season Climbing Report, 530/926-5555; Shasta Mountain Guides, 530/926-3117 or www.shastaguides.com.

29 SHASTA SUMMIT TRAIL
14 mi/1.5 days   👣5 ⛰10

on the southern slope of Mount Shasta in the Shasta-Trinity National Forest

Map 2.2, page 66   **BEST** (

The hike to the top of 14,179-foot Mount Shasta is one of America's epic treks. Your challenge is to climb 7,229 feet over ice, snow, and rock while trying to suck what little oxygen you can out of the thin air. It may be the greatest adventure in the West that most hikers in good condition have an honest chance of achieving.

Timing is everything. Time your trip for when the wind is down on top, the summit is clear, no thunderstorms, and the route has plenty of snow, which provides an excellent climbing surface (where you wear crampons) and acts as a mortar for holding boulders in place.

The trip starts out of Bunny Flat at 6,950 feet, leads through a forest of Shasta red firs, climbs to where the trail intersects with the route out of Sand Flat, then turns right and rises to Horse Camp, at an elevation of 7,800 feet and a distance of 1.8 miles. There's a hiker's cabin, called the Sierra Club Hut, on the left, an incredible spring with sweet-tasting water on the right—it's a must to fill up your water bottles here—and a short walk to environmental toilets to your right. Most people camp one night at Horse Camp and then leave very early the next morning for the summit.

After filling your canteens at the spring, start hiking the Summit Trail. Make your first steps across a series of large stones called Olberman's Causeway. From here, the trail quickly rises above timberline, gaining 1,000 feet per mile for six miles, and after a short time, it becomes a faint path. One route ventures to your left and is routed, including a span of switchbacks, up to Helen Lake, a flat spot for a trail camp. Another route crosses a subridge to your right and then you are routed up Avalanche Gulch, with Red Bank looming directly overhead.

Expect snow and ice, that's when the climbing is best, and you will stop and strap your crampons onto your boots. The walking is easy with crampons. The trail climbs up Avalanche Gulch, and some people stop to make trail camps at a flat spot called Helen Lake, at 10,440 feet. Hikers not acclimated to high altitudes may begin experiencing some dizziness, but there's no relief in sight. At this point, the hike gets steeper (about a 35-degree slope), and some give up before reaching Red Bank—a huge, red, volcanic outcrop at about 12,500 feet. At Red Bank, depending on how much snow is on the mountain, you might find a narrow and steep rock/ice chute. I prefer this route, though you'll need your ice ax in order to pull your way through, and where a slip is certain without crampons. In high snow years, the chute is filled with snow and the climb continues ahead at steep grade. There are two other routes as well: one very steep ascent to your left, another that circles The Thumb to your right, but in the latter, you will pass a crevasse that should not be circumvented without an experienced guide to keep you safe.

When you emerge atop Red Bank, you are nearly 13,000 feet high, at the foot of a glacier field and Misery Hill, so named because it's a long, slow climb through snow in spring and scree in summer. It's a myth that a lot of people actually mistake it for the peak—if you were that off base, you'd never make it this far. Once atop Misery Hill, you'll see the true Shasta Summit, a massive pinnacle of lava that seems to jut straight up into the air. Cross a sun-cupped glacier field to reach the pinnacle and there you will see the trail routed up to the top. With a final push, follow the trail, grabbing rocks to help pull you up and sucking the thin air, and with a few last steps, you'll be on top,

at 14,179 feet. On clear days you can see hundreds of miles in all directions, and the sky is a deeper cobalt blue than you ever imagined. On top, you'll sign your name in a logbook in an old rusted metal box, then take in the grand wonders surrounding you. It's a remarkable trip, one that can inspire some people to keep their bodies in good enough shape to make the trip every year.

About half the people who try to climb Mount Shasta don't make it. The number one reason is because they are stopped by bad weather. High winds above 12,000 feet are common in May and June. In late summer, typically mid-August through early October, there is a danger from tumbling boulders. Snow acts as a mortar and holds the volcanic landscape together. Most hikers in good condition who start the trip very early and have the proper equipment can summit, especially in July, when the weather and climbing conditions are often best. Early? You should depart from Bunny Flat by 3am, or hike in a day early, set up a base camp at Horse Camp (at tree line), and start no later than 4am. Another strategy that works is to

© TOM STIENSTRA

Shasta Summit Trail

set up a base camp higher on the mountain, at Helen Lake, or in high snow years at the flat spot on Green Butte to climb Green Butte Ridge (it is not passable is low snow years). For equipment, you'll need a day pack with warm clothes, a windbreaker, two canteens of water, food, and an ice ax and crampons are mandatory. Refill your canteen wherever you find a rivulet of water (it's occasionally possible at Red Bank); rangers recommend using a water filter.

It's an absolute must to make an early start. In the hot summer months, towering cumulus clouds sometimes form on Mount Shasta during the afternoon, and by then you'll want to be making the trip down. If towering cumulonimbus begin forming by noon, intense thunderstorms are possible by midafternoon.

All hikers must pack out their waste. Special waste pack-out bags are available at no charge at the trailhead and at the Mount Shasta Ranger Station in Mount Shasta.

The biggest danger and largest number of injuries on Mount Shasta come not from falling, but from being hit by tumbling boulders. In fact, our former research assistant, Robyn Brewer, was struck in the foot by a boulder in her first attempt at climbing Shasta. She was hit so hard that it knocked her hiking boot off, breaking her foot and requiring an emergency helicopter airlift out for medical treatment. Always keep a good distance between you and your hiking partners, don't hike in a vertical line, and if a rock comes bouncing down, always shout, "Rock! Rock!" Some guides recommend wearing helmets. By the way, Robyn returned to Mount Shasta the following two years and made it to the top on both trips.

The mountain is best hiked when it still has a good coating of snow and ice, which provide excellent footing with crampons. When the snow and ice melt off in late fall, tromping through the small volcanic rocks is like slogging in mushy sand, and there is the additional problem of boulder falls.

Drink lots of water. In high altitudes, dehydration is a common problem and can result in early exhaustion and extreme vulnerability to mountain sickness.

When you drive into the town of Mount Shasta, at the corner of Lake and Main Street, the main intersection in downtown Mount Shasta, you'll see Shasta Mountain Guides on the right, and the Fifth Season, which provides rental equipment, on the left.

User Groups: Hikers only. No dogs, horses, or mountain bikes. No wheelchair facilities.

Permits: Parking and access are free. A free wilderness permit is required for both day use and overnight use. A $25 Summit Permit, good for three days, is required for hikers climbing over 10,000 feet in elevation. An annual Summit Pass is available for $30. All climbers are required to pack out waste and must bring a pack-out bag.

Maps: For a map, ask the U.S. Forest Service for Shasta-Trinity National Forest or Mount Shasta Wilderness. For a topographic map, ask the USGS for Mount Shasta.

Directions: From Redding, take I-5 north to the exit for Central Mount Shasta. Take that exit to the stop sign at Lake Street. Turn right and drive one mile east (through town) on Lake Street, and then bear left as it merges with Washington Drive (and becomes Everitt Memorial Highway). Continue on Washington/Everitt Memorial Highway (past the high school on the right) and drive 11.1 miles to Bunny Flat. As you drive in, the trailhead is on the left, next to the restroom.

Contact: Shasta-Trinity National Forest, Mount Shasta Ranger District, Mount Shasta, 530/926-4511, www.fs.usda.gov/stnf; Fifth Season Climbing Report, 530/926-5555; Shasta Mountain Guides, 530/926-3117 or www.shastaguides.com.

30 GRAY BUTTE
2.8 mi/1.75 hr

from Ski Bowl on the southern slope of Mount Shasta in Mount Shasta Wilderness

Map 2.2, page 66   BEST (

This is a great day hike. It's easy, unique, and with a great pay-off for those who don't mind a short rock climb to a perch atop Gray Butte. Start at the old Ski Bowl, on the right of the road at the Squaw Creek Trailhead (a mile past Panther Meadows and near the end of paved, two-lane Everitt Memorial Highway). This hike is a short one, from Ski Bowl to Gray Butte and back.

From the trailhead, head southeast on a clear route across a volcanic scree, just above tree line. You'll see a sculpted volcanic valley called The Gate. Some mountain visitors consider this to be the mountain's sacred portal to the spiritual dimension. Gray Butte looms above to your right. Reaching the top (at 8,119 feet) requires a scramble over sharp-edged volcanic rock (if you wear rings on your fingers, they will scuff the exposed bottom side). But the scramble is well worth it: There is a perfect lookout to the south, with Castle Crags, Mount Lassen, and the drop-off in the Sacramento Valley, all prominent.

User Groups: Hikers only. Dogs are allowed at Gray Butte, but not beyond and are not advised. No horses or mountain bikes. No wheelchair facilities.

Permits: Parking and access are free. A free wilderness permit is required for both day use and overnight use. A $25 Summit Permit, good for three days, is required for hikers climbing over 10,000 feet in elevation. An annual Summit Pass is available for $30. All climbers are required to pack out waste and must bring a pack-out bag.

Maps: For a map, ask the U.S. Forest Service for Shasta-Trinity National Forest or Mount Shasta Wilderness. For a topographic map, ask the USGS for Mount Shasta.

Directions: From Redding, take I-5 north to the exit for Central Mount Shasta. Take that exit to the stop sign at Lake Street. Turn right and drive one mile east (through town) on Lake Street, and then bear left as it merges with Washington Drive (and becomes Everitt Memorial Highway). Continue on Washington/Everitt Memorial Highway (past the high school on the right) and drive 11.1 miles to Bunny Flat (restroom available), and then continue 2.5 miles (past the entrance spur to Panther Meadows) to the trailhead on the right.

Contact: Shasta-Trinity National Forest, Mount Shasta Ranger District, Mount Shasta, 530/926-4511, www.fs.usda.gov/stnf; Fifth Season Climbing Report, 530/926-5555; Shasta Mountain Guides, 530/926-3117 or www.shastaguides.com.

31 GREEN BUTTE RIDGE
4.4 mi/4.0 hr

on the southern slope of Mount Shasta

Map 2.2, page 66

In the big snow years, this is our favorite trek on Mount Shasta. You have a towering view down into canyons on each side of you, and beyond to Castle Crags and miles of wildlands. Yet it is also one of the most overlooked. Green Butte, a huge rock outcrop set at 9,200 feet, is your destination. From Bunny Flat at 6,950 feet, it means a climb of 2,250 feet in a little over two miles. In the big snow years, a climber's route will be available across the top of the knife-edge ridge, a great route to The Thumb and beyond to the summit.

From the Bunny Flat trailhead, just about everybody hikes to Horse Camp. Instead, there is an unsigned cut-off to the right that climbs through forest and connects to Green Butte Ridge. You end up with a towering view over Lake Siskiyou and beyond to the top of Castle Crags. From here, in winter, many will snowboard back down. Most use split boards. This one is a 10, an unforgettable trek, and though you earn every step, the pay-offs are world-class in scope.

In big snow years, this is a great route to

summit. As you climb on the ridge, you will tower over Avalanche Gulch to your left, the old Mount Shasta Ski Bowl to your right. It leads up to The Thumb, where you cross above Red Banks and join the main route up Misery Hill.

The route is well protected from spring winds. It can blow 80 mph across Misery Hill and you'll feel only a light breeze here until you top 10,000 feet.

User Groups: Hikers only. Dogs are permitted in Old Ski Bowl, but not beyond into Mount Shasta Wilderness. No horses or mountain bikes. No wheelchair facilities.

Permits: Parking and access are free. A free wilderness permit is required for both day use and overnight use. A $25 Summit Permit, good for three days, is required for hikers climbing over 10,000 feet in elevation. An annual Summit Pass is available for $30. All climbers are required to pack out waste and must bring a pack-out bag.

Maps: For a map, ask the U.S. Forest Service for Shasta-Trinity National Forest or Mount Shasta Wilderness. For a topographic map, ask the USGS for Mount Shasta.

Directions: From Redding, take I-5 north to the exit for Central Mount Shasta. Take that exit to the stop sign at Lake Street. Turn right and drive one mile east (through town) on Lake Street, and then bear left as it merges with Washington Drive (and becomes Everitt Memorial Highway). Continue on Washington/Everitt Memorial Highway (past the high school on the right) and drive 11.1 miles to Bunny Flat. As you drive in, the trailhead is on the left, next to the restroom.

Contact: Shasta-Trinity National Forest, Mount Shasta Ranger District, Mount Shasta, 530/926-4511, www.fs.usda.gov/stnf; Fifth Season Climbing Report, 530/926-5555; Shasta Mountain Guides, 530/926-3117 or www.shastaguides.com.

32 BREWER CREEK TRAILHEAD

4.2 mi/3.0 hr

on the northeast slope of Mount Shasta

Map 2.2, page 66

It's so quiet here that you can practically hear the wildflowers bloom. We've hiked the north slope of Shasta out of the Brewer Creek trailhead several times and often not seen another person. The trip makes for a good day hike in the Mount Shasta Wilderness. The trailhead is set near Brewer Creek (at 7,200 feet), hence the name. The drive in is long, and because of that, many prefer Clear Creek Trailhead and its views of Mud Creek Falls and Ash Creek Falls to this trailhead.

After a short walk through a section of forest that was selectively logged many years ago, you'll enter the Shasta Wilderness and be surrounded by old-growth firs, many scraggly from enduring harsh winters and the short growing season. Here the trail climbs more. It's a steady climb up through forest, with gradual switchbacks as it goes. When you near tree line, at 7,700 feet, the trail turns to the left and begins to lateral across the mountain. It's 2.1 miles to timberline from the trailhead, and most people hike to this point, then turn back. The trail becomes a route, and at times seems to disappear. You can add a mile or two by climbing a wide, volcanic slope with good footing all the way, and rise to 9,500 feet. This is a great spot for a picnic, provides sweeping views, and may inspire dreams of the day you'll next climb all the way to the top of Shasta.

Special note: Mountaineers who try to climb Shasta from this trailhead have only one good route from the point where the trail meets tree line, which is to head to the right up and over Hotlum Glacier. This route is extremely difficult, very steep, and dangerous. Only mountaineers with guides or considerable experience glacier-trekking should attempt this route to the summit.

User Groups: Hikers only. No dogs, horses, or mountain bikes. No wheelchair facilities.

Permits: Parking and access are free. A free wilderness permit is required for both day use and overnight use. A $25 Summit Permit, good for three days, is required for hikers climbing over 10,000 feet in elevation. An annual Summit Pass is available for $30. All climbers are required to pack out waste and must bring a pack-out bag.

Maps: For a map, ask the U.S. Forest Service for Shasta-Trinity National Forest or Mount Shasta Wilderness. For a topographic map, ask the USGS for Mount Shasta.

Directions: From Redding, take I-5 north for 58 miles to the Highway 89/McCloud-Reno exit. Bear right on Highway 89 and drive nine miles to McCloud, then continue for another 2.8 miles to Pilgrim Creek Road. Turn left on Pilgrim Creek Road and drive 5.3 miles (becomes Forest Road 13) and continue another two miles to Forest Road 19. Continue on Forest Road 19/Military Pass Road for seven miles to Forest Road 42N02. Turn left on 42N02 and drive four miles (signed, stay on 42N02 at junctions) to trailhead parking area. High-clearance vehicles are recommended; four-wheel drive is helpful.

Contact: Shasta-Trinity National Forest, Mount Shasta Ranger District, Mount Shasta, 530/926-4511, www.fs.usda.gov/stnf; McCloud Ranger District, 530/964-2184; climbing report 530/926-5555.

33 CLEAR CREEK TRAILHEAD/MUD CREEK FALLS

4.0 mi/2.5 hr

on the southeast slope of Mount Shasta

Map 2.2, page 66

A short walk on the remote southeast flank of Mount Shasta can provide entry to a land of enchantment. From Clear Creek Trail, you get a great day hike that features an overlook of deep canyons, views of glaciers, and Mount Shasta's prettiest waterfall, Mud Creek Falls (and for those with the zest for it, nearby Ash Creek

Falls). The drive in is well signed and much closer from Highway 89 than the drive to the distant Brewer Creek Trailhead.

At the parking area, the trail starts just to the left of the restroom (many years ago, the trail instead followed an old overgrown jeep road from the upper end of the parking area; that is now reclaimed by a young forest and the going is very slow, where you must pass many downed trees). The trail is routed along a ridge as you climb on an even grade through forest. As you near tree line, you'll see the edge of a canyon rim to your left. At a break in the trees on your left, look up the canyon, you'll see the sensational Mud Creek Falls, roughly 125 feet high, directly ahead, though from a distance. This is the pay-off for day hikes.

If you want more, you can continue up-slope about a mile to a meadow, creek, and campsite that summit hikers use as a base camp. This is a launch point, not an end point. The route here includes an open crossing on the side of the Wintun Glacier, scary for most, where a slip means a long fall. Only mountaineers with guides or considerable experience glacier-trekking should attempt this route to the summit.

There's another option for those who want to trek the sub-alpine region of giant Shasta. With a topo map, the ambitious can venture off trail to find and see nearby Ash Creek Falls. Mud Creek Falls and Ash Creek Falls are best viewed in early summer, when snowmelt is peaking and runoff is high. They are both gorgeous.

This area is rich in natural history. The canyon was carved by a glacier and is still fed with water from the towering, fractured Konwakiton Glacier, which runs the color of volcanic silt. There are several glaciers directly above your vantage point, which feed the canyon's erosive silt into Mud Creek.

User Groups: Hikers only. No dogs, horses, or mountain bikes. No wheelchair facilities.

Permits: Parking and access are free. A free wilderness permit is required for both day use and overnight use. A $25 Summit Permit, good for three days, is required for hikers climbing over 10,000 feet in elevation. An annual

Summit Pass is available for $30. All climbers are required to pack out waste and must bring a pack-out bag.

Maps: For a map, ask the U.S. Forest Service for Shasta-Trinity National Forest or Mount Shasta Wilderness. For a topographic map, ask the USGS for Mount Shasta.

Directions: From Redding, take I-5 north for 47 miles to the Highway 89/McCloud-Reno exit. Bear right on Highway 89 and drive nine miles to McCloud, then continue for another 2.8 miles to Pilgrim Creek Road. Turn left on Pilgrim Creek Road (Forest Road 13) and drive five miles (paved) to Widow Springs Road (Forest Road 41N15). Turn left and drive about five miles to Forest Road 31. Cross this road (still Forest Road 31) for 0.1 mile to a junction, stay left, and continue 0.5 mile to Forest Road 4N125. Turn left on Forest Road 4N125 and drive 2.2 miles to the parking area and trail. The road is well signed. High-clearance, four-wheel-drive vehicles recommended (as you near the trailhead, the road becomes steep, often with deep dust in late summer that can feel like snow under your tires).

Contact: Shasta-Trinity National Forest, Mount Shasta Ranger District, Mount Shasta, 530/926-4511, www.fs.usda.gov/stnf; McCloud Ranger District, 530/964-2184; climbing report 530/926-5555.

34 ETNA SUMMIT TO GRIDER CREEK (PCT)

49.0 mi one-way/4 days 3 ▲10

from Etna Summit into the Marble Mountain Wilderness west of Etna

Map 2.2, page 66

The Etna Summit is one of the major access points for the Pacific Crest Trail in Northern California. There is a good, safe parking area (with a nice view), and at an elevation of 5,492 feet, you don't have to start your hike with a wicked climb that is demanded at so many other PCT trailheads. From Etna Summit, the trail starts by crossing rugged, dry, and often

hot terrain that is best dealt with in the morning. You'll reach Shelly Lake about eight miles in. Note that there is no water available along this route until Shelly Lake. The campground at Shelly Meadows is a good first-night stopover. From there, an excellent second-day destination is the Marble Valley, about another 10 miles north, with camping in the nearby Sky High Lakes Basin. The next 20 miles of trail cross through and out of the Marble Mountains. You'll pass Marble Mountain (a side trip to the Marble Rim is mandatory), Paradise Lake (many visitors will make camp here), and Kings Castle. As you face the lake, a spring is located to the left of the campsites in a small ravine at the head of the lake. Most of the trail here is above tree line, with outstanding lookouts at several points, including a great vista from Marble Rim. Moving onward, the trail follows Big Ridge to Buckhorn Mountain (6,908 feet), continues past Huckleberry Mountain (6,303 feet), and then drops down to the headwaters of Grider Creek, the next major trailhead access point. As you head north, the trail becomes less and less traveled.

To pick up the next trail heading north, see the *Grider Creek to Seiad Valley (PCT)* hike in this chapter. If you are walking this trail in reverse, see the *Cecilville Road to Russian Wilderness (PCT)* hike in this chapter to continue south.

User Groups: Hikers, dogs, and horses. No mountain bikes. No wheelchair facilities.

Permits: Campfire permits (free) are required for campfires and stoves. Parking and access are free.

Maps: A trail information sheet can be obtained by contacting the Salmon River Ranger District. For a map, ask the U.S. Forest Service for Klamath National Forest or Marble Mountain Wilderness. For a topographic map, ask the USGS for Eaton Peak.

Directions: From Redding, take I-5 to Yreka and the exit for Highway 3/Fort Jones. Take that exit to the stop sign, turn left, and drive a short distance to the lighted intersection. Turn left on Highway 3 and drive 28 miles to Etna.

Turn west on Etna-Somes Bar Road (called Main Street in town) and drive 10.5 miles to Etna Summit. The parking area is on the left.

Contact: Klamath National Forest, Salmon/ Scott River Ranger District, Fort Jones, 530/468-5351, www.fs.usda.gov/klamath.

35 TAYLOR LAKE TRAIL
1.0 mi/0.5 hr

from Etna Summit into the Russian Wilderness west of Etna

Map 2.2, page 66   **BEST**

Taylor Lake is proof that wildernesslike lakes can be accessible by wheelchair. The trail is made of hard-packed dirt and is wheelchair-accessible, though wheelchairs with wide wheels are recommended. For those with boots instead of wheels, it's about a 10-minute walk to Taylor Lake, a long, narrow lake set on the northern end of the Russian Wilderness. Trout fishing is often very good here, and the walk is short enough for hikers to bring along a small raft or float tube. The region directly above the lake toward Big Blue Lake and beyond in the Russian Wilderness will show evidence of a significant forest fire burn.

For a side-trip option, the Pacific Crest Trail runs east just above the lake. There is a very steep cut-off trail that climbs from the lake up to the PCT.

User Groups: Hikers, wheelchairs, dogs, and horses. No mountain bikes.

Permits: No permits are required for day use. A campfire permit (free) is required for campfires and stoves. Parking and access are free.

Maps: A trail information sheet can be obtained by contacting the Salmon Ranger District. For a map, ask the U.S. Forest Service for Klamath National Forest or Marble Mountain Wilderness. For a topographic map, ask the USGS for Eaton Peak.

Directions: From Redding, take I-5 to Yreka and the exit for Highway 3/Fort Jones. Take that exit to the stop sign, turn left, and drive a short distance to the lighted intersection. Turn

left on Highway 3 and drive 28 miles southwest to Etna. Turn west (right) on Etna-Somes Bar Road (called Main Street in town) and drive 10.25 miles (over the top of the Etna Summit and down the other side) to Forest Road 41N18 (a signed access road). Turn left and continue to the trailhead.

Contact: Klamath National Forest, Salmon/ Scott River Ranger District, Fort Jones, 530/468-5351, www.fs.usda.gov/klamath.

36 STATUE LAKE
6.0 mi/4.0 hr

in the Russian Wilderness west of Etna

Map 2.2, page 66

Statue Lake earned its name from the unique granite sculptures that frame the back wall of the lake. When you first arrive at the small lake, it's a gorgeous yet solemn sight, one of nature's mountain temples. No place else looks like this. Some of the granite outcrops look like fingers sculpted with a giant chisel. There is a small primitive campsite on a granite overlook, from which you can often see small brook trout rising to feed in the lake.

After parking at the Music Creek trailhead, start the trip by hiking up a moderate grade and climbing about a mile through burned-out forest to the Pacific Crest Trail. Turn right and hike on the PCT for about 1.5 miles, an easy walk in the forest. When you reach a small spring creek, stop and fill your canteens, then leave the trail and head uphill. There is no trail or sign. This is an off-trail trek where you read a topo map and match it up with the landscape. Well worth it. It's about a 30-minute, cross-country hike to the lake, and the last 10 minutes is over a large field of boulders. The region shows evidence of a significant forest fire burn, but the small Statue Lake itself is untouched.

User Groups: Hikers only. Dogs are permitted but not advised because of the route crossing a boulder field. No horses or mountain bikes. No wheelchair facilities.

Permits: No permits are required for day use.

A campfire permit (free) is required for campfires and stoves. Parking and access are free.

Maps: A trail information sheet can be obtained by contacting the Salmon Ranger District. For a map, ask the U.S. Forest Service for Klamath National Forest or Marble Mountain Wilderness. For a topographic map, ask the USGS for Sawyers Bar.

Directions: From Redding, take I-5 to Yreka and the exit for Highway 3/Fort Jones. Take that exit to the stop sign, turn left, and drive a short distance to the lighted intersection. Turn left on Highway 3 and drive 28 miles southwest to Etna. Turn west on Etna-Somes Bar Road (called Main Street in town), drive over Etna Summit, and continue down the other side to Forest Road 40N54 (just before the Salmon River Bridge). Turn left on Forest Road 40N54 and drive eight miles to the Music Creek trailhead. (A sign that says Pacific Crest Trail is usually posted. The sign for Music Creek trailhead is repeatedly stolen.)

Contact: Klamath National Forest, Salmon/Scott River Ranger District, Fort Jones, 530/468-5351, www.fs.usda.gov/klamath.

37 TRAIL CREEK ROUTE

7.0 mi/2 days 4 △6

in the Russian Wilderness west of Callahan

Map 2.2, page 66

The Trail Creek "Trail" is no longer an official trail. Outside of us, few tried hiking it. The Forest Service has decommissioned it, which means no trail maintenance is performed. It is now more of a route, one that leads into the Russian Wilderness. We found it a quick, yet very steep, way to gain access to Syphon Lake and the Russian Wilderness. The Trail Creek Route starts out as more of an old jeep road, involving a steep climb and drop, and then a short cross-country jaunt. (When you finish, you could always write the book, *My Life as a Jeep*.) From Trail Creek Campground to the PCT, you are unlikely to see anybody but your companions, and that's a plus. This is also a

good route with dogs, because you won't see a soul.

The trailhead is located a short distance up a gravel road across from Trail Creek Campground (located along Cecilville-Callahan Road). For the first 1.5 miles, the trail ventures steeply up on an old fire lane. It continues to climb, and as you near the crest, you'll junction with the Pacific Crest Trail. Turn left on the PCT, and then just five minutes later, turn at a signed junction to Syphon Lake. This is a good first night's camp. Russian or Waterdog Lakes are good second-day destinations.

Once you hit the high country, the lakes are very beautiful, especially Russian Lake, which is excellent for swimming. Because the wilderness here is small, it does not take many people hiking in to take up the campsites. Expect occasional cow sightings in midsummer near Syphon Lake. The Russian Wilderness is a place so pristine and so small that it just can't handle many visitors. If you go, walk softly, and treat the fragile area with care.

For most, the trailhead for the Pacific Crest Trail off the Cecilville-Callahan Road is by far preferable. This provides a much easier route into the southern portion of the Russian Wilderness, but it will add 10 miles to your round-trip. That's the attraction of starting here instead.

User Groups: Hikers, dogs, and horses. Mountain bikes allowed only outside of the wilderness border. No wheelchair facilities.

Permits: A wilderness permit is required for hikers planning to camp. Parking and access are free.

Maps: For a map, ask the U.S. Forest Service for Klamath National Forest. For topographic maps, ask the USGS for Deadman Peak and Eaton Peak.

Directions: From Redding, drive north on I-5 for 70 miles. Just past Weed, take the Edgewood exit. At the stop sign, turn left and drive through the underpass to another stop sign. Turn right on Old Highway 99 and drive six miles to Gazelle. Turn left at Gazelle on

Gazelle-Callahan Road and drive about 20 miles to Callahan. From Callahan on Highway 3, turn west on County Road 402 (Cecilville Road) and drive 17 miles to Trail Creek Campground. The trail has been decommissioned. Across from the campground, a route heads north from a gravel road.

Contact: Klamath National Forest, Salmon/ Scott River Ranger District, Fort Jones, 530/468-5351, www.fs.usda.gov/klamath.

38 CECILVILLE ROAD TO RUSSIAN WILDERNESS (PCT)

3.0 mi one-way/1 day 🚶3 ⛰7

from Cecilville Road west of Callahan to the southern border of the Russian Wilderness

Map 2.2, page 66

Most hikers use this as a jump-off spot to the Russian Wilderness. This involves a long, steady climb up to the southern border of the Russian Wilderness. A good destination to the south is the short hike to Hidden Lake or South Fork Lakes.

Those venturing onward along the PCT will then enter a complex landscape matrix that includes the headwaters of the Scott, Salmon, and Trinity Rivers, along with the beautiful scenery that such diversity creates.

Either way, you start from the bottom of the canyon at the North Fork Scott River, so you'll face a climb no matter what your destination.

To pick up the next trail heading north (actually, in this case, heading west), see the *Etna Summit to Grider Creek (PCT)* hike in this chapter. If you are walking this trail in reverse, see the *Scott Mountain to Cecilville Road (PCT)* hike in this chapter to continue east.

User Groups: Hikers, dogs, and horses. No mountain bikes. No wheelchair facilities.

Permits: No permits are required for this section. Parking and access are free.

Maps: For topographic maps, ask the USGS for Deadman Peak and Eaton Peak.

Directions: From Redding, drive north on I-5 for 70 miles. Just past Weed, take the Edgewood exit. At the stop sign, turn left and drive through the underpass to another stop sign. Turn right on Old Highway 99 and drive six miles to Gazelle. Turn left at Gazelle on Gazelle-Callahan Road and drive about 20 miles to Callahan. From Callahan, turn west on Cecilville Road (County Road 402, narrow at times) and drive 11.5 miles to the Cecilville Summit. Parking is limited here; a larger parking area is located just past Cecilville Summit at the Carter Meadows trailhead (it will add 0.25 mile to your hike).

Contact: Klamath National Forest, Salmon/ Scott River Ranger District, Fort Jones, 530/468-5351, www.fs.usda.gov/klamath.

39 TRAIL GULCH LAKE/ LONG GULCH LAKE LOOP

9.1 mi/2 days 🚶3 ⛰9

in the Trinity Alps Wilderness west of Callahan

Map 2.2, page 66

This is a beautiful weekend trek with two gorgeous lakes in the Trinity Alps. It's a nine-mile round-trip with an elevation gain of roughly 2,400 feet. When you look at the map, you might think it makes more sense to do Long Gulch Lake first, then Trail Gulch, but we have recommended this route for many years and it still works the best.

The Trail Gulch Trail rises along Trail Gulch Creek, steeply at times, but in just 2.25 miles, you'll arrive at Trail Gulch Lake. That makes it close enough to go in and out in a day, or better yet, you can make it a good weekend overnighter without tremendous strain. Trail Gulch Lake is 14 acres and 21 feet deep. It is set northeast of Deadman Peak (7,741 feet). The fishing at Trail Gulch Lake is often good for small trout. Long Gulch Lake is just another three miles from Trail Gulch Lake, another gorgeous lake nestled in forest and backed on its far side by a towering sloped wall.

User Groups: Hikers, dogs, and horses. No mountain bikes. No wheelchair facilities.

Permits: A wilderness permit is required for hikers planning to camp. Parking and access are free.

Maps: For a map, ask the U.S. Forest Service for Klamath National Forest or Trinity Alps Wilderness. For topographic maps, ask the USGS for Deadman Peak and Billys Peak.

Directions: From Redding, drive north on I-5 for 70 miles. Just past Weed, take the Edgewood exit. At the stop sign, turn left and drive through the underpass to another stop sign. Turn right on Old Highway 99 and drive about six miles to Gazelle. Turn left on Gazelle-Callahan Road and drive about 20 miles to Callahan. From Callahan, turn west on County Road 402 (Cecilville Road) and drive 11 miles. Turn left on Forest Road 39N08 and drive 1.5 miles to the trailhead.

Contact: Klamath National Forest, Salmon/Scott River Ranger District, Fort Jones, 530/468-5351, www.fs.usda.gov/klamath.

40 SCOTT MOUNTAIN TO CECILVILLE ROAD (PCT)

18.0 mi one-way/2 days 🚶4 ⛰10

from Highway 3 at Scott Mountain Campground

Map 2.2, page 66

A number of wilderness lakes in the Trinity Alps that can that can be reached by side-trip hikes make this section of the PCT appealing. It draws many for trips of a weekend up to a week. From the camp at Scott Mountain, the trail is routed west for five miles, where the first of a series of lakes is within 0.5 mile of the trail. They include Upper Boulder, East Boulder, Mid Boulder, and Telephone Lakes—all quite pretty and accessible from the main trail. After hiking past Eagle Peak, set at 7,789 feet, you'll pass additional short cutoffs that are routed to West Boulder, Mavis, and Fox Creek Lakes. Hikers often camp at one of these lakes before the steep drop down to the South Fork Scott River and heading north into the Russian Wilderness.

To pick up the next trail heading north

(actually, in this case, heading west), see the *Cecilville Road to Russian Wilderness (PCT)* hike in this chapter. If you are walking this trail in reverse, see the *Mumbo Basin to Scott Mountain (PCT)* hike in this chapter to continue south.

User Groups: Hikers, dogs, and horses. No mountain bikes. No wheelchair facilities.

Permits: A wilderness permit is required for camping in the Trinity Alps Wilderness. Contact the Weaverville Ranger District for information.

Maps: For topographic maps, ask the USGS for Scott Mountain, Tangle Blue Lake, Billys Peak, and Deadman Peak.

Directions: From Callahan, drive south on Highway 3 about seven miles to the trailhead, at Scott Mountain Campground.

Contact: Shasta-Trinity National Forest, Weaverville Ranger Station, Weaverville, 530/623-2121, www.fs.usda.gov/stnf.

41 CORY PEAK/KANGAROO LAKE TRAILHEAD

3.0 mi/2.25 hr 🚶3 ⛰9

in Klamath National Forest east of Callahan

Map 2.2, page 66 **BEST (**

From the lake, a spur trail rises steeply to the Pacific Crest Trail. Turn left and the PCT rises steeply to the rim overlooking the lake. You climb about 800 feet in 1.5 miles. A nearby scramble to Cory Peak, at 7,737 feet, provides a 360-degree view. This is a great trail-style picnic site. All of Northern California's prominent mountain peaks are in view here, and immediately below you, to the west, is Kangaroo Lake, like a large sapphire. Backpackers can extend this trip eastward four miles on the Pacific Crest Trail past Robbers Meadow to Bull Lake, a small lake in a remote, sparse setting.

The early section of this trail is called the Fen Trail, but most use it to get to the rim above the lake for the big views.

Kangaroo Lake is one of the most easily reached pristine mountain lakes, with a campground, wheelchair-accessible fishing, and PCT trailhead located near the campground. Getting here may feel remote, but the road, Rail Creek Road, is paved all the way. It leads to a parking area set adjacent to the walk-in campground and trailhead for the short walk to the lake. The trailhead is located just downhill from the parking area. Some will start at the campground and then intersect it, and make a left turn toward Cory Peak.

The lake covers only 21 acres, but often produces large brook trout. In an unsolved conflict, most hikers call this the Kangaroo Lake trailhead, while some Forest Service rangers refer to it as the Fen Trailhead.

User Groups: Hikers, dogs, horses, and mountain bikes. Fishing is wheelchair-accessible.

Permits: No permits are required. Parking and access are free.

Maps: A trail guide can be obtained by contacting Klamath National Forest. For a map, ask the U.S. Forest Service for Klamath National Forest. For a topographic map, ask the USGS for Scott Mountain.

Directions: From Redding, drive north on I-5 for 70 miles. Just past Weed, take the Edgewood exit. At the stop sign, turn left and drive through the underpass to another stop sign. Turn right on Old Highway 99 and drive about six miles to Gazelle. Turn left on Gazelle-Callahan Road and drive over the summit. Continue down the other side of the mountain about five miles to Rail Creek Road. Turn left on Rail Creek Road and drive seven miles to where the road dead-ends, at the parking area for Kangaroo Lake. As you drive up, look for the trail to the right of the campground.

Contact: Klamath National Forest, Salmon/Scott River Ranger District, Fort Jones, 530/468-5351, www.fs.usda.gov/klamath.

42 MOUNT EDDY TRAIL
11.0 mi/2.25 hr

Parks Creek Trailhead in Shasta-Trinity National Forest west of Mount Shasta

Map 2.2, page 66   **BEST (**

The trip to the top of Mount Eddy is one of the best one-day mountain climbs in California. It requires a round-trip of about 11 miles, with a climb of 2,200 feet. Though most of it is rhythmic, there are two steep sections, including a long stretch of switchbacks to make the summit.

In the north state, 14,179-foot Mount Shasta looms over everything for a radius of 75 miles. The summit of Mount Eddy is where you get the best view of giant Shasta. Mount Eddy is located directly to the west of Mount Shasta in Siskiyou County, with I-5 running down the valley between them. If you've ever cruised I-5, you've probably already seen it, even if it barely registered in the shadow of nearby Shasta.

The trip starts at a trailhead for the Pacific Crest Trail (known locally at the Parks Creek Trailhead) with an easy hike to Deadfall Lake. The walking starts off as easy and rhythmic, where you poke in and out of forest of mostly Douglas fir, with occasional visits from golden-mantled ground squirrels. It stays like this for just under three miles, gaining just 450 feet, when you reach a junction with the Mount Eddy Trail on your left and the Pacific Crest Trail on your right, at the foot of Middle Deadfall Lake (set just over a short rise). Turn left and start to climb. Once you pass Middle Deadfall Lake (7,300 feet), the climb becomes steeper, where you rise up 600 feet past the Upper Deadfall Lakes. The trail skirts the upper lake, nestled against the back face of Mount Eddy, and climbs to the ridge that overlooks the Deadfall Lakes Basin. The long-distance views to the west are breathtaking, and to soak them up, the ridge top makes for a natural rest stop.

From here the trail rises above treeline, and then climbs another 900 feet in less than a mile, with seven switchbacks routed up a

© TOM STIENSTRA

Mount Eddy Trail

barren slope. In the process, there is no hint of the coming view of Mount Shasta. Then, suddenly, just as you gain the top of Mount Eddy, the entire western exposure of Mount Shasta comes into view, a stunning moment with an additional 125 miles of scenic points stretching into the distance. Looking down to the east, you can see how the giant Shasta rises 11,000 feet from the 3,000-foot elevations of the valley below, a euphoric moment.

To turn this into an overnighter, there are several backpacking sites at Middle Deadfall Lake, both at the foot of the lake (popular with locals) and at the far end of the lake. A better choice is to climb up to the Upper Deadfall Lake, where there are a few pristine sites at the far end of the lake, to the left of the Mount Eddy Trail.

There is one continuing problem on this route. On a regular basis, mountain bikers illegally ride the Pacific Crest Trail here (which overlaps this route for three miles) between the trailhead above Gumboot Lake, to the north, and the Parks Creek trailhead, to the south.

Bikes are banned from the entire length of the PCT, of course.

User Groups: Hikers, dogs, and horses. No mountain bikes. No wheelchair facilities.

Permits: A campfire permit (free) is required for overnight use. Parking and access are free.

Maps: For a map, ask the U.S. Forest Service for Shasta-Trinity National Forest. For a topographic map, ask the USGS for Mount Eddy.

Directions: From Redding, drive north on I-5 for 70 miles. Just past Weed, take the Edgewood exit. At the stop sign, turn left and drive through the underpass to another stop sign. Turn right on Old Highway 99 and drive 0.5 mile to Stewart Springs Road. Turn left on Stewart Springs Road and drive to the road's end, at Stewart Springs Resort. Bear right on Forest Road 17 (Parks Creek Road) and drive nine miles to the Deadfall Lakes parking area, at the summit. The trailhead is at the south side of the parking area. Take the Pacific Crest Trail, heading south.

Contact: Shasta-Trinity National Forest, Mount Shasta Ranger District, Mount Shasta, 530/926-4511, www.fs.usda.gov/stnf.

43 TOAD LAKE TRAIL
1.5 mi/2 days 🏃1 ▲8

in Shasta-Trinity National Forest west of
Mount Shasta

Map 2.2, page 66 **BEST (**

You might be wondering why a 1.5-mile round-trip hike, with a difficulty rating of only 1, is projected as a two-day trip. The reason is the drive to the trailhead. It's an endless, twisting road that winds its way up the Middle Fork drainage of the Sacramento River, rising up along the west flank of Mount Eddy. It's too much driving, for most, to go up and back in a day (and on the way in, keep your tongue in your mouth, because the ride is so jarring that you might bite off the end of it when you hit a big pothole). Once parked, you'll immediately notice the perfect calm, and then, with a 15-minute walk to the lake (at 6,950 feet), you'll be furnished with a picture-perfect lakeside campsite. The lake covers 23 acres, provides excellent swimming, fair fishing for small trout (sometimes a bit weedy in late summer), and great side trips.

Side trip: The best side trip is the one-mile hike from Toad Lake to Porcupine Lake, an idyllic, pristine small lake near the PCT. To get there from Toad Lake, first walk to the backside of Toad Lake. Then look for an unsigned route (it looks kind of like a game trail) that is routed up the slope on the backside of the lake. That route ventures upslope, and on top, junctions with the Pacific Crest Trail. Turn left and then walk south for 0.25 mile on the PCT to the Porcupine Lake cutoff, on the right. Gorgeous.

User Groups: Hikers, dogs, and horses. No mountain bikes allowed on the Pacific Crest Trail. No wheelchair facilities.

Permits: No permits are required. Parking and access are free.

Maps: For a map, ask the U.S. Forest Service for Shasta-Trinity National Forest. For a topographic map, ask the USGS for Mount Eddy.

Directions: From Redding, take I-5 north to the exit for Central Mount Shasta. Take that exit to the stop sign. At the stop sign, turn left and drive 0.5 mile to Old Stage Road. Turn left on Old Stage Road and drive 0.25 mile to a fork with W. A. Barr Road. Stay to the right at the fork and drive two miles, cross Box Canyon Dam at Lake Siskiyou, and continue around the lake on W. A. Barr Road (which becomes Forest Road 26/South Fork Road). Continue four miles past the Lake Siskiyou Camp resort, cross an unnamed concrete bridge, and look for a dirt road on the right (signed Toad Lake/Morgan Meadows). Turn right and drive 0.2 mile to the first fork, bear left, and drive 11 miles to the lake trailhead parking area. The road is very rough and twisting, and for the last 0.5 mile, a high-clearance, four-wheel-drive vehicle is recommended. It is a 0.5-mile walk from the parking area to the lake.

Contact: Shasta-Trinity National Forest, Mount Shasta Ranger District, Mount Shasta, 530/926-4511, www.fs.usda.gov/stnf.

44 SISSON-CALLAHAN
14.0 mi one-way/2 days 🏃5 ▲8

in Shasta-Trinity National Forest near Lake
Siskiyou west of Mount Shasta

Map 2.2, page 66

The Sisson-Callahan Trail is something of a legend in the Mount Shasta area. For many years, few made this trek. It is getting revived by locals with an interest in history and unique hikes. This route is long, steep, and hot, climbing 5,000 feet over the course of nine miles to the top of Mount Eddy (at 9,025 feet), then down nearly 2,000 feet in two miles to Deadfall Lakes for the nearest campsite. Long ago, it was a well-traveled route up the east flank of Mount Eddy, over the top (through a saddle below the summit), and down to Deadfall Lakes. But with a much easier route available from the Deadfall Lakes trailhead, this trail is passed over. It is now something of a historic landmark.

The Sisson-Callahan Trail starts as an old logging road on the back side of Lake Siskiyou, not far from the mountain bike route that circles (with a jog at the campground) Lake

Siskiyou. The trail climbs up a canyon past meadows, then gains a ridge. It is not designated as wilderness, but after an hour, you will see not see another soul and the land takes on a wilderness feel. The great scenic beauty doesn't start until you've climbed several thousand feet, and by then you'll care more about how much water is left in your canteen than about the incredible sweeping view of Mount Shasta to the east. As you get near the Trinity Divide, you'll face some killer switchbacks to reach the Eddy Ridge. As you reach the Eddy crest, look close and you will find an old metal sign for a former route for the Pacific Crest Trail; it might be 50 or 60 years old (perhaps older, best we could gauge).

From here it is mandatory to hike the switchbacks up to the Mount Eddy Summit. After that, it's a 1,750-foot descent to Middle Deadfall Lake, where you make camp. Your hiking reward comes the next morning, when, after lounging around at Lower Deadfall Lake, you walk out three nearly level miles to the Park Creek/PCT trailhead, then catch your shuttle ride back to Mount Shasta. All in all, this is a genuine butt-kicker of a trail. Unless you want to do a hike that no one else does, a much better route to the Deadfall Lakes and Mount Eddy is from the Parks Creek trailhead.

User Groups: Hikers, dogs, horses, and mountain bikes (very difficult; legal for trail, but not recommended). No wheelchair facilities.

Permits: No permits are required. Parking and access are free.

Maps: For a map, ask the U.S. Forest Service for Shasta-Trinity National Forest. For topographic maps, ask the USGS for Mount Shasta city and Mount Eddy.

Directions: From Redding, take I-5 north to the exit for Central Mount Shasta city. Take that exit to the stop sign. Turn left and drive 0.5 mile to Old Stage Road. Turn left on Old Stage Road and drive 0.25 mile to a fork with W. A. Barr Road. Stay to the right at the fork and drive two miles to North Shore Road (if you cross the dam at Lake Siskiyou, you have gone too far). Turn right on North Shore (which

becomes Forest Road 40N27/Deer Creek Road) and drive four miles, across the bridge on Deer Creek to the next major junction, Forest Road 40N27C. Turn left on Forest Road 40N27C and park along the edge of the road before the ford on the North Fork Sacramento. (The water here is sometimes deeper than it looks; don't be tempted to drive it.) The Sisson-Callahan Trail (which first appears as a road) starts on the other side of the ford, on an old logging skid road that goes to the right. Within 0.5 mile, it turns into a trail.

Contact: Shasta-Trinity National Forest, Mount Shasta Ranger District, Mount Shasta, 530/926-4511, www.fs.usda.gov/stnf.

45 HEART LAKE TRAIL
3.0 mi/2.25 hr   2   10

at Castle Lake in Shasta-Trinity National Forest west of Mount Shasta

Map 2.2, page 66

This is the best site for a photo of Mount Shasta. If you want a calendar-quality photograph, trek to Heart Lake. Then scramble up the back wall and you'll get a breathtaking view of Mount Shasta with this heart-shaped alpine pond in the foreground. (Also note that the best drive-to spot anywhere for photographs of Mount Shasta is on Castle Lake Road at a turnout about one mile downhill from the Castle Lake parking area.)

Funny thing is, a lot of people can't find little Heart Lake. To start, at the parking area for pretty Castle Lake, look for the trailhead on the left side of the lake. You will cross the outlet stream. The trail then rises up along the slope just left of the lake. Below to your right is Castle Lake, a pretty sight that's set in a rock bowl with a high back wall. The trail rises up, steep in a few spots, to a saddle at 5,900 feet. At the saddle, bear uphill to the right on the faint trail. If you have the ability to envision wild landscapes, look for the wall and terrace above you, a bit to the right. The hike then becomes an easy scramble. Keep an eye out for faint routes that lead to the lake. It is nestled over a lip at 6,050 feet, tucked away in a pocket. Because the lake is small, the water warms up by midsummer, making it great for wading or a quick dip (but it's too small to really swim). The view is a real stunner.

The tale of Castle Lake, set at an elevation of 5,450 feet, is that the water is like none other in the world, which has led some people to jump into the lake for complete renewal. In reality, the water is so pure, containing few nutrients of any kind, that UC Davis has a water-sampling station here in an ongoing comparison study with Lake Tahoe.

User Groups: Hikers and dogs. Not suitable for horses or mountain bikes. No wheelchair facilities.

Permits: No permits are required. Parking and access is free.

Maps: For a map, ask the U.S. Forest Service for Shasta-Trinity National Forest or Castle Crags Wilderness. For a topographic map, ask the USGS for Mount Shasta city.

Directions: From Redding, take I-5 north to the exit for Central Mount Shasta city. Take that exit to the stop sign. Turn left and drive 0.5 mile to Old Stage Road. Turn left on Old Stage Road and drive 0.25 mile to a fork with W. A. Barr Road. Stay to the right at the fork and drive two miles, cross Box Canyon Dam at Lake Siskiyou, and continue 0.5 mile to Castle Lake Road. Turn left and drive 7.5 miles to the parking area at the end of the road, at Castle Lake. The trailhead begins on the eastern end of the parking lot.

Contact: Shasta-Trinity National Forest, Mount Shasta Ranger District, Mount Shasta, 530/926-4511, www.fs.usda.gov/stnf.

46 MIDDLE FALLS TRAIL
0.5-3.0 mi/0.5-1.5 hr 🏃1 ⛰10

at Fowler's Camp in Shasta-Trinity National Forest east of McCloud

Map 2.2, page 66

Middle Falls, on the McCloud River, is one of the prettiest waterfalls in Northern California. It is a wide and tall cascade of water that pours over a 50-foot cliff into a deep pool in a rock bowl. This hike is an easy walk on a paved trail. You can start at an overlook above Middle Falls (parking nearby), at a trailhead near the restroom at Fowlers Campground, or at the parking lot for Lower Falls. We suggest you start at Lower Falls and skirt the left side of the McCloud River to enjoy the full exposure of the river, all three waterfalls, and the experience of it.

Lower Falls is a chute-type waterfall, visible with a short walk from the paved parking area. From here, hike up the trail and enjoy the beautiful McCloud River. As you pass Fowlers Campground, the trail routes into forest with the gorgeous river off to your right. You'll round a bend, probably hearing the waterfall before you see it, and then suddenly, there it is, this wide sheet of falling water. It's something like a miniature Niagara Falls. The trail runs near a boulder field on the outer reaches of the plunge pool. On summer weekends, teenagers climb to the rim above the falls, then plunge 50 feet into the pool like human missiles. It's a dangerous venture that we don't recommend. (At high flow, we've also seen kayakers run over the top.)

The trail switchbacks up to the rim overlooking Middle Falls, then extends upstream to staircase-like Upper Falls. There is only one good spot to see Upper Falls. Instead, the trail runs near its brink, where water shoots past. It is also possible to drive to a parking area near the brink of the falls, reducing the hike to about 50 yards. A restroom is available at the parking area.

There is one frustrating element. Because the falls have become easy to reach, you get the bad with the good—visitors litter this spot, or worse, they discard cigarette butts on the trail. We try to reverse this offensive practice by packing out any trash that we see.

User Groups: Hikers and dogs. No horses or mountain bikes. The paved path from Lower Falls to Middle Falls is wheelchair-accessible.

Permits: No permits are required. Parking and access are free.

Maps: For a map, ask the U.S. Forest Service for Shasta-Trinity National Forest. For a topographic map, ask the USGS for McCloud.

Directions: From Redding, take I-5 north for 47 miles to the Highway 89/McCloud-Reno exit. Bear right on Highway 89 and drive nine miles to McCloud. Continue southeast on Highway 89 for five miles to the sign for Fowler's Campground and Forest Road 39N28. Turn right and drive one mile to a fork.

To reach Lower Falls: At the fork, turn right and drive to the parking area and overlook.

To reach Middle Falls Trailhead: Bear left at the fork for Fowler's Campground, drive through the campground to the restroom, and park. The trailhead is across the road from the restroom.

Contact: Shasta-Trinity National Forest, McCloud Ranger District, McCloud, 530/964-2184, www.fs.usda.gov/stnf.

47 CARIBOU LAKES TRAIL
18.0 mi/2 days 🥾3 ⛺9

in the Trinity Alps Wilderness northwest of Trinity Lake

Map 2.2, page 66

The Caribou Lakes Basin provides the classic Trinity Alps scene: three high mountain lakes, beautiful and serene, with the back wall of the Sawtooth Ridge casting a monumental backdrop on one side, and on the other side, a drop-off and great views of a series of mountain peaks and ridgelines. Sunsets are absolutely remarkable when viewed from here. The centerpiece is Caribou Lake, the largest lake in the Trinity Alps Wilderness. Because it's a nine-mile hike to the Caribou Lakes Basin, this often makes for a first night's camp for week-long treks into this section of the Trinity Alps Wilderness.

The trail starts at the bottom of the Salmon River, however, and like all trails that start at the bottom of canyons, it means you begin the trip with a terrible climb that never seems to end, especially on hot summer afternoons. Plan

Middle Falls Trail

on drinking a full canteen of water, and be certain not to miss the natural spring located near the crest, just off to the right (look for the spur-like footpath that leads to it). After reaching the crest, the trail travels counterclockwise around the mountain for several hours en route, then drops into the Caribou Lakes Basin. Ignore your urge to stop at the first lake, because the best campsites, swimming, and views are from last lake of the circuit, Caribou Lake. Because this is a popular destination, fishing is often poor.

User Groups: Hikers and dogs. Horses are permitted but not recommended. No mountain bikes. No wheelchair facilities.

Permits: A wilderness permit is required for camping.

Maps: For a map, ask the U.S. Forest Service for Klamath National Forest or Trinity Alps Wilderness. For a topographic map, ask the USGS for Caribou Lakes.

Directions: From Weaverville, take Highway 3 north past Trinity Lake and continue to Coffee Creek Road/County Road 104 (located near the Coffee Creek Ranger Station). Turn left and drive 17 miles to the trailhead at the end of the road, at Big Flat Campground.

Contact: Shasta-Trinity National Forest, Weaverville Ranger Station, Weaverville, 530/623-2121, www.fs.usda.gov/stnf; Klamath National Forest, Salmon/Scott River Ranger District, Fort Jones, 530/468-5351, www.fs.usda.gov/klamath.

trailheads on Coffee Creek Road, this one is often overlooked. The trail starts near an old sawmill along Coffee Creek, heads south (to the left), and in less than a mile starts the climb adjacent to Union Creek (on your right). Like most hikes that start at a streambed, you pay for your pleasure, going up, not down. After about two miles, the trail crosses Union Creek and continues on for a few miles, now with the stream on the left. Most of the walk is in forest with good shade. You'll pass a trail junction for Bullards Basin, and about 0.5 mile later, turn right on the cutoff trail to Union Lake. The lake is long and shallow, with good swimming in summer. With Union Lake as a base camp, other lakes within range by day hikes are Landers and Foster Lakes.

User Groups: Hikers, dogs, and horses. No mountain bikes. No wheelchair facilities.

Permits: A wilderness permit is required for hikers planning to camp.

Maps: For a map, ask the U.S. Forest Service for Shasta-Trinity National Forest or Trinity Alps Wilderness. For a topographic map, ask the USGS for Caribou Lakes.

Directions: From Weaverville, take Highway 3 north past Trinity Lake and continue to Coffee Creek Road/County Road 104 (located near the Coffee Creek Ranger Station). Turn left and drive about 10 miles to the trailhead, on the left.

Contact: Shasta-Trinity National Forest, Weaverville Ranger Station, Weaverville, 530/623-2121, www.fs.usda.gov/stnf.

48 UNION LAKE TRAIL
12.0 mi/2 days   🚶3 ⛰9

in the Trinity Alps Wilderness northwest of Trinity Lake

Map 2.2, page 66

Union Lake is a blue gem nestled in a granite basin below sloped alpine granite Red Rock Mountain. The hike in and out is a good weekend affair, but most visitors are backpackers who are using the camp at the lake as a first-day destination for a multiday trip. Of the

49 BIG BEAR LAKE TRAIL
10.0 mi/2 days   🚶3 ⛰8

in the Trinity Alps Wilderness south of Callahan

Map 2.2, page 66

The five-mile hike up to Big Bear Lake, a large lake by wilderness standards, beautiful by anybody's standards, can make for a weekend backpack trip. The hike is steep, with little shade. The trail ends at the lake, so if the lakeside campsites are already taken when you arrive, you're out of luck for a quality place to camp. The trailhead is easy to reach, located just off Highway 3 north of Trinity Lake. The route is simple but not easy. It follows Bear Creek for the entire route, with one stream crossing, and climbs all the way. The trail is steep, popular, and beautiful. Once you reach the lake, a bonus is the side trip to the Wee Bear Lakes. From the outlet of Big Bear, take the easterly ridge, which takes about a mile of scrambling cross-country to reach the basin with the Wee Bears, as we call them.

User Groups: Hikers and dogs. Horses are allowed but not recommended. No mountain bikes. No wheelchair facilities.

Permits: A wilderness permit is required for hikers planning to camp in the wilderness.

Maps: For a map, ask the U.S. Forest Service for Shasta-Trinity National Forest. For a topographic map, ask the USGS for Tangle Blue Lake.

Directions: From Redding, take I-5 to Yreka and the exit for Highway 3/Fort Jones. Take that exit to the stop sign, turn left, and drive a short distance to the lighted intersection. Turn left on Highway 3 and drive about 40 miles to Callahan. Continue south on Highway 3 for about 13 miles to Bear Creek Loop Road. Turn right and drive a short distance (on an unpaved road) to the signed trailhead (located near the Bear Creek road crossing).

Contact: Shasta-Trinity National Forest, Weaverville Ranger Station, Weaverville, 530/623-2121, www.fs.usda.gov/stnf.

50 MUMBO BASIN TO SCOTT MOUNTAIN (PCT)

35.0 mi one-way/4 days 🥾3 ⛰10

in Shasta-Trinity National Forest from Gumboot trailhead to Scott Mountain

Map 2.2, page 66

This section of the PCT starts at a popular trailhead and quickly jumps northward into remote, beautiful country. The first highlight, only a mile up the trail, is the view below, to the left of secluded Picayune Lake. The trail then heads on, passing little yet pristine Porcupine Lake (no easy access from PCT). The trail then heads over the rim and skirts below Middle Deadfall Lake (just over the rise to your right), a popular site for easy backpack trips. From Deadfall Lakes, the trail continues as an easy jaunt to the Parks Creek Trailhead and crosses a paved road. It then eventually descends and curves around the headwaters of the Trinity River, then climbs back up Chilcoot Pass and past Bull Lake. From here, it's a 10-mile pull to the Scott Mountain Summit trailhead (see the *Cecilville Road to Russian Wilderness (PCT)* hike in this chapter).

If you are walking this trail in reverse, see the *Castle Crags to Mumbo Basin (PCT)* hike in this chapter to continue south.

User Groups: Hikers, dogs, and horses. No mountain bikes. No wheelchair facilities.

Permits: No permits are required. Parking and access are free.

Maps: For topographic maps, ask the USGS for Mumbo Basin, South China Mountain, and Scott Mountain.

Directions: From Redding, take I-5 north to the exit for Central Mount Shasta city. Take that exit to the stop sign. Turn left and drive 0.5 mile to Old Stage Road. Turn left on Old Stage Road and drive 0.25 mile to a fork with W. A. Barr Road. Stay to the right at the fork and drive two miles, cross Box Canyon Dam at Lake Siskiyou, and continue around the lake on W. A. Barr Road (which becomes Forest Road 26/ South Fork Road). Continue four miles past the Lake Siskiyou Camp resort and continue up the canyon for 12.5 miles to Gumboot Lake Road. Bear right, staying on Forest Road 26, and continue 2.5 miles to the ridge and the parking area and trailhead.

Contact: Shasta-Trinity National Forest, Mount Shasta Ranger District, Mount Shasta, 530/926-4511, www.fs.usda.gov/stnf.

51 GUMBOOT OVERLOOK CRAG

1.5 mi/1.5 hr

in Shasta-Trinity National Forest west of Mount Shasta

Map 2.2, page 66

This is an off-trail trek for people who like to scramble to ridges for views. If you must always have a trail to hike on, well, this trip is not for you. But if you don't mind a little cross-country scramble to a mountain rim, then a short cutoff to a peak with spectacular views of Gumboot Lake and Mount Shasta beyond, sign up for this hike.

The trip starts at Gumboot Lake (6,050 feet elevation), a pretty lake in the Trinity-Divide. As you face the lake, look for a fisherman's trail on the right. It leads in a half circle around the lake. At the back of the lake, break off to the right of the trail and start climbing the slope, where you head up toward the ridge that is a backdrop for the basin. A little less than halfway to the top, you'll pass Little Gumboot Lake and after that, you will scramble your way to the ridge, where you'll intersect with the Pacific Crest Trail. If you are comfortable off trail, the difficulty is a 3; if not, a 5. Head to the left for a short distance, then break off the trail again, this time to the left, heading on the mountain spine toward the peak that towers over Gumboot Lake, with Mount Shasta as the backdrop off to the east. This is Gumboot Overlook Crag, your destination. The world may not be perfect, but from this lookout, it comes close.

User Groups: Hikers and dogs only. No horses or mountain bikes. No wheelchair facilities.

Permits: No permits are required. Parking and access are free.

Maps: For a map, ask the U.S. Forest Service for Shasta-Trinity National Forest. For a topographic map, ask the USGS for Mumbo Basin.

Directions: From I-5 at Mount Shasta city, take the Central Mount Shasta exit. At the stop sign, turn west and drive 0.5 mile to Old Stage Road. Turn left on Old Stage Road and drive 0.25 mile to a fork with W. A. Barr Road. Stay to the

right at the fork and drive two miles, cross Box Canyon Dam at Lake Siskiyou, and continue around the lake on W. A. Barr Road (which becomes Forest Road 26/South Fork Road). Continue four miles past the Lake Siskiyou Camp resort and continue up the canyon to Gumboot Lake Road (Forest Road 40N37). Bear left on Gumboot Lake Road and drive 0.5 mile to the parking area near the shore of the lake.

Contact: Shasta-Trinity National Forest, Mount Shasta Ranger District, Mount Shasta, 530/926-4511, www.fs.usda.gov/stnf.

52 TAMARACK LAKE TRAILHEAD

5.0 mi/4.0 hr

in Shasta-Trinity National Forest southwest of Mount Shasta

Map 2.2, page 66

Tamarack Lake is a beautiful alpine lake and a place of remarkable serenity so pretty that it can feel sacred. Set high in the Trinity Divide at 6,000 feet, this jewel sits nestled in a high basin and backed by a mountain wall. The route in is on an old jeep road. From the trailhead at 5,232 feet, you are routed south up to a sub-ridge at 5,600 feet, then past a meadow. At the first of two smaller lakes, the Twin Lakes, bear left past both lakes. The route then climbs another short ridge to arrive at Tamarack Lake at 5,962 feet. From the back (southern) side of Tamarack, there is a great view of Grey Rocks, a series of dark, craggy peaks. Hit it right, with nobody else around, and this place will have you thanking a higher power for the privilege of breathing the air here.

User Groups: Hikers and dogs. Not suitable for horses or mountain bikes. No wheelchair facilities.

Permits: No permits are required.

Maps: For a map, ask the U.S. Forest Service for Shasta-Trinity National Forest. For a topographic map, ask the USGS for Chicken Hawk Hill.

Directions: From Redding, take I-5 north for

about 50 miles to the exit for Castella/Castle Crags State Park. Take that exit to the stop sign, turn left and drive west on Castle Creek Road. Continue past the park (the road becomes Forest Road 25/Whalen Road) and continue 12.5 miles on to Forest Road 38N17 (Tamarack Road). Turn left on Forest Road 38N17 and drive about three miles (near the second crossing of Twin Lakes Creek) to a very rough jeep road on your right. Park in the vicinity, on the shoulder; do not block the road. The jeep road is the trailhead. Note: A handful of off-road drivers with specialized vehicles occasionally drive the jeep road to Tamarack Lake.

Contact: Shasta-Trinity National Forest, Mount Shasta Ranger District, Mount Shasta, 530/926-4511, www.fs.usda.gov/stnf.

53 ROOT CREEK TRAIL
2.3 mi/1.75 hr 🥾1 ⛰7

in Castle Crags State Park south of Mount Shasta

Map 2.2, page 66

Castle Crags State Park features a series of huge granite spires that tower over the Sacramento River Canyon, the kind of sight that can take your breath away the first time you see it from I-5. That sight inspires a lot of people to take one of the hikes at the park, and while most don't have the time, energy, or body conditioning to complete Castle Crags Trail, Root Creek Trail is a good second choice.

As you drive up the access road, look for the signed trailhead to the left, just as you arrive at the parking area. The elevation is 2,500 feet at the trailhead. Start at this trailhead, which is signed for Castle Crags Trail, and walk 0.25 mile to a trail junction. Turn right on Root Creek Trail. From here, the trail is routed through a thick, cool forest, an easy walk that most visitors overlook. It continues to Root Creek, a pretty, babbling stream. You'll see some vintage pipes, valves, and infrastructure when this was the water intake for a small settlement located below down the canyon. Those

with canyoneering skills should trek upstream; on the right side of the stream, look for a series of small pool-and-drop waterfalls (and one a bit larger) that few know about.

User Groups: Hikers only. No dogs, horses, or mountain bikes. No wheelchair facilities.

Permits: No permits are required. A state park entrance fee of $8 is charged for each vehicle.

Maps: A trail map can be obtained for a fee by contacting Castle Crags State Park. For a topographic map, ask the USGS for Dunsmuir.

Directions: From Redding, take I-5 north for 46 miles to the exit for Castella/Castle Crags State Park. Take that exit to the stop sign, turn left and drive west on Castle Creek Road. Continue (past a gas station and store on the left) for 0.25 mile to the park entrance on the right. Turn right and drive to the kiosk. Just past the kiosk, bear right and drive two miles (past the campground) to the parking area for Vista Point. From the parking area, walk a short distance west down the entrance road to the signed trailhead on the north side (right side, when walking back).

Contact: Castle Crags State Park, Castella, 530/235-2684, www.parks.ca.gov.

54 CASTLE CRAGS TO MUMBO BASIN (PCT)
25.0 mi one-way/2 days 🥾4 ⛰10

from Castle Crags State Park west into Shasta-Trinity National Forest

Map 2.2, page 66

This is a key juncture for the PCT, where the trail climbs out of a river canyon and back to high ridgelines. It's in a classic region, the Trinity Divide, known for lakes sculpted in granite and sweeping views of Mount Shasta. From the start, the trail runs beneath the spires of Castle Crags, a setting that can astonish newcomers. From the Sacramento River at Castle Crags, at an elevation of 2,000 feet, the trail laterals up the north side of Castle Creek Canyon, rising just below the base of the awesome crags. In wet years, you will pass beautiful Burstarse

Falls on the right. The trail finally hits the rim at the backside of Castle Ridge. Then it follows the rim in a half circle to the west, to the Seven Lakes Basin and beyond to the Mumbo Basin and the Gumboot Lake trailhead. The final five miles of this segment pass by a dozen pristine mountain lakes, but most are well off the trail.

To continue north on the PCT, see the *Mumbo Basin to Scott Mountain (PCT)* hike in this chapter. If you are walking this trail in reverse, see the *Ash Camp to Castle Crags Wilderness (PCT)* hike in this chapter to continue south.

User Groups: Hikers only. No dogs, horses, or mountain bikes. No wheelchair facilities.

Permits: No permits are required. A state park entrance fee of $8 is charged for each vehicle if you drive through the park entrance.

Maps: A trail map can be obtained for a fee by contacting Castle Crags State Park. For topographic maps, ask the USGS for Dunsmuir, Seven Lakes Basin, and Mumbo Basin.

Directions: From Redding, take I-5 north for 46 miles to the exit for Castella/Castle Crags State Park. Take that exit to the stop sign, turn left and drive west on Castle Creek Road. Continue (past a gas station and store on the left) for 0.25 mile to the park entrance on the right. Turn right and drive to the kiosk. Just past the kiosk, bear right and drive two miles (past the campground) to the parking area for Vista Point. From the parking area, walk a short distance west down the entrance road to the signed trailhead on the north side (right side, when walking back).

Contact: Castle Crags State Park, Castella, 530/235-2684, www.parks.ca.gov.

55 CRAGS TRAIL TO CASTLE DOME

6.5 mi/4.0 hr   👣 5   ⛰ 10

in Castle Crags State Park south of Mount Shasta

Map 2.2, page 66

From Vista Point in Castle Crags State Park,

hikers can gaze up at the fantastic crags and spot Castle Dome (at 4,966 feet), the leading spire on the crags' ridge. This high, rounded, missile-shaped piece of rock is your destination on Castle Crags Trail. If you're out of shape, be warned: This climb is a butt-kicker, where you climb all the way, often like a workout on a Stairmaster, until you reach the ridge.

As you drive up to the parking area, you will see the signed trailhead on your left (just before the parking lot). The elevation is 2,500 feet. Start by taking Castle Crags Trail for 0.25 mile; when you reach a three-trail junction, continue on Castle Crags Trail. Here the trail launches off, rising through a thick forest. It climbs steeply at times before eventually turning to the right. It emerges from the forest. Once above tree line, the views of the Sacramento River Canyon far below get better with each rising step. In spring, snow and ice fields are common this high. The trail goes onward, always climbing, and eventually you will reach a saddle at the foot of Castle Dome, where a few trees have somehow gained toeholds (you cannot climb Castle Dome without ropes and high-level rock-climbing skills). Continue on, the best is just ahead. The trail wends its way into the ridge interior of the crags. To your right, you can scramble off trail up to a notch, where you get a divine perch to gaze north at Mount Shasta. It will be a moment you'll prize forever.

The views and photographs are eye-popping, making it a must-do for those who rate their hikes based on the lookouts. However, not all of the trip is pristine; unfortunately, highway noise emerges from the canyon, as well as that of the inevitable freight train. At the summit rim, there isn't a hint of that.

User Groups: Hikers only. No dogs, horses, or mountain bikes. No wheelchair facilities.

Permits: No permits are required. A state park entrance fee of $8 is charged for each vehicle.

Maps: A trail map can be obtained for a fee by contacting Castle Crags State Park. For a topographic map, ask the USGS for Dunsmuir.

Directions: From Redding, take I-5 north for 46 miles to the exit for Castella/Castle Crags

State Park. Take that exit to the stop sign, turn left and drive west on Castle Creek Road. Continue (past a gas station and store on the left) for 0.25 mile to the park entrance on the right. Turn right and drive to the kiosk. Just past the kiosk, bear right and drive two miles (past the campground) to the parking area for Vista Point. From the parking area, walk a short distance west down the entrance road to the signed trailhead on the north side (right side, when walking back).

Contact: Castle Crags State Park, Castella, 530/235-2684, www.parks.ca.gov.

56 ASH CAMP TO CASTLE CRAGS WILDERNESS (PCT)
30.0 mi one-way/2 days 🥾4 ⛺10

from Ash Camp on the McCloud River west into Castle Crags State Park

Map 2.2, page 66

Of the hundreds of rivers along the Pacific Crest Trail, the McCloud River is one of the most prized. This segment of the PCT starts right alongside the lush McCloud River at Ash Camp, set at about 3,000 feet. The trail is then routed downstream above the McCloud River for 2.5 miles, then is routed away from it. Eventually you cross Squaw Valley Creek and then climb steeply to top Girard Ridge (at 4,500 feet), a long and dry climb. But when you top the final ridge above the Sacramento River Canyon, that is when Mount Shasta, Black Butte, and Castle Crags suddenly emerge into view. After traversing the ridge for a few miles, the trail suddenly drops and cascades down to the Sacramento River Canyon at Soda Creek. Your toes will be jamming into your boots as you head downhill. At the river you might stop to soak your feet before picking up and heading west to start the climb into Castle Crags State Park.

To continue north on the PCT, see the *Castle Crags to Mumbo Basin (PCT)* hike in this chapter. If you are walking this trail in reverse, see the *McArthur-Burney Falls Memorial State Park to Ash Camp (PCT)* hike, in the *Lassen and Modoc* chapter, to continue south.

User Groups: Hikers, dogs, and horses. No mountain bikes. No wheelchair facilities.

Permits: Wilderness permits are required only in Castle Crags Wilderness.

Maps: For topographic maps, ask the USGS for Shoeinhorse Mountain, Yellowjacket Mountain, and Dunsmuir.

Directions: From Redding, take I-5 north for 47 miles to the Highway 89/McCloud-Reno exit. Bear right on Highway 89 and drive nine miles to McCloud and Squaw Valley Road. Turn right on Squaw Valley Road, and drive about five miles (Squaw Valley Road becomes Forest Road 11/Hawkins Creek Road). Continue on Forest Road 11, keeping right past the McCloud boat ramp, and continue over the McCloud Dam. Turn right (still Forest Road 11) and drive down the canyon for one mile. At the turnoff for Ash Camp, bear right and drive a short distance to the parking area.

Contact: Shasta-Trinity National Forest, McCloud Ranger District, McCloud, 530/964-2184, www.fs.usda.gov/stnf.

57 MCCLOUD NATURE TRAIL
5.0 mi/2.5 hr 🥾1 ⛺9

at Nature Conservancy on the McCloud River south of McCloud

Map 2.2, page 66   **BEST (**

Have you ever yearned for a place where old trees are left standing, deer and bobcats roam without fear, and a crystal-perfect river flows free in an untouched canyon? The McCloud River Preserve is such a place, and because it's managed by the Nature Conservancy, it will always remain that way. Although the lower McCloud River is best known for its fly-fishing for trout, there's an excellent hiking trail that runs alongside the river that spans 2.5 miles from the parking area on downstream. After parking, the trail is routed along the river, with a rocky trail for 100 yards, and then ventures into forest and emerges at a cabin managed for the McCloud River Preserve for the Nature Conservancy. The trail then runs along the river, with one climb and drop, for 2.25 miles. A highlight, about two miles in, is where the river plunges into a series of deep holes and gorges. Few go past this point. At the end of the trail, the river is blocked by a yellow nylon rope, with some poison oak in the vicinity here, to indicate the end of the property owned by the Nature Conservancy.

If you camp at nearby Ah-Di-Na Campground, another trail runs upstream along the McCloud River, but does not connect to this featured stretch. The McCloud Nature Trail starts a full mile downstream by road from Ah-Di-Na.

User Groups: Hikers only. No dogs, horses, or mountain bikes. No wheelchair facilities.

Permits: No permits are required. Parking and access are free.

Maps: For a map, ask the U.S. Forest Service for Shasta-Trinity National Forest. For a topographic map, ask the USGS for Lake McCloud.

Directions: From Redding, take I-5 north for 47 miles to the Highway 89/McCloud-Reno exit. Bear right on Highway 89 and drive nine miles to McCloud at Squaw Valley Road. Turn right on Squaw Valley Road and drive 11.5 miles (at 5 miles, the road passes from Siskiyou County into Shasta County and becomes Forest Road 11. It then crosses a cattle guard and continues to McCloud Reservoir. At the reservoir, turn right and continue) to Battle Creek Cove and Forest Road 38N53/Ah-Di-Na Road (a dirt road) on the right. Turn right and drive seven miles (dusty, often bumpy, continue past Ah-Di-Na Campground) to the road's end, at Fisher Creek and trailhead. The Nature Conservancy boundary is 0.5 mile downstream.

Contact: Shasta-Trinity National Forest, McCloud Ranger District, McCloud, 530/964-2184, www.fs.usda.gov/stnf.

58 NEW RIVER TRAILHEAD
24.0 mi/3 days ⛰3 ⛺6

in the Trinity Alps Wilderness east of Willow Creek

Map 2.3, page 67

This route is a little-used rarity in the Trinity Alps Wilderness: a trail that features small streams, not high mountain lakes. In addition, there is damage from forest fires in the area. But if you want to be by yourself, this is the place. The highlights are the headwaters of the New River (a tributary to the Trinity River), the history of the area, and Mary Blaine Meadow.

The trail starts right along the New River, the site of one of California's last runs of summer steelhead. You'll hike about three miles before the junction with the Slide Creek Trail. Slide Creek Trail is 9.5 miles and passes Mary Blaine Meadow, the final destination of this hike (just a half mile before Slide Creek Trail ends at Salmon Summit Trail). The meadow is set below Mary Blaine Mountain, and to the north, Dees Peak. The whole region is cut with small streams in crevices and canyons.

User Groups: Hikers, dogs, and horses. No mountain bikes. No wheelchair facilities.

Permits: A wilderness permit is required for hikers planning to camp.

Maps: For a map, ask the U.S. Forest Service for Shasta-Trinity National Forest or Trinity Alps Wilderness. For topographic maps, ask the USGS for Jim Jam Ridge, Dees Peak, and Trinity Mountain.

Directions: From Weaverville, take Highway 299 west 45 miles to Denny Road. Turn north (right) on County Road 402 (Denny Road) and drive about 21 miles. Turn left on Forest Road 7N15 and drive four miles north to the trailhead parking area. The trailhead is at Hawkins Bar.

Contact: Shasta-Trinity National Forest, Weaverville Ranger Station, Weaverville, 530/623-2121, www.fs.usda.gov/stnf.

59 EAST FORK LOOP

20.0 mi/3 days   3 △7

in the Trinity Alps Wilderness east of Willow Creek

Map 2.3, page 67

Where else can you hike 20 miles with a chance of not seeing anybody? The East Fork trailhead provides access to one of the more primitive, less-traveled regions of the Trinity Alps Wilderness. It's an area known for streams and forests in the lower reaches and bare limestone ridges in the higher reaches, with a mosaic of forest fire damage in the region from several fires. The trip starts at East Fork trailhead, adjacent to the East Fork New River. It climbs along this watershed and, after two miles, turns before coming to Pony Creek. In the next six miles, which include sections that are quite steep, the trail climbs to Limestone Ridge, near little Rattlesnake Lake. At Limestone Ridge, turn right on New River Divide Trail and head south for six miles, passing Cabin Peak at 6,870 feet and arriving at White Creek Lake.

To complete the loop, turn right on the trail at White Creek Lake and start the trip back, descending most of the way. The trail goes past Jakes Upper Camp and Jakes Lower Camp before linking up again with East Fork Trail for the jog back to the parking area.

User Groups: Hikers, dogs, and horses. No mountain bikes. No wheelchair facilities.

Permits: A wilderness permit is required for hikers planning to camp.

Maps: For a map, ask the U.S. Forest Service for Shasta-Trinity National Forest or Trinity Alps Wilderness. For a topographic map, ask the USGS for Jim Jam Ridge.

Directions: From Weaverville, turn west on Highway 299 and drive 45 miles to Denny Road. Turn north on County Road 402 (Denny Road) and drive 22 miles (the last four miles of the road become unpaved Forest Road 7N01) to the trailhead parking area. The trailhead is at Hawkins Bar.

Contact: Shasta-Trinity National Forest, Weaverville Ranger Station, Weaverville, 530/623-2121, www.fs.usda.gov/stnf.

60 BURNT RANCH FALLS

1.25 mi/1.0 hr   1 △8

in Shasta-Trinity National Forest on Highway 299 east of Willow Creek

Map 2.3, page 67

Burnt Ranch Falls isn't a spectacular cascade of water like other, more famous waterfalls, but it is the center of a very pretty, easy-to-reach scene on the Trinity River. It's a relatively small but wide waterfall, composed of about 10 feet of rock that creates a natural barrier for migrating salmon and steelhead during low-water conditions. Thus the highlight comes when river flows rise a bit in the fall, so that you can watch the spectacular sight of salmon and steelhead jumping and sailing through the air to get over and past the falls. Timing is best in fall and early winter, when the season's first rains attract the fish upstream.

The trip starts at the Burnt Ranch Campground. The trail is a short but steep 0.75-mile jaunt. When you arrive at the river, walk out a short way on the rocky spot to watch the fish jump. The setting, in an area along Highway 299, has a magnificent natural landscape. When you look up from the river, the Trinity Canyon walls look like they ascend into the sky. Unlike most waterfalls, Burnt Ranch Falls is a far less compelling scene at high water. During high, turbid flows, it becomes much more difficult to see fish jumping past the falls. See a fish and this one is a 10.

User Groups: Hikers and dogs. No horses or mountain bikes. No wheelchair facilities.

Permits: No permits are required.

Maps: For a map, ask the U.S. Forest Service for Shasta-Trinity National Forest. For a topographic map, ask the USGS for Ironed Mountain.

Directions: From Weaverville, drive west on Highway 299 to Burnt Ranch. From Burnt Ranch, continue 0.5 mile west on Highway 299

to Burnt Ranch Campground and the trailhead, on the right.

Contact: Shasta-Trinity National Forest, Weaverville Ranger Station, Weaverville, 530/623-2121, www.fs.usda.gov/stnf.

61 NEW RIVER DIVIDE TRAIL
30.0 mi/3 days   3 7

in the Trinity Alps Wilderness north of Trinity River's Big Bar

Map 2.3, page 67

The New River Divide Trail provides access to the Limestone Ridge of the Trinity Alps, taking a ridgeline route most of the way. This is an area known for having lookouts from mountain rims, the headwaters of many small feeder streams, and few people. The trip starts at the Green Mountain trailhead, at an elevation of 5,052 feet, and in the first three miles, the route skirts the southern flank of Brushy Mountain, past Panther Camp and Stove Camp, and along the eastern flank of Green Mountain. As the trail climbs toward the Limestone Ridge, you'll find yourself perched on a divide, where the streams on each side pour into different watersheds. Eventually the trail rises all the way to Cabin Peak (at 6,870 feet) and beyond to little Rattlesnake Lake, a one-way distance of about 15 miles. Some of the area, especially off to the north, has evidence of past forest fires.

User Groups: Hikers, dogs, and horses. No mountain bikes. No wheelchair facilities.

Permits: A wilderness permit is required. Parking and access are free.

Maps: For a map, ask the U.S. Forest Service for Shasta-Trinity National Forest or Trinity Alps Wilderness. For a topographic map, ask the USGS for Del Loam.

Directions: From Weaverville, drive west on Highway 299 for 28 miles to French Creek Road (Forest Road 5913). Turn north (right) and drive seven miles (the road becomes Forest Road 5N04). Continue straight for four miles to the trailhead, at the Green Mountain parking area.

Contact: Shasta-Trinity National Forest, Big Bar Ranger Station, Big Bar, 530/623-6106, www.fs.usda.gov/stnf.

62 CANYON CREEK LAKES TRAILHEAD
16.0 mi/2 days   4 10

in the Trinity Alps Wilderness north of Weaverville

Map 2.3, page 67

This is the kind of place where wilderness lovers think they can find religion. But what they find, guaranteed, are tons of other people: Expect about 50 other hikers on weekdays and 200 to 300 on weekends. The destination is Canyon Creek Lakes, set high in a mountain canyon, framed by Sawtooth Mountain to the east and a series of high granite rims to the north. The route in is no mystery; it's a climb of 3,100 feet over the course of eight miles. The trail heads straight upstream along Bear Creek for about 0.25 mile, crossing Bear Creek before continuing along Canyon Creek. Four miles out, you'll reach the first of four waterfalls. The first is the smallest, then they get progressively taller, and all are gorgeous. After the last waterfall, walk 0.5 mile to reach Lower Canyon Creek Lake, seven miles out from the trailhead. From this place, which is now largely above tree line, cross Stonehouse Gulch to reach the first of two lakes. The trail skirts the left side of the first of the Canyon Creek Lakes, then in 0.5 mile, it arrives at the head of the larger one. From Lower Canyon Creek Lake, the trail turns to the right away from the lake. Follow the cairns to bear to the right, rather than the trail that runs along the shore of Lower Lake and ends in brush.

These lakes are like jewels set in the bottom of a gray, stark, high mountain canyon, and once you've seen them, you'll have their picture branded permanently in your mind. This has become a special weekend favorite for hikers from Eureka and Redding.

User Groups: Hikers, dogs, and horses. No mountain bikes. No wheelchair facilities.

Permits: A wilderness permit is required for hikers planning to camp.

Maps: For a map, ask the U.S. Forest Service for Shasta-Trinity National Forest or Trinity Alps Wilderness. For a topographic map, ask the USGS for Dedrick.

Directions: From Weaverville, drive west on Highway 299 for eight miles to Junction City and Canyon Creek Road. Turn north on Canyon Creek Road and drive 13 miles to the trailhead, at the end of the road (0.75 mile past Ripstein Campground).

Contact: Shasta-Trinity National Forest, Weaverville Ranger Station, Weaverville, 530/623-2121, www.fs.usda.gov/stnf.

63 SOUTH FORK NATIONAL RECREATION TRAIL

5.0 mi/2.5 hr 👫2 🛖6

in Shasta-Trinity National Forest east of Ruth Lake on Highway 36

Map 2.3, page 67

This remote trail is best known for following along the South Fork Trinity River and heads south toward the Yolla Bolly Wilderness. This is best accessed as an early-season trail, when so many other mountain routes are still snowbound. Mountain bikers and equestrians often share the trail on warm spring weekends. There are no lakes anywhere near the trail, and for the most part, the trail just meanders along, with that stream nearby providing a constant point of reference.

Even the trailhead, a short drive out of the Hell Gate Campground, is remote and obscure. Immediately, the trail picks up the stream, and in less than an hour, you might even feel as if you've discovered your own private little universe. How far might you go? For many, an hour in, an hour out, is plenty. Locations along the creek include Collins Creek (0.3 mile), Farley Creek (0.9), Marie Creek (2.5), Steel Mule Bridge (2.8), Silver Creek (6.2), and Smokey Creek and the site of an old ranger station (7.2). Hikers can keep going about 10 miles farther one-way to the trail's end at Double Cabin site, where you can leave a shuttle car and make this a one-way trip. In summer, the temperatures can really smoke out here and the stream is your savior. Note that the trail crosses private property several times; stay on the trail, respect property rights, and help keep this trail open.

User Groups: Hikers and dogs. No horses or mountain bikes. No wheelchair facilities.

Permits: Campfire permits are required for overnight use. Parking and access are free.

Maps: For a map, ask the U.S. Forest Service for Shasta-Trinity National Forest. For a topographic map, ask the USGS for Forest Glen.

Directions: From Red Bluff, take Highway 36 (very twisty) west and drive 47 miles to Platina and continue to the junction with Highway 3. Continue west on Highway 36 for 10 miles to the Hell Gate Campground (on the left) and Forest Road 1526. Turn left on Forest Road 1526 and drive to the trailhead.

Contact: Shasta-Trinity National Forest, Hayfork Ranger Station, Hayfork, 530/628-5227, www.fs.usda.gov/stnf.

64 BLACK ROCK LAKE TRAIL

4.5 mi/3.0 hr 👫2 🛖8

on the northern boundary of the Yolla Bolly Wilderness west of Red Bluff

Map 2.3, page 67

This 2.25-mile hike from the Stuart Gap trailhead to Black Rock Lake is one of the best day hikes in the Yolla Bolly Wilderness. One of the highlights comes in mid- to late June, when the wildflower blooms are absolutely beautiful. From the trailhead at 5,600 feet at the northern tip of the wilderness, start by hiking about a mile on the Pettyjohn Trail. It is set along the northwestern flank of North Yolla Bolly Mountain (7,863 feet) and is routed toward Pettyjohn Basin. When you reach the Black Rock Lake Trail, turn right on it and tromp another 1.25 miles to the lake. The trail contours through open stands of pine and fir and some small meadows. Small Black Rock Lake is set just below Black Rock Mountain (7,755 feet), and is ideal for swimming.

There are many other excellent day hikes from this trailhead: Yolla Bolly Lake, Black Rock Mountain (great views), North Yolla Bolly Mountain (more sweeping vistas), and Cedar Basin (several creeks). Any of these make for good days, remote and quiet. The trailhead can also be used as a jump-off spot for a hike straight south on Pettyjohn Trail into the wilderness interior.

User Groups: Hikers, dogs, and horses. No mountain bikes. No wheelchair facilities.

Permits: A campfire permit is required for hikers planning to camp.

Maps: For a map, ask the U.S. Forest Service for Shasta-Trinity National Forest or Yolla Bolly Wilderness. For a topographic map, ask the USGS for North Yolla Bolly.

Directions: From Red Bluff, take Highway 36 (very twisty) west and drive 47 miles to Platina. Continue west on Highway 36 for 11 miles to Forest Road 30 (Wildwood-Mad River Road). Turn left (south) and drive nine miles to Forest Road 35. Turn left (east) on Forest Road 35 and drive 10 miles to the intersection of several roads. Take the signed fork for Stuart Gap trailhead and drive 1.8 miles (unpaved) to the trailhead parking area. Hike on Pettyjohn Trail for one mile to reach Black Rock Lake Trail.

Contact: Shasta-Trinity National Forest, Yolla Bolly and Hayfork Ranger Station, Hayfork, 530/628-5227, www.fs.usda.gov/stnf.

65 SWIFT CREEK TRAIL TO GRANITE LAKE
12.0 mi/2 days   🥾4 ⛰9

in the Trinity Alps Wilderness west of Trinity Center

Map 2.4, page 68

When hikers scan wilderness maps, they often search for trails that are routed a short distance to a beautiful lake for a first night's camp. That's exactly what you get at Granite Lake. The trip in to Granite Lake is only about six miles, but it's anything but easy. From the trailhead, start by tracing the right side of Swift Creek. One mile in, the Granite Lake Trail splits off. Just beyond the confluence of Swift and Granite Creeks, you cross the stream to the left. This trail runs along the right side of Granite Creek for four miles and includes a very steep section in the final mile that will have you wondering why you ever thought this was going to be such a short, easy trip. Four miles in, you'll get your sighting of Bear Basin. Finally you'll rise to Gibson Meadow and just beyond, Granite Lake, a gorgeous sight below Gibson Peak. For a natural mountain lake, it's a fair size, with good swimming during the day and trout fishing in the evening. This is a popular spot, so plan on company. The lake is nestled amid towering granite.

One important note on the way in: For the most part, the creek is not accessible as a water source, so monitor your canteen level.

User Groups: Hikers, dogs, and horses. No mountain bikes. No wheelchair facilities.

Permits: A wilderness permit is required for hikers planning to camp.

Maps: For a map, ask the U.S. Forest Service for Shasta-Trinity National Forest or Trinity Alps Wilderness. For topographic maps, ask the USGS for Covington Mill and Trinity Center.

Directions: From Weaverville, take Highway 3 north for 28 miles to Trinity Center and Swift Creek Road. Turn left and drive 6.8 miles to the parking area, at the wilderness border.

Contact: Shasta-Trinity National Forest, Weaverville Ranger Station, Weaverville, 530/623-2121, www.fs.usda.gov/stnf.

66 LONG CANYON TRAILHEAD
16.0 mi/2 days   🥾4 ⛰9

in the Trinity Alps Wilderness northwest of Trinity Lake

Map 2.4, page 68

Your mission, should you choose to accept it, is the 6.5-mile, largely uphill hike to the west side of Gibson Peak, where Deer Lake, Summit Lake, Luella Lake, Diamond Lake, and Siligo Peak can provide days of side-trip destinations. From the trailhead, the trip starts by tracing along the East Fork Stuart Fork, a feeder creek to Trinity Lake. After two miles you'll arrive at a fork in the trail. Take the right fork (the left fork is routed to Bowerman Meadows and little Lake Anna), which climbs farther along the stream and then traces the southern flank of Gibson Peak. At times the trail is steep in this area, but finally you'll pass Gibson Peak, and Siligo Peak will come into view. The trail also intersects a loop trail that circles Siligo Peak and provides access to four high mountain lakes. Summit Lake is the favorite. Spring wildflowers are spectacular.

User Groups: Hikers, dogs, and horses. No mountain bikes. No wheelchair facilities.

Permits: A wilderness permit is required for hikers planning to camp.

Maps: For a map, ask the U.S. Forest Service for Shasta-Trinity National Forest or Trinity Alps Wilderness. For a topographic map, ask the USGS for Covington Mill.

Directions: From Weaverville, take Highway 3 north to Covington Mill and Forest Road 115. Turn left and drive for 2.5 miles to the trailhead.

Contact: Shasta-Trinity National Forest, Weaverville Ranger Station, Weaverville, 530/623-2121, www.fs.usda.gov/stnf.

67 STUART FORK TRAILHEAD

28.0 mi/4 days   👣5 ⛰10

in the Trinity Alps Wilderness northwest of Trinity Lake

Map 2.4, page 68

Don't say we didn't warn you: This trail doesn't have a difficulty rating of five for nothing. The hike requires an endless climb—very steep at times, particularly as you near the Sawtooth Ridge—spanning nearly 14 miles to Emerald Lake. The first nine miles are easy, and it will

have you thinking that this hike is a piece of cake—long, but easy. But surprise! The last five miles from Morris Meadows are the killer. But after arriving and resting up for a night, you'll find that ecstasy follows. Emerald Lake is one of three lakes set in line in a canyon below the Sawtooth Ridge; the others on this side of the ridge are Sapphire and Mirror. The surroundings are stark and prehistoric, and the lakes are gemlike, blue, and clear, with big rainbow trout and water that is perfect for refreshing swims. From Emerald Lake, the trail continues a mile to Sapphire Lake. From Sapphire, it's an off-trail scramble, often across big boulders, as you climb another mile to reach Mirror Lake. The entire scene is surreal.

Note: On the way to Emerald Lake, you might notice a cutoff trail to the right. On your trail map, you'll notice that it crosses the Sawtooth Ridge and leads in to the acclaimed Caribou Lakes Basin. On the map it appears to be a short, easy trip, but in reality, it involves a terrible climb with more than 100 switchbacks. Don't say you weren't warned.

User Groups: Hikers, dogs, and horses. No mountain bikes. No wheelchair facilities.

Permits: A wilderness permit is required for hikers planning to camp.

Maps: For a map, ask the U.S. Forest Service for Shasta-Trinity National Forest or Trinity Alps Wilderness. For a topographic map, ask the USGS for Covington Mill.

Directions: From Weaverville, take Highway 3 north to Trinity Lake and Trinity Alps Road. Turn left on Trinity Alps Road and drive 2.5 miles to the trailhead at Bridge Camp.

Contact: Shasta-Trinity National Forest, Weaverville Ranger Station, Weaverville, 530/623-2121, www.fs.usda.gov/stnf.

68 HIRZ BAY TRAIL

3.2 mi/1.75 hr 🏃1 ⛺8

on the McCloud arm of Shasta Lake north of Redding

Map 2.4, page 68

This trail, along a remote section of Shasta Lake, is best in spring when the temperatures are ideal, the lake is highest, the oaks are budding, and wildlife is abundant. Start at Dekkas Rock day-use area, located on the upper McCloud River Arm of Shasta Lake, near Hirz Bay. From Dekkas Rock, the trail traces the shoreline of the lake, in and out along small coves and creek inlets. Straight across the lake are pretty views of the deep coves at Campbell Creek and Dekkas Creek, of unique limestone outcrops, and of Minnesota Mountain (at 4,293 feet).

User Groups: Hikers and leashed dogs. No mountain bikes or horses. No wheelchair facilities.

Permits: No permits are required. Free at Dekkas Rock day-use area. A parking fee of $10 per vehicle is charged if parking at the Hirz Bay boat launch.

Maps: For a map, ask the U.S. Forest Service for Shasta-Trinity National Forest. For a topographic map, ask the USGS for O'Brien.

Directions: From Redding, take I-5 north to Shasta Lake and the exit for Salt Creek/Gilman Road. Take that exit and drive east on Gilman Road/County Road 7H009 for 10 miles (past the access road for Hirz Bay boat launch and campground) and then continue two miles to the Dekkas Rock day use area.

Contact: Shasta-Trinity National Forest, Shasta Lake Ranger District, Redding, 530/275-1587; Shasta Lake Visitors Center, 530/275-1589, www.fs.usda.gov/stnf.

69 GREENS CREEK BOAT-IN TRAIL

1.0 mi/1.0 hr 🏃3 ⛺8

on the McCloud arm of Shasta Lake north of Redding

Map 2.4, page 68

Your reward is a towering view of Shasta Lake, unique and special. Now get this: 1. Almost no one hikes this entire trail. 2. Almost no one hikes part of this trail. 3. Almost no one even knows about this trail.

Why? Because even with two million people estimated to visit Shasta Lake every year, the only way to access this trail is from a boat-in campsite at Greens Creek, on the east side of the McCloud arm of the lake. At the back of the cove at Greens Creek, you'll find a small U.S. Forest Service billboard posted with recreation guide sheets, and behind it are the campground and trailhead. Yet it is one of our favorites.

There are many fascinating side trips on the steep climb up toward a saddle between Town Mountain, at 4,325 feet, and Horse Mountain, at 4,025 feet. The trail enters an oak and madrone forest that is interspersed with limestone formations. The latter are worth exploring, and if you spend enough time hiking and investigating, you may find some small caves. Most people are inspired to hike just high enough to get a good clear view of the lake below.

User Groups: Hikers and leashed dogs. No horses or mountain bikes. No wheelchair facilities.

Permits: No permits are required. A parking fee of $10 per vehicle is charged at boat ramps.

Maps: For a map, ask the U.S. Forest Service for Shasta-Trinity National Forest. For a topographic map, ask the USGS for O'Brien.

Directions: First, load your boat: From Redding, take I-5 north to Shasta Lake and the exit for Salt Creek/Gilman Road. Take that exit and drive east on Gilman Road/County Road 7H009 for 10 miles to the access road for Hirz Bay boat launch. Launch your boat and drive out in the McCloud arm of Shasta Lake toward the Shasta Caverns. Turn left at Greens

Creek Cove and land your boat at Greens Creek Boat-In Campground. A billboard is at the back of the cove near the trailhead.

Nearby boat ramps: Bailey Cove (lake must be 73 percent full or higher).

Contact: Shasta-Trinity National Forest, Shasta Lake Ranger District, Redding, 530/275-1587; Shasta Lake Visitors Center, 530/275-1589, www.fs.usda.gov/stnf.

70 BAILEY COVE LOOP TRAIL
2.8 mi/1.5 hr   👫2 ⛰7

on the McCloud arm of Shasta Lake north of Redding

Map 2.4, page 68

The McCloud River arm is the prettiest part of giant Shasta Lake. The mountain canyon features towering limestone formations and the lake's clear, emerald waters. This trail provides a great view of these phenomena, as well as a close-to-the-water loop hike on one of the lake's peninsulas.

From the trailhead, start by hiking on the left fork, which travels out along Bailey Cove. As you continue, the trail is routed in a clockwise direction, first along the McCloud arm of the lake, then back to the parking area along John's Creek Inlet. When you reach the mouth of Bailey Cove, stop and enjoy the view. Directly across the lake are the limestone formations, featuring North Gray Rocks (at 3,114 feet) and topped by Horse Mountain (at 4,025 feet). The famous Shasta Caverns are located just below North Gray Rocks. This hike is best done in May and June, when the lake is at its highest levels. In late summer or fall, when the levels are down, you'll be looking out at a lot of red dirt. Watch out for the poison oak just off the trail.

User Groups: Hikers and leashed dogs. No mountain bikes or horses. No wheelchair facilities.

Permits: No permits are required. A parking fee of $6 per vehicle is charged.

Maps: For a map, ask the U.S. Forest Service

for Shasta-Trinity National Forest. For a topographic map, ask the USGS for O'Brien.

Directions: From Redding, take I-5 north to Shasta Lake and the exit for O'Brien/Shasta Caverns. Take that exit and turn east on Shasta Caverns Road and drive 0.1 mile to the sign for Bailey Cove Boat Ramp. Bear right at the sign and drive 0.5 mile to the day-use parking area.

Contact: Shasta-Trinity National Forest, Shasta Lake Ranger District, Redding, 530/275-1587; Shasta Lake Visitors Center, 530/275-1589, www.fs.usda.gov/stnf.

71 WATERS GULCH OVERLOOK
3.8 mi/2.0 hr   👫2 ⛰7

at Packers Bay on Shasta Lake north of Redding

Map 2.4, page 68

Shasta Lake is so big—the biggest reservoir in California—that it can be difficult to know where to start in your mission to explore it. A good answer is right here on the Waters Gulch Loop. It connects to the Overlook Trail, a cut-off of 0.8 mile that climbs atop a small mountain and furnishes a view of the main lake. The trailhead is at Packers Bay, which is easily accessible off I-5. From the trailhead at the parking area, walk down the road and start hiking the trail from the Packer's Bay boat-ramp parking lots, and then finish back at the trailhead parking areas. This provides the best loop hike for this site. Highlights of this trip include a route that extends onto one of the lake's peninsulas; Waters Gulch; a cove on the main Sacramento River arm of the lake; and several lookout points. Although there are many drive-to areas with lake views—most people join the crowd at the dam—you can get a little seclusion here as well.

User Groups: Hikers and leashed dogs. No horses or mountain bikes. No wheelchair facilities.

Permits: No permits are required. Parking and access are free.

Maps: For a map, ask the U.S. Forest Service for Shasta-Trinity National Forest. For a topographic map, ask the USGS for O'Brien.

Directions: From Redding, take I-5 north to Shasta Lake and the exit for Packers Bay. Take the exit and drive southwest on Packers Bay Road for one mile to the trailhead, on the right (0.25 mile before the boat ramp).

Contact: Shasta-Trinity National Forest, Shasta Lake Ranger District, Redding, 530/275-1587; Shasta Lake Visitors Center, 530/275-1589, www.fs.usda.gov/stnf.

72 BOULDER CREEK FALLS
2.0 mi/1.0 hr   🏃1 ⛰10

at Whiskeytown Lake National Recreation Area west of Redding

Map 2.4, page 68

Boulder Creek Falls is a 138-foot tall waterfall set in a deep ravine. At the top, the waterfall starts as a narrow cascade where the water builds speed. It then widens into a 28-foot cataract, a gentler rush of water over boulders. You get a full frontal for great photos. There are two ways to get here, and, of course, we picked the short, easier hike with the more difficult drive to the trailhead. At the parking area, the trailhead is well signed. The route starts on dirt road, a former logging road, and is routed into a hardwood forest. It's an easy walk to a creek with a well-signed spur to the waterfall. Turn right at the spur, and it's another 0.1 mile along the creek to the plunge pool. A four-wheel-drive vehicle is advised to reach this trailhead. If you do not have an aggressive vehicle, another trailhead to Boulder Creek Falls is available along the lake on South Shore Drive; from there, it is a 5.5-mile round-trip.

User Groups: Hikers, mountain bikes, dogs, and horses. No wheelchair facilities.

Permits: A parking fee of $10 per vehicle, good for a week, is charged.

Maps: For a detailed trail map, contact Whiskeytown National Recreation Area. For a topographic map, ask the USGS for Igo.

Directions: Take I-5 to Redding and the exit for Highway 44 West. Take that exit, merge onto 44W and drive 1.2 miles (into town) to Highway 273/N. Pine Street (large signs for 299/Weaverville-Eureka). Turn right on North Pine and drive 500 feet to the first left, for Eureka Way (signed for 299/Weaverville-Eureka). Turn left on Eureka Way and drive 7.7 miles (becomes Highway 299) to Whiskeytown Lake (signed for Visitor Center) on left.

To the waterfall: From the Whiskeytown Visitors Center, return to the junction with Highway 299. Turn left and drive 7.1 miles to a left turn for South Shore Drive/Carr Powerhouse. Turn left and drive 0.5 mile to Mill Creek Road (a steep dirt road on right). Turn right (four-wheel drive advised) and drive 1.8 miles to the end of the road. A parking area and the signed trailhead are on the gated road on the right.

Option: For another trailhead with a paved road, from the turnoff on South Shore Drive, drive 5.3 miles to Brandy Creek; requires a 5.5-mile round-trip hike.

Contact: Whiskeytown National Recreation Area, Whiskeytown, 530/246-1225, www.nps.gov/whis.

73 DAVIS GULCH TRAIL
3.3 mi one-way/3.5 hr   🏃1 ⛰7

at Whiskeytown Lake National Recreation Area west of Redding

Map 2.4, page 68

The Davis Gulch Trail is Whiskeytown Lake's easiest hike that you can do as a one-way descent, with a shuttle car at the end. Or you can drop off your kids, go have fun with something more serious, and pick them up later at the end. This meandering route along the southwest end of the lake starts out at 1,414 feet (at an information billboard along an access road) and winds its way down to the Brandy Creek Picnic Area, at 1,240 feet. It is a moderate descent on a wide, flat footpath surrounded mostly by oak and manzanita. Along the way, there are many good views of Whiskeytown Lake. The trail spans 3.3 miles and dead-ends. With two vehicles, it is possible to make it a one-way hike with a shuttle and then (better yet) hike the whole route downhill.

User Groups: Hikers and dogs. No horses or mountain bikes. No wheelchair facilities.

Permits: A parking fee of $10 per vehicle, good for a week, is charged.

Maps: For a detailed trail map, contact Whiskeytown National Recreation Area. For a topographic map, ask the USGS for Igo.

Directions: Take I-5 to Redding and the exit for Highway 44 West. Take that exit, merge onto 44W, and drive 1.2 miles (into town) to Highway 273/N. Pine Street (large signs for 299/Weaverville-Eureka). Turn right on North Pine and drive 500 feet to first left, for Eureka Way (signed for 299/Weaverville-Eureka). Turn left on Eureka Way and drive 7.7 miles (becomes Highway 299) to Whiskeytown Lake (signed for Visitor Center) on left. From the visitors center, continue on J. F. Kennedy Memorial Drive for three miles to the Davis Gulch trailhead, on the right. To reach the Brandy Creek Picnic

Area (and end of the trail), continue three more miles on J. F. Kennedy Memorial Drive.

Contact: Whiskeytown National Recreation Area, Whiskeytown, 530/246-1225, www.nps.gov/whis.

74 WHISKEYTOWN FALLS
3.4 mi/2.5 hr   🥾3 ⛰10

at Whiskeytown Lake National Recreation Area west of Redding

Map 2.4, page 68   **BEST (**

The viewing areas for Whiskeytown Falls are set in a rock staircase, with a railing for safety, just to the left of the cascades. You rise up to a series of perches, including Photographer's Ledge, and above that, Artist's Ledge. These are among the best waterfall views in the state, so close you can often taste the water as it surges past. The waterfall is estimated at 220 feet tall, top to bottom. You can feel a rush of cool air pushed by the blast of water.

From the metal railing, the water sails past you just a few feet distant and then rockets over

lower cascade of Whiskeytown Falls

© TOM STIENSTRA

a brink into a foaming white cascade. It thunders down the canyon. Above you are a series of four giant steps where the water carves mosaics down the rock faces. Below you, a white torrent pounds to the final ledge—and then over the top and pours like an angled fountain into the final plunge pool. Whiskeytown Falls is the prettiest waterfall in California that relatively few have seen.

It's only a 1.7-mile hike one-way, a short yet aerobic climb most of the way, where you arrive at the final cascade and a staircase built into the rock just to the left of the waterfall. The moments here, one after another, are touched by how this place makes you feel as much as what you see. It starts out as a mild walk on a trail over a sandstone-based terrain. The route leads to Crystal Creek, over a bridge and beyond to a junction (with the Mill Creek Trail). You bear right, signed for Whiskeytown Falls, and you're on your way. From the junction, it's about a half-hour aerobic climb, with several concrete benches positioned as rest stops, past a picnic area and then into the canyon. The first view is of the lower cascade. This seems to be the most popular site for a photo, but it represents only a small piece of the entire falls. If you own a quality camera, bring a tripod and set a slow shutter speed to capture the soft, blurred rush of moving water down the cascade.

User Groups: Hikers, mountain bikes, and horses are permitted up to picnic area. Hikers only allowed after this point. No dogs. No wheelchair facilities.

Permits: A parking fee of $10 per vehicle, good for a week, is charged. A self-pay station is available at the trailhead.

Maps: For a trail map/brochure, contact Whiskeytown National Recreation Area. For a topographic map, ask the USGS for Igo.

Directions: Take I-5 to Redding and the exit for Highway 44 West. Take that exit, merge onto 44 West and drive 1.2 miles (into town) to Highway 273/N. Pine Street (large signs for 299/Weaverville-Eureka). Turn right on North Pine and drive 500 feet to first left for Eureka Way (signed for 299/Weaverville-Eureka).

Turn left on Eureka Way and drive 7.7 miles (becomes Highway 299) to Whiskeytown Lake (signed for Visitor Center) on left.

From visitors center, return a short distance to Highway 299. Turn left on 299 and drive west 8.4 miles to Crystal Creek Road. Turn left and drive 3.7 miles (paved) to parking and trailhead on left.

Contact: Whiskeytown National Recreation Area, Whiskeytown, 530/246-1225, www.nps.gov/whis.

75 BRANDY CREEK FALLS
3.0 mi/2.0 hr   3   9

at Whiskeytown Lake National Recreation Area west of Redding

Map 2.4, page 68

Brandy Creek Falls is a cascade chute with a series of pool-and-drops that pour into a big pool. It is spectacular at high water, a cataract where all the waterfall pools are connected into a massive whitewater flow. At low water, it splits into two thin cascades with a series of small drops. This is not a Yosemite-like freefall and the trailhead is still fairly obscure. It's a 1.5-mile hike to get there, with a 500-foot climb.

From the trailhead, you'll cross a creek in 0.5 mile. There is a large debris field of logs and boulders in the creek, the result of the 1977 flood. Continue on and in another 0.25 mile, you will reach a junction with the Rich Gulch Trail. Though you pass this by and continue ahead, note that the trail narrows here and is accessible only for hikers. From here to the falls, the trail enters the Brandy Creek Canyon with fern grottoes and clifflike dropoffs. It can be slippery, but the route heads right along the cascade. As you forge on, you will find steps cut in rock that will lead you past five pools and falls that run about 50 feet. Very special stuff.

User Groups: Hikers only. No mountain bikes, dogs, or horses. No wheelchair facilities.

Permits: A parking fee of $10 per vehicle, good for a week, is charged.

Maps: For a detailed trail map, contact

Whiskeytown National Recreation Area. For a topographic map, ask the USGS for Igo. Take I-5 to Redding and the exit for Highway 44 West. Take that exit, merge onto 44W and drive 1.2 miles (into town) to Highway 273/N. Pine Street (large signs for 299/Weaverville-Eureka). Turn right on North Pine and drive 500 feet to first left for Eureka Way (signed for 299/Weaverville-Eureka). Turn left on Eureka Way and drive 7.7 miles (becomes Highway 299) to Whiskeytown Lake (signed for Visitor Center) on left.

From the visitors center, continue south on Kennedy Memorial Drive to a fork. Bear right at the fork, cross over the dam, and continue past the Brandy Creek area to Shasta Bally Road. Turn left and drive 2.5 miles on the dirt road to a junction. Turn left and drive 0.75 mile to a small parking area. The signed trailhead is 150 feet up the road.

Contact: Whiskeytown National Recreation Area, Whiskeytown, 530/246-1225, www.nps.gov/whis.

76 SYD CABIN RIDGE TRAIL
8.0 mi/2 days   👫3   ▲7

on the eastern boundary of the Yolla Bolly Wilderness west of Red Bluff

Map 2.4, page 68

Not many people hike into the Yolla Bolly Wilderness, set up a camp, then hike back out the next day. But here is a chance to do exactly that. The trailhead is at the Tomhead Saddle, located just west of Tomhead Mountain, at an

elevation of 6,757 feet. From here, hike past Tomhead Spring on Syd Cabin Ridge Trail, then drop down into Hawk Camp. Set just below the confluence of three feeder streams, Hawk Camp is a spot to overnight. On the way back, expect a steady climb with no water between Tomhead Spring and Hawk Camp. If you plan on extending your trip for several days into the wilderness, a network of trails intersects just beyond Hawk Camp, but note that a stream crossing is required. The Yolla Bolly Wilderness is one of the least-used significant wilderness areas in California.

User Groups: Hikers, dogs, and horses. No mountain bikes. No wheelchair facilities.

Permits: A campfire permit is required for hikers planning to camp.

Maps: For a map, ask the U.S. Forest Service for Shasta-Trinity National Forest or Yolla Bolly Wilderness. For a topographic map, ask the USGS for North Yolla Bolly.

Directions: From Red Bluff, turn west on Highway 36 (twisty) and drive about 13 miles to Cannon Road. Turn left (south) on Cannon Road and go approximately five miles to Pettyjohn Road. Turn right (west) on Pettyjohn Road and drive to Forest Road 27N06. Turn left (south) on Forest Road 27N06 and continue three miles to the parking area at Tomhead Saddle Campground. From Highway 36, this route is a dirt road all the way in. A high-clearance vehicle is recommended. In storms, it can also be slippery when wet.

Contact: Shasta-Trinity National Forest, Yolla Bolly and Hayfork Ranger Station, Hayfork, 530/628-5227, www.fs.usda.gov/stnf.

LASSEN AND MODOC

At 10,457 feet, Mount Lassen's domed summit is visible for more than 100 miles. It blew its top in 1914, with continuing eruptions through 1918. Now dormant, the volcanic-based geology—pumice boulders, volcanic rock, and spring-fed streams from underground lava tubes—dominates this landscape. Lassen Volcanic National Park is one of the few national parks where you can enjoy the wilderness in relative solitude. The best hikes are the Summit Climb and Bumpass Hell. Highlights include canoeing and fly-fishing at Fall River, Big Lake, and Ahjumawi State Park. McArthur-Burney Falls State Park, along with the Pit River and Lake Britton, make the best destinations for families. In remote Modoc County, Lava Beds National Monument boasts caves and lava tubes, including the 6,000-foot Catacomb Tunnel. Nearby is pretty Medicine Lake, formed in a caldera, which provides good exploring.

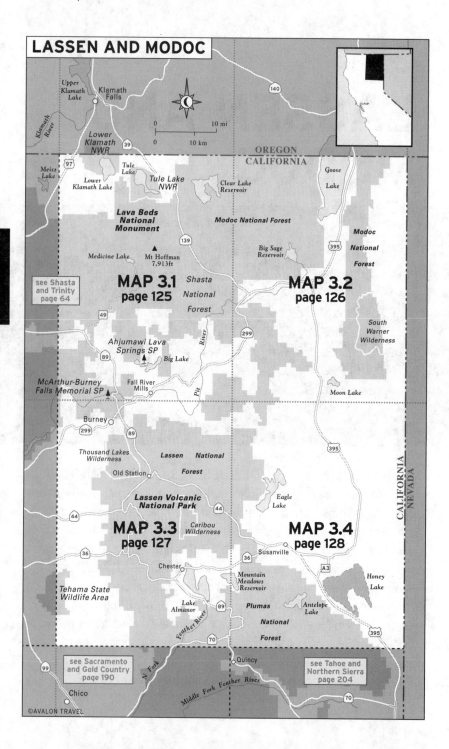

LASSEN AND MODOC

Upper Klamath Lake
Klamath Falls
140
OREGON
CALIFORNIA

Klamath River

Lower Klamath NWR
39
97

N
0   10 mi
0   10 km

Meiss Lake
Lower Klamath Lake
Tule Lake
Tule Lake NWR
Clear Lake Reservoir
Goose Lake

Lava Beds National Monument

Medicine Lake
▲ Mt Hoffman 7,913ft
139

Big Sage Reservoir
395

Modoc National Forest

Modoc National Forest

Modoc National Forest

see Shasta and Trinity page 64

MAP 3.1 page 125

Shasta National Forest

MAP 3.2 page 126

South Warner Wilderness

49

Ahjumawi Lava Springs SP
▲
89
Big Lake

River

299

McArthur-Burney Falls Memorial SP
Fall River Mills
Pit River

Moon Lake

Burney
299
89

Thousand Lakes Wilderness

Lassen National Forest

Old Station

395

Lassen Volcanic National Park
44

Eagle Lake

44
Caribou Wilderness

MAP 3.3 page 127

MAP 3.4 page 128

36

36
Susanville
A3

Chester

Honey Lake

Tehama State Wildlife Area

Mountain Meadows Reservoir

Lake Almanor
89

Antelope Lake

Plumas

Feather River
70

National

Forest

395

CALIFORNIA
NEVADA

see Sacramento and Gold Country page 190

N Fork

Quincy

see Tahoe and Northern Sierra page 204

99

Chico
©AVALON TRAVEL

Middle Fork Feather River

70

Map 3.1

Sites 1-11
Pages 129-136

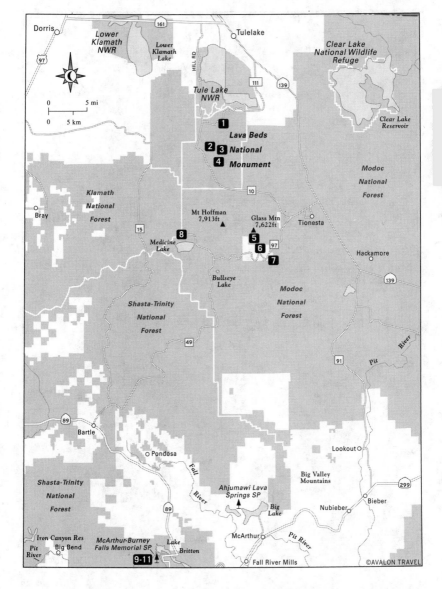

Map 3.2

Sites 12-20
Pages 136-141

©AVALON TRAVEL

Map 3.3

Sites 21-52
Pages 141-161

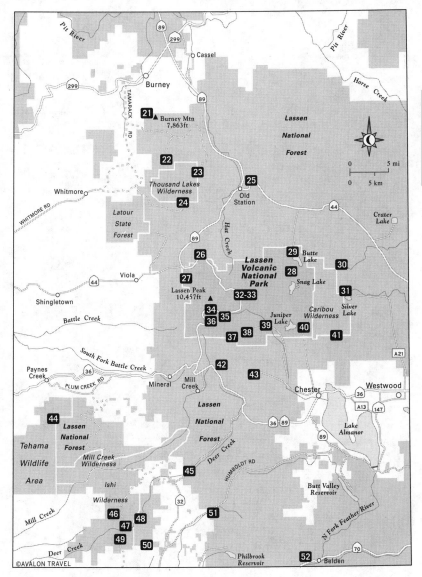

Map **3.4**

Site 53
Page 161

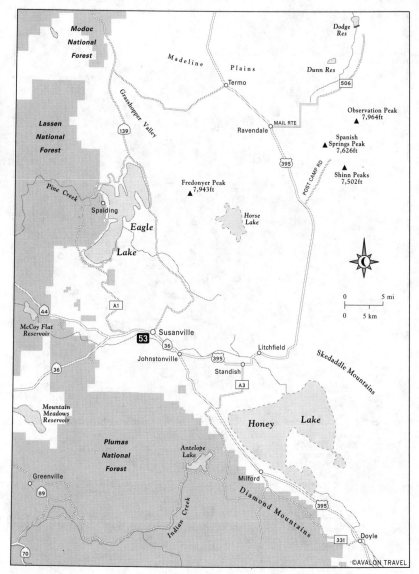

Modoc
National
Forest

Dodge
Res

Madeline Plains

Dunn Res

Termo

506

Grasshopper Valley

Lassen
National
Forest

139

MAIL RTE

Observation Peak
▲ 7,964ft

Ravendale

Spanish
▲ Springs Peak
7,626ft

395

Shinn Peaks
▲ 7,502ft

POST CAMP RD

Pine Creek

Fredonyer Peak
▲ 7,943ft

Spalding

Eagle

Horse
Lake

Lake

0   5 mi

0   5 km

44

A1

McCoy Flat
Reservoir

53 Susanville

36

Johnstonville

395

Litchfield

Standish

Skedaddle Mountains

36

A3

Mountain
Meadows
Reservoir

Honey   Lake

Plumas
National
Forest

Antelope
Lake

Greenville

89

Milford

Diamond Mountains

395

Indian Creek

70

331   Doyle

©AVALON TRAVEL

1 CAPTAIN JACK'S STRONGHOLD

1.7 mi/1.5 hr 👫1 ⛰8

in Lava Beds National Monument south of Klamath Wildlife Refuge

Map 3.1, page 125 **BEST (**

Captain Jack's Stronghold provides a history lesson and an introduction to the Lava Beds National Monument. It's an easy walk on a clear trail amid a volcanic plateau, with a few trenches, dips, and rocks. From this trailhead, there are actually two loop trails available, including a shorter route that is just 0.5 mile long. The general terrain is level, with a trailhead elevation of 4,047 feet and a high point of 4,080 feet.

Captain Jack was a Modoc warrior who fought U.S. troops attempting to relocate Native Americans off their lands and onto a reservation. His hiding place in this natural lava fortress was betrayed by his own troops, and in 1873, Captain Jack was finally captured and hanged, and this site was later named for him.

Note that during the winter, this is an outstanding area to see mule deer. Many of the famous photographs of big bucks in California were taken in this area. The wildlife viewing is best at the onset of winter, after the first inch or two of snow has fallen. In addition, a good nearby side trip is Tule Lake, a favorite wintering area for waterfowl and bald eagles.

User Groups: Hikers only. No dogs, horses, or mountain bikes. No wheelchair access.

Permits: No permits are required. A park entrance fee of $15, good for seven days, is charged per vehicle.

Maps: A free brochure is available by contacting Lava Beds National Monument. For a topographic map, ask the USGS for Captain Jack's Stronghold.

Directions: From Redding, take I-5 north for 68 miles to the exit for Central Weed/Highway 97-Klamath Falls. Take that exit to the stop sign, turn right and drive one mile through town to the junction with Highway 97. Bear right on Highway 97 and drive 54 miles to Highway 161. Turn right (east) on Highway 161 and drive 20 miles to Hill Road. Turn right (south), drive 18 miles to the visitors center, and look for the main road of the Lava Beds National Monument (it's unnamed). Turn north and drive 13 miles on the main monument road to the Captain Jack's Stronghold access road. Turn right and drive to the trailhead.

Contact: Lava Beds National Monument, Tulelake, 530/667-8113, www.nps.gov/labe.

2 WHITNEY BUTTE TRAIL

6.8 mi/4.0 hr 👫2 ⛰8

in Lava Beds National Monument south of Klamath Wildlife Refuge

Map 3.1, page 125

The Whitney Butte Trail is one of three wilderness trails in Lava Beds National Monument, and for many, it's the best of the lot. From the top of Whitney Butte, 5,004 feet, a cinder cone, the views are spectacular across the volcanic landscape. The trailhead, 4,880 feet, is at Merrill Ice Cave. The trail goes west for two miles near the edge of Whitney Butte to a trail junction. Turn left and walk 1.2 miles to the end of the trail at the edge of the Callahan Lava Flow. Be sure to climb Whitney Butte. This area bears a resemblance to the surface of the moon, and skilled photographers who know how to use sunlight to their advantage can take black-and-white pictures that can fool most people into thinking they are looking at a lunar surface. Most people arrive just to see the Merrill Ice Cave (which is actually a lava tube) at the beginning of the hike. If you plan to explore the cave, bring plenty of flashlight power, a hard hat, and kneepads. The views are often spectacular across the volcanic landscape to 14,179-foot Mount Shasta.

User Groups: Hikers and horses. No dogs or mountain bikes. No wheelchair facilities.

Permits: No permits are required. A park entrance fee of $15, good for seven days, is charged per vehicle.

Maps: A free brochure is available by contacting Lava Beds National Monument. For a topographic map, ask the USGS for Schonchin Butte.

Directions: From Redding, take I-5 north for 68 miles to the exit for Central Weed/Highway 97-Klamath Falls. Take that exit to the stop sign, turn right and drive one mile through town to the junction with Highway 97. Bear right on Highway 97 and drive 54 miles to Highway 161. Turn right (east) on Highway 161 and drive 20 miles to Hill Road. Turn right (south), drive 18 miles to the visitors center, and look for the main road of the Lava Beds National Monument (it's unnamed). From the visitors center, turn north on the monument main road and drive 1.2 miles north to the turnoff for Merrill Ice Cave. Turn left and drive 0.7 mile to the parking lot and trailhead, at the end of the road.

Contact: Lava Beds National Monument, Tulelake, 530/667-8113, www.nps.gov/labe.

3 THOMAS WRIGHT BATTLEFIELD TRAIL/ BLACK CRATER

2.2 mi/1.0 hr

in Lava Beds National Monument south of Tulelake Wildlife Refuge

Map 3.1, page 125

One trail, two pay-offs. After just 0.25 mile on this trail, hikers reach a short spur to the awesome Black Crater. In the world of volcanic geology, this is a spatter cone. It feels as if you are looking into the bowels of the earth. When ready, return to the main trail. It's an easy glide along lava fields, but note: As you continue on, you might even get the sense that ghosts are shadowing your footsteps. That is because some say this area is haunted by the ghosts of Modoc Indians, who fought troops in several violent battles for custody of the land. Though the Modoc warriors eventually lost that war, some say they actually won in the long run, since their spirits haunt modern-day visitors. At the end of the trail are interpretive signs that explain the Thomas Wright battlefield site. For an

Catacombs Cave on the Whitney Butte Trail

© TOM STIENSTRA

excellent side trip from here, continue off trail, clambering up to the Hardin Butte, a 130-foot climb, for a view. The butte sits on the western edge of the huge Schonchin Lava Flow.

User Groups: Hikers only. No dogs, horses, or mountain bikes. No wheelchair facilities.

Permits: No permits are required. A park entrance fee of $15, good for seven days, is charged per vehicle.

Maps: A free brochure is available by contacting Lava Beds National Monument. For a topographic map, ask the USGS for Captain Jack's Stronghold.

Directions: From Redding, take I-5 north for 68 miles to the exit for Central Weed/Highway 97-Klamath Falls. Take that exit to the stop sign, turn right and drive one mile through town to the junction with Highway 97. Bear right on Highway 97 and drive 54 miles to Highway 161. Turn right (east) on Highway 161 and drive 20 miles to Hill Road. Turn right (south) and drive five miles to the trailhead on the left (the visitors center is another five miles south).

Contact: Lava Beds National Monument, Tulelake, 530/667-8113, www.nps.gov/labe.

4 SCHONCHIN BUTTE TRAIL
1.8 mi/1.0 hr

in Lava Beds National Monument south of Tulelake Wildlife Refuge

Map 3.1, page 125

This is a short hike, but for many, it's a butt-kicker. A portion of it is quite steep—enough to get most folks wheezing like old steam locomotives. The trail climbs 600 feet, from a trailhead elevation of 4,700 feet to the lookout at 5,300 feet. There are benches along the trail in case you need to catch your breath. Schonchin Butte has an old fire lookout, and the views are spectacular, of course, especially of the Schonchin Lava Flow to the northeast. Because of the proximity to the visitors center, as well as the short distance involved, many visitors make the tromp to the top. After completing

this trip, always explore some of the caves in the matrix of underground lava tubes. You need a hard hat and flashlight to do it (available for a fee at the visitors center). For extensive caving, always wear kneepads. There are more than 700 caves in a five-mile radius, including 15 with signed entrances on the Cave Loop.

User Groups: Hikers only. No dogs, horses, or mountain bikes. No wheelchair facilities.

Permits: No permits are required. A park entrance fee of $15, good for seven days, is charged per vehicle.

Maps: A free brochure is available by contacting Lava Beds National Monument. For a topographic map, ask the USGS for Schonchin Butte.

Directions: From Redding, take I-5 north for 68 miles to the exit for Central Weed/Highway 97-Klamath Falls. Take that exit to the stop sign, turn right and drive one mile through town to the junction with Highway 97. Bear right on Highway 97 and drive 54 miles to Highway 161. Turn right (east) on Highway 161 and drive 20 miles to Hill Road. Turn right (south), drive 18 miles to the visitors center, then look for the main (unnamed) road for the Lava Beds National Monument. Turn north and drive 2.3 miles to the turnoff for Schonchin Butte. Turn right at the sign for Schonchin Butte and drive about one mile on a gravel road to the trailhead.

Contact: Lava Beds National Monument, Tulelake, 530/667-8113, www.nps.gov/labe.

5 MEDICINE LAKE SHORELINE
1.0 mi/1.0 hr

in Modoc National Forest northeast of Mount Shasta

Map 3.1, page 125

When you stand on the shore of Medicine Lake, it might be difficult to believe that this was once the center of a volcano. The old caldera is now filled with water and circled by conifers, and the lake is clear and crisp. Set at 6,700 feet, it's a unique and popular destination for camping, boating, and fishing. At some point in their stay, most campers will take a morning or afternoon to walk around the lake. Although there is no specific trail, the route is clear enough. There is a sense of timelessness here. Although its geology is comparable to Crater Lake in Oregon, Medicine Lake is neither as deep nor as blue. But a bonus here is the good shore fishing for large brook trout, often in the 12- to 14-inch class, buoyed by the large stocks of trout. There are also many excellent nearby side trips. They include the ice caves (along the access road on the way in); a great mountaintop lookout from Little Mount Hoffman, Little Medicine Lake (very deep, good fishing), and nearby little Bullseye and Blanche Lakes.

User Groups: Hikers, dogs, horses, and mountain bikes. There are wheelchair facilities at the beach and the boat ramp.

Permits: No permits are required. Parking and access are free unless you're camping.

Maps: A free brochure on the Medicine Lake Highlands is available by contacting the Doublehead Ranger District. For a map, ask the U.S. Forest Service for Modoc National Forest. For a topographic map, ask the USGS for Medicine Lake.

Directions: From Redding, take I-5 north for 58 miles to the exit for Highway 89. Bear right at that exit and drive 26.5 miles to Harris Springs Road. Turn left on Harris Springs Road and drive 4.4 miles to Medicine Lake Road. Turn right on Medicine Lake Road and drive 27.5 miles (paved, but narrow at times) to the turnoff for Medicine Lake. Turn left and drive 0.3 mile to a T. Turn left at the T for beach and boat ramp. Turn right at the T for campgrounds, Little Medicine Lake, and Hoffman Lookout. For a shoreline walk, turn left to the boat ramp, and then walk to the right along the swimming beach.

Contact: Modoc National Forest, Doublehead Ranger District, Tulelake, 530/667-2246, www.fs.usda.gov/modoc.

6 LITTLE GLASS MOUNTAIN
0.5 mi/2.0 hr 🥾3 ⛰10

in Modoc National Forest east of Medicine Lake

Map 3.1, page 125

Little Glass Mountain is a spectacular volcanic "glass flow" that covers a square mile in the Medicine Lake Highlands. It was created when glassy dacite and rhyolitic obsidian flowed from the same volcanic vent without mixing, creating a present-day phenomenon that exhibits no modification from weather, erosion, or vegetation. It's about 100 feet high. There are no designated trails on Glass Mountain, so visitors just wander about, inspecting the geologic curiosities as they go. Take care to stay clear of the obsidian, which is quite slippery and can have arrowhead-sharp edges. Don't walk on it, and don't handle it. Be sure to stay on the gray-colored dacite instead. Got it? Stay on the gray stuff. Stay off the black stuff. The mountain was formed 1,000 years ago as a lava flow. If you wear rings, you will scuff the bottom of the ring with lava when you grab for hand holds. A panoramic view of Little Glass Mountain backed by Mount Shasta is available at the Little Mount Hoffman Lookout near Medicine Lake.

Note: In some previous editions of this book, we sent readers to Glass Mountain, a mistake (much of the obsidian there appears to have been excavated, and a road bisects some of the flow); if you love unique volcanics, Little Glass Mountain is the one you want to see.

User Groups: Hikers and dogs. The terrain is not suitable for horses or mountain bikes. No wheelchair facilities.

Permits: No permits are required. Parking and access are free.

Maps: A free brochure on the Medicine Lake Highlands is available by contacting the Doublehead Ranger District. For a map, ask the U.S. Forest Service for Modoc National Forest. For a topographic map, ask the USGS for Medicine Lake.

Directions: From Redding, take I-5 north for 58 miles to the exit for Highway 89. Bear right at that exit and drive 26.5 miles to Harris Springs Road. Turn left on Harris Springs Road and drive 4.4 miles (turnoff to Medicine Lake Road on right), and continue straight on Harris Spring Road for 7.9 miles to Forest Road 44N05. Turn right and drive 0.6 miles to Forest Road 43N77 and continue for 0.5 mile to the foot of Little Glass Mountain. Park and trek in the volcanic landscape.

Contact: Modoc National Forest, Doublehead Ranger District, Tulelake, 530/667-2246, www. fs.usda.gov/modoc.

7 BURNT LAVA FLOW
1.0 mi/1.5 hr

in Modoc National Forest south of Medicine Lake

Map 3.1, page 125

The Burnt Lava Flow is called a land of "rocks that float and mountains of glass." It may seem as if you're exploring some prehistoric area that resembles the moon. But get this: The lava formation is only a few hundred years old, the youngest flow in the Medicine Lake Highlands. It's located south of Glass Mountain and covers some 8,760 acres, with little islands of forest amid the bare, jet-black lava flow. High Hole Crater, located at the north end, rises up 386 feet above the base layer of the flow, and is about 150 feet deep. There is no trail, so pick any direction—most visitors go from tree island to tree island. There are a few weird spots where the ground can be like quicksand when dry and like wet concrete when wet. Just walk around those spots, staying on the hard, black lava flow. When we took an aerial survey of the area, the Burnt Lava Flow was one of the most fascinating portions of the entire region. On foot, it's even stranger.

User Groups: Hikers and dogs. The terrain is not suitable for mountain bikes or horses. No wheelchair facilities.

Permits: No permits are required. Parking and access are free.

Maps: For a map, ask the U.S. Forest Service for

Modoc National Forest. For a topographic map, ask the USGS for Porcupine Butte.

Directions: From Redding, take I-5 north for 58 miles to the exit for Highway 89. Bear right at that exit and drive 26.5 miles to Harris Springs Road. Turn left on Harris Springs Road and drive 4.4 miles to Medicine Lake Road. Turn right on Medicine Lake Road and drive 19.6 miles (paved, but narrow at times) to the turnoff for Burnt Lava Flow (straight would instead take you to Medicine Lake). Turn right and drive 4.1 miles to Forest Road 43N17. Turn right and drive 1.7 miles to the foot of the Burnt Lava Flow Geologic Area.

Contact: Modoc National Forest, Doublehead Ranger District, Tulelake, 530/667-2246, www. fs.usda.gov/modoc.

8 MEDICINE LAKE GLASS FLOW
1.0 mi/1.0 hr

in Modoc National Forest north of Medicine Lake

Map 3.1, page 125

First, a good story: In 1965, the Medicine Lake Glass Flow was selected by the Manned Spacecraft Center for study by astronauts preparing for the first manned trip to the moon. It feels much the same today as you make your visit. The Medicine Lake Glass Flow Geologic Area covers 570 acres. It has no designated trails. You can explore in any direction you wish, where you probe about the stony-gray dacite, which runs 50-150 feet deep. This part of the Medicine Lake Highlands is located about a mile north of Medicine Lake. It is set within the caldera of the Medicine Lake Volcano. Before the first lunar landing, many originally believed this area to resemble the surface of the moon. Most people will just poke around for an hour or two, take a few pictures, and leave, saying they've never seen anything like it.

User Groups: Hikers and dogs. The terrain is not suitable for mountain bikes or horses. No wheelchair facilities.

Permits: No permits are required. Parking and access are free.

Maps: A free brochure on the Medicine Lake Highlands is available by contacting the Doublehead Ranger District. For a map, ask the U.S. Forest Service for Modoc National Forest. For a topographic map, ask the USGS for Medicine Lake.

Directions: From Redding, take I-5 north for 58 miles to the exit for Highway 89. Bear right at that exit, merged with Highway 89, and drive 26.5 miles to Harris Springs Road. Turn left on Harris Springs Road and drive 4.4 miles to Medicine Lake Road. Turn right on Medicine Lake Road and drive 27.5 miles (paved, but narrow at times) to the turnoff for Medicine Lake. Turn left and drive 0.3 mile to a T. At the T, turn right and drive (slow) past the campgrounds and Little Medicine Lake for 1.5 miles to a junction with Lava Beds/Forest Road 44N75. Turn right on Forest Road 44N75 and drive 1.2 miles to the foot of the Medicine Lake Glass Flow on the right. There are no designated trailheads or trails.

Contact: Modoc National Forest, Doublehead Ranger District, Tulelake, 530/667-2246, www. fs.usda.gov/modoc.

🟦 BURNEY FALLS LOOP TRAIL

1.2 mi/0.5 hr   🏃1 ⛰10

in McArthur-Burney Falls Memorial State Park north of Burney

Map 3.1, page 125   BEST (

Spectacular Burney Falls is one of the prettiest waterfalls in the north state. The trip starts by taking in Burney Falls at a lookout point for the full frontal. This is the eye-popping 129-foot waterfall. If you look close, you will see that the surrounding moss-covered canyon wall is a mosaic of oozing water. That is because lava tubes feed underground water through the basalt rock: 100 million gallons a day, year-round—making it an endless freshwater fountain. The waterfall plunges over the brink in two pieces, split at the rim by a small bluff, where two trees have managed toeholds (although the river flows over the top of them during high water from the spring snowmelt). From a parking lot, it's a 100-foot walk to the overlook. This spot also marks the start of Burney Falls Loop Trail, an easy 1.2-mile loop around the waterfall and back.

At the start of the trail, you descend 200 feet and skirt the plunge pool of the waterfall. Then the trail is routed downstream along Burney Creek and crosses a wood bridge. You then hike upstream back to the waterfall for more fantastic views. At one spot, you are situated directly adjacent to the water's cascade for mid-level flows. The trail climbs up past the brink of the falls and continues upstream along Burney Creek. It then crosses another bridge. Look up to your left here to the treetops, where a mated pair of bald eagles tend a nest atop a towering pine. The trail then returns to the falls overlook. It's also a self-guided nature trail, but rather than having to carry a brochure with you, you can just read the small signs that explain the featured sites.

User Groups: Hikers only. No dogs, horses, or mountain bikes. There is paved wheelchair access at the falls overlook point, at the beginning of the trail.

Permits: No permits are required. A state park day-use fee of $8 is charged for each vehicle.

Maps: A trail guide is available for a fee at the state park. For a topographic map, ask the USGS for Burney Falls.

Directions: From Redding, take Highway 299 east for 50 miles to Burney and continue five miles to the junction with Highway 89. Turn left (north) and drive 5.8 miles to the state park entrance on the left. At the entrance station, continue straight for a short distance and park in the main lot on the right. The trailhead is across the road at the falls overlook.

Contact: McArthur-Burney Falls Memorial State Park, Burney, 530/335-2777, www.parks. ca.gov.

© TOM STIENSTRA

Burney Falls Loop Trail

10 RIM TRAIL

3.0 mi/1.75 hr 👫₁ ⛰₇

at Lake Britton in McArthur-Burney Falls
Memorial State Park north of Burney

Map 3.1, page 125

The Rim Trail provides an easy walk for campers at McArthur-Burney Falls Memorial State
Park. The trail starts at the campground and
is routed to the rim of Lake Britton, a distance
of 1.5 miles. It's an easy walk, and pretty too,
heading first through forest, then emerging in
a pretty cove, with PG&E's Camp Britton across
the water. From here, the trail traces the shore
of Lake Britton, a sheltered area of the lake, and
leads to the road. It's another minute to the little marina on the left, with kayak and paddle-
boat rentals, or to the swimming beach on the
right. The lake is kept full nearly year-round,
even in drought years. In recent summers, algae
has been a problem for swimmers.

User Groups: Hikers only. No dogs, horses, or
mountain bikes. No wheelchair facilities.

Permits: No permits are required. A state park
day-use fee of $8 is charged for each vehicle.

Maps: A trail guide is available for a fee at
the state park. For a topographic map, ask the
USGS for Burney Falls.

Directions: From Redding, take Highway 299
east for 50 miles to Burney and continue five
miles to the junction with Highway 89. Turn
left (north) and drive 5.8 miles to the state park
entrance on the left. At the entrance station,
continue straight for a short distance and park
in the main lot on the right. The trailhead is
across the road at the falls overlook.

Contact: McArthur-Burney Falls Memorial
State Park, Burney, 530/335-2777, www.parks.
ca.gov.

11 MCARTHUR-BURNEY FALLS MEMORIAL STATE PARK TO ASH CAMP (PCT)

52.0 mi one-way/4 days

from McArthur-Burney Falls Memorial State Park west into Ash Camp in Shasta-Trinity National Forest

Map 3.1, page 125

For PCT hikers, it may be difficult to leave the woods, waters, and aura of McArthur-Burney Falls Memorial State Park, but off you go, facing dry country and some of Northern California's least-used portions of the Pacific Crest Trail. Typically the only hikers who complete this section are the ones hiking the entire route from Mexico to Canada; they're virtually forced to endure it.

From Burney Falls, the PCT heads west, touching the Pit River arm of Lake Britton, and then continues forward into Lassen Volcanic National Park, crossing into Shasta-Trinity National Forest and up to Grizzly Peak. Much of this route is across dry, hot, exposed slopes, where the trail has deteriorated in many spots due to the encroachment of brush and the zero trail maintenance by the U.S. Forest Service. Fire damage is a problem too, in Lassen Volcanic National Park and the vicinity. Knowing you're smack between the lush beauty of Burney Falls (behind you) and the McCloud River (ahead of you) can make dealing with the present landscape a frustrating encounter. Always fill your canteens with water wherever you find it, and don't hesitate to make a camp if, late in the day, you find even a small flat spot with water nearby. In extremely dry years it's possible to travel this entire stretch without finding any water.

After the hot climb near Grizzly Peak, most hikers will want to make a lightning-fast descent to the Eden of the McCloud River at Ash Camp. But hold your horses. As long as you've come this far, make the short side trip up to Grizzly Peak, and while you're looking at the incredible view of Mount Shasta and the McCloud Flats, congratulate yourself for completing such a terrible hike. Considering the PCT is the feature national recreation trail in America, this stretch is an embarrassment to the U.S. Forest Service and an abomination to hikers. It's almost as bad as the choice to route the PCT on the Hat Creek Rim.

To continue north on the PCT, see the *Ash Camp to Castle Crags Wilderness (PCT)* hike in the *Shasta and Trinity* chapter. If you are walking this trail in reverse, see the *Hat Creek Rim to McArthur-Burney Falls Memorial State Park (PCT)* hike in this chapter to continue south.

User Groups: Hikers, dogs (except in the state park boundaries), and horses. No mountain bikes. No wheelchair facilities.

Permits: A campfire permit (free) is required. A fee of $8 is charged per vehicle at the state park.

Maps: For USGS topographic maps, ask for Burney Falls, Skunk Ridge, and Grizzly Peak.

Directions: From Redding, take Highway 299 east for 50 miles to Burney and continue five miles to the junction with Highway 89. Turn left (north) and drive 5.8 miles to the state park entrance on the left. At the entrance station, continue straight for a short distance and park in the main lot on the right.

Contact: McArthur-Burney Falls Memorial State Park, Burney, 530/335-2777, www.parks. ca.gov.

12 HI GRADE NATIONAL RECREATION TRAIL

1.1 mi/0.5 hr

in Modoc National Forest east of Goose Lake

Map 3.2, page 126

The Hi Grade National Recreation Trail is actually 5.5 miles long, but only 1.1 miles are specifically designed for hiking. The remainder of this trail is an old jeep road designated for four-wheel drive use, one of the only national four-wheel-drive trails in the state. Of course, you can still hike all of it, but it's better to use four-wheeling to get out there, then hike the final mile to get way out there. As you go, watch for signs of old, abandoned mining operations, because gold was discovered here. They never found enough to cause any outpouring of gold miners, though, and the result is a sparsely populated county, with this area being abandoned completely. The surrounding habitat is a mix of high desert and timber, although the trees tend to be small.

A good side trip from the nearby Buck Creek Ranger Station is to Fandango Pass, where there are nice views to the east of Surprise Valley and the Nevada Mountains. This is where a group of immigrants arrived, topped the ridge, looked west, saw Goose Lake, and shouted, "Aha! The Pacific Ocean! We have arrived!" So they started dancing the fandango. That's how the mountain pass got its name. As lore has it, the local natives then massacred them.

User Groups: Hikers, dogs, horses, and mountain bikes. No wheelchair facilities.

Permits: No permits are required. Parking and access are free.

Maps: For a map, ask the U.S. Forest Service for Modoc National Forest. For topographic maps, ask the USGS for Mount Bidwell and Willow Ranch.

Directions: From Redding, take Highway 299 east for 146 miles to Alturas and the junction with U.S. 395. Turn north on U.S. 395 and drive about 35 miles to Forest Road 9. Turn right on Forest Road 9 and drive 4.5 miles to Buck Creek Ranger Station. At the Buck Creek Ranger Station, turn left on Forest Road 47N72 and drive about six miles to the trailhead. Four-wheel-drive vehicles are required.

Contact: Modoc National Forest, Warner Mountain Ranger District, Cedarville, 530/279-6116, www.fs.usda.gov/modoc.

Lake is the most popular hike in the South Warner Wilderness. That still doesn't mean you'll run into other people or horses, because the Warners are a remote, lonely place rarely visited by hikers from the Bay Area, Sacramento, or Los Angeles. Patterson Lake is set in a rock basin at 9,000 feet, just below Warren Peak (9,718 feet), the highest lake in the wilderness and the highlight destination for most visitors. The Pepperdine trailhead (at 6,900 feet) is located just beyond Porter Reservoir, where a primitive campground and a horse corral are available. The hike is a sustained climb, gaining 2,100 feet, passing to the right of Squaw Peak (8,646 feet) and then tiny Cottonwood Lake. From Squaw Peak, looking east, you'll feel as if you're looking across hundreds of miles of a stark, uninhabited landscape.

User Groups: Hikers, dogs, and horses. No mountain bikes. No wheelchair facilities.

Permits: A campfire permit (free) is required. Parking and access are free.

Maps: For a map, ask the U.S. Forest Service for Modoc National Forest or South Warner Wilderness. For a topographic map, ask the USGS for Warren Peak.

Directions: Take U.S. 395 to the south end of Alturas and to County Road 56. Turn east on County Road 56 and drive 13 miles to the Modoc National Forest boundary and Parker Creek Road. Turn left and drive six miles on Parker Creek Road, to the sign for Pepperdine Campground. Turn right and drive to the trailhead.

Contact: Modoc National Forest, Warner Mountain Ranger District, Cedarville, 530/279-6116, www.fs.usda.gov/modoc.

13 PEPPERDINE TRAILHEAD
12.0 mi/2 days   🥾3 ⛰9

on the northern boundary of the South Warner Wilderness east of Alturas

Map 3.2, page 126

The six-mile trip on Summit Trail to Patterson

14 PINE CREEK TRAILHEAD
4.0 mi/3.0 hr   🥾3 ⛰8

on the northwestern boundary of the South Warner Wilderness east of Alturas

Map 3.2, page 126

This is one of the great short hikes anywhere.

The Pine Creek Trail is a magnificent traipse into the beautiful South Warner Wilderness.

The trail starts along the south fork of Pine Creek, about 6,800 feet in elevation, then heads straight east into the wilderness, climbing the lush western slopes. In the course of two miles, the trail rises 1,000 feet to the Pine Creek Basin. Along the trail are several small lakes, the largest being the two set right along the trail as you enter the basin. Above you is a stark, volcanic-faced rim with few trees, where the headwaters of eight small creeks start from springs, pour down the mountain, join, and then flow into several small lakes. To lengthen the hike, go on to Patterson Lake, a gorgeous mountain lake surrounded by towering rock walls; the round-trip is 11 miles.

Modoc County is the least-populated and least-known region of California, with only 10,000 residents sprinkled across a huge area. Yet there are many outstanding adventures available here.

User Groups: Hikers, dogs, and horses. No mountain bikes. No wheelchair facilities.

Permits: No permits are required. Parking and access are free.

Maps: For a map, ask the U.S. Forest Service for Modoc National Forest or South Warner Wilderness. For a topographic map, ask the USGS for Eagle Peak.

Directions: Take U.S. 395 to the south end of Alturas and to County Road 56. Turn east on County Road 56 and drive 13 miles to the Modoc National Forest boundary and West Warner Road. Turn right (south) on West Warner Road and go about 10 miles to the sign for the Pine Creek trailhead. Turn left (east) and head 1.75 miles to the parking area. The road is unpaved for the last 12 miles.

Contact: Modoc National Forest, Warner Mountain Ranger District, Cedarville, 530/279-6116, www.fs.usda.gov/modoc.

15 SOUP SPRING TRAILHEAD

3.0 mi/2.0 hr

on the western boundary of the South Warner Wilderness east of Alturas

Map 3.2, page 126

Mill Creek is a small, pristine trout stream that brings the lonely Warner Mountains to life. It's a short hike to get here, up a hill and then down, heading into a valley. On this valley floor, you'll find Mill Creek, only a 1.5-mile walk out of the Soup Spring trailhead. Mill Creek is a great spot for a picnic lunch or a high-finesse fishing trip. The trout are extremely sensitive, so anything clumsy—like letting your shadow hit the water or clanking your boots on the shore—will spook them off the bite. The trout are small, dark, and chunky, unlike any seen elsewhere.

Some hikers use Slide Creek Trail as a way of climbing up near the Warner Rim and to the intersection with the Summit Trail, the feature hike in the South Warner Wilderness. That makes sense, as there is a primitive campground and corral at the trailhead; then it's a four-mile romp uphill to the Summit Trail junction. It includes a 1,000-foot climb on the way, with the trail routed up the Slide Creek Canyon over the last two miles.

User Groups: Hikers, dogs, and horses. No mountain bikes. No wheelchair facilities.

Permits: No permits are required. Parking and access are free.

Maps: For a map, ask the U.S. Forest Service for Modoc National Forest or South Warner Wilderness. For a topographic map, ask the USGS for Eagle Peak.

Directions: From Alturas, take U.S. 395 south for 18.5 miles to Likely and Jess Valley Road (County Road 64). Turn east on Jess Valley Road and drive nine miles to West Warner Road (Forest Road 5). Turn left on West Warner Road (Forest Road 5) and drive 4.5 miles to Soup Loop Road (Forest Road 40N24). Turn right and drive six miles (a gravel road) to the campground parking lot, on the right.

Contact: Modoc National Forest, Warner

Mountain Ranger District, Cedarville, 530/279-6116, www.fs.usda.gov/modoc.

16 MILL CREEK FALLS TRAILHEAD
0.5 mi/0.5 hr   👣1 ⛰9

on the southwestern boundary of the South Warner Wilderness east of Alturas

Map 3.2, page 126

The short, easy walk from the Mill Creek Falls trailhead to Clear Lake leads to one of the prettiest spots in Modoc County. It's 0.5 mile to Mill Creek Falls and another 0.5 mile to Clear Lake. At the fork, bear left for the waterfalls, or bear right for the lake. Most hikers will take in both. The trail skirts along the perimeter of a pretty lake set at 6,000 feet. Of the lakes and streams in the Warners, it's Clear Lake that has the largest fish, with brown and rainbow trout ranging to more than 10 pounds. There just aren't many of them. Backpackers can head onward from Clear Lake on Poison Flat Trail, but expect a very steep howler of a climb before intersecting with Mill Creek Trail.

User Groups: Hikers, dogs, and horses. Some wheelchair-accessible facilities are available at the nearby campground, but there is no wheelchair access on this trail. No mountain bikes.

Permits: No permits are required. Parking and access are free.

Maps: For a map, ask the U.S. Forest Service for Modoc National Forest or South Warner Wilderness. For a topographic map, ask the USGS for Eagle Peak.

Directions: From Alturas, take U.S. 395 south for 18.5 miles to Likely and Jess Valley Road (County Road 64). Turn east on Jess Valley Road and drive nine miles to a fork. At the fork, bear left on Forest Road 5 and drive 2.5 miles to Forest Road 40N46. Turn right and drive two miles to the trailhead.

Contact: Modoc National Forest, Warner Mountain Ranger District, Cedarville, 530/279-6116, www.fs.usda.gov/modoc.

17 EMERSON TRAILHEAD
7.0 mi/2 days   👣5 ⛰9

on the eastern boundary of the South Warner Wilderness east of Alturas

Map 3.2, page 126

Don't be yelpin' about the dreadful climb up to North Emerson Lake, because we're warning you right here, loud and clear, that it qualifies as a first-class butt-kicker. A "kill-me, eat-me" kind of hike. If you choose to go anyway, well, you asked for it. The trail climbs 2,000 feet in 3.5 miles, but much of that is in a hellish 0.5-mile stretch that'll have you howling for relief. Your reward is little North Emerson Lake at 7,800 feet, a wonderland in a rock bowl with a high sheer back wall.

The Emerson trailhead, the most remote of those providing access to the Warners, is located on the east side of the mountain rim, near stark, dry country. A primitive campground is available at the trailhead. Out of camp, take North Emerson Trail. And while you're at it, get yourself in the right frame of mind to cheerfully accept that you'll be getting your butt kicked. But rest assured that North Emerson Lake is worth every step. You also get incredible long-distance views across the desert to the east.

User Groups: Hikers, dogs, and horses. No mountain bikes. No wheelchair facilities.

Permits: A campfire permit (free) is required. Parking and access are free.

Maps: For a map, ask the U.S. Forest Service for Modoc National Forest or South Warner Wilderness. For a topographic map, ask the USGS for Emerson Peak.

Directions: From Alturas, take Highway 299 east for 22 miles to Cedarville and County Road 1. Turn right (south) on County Road 1 and go about 16 miles to Eagleville and continue another 1.5 miles south on County Road 1 to Emerson Road. Turn right on Emerson Road and go three miles to the trailhead. Emerson Road is very steep and is slippery when wet or icy. Four-wheel drive advised.

Contact: Modoc National Forest, Warner

Mountain Ranger District, Cedarville, 530/279-6116, www.fs.usda.gov/modoc.

18 EAST CREEK LOOP

15.0 mi/2 days ♙ 3 ⛰ 7

on the southern boundary of the South Warner Wilderness east of Alturas

Map 3.2, page 126

The East Creek Loop is a favorite loop hike in the Warner Mountains. It can be completed in a weekend, not including driving time, and provides a capsule look at the amazing contrasts of the Warners. The hike includes small, seemingly untouched streams, as well as high, barren mountain rims.

To start this trip, take the East Creek Trail, elevation 7,100 feet. It is routed 5.5 miles north into the wilderness. Just before the junction with Poison Flat Trail, a spring is located on the left side of the trail. Don't miss it—you'll need the water for the upcoming climb. Turn right at the junction with Poison Flat Trail to make the 800-foot climb above tree line, and turn right again on Summit Trail. The loop is completed by taking Summit Trail back south, crossing high, stark country—most of it more than 8,000 feet in elevation. In the last two miles, the trail drops sharply, descending 1,000 feet on the way to Patterson Campground, which marks the end of the loop trail. Reaching the parking area at the East Creek trailhead requires a 0.5-mile walk on the forest road.

User Groups: Hikers, dogs, and horses. No mountain bikes. No wheelchair facilities.

Permits: A campfire permit (free) is required. Parking and access are free.

Maps: For a map, ask the U.S. Forest Service for Modoc National Forest or South Warner Wilderness. For a topographic map, ask the USGS for Emerson Peak.

Directions: From Alturas, take U.S. 395 south for 18.5 miles to Likely and Jess Valley Road (County Road 64). Turn east on Jess Valley Road and drive nine miles to South Warner Road (Forest Road 64). Turn right and drive southeast (heading toward Patterson Campground) to the access road for East Creek Trail. Turn left and drive a short distance to the parking area.

Contact: Modoc National Forest, Warner Mountain Ranger District, Cedarville, 530/279-6116, www.fs.usda.gov/modoc.

19 SUMMIT LOOP

45.0 mi/4 days ♙ 4 ⛰ 10

on the southern boundary of the South Warner Wilderness east of Alturas

Map 3.2, page 126

The Summit Loop is the backpacking trek that most hikers yearn to take someday. If you are one of the lucky few to get here, you'll find this hike traverses both sides of the Warner ridge, providing an intimate look at a diverse place. The west side of the Warner Mountains is a habitat filled with small pine trees, meadows, and the headwaters of many small streams. The east side, however, is stark and rugged, with great long-distance lookouts to the east across high desert and miles of sagebrush and juniper.

Start the trip at the Patterson Camp trailhead (at 7,200 feet). From here the trail climbs quickly, rising to 8,200 feet in two miles, accessing high, barren country. Great views abound from here as hikers head north. Then, to reach the north end of the wilderness, take the turn at Owl Creek Trail and hike to Linderman Lake, set at the foot of Devils Knob (8,776 feet). Continue past Squaw Peak (8,646 feet). To return in a loop, make the hairpin left turn at Summit Trail and walk back on the mostly lush western slopes of the Warners. Highlights on the return loop segment include Patterson Lake, 9,000 feet, the headwaters of Mill Creek and North Fork East Creek, and many beautiful and fragile meadows. The trail ends at the East Creek parking area, a 0.5-mile walk from the Patterson Camp trailhead.

Savor every moment of this trip—it's one of the greatest little-known hikes anywhere in the United States. The Warner Mountains have a mystique about them, a charm cultivated by the thoughts of hikers who dream of an area where the landscape is remote and untouched, and the trails are empty. However, only rarely do they get around to it. For most, the Warners are just too remote and too far away, and the trip requires too much time.

User Groups: Hikers, dogs, and horses. No mountain bikes. No wheelchair facilities.

Permits: A campfire permit (free) is required. Parking and access are free.

Maps: For a map, ask the U.S. Forest Service for Modoc National Forest or South Warner Wilderness. For a topographic map, ask the USGS for Emerson Peak.

Directions: From Alturas, take U.S. 395 south for 18.5 miles to Likely and Jess Valley Road (County Road 64). Turn east on Jess Valley Road and drive nine miles to South Warner Road (Forest Road 64). Turn right and drive 16 miles to Patterson Campground. The trailhead is at the camp.

Contact: Modoc National Forest, Warner Mountain Ranger District, Cedarville, 530/279-6116, www.fs.usda.gov/modoc.

20 BLUE LAKE LOOP NATIONAL RECREATION TRAIL

2.0 mi/1.25 hr   🏃₁ ⛰₇

at Blue Lake in Modoc National Forest southeast of Alturas

Map 3.2, page 126

Blue Lake is the prettiest lake you can reach with a car in Modoc County. The Blue Lake Loop National Recreation Trail is simply a trail around the lake. With a campground at the lake, this trail makes a good side trip for overnight visitors. In addition, a fishing pier and wheelchair-accessible restroom are available. Most visitors are here to camp, boat, and fish. Some of the surrounding forest has evidence of a past fire in the area.

User Groups: Hikers and dogs. The fishing pier and restroom are wheelchair-accessible. No horses or mountain bikes.

Permits: No permits are required. Parking and access are free.

Maps: For a map, ask the U.S. Forest Service for Modoc National Forest. For a topographic map, ask the USGS for Jess Valley.

Directions: From Alturas, take U.S. 395 south for 18.5 miles to Likely and Jess Valley Road (County Road 64). Turn east on Jess Valley Road (County Road 64) and drive nine miles to a fork. When the road forks, bear right on Blue Lake Road (Forest Road 64) and drive seven miles to Forest Road 39N30 (signed for Blue Lake). Turn right and drive to the parking area.

Contact: Modoc National Forest, Warner Mountain Ranger District, Cedarville, 530/279-6116, www.fs.usda.gov/modoc.

21 BURNEY MOUNTAIN SUMMIT

0.25-8.0 mi/0.25-3.0 hr   🏃₁ ⛰₉

in Lassen National Forest south of Burney

Map 3.3, page 127

The view is just so good from the top of Burney Mountain (elevation 7,863 feet) that the trip had to be included in this book. If you drive to the summit, the "hike" consists of just moseying around and gazing off in all directions. There is a fire lookout on top of the mountain. Occasionally, tours are available. Burney Mountain often gets lost in the shadow of its big brothers, Mount Lassen and Mount Shasta, but of the three, the view just might be best from Burney. That's because a view of Lassen or Shasta offers impressive panoramas that just can't be duplicated.

If you show up in the winter or after 6pm, when the access road is gated, or if you simply want the exercise, it's a four-mile hike up the road to the top of the mountain.

User Groups: Hikers, dogs, horses, and mountain bikes. No wheelchair facilities.

Permits: No permits are required. Parking and access are free.

Maps: For a map, ask the U.S. Forest Service for Lassen National Forest. For topographic maps, ask the USGS for Burney Mountain West and Burney Mountain East.

Directions: From Redding, take Highway 299 east for 50 miles to Burney and continue five more miles east to Highway 89. Turn south (right) on Highway 89 and drive 10.5 miles to Forest Road 26/Forest Road 34N19 (signed). Turn right on Forest Road 26 and drive 10 miles to Forest Road 34N23. Turn right and drive seven miles to the mountain summit. Note that the summit access road is blocked by a gate at 6pm each day and throughout winter. You can park at the gate and hike to the top.

Contact: Lassen National Forest, Hat Creek Ranger District, Falls River Mills, 530/336-5521, www.fs.usda.gov/lassen.

22 CYPRESS TRAILHEAD
6.0 mi/1 day

on the north boundary of the Thousand Lakes Wilderness north of Lassen Volcanic National Park

Map 3.3, page 127

The relocation of the Tamarack Trailhead means that the Cypress Trailhead is no longer the top starting point for the Thousand Lakes Wilderness. The wilderness is located at 5,400 feet, with many small lakes sprinkled about in a radius of just two miles. But getting here involves a climb of more than 1,000 feet. The primary destination is Lake Eiler, a round-trip of six miles, though it is 9.9 miles if you also hike around the lake and return to the trailhead. It is the largest lake in this region, set just below Eiler Butte. But a network of trails here connects to other lakes, so an option is to keep on going for an overnighter. From the south side of Eiler Lake, the trail loops deeper into the wilderness in a clockwise arc. It passes near several other lakes, including Box and Barrett Lakes. Both of these provide good fishing for small trout.

This wilderness is not called "Thousand Lakes" because there are a lot of lakes. After heavy rains or snowmelt, there are thousands of little pockets of water-breeding mosquitoes here in spring. And *that* is how it was named.

User Groups: Hikers, dogs, and horses. No mountain bikes. No wheelchair facilities.

Permits: No permits are required. Parking and access are free.

Maps: For a map, ask the U.S. Forest Service for Lassen National Forest. A wilderness trail map is available for a fee from the Hat Creek Ranger District. For topographic maps, ask the USGS for Thousand Lakes Valley and Jacks Backbone.

Directions: From Redding, take Highway 299 east for 50 miles to Burney and continue east five miles to Highway 89. Turn right (south) on Highway 89 and drive 10.5 miles to Forest Road 26 (Forest Road 34N19). Turn west on Forest Road 26 (Forest Road 34N19) and drive 8.5 miles to Forest Road 34N60. Turn left and drive 2.5 miles to the parking area.

Contact: Lassen National Forest, Hat Creek Ranger District, Falls River Mills, 530/336-5521, www.fs.usda.gov/lassen.

23 TAMARACK TRAILHEAD/ LAKE EILER
7.0 mi/3.5 hr

on the east boundary of the Thousand Lakes Wilderness north of Lassen Volcanic National Park

Map 3.3, page 127

From the Tamarack Trailhead, it's a 3.5-mile walk with a 400-foot climb to Lake Eiler. The lake is gorgeous, but note that the Eiler fire burned much of the national forest in the vicinity. Most visitors will do this as a weekend trip, or locals will venture in as a day trip; have a picnic, swim, or fish, and then return.

If you are setting out on a multiday backpacking trek, then go onward to several other wilderness lakes. The trail is then routed into the northwestern interior of the Thousand Lakes Wilderness. After two miles, you'll reach a fork in the trail; turn left (south) to reach Barrett Lake in just another mile of hiking.

Note that there is a complex trail network in this area with many junctions, creating a situation in which backpackers can invent their own multiday route. From Barrett Lake, other attractive destinations include Durbin Lake, 0.5 mile to the south, and Everett and Magee Lakes, another (very challenging) 2.7 miles away.

User Groups: Hikers, dogs, and horses. No mountain bikes. No wheelchair facilities.

Permits: No permits are required. Parking and access are free.

Maps: For a map, ask the U.S. Forest Service for Lassen National Forest. A wilderness trail map is available for a fee from the Hat Creek Ranger District. For topographic maps, ask the USGS for Thousand Lakes Valley and Jacks Backbone.

Directions: From Redding, take Highway 299 east for 50 miles to Burney and continue east five miles to Highway 89. Turn right (south) on Highway 89 and drive about 14 miles to Forest Road 33N25. Turn west on Forest Road 33N25 and drive 7.5 miles to a Y junction. Turn right and drive just about 1.5 miles to the trailhead (the new route is well signed).

Contact: Lassen National Forest, Hat Creek Ranger District, Falls River Mills, 530/336-5521, www.fs.usda.gov/lassen.

24 BUNCHGRASS TRAILHEAD
8.0 mi/2 days 👥2 ⛰️7

on the south boundary of the Thousand Lakes Wilderness north of Lassen Volcanic National Park

Map 3.3, page 127

This trailhead is obscure and difficult to reach, and because of that, few visitors choose it as a jump-off spot for their treks. The trailhead is the southernmost access point to the Thousand Lakes Wilderness. The destination is Durbin Lake, a four-mile hike one-way, which can make for a destination for a weekend backpack trip. The trailhead elevation is 5,680 feet, and

from here, it's a fair walk in, up and down. The landscape is a mix of lodgepole pine and open terrain. If you're not in shape, you'll know it well before you reach the lake. You'll come to Hall Butte (at 7,187 feet) and then Durbin Lake. A side-trip option is to climb Hall Butte. Break off the trail at three miles in, for a 0.5-mile tromp to the top with no trail.

User Groups: Hikers, dogs, and horses. No mountain bikes. No wheelchair facilities.

Permits: A campfire permit (free) is required. Parking and access are free.

Maps: For a map, ask the U.S. Forest Service for Lassen National Forest. A wilderness trail map is available for a fee from the Hat Creek Ranger District. For topographic maps, ask the USGS for Thousand Lakes Valley and Jacks Backbone.

Directions: From Redding, take Highway 299 east for 50 miles to Burney and continue east five miles to Highway 89. Turn right (south) on Highway 89 and drive 31 miles to Forest Road 16 (Forest Road 33N16). Turn right on Forest Road 16 and drive seven miles to Forest Road 32N45. Turn right on Forest Road 32N45 and drive two miles to Forest Road 32N42Y (which is very steep). Turn left and head to the parking area, at the end of the road.

Contact: Lassen National Forest, Hat Creek Ranger District, Falls River Mills, 530/336-5521, www.fs.usda.gov/lassen.

25 HAT CREEK RIM TO MCARTHUR-BURNEY FALLS MEMORIAL STATE PARK (PCT)
40.0 mi one-way/3 days 👥5 ⛰️8

from the Highway 44 parking area north to McArthur-Burney Falls Memorial State Park

Map 3.3, page 127

This section of the PCT includes the infamous 27-mile section without water. Unless you are through-hiking the entire PCT, there is no reason to suffer this ignominy. Yet this 40-mile section also features Hat Creek, Baum Lake, Crystal Lake, and spectacular Burney Falls.

The good news is that a trail angel has been providing a water cache at about midpoint on the Hat Creek Rim, where he drives in on a Forest Service road that crosses the PCT here. We've seen many PCT hikers cheat by hitchhiking past this section on Highway 89, but with a water cache, there is no reason to do that, and defeats the purpose of the challenge of a thru-hike on the PCT.

From the trailhead at Highway 44, the trail passes through the wooded watershed of Hat Creek to a long, shadeless section that will have you counting the drops of water in your canteen. This is the Hat Creek Rim section of the PCT, the roughest section of the entire route from Mexico to Canada, with no water available for 27 miles of trail. A single drop of water will be valued more than a $10,000 bill.

After departing from Hat Creek, the PCT heads past Baum and Crystal Lakes. You cross Highway 299, and from there, it's an eight-mile romp to McArthur-Burney Falls State Park and its breathtaking 129-foot waterfall.

To continue north on the PCT, see the *McArthur-Burney Falls Memorial State Park to Ash Camp (PCT)* hike in this chapter. If you are walking this trail in reverse, see the *Lassen Volcanic National Park to Highway 44 (PCT)* hike in this chapter to continue south.

User Groups: Hikers, dogs (except in the state park boundaries), and horses. No mountain bikes. No wheelchair facilities.

Permits: A campfire permit (free) is required. A state park entrance fee of $8 is charged per vehicle.

Maps: For topographic maps, ask the USGS for Cassel, Dana, Old Station, Murken Bench, Hogback Ridge, and Burney Falls.

Directions: From Redding, take Highway 44 east for 60 miles to Highway 89/44. Turn left (north) on Highway 89/44 and drive 13 miles to Old Station and continue a short distance to Highway 44. Turn right (east) on Highway 44 and drive 0.25 mile beyond the Old Station Post Office to Forest Road 32N20. Turn right on Forest Road 32N20. The trail crosses the road about 0.5 mile from the junction of Highway

44 and Forest Road 32N20. If you have horses and need to park a horse trailer, use Mud Lake trailhead, located three miles from the junction of Highway 89 and Highway 44.

Contact: Lassen National Forest, Hat Creek Ranger District, Falls River Mills, 530/336-5521, www.fs.usda.gov/lassen.

🗳26 NOBLES EMIGRANT TRAIL
5.0 mi/3.0 hr   🚶2 ⛰8

from the Manzanita Lake Trailhead in Lassen Volcanic National Park east of Red Bluff

Map 3.3, page 127

The trail, with its easy, moderate grade, passes first through an old forest with towering firs, cedars, and pines. About 2.5 miles in, you'll arrive at Lassen's strange Dwarf Forest. Not only will you be surrounded by stunted trees, but you also get views of Chaos Crags, a jumble of pinkish rocks constituting what's left of an old broken-down volcano. Many visitors hike to this point, then turn around and return to the campground.

The most difficult part of this hike is the first two steps. Why? Because the trailhead is set near the northern park entrance amid a number of small roads and a maintenance area, and despite a trail sign, many visitors can't find it and give up. It's worth the search, because it's a great day hike for campers staying at Manzanita Lake.

It's a historic trail, of course, that follows part of a historical route that was originally an east-west portion of the California Trail, used by emigrants in the 1850s. There is no water available on the trail, so be sure to have at least one filled canteen per hiker. Because of the moderate slope, this trail is an ideal cross-country ski route in the winter months.

User Groups: Hikers and horses. No dogs or mountain bikes. No wheelchair facilities.

Permits: A park entrance fee of $20, good for a week, is charged for each vehicle.

Maps: Trail maps are available for a fee from park visitors stations and at Lassen Loomis

Museum Association. For a map, ask the U.S. Forest Service for Lassen National Forest. For a topographic map, ask the USGS for Manzanita Lake.

Directions: From Redding, take Highway 44 east for 46 miles to the junction with Highway 89. Turn right (south) on Highway 89 and drive one mile to the park entrance station. Continue on the main park road (Lassen Park Highway/Highway 89) for 0.5 mile to the turn-off for Manzanita Lake. The trailhead is across the road from Manzanita Lake, just past the Loomis Museum.

Contact: Lassen Volcanic National Park, Mineral, 530/595-4480, www.nps.gov/lavo; Lassen Loomis Museum Association, Mineral, www.lassenassociation.org.

27 MANZANITA LAKE TRAIL
1.5 mi/1.0 hr   🚶1 ⛰8

at the northern entrance to Lassen Volcanic National Park on Highway 44

Map 3.3, page 127

There's no prettier lake that you can reach by car in Lassen Volcanic National Park than Manzanita Lake. That is why many consider the campground here an ideal destination. With 179 sites, it's the largest camp in the park, and it's easy to reach, located just beyond the entrance station at the western boundary of the park. The trail simply traces the shoreline of this pretty lake at a 5,950-foot elevation and is easily accessible from either the parking area just beyond the entrance station or from the campground. Rental park model-style camping cabins are available in forest near the lake, and along the shore below the cabins are kayak rentals. Nearby Reflection Lake, located just across the park's entrance road, provides a side trip; that adds about a half mile. Note that the fishing at Manzanita Lake is catch-and-release only, where anglers must use artificials, that is, do not use bait, and pinch down your barbs.

User Groups: Hikers only. No dogs, horses, or mountain bikes. No wheelchair facilities.

Permits: A park entrance fee of $20, good for a week, is charged for each vehicle.

Maps: Trail maps are available for a fee from park visitors stations and at Lassen Loomis Museum Association. For a map, ask the U.S. Forest Service for Lassen National Forest. For a topographic map, ask the USGS for Manzanita Lake.

Directions: From Redding, take Highway 44 east for 46 miles to the junction with Highway 89. Turn right (south) on Highway 89 and drive one mile to the park entrance station. Continue on the main park road (Lassen Park Highway/Highway 89) for 0.5 mile, to the turnoff for Manzanita Lake Campground. Turn right and drive 0.5 mile to the day-use parking area.

Contact: Lassen Volcanic National Park, Mineral, 530/595-4480, www.nps.gov/lavo; Lassen Loomis Museum Association, Mineral, www.lassenassociation.org.

28 CINDER CONE TRAIL
4.0 mi/3.0 hr   🚶3 ⛰9

from Butte Lake Trailhead in Lassen Volcanic National Park

Map 3.3, page 127

Huge chunks of Lassen Volcanic National Park are overlooked by visitors simply because access is not along the Lassen Park Highway. Butte Lake and the Cinder Cone Trail (and the next hike, the Prospect Peak Trail), set in the northeastern corner of the park, are such areas. When you arrive by car, you'll find a pretty campground on your right, then Butte Lake on your left, and just beyond, the end of the road and the trailhead. The trailhead for Nobles Emigrant Trail/Cinder Cone Trail is set at an elevation of 6,100 feet. The trail starts out easy, and for a few stretches in the first half mile, the surface can have short stretches of sand. It heads southwest through forest. At 1.5 miles, you'll reach the Cinder Cone cutoff, and there, everything suddenly changes. The last 0.5 mile rises to the top of the Cinder Cone, a short but very intense climb of 800 feet to the summit rim at 6,907 feet. The views are unforgettable, especially south to the Painted Dunes and Fantastic Lava Beds. This is a classic volcanic landscape. The cinder cone itself looks like a moon crater.

User Groups: Hikers only. No dogs, horses, or mountain bikes. No wheelchair facilities.

Permits: No permits are required. A park entrance fee of $20, good for a week, is charged for each vehicle.

Maps: Trail maps are available for a fee from park visitors stations and at Lassen Loomis Museum Association. For a map, ask the U.S. Forest Service for Lassen National Forest. For a topographic map, ask the USGS for Prospect Peak.

Directions: From Redding, take Highway 44 east for 60 miles to Highway 89/44. Turn left (north) on Highway 89/44 and drive 13 miles to Old Station and continue a short distance to Highway 44. Turn right (east) on Highway 44 and drive 10 miles to Butte Lake Road (Forest Road 32N21). Turn right (south) on Butte Lake Road (Forest Road 32N21) and drive six miles to Butte Lake (pass the campground on the right, boat ramp on the left) and continue to the end of the road, parking, and trailhead.

Contact: Lassen Volcanic National Park, Mineral, 530/595-4480, www.nps.gov/lavo; Lassen Loomis Museum Association, Mineral, www.lassenassociation.org.

29 PROSPECT PEAK TRAIL
7.0 mi/4.5 hr   👣 4 ⛺ 10

at Butte Lake in Lassen Volcanic National Park

Map 3.3, page 127

Your rewards on this trail are a series of great views in Lassen Volcanic National Park and a trail that gets little use. We've never seen anybody else here or a single piece of litter. The trailhead (Nobles Emigrant Trail), at 6,100 feet, is located past Butte Lake. After less than 0.5 mile (flat, wide, and sandy), you'll turn right at the junction with Prospect Peak Trail. The trail immediately starts to climb. Get used to it, because there's no respite. It climbs more than 2,200 feet over the course of just 3.3 miles. Views emerge below of Butte Lake, Snag Lake,

Cinder Cone Trail

© TOM STIENSTRA

the Fantastic Lava Beds, Cinder Cone, and then to the volcanic rim on the horizon crowned by 10,457-foot Lassen Peak. It finally tops the summit at 8,338 feet. It's a flat-top summit, not a peak. The best view is not from the actual peak, but from the left of the summit where you can best see Lassen Peak, Mount Hoffman, and Crater Butte, along with thousands and thousands of acres of national forest to the north. Since the snowmelt occurs earlier here than in the rest of the park, this trip makes a perfect hike in the early to mid-spring, when the air is still cool. If you wait until summer, you'll find this a dry, forsaken place. Hiking to the top of most mountains requires a long, grinding climb. Gaining the summit of Prospect Peak is somewhat different. Long? No. Grinding? Yep.

User Groups: Hikers only. No dogs, horses, or mountain bikes. No wheelchair facilities.

Permits: No permits are required. A park entrance fee of $20, good for a week, is charged for each vehicle.

Maps: Trail maps are available for a fee from park visitors stations and at Lassen Loomis Museum Association. For a map, ask the U.S. Forest Service for Lassen National Forest. For a topographic map, ask the USGS for Prospect Peak.

Directions: From Redding, take Highway 44 east for 60 miles to Highway 89/44. Turn left (north) on Highway 89/44 and drive 13 miles to Old Station and continue a short distance to Highway 44. Turn right (east) on Highway 44 and drive 10 miles to Forest Road 32N21. Turn right (south) on Forest Road 32N21 and drive seven miles to Butte Lake (pass the campground on the right, boat ramp on the left) and continue to the end of the road, parking, and trailhead.

Contact: Lassen Volcanic National Park, Mineral, 530/595-4480, www.nps.gov/lavo; Lassen Loomis Museum Association, Mineral, www.lassenassociation.org.

30 CONE LAKE TRAILHEAD
4.0 mi/2.5 hr   👫2 ⛰8

on the boundary of Caribou Wilderness east of Lassen Volcanic National Park

Map 3.3, page 127

Triangle Lake is the prize destination with only a two-mile hike in the northern Caribou Wilderness near Black Butte. The trailhead is located at tiny Cone Lake, just outside the wilderness. From here, you walk for nearly a mile before passing the wilderness boundary, which is clearly marked. At that point, you can sense the change in features, as the land becomes wild and untouched. Continue one mile south to Triangle Lake, which provides good fishing during the evening for pan-sized trout. If you want more, you can get more. For an overnighter, the best campsites are on the west side of the lake.

At Triangle Lake, the trail forks and you can continue your adventure. The right fork is routed right into Lassen Volcanic National Park, a distance of only 1.5 miles, from which you can access Widow Lake. A free wilderness permit is required from Lassen Volcanic National Park for overnight use. The left fork, on the other hand, leads to Twin Lakes over the course of just 0.5 mile.

User Groups: Hikers, dogs, and horses. No mountain bikes. No wheelchair facilities.

Permits: No permits are required for day use. Campfire permits are required for overnight use. Parking and access are free.

Maps: A trail map is available for a fee from the Almanor Ranger District. For a map, ask the U.S. Forest Service for Lassen National Forest or Caribou Wilderness. For a topographic map, ask the USGS for Bogard Buttes.

Directions: From Redding, take Highway 44 east for 60 miles to Highway 89/44. Turn left (north) on Highway 89/44 and drive 13 miles to Old Station and continue a short distance to Highway 44. Turn right (east) on Highway 44 and drive 30 miles to Bogard Work Station and continue a short distance to Forest Road 10 on the right. Turn right on Forest Road 10 and drive 5.9 miles to Forest Road 32N09. Turn right (still Forest Road 32N09) and drive one mile to Cone Lake Road. Turn left on Cone Lake Road (still Forest Road 32N09) and drive 1.7 miles to the Cone Lake trailhead. Note that from Highway 44, the roads are unpaved to the trailhead.

Contact: Lassen National Forest, Almanor Ranger District, Chester, 530/258-2141, www.fs.usda.gov/lassen.

31 CARIBOU LAKE TRAILHEAD

12.0 mi/2 days   3   9

on the boundary of Caribou Wilderness east of Lassen Volcanic National Park

Map 3.3, page 127

From the Caribou Lake Trailhead, you get wilderness access to an array of pretty mountain lakes. Rarely are so many wilderness lakes this close to a trailhead. The trip starts at Caribou Lake (low lake levels are often a problem in late summer and fall), where the trail heads west. In no time you pass all kinds of tiny lakes. The first one, Cowboy Lake, is only 0.25 mile down the trail. In another 15 minutes, you'll come to Jewel Lake, which is one of our favorites, and often the prettiest. This procession of lakes never seems to stop. Eleanor Lake is next. Then, two miles in, turn left at the fork and you pass Black Lake, North and South Divide Lakes, and farther on, Long Lake. Long Lake is six miles from the trailhead and makes a great two-day backpacking adventure. The Caribou Wilderness is quite small, just nine miles from top to bottom, and only five miles across, with elevations ranging 5,000-7,000 feet. This trip provides a visit to the best of it.

User Groups: Hikers, dogs, and horses (a horse corral is available at the trailhead). No mountain bikes. No wheelchair facilities.

Permits: A campfire permit (free) is required. Parking and access are free.

Maps: A trail map is available for a fee from the Almanor Ranger District. For a map, ask the U.S. Forest Service for Lassen National Forest or Caribou Wilderness. For a topographic map, ask the USGS for Red Cinder.

Directions: From Red Bluff, take Highway 36 east and drive 82 miles to Westwood (east of Lake Almanor) and Mooney Road/County Road 21. Turn left on Mooney Road/County Road A21 and go 13.9 miles to Silver Lake Road. Turn left on Silver Lake Road and drive five miles to a Y with Forest Road 10. Bear right on Forest Road 10 and drive 0.25 mile to a fork with Forest Road 31N18. Turn right on Forest Road 31N18 and drive 0.8 mile (at 0.2 mile, requires a left turn, same road) to Caribou Lake and the trailhead.

Contact: Lassen National Forest, Almanor Ranger District, Chester, 530/258-2141, www.fs.fed.us/r5.

32 ECHO AND TWIN LAKES

8.0 mi/5.5 hr   2   10

in Lassen Volcanic National Park east of Red Bluff

Map 3.3, page 127   BEST (

You get it all on this hike to Lower Twin Lake: beautiful lakes, forest, meadows, and wildflowers. The route provides testimony to the beauty of the Lassen Wilderness. The trailhead elevation is 7,000 feet. The trail starts on the north side of Summit Lake. Right off, the trail climbs 500 feet in the first mile. After this climb, the rest of the hike will be a breeze. You'll arrive at Echo Lake in just another mile and at Upper Twin and Lower Twin in the next two miles, dropping 500 feet on your way. Views of Lassen Peak are spectacular. It's all very pretty and is a great bonus for Summit Lake campers. For campers staying at one of the Summit Lake campgrounds, it makes an outstanding day hike or an easy overnighter for backpackers. If you are not camping, start at the day-use area near the North Summit Lake Campground.

User Groups: Hikers and horses. No dogs or mountain bikes. No wheelchair facilities.

Permits: No permits are required. A park

entrance fee of $20, good for a week, is charged for each vehicle.

Maps: Trail maps are available for a fee at park visitors stations and at Lassen Loomis Museum Association. For a map, ask the U.S. Forest Service for Lassen National Forest. For a topographic map, ask the USGS for Reading Peak.

Directions: From Redding, take Highway 44 east for 46 miles to the junction with Highway 89. Turn right (south) on Highway 89 and drive one mile to the park entrance station. Continue on the main park road (Lassen Park Highway/Highway 89) for 12 miles to the turnoff for Summit Lake North Campground. Turn left and park in the day-use area near the lake. Look for the boardwalk that leads to a trail sign, then turn left and start your hike.

Contact: Lassen Volcanic National Park, Mineral, 530/595-4480, www.nps.gov/lavo; Lassen Loomis Museum Association, Mineral, www.lassenassociation.org.

33 SUMMIT LAKE LOOP
0.5 mi/0.5 hr   🚶1 ⛺8

in Lassen Volcanic National Park east of Red Bluff

Map 3.3, page 127

Summit Lake is a beautiful spot where deer visit almost every summer evening. Nearby campgrounds on both sides of the lake (north and south) are set in conifers, with a pretty meadow just south of the lake along Kings Creek. This hike is a simple walk around Summit Lake. From the South Summit Lake Campground, the trail starts next to a day-use parking area, near the campground entrance road, and leads a short distance to the shore of the lake and the trail. From the North Summit Lake Campground, there is an area for kayak launching along the shore, and from there, you can walk to your right. The pretty walk is best taken at dusk, when the changing evening colors reflect a variety of tints across the lake surface. The best place to see wildlife, especially deer, is in the meadow adjacent to Kings Creek, the lake's outlet stream. The elevation is 7,000

© TOM STIENSTRA

Summit Lake Loop

feet. This trail was once a "fisherman's trail." No more. No lakes in Lassen Volcanic National Park are stocked with trout and the fishing is terrible.

User Groups: Hikers and horses. No dogs or mountain bikes. No wheelchair facilities.

Permits: No permits are required. A park entrance fee of $20, good for a week, is charged for each vehicle.

Maps: Trail maps are available for a fee at park visitors stations and at Lassen Loomis Museum Association. For a map, ask the U.S. Forest Service for Lassen National Forest. For a topographic map, ask the USGS for Reading Peak.

Directions: From Redding, take Highway 44 east for 46 miles to the junction with Highway 89. Turn right (south) on Highway 89 and drive one mile to the park entrance station. Continue on the main park road (Lassen Park Highway/Highway 89) for 12 miles to the turnoff for Summit Lake North Campground. Turn left and park in the day-use area near the lake.

Contact: Lassen Volcanic National Park, Mineral, 530/595-4480, www.nps.gov/lavo; Lassen Loomis Museum Association, Mineral, www.lassenassociation.org.

34 LASSEN PEAK TRAIL
5.0 mi/4.0 hr   👫4 ⛰10

in Lassen Volcanic National Park east of Red Bluff

Map 3.3, page 127   **BEST (**

When you gain the rim of the caldera at Lassen Peak, you realize in a flash why you came this far. As you top the rise, hardened lava flows extend in the caldera in front of you, a jumble of crags and craters crowned by the plug-dome summit at 10,457 feet. The air is cool and clear, the sky cobalt blue. About 100 miles to the north, Mount Shasta rises like a diamond in a field of coal. Far below to the southeast, giant Lake Almanor looks like a sapphire nestled in a sea of conifers. After six years, the trail to Lassen Peak reopened in 2015 after being reconstructed and stabilized. It's again among a handful of world-class hikes to mountaintops that can be completed by most people in reasonable physical condition as a day hike: 2.5 miles with a 2,000-foot elevation gain, five miles in all.

The trailhead is located at an elevation of 8,500 feet along the Lassen Park Highway, with a large parking lot and several restrooms, but no drinking water (so bring your own). When you peer up, you look across the steep slopes of dacite that lead to the crag rim of the caldera, and while 2,000 feet up, it seems in close range. The first 1.3 miles are routed up the backside of a sub-ridge up to Grandview, where you can see Lake Helen below to the south, and across to the southeast to Lake Almanor. This is where the rebuilt trail starts. Trail crews constructed a series of rock stairs at several areas that had been vulnerable to rock slides. The route follows the ridge much as previously, but in several sections, the rock stairs and reinforcement walls are now in place. New interpretive signs also have been installed.

With each step you climb, the views get better. You get a lookout for nearby 9,239-foot Mount Brokeoff, a panorama of the scope of the caldera of the giant 500,000-year-old Tehama Volcano, and to the north, across the 32,000-acre burn zone of the Eiler Fire in 2014. That is just a sideshow once you make the rim. In the caldera of Lassen Peak, the jumbled volcanics span more than a quarter mile. It's a perfect spot to crown the day with a trail lunch and a view. Youngsters could play for hours in the volcanic crags.

The ambitious can instead walk north across a snowfield toward the summit peak. At the foot of the plug dome, the trail then forks. The right fork leads to several perches near the top with fantastic views for a seat and a trail lunch. The left fork is routed around the backside of the summit, where you can then rock climb to gain a perch on one of the pinnacles. Lassen Peak is a huge volcanic flume with hardened lava flows, craters, outcrops, and extraordinary views in all directions.

Note: Winds are common at Lassen Peak,

especially on summer afternoons. Hikers should stash a windbreaker in their daypacks. In addition, if you see cumulus clouds starting to form on the rim, common on summer afternoons, don't go. Quick-forming thunderstorms with lightning are also common on hot afternoons. It's always a mistake to suddenly climb the summit without planning the trip. Stay at lower elevations if there's any chance of lightning activity.

User Groups: Hikers only. No dogs, horses, or mountain bikes. No wheelchair facilities.

Permits: No permits are required. A park entrance fee of $20, good for a week, is charged for each vehicle.

Maps: Trail maps are available for a fee at park visitors stations and at Lassen Loomis Museum Association. For a map, ask the U.S. Forest Service for Lassen National Forest. For a topographic map, ask the USGS for Lassen Peak.

Directions: From Red Bluff, take Highway 36 east and drive 47 miles to the junction with Highway 89. Turn north (left) on Highway 89 and continue 4.5 miles to the park entrance. Continue seven miles on the main park road (Lassen Park Highway/Highway 89) to the parking area and store on the left. The trailhead is at the west end of the parking lot.

Contact: Lassen Volcanic National Park, Mineral, 530/595-4480, www.nps.gov/lavo; Lassen Loomis Museum Association, Mineral, www.lassenassociation.org.

large basin nestled between Reading Peak and Lassen Peak. You make a short, steep climb to Terrace Lake, and then a 0.25-mile junket to skirt the southeast shoreline of Shadow Lake (which is at least three times the size of Terrace Lake). The lakes are set just north of Reading Peak, 8,701 feet. From Shadow Lake, add 0.75 mile to reach Cliff Lake (7,250 feet), another beautiful spot.

User Groups: Hikers only. No dogs, horses, or mountain bikes. No wheelchair facilities.

Permits: No permits are required. A park entrance fee of $20, good for a week, is charged for each vehicle.

Maps: Trail maps are available for a fee at park visitors stations and at Lassen Loomis Museum Association. For a map, ask the U.S. Forest Service for Lassen National Forest. For a topographic map, ask the USGS for Reading Peak.

Directions: From Red Bluff, take Highway 36 east and drive 47 miles to the junction with Highway 89. Turn north (left) on Highway 89 and continue 4.5 miles to the park entrance. Continue nine miles on the main park road (Lassen Park Highway/Highway 89) to the parking area and trailhead, on the left (two miles past the parking area for Lassen Summit).

Contact: Lassen Volcanic National Park, Mineral, 530/595-4480, www.nps.gov/lavo; Lassen Loomis Museum Association, Mineral, www.lassenassociation.org.

35 SHADOW LAKE TRAIL
1.6 mi/1.0 hr   👫2 ⛰9

in Lassen Volcanic National Park east of Red Bluff

Map 3.3, page 127

A hike of less than a mile on this trail will take you past little Terrace Lake (7,800 feet) and then shortly after to Shadow Lake (7,600 feet). It's rare to reach such a pretty lake surrounded by wildlands in such a short distance. From Shadow Lake, the views are excellent of Lassen Peak. The trail is routed through the

36 BUMPASS HELL TRAIL
3.0 mi/2.0 hr   👫2 ⛰10

in Lassen Volcanic National Park east of Red Bluff

Map 3.3, page 127

This is the most popular trail in Lassen Volcanic National Park. Bumpass Hell is like a walk into a prehistoric past, complete with steam vents, boiling mud pots, and natural furnaces. It's all set amid volcanic rock in a large basin, and for some, it might feel as if at any moment, a T. rex might charge around the bend and munch a few tourists. It's the park's largest thermal area.

The elevation at the trailhead is 8,200 feet. The trail starts with a gradual 500-foot climb. You pass an excellent interpretive sign at an overlook that explains the origin and size of the gigantic Tehama Volcano. (Be sure to stop at the park information sign; the steel map shows just how big the Tehama Volcano was, all the way to Mount Brokeoff.) The trail continues in the first mile to a ridge that overlooks the thermal area, an excellent lookout for a photo. You then descend 250 feet into the thermal basin. Wood walkways are routed past the best sites, with several platform decks for lookouts. Exhibits explain the area. There are usually large numbers of tourists at Bumpass Hell, but it works. The basin sits in a pocket just below Bumpass Mountain (8,753 feet).

It is called "Bumpass" Hell because back in the old days, a guy named Bumpass slipped into the boiling water, scalded his feet, and in the ensuing newspaper report, the writer called the place "Bumpass's Hell," and the name stuck.

User Groups: Hikers only. No dogs, horses, or mountain bikes. No wheelchair facilities.

Permits: No permits are required. A park entrance fee of $20, good for a week, is charged for each vehicle.

Maps: Trail maps are available for a fee from park visitors stations and at Lassen Loomis Museum Association. For a topographic map, ask the USGS for Lassen Peak.

Directions: From Red Bluff, take Highway 36 east and drive 47 miles to the junction with Highway 89. Turn north (left) on Highway 89 and drive 4.5 miles to the park entrance. Continue six miles on the main park road (Lassen Park Highway/Highway 89) to the trailhead, on the right.

Contact: Lassen Volcanic National Park, Mineral, 530/595-4480, www.nps.gov/lavo; Lassen Loomis Museum Association, Mineral, www.lassenassociation.org.

37 DRAKE LAKE TRAIL

4.5 mi/2.75 hr   👣3 ⛰6

at Drakesbad in Lassen Volcanic National Park

Map 3.3, page 127

The appeal of Drake Lake is that it is the closest lake to Drakesbad. If you're camping or staying at the lodge, you'll see the lake on the map and might wonder what it's like. Drake Lake is a somewhat swampy sub-alpine lake that brightens a largely dry hillside, where deer are often more plentiful than people. It is set in a remote forested pocket, very secluded. From the trailhead at Drakesbad, at about 5,650 feet, it's about an 800-foot climb over the course of two miles to Drake Lake (6,482 feet). Midway up the grade, the hike becomes steep and stays that way for nearly 45 minutes.

The lake is the payoff—emerald green and circled by firs. After you catch your breath, you may feel like jumping in and cooling off, particularly if it's a hot summer day. Well, we've got news for you: In early summer, the water is still ice cold, and just when you realize that, a battalion of mosquitoes will show up and start feasting on all your bare, sumptuous flesh. Then what? Jump in and freeze your buns? Stand there and get devoured? Heck no, you'll have your clothes back on in record time.

User Groups: Hikers only. Horses are allowed on a portion of the trail. No dogs or mountain bikes. No wheelchair facilities.

Permits: No permits are required. A park entrance fee of $20, good for a week, is charged for each vehicle.

Maps: Trail maps are available for a fee from park visitors stations and at Lassen Loomis Museum Association. For a topographic map, ask the USGS for Reading Peak.

Directions: From Red Bluff, take Highway 36 east and drive 47 miles to the junction with Highway 89. Do not turn. Continue east on Highway 36 toward Lake Almanor and to Chester and Feather River Drive. Turn left on Feather River Drive and drive 0.75 mile. Bear left for Drakesbad and Warner Valley, and drive six miles to Warner Valley Road. Turn right and drive 11 miles to Warner Valley Campground. Continue for 0.5 mile to the trailhead, on the left. The last 3.5 miles is unpaved, and there is one steep hill that can be difficult for trailers or RVs.

Contact: Lassen Volcanic National Park, Mineral, 530/595-4480, www.nps.gov/lavo; Lassen Loomis Museum Association, Mineral, www.lassenassociation.org.

38 DEVILS KITCHEN TRAIL
4.4 mi/2.5 hr   🏃2 ⛰8

at Drakesbad in Lassen Volcanic National Park

Map 3.3, page 127

Drakesbad is the undiscovered Lassen—beautiful, wild, and remote. The area gets missed by many because access is obscure and circuitous: out of Chester en route to the Warner Valley Campground and nearby trailhead, and not from the Lassen's Park Highway. There's no way to get here when entering from either of the main Lassen park entrances. But those who persevere will find a quiet paradise, along with this easy trip to Devils Kitchen, a unique geologic thermal area. The trail is an easy hike, heading west above Hot Springs Creek. The elevation at the trailhead is 5,650 feet, with a gradual climb of 300 feet. After two miles it ventures into this barren pocket of steaming vents, boiling mud pots, and fumaroles. You'll immediately see why it was tagged Devils Kitchen. It is not as dramatic as Bumpass Hell, but you have a chance here of getting it to yourself. Stay on the trail, of course.

User Groups: Hikers only. Horses are allowed on a portion of the trail. No dogs or mountain bikes. No wheelchair facilities.

Permits: No permits are required. A park entrance fee of $20, good for a week, is charged for each vehicle.

Maps: Trail maps are available for a fee from park visitors stations and at Lassen Loomis Museum Association. For a topographic map, ask the USGS for Reading Peak.

Directions: From Red Bluff, take Highway 36 east and drive 47 miles to the junction with Highway 89. Do not turn. Continue east on Highway 36 toward Lake Almanor and to Chester and Feather River Drive. Turn left on Feather River Drive and drive 0.75 mile. Bear left for Drakesbad and Warner Valley, and drive six miles to Warner Valley Road. Turn right and drive 11 miles to Warner Valley Campground. Continue 0.5 mile to the trailhead, on the left. The last 3.5 miles are unpaved, and there is one steep hill that can be difficult for trailers or RVs.

Contact: Lassen Volcanic National Park, Mineral, 530/595-4480, www.nps.gov/lavo; Lassen Loomis Museum Association, Mineral, www.lassenassociation.org.

39 LASSEN VOLCANIC NATIONAL PARK TO HIGHWAY 44 (PCT)
32.0 mi one-way/3 days   🏃3 ⛰9

in Lassen Volcanic National Park

Map 3.3, page 127

Start at Warner Valley (at 5,680 feet), at Hot Springs Creek, and then head north into mostly remote terrain in Lassen Volcanic National Park. The trail is routed across Grassy Swale, past Swan Lake, and on to Lower Twin Lake (seven miles in), a pretty lake circled by conifers.

From here, the trail heads north through a strange but compelling volcanic area. It skirts the western flank of Fairfield Peak (7,272 feet) and then heads onward. It turns west past Soap Lake and Badger Flat, and continues out past the park's boundary. The area in the northeast region of the park has significant forest fire damage that extends north toward Burney.

As you hike toward Highway 44, you'll be lateraling Badger Mountain (6,973 feet) to your right, with the Hat Creek drainage off to your immediate left. In this latter stretch of trail, you'll cross no major lakes or streams (plan your water well). You forge on through the national forest, which is mostly second-growth, crossing a few roads along the way. In the spring, wildflowers are exceptional near the Hat Creek area. Several primitive U.S. Forest Service campgrounds are located on the trail about 10 miles north of the border of Lassen Volcanic National Park.

To continue north on the PCT, see the *Hat Creek Rim to McArthur-Burney Falls Memorial State Park (PCT)* hike in this chapter.

User Groups: Hikers and horses. No dogs or mountain bikes are allowed in the Lassen Volcanic National Park section of the hike. No wheelchair facilities.

Permits: A wilderness permit (free) is required for hikers planning to camp in the Lassen Volcanic National Park backcountry and for equestrians. You may not camp with horses in the national park's backcountry, but a horse corral is available by reservation for overnighters at Summit Lake and Juniper Lake, and a small corral is located near the park's northern boundary for exclusive use by those on the Pacific Crest Trail. A park entrance fee of $20, good for a week, is charged for each vehicle.

Maps: For topographic maps, ask the USGS for Reading Peak, West Prospect Peak, and Old Station.

Directions: From Red Bluff, take Highway 36 east and drive 47 miles to the junction with Highway 89. Do not turn. Continue east on Highway 36 toward Lake Almanor and to Chester and Feather River Drive. Turn left (north) and drive 0.75 mile to Warner Valley Road (signed to Juniper Lake and Drakesbad). Turn left and drive six miles to Warner Valley Road. Turn right and drive 11 miles (on an improved dirt road) to the Warner Valley Campground and trailhead, on the right.

Contact: Lassen Volcanic National Park, Mineral, 530/595-4480, www.nps.gov/lavo; Lassen National Forest, Hat Creek Ranger District, Falls River Mills, 530/336-5521, www.fs.fed.us/r5.

40 JUNIPER LAKE TRAILHEAD/ INSPIRATION POINT

1.4 mi/2.0 hr 🏃3 ⛰10

in Lassen Volcanic National Park north of Lake Almanor

Map 3.3, page 127

Your pay-off is 7,200-foot Inspiration Point for panoramic views across the park's backcountry to Lassen Peak. The trailhead is 50 feet east from the parking area at the Juniper Lake picnic area. The trail is steep. It climbs 400 feet in 0.7 mile through both forest and patches of meadow to the summit. Your reward is spectacular views: Lassen Peak, flat-topped Prospect Peak, below to the Cinder Cone, and Mount Harkness.

User Groups: Hikers and horses. No dogs or mountain bikes. No wheelchair facilities.

Permits: For overnight use, a wilderness permit (free) is required. A park entrance fee of $20, good for a week, is charged for each vehicle.

Maps: Trail maps are available for a fee from park visitors stations and at Lassen Loomis Museum Association. For a topographic map, ask the USGS for Mount Harkness.

Directions: From Red Bluff, take Highway 36 east and drive 47 miles to the junction with Highway 89. Do not turn. Continue east on Highway 36 toward Lake Almanor and to Chester and Feather River Drive. Turn left on Feather River Drive and drive 0.75 mile to a Y. Bear right at the Y to Juniper Lake Road and drive 13 miles to the Snag Lake trailhead, near the ranger station. The access road is rough. Trailers and RVs are not recommended.

Contact: Lassen Volcanic National Park, P.O. Box 100, Mineral, CA 96063, 530/595-4480, www.nps.gov/lavo; Lassen Loomis Museum Association, P.O. Box 220, Mineral, CA 96063, www.lassenassociation.org.

41 HAY MEADOWS TRAIL TO LONG LAKE

8.0 mi/1-2 days

on the boundary of Caribou Wilderness north of Lake Almanor

Map 3.3, page 127

You get an easy walk in beautiful country that passes one little lake after another until your pay-off destination for your camp or day hike with a picnic, Long Lake. What you'll find is that nestled between South Caribou Peak and Black Cinder Rock is a little alpine pocket where dozens of small lakes are sprinkled about the southern Caribou Wilderness. It's a slice of paradise. The trail out of Hay Meadows is a loop that crosses right through these lakes: They include Beauty, Long, Posey, and Evelyn.

After arriving at the trailhead at Hay Meadow, the trip starts easily enough, first crossing Hay Meadows. In another mile, you'll reach Beauty Lake, the first of the four lakes on this loop hike. They are all good for swimming, although a bit cold, and Beauty and Posey have the best trout fishing.

For backpackers, you can extend your trek by venturing up to Hidden Lakes, a series of several small but pretty waters, set just below South Caribou Mountain.

User Groups: Hikers, dogs, and horses (a horse corral is available at the trailhead). No mountain bikes. No wheelchair facilities.

Permits: A campfire permit (free) is required. Parking and access are free.

Maps: A trail map is available for a fee from the Almanor Ranger District. For a map, ask the U.S. Forest Service for Lassen National Forest or Caribou Wilderness. For a topographic map, ask the USGS for Red Cinder.

Directions: From Red Bluff, take Highway 36 east and drive 47 miles to the junction with Highway 89. Do not turn. Continue east on Highway 36 toward Lake Almanor and to Chester. In Chester, continue east on Highway 36 for five miles to Forest Road 10. Turn north on Forest Road 10 and drive 9.5 miles to Forest Road 30N25. Turn left on Forest Road 30N25 and drive to the trailhead.

Contact: Lassen National Forest, Almanor Ranger District, Chester, 530/258-2141, www.fs.usda.gov/lassen.

42 SPENCER MEADOW TRAIL/CANYON CREEK FALLS

10.8 mi/1 day

in Lassen National Forest south of Lassen Volcanic National Park

Map 3.3, page 127

This hike has national park-like qualities, with a trail through forests and across gorgeous meadows, a waterfall, and big-time views. Yet it is outside the nearby Lassen Volcanic National Park, and for that reason is overlooked by tourists. The trailhead is right along Highway 36 and the route climbs 2,000 feet.

Start the trip by taking the trail straight north toward Lassen on the Spencer Meadow Trail. At 2.3 miles, you'll reach a fork (for an all-day loop hike); turn left. When the forest breaks into meadow, you get a view of Mount Brokeoff. Roughly three miles from the turn at the fork, map in hand, you'll find a spur on the left (note: no trail sign), which leads to an overlook of 50-foot Canyon Creek Falls. For waterfall lovers, this is the destination.

Note: The ambitious can return to the main trail, and instead of heading back, continue on a full loop, 13 miles, routed to Spencer Meadow and back. Campsites are available on the edge of the meadow.

User Groups: Hikers, dogs, horses, and mountain bikes. No wheelchair facilities.

Permits: No permits are required for day use. Campfire permits are required for overnight use. Parking and access are free.

Maps: A trail map is available for a fee from the Almanor Ranger District. For a map, ask the U.S. Forest Service for Lassen National Forest. For a topographic map, ask the USGS for Childs Meadows.

Directions: From Red Bluff, take Highway 36 east for 43 miles to Mineral, then continue east on Highway 36 for about seven miles to the trailhead parking area on the left.

Contact: Lassen National Forest, Almanor Ranger District, Chester, 530/258-2141, www. fs.usda.gov/lassen.

43 DOMINGO SPRING CAMPGROUND TO WARNER VALLEY (PCT)

11.0 mi one-way/1 day

at the Domingo Spring Trailhead in Lassen National Forest west of Lake Almanor

Map 3.3, page 127

From Domingo Spring, the Pacific Crest Trail runs straight north through Lassen National Forest and into Lassen Volcanic National Park. As you enter the park boundary, you'll pass Little Willow Lake (not much to it) on the left. In two miles, you'll reach Boiling Springs Lake with the Warner Valley Campground (on the right) and the Drakesbad Guest Ranch (on the left).

To continue north on the PCT, see the *Lassen Volcanic National Park to Highway 44 (PCT)* hike in this chapter.

User Groups: Hikers and horses. No mountain bikes or dogs (in a national park). No wheelchair facilities.

Permits: A campfire permit (free) is required. Parking and access are free.

Maps: For a map, ask the U.S. Forest Service for Lassen National Forest. For a topographic map, ask the USGS for Stover Mountain.

Directions: From Red Bluff, take Highway 36 east and drive 47 miles to the junction with Highway 89. Do not turn. Continue east on Highway 36 toward Lake Almanor and to Chester and Feather River Drive. Turn left (north) and drive 0.75 mile to Warner Valley Road (signed Juniper Lake and Drakesbad). Turn left and drive to Old Red Bluff Road (County Road 311) and go three miles to the parking area at Domingo Spring Campground.

Contact: Lassen National Forest, Almanor Ranger District, Chester, 530/258-2141, www. fs.usda.gov/lassen.

44 MCCLURE TRAIL

9.0 mi/1 day

in the Tehama Wildlife Area east of Red Bluff

Map 3.3, page 127

If you love foothill oak wildlands, this is the trek for you. In spring, when the oaks first bud and the hills are glowing, the Tehama Wildlife Area is at its prettiest. The landscape includes a stream, abundant vegetation, and at times, plenty of birds and animals.

This trail accesses the best of the wildlife area. From the McClure trailhead, hike down a steep canyon to Antelope Creek. The canyon is buffered by riparian vegetation. In late winter and spring, the canyon's adjoining hillsides come alive in green, and all wildlife seems to prosper. The stream is very pretty, and fishing is catch-and-release only with the use of artificials. The hike can be cut short, of course, and you do not need to walk the entire 4.5 miles out and back.

The area is huge, covering 44,862 acres, and is popular in the fall during hunting season for deer and wild pigs. Deer are abundant in late fall and often migrate in after the hunting season is over. There are also lots of squirrels, hawks, and rattlesnakes. Low numbers of wild pigs roam the canyons but are never seen from trails. This area is also very popular with turkey hunters in season.

User Groups: Hikers and dogs. Mountain bikes and horses permitted but not recommended because of terrain. No wheelchair facilities.

Permits: A campfire permit (free) is required for overnight use. Parking and access are free.

Maps: For a free map, contact the Tehama Wildlife Area. For a map, ask the U.S. Forest Service for Lassen National Forest. For a topographic map, ask the USGS for Dewitt Peak.

Directions: From Red Bluff, take Highway

36 east and drive 20 miles to Paynes Creek and Plum Creek Road. Turn right (south) on Plum Creek Road and go to Ishi Conservation Camp and continue about 2.5 miles south to High Trestle Road and follow it to Hogsback Road. Park across from the intersection of High Trestle and Hogsback Roads, and walk about 0.25 mile on the dirt road to the trailhead.

Access note: Access to the Tehama Wildlife Area is closed to the public from February to the first Saturday in April. Access is also restricted for a short period during deer season in late September.

Contact: Lassen National Forest, Almanor Ranger District, Chester, 530/258-2141, www.fs.usda.gov/lassen; Department of Fish and Game, Tehama Wildlife Area, Paynes Creek, 530/597-2201; Department of Fish and Game, Region 1 Headquarters, 530/225-2300, www.dfg.ca.gov.

45 DEER CREEK TRAIL
1.0-8.0 mi/1 day

in Lassen National Forest west of Lake Almanor

Map 3.3, page 127   **BEST (**

The Deer Creek Trail has all the ingredients to make it ideal for a trout angler, an explorer, or somebody just looking for a dunk on a hot day. The gorgeous stream runs right alongside the trail, with good access throughout and fish (often plenty of them) in the summer months.

From the parking area, look for the trail on the left side of the road. Start by hiking downstream. The trail is routed downstream along the river for about 10 miles. Rarely does anybody ever walk all the way to the end. Instead they take their time, perhaps fishing or swimming along the way.

In summer, Deer Creek is cold and clear, tumbling its way over rocks and into pools, with trout seemingly in every one. California Department of Fish and Game rules mandate catch-and-release fishing with artificials with a single barbless hook for most of the river. This trail has also become popular among mountain bikers. Most are courteous to hikers, and on a single-track trail, that's important. An interesting note is that the canyon rim is made up of a series of volcanic crags and basalt spires. For swimmers, the cold water can provide a rush on summer days where temperatures commonly reach the 90s and 100s, and you can expect significant anatomical changes, male and female alike.

User Groups: Hikers, dogs, and horses. Mountain bikes aren't advised. No wheelchair facilities.

Permits: No permits are required. Parking and access are free.

Maps: A trail map is available for a fee from Almanor Ranger District. For a map, ask the U.S. Forest Service for Lassen National Forest. For a topographic map, ask the USGS for Onion Butte.

Directions: From Chico, take Highway 32 northeast for 40 miles (it becomes narrow and twisty). Just after crossing a small, red, metal bridge (locals call it the Red Bridge) that crosses Deer Creek, park on the right (south) side of the road, where there's a dirt pullout. The trailhead is just up from the bridge, on the left (north) side of the road.

Contact: Lassen National Forest, Almanor Ranger District, Chester, 530/258-2141, www.fs.usda.gov/lassen.

46 RANCHERIA TRAIL TO MILL CREEK
4.0 mi/2.75 hr

in the Ishi Wilderness east of Red Bluff

Map 3.3, page 127

The pay-off is Mill Creek, a gorgeous foothill stream set at the bottom of a deep foothill canyon in the Ishi Wilderness. The trail starts by following an old jeep road, then leaves the road at a fence line off to the right. If it's hot, which is typical here most of the year, you'll already be reaching for your canteen. The trail then drops like a cannonball for 1,000 feet into the Mill Creek Canyon. This canyon is a surprising and awesome habitat with some of the prettiest areas of the Ishi Wilderness. Some of the volcanic rock formations and canyon rims are awesome. The fishing is also often good. Rules mandate catch-and-release with the use of artificials.

There is a problem, of course, and this is it: Shadowing your trek and enjoyment of the Mill Creek Canyon is the knowledge that you have to climb back out. To make it out before sunset, that climb will likely be during the late afternoon, the hottest part of the day. By the time you reach the car, your butt will be thoroughly kicked.

Also note that the trailhead access road is quite rough, impassable for most cars, and that's just a prelude to what lies ahead.

User Groups: Hikers, dogs, and horses. No mountain bikes. No wheelchair facilities.

Permits: A campfire permit (free) is required for overnight use. Parking and access are free.

Maps: A trail map is available for a fee from Almanor Ranger District. For a map, ask the U.S. Forest Service for Lassen National Forest or Ishi Wilderness. For topographic maps, ask the USGS for Panther Spring and Butte Meadows.

Directions: From Red Bluff, take Highway 36 east and drive 20 miles to Paynes Creek and continue to Little Giant Mill Road. Turn right (south) on Little Giant Mill Road (Road 202) and drive seven miles to Ponderosa Way. Turn south and drive about 10 miles to Forest Road 28N57. Turn right (west) and follow the Peligreen Jeep Trail for two miles to the Rancheria trailhead. The last two miles of road are suitable only for four-wheel-drive vehicles.

Contact: Lassen National Forest, Almanor Ranger District, Chester, 530/258-2141, www.fs.usda.gov/lassen.

47 LOWER MILL CREEK

13.0 mi/1 day

in the Ishi Wilderness east of Red Bluff

Map 3.3, page 127

If you have time for only one trail in the Ishi Wilderness, the trail to Lower Mill Creek is the one to pick. That goes whether you want to invest just an hour or a full day, because any length of trip can be a joy here. The trail parallels Mill Creek for 6.5 miles to its headwaters at Papes Place. You get magnificent scenery in this foothill canyonland and many good fishing and swimming holes along the way. This is a dramatic foothill canyon, and as you stand along the stream, the walls can seem to ascend into heaven. It's a land shaped by thousands of years of wind and water.

Note: Directly across from the trailhead, on Ponderosa Way, is another trailhead, this one for a route that follows Upper Mill Creek into Lassen National Forest. Although not as spectacular as Lower Mill Creek, it provides a good option for hiking, fishing, and swimming. Note that fishing is restricted to catch-and-release and the use of artificials.

Note: A trail map is strongly advised for those hiking in the Ishi Wilderness.

User Groups: Hikers, dogs, and horses. No mountain bikes. No wheelchair facilities.

Permits: A campfire permit (free) is required for overnight use. Parking and access are free.

Maps: A trail map is available for a fee from Almanor Ranger District. For a map, ask the U.S. Forest Service for Lassen National Forest or Ishi Wilderness. For topographic maps, ask the USGS for Panther Spring and Butte Meadows.

Directions: From Red Bluff, take Highway 36 east and drive 20 miles to Paynes Creek, and continue to Little Giant Mill Road. Turn right (south) on Little Giant Mill Road (Road 202) and drive seven miles to Ponderosa Way. Turn south at Ponderosa Way and drive about 17 miles to the Mill Creek trailhead. The access road is a slow go.

Contact: Lassen National Forest, Almanor

Ranger District, Chester, 530/258-2141, www. fs.usda.gov/lassen.

48 MOAK TRAIL
14.0 mi/1.5 days 👣2 ⛰7

in the Ishi Wilderness east of Red Bluff

Map 3.3, page 127

In the spring in the Ishi, the foothill country is loaded with wildflowers and tall, fresh grass. The views of the Sacramento Valley are spectacular. The Moak Trail is located on the eastern border of the Ishi Wilderness and is routed into the wilderness center. The trail includes a poke-and-probe section over a lava-rock boulder field, and there are good trail camps at Deep Hole (2,800 feet) and Drennan. It's an excellent weekend trip, including a loop route by linking Moak Trail with Buena Vista Trail, most of it easy walking. Hit it right in the spring, and Moak Trail could be the best overnight hike in California's foothill country. Hit it wrong in the summer, and you'll wonder what you did to deserve such a terrible fate. Alas, if you try this trip in the summer or fall, you'll need to have your gray matter examined at Red Bluff General. No wildflowers, no shade, 100-degree temperatures, and as for water, you're dreamin'.

Note: A trail map is strongly advised for those hiking in the Ishi Wilderness.

User Groups: Hikers, dogs, and horses. No mountain bikes. No wheelchair facilities.

Permits: A campfire permit (free) is required for overnight use. Parking and access are free.

Maps: A trail map is available for a fee from Almanor Ranger District. For a map, ask the U.S. Forest Service for Lassen National Forest or Ishi Wilderness. For topographic maps, ask the USGS for Panther Spring and Butte Meadows.

Directions: From Red Bluff, take Highway 36 east and drive 20 miles to Paynes Creek, and continue to Little Giant Mill Road. Turn right (south) on Little Giant Mill Road (Road 202) and drive seven miles to Ponderosa Way. Turn south at Ponderosa Way and drive about 24 miles to the Moak trailhead.

Contact: Lassen National Forest, Almanor Ranger District, Chester, 530/258-2141, www. fs.usda.gov/lassen.

49 DEER CREEK TRAIL
14.0 mi/1.5 days 👣2 ⛰9

in the Ishi Wilderness east of Red Bluff

Map 3.3, page 127

The Deer Creek Trail is the most popular hike in the Ishi Wilderness, and that's no accident. Even if you cut the trip short to just an hour or two, the hike is a pleasurable romp. The trail runs midway up open slopes, offering spectacular views of Deer Creek Canyon's basalt cliffs and spires, and of the stream below.

The trailhead is at the southeast border of the wilderness. Right from the start, it's routed along the north shore of Deer Creek. Iron Mountain (at 3,274 feet) is located to the immediate north. The trail continues along the stream into the wilderness interior. It skirts past the northern edge of what is called the Graham Pinery, a dense island of ponderosa pine growing on a mountain terrace. A bonus is good bird-watching for hawks, eagles, and falcons at the rock cliffs, and looking for a large variety of wildlife, including rattlesnakes (here's your warning) and lots of squirrels and quail. Trout fishing can be decent near Potato Patch and Alder Creek Campgrounds. Below Potato Patch Campground, fishing is catch-and-release only with the use of artificials.

Note: A trail map is strongly advised for those hiking in the Ishi Wilderness.

User Groups: Hikers, dogs, and horses. No mountain bikes. No wheelchair facilities.

Permits: A campfire permit (free) is required for overnight use. Parking and access are free.

Maps: A trail map is available for a fee from Almanor Ranger District. For a map, ask the U.S. Forest Service for Lassen National Forest or Ishi Wilderness. For topographic maps, ask the USGS for Panther Spring and Butte Meadows.

Directions: From Red Bluff, take Highway 36 east and drive 20 miles to Paynes Creek, and continue to Little Giant Mill Road. Turn right (south) on Little Giant Mill Road (Road 202) and drive seven miles to Ponderosa Way. Turn south at Ponderosa Way and drive about 26 miles to the Deer Creek trailhead.

Contact: Lassen National Forest, Almanor Ranger District, Chester, 530/258-2141, www. fs.usda.gov/lassen.

50 DEVILS DEN TRAIL
9.0 mi/1 day 🏃4 ⛰7

in the Ishi Wilderness east of Red Bluff

Map 3.3, page 127

The Devils Den Trail runs on the opposite side of Deer Creek from the Deer Creek Trail (see hike listing in this chapter). The trailhead is less than a half mile from the Deer Creek trailhead, but that is where the similarities end. The trail starts easy. It is routed along Deer Creek for the first mile (trout fishing here is restricted to catch-and-release and the use of artificials). Enjoy yourself, because what follows is not exactly a picnic. The trail turns left and climbs up Little Pine Creek all the way to the ridge top, with the last mile on an old, hot, and chunky abandoned road. Along the way, the vegetation changes from riparian along the creek to woodland on the slopes, then chaparral on the ridge. A series of small volcanic spires and formations spike the Deer Creek Rim, in some cases, they look like they are from another planet. In addition, an island of conifers, the Graham Pinery, is available for viewing with a 0.25-mile side trip. Many do this hike just for this opportunity. Note: Always bring a water filtration pump to fill your canteen at Deer Creek.

The main attractions here are: 1) nobody else is usually around; 2) Deer Creek; 3) nobody else is usually around; 4) the Graham Pinery; 5) nobody else is usually around; 6) the volcanic rim; 7) nobody else is usually around.

Note: A trail map is strongly advised for those hiking in the Ishi Wilderness.

User Groups: Hikers, dogs, and horses. No mountain bikes. No wheelchair facilities.

Permits: A campfire permit (free) is required for overnight use. Parking and access are free.

Maps: A trail map is available for a fee from Almanor Ranger District. For a map, ask the U.S. Forest Service for Lassen National Forest or Ishi Wilderness. For topographic maps, ask the USGS for Panther Spring and Butte Meadows.

Directions: From Red Bluff, take Highway 36 east and drive about 20 miles to Paynes Creek and then continue to Little Giant Mill Road. Turn right (south) on Little Giant Mill Road (Road 202) and drive seven miles to Ponderosa Way. Turn south at Ponderosa Way and drive 32.5 miles to the Devils Den trailhead (just south of the Deer Creek trailhead).

Contact: Lassen National Forest, Almanor Ranger District, Chester, 530/258-2141, www. fs.usda.gov/lassen.

51 HUMBOLDT SUMMIT TO DOMINGO SPRINGS (PCT)
28.0 mi one-way/2 days 🏃3 ⛰6

at Humboldt Summit in Lassen National Forest

Map 3.3, page 127

The idea of back-to-back 14-mile days to get through this chunk of trail may not appeal to weekend hikers, especially while carrying full-weight expedition packs. But that's standard for most hikers on this stretch of PCT. Some may even try to do it in a day, with little here to tarry for and with Lassen Volcanic National Park beckoning ahead. The trail starts just below Humboldt Peak, at 7,087 feet, and heads north along the ridgeline. For the most part, the trail is routed past Butt Mountain (7,866 feet) and down to Soldier Meadows. A spring and stream make this a delightful stop before crossing Highway 36, forging onward another three miles to the Stove Springs Campground. The trail then skirts around the western flank of North Stover Mountain and drops down to Domingo Springs, where another campground is available.

To continue north on the PCT, see the *Domingo Springs to Lassen Volcanic National Park (PCT)* hike in this chapter. If you are walking this trail in reverse, see the *Feather River to Humboldt Summit (PCT)* hike in this chapter to continue south.

User Groups: Hikers, dogs, and horses. No mountain bikes. No wheelchair facilities.

Permits: A campfire permit (free) is required. Parking and access are free.

Maps: For a map, ask the U.S. Forest Service for Lassen National Forest. For topographic maps, ask the USGS for Humboldt Peak and Stover Mountain.

Directions: From Red Bluff, take Highway 36 east and drive 47 miles to the junction with Highway 89. Turn south on Highway 89 and drive four miles to County Road 308 (Humboldt Road). Turn right and drive 15 miles to the trailhead parking area.

Contact: Lassen National Forest, Almanor Ranger District, Chester, 530/258-2141, www.fs.usda.gov/lassen.

runs adjacent to the trail for eight miles. Then later, there's a short crossing over the headwaters of Willow Creek. Some might prefer to take three days instead of two to hike this section, but with the stunning Lassen Volcanic National Park looming ahead, most hikers are willing to put in long days to get through this area.

To continue north on the PCT, see the *Humboldt Summit to Domingo Springs (PCT)* hike in this chapter. If you are walking this trail in reverse, see the *Bucks Summit to Feather River (PCT)* hike, in the *Sacramento and Gold Country* chapter, to continue south.

User Groups: Hikers, dogs, and horses. No mountain bikes. No wheelchair facilities.

Permits: A campfire permit (free) is required. Parking and access are free.

Maps: For a map, ask the U.S. Forest Service for Plumas National Forest. For topographic maps, ask the USGS for Belden and Humboldt Peak.

Directions: From Quincy, drive west on Highway 70 about 26 miles to the trailhead, at the roadside rest area at Belden.

Contact: Plumas National Forest, Mount Hough Ranger District, Quincy, 530/283-0555, www.fs.usda.gov/lassen.

52 FEATHER RIVER TO HUMBOLDT SUMMIT (PCT)
26.0 mi one-way/2 days　🏃4 ⛰6

at the Belden Trailhead on Highway 70 in Plumas National Forest

Map 3.3, page 127

The trail is not only rough from Belden to Humboldt Summit, it's not particularly pretty either, especially compared to the nearby wilderness. The climb is a dry slice of rattlesnake country. From the North Fork Feather River at Belden (elevation 2,310 feet), the PCT climbs 4,777 feet over the course of this two-day thumper to Humboldt Summit, at 7,087 feet. There are no lakes along this trail, only a few small water holes requiring short side trips. Instead, the prettiest sections are along streams, the first being Chips Creek, which

53 BIZZ JOHNSON
1.0-26.0 mi one-way/0.5 hr-3 days

🏃1 ⛰7

west of Susanville

Map 3.4, page 128

This is the best mountain bike trail in California that nobody knows about, the 26.6-mile Bizz Johnson Trail. For biking, it's a 10. For hiking, it's OK for short day trips, in and out. It can be euphoric as a bike ride with views, tunnels, trestles, forest, and a 1 percent grade.

The Bizz Johnson Trail can be okay for day-trip walks, with trailhead access spaced five to seven miles apart. People can hike or bike different portions of the trail. You don't have to complete the entire route, of course. The seven-mile stretch west of Susanville is the most popular stretch of the 25-mile route. The biggest problem is your trip can feel like the endless hike to nowhere.

The trailhead is at 4,200 feet, and the high point of the route is at 5,600 feet at Westwood Junction. The trail traces the old Fernley and Lassen railroad line, a branch line of the South Pacific Railroad. It is routed in the Susan River Canyon along the Susan River for 15 miles, then from the Susanville Railroad Depot to the Mason Station trailhead five miles north of Westwood. The surface is a mixture of compacted dirt and small gravel. The trail features beautiful views in many areas and passes through two old railroad tunnels and 11 old railroad bridges. You won't cross any developed areas.

In the 1960s, when Shasta legend John Reginato heard that Southern Pacific was going to abandon a rail line between Westwood and Susanville, he urged that it be converted to a hiking trail. It took many years, but the idea eventually struck home, and the Bureau of Land Management worked with the U.S. Forest Service to develop and refine it.

The one negative: Like most rails-to-trails projects, it's way too wide.

In the winter, it makes a great trip on cross-country skis or on a snowmobile (snowmobiling is allowed on the western half of the trail, from Mason Station to just beyond Westwood Junction).

User Groups: Hikers, dogs (must be leashed near Susanville), horses, and mountain bikes. Wheelchair-accessible from Susanville and Hobo Camp trailhead.

Permits: No permits are required. Parking and access are free.

Maps: For a free brochure, contact the Bureau of Land Management. For a map, ask the U.S. Forest Service for Lassen National Forest. For topographic maps, ask the USGS for Westwood East, Fredonyer Pass, and Susanville.

Directions: From Susanville, take Highway 36 to Weatherlow Street. Turn on Weatherlow (it becomes Richmond Road) and drive 0.5 mile to the Susanville Depot Visitors Center and the trailhead, on the right.

Alternate trailhead: From Westwood, take Highway 36 to County Road A21. Turn north and drive three miles to a signed trailhead access road (dirt). Turn right and drive 0.4 mile to the trailhead, on the left.

Contact: Lassen Land & Trails Trust, 530/257-3252, www.lassenlandandtrailstrust.org; Lassen National Forest, Eagle Lake Ranger District, Susanville, 530/257-4188, www.fs.usda.gov/lassen; Bureau of Land Management, Eagle Lake Field Office, Susanville, 530/257-0456, www.blm.gov/ca/.

MENDOCINO AND WINE COUNTRY

© SABRINA YOUNG

The Mendocino coast is dramatic and remote with several stellar state parks, while Sonoma Valley produces some of the most popular wines in the world. The Mendocino coast features a series of romantic hideaways and excellent adventuring and hiking. The Fort Bragg area has three state parks, with outstanding recreation, including several easy hikes, many amid redwoods and along pretty streams. (For overnight hikes in a state park on a summer weekend, campsite reservations are required far in advance.) A driving tour of Highway 1 along this section of the coast is the fantasy of many. Along the twists and turns of the road are dozens of hidden beaches and untouched coastline to stop and explore. The prize spots are MacKerricher State Park, Salt Point State Park, and Anchor Bay. Inland, you'll find pockets of redwoods near Guerneville, Philo, and Calistoga.

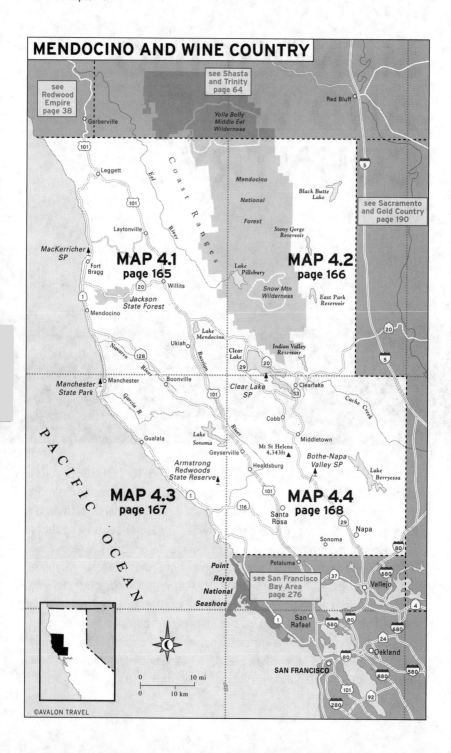

MENDOCINO AND WINE COUNTRY

see Redwood Empire page 38

see Shasta and Trinity page 64

Red Bluff

Yolla Bolly Middle Eel Wilderness

Garberville

see Sacramento and Gold Country page 190

Leggett

Mendocino

National

Forest

Black Butte Lake

Coast Ranges

Eel River

Stony Gorge Reservoir

MacKerricher SP

Laytonville

MAP 4.1 page 165

MAP 4.2 page 166

Fort Bragg

Willits

Lake Pillsbury

Snow Mtn Wilderness

East Park Reservoir

Jackson State Forest

Mendocino

Navarro River

Ukiah

Lake Mendocino

Clear Lake

Indian Valley Reservoir

Boonville

Russian River

Clearlake

Manchester State Park

Manchester

Garcia R.

Clear Lake SP

Cache Creek

Gualala

Lake Sonoma

Cobb

Geyserville

Mt St Helena 4,343ft

Middletown

Bothe-Napa Valley SP

Lake Berryessa

MAP 4.3 page 167

Armstrong Redwoods State Reserve

Healdsburg

MAP 4.4 page 168

PACIFIC OCEAN

Santa Rosa

Napa

Sonoma

Point

Reyes

National

Seashore

Petaluma

see San Francisco Bay Area page 276

Vallejo

San Rafael

Oakland

SAN FRANCISCO

0   10 mi
0   10 km

©AVALON TRAVEL

Map 4.1

**Sites 1-10
Pages 169-174**

Map 4.2

Sites 11-15
Pages 175-177

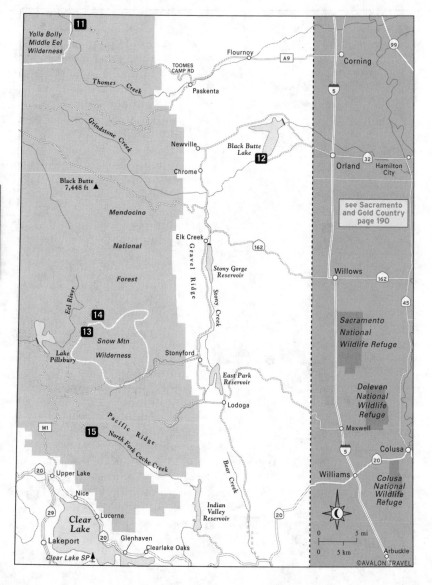

Map 4.3

Sites 16-22
Pages 177-181

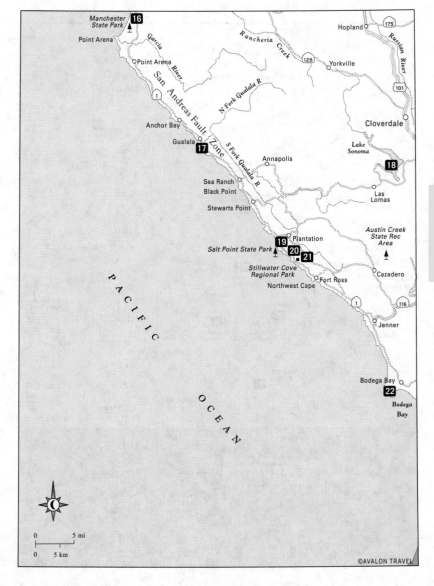

Map 4.4

Sites 23-31
Pages 181-187

1 LOST COAST TRAIL/ SINKYONE TRAILHEAD

16.7 mi one-way/2 days 🥾3 ⛰10

in Sinkyone Wilderness State Park

Map 4.1, page 165 **BEST (**

This remote and rugged wilderness of Northern California coastline, covering more than 7,000 acres, is now protected forever as Sinkyone Wilderness State Park. It was once one of the least traveled jewels of California. No more. It has become fairly popular for trekkers looking for the wild side, despite few directional signs along roads, no highways leading here, and virtually no park promotion. The primitive, steep, and unforgiving terrain provides a rare coastal wilderness experience. The best way to explore it is on Lost Coast Trail, which is best hiked north to south to keep the north winds out of your face. A shuttle service is available for a fee through Lost Coast Trail Transport Service.

Day 1: From the northern trailhead at Orchard Camp, Lost Coast Trail starts out flat and pleasant, arcing around Bear Harbor Cove. From here the trail climbs 800 feet and then back down, passing through a redwood grove and also breaking out for sweeping coastal views. Enjoy them, because the hike gets more difficult, including a steep climb up, over, and down a mountain. The trail finally descends into Little Jackass Creek Camp, which is set beside a small stream 10.5 miles from your start.

Day 2: The closeout of a two-day hike should always be as enjoyable as possible, and so it is here, with divine views in many spots along the 6.5-mile route. Alas, there's usually payment for views, and that comes in the form of several rugged climbs in the park's most remote sections. After climbing to nearly 1,000 feet, the trail ends with an 800-foot downgrade over the last mile, descending to the Usal Campground parking area.

Notes: All food must be bear-proofed. Dogs are permitted only at car camps. At the northern boundary of the Sinkyone Wilderness, this trail continues north into the King Range National Conservation Area, where it's routed for another 30 miles to the mouth of the Mattole River (see the listing for *Lost Coast Trail/Mattole Trailhead* in the *Redwood Empire* chapter).

User Groups: Hikers only. Horses allowed only on the section of trail between the trailhead at the park entrance and Wheeler Camp. No dogs or mountain bikes. No wheelchair facilities.

Permits: No permits are required. Parking and access are free unless you plan to camp.

Maps: A trail map and brochure is available for a fee from Sinkyone Wilderness State Park. For topographic maps, ask the USGS for Petrolia, Cooskie Creek, Shubrick Peak, Bear Harbor, and Shelter Cove.

Directions: From Garberville, take U.S. 101 north to the exit for Redway. Take that exit to Briceland Road. Turn left (west) on Briceland Road and drive 17 miles to Whitethorn. Continue six miles to the Four Corners Fork then another six miles (the road turns to gravel) to the Needle Rock Ranger Station. Continue past the ranger station to the visitors center and park at Orchard Camp. Be aware that the access road is unpaved, that it may close unexpectedly in the winter, and that four-wheel-drive vehicles are often required in wet weather. There are few signs pointing the way to the park, and when they are posted, they are often stolen. Trailers and RVs are not recommended.

Contact: Sinkyone Wilderness State Park, 707/986-7711, www.parks.ca.gov; Lost Coast Trail Transport Service, 707/986-9909, www.lostcoasttrail.com; Lost Coast Shuttle, 707/986-7437, www.lostcoastshuttle.com.

2 SOLDIER RIDGE TRAIL

11.2 mi/2 days 🥾3 ⛰8

on the boundary of Yolla Bolly Wilderness west of Red Bluff

Map 4.1, page 165

This wilderness trail features three linked segments: Soldier Ridge Trail, Minnie Lake Trail, and Kingsley Lake Trail. In the process, this combines for a 5.6-mile walk to your destination, Kingsley Lake. The rugged climb on Soldier Ridge Trail to get there, along with the charm of this little lake, makes for an overnighter. It's a long drive in the middle of nowhere just to reach the trailhead, and then when you get there, you'll face a daunting 3.5-mile climb up the spine of Soldier Ridge toward the Yolla Bolly Crest. At the crest are three mountains lined in a row: Sugarloaf Mountain (elevation 7,367 feet), Solomon Peak (7,581 feet), and Hammerhorn Mountain (7,567 feet). The trail crosses a saddle between Sugarloaf Mountain and Solomon Peak, then drops down to little Kingsley Lake, which is created from the headwaters of Thomes Creek. All is quiet and peaceful here.

User Groups: Hikers, dogs, and horses. No mountain bikes. No wheelchair facilities.

Permits: A campfire permit is required for hikers planning to camp. Parking and access are free.

Maps: For a map, ask the U.S. Forest Service for Mendocino National Forest or Yolla Bolly Wilderness. For a topographic map, ask the USGS for South Yolla Bolly.

Directions: From Willits, drive north on U.S. 101 for 13 miles to Longvale and Highway 162. Turn east on Highway 162 and drive 30 miles to the turnoff for Highway 162 East. Turn right and drive nine miles to the Eel River Bridge and Forest Road M1 (Indian Dick Road). At the bridge, turn left (north) onto Forest Road M1 and drive 27 miles to the trailhead, at the end of the road.

Contact: Mendocino National Forest, Covelo Ranger District, Covelo, 707/983-6118, www.fs.usda.gov/mendocino.

3 WRIGHTS VALLEY TRAIL
8.0 mi/4.5 hr   🏃2 ⛺7

on the boundary of Yolla Bolly Wilderness west of Red Bluff

Map 4.1, page 165

The Rock Cabin Trail (also known as the River Trail) extends north into the Yolla Bolly Wilderness and up, over, and down a short ridge before pouring into Wrights Valley. About halfway in, the River Trail jumps to Wrights Valley Trail. It's about a four-mile trip one-way to your destination. Here you'll find the headwaters of the Middle Fork Eel River, one of the prettiest streams in the wilderness. The trail is well marked and includes two creek crossings and a pretty waterfall. The Yolla Bollys provide few lakes, but the Middle Fork awaits you. In order to protect steelhead, no fishing is allowed.

Note: Little Henthorne Lake, complete with two wilderness cabins, is located 2.5 miles from the Rock Cabin trailhead. Resist the urge to visit. This is maintained as private property. Hikers are often tempted to hike in via a very faint cowboy trail (with a river crossing) and camp here illegally.

User Groups: Hikers, dogs, and horses. No mountain bikes. No wheelchair facilities.

Permits: A campfire permit is required for hikers planning to camp. Parking and access are free.

Maps: For a map, ask the U.S. Forest Service for Mendocino National Forest or Yolla Bolly Wilderness. For a topographic map, ask the USGS for South Yolla Bolly.

Directions: From Willits, drive north on U.S. 101 for 13 miles to Longvale and Highway 162. Turn east on Highway 162 and drive 30 miles to the turnoff for Highway 162 East. Turn right and drive nine miles to the Eel River Bridge and Forest Road M1 (Indian Dick Road). At the bridge, turn left (north) onto Forest Road M1 and drive 24 miles to Forest Road 25N15C. Turn left on Forest Road 25N15C and drive 0.75 mile to the turnoff for the Rock Cabin trailhead. Turn left and drive 0.25 mile to the trailhead, at the end of the road.

Contact: Mendocino National Forest, Covelo Ranger District, Covelo, 707/983-6118, www.fs.usda.gov/mendocino.

4 BRUHEL POINT TIDEPOOLS
0.5 mi/0.5 hr   🏃1 ⛰10

on the Mendocino coast north of Fort Bragg

Map 4.1, page 165

Some of the best tidepools on the Pacific Coast can be found in Mendocino. One of the best of the best is here, located just south of Bruhel Point. When you first arrive, you'll find a Caltrans roadside vista point (no overnight parking), restrooms, and a beach access trail. This is your calling. The trail is routed north toward Bruhel Point. And much of it is set along the edge of ocean bluffs. Do not make your own descent down the bluff. Instead take only the cutoff trails, which lead to the best tidepool areas. Time your trip during a low tide, or better yet, a minus low tide. That is when the ocean pulls back, leaving a series of holes and cuts in a rock basin that remain filled with water, providing the perfect habitat and viewing areas for all kinds of tiny marine life.

User Groups: Hikers and dogs. Not suitable for mountain bikes or horses. No wheelchair facilities.

Permits: No permits are required. Parking and access are free.

Maps: For a topographic map, ask the USGS for Inglenook.

Directions: From Westport, drive south on Highway 1 about two miles to milepost marker 74.09 and park at the Caltrans Vista Point parking lot. The tidepools are a short walk.

Contact: None.

5 LAKE CLEONE TRAIL
1.2 mi/0.5 hr   🏃1 ⛰9

in MacKerricher State Park north of Fort Bragg

Map 4.1, page 165

The loop trail around Lake Cleone is not only easy but also definitely something special. Mrs. MacKerricher aptly named the trail Cleone, which means "gracious" or "beautiful" in Greek. The route includes several sections on raised wooden walkways, which provide routes through marshy areas. In the winter months, the southern part of the trail (without the boardwalk) can be flooded. Be sure to wear your high boots in the rainy season.

In some spots, the trail burrows like a tunnel through a variety of trees and lush vegetation. At others, it provides many glimpses of pretty Lake Cleone. It loops all the way around the lake, which is almost always full. The beautiful Pacific Ocean looms just beyond to the west, a cypress grove is to the south, and a marsh is to the east. The boardwalk is wheelchair-accessible. MacKerricher State Park is filled with many enticing highlights. It is also one of the few state parks with free day-use access.

Side trip: From the parking lot adjacent to the lake, you can walk under the built-up foundation of an old railroad line (now a bicycle trail called Old Haul Road) and connect to Headlands Trail. This is a must-do. It's an easy short walk, much of it on a raised walkway that leads to a series of tidepools and the best seal- and whale-watching station on the coast.

User Groups: Hikers, leashed dogs, and wheelchairs (the trail is partially wheelchair-accessible). No horses or mountain bikes. Horse trails and mountain bike routes are available elsewhere in the state park.

Permits: No permits are required. Parking and access are free.

Maps: A brochure and trail map is available for a fee at MacKerricher State Park. For a topographic map, ask the USGS for Inglenook.

Directions: From Fort Bragg drive north on Highway 1 for three miles to the park entrance. Turn left and drive to the parking area beside the lake. The trailhead is on the east side of the parking lot.

Contact: MacKerricher State Park, Mendocino, 707/964-9112, www.parks.ca.gov.

6 CHAMBERLAIN CREEK WATERFALL TRAIL

0.5 mi/0.5 hr   👥2 ⛰10

in Jackson State Forest east of Fort Bragg

Map 4.1, page 165

Chamberlain Creek Falls is a surprise 50-foot waterfall set in a canyon framed by redwoods, well secluded in Jackson State Forest. Time it in the spring after a period of heavy rain and this one is a 10, where you'll find a silvery stream emerging from the greenery in a chutelike cataract over the brink. It's off the Mendocino grid and set back off an old logging road. The trail is short, little known to outsiders, and beautiful. This access road (gravel/dirt), by the way, can get muddy in the winter and extremely dusty in the summer. After parking, you'll find the trail routed a short distance down the canyon to the stream, starting with a short series of steps. The trail simply heads down the canyon directly to the base of the waterfall. Jackson State Forest is overlooked by most visitors, despite the beauty of the area and the popularity of the Mendocino coast. That means you'll most likely have the place to yourself. Jackson State Forest is the largest of Cal Fire's eight demonstration state forests at 48,652 acres.

User Groups: Hikers and dogs. No horses or mountain bikes. No wheelchair facilities.

Permits: No permits are required. Parking and access are free.

Maps: For a free trail map, contact Jackson Demonstration State Forest. For a topographic map, ask the USGS for Northspur.

Directions: From Willits, take Highway 20 west for 17 miles to Forest Road 200, a dirt road just before the Chamberlain Creek bridge. Turn right on Road 200 and drive one mile to a fork. Bear left and drive 3.5 miles. Look for a parking pullout and park on the side of the road. The trailhead is on the left. In the heaviest rainy season, note that State Forest Road 200 is sometimes closed due to weather; call ahead for the status.

Contact: Jackson Demonstration State Forest, Fort Bragg, 707/964-5674, www.fire.ca.gov.

7 FALLS LOOP TRAIL

7.0 mi/4.0 hr   👥2 ⛰10

in Russian Gulch State Park south of Fort Bragg

Map 4.1, page 165

A 35-foot waterfall in deep forest makes this walk one of the prettiest on the Mendocino coast. Most of the year, this waterfall is a narrow silvery stream that pours atop and across a boulder. In winter it can build into a more powerful chute and land in the rock basin with surging splashes. It's way better at high flows, of course.

The route is simple. Take North Trail for 2.5 miles out to its junction with Falls Loop Trail (see note for bikers). This seems nearly flat, with only a slight grade. At that junction, turn left and hike less than a mile, some of it a 150-foot climb, to reach the falls. Even in the summer months, this is a pretty, if narrow, silver cascade, streaming 20 feet across a granite boulder and down into a pool. The entire trip has very little elevation gain. It's an easy walk out to Falls Loop Trail, then only a 200-foot gain to reach the waterfall. As you go, you'll delve deeper and deeper into dense forest, and although a lot of the old growth was taken a long time ago, much is still divine.

Note: A paved bicycle trail runs parallel to North Trail and makes a great bike trip. But please note that bikes are not permitted on the dirt Falls Loop Trail. Bike racks are available at the intersection of these two trails, meaning bikers can make the trip to the falls with only a one-mile hike. In other words, ride to the Falls Loop Trail junction, park your bike, and walk one mile from there. This bike trail is also wheelchair-accessible. A large number of people also walk the bike trail, a five-mile round-trip.

User Groups: Hikers only. No mountain bikes, dogs, or horses. However, a paved trail for bicycles and wheelchairs is routed 2.5 miles to the trailhead of Falls Loop Trail.

Permits: No permits are required. A state park entrance fee of $8 is charged for each vehicle.

Maps: A brochure and trail map is available for a fee at Russian Gulch State Park. For a topographic map, ask the USGS for Mendocino.

Directions: From Fort Bragg, take Highway 1 south for six miles to the Russian Gulch State Park entrance. Turn right and drive a very short distance to the state park entrance. After passing the kiosk, travel down the hill and to the bridge. Turn left and drive past the campsites to the trailhead.

Contact: Russian Gulch State Park, Mendocino, 707/937-5804, www.parks.ca.gov.

8 FERN CANYON TRAIL
8.1 mi/5.0 hr

in Van Damme State Park south of Mendocino

Map 4.1, page 165

This beautiful streamside walk amid coastal redwoods is one of the most popular trails on the Mendocino coast. In spring, this one is a 10. The trail starts at the bottom of a canyon along the Little River and heads upstream, rising gently along the way, with a series of little bridges that crisscross the water. The creek is pretty and often clear, the forest canopy towers, and the understory of fern and sorrel is lush. Most people hike 2.3 miles (paved all the way) out to the junction of Loop Trail and then turn around and head back. Visitors can add on a three-mile loop, including a visit to the Pygmy Forest. This is where an elevated wood walkway is routed amid this unusual setting. Some people love this, for others, it's no big deal, and there is a closer trailhead on a back road to the Pygmy Forest that you can drive to.

Note that heavy rains can flood out the trail and wash out the bridges. Also note that if you're a cheapskate, you can avoid paying the park entrance fee by parking in the beach parking lot next to the park entrance and walking in.

Note: This Fern Canyon Trail is not to be confused with the Fern Canyon Loop Trail on the Humboldt coast in the *Redwood Empire* chapter.

User Groups: Hikers only. No dogs or horses. Wheelchairs and mountain bikes are allowed only on the first 2.3 miles of the trail.

Permits: No permits are required. A state park entrance fee of $8 is charged for each vehicle. Beach parking is free.

Maps: A brochure and trail map is available for a fee at Van Damme State Park. For a topographic map, ask the USGS for Mendocino.

Directions: From Mendocino, take Highway 1 south for 2.5 miles to the park entrance. Turn left and drive 0.75 mile (signed) to the trailhead parking near the campground. Campers start near campsite 26.

Contact: Van Damme State Park, Mendocino, 707/937-5804, www.parks.ca.gov.

9 GLEN EDEN TRAIL
3.0-10.5 mi/1.0-5.0 hr

in Cow Mountain Recreation Area east of Ukiah

Map 4.1, page 165

This trail will have you sweating like Charles Manson's cellmate. The Glen Eden Trail is not

Fern Canyon Trail

© SABRINA YOUNG

only difficult to find (follow the directions precisely), but has several steep sections and is typically quite hot from late spring through summer and fall. The Glen Eden Trail eventually crosses Mendo Rock Road (this provides another trailhead possibility) and continues up to a series of great overlooks of Clear Lake. The views of Clear Lake and the Mayacamas Range are outstanding. To return, retrace your route. Few make the entire trip, but instead they just hike out to a good lookout and then return. The chaparral-covered slopes are peppered with pine and oak, with many miles of trails and fire roads. But it's extremely rare to see other hikers. No off-road vehicles are allowed, unlike the southern portion of the Cow Mountain Recreation Area.

The 52,000-acre Cow Mountain Recreation Area is named for the longhorn cattle that once roamed wild in this area.

User Groups: Hikers, dogs, and horses. Mountain bikes are prohibited on the first 2.5 miles of trail, after which public property starts and bicycles are allowed. Bikers should access Glen Eden Trail from other trailheads on Bureau of Land Management (BLM) land.

Permits: No permits are required. Parking and access are free.

Maps: For a free trail map of the Cow Mountain Recreation Area, contact the Bureau of Land Management. For a topographic map, ask the USGS for Cow Mountain.

Directions: From Ukiah, take U.S. 101 north for five miles to Highway 20. Turn east on Highway 20 and drive 14.6 miles (past Blue Lakes) to Scotts Valley Road. Turn right and drive 2.6 miles to the trailhead and parking.

Contact: Bureau of Land Management, Ukiah Field Office, Ukiah, 707/468-4000, www.blm. gov/ca.

🔟 BIG HENDY GROVE/ HERMIT'S HUT TRAIL

1.0 mi/0.5 hr   🥾1 ⛰7

in Hendy Woods State Park in Mendocino National Forest

Map 4.1, page 165

This easy and short walk through an ancient redwood forest can have you smiling for days. Hendy Woods is located in the redwood-filled canyon of the Navarro River, which flows to the sea on the Mendocino coast. Although the park covers 845 acres, the two old-growth redwood groves, Little Hendy (20 acres) and Big Hendy (80 acres), are most compelling.

When you first arrive, you'll be stunned at the sudden interface of the foothill grasslands with redwoods. At Big Hendy, start by taking the 0.5-mile Discovery Trail, which leaves the grasslands and enters the redwood grove on a dirt path. Suddenly you'll be walking among towering redwoods, moss-covered stumps, and a sprinkling of giant fallen trees, all set amid ferns and sorrel. A great side trip is to walk uphill on the cutoff trail to the old hermit's hut in a hollowed-out tree stump, where one of the last of the real hermits lived for years.

User Groups: Hikers and wheelchairs. No dogs, horses, or mountain bikes.

Permits: No permits are required. A state park entrance fee of $8 is charged for each vehicle.

Maps: A brochure and trail map is available for a fee at Hendy Woods State Park. For a topographic map, ask the USGS for Philo.

Directions: From Mendocino, take Highway 1 south for about five miles to Highway 128. Turn east on Highway 128 and drive about 20 miles to Philo Greenwood Road. Turn south (right) and drive 0.5 mile to the entrance of Hendy Woods State Park, on the left. The trailhead begins just off the parking area.

Contact: Hendy Woods State Park, Mendocino District, Mendocino, 707/895-3141, www.parks. ca.gov.

11 IDES COVE NATIONAL RECREATION TRAIL

10.5 mi/5.5 hr 　　🚶3 ⛰7

on the boundary of Yolla Bolly Wilderness west of Red Bluff

Map 4.2, page 166

At 8,092 feet, South Yolla Bolly Mountain is the highest point in this wilderness. The Ides Cove National Recreation Trail skirts this mountain as part of one of the top one-day loop trails available in the Yolla Bollys. A bonus is that a shorter loop hike (3.5 miles) is also available. From the Ides Cove trailhead, the trail drops down to the headwaters of Slide Creek and heads out to the foot of Harvey Peak, at 7,361 feet. This is the halfway point and a good spot for lunch. The trail turns sharply and is routed back along the flank of the South Yolla Bolly Mountains. On the way, it passes both Long and Square Lakes, which are both tiny water holes with small brook trout.

A free, primitive campground with two sites is available at the trailhead. Horse facilities are nearby, but not at the trailhead. The trail gets only light use.

User Groups: Hikers, dogs, and horses. No mountain bikes. No wheelchair facilities.

Permits: A campfire permit is required for hikers planning to camp.

Maps: For a map, ask the U.S. Forest Service for Mendocino National Forest or Yolla Bolly Wilderness. For a topographic map, ask the USGS for South Yolla Bolly.

Directions: From Redding, take I-5 south to Corning and the exit for Corning Road/ Paskenta Road. Take that exit, turn west on Paskenta Road and drive about 20 miles to Paskenta. In the town of Paskenta, Corning/ Paskenta Road will split, becoming Round Valley Road on the left and County Road M2/ Toomes Creek Road straight ahead. Continue straight on County Road M2/Toomes Creek Road for 20 miles to Cold Springs Ranger Station and County Road M22. Turn right on County Road M22 and drive about 15 miles to the trailhead.

Contact: Mendocino National Forest, Stonyford Work Center, Stonyford, 530/963-3128, www.fs.usda.gov/mendocino.

12 BIG OAK TRAIL

1.0 mi/0.5 hr 　　🚶1 ⛰6

at the head of Black Butte Reservoir west of Orland

Map 4.2, page 166

The Big Oak Trail is routed through a riparian area in the Stony Creek drainage above the head of Black Butte Reservoir. The habitat is constantly changing here based on creek flows and temperatures. The route is an easy jaunt. The riparian habitat here can make it an area to see wildlife in the sparse foothills of the Sacramento Valley. It has become part of California's Watchable Wildlife system. The best time for hiking is at dusk, when the temperatures are more moderate and the best chance to see emerging wildlife occurs. This hike is not without a few potential problems. It's too hot in the summer, and that's when most people have time to visit the area.

User Groups: Hikers, dogs, and mountain bikes. No horses. No wheelchair facilities.

Permits: No permits are required. Parking and access are free.

Maps: For a topographic map, ask the USGS for Julian Rocks.

Directions: Take I-5 to Orland and the exit for Black Butte Lake. Take that exit, turn west on Newville Road (County Road 200) and drive 10 miles to County Road 206. Turn left on County Road 206 and drive to County Road 200A. Bear left on County Road 200A and drive to the lake and trailhead.

Contact: U.S. Army Corps of Engineers, Black Butte Lake, Orland, 530/865-4781, www.spk. usace.army.mil.

13 MIDDLE FORK FALLS LOOP

4.4 mi/3.0 hr   🏃3 ⛰9

on the boundary of Snow Mountain Wilderness in Mendocino National Forest

Map 4.2, page 166

Very few people know about the Snow Mountain Wilderness, and far fewer know about this loop trail that traverses the region's most treasured areas. Double-peaked Snow Mountain itself is the big ridge located about midway between I-5 at Willows and U.S. 101 at Willits. This trail starts at the northern boundary of the wilderness at the West Crockett trailhead (just west of Crockett Peak). Start by hiking two miles to get into Middle Fork Creek. The trail connects there with a spur trail to the waterfall. Take that spur 0.2 mile to the waterfall.

To turn this into a major loop, take the main trail uphill, a significant climb, to reach a small loop set between East Snow Mountain (7,056 feet) and West Snow Mountain (7,038 feet). To return, take North Ridge Trail, which drops down from Snow Mountain and traces the Middle Fork of Stony Creek for a good portion of the route back to the parking area; 13 miles.

This is a good hike in late winter or spring, but much of this area can be quite dry and hot in midsummer, especially on the North Ridge. From late spring through fall, rattlesnakes are common. Hikers should always be certain to carry a lot of water here, twice as much as usual.

User Groups: Hikers, dogs, and horses. No mountain bikes. No wheelchair facilities.

Permits: A campfire permit is required for hikers planning to camp. Parking and access are free.

Maps: For a map, ask the U.S. Forest Service for Mendocino National Forest. For topographic maps, ask the USGS for Crockett Peak and St. John Mountain.

Directions: Take I-5 to Willows and the exit for Highway 162. Take that exit, turn west on Highway 162 and drive 21 miles to a T junction (signed Elk Creek). Turn left and drive one mile through the town of Elk Creek to Ivory Mill Road. Turn right on Ivory Mill Road (Road 308) and drive 15 miles to Forest Road M3. Turn left on Forest Road M3 and drive 15.5 miles to the signed turnoff for West Crockett trailhead. Turn left and drive 0.5 mile to the trailhead.

Contact: Mendocino National Forest, Stonyford Work Center, Stonyford, 530/963-3128, www.fs.usda.gov/mendocino.

14 BEAR WALLOW TRAILHEAD

3.25 mi/1.75 hr   🏃2 ⛰7

on the boundary of Snow Mountain Wilderness in Mendocino National Forest

Map 4.2, page 166

Every wilderness has secret spots. So it is here in the Snow Mountain Wilderness. On a hot summer day when every drop of water is counted as if it were liquid gold, you'll find a simple paradise on this short walk to the headwaters of a tiny fork of Bear Wallow Creek.

Your destination is a pretty section of Bear Wallow Creek, a small feeder stream to the middle fork of Stony Creek. The hike starts at the Bear Wallow trailhead near the Windy Point Campground. The trail is routed straight east on Bear Wallow Trail for a little more than a mile. About 1.5 miles in, start looking for a spur trail on the right side, and when you see it, take it. This spur drops a short distance down to the source of the north fork of Bear Wallow Creek. If you think there are too many people in the world, just come here and look around.

User Groups: Hikers, dogs, and horses. No mountain bikes. No wheelchair facilities.

Permits: A campfire permit is required for hikers planning to camp. Parking and access are free.

Maps: For a map, ask the U.S. Forest Service for Mendocino National Forest. For topographic maps, ask the USGS for Crockett Peak and St. John Mountain.

Directions: Take I-5 to Willows and the exit for Highway 162. Take that exit, turn west on

Highway 162 and drive 21 miles to a T junction (signed Elk Creek). Turn left and drive 1.3 miles through the town of Elk Creek to Road 308/Ivory Mill Road. Turn right on Ivory Mill Road (Road 308) and drive 15 miles to Forest Road M3 (well signed). Turn left on Forest Road M3 and drive 13.4 miles to the trailhead.

Contact: Mendocino National Forest, Stonyford Work Center, Stonyford, 530/963-3128, www.fs.usda.gov/mendocino.

15 SUMMIT SPRINGS TRAILHEAD/WEST SNOW MOUNTAIN LOOP

12 mi/1 day

on the boundary of Snow Mountain Wilderness in Mendocino National Forest

Map 4.2, page 166

This trail includes two killer climbs, a wonderful little spring along the trail, and the ascent of West Snow Mountain, at 7,038 feet, for a panorama. Still interested? Then read on. The trail starts at the Summit Spring trailhead (there's a small, primitive trailhead camp with a pit toilet and an unreliable spring). In the first two miles, you get a no-fun clamber up to High Rock. At the trail junction here, turn right on Box Spring Loop Trail and hike past the headwaters of Trout Creek to Box Spring, located just to the right of the trail, near another trail junction. In hot weather (typically all summer), this spot is paradise. Turn left and make the three-mile climb up West Snow Mountain. You will grunt and thump it out every step of the way. At the top, enjoy this victory for a while before dropping back down for the final three miles to the trailhead and parking area.

Do you yearn for the passion of the mountain experience? Do you crave the zest of life when you have a bad case of dry mouth and discover a mountain spring? Is the price of a climb worth it for the mountaintop payoff? Are you nuts? You need to answer yes, yes, yes, and yes to be ready for this loop hike.

User Groups: Hikers, dogs, and horses. No mountain bikes. No wheelchair facilities.

Permits: A campfire permit is required for hikers planning to camp. Parking and access are free.

Maps: For a map, ask the U.S. Forest Service for Mendocino National Forest. For a topographic map, ask the USGS for Fouts Springs.

Directions: Take I-5 to the exit for Maxwell (north of Williams, south of Willows). Take that exit to Maxwell-Sites Road, turn west, and drive to Sites and Sites-Lodoga Road. Turn left on Sites-Lodoga Road and drive to Lodoga and Lodoga-Stonyford Road. Turn left and loop around East Park Reservoir to reach Stonyford and Fouts Spring Road (Road M10). Turn west and drive 25 miles to a signed access road for Summit Spring trailhead. Turn right and drive 1.5 miles to the parking area and trailhead, at the end of the road.

Contact: Mendocino National Forest, Stonyford Work Center, Stonyford, 530/963-3128, www.fs.usda.gov/mendocino.

16 ALDER CREEK TRAIL

4.0 mi/1.75 hr

in Manchester State Park north of Point Arena

Map 4.3, page 167

The Alder Creek Trail starts by the park headquarters for Manchester State Park. The trail is routed past Lake Davis to the beach, then continues north along the beach to the mouth of Alder Creek. This is a coastal lagoon that attracts many species of shorebirds, including, though rarely, whistling swans. It's also the area where the San Andreas Fault heads off from land into the sea.

Time it right here and all can seem perfect. Manchester State Park has two moods: one is sweet and one is foul. In late summer, fall, and late winter, radiant sunbeams set the Mendocino coast aglow, making for flawless beach walks. But in early summer, winds often blast out of the northwest and it can feel as if your head could blow off. Good thing it's attached at the neck (well, at least for most people). In midsummer, fog smothers the coast about every morning.

User Groups: Hikers and horses. No dogs. The terrain isn't suitable for mountain bikes. No wheelchair facilities.

Permits: No permits are required. Parking and access are free.

Maps: A brochure and trail map is available for a fee at Manchester State Park. For a topographic map, ask the USGS for Point Arena.

Directions: From Point Arena, take Highway 1 north for five miles to Kinney Lane. Turn left and drive one mile to the park entrance, on the right.

Contact: Manchester State Park, 707/882-2463, Mendocino, 707/937-5804, www.parks.ca.gov.

17 HEADLANDS LOOP

1.5 mi/0.75 hr

in Gualala Point Regional Park on the Sonoma coast

Map 4.3, page 167

The Headlands (to beach) Loop is an easy, short walk. It provides coastal views with a short cutoff on a spur trail. It also furnishes a lookout over the Gualala River and a route amid giant coastal cypress trees. From the visitors center, the trail is routed along the Gualala River and then turns and loops to the left. Here you can take the short cutoff trail that leads to the beach. On the way back, the trail traces the ocean bluffs for a short spell. For coastal views, take the spur trail to a lookout. Then the main trail turns inland and returns to the visitors center. Bonuses here include excellent whale-watching during the winter and good wildflower blooms on the grassy hillsides in spring. It is mostly level. The trailhead elevation is 250 feet.

User Groups: Hikers and dogs. No horses.

Permits: No permits are required. There is a parking fee of $7 per vehicle.

Maps: For a topographic map, ask the USGS for Gualala.

Directions: From Gualala, drive south on Highway 1 for 0.25 mile (over the Gualala River) and turn west into the park entrance. Continue to the visitors center.

Contact: Gualala Point Regional Park, Gualala, CA 95445, 707/785-2377, http://parks.sonomacounty.ca.gov.

18 LAKE SONOMA SOUTHLAKE TRAIL

5.2 mi/2.0 hr

at Lake Sonoma northwest of Healdsburg

Map 4.3, page 167

This trail provides the best introduction to Lake Sonoma, unless, that is, you have a boat and take advantage of the boat-in campsites. The Southlake Trail starts off of Stewart's Point Road below the Overlook. The short trail at the Overlook provides spectacular views of the lake. But that's what you get on this trail almost the entire way. The trail winds along the southwestern portion of Warm Springs Arm through gray pine and madrone woodlands. It traces alongside the lake, enters and exits a series of small groves, and extends along the lake's fingers. At 2.7 miles, you'll reach Quicksilver Campground—it's the easiest hike to any lakeside campground at Lake Sonoma. A few trails bisect the route and extend into more-remote surrounding country, allowing ambitious hikers to create longer adventures. When you've had enough, just turn back.

The trail is not very steep, but does have some changes in elevation. It features sun exposure, making it great for wildflowers in the spring but very hot on summer afternoons. Most of the habitat is oak grasslands, and on rare occasion you may see deer, and in summer, rattlesnakes.

User Groups: Hikers, dogs, and horses. No mountain bikes. No wheelchair facilities.

Permits: No permits are required. Parking and access are free.

Maps: For a free map, go to the visitors center or contact the U.S. Corps of Engineers. For a topographic map, ask the USGS for Warm Springs Dam.

Directions: From Santa Rosa, take U.S. 101 north for 12 miles to the exit for Healdsburg and Dry Creek Road. Take that exit, turn left on Dry Creek Road and drive about 11 miles (crossing Dry Creek; Dry Creek Road becomes Skaggs Springs Road; continue past visitors center) to Skaggs Springs-Stewarts Point Road. Turn left and drive 0.25 mile to a trailhead spur road. Turn right and drive a short distance to the trailhead on the left.

Contact: U.S. Army Corps of Engineers, Lake Sonoma, Geyserville, 707/431-4590; visitors center 707/431-4533, www.spn.usace.army.mil.

19 SALT POINT BLUFF TRAIL
3.5 mi/1.5 hr   🥾1   ⛰10

in Salt Point State Park north of Jenner

Map 4.3, page 167

The dramatic, rocky shoreline of Salt Point State Park is memorable to anyone who has seen it. This trail provides the best look at it, including some simply awesome views from a 100-foot-high ocean bluff. The trailhead is at the parking area set near the tip of Salt Point. From here, hike north over Warren Creek, a seasonal stream, and then continue across the bluffs. You can practically feel the crashing of ocean breakers below you, the spray rocketing skyward. The trail eventually winds around and down to Stump Beach Cove, a pretty, sandy beach where the calm waters are in sharp contrast to the nearby mauling ocean breakers. Salt Point State Park is known for excellent sport abalone diving in season, and also for providing a marine reserve, Gerstle Cove, where no form of marine life may be taken or disturbed. This park is stellar.

User Groups: Hikers only. Horses are allowed on designated trails only, and mountain bikes are allowed only on fire roads. One trail (Gerstle Cove) is paved for wheelchairs for 100 yards out to Salt Point. No dogs.

Permits: No permits are required. A state park day-use fee of $8 is charged per vehicle.

Maps: A trail map is available for a fee from

© SABRINA YOUNG

Salt Point Bluff Trail

Salt Point State Park. For a topographic map, ask the USGS for Plantation.

Directions: From Santa Rosa, take U.S. 101 north to the exit for River Road. Take that exit, turn left on River Road and drive 13 miles to Highway 116 and Guerneville. Turn right on Highway 116 and drive to Highway 1 at Jenner. Turn north on Highway 1 and drive 20 miles (nine miles past Fort Ross) to the park entrance. Turn left (west) and drive to the entrance kiosk. The trailhead is at the Salt Point parking area.

Contact: Salt Point State Park, Jenner, 707/847-3221, www.parks.ca.gov.

20 SENTINEL ROCK/ FISK MILL COVE
4.0 mi/2.5 hr   🏃1 ⛰10

in Salt Point State Park north of Jenner

Map 4.3, page 167

Fisk Mill Cove is a beautiful spot at Salt Point State Park. It provides a great whale-watching spot. The best strategy is to enter the trail at the north end and then venture to the wooden deck at Sentinel Rock. Take in the sweeping views across the ocean and below to Fisk Mill Cove. From here, the trail ventures south two miles to Stump Beach Cove. When you roam about at the park, always keep an eye out. On the coastal bluffs, this is one of the better locations anywhere for a chance to see a badger.

User Groups: Hikers only. Horses are allowed on designated trails only, and mountain bikes are allowed only on fire roads. No dogs.

Permits: No permits are required. A state park day-use fee of $8 is charged per vehicle.

Maps: A trail map is available for a fee from Salt Point State Park. For a topographic map, ask the USGS for Plantation.

Directions: From Santa Rosa, take U.S. 101 north to the exit for River Road. Take that exit, turn left on River Road and drive 13 miles to Highway 116 and Guerneville. Turn right on Highway 116 and drive to Highway 1 at Jenner. Turn north on Highway 1 and drive 20 miles (nine miles past Fort Ross) to the park entrance.

Continue north (past main park entrance on your left) for about three miles to signed parking area on left for Sentinel Rock (and on right for Kruse Rhododendron State Natural Reserve). Turn left to parking and trailhead.

Contact: Salt Point State Park, Jenner, 707/847-3221, www.parks.ca.gov.

21 STOCKOFF CREEK LOOP
1.25 mi/0.75 hr   🏃1 ⛰8

in Stillwater Cove Regional Park north of Jenner

Map 4.3, page 167

The trailhead is located at the day-use parking lot, and after starting the walk, you'll enter a gorgeous forest of firs and redwoods. You then come to the Loop Trail junction, where you turn right. The trail is then routed along the creek, crosses a few bridges, and eventually rises above the watershed and loops back through forest to the parking area. It's an easy, pretty, and secluded loop hike.

Must-do side trip: Cross Highway 1 to see Stillwater Cove, a dramatic rock-strewn shore. Highway 1 is one of the top tourist drives in the United States, which explains why the coastal state parks get such heavy use in the summer months. This little regional park, however, is sometimes overlooked by out-of-state traffic.

User Groups: Hikers and dogs. No horses or mountain bikes. No wheelchair facilities.

Permits: No permits are required. A day-use fee of $7 is charged for each vehicle.

Maps: For a free brochure, contact Stillwater Cove Regional Park. For a topographic map, ask the USGS for Plantation.

Directions: From Santa Rosa, take U.S. 101 north to the exit for River Road. Take that exit, turn left on River Road and drive 13 miles to Highway 116 and Guerneville. Go right on Highway 116 and drive to Highway 1. Turn right and head north, past the town of Jenner, for 16 miles to the park entrance, on the right at mile marker 37.01.

Contact: Stillwater Cove Regional Park,

County of Sonoma, Santa Rosa, 707/847-3245; Regional Parks Department, 707/565-2041, http://parks.sonomacounty.ca.gov.

22 BODEGA HEAD LOOP
1.5 mi/1.0 hr

on the Sonoma coast west of Bodega Bay

Map 4.3, page 167

Pick a calm, clear evening with scarcely a breeze and the view here at sunset can be so poignant that it can touch your heart at the memories of all the things you've let slip through your fingers. It's that kind of place. The short loop hike at Bodega Head will provide an introduction to one of California's great coastal areas for an easy hike and views that can set off feelings that you will never forget. The trail starts at the east parking lot, and in just 1.5 miles, you get views of cliffs and untouched beaches. And then it is on southward for views of the sea and beyond. For a side trip, take a short tromp on a spur trail to the tip-top of Bodega Head for 360-degree views. Rarely does the ocean seem so vast as it does here. The North Farallon Island looks like you could reach it with a running leap. A few notes about the weather: In spring and early summer, the wind can really howl out of the northwest. In late summer, fall, or late winter, between storms, Bodega Bay gets its warmest, and often most wind-free, weather. Whale-watching is great from January through April. But it's the sunsets here that you'll never forget.

User Groups: Hikers only. No horses, dogs, or mountain bikes. No wheelchair facilities.

Permits: No permits are required. Parking and access are free.

Maps: A trail map and brochure are available for a fee from Sonoma Coast State Beach.

Directions: Take U.S. 101 to Petaluma and the exit for East Washington. Take that exit to East Washington. Turn west and drive through Petaluma (it becomes Bodega Avenue) for about 10 miles to Valley Ford Road. Bear right and drive 7.5 miles to Highway 1. Turn north on Highway 1 and drive nine miles to Bodega Bay

and continue to East Shore Road. Turn left on East Shore Road and drive less than 0.5 mile to a stop sign at Bay Flat Road. Turn right and drive five miles around Bodega Bay (the road turns into West Side Road). Continue past Spud Point Marina and drive to the Bodega Head parking area.

Contact: Sonoma Coast State Beach, Bodega Bay, 707/875-3483, www.parks.ca.gov.

23 BLUE RIDGE TRAIL TO FISKE PEAK
8.0 mi/4.0 hr

north of Lake Berryessa

Map 4.4, page 168

You climb 2,100 feet in four miles to gain the ridge at Fiske Peak. In the process, your pay-off is a fantastic view into the Cache Creek Canyon, Capay Valley, and to the county's peaks. The hike starts along Rayhouse Road/Road 40 (see directions). It starts as a road a short ways to a sign for the Blue Ridge Trail. Thus your adventure begins, and in turn, so does the climb. It's an aerobic thumper for three miles to the ridge; Fiske Peak isn't really much of a peak, and you have to continue about 15 minutes to find it. The Blue Ridge climbs the hilltop rim that splits Yolo and Napa Counties. In spring wildflowers are ablaze and bushes and trees in full bloom, and clear skies provide long-distance views. You'll see songbirds, swallows, falcons, and eagles flitting, hovering, and soaring. There is also a good share of lizards and rattlesnakes.

User Groups: Hikers and dogs. Horses and mountain bikes, while allowed, aren't recommended because of the steep, rocky terrain. No wheelchair facilities.

Permits: No permits are required. Parking and access are free.

Maps: For a free primitive trail map, contact the Bureau of Land Management. For a topographic map, ask the USGS for Glascock.

Directions: From Sacramento, take I-5 north to Woodland and the exit for Highway 16. Take that exit, turn west on Highway 16 and drive about 45 miles (into the Capay Valley along Cache Creek) to County Road 40 (near Yolo County Park). Turn left on County Road 40 (a gravel road) and drive 0.25 mile and look for a concrete bridge (low water crossing). Continue over the bridge and drive 200 yards and look for the trailhead on the left. Park in the unpaved area near Cache Creek and walk down the dirt road through a meadow to the trailhead. In the winter, the dirt road is blocked by a locked gate; park instead at Lower Yolo County Park and walk down to the trailhead. Note that during the winter, the bridge is at times impassable due to high water.

Contact: Bureau of Land Management, Ukiah Field Office, Ukiah, 707/468-4000, www.ca.blm.gov.

24 GILLIAM CREEK TRAIL
8.9 mi/1 day   🚶3 ⛰8

in Austin Creek State Recreation Area north of Guerneville

Map 4.4, page 168

The Gilliam Creek Trail is very pretty in late winter and spring. For much of the route, the trail parallels Gilliam Creek amid shaded oak woodlands. The area has more of a wilderness feel than most parks in this habitat because you drive through redwoods to get here, and in addition, the final 2.5 miles of access road is narrow and twisty. The trailhead elevation is 1,100 feet. You contour across the slope, then drop down to the headwaters of Schoolhouse Creek, at 400 feet. The trail then follows the stream, past the confluence with Gilliam Creek, and extends 3.7 miles into the backcountry, all the way down to an elevation of 200 feet. At the confluence of East Austin Creek, the best way to do it is to turn right and hike deeper into wild, hilly country along the stream. Then return on the loop on East Austin Creek Trail, a fire road with a—yep, by now you should have figured this out—long climb. At this point, you may ask, "Are we having fun yet?" Visitors who

love Armstrong Redwoods tend not to speak of the adjoining Austin Creek Recreation Area with any terms of endearment.

The rolling hills, open forests, and stream-side riparian habitat in Austin Creek State Recreation Area can seem a million miles away from the forests of Armstrong Redwoods. Yet the two parks together actually form 6,488 acres of contiguous parkland. While most tourists are walking around the redwoods at Armstrong, this trail offers a quiet and ambitious alternative.

User Groups: Hikers and horses (no horses permitted during wet weather). Mountain bikes permitted on fire roads. No dogs. No wheelchair facilities.

Permits: No permits are required. A state park day-use fee of $8 is charged for each vehicle. A senior discount is available.

Maps: A trail map is available for a fee from Armstrong Redwoods State Reserve. For a topographic map, ask the USGS for Guerneville.

Directions: From Santa Rosa, take U.S. 101 north to the exit for River Road. Take that exit, turn left on River Road and drive 13 miles to Highway 116 and Guerneville. Turn right on Highway 116 and drive a short distance to Armstrong Woods Road. Turn right (north) on Armstrong Woods Road and drive into Armstrong Redwoods State Reserve entrance, then continue about four miles into adjoining Austin Creek Recreation Area and to the trailhead. The last 2.5 miles are twisty and narrow; no trailers or vehicles more than 20 feet long are permitted.

Contact: Armstrong Redwoods State Reserve, Guerneville, 707/869-2015, www.parks.ca.gov.

25 EAST RIDGE TRAIL
6.8 mi/4.0 hr   🚶3 ⛰7

in Armstrong Redwoods State Natural Reserve north of Guerneville

Map 4.4, page 168

The East Ridge Trail rises 1,400 feet over the course of 3.4 miles. Your reward is a series of lookouts over the top of a sea of redwoods below. The trailhead is at an elevation of 200 feet, adjacent to Fife Creek. The route climbs gradually at first, then in the first 0.5 mile rises to cross the headwaters of Fife Creek, at an elevation of 600 feet. Your climb has only just begun, and if you're already running out of gas, you'd best head back. The trail continues climbing all the way, contouring its way up toward McCray Mountain (1,940 feet), and tops out at a service road at 1,600 feet.

For short strolls through the park's redwoods, take the Discovery Trail or Armstrong Nature Trail in Armstrong Redwoods.

User Groups: Hikers and horses. No dogs or mountain bikes. No wheelchair facilities.

Permits: No permits are required. A state park day-use fee of $8 is charged for each vehicle. A senior discount is available.

Maps: A trail map is available for a fee from Armstrong Redwoods State Reserve. For a topographic map, ask the USGS for Guerneville.

Directions: From Santa Rosa, take U.S. 101 north to the exit for River Road. Take that exit, turn left on River Road and drive 13 miles to Highway 116 and Guerneville. Go right on Highway 116 and drive a short distance to Armstrong Woods Road. Turn right (north) on Armstrong Woods Road and drive 2.5 miles to the Armstrong Redwoods State Reserve entrance. The trailhead is adjacent to the visitors center.

Contact: Armstrong Redwoods State Natural Reserve, Guerneville, 707/869-2015, www.parks.ca.gov.

26 MOUNT ST. HELENA TRAIL

10.2 mi/4.5 hr

🥾 4 ⛰️ 10

in Robert Louis Stevenson State Park north of Calistoga

Map 4.4, page 168

Mount St. Helena is Sonoma County's highest mountain. This is the peak that strikes such a memorable silhouette when viewed from the

Bay Area. This trail climbs to the 4,343-foot summit and requires an ascent of 2,068 feet over the course of five miles. On the crystal days of early spring, the views can make life seem complete. On the best days, 150 miles to the east, you can see the snow glisten white on the Sierra Crest. Closer to home, Mount Tamalapis and Mount Diablo rise up to the south in the Bay Area. Lake Berryessa is below to the east and the Napa Valley plunges to the south. Several times in the spring, we've seen the clear outline of Lassen Peak to the northeast.

The Mount St. Helena trail starts along Highway 29 at the ridge above the Calistoga Valley. From the trailhead, the route emerges from oak woodlands on a dirt service road. The climb is a steady pull, with two steep spots. Four miles in, continue straight at a junction to the North Peak (a left will take you instead to 4,003-foot South Peak).

Strong hikers will make the summit in about 2.5 to 3 hours, with the last half hour strenuous, and then for the easy return trip, sail down in about 1.5 to 2 hours. In spring, bring a windbreaker for often chilly breezes out of the north on top, and a change of shirt; you will likely sweat through whatever you are wearing on the climb, especially if you carry a pack.

Visibility is best in spring, when north winds clear the air, showcasing remarkable views in all directions. Bill Grummer, a ranger pal, claims that on the best days visitors can see Mount Shasta (192 miles away), but so far we haven't had that experience. However, it is documented that in the late 19th century, surveyors sent signals back and forth between here and Mount Shasta, setting a record for longest signal distance. On other stellar days, you can see the Farallon Islands, 25 miles offshore from San Francisco, and a glimpse of the city itself (but not the Golden Gate Bridge).

History lesson: The park is named "Robert Louis Stevenson State Park" because in 1880, this is where Stevenson, the author of *Treasure Island*, spent his summer honeymoon in a cabin (long since gone). The cabin site is off a spur (hikers only), 1.5 miles in, marked along the trail to the top.

In the summer, the hike can be pure hell: Much of the trail is actually a fire road with little shade, there's no water anywhere along the route, and the heat commonly blazes in the 90s and 100s out here.

After logging weather records for years, we have found the most likely time for Mount St. Helena to receive snow is just before a full moon in February.

User Groups: Hikers only on single-track trail. Mountain bikes allowed on a nearby fire road 0.25 mile north on Highway 29. No dogs or horses. No wheelchair facilities.

Permits: No permits are required. Parking and access are free.

Maps: A brochure and map are available at the park for a fee. For topographic maps, ask the USGS for Detert Reservoir and Mount St. Helena.

Directions: From Calistoga, take Highway 29 north for eight miles to the parking area at the highway summit, signed Robert Louis Stevenson State Park. The trailhead is next to the parking area. You can park on the east or west side of the road. The trail is located on the west side of the road (the trailhead is not signed from the road).

Contact: Robert Louis Stevenson State Park, c/o Bothe-Napa Valley State Park, 707/942-4575; www.parks.ca.gov; Calistoga info, 866/306-5588, www.visitcalistoga.com.

27 PALISADES TRAIL
4.0-9.5 mi one-way/2.0-4.0 hr

👥3 ⛰9

near Calistoga

Map 4.4, page 168

This trip can be done three ways: A 4-mile round-trip to Table Rock and back, an 8-mile round-trip to the southern edge of the Palisades and back (recommended), or a wild 9.5-mile one-way trek (with a shuttle car) down to the valley. The Palisades? Aren't the Palisades a glacier-carved series of 14,000-foot peaks in the Sierra Nevada? Well, yep, but Napa County's Palisades are nearly as dramatic and accessible year-round: It's a stunning, mile-long volcanic wall set along a ridge that overlooks Calistoga and the Napa Valley. The Palisades are dramatic up close and personal, and provide gorgeous long-distance views. In addition, this trail is one of the best near Calistoga for seeing raptors, including a chance to spot peregrine falcons, and also for wildflowers, particularly bitterroot.

From Calistoga, it's a twisty, eight-mile drive up Highway 29 to the parking area and trailhead, the same staging area used for the Mount St. Helena Trail. It is signed Robert Louis Stevenson State Park. To hike to Table Rock and the Palisades, the trailhead is on the right (southeast) side of the road.

From the southeast side of the parking area (elevation 2,250 feet), you start this hike on the Table Rock Trail. It's about two miles to Table Rock (2,465 feet), just enough of a climb to get you above the canyon woodlands. Some enjoy the views from atop Table Rock, have a picnic, and then head back to the car. But the trip gets better by continuing on the Palisades Trail. This drops down to Lasky Point (2,045 feet), and then climbs back up for about two miles along the base of the Palisades (2,930 feet). The trail is spectacular, set just beneath the sheer volcanic cliffs along the ridge. At 3.9 miles in, you will reach the junction of Historic Oat Hill Mine Road, a long-abandoned, rocky jeep road. Most people turn around and head back from here.

Oat Hill Mine Road is the route down to the valley for a one-way hike with a shuttle. But it plummets 2,000 feet over 4.5 miles, some of it rocky, and can be a thigh-burning, knee-wrenching, toe-jamming experience that's only for the deranged (like us, for instance).

Calistoga is one of the best decompression chambers designed by mankind. But after a day or two of getting turned into Jell-O by soaks in steaming mineral water, massages, and mud baths, you can be brought back to life by the electrifying hike to the Palisades.

The best time for this getaway is from mid-March through mid-May, when the foothills are green, the skies are often crystal-clear, and the morning air is still cool. There is no drinking water available anywhere on the trail. Rangers warn not to leave valuables in your car (covering them with a jacket or blanket isn't enough, either).

User Groups: Hikers only. No dogs, horses, or mountain bikes. No wheelchair facilities.

Permits: Parking and access are free.

Maps: A brochure and map are available for a fee at the park or by mail. For topographic maps, ask the USGS for Detert Reservoir and Mount St. Helena.

Directions: From Calistoga, take Highway 29 north for eight miles to the parking area at the highway summit, signed Robert Louis Stevenson State Park. The trailhead is on the right (southeast) side of the road.

Contact: Robert Louis Stevenson State Park, c/o Bothe-Napa Valley State Park, Calistoga, 707/942-4575, www.parks.ca.gov.

28 COYOTE PEAK/ REDWOOD TRAIL LOOP

4.4 mi/3.0 hr 🏃2 ⛰8

in Bothe-Napa Valley State Park south of Calistoga

Map 4.4, page 168

The best way to see the surprise redwoods and pretty creek at Bothe-Napa Valley State Park is on the Coyote Peak/Redwood Trail Loop. Start just past the Ritchey Creek Campground turnoff, near the picnic area. The first 0.5 mile is on the Ritchey Canyon Trail, a very pretty stretch of trail along beautiful Ritchey Creek. Then bear left on the Redwood Trail. You'll be surrounded by some of the park's highest stands of redwoods. The trail continues along Ritchey Creek for 0.25 mile, then connects to the Coyote Peak Trail. Take the Coyote Peak Trail, which rises quickly, skirting the northern

flank of Coyote Peak. (A short spur trail will take you all the way to the top, elevation 1,170 feet.) Then the trail drops down the other side of the hill and intersects with South Fork Trail, which heads all the way back down to Ritchey Creek. From the trailhead to the end of the hike, the elevation gain is roughly 800 feet, totaling the up-and-downs.

Who ever heard of redwoods in the Napa Valley? Who ever heard of a mountain peak there, too? Only those who also know of Bothe-Napa Valley State Park, which is like an island of wildland in a sea of winery tourist traffic. Bothe-Napa has some of the most easterly stands of coastal redwoods, plus Douglas fir and an excellent lookout from Coyote Peak, all quite a surprise for newcomers. Note that temperatures can be extremely hot in the summer—as high as 105 degrees in unshaded areas—but you'll find a cool paradise along Ritchey Creek.

User Groups: Hikers only. Horses permitted on some designated trails. Mountain bikes allowed on fire roads and designated trails but not on most of this described loop. No dogs. No wheelchair facilities.

Permits: No permits are required. A state park fee of $8 is charged per vehicle.

Maps: A brochure and trail map are available for a fee. For a topographic map, ask the USGS for Calistoga.

Directions: From Calistoga, take Highway 29 south for about five miles to the park entrance on the right side of the road. Turn right and drive past the entrance station to just past the Ritchey Creek Campground turnoff (near the picnic area), where there is trailhead parking.

Contact: Bothe-Napa Valley State Park, Calistoga, 707/942-4575, www.parks.ca.gov.

29 SPRING LAKE TRAIL

2.0 mi/1.0 hr 🏃1 ⛰6

in Spring Lake Regional Park in Santa Rosa

Map 4.4, page 168

Spring Lake is Santa Rosa's backyard fishing

hole, a popular place for trout fishing, an evening picnic, or a short hike. For newcomers, we suggest you take the walk along the west shore of Spring Lake. From the parking area, start this trip by walking along the shore to Spring Lake's west dam. Then turn left and head into adjoining Howarth Park and on to Lake Ralphine. It's an easy, enjoyable stroll. The lake is stocked with trout in winter and spring, and it provides a fair fishery for bass in the summer. The lake is fun and quiet, with boats restricted to electric motors; no gas motors are allowed. The elevation is 300 feet, and the trail is mostly level.

User Groups: Hikers and dogs. Horses are allowed only on designated trails. The park has 2.3 miles of trail that are paved for wheelchair and bicycle use.

Permits: No permits are required. There is a parking fee of $7 per vehicle.

Maps: A free trail map is available from Spring Lake Regional Park. For a topographic map, ask the USGS for Santa Rosa.

Directions: From Santa Rosa, take Highway 12 east (it becomes Hoen Avenue) to Newanga Avenue. Turn left on Newanga Avenue and drive 0.5 mile to the park entrance. The various trailheads are well marked and easily accessible from the parking area at the lake.

Contact: Spring Lake Regional Park, c/o Sonoma County Regional Parks, Santa Rosa, 707/539-8092; Sonoma County Regional Parks Department, 707/565-2041, http://parks.sonomacounty.ca.gov.

30 BALD MOUNTAIN LOOP
8.2 mi/1 day   🚶3 ⛰️8

in Sugarloaf Ridge State Park north of Sonoma

Map 4.4, page 168

Bald Mountain, elevation 2,729 feet, overlooks the Napa Valley, with Mount St. Helena to the north. The old mountain is the centerpiece of Sugarloaf Ridge State Park, a 4,020-acre park featuring redwoods in the Sonoma Creek watershed, open meadows peppered with oaks on the hilltops, and some chaparral on ridges. On clear days from the summit, you can see portions of the San Francisco Bay Area and then be thankful you're here instead.

The most ambitious hike in the park is the Bald Mountain Loop, an 8.2-mile trek. The trail starts at the parking lot and then is routed into a loop by linking the Bald Mountain, Gray Pine, Brushy Peaks, and Meadow Trails. Many less-demanding hikes are available in the park, but this route will give hikers the greatest sense of the park's wildest lands. It's best hiked in the spring, when the air is still cool, the hills are green, and the wildflowers are in bloom.

There's a bonus as well: When Sonoma Creek is really flowing, a 25-foot waterfall set in a wooded canyon tumbles downstream from the campground; a short trail is available from the park's entrance road, located at an unsigned turnout on the road's shoulder. A more formal route to the waterfall is on Canyon Trail.

User Groups: Hikers only. Horses are allowed on trails in summer and on fire roads in the park in winter. No dogs. No wheelchair facilities.

Permits: No permits are required. A state park day-use fee of $8 is charged for each vehicle.

Maps: A trail map and brochure are available for a fee from Sugarloaf Ridge State Park. For a topographic map, ask the USGS for Kenwood.

Directions: From Santa Rosa, take Highway 12 east through Kenwood to Adobe Canyon Road. Turn left on Adobe Canyon Road and drive 3.5 miles to the main park entrance at the end of the road.

Contact: Sugarloaf Ridge State Park, 2605 Adobe Canyon Road, Kenwood, CA 95452, 707/833-5712, www.parks.ca.gov.

31 RIDGE TRAIL/NORTH SONOMA MOUNTAIN

8.0 mi/3.5 hr   👫3 ⛰8

in Sonoma Mountain Regional Park east of Rohnert Park

Map 4.4, page 168

From the Ridge Trail on North Sonoma Mountain, you will discover why the newest park in the greater Bay Area can appeal to anybody across the region. Two miles in, you emerge above a hardwood forest for a towering view across Santa Rosa and beyond. To the north is Bennett Valley and Sonoma Valley, backed by a horizon of peaks: Taylor Mountain, Bennett Peak, Hood Mountain, Sugarloaf Ridge, and Mount St. Helena. You'll never forget it. It will change how you feel how Sonoma County and the wine country.

This new trail was opened in 2015, part of a new stretch of the Bay Ridge Trail, which links North Sonoma Mountain to Jack London State Park. From parking lot to parking lot, you can now complete an eight-mile trek, one-way with a shuttle car. Another highlight is the first public access to the north side of Sonoma Mountain.

To get to the trailhead, you drive out of Petaluma to Penngrove and then to the northern flank of Sonoma Mountain.

The marquee trail is the Ridge Trail, which starts at about 1,000-foot elevation. The trail starts near the South Fork Matanzas Creek, a riparian zone with redwoods and fern understory, always a surprise to newcomers. At the footbridge for the Ridge Trail, two picnic tables are available along Matanzas Creek. About a half-mile in, you get views of nearby fields and beyond to Bennett Peak, and then enter oak woodlands. You then start to climb, about 700 feet over the span of about 1.5 miles, and emerge for sweeping lookouts across Santa Rosa far below and to a ridge-lined horizon with many famous peaks. The silhouette of 4,341-foot Mount St. Helena in the Mayacamas Mountain is the classic landmark for the region. So is Sugarloaf Ridge to the east, the familiar mountain that crowns Sugarloaf Ridge State Park.

As parkland, the headwaters of Matanzas Creek, a surprise grove of redwoods and a large swath of oak woodlands, will now be protected. It will also provide a contiguous wildlife corridor. On the ground, mountain lions and bobcats are at the top of the food chain, and in the air, you might see golden eagles, falcons, and hawks.

User Groups: Hikers and horses only. No dogs or mountain bikes. No wheelchair facilities.

Permits: A parking fee of $7 is charged each vehicle at a self-pay station; free for Sonoma County Regional Park members.

Maps: Small map available at trailhead kiosk; PDF online at http://parks.sonomacounty.ca.gov/.

Directions: From San Francisco, take U.S. 101 north to Petaluma and continue to the exit for Old Redwood Highway (toward Penngrove). Take that exit to Old Redwood Highway. Turn right and drive 1.5 miles to Petaluma Hill Road. Turn right and drive 2.3 miles to Roberts Road. Turn right and drive 1.3 miles, and continue onto Pressley Road and drive 2.9 miles to Sonoma Mountain Road. Turn right onto Sonoma Mountain Road and continue to park entrance on the right.

Contact: Sonoma County Regional Parks, 707/565-2041, http://parks.sonomacounty.ca.gov.

SACRAMENTO AND GOLD COUNTRY

© TOM STIENSTRA

The Sacramento Valley is a landscape filled with rivers—the Sacramento, Feather, Yuba, American, and Mokelumne—providing both recreation and habitat for wildlife refuges. This is an area for California history buffs, with Placerville KOA and nearby Malakoff Diggins State Historic Park in the center of some of the state's most extraordinary history: the gold rush era. The highlight of foothill country is its series of great lakes—Camanche, Rollins, Oroville—for water sports, fishing, and recreation. In the Mother Lode country, three lakes—Camanche, Amador, and Pardee—are outstanding for fishing. Spring and fall are gorgeous, as are summer evenings, but there are always periods of 100°F-plus temperatures in the summer. But that's what gives these lakes and rivers such appeal. On a hot day, jumping into a cool lake is more valuable than gold.

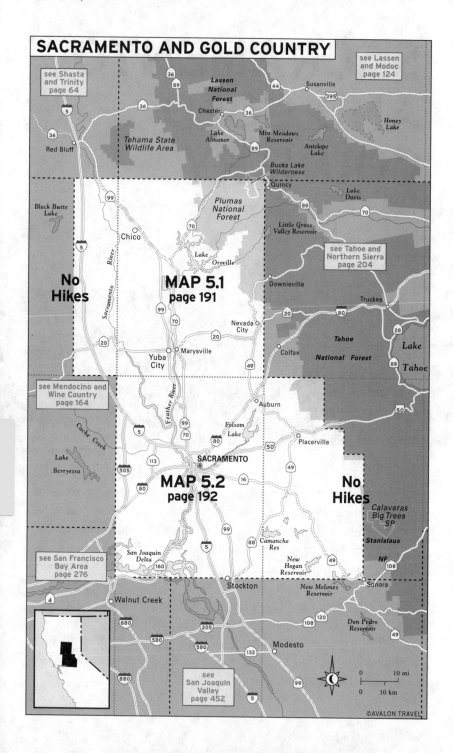

SACRAMENTO AND GOLD COUNTRY

see Shasta and Trinity page 64

see Lassen and Modoc page 124

Lassen National Forest

36
89

44

Susanville

395

Chester

36

36

Red Bluff

36

Tehama State Wildlife Area

Lake Almanor

Mtn Meadows Reservoir

Antelope Lake

Honey Lake

89

Black Butte Lake

99

Bucks Lake Wilderness

Quincy

Plumas National Forest

Lake Davis

70

Chico

70

Little Grass Valley Reservoir

89

No Hikes

Sacramento River

Lake Oroville

MAP 5.1 page 191

Downieville

see Tahoe and Northern Sierra page 204

99

70

Nevada City

20

Truckee

80

28

Marysville

20

49

Colfax

Tahoe National Forest

89

Lake Tahoe

Yuba City

see Mendocino and Wine Country page 164

Feather River

Auburn

50

5

99

70

Folsom Lake

Placerville

Cache Creek

80

113

SACRAMENTO

50

49

No Hikes

Lake Berryessa

505

MAP 5.2 page 192

16

Calaveras Big Trees SP

80

Stanislaus NF

see San Francisco Bay Area page 276

99

5

88

Camanche Res

49

108

San Joaquin Delta

160

New Hogan Reservoir

Stockton

New Melones Reservoir

Sonora

4

Walnut Creek

680

205

108

120

Don Pedro Reservoir

49

580

580

132

Modesto

880

see San Joaquin Valley page 452

5

99

0   10 mi

0   10 km

©AVALON TRAVEL

Map 5.1

Sites 1-8
Pages 193-197

5.2

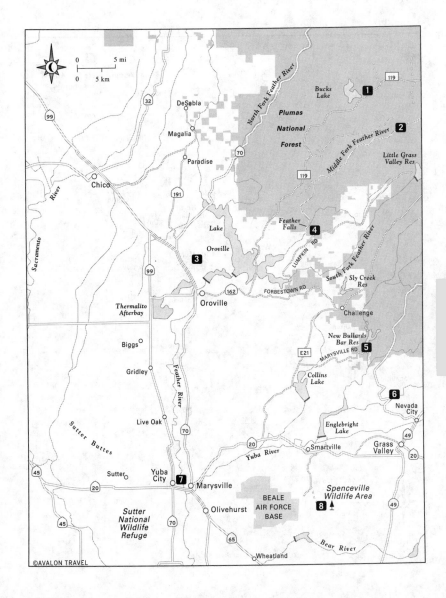

Map 5.2

Sites 9-13
Pages 198-201

1 BUCKS SUMMIT TO FEATHER RIVER (PCT)

20.0 mi one-way/2 days 🚶3 ⛰8

at Bucks Summit Trailhead at the southern boundary of the Bucks Lake Wilderness west of Quincy

Map 5.1, page 191

It's 20 miles from Bucks Summit to Belden, all of it on the Pacific Crest Trail through the Bucks Lake Wilderness. The trail passes across a granitic-based alpine area, where forest is interspersed with glacier-smoothed rock peaks. The trailhead is at Bucks Summit (elevation 5,531 feet), and from here, the route generally follows the ridgeline for many miles, climbing to the southern flank of Mount Pleasant, at 6,924 feet. Along the way, you'll see a short spur trail to little Rock Lake. The trail heads past Three Lakes, where another spur trail provides another option, this one to Kellogg Lake. From here, the trail begins descending and then drops very sharply all the way down to 2,310 feet, to the North Fork Feather River at Belden.

To continue north on the Pacific Crest Trail (PCT), see the *Feather River to Humboldt Summit (PCT)* hike, in the *Lassen and Modoc* chapter. If you are walking this trail in reverse, see the *Fowler Peak to Bucks Summit (PCT)* hike, in the *Tahoe and Northern Sierra* chapter, to continue south.

User Groups: Hikers, dogs, and horses. No mountain bikes. No wheelchair access.

Permits: A wilderness permit (free) is required. Parking and access are free.

Maps: For a map, ask the U.S. Forest Service for Plumas National Forest. For a topographic map, ask the USGS for Bucks Lake.

Directions: Take Highway 89 to Quincy and Bucks Lake Road. Turn west on Bucks Lake Road and drive about 11 miles to the trailhead, at Bucks Summit.

Contact: Plumas National Forest, Mount Hough Ranger District, Quincy, 530/283-0555, www.fs.usda.gov/plumas.

2 HARTMAN BAR NATIONAL RECREATION TRAIL

4.4 mi/3.0 hr 🚶5 ⛰8

in Plumas National Forest east of Lake Oroville

Map 5.1, page 191

Hikers often pay for their pleasure. This hike involves two installments. The trail descends from the Hartman Ridge down the canyon to Hartman Bar on the Middle Fork Feather River. Going down will have your toes jamming into your boots, and the trip back can have your heart firing off like cannon shots. But waiting for you is the Middle Fork Feather, one of the prettiest streams around, and with some of the best trout fishing as well. In fact, of the hundreds of trout streams in California, the Middle Fork Feather is clearly in the top five. If you don't like to fish but would rather explore farther, a footbridge crosses the stream and climbs the other side of the canyon, meeting Catrell Creek at 0.5 mile. If you want to split the trip into two days and camp, the primitive Dan Beebe Camp is available along the river.

User Groups: Hikers, dogs, and horses. A horse corral is at the trailhead. Mountain bikes not recommended. No wheelchair facilities.

Permits: No permits are required. Parking and access are free.

Maps: For a map, ask the U.S. Forest Service for Plumas National Forest. For topographic maps, ask the USGS for Cascade and Haskins Valley.

Directions: From Oroville, drive east on Highway 162 for eight miles to Highway 174/Forbestown Road (and a junction signed Challenge/LaPorte). Turn right on Forbestown Road and drive east to Highway 120 (Quincy-LaPorte Road). Turn left and drive past LaPorte to Little Grass Valley Road. Turn left and drive a short distance to Black Rock Campground. Turn left on Forest Road 94 and drive 10 miles to Forest Road 22N42Y. Turn right and drive 0.25 mile to the parking area, at the end of the road.

Contact: Plumas National Forest, Feather River Ranger District, Oroville, 530/534-6500, www.fs.usda.gov/plumas.

3 NORTH TABLE MOUNTAIN
3.2 mi/2.5 hr 🚶3 ⛰️8

near Lake Oroville

Map 5.1, page 191

Table Mountain, with its amazing chasms and canyon, is not a mountain at all. It is a flat-topped ridge splayed by a series of dramatic gorges and a deep canyon. In spring after a heavy rain, the aquifer here can pump enough water to create a series of waterfalls in the gorges. The trail starts from the northwest corner of the Table Mountain trailhead then travels 1.6 miles to a rim. You get a sweeping view of Mill Creek and the surrounding Land of Ishi. The top of Table Mountain is on private property and you'll see the markers.

User Groups: Hikers, dogs, and horses. No mountain bikes. No wheelchair facilities.

Permits: Parking and access are free.

Maps: A trail map is available for a fee from Almanor Ranger District. For a map, ask the U.S. Forest Service for Lassen National Forest or Ishi Wilderness. For topographic maps, ask the USGS for Panther Spring and Butte Meadows.

Directions: From Sacramento, take Highway 70 north to Oroville and the exit for Grand Avenue. Turn right (east) and drive 1 mile to Table Mountain Boulevard. Turn left on Table Mountain Boulevard and go 0.1 mile to Cherokee Road. Turn right on Cherokeee Road and drive 6.3 miles to reserve. Formal access is through a small parking lot on the western side of Cherokee Road.

Contact: North Table Mountain Ecological Reserve, Department of Fish and Wildlife, Lands Program, 916/445-0411, www.wildlife.ca.gov.

4 FEATHER FALLS LOOP
9.5 mi/4.0 hr 🚶3 ⛰️10

in Plumas National Forest east of Lake Oroville

Map 5.1, page 191 **BEST ☾**

At Feather Falls, euphoria happens. From the viewing deck, perched on a knife-edged outcrop, you can take in a full frontal of 410-foot Feather Falls. Pounding water reverberates against the high walls and thunders down the canyon. It's so perfect that it can seem surreal, like it's a movie set. The side trip to the brink of the waterfall can then snap you back into the moment. From a boulder near the rim, you can watch a churning fountain of white water surge past you through a rocky gorge, pound down a chute, and then pour over the top. The air tastes clean and sparkles from the refracted mist.

The hike is not steep or hard, just long. Right from the start, the walking is easy and rhythmic. You start by sailing down a hill to a fork. Take the left fork. Just above the trail on your left, explorer types will find Indian grinding mortars in the large sandstone outcrops. You then head down the canyon, in forest, for a mile to the new bridge at Frey Creek (in a snowstorm, a tree fell on the old bridge and destroyed it). In winter, there can be unbelievable millions of migratory ladybugs at the creek. You then climb out of the canyon and hit the main trail. Turn left.

Across the main canyon, Bald Rock Dome emerges into view. It towers over the canyon like a monolith out of Yosemite. Then ahead, you will hear the thundering crash of water before you see it. At first, all you get are filtered glimpses of silver. At a signed cut-off, you turn left, and ahead, can see how a bridged catwalk leads out to the viewing deck, perched on an outcrop. Then, from the platform, you get a full frontal of Feather Falls, top to bottom. You can see straight across the canyon and watch a silver chute gush through a gorge to the brink, then sail over the top into a white plume, feathered at the edges. Awesome.

From the deck, you return to the main trail. Turn left and it's a half-mile hike to the brink. Along the stream that feeds the waterfall, you'll find several short, unsigned cut-offs down to view spots. The river pours clear and swirling through a series of pools, then churns and boils into a set of plunge pools. On a promontory rock that overlooks the brink, the Forest Service has put up a high cyclone fence to keep people from falling over the side. It's easy to spend a lot of time out here, poking around, looking for new vantage points, or just sitting a bit to watch the water go by.

On the return trip to the parking lot, to complete the loop, stay left on the main trail at the fork (right will head down to the bridge at Frey Creek). This is an easy leg stroker, with a pretty vantage point of upper Frey Cascade.

Note: For many years, Feather Falls was reported as 640 feet, the sixth highest waterfall outside of Yosemite, according to an information sheet published by the U.S. Forest Service. Several waterfall hunters, including Bryan Swan, Dean Goss, and Leon Turnbull, measured it using a laser rangefinder and clinometer and verified it at 410 feet.

User Groups: Hikers and dogs. Horses and mountain bikes permitted but not recommended. No wheelchair facilities.

Permits: No permits are required. Parking and access are free.

Maps: For a map, ask the U.S. Forest Service for Plumas National Forest or Middle Fork Feather River. For a topographic map, ask the USGS for Brush Creek.

Directions: Drive to Oroville and the exit for Oro Dam Blvd./Highway 162. Take that exit and turn east on Oro Dam Blvd./Olive Highway and drive for 1.7 miles to a stoplight (signed for Olive Highway). Turn right (still Olive Highway) and drive 6.6 miles to Forbestown Road. Turn right on Forbestown Road and go 6.2 miles to Lumpkin Road. Turn left on Lumpkin and drive 11.3 miles to signed turn for Feather Falls. Turn left and drive 1.5 miles to parking, trailhead, and campground.

Contact: Plumas National Forest, Feather River Ranger District, Oroville, 530/534-6500, www.fs.usda.gov/plumas.

Feather Falls Loop

5 BULLARDS BAR TRAIL
1-13.5 mi/0.5 hr-1 day 🥾1 ⛰7

on Bullards Bar Reservoir in Tahoe National Forest

Map 5.1, page 191

Visitors to the Dark Day Picnic Area take this trail above the shore of Bullards Bar Reservoir to Vista Point. Most folks just walk to Vista Point, then turn back. The view overlooks the lower end of the lake and the dam. You can also drive to a parking area near Vista Point and then use that as a trailhead to access the Bullards Bay Trail and hike up toward the head of the lake. This trail connects to a network of other trails that make up 23 miles of trails in this area. These include Rebel Ridge Trail, 7-Ball Trail, and 8-Ball Trail.

User Groups: Hikers, dogs, horses, and mountain bikes. No wheelchair facilities.

Permits: No permits are required. Parking and access are free.

Maps: For a map, ask the U.S. Forest Service for Tahoe National Forest. For topographic maps, ask the USGS for Camptonville and Challenge.

Directions: From Marysville, take Highway 20 east for 12 miles to Marysville Road. Turn left on Marysville Road (signed for Bullards Bar Reservoir) and drive 10 miles to Old Marysville Road. Turn right and drive 14 miles, over the dam, and continue four miles to Dark Day Road. Turn left and drive to the picnic area and trailhead.

Contact: Tahoe National Forest, Nevada City/Downieville Ranger Districts, North Yuba Ranger Station, Camptonville, 530/288-3231, www.fs.usda.gov/tahoe.

6 SOUTH YUBA INDEPENDENCE TRAIL
1.0-9.0 mi/0.5-3.0 hr   🥾1 ⛰8

near Nevada City

Map 5.1, page 191   **BEST (**

This trail is routed for 4.5 miles in and out of forest and riparian habitat with views of the Yuba River Canyon and the South Yuba river. The recommended trailhead is set at midtrail along Highway 49. That gives you the option of hiking either direction. A waterfall with a nearby water flume is a unique side attraction. From the trailhead, hike to the west to visit Rush Creek Falls and spectacular Flume 28, one mile from the trailhead. The path was originally a canal route, built in 1859 to carry water from the Yuba to a hydraulic mining site in Smartville.

This is considered the nation's first wheelchair-accessible wilderness trail; the wheelchair-accessible portion is a seven-mile round-trip. Occasionally, guided walks and gold panning demonstrations are available. In spring, we've seen guided wildflower walks as well.

User Groups: Hikers, dogs, and wheelchairs. No horses or mountain bikes.

Permits: No permits are necessary. Parking and access are free.

Maps: A brochure and map are available at the trailhead or from the Bridgeport Ranger

Station. For a topographic map, ask the USGS for Nevada City.

Directions: From Auburn, drive north on Highway 49 for 27 miles to Nevada City. Continue on Highway 49 for six miles past Nevada City to the trailhead parking area, along the highway on the right, located just before the South Yuba River Bridge. If you reach the bridge, you have gone too far.

Contact: South Yuba River State Park, 530/432-2546, www.parks.ca.gov.

7 NORTH BUTTE/ SUTTER BUTTES
3.0 mi/2.0 hr   🥾3 ⛰10

at Sutter Buttes near Yuba City

Map 5.1, page 191

From a lava pinnacle atop the Smallest Mountain Range in the World, you get a hawk's-eye view of land few have seen. This is at the Sutter Buttes, located about an hour north of Sacramento, one of California's last lands of mystery. Since it is surrounded by private land, few have trekked the Sutter Buttes and almost no one has seen Peace Valley, new state land that could become a park. To hike the Sutter Buttes, the access is with guided group walks with the Sutter Buttes Land Trust. Great folks and well worth it.

The best trip is a three-mile round-trip hike to the North Butte. It starts as an easy walk, meandering up through a valley to a sub-ridge, with a 1,000-foot climb off-trail in the last 0.5 mile. A short way in, you will see an Indian grinding rock along a dry creek bed where ancient mortars had been hollowed out in the stone. From here, hike up the valley. It's common to spot red-tailed hawks, vultures, harriers, and deer. The lucky few see fox, bobcat, owls, or golden eagles. There is no trail amid the volcanic crags, scree, and brush for the final 0.5-mile push to the summit. Instead, pick your way up to the 1,863-foot North Butte summit. From the top, you can scan across the multiple peaks, crowned by the South Butte at

2,117 feet. Despite some 38.3 million people living in California, only a scant few know this experience.

The Maidu called the Sutter Buttes "Esto Yamini," which means "Middle Mountain," and that's how the Foundation got its name. Trips are best in fall, winter, and early spring. Some may also wonder how the Sutter Buttes qualifies as "The Smallest Mountain Range in the World." The answer is that land has to have an elevation of at least 2,000 feet to qualify as a mountain. At 2,117 feet, the Sutter Buttes just barely qualify as a mountain range. There is no drive-up public access. The only trail access is through guided trips with the Middle Mountain Foundation.

User Groups: Hikers only. No dogs, horses, or mountain bikes. No wheelchair facilities.

Permits: Advance reservations for guided group hikes are required at 530/671-6116. Most trips cost $35 (suggested donation). Roughly 10-20 participants are allowed on most hikes.

Maps: A brochure and map are available from trip leaders upon meeting at the Sutter County Museum.

Directions: Hiking groups meet at the Sutter County Museum in Yuba City. Directions are provided when the reservation is confirmed. After orientation, drivers will lead the route past several locked gates to the trailhead in Sutter Buttes.

Contact: Sutter Buttes Land Trust, Yuba City, 530/755-3568; hike info, 530/671-6116, www.middlemountainhikes.org.

8 SHINGLE FALLS (FAIRY FALLS) LOOP

5.0 mi/2.5 hr

in Spenceville Wildlife Area near Smartville

Map 5.1, page 191

This is a pretty spot of surprise in the foothills of the Sacramento Valley. The falls are called Shingle Falls, Fairy Falls, Dry Creek Falls, and Beale Falls. By any name, it is a surprise destination in the oak woodlands east of Lincoln.

From the parking area and trailhead, walk across a worn-out bridge to a fire road. Turn right on the fire road and walk a short distance to a fork. For the recommended five-mile loop, turn left. It's a steady climb to a ridge, and in hot weather, rates a 3, not a 2. You'll continue to a junction, where you turn right (there is a small sign) under a grove, through a gate, and you'll continue down toward the bottom of a gorge to a rock-edge view of the Upper Falls. Downstream, about 100 yards, you'll find a smaller waterfall. Rock trekkers can climb down to the plunge pool. There's also some swimming/wading holes along the stream.

To return, a road is routed right along the river, downstream, and reaches the fork/road junction. Turn left and it's a short distance back to the old bridge, which you cross again to reach parking.

Wild turkeys are common sightings. Best time to hike the trail? December through April, when the hills are saturated, the aquifer is flushed, and the waterfall is pumping. In turkey season, the Department of Fish and Game conducts a permit system for turkey hunting and hiking is not permitted. Seasonal hunting may be permitted for other species September-January.

User Groups: Hikers and dogs. Horses and mountain bikes not allowed on this trail. Horses allowed on marked trails and service roads elsewhere in the wildlife area. Mountain bikes are allowed only on service roads. No wheelchair facilities.

Permits: No permits are necessary. Parking and access are free. Organized groups must obtain a free permit.

Maps: Free maps of Spenceville Wildlife Area are available at information signposts in the refuge. For a topographic map, ask the USGS for Camp Far West.

Directions: From Marysville, take Highway 20 east for 15 miles to Smartville Road (just east and opposite a CDF fire station). Turn right (south) on Smartville Road and enter the wildlife area. At 0.9 mile, bear left at a fork (the road is signed Chuck Yeager) and continue about four miles to Waldo Road (gravel). Turn left on Waldo Road and drive 2.1 miles to Spenceville Road. Turn left and drive two miles to the end of the road, at a closed bridge. Park, walk across the bridge, and begin the hike.

Contact: Spenceville Wildlife Area, c/o Oroville Wildlife Area, Department of Fish and Game, Oroville, 530/538-2236, www.wildlife. ca.gov.

9 HIDDEN FALLS LOOP
5.1 mi/2.25 hr   🥾2 ⛰️9

Hidden Falls Regional Park near Auburn

Map 5.2, page 192

This is a great hike for people who love canyons with rushing water. This loop includes trail along two separate creeks, their confluences, two waterfalls, and several gorgeous pools. From the parking area, look for the picnic table near the trailhead. Turn right and take the Poppy Trail down into the ravine, following several switchbacks for one mile. After arriving at Deadman Creek, walk over a bridge that leads to a service road and continue a short distance to the Blue Oak Loop Trail on the right. The Blue Oak Loop Trail will route you 0.5-mile up canyon and then left up a short ridge, where you will cross a road. Continue straight for 0.7 mile on the Seven Pools Vista down to a lookout (the trail turns sharply left) over Coon Creek. Continue along Coon Creek, where junctions with the Seven Pools Loop and the Canyon View Trail appear in about one mile. Continue past Canyon View Falls, the Canyon View Bridge, and beyond to a spur on the right for Hidden Falls. Return by hiking up the Hidden Falls Access Trail and climbing out on Poppy Trail. This is one of the best trips in the Sierra foothills.

User Groups: Hikers, dogs, horses, and mountain bikes. A short trail near parking is partially wheelchair accessible.

Permits: Parking and access are free. The parking lot can fill on good-weather weekends in spring and fall.

Maps: A trail map is posted at billboard near trailhead and is available online.

Directions: Take I-80 to Auburn and the exit for Highway 49 North. Turn north and drive 2.8 miles (get in left lane) to Atwood. Turn left at Atwood and drive 17 miles to Mount Vernon Road. Continue straight on Mount Vernon Road for 2.7 miles to Mears Drive. Turn right on Mears and drive 1 mile (turning left) to the park entrance.

Contact: Hidden Falls Regional Park, Placer County Parks and Recreation, 530/889-4016, www.placer.ca.gov.

10 CODFISH CREEK TRAIL
3.0 mi/1.5 hr   🥾2 ⛰️8

in Auburn State Recreation Area

Map 5.2, page 192

The Codfish Creek Trail follows an old mining route downstream along the North Fork American River along its edge, then cuts up the canyon of Codfish Creek. The highlight here is 60-foot Codfish Falls. The trail begins at the north side of the bridge, on Ponderosa Way, and heads downstream on sunny and exposed slopes. The path brings visitors to a series of cascades on Codfish Creek. At 1.2 miles, the trail turns right and leads upstream along Codfish Creek, heading away from the river, for canyon views. In March, April, and early May, you get the triple bonus of a full-flowing waterfall, lots of blooming wildflowers, and big canyon views.

User Groups: Hikers and dogs. No horses or mountain bikes. No wheelchair facilities.

Permits: No permits are necessary. Parking and access are free.

Maps: For a national forest map, which includes Auburn State Recreation Area lands, ask the U.S. Forest Service for Tahoe National Forest. For a topographic map, ask the USGS for Colfax.

Directions: From Sacramento, take I-80 east for 40 miles (past Auburn) to Weimar and the Weimar Crossroad exit. Take that exit, then a right at the fork off the off-ramp at Canyon Way (which becomes Ponderosa Way) and drive 5.5 miles (the road turns to dirt) to a bridge at the American River. Park near the bridge on the south side of the road (the side closest to the river) and look for the trailhead, on the north side of the bridge; the trail heads downstream past the beach area. A high-clearance vehicle is recommended and four-wheel drive is helpful.

Contact: Auburn State Recreation Area, Auburn, 530/885-4527, www.parks.ca.gov.

11 RIVERBANK TRAIL
3.5 mi/2.0 hr
🏃1 📷7

at Dry Creek Community Park near Roseville

Map 5.2, page 192

This local park provides a quick respite in Roseville. The trail runs along pretty Dry Creek, the centerpiece of Dry Creek Community Park. After significant rains in early spring, the riparian zone glows neon green as the creek forms a pretty stream. At the start, look for a paved bike trail and a dirt hiking trail. Turn right for the dirt trail routed toward Dry Creek. In the first stretch, you will walk near the river and past pools. You then get routed away from the creek, eventually arriving near a golf course on the right; continue a bit farther to a spur trail downstream.

User Groups: Hikers, dogs, and horses. A separate paved path is provided for bikes and wheelchairs.

Permits: Parking and access are free.

Maps: A trail map is available for a fee from Almanor Ranger District. For a map, ask the U.S. Forest Service for Lassen National Forest or Ishi Wilderness.

Directions: From Sacramento, take I-80 east to exit 98 (near Citrus Heights) for Greenback Lane. Take that exit for 0.3 mile and get in one of the two left lanes to access Greenback Lane. Turn left and go 0.1 mile and then continue onto Elkhorn Boulevard for 1.7 miles to Walerga Road. Turn right and drive 2.8 miles to the park.

Contact: Dry Creek Community Park, Placer County Parks and Recreation, 530/889-4016, www.placer.ca.gov.

12 AMERICAN RIVER PARKWAY
0.25-32.0 mi one-way/0.5 hr-2 days
🏃1 📷7

along the American River from Sacramento to Folsom

Map 5.2, page 192   **BEST (**

The American River Parkway and Jedediah Smith Memorial Trail is the famous paved 32-mile path along the American River that links Folsom Lake on downstream past Fair Oaks, Rancho Cordova, and Sac State en route to Old Town Sacramento and Discovery Park. More than five million people use this trail every year. We admit this is the one trail we did not hike at all, but rather rode it out on a bike, a one-day trip with a shuttle car. There are 15 access points, of course, for short walks with river views. The prettiest stretch spans from Folsom Lake down past the dam into a riparian zone toward Nimbus.

Spring and fall are when the American River is prettiest. In spring, the trees and grass are green, the water is rolling fresh, and by May, schools of shad are swimming upstream. Come autumn, the leaves of the adjacent trees turn bright colors, lighting up the river. In the intervening summer months, 100-degree temperatures keep trail use low during the day, but when evening shade emerges, so do joggers and walkers.

There are actually two parallel trails, one paved for bicyclists and in-line skaters only, and a dirt trail for horses (note that there is no shoulder on the horse trail). Walkers and joggers should stay off the paved portion, and should instead use the dirt trail or the shoulder of the bike trail.

Note: In-line skates or roller skates are allowed on the state park and county park portions of trail. The state park portion is two separate trails most of the route, but a 0.5-mile section is shared. All nine miles of state trail are paved, and wheelchairs are allowed. Elsewhere, wheelchairs are allowed on the actual trail, and wheelchair-accessible restrooms, fishing areas, and picnic grounds are available along the way.

User Groups: Hikers, dogs, mountain bikes, in-line skates, roller skates, and horses allowed, but horses are not advised. (See the note about restrictions for mountain bikes and hikers.)

Permits: No permits are required. Folsom Lake State Recreation Area at the head of the Parkway charges a fee of $12 per vehicle at Beals Point; $10 at other state park access areas.

Maps: A trail map is available for a fee at the county parks department. For topographic maps, ask the USGS for Sacramento East, Carmichael, Citrus Heights, and Folsom.

Directions: The trail begins at Folsom Lake Recreation Area and ends at Discovery Park in Sacramento. From Sacramento, take U.S. 50 east for 18.4 miles to Exit 23 for Folsom Boulevard. Take that exit, go 0.2 mile, then bear left to take the ramp toward Folsom and Folsom Boulevard. Turn left on Folsom

Boulevard and drive 3.6 miles, then continue straight (becomes Folsom-Auburn Boulevard) and go 2.0 miles to the park entrance. Park near the boat ramp.

Contact: County of Sacramento, Parks and Recreation Division, Park Ranger Section, Sacramento, www.regionalparks.saccounty. net; rangers, 916/875-7275; Folsom Lake State Recreation Area, 916/988-0205, www.parks. ca.gov.

13 COSUMNES RIVER TRAIL
3.3 mi/2.0 hr   🏃1 ⛰8

in Cosumnes River Preserve near Galt

Map 5.2, page 192

The River Walk Trail is an easy 3.3-mile trip from start to finish; it's nearly flat and routed amid the preserved diversity of habitats for the chance to see birds and wildlife. The habitat changes quickly, so if you want to see wildlife, be ready. Bring binoculars and keep quiet; young adults who shout and hoot have about as much chance at sighting a sandhill crane as a polar bear in the desert. The Cosumnes River flows through one of the richest landscapes in the Delta, a mix of wetlands, riparian woodlands, river cuts, and sloughs that provides habitat for thousands of waterfowl, songbirds, hawks, and falcons. Coyote, fox, raccoon, otters, rabbits, and deer are common sightings. This is a great getaway for bird- and wildlife-watching, driving tours, easy walks, and hand-powered boating—either bring your own kayak or canoe or book a kayak trip with an outfitter. Free, guided walking tours are also available. The marsh often comes to life at dawn and dusk.

User Groups: Hikers only. No mountain bikes, dogs, or horses.

Permits: No permits are necessary. Parking and access are free; donations accepted.

Maps: A brochure and map are available at the visitors center.

Directions from Antioch: From Antioch, take Highway 160 (signed for Stockton/Rio

© TOM STIENSTRA

American River

Vista) and drive for 18.8 miles to Isleton (becomes Isleton Rd.) and continue eight miles to River Road (cross the bridge at Georgiana Slough). Turn right on River Road and drive (becomes Walnut Grove-Thornton Road) eight miles to Thornton (just after you cross I-5) and Thornton Road. Turn left on Thornton Road and drive 2.3 miles (you will cross a bridge over the Mokelumne River, becomes Franklin) and continue 0.7 mile to the preserve entrance on right (signed). Turn right and continue short distance to visitors center.

Directions from Sacramento: From Sacramento, take I-5 south to the Twin Cities Road exit (marked with a binoculars sign for wildlife viewing, about midway between Stockton and Sacramento). Take the Twin Cities Road exit and go east for exactly one mile, to the first stop sign at Franklin. Turn right on Franklin and drive 1.7 miles. Look for the visitors center on the left side of Franklin and park in the parking lot just past the visitors center.

Directions from Stockton: From Stockton, take I-5 north to the Thornton-Walnut Grove Road exit. Take that exit and go east to Thornton Road (just after a gas station). Turn left on Thornton and drive two miles (it becomes Franklin Blvd.) and continue over the Thornton-Franklin Bridge to parking and the visitors center.

Contact: Cosumnes River Preserve, Galt, 916/684-2816, www.cosumnes.org.

TAHOE AND NORTHERN SIERRA

Mount Tallac affords a view across Lake Tahoe like no other: a cobalt-blue expanse of water bordered by mountains that span miles of Sierra wildlands. The Tahoe area has a wide range of scenic hikes with access to hundreds of lakes. The best for scenic beauty are Echo Lakes, Donner, Fallen Leaf, Sardine, Caples, Loon, and Union Valley. The north end of the Northern Sierra starts near Bucks Lake and extends to Bear River Canyon. In between are the Lakes Basin Recreation Area in southern Plumas County; the Crystal Basin in the Sierra foothills west of Tahoe; Lake Davis near Portola; and the Carson River Canyon and Hope Valley south of Tahoe. It's true that people come here in droves, but if you're willing to hunt a bit, there are trails you can share with only chipmunks.

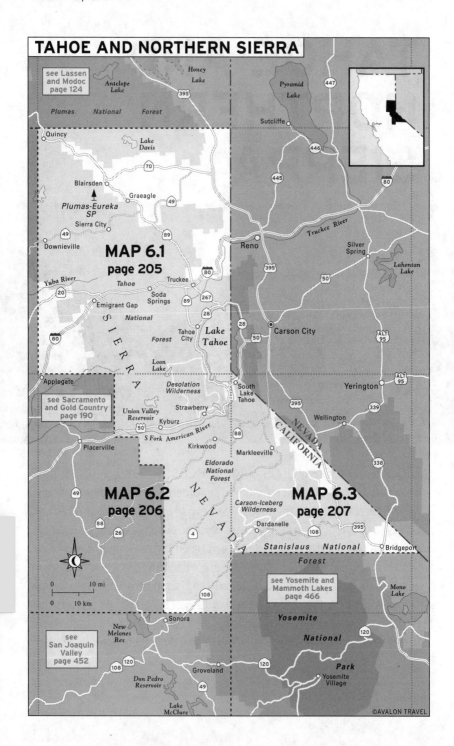

TAHOE AND NORTHERN SIERRA

see Lassen and Modoc page 124

Antelope Lake

Honey Lake

Pyramid Lake

447

Sutcliffe

Plumas National Forest

395

Quincy

Lake Davis

70

446

445

Blairsden

Graeagle

49

Plumas-Eureka SP

Sierra City

89

80

Silver Spring

Lahontan Lake

Truckee River

Downieville

Reno

MAP 6.1
page 205

395

Yuba River

20

Tahoe

Truckee

Soda Springs

89

267

50

Carson City

ALT 95

Emigrant Gap

28

80

S I E R R A

National

28

Tahoe City

Lake Tahoe

50

Loon Lake

Forest

ALT 95

Applegate

Desolation Wilderness

South Lake Tahoe

Yerington

see Sacramento and Gold Country page 190

Union Valley Reservoir

Strawberry

339

50

Kyburz

S Fork American River

88

Wellington

Placerville

Kirkwood

Markleeville

338

395

49

Eldorado National Forest

MAP 6.2
page 206

88

26

N E V A D A

Carson-Iceberg Wilderness

MAP 6.3
page 207

4

Dardanelle

108

395

Bridgeport

0   10 mi
0   10 km

Stanislaus National

Forest

see Yosemite and Mammoth Lakes page 466

Mono Lake

108

Sonora

Yosemite

120

see San Joaquin Valley page 452

New Melones Res

National

108 120

Groveland

120

Park

49

Yosemite Village

Don Pedro Reservoir

Lake McClure

©AVALON TRAVEL

Map 6.1

Sites 1-44
Pages 208-234

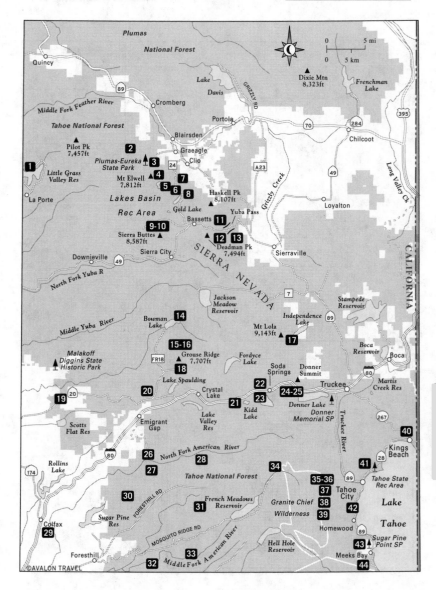

Map 6.2
Sites 45-77
Pages 234-258

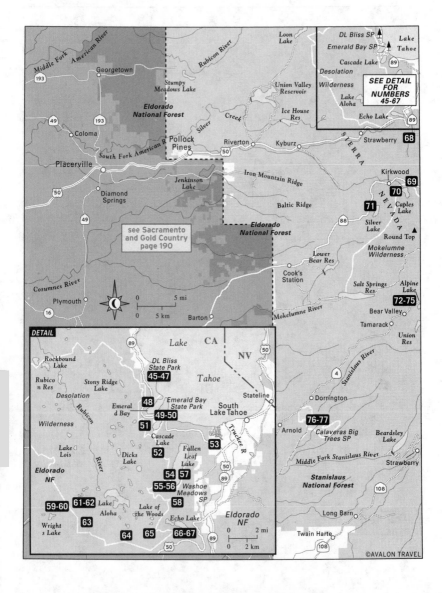

Map 6.3

Sites 78-103
Pages 258-273

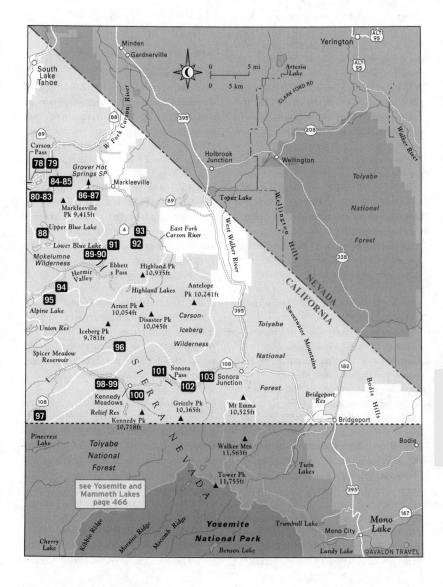

1 FOWLER PEAK TO BUCKS SUMMIT (PCT)

26.0 mi one-way/3 days 🏃4 ⛰6

at Fowler Peak north of Little Grass Valley Reservoir in Plumas National Forest

Map 6.1, page 205

Most Pacific Crest Trail (PCT) hikers will sprint through this section of trail. From Fowler Peak trailhead, it passes through Plumas National Forest country until reaching the southern border of the Bucks Lake Wilderness. It starts quite nicely, where you drop down to the Middle Fork Feather River (3,180 feet), a great trout stream with an excellent footbridge to get you across a gorge. We suggest you linger here and soak it in. Enjoy it, because the rest of this route won't exactly have you writing postcards home. It climbs from the Middle Fork Feather to 6,955-foot Lookout Rock, a long, dry pull, and then drops down to Bucks Creek. Most of this region is dry rattlesnake country, so watch your step, and time your water stops.

To continue north on the PCT, see the *Bucks Summit to Feather River (PCT)* hike in the *Sacramento and Gold Country* chapter. If you are walking this trail in reverse, see the *Yuba River to Fowler Peak (PCT)* hike in this chapter to continue south.

User Groups: Hikers, dogs, and horses. No mountain bikes. No wheelchair access.

Permits: A wilderness permit (free) is required. Parking and access are free.

Maps: For a map, ask the U.S. Forest Service for Tahoe and Plumas National Forests. For topographic maps, ask the USGS for Onion Valley, Dogwood Peak, and Bucks Lake.

Directions: From Oroville, take Highway 162 east for eight miles to Highway 174 (Forbestown Road and the junction signed Challenge/LaPorte). Turn right on Forbestown Road and drive east to Highway 120/Quincy-LaPorte Road. Turn left and drive past LaPorte to Little Grass Valley Road. Turn left on Little Grass Valley Road and drive to Black Rock Campground and Forest Road 94. Bear left on

Forest Road 94 and drive three miles to Forest Road 22N27. Turn right and drive four miles to the parking area.

Contact: Plumas National Forest, Feather River Ranger District, 530/534-6500, www.fs.usda.gov/plumas.

2 EUREKA PEAK LOOP

3.0 mi/2.0 hr 🏃3 ⛰10

in Plumas-Eureka State Park east of Quincy

Map 6.1, page 205

From Eureka Peak (elevation 7,447 feet), you get a panoramic view of the north Sierra that includes all the peaks of the Lakes Basin National Recreation Area and beyond. Mount Elwell (7,818 feet) is the most prominent to the south, Plumas National Forest to the north, and the west is crowned by Blue Nose Mountain (7,290 feet), Stafford Mountain (7,019 feet), and Beartrap Mountain (7,232 feet). It's the vista that compels people to make the climb—a serious three-mile loop, and the first half is an hour-long huff-and-puff to the top. The trailhead starts at a parking area near the dam at Eureka Lake (elevation 6,300 feet). If you bear left at a fork on the way up, you will hike past False Peak to the left and then up to Eureka Peak, and can turn it into a loop. It then climbs 1,150 feet to the top. Bring plenty of water and snacks to enjoy from the summit. At rare times (usually at night for illegal campers), the ranger closes the gate to Eureka Lake, which adds 1.2 miles to the hike on each end.

User Groups: Hikers only. No dogs, horses, or mountain bikes. No wheelchair facilities.

Permits: No permits are required, $8 day-use and parking.

Maps: A brochure and trail map is available for a fee from Plumas-Eureka State Park. For a topographic map, ask the USGS for Johnsville.

Directions: From Sacramento, take I-80 east for 97 miles to Truckee and the exit for Donner Pass Road/Highway 89 North. Take that exit to the traffic circle, then take the second exit for 0.2 mile to another traffic circle. Take the third exit on that traffic circle to Highway 89 and drive 22.6 miles to Sierraville and a junction for Highway 49/Highway 89 (signed for Quincy/Downieville). Turn left (signed 49/89) and drive 4.9 miles to a turnoff for Highway 89. Turn right on Highway 89 and drive 17 miles to Johnsville Road. Turn left and drive 5.1 miles to Johnsville-McCrea Road. Turn left and drive 0.5 mile to the park entrance. From the kiosk, continue to the parking area; the trailhead is near the dam at Eureka Lake.

Contact: Plumas-Eureka State Park, 530/836-2380, www.parks.ca.gov.

🖪 GRASS LAKE TRAIL/ LITTLE JAMISON CREEK
3.5 mi/2.0 hr   🏃2 ⛰8

in Plumas-Eureka State Park east of Quincy

Map 6.1, page 205

From the trailhead at the Jamison Mine building, take the Grass Lake Trail. It follows along Little Jamison Creek. You'll find a short spur trail to Little Jamison Falls. That's a must-do, of course. Back on the trail, you will climb 1.75 miles to Grass Lake. The trail skirts the east side of the lake. For those on a day hike, this is far enough: a good trail from a historic site, a waterfall, a lake, and a picnic.

You can forge onward. It's another two miles to Jamison Lake, and with the trail climbing more steeply you can continue to spur trails for several lakes—Rock, Jamison, and Smith Lakes—and beyond to other nearby trails listed in the section. That includes Smith Lake and Mount Elwell. Note that the first half mile of trail is located in the state park, and the remainder is in Plumas National Forest.

User Groups: Hikers, dogs, horses, and mountain bikes. No wheelchair facilities.

Permits: No permits are required; $8 day use and parking.

Maps: A brochure and trail map is available for a fee from Plumas-Eureka State Park. For a topographic map, ask the USGS for Johnsville.

Directions: From Sacramento, take I-80 east for 97 miles to Truckee and the exit for Donner Pass Road/Highway 89 North. Take that exit to the traffic circle, then take the second exit for 0.2 mile to another traffic circle. Take the third exit on that traffic circle to Highway 89 and drive 22.6 miles to Sierraville and a junction for Highway 49/Highway 89 (signed for Quincy/Downieville). Turn left (signed 49/89) and drive 4.9 miles to a turnoff for Highway 89. Turn right on Highway 89 and drive 17 miles to Johnsonville Road. Turn left on Johnsonville Road and drive 4.6 miles to Jamison Mine Road. Turn left and drive 0.7 mile to the Jamison Mine Complex. The trailhead starts at the far end of the parking lot.

Contact: Plumas-Eureka State Park, 530/836-2380, www.parks.ca.gov.

🖪 MOUNT ELWELL TRAIL
6.0 mi/3.5 hr   🏃3 ⛰10

at Smith Lake in Lakes Basin National Recreation Area south of Quincy

Map 6.1, page 205

This is one of the great hikes in the north Sierra. From atop Mount Elwell (7,822 feet), you're surrounded by the Lakes Basin National Recreation Area, a wildland filled with alpine lakes and granite peaks. You'll find yourself dreaming of the days when you might visit them. This trail is a good way to start. It begins at the Smith Lake trailhead and passes near Smith Lake (6,079 feet) on Smith Lake Trail, climbing all the way, 2,018 feet over the course of three miles.

A variety of routes connect to the final ascent. The Smith Lake Trailhead is an excellent choice; many believe the best trailhead is at Lake Basin Campground near site 15, while others leave from Gray Eagle Lodge via Long Lake. Plan for a 6-7-mile round-trip hike with a challenging 2,000-foot-plus elevation gain in two climbs. The final ascent is a panorama you'll never forget. Long Lake sits at the foot of Mount Elwell and is one of the prettiest lakes anywhere.

User Groups: Hikers, dogs, mountain bikes, and horses. No wheelchair facilities.

Permits: No permits are required. Parking and access are free.

Maps: A trail map is available for a fee at the Beckwourth Ranger District. For a map, ask the U.S. Forest Service for Plumas National Forest. For a topographic map, ask the USGS for Gold Lake.

Directions: From Sacramento, take I-80 east for 97 miles to Truckee and the exit for Donner Pass Road/Highway 89 North. Take that exit to the traffic circle, then take the second exit for 0.2 mile to another traffic circle. Take the third exit on that traffic circle to Highway 89 and drive 22.6 miles to Sierraville and a junction for Highway 49/Highway 89 (signed for Quincy/Downieville). Turn left (signed 49/89) and drive 4.9 miles to a turnoff for Highway 89. Turn right on Highway 89 and drive 15.3 miles to the Gold Lake Highway. Turn left on the Gold Lake Highway and drive five miles to the sign for Gray Eagle Lodge. Turn right and drive 0.4 mile to a fork. Bear right a short distance to Smith Lake and the trailhead.

Contact: Plumas National Forest, Beckwourth Ranger District, 530/836-2575, www.fs.usda. gov/plumas.

⑤ LONG LAKE
2.5 mi/1.5 hr

north of Sierra City

Map 6.1, page 205

Long Lake is a celestial-level setting in the heavenly Lakes Basin National Recreation Area. It's big, gorgeous, often cobalt blue, and nestled at the foot of Mount Elwell. The trailhead for this hike is located at the Lakes Basin Campground (elevation 6,300 feet) near site 15. From here, the trail is clear and well maintained but requires a short huff-and-puff of a mile. Here you'll see the turnoff for a 0.25-mile spur trail to Long Lake. The trail skirts along the southeast shoreline. For an easy walk and a trail picnic at a gorgeous destination, this is it.

Most hikers will want to continue on to several other lakes and destinations nearby. It is one mile to little Silver Lake, 0.75 mile to Cub Lake, and another 0.5 mile to Little Bear and Big Bear Lakes,

Note: Camping is permitted only at the Lakes Basin Campground. No camping is permitted at either Long or Silver Lakes.

User Groups: Hikers, dogs, mountain bikes, and horses. No wheelchair facilities.

Permits: No permits are required. Parking and access are free.

Maps: A trail map is available for a fee at the Beckwourth Ranger District. For a map, ask the U.S. Forest Service for Plumas National Forest. For a topographic map, ask the USGS for Gold Lake.

Directions: From Sacramento, take I-80 east for 97 miles to Truckee and the exit for Donner Pass Road/Highway 89 North. Take that exit to the traffic circle, then take the second exit for 0.2 mile to another traffic circle. Take the third exit on that traffic circle to Highway 89 and drive 22.6 miles to Sierraville and a junction for Highway 49/Highway 89 (signed for Quincy/Downieville). Turn left (signed 49/89) and drive 4.9 miles to a turnoff for Highway 89. Turn right on Highway 89 and drive 15.3 miles to the Gold Lake Highway. Turn left on the Gold Lake Highway and drive about six miles until you see the sign for the Lakes Basin Campground. The trailhead is near site 15.

Contact: Plumas National Forest, Beckwourth Ranger District, 530/836-2575, www.fs.usda. gov/plumas.

⑥ ROUND LAKE TRAILHEAD
1.4 mi/1.0 hr

on the southern boundary of Lakes Basin National Recreation Area north of Sierra City

Map 6.1, page 205

The 0.7-mile hike to Big Bear Lake is an easy, popular, and pretty walk. For visitors who stay at Gold Lake Lodge, it's always a must-do. The trailhead is located alongside the parking lot next to the road to the lodge; the trail is a closed road to Round Lake. It becomes a trail within a few hundred yards when routed west to Big Bear Lake, the first in a series of nearby beautiful alpine lakes in the Lakes Basin National Recreation Area. Although most day users return after a picnic at Big Bear Lake, the trip can easily be extended, either west to Round Lake or Silver Lake or north to Long Lake.

User Groups: Hikers, dogs, mountain bikes, and horses. No wheelchair facilities.

Permits: No permits are required. Parking and access are free.

Maps: A trail map is available for a fee from Beckwourth Ranger District. For a map, ask the U.S. Forest Service for Plumas National Forest. For a topographic map, ask the USGS for Gold Lake.

Directions: From Sacramento, take I-80 east for 97 miles to Truckee and the exit for Highway 89 North. Take that exit to the traffic circle, then take the third exit to Highway 89 and drive 22.6 miles to a junction for Highway 49/Highway 89 (signed for Quincy/Downieville). Turn left and drive 17.8 miles (stay on 49 at junctions) to Bassetts and the Gold Lake Highway. Turn right and drive 7.9 miles to the exit on left for Gold Lake Lodge and trailhead.

Contact: Plumas National Forest, Beckwourth Ranger District, 530/836-2575, www.fs.usda. gov/plumas.

7 FRAZIER FALLS TRAIL
1.0 mi/1.0 hr   🏃‍♂️1   ⛰️10

north of Sierra City

Map 6.1, page 205

Frazier Falls is a 178-foot, silver-tasseled waterfall that tumbles out of a chute into a rocky basin. It is like a miniature version of Feather Falls (near Lake Oroville). The trail is a 0.5-mile romp on a gentle route that leads to the scenic, fenced overlook of the falls. The best time to visit is early summer, when snowmelt from the high country peaks fills Frazier Falls

like a huge fountain. In addition, wildflowers along the trail in early summer add a splash of color, with violet lupine the most abundant. The road to the trailhead is paved all the way, the hike is easy, the falls are beautiful, and as you might expect, thousands of people make the trip every summer.

User Groups: Hikers, wheelchairs, and dogs. No ATVs, mountain bikes, or horses. Wheelchair facilities are available.

Permits: No permits are required. Parking and access are free.

Maps: A trail map is available for a fee from Beckwourth Ranger District. For a map, ask the U.S. Forest Service for Plumas National Forest. For a topographic map, ask the USGS for Gold Lake.

Directions: From Sacramento, take I-80 east for 97 miles to Truckee and the exit for Donner Pass Road/Highway 89 North. Take that exit to the traffic circle, then take the second exit for 0.2 mile to another traffic circle. Take the third exit on that traffic circle to Highway 89 and drive 22.6 miles to Sierraville and a junction for Highway 49/Highway 89 (signed for Quincy/Downieville). Turn left (signed 49/89) and drive 4.9 miles to a turnoff for Highway 89. Turn right on Highway 89 and drive 15.3 miles to the Gold Lake Highway. Turn left on the Gold Lake Highway and drive 1.7 miles to Frazier Creek Road. Turn left and drive 3.9 miles to the trailhead.

Note: If you continue west on Gold Lake Highway for several miles, you will see another trailhead sign for Frazier Falls; it can also be reached on this route, but the road is unpaved.

Contact: Plumas National Forest, Beckwourth Ranger District, 530/836-2575, www.fs.usda. gov/plumas.

8 HASKELL PEAK TRAIL
3.0 mi/2.0 hr   🏃‍♂️3   ⛰️10

north of Highway 49 in Tahoe National Forest

Map 6.1, page 205

Haskell Peak is one of the great but little-known

lookouts. On clear days, visitors can see many mountains both nearby and distant, including Mount Shasta and Mount Lassen, in Northern California; Mount Rose, in Nevada; and the closer Sierra Buttes. To get this view requires a 1,100-foot climb over the course of 1.5 miles, where you top out at the 8,107-foot summit. The trail climbs at a decent, steady grade through heavy forest for the first mile. It then flattens and reaches an open area, where Haskell Peak comes into view. From here it's only a 0.25-mile (but very steep) climb to the top. You'll discover that Haskell Peak is the flume of an old volcano and has many unusual volcanic-rock formations. A fire lookout was once perched here, but it's gone now. Elevations range from 7,000 to 8,107 feet.

User Groups: Hikers, dogs, horses, and mountain bikes. No wheelchair facilities.

Permits: No permits are required. Parking and access are free.

Maps: For a map, ask the U.S. Forest Service for Tahoe National Forest. For a topographic map, ask the USGS for Clio.

Directions: From Sacramento, take I-80 east for 97 miles to Truckee and the exit for Donner Pass Road/Highway 89 North. Take that exit to the traffic circle, then take the second exit for 0.2 mile to another traffic circle. Take the third exit on that traffic circle to Highway 89 and drive 22.6 miles to Sierraville and a junction for Highway 49/Highway 89 (signed for Quincy/Downieville). Turn left and drive 17.8 miles (stay on 49 at junctions) to Bassetts and the Gold Lake Highway. Turn right and drive 3.7 miles to Forest Road 9 (Haskell Peak Road). Turn right and drive 8.4 miles. The trailhead is on the left; parking is available on either side of the road.

Contact: Tahoe National Forest, Yuba Ranger District, 530/288-3231 or 530/478-6253 (voice), www.fs.usda.gov/tahoe.

⑨ DEER LAKE TRAIL

5.0 mi/3.5 hr

west of Packer Lake in Tahoe National Forest

Map 6.1, page 205

Most lakes are green, but Deer Lake is azure blue. With the spectacular Sierra Buttes in the background, this trip is popular. It gets some of the heaviest use of any trail in this section of Tahoe National Forest. It's a 2.5-mile hike to the lake where you climb 1,000 feet and top out at 7,110 feet.

From the trailhead, you'll climb through a basin and get a sweeping view of the massive Sierra Buttes and the surrounding forested slopes. As you head on, you'll cross a signed spur trail, a 0.25-mile route to Grass Lake. Most take the detour, and for some, this alone is enough of a trip. Deer sightings are common here. Then, back on the trail to Deer Lake, it's onward, over the ridge and down to Deer Lake. On warm evenings, the brook trout can leave tiny circles while feeding on surface insects. This hike has it all and that's why it often includes so many other people.

User Groups: Hikers, dogs, horses, and mountain bikes. No wheelchair facilities.

Permits: No permits are required. Parking and access are free.

Maps: A trail map is available for a fee at the Downieville Ranger District. For a map, ask the U.S. Forest Service for Tahoe National Forest. For a topographic map, ask the USGS for Sierra City.

Directions: From Sacramento, take I-80 east for 97 miles to Truckee and the exit for Donner Pass Road/Highway 89 North. Take that exit to the traffic circle, then take the second exit for 0.2 mile to another traffic circle. Take the third exit on that traffic circle to Highway 89 and drive 22.6 miles to Sierraville and a junction for Highway 49/Highway 89 (signed for Quincy/Downieville). Turn left (signed 49/89) and drive 17.8 miles (stay on 49 at junctions) to Bassetts and the Gold Lake Highway. Turn right (north) on to Gold Lake Highway and drive 1.4 miles to Sardine Lake Road. Turn left on Sardine Lake

Road and drive a short distance. Cross the Salmon Creek Bridge and continue 0.3 mile to Packer Lake Road. Turn right on Packer Lake Road and drive 2.5 miles to the trailhead. Parking is available in the Packsaddle camping area just opposite the trailhead.

Contact: Tahoe National Forest, Yuba Ranger District, 530/288-3231 or 530/478-6253 (voice), www.fs.usda.gov/tahoe.

10 SIERRA BUTTES TRAIL
5.0 mi/3.5 hr   🚶4 ⛰10

near Packer Lake in Tahoe National Forest

Map 6.1, page 205

The sensation can feel like you are walking on air. Many get dizzy. Some are afraid to look down. Most all feel a sense of rapture. This is your pay-off at the 8,587-foot Sierra Buttes and its lookout station. A small grated walkway extends around the lookout, where you can look straight down, past your boots and into the open air below. You are atop a pinnacle that is roughly 5,000 feet over Sierra City on one side, 2,800 feet over Sardine Lakes on the other.

The 360-degree view is one of the best you can get with a short hike, but that's not what will stay with you for years. You will remember the act of faith required to traverse a set of metal stairways and grated deck that jut out over open space. Only the daring will look down to see the plummeting open space below. Put this one on your must-do list. The Sierra Buttes are a series of towering crags located in Tahoe National Forest that loom above the Yuba River Canyon, Sierra City and Highway 49.

It's a one-way hike of 2.5 miles, by my estimate, with a climb of about 2,400 feet. I did it in an hour, 10 minutes, with a steady, rhythmic pace that I estimated at a little less than my normal 2.5 mph (note: the Forest Service says it is 3.3 miles one-way, but I believe that is the distance of an adjacent jeep trail, and a hiking blogger says I am wrong and it's 3.5 miles; nope, I'm not that fast uphill).

The parking area and trailhead is at about 6,200 feet, where trail starts as an old jeep road (a designated OHV route is off to the right). You begin to climb right away. After making your way up to a ridge, it becomes a single-track hiking path, shaded below old-growth whitebark pine. At a few openings in the forest ahead of you, you can see how the route follows the ridge and rises to the southern spine of the buttes. In about a mile, look for a huge boulder field on your left. An unsigned cut-off spur leads about 30 yards to your first gorgeous lookout, of Young America Lake directly below and beyond to Upper and Lower Sardine Lake, backed by an overview of Mount Elwell and the Lakes Basin.

From here, the climb gets steeper. It's a short trip, so those not used to the grade or altitude can take plenty of time. Near tree line, the trail emerges and hits the old jeep road, the one used in the 1960s when the lookout was constructed, and you turn left, then know you are getting close. The trail bounds, rises, and carves its way through the lower buttes. To the distant north, 10,457-foot Lassen Peak comes into view. You continue up the trail, round a bend, and suddenly the lookout, top pinnacle, and the series of metal stairs are in front of you.

At the stairs, some people have no trouble bounding right up. Others need a steadying hand of comfort from behind. Some look down. Others? No way. The stairs jangle and rattle as you climb; you might hear a little voice in the back of your head daring you to look down. At one spot, where a set of stairs extends over open air, you realize why this hike is an act of faith. The final set of stairs give you access to the grated catwalk deck around the lookout building, perched on the top of a crag. It can be eerie to peer down through the grate in some spots and see nothing but air so far below. Some get vertigo from the spatial disorientation and will suddenly grab on to the building or whoever is standing next to them. The view is fantastic. Directly below to the west, the Yuba River Canyon drops 5,000 feet in 10 miles and leads out toward the Sacramento Valley. To the south, you can scan across gorgeous French Meadows Reservoir, Grouse Ridge, and the Bowman Lakes, and to the distant snowy crest of the Crystal Basin on the edge of Tahoe. Below to the east is the showstopper, the Sardine Lakes.

As pretty as it is, what you will remember at the Sierra Buttes Lookout is not the view. It's the edge-of-the world, fear-edged euphoria. The experience can open your pores and make every cell in your body feel alive.

User Groups: Hikers, dogs, and horses. No mountain bikes (except on jeep trail). No wheelchair access.

Permits: No permits are required. Parking and access are free.

Maps: A trail map is available for a fee from the Downieville Ranger District. For a map, ask the U.S. Forest Service for Tahoe National Forest. For a topographic map, ask the USGS for Sierra City.

Directions: From Sacramento, take I-80 east for 97 miles to Truckee and the exit for Highway 89 North. Take that exit to the traffic circle, then take the third exit to Highway 89 and drive 22.6 miles to a junction for Highway 49/Highway 89 (signed for Quincy/Downieville). Turn left and drive 17.8 miles (stay on 49 at junctions) to Bassetts and the Gold Lake Highway. Turn right and drive 1.4 miles to Sardine Lake/Packer Lake Road. Turn left and drive a short distance to a junction signed Sardine Lakes ahead, Packer Lake to right. Turn right on Packer Lake Road. Continue past turnoff for Packer Lake and bear left at a fork (still paved), following the signs to a trailhead for the Pacific Crest Trail (do not bear right at a jeep road). Continue as road becomes dirt (OK for cars) to a parking area on left at trailhead. Parking and trailhead signed.

Contact: Tahoe National Forest, Yuba Ranger District, 530/288-3231 or 530/478-6453 (voice), www.fs.usda.gov/tahoe.

11 CHAPMAN CREEK TRAIL
3.0 mi/2.0 hr

east of Sierra City in Tahoe National Forest

Map 6.1, page 205

Chapman Creek is a babbling brook that you can walk alongside, or you can stop to picnic near it, fish a little in it, or do absolutely nothing. That's right, nothing. It's that kind of place. The trailhead, elevation 5,840 feet, is set at a campground, which provides easy access. Outside of campers, few others know of it. The trail winds easily along the contours of Chapman Creek under the canopy of a dense forest, rising gently along the way. It climbs to 6,400 feet, 560 feet in a span of 1.5 miles. The river is the lifeblood for a variety of birds and wildlife, but few visitors make the trip for that reason. Rather they come to stroll and let their minds wander and be free.

User Groups: Hikers, dogs, horses, and mountain bikes. No wheelchair facilities.

Permits: No permits are required. Parking and access are free.

Maps: For a map, ask the U.S. Forest Service for Tahoe National Forest. For a topographic map, ask the USGS for Sierra City.

Directions: From Sacramento, take I-80 east for 97 miles to Truckee and the exit for Donner Pass Road/Highway 89 North. Take that exit to the traffic circle, then take the second exit for 0.2 mile to another traffic circle. Take the third exit on that traffic circle to Highway 89 and drive 22.6 miles to Sierraville and a junction for Highway 49/Highway 89 (signed for Quincy/Downieville). Turn left on Highway 49 and drive over Yuba Pass; continue for four miles to the Chapman Creek Campground, on the right. The trailhead and a parking area are located at the north end of the campground.

Contact: Tahoe National Forest, Yuba Ranger District, 530/288-3231 or 530/478-6453 (voice), www.fs.usda.gov/tahoe.

12 WILD PLUM LOOP/ HAYPRESS CREEK

6.0 mi/1 day   🥾3 ⛰️8

east of Sierra City in Tahoe National Forest

Map 6.1, page 205

A canyon with a hidden stream and a waterfall surrounded by old-growth red fir make this a hike for the properly inspired. Why must you be properly inspired? The route to the trailhead causes it to get missed. In addition, the trail climbs from 4,400 feet up Haypress Creek to 5,840 feet, a 1,440-foot rise over just three miles. The trail starts out almost flat for the first 0.5 mile, and then it crosses over Haypress Creek on a footbridge. There's an excellent view of the Sierra Buttes in this area. Continue on Haypress Creek Trail, where you rise past a rocky area and into a once-logged forest. The trail soon enters an old-growth forest. It then contours along Haypress Canyon, and then passes by a pretty waterfall. This hike makes a great day trip with a picnic lunch, and trail use is typically quite light. Note that on the return trip, you turn right on the Pacific Crest Trail to complete the loop. Walk 0.5 mile and turn left at the Wild Plum Loop sign to return.

User Groups: Hikers, dogs, and horses. No mountain bikes. No wheelchair facilities.

Permits: No permits are required. Parking and access are free.

Maps: For a map, ask the U.S. Forest Service for Tahoe National Forest. For a topographic map, ask the USGS for Haypress Valley.

Directions: From Sacramento, take I-80 east for 97 miles to Truckee and the exit for Donner Pass Road/Highway 89 North. Take that exit to the traffic circle, then take the second exit for 0.2 mile to another traffic circle. Take the third exit on that traffic circle to Highway 89 and drive 22.6 miles to Sierraville and a junction for Highway 49/Highway 89 (signed for Quincy/Downieville). Turn left on Highway 49 and drive 12 miles (past Bassetts) to Wild Plum Road (near the eastern end of Sierra City) at the sign for Wild Plum Campground. To then reach the trailhead, drive one mile on this road to the Wild Plum trailhead parking area. Walk through the campground to its upper loop, walk around a locked gate, and continue up the road 0.25 mile to the Wild Plum Loop Trail Sign. Walk 0.25 mile to the intersection with the Pacific Crest Trail, turn left, and cross a bridge over Haypress Creek. Continue for 200 yards to the trailhead, on the right.

Contact: Tahoe National Forest, Yuba Ranger District, 530/288-3231 or 530/478-6253 (voice), www.fs.usda.gov/tahoe.

13 YUBA RIVER TO FOWLER PEAK (PCT)

51.0 mi one-way/4 days   🥾4 ⛰️9

in Tahoe National Forest, off Highway 49 east of Sierra City

Map 6.1, page 205

To continue north on the PCT, see the *Fowler Peak to Bucks Summit (PCT)* hike in this chapter. If you are walking this trail in reverse, see the *Donner Pass to the Yuba River (PCT)* hike in this chapter.

User Groups: Hikers, dogs, and horses. No mountain bikes. No wheelchair access.

Permits: A wilderness permit (free) is required. Parking and access are free.

Maps: For a map, ask the U.S. Forest Service for Tahoe National Forest. For topographic maps, ask the USGS for Haypress Valley, Sierra City, Mount Fillmore, and Onion Valley.

Directions: From Sacramento, take I-80 east for 97 miles to Truckee and the exit for Donner Pass Road/Highway 89 North. Take that exit to the traffic circle, then take the second exit for 0.2 mile to another traffic circle. Take the third exit on that traffic circle to Highway 89 and drive 22.6 miles to Sierraville and a junction for Highway 49/Highway 89 (signed for Quincy/Downieville). Turn left on Highway 49 and drive 12 miles (past Bassetts) to near the eastern end of Sierra City. Look for the Pacific Crest Trail access sign and park on the right (north) side of the road.

Contact: Tahoe National Forest, Yuba Ranger

District, 530/288-3231 or 530/478-6253 (voice), www.fs.usda.gov/tahoe.

14 GROUSE RIDGE TO GLACIER LAKE
8.0 mi/4.0 hr   🏃3   ⛰9

in Tahoe National Forest north of Emigrant Gap

Map 6.1, page 205

The prize destination is a hidden, pristine lake called Glacier Lake, set at the foot of an awesome volcanic massif called Black Butte. Highlights include beautiful sweeping views of the Sierra and the opportunity for side trips to several other lakes. A round-trip from the trailhead to Glacier Lake and back is just under seven miles. It is one of the highlights of the Bowman Lakes Recreation Area, generally ranging 5,000-7,500 feet in elevation, featuring Sierra granite, pines, and dozens of alpine lakes.

It's a bumpy drive up past a small campground to the Grouse Ridge Trailhead and parking area. From the trailhead, the hike starts on an exposed ridge. Within just a few minutes, two gorgeous azure-blue lakes come into view to your left, Milk Lake and Round Lake. Many creep over to the ridge to get a better look. Then, back on the trail, another pretty lake can be spotted off to your right, Sanford Lake. The trail then descends quickly into a forested valley, where you arrive at an unsigned trail junction (out of curiosity, we explored this and found it led down a canyon to pretty Downey Lake. This alone is a good trip, an easy 20-minute jaunt to get there). Continuing north, you pass a signed trail junction on your left (which is routed west down to Round Lake, Milk Lake, and then Carr and Feely lakes), and then to a trail cut-off on your right—this is your turn for Glacier Lake.

This cut-off trail passes through a series of meadows and stands of pines, rising steadily along the way, with exposed Sand Ridge (fantastic wildflowers in mid-June) directly off to your left. Eventually you will spot Black Butte, the craggy ridge set on the nearby horizon ahead, and realize that Glacier Lake, your destination, is set right at the foot of it. You will top a ridge and come across a series of small camping flats, popular in July and August, and descend to lake's edge, an elevation of 7,500 feet. This is a small and pristine setting, with the lake's clear, calm waters providing a sharp contrast to the high backdrop of the Buttes, brown, black, and craggy, even crumbling in spots.

User Groups: Hikers, dogs, horses, and mountain bikes. No wheelchair facilities.

Permits: A campfire permit (free) is required for overnight use. Parking and access are free.

Maps: For a map, ask the U.S. Forest Service for Tahoe National Forest. For topographic maps, ask the USGS for Cisco Grove and English Mountain.

Directions: From Sacramento, take I-80 east past Emigrant Gap to the exit for Highway 20. Take that exit and go west four miles to Bowman Lake Road (Forest Road 18). Turn right on Bowman Lake Road and drive about five miles to Grouse Ridge Road. Turn right and go six miles (often rough) to a fork at Grouse Ridge. At the fork, bear right to the campground or bear left to the trailhead. A four-wheel-drive, high-clearance vehicle is recommended.

Contact: Tahoe National Forest, Nevada City Ranger District, 530/265-4531, www.fs.usda.gov/tahoe; Big Bend Visitors Center, 530/426-3609.

15 LINDSEY LAKES TRAIL
7.0 mi/3.0 hr   🏃2   ⛰7

in Tahoe National Forest north of Emigrant Gap

Map 6.1, page 205

The highlight of Lindsey Lakes Trail is that it intersects with other trails, including the beautiful Grouse Ridge Trail, and is set in a gorgeous landscape that features Sierra alpine beauty. But the trail itself from Lindsey Lakes to Rock Lake is a service road closed to public vehicle traffic, so you're hiking up a road. This 3.5-mile trail dead-ends after climbing past the three Lindsey Lakes, and it offers a great optional side trip. From the trailhead at Lower Lindsey Lake (elevation 6,160 feet), hike up to the other lakes on a short trail (it's quite steep in several places) before you top out at 6,400 feet. The route gets medium use and accesses good swimming holes with cold water, but the fishing is poor. A side trip from the Lindsey Lakes Trail is Crooked Lakes Trail (excellent).

User Groups: Hikers, dogs, and horses. Mountain bikes not advised. No wheelchair facilities.

Permits: No permits are required. Parking and access are free.

Maps: For a map, ask the U.S. Forest Service for Tahoe National Forest. For topographic maps, ask the USGS for English Mountain and Graniteville.

Directions: From Sacramento, take I-80 east past Emigrant Gap to the exit for Highway 20. Take that exit and go west four miles to Bowman Lake Road (Forest Road 18). Turn right on Bowman Lake Road and drive 8.5 miles to a junction signed Lindsey Lake, Feely Lake, Carr Lake. Turn right (dirt, some rocks, passable for cars, SUV recommended) and drive four miles (at fork, turn left for Lindsey Lake, right for Carr and Feeley Lakes). Turn left and drive about a mile to Lindsey Lake and trailhead. The last half-mile of road can be rough; high-clearance vehicles are advised.

Contact: Tahoe National Forest, Nevada City Ranger District, 530/265-4531, www.fs.usda.gov/tahoe; Big Bend Visitors Center, 530/426-3609.

16 CARR/FEELY TRAILHEAD TO PENNER LAKE

6.0 mi/3.0 hr 👣3 ⛰10

at Carr Lake in Tahoe National Forest north of Emigrant Gap

Map 6.1, page 205

The Bowman Lakes Recreation Area is best known for the popular Carr Lake Trailhead (crowded on summer weekends), which provides easy access to Carr Lake and Feeley Lake, and then launches into wildlands to gorgeous Island Lake and stunning Penner Lake, an easy six-mile round-trip. Dozens of small lakes are within reach on the Crooked Lakes Trail, Grouse Ridge Trail and others. Milk Lake, for instance, is also gorgeous. The area feels like wilderness, but is not designated as wilderness. Mountain bikes are permitted on trails, though until all the snow melts off and surface dries out, conditions are poor for biking.

From the park area, walk back a short distance and turn right for a short climb past Carr Lake on the right. You emerge above Carr and Feely Lake (6,720 feet) comes into view on the left. The trail runs along the right side of Feely and then enters forest. It's a gentle climb then to Island Lake, named for the little rock "islands," as they call them, to the junction of the Crooked Lakes Trail (signed). Take the Crooked Lakes Trail through a fir forest for 1.5 miles, which includes a short climb, to Penner Lake. Penner Lake (along with Milk) is one of the prettiest lakes in the area. The ambitious can continue another mile to Upper Rock Lake.

User Groups: Hikers, dogs, mountain bikes, and horses. No wheelchair facilities.

Permits: No permits are required. Parking and access are free.

Maps: For a map, ask the U.S. Forest Service for Tahoe National Forest. For topographic maps, ask the USGS for English Mountain and Graniteville.

Directions: From Sacramento, take I-80 east past Emigrant Gap to the exit for Highway 20. Take that exit and go west four miles to Bowman Lake Road (Forest Road 18). Turn right on Bowman Lake Road and drive 8.5 miles to a junction signed Lindsey Lake, Feely Lake, Carr Lake. Turn right (dirt, some rocks, passable for cars, SUV recommended) and drive four miles (at fork, turn left for Lindsey Lake, right for Carr and Feeley Lakes). Turn right and drive about a mile to the parking area for Carr Lake and trailhead. The last half-mile of road can be rough; high-clearance vehicles are advised, four-wheel drive is better.

Contact: Tahoe National Forest, Nevada City Ranger District, 530/265-4531, www. fs.usda.gov/tahoe; Big Bend Visitors Center, 530/426-3609.

17 DONNER PASS TO THE YUBA RIVER (PCT)

38.0 mi one-way/3 days 👥3 ⛺7

from Highway 80 to Highway 49 in Tahoe National Forest

Map 6.1, page 205

This is not one of the more glamorous sections of the Pacific Crest Trail. But it is still good. For the most part, the PCT here follows a crest that connects a series of small mountaintops before dropping down to Jackson Meadow Reservoir and Highway 49. Some good views are to be had on the first leg of the trail, so many that some PCT hikers begin to take them for granted after a while. The trail is routed past Castle Peak (elevation 9,103 feet), Basin Peak (9,015 feet), and Lacey Mountain (8,214 feet). Most can cover this much terrain for an ambitious first day, perhaps with stops at Paradise Lake or White Rock Lake. As the trail drops to Jackson Meadow Reservoir, the views end, but in time you'll catch sight of the lake; surrounded by firs, it is quite pretty. The PCT then skirts the east side of the reservoir, passes several drive-to campgrounds, heads through Bear Valley (not *the* Bear Valley), and drops steeply to Milton Creek and four miles beyond that to Loves Falls at Highway 49.

To continue north on the PCT, see the *Yuba River to Fowler Peak (PCT)* hike in this chapter. If you are walking this trail in reverse, see the *Barker Pass to Donner Pass (PCT)* hike in this chapter.

back side approach to Castle Peak

© TOM STIENSTRA

User Groups: Hikers, dogs, and horses. No mountain bikes. No wheelchair facilities.

Permits: A campfire permit (free) is required for overnight use. Parking and access are free.

Maps: For a map, ask the U.S. Forest Service for Tahoe National Forest. For topographic maps, ask the USGS for Norden, Soda Springs, Webber, Haypress Valley, Independence Lake, and English Mountain.

Directions: From Auburn, take I-80 east to the Boreal/Donner Summit and the signed exit for Pacific Crest trailhead parking area. Take that exit to parking. There is no hiker parking in the Donner Summit rest area.

Contact: Tahoe National Forest, Sierraville Ranger District, 530/994-3401, www.fs.usda. gov/tahoe.

18 GLACIER LAKE FROM CARR LAKE

10.0 mi/1 day

in Tahoe National Forest north of Emigrant Gap

Map 6.1, page 205

In just a few hours you can be transported to heaven. Some people, however, call it the Bowman Lakes Recreation Area. It is a five-mile hike with a 1,500-foot climb to reach Glacier Lake (7,000 feet). You pass lake after lake and then end up at a pristine setting with a high back wall. The small lake is set in a rock-bound bowl with the Black Buttes looming nearby. The tree cover is sparse, and the rock cover is abundant.

Start your hike from the trailhead at Carr Lake. You then pass Carr Lake on the right, Feely Lake on the left, and then Island and Round Lake. You'll drop down into forest and meadow landscape and reach a trail junction (right leads up to Grouse Ridge, another trailhead where you can start this trip). At the junction, continue east on Glacier Lake Trail. You will continue through a meadow and some forest. Here you start a gradual climb, passing a small lake before entering a rocky area and then

dropping down to the pretty lake. Several backpacking campsites are available.

Some maps of Tahoe National Forest do not show the direct route to Glacier Lake. Our route climbs up through a beautiful canyon. One map I saw, on the other hand, shows the trail routed up a hot, exposed route on Sandy Ridge off to the left.

User Groups: Hikers, dogs, and horses. Mountain bikes not advised. No wheelchair facilities.

Permits: No permits are required. Parking and access are free.

Maps: For a map, ask the U.S. Forest Service for Tahoe National Forest. For topographic maps, ask the USGS for Cisco Grove and English Mountain.

Directions: From Sacramento, take I-80 east past Emigrant Gap to the exit for Highway 20. Take that exit and go west four miles to Bowman Lake Road (Forest Road 18). Turn right on Bowman Lake Road and drive 8.5 miles to a junction signed Lindsey Lake, Feely Lake, Carr Lake. Turn right (dirt, some rocks, passable for cars, SUV recommended) and drive four miles (at fork, turn left for Lindsey Lake, right for Carr and Feeley Lakes). Turn right and drive about a mile to the parking area for Carr Lake and trailhead. The last half-mile of road can be rough; high-clearance vehicles are advised, four-wheel drive is better.

Contact: Tahoe National Forest, Nevada City Ranger District, 530/265-4531, www. fs.usda.gov/tahoe; Big Bend Visitors Center, 530/426-3609.

19 PIONEER TRAIL/ OMEGA OVERLOOK

1.0 mi/0.5 hr

east of Nevada City, off of Highway 20 in Tahoe National Forest

Map 6.1, page 205

The Caltrans Omega Overlook provides a view over the South Yuba River Canyon and beyond, as well as a historic site of a huge hydraulic gold-mining operation. There is a parking area, a restroom, and a viewing area. It is also a primary trailhead for the 24-mile Pioneer Trail. The Pioneer Trail is like taking a history lesson. You trace the route of the first wagon road, opened by emigrants and gold seekers in 1850. The trail is better suited for mountain biking. In fact, it has become almost an exclusive biking trip, but its historical significance still merits its inclusion in this book.

Significant sites are Central House (once a stagecoach stop) and White Cloud and Skillman Flat (former mill sites, one burned down).

A high percentage of mountain bikers seem to use the one-way trip downhill from Omega to Five Mile House, with a shuttle. When encountering other trail users, all need to remember to demonstrate the utmost courtesy.

User Groups: Hikers, dogs, mountain bikes, and horses. No wheelchair facilities.

Permits: A campfire permit (free) is required for overnight use. Parking and access are free.

Maps: For a map, ask the U.S. Forest Service for Tahoe National Forest. For a topographic map, ask the USGS for Washington.

Directions: From Nevada City, take Highway 20 east and drive for 16.9 miles to Omega Overlook on the left. Turn left and drive a short distance to parking.

Contact: Tahoe National Forest, Nevada City Ranger District, 530/265-4531, www.fs.usda.gov/tahoe; Big Bend Visitors Center, 530/426-3609.

20 SIERRA DISCOVERY TRAIL
1.0 mi/0.5 hr 🏃1 ⛰8

off Highway 20 near Lake Spaulding

Map 6.1, page 205   BEST (

Many short interpretive trails are long on words in brochures and short on beauty. Not this one. It provides glimpses of a series of gorgeous sites amid a forest of pines and cedars, with a pay-off of a pretty stream and small waterfall. Much of the trail is soil cement or compressed gravel. It is designed as an interpretive loop walk, with information about ecosystems, wildlife, geology, and cultural history available. What sets it apart is the pretty Bear River and its rich forest.

User Groups: Hikers, dogs, and wheelchairs (with assistance). No horses or mountain bikes. Dogs permitted, but rangers strongly discourage bringing them on this trail.

Permits: No permits are necessary. Parking and access are free.

Maps: For a topographic map, ask the USGS for Blue Canyon.

Directions: From Sacramento, take I-80 east past Emigrant Gap to the exit for Highway 20. Take that exit and go west four miles to Bowman Lake Road (Forest Road 18). Turn right on Bowman Lake Road and drive 0.6 mile to the Sierra Discovery Trail parking lot on the left.

Contact: Pacific Gas & Electric, 916/386-5164, www.pge.com./recreation.

21 LOCH LEVEN LAKES
7.2 mi/4.0 hr 🏃3 ⛰8

south of Cisco Grove in Tahoe National Forest

Map 6.1, page 205

Most people would like to know what heaven is like. This trip to Loch Leven Lakes won't be your final resting place, yet it provides a glimpse of what heaven might resemble. Although there is some road noise at the beginning of this trip, the end is well worth it. You get sweeping vistas of ridges and valleys, gorgeous high alpine meadows, and glaciated mountain terrain with a series of pretty lakes.

The trail starts at 5,680 feet, then works its way upward on a moderate grade to the southwest. Granite outcrops are numerous, and huge boulders (deposited by receding glaciers) lie sprinkled among Jeffrey pine and lodgepole pine. The trail crosses a creek and railroad tracks, then climbs through a cool forest. Here the trail becomes steeper, where you climb 800 feet in 1.25 miles. It then tops the summit and descends gently to Lower Loch Leven Lake (2.5 miles from the trailhead). Many people stop here, content to just take in the surroundings. But you can forge on for another mile, circling Middle Loch Leven Lake (2.8 miles from the trailhead) and heading east up to High Loch Leven Lake (3.6 miles from the trailhead), at 6,800 feet. At the south end of Lower Loch Leven Lake, turn left at the trail junction to see Middle and High Loch Leven Lakes (turning right at the junction will route you to Salmon Lake, a less-crowded alternative). Once you've come this far, beautiful High Loch Leven is an easy trip and a must-do.

But this hike is not without frustration: The first hour involves a continuous climb, with the echo of I-80 traffic in the background. You do not escape the noise until you top the ridge. Elevations range 5,680-6,850 feet at the ridge, a gain of 1,070 feet. With access so easy off I-80, the area can become inundated with people on summer weekends. With no trailhead quota, the numbers can affect the sense of wilderness.

User Groups: Hikers, dogs, and horses. Mountain bikes not advised. No wheelchair facilities.

Permits: No permits are required. Parking and access are free.

Maps: For a map, ask the U.S. Forest Service for Tahoe National Forest. For a topographic map, ask the USGS for Cisco Grove.

Directions: From Sacramento, take I-80 east for 70 miles into the Sierra Nevada and to exit 165 toward Cisco Grove. Take that exit a short distance to Hampshire Rocks Road. Turn left on Hampshire Rocks Road and drive (well signed) 0.2 mile to the Big Bend Visitors Center on the right. The parking area and trailhead is located about 0.2 mile east of the visitors center. The trailhead is on the opposite side of the road from the parking area.

Contact: Big Bend Visitors Center, 530/426-3609, www.fs.usda.gov/tahoe.

22 LOWER LOLA MONTEZ LAKE

6.0 mi/3.0 hr   🏃2 ⛰8

in Tahoe National Forest near Soda Springs

Map 6.1, page 205

If timing is everything in love and the outdoors, then time this trip for the shoulder seasons, spring or fall. In summer, mountain bikers take over this trail. Traffic is high on weekends. Lower Lola Montez is a beautiful alpine lake set at 7,200 feet. Start at Toll Mountain Estates, a private community. The first 0.25 mile is on single track. Then you reach a dirt road and turn right, cross Castle Creek, and continue until the road becomes single track again. The route is marked all the way, and with all the people who ride this in summer, it's an easy track to follow.

User Groups: Hikers, dogs, horses, and mountain bikes. No wheelchair facilities.

Permits: No permits are required. Parking and access are free.

Maps: For a map, ask the U.S. Forest Service for Tahoe National Forest. For topographic maps, ask the USGS for Soda Springs and Norden.

Directions: From Auburn, take I-80 east for 55 miles to Soda Springs. Take the Soda Springs/Norden exit and cross the overpass to the north side of the freeway. Follow the paved road east, past the fire station, for 0.3 mile to the trailhead parking area.

Contact: Tahoe National Forest, Truckee Ranger District, 530/587-3558, www.fs.usda.gov/tahoe; Big Bend Visitors Center, 530/426-3609.

23 PALISADE CREEK TRAIL TO HEATH FALLS

10.0 mi/6.0 hr   🏃3 ⛰10

in Tahoe National Forest near Soda Springs

Map 6.1, page 205

The hike to Heath Falls is like going on vacation on your credit card. You can have all the fun you want, but when you return home, you have to pay up. That's because the trip to the Heath Falls Overlook is downhill nearly all the way, where you descend 1,700 feet over five miles. Stunning alpine scenery will have you smiling the whole time. The return trip is a long and steady five-mile climb back uphill, so be sure you have plenty of trail snacks, water, and energy left for it.

The trail begins at the dam between the two Cascade Lakes, the first of many lakes you'll see on this trip. The big hunk of imposing rock you have to walk around is 7,704-foot Devils Peak. Take the right fork signed for the North Fork American River, and get ready for a steady diet of granite, lakes, and vistas. At 2.2 miles, the trail leaves the rocks behind and enters the forest, switchbacking downhill for two miles to the Palisade Creek Bridge. Look for an un-signed junction 300 yards beyond it, where Heath Falls Overlook Trail heads east. Follow it for 0.5 mile to the trail's end, at a vista of the American River's Heath Falls. After you enjoy the falls overlook, you've got to make the long climb home. Hope you have at least one Clif Bar left.

User Groups: Hikers, dogs, and horses. No mountain bikes. No wheelchair facilities.

Permits: No permits are required. Parking and access are free.

Maps: For a map, ask the U.S. Forest Service for Tahoe National Forest. For topographic maps, ask the USGS for Soda Springs and Norden.

Directions: From Sacramento, take I-80 east for 79 miles to exit 174 for Soda Springs/Norden. Take that exit for 0.2 mile to Donner Pass Road. Turn right on Donner Pass Road and drive 0.7 mile to Soda Springs Road. Turn right and drive 0.9 mile to Pahatsi Road. Turn right and drive 0.2 mile (turns to dirt, becomes Kidd Lakes Road) and continue straight for 3.8 miles (you pass Kidd Lake on your left and the Royal Gorge Devils Lookout Warming Hut on your right) to a fork. After the warming hut, take the left fork and drive 0.5 mile to the trail-head, signed as Palisade Creek Trail, on the north side of Cascade Lakes.

Contact: Tahoe National Forest, Truckee Ranger District, 530/587-3558, www.fs.usda.gov/tahoe; Big Bend Visitors Center, 530/426-3609.

24 WARREN LAKE
14.0 mi/2 days

in Tahoe National Forest near Donner Summit

Map 6.1, page 205

The first 1.6 miles of this trail follow the same route as the Summit Lake Trail (see listing), along the PCT access trail and through the tunnel underneath I-80 to a fork. To reach Warren Lake, take the left fork (the right fork goes to Summit Lake). Whereas Summit Lake Trail is an easy stroll, the Warren Lake Trail climbs 1,500 feet and then drops 1,500 feet, which you must repeat on the return trip. The elevation change means you part company with most casual hikers.

From the fork, the route climbs through lodgepole pine and red fir forest to a saddle at three miles, where there are excellent views of much of the landscape you will hike through. The trail drops gently over the next 3.5 miles, into a wide valley basin that has a mix of volcanic and glaciated rocks. Wildflowers abound on the valley floor. After a brief climb to a ridge, the final mile is a steep descent, where you plummet 1,000 feet to Warren Lake. You'll find many campsites on the lake's west and south sides.

For Day 2, note that just before you reach the top of the ridge, about 1.3 miles from Warren Lake, there is a left spur trail that leads to Devils Oven Lake. It's a good day hike for Day 2.

User Groups: Hikers, dogs, horses, and mountain bikes. No wheelchair facilities.

Permits: No permits are required. Parking and access are free.

Maps: For a map, ask the U.S. Forest Service for Tahoe National Forest. For a topographic map, ask the USGS for Norden.

Directions: From Sacramento, take I-80 east for 86 miles to exit 176 for Castle Peak/Boreal Ridge Road exit (just west of Donner Summit).

Take that exit and turn right, go a very short distance, and then immediately turn left, and drive 0.4 mile to the trailhead for Donner Summit and the Pacific Crest Trail.

Contact: Tahoe National Forest, Truckee Ranger District, 530/587-3558, www. fs.usda.gov/tahoe; Big Bend Visitors Center, 530/426-3609.

25 SUMMIT LAKE TRAIL
4.0 mi/2.0 hr

in Tahoe National Forest near Donner Summit

Map 6.1, page 205

The Summit Lake Trail is a quick and easy leg-stretcher and a great hike for families. It leads two miles to a pretty alpine lake at 7,400 feet. It is crowded on weekends, plus those who are not fit complain that the short climb is harder than they expected. Start the trip at the PCT trailhead. Head east, where you roughly parallel the freeway. A half mile in, watch for an intersection. You must turn left and follow the PCT Access Trail north (signed for Castle Pass and Peter Grubb Hut) through a tunnel underneath I-80 (it's not as bad as it sounds). Once you're on the north side of the freeway, you'll reach a fork. Bear right for Summit Lake and Warren Lake, then start to climb a bit. The trail alternates through fir forest and occasional open ridges, with some excellent views to the south and east. At 1.6 miles, you'll see another trail fork: Warren Lake to the left, and Summit Lake to the right. Bear right, and finish out your walk to the lake's edge.

User Groups: Hikers, dogs, horses, and mountain bikes. No wheelchair facilities.

Permits: No permits are required. Parking and access are free.

Maps: For a map, ask the U.S. Forest Service for Tahoe National Forest. For a topographic map, ask the USGS for Norden.

Directions: From Sacramento, take I-80 east for 86 miles to exit 176 for Castle Peak/Boreal Ridge Road exit (just west of Donner Summit). Take that exit and turn right, go a very short

distance, and then immediately turn left, and drive 0.4 mile to the trailhead for Donner Summit and the Pacific Crest Trail.

Contact: Tahoe National Forest, Truckee Ranger District, 530/587-3558, www. fs.usda.gov/tahoe; Big Bend Visitors Center, 530/426-3609.

26 EUCHRE BAR TRAIL
10.5 mi/2 days

on the North Fork American River near Baxter in Tahoe National Forest

Map 6.1, page 205

This is an old mining trail, so steep with a 2,000-foot descent on the way in. For the trip back out of the canyon, it qualifies as a kill-me, eat-me hike. Yet it comes with access to a cool suspension bridge and a beautiful section of the North Fork American River. From the trailhead, the route winds steeply down to the river and Euchre Bar near Rawhide, where a suspension footbridge crosses the water. The trail then leads upriver for 2.4 miles, along an excellent stretch of water for fishing, camping, panning for gold, and swimming (cold). The trail extends along the river for 5.3 miles.

User Groups: Hikers, dogs, and horses. Mountain bikes not advised. No wheelchair facilities.

Permits: Campfire permits are required for overnight use. Parking and access are free.

Maps: For a map, ask the U.S. Forest Service for Tahoe National Forest. For topographic maps, ask the USGS for Dutch Flat and Westville.

Directions: From Sacramento, take I-80 east for 51 miles to exit 146 for Alta. Take that exit 0.2 mile to Morton. Turn right on Morton, drive 100 feet to Casa Loma Road, then turn left on Casa Loma and drive three miles (requires several jogs, becomes rough, high-clearance recommended, four-wheel drive advised near end) to the trailhead.

Contact: Tahoe National Forest, Nevada City Ranger District, 530/265-4531, www.fs.usda. gov/tahoe.

27 ITALIAN BAR TRAIL

4.5 mi/3.5 hr   🥾5   ⛰8

near the North Fork American River in Tahoe
National Forest

Map 6.1, page 205

Miners in the 1850s were like mountain goats.
Like any good goat, they knew the most direct
route between two points was a straight line.
As a result, this route—which miners once used
to reach the North Fork American River—is
almost straight down going in and straight up
coming out, gaining 3,000 feet in elevation over
the course of 2.25 miles. The grade was measured at 35 percent at its steepest slopes (from
4,834 to 2,447 feet). As you head down from the
trailhead at 5,400 feet, you get little help from
switchbacks. The trail ends at the river, and
from there, you must scramble and hop from
rock to rock along the riverbanks. Eventually
you end up at a secluded spot where all seems
perfect—until you start the hike back. When
you face the 3,000-foot climb out, you will wonder how you ever talked yourself into doing this
hike.

User Groups: Hikers, dogs, and horses.
Mountain bikes not advised. No wheelchair
facilities.

Permits: No permits are required. Parking and
access are free.

Maps: For a map, ask the U.S. Forest Service for
Tahoe National Forest. For a topographic map,
ask the USGS for Westville.

Directions: Take I-80 to Auburn and the exit
for Foresthill/Foresthill Road. Take that exit,
turn east on Foresthill Road, and drive 15.5
miles to Foresthill (and the Forest Service district office). Continue on Foresthill Road for
14.5 miles to Humbug Ridge Road (Forest Road
66). Turn left and drive three miles north to the
trailhead. Four-wheel-drive, high-clearance vehicles are advised.

Contact: American River Ranger District,
530/367-2224, www.fs.usda.gov/tahoe.

28 MUMFORD BAR TRAIL

7 mi/1 day   🥾5   ⛰8

near the North Fork American River in Tahoe
National Forest

Map 6.1, page 205

This trail spans 5,377 to 2,632 feet to the North
Fork American, a descent of 2,745 feet in 3.5
miles. Of the steep trails that plummet into the
canyon of the North Fork American, this seems
to be the most popular. On the way down, you
get pretty views of the river canyon, and then of
Royal Gorge. It leads down to the Mumford Bar
Cabin, restored for viewing. You can continue
upstream from here on the American River
Trail. However, there has been significant fire
damage to the American River Trail, which
has been removed from this edition along with
nearby Beacroft and Sailor Flat Trails.

User Groups: Hikers, dogs, and horses.
Mountain bikes are not advised. No wheelchair facilities.

Permits: No permits are required. Parking and
access are free.

Maps: For a map, ask the U.S. Forest Service for
Tahoe National Forest. For topographic maps,
ask the USGS for Duncan Peak and Westville.

Directions: Take I-80 to Auburn and the exit
for Foresthill/Foresthill Road. Take that exit,
turn east on Foresthill Road, and drive 15.5
miles to Foresthill (and the Forest Service district office). Continue another 17 miles northeast (the road becomes Foresthill Divide Road)
to the Mumford Bar Campground. Turn left
and drive through the campground and access
a road (becomes passable only for four-wheel-
drive vehicles; others should park in the developed area on top) and continue to the trailhead.

Contact: Tahoe National Forest, Foresthill
Ranger District, 530/367-2224, www.fs.usda.
gov/tahoe.

29 STEVENS TRAIL
9.0 mi/5.0 hr   🚶2 ⛺8

near Colfax

Map 6.1, page 205

The Stevens Trail is a surprise to many. The trailhead is right aside I-80. Yet it leaves the noisy highway traffic behind in Colfax and runs 4.5 miles down into the canyon of the North Fork American River. The features here are gentle terrain and long-distance canyon and stream views.

The parking area has a big trailhead sign and this has become a very popular trail. You descend 1,200 feet over the course of 4.5 miles if you choose to head all the way to the river. From the ridge, continue on a gentle downhill path, where the return trip is up but is well graded and not too difficult for most hikers. In wet years, there can be some small waterfalls. About two miles in, the trail splits; the upper trail (hikers only) leads to a creek crossing—little pool-and-drop cascades—and then rejoins with the main trail.

You can also see the railroad line that was built by Chinese laborers dangling in rope-strung baskets from the cliffs above. In the spring, you will also pass blooming wildflowers and buckeye trees. This trail is registered as a National Historic Trail. It was originally part of a livery trail from the town of Iowa Hill to Colfax. The entire historic route is no longer connected, with no bridge over the river, and the trail gone beyond that anyway. The biggest problem here is timing. This is no fun on a summer afternoon, with 90-degree temperatures and an afternoon climb out of a canyon.

Note: Mountain lion encounters have occurred on this trail.

User Groups: Hikers, dogs, horses, and mountain bikes. No wheelchair facilities.

Permits: No permits are necessary. Parking and access are free.

Maps: For a topographic map, ask the USGS for Colfax.

Directions: From Sacramento, drive east on I-80 for four miles to Colfax and the exit signed Colfax-Grass Valley/Highway 174. Take that exit and drive a short distance (on the southeast side of I-80) to a stop sign at North Canyon (a frontage road). Turn left at North Canyon Way and drive one mile to the trailhead parking area. On weekends in spring, the parking lot can fill. Park on the road's shoulder and do not block the lanes.

Contact: Bureau of Land Management, Mother Lode Field Office, 916/941-3101, www.blm.gov/ca.

30 GREEN VALLEY TRAIL
5.2 mi/1 day   🚶5 ⛺8

on the North Fork American River near Sugar Pine Reservoir

Map 6.1, page 205

The trip starts at a little-known trailhead near Sugar Pine Reservoir, beyond the Sugarpine Dam (elevation 4,080 feet). From there, Green Valley Trail is steep and often rocky. It descends 2,240 feet in 2.25 miles before reaching the river. We do not advise extending your trip from here. It is possible to continue downriver a short way, or to cross the river (good luck) and hike upstream into Green Valley. However, these sections of the trail are in very poor condition, and the upstream route crosses private property owned by people who do not take kindly to visitors.

The end point is a site along the North Fork America. Fishing is decent. At some point, you'll just want to watch the water go by, and try to forget what you have to do to return to your car. The price is steep. Run out of water on a hot day and the return trip will put you through more punishment than is typically handed out at Folsom Prison.

User Groups: Hikers, dogs, and horses. Mountain bikes are not advised. No wheelchair facilities.

Permits: No permits are required. Parking and access are free.

Maps: For a map, ask the U.S. Forest Service for

Tahoe National Forest. For a topographic map, ask the USGS for Dutch Flat.

Directions: Take I-80 to Auburn and the exit for Foresthill/Foresthill Road. Take that exit, turn east on Foresthill Road, and drive 15.5 miles to Foresthill (and the Forest Service district office). Continue another 10 miles (it becomes Foresthill Divide Road, then Forest Road 10/Sugar Pine Road) and continue five miles (cross Sugar Pine Dam). From the dam, continue one mile to Elliot Ranch Road (just past the entrance to Sugar Pine Campground, on the right). Turn north on Elliot Ranch Road and drive three miles to the trailhead on the left. High-clearance vehicles required, four-wheel drive advised.

Contact: Tahoe National Forest, Foresthill Ranger District, 530/367-2224, www.fs.usda.gov/tahoe.

31 FOREST VIEW LOOP TRAIL
1.0 mi/0.5 hr   🏃1 ⛰9

in Tahoe National Forest east of Foresthill

Map 6.1, page 205

This is an easy, short loop trail that is routed through California's northernmost grove of sequoias. It is set at 5,200 feet on Mosquito Ridge Road. The trail meanders through virgin old-growth forest, home to a half dozen monster-sized trees. Along the 0.5-mile Big Trees Interpretive Trail are 16 stops marked with numbers that coincide with numbered listings in a brochure that's available at the trailhead, allowing visitors to take an interesting and informative self-guided tour of the history of these massive trees. Linked with Forest View Trail, the entire loop can extend 1.5 miles. Despite the long drive to the trailhead on Mosquito Ridge, the trail gets quite a bit of use. The drive in provides views of an expansive foothill landscape before entering the conifers.

User Groups: Hikers and dogs. No horses or mountain bikes. No wheelchair facilities.

Permits: No permits are required. Parking and access are free.

Maps: Free interpretive brochures are available at the trailhead. For a map, ask the U.S. Forest Service for Tahoe National Forest. For a topographic map, ask the USGS for Greek Store.

Directions: Take I-80 to Auburn and the exit for Foresthill/Foresthill Road. Take that exit, turn east on Foresthill Road, and drive 15.5 miles to Foresthill (and the Forest Service district office), and then continue 1.2 miles to Mosquito Ridge Road. Turn right (east) on Mosquito Ridge Road and drive 24 miles to Forest Road 16. Turn right and drive 0.5 mile to parking and the trailhead.

Contact: Tahoe National Forest, Foresthill Ranger District, 530/367-2224, www.fs.usda.gov/tahoe.

32 WESTERN STATES TRAIL: DEADWOOD TO ELDORADO CREEK
5.9 mi/3.0 hr   🏃3 ⛰7

in Tahoe National Forest east of Foresthill

Map 6.1, page 205

The Western States Trail is best known for long-distance, competitive runs and equestrian rides. At times, mountain bikers take over the trail as well. This section captures one of the better sections for hikers. From Deadwood (a historic cemetery), you drop about 2.5 miles down to Eldorado Creek and reach a bridge. This is a decent spot for swimming on a midsummer afternoon, or fishing for trout on early summer evening. The trail continues over the bridge and climbs 1,600 feet to Michigan Bluff. Few do this. If you have to go up, most just want to do it once, and that's back to your car. The Michigan Bluff Trail is a section of the Western States Trail, which spans from Squaw Valley to Auburn.

User Groups: Hikers, dogs, horses, and mountain bikes. No wheelchair facilities.

Permits: No permits are required. Parking and access are free.

Maps: For a map, ask the U.S. Forest Service for Tahoe National Forest. For a topographic map, ask the USGS for Michigan Bluff.

Directions: Take I-80 to Auburn and the exit for Foresthill/Foresthill Road. Take that exit, turn east on Foresthill Road, and drive 15.5 miles to Foresthill (and the Forest Service district office). Continue northeast (it becomes Foresthill Divide Road) for 17 miles to Deadwood Ridge Road. Turn right (becomes dirt) and continue to the junction at Deadwood Cemetery. Park in the pullout. The road degrades quickly. High-clearance vehicles recommended.

Contact: Tahoe National Forest, Foresthill Ranger District, 530/367-2224, www.fs.usda.gov/tahoe.

33 GROUSE FALLS
1.0 mi/0.5 hr   🥾1 ⛰10

in Tahoe National Forest near Foresthill

Map 6.1, page 205   BEST (

Some waterfalls are simply mind-boggling in their beauty, and some provide the centerpiece of a beautiful setting. Grouse Falls is one of the latter. The hike is a 15-minute walk through old-growth forest to a viewing deck. From here you're looking out over a deep and wide canyon. The waterfall is about 0.5 mile away across the canyon. It's several hundred feet long, and when it's running full, it can seem like a scene out of Yosemite. The overlook is a wooden platform with benches where you can sit and admire the beauty. You don't see or hear immense Grouse Falls until just before you come out to the overlook, and when you do, it can be a shock to your system. You need a tripod and long lens to best capture it in a photograph.

User Groups: Hikers, dogs, horses, and mountain bikes. No wheelchair facilities.

Permits: No permits are necessary. Parking and access are free.

Maps: For a map, ask the U.S. Forest Service for Tahoe National Forest. For a topographic map, ask the USGS for Michigan Bluff.

Directions: Take I-80 to Auburn and the exit for Foresthill/Foresthill Road. Take that exit, turn east on Foresthill Road, and drive 15.5 miles to Foresthill (and the Forest Service district office). Continue 1.2 miles to Mosquito Ridge Road. Turn right on Mosquito Ridge Road and drive 19.2 miles (the road becomes Foresthill Divide Road) to Peavine Ridge Road/Road 33. Turn left and drive 5.5 miles to a spur road for Grouse Falls. Turn left and go 0.5 mile to parking and the trailhead.

Contact: Tahoe National Forest, Foresthill Ranger District, 530/367-2224, www.fs.usda.gov/tahoe.

34 WESTERN STATES TRAIL/ MCGUIRE SEGMENT
7.4 mi/2.0 hr   🥾2 ⛰8

at French Meadows Reservoir in Tahoe National Forest

Map 6.1, page 205

The McGuire Trail has become a favorite side trip for families visiting or camping at French Meadows Reservoir (elevation 5,290 feet). The highlights are sweeping views of the lake below. The trailhead is located near the boat ramp, at the upper parking lot next to the restroom. From here, the trail traces the north shore of the lake, and in the process, is routed in and out of forest. It then rises up an easy grade to the top of Red Star Ridge (5,600 feet) and provides good views of the reservoir below. French Meadows is a beautiful and large lake, covering nearly 2,000 acres when full. It is stocked each year with trout that join a healthy population of resident brown trout and holdovers from stocks of rainbow trout from prior years. Water drawdowns are a common problem in late summer, as they expose many stumps and boulders, which can be a navigational hazard for boaters.

User Groups: Hikers, dogs, horses, and mountain bikes. No wheelchair facilities.

Permits: No permits are required. Parking and access are free.

Maps: For a map, ask the U.S. Forest Service for

Tahoe National Forest. For a topographic map, ask the USGS for Bunker Hill.

Directions: Take I-80 to Auburn and the exit for Foresthill/Foresthill Road. Take that exit, turn east on Foresthill Road, and drive 15.5 miles to Foresthill (and the Forest Service district office). Continue 1.2 miles to Mosquito Ridge Road. Turn right on Mosquito Ridge Road and drive 38 miles to the French Meadows Reservoir Dam. Cross the dam, turn left (still Mosquito Ridge Road), and drive 5.5 miles (turn left at the intersection where the pavement ends, signed for boat ramp) to the trailhead, near McGuire Boat Ramp. The trailhead is located at the upper parking lot next to the restroom.

Contact: Tahoe National Forest, Foresthill Ranger District, 530/367-2224, www.fs.usda.gov/tahoe.

35 GRANITE CHIEF TRAIL TO TINKER KNOB

14.0 mi/2 days 　　　　**4**　**10**

in Tahoe National Forest near Squaw Valley

Map 6.1, page 205

Tinker Knob is not an easy summit to attain, but those who reach it always remember it. The hike starts at the Squaw Valley Fire Station, elevation 6,200 feet. That much is easy. The Granite Chief Trail climbs 2,000 feet over a span of 3.5 miles to the Pacific Crest Trail. Most of the climb is forested, but there are occasional openings with views of Lake Tahoe and surrounding peaks. Many hikers choose to "cheat " and ride the tram at Squaw Valley to reach the PCT, then start hiking around from there.

When, at last, you gain the PCT (at 8,200 feet), turn right (north) toward Tinker Knob. It's another 3.5 miles, most of it on an easier, winding grade along the top of a ridge. Yet there is a surprising, cruel stretch where you must drop downhill and then climb up again. The last section of trail is a series of switchbacks up to the Tinker Knob Saddle, then it's a brief 0.25-mile climb to the summit of Tinker Knob, at 8,950 feet. You like views? How about this one: a head-swiveling vista of Anderson Peak, Painted Rock, Silver Peak, the American River Canyon, Donner Lake, and Lake Tahoe.

One-way option with a shuttle: To make this a one-way trip of 11 miles, it can be done with a partner and a shuttle car. Leave one car at the Coldstream trailhead near Donner Memorial State Park. (It's at the horseshoe bend in the railroad tracks at the end of Coldstream Creek access road.) The Coldstream Trail meets the PCT just below the summit of Tinker Knob. After you gain the summit via the route described above, follow Coldstream Trail four miles down to its trailhead.

User Groups: Hikers, dogs, horses, and mountain bikes. No wheelchair facilities.

Permits: No permits are required. Parking and access are free.

Maps: For a map, ask the U.S. Forest Service for Tahoe National Forest. For topographic maps, ask the USGS for Tahoe City and Granite Chief.

Directions: From Truckee, take Highway 89 south and drive about eight miles to Squaw Valley Road. Turn right on Squaw Valley Road and drive 2.2 miles to the Squaw Valley Fire Station. The trail begins on its east side. You must leave your car in the large parking lot by the ski lift buildings, not by the fire station. Walk back across the bridge to the trailhead.

Contact: Tahoe National Forest, Truckee Ranger District, 530/587-3558, www.fs.usda.gov/tahoe.

36 GRANITE CHIEF TRAIL TO EMIGRANT PASS

12.0 mi/7.0 hr 　　　　**4**　**9**

in Tahoe National Forest near Squaw Valley

Map 6.1, page 205

The Granite Chief Trail begins at the Squaw Valley Fire Station (at 6,200 feet) and climbs, climbs, and climbs some more until it reaches the Pacific Crest Trail, some 2,000 feet and 3.5 miles later. This is why many hikers choose to ride the tram at Squaw Valley to reach the PCT, then start hiking around from there. But not you? You like a challenge, right? Well, in either case, see you at the top.

When you reach the PCT, turn left (south) toward Twin Peaks. The view of Lake Tahoe and its cobalt blue waters is stunning. Still ascending, hike for one mile on the PCT to the eastern flank of Granite Chief Peak (elevation 9,086 feet). Finally you begin to descend, and in one more mile you reach an intersection with Western States Trail. Turn left and take a 0.5-mile walk to visit the Watson Monument, a stone marker at Emigrant Pass. In early summer, you probably won't stay long if you arrive in the afternoon: Although the views are lovely, the wind is usually fierce by midday.

User Groups: Hikers, dogs, horses, and mountain bikes. No wheelchair facilities.

Permits: No permits are required. Parking and access are free.

Maps: For a map, ask the U.S. Forest Service for Tahoe National Forest. For topographic maps, ask the USGS for Tahoe City and Granite Chief.

Directions: From Truckee, take Highway 89 south and drive about eight miles to Squaw Valley Road. Turn right on Squaw Valley Road and drive 2.2 miles to the Squaw Valley Fire Station. The trail begins on its east side. You must leave your car in the large parking lot by the ski lift buildings, not by the fire station. Walk back across the bridge to the trailhead.

Contact: Tahoe National Forest, Truckee Ranger District, 530/587-3558, www.fs.usda.gov/tahoe.

FIVE LAKES
5.0 mi/2.0 hr   🏃2 ⛰9

in the Granite Chief Wilderness near Alpine Meadows

Map 6.1, page 205

In a hike of just an hour or so, there's a place at north Tahoe where you can reach a series of five wilderness lakes nestled in granite amid a pine forest. It's called the Five Lakes Trail and it's one of the best short day hikes in California.

It attracts a lot of folks in summer. Try it when the snow melts in spring and you can still have it to yourself. The trailhead is located near Alpine Meadows Ski Area, with a sign, billboard, and map. The hike is 2.5 miles one-way with a 1,000-foot climb into the Granite Chief Wilderness. At the trailhead, you park right on the road's shoulder, and you'll almost always see other cars marking the spot.

The first half-mile of trail climbs right off, and if you are not acclimated to the elevation, it may take a while to catch your second wind. No problem. The trip is short, so if you need to, take your time. The climb eventually steadies out and most will find a nice rhythm as you rise up the flank of the canyon. At one point, you pass a series of ski lift support structures for Alpine Meadows and can see up to the ridge to 8,637-foot Ward Peak. Much of the climb is amid exposed granite and manzanita, so it is exposed for big canyon views. At about two miles, you pop over the ridge and pass the boundary for the Granite Chief Wilderness. When you top the ridge at 7,400 feet, the trail then feeds you to a series of five pristine lakes linked by a mosaic of paths. It's a short walk beyond to the first lake on the left. The fun is just beginning. A short strait connects two of the biggest lakes, my favorites. At the biggest of them, a granite slab on one side, boulders and forest on the other, edges clear blue water. The ambitious can hike on and link up with the Pacific Crest Trail. Most have a trail picnic aside their favorite lake, then return.

User Groups: Hikers, dogs, and horses. No mountain bikes. No wheelchair facilities.

Permits: No permits are required for day hiking. Parking and access are free.

Maps: For a map, ask the U.S. Forest Service for Tahoe National Forest. For topographic maps, ask the USGS for Tahoe City and Granite Chief.

Directions: From Sacramento, take I-80 east for 90 miles to Truckee and Exit 185 for Highway 89. Take that exit, turn right, arc slightly on the roundabout, then continue on 89 and drive 9.8 miles (past exit for Squaw Valley) to Alpine Meadows Road. Turn right and drive

2.5 miles to the trailhead on the right (look for parked cars along road; billboard and sign at trailhead).

Contact: Tahoe National Forest, Truckee Ranger District, 530/587-3558, www.fs.usda.gov/tahoe.

38 WARD CREEK TRAIL
6.0 mi/3.0 hr ⠀⠀ 👥1 ⛰9

in Tahoe National Forest near Tahoe City

> **Map 6.1, page 205**

Ward Creek Trail is tame compared to some of the more famous hikes at Lake Tahoe. There's no stellar waterfall, no drop-dead gorgeous lake views, and no towering granite monoliths. But then again, there are no crowds either. For many, the trade-off is a good one. The route passes through fields of mule's ears and forests of sugar pines, with enough open sections to provide wide-open views of the surrounding mountain ridges.

The trail begins as an old dirt road, paralleling Ward Creek for 1.5 miles to a washed-out bridge and a Road Closed sign. Cross the creek on logs and continue hiking, now on a single track. The trail climbs a little higher above Ward Creek, then enters a dense, lovely pine forest. You can go as far as you like (the trail continues to Twin Peaks, 5.3 miles from the trailhead). For the mileage suggested, turn around when you are about 0.5 mile into the trees and take an easy stroll home.

User Groups: Hikers, dogs, horses, and mountain bikes. No wheelchair facilities.

Permits: No permits are required. Parking and access are free.

Maps: For a map, ask the U.S. Forest Service for Lake Tahoe Basin Management Unit. For a topographic map, ask the USGS for Tahoe City.

Directions: From Truckee, take Highway 89 south and drive to Tahoe City. Turn right on Highway 89 and drive two miles to Pineland Drive (just north of Kilner Park). Turn right on Pineland Drive and go 0.5 mile to Twin Peaks Drive. Turn left and drive 1.7 miles. (Twin Peaks Drive becomes Ward Creek Boulevard.) At 1.7 miles, park in the pullout on the left side of the highway and begin hiking at the gated dirt road, Forest Service Road 15N62. If the gate is open, you can drive inside and park along the dirt road.

Contact: Lake Tahoe Basin Management Unit, South Lake Tahoe, 530/543-2600, www.fs.usda.gov/ltbmu; visitors center (open daily mid-June-Sept., Sat.-Sun Memorial Day-mid-Oct.), 530/543-2674.

39 ELLIS PEAK TRAIL
6.0 mi/3.5 hr ⠀⠀ 👥3 ⛰10

in Tahoe National Forest near Tahoe City

> **Map 6.1, page 205**

Some people will spend a week hiking 100 miles to get what is already available in three miles and a few hours at 8,740-foot Ellis Peak. Of the dozen or so landmark peaks that surround Lake Tahoe, Ellis Peak requires one of the shortest hikes, especially compared to renowned Tallac, Freel, and Pyramid. Ellis sits on the threshold of world-class greatness; at the top, it can be difficult to decide which way to face. One side towers over north Lake Tahoe, while the other looks across a false summit and Desolation Wilderness. The Crystal Range and Loon Lake lie below to the southwest, the Granite Chief Wilderness to the northwest. Everywhere you look are miles of spectacular high Sierra grandeur.

This six-mile, round-trip hike has a total elevation gain of roughly 1,500 feet. If there's a catch, you'll find out right off. The trail is hardly graded, but is steep in two spots. In the first mile, you'll climb about 800 feet through forest. As you emerge at a sub-ridge, notice a notch in the cliff on your left—you can peer down through a plummeting drop and see the parking area and your car below. That gives you a sense of how steep the trail is. A nearby clearing blooms with rafts of mule's ears at your feet; off to the right is beautiful Loon Lake in the Crystal Basin. Once you top the first sub-ridge, the trail contours along the ridge, then sails down to a mountain saddle. It then climbs again and gains Knee Ridge. You will cross an OHV road, with oft-mosquito-y Ellis Lake a 0.5-mile side trip to your left. The primary trail is straight ahead.

From the Ellis Lake junction, it's another 0.5-mile climb to the top. You emerge on an old dirt road for a bit to see a false summit directly ahead. Resist the urge to climb it. Instead, stay right and follow the trail as it rings in a half circle, where it leads up another 0.25 mile to the top of Ellis Peak. After scrambling to the top of that pinnacle, it feels like you are on top of the world. Some of the rocks make perfect chairs; sit and take in the views—the expansive Tahoe blue on one side, what seems like an infinity of wilderness on the other.

User Groups: Hikers. Dogs and horses permitted, but not advised; only water at Ellis Lake. No mountain bikes (OHV route available 0.5 mile down road on left). No wheelchair facilities.

Permits: No permits are required. Parking and access are free.

Maps: For a map, ask the U.S. Forest Service for Lake Tahoe Basin Management Unit. For a topographic map, ask the USGS for Homewood.

Directions: Drive to Sacramento, then continue on I-80 east for 90 miles to Truckee and Exit 185 for Highway 89 South. Take that exit to a traffic circle, turn right, drive short distance to 89 South, and continue 13.5 miles to Tahoe City. Turn right (still 89) and drive 4.3 miles and look for sign on right for Kaspian Campground, and just beyond, Barker Pass Road/Forest Road 3 (unsigned). Turn right and drive seven miles (paved, watch for road bikes) into national forest. When road turns to dirt, drive short distance to Barker Pass, trailhead on left, and park along shoulder. Trailhead is signed.

Contact: Lake Tahoe Basin Management Unit, South Lake Tahoe, 530/543-2600, www.fs.usda.gov/ltbmu; visitors center (summer only), 530/543-2674.

🔟 STATELINE LOOKOUT
1.0 mi/0.5 hr

off Highway 28 near Crystal Bay

Map 6.1, page 205

At this lookout above Tahoe at North Shore (elevation 7,014 feet), you can check out the views with telescopes. Or, hey, forget the telescopes and just look with your own eyes. Either way, the view is unforgettable. A short self-guided historical trail is also available. You can learn all about the cultural history of North Shore, which includes stories of timber, railroads, casinos, and resorts. But what you remember, of course, is the world-class view across Lake Tahoe and beyond to its mountain rim.

For years we avoided this trail because we thought it was just a tourist attraction, located at the lookout tower that straddles the Nevada and California state line. It turns out that *we* were the dumb tourists, because this little trail is great.

User Groups: Hikers, wheelchairs, and dogs. No horses or mountain bikes.

Permits: No permits are required. Parking and access are free.

Maps: For a map, ask the U.S. Forest Service for Lake Tahoe Basin Management Unit. For a topographic map, ask the USGS for Kings Beach.

Directions: From Truckee, take Highway 89 south and drive to Tahoe City and Highway 28. Turn left on Highway 28 and drive six miles to Reservoir Drive (just east of the old Tahoe Biltmore Casino). Turn left (north) and drive to Lake View Avenue. Turn right and drive through a residential area and continue to Forest Service Road 1601 (at an unmarked iron gate). Turn left on Forest Service Road 1601, park at the gate, and walk 0.5 mile to the lookout. Parking is limited. Do not look for a sign along Highway 28 that says "Stateline Lookout, " because it doesn't exist.

Contact: Lake Tahoe Basin Management Unit, South Lake Tahoe, 530/543-2600, www.fs.usda.gov/ltbmu; visitors center (open daily mid-June through September; weekends Memorial Day through mid-October), 530/543-2674.

41 BURTON CREEK LOOP
4.3 mi/2.5 hr

off Highway 28 near Tahoe City

Map 6.1, page 205

Burton Creek is Lake Tahoe's second-largest state park. You might wonder why few people have ever heard of it. It's because the park has no visitors center, no campground, no entrance kiosk, and, unfortunately, no trail signs or official map. What really matters is that it has no crowds, a major bonus at Lake Tahoe. Yet the park spans more than 2,000 acres and is classified as an "undeveloped park. "

A five-mile loop trip is possible in the park. Start at the trailhead on the west side of North Tahoe High School. From there it's 0.4 mile to a trail junctions that rings the Burton Creek Natural Preserve. Burton Creek runs through its center. Turn right at that junction and complete the oblong loop along the riparian creek zone, a distance of 3.9 miles, to return to the junction. You will wander through a mix of fir and pine forest, open meadows, and creekside riparian habitat. Although the trail is not signed, there are numbers painted at most intersections, which help you stay on track. There are a series of spur trails (with numbers) that lead to other trailheads.

User Groups: Hikers, leashed dogs, horses, and mountain bikes. No wheelchair facilities.

Permits: No permits are required. Parking and access are free.

Maps: PDF at website. For a topographic map, ask the USGS for Tahoe City.

Directions: From Truckee, take Highway 89 south and drive to Tahoe City and Highway 28. Turn left on Highway 28 and drive 2.3 miles to Old Mill Road. Turn left and drive 0.4 mile to Polaris Road. Turn left on Polaris Road and drive 0.5 mile to North Tahoe High School and the dirt road by the school parking lot. Park alongside the dirt road. Be careful not to block the gate.

Contact: Burton Creek State Park, 530/583-3074 or 530/525-7232, www.parks.ca.gov.

42 BARKER PASS TO DONNER PASS (PCT)
31.4 mi one-way/3 days

from Barker Pass to Donner Pass

Map 6.1, page 205

The trailhead at Barker Pass (7,650 feet), is one of the best. It provides direct access to the Granite Chief Wilderness to the north or the Desolation Wilderness to the south. For PCT hikers who are heading north, the trip starts with a climb of 800 feet to enter Granite Chief. Once on the ridge, you're rewarded with 360-degree views of this high-mountain landscape, a mix of volcanic rock and granite ridges, much of it above tree line. Though hikers don't face the long, sustained climbs so common in the southern Sierra, it's enough of a roller-coaster ride to require hikers to be in excellent shape. The trail cuts the flank of Ward Peak, at 8,470 feet, then switchbacks steeply down to Five Lakes and Five Lakes Creek (where there's an opportunity to camp). The trail then continues up and down canyons all the way to Donner Pass. You can expect to see lots of hikers, because along the way, you'll pass near two ski resorts (Alpine Meadows and Squaw Valley), where hikers can use the ski lifts in the summer to gain easy elevation to the ridgeline, rather than having to grind out long, all-day climbs. Before making the final leg of this section to Donner Pass, a descent of more than 1,000 feet, hikers can enjoy breathtaking views of Donner Lake and the miles of surrounding high country.

To continue north on the PCT, see the *Donner Pass to the Yuba River (PCT)* hike in this chapter. If you are walking this trail in reverse, see the *Echo Lakes Resort to Barker Pass (PCT)* hike in this chapter.

User Groups: Hikers, dogs, and horses. No mountain bikes. No wheelchair facilities.

Permits: A backcountry permit is required for traveling through various wilderness and special-use areas that the trail traverses. In addition, a campfire permit is required for the use of portable camp stoves or the building of campfires (where allowed). To make it simple, you can contact the national forest, Bureau of Land Management (BLM), or national park office at your point of entry for a combined permit that is good for traveling through multiple-permit areas during your dates of travel.

Maps: For topographic maps, ask the USGS for Emerald Bay, Rockbound Valley, Homewood, Tahoe City, Granite Chief, and Norden.

Directions: To reach the Barker Pass trailhead: From Truckee, take Highway 89 south and drive to Tahoe City. Turn right on Highway 89 and drive south to Kaspian Picnic Grounds (0.5 mile north of Tahoe Pines) and Forest Road 15N03. Turn right (west) and drive seven miles to the trailhead.

For the Donner Pass trailhead: From Truckee, drive west on I-80 and exit at Castle Peak Area/Boreal Ridge, just west of the Donner Summit roadside rest area. The sign for the Pacific Crest trailhead is what you're looking for, and it's located on the south side of the highway.

Contact: Tahoe National Forest, Truckee Ranger District, 530/587-3558, www.fs.usda. gov/tahoe; Lake Tahoe Basin Management Unit, South Lake Tahoe, 530/543-2600, www. fs.usda.gov/ltbmu; visitors center (open daily mid-June-Sept., Sat.-Sun. Memorial Day-mid-Oct.), 530/543-2674.

43 GENERAL CREEK TO LILY POND
7.0 mi/3.5 hr 🏃1 ⚠7

in Ed Z'berg Sugar Pine Point State Park near Lake Tahoe

Map 6.1, page 205

Lily Pond, a marshy, serene spot, rare for the high Sierra, provides serenity to go with its uniqueness. The only problem is the trail is a dirt road. This hike starts in Sugar Pine Point State Park. You start by walking along a flat, open stretch of General Creek. You then hike gently uphill through the forest to the Lily Pond. At 2.5 miles from the campground, at the

far end of the loop, you'll see the single-track turnoff signed for Lily Pond and Lost Lake. It's a one-mile hike through a rocky, dense forest to the pond, which is indeed covered with lilies. On your return, you can always take the south side of the loop for variety, then turn left on the bridge over General Creek to return to the start of the loop.

There are a couple key factors to enjoying this walk: If you're not staying in the General Creek Campground, the day-use parking area is more than 0.5 mile from site 149, where the trail begins. To make this walk to the trailhead more pleasant, be sure to take the single-track trail from the parking lot instead of walking along the paved camp road. The trail is somewhat hidden from view, so if you don't see it, ask the attendant in the entrance kiosk where it is. Next, when you finally meet up with the loop, be sure to take the north side of it, which is prettier than the south side, with lots of big sugar pines interspersed with Jeffreys and lodgepoles. The south side is mostly open meadows. A little history: This was the site of the 1960 Olympics biathlon. Nowadays in winter, the trail is part of a popular cross-country skiing loop.

User Groups: Hikers and mountain bikes. No dogs or horses. No wheelchair facilities.

Permits: No permits are required. A day-use fee of $8 is charged per vehicle.

Maps: A map of Sugar Pine Point State Park is available for a fee at the entrance station, PDF at website. A Lake Tahoe map is available for a fee from Tom Harrison Maps. For a topographic map, ask the USGS for Homewood.

Directions: From Truckee, take Highway 89 south and drive to Tahoe City. Turn right on Highway 89 and drive south eight miles to the General Creek Campground entrance on the right. Turn right and park in one of the day-use areas by the entrance kiosk, then walk into the campground to site 149 and the start of the trail. You can walk into the camp on the park road or take the single-track trail that leads from the parking lot.

Contact: Ed Z'berg Sugar Pine Point State

Park, Tahoma, 530/525-7982, www.parks.ca.gov.

44 MEEKS CREEK TRAIL TO RUBICON LAKE

15.0 mi/1-2 days   🏃3   ⛰9

in the Desolation Wilderness

Map 6.1, page 205

This trek into the Desolation Wilderness is a moderate-level backpacking trip that's loaded with alpine lakes and classic Tahoe scenery. In summer, plan on sharing the trail with lots of other folks. The trip starts as you hike on a closed dirt road (Road 14N42) that leads from the Desolation Wilderness sign near Meeks Bay for 1.3 level miles to a trail sign for Phipps Pass and Tahoe-Yosemite Trail. Bear right here and begin the gradual climb to a chain of alpine lakes. You hike parallel to Meeks Creek on a gently climbing trail, and pass the wilderness boundary at 2.5 miles. You're in forest most of the time, so don't expect a lot of panoramic views, but then again, don't expect any brutal, sunny, exposed ascents. Cross Meeks Creek and continue straight to Lake Genevieve, at 4.5 miles. The lake is shallow but provides swimming. The trail then climbs up to larger Crag Lake, then continues to climb farther to small, lily-covered Shadow Lake. (A right fork beyond Crag Lake leads to small Hidden Lake, less than 0.25 mile off the main trail; it's a good side trip.) From Shadow Lake, it's a mile farther to Stony Ridge Lake, the largest of this series of lakes, and then yet another mile to gorgeous Rubicon Lake, 7.5 miles from the trailhead and with a total elevation gain of only 2,000 feet. The main steep stretch is right at the end, between Stony Ridge Lake and Rubicon Lake. Campsites can be found at most all of the lakes, but Rubicon Lake is the preferred site, since it's the most scenic of the group.

User Groups: Hikers, dogs, and horses. No mountain bikes. No wheelchair facilities.

Permits: Permits are required year-round for both day and overnight use. Day hikers may obtain a free permit from a ranger station or may self-issue at most major trailheads. Backpackers camping in Desolation Wilderness are subject to trailhead quotas. There is a $5 reservation fee, plus $5 per person for one night, $10 per person for two or more nights up to 14 days (nonrefundable); reserve at www.recreation.gov. Children ages 12 and under are free. Golden Passes do not apply to personal-use permits. For groups, the cost of a single permit will not exceed $100.

Maps: For a map, ask the U.S. Forest Service for Desolation Wilderness or Lake Tahoe Basin Management Unit. A Lake Tahoe or Desolation Wilderness map is also available from Tom Harrison Maps. For topographic maps, ask the USGS for Homewood and Rockbound Valley.

Directions: From Truckee, take Highway 89 south and drive to Tahoe City. Turn right on Highway 89 and drive south for 10 miles to Meeks Bay Resort. Look for a small dirt parking lot across from the resort, on the west side of the highway, and park there. The trailhead is well marked.

Contact: Lake Tahoe Basin Management Unit, South Lake Tahoe, 530/543-2600, www.fs.usda.gov/ltbmu; visitors center (open daily mid-June-Sept., Sat.-Sun. Memorial Day-mid-Oct.), 530/543-2674.

45 RUBICON AND LIGHTHOUSE LOOP

2.0 mi/1.0 hr   🏃1   ⛰10

in D. L. Bliss State Park on the west shore of Lake Tahoe

Map 6.2, page 206

When you visit South Lake Tahoe, this is one of the must-sees, must-dos. The trail edges along the steep cliffs on the west side of the lake and provides a panorama across Lake Tahoe. You can also turn it into an excellent short loop. The Rubicon Trail starts at Calawee Cove Beach. The trail is cut into a slope that faces the lake, at times with 100-foot drop-offs straight down to Lake Tahoe. Cable-type rails are in place in some sections for safety. Hike 0.25 mile to a spur trail that leads to the old lighthouse; there's no view, but check out the remains of a 1916 lighthouse. Then continue beyond it for another 0.5 mile. Every step of the way, the lake and mountain views are mind-boggling. You'll arrive at the trail junction. Bear right and walk to a parking lot, where you can pick up Lighthouse Trail and loop back to Calawee Cove Beach. If you want to see those lake vistas one more time, forget about the loop and just head back the way you came. Not everybody is up for hiking the entire length of the Rubicon Trail, but this hike provides a sample of the spectacular views.

User Groups: Hikers only. No dogs, horses, or mountain bikes. No wheelchair facilities.

Permits: No permits are required. A day-use fee of $10 is charged per vehicle.

Maps: A map of D. L. Bliss State Park is available for a fee at the entrance station. A Lake Tahoe map is available for a fee from Tom Harrison Maps. For a topographic map, ask the USGS for Emerald Bay.

Directions: From South Lake Tahoe, take Highway 89 north past Emerald Bay and continue a short distance to the entrance road for D. L. Bliss State Park. Turn right and drive 0.5 mile to the entrance station and continue for 0.7 mile to a fork. Turn right and drive another 0.7 mile to Calawee Cove Beach and the parking lot. The Rubicon Trail begins on the far side of the lot. If this lot is full, you will have to use one of the other day-use parking lots in the park.

Contact: D. L. Bliss State Park, 530/525-7277 (summer) or 530/525-3345, www.parks.ca.gov.

46 RUBICON TRAIL
9.0 mi/5.0 hr   🚶2 ⛰10

in D. L. Bliss State Park on the west shore of Lake Tahoe

Map 6.2, page 206   **BEST (**

The Rubicon Trail is the premier easy day hike at Lake Tahoe. If you want the best scenery that Lake Tahoe offers, this is the trail. There is one little problem on pretty summer days. Right: It's you and often a zillion other hikers who want the same thing. If possible, walk this trail in the off-season; September, for instance, is great—and do it on a weekday. At dawn or dusk in summer, the trail, views, and experience can seem like a miracle. You get eye-popping scenery as you gaze out across the surface and deep into the depths of sparkling, clear, 12-mile-wide Lake Tahoe and beyond to the rim of mountains that surround it.

The trailhead is at the far side of the parking lot for Calawee Cove Beach. A short distance after you start, be sure to take the left fork, which will keep you on Rubicon Trail. The trail stays close to the lake edge and has very little elevation change, just some mild ups and downs, holding steady near 6,300 feet. Highlights include Rubicon Point, Emerald Point, Emerald Bay and Fannette Island, Vikingsholm Castle, and Eagle Point. If you stop for a picnic, don't be surprised if several little chipmunklike ground squirrels visit you, hoping for a hand-out.

An option is to hike the trip in the opposite direction. That, is, you can start and end your Rubicon hike at Vikingsholm. To do that, park at the Emerald Bay Overlook parking lot, hike down to Vikingsholm, and then head north to the boat-in campground and beyond. Finding a parking spot at the Overlook in summer, unless you arrive very early, can be like searching for a polar bear in the desert. You'll add on nearly two miles round-trip getting from the parking lot to Vikingsholm, during which there is a 600-foot elevation change. Regardless, some prefer this.

User Groups: Hikers only. No dogs, horses, or mountain bikes. No wheelchair facilities.

Permits: No permits are required. A day-use fee of $10 is charged per vehicle.

Maps: A map of D. L. Bliss State Park is available for a fee at the entrance station. A Lake Tahoe map is available for a fee from Tom Harrison Maps. For a topographic map, ask the USGS for Emerald Bay.

Directions: From South Lake Tahoe, take

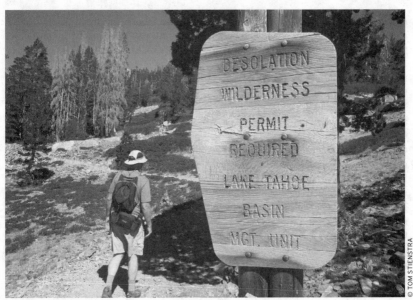

Desolation Wilderness

Highway 89 north past Emerald Bay and continue a short distance to the entrance road for D. L. Bliss State Park. Turn right and drive 0.5 mile to the entrance station, then continue for 0.7 mile to a fork. Turn right and drive another 0.7 mile to Calawee Cove Beach and the parking lot. The Rubicon Trail begins on the far side of the lot. If this lot is full, you will have to use one of the other day-use parking lots in the park.

Contact: D. L. Bliss State Park, 530/525-7277 (summer) or 530/525-3345, www.parks.ca.gov.

47 BALANCING ROCK
1.0 mi/0.5 hr 👣1 ⛰8

in D. L. Bliss State Park on the west shore of Lake Tahoe

Map 6.2, page 206

The Balancing Rock is a big hunk of granite that has been a curiosity for eons at Lake Tahoe. It's a 130-ton rock that sits balanced on a small rock pedestal, like a giant golf ball on an itty-bitty golf tee. At one angle, it seems impossible.

This is a short, easy interpretive trail that is routed to it. The trail's interpretive brochure explains that erosion will eventually wear away the pedestal and cause the Balancing Rock to lose its balance. Tahoe lovers have been awaiting this event forever, and it still hasn't happened. In addition to Balancing Rock, the trail shows off many of the plants and trees of the Tahoe area. It's a good learning experience for both kids and adults.

User Groups: Hikers only. No dogs, horses, or mountain bikes. No wheelchair facilities.

Permits: No permits are required. A day-use fee of $10 is charged per vehicle.

Maps: A map of D. L. Bliss State Park is available for a fee at the entrance station. A Lake Tahoe map is available for a fee from Tom Harrison Maps. For a topographic map, ask the USGS for Emerald Bay.

Directions: From South Lake Tahoe, take Highway 89 north past Emerald Bay and continue a short distance to the entrance road for D. L. Bliss State Park. Turn right and drive 0.5 mile to the entrance station, then continue for

0.7 mile to a fork. Turn left and drive 0.25 mile to the Balancing Rock parking lot, on the left.

Contact: D. L. Bliss State Park, 530/525-7277 (summer) or 530/525-3345, www.parks.ca.gov.

48 VIKINGSHOLM

2.0 mi/1.0 hr   🚶2 ⛰9

in Emerald Bay State Park on the west shore of Lake Tahoe

Map 6.2, page 206

Start this trip at dawn and you'll have paradise in your grasp. Start it on a summer day, and grasping a parking spot at the Emerald Bay Overlook will seem like the impossible dream. This walk is a one-mile traipse on a dirt road with a 500-foot descent to Vikingsholm, a Viking castle built by an heiress in 1929. The beauty lies in the scenery spread out before you as you hike downhill. You'll see spectacular Fannette Island and the deep blue waters of Emerald Bay. The route also ventures through old-growth cedar and pine forest. You then arrive at Lake Tahoe's coveted sandy shoreline. Although visitors have to pay a buck to tour the inside of the castle, you can hike to it for free and add on a side trip to the base of 150-foot Eagle Falls, situated 0.25 mile from Vikingsholm. For many people, the surprise on this trail is that the return hike has a 500-foot elevation gain. What, you mean we have to breathe hard?

Note: Arrive early. By midmorning on summer weekends, visitors can be forced to park up to two miles away.

User Groups: Hikers only. No dogs, horses, or mountain bikes. No wheelchair facilities.

Permits: No permits are required. A fee of $10 is charged per vehicle, $5 per person to tour the inside of the castle.

Maps: A map of Emerald Bay and D. L. Bliss State Parks is available for a fee at the visitors center at Vikingsholm. A Lake Tahoe map is available for a fee from Tom Harrison Maps. For a topographic map, ask the USGS for Emerald Bay.

Directions: From South Lake Tahoe, take Highway 89 north and drive nine miles to the Emerald Bay Overlook parking lot on the east side of Highway 89. The trail begins from the lakeside of the parking lot.

Contact: Emerald Bay State Park, 530/525-7232, visitors center, 530/525-3345, www.parks.ca.gov.

49 UPPER EAGLE FALLS AND EAGLE LAKE

2.0 mi/1.0 hr   🚶2 ⛰9

off Highway 89 near South Lake Tahoe

Map 6.2, page 206

This is one of the three most popular walks in the Tahoe region, right there with the nearby walk down to Vikingsholm and the Rubicon Trail. The trailhead is at the Eagle Falls Picnic Area. Near the restroom, you'll see the sign that points the way to the Upper Eagle Falls Trail. It is something of a "designer" path, where natural granite is cut into flagstonelike stairs and an elaborate wooden bridge escorts visitors over the top of the falls. It's a beautiful walk, best taken early in the morning and during the week, when the masses aren't around. The waterfall pours right under the hikers' bridge. Just beyond the bridge, the designer aspect of the trail ends as you enter the Desolation Wilderness. From here, it's a 400-foot climb in less than a mile to reach pretty Eagle Lake, surrounded by granite cliffs. People fish and picnic here; some even try to swim in the icy water.

If you want to see the "other" Eagle Falls, the one that drops right along Highway 89, see the listing in this chapter.

User Groups: Hikers and dogs. No horses or mountain bikes. No wheelchair facilities.

Permits: Day hikers must fill out a free permit at the wilderness trailhead. A $5 parking fee is charged per vehicle.

Maps: For a map, ask the U.S. Forest Service for Desolation Wilderness or Lake Tahoe Basin Management Unit. A Lake Tahoe map is available for a fee from Tom Harrison Maps. For a topographic map, ask the USGS for Emerald Bay.

Directions: From South Lake Tahoe, take Highway 89 north and drive 8.5 miles to the Eagle Falls Picnic Area and trailhead. Turn left into the parking area or park in the roadside pullout just north of the picnic area on the west side of Highway 89.

Contact: Lake Tahoe Basin Management Unit, South Lake Tahoe, 530/543-2600, www.fs.usda.gov/ltbmu; visitors center (open daily mid-June-Sept., Sat.-Sun. Memorial Day-mid-Oct.), 530/543-2674.

50 VELMA LAKES
10.0 mi/5.0 hr

in the Desolation Wilderness

Map 6.2, page 206

The Velma Lakes are classic Desolation: gorgeous, alpine jewels. This route follows the trail to Eagle Falls and Eagle Lake (see listing in this chapter) for the first mile, then climbs through a rugged, glaciated landscape, with only occasional hardy lodgepole pines and twisted junipers providing meager shade. The lack of trees and the abundance of rock mean wide-open views and plenty of granite drama: Welcome to the Sierra high country.

The trailhead is at the Eagle Falls Picnic Area. Near the restroom, you'll see the sign that points the way to the Upper Eagle Falls Trail. At three miles (you intersect the trail that heads left to Dicks Lake), stay right for Velma Lakes. In one mile, your trail heads directly to Middle Velma Lake, the most popular of the lakes. It has several granite islands sprinkled in cobalt blue water. It's popular for swimming, though often cold.

Just before Middle Velma Lake, you can take a left cutoff and head south to Upper Velma Lake in 0.5 mile. Another option is to take the trail, on your right, north along a creek, also 0.5 mile, to Lower Velma Lake. Remember to bring your sunscreen because the rocky trail to the Velma Lakes is exposed and open.

You can also begin the Velma Lakes hike from the trailhead at Bayview Campground. You will miss out on seeing Eagle Lake and a world-class view of Tahoe.

User Groups: Hikers and dogs. No horses or mountain bikes (the Bayview Trail provides access for horses; contact Tahoe Basin National Forest). No wheelchair facilities. To reach Velma Lakes, equestrians must access from another trailhead; Bayview trailhead is the best for this.

Permits: Permits are required year-round for both day and overnight use. Day hikers may obtain a free permit from a ranger station or may self-issue at most major trailheads. Backpackers camping in Desolation Wilderness are subject to trailhead quotas. There is a $5 reservation fee, plus $5 per person for one night, $10 per person for two or more nights up to 14 days (nonrefundable); reserve at www.recreation.gov. Children ages 12 and under are free. For groups, the cost of a single permit will not exceed $100. A $5 parking fee is charged per vehicle.

Maps: For a map, ask the U.S. Forest Service for Desolation Wilderness or Lake Tahoe Basin Management Unit. A Lake Tahoe or Desolation Wilderness map is available from Tom Harrison Maps. For topographic maps, ask the USGS for Emerald Bay and Rockbound Valley.

Directions: From South Lake Tahoe, take Highway 89 north and drive 8.5 miles to the Eagle Falls Picnic Area and trailhead. Turn left into the parking area or park in the roadside pullout just north of the picnic area, on the west side of Highway 89.

Contact: Lake Tahoe Basin Management Unit, South Lake Tahoe, 530/543-2600, www.fs.usda.gov/ltbmu; visitors center (open daily mid-June-Sept., Sat.-Sun. Memorial Day-mid-Oct.), 530/543-2674.

51 CASCADE FALLS

2.0 mi/1.0 hr

off Highway 89 near South Lake Tahoe

Map 6.2, page 206

This trail is the best easy hike at Lake Tahoe. The one-mile trail leads to the brink of a stunning 200-foot cascade that drops into the southwest end of Cascade Lake. The trip is short and flat enough for almost anybody to make the trip, including young children, yet it still feels like wilderness.

From the trailhead at Bayview Campground, take the left fork signed for Cascade Falls. In five minutes, you get tremendous views of Cascade Lake (elevation 6,464 feet) below to your left. It isn't long and you start to hear and see the falls. The trail disintegrates as it nears the waterfall's edge, and hikers with children shouldn't get too close. Truth is, the best views are actually farther back on the trail. Upstream of the falls are some lovely pools surrounded by wide shelves of granite. Make sure you visit in spring or early summer, when the waterfall is flowing full and wide, because by August, it loses its drama.

User Groups: Hikers and dogs. No horses or mountain bikes. No wheelchair facilities.

Permits: No permits are required. Parking and access are free.

Maps: For a map, ask the U.S. Forest Service for Lake Tahoe Basin Management Unit. A Lake Tahoe map is available for a fee from Tom Harrison Maps. For a topographic map, ask the USGS for Emerald Bay.

Directions: From South Lake Tahoe, take Highway 89 north and drive 7.5 miles to the Bayview Campground. Turn left and drive to the far end of the campground to the trailhead parking area. If it's full, park on the shoulder of Highway 89 near the entrance to the campground.

Contact: Lake Tahoe Basin Management Unit, South Lake Tahoe, 530/543-2600, www.fs.usda.gov/ltbmu; visitors center (open daily mid-June-Sept., Sat.-Sun. Memorial Day-mid-Oct.), 530/543-2674.

52 MOUNT TALLAC (TALLAC TRAILHEAD)

9.0 mi/6.0 hr

in the Desolation Wilderness near Fallen Leaf Lake

Map 6.2, page 206

First, a word of warning: If you are hiking Mount Tallac for the first time, start instead from the Glen Alpine Trailhead. That already accomplished, and you want a steeper challenge, then the Mount Tallac Trailhead is for you. Mount Tallac towers over Lake Tahoe and provides one of the most beautiful lookouts in North America. From the 9,375-foot summit, you look down on Fallen Leaf Lake, Cascade Lake, Emerald Bay, Lake Tahoe, and beyond to Mount Rose on the eastern Tahoe rim. To the west you can see across miles of Desolation Wilderness.

From this trailhead, you pay dearly for it: You climb 2,600 feet over the final three miles, plus another 900-foot climb in the first 1.5 miles. From the trailhead, you make the first butt-kicker climb for 1.7 miles to Floating Island Lake. You get excellent views of Fallen Leaf Lake and Lake Tahoe along the way. Then it's another 0.7 mile to a trail junction just before Cathedral Lake, where a trail from Fallen Leaf Lake joins this trail. Cathedral Lake is a good rest stop before making the final ascent to the top of Mount Tallac, a 2.4-mile butt-kicker of a climb on a rocky trail. It's made somewhat easier by a continuous and inspiring parade of vistas, including long-distance looks at Gilmore Lake, Susie Lake, and Lake Aloha. The trail ends 0.25 mile below the summit, where it meets the other Mount Tallac trail that emerges from Gilmore Lake. Bear right, and boulder hop your way to the top.

The return trip down is terrible for many, a knee-screaming, toe-jamming affair that will have some questioning the purpose of life.

User Groups: Hikers and dogs. No horses or mountain bikes. No wheelchair facilities.

Permits: Permits are required year-round for both day and overnight use. Day hikers may obtain a free permit from a ranger station or may self-issue at most major trailheads. Backpackers camping in Desolation Wilderness are subject to trailhead quotas. There is a $5 reservation fee, plus $5 per person for one night, $10 per person for two or more nights up to 14 days (nonrefundable); reserve at www.recreation.gov. Children ages 12 and under are free. Golden Passes do not apply to personal-use permits. For groups, the cost of a single permit will not exceed $100.

Maps: For a map, ask the U.S. Forest Service for Desolation Wilderness. A Lake Tahoe or Desolation Wilderness map is also available for a fee from Tom Harrison Maps. For a topographic map, ask the USGS for Emerald Bay.

Directions: From South Lake Tahoe, take Highway 89 north and drive 3.8 miles to the signed turnoff for Mount Tallac and Camp Concord (on the left, across the highway from the sign for Baldwin Beach). Drive 0.4 mile to the trailhead entrance road on the left. Turn left and drive 0.6 mile to the trailhead.

Contact: Lake Tahoe Basin Management Unit, South Lake Tahoe, 530/543-2600, www.fs.usda.gov/ltbmu; visitors center (open daily mid-June-Sept., Sat.-Sun. Memorial Day-mid-Oct.), 530/543-2674.

53 RAINBOW AND LAKE OF THE SKY TRAILS
0.5 mi/0.5 hr 🚶1 ⛰8

in Tahoe National Forest near South Lake Tahoe

Map 6.2, page 206 BEST (
At the Lake Tahoe Visitors Center, several short interpretive walks are available. The best are the Rainbow Trail and Lake of the Sky Trail. You can hike them both from the same starting point at the visitors center and combine an interesting nature lesson with a walk along Lake Tahoe's shoreline for exceptional scenery and views.

Start with Rainbow Trail, which leads from the visitors center's west side and takes you to Taylor Creek and its Stream Profile Chamber. The creek is where thousands of kokanee salmon come to spawn in the fall. You can view the fish through the glass walls of the profile chamber. You can also see them the ordinary way, just by peering into the creek as you walk. Then loop back to the visitors center and pick up Lake of the Sky Trail. You'll pass by Taylor Creek Marsh on your way to Tallac Point and Tahoe's shoreline. In summer, people go swimming at this sandy stretch of beach.

User Groups: Hikers and wheelchair users. No dogs, horses, or mountain bikes.

Permits: No permits are required. Parking and access are free.

Maps: For a map, ask the U.S. Forest Service for Lake Tahoe Basin Management Unit. A free forest recreation newspaper is also available. A Lake Tahoe map is available for a fee from Tom Harrison Maps. For a topographic map, ask the USGS for Emerald Bay.

Directions: From South Lake Tahoe, take Highway 89 north and drive three miles to the Lake Tahoe Visitors Center turnoff, on the right. Turn right and drive to the visitors center parking lot, where the trails begin.

Contact: Lake Tahoe Basin Management Unit, South Lake Tahoe, 530/543-2600, www.fs.usda.gov/ltbmu; visitors center (open daily mid-June-Sept., Sat.-Sun. Memorial Day-mid-Oct.), 530/543-2674.

54 MOUNT TALLAC LOOP (GLEN ALPINE TRAILHEAD)
11.6 mi/7.5 hr 🚶4 ⛰10

in the Desolation Wilderness near Fallen Leaf Lake

Map 6.2, page 206
Your first steps on Mount Tallac are flamed by a craving for one of the greatest 360-degree views in North America. They are also tempered by the challenge of a 3,175-foot climb in 5.8 miles (one-way) to reach the summit. Tallac towers over Lake Tahoe, where the lake

and sky seem to merge into a cobalt-blue spectacle. Once at the top at 9,735 feet, you can then turn to the west and take in the granite, ice, and lakes of the vast Desolation Wilderness. In all, the scope covers more than 5,000 square miles of Tahoe paradise.

There are two routes up. The preferred route starts from the Glen Alpine Trailhead, located just beyond the head of Fallen Leaf Lake. The trek comes in three stages. The trail starts easy and flat, and in the first mile, becomes a vintage road made of rocks that leads to a former historic camp and a few old cabins. On your left, you pass gorgeous Glen Alpine Falls, best seen when flush with runoff from snowmelt. The air is scented with pine duff, and for those who are imprinted by Tahoe, the familiar tang in the air can make you feel like you are home again. You'll pass a sign that marks the entry point for Desolation Wilderness (a threshold moment) before climbing up Glen Alpine Canyon. Most make quick work of the first 1.7 miles to a trail junction, signed for Grass Lake on your left and Gilmore Lake on your right.

The second stage of the hike rises out of the canyon 2.6 miles to Gilmore Lake. It's a steady climb all the way, where trail builders installed enough switchbacks to keep the grade just right; we never went aerobic at any point, just walked right up. Even in early August, it is common to see tons of wildflowers, with lots of lupine, mule's ear, paintbrush, and rafts of corn lilies. Creeks are flush with clear, cold water, and miniature waterfalls. At times in late spring, if you stand too long to enjoy them, mosquitoes and biting flies will want to see how you taste, a small price to pay for beauty in the high country. Gilmore Lake, nestled in a basin at 8,290 feet at the foot of Tallac's backside, is a perfect stop for a rest or snack, with a confluence of trails to meet other hikers. Some will make camp here. It's one of the better lakes in Desolation to fish. At dusk, the trout rise to the surface to feed and can sound like little popguns going off.

The third stage is the last stretch to the summit, where you climb 1,445 feet in 1.6 miles. As you leave Gilmore, the climb is easy and the hillside is buried in greenery and tons of wildflowers. Soon enough, though, it gets steeper, and most will puff their way above tree line. The last 0.5 mile is the steepest as you approach the cragged rim. In the final steps, you reach the mountain crest and the Tahoe basin is unveiled before you. The trail diminishes in the rock, but you can still make out a faint route that leads to the true summit. One of the most eye-popping views in North America is yours.

On top, there is a single rock perch that crowns Tallac's summit. Nearby, there are many slabs that seem built for you to take a seat, slow the world down, and take it all in. Pray for a clear day with no haze. Directly below you, the slope plummets 3,000 feet to Fallen Leaf Lake near your starting point. The view then extends across a sea of pines and aspens to Cascade Lake, Emerald Bay, and Lake Tahoe. The lake is so big and so deep blue that for many it evokes emotion that can last for years. The eastern horizon is topped by Monument Peak, Freel Peak, and Mount Rose in Nevada. The view to the west into Desolation is equally profound, across distant Aloha Lake to huge snow-packed slopes that reach up to Pyramid Peak, Mount Price, and the rim that crests the Crystal Basin.

If you have only one mountain to climb and one view to take in, this can often be the best choice.

User Groups: Hikers and dogs. No horses or mountain bikes. No wheelchair facilities.

Permits: Permits are required year-round for both day and overnight use. Day hikers may obtain a free permit from a ranger station or may self-issue at most major trailheads. Backpackers camping in Desolation Wilderness are subject to trailhead quotas. There is a $5 reservation fee, plus $5 per person for one night, $10 per person for two or more nights up to 14 days (nonrefundable); reserve at www.recreation. gov. Children ages 12 and under are free. Golden Passes do not apply to personal-use permits. For groups, the cost of a single permit will not exceed $100.

Maps: For a map, ask the U.S. Forest Service for Desolation Wilderness. A Lake Tahoe or Desolation Wilderness map is also available for a fee from Tom Harrison Maps. For a topographic map, ask the USGS for Echo Lake.

Directions: From South Lake Tahoe, take Highway 89 north and drive 2.9 miles to Fallen Leaf Lake Road. Turn left and drive 4.8 miles on a narrow road (go slow, be ready for oncoming cars) past the Fallen Leaf Marina to a fork. Take the left fork on Road 1216, signed for Lily Lake and the Desolation Wilderness. Drive 0.7 mile to road's end, parking, and the trailhead.

Contact: Lake Tahoe Basin Management Unit, South Lake Tahoe, 530/543-2600, www. fs.usda.gov/ltbmu; visitors center (open daily mid-June-Sept., Sat.-Sun. Memorial Day-mid-Oct.), 530/543-2674.

55 GILMORE LAKE
7.6 mi/4.0 hr 🥾3 ⛰️9

in the Desolation Wilderness near Fallen Leaf Lake

Map 6.2, page 206

If you only have time to day-hike to one destination near South Lake Tahoe, Gilmore Lake is an excellent choice. Everything about it is a classic Lake Tahoe and Desolation Wilderness trip, a collection of the best the area has to offer. You get to visit a scenic alpine lake, and along the way, you are treated to fields of wildflowers, mountain vistas, forests, and more. The only thing you don't get are views of Lake Tahoe. Of course, we're not the only ones who like this trail, so all the usual disclaimers apply about timing your trip for the off-season or during the week.

With that said, take off from the Glen Alpine trailhead and hike up the road past the vintage cabin settlement on the right. The rocky road eventually becomes a rocky trail. This cobblestone-like stretch is by far the worst part of the hike; the rocks make it rough going for hikers' ankles and knees. At 1.5 miles in, you will reach a junction with the Grass Lake Trail. Bear

right for Gilmore Lake. The trail surface improves dramatically. You then start a steady, rhythmic climb. In the next 1.5 miles, you'll pass a series of trail junctions (paths lead off to the left, to Susie and Heather Lakes). Bear right for Gilmore Lake, the largest lake in this area. You'll reach it at 3.5 miles, with a total 1,700-foot elevation gain. Despite the fact that many people cruise by Gilmore Lake each day on their way to climb Mount Tallac, few take the time to hang out for long by the lake's sapphire-blue waters. The lake, ringed by grassy, flower-filled meadows, manages to stay pristine.

User Groups: Hikers and dogs. No horses or mountain bikes. No wheelchair facilities.

Permits: Permits are required year-round for both day and overnight use. Day hikers may obtain a free permit from a ranger station or can self-issue at the Glen Alpine trailhead. Backpackers camping in Desolation Wilderness are subject to trailhead quotas. There is a $5 reservation fee, plus $5 per person for one night, $10 per person for two or more nights up to 14 days (nonrefundable); reserve at www. recreation.gov. Children ages 12 and under are free. Golden Passes do not apply to personal-use permits. For groups, the cost of a single permit will not exceed $100.

Maps: For a map, ask the U.S. Forest Service for Desolation Wilderness. A Lake Tahoe or Desolation Wilderness map is also available for a fee from Tom Harrison Maps. For a topographic map, ask the USGS for Emerald Bay.

Directions: From South Lake Tahoe, take Highway 89 north and drive 2.9 miles to Fallen Leaf Lake Road. Turn left and drive 4.8 miles on a narrow road past the Fallen Leaf Marina to a fork. Take the left fork on Road 1216, signed for Lily Lake and the Desolation Wilderness. Drive 0.7 mile to the trailhead, at the road's end.

Contact: Lake Tahoe Basin Management Unit, South Lake Tahoe, 530/543-2600, www. fs.usda.gov/ltbmu; visitors center (open daily mid-June-Sept., Sat.-Sun. Memorial Day-mid-Oct.), 530/543-2674.

56 SUSIE AND HEATHER LAKES
10.0 mi/5.0 hr   👣3 ⛰9

in the Desolation Wilderness near Fallen Leaf Lake

Map 6.2, page 206

It doesn't take a long expedition to see the rugged alpine beauty of Desolation Wilderness. This trip, a day hike to Susie and Heather Lakes, is a perfect example. Start at the Glen Alpine trailhead. The trail to Susie and Heather Lakes begins as a rocky road. You will pass a waterfall on Glen Alpine Creek and a vintage resort, now something of a ghost town, on the right. At 1.2 miles, you'll see a sign for Gilmore, Susie, and Grass Lakes. Here you start to climb, steady and rhythmic (you'll pass a short cutoff on the left to little Grass Lake, which adds one mile to your trip each way). Continue straight, signed for Susie, Heather, and Aloha Lakes. At four miles, you'll reach the eastern shore of Susie Lake. The route runs along Susie Lake, and continues to its southern edge, and then it is another mile to Heather Lake. The granite-lined lake is deep and wide, and is set in a landscape of classic high Sierra scenery. There you go. Everything you could ask for in just a day.

User Groups: Hikers, dogs, and horses. No mountain bikes. No wheelchair facilities.

Permits: Permits are required year-round for both day and overnight use. Day hikers may obtain a free permit from a ranger station or may self-issue the Glen Alpine trailhead. Backpackers camping in Desolation Wilderness are subject to trailhead quotas. There is a $5 reservation fee, plus $5 per person for one night, $10 per person for two or more nights up to 14 days (nonrefundable); reserve at www.recreation.gov. Children ages 12 and under are free. Golden Passes do not apply to personal-use permits. For groups, the cost of a single permit will not exceed $100.

Maps: For a map, ask the U.S. Forest Service for Desolation Wilderness. A Lake Tahoe or Desolation Wilderness map is also available for a fee from Tom Harrison Maps. For a topographic map, ask the USGS for Emerald Bay.

Directions: From South Lake Tahoe, take Highway 89 north and drive 2.9 miles to Fallen Leaf Lake Road. Turn left and drive 4.8 miles on a narrow road (go slow, watch for oncoming vehicles) past the Fallen Leaf Marina to a fork. Take the left fork on Road 1216, signed for Lily Lake and the Desolation Wilderness. Drive 0.7 mile to the trailhead, at the road's end.

Contact: Lake Tahoe Basin Management Unit, South Lake Tahoe, 530/543-2600, www.fs.usda.gov/ltbmu; visitors center (open daily mid-June-Sept., Sat.-Sun. Memorial Day-mid-Oct.), 530/543-2674.

57 FALLEN LEAF LAKE TRAIL
2.0 mi/1.0 hr   👣1 ⛰9

near South Lake Tahoe

Map 6.2, page 206   **BEST (**

Fallen Leaf Lake, at 6,400 feet in elevation, is the second-largest lake in the Tahoe Basin. Many call it one of the prettiest. Most of its shorefront lands are privately owned. But this path allows you access to the area that is public. This is a short, mostly flat trail that leads to the lake and then along its northern edge to the dam, which you can walk across. Much of the trail hugs the lake's shoreline, so you can look out across the blue water and take in deep inside the feeling that comes with deep, sapphire waters. You also get excellent views of Glen Alpine Canyon and Mount Tallac. In the fall, the shoreline of Fallen Leaf Lake is one of the best spots near Tahoe to admire the quaking aspens as they turn from yellow to gold. Campers staying at Fallen Leaf Lake Campground can access this trail from their tents.

User Groups: Hikers, dogs, horses, and mountain bikes. No wheelchair facilities.

Permits: No permits are required. Parking and access are free.

Maps: For a map, ask the U.S. Forest Service for Lake Tahoe Basin Management Unit. A Lake Tahoe map is available for a fee from Tom

Harrison Maps. For a topographic map, ask the USGS for Emerald Bay.

Directions: From South Lake Tahoe, take Highway 89 north and drive 2.9 miles to Fallen Leaf Lake Road. Turn left and drive 0.8 mile to the Fallen Leaf Lake dirt parking area on the right. It is not signed.

Contact: Lake Tahoe Basin Management Unit, South Lake Tahoe, 530/543-2600, www. fs.usda.gov/ltbmu; visitors center (open daily mid-June-Sept., Sat.-Sun. Memorial Day-mid-Oct.), 530/543-2674.

58 ANGORA LAKES TRAIL
1.0 mi/0.5 hr   🚶1 ⛰8

at Angora Lake near South Lake Tahoe in Tahoe National Forest

Map 6.2, page 206   **BEST (**

Upper Angora Lake is a pristine jewel backed by a high granite wall. From the parking lot, hike uphill on the signed dirt road, and in 15 minutes, you'll be looking at Lower Angora Lake off to the left, which has a few cabins on its far side. Continue beyond its edge another 0.25 mile and, voilà, you reach the upper lake and Angora Lakes Resort, built in 1917. Although the resort cabins are always rented way in advance, day users can buy lemonade and sit at a picnic table to watch the action, or take part in it at the small, picturesque lake. Action? What action? Rowboats can be rented for a few bucks for a romantic cruise about the little lake. In mid-summer, toddlers wade around at the shallow beach area, and plenty of folks just plunk themselves down along the shoreline to stare at the bowl-shaped, glacial cirque lake. It has a high granite wall on its far side, where in early summer a waterfall of snowmelt flows down to the lake. The Angora Lakes are extremely popular with children's day camps and groups, and on some days, the little ones outnumber the old folks.

User Groups: Hikers, dogs, horses, and mountain bikes. No wheelchair facilities.

Permits: No permits are required. A parking fee of $7 is charged per vehicle.

Maps: For a map, ask the U.S. Forest Service for Lake Tahoe Basin Management Unit. A Lake Tahoe map is available for a fee from Tom Harrison Maps. For a topographic map, ask the USGS for Echo Lake.

Directions: From South Lake Tahoe, take Highway 89 north and drive 2.9 miles to Fallen Leaf Lake Road. Turn left and drive two miles to a fork. Turn left and drive 0.5 mile to Forest Road 12N14. Bear right on Forest Service Road 12N14 and drive 2.3 miles (great views to the right) to the road's end and the trailhead.

Contact: Lake Tahoe Basin Management Unit, South Lake Tahoe, 530/543-2600, www.fs.usda. gov/ltbmu; visitors center, (open only in summer), 530/543-2674; Angora Lakes Resort, 530/541-2092, www.angoralakesresort.com.

59 ROCKBOUND PASS AND LAKE DORIS
12.0 mi/6.0 hr-2 days   🚶3 ⛰9

in the Desolation Wilderness

Map 6.2, page 206

To make the epic trip to 8,650-foot Rockbound Pass, for the first 1.9 miles, follow the trail notes for the route to Gertrude and Tyler Lakes (see listing in this chapter). Then bear left to stay on the Rockbound Pass Trail. You then hike through mixed conifers to get your first glimpse of Rockbound Pass at 2.5 miles, a distant notch in the mountains to the north. To reach it, you then must descend a bit and cross the Jones Fork of Silver Creek, then parallel the stream on its course from Maud Lake. This becomes very rocky terrain. In some places, the trail is even blasted out of granite. At 4.5 miles, you'll reach the western shore of Maud Lake, elevation 7,700 feet. Many backpackers make camp here, while day hikers continue the ascent to the pass. It's not much farther; after a steady climb, you gain its wide summit at 5.9 miles. The views of Desolation Wilderness open wide, including views below on one side at Maud Lake and ahead to Lake Doris. Up on top at the pass, the winds can howl, especially in the spring. If that's the case, descend 0.5 mile to Lake Doris, just to the left of the trail, where you can make camp, or if you're day hiking, just hang out and rest. The total elevation gain on this trip is 1,700 feet, plus a short descent to Lake Doris.

User Groups: Hikers, dogs, and horses. No mountain bikes. No wheelchair facilities.

Permits: Permits are required year-round for both day and overnight use. Day hikers may obtain a free permit from a ranger station or may self-issue at most major trailheads. Backpackers camping in Desolation Wilderness are subject to trailhead quotas. There is a $5 reservation fee, plus $5 per person for one night, $10 per person for two or more nights up to 14 days (nonrefundable); reserve at www.recreation.gov. Children ages 12 and under are free. Golden Passes do not apply to personal-use permits. For groups, the cost of a single permit will not exceed $100.

Directions: From Placerville, take Highway 50 east for 30 miles to Kyburz and continue five miles to the signed turnoff for Wrights Lake on the north side of the highway (about 21 miles west of South Lake Tahoe). Turn left (north) on Wrights Lake Road and drive eight miles to Wrights Lake Visitors Center. Continue straight for 0.5 mile to the Rockbound trailhead (on the way to Dark Lake).

Contact: Eldorado National Forest, Pacific Ranger District, 530/644-2349, www.fs.usda.gov/eldorado.

60 GERTRUDE AND TYLER LAKES

9.0 mi/5.0 hr or 2 days 🏃4 ⛰9

in the Desolation Wilderness

Map 6.2, page 206

There's a ton of stellar hiking to be accomplished in the Wrights Lake area. The trip to Gertrude and Tyler Lakes stands out as one of the best day hikes. It provides great scenery, a good workout, and a chance to practice your cross-country skills on the way to Tyler Lake. A clearly defined trail leads to pretty Gertrude Lake. But Tyler Lake, higher and lovelier, is found only by those who forge their own way. That makes for a fun little adventure if you desire.

Begin on Rockbound Pass Trail, where you pass Beauty Lake 0.5 mile out. You then continue on an easy path until 1.9 miles in, where you'll see a sign for Tyler Lake. Bear right and prepare to work a lot harder for the rest of the hike. One memorable 0.5-mile stretch goes straight uphill and will cause you to question your sanity; definitely a kill-me, eat-me kind of moment. The worst part doesn't last long, and the views of the spectacular peaks of the Crystal Range will reward you. At 3.5 miles, you'll reach a spur trail on the left that can be difficult to spot (a 100-yard walk leads to the grave of William Tyler, a rancher who died here in a blizzard in the 1920s). A half mile beyond this cutoff is Gertrude Lake, at 8,000 feet.

Note that just past the faint cutoff trail to the grave, there is a near-invisible fork on the right. That is the start of an unmaintained trail to Tyler Lake. Tyler is set 400 feet higher than Gertrude Lake. If you miss the trail turnoff, watch for occasional rock cairns and keep an eye on your trail map; Tyler Lake lies 0.5 mile southeast of Gertrude Lake.

Of the two lakes, Tyler is more beautiful, set in a granite basin with a few sparse pines on its shores. Because it's slightly difficult to locate, you have an excellent chance at solitude at Tyler Lake, even on summer weekends.

User Groups: Hikers, dogs, and horses. No mountain bikes. No wheelchair facilities.

Permits: Permits are required year-round for both day and overnight use. Day hikers may obtain a free permit from a ranger station or may self-issue at most major trailheads. Backpackers camping in Desolation Wilderness are subject to trailhead quotas. There is a $5 reservation fee, plus $5 per person for one night, $10 per person for two or more nights up to 14 days (nonrefundable); reserve at www.recreation.

gov. Children ages 12 and under are free. Golden Passes do not apply to personal-use permits. For groups, the cost of a single permit will not exceed $100.

Maps: For a map, ask the U.S. Forest Service for Desolation Wilderness or Eldorado National Forest. A Lake Tahoe or Desolation Wilderness map is also available from Tom Harrison Maps. For topographic maps, ask the USGS for Pyramid Peak and Rockbound Valley.

Directions: From Placerville, take Highway 50 east for 30 miles to Kyburz and continue five miles to the signed turnoff for Wrights Lake (about 21 miles west of South Lake Tahoe). Turn left (north) on Wrights Lake Road and drive eight miles to Wrights Lake Visitors Center. Continue straight past the visitors center for 0.5 mile to the Rockbound trailhead (on the way to Dark Lake).

Contact: Eldorado National Forest, Pacific Ranger District, 530/644-2349, www.fs.usda. gov/eldorado.

61 TWIN AND ISLAND LAKES
6.4 mi/4.0 hr or 2 days   👫3 ⛰10

in the Desolation Wilderness

Map 6.2, page 206

The hike to Twin and Island Lakes is hands-down the most scenic in the gorgeous Wrights Lake area. Of the entire Desolation Wilderness, you get the most striking views on the hike. You'll have miles of solid granite under your feet. The trail is extremely well marked, and its moderate grade is suitable for all types of hikers. Start at the Twin Lakes trailhead. The first 1.2 miles features a gentle climb to the intersection with the trail to Grouse, Hemlock, and Smith Lakes. Bear left for Twin Lakes and climb up over the granite for 0.75 mile, when you crest a ridge and start to descend. The vistas of jagged Crystal Range peaks to the northeast make an awesome backdrop. At 2.5 miles, you'll reach the dam at Lower Twin Lake. Cross it and continue hiking along the lake's northwest shore to tiny Boomerang Lake, at three miles.

The lake is shaped like its name and is shallow enough to provide warm water for swimming. Another 0.25 mile on the trail brings you to the south end of Island Lake, where the vistas of the Crystal Range are the best of the trip. If you ever wanted to sell somebody on the beauty of the Northern Sierra, this trail would be the place to do it.

The only downer on the trip to Twin and Island Lakes is the sheer number of people who make this journey every day during the summer months.

User Groups: Hikers, dogs, and horses. No mountain bikes. No wheelchair facilities.

Permits: Permits are required year-round for both day and overnight use. Day hikers may obtain a free permit from a ranger station or may self-issue at most major trailheads. Backpackers camping in Desolation Wilderness are subject to trailhead quotas. There is a $5 reservation fee, plus $5 per person for one night, $10 per person for two or more nights up to 14 days (nonrefundable); reserve at www.recreation. gov. Children ages 12 and under are free. Golden Passes do not apply to personal-use permits. For groups, the cost of a single permit will not exceed $100.

Maps: For a map, ask the U.S. Forest Service for Eldorado National Forest or Desolation Wilderness. A Lake Tahoe or Desolation Wilderness map is also available for a fee from Tom Harrison Maps. For a topographic map, ask the USGS for Pyramid Peak.

Directions: From Placerville, take Highway 50 east for 30 miles to Kyburz and continue five miles to the signed turnoff for Wrights Lake (about 21 miles west of South Lake Tahoe). Turn left (north) on Wrights Lake Road and drive eight miles to Wrights Lake Visitors Center. Turn right and continue one mile beyond the campground to the end of the road and the Twin Lakes trailhead.

Contact: Eldorado National Forest, Pacific Ranger District, 530/644-2349, www.fs.usda. gov/eldorado; Lake Tahoe Basin Management Unit, South Lake Tahoe, 530/543-2600, www. fs.usda.gov/ltbmu; visitors center (open daily mid-June-Sept., Sat.-Sun. Memorial Day-mid-Oct.), 530/543-2674.

62 GROUSE, HEMLOCK, AND SMITH LAKES

6.0 mi/3.0 hr or 2 days 🏃4 ⛰10

in the Desolation Wilderness

Map 6.2, page 206

The Crystal Basin area is a magical place on the western edge of the Desolation Wilderness. The high peaks of the Crystal Range overlook the basin and its multitude of lakes. Several excellent day hikes and backpacking trips are possible in this area, most of which begin from popular Wrights Lake Campground. Of those, the trip to Grouse, Hemlock, and Smith Lakes is a favorite. That is despite a relentless climb required to reach all three lakes. From the parking area, start this trip on the Twin Lakes Trail. It arcs past a meadow and then enters a pine and fir forest that is interspersed with stretches of granite. At a trail junction 1.2 miles out, head right for Grouse, Hemlock, and Smith Lakes. Small and pretty Grouse Lake is a one-mile, heart-pumping climb away, with many fine glances back at Wrights Lake and Icehouse Reservoir as you ascend. Many backpackers camp at Grouse Lake (look for wood posts that indicate designated campsites, and note that camping within 500 feet of Grouse Lake and its tributaries is prohibited). More hardy types and day hikers should head for Hemlock and Smith Lakes, farther uphill. The lakes get progressively prettier as you go, but the ascent gets steeper, too. Tiny Hemlock Lake is only 0.5 mile from Grouse Lake, and it boasts a spectacular rockslide on one shoreline and many scrawny hemlock trees on the other. Smith Lake lies another 0.5 mile beyond, way up high near tree line, at 8,700 feet, and it's a stunner.

User Groups: Hikers, dogs, and horses. No mountain bikes. No wheelchair facilities.

Permits: Permits are required year-round for both day and overnight use. Day hikers may obtain a free permit from a ranger station or may

self-issue at most major trailheads. Backpackers camping in Desolation Wilderness are subject to trailhead quotas. There is a $5 reservation fee, plus $5 per person for one night, $10 per person for two or more nights up to 14 days (nonrefundable); reserve at www.recreation. gov. Children ages 12 and under are free. Golden Passes do not apply to personal-use permits. For groups, the cost of a single permit will not exceed $100.

Maps: For a map, ask the U.S. Forest Service for Eldorado National Forest or Desolation Wilderness. A Lake Tahoe or Desolation Wilderness map is also available for a fee from Tom Harrison Maps. For a topographic map, ask the USGS for Pyramid Peak.

Directions: From Placerville, take Highway 50 east for 30 miles to Kyburz and continue five miles to the signed turnoff for Wrights Lake (about 21 miles west of South Lake Tahoe). Turn left (north) on Wrights Lake Road and drive eight miles to Wrights Lake Visitors Center. Turn right and continue one mile beyond the campground to the end of the road and the Twin Lakes trailhead.

Contact: Eldorado National Forest, Pacific Ranger District, 530/644-2349, www.fs.usda. gov/eldorado; Lake Tahoe Basin Management Unit, South Lake Tahoe, 530/543-2600, www. fs.usda.gov/ltbmu; visitors center (open daily mid-June-Sept., Sat.-Sun. Memorial Day-mid-Oct.), 530/543-2674.

63 LYONS CREEK TRAIL TO LAKE SYLVIA

9.0 mi/4.5 hr or 2 days 🏃3 ⛰9

in the Desolation Wilderness

Map 6.2, page 206

There are no easy hikes in the Wrights Lake area. This trek to Lake Sylvia (and Lyons Lake for the ambitious), on the other hand, requires one of the lesser climbs: "only" a 1,700-foot elevation gain to visit two beautiful lakes. The trip's total mileage is long, but the grade is steady, that is, except for the final 0.5 mile to Lyons Lake.

From the trailhead, you start by hiking on the south side of Lyons Creek for four miles. You'll pass through woods and meadows, then cross the stream, and in 0.1 mile, reach a junction. Lake Sylvia is 0.5 mile to the right. Lyons Lake is to the left and steeply uphill. Take your pick, or better yet, go see both. Lake Sylvia is shadowed by Pyramid Peak and has good campsites along its shoreline. Lyons Lake requires a nasty 450-foot climb in 0.5 mile, but its superior scenery makes it well worth the effort.

If you're fond of walking along pretty streams, where you are accompanied by the gurgle and babble of a creek as you hike, you'll love this hike. In addition, wildflowers proliferate in early summer, and views of Pyramid Peak (just shy of 10,000 feet in elevation) inspire you as you gently ascend.

Because this trailhead is a few miles distant from popular Wrights Lake Campground, it gets far fewer visitors than the trails that start right out of camp.

User Groups: Hikers, dogs, and horses. No mountain bikes. No wheelchair facilities.

Permits: Permits are required year-round for both day and overnight use. Day hikers may obtain a free permit from a ranger station or may self-issue at most major trailheads. Backpackers camping in Desolation Wilderness are subject to trailhead quotas. There is a $5 reservation fee, plus $5 per person for one night, $10 per person for two or more nights up to 14 days (nonrefundable); reserve at www.recreation. gov. Children ages 12 and under are free. Golden Passes do not apply to personal-use permits. For groups, the cost of a single permit will not exceed $100.

Maps: For a map, ask the U.S. Forest Service for Eldorado National Forest or Desolation Wilderness. A Lake Tahoe or Desolation Wilderness map is also available for a fee from Tom Harrison Maps. For a topographic map, ask the USGS for Pyramid Peak.

Directions: From Placerville, take Highway 50 east for 30 miles to Kyburz and continue five miles to the signed turnoff for Wrights Lake (about 21 miles west of South Lake Tahoe). Turn left (north) on Wrights Lake Road and drive four miles to the signed spur for the Lyons Creek Trail. Turn right and drive a short distance to the trailhead.

Contact: Eldorado National Forest, Pacific Ranger District, 530/644-2349, www.fs.usda. gov/eldorado; Lake Tahoe Basin Management Unit, South Lake Tahoe, 530/543-2600, www. fs.usda.gov/ltbmu; visitors center (open daily mid-June-Sept., Sat.-Sun. Memorial Day-mid-Oct.), 530/543-2674.

64 HORSETAIL FALLS VISTA
2.0 mi/1.0 hr   🏃1 ⛰9

in Eldorado National Forest near South Lake Tahoe

Map 6.2, page 206

This is the famous side trip for people driving to and from Tahoe on U.S. 50. Although the trail doesn't go all the way to the base of Horsetail Falls, it provides many excellent views of it, as well as of Pyramid Creek's glacier-carved canyon. Lower Horsetail Falls is about 90 feet high. About 15,000 people each summer glimpse the falls from their cars, then pull over at the giant parking lot by the trailhead and hike this trail to get closer to it. You are routed past a gorgeous stretch of Pyramid Creek called the Cascades. The trail stays outside the wilderness boundary, and provides a safe and easy alternative for casual visitors, points of conflict in the past.

The trail has been a source of controversy because the waterfall itself is located within the Desolation Wilderness boundary on a rough but serviceable route. Yet the first mile of trail is outside the wilderness boundary and is easily accessible from the highway. Over the years, that first easy mile has encouraged many inexperienced visitors to try to hike to the falls, resulting in numerous accidents and even deaths from falls on the slippery rocks where the trail disappears.

The Forest Service carried out the wilderness mandate by not making mechanical alterations to the trail, such as building bridges or blasting an obvious path into the granite. Instead, to decrease the frequent injuries, rangers provided oversight to build the 1.5-mile Pyramid Creek Loop Trail. It is made specifically for day users who just want to see Horsetail Falls and spectacular, granite-lined Pyramid Creek. The Pyramid Creek Loop takes off from the main trail about 0.5 mile in. Problem solved.

User Groups: Hikers and dogs. No horses or mountain bikes. No wheelchair facilities.

Permits: No permits are required if you stay out of the wilderness boundary. Parking is $5 per vehicle.

Maps: For a map, ask the U.S. Forest Service for Eldorado National Forest. A Lake Tahoe map is available for a fee from Tom Harrison Maps. For a topographic map, ask the USGS for Echo Lake.

Directions: From Placerville, take Highway 50 east to Strawberry (about 20 miles from South Lake Tahoe) and continue about three miles to Twin Bridges and a large pullout on the north side of the highway (0.5 mile west of the turnoff for Camp Sacramento). Park in the designated parking lot for the signed trailhead.

Contact: Eldorado National Forest, Pacific Ranger District, 530/644-2349, www.fs.usda.gov/eldorado.

65 RALSTON PEAK
8.0 mi/5.0 hr

in the Desolation Wilderness near South Lake Tahoe

Map 6.2, page 206

From Ralston Peak's 9,235-foot summit, you get an eye-popping view of Lake Tahoe, Fallen Leaf Lake, Carson Pass, Echo Lakes, and below you (to the north), Ralston Lake. This is simply a spectacular lookout. To get it, you may also find that your butt gets kicked. From trailhead to summit, you ascend from 6,400 to 9,240 feet over the course of four miles. The route has a little of everything: dense forest, open manzanita-covered slopes, meadows, and granite ridges. It also has lots of one thing: elevation gain.

To start, from the east side of the parking area, you walk north up the paved road for 200 yards and look for the trail that leads off on the left. This is your launch point. You then climb upward through nonstop trees and nonstop switchbacks for a mile, then enter a more open area as you pass the wilderness boundary sign at 1.5 miles. The views start to widen. Your lungs request a lunch break, but they don't get one until 2.5 miles up, when you finally gain the ridge. A half mile later, the break is over, and you climb again, this time to another ridge at 3.5 miles, covered in meadow grasses and wildflowers. You'll reach a trail on your right that leads to the summit. Part ways with the main trail, and in 0.5 mile, you scramble over jumbled rock to gain the 9,235-foot summit. Enjoy the panorama. You have earned it.

User Groups: Hikers and dogs. No horses or mountain bikes. No wheelchair facilities.

Permits: Permits are required year-round for both day and overnight use. Day hikers may obtain a free permit from a ranger station or may self-issue at most major trailheads. Backpackers camping in Desolation Wilderness are subject to trailhead quotas. There is a $5 reservation fee, plus $5 per person for one night, $10 per person for two or more nights up to 14 days (nonrefundable); reserve at www.recreation.gov. Children ages 12 and under are free. Golden Passes do not apply to personal-use permits. For groups, the cost of a single permit will not exceed $100.

Maps: For a map, ask the U.S. Forest Service for Eldorado National Forest or Desolation Wilderness. A Lake Tahoe or Desolation Wilderness map is also available for a fee from Tom Harrison Maps. For a topographic map, ask the USGS for Echo Lake.

Directions: From Placerville, take Highway 50 east to Twin Bridges and then continue 1.5 miles to Camp Sacramento and the turnoff. There is a parking area off the north side of

U.S. 50 and a sign for Ralston Trail to Lake of the Woods.

From South Lake Tahoe, take Highway 89 south for five miles to Highway 50. Turn right (west) on U.S. 50 and drive about 14 miles to the turnoff for Camp Sacramento (if you reach Twin Bridges, you've gone 1.5 miles too far west).

Contact: Eldorado National Forest, Pacific Ranger District, 530/644-2349, www.fs.usda.gov/eldorado; Lake Tahoe Basin Management Unit, South Lake Tahoe, 530/543-2600, www.fs.usda.gov/ltbmu; visitors center (open daily mid-June-Sept., Sat.-Sun. Memorial Day-mid-Oct.), 530/543-2674.

66 BOAT TAXI TO LAKE ALOHA
6.0-12.0 mi/3.5-6.0 hr

in the Desolation Wilderness

Map 6.2, page 206

This is a sensational trip, one of the great boat-and-hike adventures in California. You start with a boat taxi across the two Echo Lakes and get dropped off at the trailhead for the Pacific Crest Trail. Then it's an easy climb to great views with a series of spur trails to beautiful alpine lakes in Desolation Wilderness, crowned by Lake Aloha in Desolation Valley.

From the hiker's parking lot, walk 0.25 mile downhill to the resort and the boat launch area, at the edge of Echo Lake. The boat taxi leaves at frequent intervals (or whenever more than two people show up) from 8am to 6pm daily all summer. The trip costs $12 each way. The boat carries hikers two miles to the far end of Upper Echo Lake, and the boat ride is unique, too, where you pass many lovely lakeside cottages. You arrive at the border of the Desolation Wilderness, fresh, rested, and ready. If you instead hike the PCT both coming and going, it will add five miles to the trip.

From the boat taxi drop-off point, gain the main trail (Pacific Crest Trail) and head to your left. It's a 3.5-mile hike to the eastern edge of Lake Aloha. You start with a steady climb up to a ridge. Be sure to stop and turn around to enjoy the stunning lake view. After topping the ridge, the hike is an easy saunter. You'll pass several signed junctions with numerous trails along the way, all of which lead to various lakes in very short distances. Your best bet is to stay on the main path for Lake Aloha, then take some of the cutoffs to neighboring lakes on your way back. When you reach Lake Aloha's shore, hike along its beautiful north side for a distance, admiring the rocky coves and islands of the giant, shallow lake. At one time, Lake Aloha was several small lakes. They were dammed with a unique rock wall to create this huge body of water. The effect is a bit surreal, although beautiful. The lake's elevation is 8,116 feet.

On the trip back, take one or more of the signed trail junctions and visit Lake of the Woods, Lake Lucille, Lake Margery, Tamarack Lake, or Ralston Lake. All are less than one mile off the Lake Aloha Trail. Tamarack Lake is the best for scenery; Lake of the Woods is the best for fishing.

On the return trip, some bypass the boat taxi and continue on the Pacific Crest Trail back to the parking area. That will add 2.5 miles to your trip. The trail rises well above the lake, and eventually you will pass a series of vacation homes.

User Groups: Hikers and dogs (not advised because sharp rocks can bruise their foot pads). No horses or mountain bikes. No wheelchair facilities.

Permits: Boat taxi (not required) is $12 per hiker one-way, $5 for dogs. Permits are required year-round for both day and overnight use. Day hikers may obtain a free permit from a ranger station or may self-issue at most major trailheads. Backpackers camping in Desolation Wilderness are subject to trailhead quotas. There is a $5 reservation fee, plus $5 per person for one night, $10 per person for two or more nights up to 14 days (nonrefundable); reserve at www.recreation.gov. Children ages 12 and under are free. Golden Passes do not apply to personal-use permits. For groups, the cost of a single permit will not exceed $100.

Maps: For a map, ask the U.S. Forest Service for Desolation Wilderness. A Lake Tahoe or Desolation Wilderness map is also available for a fee from Tom Harrison Maps. For a topographic map, ask the USGS for Echo Lake.

Directions: From Placerville, take Highway 50 east for 46 miles to Echo Summit (and Sierra at Tahoe Ski Resort) and then continue east on Highway 50 for 1.8 miles to Johnson Pass Road and a signed turnoff (brown sign) for Berkeley Camp/Echo Lake (one mile west of Echo Summit). Turn left and drive 0.5 mile to Echo Lakes Road. Turn left and drive one mile to a series of parking lots located 0.25 mile before the road ends at Echo Lakes Resort. Hikers not staying at the resort must park in one of the upper lots or alongside the road, not in the main lower lot by the resort, and walk down to the marina, boat taxi, or trailhead.

From South Lake Tahoe: Take Highway 89 south for five miles to U.S. 50. Turn right (west) on U.S. 50 and drive 5.5 miles to the signed turnoff for Echo Lakes on the right (one mile west of Echo Summit). Turn right and drive 0.5 mile to Echo Lakes Road. Turn left and drive one mile to a series of parking lots located 0.25 mile before the road ends at Echo Lakes Resort.

Contact: Echo Lakes Chalet, 530/659-7207, www.echochalet.com; Eldorado National Forest, Pacific Ranger District, 530/644-2349, www.fs.usda.gov/eldorado; Lake Tahoe Basin Management Unit, South Lake Tahoe, 530/543-2600, www.fs.usda.gov/ltbmu; visitors center (open daily mid-June-Sept., Sat.-Sun. Memorial Day-mid-Oct.), 530/543-2674.

67 ECHO LAKES RESORT TO BARKER PASS (PCT)

32.3 mi one-way/3 days 🥾4 ⛰️9

from Echo Lake to Forest Road 3 near Barker Pass

Map 6.2, page 206

The Desolation Wilderness (and the neighboring Granite Chief Wilderness) are filled with sculpted granite domes and hundreds of gemlike lakes. All is pristine, yet access is also quite easy, making this, along with the John Muir Trail, the most heavily used section of the PCT. The trip starts at Echo Lake (elevation 7,400 feet), climbs through pines past Upper Echo Lake, and then continues up and north toward Triangle Lake, one of dozens of lakes you pass on your northward route. They come and go in spectacular fashion: Lake Margery, Lake Aloha, and then Heather, Susie, and Gilmore Lakes, and finally Dicks Lake (at 9,380 feet). There are so many, in fact, that you can plan on a perfect campsite near a lake every night, providing you don't mind the company of other hikers drawn by classic beauty. The views are dramatic as well, across miles and miles of the glacial-carved granite, all of it marvelous high Sierra landscape. As you continue, you'll discover Upper and Middle Velma Lakes, both very pretty and with good fishing. The trail skirts the ridgeline, keeping the higher knobs to the east as it gradually descends toward Richardson Lake, just beyond the Desolation Wilderness boundary, ready now to enter the Granite Chief Wilderness to the north.

To continue north on the PCT, see the *Barker Pass to Donner Pass (PCT)* hike in this chapter. If you are walking this trail in reverse, see the *Carson Pass to Echo Lakes Resort (PCT)* hike in this chapter.

User Groups: Hikers, dogs, and horses. No mountain bikes. No wheelchair facilities.

Permits: A backcountry permit is required for traveling through various wilderness and special-use areas the trail traverses. In addition, a campfire permit is required for the use of portable camp stoves or the building of campfires where allowed. To make it simple, you can contact the national forest, Bureau of Land Management (BLM), or national park office at your point of entry for a combined permit that is good for traveling through multiple-permit areas during your dates of travel.

Maps: For topographic maps, ask the USGS

for Echo Lake, Emerald Bay, and Rockbound Valley.

Directions: From Placerville, take Highway 50 east for 46 miles to Echo Summit (and Sierra at Tahoe Ski Resort) and then continue east on Highway 50 for 1.8 miles to Johnson Pass Road and a signed turnoff (brown sign) for Berkeley Camp/Echo Lake (one mile west of Echo Summit). Turn left and drive 0.5 mile to Echo Lakes Road. Turn left and drive one mile to a series of parking lots located 0.25 mile before the road ends at Echo Lakes Resort. Hikers not staying at the resort must park in one of the upper lots or alongside the road, not in the main lower lot by the resort, and walk down to the marina, boat taxi, or trailhead.

From South Lake Tahoe: Take Highway 89 south for five miles to U.S. 50. Turn right (west) on U.S. 50 and drive 5.5 miles to the signed turnoff for Echo Lakes on the right (one mile west of Echo Summit.) Turn right and drive 0.5 mile to Echo Lakes Road. Turn left and drive one mile to parking 0.25 mile above Echo Lakes Resort.

To reach the Barker Pass trailhead from Tahoe Pines on Highway 89, head north for 0.5 mile to the Kaspian Picnic Grounds and then bear left (west) for seven miles on Forest Service Road 15N03.

Contact: Echo Lakes Chalet, 530/659-7207, www.echochalet.com; Lake Tahoe Basin Management Unit, South Lake Tahoe, 530/543-2600, www.fs.usda.gov/ltbmu; visitors center (open daily mid-June-Sept., Sat.-Sun. Memorial Day-mid-Oct.), 530/543-2674.

68 DARDANELLES LAKE AND ROUND LAKE
7.6 mi/4.5 hr 🏃3 ⛰9

in Meiss Country south of Lake Tahoe

Map 6.2, page 206

Dardanelles Lake is nestled at an elevation of 7,740 feet, set in a pocket with a granite backdrop. It's striking and gorgeous. This trek provides a tour into "Meiss Country," that large and wonderful roadless area south of Lake Tahoe. The forces that shaped the land, ice

Echo Lakes

© TOM STIENSTRA

(glaciers) and fire (volcanic action), have made their presence clearly visible.

The route to Dardanelles Lake and Round Lake, along the Tahoe Rim Trail, starts out steep but gets easier as it goes. From the parking lot, the trail heads south, and in about 100 yards crosses Highway 89, then makes an initial climb through fir and pine forest to Big Meadow. The meadow makes lovely, level walking for 0.25 mile; then it's back into the trees. Follow the trail signs for Round Lake until you complete a steep, short descent at two miles out. At the bottom of the hill, at Meiss Meadow Trail toward Christmas Valley, turn sharply right. Walk less than 0.25 mile, then turn left and cross a creek for the final 1.2 miles to Dardanelles Lake. It's good for swimming, fishing, and picnicking. If you time your trip for autumn, you'll be treated to a marvelous color display from the aspens and alders that grow along this trail's many streams.

On your return, retrace your steps to the junction at the bottom of the hill, then hike 0.75 mile in the opposite direction to visit Round Lake. Although not quite as scenic as Dardanelles Lake, Round Lake provides a stark, fascinating contrast to its neighbor: It is surrounded by volcanic rock formations, not granite cliffs.

Note that this trail is open to mountain bikers. On weekdays you might not see a single bike, but on weekends you'll see plenty.

User Groups: Hikers, dogs, horses, and mountain bikes. No wheelchair facilities.

Permits: No permits are required. Parking and access are free.

Maps: For a map, ask the U.S. Forest Service for Lake Tahoe Basin Management Unit. A Lake Tahoe map is available for a fee from Tom Harrison Maps. For a topographic map, ask the USGS for Echo Lake.

Directions: From South Lake Tahoe, take Highway 89 south for five miles to Meyers and the junction with Highway 89, and then continue south on Highway 89 for five more miles to the Big Meadow trailhead parking area on the northwest side of the road. Turn left off the

highway, then bear left and park near the restrooms. The trail begins from the south side of the parking lot loop and crosses Highway 89 in about 100 yards.

Contact: Lake Tahoe Basin Management Unit, South Lake Tahoe, 530/543-2600, www. fs.usda.gov/ltbmu; visitors center (open daily mid-June-Sept., Sat.-Sun. Memorial Day-mid-Oct.), 530/543-2674.

69 LAKE MARGARET
4.6 mi/3.0 hr   🏃1 ⛰9

near Carson Pass and Kirkwood Lake

Map 6.2, page 206   **BEST (**

Can you imagine a hike to an alpine lake with only a 500-foot elevation gain? It might seem too good to be true, but here you are. If you need an easy-trail fix, Lake Margaret should do the trick.

The trail undulates gently, never gaining or losing more than a couple hundred feet. The first stretch is actually downhill. Then the path climbs gently over a small ridge and then descends again over granite slabs, where the route is marked with cairns. You'll cross branches of Caples Creek twice in the first mile. At 1.5 miles, the trail passes by a couple of tiny ponds. At two miles out, after crossing another creek, you'll find yourself in a lovely grove of aspens and knee-high wildflowers. At 2.3 miles, after about an hour of walking and only a minor expenditure of energy, you'll reach the granite shoreline of Lake Margaret. Swimming is excellent. A few tiny islands and many shoreline boulders make fine sunbathing spots. Figure on staying awhile. The lake's elevation is 7,500 feet.

Note that although most of the trails in the Carson Pass area are famous for wildflowers, the proximity of several small streams makes the bloom especially showy on this path. The peak wildflower season is from mid-June to mid-August.

User Groups: Hikers, leashed dogs, horses, and mountain bikes. No wheelchair facilities.

Permits: No permits are required. Parking and access are free.

Maps: For a map, ask the U.S. Forest Service for Eldorado National Forest or Mokelumne Wilderness. For a topographic map, ask the USGS for Caples Lake.

Directions: From South Lake Tahoe, take Highway 89 south for five miles to Meyers and the junction with Highway 89, and then continue south on Highway 89 for 11 miles to Highway 88. Turn west on Highway 88 and drive 14.5 miles to the Lake Margaret sign, on the north side of the road (5.5 miles west of Carson Pass Summit, and 5.5 miles east of Silver Lake.) Turn north and park at the trailhead parking area.

Contact: Eldorado National Forest, Amador Ranger District, 209/295-4251, www.fs.usda.gov/eldorado.

70 CAPLES LAKE TRAILHEAD TO EMIGRANT LAKE
8.0 mi/4.0 hr or 2 days   🥾3 ⛰9

in the Mokelumne Wilderness near Caples Lake

Map 6.2, page 206

A climb of less than 1,000 feet leads to gorgeous Emigrant Lake at an elevation of 8,600 feet. The trail starts at the spillway at Caples Lake, along the lake's south side, and follows a historic emigrant route. The first two miles are right along the lake's edge, where you climb gently above the shoreline, always in the shade of big conifers. You continue along Emigrant Creek to a stream crossing at 3.5 miles, followed by another crossing. Most of the trail's ascent is packed into the last 1.8 miles. A few switchbacks ultimately carry you up to Emigrant Lake, a beautiful cirque lake. Covered Wagon Peak and Thimble Peak, at 9,500 feet, rise above the scene. The trail's total elevation gain is less than 1,000 feet, making this an easy day hike for most, even with its eight-mile distance.

The trailhead at Caples Lake is often jam-packed with backpackers, so do yourself a favor: visit here midweek or in the off-season, or make your trip a day hike instead of an overnighter. Why is this trail so popular? It's gorgeous and easy compared to other Sierra treks.

User Groups: Hikers, leashed dogs, and horses. No mountain bikes. No wheelchair facilities.

Permits: No day-hiking permits are required. A free wilderness permit is required for overnight stays; it is available from the Amador Ranger Station, the Carson Pass Information Station, or the Eldorado Information Center. Maximum group size for day use is 12. Maximum group size for overnight use is eight. No self-registration is available at the trailhead.

Maps: For a map, ask the U.S. Forest Service for Eldorado National Forest or Desolation Wilderness. For a topographic map, ask the USGS for Caples Lake.

Directions: From South Lake Tahoe, take Highway 89 south for five miles to Meyers and the junction with Highway 89, and then continue south on Highway 89 for 11 miles to Highway 88. Turn west on Highway 88 and drive 14 miles (five miles west of Carson Pass) to the west side of Caples Lake and the trailhead parking area.

Contact: Eldorado National Forest, Amador Ranger District, 209/295-4251, www.fs.usda.gov/eldorado.

71 MINKALO TRAIL
7.0 mi/3.5 hr   🥾2 ⛰8

near Silver Lake

Map 6.2, page 206

The Minkalo Trail is your best bet from Silver Lake. The trail leads to Granite Lake in one mile and to Plasse's Resort, on the south side of the lake, in three miles. Why not hike to both, then buy a pizza or a Clif Bar at Plasse's Resort Trading Post to fuel up for the hike back to the Minkalo trailhead?

Silver Lake is located at an elevation of 7,300 feet along Highway 88. The trailhead is located near the Kit Carson Lodge (see directions). The trail starts out rocky and stays that way for the first 0.25 mile. Cross a bridge over Squaw Creek to a right fork that leads to Plasse's Resort. Take the left fork first, which heads to Granite Lake. It takes about a 20-minute walk with a moderate climb. It's a pretty lake and good for swimming. After you've visited, return to the trail junction and hike south, soon coming close to the edge of Silver Lake. The trail then provides pretty lake views, including long looks at Treasure Island, Silver Lake's island. It takes about an hour to reach the campground at Plasse's, an excellent place for horse lovers (and pizza lovers).

User Groups: Hikers, leashed dogs, horses, and mountain bikes. No wheelchair facilities.

Permits: No permits are required. Parking and access are free.

Maps: For a map, ask the U.S. Forest Service for Eldorado National Forest, or Desolation Wilderness. For a topographic map, ask the USGS for Caples Lake.

Directions: From South Lake Tahoe, take Highway 89 south for five miles to Meyers and the junction with Highway 89, and then continue south on Highway 89 for 11 miles to Highway 88. Turn right (west) on Highway 88 and drive 15.5 miles (10.8 miles west of Carson Pass) to the turnoff for Kit Carson Lodge on the north side of the road. Turn north and drive past Kit Carson Lodge, go left at the first fork, and go right at the second fork, to the parking for Minkalo Trail. (It's a total of 1.4 miles from Highway 88.) Walk back down the road for about 40 yards to find the trailhead.

Contact: Eldorado National Forest, Amador Ranger District, 209/295-4251, www.fs.usda.gov/eldorado.

72 OSBORNE HILL
2.6 mi/1.5 hr   👣1 ⛰7

on Highway 4 near Lake Alpine

Map 6.2, page 206

We like the way Lake Alpine looks from close up on Lakeshore Trail, but then again, we like the way Lake Alpine looks from far up on Osborne Hill, also known as Osborne Point. A short, healthy climb brings you to the point, from which you can look down at the lake and beyond into the Carson-Iceberg Wilderness. The trail ends there but connects to Emigrant West Trail if you wish to hike farther. In spring, if you're itching for winter to be over so you can go hiking, Highway 4 is kept open as far as Silvertip Campground, but not always farther east. Thus if the snow is dwindling, you'll have access to this trailhead often long before you can access the others near Lake Alpine.

User Groups: Hikers, dogs, horses, and mountain bikes. No wheelchair facilities.

Permits: No permits are required. Parking and access are free.

Maps: For a map, ask the U.S. Forest Service for Stanislaus National Forest. For a topographic map, ask the USGS for Tamarack.

Directions: From Angels Camp, take Highway 4 east for 40 miles to Bear Valley. Set your odometer at Bear Valley and drive east on Highway 4 for three miles to the Osborne Ridge trailhead (just east of Silvertip Campground). Take the trail that leads from the south side of the road.

Contact: Stanislaus National Forest, Calaveras Ranger District, 209/795-1381, www.fs.usda.gov/stanislaus.

73 LAKESHORE TRAIL AND INSPIRATION POINT
4.0 mi/2.0 hr

on Highway 4 near Lake Alpine

Map 6.2, page 206

It's hard to say which trail is better, Lakeshore Trail or Inspiration Point Trail. To solve the dilemma, hike both of them together. The trip starts with a short walk down a dirt road; then turn right onto a single track. After 10 minutes of hiking through a thick lodgepole pine forest peppered with tiny pinecones, you're at the edge of Lake Alpine, elevation 7,350 feet. Follow the trail to your left, and in another 10 minutes, you reach a left fork for Inspiration

Point (Lakeshore Trail continues straight). You'll want to head out and back on both trails; it makes no difference which one you take first.

The Lakeshore Trail is flat and stays within 100 feet of the water's edge, offering many pretty lake views. Eventually the trail meets up with Slick Rock, a four-wheel-drive road, but there's no need to go that far. Just walk a mile or so to the dam, and then turn around and head back. The Inspiration Point Trail, on the other hand, is more of a workout: a steep one-mile climb to the summit at Inspiration Point, from which you can see for miles. Pick a clear day, and you'll be pointing out Lake Alpine, Elephant Rock, the Dardanelles, and Spicer Meadow Reservoir.

User Groups: Hikers, dogs, and horses. No mountain bikes. No wheelchair facilities.

Permits: No permits are required. Parking and access are free.

Maps: For a national forest map, ask for Stanislaus National Forest. For a topographic map, ask the USGS for Spicer Meadow Reservoir.

Directions: From Angels Camp, take Highway 4 east for 40 miles to Bear Valley. Set your odometer at Bear Valley and drive east on Highway 4 for 4.3 miles to the Lake Alpine East Shore trailhead turnoff, on the right. Turn right, drive 0.25 mile, and turn right again and drive 0.1 mile past Pine Marten Campground to the signed parking area and the trailhead.

Contact: Stanislaus National Forest, Calaveras Ranger District, 209/795-1381, www.fs.usda.gov/stanislaus.

74 DUCK LAKE
3.0 mi/1.5 hr

in the Carson-Iceberg Wilderness off Highway 4 near Lake Alpine

Map 6.2, page 206

The trailhead at Silver Valley Campground is the start of the route to Duck Lake. It's also one of the busiest trailheads into the Carson-Iceberg Wilderness. The trip to Duck Lake is a great easy hike for families or people just in the mood for a stroll (the more ambitious can continue past the lake on an eight-mile round-trip to Rock Lake). It's only one mile to reach Duck Lake, but once you're there, you'll want to walk the loop trail around its perimeter, which adds another mile to your trip. The area is the site of a historic cow camp, where animals have grazed since the late 19th century. You can examine what's left of a few early-20th-century cowboy cabins.

User Groups: Hikers, dogs, and horses. No mountain bikes. No wheelchair facilities.

Permits: No day-use permits are required. Parking and access are free.

Maps: For a map, ask the U.S. Forest Service for Stanislaus National Forest or Carson-Iceberg Wilderness. For a topographic map, ask the USGS for Spicer Meadow Reservoir.

Directions: From Angels Camp, take Highway 4 east for 40 miles to Bear Valley. Set your odometer at Bear Valley and drive east on Highway 4 for 4.3 miles to the Lake Alpine East Shore trailhead turnoff on the right. Turn right and continue straight to Silver Valley Campground and the Silver Valley trailhead.

Contact: Stanislaus National Forest, Calaveras Ranger District, 209/795-1381, www.fs.usda.gov/stanislaus.

75 WOODCHUCK BASIN TO WHEELER LAKE
6.4 mi/3.5 hr   🥾3 ⛰️8

in the Mokelumne Wilderness off Highway 4 near Lake Alpine

Map 6.2, page 206

Your goal is little Wheeler Lake, a fine overlooked lake (and we'll explain why). Start at the Woodchuck Basin Trailhead, elevation 7,800 feet. The trail leads into the Mokelumne Wilderness, and after you climb uphill for 1.7 forested miles, you reach a junction where you can go left for Underwood Valley or right for tiny Wheeler Lake. Bear right, pass a Mokelumne Wilderness sign, and in moments, you plummet 1,000 feet in a 1.5-mile descent to Wheeler Lake. Think it over before you go, because you'll need to regain those 1,000 feet on the way home. That's why many choose not to do this hike. But if you're willing to take the plunge, you're treated to a picturesque, tree- and granite-lined lake, where you can pass the afternoon with little fear that you'll be bugged by a busload of other hikers.

User Groups: Hikers, leashed dogs, and horses. No mountain bikes. No wheelchair facilities.

Permits: No permits are required. Parking and access are free.

Maps: For a map, ask the U.S. Forest Service for Stanislaus National Forest or Mokelumne Wilderness. For a topographic map, ask the USGS for Spicer Meadow Reservoir.

Directions: From Angels Camp, take Highway 4 east for 40 miles to Bear Valley. Set your odometer at Bear Valley and drive east on Highway 4 for 5.5 miles to the Woodchuck Basin trailhead on the left. Turn left and drive 0.25 mile to the parking area.

Contact: Stanislaus National Forest, Calaveras Ranger District, 209/795-1381, www.fs.usda. gov/stanislaus.

North Grove Loop

76 DISCOVERY STUMP/ NORTH GROVE LOOP

1.0 mi/0.5 hr

in Calaveras Big Trees State Park

Map 6.2, page 206

The giant sequoia that nobody forgets is what is called the "Discovery Stump. " Others just call it "The Big Stump. " It's the most popu- lar spot in the park. Start at the visitors center, then walk south a short distance past the camp- fire center, to the stump. It is 24 feet in diam- eter. Everybody gets their picture taken on it. Here's the story: Back in the day, a gent wanted to prove how big the trees were to folks on the East Coast, so naturally, he cut the biggest one down, collected the bark and wasted the wood, then took it by railroad to the World's Fair and reassembled it to prove how big it was. Except everybody thought it was a hoax. Then, shortly thereafter, the bark collection was burned in a fire. Surprised the guy didn't shoot a Bigfoot while he was at it? The giant stump has been used for just about everything, including a dance floor. According to projections, if it had been allowed to grow, it would be bigger than the General Sherman Tree in Sequoia National Park, the largest living thing by volume on the planet.

Once you have seen The Big Stump, which is what we call it, return to the North Grove Loop. It is routed in a loop in a grove of giant sequoias that include several mammoth-sized trees and the Pioneer Cabin Tree. The trail goes right through a cut-off in the Pioneer Cabin Tree, but truth is, the tree is not a tree, but an elon- gated stump; you can frame pictures to make it look alive by not showing the top.

The easy trail is routed among the giant se- quoias, near Big Tree Creek, and back, easy, short and pretty. These trees, of course, are known for their tremendous diameter: It can take a few dozen people, linking hands, to en- circle one. This trip is actually best in winter after fresh snowfall, when your footsteps are the only signs of life, and it feels like you are in a time machine. This trail gets very heavy use.

User Groups: Hikers and wheelchairs. No dogs, horses, or mountain bikes.

Permits: No permits are required. A state park entrance fee of $10 is charged each vehicle.

Maps: A brochure and trail map is available for a fee at Calaveras Big Trees State Park. For a topographic map, ask the USGS for Dorrington.

Directions: From Angels Camp, take Highway 4 east for 23 miles to Arnold, and then continue for four miles to the park entrance. The trailhead is adjacent to the park entrance.

Contact: Calaveras Big Trees State Park, 209/795-2334, visitors center, 209/795-3840, www.parks.ca.gov.

77 SOUTH GROVE LOOP
5.0 mi/3.0 hr   👣2 ⛰8

northeast of Arnold on Highway 4

Map 6.2, page 206

The two largest sequoias in Calaveras Big Trees State Park are found on a spur trail of this hike, and that makes it a must-do for visitors. But so many tourists are content to just walk the little trail at the North Grove, look at the giant stump and take the trail through the walk-thru tree, and then hit the road. Why rush? As long as you're at the park, take the South Grove Loop. The loop itself is 3.5 miles long, but the highlight is a spur trail that branches off 0.75 mile to the Agassiz Tree and the Palace Hotel Tree, two monster-sized specimens. For a great photograph, have someone take a picture of you standing at the base of one of these trees; you will look like a Lilliputian from *Gulliver's Travels.*

User Groups: Hikers only. No dogs, horses, or mountain bikes. No wheelchair facilities.

Permits: No permits are required. A state park entrance fee of $10 is charged each vehicle.

Maps: A brochure and trail map is available for a fee at Calaveras Big Trees State Park. For

a topographic map, ask the USGS for Boards Crossing.

Directions: From Angels Camp, take Highway 4 east for 23 miles to Arnold, and then continue for four miles to the park entrance. Turn right into the park entrance, then drive down the parkway for nine miles to the trailhead, on the right. Note: The road is closed in winter.

Contact: Calaveras Big Trees State Park, 209/795-2334; Columbia State Park, 209/532-0150, www.parks.ca.gov.

78 CARSON PASS TO ECHO LAKES RESORT (PCT)
15.8 mi one-way/1-2 days   👣4 ⛰10

from Carson Pass at Highway 88 north to Echo Lake near U.S. 50, just south of Lake Tahoe

Map 6.3, page 207   **BEST (**

When you've hiked on the Pacific Crest Trail for weeks, the first glimpse of Lake Tahoe in the distance can seem like a privileged view into heaven. I'll never forget it. That view is just a few miles from Ebbetts Pass. You start by hiking over a short mountain rim (nice view to the west of Caples Lake) and then you drop into the headwaters of the Truckee River. As you look northward after making the rim, Lake Tahoe suddenly comes into view. It's like having a divine vision. And finally there is water available from several small creeks as you walk into the Truckee headwaters. At the same time, you will be greeted by a high meadow surrounded by a light forest. All seems right with the world again. With Echo Lakes Resort within one day's hiking time, you will be amazed at how inspired (and fast) you can get on this section of trail. It's very pretty, weaving through lush canyons and along creeks, eventually reaching beautiful and tiny Showers Lake. Here the trail seems to drop off to never-never land; it descends quickly and steeply in the march toward Tahoe. Contentment reigns. When you reach Little Norway, however, reality sets in. Cars are everywhere. The trail suddenly grinds down amid cabins and vacation property. There's one last hill to climb, a real half hour of frustration–you're ready for your reward at the store—and then the PCT drops quickly to the parking lot for Echo Lakes.

To continue north on the PCT, see the *Echo Lakes Resort to Barker Pass (PCT)* hike in this chapter. If you are walking this trail in reverse, see the *Blue Lakes Road to Carson Pass (PCT)* hike in this chapter.

User Groups: Hikers, dogs, and horses. No mountain bikes. No wheelchair facilities.

Permits: A backcountry permit is required for traveling through various wilderness and special-use areas that the trail traverses. In addition, a campfire permit is required for the use of portable camp stoves or the building of campfires where permitted. To make it simple, you can contact the national forest, Bureau of Land Management (BLM), or national park office at your point of entry for a combined permit that is good for traveling through multiple-permit areas during your dates of travel.

Maps: For national forest maps, ask for Lake Tahoe Basin Management Unit, Tahoe National Forest, Eldorado National Forest, and Stanislaus National Forest. For topographic maps, ask the USGS for Carson Pass, Caples Lake, and Echo Lake.

Directions: To reach the Carson Pass trailhead: From South Lake Tahoe, take Highway 89 south for five miles to Meyers and the junction with Highway 89, and then continue south on Highway 89 for 11 miles to Highway 88. Turn right (west) on Highway 88 and drive 10 miles to Carson Pass.

For the Echo Lakes Resort trailhead: From South Lake Tahoe, take Highway 89 south for five miles to U.S. 50. Turn right (west) on U.S. 50 and drive 5.5 miles to the signed turnoff for Echo Lakes on the right (one mile west of Echo Summit). Turn right and drive 0.5 mile to Echo Lakes Road. Turn left and drive one mile to a series of parking lots located 0.25 mile before the road ends at Echo Lakes Resort. Hikers not staying at the resort must park in one of the upper lots or alongside the road, not in the main lower lot by the resort, and walk down to the marina, boat taxi, or trailhead.

Contact: Eldorado National Forest, Amador Ranger District, 209/295-4251, www.fs.usda.gov/eldorado; Lake Tahoe Basin Management Unit, South Lake Tahoe, 530/543-2600, www.fs.usda.gov/ltbmu; visitors center (open daily mid-June-Sept., Sat.-Sun. Memorial Day-mid-Oct.), 530/543-2674.

79 CARSON PASS TO SHOWERS LAKE
10.0 mi/6.0 hr

near Caples Lake in Meiss Country

Map 6.3, page 207

Here's a day hike on the Pacific Crest Trail into the land of Meiss Country, that is, the headwaters for the Upper Truckee River. Start this trip at the PCT trailhead on the north side of Carson Pass. You head uphill where you climb through Meiss Pass and then drop into a huge valley basin. Views along the way include Mount Round Top, Elephant Back, and Red Lake Peak, and expand to distant, far-off Lake Tahoe to the north. It's 2.9 miles to a fork with the Tahoe Rim Trail (TRT), just beyond a crossing of Upper Truckee River (little more than a creek here). While stopping to pump a canteen's worth of water here, we've had hummingbirds come up and eye us from a foot away.

At the fork, stay left on the PCT and TRT, and cross the river again on your way to Showers Lake, 2.1 miles farther. The last half mile of trail is a 350-foot descent to Showers Lake, with 9,590-foot Little Round Top poking up above it to the west. The trail leads along the east side of the lake, where campsites can be found. The lake is set at 8,790 feet and is the highest lake in the Upper Truckee River Basin. It's very pretty.

By the way, at that fork, the right fork leads 2.2 miles to Round Lake, Meiss Country's largest lake and a popular destination,

This trip is popular with the horsey set. A separate trail leads to Showers Lake from

Schneider Camp, a large horse camp, so weekends bring a fair amount of horse traffic. Also note that the trip begins in Eldorado National Forest, but two-thirds of the trail is within jurisdiction of the Lake Tahoe Basin Management Unit.

Note that no bikes are permitted on the PCT, but we've seen plenty of tire tread here on the trail.

User Groups: Hikers, leashed dogs, and horses. No mountain bikes. No wheelchair facilities.

Permits: No permits are required. A $5 parking fee is charged per vehicle.

Maps: For a map, ask the U.S. Forest Service for Eldorado National Forest or Mokelumne Wilderness. For topographic maps, ask the USGS for Caples Lake and Carson Pass.

Directions: From South Lake Tahoe, take Highway 89 south for five miles to Meyers and the junction with Highway 89, and then continue south on Highway 89 for 11 miles to Highway 88. Turn west on Highway 88 and drive 10 miles to Carson Pass Summit. The parking area and Meiss trailhead are on the right (north), across the highway from (and slightly west of) the Carson Pass Information Station.

Contact: Eldorado National Forest, Amador Ranger District, Pioneer, 209/295-4251 www.fs.fed.us/r5.

80 WOODS LAKE TO WINNEMUCCA LAKE

3.0 mi/1.5 hr

in the Mokelumne Wilderness near Carson Pass

Map 6.3, page 207   BEST (

Woods Lake is a little magical spot where you can drive right up, walk a few feet to the water's edge, and plunk in your fishing line. It's also the trailhead for numerous great hikes into the Mokelumne Wilderness, including this easy trip to deep blue Winnemucca Lake, set at the base of Mount Round Top (elevation 10,381 feet). From Woods Lake, the trip starts where you walk amid big conifers until you come out to a glacial moraine. A view emerges of Mount Round Top, a huge old volcanic vent. It's a stunning sight, and in an average winter, collects massive amounts of snow. In early summer, wildflowers bloom in profusion on the open slopes surrounding the path. From Woods Lake, it is only 1.5 miles of gentle to moderate climbing to reach the edge of Winnemucca Lake, nestled at the foot of Mount Round Top.

The land here has been formed by volcanic action, so as you walk, wide-traveled hikers may have to remember that you aren't at Lassen Peak or Mount Shasta. The beauty attracts a ton of people, often 200 to 300 on summer weekends.

The peak season for wildflowers is mid-June to mid-August, at its very best in mid-to-late July. If you hiked this trail in years past, you may remember that it once started by crossing a footbridge. That is no longer true.

User Groups: Hikers, leashed dogs, and horses. No mountain bikes. No wheelchair facilities.

Permits: A free wilderness permit is required for overnight stays; it is available from the Amador Ranger Station, the Carson Pass Information Station, or the Eldorado Information Center. A parking fee of $5 is charged, good for overnight use.

Maps: For a map, ask the U.S. Forest Service for Mokelumne Wilderness or Eldorado National Forest. For topographic maps, ask the USGS for Caples Lake and Carson Pass.

Directions: From South Lake Tahoe, take Highway 89 south for five miles to Meyers and the junction with Highway 89, and then continue south on 89 for 11 miles to Highway 88. Turn right (west) on Highway 88 and drive 12 miles to the Woods Lake Campground turnoff, on the south side of the road (1.5 miles west of Carson Pass Summit). Turn left and drive one mile to the trailhead parking area (0.5 mile before reaching Woods Lake).

Contact: Eldorado National Forest, Amador Ranger District, 209/295-4251, www.fs.usda.gov/eldorado.

81 WOODS LAKE TRAILHEAD TO ROUND TOP LOOP

6.6 mi/4.0 hr   🥾4 ⛰10

in the Mokelumne Wilderness near Carson Pass

Map 6.3, page 207

The mission on this hike is to connect the trailhead from Woods Lake to Winnemucca Lake and beyond to the top of 10,380-foot Mount Round Top. Your reward is a 10. You pay a bit for your pleasure. Start at the Woods Lake Trailhead, and take the Winnemucca Lake Trail for the first 1.5 miles to Winnemucca's edge, as described in the previous hike. Then bear right and cross the stream on the west side of the lake. It's then one mile, uphill, to Round Top Lake, steep enough to get you puffing. The gorgeous volcanic scenery makes it all worthwhile. Round Top Lake is set below The Sisters, two peaks that are both over 10,000 feet high. You also have views of Mount Round Top and Fourth of July Peak. It's incredibly dramatic.

From the eastern edge of Round Top Lake, you'll see a path that is routed up the side of Mount Round Top. The grade is brutal, but when you reach the top after a final rocky scramble, you have a stunning view of The Dardanelles, Lake Tahoe, Caples Lake, Woods Lake, Round Top Lake, Winnemucca Lake, and Frog Lake. Summit City Canyon, 3,000 feet below the south side of Round Top, is stunning. At 10,380 feet, Mount Round Top is the highest peak in the Carson Pass area and is the finest place for a bird's-eye view. The summit is more like a knife-thin, rocky ridge, so watch your footing. This is not a place for children or inexperienced hikers.

After your summit visit, return downhill to Round Top Lake to finish out your loop. Follow the lake's outlet creek on Lost Cabin Mine Trail for two miles back to Woods Lake Campground; then wind your way through the camp back to the Woods Lake Picnic Area, where you left your car.

User Groups: Hikers, leashed dogs, and horses. No mountain bikes. No wheelchair facilities.

Permits: A free wilderness permit is required for overnight stays; it is available from the Amador Ranger Station, the Carson Pass Information Station, or the Eldorado Information Center. A parking fee of $5 is charged, good for overnight use.

Maps: For a map, ask the U.S. Forest Service for Mokelumne Wilderness or Eldorado National Forest. For topographic maps, ask the USGS for Caples Lake and Carson Pass.

Directions: From South Lake Tahoe, take Highway 89 south for five miles to Meyers and the junction with Highway 89, and then continue south on Highway 89 for 11 miles to Highway 88. Turn right (west) on Highway 88 and drive 12 miles to the Woods Lake Campground turnoff, on the south side of the road (1.5 miles west of Carson Pass Summit). Turn left and drive 1.5 miles to the trailhead parking area, by the picnic area at Woods Lake.

Contact: Eldorado National Forest, Amador Ranger District, 209/295-4251, www.fs.usda.gov/eldorado.

82 WOODS LAKE TRAILHEAD TO FOURTH OF JULY LAKE

8.8 mi/4.5 hr or 2 days   🥾4 ⛰9

in the Mokelumne Wilderness near Caples Lake

Map 6.3, page 207

In some parts of California, the idea of 200 to 300 hikers on a wilderness trail in a single day on a summer weekend is mind-boggling. Yet that is what you get here. Carson Pass and Woods Lake are stellar trailheads, and with several lakes and Mount Round Top so close, the crowds thus arrive. So timing becomes key, along with deciding which way to go. There are so many ways from so many trailheads, including ones at Carson Pass and Upper Blue Lake.

The shortest and most direct route is from Woods Lake trailhead, located 0.5 mile before the Woods Lake Campground and picnic area. This includes a nice stopover at Round Top Lake, two miles in. You pass some old mining cabins before you enter the wilderness boundary. Pass the eastern flank of 9,000-foot Black Butte, an old volcanic vent that is similar in appearance to Mount Round Top a few miles to the east. In less than an hour, you arrive at Round Top Lake, a worthy destination in itself and a good spot for a snack break beneath the sturdy shoulders of the two peaks of The Sisters. It's only two more miles to Fourth of July Lake, but they are steep and downhill (which means you must climb back out on the way home). This is actually good news: It means you will leave the majority of the crowds behind. Most people give up at Fourth of July Saddle, a rocky overlook that sits 1,000 feet above the lake. In addition to the tough grade, the route is often dusty. At the lake, fishing is good for brook trout, and many campsites can be found near its edge. Late in the summer, a sandy beach gets exposed, good for swimmers.

User Groups: Hikers, leashed dogs, and horses. No mountain bikes. No wheelchair facilities.

Permits: A free wilderness permit is required for overnight stays; it is available from the Amador Ranger Station, the Carson Pass Information Station, or the Eldorado Information Center. A parking fee of $5 is charged, good for overnight use.

Maps: For a map, ask the U.S. Forest Service for Eldorado National Forest or Mokelumne Wilderness. For a topographic map, ask the USGS for Caples Lake.

Directions: From South Lake Tahoe, take Highway 89 south for five miles to Meyers and the junction with Highway 89, and then continue south on Highway 89 for 11 miles to Highway 88. Turn right (west) on Highway 88 and drive 12 miles to the Woods Lake Campground turnoff, on the south side of the road (1.5 miles west of Carson Pass Summit). Turn left and drive one mile to the trailhead (0.5 mile before the campground and picnic area).

Contact: Eldorado National Forest, Amador Ranger District, 209/295-4251, www.fs.usda.gov/eldorado.

83 FROG LAKE

1.8 mi/1.0 hr   🏃1 ⛰9

in the Mokelumne Wilderness near Carson Pass

Map 6.3, page 207

Any hiking trip from the Carson Pass trailhead is going to be packed with people. So it is here, with 200-plus people out on weekends. That known, this trail is educational and beautiful. The short walk to Frog Lake is suitable even for small children (and if you're more ambitious, you can continue another 1.5 miles to beautiful Winnemucca Lake). At Frog Lake, you are provided with a fascinating look at Elephant Back (elevation 9,585 feet), which looks exactly like its name. It's a lava dome, a round mass of solid lava. The lake is a beautiful turquoise color, perfect for picnicking, although because the area is rather open and exposed, the wind sometimes blows with ferocity.

Plenty of people take this walk in early summer to see the wildflowers, especially lupine and Indian paintbrush, from mid-June to mid-August (best in late July). A huge patch of wild iris also blooms alongside Frog Lake. It's a sight to behold. There are many other species of wildflowers here. An identification sheet is posted at the billboard near the trailhead and at the visitors center.

At the visitors center, you can learn about Kit Carson, the great explorer for whom this pass was named, and you can learn about the geologic forces that shaped this region, which is called the Round Top Geologic Area. Evidence of both glacial and volcanic action can be seen with every step you take.

User Groups: Hikers, leashed dogs, and horses. No mountain bikes. No wheelchair facilities.

Permits: A free wilderness permit is required for overnight stays between April 1 and November 30; it is available from the Amador Ranger Station, the Carson Pass Information Station, or the Eldorado Information Center. A $5 parking fee is charged per vehicle.

Maps: For a map, ask the U.S. Forest Service for Eldorado National Forest or Mokelumne

Wilderness. For a topographic map, ask the USGS for Carson Pass.

Directions: From South Lake Tahoe, take Highway 89 south for five miles to Meyers and the junction with Highway 89, and then continue south on Highway 89 for 11 miles to Highway 88. Turn right (west) on Highway 88 and drive 10 miles to Carson Pass Summit. The parking area and trailhead are on the left, by the Carson Pass Information Station.

Contact: Eldorado National Forest, Amador Ranger District, 209/295-4251, www.fs.usda.gov/eldorado.

84 RAYMOND LAKE

11.0 mi/1-2 days   🥾3 ⛰️9

in the Mokelumne Wilderness near Blue Lakes

Map 6.3, page 207

Raymond Lake is a popular weekend trip despite the 3,000-foot climb. The pretty campsites at the little lake are used by PCT hikers and weekenders who make this a two-day in-and-outer. That is, about five miles in and about five miles out, and that's why it works, especially for couples or young families new to backpacking. The lake is about 10 acres in size and is set at 9,000 feet, with several small campsites sprinkled near the lake. The trail starts near Wet Meadows Reservoir and heads east from the access road on the Pacific Crest Trail. It follows the PCT for 4.5 miles, a moderate ascent, to the junction with the Raymond Lake Trail. Turn right for the final mile. This final stretch is only a mile but is a butt-kicker, mostly because you're already getting tired when you begin it. The lake is set below 10,000-foot Raymond Peak, an alpine peak.

User Groups: Hikers, dogs, and horses. No mountain bikes. No wheelchair facilities.

Permits: A free wilderness permit is required for overnight stays; it is available on the wilderness bulletin board at the trailhead, from the ranger station in Markleeville, the Carson Pass Information Station, or the Carson Ranger district in Carson City. Groups are limited to

12, and no campfires are permitted above 8,000 feet.

Maps: For a map, ask the U.S. Forest Service for Humboldt-Toiyabe National Forest, Carson District. For topographic maps, ask the USGS for Pacific Valley and Ebbetts Pass.

Directions: From South Lake Tahoe, take Highway 89 south for five miles to Meyers and the junction with Highway 89, and then continue south on Highway 89 for 11 miles to Highway 88. Turn right (west) on Highway 88 and drive 2.5 miles to the Blue Lakes turnoff, on the south side of the road. Turn south and drive 11 miles to the left turnoff for Tamarack Lake and Wet Meadows. Bear left and drive three miles to the left turnoff for Lower Sunset Lake. Turn left and drive a short distance to the trailhead.

Contact: Humboldt-Toiyabe National Forest, 775/331-6444, www.fs.usda.gov/htnf.

85 BLUE LAKE DAM TO GRANITE LAKE

4.0 mi/2.0 hr   🥾1 ⛰️9

in the Mokelumne Wilderness near Blue Lakes

Map 6.3, page 207

The trip starts at the dam at Upper Blue Lake. A well-signed and meandering route ventures one mile to enter the Mokelumne Wilderness. Another mile beyond the wilderness boundary is Granite Lake. To reach it requires a total 550-foot climb, but the trail is well graded and some will barely notice they are climbing. Note that a quarter mile past the boundary sign, you'll see a large pond, but don't mistake that for Granite Lake, which is another 20 minutes farther on the trail. When you arrive, you'll find this small lake set in a granite pocket. Don't be concerned if there are lots of cars in the dam parking lot. Most of them belong to anglers, not hikers.

User Groups: Hikers, leashed dogs, and horses. No mountain bikes. No wheelchair facilities.

Permits: A free wilderness permit is required for overnight; it is available from the Amador

Ranger Station, the Carson Pass Information Station, or the Eldorado Information Center.

Maps: For a map, ask the U.S. Forest Service for Eldorado National Forest. For a topographic map, ask the USGS for Pacific Valley.

Directions: From South Lake Tahoe, take Highway 89 south for five miles to Meyers and the junction with Highway 89, and then continue south on Highway 89 for 11 miles to Highway 88. Turn right (west) on Highway 88 and drive 2.5 miles to the Blue Lakes turnoff, on the south side of the road. Turn south and drive 12 miles to the fork at Lower Blue Lake. Turn right and drive 1.5 miles to the dam by Upper Blue Lake, shortly past Middle Creek Campground; turn left into the parking area. The Grouse Lake Trail leads to Granite Lake from the west side of the parking area.

Contact: Eldorado National Forest, Amador Ranger District, 209/295-4251, www.fs.usda.gov/eldorado.

86 HOT SPRINGS CREEK WATERFALL

3.0 mi/1.5 hr

in Grover Hot Springs State Park near Markleeville

Map 6.3, page 207

Your goal is a 50-foot waterfall, best in spring and early summer, of course. The route is a bit tricky, but even without a waterfall, this would be a great trail to walk. The route starts from just beyond the campgrounds in Grover Hot Springs State Park, an elevation of 5,900 feet. From here, you hike on the Burnside Lake and Charity Valley Trails for 0.5 mile, then reach a fork signed for the waterfall. Turn left at the fork, and in the process, some newcomers get confused where you reach a jumbled pile of boulders on the trail. Simply go up and over them. Hot Springs Canyon gradually narrows on its way to the falls, and when you near the creek's edge, you might see small trout swimming in its pools. You then arrive at the waterfall, perched at an elevation of 6,200 feet.

Technically it is outside of state parkland and in Humboldt-Toiyabe National Forest, so you'll see backpackers' campfire rings on the cliff above the falls.

Highlights of the trail include the giant Jeffrey pines of Hot Springs Valley, enclosed by rocky cliffs and 10,000-foot peaks.

User Groups: Hikers and leashed dogs (not recommended). No horses or mountain bikes. No wheelchair facilities.

Permits: No permits are required. A day-use fee of $8 is charged per vehicle; there is a fee of $7 per person for use of the hot springs pool.

Maps: A map of Grover Hot Springs State Park is available for a fee at the entrance station. For a topographic map, ask the USGS for Markleeville.

Directions: From South Lake Tahoe, take Highway 89 south for five miles to Meyers and the junction with Highway 89, and then continue south on Highway 89 for 11 miles to Highway 88. Turn left on Highway 88/89 and drive 13 miles to Markleeville at Hot Springs Road. Turn right (west) on Hot Springs Road and drive 3.5 miles to the state park entrance. The signed trailhead is 0.25 mile beyond the entrance station and campground turnoffs, at a gated dirt road.

Contact: Grover Hot Springs State Park, 530/694-2248, pool information 530/694-2249, www.parks.ca.gov.

87 GROVER HOT SPRINGS TO BURNSIDE LAKE

8.4 mi/5.0 hr

in Humboldt-Toiyabe National Forest near Markleeville

Map 6.3, page 207

From Grover Hot Springs State Park, at 5,900 feet, the Burnside Lake Trail leaves in elevation and climbs west to Burnside Lake, at 8,160 feet, a gain of 2,260 feet. The climb is spaced out over four miles, so it's a steady workout to the lake. Along the way, you pass tall and majestic sugar pines and rocky outcrops, with

10,023-foot Hawkins Peak and 9,417-foot Markleeville Peak towering over the scene. The lake is about 10 surface acres and is popular for trout fishing. Although you can start hiking on the trail from Hot Springs Road shortly before the state park entrance, it's best to start from the trailhead at the park. That shaves one mile off your trip, but also when you return from your hike, you can take a dip in the 102- to 104-degree hot springs. At first you may encounter mountain bikers on the trail; they will soon branch off on their way to Charity Valley, a great mountain bike trek.

User Groups: Hikers, dogs, horses, and mountain bikes. No wheelchair facilities.

Permits: No permits are required. A day-use fee of $8 is charged per vehicle at Grover Hot Springs State Park; there is a fee of $7 per person for use of the hot springs pool.

Maps: For a map, ask the U.S. Forest Service for Humboldt-Toiyabe National Forest, Carson District. A map of Grover Hot Springs State Park is available for a fee at the entrance station. For a topographic map, ask the USGS for Markleeville.

Directions: From South Lake Tahoe, take Highway 89 south for five miles to Meyers and the junction with Highway 89, and then continue south on Highway 89 for 11 miles to Highway 88. Turn left on Highway 88/89 and drive 13 miles to Markleeville at Hot Springs Road. Turn right (west) on Hot Springs Road and drive 3.5 miles to the state park entrance. The signed trailhead is 0.25 mile beyond the entrance station and campground turnoffs, at a gated dirt road. Another trailhead is located outside the state park on Hot Springs Road, 0.75 mile before the state park entrance, and is signed for Charity Valley and gets heavy mountain bike use.

Contact: Grover Hot Springs State Park, Markleeville, 530/694-2248 or 530/525-7232, www.parks.ca.gov; Humboldt-Toiyabe National Forest, 775/331-6444, www.fs.usda.gov/htnf.

88 BLUE LAKES ROAD TO CARSON PASS (PCT)

12.0 mi one-way/1 day 🏃4 ⛰9

from Blue Lakes Road north to Carson Pass and Highway 88

Map 6.3, page 207

Many hikers underestimate the climb over Elephant Back to reach Carson Pass. After all, on a map, it doesn't look like much, and from a distance, as you size it up, it looks easy enough. Wrong. It's a long, grueling pull. The trip out of Blue Lakes starts easily, with a dirt road often in view and adding a bit of early angst to the affair. As you go, you keep wondering when the climb will start. Well, eventually it does, and, alas, it takes a couple of hours, a long, steady march. After topping the Elephant Back, the route drops down to Carson Pass at a rest stop, where you'll likely meet humanity, but believe it or not, no water! When we hiked from Yosemite to Tahoe, this was the worst shock of the trip. Conserve yours if you plan to go onward, because it takes another hour of hiking before you'll reach the next trickle.

To continue north on the PCT, see the *Carson Pass to Echo Lakes Resort (PCT)* hike in this chapter. If you are walking this trail in reverse, see the *Ebbetts Pass to Blue Lakes Road (PCT)* hike in this chapter.

User Groups: Hikers, dogs, and horses. No mountain bikes. No wheelchair access.

Permits: A backcountry permit is required for traveling through various wilderness and special-use areas that the trail traverses. In addition, a campfire permit is required for the use of portable camp stoves or the building of campfires where allowed. To make it simple, you can contact the national forest, Bureau of Land Management (BLM), or national park office at your point of entry for a combined permit that is good for traveling through multiple-permit areas during your dates of travel.

Maps: For a map, ask the U.S. Forest Service for Lake Tahoe Basin Management Unit, Tahoe National Forest, Eldorado National Forest, and Stanislaus National Forest. For topographic maps, ask the USGS for Pacific Valley and Carson Pass.

Directions: To reach the Blue Lakes Road trailhead from the Highway 88/89 junction at Hope Valley, go west on Highway 88 to Blue Lakes Road and turn left. Stay on Blue Lakes Road for 11 miles to the trailhead parking, just before reaching Blue Lakes.

For the Carson Pass trailhead from the Highway 88/89 junction at Hope Valley, go west on Highway 88 to Carson Pass.

Contact: Eldorado National Forest, Amador Ranger District, 209/295-4251, www.fs.usda.gov/eldorado.

89 KINNEY LAKES
5.0 mi/2.5 hr

in Humboldt-Toiyabe National Forest near Ebbetts Pass

Map 6.3, page 207

From the Ebbetts Pass trailhead, Kinney Lakes is an easy tromp north on the Pacific Crest Trail. You pass little Sherrold Lake on the way to Upper Kinney Lake (which is actually a reservoir).

You start hiking at 8,700 feet at the pass, so even though this trail has an easy to moderate grade, your lungs are getting a workout. The trail leads through a landscape of big conifers with little undergrowth, typical of the high country. When the trees thin out, your views open wide. Raymond Peak and Reynolds Peak rule the skyline. At 1.6 miles, you reach a signed junction for Upper and Lower Kinney Lakes, and you can take your pick as to which one to visit first. The Pacific Crest Trail leads directly to the upper lake, while the lower lake must be visited by following an eastward fork from the PCT. The upper lake, though smaller, is the prettier of the two.

User Groups: Hikers, dogs, and horses. No mountain bikes. No wheelchair facilities.

Permits: Wilderness permits are required for overnight use. No campfires are allowed above 8,000 feet. Parking and access are free.

Maps: For a map, ask the U.S. Forest Service for Humboldt-Toiyabe National Forest, Carson District. For a topographic map, ask the USGS for Ebbetts Pass.

Directions: From Angels Camp, drive east on Highway 4 for about 40 miles to Bear Valley. Set your odometer at Bear Valley, and drive 15 miles farther east on Highway 4 to Ebbetts Pass and the trailhead parking area. The trail is on the north side of the road.

If you are coming from Markleeville, drive south on Highway 89/Highway 4 for 15 miles to Ebbetts Pass.

Contact: Humboldt-Toiyabe National Forest, 775/331-6444, www.fs.usda.gov/htnf.

90 EBBETTS PASS TO BLUE LAKES ROAD (PCT)
17.7 mi one-way/1 day

from Highway 4 near Ebbetts Pass to Blue Lakes Road south of Carson Pass and Highway 88

Map 6.3, page 207

As you leave Ebbetts Pass and head north, you'll cross a series of fantastic volcanic formations in the Mokelumne Wilderness. The country here may look stark from a distance, but it is loaded with tiny wildflowers in every ravine. The trail is easy without a lot of climb and descent, then repeat; and a lot of hikers make great time in this area. The lack of available water can become a concern. Tank up whenever you get the chance, such as at Eagle Creek below Reynold Peak (9,690 feet). The Mokelumne Wilderness is a relative breeze, and you'll find yourself approaching civilization at a series of small lakes in Tahoe National Forest. The trail rises up a stark, wind-blown, sandy ridge, with excellent views of the Blue Lakes, but again, there is no water for several miles until you drop down near Lost Lake. You'll actually cross several roads on this stretch of trail, and maybe even see a car, a moment of irony for long-distance PCT hikers. But the going is easy; we think this is one of the fastest sections of the PCT in the central Sierra. To continue north on the PCT, see the *Blue Lakes Road to Carson Pass (PCT)* hike in this chapter.

User Groups: Hikers, dogs, and horses. No mountain bikes. No wheelchair facilities.

Permits: A backcountry permit is required for traveling through various wilderness and special-use areas that the trail traverses. In addition, a campfire permit is required for the use of portable camp stoves or the building of campfires (where permitted). To make it simple, you can contact the national forest, Bureau of Land Management (BLM), or national park office at your point of entry for a combined permit good for traveling through multiple-permit areas during your dates of travel.

Maps: For a map, ask the U.S. Forest Service for Lake Tahoe Basin Management Unit, Tahoe National Forest, Eldorado National Forest, and Stanislaus National Forest. For topographic maps, ask the USGS for Ebbetts Pass, Pacific Valley, and Carson Pass.

Directions: To reach the Ebbetts Pass trailhead from Angels Camp, head east on Highway 4 to Ebbetts Pass.

To reach the Blue Lakes Road trailhead from the Highway 88/89 interchange at Hope Valley, head west on Highway 88 to Blue Lakes Road and turn left. Stay on Blue Lakes Road to the trailhead parking area, just before reaching Blue Lakes.

Contact: Eldorado National Forest, Amador Ranger District, 209/295-4251, www.fs.usda.gov/eldorado.

91 NOBLE LAKE

9.0 mi/4.5 hr

in Humboldt-Toiyabe National Forest near Ebbetts Pass

Map 6.3, page 207

Noble Lake lies just outside of the Carson-Iceberg Wilderness. You can best reach it with a gentle route from Ebbetts Pass.

From Ebbetts Pass (elevation 8,700 feet), there's a 1,200-foot climb to the lake at 9,440

feet (which includes some ups and downs). The lake is a fine spot for camping or just spending an afternoon. It is not pristine gorgeous, but is an 8, classic high Sierra, with big conifers, snowcapped peaks, hard granite, and lush meadows.

From the trailhead parking area, the route follows a short 0.25-mile spur trail that climbs a short distance, then connects to the Pacific Crest Trail. You head south, of course, first climbing to a short ride, and then you make a long descent into Noble Canyon. At three miles, you will cross Noble Creek and then climb again to a high meadow. Soon you can see Noble Lake; the main lake is to the right of the trail, but a smaller, unnamed lake is to the left, about 650 feet off the trail. Both have decent campsites and many good rocks to sit on and relax.

A boulder field above the campsites is loaded with ground squirrels, and if you hike overnight here with a dog, the squirrels will drive your dog crazy. I don't think Bart-Dog went to sleep the whole night. This lake is excellent for swimming but poor for fishing. For camping, group size is limited to 15 people, and a 100-foot setback from the lake is required.

User Groups: Hikers, dogs, and horses. No mountain bikes. No wheelchair facilities.

Permits: No day-hiking permits are required. A free wilderness permit is available at the trailhead (self-issue). Parking and access are free.

Maps: For a map, ask the U.S. Forest Service for Humboldt-Toiyabe National Forest, Carson District. For a topographic map, ask the USGS for Ebbetts Pass.

Directions: From Angels Camp at the intersection of Highways 4 and 49, go east on Highway 4 for 40 miles to Bear Valley. Set your odometer at Bear Valley, and drive 15 miles farther east on Highway 4 to Ebbetts Pass and the trailhead parking area (located just east of Ebbetts Pass; do not park on Highway 4). The trailhead is on the south side of the road.

Contact: Humboldt-Toiyabe National Forest, 775/331-6444, www.fs.usda.gov/htnf.

92 WOLF CREEK TRAIL TO WOLF CREEK FALLS

9.6 mi/5.0 hr   🥾2 ⛰8

in the Carson-Iceberg Wilderness near Markleeville

Map 6.3, page 207

When fed by snowmelt, Wolf Creek Falls thunders over a volcanic cliff. That's your pay-off, and amid the crowds in the Tahoe region, there's a good chance you'll have it to yourself. The trailhead is at an elevation of 6,480 feet. The trail is an old jeep road that is routed along Wolf Creek, uphill through forest, and in turn, provides shade most of the way. Wolf Creek is very pretty, especially when the sun catches it just right. Hike 4.3 miles out to a fork for the steep Bull Canyon Trail to Bull Lake. Bear left and continue 0.5 mile to Wolf Creek Falls. The waterfall is located just off the trail to the left, about 50 yards beyond where the trail passes through a cattle fence. For waterfall lovers, this one is impressive early in the summer.

User Groups: Hikers, dogs, and horses. No mountain bikes. No wheelchair facilities.

Permits: A free wilderness permit is required for overnight stays; it is available at the trailhead. Parking and access are free.

Maps: For a map, ask the U.S. Forest Service for Humboldt-Toiyabe National Forest, Carson District, and Carson-Iceberg Wilderness. For a topographic map, ask the USGS for Wolf Creek.

Directions: From South Lake Tahoe, take Highway 89 south for five miles to Meyers and the junction with Highway 89, and then continue south on Highway 89 for 11 miles to Highway 88. Turn left on Highway 88/89 and drive 13 miles to Markleeville. From Markleeville, continue south on Highway 89 for four miles to Monitor Pass Junction and Highway 4. Bear right (south) on Highway 4 and drive 2.5 miles to the signed turnoff for Wolf Creek, on the left. Turn left (south) and drive 4.9 miles to the trailhead, about 100 yards before the end of the road.

Contact: Humboldt-Toiyabe National Forest, 775/331-6444, www.fs.usda.gov/htnf.

93 EAST CARSON RIVER TRAIL

4.0 mi/2.0 hr   🥾2 ⛰7

in the Carson-Iceberg Wilderness near Markleeville

Map 6.3, page 207

The East Carson River Trail can be your salvation in spring when there's still too much snow around Ebbetts Pass. Trailhead elevation is only 6,240 feet at the north side of Wolf Creek Meadows (private property), which means it's snow-free before other nearby areas. At the start, you hike uphill a short distance to a trail junction and the boundary sign for the Carson-Iceberg Wilderness. Turn left (the right fork is the High Trail northern terminus). An interesting journey is 1.5 miles to Wolf Creek Lake (sometimes dry) and Railroad Canyon, the site of 19th-century logging operations.

User Groups: Hikers, dogs, and horses. No mountain bikes. No wheelchair facilities.

Permits: A free wilderness permit is required for overnight stays; it is available at the trailhead. Parking and access are free.

Maps: For a map, ask the U.S. Forest Service for Humboldt-Toiyabe National Forest, Carson District, and Carson-Iceberg Wilderness. For a topographic map, ask the USGS for Wolf Creek.

Directions: From South Lake Tahoe, take Highway 89 south for five miles to Meyers and the junction with Highway 89, and then continue south on Highway 89 for 11 miles to Highway 88. Turn left on Highway 88/89 and drive 13 miles to Markleeville. Continue south on Highway 89/Highway 4 for 7.5 miles to the signed turnoff for Wolf Creek on the left. Turn left (east) and drive 3.5 miles to the left turnoff signed for East Carson River Trail. Turn left and drive one mile to the road junction to Dixon Mine. Turn right and drive 0.25 mile to the trailhead.

Contact: Humboldt-Toiyabe National Forest, 775/331-6444, www.fs.usda.gov/htnf.

94 MOSQUITO LAKES TO HEISER LAKE
4.8 mi/2.5 hr 🥾3 ⛰9

in the Carson-Iceberg Wilderness near Ebbetts Pass

Map 6.3, page 207

The trailhead at Mosquito Lakes, perched at an elevation of 8,000 feet on Highway 4, is gorgeous. You know you're in for a good trip when the trailhead is located at such a pretty spot. And so it is here. The trail climbs and descends, then climbs and descends some more, mostly heading in a straight-line course due south to Heiser Lake. It's one of those rare trails where you've got to work equally hard whether on the way in or on the way out. Two miles in, at a junction with the trail from Bull Run Lake, bear left and finish out the last 0.5 mile to Heiser Lake, set at 8,300 feet. The lake is granite bound, with a couple of tiny islands sticking out of its shallow waters. Quiet, pristine, gorgeous.

User Groups: Hikers, dogs, and horses. No mountain bikes. No wheelchair facilities.

Permits: No day-hiking permits are required. Parking and access are free.

Maps: For a map, ask the U.S. Forest Service for Stanislaus National Forest and Carson-Iceberg Wilderness. For topographic maps, ask the USGS for Pacific Valley and Spicer Meadow Reservoir.

Directions: From Angels Camp, take Highway 4 east for 40 miles to Bear Valley. Set your odometer at Bear Valley and drive 10 miles farther east on Highway 4 to the Mosquito Lakes trailhead and Heiser Lake Trail. Park on the right (south) side of the road, across from the campground; there is only enough space for a few cars.

Contact: Stanislaus National Forest, Calaveras Ranger District, 209/795-1381, www.fs.usda.gov/stanislaus.

95 BULL RUN LAKE
7.0 mi/4.0 hr 🥾2 ⛰9

in the Carson-Iceberg Wilderness near Ebbetts Pass

Map 6.3, page 207

The hike to Bull Run Lake can be a side trip or an option to nearby Heiser Lake (see previous listing). The lake is set at 8,300 feet and is a fine reward for your effort. It is gorgeous, set in a steep-walled granite bowl. Plus, this trail to Bull Run Lake is well graded, with one steep section in the last 0.5 mile. The trailhead is set at 7,800 feet. The first 1.3 miles are almost level, traveling slightly downhill through a grassy meadow that is filled with wildflowers in the early summer and turns golden by September. After that, you start to climb, mostly through pine forest and over stretches of granite with trail cairns. At 2.2 miles, watch for a trail junction. Turn right for Bull Run Lake (straight ahead, on the other hand, is Heiser Lake). After a brief flat stretch, prepare for a final mile of climbing, with the last part the steepest.

On summer weekends, you might have to share the trail to Bull Run Lake with some horses. After all, their owners like the big parking lot at the trailhead, large enough for horse trailers. Maybe you should pack along a few extra apples or carrots, eh?

User Groups: Hikers, dogs, and horses. No mountain bikes. No wheelchair facilities.

Permits: No day-hiking permits are required. Parking and access are free.

Maps: For a map, ask the U.S. Forest Service for Stanislaus National Forest or Carson-Iceberg Wilderness. For topographic maps, ask the USGS for Pacific Valley and Spicer Meadow Reservoir.

Directions: From Angels Camp, take Highway 4 east for 40 miles to Bear Valley. Set your odometer at Bear Valley and drive 8.5 miles farther east on Highway 4 to the Stanislaus Meadow turnoff, on the right (Road 8N13). Turn right and drive a short distance to the trailhead parking area.

Contact: Stanislaus National Forest, Calaveras

Ranger District, 209/795-1381, www.fs.usda. gov/stanislaus.

96 CLARK FORK TO BOULDER LAKE

8.0 mi/4.0 hr

in the Carson-Iceberg Wilderness on Clark Fork Stanislaus River

Map 6.3, page 207

The pay-offs on this hike include a trail along the beautiful Clark Fork Stanislaus River and then a climb along a pretty creek to little Boulder Lake. The trailhead is at Iceberg Meadow. You immediately enter the Carson-Iceberg Wilderness at the base of imposing Iceberg Peak. The trail starts where you hike upstream on the northern edge of the Clark Fork. This is a good trout stream, and through early summer, wildflowers are abundant amid a mixed forest of white firs and Jeffrey pines. At the water's edge, the trees are leafier, including cottonwoods and aspens. At 2.5 miles you reach a junction near Boulder Creek. To reach Boulder Lake, turn left (straight takes you along the Clark Fork). The trail then climbs, steep at times, for 1.5 miles uphill to tiny Boulder Lake. It's a good workout to a pretty destination.

User Groups: Hikers, dogs, and horses. No mountain bikes. No wheelchair facilities.

Permits: A free wilderness permit is required for overnight stays and is available from the Summit Ranger Station. Parking and access are free.

Maps: For a map, ask the U.S. Forest Service for Stanislaus National Forest or Carson-Iceberg Wilderness. For a topographic map, ask the USGS for Donnell Lake.

Directions: From Sonora, take Highway 108 east for 46 miles to the left turnoff for Clark Fork Road (about 17 miles east of Strawberry). Turn left and follow Clark Fork Road for about seven miles to its end, at the Clark Fork trailhead at Iceberg Meadow.

Contact: Stanislaus National Forest, Summit

Ranger District, 209/965-3434, www.fs.usda. gov/stanislaus.

97 TRAIL OF THE GARGOYLES

3.0 mi/1.5 hr

near Strawberry and Pinecrest Lake in Stanislaus National Forest

Map 6.3, page 207   **BEST (**

If this trail was called "Edge of the World, " it would give you just what you might expect. The trailhead is in the middle of a 1.5-mile trail, which means you'll walk out and back in both directions. It starts out nondescript, but that quickly changes. The gargoyles—odd rock formations—soon line the trail, perched at the edge of a cliff at 7,400 feet in elevation. You walk just inches away from what appears to be the edge of the world, with only thin air between you and the densely forested basin several hundred feet below. It's an easy and nearly flat trail, but if you have kids, or adults that act like kids, keep an eye on them.

User Groups: Hikers and leashed dogs. No horses or mountain bikes. No wheelchair facilities.

Permits: No permits are required. Parking and access are free.

Maps: For a map, ask the U.S. Forest Service for Stanislaus National Forest. For a topographic map, ask the USGS for Pinecrest.

Directions: From Sonora, take Highway 108 east for 32 miles to Strawberry, and then continue east 2.4 miles to Herring Creek Road (Forest Road 4N12). Turn right on Herring Creek Road and drive 6.7 miles to an often-unsigned turnoff on the left. Turn left and drive 0.2 mile to the trailhead.

Contact: Stanislaus National Forest, Summit Ranger District, 209/965-3434, www.fs.usda. gov/stanislaus.

98 COLUMNS OF THE GIANTS
0.5 mi/0.5 hr 🏃1 ⛰8

near Dardanelle

Map 6.3, page 207

This is the central Sierra's answer to Devils Postpile National Monument. The Columns of the Giants features rock columns that are 30-40 feet in height and 3-4 feet in diameter. Although many are still standing tall or at least at an angle, others have shattered into thousands of pieces, creating a giant pile of rubble, at times just a jumbled heap of rocks. An interpretive trail sign explains that underneath this rock pile is evidence of the last small ice age in the Sierra, frozen remnants of ice fields that are replenished each year by winter snow and cold. The rock formations at the end of the Columns of the Giants geological trail were formed 150,000 years ago, when a series of volcanic eruptions occurred. The lava flow cooled rapidly, probably during cold weather, and cracked into narrow, hexagonal, basalt columns. Make sure you bring your camera.

User Groups: Hikers and leashed dogs. No horses or mountain bikes. No wheelchair facilities.

Permits: No permits are required. Parking and access are free.

Maps: For a map, ask the U.S. Forest Service for Stanislaus National Forest. For a topographic map, ask the USGS for Dardanelle.

Directions: From Sonora, take Highway 108 east for 50 miles to Pigeon Flat Campground (two miles east of Dardanelle) on the south side of the highway. If you're traveling west on Highway 108, the campground is 12.6 miles west of Sonora Pass. Park in the day-use parking lot just outside the camp.

Contact: Stanislaus National Forest, Summit Ranger District, 209/965-3434, www.fs.usda.gov/stanislaus.

99 KENNEDY LAKE
14.8 mi/2 days 🏃3 ⛰8

in the Emigrant Wilderness near Dardanelle

Map 6.3, page 207

Follow the trail notes to Relief Reservoir (see listing in this chapter), but at 2.6 miles, take the left fork for Kennedy Lake. The trail climbs for another 1.6 miles, then goes flat for the final 3.2 miles to the lake. It's an easy two-day backpack trip, with low mileage and only a 1,200-foot elevation gain. Note that all the campsites are set downstream of the lake rather than along its shoreline.

If the number of cars in the Kennedy Meadows parking lot scares you, take heart. Many of them belong to people day hiking to fish at Relief Reservoir. If you have the time and inclination for a longer trip to Kennedy Lake, you will leave a lot of your fellow hikers behind. Even so, don't expect solitude. You'll likely share the lake with other backpackers, horse packers, and grazing cows.

User Groups: Hikers, leashed dogs, and horses. No mountain bikes. No wheelchair facilities.

Permits: A free wilderness permit is required for overnight stays and is available from the Summit Ranger Station. Parking and access are free.

Maps: For a map, ask the U.S. Forest Service for Stanislaus National Forest or Emigrant Wilderness. For a topographic map, ask the USGS for Sonora Pass.

Directions: From Sonora, take Highway 108 east for 55 miles to the turnoff for Kennedy Meadows (six miles east of Dardanelle) on the south side of the highway. Turn right and drive one mile to the large parking area. If you're traveling west on Highway 108, the Kennedy Meadows turnoff is 9.1 miles west of Sonora Pass.

Contact: Stanislaus National Forest, Summit Ranger District, 209/965-3434, www.fs.usda.gov/stanislaus.

100 RELIEF RESERVOIR

6.0 mi/3.0 hr   🏃3 ⛰8

on the edge of the Emigrant Wilderness near
Dardanelle

Map 6.3, page 207

At Kennedy Meadows along Highway 108, the
trips starts from a mammoth trailhead and
parking lot. At peak use, the number of vehicles
might have you shaking your head. Many visitors take the three-mile trip to Relief Reservoir
(elevation 7,200 feet), a PG&E lake, to do a little fishing, then hike back out. The Emigrant
Wilderness is best known for its miles of high
granite and small lakes in deep pockets. Relief
Reservoir is the most popular.

The route is called the Huckleberry Trail and
leads along the Stanislaus River. It passes the
boundary for the Emigrant Wilderness at one
mile, then skirts its edge. You will quickly understand why this trip is so popular. The river
canyon gets more and more beautiful as you
head deeper into it. The trail had to be blasted
into the steep granite slopes. At 2.6 miles, you
will pass a turnoff (on the left for Kennedy
Creek and Kennedy Lake), and then proceed
straight for another 0.5 mile to an overlook
of Relief Reservoir. It's a steep drop down to
the water's edge in the last 0.25 mile, which,
of course, must be regained on the return trip.

At times, horses can chop up the trail, and
the route is overused; a trail quota would help.
Some weekends it seems you must pull off the
path repeatedly to let horses pass.

User Groups: Hikers, leashed dogs, and horses.
No mountain bikes. No wheelchair facilities.

Permits: No day-use permits are required.
Parking and access are free.

Maps: For a map, ask the U.S. Forest Service
for Stanislaus National Forest or Emigrant
Wilderness. For a topographic map, ask the
USGS for Sonora Pass.

Directions: From Sonora, take Highway 108
east for 55 miles to the Kennedy Meadows turnoff (six miles east of Dardanelle) on the south
side of the highway. Turn right and go one mile
to the well-signed parking area. Day hikers

can park 0.5 mile farther down the road, near
Kennedy Meadows Resort. If you're traveling
west on Highway 108, the Kennedy Meadows
turnoff is 9.1 miles west of Sonora Pass.

Contact: Stanislaus National Forest, Summit
Ranger District, 209/965-3434, www.fs.usda.
gov/stanislaus.

101 SARDINE FALLS

2.0 mi/1.0 hr   🏃1 ⛰8

near Sonora Pass

Map 6.3, page 207

The goal is Sardine Falls, a gorgeous waterfall that cascades over a brink and sails down
into a ravine and through forest. There is no
formal trail along Highway 108 or sign that
says "Sardine Falls. " I always called it Sonora
Pass Falls until I was told differently. You can
glimpse the falls from Highway 108, and east of
Sonora Pass, you'll see pullouts and what looks
like old jeep roads. This is it. From parking,
head across the northwest side of the meadow.
Look for a route that is signed Route Closed to
Motorized Vehicles; it's the most direct path.
Cross Sardine Creek, which parallels Highway
108, and walk up the right side of larger McKay
Creek. After climbing uphill over a rise, you'll
hear and then see Sardine Falls, gracefully
framed by a few sparse lodgepole pines. During
peak snowmelt, a great find.

User Groups: Hikers, leashed dogs, and horses.
No mountain bikes. No wheelchair facilities.

Permits: No permits are required. Parking and
access are free.

Maps: For a map, ask the U.S. Forest Service for
Humboldt-Toiyabe National Forest, Bridgeport
District. For a topographic map, ask the USGS
for Pickel Meadow.

Directions: From the junction of U.S. 395 and
Highway 108, take Highway 108 west and drive
12.5 miles (2.5 miles east of Sonora Pass) and
park along the road in the gravel pullouts near
the overgrown jeep roads on the northwest side
of the meadow.

Contact: Humboldt-Toiyabe National Forest,

Bridgeport Ranger District, 760/932-7070, www.fs.usda.gov/htnf.

102 SONORA PASS TO EBBETTS PASS (PCT)
30.8 mi one-way/3 days 🏃5 ⛰10
from Highway 108 at Sonora Pass north to Highway 4 near Ebbetts Pass

Map 6.3, page 207

This section of the Pacific Crest Trail does not have the glamorous reputation of the stretch of trail in the southern Sierra. For those of us who have hiked it, it's just as compelling. From Sonora Pass, you're forced to climb out for a good hour or two. Then you'll rise over Wolf Creek Gap (10,300 feet, the highest, most northern point on the PCT) and make the easy drop down along pretty Wolf Creek and to the Carson Canyon. This is the start of the Carson-Iceberg Wilderness, a giant swath of land that is a rare, unpeopled paradise. The Sierra riparian zones here are lined with flowers, seemingly all kinds and all colors, often in luxuriant beds of greenness. The PCT climbs out of Carson Canyon around Boulder Peak, then down and up two more canyons. All the while, you keep crossing creeks filled with natural gardens. You wind your way across and through these areas and eventually climb a ridge, then head down, steeply at times, to Ebbetts Pass. There's no water here. No problem. A short half-hour climb and you can be pumping water, and maybe setting up camp too, at little Sherrold Lake, not far from the edge of the Mokelumne Wilderness.

To continue north on the PCT, see the *Ebbetts Pass to Blue Lakes Road (PCT)* hike in this chapter.

User Groups: Hikers, dogs, and horses. No mountain bikes. No wheelchair facilities.

Permits: A wilderness permit is required for traveling through various wilderness and special-use areas the trail traverses. Contact the Stanislaus National Forest to obtain a permit that is good for the length of your trip.

Maps: For topographic maps, ask the USGS for Pickel Meadow, Disaster Peak, Dardanelles Cone, and Ebbetts Pass.

Directions: From Sonora, take Highway 108 east to Sonora Pass to the parking area and trailhead (south side of parking area).

Contact: Stanislaus National Forest, Summit Ranger District, 209/965-3434, www.fs.usda.gov/stanislaus.

103 SECRET AND POORE LAKES
6.5 mi/3.5 hr 🏃3 ⛰9
near Sonora Pass

Map 6.3, page 207

This hike rates a solid 8, but we nudged it up after discovering one of the most spectacular waterfalls in the Sierra above Poore Lake. This 6.5-mile loop trip begins at a footbridge over West Walker River at Leavitt Meadows Campground. After 0.25 mile, take the left fork for Secret Lake (this is no secret and you won't be alone here, most likely). Climb for nearly two miles through sage and Jeffrey pines, then descend 0.5 mile to Secret Lake. Much larger Poore Lake is visible over your left shoulder. Take a break at Secret Lake, then continue around the right side of the lake, hiking through sparse junipers and pines for 0.5 mile to the left turnoff for Poore Lake. Turn left for the final 0.75 mile to the large lake; this last section is the roughest. In spring, look for the waterfall above the lake.

When you are ready to return, retrace your steps to the junction. From the junction, you can loop back to the campground on a lower trail that follows closer to the West Walker River through Leavitt Meadow.

Notes: If Poore Lake turns out to be less than what you envisioned, you can always hike beyond the return loop junction to little Roosevelt Lake. No mountain bikes are permitted beyond Poore Lake, so that means Roosevelt Lake is free of them, at least in theory. In addition, there is no bridge available for off-road vehicles, so though this area was once an OHV spot, it is no longer. Finally, a nearby U.S. Marine training facility means it is possible you may see groups dressed in camo outfits running along the road. They do not fire their weapons here and they almost never enter the forest.

User Groups: Hikers, dogs, horses, and mountain bikes. No wheelchair facilities.

Permits: No day-use permits are required. Campfire permits required for overnight use. Parking and access are free.

Maps: For a map, ask the U.S. Forest Service for Humboldt-Toiyabe National Forest, Bridgeport District. For a topographic map, ask the USGS for Pickel Meadow.

Directions: From the junction of U.S. 395 and Highway 108, take Highway 108 west for seven miles to Leavitt Meadows Campground, on the south side of the road. If you are coming from the west, the camp is eight miles east of Sonora Pass. Day hikers may park inside the campground; backpackers must park 0.25 mile west of the camp on Highway 108.

Contact: Humboldt-Toiyabe National Forest, Bridgeport Ranger District, 760/932-7070, www.fs.usda.gov/htnf.

SAN FRANCISCO BAY AREA

© TOM STIENSTRA

The Bay Area is home to 150 significant parks (including 12 with redwoods), 7,500 miles of hiking and biking trails, 45 lakes, 25 waterfalls, 100 miles of coast, mountains with incredible lookouts, bays with islands, and, in all, 1.2 million acres of greenbelt with hundreds of acres being added each year. Bay area hikes cover Angel Island, Point Reyes National Seashore, the Marin Headlands, Sunol-Ohlone Wilderness, Butano Redwoods State Park, and Big Basin Redwoods State Park. These parks offer trails of all lengths—from weekend strolls to long-distance hikes with campgrounds like the Coast Trail and the Skyline-to-the-Sea. Demand at these parks is high, so plan ahead. But if you visit at nonpeak times (Mon.-Thurs.), it's like having the trail to yourself.

SAN FRANCISCO BAY AREA

©AVALON TRAVEL

PACIFIC OCEAN

MAP 7.1
page 277

MAP 7.3
page 278

MAP 7.4
page 280

MAP 7.2
page 279

San Pablo Bay

San Francisco Bay

Suisun Bay

San Joaquin River

Olema
Bolinas
Petaluma
San Rafael
Pacifica
San Francisco
Richmond
Berkeley
Oakland
Vallejo
Suisun City
Concord
Danville
Pittsburg
Rio Vista
Woodside
Redwood City
Hayward
Livermore
Pescadero
Fremont
San Jose
Stockton
Manteca
Santa Cruz
Morgan Hill
Gilroy
Santa Nella
Camanche Lake
San Luis Reservoir

see Sacramento
and Gold Country
page 190

see San Joaquin Valley
page 452

0   10 mi
0   10 km

Map 7.1

Sites 1-60 **Pages 281-321**

NORTH BAY

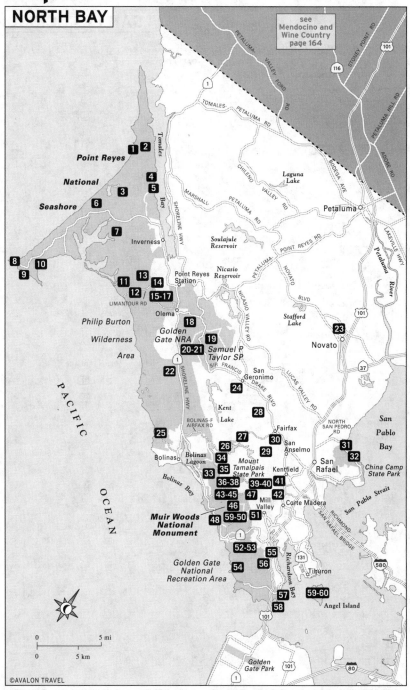

see Mendocino and Wine Country page 164

Map 7.2

Sites 61-106

Pages 322-355

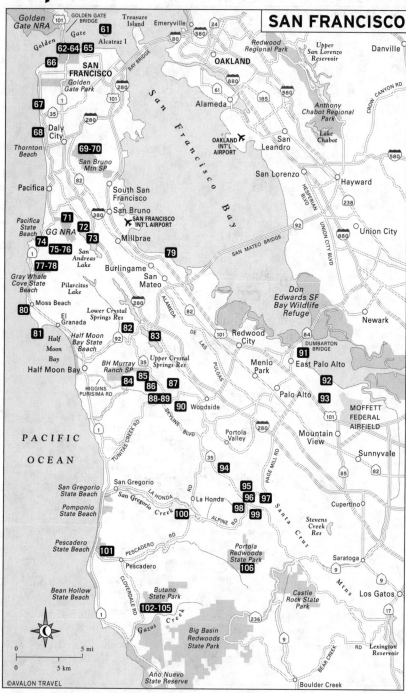

SAN FRANCISCO

©AVALON TRAVEL

Map 7.3

Sites 107-156   **Pages 355-392**

Map 7.4   Sites 157-193   Pages 394-421

@AVALON TRAVEL

PACIFIC OCEAN

0 — 5 km
0 — 5 mi

Pescadero

Pigeon Point

Año Nuevo State Reserve

Point Año Nuevo

161

162

Davenport

Butano State Park

160

Big Basin Redwoods State Park

163-165

Portola Redwoods SP

166

STATE PARK RD

38

SKYLINE BLVD

Santa Cruz

Monterey Bay

Aptos

1

Felton

Ben Lomond

Boulder Creek

9

236

9

Castle Rock State Park

168-169

167

170

Sanborn-Skyline County Park

183-184

Scotts Valley

181-182

17

Santa Cruz Mountains

176

174

9

Saratoga

Cupertino

280

85

101

Sunnyvale

177

175

Los Gatos

SAN TOMAS

17

EXPY

Santa Clara

158

237

178

85

87

280

San Jose

Milpitas

880

157

Watsonville

see Monterey and Big Sur page 424

185

186

152

WATSONVILLE RD

Morgan Hill

180

179

ALMADEN EXPY

MONTEREY HWY

101

Santa Clara Valley

171

FELTER RD

130

159

680

Joseph D Grant County Park

172-173

Calaveras Reservoir

Gilroy

152

LEAVESLEY RD

NEW AVE

193

GILROY HOT SPRINGS RD

Coyote Lake

187

EAST DUNNE AVE

Anderson Lake County Park

Anderson Lake

188-189

190-191

Henry W Coe State Park

To Bell Station and Highways 152/156

192

MOUNT HAMILTON RD

Diablo Range

see San Joaquin Valley page 452

SOUTH BAY

1 MCCLURES BEACH TRAIL
1.0 mi/0.5 hr
🚶1 ⛰7

in Point Reyes National Seashore

Map 7.1, page 277

An easy 0.5-mile downhill walk will lead you to McClures Beach. You'll find tidepools to the south and beachfront to the north. The best time to visit is during minus low tides, when the ocean rolls back and unveils acres of beach and a small collection of tidepools to the nearby south. Beachcombing along McClures Beach and Driftwood Beach (to the immediate north) during these low tides also can unveil unusual finds, although park rules prohibit you from taking anything. In fall and early winter, the sunsets here can be spectacular, especially when refracted light through layers of cirrus can make the sky look like a scene from *The Ten Commandments*. In summer, however, this is one of the foggiest places on the Pacific Coast. McClures Beach is an easy-to-reach spot that is often overlooked in the divine panorama of Point Reyes. It sits in the shadow of nearby Pierce Ranch, with its 500-strong elk herd. Many visitors never drive to the road's end to the trailhead to McClures Beach, except perhaps to use the restrooms, and can then find the trailhead by accident.

Note: During periods of big ocean swells, tidepooling at this beach can be dangerous, as incoming tides can cut you off, leaving no way to escape. Consult a tide table, and never turn your back on the waves.

User Groups: Hikers only. No dogs, horses, or mountain bikes. No wheelchair facilities.

Permits: No permits are required. Parking and access are free.

Maps: For a free map, write to Point Reyes National Seashore. For a topographic map, ask the USGS for Tomales.

Directions: From the Golden Gate Bridge, take U.S. 101 north for 7.5 miles to the exit for Sir Francis Drake Boulevard. Turn west and drive 20 miles to Olema and Highway 1. Turn right on Highway 1 and drive about 100 yards to Bear Valley Road. Turn left on Bear Valley Road and drive 2.4 miles to Sir Francis Drake. Turn left on Sir Francis Drake and drive 5.6 miles to Pierce Point Road. Bear right and drive nine miles to Pierce Ranch, then turn left and drive 0.5 mile to the parking area and the trailhead.

Contact: Point Reyes National Seashore, Bear Valley Visitors Center, 415/464-5100, www.nps.gov/pore.

2 TOMALES POINT TRAIL
6.0 mi/3.5 hr
🚶2 ⛰10

in Point Reyes National Seashore

Map 7.1, page 277   BEST (

This is the best hike in California for wildlife watching. Imagine meeting up with an elk that stands five feet at the shoulders and has antlers that practically poke holes in the clouds. You have a better chance to see and photograph elk here than anyplace else in California. Over the years, the elk herd has averaged 450 animals. It peaked at 540 in fall 2012, but drought and fences, which kept elk from expanding their range to find water, reduced the herd to 286. The end of drought and herd expansion elsewhere in the park will likely bring the numbers back. We have seen as many as 200 elk on a single trip. On another, we counted 13 elk, six deer, three rabbits, and a fox—all within a two-hour span.

This hike starts on the main trail at the north end of the parking lot, just to the left of the ranch. The route has a flat walking surface and easy grades, and is flanked much of the way to the west by the Pacific Ocean and to the east by Tomales Bay, both beautiful sights. About a mile in, elk paths cut into grass and low brush off to the right. The best suggestion is to trace out one or more of these elk trails. This provides numerous off-trail side trips where you can discover more beautiful views and elk. If you break off to the right and make the easy, short climb to a ridge, you can then turn left for a short walk to an overlook of a canyon that plunges down to Tomales Bay. This is not only gorgeous, but one of the better habitats for elk;

you can often see harems with a bull anywhere from the rim on down to just above the beach and cove.

Most people make this a five-mile round-trip. They hike north on the main trail to the top of a grade, a great lookout of Dillon Beach and Bodega Bay. The reason most people turn around here is that the trail descends several hundred feet, so if they continue north, it means an additional climb on the way back. It is six miles, but for most, it's an easy six. In summer, wind and fog occasionally take over.

In the evening (and in the fall, when the bulls collect harems), the herd will also often congregate near a watering area set in a valley about three miles from the trailhead, and also in the deep valley that opens up Tomales Bay. For a bonus, continue hiking the extra 0.5 mile past the elk watering area all the way to Tomales Point.

Note: It is a violation of federal law to herd, chase, or otherwise harass elk.

User Groups: Hikers and horses. Nearby Pierce Ranch (a former working ranch) is accessible to wheelchairs, but Tomales Point Trail is not. No dogs or mountain bikes.

Permits: No permits are required. Parking and access are free.

Maps: For a free map, write to Point Reyes National Seashore. For a topographic map, ask the USGS for Tomales.

Directions: From the Golden Gate Bridge, take U.S. 101 north for 7.5 miles to the exit for Sir Francis Drake Boulevard. Turn west and drive 20 miles to Olema and Highway 1. Turn right on Highway 1 and drive about 100 yards to Bear Valley Road. Turn left on Bear Valley Road and drive 2.4 miles to Sir Francis Drake. Turn left on Sir Francis Drake and drive 5.6 miles to Pierce Point Road. Bear right and drive nine miles to the Pierce Ranch parking area and the trailhead.

Contact: Point Reyes National Seashore, Bear Valley Visitors Center, 415/464-5100, www.nps.gov/pore.

3 ABBOTTS LAGOON TRAIL
3.2 mi/1.5 hr 🏃1 ⛰9

in Point Reyes National Seashore

Map 7.1, page 277   **BEST (**

Two hours at Abbotts Lagoon—a pretty coastal pond with adjacent grasslands on one side and wilderness-style beach on the other—can give you a glow that lasts for weeks. Yet many drive right past the trailhead while en route to Pierce Ranch to see the elk. You can do both. From the parking area it's a 1.6-mile walk, one-way, to the beach. It's gorgeous every step of the way, especially during a series of warm, clear days. The trail descends through coastal foothills, a working ranch to your left, grasslands and wetlands to your right. The walking is easy. About a mile in, you'll reach a bridge. The trail then skirts the shoreline of Abbots Lagoon to your left as you emerge in sand dunes. The trail ends at a wilderness beach where you can stop and have a picnic, or continue for miles.

This is a diverse habitat matrix that can support waterfowl that require freshwater, migratory shorebirds, and songbirds that love the mix of coastal grasslands and a pond. If you see red-winged blackbirds, stop at the bench and listen to their call, perhaps the sweetest sound in nature.

User Groups: Hikers and mountain bikes (bikers on the first mile only; do not cross the bridge). The first portion of the trail is wheelchair accessible with assistance. No dogs or horses.

Permits: No permits are required. Parking and access are free.

Maps: For a free map, write to Point Reyes National Seashore. For a topographic map, ask the USGS for Drakes Bay.

Directions: From the Golden Gate Bridge, take U.S. 101 north for 7.5 miles to the exit for Sir Francis Drake Boulevard. Turn west and drive 20 miles to Olema and Highway 1. Turn right on Highway 1 and drive about 100 yards to Bear Valley Road. Turn left on Bear Valley Road and drive 2.4 miles to Sir Francis Drake. Turn left on Sir Francis Drake and drive 5.6 miles to Pierce Point Road. Bear right and drive 3.3 miles to a small parking area with restrooms. The trailhead is on the left side of the road.

Contact: Point Reyes National Seashore, Bear Valley Visitors Center, 415/464-5100, www.nps. gov/pore.

4 MARSHALL BEACH TRAIL
2.8 mi/1.5 hr 🚶1 ⛰9

in Point Reyes National Seashore

Map 7.1, page 277

Marshall Beach is one of the more secluded beaches in Marin County. This pretty spot is set in a gorgeous cove along Tomales Bay. The water is often calm and pretty, sheltered from north winds by Inverness Ridge. The trailhead tends to be overlooked, because there are no signs directing hikers to it until you reach the trailhead itself. The hike is 1.4 miles one-way. You take an easy descent down into a gulch, and then to the cove that helps shelter the beach. It's the kind of place where you can just sit and watch the water lap gently at the shore. During the week, you can often have the spot all to yourself. In terms of the public's recognition, Marshall Beach is overshadowed by nearby Tomales Bay State Park.

User Groups: Hikers, horses, and mountain bikes. No dogs. No wheelchair facilities.

Permits: No permits are required. Parking and access are free.

Maps: For a free map, write to Point Reyes National Seashore. For a topographic map, ask the USGS for Tomales.

Directions: From the Golden Gate Bridge, take U.S. 101 north for 7.5 miles to the exit for Sir Francis Drake Boulevard. Turn west and drive 20 miles to Olema and Highway 1. Turn right on Highway 1 and drive about 100 yards to Bear Valley Road. Turn left on Bear Valley Road and drive 2.4 miles to Sir Francis Drake. Turn left on Sir Francis Drake and drive 5.6 miles to Pierce Point Road. Bear right and drive 1.3 miles (just past the entrance road for Tomales Bay State Park, on the right) to Duck Cove/

Marshall Beach Road. Turn right and drive 2.6 miles (bear left at the fork) to the parking area for Marshall Beach Trail.

Contact: Point Reyes National Seashore, Bear Valley Visitors Center, 415/464-5100, www.nps. gov/pore.

5 JEPSON/JOHNSTONE TO PEBBLE BEACH
4.5 mi/2.5 hr 🚶2 ⛰9

in Tomales Bay State Park

Map 7.1, page 277

This is an easy, pretty walk to a gorgeous picnic area and beach. Look for the trailhead for the Jepson Trail on the right of parking. The Jepson Trail is routed into a lush coastal forest and out the other side (past a few trail junctions and a private road) for about a mile to the Johnstone Trail. Turn left and you descend another mile to the cut-off spur for Pebble Beach on the right. You can often have it to yourself.

If you fall in love with Tomales Bay State Park, there are several must-do trips. The highlights include: Hearts Desire Beach, Indian Beach, Shell Beach, beautiful water views, and the chance to hand-launch kayaks or canoes. A walk to Indian Beach can be one of the best treasure hunts in the Bay Area. From the parking area, the trail meanders along the pretty shore of Tomales Bay. According to Carlos Porrata, head ranger at the park, this is where visitors have found perfectly crafted arrowheads, ancient bowls, and other Native American artifacts. It is illegal, of course, to take any artifact or disturb any archaeological site, and any finds must be immediately reported.

If you have a car-top boat that can be launched by hand, such as a canoe or kayak, then don't leave it behind. Tomales Bay often provides the best flat-water paddling in the Bay Area. If you paddle north along the western shore, you can often spot many elk in shoreline ravines.

Tomales Bay State Park is lost in the

overwhelming shadow of the adjacent Point Reyes National Seashore. In addition, visiting Point Reyes is free, and this park costs $8 per vehicle, so many choose not to make the trip. Yet this is a great park with stellar destinations.

User Groups: Hikers only. The park headquarters is wheelchair accessible, but the trail is not. No dogs, horses, or mountain bikes.

Permits: A day-use fee of $8 is charged at the entrance station.

Maps: A brochure and map are available for a fee at the entrance station to Tomales Bay State Park. For a topographic map, ask the USGS for Tomales.

Directions: From San Francisco, take U.S. 101 north over Golden Gate Bridge into Marin and continue 7.5 miles to Sir Francis Drake Boulevard. Take that exit west and drive 20 miles to Highway 1. Turn right on Highway 1 and drive 100 yards to Bear Valley Road. Turn left on Bear Valley Road and drive two miles to Sir Francis Drake Highway. Turn left on Sir Francis Drake Highway and drive 5.6 miles to Pierce Point Road. Bear right on Pierce Point Road and drive 1.2 miles to the entrance road on the right for Tomales Bay State Park (well signed). Turn right and drive 1.5 miles to the parking area and the trailhead at Hearts Desire Beach.

Contact: Tomales Bay State Park, Inverness, 415/669-1140 or 415/898-4362; Marin District Headquarters, 415/898-4362, www.parks.ca.gov.

6 SOUTH BEACH TRAIL
0.1-20.0 mi/0.25 hr-1 day 👥2 ⛰6

in Point Reyes National Seashore

Map 7.1, page 277

The Point Reyes beach extends for nearly 10 miles, all of it pristine with white, foaming surf that rolls on endlessly. If you desire miles of untouched beachfront, you've come to the right place. An initial short trail leads from the parking area to South Beach, about three miles north of the Point Reyes Lighthouse. For the best stroll, walk south for about a mile to an expanse of sand dunes. Or walk as far as you'd like and turn around. It is wise to call ahead for weather conditions, as low fog is common, especially during the summer, and strong winds out of the northwest are typical on spring and early-summer afternoons. The beach makes a good picnic site and is one of the few places at Point Reyes where you can take a leashed dog.

A word of warning: Do not swim or bodysurf here. This stretch of coast is known for its treacherous undertow, the kind that can trap even the strongest swimmers, pulling people under and pushing them out to sea, despite their attempts to swim back to the beach.

User Groups: Hikers, dogs, and horses. No mountain bikes. No wheelchair facilities. Note that dogs may not be allowed if marine mammals are present.

Permits: No permits are required. Parking and access are free.

Maps: For a free map, write to Point Reyes National Seashore. For a topographic map, ask the USGS for Drakes Bay.

Directions: From the Golden Gate Bridge, take U.S. 101 north for 7.5 miles to the exit for Sir Francis Drake Boulevard. Turn west and drive 20 miles to Olema and Highway 1. Turn right on Highway 1 and drive about 100 yards to Bear Valley Road. Turn left on Bear Valley Road and drive 2.4 miles to Sir Francis Drake. Turn left on Sir Francis Drake and drive 11.6 miles to the access turnoff for the South Beach parking lot, on the right. Turn right and drive to the parking lot for South Beach.

Contact: Point Reyes National Seashore, Bear Valley Visitors Center, 415/464-5100, www.nps.gov/pore.

7 ESTERO TRAIL
7.8 mi/3.5 hr 👥2 ⛰9

in Point Reyes National Seashore

Map 7.1, page 277

The Estero Trail is one of the best hikes for most people at Point Reyes National Seashore.

The Estero Trail crosses a valley, parallels a bay, ascends a ridge, and leads down to the waterfront, where a perfect, quiet picnic spot awaits. It's an ideal first hike for newcomers. After parking, Estero Trail starts by dropping down into a small valley, where you cross a narrow inlet of Home Bay. The surroundings include pretty, low-lying coastal foothills set at the threshold of Drakes Estero, a drop-dead beautiful tidal lagoon. From here, the trail rises gently along the southeastern flank of the Estero. At 2.4 miles in, you will reach a trail junction. Continue straight on Sunset Beach Trail, where it is an easy 1.5-mile glide down to Sunset Beach. This is a great picnic site for a trail lunch, set inside the mouth of the Estero, about a mile from the Pacific Ocean. This makes it a 7.8-mile round-trip.

There is an option to extend your trip. When you reach the trail junction with Sunset Beach Trail (straight), an option is to instead turn left (south). A 15-minute climb will take you to a short ridge and the junction of Drakes Head Trail. Here you get a sweeping view of Drakes Bay, Estero de Limantour, and more foothills.

User Groups: Hikers, horses, and mountain bikes. The first two miles are wheelchair-accessible, with assistance. No dogs.

Permits: No permits are required. Parking and access are free.

Maps: For a free map, write to Point Reyes National Seashore. For a topographic map, ask the USGS for Drakes Bay.

Directions: From the Golden Gate Bridge, take U.S. 101 north for 7.5 miles to the exit for Sir Francis Drake Boulevard. Turn west and drive 20 miles to Olema and Highway 1. Turn right on Highway 1 and drive about 100 yards to Bear Valley Road. Turn left on Bear Valley Road and drive 2.4 miles to Sir Francis Drake. Turn left on Sir Francis Drake and drive 7.5 miles to Estero Road, on the left. Turn left and drive one mile to the parking area.

Contact: Point Reyes National Seashore, Bear Valley Visitors Center, 415/464-5100, www.nps.gov/pore.

8 POINT REYES LIGHTHOUSE
0.8 mi/0.5 hr 🏃1 ⛰8

in Point Reyes National Seashore

Map 7.1, page 277

In winter, there may be no better place on land from which to watch migrating whales. Year-round, the lookout from Point Reyes Lighthouse can provide the kind of view to ignite the inspiration you may need to start a challenging project (like, say, writing a book). The half-mile walk is more rigorous than many expect. On the way in, you descend 308 steps to a bluff-top lookout where a front-of-the-rail view provides world-class moments. At the lighthouse, a railing at the point provides a perch for stunning ocean views. You can see for miles across the Pacific. On a good day, you might see 5 to 10 whale spouts, and if lucky, a breech or tail salute. On the way back, the climb up those 308 steps, equivalent to 30 stories on a high rise, can catch some by surprise.

To see whales, scan the ocean for what looks like a little puff of smoke on the water's surface: a whale spout. When you find one, zoom in closer. The Great Whale Highway is located just offshore of Point Reyes. On clear weekends, particularly in winter, the place can be crowded. A fence on the edge of the cliff keeps visitors from falling overboard from one of the most dramatic coastal lookouts anywhere. Sunsets here are unforgettable. A shuttle bus is required (see below) on good-weather Sundays in winter and early spring.

User Groups: Hikers and mountain bikes (bikes are restricted from the stairs and not advised). No dogs or horses.

Permits: No permits are required. Parking and access are free.

Maps: For a free map, write to Point Reyes National Seashore. For a topographic map, ask the USGS for Drakes Bay.

Directions: From the Golden Gate Bridge, take U.S. 101 north for 7.5 miles to the exit for Sir Francis Drake Boulevard. Turn west and drive 20 miles to Olema and Highway 1. Turn right on Highway 1 and drive about 100 yards to Bear

Valley Road. Turn left on Bear Valley Road and drive 2.4 miles to Sir Francis Drake. Turn left on Sir Francis Drake and drive 17.6 miles. At the T (left goes to Chimney Rock Headlands), continue straight ahead to the parking area for the Point Reyes Lighthouse.

Shuttle bus: On good weather weekends and holidays in winter (late Dec.-mid-Apr.) a shuttle bus is required. Tickets are at Drakes Beach Visitors Center (9:30am-3:30pm, $5). Drive to the South Beach Junction, where the road is blocked. Park and take shuttle bus. The shuttle buses run approximately every 20 minutes, 9:30am-3:30pm. A shuttle bus is not usually required on weekdays or bad weather weekends.

Contact: Point Reyes National Seashore, Bear Valley Visitors Center, 415/464-5100, www.nps.gov/pore.

9 CHIMNEY ROCK TRAIL
2.8 mi/1.25 hr   👣1   ⛰10

in Point Reyes National Seashore

Map 7.1, page 277   **BEST (**

Note: In March 2015, a portion of the Arch Rock overlook collapsed. The part of the trail leading up to Arch Rock remains closed.

This is one of the most eye-popping easy hikes in California. The trail starts at the south end of the parking lot, next to a park billboard, on a path that is largely sheltered by the towering headlands ridge to your right. In minutes, you will pass through a cypress forest and then emerge for pretty views of Drakes Bay off to your left. The trail then rises along an isthmus, with cliffs on each side. The ocean is on the right and Drakes Bay is on the left. The trail curves and rises up to the Chimney Rock Headlands, 0.5 mile in. Be sure to turn and look back for a fantastic 180-degree sweep, with the Pacific now on your left, Drakes Bay on your right. Often there are awesome winds that sweep up the cliffs here. The perch is sensational for views, with sightings of whale spouts in winter, the Farallon Islands, and then across the Headlands to the north. Looking back to

the east, you can take in the calm waters of Drakes Bay and beyond to Drakes Estero, Limantour, and Inverness Ridge. The main trail continues south to a lookout of a series of rock stacks that emerge from the ocean just beyond land's end. The biggest is Chimney Rock. One of the rock formations has a bridged archway where a surging ocean foams through the center, a phenomenon.

In peak spring season, you can often see unbelievable diversity of wildflowers on the lee side of the headlands on the Chimney Rock Trail, including rafts of Douglas iris and good numbers of checkerbloom. Because of exposure to wind, wildflowers tend to dry out sooner here than at more protected areas, but they are spectacular when you hit it right.

User Groups: Hikers and mountain bikes. The first 0.25 mile of the trail is wheelchair-accessible. No dogs or horses.

Permits: No permits are required. Parking and access are free.

Maps: For a free map, write to Point Reyes National Seashore. For a topographic map, ask the USGS for Drakes Bay.

Directions: From the Golden Gate Bridge, take U.S. 101 north for 7.5 miles to the exit for Sir Francis Drake Boulevard. Turn west and drive 20 miles to Olema and Highway 1. Turn right on Highway 1 and drive about 100 yards to Bear Valley Road. Turn left on Bear Valley Road and drive 2.4 miles to Sir Francis Drake. Turn left on Sir Francis Drake and drive 17.4 miles toward the Point Reyes Lighthouse to a fork with Chimney Rock Road on the left. Turn left and drive one mile to the parking area and trailhead.

Shuttle bus: On good weather weekends and holidays in winter, usually late December to mid-April, a shuttle bus is required. Tickets are at Drakes Beach Visitors Center (9:30am-3:30pm, $5). Drive to the South Beach Junction, where the road is blocked. Park and take shuttle bus. The shuttle buses run approximately every 20 minutes, 9:30am-3:30pm A shuttle bus is not usually required on weekdays or bad weather weekends.

Contact: Point Reyes National Seashore, Bear Valley Visitors Center, 415/464-5100, www.nps. gov/pore.

10 SIR FRANCIS DRAKE TRAIL

1.9 mi/1.0 hr 🥾1 ⛰️8

in Point Reyes National Seashore

Map 7.1, page 277

This spot is not exactly a secret. In fact, you might as well stand on the Golden Gate Bridge with a megaphone and announce its existence to the world. At the trailhead, for instance, you will discover a large parking lot and visitors center, complete with exhibits, maps, and books (maybe even this one, and if not, ask why; after all, we've hiked every trail in the park). The trail traces the back of the arcing beaches along Drakes Bay and provides scenic lookouts onto the bay's protected waters. The trail continues to the mouth of Drakes Estero, then returns via an inland loop that includes a short climb up, then down to a waterfront bluff. This is one of the more popular hikes at Point Reyes National Seashore, and why not? It is an easy walk, provides great scenic beauty, and traces three habitats: beach frontage, the mouth of a lagoon, and hillside bluffs.

User Groups: Hikers and mountain bikes. No dogs or horses. No wheelchair facilities.

Permits: No permits are required. Parking and access are free.

Maps: For a free map, write to Point Reyes National Seashore. For a topographic map, ask the USGS for Drakes Bay.

Directions: From the Golden Gate Bridge, take U.S. 101 north for 7.5 miles to the exit for Sir Francis Drake Boulevard. Turn west and drive 20 miles to Olema and Highway 1. Turn right on Highway 1 and drive about 100 yards to Bear Valley Road. Turn left on Bear Valley Road and drive 2.4 miles to Sir Francis Drake. Turn left on Sir Francis Drake, drive 11.1 miles, and look for the sign indicating a left turn to a visitors center. Turn left and drive 1.2 miles to

the parking lot at the Kenneth Patrick Visitors Center and the trailhead.

Contact: Point Reyes National Seashore, Bear Valley Visitors Center, 415/464-5100, www.nps. gov/pore.

11 SKY TRAIL TO PALOMARIN

15.3 mi one-way/ 2 days 🥾3 ⛰️10

in Point Reyes National Seashore

Map 7.1, page 277

With a slight change of approach, one of the Bay Area's greatest overnight hikes can be made even greater. You do it by taking Sky Trail to Palomarin, with a shuttle car for a one-way hike. This trip starts on a Saturday at the Sky Trailhead and parking lot, where you hike 7.1 miles to Glen Camp and spend the night. The next day, complete the route where you hike 8.2 miles out to Palomarin and your shuttle car. It splits the weekend into two even days, unlike the famed Coast Trail route. In addition, your best chance these days of getting a campsite on a Saturday night is at Glen Camp, with Wildcat sold out fast, spring through fall.

On Day 1, hike 7.1 miles to Glen Camp. Don't get disgruntled over the first 15 minutes, where the trail is routed up to the ridge on a service road, no views (but pretty bracken ferns and forget-me-nots). At 1.3 miles, you emerge at Sky Camp at 1,000 feet elevation, and with a short walk to the adjacent hill, the eye-popping views are revealed to the west. The expanse of Drakes Bay below is stunning, along with Arch Rock, Drakes Beach, Chimney Rock, and Point Reyes, from left to right. The views then sparkle for much of the hike, with the route occasionally passing through old-growth bishop pines. Over and over, you emerge for views below of Sculptured Beach, Point Resistance, and Arch Rock. Eventually you top out at Glen Camp. Be sure to bring a light tent. Morning fog can be wet.

On Day 2, hike 8.2 miles from Glen Camp to the end of the trail at Palomarin Trailhead and your shuttle car. The day starts where you sail downhill and take in pretty views of Wildcat Valley, ocean breakers, and Wildcat Beach, and then connect with the Coast Trail. It is 0.8 mile to the Coast Trail, and then another 1.1 miles to Wildcat Camp.

Note about Alamere Falls: It was 50-50 whether to include this short portion about the Alamere Falls spur. From Wildcat Camp, as you head south, near the wood bridge over Alamere Creek, there is an unsigned cut-off on the right; this is the route to the brink of Alamere Falls (rains revive it in winter and spring). The park closed this unofficial route, though many still figure out a way to get past the closure sign and trek the short distance to the brink of the falls. Officially, it is not a trail and rangers do not want you on it. To get a full front view of Alamere Falls, from Wildcat Camp, descend to the beach and hike south one mile.

From the bridge at Alamere Creek, it is 3.6 miles to the end of the trail and the parking lot at Palomarin. In the process, the route contours south in and out of coastal valleys, where you pass Wildcat Lake, Pelican Lake, and Bass Lake, all gorgeous en route to the trail's end. On a fresh, clear April weekend, this is one of the best ways to celebrate the coronation of spring.

User Groups: Hikers only. No wheelchair facilities.

Permits: Parking and access are free. Reservations and permit required for camping. Reserve at www.recreation.gov; $20 per night for up to six per site. Garbage must be packed out.

Maps: For a free map, write to Point Reyes National Seashore. For a topographic map, ask the USGS for Drakes Bay.

Directions: To Bear Valley Visitors Center: From the Golden Gate Bridge, take U.S. 101 north for 7.5 miles to the exit for Sir Francis Drake Boulevard. Turn west and drive 20 miles to Olema and Highway 1. Turn right on Highway 1 and drive about 100 yards to Bear Valley Road. Turn left and drive 0.7 mile to the Seashore Information sign and access road for Bear Valley Visitors Center. Turn left and go a short distance to the visitors center (campers must pick up permits in person).

To Sky Trailhead: From Bear Valley Visitors Center, exit parking lot to Bear Valley Road. Turn left and drive a short distance to Sir Francis Drake Boulevard. Turn left on Bear Valley Road and drive two miles to Limantour Road. Turn left on Limantour and drive a little over three miles on access road to the Sky Trail parking and trailhead on the left.

Visitors center to Palomarin: From the visitors center, exit the parking lot to Bear Valley Road, turn right, and go 0.5 mile to Highway 1. Turn right and drive 9.3 miles to Olema-Bolinas Road on the right (the sign is always stolen; if you reach Bolinas Lagoon, turn around on Highway 1 and look for the road on left). Turn right and go 1.3 miles to the junction with Horseshoe Hill Road. Turn left (still Olema-Bolinas Road) and go 0.5 mile to Mesa Road. Turn right and go 4.8 miles (pass an antenna farm called The Towers) to the parking area.

Contact: Point Reyes National Seashore, Bear Valley Visitors Center, 415/464-5100, www.nps. gov/pore.

12 SKY TRAIL LOOP

9.6 mi/4.0 hr   🚶3   ⛰️10

in Point Reyes National Seashore

Map 7.1, page 277

Hit it right on a clear day and it can feel like you have a foothold in the heavens on the Point Reyes Sky Trail. From the trailhead at the parking area on Limantour Road, you pass around a gate to hike up a service road edged by cypress and, in the spring, occasional patches of forget-me-nots in the shade. The trail climbs, from gentle to moderate, to the south for 0.8 mile to a junction with the Fire Lane Trail (on the right). Ignore that and continue on the service road for another half mile to the Sky Camp. In the process, you will walk along the edge of the burn zone of the 1995 fire, with remnants of that event still visible.

Notice the mix of fresh-sprouted grass, wild-flowers, and young pines, and old cypress and pine that the fire missed, and the sprinkling of blackened tree skeletons that still stand. As you near Sky Camp, the views start to open up. When you reach the camp, look to your right for the nearby short hill to gain the best perch for the jaw-dropping view of Drakes Bay. This 1,000-foot ridgeline perch towers over Drakes Bay and the Pacific Ocean. Plunging below at your boot tips are miles of foothills reborn. Scan from right to left taking in Point Reyes, Chimney Rock, and the curving Limantour Beach to Arch Rock. You can simply turn back for a 2.6-mile romp (mostly downhill on the return).

Better yet, extend the trek to create a spectacular loop, down to the beach and then back up, for a 9.6-mile round-trip. From Sky Camp, stay on the Sky Trail along Inverness Ridge, sheltered by old-growth pines and firs, south to the Woodward Valley Trail. Turn right and sail down Woodward Valley Trail, with jaw-dropping views of the ocean, down to the Coast Trail. On the way down, you may experience the unbelievable feeling that you can sense the earth's curve on the distant horizon. Turn right on the Coast Trail, and in less than a mile, you'll pass Coast Camp, a good spot for your picnic for the day. Then continue ahead into a valley to the Laguna Trail/Fire Trail. Turn right. It's quite steep in a few spots back up to Sky Trail. Back on top, to complete the trip, turn left on Sky Trail and sail back to the parking area. This is one of the best coastal routes in California.

User Groups: Hikers only. Bikes and horses permitted to Sky Camp. No wheelchair facilities.

Permits: No permits are required. Parking and access are free. Permits are required to camp at Sky Camp. Reserve at www.recreation.gov; $20 per night for up to six per site; 11 campsites with picnic table, fire grills (charcoal only), drinking water, pit toilet. Garbage must be packed out.

Maps: For a free map, write to Point Reyes

Sky Trail Loop

© TOM STIENSTRA

National Seashore. For a topographic map, ask the USGS for Drakes Bay.

Directions: From the Golden Gate Bridge, take U.S. 101 north for 7.5 miles to the exit for Sir Francis Drake Boulevard. Turn west and drive 20 miles to Olema and Highway 1. Turn right and drive about 100 yards to Bear Valley Road. Turn left and drive 0.7 mile to the Seashore Information sign and access road for Bear Valley Visitors Center. Turn left and head a short distance to the visitors center (campers must pick up permits in person). From Bear Valley Visitors Center, return to Bear Valley Road. Turn left and drive 1.3 miles to Limantour Road (signed Hostel and Limantour Beach). Turn left and drive 3.4 miles to the access road on the left for Sky Trail. Turn left and drive a short distance to the parking area.

Contact: Point Reyes National Seashore, Bear Valley Visitors Center, 415/464-5100, www.nps.gov/pore.

13 COAST TRAIL

16.1 mi one-way/2-plus days

🚶3 ⛰10

in Point Reyes National Seashore

Map 7.1, page 277   BEST (

Of the handful of overnight hiking trips available in the Bay Area, Coast Trail provides the most extended tour into a land of charm. This continuous backcountry route is 16.1 miles long, one-way, enough to allow lingering hikers to spend a weekend at it, and short enough for the ambitious to tackle in a single day. The trail offers camps at ocean bluffs, a beach with sculptured rocks and tidepools, bluff-top lookouts with a chance to see passing whales, a rare waterfall from an ocean bluff that pours like a fountain to a beach and then runs into the ocean, and coastal freshwater lakes. There are only a few catches: You need a hiking partner who will double as a shuttle driver so you can leave a car at each end of the trail. You'll need to come prepared to cook your food using a small backpack stove, not a campfire. Tents are recommended, because the coastal weather is the most unpredictable in the Bay Area—clear, calm, and warm one day, then suddenly foggy, windy, moist, and clammy the next.

The trailhead for Coast Trail is at the Point Reyes Hostel, from where you will hike north to south, and keep the wind at your back and out of your face. The first camp, Coast Camp, is an easy 2.8 miles, ideal for those who head out on a Friday evening after work. As you hike in, you'll have a panoramic view of the coastal foothills that were burned in the wildfire of October 1995 and since reborn. The campground and trail were untouched. The sound of ocean waves will send you to sleep the first night, or, in some sensitive cases, might keep you awake.

If you try to hike the Coast Trail in two days, you will face a first-day tromp of 10.6 miles, direct to Wildcat Camp. Because of the additional time spent getting camping permits at the Bear Valley Visitors Center and setting up a shuttle car at the trail's end at Palomarin, most hikers get a late start, which means facing a late arrival at Wildcat. One option is to start instead at Sky Trail off Limantour Road and spend the night at Glen Camp (see the listing for *Sky Trail to Palomarin* in this chapter).

From Coast Camp, the next day you will hike south, getting glimpses along the way of Sculptured Beach, with its magnificent rock stacks and tunnels. The cut-off trail to Arch Rock is closed after the collapse in 2015. You'll see and pass Sculptured Beach, Kelham Beach (trail repaired), and Arch Rock. The Coast Trail continues south to Wildcat Camp, set on a bluff overlooking the ocean. That makes day two a hike of 7.8 miles. It's an additional mile, one-way, to walk south on the beach for a view of Alamere Falls.

On day three, figure on a 5.5-mile closeout with plenty of great sideshows. You will hike past a series of coastal lakes, nearby Wildcat Lake and little Ocean Lake. After climbing to a short ridge, you will skirt above Pelican Lake and along the northern shore of Bass Lake. The trail then heads up a coastal hill, tops out at 563 feet, and then laterals down a canyon and back to ocean bluffs. Following the trail, you turn south and in a mile arrive at the Palomarin trailhead. You will be ready to reach your shuttle car and head for the barn. This is one of the Bay Area's greatest hikes. For many who want only the best, this is on their must-do list on a clear, warm coastal day at peak spring or fall. For camping reservations, make your dates when they first become available at www.recreation.gov.

User Groups: Hikers and horses. Mountain bikes permitted only from the Laguna trailhead to the Coast Campground and otherwise prohibited. Partially accessible to wheelchair users who have assistance. No dogs.

Permits: Parking and access are free. Reservations and a permit are required for camping. Reserve at www.recreation.gov; $20 per night for up to six per site. Garbage must be packed out.

Maps: For a free map, write to Point Reyes

National Seashore. For a topographic map, ask the USGS for Drakes Bay.

Directions: To Bear Valley Visitors Center: From the Golden Gate Bridge, take U.S. 101 north for 7.5 miles to the exit for Sir Francis Drake Boulevard. Turn west and drive 20 miles to Olema and Highway 1. Turn right and drive about 100 yards to Bear Valley Road. Turn left and drive 0.7 mile to the Seashore Information sign and access road for Bear Valley Visitors Center. Turn left and head a short distance to the visitors center (campers must pick up permits in person).

To Coast Trail trailhead: After getting a camping permit at Bear Valley Visitors Center, leave the parking lot and take the access road to Bear Valley Road. Turn left and drive to Limantour Road. Turn left and drive six miles, looking for the signed turn on the left for Point Reyes Hostel. Turn left on the access road for the Point Reyes Hostel and continue to where road ends at the parking lot. After parking, hike back to the hostel and look for the trailhead on the left (west, across the road from the hostel).

Visitors center to Palomarin: Exit the parking lot to Bear Valley Road, turn right and go 0.5 mile to Highway 1. Turn right and drive 9.3 miles to Olema-Bolinas Road on the right (the sign is always stolen; if you reach Bolinas Lagoon, turn around and look for the road on left). Turn right and go 1.3 miles to junction with Horseshoe Hill Road. Turn left (still Olema-Bolinas Road) and go 0.5 mile to Mesa Road. Turn right and go 4.8 miles (pass an antenna farm called The Towers) to the parking area.

Contact: Point Reyes National Seashore, Bear Valley Visitors Center, 415/464-5100, www.nps.gov/pore.

14 LAGUNA LOOP TRAIL
5.5 mi/2.5 hr 🥾2 ⛺8

in Point Reyes National Seashore

Map 7.1, page 277

The Laguna Loop Trail can make for a great Sunday morning walk. The trailhead is just 0.2 mile down the road from the Point Reyes Hostel, adjacent to the park's Environmental Education Center. From there, the trail continues 1.8 miles up to Inverness Ridge, with great views of Drakes Bay along the way. At the ridge, turn right and hike 0.7 mile toward Mount Wittenberg, which at 1,407 feet is the highest point at Point Reyes National Seashore. On the north flank of Mount Wittenberg, hikers should turn right on the Fire Lane Trail, which loops back around for three miles to the Laguna trailhead. This excellent loop hike entails a bit of a climb and offers Pacific lookouts, yet it is short enough to complete in a few hours. You'll also get a view of the foothills reborn since the legendary wildfire of 1995.

User Groups: Hikers and horses. Mountain bikes are permitted only from the Laguna trailhead to the Coast Campground and are otherwise prohibited. No dogs. No wheelchair facilities.

Permits: No permits are required. Parking and access are free.

Maps: For a free map, write to Point Reyes

Laguna Loop Trail, Inverness Ridge

© TOM STIENSTRA

National Seashore. For a topographic map, ask the USGS for Inverness.

Directions: From the Golden Gate Bridge, take U.S. 101 north for 7.5 miles to the exit for Sir Francis Drake Boulevard. Turn west and drive 20 miles to Olema and Highway 1. Turn right and drive about 100 yards to Bear Valley Road. Turn left at Bear Valley Road and drive two miles to Limantour Road. Turn left and drive six miles. Turn left on the access road for the Point Reyes Hostel and drive 0.2 mile past the hostel to the parking area and trailhead (on the right side of the road).

Contact: Point Reyes National Seashore, Bear Valley Visitors Center, 415/464-5100, www.nps. gov/pore.

15 MOUNT WITTENBERG LOOP
4.5 mi/2.5 hr　　　　　🚶3 ⛰9

in Point Reyes National Seashore near Olema

Map 7.1, page 277

One little turn off a major trail can lead to a landscape where hiking dreams come true. The Mount Wittenberg Loop is such a trek, one of the best short hikes in the Point Reyes National Seashore. The trail provides a route through deep forest, a climb with a steady grade, and then magnificent lookouts of Drakes Bay to the west and the Olema Valley to the east. The destination is the flank of Mount Wittenberg (at 1,407 feet, the highest in the park), but the best views are from the ridge just west of the rounded summit (not at the summit). After parking at the huge parking lot at Bear Valley Visitors Center, look for the trailhead for Bear Valley Trail at the south end of the parking area. This has long been one of the heaviest used trails in the Bay Area, and hence comes the trick: Hike on Bear Valley Trail for just 0.2 mile! On your right, look for the cut-off route for the Sky Trail. Bear right at the cutoff, and from here, it is a 1.4-mile hike with a climb of 1,200 feet. It's a steady grade and hikers in decent condition can easily handle it. You'll

pass through old-growth forest and lush ravines, with occasional peephole-like lookouts to Olema Valley. It rises to the foot of Mount Wittenberg (and with another 100-foot climb, a cutoff trail takes hikers to the rounded summit). The views are not the greatest from the top, but instead from just nearby on Sky Trail. At Sky Trail, walk southwest 0.4 mile to the junction with Meadow Trail. In the process, there are dramatic views of Drakes Bay to the west and some hidden meadows to the east. You'll also have a panoramic shot of the coastal foothills. From Meadow Trail, turn left and you will glide downhill for 1.5 miles back down to Bear Valley Trail. The trail widens and flattens, and you'll see people again, then you walk out 0.8 mile to the parking lot. There you have it: To paradise and back in just a few hours.

User Groups: Hikers and horses. No dogs or mountain bikes. No wheelchair facilities.

Permits: No permits are required. Parking and access are free.

Maps: For a free map, write to Point Reyes National Seashore. For a topographic map, ask the USGS for Inverness.

Directions: From the Golden Gate Bridge, take U.S. 101 north for 7.5 miles to the exit for Sir Francis Drake Boulevard. Turn west and drive 20 miles to Olema and Highway 1. Turn right and drive about 100 yards to Bear Valley Road. Turn left and drive 0.7 mile to sign for Seashore Information and road on left. Turn left and drive to the parking lot for the Bear Valley Visitors Center. The trailhead is at the south end of the parking lot.

Contact: Point Reyes National Seashore, Bear Valley Visitors Center, 415/464-5100, www.nps. gov/pore.

16 BEAR VALLEY TRAIL
8.2 mi/4.0 hr　　　　　🚶1 ⛰7

in Point Reyes National Seashore near Olema

Map 7.1, page 277

This is one of the most popular trails in the park. It starts at the south end of the parking lot at the main visitors center and follows a heavily used service road through pretty forest. It leads past Divide Meadow to Bear Valley, then down along Coast Creek to the beach, a highlight.

User Groups: Hikers, mountain bikes (first three miles only), and horses (weekdays only). The 1.5-mile trail to Divide Meadow is wheelchair-accessible but requires a significant amount of assistance. No dogs.

Permits: No permits are required. Parking and access are free.

Maps: For a free map, write to Point Reyes National Seashore. For a topographic map, ask the USGS for Inverness.

Directions: From the Golden Gate Bridge, take U.S. 101 north for 7.5 miles to the exit for Sir Francis Drake Boulevard. Turn west and drive 20 miles to Olema and Highway 1. Turn right and drive about 100 yards to Bear Valley Road. Turn left and drive 0.7 mile to the sign for Seashore Information and a road on the left. Turn left and drive to the parking lot for the Bear Valley Visitors Center.

Contact: Point Reyes National Seashore, Bear Valley Visitors Center, 415/464-5100, www.nps. gov/pore.

17 EARTHQUAKE TRAIL
1.2 mi one-way/0.75 hr 👫1 ⛰7

in Point Reyes National Seashore near Olema

Map 7.1, page 277

The trailhead is located right next to the picnic area at the Bear Valley Visitors Center. That makes this a popular easy walk. The geology also fascinates many. It is one of the world's classic examples of an earthquake fault line: the San Andreas Fault. Because we like big views, waterfalls, and wildflowers, it doesn't quite flip our pancake, but it does provide one of the best lessons you can get from the University of Nature.

The trail starts at the Bear Valley Picnic Area. It's a short, paved loop.

User Groups: Hikers and horses. No dogs or mountain bikes. No wheelchair facilities.

Permits: No permits are required. Parking and access are free.

Maps: For a free map, write to Point Reyes National Seashore. For a topographic map, ask the USGS for Inverness.

Directions: From the Golden Gate Bridge, take U.S. 101 north for 7.5 miles to the exit for Sir Francis Drake Boulevard. Turn west and drive 20 miles to Olema and Highway 1. Turn right and drive about 100 yards to Bear Valley Road. Turn left and drive 0.7 mile to the sign for Seashore Information and a road on the left. Turn left and drive to the parking lot for the Bear Valley Visitors Center.

Contact: Point Reyes National Seashore, Bear Valley Visitors Center, 415/464-5100, www.nps. gov/pore.

18 BOLINAS RIDGE
10.5 mi one-way/4.5 hr 👫3 ⛰9

in Marin County west of San Rafael

Map 7.1, page 277

The Bolinas Ridge Trail spans 10.5 miles (one-way) from Sir Francis Drake Boulevard south to Bolinas-Fairfax Road in west Marin County. From Bolinas Ridge, you start with hilltop views across the foothill grasslands and valleys and beyond to the Marin coast. It can be a good short walk, a better hike, and for ambitious mountain bikers, a sensational 20-mile loop with several cut-offs available for shorter options.

From the trailhead at Sir Francis Drake, the trail undulates up and down the foothills, with an overall climb of about 750 feet in six miles. You get views of Olema Valley, the San Andreas Rift Zone and beyond south to Bolinas Lagoon. Some just venture south for a few miles, then turn around when ready for a mostly downhill glide. If you continue south, the route descends, steeply at times, into redwoods. Most of the trail is an abandoned ranch road. The trail is routed for about five miles through open grasslands with lots of cows and several gates. Do not go off trail, where ticks wait perched on the high grass to ambush you if you (or your dog) brush by.

Note: You can also start the trip from Samuel P. Taylor State Park, where secure parking is available. To do this, you connect out of Samuel P. Taylor on the Jewell Trail; but the Jewell Trail was closed by a washout in 2015 and will need to be restored and reopened before this route is accessible again.

User Groups: Hikers, dogs, horses, and mountain bikes. No wheelchair facilities.

Permits: No permits are required. Parking and access are free.

Maps: For a free map, write to Point Reyes National Seashore. For topographic maps, ask the USGS for Inverness, San Geronimo, and Bolinas.

Directions: From San Francisco, take U.S. 101 north over the Golden Gate Bridge and continue 8.7 miles to Larkspur and the exit for San Anselmo/Sir Francis Drake West. Take that exit, drive 0.4 mile, and merge onto Sir Francis Drake. Drive 19.4 miles, past Samuel P. Taylor State Park, to the trailhead on the left (if you reach Olema, you missed it: the trailhead is back one mile). Park on the shoulder.

Contact: Golden Gate National Recreation Area, Fort Mason, San Francisco, 415/561-4700, www.nps.gov/goga.

19 BARNABE PEAK LOOP
5.5 mi/3.5 hr

in Samuel P. Taylor State Park west of San Rafael

Map 7.1, page 277

The traditional route to 1,466-foot Barnabe Peak and its amazing views of the coast will be closed at least to 2018, and perhaps beyond that (and we'll explain why shortly). The Barnabe Fire Road provides a 5.5-mile loop with a 1,300-foot climb to the top. From the summit, you get a sweeping lookout that spans from Mount Tamalpais to Point Reyes. An old lookout tower is positioned here, but there is no access. Most will plan a picnic at the base of the old tower.

You can still make the hike, just on a fire road instead of a trail. If you've done Barnabe in the past, you start at a new trailhead. Park at the Azalea Picnic Area, a day-use area inside the main entrance to Samuel P. Taylor State Park. Then walk toward the dump station, and take the North Creek Trail for about two minutes to the bridge for Lagunitas Creek, and then cross Sir Francis Drake Boulevard. On the north side of Sir Francis Drake, you'll see the Madrone Group Campground, and from there, the Barnabe Fire Road. Now you're on your way.

Bill's Trail out of Devil's Gulch to Stairstep Falls and Barnabe Peak is closed to renovation through at least 2018, and perhaps beyond that. Because of issues with endangered species, including the spotted owl, trail work can only be completed here when the work of trail crews will have no effect on owls that are calling for mates, nesting, or rearing young.

Samuel P. Taylor State Park is located along Sir Francis Drake Boulevard in western Marin, best known for its stand of redwoods and the lush undergrowth in the canyon along the headwaters of Lagunitas Creek. The park covers 2,700 acres and features excellent hiking, biking, and camping.

User Groups: Hikers, dogs, and mountain bikes (bikes are not permitted on spur trails). No horses.

Permits: A state park day-use fee of $8 per vehicle is charged at the entrance station.

Maps: A brochure and map are available for a fee at the entrance station to Samuel P. Taylor State Park. For a topographic map, ask the USGS for San Geronimo.

Directions: To park headquarters: From the Golden Gate Bridge, take U.S. 101 north for 7.5 miles to the exit for Sir Francis Drake Boulevard. Take that exit west and drive 14.5 miles to the park entrance, on the left.

Contact: Samuel P. Taylor State Park, Lagunitas, 415/488-9897; Marin District Headquarters, 415/898-4362, www.parks.ca.gov.

20 PIONEER TREE TRAIL
1.6 mi/0.75 hr   🥾2 ⛰7

in Samuel P. Taylor State Park west of San Rafael

Map 7.1, page 277

If you like big trees and a simple, short walk, the Pioneer Tree Trail in Samuel P. Taylor State Park will provide it. In just 0.5 mile, you will walk amid the park's prize grove of old-growth coastal redwoods, the species that produces the tallest trees in the world. Park at the Redwood Grove Group Picnic Area. Walk 0.1 mile on the Cross Marin Trail to the Pioneer Tree Trailhead on the right. From here, it's 0.25-mile into the heart of the grove of old-growth. The trail then turns left sharply, and you walk another 0.25 mile. When you run out of big trees, most turn around and return at this point.

If you continue on, you will eventually reach a spur for the Pioneer Trail, less impressive than the behemoths in the Santa Cruz Mountains, and reach the Cross Marin Trail along Lagunitas Creek. Turn left and go 0.6 mile to reach your starting point, the picnic area. That is a 2.7-mile loop.

User Groups: Hikers only. No dogs, horses, or mountain bikes.

Permits: A state park day-use fee of $8 per vehicle is charged at the entrance station.

Maps: A brochure and map are available for a fee at the entrance station to Samuel P. Taylor State Park. For a topographic map, ask the USGS for San Geronimo.

Directions: From the Golden Gate Bridge, take U.S. 101 north for 7.5 miles to the exit for Sir Francis Drake Boulevard. Take that exit west and drive 14.5 miles to the park entrance, on the left. Park at the Redwood Grove Group Picnic Area.

Contact: Samuel P. Taylor State Park, Lagunitas, 415/488-9897; Marin District Headquarters, 415/898-4362, www.parks.ca.gov.

21 KENT DAM TRAIL
1.8 mi/1.0 hr   🥾1 ⛰6

in northwest Marin County west of San Rafael

Map 7.1, page 277

Kent Lake is nearly four miles long, with an additional large arm extending east into Big Carson Creek. Only hikers and mountain bikers see it. Start by parking along Sir Francis Drake Boulevard at Shafter Bridge. Hike past the gate on Lower Peters Creek Dam Road (Lagunitas Creek to your right) to a junction (San Geronimo Ridge Road on your left, an excellent mountain bike ride), and continue ahead (at a spur, stay left on the main road). The road bends like a horseshoe, first to the left, then ahead, and then to the right as it rises up to Peters Dam. When the lake first emerges into view, it is an amazing sight, especially when the lake fills in late winter. Emerald water fills a long canyon, bordered on each side by rising slopes filled with conifers. Most people are astounded the first time they see Kent Lake, for they have no idea such a huge lake is tucked away in a Marin canyon. The road continues along the east side of the lake and then eventually rises up into forested slopes to a network of fire roads.

User Groups: Hikers, dogs, and mountain bikes. No horses. No wheelchair facilities.

Permits: No permits are required. Groups are limited to 19 people. Parking and access are free.

Maps: This trail is included on a free map of Point Reyes National Seashore (see address below). For topographic maps, ask the USGS for San Geronimo and Bolinas.

Directions: From the Golden Gate Bridge, take U.S. 101 north for 7.5 miles to the exit for Sir Francis Drake Boulevard. Take that exit west and drive about 12 miles to Shafter Bridge. Park here and look for the locked gate at the entrance to the trailhead (Lower Peters Creek Dam Road).

Contact: Sky Oaks Ranger Station, 415/945-1181; Marin Municipal Water District, 415/945-1195, www.marinwater.org.

22 OLEMA VALLEY

3.0 mi/1.25 hr

in Point Reyes National Seashore south of Olema

Map 7.1, page 277

Olema Valley is a mix of lush meadows and forests that roughly traces the San Andreas Fault. The trailhead is at Five Brooks. Take the Stewart Trail, a road that runs past a duck pond, and then which junctions quickly with the Olema Valley Trail. The meadow area attracts a lot of deer, morning and evening. It's 1.3 miles, which includes a short climb, to the headwaters of Pine Gulch Creek. From there, most continue a short distance, and then return when ready. An option is to continue southward for four miles or more to Olema Creek and along the San Andreas Fault. In wet weather, the creeks often flood the trail. If that is a concern, wear waterproof boots in winter. In summer, this has become a popular mountain bike route.

User Groups: Hikers, horses, and mountain bikes. No dogs. No wheelchair facilities.

Permits: No permits are required. Parking and access are free.

Maps: For a free map, write to Point Reyes National Seashore. For a topographic map, ask the USGS for Bolinas.

Directions: From the Golden Gate Bridge, take U.S. 101 north for 7.5 miles to the exit for Sir Francis Drake Boulevard. Turn west and drive 20 miles to Olema and Highway 1. Turn left on Highway 1 and drive 3.6 miles to the access road for Five Brooks trailhead on the right (west). Turn right and drive to parking and continue to the Stewart Trail and the duck pond.

Contact: Point Reyes National Seashore, Bear Valley Visitors Center, 415/464-5100, www.nps.gov/pore.

23 MOUNT BURDELL

5.8 mi/3.0 hr

in Olompali State Historic Park near Novato

Map 7.1, page 277

The pay-off at Olompali State Historic Park is the big view from the upper slopes and summit of 1,558-foot Mount Burdell as you tower over the expanse of San Pablo Bay. Below are the wetlands of Bahia Marsh and the Petaluma River near the Gnoss Field Airport. You can see the Sonoma Mountains to the north, across the bay to Carquinez Bridge to the east. It's a 5.8-mile round-trip to Burdell summit, a 1,500-foot climb. The hike is routed through pretty woodlands, up well-graded switchbacks, and emerges in grasslands with a picnic site on top. The habitat supports tons of deer and wild turkey.

Note: No mountain bikes or dogs are permitted at Olompali State Historic Park, yet they are allowed at adjoining Mount Burdell Open Space Preserve. Near the summit, a trail connects the two parks, and if you see bikes or dogs, that is where they are coming from.

User Groups: Hikers. No dogs, horses, or mountain bikes. No wheelchair facilities on Mount Burdell Trail, but they are available near the parking area.

Permits: No permits are required. There is an $8 parking fee.

Maps: A trail map is posted at information billboard near the parking area. For a topographic map, ask the USGS for Burdell.

Directions: From San Francisco, take U.S. 101 north for about 25 miles (past Highway 37 on right) to Exit 463 for Atherton Avenue/San Marin Drive. Take that exit to Atherton. Turn left on Atherton and go 0.2 mile (cross the overpass over 101) to Redwood Boulevard. Turn right and drive 2.7 miles on Redwood (a frontage road, just west of 101) to the park entrance on the left.

Contact: Olompali State Historic Park, 415/892-3383, www.parks.ca.gov.

24 GREEN HILL/SAN GERONIMO RIDGE

4.0 mi one-way/ 2.5 hr 🏃3 ⛰8

in Giacomini Open Space, Marin

Map 7.1, page 277

Giacomini Open Space is a hidden preserve that provides a gateway to 25,000 acres of wildlands. It is located east of Fairfax on the flank of San Geronimo Ridge, at the foot of Marin's Mount Tamalpais. The drive in makes it off the radar for just about everybody but locals, and that makes it special, too. In two miles, you are transported from city driving (Sir Francis Drake) to a little-known, primitive country road (Conifer Way) and a surprise gated trailhead at Conifer Fire Road. This provides one of the fastest transformations from urban to wild in the Bay Area.

From the gate (880 feet elevation), head up Conifer Road for 0.7 mile to a forked junction. Right goes to Green Hill (1,418 feet, four-mile round-trip) for big views. You're on fire roads. You emerge on top with a panorama across the wooded watershed lands.

The ambitious few can continue on, but you pay a price coming back. It's 5.4 miles one-way, where you climb roughly 600 feet to ridge top, then descend 1,000 feet to Peters Dam at Kent Lake (see previous hike). With a shuttle car at Shafter Bridge, you can make this a tremendous one-way that nobody does.

Giacomini Open Space encompasses 1,500 acres on the flanks of San Geronimo Ridge Fire Road. It adjoins Marin Watershed lands, and on the ridge, you get views of Kent Lake and across west Marin. A network of fire roads for mountain biking connects to the watershed lands and to other preserves.

User Groups: Hikers, mountain bikes, dogs and horses. Limited wheelchair facilities.

Permits: No permits are required. Parking and access are free.

Maps: A sheet map is available from Bay Ridge Trail Council. For topographic maps, ask the USGS for San Geronimo.

Directions: From San Francisco, take U.S. 101 north over the Golden Gate Bridge and continue 9.4 miles to Exit 450B (for San Anselmo and Sir Francis Drake Boulevard). Take that exit and drive 0.5 mile to the merge with Sir Francis Drake, then continue 9.5 miles (past Fairfax, near Woodacre) to Railroad Avenue. Turn left on Railroad and go 0.7 mile to Carson Road. Turn right and drive up the hill (becomes narrow and curvy) for one mile to Conifer Way. Turn left (very sharp) and go 0.2 mile (slow) to end of road, limited parking, gate, and trailhead.

Contact: Marin County Open Space District, 415/ 499-6387, www.marincountyparks.org.

25 ALAMERE FALLS TRAIL

13.0 mi/1 day 🏃2 ⛰10

in Point Reyes National Seashore northwest of Bolinas

Map 7.1, page 277

Alamere Falls tumbles over an ocean bluff, then cascades 40 feet to the beach below and into the Pacific Ocean. It is stunning, beautiful, and constantly changing as the rains come and go. There's one catch: This trip used to be 8.4 miles, but a trail closure now makes it 13 miles, though a lot of people break the rules (and we'll get to that).

From the Palomarin Trailhead, follow the southern end of the Coast Trail as it starts out on a service road that contours along the coastal foothills. At times you'll tower over the ocean and on clear days, the Farallon Islands look close enough to reach with a jump. The trail follows along the ocean for about a mile, then dips down into a ravine to climb out 500 feet to a sub-ridge and trail junction. Stay left on the Coast Trail for two miles, gently descending past pretty Bass Lake. A mile later, you'll hike along a sub-ridge that overlooks Pelican Lake, a bit bigger than Bass Lake and also gorgeous. This is an excellent area for wildflowers and for sighting deer and birds. After passing Pelican Lake, the route continues north and arrives at a small bridge at Alamere Creek. You can get a ticket if you trek off-trail and follow the creek downstream to the brink of the falls.

You then continue another 1.3 miles to Wildcat Camp, where you drop down to the wilderness beach. It's a mile south along the beach to the base of Alamere Falls for a full frontal, the best views and photo ops. Even with light flows in Alamere Creek, this is one of the Bay Area's most beautiful waterfalls. After toppling over a rocky brink to the beach 40 feet below, the water cuts an ever-changing mosaic in the sand before running into the ocean. At moderate or high flows, it charges over the cliff in a wide sheet of whitewater. At these times, it is one of the prettiest coastal waterfalls anywhere in the world.

Trail spur conflict: From the Coast Trail, next to the wood bridge over Alamere Creek, there is an unsigned cut-off spur on the right; this is the historic route to the brink of Alamere Falls. The park closed this unofficial route, though many still figure out a way to get past the closure sign and trek the short distance to the brink of the falls. Officially, it is not a trail and rangers do not want you on it.

User Groups: Hikers and horses. No dogs or mountain bikes. No wheelchair facilities.

Permits: No permits are required. Parking and access are free.

Maps: For a free map, write to Point Reyes National Seashore. For topographic maps, ask the USGS for Bolinas and Double Point.

Directions: From San Francisco, take U.S. 101 north over the Golden Gate Bridge and continue nine miles to Exit 450B for Sir Francis Drake Boulevard/San Anselmo. Take that exit (stay in the second lane from the right), continue to Sir Francis Drake, and drive 21 miles to Highway 1. Turn left and drive nine miles to Olema-Bolinas Road on the right (the sign is always stolen; if you reach Bolinas Lagoon, turn around and look for a road on the left). Turn right and go 1.3 miles to the junction with Horseshoe Hill Road. Turn left (still Olema-Bolinas Road) and go 0.5 mile to Mesa Road. Turn right and go 4.8 miles (past an antenna farm called The Towers) to the parking area.

Note: Those familiar with the area can take Highway 1 on the Marin coast past Bolinas Lagoon to an unsigned turn on the left (Olema-Bolinas Road). This saves about 40 minutes.

Contact: Point Reyes National Seashore, Bear Valley Visitors Center, 415/464-5100, www.nps.gov/pore.

26 ALPINE/KENT LAKE PUMP TRAIL
2.0 mi/1.0 hr 👣1 ⛰9

on Mount Tamalpais at Alpine Lake Dam

Map 7.1, page 277

Water-watching has become a spectator sport in Marin. You'll see why if you venture out pretty Bolinas-Fairfax Road. On the right of Alpine Dam, look for the gated service road. This is the Kent Lake Pump Trail. In winter and spring, walk down a short distance to get a view of the "waterfall," a 140-foot stepped cascade, as it flows across the back of the dam and into Lagunitas Creek. In summer months, this is the start of a great, easy walk to a picnic site. On the Pump Trail, walk down into the canyon and look for a cut-off route on your left that leads down to the creek. Stay alert for the second cutoff on your left, down to the creek. Your destination is a beautiful spot along the stream, sheltered beneath a hardwood canopy. Gorgeous. For most, this is the trip, a round-trip of about two miles.

The Pump Trail seems made to order for mountain biking. It descends into the canyon, with Lagunitas Creek on your left, and within two miles, you reach the headwaters of Kent Lake (full). The road is then routed along the lake and past two feeder creeks around a deep cove; a 9.6-mile round-trip, 250-foot descent on the way in. The trail gradient is generally good, from Alpine Dam (648 feet) to Kent Lake (403 feet).

Two wildlife notes: Bear scat has been sighted and verified twice on the far reaches of the Pump Trail. Also note that in late March, April, and May, there is often an active osprey nest atop a dead snag near the end of the trail at Kent Lake.

User Groups: Hikers, dogs, horses, and mountain bikes. No wheelchair facilities.

Permits: No permits are required. Groups are limited to 19 people. Parking and access are free.

Maps: A hiking and biking map is available for a fee from the Marin Water District. For a topographic map, ask the USGS for Bolinas.

Directions: From San Francisco, take U.S. 101 over the Golden Gate Bridge and continue 7.5 miles to the exit for Sir Francis Drake Boulevard. Take that exit (toward San Anselmo) and continue 0.4 mile and merge with Sir Francis Drake Boulevard. Continue 3.5 miles (get in left lane) to Center Boulevard. Turn left on center and drive 1.7 miles into Fairfax (becomes Broadway Boulevard) to Bolinas Road. Turn left on Bolinas Road and drive 7.6 miles (becomes Bolinas-Fairfax Road, curvy) to Alpine Dam and very limited parking on shoulder on right, and Pump Trail (a gated service road) on right.

Contact: Sky Oaks Ranger Station, 415/945-1181; Marin Municipal Water District, 415/945-1195, www.marinwater.org.

27 PINE MOUNTAIN/ CARSON FALLS

3.0 mi/1.5 hr

on Mount Tamalpais west of Fairfax

Map 7.1, page 277

Carson Falls has five decks and drops that span nearly 100 feet, from top to bottom. This hike is a three-mile round-trip, rated easy. The best view is near the brink of the last waterfall. Turn and look up. You get a beautiful view upstream of four waterfalls, pool-and-drop, pouring over boulders in a deep gorge. Just below you is the rim of a 35-foot freefall. The walk to this quiet, divine spot hidden in deep valley on the north slopes of Mount Tamalpais is an easy stroll across hilly grasslands (often accompanied by a hawk or two floating about overhead), followed by a short jog down a canyon into the Carson Creek drainage.

The trailhead (at 1,078 feet) is adjacent to one of the larger parking areas along trailheads on Bolinas-Fairfax Road. After parking, cross Bolinas-Fairfax Road to reach the trailhead, Pine Mountain Road, a water district service road. The road climbs 400 feet over the course of a mile, and merges into a junction with Oat Hill Road on the crest of a hill flanked on both sides by foothill grasslands. Turn left here and in 0.25 mile you'll reach a sign for the Carson Falls turnoff on your right. Here you'll leave the fire roads and follow a trail for 0.5 mile to Carson Creek, a small bridge and the series of waterfalls.

User Groups: Hikers, dogs, and horses. Mountain bikes are allowed on Pine Mountain and Oat Hill Roads, but not on the hiking trail down to Carson Falls. No wheelchair facilities.

Permits: No permits are required. Groups are limited to 19 people. Parking and access are free.

Maps: A hiking and biking map is available for a fee from the Marin Water District. For a topographic map, ask the USGS for Bolinas.

Directions: From San Francisco, take U.S. 101 over the Golden Gate Bridge and continue 7.5 miles to the exit for Sir Francis Drake Boulevard. Take that exit (toward San Anselmo) and continue 0.4 mile and merge with Sir Francis Drake Boulevard. Continue 3.5 miles (get in left lane) to Center Boulevard. Turn left on center and drive 1.7 miles into Fairfax (becomes Broadway Boulevard) to Bolinas Road. Turn left on Bolinas Road and drive for 3.8 miles (past the golf course) to the large dirt parking area on the left. The trailhead for Pine Mountain Road and an information billboard are across the road from the parking area.

Contact: Sky Oaks Ranger Station, 415/945-1181; Marin Municipal Water District, 415/945-1195, www.marinwater.org.

28 CARSON FALLS LOOP
7.4 mi/3.5 hr   🥾3   ⛰10

on Mount Tamalpais west of Fairfax

Map 7.1, page 277

How can you take a great hike and make it better? By hiking to Carson Falls, and turning it into a stellar loop hike, sensational from late winter through spring. Start the trip by hiking up Pine Mountain Fire Road for one mile, gaining 300 feet, to the junction with Oat Hill Road. The route up provides sweeping views of surrounding foothills and beyond, including an awesome look at the remote north flank of Mount Tamalpais, and glimpses of Alpine Lake. It's common to see red-tailed hawks hunting and hovering. At the ridge and road junction, turn left at Oat Hill Road and walk 0.25 mile, or about five minutes. At the large sign for Carson Falls, turn right and leave the fire roads behind. The trail is a series of switchbacks downhill for 0.5 mile. This fern-lined stretch of single-track deposits you on a narrow, artfully constructed footbridge above Carson Falls. Cross it and work your way down on the far side of the stream to the waterfalls. The best "ah" moment is just below the midway point, where you can look up and see three pool-and-drop waterfalls and a short cascade.

It's only a three-mile trip, out and back, to Carson Falls. This is how you can extend the trip to a great 7.4-mile loop hike: From the falls, continue down the Little Carson Trail to the Kent Pump Road, bear left, and continue 1.4 miles above Kent Lake to Old Vee Road. Turn left and climb 1.2 miles up to Oat Hill Road. Turn left and hike 1.5 miles along the ridge to Pine Mountain Road. Turn right and return one mile downhill to the parking area. Rating: Fantastic.

User Groups: Hikers, dogs, horses, and mountain bikes. No wheelchair facilities. Note that mountain bikes are allowed on Pine Mountain and Oat Hill Roads, but not on the hiking trail down to Carson Falls.

Permits: No permits are required. Groups are limited to 19 people. Parking and access are free.

Maps: A hiking and biking map is available for a fee from the Marin Water District. For a topographic map, ask the USGS for Bolinas.

Directions: From San Francisco, take U.S. 101 over the Golden Gate Bridge and continue 7.5 miles to the exit for Sir Francis Drake Boulevard. Take that exit (toward San Anselmo) and continue 0.4 mile and merge with Sir Francis Drake Boulevard. Continue 3.5 miles (get in left lane) to Center Boulevard. Turn left on center and drive 1.7 miles into Fairfax (becomes Broadway Boulevard) to Bolinas Road. Turn left on Bolinas Road and drive for 3.8 miles (past the golf course) to the large dirt parking area on the left. The trailhead for Pine Mountain Road and an information billboard are across the road from the parking area.

Contact: Sky Oaks Ranger Station, 415/945-1181; Marin Municipal Water District, 415/945-1195, www.marinwater.org.

29 TWO LAKES TRAIL
5.0 mi/2.5 hr   🥾2   ⛰10

on Mount Tamalpais at Lagunitas Lake near San Anselmo

Map 7.1, page 277

This is our favorite hike at Bon Tempe and Lagunitas Lakes. Note that there is no officially named "Two Lakes Trail," so don't look for a sign. As you clear the rise, Lagunitas Lake first comes into view and the beauty hits you all at once: A pristine little lake, backed by forest and the rising slopes of the northeast face of Mount Tamalpais. This walk is pretty, easy, featuring tons of birds and maybe a turtle or two sunning on a rock or log, and can be shorted to a really easy 40-minute loop around Lagunitas (easy enough for baby strollers).

The trailhead lies at an elevation of 740 feet at the Lagunitas Picnic Area, adjacent to Lagunitas Lake, the smallest of Marin County's eight lakes. Walk past the picnic area and then hike up to the earthen dam. You'll pop out with a pretty lake view and a sign warning visitors to watch out for migrating newts. Walk around Lagunitas Lake counterclockwise, where you eventually link up with Pilot Knob Trail. Turn left, hike past the parking area, and connect with Bon Tempe Shadyside Trail. This route circles the lake (with one short juncture on the Sky Oaks Trail) and eventually leads all the way back to the parking area. As with any loop that links different trails, a map can be helpful, especially for newcomers. Pick one up at the entrance station.

User Groups: Hikers, leashed dogs. No horses or mountain bikes. Limited wheelchair facilities.

Permits: A day-use fee of $8 is charged per vehicle. A self-pay station accepts credit cards, $1, $5, and $10 bills, and cannot make change. Groups are limited to 19 people.

Maps: A hiking and biking map is available for a fee from the Marin Water District. For a topographic map, ask the USGS for Bolinas.

Directions: From San Francisco, take U.S. 101 over the Golden Gate Bridge and continue 7.5 miles to the exit for Sir Francis Drake Boulevard. Take that exit (toward San Anselmo) and continue 0.4 mile and merge with Sir Francis Drake Boulevard. Continue 3.5 miles (get in left lane) to Center Boulevard. Turn left on center and drive 1.7 miles into Fairfax (becomes Broadway Boulevard) to Bolinas Road. Turn left on Bolinas Road and drive 1.5 miles to Sky Oaks Road on left. Turn left and drive 0.5 mile to the entrance station. Then continue:

To Lagunitas Lake: From the entrance station, go 0.25 mile to a fork. Bear left and drive 1.25 miles to the parking and picnic area. Park and hike uphill on the service road to dam, lake, and trailhead.

To Bon Tempe Lake: From the entrance station, go 0.25 mile to a fork. Bear right on Bon Tempe Road and drive 0.2 mile to the parking area. Walk a short distance to the dam/spillway for lake access and the nearby trailhead.

Contact: Sky Oaks Ranger Station,

415/945-1181; Marin Municipal Water District, 415/945-1195, www.marinwater.org.

30 DEER PARK TRAIL/ BALD HILL

2.0 mi/1.25 hr

on Mount Tamalpais near San Anselmo

Map 7.1, page 277

The trailhead at Deer Park is one of the most popular in the sphere of influence of Mount Tamalpais. The Deer Park Trail provides nature, peace, and a 350-foot climb in a mile. Pleasure you will get. The trail rises up the slopes of Bald Hill and the views open up around you. It is also common to see deer in this area, and wildflower blooms are quite good in the spring. This is also one of the areas where bear scat was sighted and verified. If you want even more, you'll have an opportunity to link up with a mosaic of other trails in the area.

User Groups: Hikers only. No dogs, horses, or mountain bikes. No wheelchair facilities.

Permits: No permits are required. Groups are limited to 19 people. Parking and access are free.

Maps: A hiking and biking map is available for a fee from the Marin Water District. For a topographic map, ask the USGS for San Rafael.

Directions: From San Francisco, take U.S. 101 over the Golden Gate Bridge and continue 7.5 miles to the exit for Sir Francis Drake Boulevard. Take that exit (toward San Anselmo) and continue 0.4 mile and merge with Sir Francis Drake Boulevard. Continue 3.5 miles (get in left lane) to Center Boulevard. Turn left on center and drive 1.7 miles into Fairfax (becomes Broadway Boulevard) to Bolinas Road. Turn left on Bolinas Road and drive 0.5 mile to Porteous Avenue. Turn left on Porteous Avenue and continue to Deer County Park. If you walk behind the school on the left, and completely pass it, the trailhead will be on your left.

Contact: Marin County Parks and Open Space

District, 415/499-6387, www.marincountyparks.org.

31 SHORELINE TRAIL
5.0 mi/2.5 hr   🚶1 ⛰7

in China Camp State Park east of San Rafael

Map 7.1, page 277

China Camp is located on the shore of San Pablo Bay. The park provides sensational water views, picnic sites on bluffs overlooking the shore, great mountain biking, hikes through the woods to world-class lookouts, cultural history, camping, wetlands for birds, and a nearby fishing pier. The Shoreline Trail can provide an introduction. From the trailhead, the trail meanders along the shore of San Pablo Bay, bordered by undisturbed hills on one side and waterfront on the other. The first mile provides good lookouts across the bay; the last 0.5 mile crosses a meadow, then runs adjacent to tidal areas, marshes, and wetlands that are home to many species of waterfowl. The hike doesn't involve serious elevation gains or losses, so you won't face any surprise climbs.

User Groups: Hikers, horses, and mountain bikes. No dogs. No wheelchair facilities.

Permits: No permits are required. A state park day-use fee of $5 per vehicle is charged at the entrance station. Get receipt to park at different sites.

Maps: A brochure and map are available for a fee at park headquarters or by contacting the state parks district office. For a topographic map, ask the USGS for San Quentin.

Directions: Take U.S. 101 to San Rafael and the exit for North San Pedro. Take that exit and drive east four miles to park. At the fork (with a kiosk and campground on right), stay left and drive one mile (past the picnic areas on the left) to the ranger station, on the right, and the trailheads.

Alternate directions if arriving from the south/San Francisco: From the Golden Gate Bridge, continue north on U.S. 101 for 11.5 miles and the exit for Central San Rafael. Take

that exit for 0.2 mile to (second right) 2nd Street. Turn right at Second Street and drive (becomes 3rd Street) 0.7 mile (shopping center on right) and continue ahead 5.2 miles (slow down, speed trap at curves, then you'll pass Loch Lomond on right) to park entrance; trailheads, campground on left access roads, blufftop picnic sites on right.

Contact: China Camp State Park, 415/456-0766; California State Parks, Marin District, 415/898-4362, www.parks.ca.gov.

32 PATRICK'S POINT
5.0 mi/2.5 hr   🚶3 ⛰10

in China Camp State Park east of San Rafael

Map 7.1, page 277

A stroke of genius by a state park ranger has created the Bay Area's greatest new lookout. In this case, the strokes of genius were made by a chainsaw. Ranger Patrick Robards, a fire science specialist, ordered a hilltop grove of eucalyptus taken out at China Camp State Park. The result at this spot is a jaw-dropping, five-bridge view of the bay and the region's mountain peaks, as well as a Marin-360 that will have you wishing your neck could full-pivot swivel. So, we named the spot Patrick's Point, and the name has stuck.

This trip starts with the drive on North San Pedro Road from San Rafael out to the Marin shoreline along San Pablo Bay. When you reach a fork to a ranger kiosk, instead stay left on the main road (turning right to the kiosk will take you to the park's campground entrance). Continue on the main road past the sensational picnic areas (on the left, at water's edge) to the turnoff on the right to the ranger station. This is your starting point. From here, it is a 2.5-mile loop with a 500-foot climb to McNear's Ridge and Patrick's Point.

Near the ranger station, with the park map in hand, start at the Shoreline trailhead. Take the Shoreline Trail north (you'll have good views of the San Pablo Bay shore) to the Oak Ridge Trail. Turn left on the Oak Ridge Trail and climb steadily to a junction with the McNear's Fire Trail. Turn right and you pop out on top. Note that on the park map, the lookout is not marked.

What a view: On clear days, you can see the Bay Bridge, the Richmond-San Rafael Bridge, the Carquinez Bridge, the Benicia Bridge, and the tops of the Golden Gate Bridge. We've seen crystal-clear days from this lookout where it seemed you could take a running start and then leap across the bay and land on Point Pinole.

User Groups: Hikers, horses, and mountain bikes. No dogs. No wheelchair facilities.

Permits: No permits are required. A fee of $5 per vehicle is charged at China Camp Village. Get receipt to park at different sites.

Maps: A brochure and map are available for a fee at park headquarters or by contacting the state parks district office. For a topographic map, ask the USGS for San Quentin.

Directions: Take U.S. 101 to San Rafael and the exit for North San Pedro. Take that exit and drive east four miles to park. At the fork (with a kiosk and campground on right), stay left and drive one mile (past the picnic areas on the left) to the ranger station, on the right, and the trailheads.

Alternate directions if arriving from the south/San Francisco: From the Golden Gate Bridge, continue north on U.S. 101 for 11.5 miles and the exit for Central San Rafael. Take that exit for 0.2 mile to (second right) 2nd Street. Turn right at Second Street and drive (becomes 3rd Street) 0.7 mile (shopping center on right) and continue ahead 5.2 miles (slow down, speed trap at curves, then you'll pass Loch Lomond on right) to park entrance; trailheads, campground on left access roads, blufftop picnic sites on right.

Contact: China Camp State Park, 415/456-0766; California State Parks, Marin District, 415/898-4362, www.parks.ca.gov.

33 MARTIN GRIFFIN PRESERVE/AUDUBON CANYON RANCH TRAIL
0.4 mi/0.25 hr 🥾2 ⛰️10

in Martin Griffin Preserve near Bolinas Lagoon

Map 7.1, page 277   **BEST (**

In most years, Audubon Canyon is a slice of paradise. This is the number one habitat on the Pacific Coast to view herons and egrets, those large, graceful seabirds, as they court, mate, nest, and rear their young. In some years, though, usually in drought, the birds have not shown up in significant enough numbers to make the trip, and worse, to open the property to the public.

From headquarters, the hike is short with a 200-foot climb that requires about 20 minutes to reach the canyon overlook. Benches are provided for rest stops. Scopes are installed at the top to peer across the valley and zero in on the giant nests in the redwoods. Bird-watchers might want to repeat this great trip again and again, tracking the mating process of the great birds. The ritual starts when the male offers the female a twig. If the offer is accepted, the two then build a nest together. If rebuffed, the male then seeks another mate. Not much different than humans, eh? May and June are usually the best times to come. In May, the eggs start hatching, and by June, there can be as many as 200 hatchlings in the different nests. They eagerly await breakfast, lunch, and dinner, which are provided when their huge parents return from Bolinas Lagoon and vomit the goodies all over the nest. Hey, what's for dessert? First flight is an amazing event, when the young birds are given the heave-ho and have about 100 feet to figure how this flying thing works.

Note: Martin Griffin Preserve was renamed to honor Marty Griffin and recognize his role in protecting the Marin coast. For 40 years, it was known as Bolinas Lagoon Preserve of Audubon Canyon Ranch. The preserve is open only on weekends and holidays (10am-4pm, mid-Mar.-mid-July).

User Groups: Hikers only. No dogs, horses, or mountain bikes. No wheelchair facilities.

Permits: Entrance to the ranch is free, but donations are requested; a $15 donation from families is suggested.

Maps: A small trail map and brochure are available at ranch headquarters. For a topographic map, ask the USGS for Bolinas.

Directions: From San Francisco, take U.S. 101 north over the Golden Gate Bridge and continue four miles to Marin and to Exit 445B for Highway 1/Stinson Beach. Take that exit and continue west for one mile to the stoplight at a T intersection (Tam Junction) for Shoreline Highway/Highway 1. Turn left on Shoreline Highway and drive 11 miles to Stinson Beach. Continue north on Highway 1 for 3.5 miles to the preserve entrance gate on the right.

Contact: Audubon Canyon Ranch, 415/868-9244, www.egret.org.

34 CATARACT FALLS
2.5 mi/1.5 hr

on Mount Tamalpais at Alpine Lake Dam

Map 7.1, page 277

Cataract Falls is not a single waterfall, but a series of cascades that rushes down a beautifully wooded canyon set in the northwest slopes of Mount Tamalpais. For those who search out the top-rated hikes, there's many a day when this trail is definitely a 10. At times, when the canyon is flush with water, it can rate as one of the best winter day hikes in California. In summer and fall, when the creek is rendered a trickle or even goes dry, it's more like a 7.

From the trailhead at the south end of Alpine Lake (elevation 644 feet), you face a 750-foot climb over the span of just a mile to reach the centerpiece falls at 1,400 feet. Some hikers take the route from the Laurel Dell trailhead, which has a 240-foot drop over 0.4 mile. The canyon's prettiest falls are at an elevation range of about 1,200 to 1,400 feet.

The trail starts by contouring along a cove of Alpine Lake. It then rises from the lake,

climbing up into a lush canyon where there seems to be one small waterfall after another. These are not big free falls like in Yosemite, but rather small cascades, surrounded by luxuriant riparian beauty. Compared to almost anywhere in the Bay Area environs after such recent heavy rains, the collective beauty can seem nonpareil.

In late winter, especially when the skies have just cleared after heavy rains, the cascades in this canyon can look like something found in Hawaii. This is particularly true when rays of sunlight catch the droplets of water just right, and the refracted light makes them sparkle. From top to bottom, there's one cascade after another, crowned by a silvery chute pouring into a plunge pool. After getting your fill of this sight, return the way you came.

The trailhead is a few hundred yards past the west side of the dam at Alpine Lake. This is the best-known fall in the region, and parking along the road is extremely limited, often making for a frustrating encounter on weekends, especially Sundays in winter after a Saturday rain.

User Groups: Hikers and dogs. No horses or mountain bikes. No wheelchair facilities.

Permits: No permits are required. Groups are limited to 19 people. Parking and access are free.

Maps: A hiking and biking map is available for a fee from the Marin Water District. For a topographic map, ask the USGS for Bolinas.

Directions: From San Francisco, take U.S. 101 over the Golden Gate Bridge and continue 7.5 miles to the exit for Sir Francis Drake Boulevard. Take that exit (toward San Anselmo) and continue 0.4 mile and merge with Sir Francis Drake Boulevard. Continue 3.5 miles (get in left lane) to Center Boulevard. Turn left on center and drive 1.7 miles into Fairfax (becomes Broadway Boulevard) to Bolinas Road. Turn left on Bolinas Road and drive eight miles, cross Alpine Dam, and continue a short distance to the trailhead on the left. Park on the road's shoulder (usually on the right); it often fills quickly on Sunday mornings in winter.

Contact: Sky Oaks Ranger Station, 415/945-1181; Marin Municipal Water District, 415/945-1195, www.marinwater.org; Mount Tamalpais State Park, 415/388-2070; California State Parks, Marin District, 415/898-4362, www.parks.ca.gov.

35 LAUREL DELL LOOP
2.5 mi/1.5 hr 🚶1 ⛰8

in Mount Tamalpais State Park

Map 7.1, page 277

Laura Dell trailhead provides the easiest route to Cataract Falls. Instead of the climb from Bolinas-Fairfax Road and Alpine Lake (see the previous listing), here you start high and glide down to the upper set of falls, then return via a gentle loop. The trailhead is at 1,640 feet. Walk down fire road 0.7 mile to the Laurel Dell picnic site, then turn left on Cataract Trail for a one-mile descent into the steep canyon to see Cataract Falls. You'll descend past a series of tiny waterfalls in a lush setting. When running at full strength, the cascades are a precious sight. The canyon's prettiest falls are at an elevation range of about 1,200 feet. Many prefer first sight of the falls as a frontal, and that's when the trailhead at Bolinas-Fairfax Road/Alpine Lake is more popular.

To do this loop, continue along the Cataract Trail to the High Marsh Trail. Turn right on the High Marsh Trail, hike onward, and turn right at any of the next three trail intersections to return to the Laurel Dell trailhead. Of the three choices, the second makes the best return loop, as the short cutoff will put you within a few hundred yards of the trailhead.

User Groups: Hikers and dogs. No horses or mountain bikes. No wheelchair facilities.

Permits: No permits are required. Parking and access are free.

Maps: A brochure and map of Mount Tamalpais State Park is available for a small fee at the visitors center or by writing to the address below. For topographic maps, ask the USGS for Bolinas and San Rafael.

Directions: From San Francisco, take U.S. 101 north over the Golden Gate Bridge and continue four miles to Marin and the exit for Highway 1/Stinson Beach. Take that exit and continue west for one mile to the stoplight at T intersection for Shoreline Highway/Highway 1. Turn left on Shoreline Highway and drive 2.6 miles to the Panoramic Highway. Bear right on Panoramic Highway and drive (at junction for Muir Woods, continue straight) 5.2 miles to Pantoll Road. Bear right on Pantoll Road and go 1.4 miles to T intersection at Rock Spring and Ridgecrest Boulevard. Turn left and drive 1.4 miles to trailhead (look for fire road) on right.

Must-do summit: From Laurel Dell, turn left on Ridgecrest and drive 4.5 miles to East Peak.

Contact: Mount Tamalpais State Park, 415/388-2070; California State Parks, Marin District, 415/898-4362, www.parks.ca.gov.

36 O'ROURKE'S BENCH / ROCK SPRINGS
0.6 mi/0.5 hr 🚶1 ⛰10

in Mount Tamalpais State Park

Map 7.1, page 277

One of the best easy walks in the Bay Area with a world-class payoff is the stroll to O'Rourke's Bench. On a clear day, the view seems to span to infinity. From this perch at 2,040 feet, coastal hills and valley plunge at your feet to the Pacific Ocean. In one turn of the head, you can take in unbelievable miles of sunlit charm, up and down the coast, across to San Francisco, and on crystal days, to the Mount Diablo summit. No matter where you live, your age or level of outdoor orientation, O'Rourke's Bench is a must-do.

The walk: From Rock Spring Parking (1,972-foot elevation), cross Ridgecrest and look for the trail on the south side of the road (at a junction with Pantoll Road). From here, it's an easy

0.3-mile walk (about 15 minutes) to the stone bench; a gentle uphill climb of 70 feet, where you emerge from the woods to the bench and lookout. You'll find a treasured plaque that says: "Give me these hills and the friends I love. I ask no other heaven. To our Dad O'Rourke, in joyous celebration of his 76th birthday, Feb. 25th, 1927. From the friends to whom he showed this heaven."

It's always good: Even when the coast is buried in fog, the lookout perch is high enough to usually be above the stratus layer. It can be like peering across the top of a gorgeous sea of fog. On clear days, the ocean can sparkle in refracted silvers. Plus it can be one of the best places anywhere to see a sunset. In addition, a network of trails provides a mosaic of connected routes out of Rock Spring, Mountain Theater, Bootjack, and Pantoll trailheads on the west flank of Mount Tamalpais.

User Groups: Hikers only. No dogs, horses, or mountain bikes. No wheelchair facilities.

Permits: No permits are required. Parking and access are free.

Maps: A hiking and biking map is available for a fee from the Marin Water District. For a topographic map, ask the USGS for San Rafael.

Directions: From San Francisco, take U.S. 101 north over the Golden Gate Bridge and continue four miles to Marin and the exit for Highway 1/Stinson Beach. Take that exit and continue west for one mile to the stoplight at T intersection for Shoreline Highway/Highway 1. Turn left on Shoreline Highway and drive 2.6 miles to the Panoramic Highway. Bear right on Panoramic Highway and drive (at junction, continue straight) 5.2 miles to Pantoll Road. At Pantoll, bear right on Pantoll Road and go 1.4 miles to Rock Spring and a T intersection with Ridgecrest Boulevard. Continue straight ahead to parking for Rock Spring Trailhead. If full, turn right on Ridgecrest and go 0.25 mile to Mountain Theater.

Contact: Mount Tamalpais State Park, 415/388-2070; California State Parks, Marin District, 415/898-4362, www.parks.ca.gov.

37 BARTH'S RETREAT
2.2 mi/1.0 hr   🚶🚶1 8

in Marin Water District

Map 7.1, page 277

From Rock Springs (1,972 feet), you'll find a trailhead at the north end of the parking lot. From here, walk 0.1 mile (you'll pass a junction/trailhead for Cataract Trail on your left), then another 0.1 mile to a fork (1,965 feet) with the Simmons Trail and a cut-off on the right that goes to parking for Mountain Theater. Continue ahead on the Simmons Trail for 0.9 mile to Barth Retreat (1,970 feet). Bring your trail lunch. This is one of Mount Tam's great walk-in picnic sites. Barth, by the way, was one Emil Barth, a prolific musician/hiker/trail-builder who constructed a camp here in the early 20th century. This route connects to an inland network of trails, from which you can explore for many treks; or simply return when ready.

User Groups: Hikers only. No dogs, horses, or mountain bikes. No wheelchair facilities.

Permits: No permits are required. Parking and access are free.

Maps: A hiking and biking map is available for a fee from the Marin Water District. For a topographic map, ask the USGS for San Rafael.

Directions: From San Francisco, take U.S. 101 north over the Golden Gate Bridge and continue four miles to Marin and the exit for Highway 1/Stinson Beach. Take that exit and continue west for one mile to the stoplight at T intersection for Shoreline Highway/Highway 1. Turn left on Shoreline Highway and drive 2.6 miles to the Panoramic Highway. Bear right on Panoramic Highway and drive (at junction, continue straight) 5.2 miles to Pantoll Road. At Pantoll, bear right on Pantoll Road and go 1.4 miles to Rock Spring and a T intersection with Ridgecrest Boulevard. Continue straight ahead to parking for Rock Spring Trailhead. If full, turn right on Ridgecrest and go 0.25 mile to parking for Mountain Theater.

Contact: Mount Tamalpais State Park,

415/388-2070; California State Parks, Marin District, 415/898-4362, www.parks.ca.gov.

38 MOUNTAIN THEATER / WEST POINT INN
3.0 mi/1.5 hr   👣1   ⛰7

in Marin Water District

Map 7.1, page 277

High on the southern slope of Mount Tamalpais, West Point Inn has provided a destination with sensational views and a quiet refuge at night for more than 100 years. From parking at Mountain Theater (elevation 2,060 feet), take the Rock Spring Trail for 1.7 miles to West Point Inn (1,785 feet). The trail is an easy glide. At one time, there were illegal mountain bikers who poached this trail, but that doesn't seem to happen much anymore. Your destination is West Point Inn. At certain lookout points from the inn, the views are great. You tower over San Francisco Bay, the Marin Headlands and across the Pacific. On late nights with a full moon, a layer of fog below can shimmer in silvers. The view nearly equals that from 2,571-foot East Peak, but without the weekend crowd around the Gardner Lookout.

It was first built in 1904 for those who rode up from Mill Valley on the "Crookedest Railroad in the World." That old railroad line is now a great mountain bike trek, and several hiking trails lead to West Point Inn as well. The inn is run as a co-op, and like a step back in time, has no electricity.

User Groups: Hikers only. No dogs, horses, or mountain bikes. No wheelchair facilities.

Permits: No permits are required. Parking and access are free.

Maps: A brochure and map of Mount Tamalpais State Park is available for a small fee at the visitors center or by writing to the address below. For a topographic map, ask the USGS for San Rafael. Much of this trail is on Marin Water District land; contact that agency to obtain a detailed map for a fee.

Directions: From San Francisco, take U.S.

101 north over the Golden Gate Bridge and continue four miles to the exit for Highway 1/ Stinson Beach. Take that exit and continue west for one mile to the stoplight at T intersection for Shoreline Highway/Highway 1. Turn left on Shoreline Highway and drive 2.6 miles to the Panoramic Highway. Bear right on Panoramic Highway and drive 5.3 miles to Pantoll. Bear right on Pantoll Road and drive 1.4 miles to a T with Ridgecrest Boulevard (Rock Spring parking and trailhead is directly ahead). Turn right on Ridgecrest and go 0.25 mile to the Mountain Theater Trailhead.

Contact: Mount Tamalpais State Park, 415/388-2070; California State Parks, Marin District, 415/898-4362, www.parks.ca.gov; Marin Municipal Water District, 415/945-1195, www.marinwater.org; West Point Inn, 415/388-9955 (not for reservations), http://westpointinn.com.

39 EAST PEAK MOUNT TAMALPAIS
0.4 mi/0.5-1.0 hr   👣1   ⛰10

in Mount Tamalpais State Park

Map 7.1, page 277   **BEST (**

Mount Tam is one of those rare spots that projects a feeling of power, and while standing on its highest point, you can sense that power flowing right through you. From Mount Tam's 2,571-foot East Peak there is no better place in the Bay Area to watch the sun set. How it makes you feel can stay with you for years. The hike is very short (after all, a parking lot is set right at the foot of the summit trail) but is quite steep. The trail rises about 330 feet to the top, at an elevation of 2,571 feet. An old lookout station is positioned at the summit, and hikers usually try to find a perch as close as possible to the top.

To the east, the bay resembles the Mediterranean Sea, like an azure pool sprinkled with islands. And at night, the lights of the bridges and the surrounding cities can give the Bay Area an almost surreal look. The true magic happens at sunset, particularly on foggy days. The peak stands well above the top of the fog layer, and when the fiery sun dips into that low stratus to the west, orange light can be refracted for hundreds of miles around. Witness this stunning sight even one time, and you will gain a new perspective about what might be possible in this world.

User Groups: Hikers only. Dogs are permitted on the paved trail but not on the mountain-top overlook. No horses or mountain bikes. No wheelchair access on the trail, but good views are available from the wheelchair-accessible parking lot.

Permits: No permits are required. A parking fee of $8 per vehicle is charged.

Maps: A brochure and map of Mount Tamalpais State Park is available for a small fee at the visitors center, located adjacent to the parking area, or by writing to the address below. For a topographic map, ask the USGS for San Rafael.

Directions: From San Francisco, take U.S. 101 north over the Golden Gate Bridge and continue four miles to the exit for Highway 1/Stinson Beach. Take that exit and continue west for one mile to the stoplight at T intersection for Shoreline Highway/Highway 1. Turn left on Shoreline Highway and drive 2.6 miles to the Panoramic Highway. Bear right on Panoramic Highway and drive 5.3 miles to Pantoll. Bear right on Pantoll Road and drive 1.4 miles to a T with Ridgecrest Boulevard. Turn right on Ridgecrest and go three miles to East Peak and parking. The road dead-ends at the parking area at the base of the summit and trailhead.

Contact: Mount Tamalpais State Park, 415/388-2070; California State Parks, Marin District, 415/898-4362, www.parks.ca.gov.

40 INSPIRATION POINT

2.6 mi/1.0 hr

in Mount Tamalpais State Park

Map 7.1, page 277

Inspiration Point provides an alternative to the East Peak of Mount Tamalapis. You can get a similar kind of magic without all the people. Park at the lot on the summit. Instead of heading up to the East Peak after parking, instead hike the fire road, Eldridge Grade. The trail wraps around the northern flank of the East Peak, then makes a hairpin turn to the left around North Knee, set at 2,000 feet. At this point, a view below of the bay comes into your scope. Inspiration Peak awaits just down the road. At the hairpin right turn, take the short cutoff trail on the left, and you will quickly reach the top at 2,040 feet. This is a vantage point for miles and miles of charmed views. All can seem enchanted. The elevation loss and gain is roughly 200 feet. Much of this trail is not on state park land but land managed by the Marin Water District.

User Groups: Hikers, dogs, and mountain bikes. No horses. No wheelchair access on the trail, but good views are available from the wheelchair-accessible parking lot.

Permits: No permits are required. A parking fee of $8 per vehicle is charged at the summit parking lot.

Maps: A brochure and map of Mount Tamalpais State Park is available for a small fee at the visitors center, located adjacent to the parking area, or by writing to the address below. For a topographic map, ask the USGS for San Rafael.

Directions: From San Francisco, take U.S. 101 north over the Golden Gate Bridge and continue four miles to the exit for Highway 1/Stinson Beach. Take that exit and continue west for one mile to the stoplight at T intersection for Shoreline Highway/Highway 1. Turn left on Shoreline Highway and drive 2.6 miles to the Panoramic Highway. Bear right on Panoramic Highway and drive 5.3 miles to Pantoll. Bear right on Pantoll Road and drive 1.4 miles to a T with Ridgecrest Boulevard. Turn right on Ridgecrest and go three miles to East Peak and parking. The road dead-ends at the parking area at the base of the summit and trailhead.

Contact: Mount Tamalpais State Park, 415/388-2070; California State Parks, Marin District, 415/898-4362, www.parks.ca.gov.

41 PHOENIX LAKE LOOP
4.5 mi/1.5 hr   👫2 ⛰9

on Mount Tamalpais near Ross

Map 7.1, page 277

Trailhead parking is terrible, but the hike is great. The latter trumps the former as the Marin Water District told us this is one of the most popular hikes in the Mount Tam watershed. The little 25-acre jewel set in a pocket just west of the town of Ross is indeed well loved. If you get a parking spot, something of a miracle on weekends, you'll see the gate, and from there, it's an 0.3-mile walk on a fire road to the spillway (pretty in winter) and on to Phoenix Lake (174 feet elevation). The trail skirts above the lake to the right. Many just go to the lake, have a picnic, sit on one of the benches, fish a little, and then head back. For a loop around the lake, continue ahead to a major junction, the Phoenix Junction, one mile in, (196 feet). Turn left on the Phoenix Ord Trail, which skirts above the southern shore of the lake for 1.1 miles, then turns left (along the shoreline) for 0.7 mile and reaches the spur that takes you back to parking. The lake is pretty, the views of the watershed are great, and in spring, this one is spectacular.

Note: From Phoenix Junction, you can instead hike straight ahead to Lagunitas and Bon Tempe Lakes, or turn right to the watershed interior and a junction called Six Points. Both are great hikes.

User Groups: Hikers, leashed dogs, horses, and mountain bikes (restricted from the lake's southern shoreline). No wheelchair facilities.

Permits: No permits are required. Groups are limited to 19 people. Parking and access are free.

Maps: A hiking and biking map is available for a fee from the Marin Water District. For a topographic map, ask the USGS for San Rafael.

Directions: From San Francisco, take U.S. 101 over the Golden Gate Bridge and continue 7.5 miles to the exit for Sir Francis Drake Boulevard. Take that exit (toward San Anselmo) and continue 0.4 mile and merge with Sir Francis Drake Boulevard. Continue west for 2.5 miles to Lagunitas Road. Turn left on Lagunitas Road and drive 1.1 miles and park along the road. Parking is extremely limited, space for about 20 cars, and is located near a residential area with No Parking signs in front of homes.

Contact: Sky Oaks Ranger Station, 415/945-1181; Marin Municipal Water District, 415/945-1195, www.marinwater.org.

42 DAWN FALLS
2.2 mi/1.0 hr

in Baltimore Canyon Open Space Preserve near Larkspur

Map 7.1, page 277

A pretty walk in the woods leads to one of Marin's romantic spots, Dawn Falls, your destination and reward in Baltimore Canyon Open Space. When refreshed by rain, Dawn Falls pours in a narrow stream over the brink and falls 25 feet in a silvery chute to the rocks below. It is named "Dawn Falls" because there are spring days when the early morning sunlight catches the water just right and refracts in color. Dry weather reduces the cascade to a trickle, and in drought, it goes dry.

From the parking area, it's a few minute's walk down to Larkspur Creek, across the bridge to the junction with the Dawn Falls Trail. Turn right and you are on your way. The trail runs along the creek at the base of Baltimore Canyon (continue straight at a trail junction), then climbs 300 feet to the falls. You emerge on the left side, with a full-frontal view.

User Groups: Hikers and dogs. No mountain bikes or horses. No wheelchair facilities.

Permits: No permits are required. Groups are limited to 19 people. Parking and access are free.

Maps: A hiking and biking map is available for a fee from the Marin Water District. For a topographic map, ask the USGS for San Rafael.

Directions: Take U.S. 101 in Marin to Corte Madera and the exit for Paradise/Tamalpais

Drive. Take that exit to Tamalpais Drive, turn west and drive about a mile to Corte Madera Avenue. Turn right and drive (the road becomes Magnolia) about 0.6 mile to Madrone Avenue (the road narrows). Turn left on Madrone Avenue and drive 0.8 mile to the trailhead, at road's end.

Contact: Marin County Parks and Open Space, 415/499-6387, www.marincountyparks.org.

43 BOOTJACK: MATT DAVIS TO WEST POINT INN
3.6 mi/2.0 hr ⚑3 ⛰9

in Mount Tamalpais State Park

Map 7.1, page 277

With the new campground at Bootjack, the Matt Davis Trail takes on new significance. The trailhead (1,400 feet) is located on the north side of the Panoramic Highway. The trail is routed to a drainage for oft-dry Rattlesnake Creek. You then hike through hardwood forest to a trail junction (1,330 feet) near Laguna Creek, 1.3 miles in, with the Nora Trail. Turn left here and climb 455 feet over the course of 0.5 mile, through a series of switchbacks, to West Point Inn. The inn and its cabins were built at the turn of the century, and like a trip in a time machine, have no electricity.

User Groups: Hikers only. No dogs, horses, or mountain bikes. No wheelchair facilities.

Permits: No permits are required. A parking fee of $8 per vehicle is charged.

Maps: A brochure and map of Mount Tamalpais State Park is available for a small fee at the visitors center or by writing to the address below. For a topographic map, ask the USGS for San Rafael.

Directions: From San Francisco, take U.S. 101 north over the Golden Gate Bridge and continue four miles to Marin and the exit for Highway 1/Stinson Beach. Take that exit and continue west for 1 mile to the stoplight at T intersection for Shoreline Highway/Highway 1. Turn left on Shoreline Highway and drive 2.6

miles to the Panoramic Highway. At Panoramic Highway, bear right and drive (at junction for Muir Woods, continue straight) 4.7 miles to Bootjack on right.

Contact: Mount Tamalpais State Park, 415/388-2070; California State Parks, Marin District, 415/898-4362, www.parks.ca.gov; reserve cabins online at http://westpointinn.com.

44 PANTOLL: MATT DAVIS/ COAST TRAIL
6.4 mi/3.0 hr ⚑2 ⛰10

on Mount Tamalpais

Map 7.1, page 277

We know people search through the book for hikes that are rated as 2s and 3s for difficulty, and 9s or 10s for scenic beauty. This is one of those hikes. Just pick a clear day. The reward is heart-touching views of the Pacific Ocean. There are places where you can stop, spread your arms wide toward the ocean, and feel as if the entire world is within your grasp. From Pantoll parking and staging area (1,500 feet), cross the road (careful on weekends) for the trailhead for the Matt Davis Trail. In turn, the Matt Davis Trail leads 1.6 miles into the woods, generally where you contour along the foothills to a trail junction (1,540 feet) with the Coast Trail. Here you turn right on the Coast Trail and climb 280 feet over the course of 1.6 miles to the Willow Camp Fire Road (1,820 feet). In the process, you will have a series of coastal lookouts to the west. The Coast Trail here generally parallels Ridgecrest Boulevard and passes just below Ballou Point. Return when ready.

User Groups: Hikers only. No dogs, horses, or mountain bikes. No wheelchair facilities.

Permits: No permits are required. A parking fee of $8 per vehicle is charged.

Maps: A brochure and map of Mount Tamalpais State Park is available for a small fee at the visitors center or by writing to the address below. For a topographic map, ask the USGS for San Rafael.

Directions: From San Francisco, take U.S. 101 north over the Golden Gate Bridge and continue four miles to Marin and the exit for Highway 1/Stinson Beach. Take that exit and continue west for one mile to the stoplight at a T intersection for Shoreline Highway/Highway 1. Turn left on Shoreline Highway and drive 2.6 miles to the Panoramic Highway. Bear right on Panoramic Highway and drive 5.2 miles to Pantoll (at the four-way junction, continue straight). Turn left into the Pantoll parking area.

Contact: Mount Tamalpais State Park, 415/388-2070; California State Parks, Marin District, 415/898-4362, www.parks.ca.gov.

45 STEEP RAVINE TRAIL
3.4 mi/1.5 hr   👫2 ⛰10

on Mount Tamalpais

Map 7.1, page 277

Just add rain, and in a hike at Steep Ravine, the divine spirit of nature will baptize you. This is the prettiest canyon in Marin and one of the prettiest walks, when wet, that is, anywhere. From Pantoll, the trailhead is at the far west end of the parking area. From here, you descend quickly, including with steps, into the lush canyon. You'll arrive at the bottom of the ravine at pretty Webb Creek. Redwoods tower over you, and at times, the forest canopy closes off the sky. In some spots, ferns line the canyon walls. The trail follows Webb Creek, crossing the stream eight times in all. In less than a mile, you'll reach a drop-off with a ladder, and in high flows, this brink produces a small but pretty waterfall. The trail continues to a historic dam, 1.7 miles in, just downstream of the junction (and bridge) with the Dipsea Trail (580 feet elevation). It's a fine picnic site. Look close and you might see small fish in the pool. Head back when ready, a climb of 920 feet in 1.7 miles.

In the most violent rainstorms, this place is a refuge of peace. This is one of the few hikes best done during a rainstorm, and if that is not for you, try to time it just after heavy rain. In the canyon, the forest canopy protects you from a direct assault from the raindrops. Everything becomes vibrant with life as it drips with water.

User Groups: Hikers only. No dogs, horses, or mountain bikes. No wheelchair facilities.

Permits: No permits are required. A parking fee of $8 per vehicle is charged.

Maps: A brochure and map of Mount Tamalpais State Park is available for a small fee at the visitors center or by writing to the address below. For a topographic map, ask the USGS for San Rafael.

Directions: From San Francisco, take U.S. 101 north over the Golden Gate Bridge and continue four miles to Marin and the exit for Highway 1/Stinson Beach. Take that exit and continue west for one mile to the stoplight at a T intersection for Shoreline Highway/Highway 1. Turn left on Shoreline Highway and drive 2.6 miles to the Panoramic Highway. Bear right on Panoramic Highway and drive 5.2 miles to Pantoll (at the four-way junction, continue straight). Turn left into the Pantoll parking area.

Contact: Mount Tamalpais State Park, 415/388-2070; California State Parks, Marin District, 415/898-4362, www.parks.ca.gov.

46 COAST VIEW TRAIL
5.2 mi/1.5 hr   👫2 ⛰9

on Mount Tamalpais

Map 7.1, page 277

The Coast View Trail out of Pantoll has been a success in its test as a new multi-use trail at Mount Tamalpais State Park. Within five minutes, by bike or on foot, you will realize that state park rangers turned what was a good idea at headquarters into a stroke of genius in the field.

After parking, elevation 1,499 feet, face the ocean with the campground on your left and look for the service road ahead and to the left that heads west (it passes just above the Steep Ravine trailhead). This is how the trip starts, on a road. You will hike (or ride) on pavement a short distance to a ranger-service area and then continue as the road turns into a dirt fire road. In another 30 seconds, you emerge at a clearing and with it, get the trail's first great lookout of the ocean and San Francisco. From here, continue straight on the fire road, heading southwest toward Muir Beach. The service road continues 0.6 mile, crosses the Dipsea Trail (1,200 feet), and then becomes a multi-use Coast View Trail. This trail is about half the width of a fire road, what mountain bikers would call a double track. It is wide enough to pass on without those surprise "showdown" moments of truth with other trail users, yet narrow enough for an intimate feel. It is an easy downhill glide two miles to a foothill ridge (and gate) that overlooks Muir Beach (it's less than another mile to Highway 1). Return when ready, a climb of about 900 feet in 2.6 miles.

User Groups: Hikers and mountain bikes. No dogs or horses. No wheelchair facilities.

Permits: No permits are required. A parking fee of $8 per vehicle is charged.

Maps: A brochure and map of Mount Tamalpais State Park is available for a small fee at the visitors center or by writing to the address below. For a topographic map, ask the USGS for San Rafael.

Directions: From San Francisco, take U.S. 101 north over the Golden Gate Bridge and continue four miles to Marin and the exit for Highway 1/Stinson Beach. Take that exit and continue west for one mile to the stoplight at a T intersection for Shoreline Highway/Highway 1. Turn left on Shoreline Highway and drive 2.6 miles to the Panoramic Highway. Bear right on Panoramic Highway and drive 5.2 miles to Pantoll (at the four-way junction, continue straight). Turn left into the Pantoll parking area.

Contact: Mount Tamalpais State Park, 415/388-2070; California State Parks, Marin District, 415/898-4362, www.parks.ca.gov.

47 MOUNTAIN HOME
2.4 mi/1.0 hr

in Mount Tamalpais State Park

Map 7.1, page 277

This 1.2-mile hike at Mount Tamalpais ends at an inn, called the Tourist Club (private), perched on a mountainside. Park at the lot at Mountain Home, along Panoramic Highway. Take Panoramic Trail 0.4 mile (it parallels Panoramic Highway) to its junction with Redwood Trail. Turn right on the Redwood Trail and then descend 0.7 mile to the Tourist Club. This route laterals across the mountain slope before it drops into a pocket.

User Groups: Hikers only. No dogs, horses, or mountain bikes. No wheelchair facilities.

Permits: No permits are required. Parking and access are free.

Maps: A brochure and map of Mount Tamalpais State Park is available for a small fee at the visitors center or by writing to the address below. For a topographic map, ask the USGS for San Rafael.

Directions: From San Francisco, take U.S. 101 north over the Golden Gate Bridge and continue four miles to Marin and the exit for Highway 1/Stinson Beach. Take that exit and continue west for one mile to the stoplight at a T intersection for Shoreline Highway/Highway 1. Turn left on Shoreline Highway and drive 2.6 miles to the Panoramic Highway. Bear right on Panoramic Highway and drive 2.6 miles to Mountain Home. The trailhead for Panoramic Trail is located on the west side of the road.

Contact: Mount Tamalpais State Park, 415/388-2070; California State Parks, Marin District, 415/898-4362, www.parks.ca.gov; Tourist Club, 415/388-9987, www.touristclubsf.org.

48 MUIR BEACH OVERLOOK AND OWL TRAIL

3.5 mi/1.5 hr　　　🥾1 ⛺10

on the Marin coast south of Stinson Beach

Map 7.1, page 277

The view from Muir Beach Overlook is drop-dead beautiful, the kind of place that will melt the steel around the most armored souls. A trip to the Overlook, a hike on the adjacent Owl Trail, and a visit to nearby Slide Ranch and the tidal reef below can be one of the best ways to capture the sparkling day on the Marin coast.

The Owl Trail starts at the north side of the parking lot (440 feet elevation) and extends past Slide Ranch to a beach with an extended tidepool reef; 3.5 miles round-trip. From the trailhead at 440 feet, you descend 240 feet in a mile through chaparral with ocean views. The trail is routed through low-lying brush, which makes wearing shorts a prickly proposition. You then arrive at Slide Ranch. Slide Ranch is a small working farm, with chickens, sheep, goats, and more (we've seen ducks here that think they are chickens), that is accessible to the public; a great family trip. You then pass giant cypress trees (where great horned owls can nest, hence the name Owl Trail) and sail down to the beach. A rope is often available to descend down a short slippery spot to the beach. At the beach during low tides, you'll find an extended tidal reef where you can rock hop, find lots of little crabs, and which makes for a good site for a picnic.

User Groups: Hikers only. No dogs, horses, or mountain bikes. The Muir Beach Overlook is wheelchair accessible, but Owl Trail is not.

Permits: No permits are required. Parking and access are free.

Maps: A brochure and map are available at the Marin Headlands Visitors Center or by contacting the Golden Gate National Recreation Area, Marin Headlands. For a topographic map, ask the USGS for Point Bonita.

Directions: From San Francisco, take U.S. 101 north over the Golden Gate Bridge and continue four miles to Marin and the exit for Highway 1/Stinson Beach. Take that exit and continue west for one mile to the stoplight at a T intersection for Shoreline Highway/Highway 1. Turn left on Shoreline Highway and drive to a signed turn for Muir Beach Overlook. Turn left at the Muir Beach Overlook and drive a short distance to the parking area. The trailhead may at first seem hidden. It is often unsigned and located at the north side of the parking area.

Contact: Muir Woods National Monument, Mill Valley, CA 94941, 415/388-2595, www.nps.gov/muwo; Golden Gate National Recreation Area, visitors center, 415/561-4700.

49 REDWOOD CREEK TRAIL

1.5 mi/1.0 hr　　　🥾1 ⛺10

in Muir Woods National Monument

Map 7.1, page 277　　　　**BEST (**

The renovated Redwood Creek Trail is now a thing of beauty. Unbelievably, thousands of people take this walk amid the giant redwoods, and yet with the new boardwalks, some paved trail, there is no damage to this beautiful landscape. From the visitors center, take the Redwood Creek Trail out along Redwood Creek for 0.5 mile to a junction with the Fern Creek Trail (more on this to come) and then continue another 0.2 mile to a bridge (actually, it is Bridge 4). Cross the bridge to the Hillside Trail, turn left and return back to the bridge (actually, Bridge 1) and the visitors center. If you have physically challenged members of your group, the loop can be cut short at two other bridges.

The Fern Creek option: You can turn this trip into a gorgeous three-mile loop and escape the crowds. From the visitors center, follow the Redwood Creek Trail to a junction with Fern Creek Trail on the right. Turn right and hike Fern Creek Trail to the junction with the Lost Trail on the right. Turn right, then climb about 500 feet up to the junction with Canopy View Trail (it used to be called Ocean View Trail). Turn right again onto Canopy View Trail and follow the trail down to return to the valley floor.

User Groups: Hikers only. No dogs (except for seeing-eye dogs), horses, or mountain bikes. The first section of the trail is wheelchair-accessible.

Permits: An entry fee of $7 per person is charged, free for 15 and under. No permits are required.

Maps: A brochure and map are available for a fee at the visitors center or by contacting Muir Woods National Monument. For a topographic map, ask the USGS for San Rafael.

Directions: From San Francisco, take U.S. 101 north over the Golden Gate Bridge and continue four miles to Marin and to Exit 445B for Highway 1/Stinson Beach. Take that exit and continue west for one mile to the stoplight at a T intersection (Tam Junction) for Shoreline Highway/Highway 1. Turn left on Shoreline Highway and drive 2.6 miles to the Panoramic Highway. Bear right on Panoramic Highway and drive 0.8 mile to a junction with Muir Woods Road. Turn left and go 1.5 miles to the park entrance road (Camp Eastwood Road). Turn right and drive 0.2 mile to the parking lot. Note that a shuttle is available in summer and may be required during high-use periods.

Contact: Muir Woods National Monument, Mill Valley, 415/388-2595, www.nps.gov/muwo; Golden Gate National Recreation Area, visitors center, 415/561-4700.

50 CANOPY VIEW TRAIL
3.4 mi/1.5 hr

in Muir Woods National Monument

Map 7.1, page 277

This trail is worth knowing. When you arrive at Muir Woods and see tour buses shooting out people like popcorn from a popping machine, you'll be glad you read this. That is because Canopy View Trail provides the best chance of getting away from the crowds. After passing the visitors center and starting down the paved path on the valley floor, turn right on Canopy View Trail. In under a minute you will enter a different world, a world of solitude, beautiful redwoods, and, alas, a steep ascent.

From the valley floor, the trail heads up the east side of the canyon on a steady grade, steep enough to get you puffing. It climbs 570 feet in 1.2 miles. You rise above the valley to where you can look down into a sea of redwoods. To complete the loop, turn left on Lost Trail, elevation 750 feet, which descends quite steeply over just 0.4 mile back to the valley floor, at 300 feet. There you turn left on Fern Creek Trail. Turn left onto the main trail to return to headquarters. It's a great escape.

Avid hikers who know the area will remember that this was once called the "Ocean View Trail," even though there was no ocean view. Some wanted the name changed to the Panoramic Trail. We like the new name, Canopy View Trail.

User Groups: Hikers only. No dogs (except for seeing-eye dogs), horses, or mountain bikes. The first section of the trail is wheelchair-accessible.

Permits: An entry fee of $7 per person is charged. No permits are required.

Maps: A brochure and map are available for a fee at the visitors center or by contacting Muir Woods National Monument. For a topographic map, ask the USGS for San Rafael.

Directions: From San Francisco, take U.S. 101 north over the Golden Gate Bridge and continue four miles to Marin and to Exit 445B for Highway 1/Stinson Beach. Take that exit and continue west for one mile to the stoplight at a T intersection (Tam Junction) for Shoreline Highway/Highway 1. Turn left on Shoreline Highway and drive 2.6 miles to the Panoramic Highway. Bear right on Panoramic Highway and drive 0.8 mile to a junction with Muir Woods Road. Turn left and go 1.5 miles to the park entrance road (Camp Eastwood Road). Turn right and drive 0.2 mile to the parking lot. Note that a shuttle is available in summer and may be required during high-use periods.

Contact: Muir Woods National Monument, Mill Valley, 415/388-2595, www.nps.gov/muwo;

Golden Gate National Recreation Area, visitors center, 415/561-4700.

51 DIPSEA TRAIL
7.5 mi one-way/3.5 hr

on Mount Tamalpais from Mill Valley to Stinson Beach

Map 7.1, page 277

In your first steps on the Dipsea Trail, you walk—or run—in the strides of ghosts, shadows, and legends, just as thousands have done over the years. The cross-country Dipsea Trail race is world-renowned as the oldest and one of the most beautiful cross-country routes anywhere. The route spans 7.5 miles from Mill Valley to Stinson Beach, crossing the south flank of Mount Tamalpais, up and down from Old Mill Park through Muir Woods and Mount Tamalpais State Park and Steep Ravine en route to the coast. The origin of the name "Dipsea" has been argued about for years, but many figure it comes from the old days when some participants jumped into the ocean to cool off after completing the trek.

The route now has classy-looking mile markers along the way, and finally, after years, many junctions have trail signs. Regardless, the trip can turn into guesswork for newcomers. First-timers should go with a hiking partner who knows the way. With a shuttle car, you're looking at 7.5 miles one-way and with all the ridges and valleys, a cumulative climb of about 4,500 feet, and then a descent to Highway 1 at Stinson Beach.

The official starting point of the race is the Mill Valley Depot, where you run a short distance down the street to Old Mill Park (elevation 120 feet). For hiking, instead park along the road at Old Mill Park (it has a restroom). At the far side of the park, you head uphill and reach the first of three sets of steps, 688 in all (formerly 671 before they were reworked). The steps are legendary among Dipsea runners. Jack Kirk, who ran the Dipsea for 67 straight years, is credited with the celebrated quote about the steps: "Old Dipsea runners never die. They just reach the 672nd step."

When the trail tops the stairs and reaches pavement, look for the arrows painted on the street to mark the way (at times, the arrows can be faint). They will route you along Sequoia Road, Walsh Drive, and then across the Panoramic Highway (elevation 560 feet) at Windy Gap. From here the trail continues across a hill peppered with expensive homes before plunging down a wooded canyon to the entrance of Muir Woods National Monument. Trail runners called this downhill plunge "Suicide."

Here, the trail signs improve. You emerge at the Muir Woods parking lot. At the bottom of the canyon, the trail crosses a temporary bridge (removed during high flows) at Redwood Creek (elevation 150 feet). You then grind out a climb in forest up past the Hogsback (elevation 730 feet), emerge past a grassland meadow, and then climb again into dense woodlands called The Rainforest. The climb gets steep as you rise through The Rainforest, up the 400-foot climb of Cardiac Hill, and then emerges at a clearing and trail junction (elevation 1,360 feet), the highest point on the route.

On clear days, this is where the ocean first comes into view. With portable restrooms, this site can provide the ideal lunch break. The major climbs are over and the ocean ahead. Unlike mono-landscapes in many areas, the Dipsea provides a mosaic of habitats, from oak woodlands, with bays, oaks, acacias and eucalyptus, into the conifers, with Douglas firs and redwoods, interspersed by meadows and riparian zones.

From that clearing with the view, you descend 1.5 miles through cathedral redwoods into Steep Ravine. The trail crosses a bridge at Webb Creek (elevation 580 feet), where everybody stops to gaze upstream at the pretty brook, edged by sword ferns, bracken ferns, and redwoods, enclosed by a towering forest canopy. Newcomers to the Dipsea may think the climbs are all done, but Insult Hill waits ahead. After that short grind, your reward is that sensational ocean views are then revealed.

Much of the descent to Stinson Beach is breathtaking, where it feels like you can open your arms wide and take in the entire expanse of the Pacific. A panorama of the ocean, Stinson Beach, and beyond to Duxbury Point comes into view. Most seem to get a second wind and rocket out of the hardwood forest. You emerge along the Panoramic Highway (a short distance from Highway 1), where there is a large dirt area for parking on the north side. You have thus completed America's landmark cross-country route. There aren't many rites of passage and this is one of them.

The length of the Dipsea has been argued over time, but Darrell White, who runs the race and is on the Dipsea Board of Directors, walked the route with GPS and a mileage wheel and verified the exact distance at 7.51 miles. In the process, he installed the mileage markers, with classy brass plates embedded in small boulders.

User Groups: Hikers only. No dogs, horses, or mountain bikes. No wheelchair facilities.

Permits: No permits required. Parking and access is free at the primary trailhead, but the trail can be accessed from Muir Woods and Mount Tamalpais State Park, where there are fees. If you start at Mount Tamalpais State Park, an $8 fee is charged per vehicle.

Maps: The Dipsea Trail crosses several jurisdictions. A brochure and map of Mount Tamalpais State Park is available for a small fee at the visitors center or by contacting Mount Tamalpais State Park. For topographic maps, ask the USGS for San Rafael and Bolinas.

Logistics: Hikers should be partnered and work out a shuttle: Drive two cars to end of trail at Panoramic Highway at Stinson Beach and park one car at dirt area on wide shoulder on north side of Panoramic Highway, located across from end of trail. Then drive other car to start of trail at Old Mill Park and park on street near park.

Directions: From San Francisco, take U.S. 101 north over the Golden Gate Bridge and continue four miles to Marin and to Exit 445B for Highway 1/Stinson Beach. Take that exit and continue west for one mile to the stoplight at a T intersection (Tam Junction) for Shoreline Highway/Highway 1. Continue straight onto Almonte Boulevard for 0.4 mile and then continue straight onto Miller Avenue for 1.8 miles (use the right lane to stay slightly left on Miller) to Throckmorton Avenue. Turn left on Throckmorton and drive 0.3 mile to the Old Mill Park on the left.

Contact: Old Mill Park, 415/388-4033, www.cityofmillvalley.org; Mount Tamalpais State Park, 415/388-2070; Muir Woods National Monument, 415/388-2595, www.nps.gov/muwo; Golden Gate National Recreation Area, 415/561-4700, www.nps.gov/goga.

52 TENNESSEE VALLEY
4.2 mi/2.0 hr   🏃1 ⛰9

in the Marin Headlands near Sausalito

Map 7.1, page 277

Tennessee Cove is a well-hidden, drop-dead gorgeous cove that extends in a sculpted curve south to Tennessee Point, with many stacks and outcrops in the tidelands to the south that catch the brunt of waves. The hike travels through Tennessee Valley (flat, paved for 0.8 mile, and very popular) and continues at a fork (trail turns to gravel, both forks reconnect in 0.6 mile), then ventures past a small marsh en route to gorgeous Tennessee Cove on the Marin coast. On the way, you are flanked by hills glowing green and peppered with wildflowers. The views of the Pacific Ocean can be gorgeous and the sunsets memorable. This trail has become a favorite for family hiking or biking trips. It is often crowded on weekends, and even on weekday afternoons when the weather is clear. You can also break off this trail to hike up on the flank of the Marin Headlands for ocean views.

User Groups: Hikers, horses, and mountain bikes. (Horses and mountain bikes must take the forked fire road.) No dogs. No wheelchair facilities.

Permits: No permits are required. Parking and access are free.

Maps: A brochure and map are available at the Marin Headlands Visitors Center or by contacting the Golden Gate National Recreation Area. For a topographic map, ask the USGS for Point Bonita.

Directions: From San Francisco, take U.S. 101 over the Golden Gate Bridge and go four miles (through the Waldo Tunnel and into Marin City) to the exit for Highway 1/Stinson Beach. Take that exit and drive 0.6 mile to Tennessee Valley Road on the left. Turn left and go two miles to the road's end, parking, and trailheads.

Contact: Marin Headlands Visitors Center, 415/331-1540; Golden Gate National Recreation Area, visitors center, 415/561-4700, www.nps.gov/goga.

53 MIWOK LOOP
3.5 mi/2.0 hr

in the Marin Headlands near Sausalito

Map 7.1, page 277

You can get one of our favorite lookouts on this trail, where you scan west from high on the Marin Headlands and across the ocean. The hike starts at the Miwok Stables (elevation 200 feet). Take the Miwok Trail, where you hike north and rise into the hills. The trail turns left and heads west 0.6 mile, where you continue to climb to the junction of Miwok Trail and Coyote Ridge Road. At this point, to make the loop hike, turn left on Ridge Road, where the trail tops out at 1,000 feet. The next mile offers spectacular views of the ocean, and every step can be special. To return to the Miwok Stables, turn left at the Fox Trail, and hike 1.1 miles; go left again on the paved Tennessee Valley Trail, and hike out the last 0.4 mile to the stables. Get yourself a clear day for the ocean views and go for it.

If you are new to the Marin Headlands, you will often see the usual parade of people on the Tennessee Valley Trail, especially on warm days. While this is one of the best easy family walks with a pay-off, there are other excellent choices available. This loop trail we created is one of them. The Miwok Loop is a nearly circular hike that traverses the pretty grasslands of the Marin Headlands. In the process, you connect a number of trails to provide for views and a workout.

Trail use is typically high on weekends, and that includes mountain bike traffic on Coyote Ridge Road. No problem. It works for everybody.

User Groups: Hikers, dogs, horses, and mountain bikes (partial access). No wheelchair facilities.

Permits: No permits are required. Parking and access are free.

Maps: A brochure and map are available at the Marin Headlands Visitors Center or by contacting the Golden Gate National Recreation Area. For a topographic map, ask the USGS for Point Bonita.

Directions: From San Francisco, take U.S. 101 over the Golden Gate Bridge and go four miles (through the Waldo Tunnel and into Marin City) to the exit for Highway 1/Stinson Beach. Take that exit and drive 0.6 mile to Tennessee Valley Road on the left. Turn left and go 1.7 miles to the road's end, parking, and trailheads.

Contact: Marin Headlands Visitors Center, 415/331-1540; Golden Gate National Recreation Area, visitors center, 415/561-4700, www.nps.gov/goga.

54 MARIN'S HILL 88
5.4 mi/2.0 hr

in the Marin Headlands near Sausalito

Map 7.1, page 277

Hill 88 is a 1,053-foot hilltop in the Marin Headlands. It towers over Rodeo Beach, with the Marin coast and ocean on one side, wilderness foothills on the other, and a pretty silhouette of Mount Tamalpais to the north, San Francisco to the south. The pay-off views and natural beauty are a 10. Yet the trip requires a climb that makes you feel that you've earned something special. That makes the trip a perfect mesh of beauty and ambition.

To get to the top, the hike is 2.7 miles with a 1,000-foot climb, steep in one spot. The trip starts as an easy walk on a gated road, the Coastal Trail. It then climbs (with pretty coastal views), and in 1.5 miles, reaches Battery Townsley (a concrete bunker, largely buried). You then climb, steep at times, up to Wolf Ridge (steep enough for the route to be stepped in spots). A spur on the right leads 0.1 mile to Hill 88. This is like a military ghost town with old gun placements on a bunker, and sensational views. When you head back, it can feel like the entire coast is at your feet. It's 5.4 miles round-trip.

An option is to turn it into a 5.5-mile loop. After your visit to Hill 88, to make the route a loop, instead turn right on Wolf Ridge. In 1.3 miles, turn right again on the Miwok Trail. It leads down to Gerbode Valley and back along Rodeo Lagoon (and the road) to parking. This is not featured because it means walking a bit along the road next to Rodeo Lagoon to get back to your parking spot.

User Groups: Hikers and horses. No mountain bikes permitted on this route at Wolf Ridge. Leashed dogs are permitted on this section of Coastal Trail and Wolf Ridge, but not on the spur to Hill 88. No wheelchair facilities.

Permits: No permits are required. Parking and access are free.

Maps: A brochure and map are available at the Marin Headlands Visitors Center or by contacting the Golden Gate National Recreation Area. For a topographic map, ask the USGS for Point Bonita.

Directions: From San Francisco, take U.S. 101 north over the Golden Gate Bridge to Marin and the exit for Alexander Avenue (just north of the bridge). Take that exit west and drive under the highway and curve south to Conzelman Road. Turn right on Conzelman and drive 1.1 miles to traffic circle at McCullough Road. Take first exit onto McCullough Road and continue 0.9 mile to Bunker Road. Turn left on Bunker Road and drive 1.8 miles (Rodeo Lagoon on left) to fork with Bunker Road on right. Continue straight ahead (becomes Mitchell Road, Fort Cronkhite on right, Rodeo Lagoon still on left) for 0.2 mile to end of road and turn right to parking lot for Rodeo Beach.

Trailhead: After parking, walk back to road. Turn right and walk short distance west to trailhead for Coastal Trail. It starts as a gated road.

Contact: Marin Headlands Visitors Center, 415/331-1540; Golden Gate National Recreation Area, visitors center, 415/561-4700, www.nps.gov/goga.

55 BOTHIN MARSH

1.0 mi/1.0 hr

in Mill Valley

Map 7.1, page 277

Bothin Marsh spans 106 acres with bridged inlets, sloughs, and tidal wetlands amid cordgrass and pickleweed that adjoin Richardson Bay. You can see shorebirds, both residents and migrants, here, and what you see often varies with tides and season; 125 bird species have been verified by photographs. From the trailhead adjacent to Almonte, the best walk is to turn left on the Mill Valley-Sausalito Path, and walk into the interior of the marsh and over a pretty bridge to Bay Front Park, with the option of continuing on the Bay Trail to Hauke Park. This is a great site for bird-watching and easy walks with water views.

User Groups: Hikers, dogs, mountain bikes, and wheelchairs. No horses.

Permits: No permits are required. Parking and access are free.

Maps: For a topographic map, ask the USGS for San Francisco North.

Directions: From San Francisco, take U.S. 101 north over the Golden Gate Bridge and continue four miles to Marin and to Exit 445B for Highway 1/Stinson Beach. Take that exit and continue west for one mile to the stoplight at a T intersection (Tam Junction) for Shoreline Highway/Highway 1. Continue straight onto

Almonte Boulevard (it becomes Miller) for one mile to trailhead/access on right (a T intersection for Almonte is adjacent to access gate).
Contact: Marin County Parks and Open Space, 415/499-6387, www.marincountyparks.org.

56 MORNING SUN TRAIL
0.6-5.2 mi/0.5-3.0 hr   🥾3 ⛰10

in the Marin Headlands near Sausalito

Map 7.1, page 277

You do this hike for one reason: the panoramic views of San Francisco Bay. There is a good parking area at the trailhead. You then climb about 400 feet and top out at 800 feet at the Alta Trail junction. The views are fantastic, where you can see across Richardson Bay to Angel Island and beyond across the Bay to the East Bay skyline. This trail didn't get its name by accident: This is one of the best places in the Bay Area to catch a sunrise. After the short but steep climb to the junction with Alta Trail (a road), turn around and take in the dawn rush. The sunrise often casts yellows and oranges across San Francisco Bay. Want more? From the Alta Trail junction, you can easily extend your trip in either direction, then turn around when ready; or create a pretty 5.2-mile loop where you link the Rodeo Valley Trail and Bobcat Trail.
User Groups: Hikers only. No dogs, horses, or mountain bikes. No wheelchair facilities.
Permits: No permits are required. Parking and access are free.
Maps: A brochure and map are available at the Marin Headlands Visitors Center or by contacting the Golden Gate National Recreation Area. For a topographic map, ask the USGS for San Francisco North.
Directions: From San Francisco, drive north on U.S. 101 through the Waldo Tunnel. Take the Spencer Avenue exit, but keep straight on the frontage road on the east side of the freeway. (Do not turn right onto Spencer Avenue.) Drive about 0.5 mile, turn left, and drive under

the freeway to the commuter parking area at the trailhead.
Contact: Marin Headlands Visitors Center, 415/331-1540; Golden Gate National Recreation Area, visitors center, 415/561-4700, www.nps.gov/goga.

57 YELLOW BLUFF TRAIL
1.5 mi/1.0 hr   🥾1 ⛰10

in the Marin Headlands near the Golden Gate Bridge

Map 7.1, page 277

This is a little piece of heaven. From your vantage point on Yellow Bluff, San Francisco can look like the Land of Oz. Yellow Bluff is located just east of the Golden Gate Bridge, the first major land point along the Marin shore at Fort Baker. You get a stunning lookout of the Golden Gate, across San Francisco Bay to the San Francisco waterfront and skyline, and the surrounding landmarks. The trail is flat, short, and unpublicized, and there are a few picnic tables nearby.

It's very easy to reach, yet missed by the tourists. From East Fort Baker, walk on the trail that heads east near the shoreline of the bay. It leads along the shore to Yellow Bluff and a picnic site. You can turn the trip into a triangular loop hike where you continue along the shore, toward Sausalito, and turn left at the trail junction to return to Fort Baker. One of the great features of this area is that it is often sunny, even when the Marin Headlands to the nearby west lie buried in fog.
User Groups: Hikers, dogs, and mountain bikes. Fort Baker is wheelchair-accessible, but the trail is not. No horses.
Permits: No permits are required. Parking and access are free.
Maps: A brochure and map are available at the East Fort Baker Visitors Center or by contacting the Golden Gate National Recreation Area, Marin Headlands. For a topographic map, ask the USGS for San Francisco North.
Directions: From San Francisco, take U.S. 101

north over the Golden Gate Bridge to Marin and stay to the right at the split. Drive a very short distance, turn left, and drive a few hundred yards to a stop sign. Turn right and drive 0.5 mile to the parking area for Fort Baker.

Contact: Marin Headlands Visitors Center, 415/331-1540; Golden Gate National Recreation Area, visitors center, 415/561-4700, www.nps.gov/goga.

58 VISTA POINT/ BATTERY SPENCER
0.5 mi/0.5 hr

in the Marin Headlands near the Golden Gate Bridge

Map 7.1, page 277

Play tourist and drive out to Battery Spencer. If the experience doesn't move you, head to the nearest emergency room and have your pulse checked. Battery Spencer is perched on a blufftop of the Marin Headlands, about eye-level with the top of the North Tower of the Golden Gate Bridge. The big pay-off is the eye-popping panorama of San Francisco. A trip here can easily be extended with a hike or scenic drive.

If parking is full when you get there, pull over and wait a minute; a spot will open up. After parking, head right toward the old concrete outbuildings and foundations for Battery Spencer. Battery Spencer was a military outpost, best known for its coastal gun battery as part of the defense to the entrance to San Francisco Bay. It's a short walk on a wheelchair-accessible pathway to the bluff-top overlook of the Golden Gate. From the bluff, you get the classic towering view across the bridge to San Francisco. On the walk back, there's a picnic bench with a view below to Fort Baker and across the bay to Angel Island and Alcatraz.

You can go the extra mile, or in this case, 2.4 miles round-trip. Look for the gated service road on the west end of Battery Spencer. It leads down 1.2 miles, with a 475-foot descent, to a pretty valley, and then to Kirby Cove. This is a gorgeous beach with the water view of the

Golden Gate Bridge. You'll also find a concrete battery, a few bluff-top tent sites, and in the valley, a campground for groups.

User Groups: Hikers and wheelchairs. No dogs, mountain bikes, or horses.

Permits: No permits are required. Parking and access are free.

Maps: A brochure and map are available at the East Fort Baker Visitors Center or by contacting the Golden Gate National Recreation Area. For a topographic map, ask the USGS for San Francisco North.

Directions: From San Francisco, take U.S. 101 north over the Golden Gate Bridge to Marin and continue 0.5 mile to the exit for Alexander Avenue. Take that exit west, keep left at the fork and drive 0.2 mile under the highway (signed for U.S. 101 South/San Francisco) and curve south to Conzelman Road, signed Marin Headlands Coastal Route. Turn right (west) on Conzelman and drive 0.3 mile to parking for Battery Spencer on left.

Contact: Marin Headlands Visitors Center, 415/331-1540; Golden Gate National Recreation Area, visitors center, 415/561-4700, www.nps.gov/goga.

59 PERIMETER TRAIL
5.0 mi/2.5 hr   🏃2 ⛰10

on Angel Island State Park

Map 7.1, page 277   **BEST (**

Pick a bright, blue-sky day at Angel Island and you get eye-popping views everywhere you turn. At the virtual center of San Francisco Bay, you are surrounded by dozens of world-renowned landmarks. If you hit it right, the view across the bay of the Golden Gate Bridge, San Francisco, and Marin Headlands can be surreal it can be so magical. You also see Raccoon Strait, Sausalito, Bay Bridge, East Bay hills, and Alcatraz.

From the ferry dock at Ayala Cove, hike out past the beach, where you turn left on a short spur to connect with the Perimeter Road. Bear right and you'll then climb easily up through eucalyptus forest. The first highlight is Camp Reynolds, a Civil War-era barracks, with a great view of the Golden Gate Bridge. From here, the road points toward San Francisco, with a fantastic view of the San Francisco waterfront and high-rises as you pass above Point Blunt. The route bears left as you pass along Fort McDowell and the East Garrison. Little known is that a secluded and gorgeous beach is hidden in a cove below the garrison. The route continues in a loop past the North Garrison Immigration Station and China Cove with views of the East Bay waterfront and foothills, and then turns again to head back to Ayala Cove.

Always hike the loop in counter-clockwise direction. The trail winds past old barracks and abandoned military buildings, climbs through lush eucalyptus forests and across high bluffs, and to lookouts. Every turn provides another awesome view.

User Groups: Hikers and mountain bikes (helmets are required for cyclists 17 years and under). The Perimeter Road is accessible to wheelchairs, but many portions are too steep for use. No dogs (except for seeing-eye dogs) or horses.

Permits: Ferry tickets include day-use fees and vary according to departure point and season; a fee is charged per bicycle. State Park annual day-use pass not accepted at Angel Island State Park.

Maps: You can purchase a brochure and topographic map for a fee at the park or by mail from the Angel Island Association. For a topographic map, ask the USGS for San Francisco North.

Directions: Ferry service to Angel Island is available from Tiburon, San Francisco, Vallejo, and Oakland/Alameda.

To the Tiburon ferry: Take U.S. 101 to Exit 447 for Highway 131 toward Tiburon Boulevard/E. Blithedale Avenue. Take that exit east for 0.3 mile to Tiburon Boulevard/ Highway 131. Turn right on Tiburon Boulevard and drive 4.3 miles to entrance and parking for Tiburon Ferry.

To the San Francisco ferry: Take U.S. 101 to the exit for Marina Boulevard exit (near the southern foot of the Golden Gate Bridge). Take that exit and drive east on Marina Boulevard toward Fisherman's Wharf. Park at a parking garage or pay lot. The ferry departs from Pier 41.

To the Vallejo ferry: Take I-80 to I-780 and drive to Curtola Parkway. Take Curtola Parkway (which becomes Mare Island Way) and continue to 495 Mare Island Way; free parking is available. The docking area is directly across from the parking lot.

To the Oakland/Alameda ferry: In Oakland drive south on I-980 to the exit for Webster. Take that exit and drive west to the ferry dock at Jack London Square. The ferry goes to San Francisco at Pier 41.

Ferries: From San Francisco: Blue & Gold Fleet (415/705-8200, www.blueandgoldfleet. com, $17, bicycles free); from Marin: Angel Island Tiburon Ferry (415/435-2131, www.angelislandferry.com, $13.50).

Contact: Angel Island State Park, 415/435-1915 or 415/435-5390 (ranger's office); California State Parks, Marin District, 415/898-4362, www.parks.ca.gov.

60 MOUNT LIVERMORE SUMMIT

4.5 mi/2.5 hr 🥾3 ⛰10

on Angel Island State Park

Map 7.1, page 277

This is one of the most dramatic urban lookouts in the world. When standing atop Mount Livermore, you will be surrounded by landmarks in every direction. At 788 feet, this is the highest point on Angel Island. The views are superb even at night, when the lights of the Golden Gate Bridge and the city glow with charm. From the visitors center, walk to the Perimeter Road and its junction with the Sunset Trail. The Sunset Trail starts where you hike west, just above the Perimeter Road (Perimeter Road is off to your right). The Sunset Trail instead bears left and climbs through a series of graded switchbacks, then turns left to rise up the south flank of the summit. After about two miles, you will reach a junction with the North Ridge Trail. Turn here and you will climb up for the final push to the top at 788 feet. The big views: Golden Gate Bridge, San Francisco waterfront, San Francisco Headlands, Marin Headlands, Raccoon Strait, Sausalito, Bay Bridge, East Bay hills, Alcatraz.

User Groups: Hikers only. No dogs (except for seeing-eye dogs), horses, or mountain bikes (they may not even be walked on this trail). No wheelchair facilities.

Permits: Ferry tickets include day-use fees and vary according to departure point and season; a fee is charged per bicycle. State Park annual day-use pass not accepted at Angel Island State Park.

Maps: You can purchase a brochure and topographic map for a fee at the park or by mail from the Angel Island Association. For a topographic map, ask the USGS for San Francisco North.

Directions: Ferry service to Angel Island is available from Tiburon, San Francisco, Vallejo, and Oakland/Alameda.

To the Tiburon ferry: Take U.S. 101 to Exit 447 for Highway 131 toward Tiburon Boulevard/E. Blithedale Avenue. Take that exit east for 0.3 mile to Tiburon Boulevard/Highway 131. Turn right on Tiburon Boulevard and drive 4.3 miles to entrance and parking for Tiburon Ferry.

To the San Francisco ferry: Take U.S. 101 to the exit for Marina Boulevard exit (near the southern foot of the Golden Gate Bridge). Take that exit and drive east on Marina Boulevard toward Fisherman's Wharf. Park at a parking garage or pay lot. The ferry departs from Pier 41.

To the Vallejo ferry: Take I-80 to I-780. Take I-780 and drive to Curtola Parkway. Take Curtola Parkway (which becomes Mare Island Way) and continue to 495 Mare Island Way, where free parking is available. The docking area is directly across from the parking lot.

To the Oakland/Alameda ferry: In Oakland drive south on I-980 to the exit for Webster. Take that exit and drive west to the ferry dock at Jack London Square. The ferry goes to San Francisco at Pier 41.

Ferries: From San Francisco: Blue & Gold Fleet (415/705-8200, www.blueandgoldfleet.com, $17, bicycles free); from Marin: Angel Island Tiburon Ferry (415/435-2131, www.angelislandferry.com, $13.50).

Contact: Angel Island State Park, 415/435-1915 or 415/435-5390 (ranger's office); California State Parks, Marin District, 415/898-4362, www.parks.ca.gov.

61 AGAVE TRAIL
1.5 mi/1.5 hr 🏃1 ⛰8

on Alcatraz Island

Map 7.2, page 278

The Agave Trail at Alcatraz Island is only open from late September to February; the trail is closed from late winter into spring and summer to protect nesting birds. Named after the agave plant, which is common here, the trail provides some of the most breathtaking views found in the Bay Area.

Start at the ferry landing on the east side of Alcatraz and follow the trail as it traces the island rim to its southern tip. It's quite wide, with a few benches and cement picnic tables situated for sweeping views of both the East Bay and San Francisco. From its southern end, the trail is routed back to the historic parade ground atop the island, where you will find some sculptural masterpieces, including 110 stone steps. The parade ground is a haven for nesting birds (this area is closed to the public each spring). Birds are thriving in the restored wildlife habitat, especially at the southern end of the island. About 10,000 marine birds live here, mainly gulls, cormorants, and egrets. With about 5,000 visitors a day in summer, that's two birds for every person—wear a hat.

The old cell block is located at the center of the island, with other buildings sprinkled along the eastern shore and on the northern tip. Ranger-led park tours are available, and visitors can rent audiotapes for a self-guided cell-house tour. Famous prisoners include The Birdman, Machine Gun Kelly, and Al Capone. The cells are only five feet by nine feet, yet because the warden ordered them painted two-tone, white over sea-foam green, they give the illusion of a much larger space.

User Groups: Hikers only. No dogs, horses, or mountain bikes. No wheelchair facilities.

Permits: No permits are required. Entry tickets include the ferryboat trip to the island and audio tours are available from Alcatraz Cruises for an additional fee. Ferries depart from Pier 31/33 in San Francisco.

Maps: A map is available at the ferry landing for a fee. For a topographic map, ask the USGS for San Francisco North.

Directions: From the Peninsula: Take U.S. 101 north to San Francisco and continue to the split with I-280 (signed Downtown SF). At the split take I-280 for 0.5 mile, keep right at the fork (signed for I-280), then continue 3.3 miles to King Street. Continue on King Street for 0.7 mile to The Embarcadero and then continue 2.1 miles to Pier 33 and nearby parking.

From the East Bay: Take the Bay Bridge to San Francisco (stay in left lanes) and the exit on the left for Harrison Street (toward Embarcadero). Take that exit for 0.4 mile (stay right) to Harrison Street. Turn right on Harrison and drive 0.3 mile to the Embarcadero. Turn left and drive 1.5 miles to Pier 33 and nearby parking.

From Marin: Take the Golden Gate Bridge to San Francisco and continue (stay left on the split for U.S. 101) about two miles to the exit for Marina Boulevard. Turn left on Marina and drive 1.1 miles to Laguna Street, and then continue on Laguna for 0.1 mile to Bay Street. Turn left on Bay Street and drive 1.4 miles to the Embarcadero and nearby parking.

Ferries: From San Francisco: Blue & Gold Fleet (415/705-8200, www.blueandgoldfleet. com, $17, bicycles free); from Marin: Angel Island Tiburon Ferry (415/435-2131, www.angelislandferry.com, $13.50).

Contact: Golden Gate National Recreation Area, 415/ 561-4900 or www.nps.gov/alcatraz; Alcatraz Cruises, 415/981-7625, www.alcatrazcruises.com.

62 COAST TRAIL/ BATTERY GODFREY

1.5 mi/1.0 hr 🥾1 ⛰10

in the Presidio

Map 7.2, page 278

This one is a 10, worth the trip no matter where you live. It's often best when turbulent skies offer textures to the setting. To your right is a magazine-cover quality view of the Golden Gate Bridge. From the Coastal Trail, the cliffs plunge below to the waterfront and beyond to the entrance of the bay, with passing ships, fishing boats, and sailboats. Directly across is the Marin Headlands, topped by Hawk Hill and edged by Point Bonita and its lighthouse.

The trip starts at Battery Godfrey in the Presidio. It is perched on a bluff west of the Golden Gate Bridge. You'll find the old concrete foundation for Battery Godfrey, fantastic views of the bridge, Marin Headlands and entrance to the bay, and a trailhead for the Coastal Trail.

From here, take the Coastal Trail toward the Golden Gate Bridge to a pay-off spot called "Overlook." A bench is set perfectly for a view of the bridge and photographs. The trail extends north a short distance to the toll plaza, where you can walk under the road to the designated Overlook above Fort Point and the southern foot of the bridge. Return when ready.

Back at Battery Godfrey, if you want to extend your trip, you can venture south on the Coastal Trail. It is routed along Lincoln Boulevard to Battery Chamberlain and Baker Beach, and then beyond to China Beach.

Battery Godfrey was a turn-of-the-century military site armed with three 12-inch guns that could fire 1,000-pound shells 10 miles.

What's left is the concrete structure that supported the cannons.

User Groups: Hikers and wheelchairs. Dogs are not advised. No horses or mountain bikes.

Permits: No permits are required. Parking and access are free.

Maps: For a free map, contact the Presidio. For a topographic map, ask the USGS for San Francisco North.

Directions: From the Peninsula: Take I-280 north to Exit 47 signed for Highway 1/Pacifica. Drive 1.1 miles to the exit for Skyline Blvd./Highway 35N and merge onto Skyline Boulevard. Continue north 4.3 miles to a stop. Turn left on Great Highway and continue north 3.5 miles to the Cliff House; the road merges with Point Lobos Avenue. Bear right and drive 0.6 miles (becoming Geary St.) and continue 0.9 mile to 26th Avenue. Turn left on 26th and go 0.5 mile to El Camino Del Mar. Turn right and drive 0.2 mile (becoming Lincoln St.); continue 1.1 miles into the Presidio and Langdon Court (for lookout, Battery Godfrey). Turn left and drive to the parking lot.

From the East Bay: Take the Bay Bridge (I-80 West) to San Francisco and the Fremont Street exit. The off-ramp merges onto Fremont Street; stay left and then continue straight to Pine Street. Turn left on Pine and drive 1.3 miles to Van Ness Avenue. Turn right on Van Ness and go 0.8 mile to Lombard/U.S. 101. Turn left on Lombard and drive three miles to Exit 439 (for Presidio). Take that exit and continue a short distance to Lincoln Boulevard. Turn right on Lincoln and go 0.3 mile (under U.S. 101) to Langdon (for lookout, Battery Godfrey) on right. Turn right and drive a short distance to park.

From Marin: Take U.S. 101 south over the Golden Gate Bridge to Exit 439 toward 25th Avenue. Take that exit and continue 0.2 mile to Lincoln Boulevard. Turn right on Lincoln and go about 500 feet to Langdon (for lookout, Battery Godfrey) on right. Turn right and drive a short distance to the parking lot.

Contact: Presidio Visitors Center, 415/561-4323, www.nps.gov/prsf.

63 ECOLOGY TRAIL TO INSPIRATION POINT

2.5 mi/1.5 hr 🏃1 ⛰10

in the Presidio

Map 7.2, page 278

The Presidio is best known for its shoreline lookouts of the Golden Gate. Instead, try this trip once and you will never forget it. The Ecology Trail is routed through Tennessee Hollow and a mixed forest, with occasional views that provide a hint to the pay-off. In less than a mile you'll reach the turnoff on your right to Inspiration Point (it can also be reached by car). The view is fantastic: You get a panorama that spans below to the Palace of Fine Arts and beyond to the San Francisco waterfront, Bay, and across to Angel Island and Alcatraz. World-class.

Then, at Inspiration Point, turn and look behind you. On the opposite side of Arguello Boulevard is a young cypress forest from which the 100-foot Goldsworthy's Spire pokes a hole in the sky. It is best accessed across the street from parking at the Presidio Café.

User Groups: Hikers and dogs. Bikes are not advised. Wheelchair access from parking at Inspiration Point.

Permits: No permits are required. Parking and access are free.

Maps: For a free map, contact the Presidio. For a topographic map, ask the USGS for San Francisco North.

Directions: From the parking lot, walk to the Inn at the Presidio on Moraga Avenue. At the corner with Hardie Avenue, turn right and walk a short distance to the trailhead.

From the Peninsula: Take U.S. 101 north to San Francisco and continue to the split with U.S. 101/Golden Gate Bridge-I-80/Bay Bridge. Stay left on U.S. 101 and follow Van Ness Avenue to Lombard Street; turn left on Lombard Street and continue to Letterman. Turn right on Letterman and drive 0.2 mile on Presidio to Funston. Turn left and drive 0.1 mile to Moraga Avenue and the trailhead adjacent to Inn at the Presidio.

From East Bay: Take the Bay Bridge to San Francisco and the exit for Fremont Street. Continue onto Front Street and follow the road a short distance to Pine Street. Turn left on Pine and drive 2.7 miles to Presidio Avenue. Turn left on Presidio and go 0.2 mile to Funston Avenue. Turn left on Funston and go 0.1 mile to Moraga Avenue. Turn right at Moraga and park in the lot on the right.

From Marin: Take the Golden Gate Bridge to San Francisco and continue to the split with U.S. 101/Marina. Stay left at the split for U.S. 101 and continue to Lombard Street. Turn right on Lombard and drive 0.3 mile to Letterman Drive. Turn right and drive 0.3 mile and continue ahead on Presidio Boulevard for 0.2 mile to Funston Avenue. Turn left on Funston and go 0.1 mile to Moraga. Turn right at Moraga (Inn at the Presidio is near the trailhead, on the left) and park in the lot on the right.

Contact: Presidio Visitors Center, 415/561-4323, www.nps.gov/prsf.

64 GOLDEN GATE BRIDGE
3.0 mi/1.25 hr   👣1 ⛰10

from San Francisco to Marin

Map 7.2, page 278

The top tourist walks in the world include the stroll to Yosemite Falls, the Redwood Creek Trail in Muir Woods, and this—the walk over the Golden Gate Bridge and back. And it makes sense: On a warm, clear day, the walk across the bridge feels like a surreal phenomenon. From the center of the bridge, the view is incomparable. Looking eastward, you can see Alcatraz, Angel Island, and the bay framed by the San Francisco waterfront and the East Bay hills. The Golden Gate Bridge is 1.2 miles long and most visitors walk halfway out, take in the view, then return to their cars (1.5-mile round-trip). If you walk from one end to the other and then return, it takes about an hour. The bridge deck is 220 feet above the water and the towers rise up 750 feet.

Parking is available at the north end of the bridge (at Vista Point) and at the south end, on each side of the toll plaza. On the San Francisco side, there is also some parking on the west side; you'll then walk through a short tunnel that runs under U.S. 101 and loops up to the pathway entrance.

From the walking lane at the center of the bridge, the view is incomparable: Looking eastward, you can see Alcatraz, Angel Island and the bay framed by the San Francisco waterfront to your right and the East Bay hills on the horizon. From the bicycle lane, you get a near-equal panorama in the other direction, of the Marin Headlands, mouth of the bay and beyond to the ocean, and the San Francisco Headlands, cliffs, and beaches to Point Lobos. Stash a windbreaker in a small pack. Even on clear days, a moist coastal breeze can cause a chill for some.

User Groups: Hikers, wheelchairs, dogs, and mountain bikes (on the west side of the bridge only). No horses.

Permits: No permits are required. Parking and access are free.

Maps: For a free map, contact the Golden Gate National Recreation Area. For a topographic map, ask the USGS for San Francisco North.

Directions: From the Peninsula: Take I-280 north to Daly City and the split with Highway 1. Stay left at the split and continue north on Highway 1 (19th Ave.) through Golden Gate Park. After passing through a tunnel, merge with U.S. 101 North (right lane). Continue 0.2 mile to the exit for Presidio/Golden Gate Bridge Vista Point. Parking and Vista Point are on the left.

From East Bay: Take the Bay Bridge to San Francisco and the exit for Fremont Street. Merge onto Fremont and go another 0.3 mile, continuing onto Front Street. Turn left on Pine Street and drive 1.4 miles to Franklin Street. Turn right on Franklin and drive 0.8 mile to Lombard/U.S. 101. Turn left on Lombard and drive 3 miles (U.S. 101) toward Golden Gate Bridge and the exit for Presidio/Golden Gate Bridge Vista Point. Parking and Vista Point are on the left.

Contact: Golden Gate National Recreation Area, Fort Mason, San Francisco, 415/561-4700, www.nps.gov/goga.

65 MARINA GREEN TO FORT POINT
3.0 mi/1.25 hr 🚶1 ⛰10

Crissy Field in San Francisco

Map 7.2, page 278

This is one of the most spectacular city walks in America. Marina Green is your launch point. From here along the Golden Gate Promenade, you get waterfront views that extend to the Golden Gate Bridge, across to Sausalito and Alcatraz. From parking, take the San Francisco Bay Trail west along Marina Green and work your way around the yacht harbors (you'll see lots of docked boats on your right) toward the St. Francis Yacht Club. Then continue toward the harbor entrance, past the Golden Gate Yacht Club, to the point at the end of the jetty and to the Wave Organ.

The Wave Organ is located at the end of the point near the mouth of the harbor. It's a wave-activated acoustic sculpture that has 25 "organ pipes," actually made out of PVC and concrete. The movement of water into the pipes sets off subtle tones that amplify water noises, best at high tides. The sound is subtle but is San Francisco cool.

From the Wave Organ, head west past the yacht harbors and pick up the Golden Gate Promenade/Bay Trail. The route (paved) runs along the bay and beachfront and continues past Crissy Field and its marsh to the Presidio, Fort Point Pier, and beyond to Fort Point at the southern foot of the Golden Gate Bridge. Along the way, you get stunning views of the Golden Gate Bridge, the Bay, and Alcatraz, along with access to the beach, restored ponds and marsh wetlands, and coastal sand dunes. For non-residents, the trip to Crissy Field is a city adventure through San Francisco past many landmarks en route to the waterfront.

User Groups: Hikers, wheelchairs, dogs, and mountain bikes. No horses.

Permits: No permits are required. Parking and access are free.

Maps: For a free map, contact the Golden Gate National Recreation Area. For a topographic map, ask the USGS for San Francisco North.

Directions: From the Peninsula: Take U.S. 101 north to San Francisco and the exit for the Central Freeway. Continue onto Octavia Boulevard and turn right on Oak Street. Turn left on Franklin Street and drive two miles to Bay Street. Turn left on Bay and go 0.3 mile to Laguna Street. Turn right on Laguna and go 0.1 mile to Marina Boulevard (street turns left) and drive ahead short distance to entrance on right to Marina Green and parking.

From the East Bay: Take Bay Bridge to San Francisco (and shortly after leaving bridge) to exit for Fremont Street. Take that exit ramp for 0.8 mile, continue onto Front Street a short distance to Pine. Turn left on Pine and drive 1.4 miles to Franklin. Turn right on Franklin and drive one mile to Bay Street. Turn left on Bay and go 0.3 mile to Laguna Street. Turn right on Laguna and go 0.1 mile to Marina Boulevard (street turns left) and drive ahead short distance to entrance on right to Marina Green and parking.

From Marin: Take Golden Gate Bridge to San Francisco and continue two miles (stay left at split on U.S. 101/Marina) onto Presidio Parkway and left turn for Marina Boulevard. Turn left on Marina and drive 0.8 mile to the entrance to Marina Green on the left and park.

Contact: Crissy Field Center, 415/561-7690; Golden Gate National Recreation Area, 415/561-4700, www.nps.gov/goga.

66 POINT LOBOS/ LANDS END TRAIL
3.0 mi/1.5 hr 🚶1 ⛰10

San Francisco headlands

Map 7.2, page 278

San Francisco's Point Lobos and Lands End

provides great views, easy adventures, and history. On any day, it is like walking amid the grandest stage. The panorama starts right along the sidewalk. Along Point Lobos Avenue, the Cliff House uphill past Louis' restaurant, you get a lookout that spans across the mouth of the bay and out to sea, to the Marin Headlands and Golden Gate Bridge. It's like a historic painting, with passing ships and fishing boats, pelicans, and cormorants. Continue uphill to Merrie Way, then turn left, that is, toward the Golden Gate.

From Merrie Way, stairs lead down to the historic Sutro Baths ruins. The foundation of the old structure and its seven swimming pools is about all that remains, and with historic photographs, you can reconstruct in your mind how it looked a century ago when thousands of people would visit on a Sunday afternoon. Along its leading edge, you get pretty ocean views where you can taste the salt air. Then return up the stairs to Merrie Way.

On the far side of Merrie Way, you'll see the trailhead for the Coastal Trail. From here, the Coastal Trail spans 1.25 miles, much of it along a former narrow-gauge rail line, on blufftops amid cypress, out to Eagles Point next to Lincoln Park. From Eagles Point, the pay-off is a view of China Beach, Baker Beach, and the coast that arcs in a curve out to the southern foot of the Golden Gate Bridge. During low tides on the Coastal Trail, look down along the cliffs and you can see relics of old shipwrecks that poke up through sea surface. A metal masthead and an engine block are the most easily identified that poke through the sea surface.

User Groups: Hikers, wheelchairs, dogs, and mountain bikes (mountain bikes must be walked through narrow sections of the trail). No horses.

Permits: No permits are required. Parking and access are free.

Maps: For a free map, contact the Golden Gate National Recreation Area. For a topographic map, ask the USGS for San Francisco North.

Directions: In San Francisco, take Geary Boulevard west. As you approach the coast, it becomes Point Lobos Avenue; look for parking near the vicinity of GGNRA trailheads and Cliff House. The stairs down to the Sutro Baths ruins and water's edge are to the left of the parking lot; the trailhead for the Coastal Trail is at the end of Merrie Way.

From the Peninsula: Take I-280 north to Exit 47 signed for Highway 1/Pacifica. Take that exit and drive 1.1 miles up the hill to the exit for Skyline Blvd./Highway 35N. Take that exit, merge onto Skyline Blvd. and continue north 4.3 miles to a stop sign (Lake Merced on right, Fort Funston on left). Turn left on Great Highway and continue north 3.5 miles north to Cliff House and where it merges with Point Lobos Ave. Continue as road curves to right to parking areas.

From the East Bay: Take I-80E into San Francisco and to the merge for U.S. 101 North/Central Freeway (also signed for Golden Gate Bridge). Take that merge to Central Freeway and go 1.1 miles (becomes Octavia Boulevard) to Fell Street. Turn left on Fell and go 1.2 miles to Masonic Avenue (just past Central). Turn right on Masonic and go 0.2 mile to Fulton Street (the third left). Turn left at Fulton and drive 3.6 miles to Great Highway. Turn right and go 0.3 mile to Point Lobos Avenue and continue short distance to parking and trailheads.

Contact: Golden Gate National Recreation Area, 415/561-4700, www.nps.gov/goga.

67 OCEAN BEACH ESPLANADE

3.0 mi/1.5 hr

on Ocean Beach along the Great Highway

Map 7.2, page 278

Ocean Beach spreads for miles along San Francisco's coastal Great Highway, from the Cliff House on south past Fort Funston to Mussel Rock. The Ocean Beach Esplanade is a paved route that borders the beach on one side and the Great Highway on the other. Here you can discover a long expanse of sand and a paved jogging trail. The nature of both the trail and the adjacent beach allows visitors to create trips of any length. The beach spans four miles, from Seal Rock (near the Cliff House) south to Fort Funston and beyond (see next hike). The huge swath of sand at Ocean Beach is popular with joggers, especially during low tides, when the hard-packed sand is uncovered. During minus low tides, this is the best area anywhere to find sand dollars; park rules prohibit picking them up. Never did understand the issue with this here; they just get ground up by the waves.

Warning: Do not swim here. There have been several drownings in this area due to riptides.

User Groups: Hikers, dogs, and horses. Partially wheelchair-accessible. No mountain bikes.

Permits: No permits are required. Parking and access are free.

Maps: For a free map, contact the Golden Gate National Recreation Area. For a topographic map, ask the USGS for San Francisco South.

Directions: In San Francisco, take Geary Boulevard west. As you approach the coast, it becomes Point Lobos Avenue. At the Cliff House, the road curves to the left and continues south as it becomes the Great Highway.

From the Peninsula: Take I-280 north to Exit 47 signed for Highway 1/Pacifica. Take that exit and drive 1.1 miles up the hill to the exit for Skyline Blvd./Highway 35N. Take that exit, merge onto Skyline Blvd. and continue north 4.3 miles to a stop sign (Lake Merced on right, Fort Funston on left). Turn left on Great Highway and drive north. Parking is available along the road on the left.

From the East Bay: Take I-80 west into San Francisco and merge onto U.S. 101 North/Central Freeway (also signed for Golden Gate Bridge). Take that exit and drive 1.1 miles onto Octavia Boulevard. Turn left on Fell Street and drive 1.2 miles to Masonic Avenue (just past Central). Turn right on Masonic and go 0.2 mile to Fulton Street (the third left). Turn left at Fulton and drive 3.6 miles to Great Highway. Turn left and look for parking along the right.

Contact: Golden Gate National Recreation Area, 415/561-4700, www.nps.gov/goga.

68 FORT FUNSTON/ SUNSET TRAIL

1.5 mi/0.5 hr

on the San Francisco coast

Map 7.2, page 278

Fort Funston is perched on San Francisco's coastal bluffs, with the Pacific on one side and Lake Merced on the other. This park is one of the most popular places in California to take dogs, and you can count on seeing plenty, up to dozens at a time. It is also the top hang-gliding spot in the Bay Area, and watching those daredevils soar is the main attraction. A viewing deck is adjacent to the parking area, where Sunset Trail begins.

Follow the wide Sunset Trail as it routes north through coastal bluffs and above sand dunes for 0.75 mile to the park's border. This is one of the most heavily used trails in the Bay Area. In fall and winter, the fog clears and the evening sunsets can make your spine tingle.

Down on the beach, you may see thick black sand unique to this part of the coast. It's not an oil spill; rather, the sand is an iron-ore derivative called magnetite. Magnetite lies in the sandstone cliff walls; as the sandstone erodes, it leaves the heavier iron-based magnetite on the beach. (If you bring a strong magnet to the beach, particles will stick to it.) Scan the cliff walls further and you might see a thick, chalky substance about a foot thick. These are veins of volcanic ash from an eruption of Mount Shasta 300 miles north; the ash made its way here via the Sacramento River and San Francisco Bay. (Former Funston ranger Steve Prokop said he once found a sabertooth tiger tooth here in a vein of volcanic ore.)

No beachcombing or collecting is permitted on Funston's beachfront. Beyond the park boundary, however, it is legal and you can often find sand dollars during low tides. From Center Hole to Mussel Rock, you can often have vast swaths of beach to yourself, especially on weekdays. Rating: Surprise discovery.

Restoration efforts here are ongoing. The Park Service replanted native flowers and plants to protect the bluffs. This has helped a colony of burrowing owls and bank swallows become re-established. You may also see red-tailed hawks.

Hang gliding: Whether you watch or take part, this is a spectacular scene. Hang gliders launch from a designated area near the bluffs, then ride the updrafts from the cliffs. When the winds are right, you might see gliders flying nearly vertical—an amazing sight—then circle in a series of dipsy-doos. This is the one sport where gravity doesn't always win, especially in the spring, when the north winds come up every afternoon.

Fort Funston gets more dogs in a week than many Bay Area parks get people in a month. The National Park Service is reviewing dog policies, including off-leash areas. If you have a dog, check posted rules before venturing out. (Note: Dogs must be on leash in some areas of Ocean Beach to protect the endangered snowy plover.)

User Groups: Hikers, dogs, and horses. Partially wheelchair-accessible (on the paved jogging route). No mountain bikes.

Permits: No permits are required. Parking and access are free.

Maps: For a free map, contact the Golden Gate National Recreation Area. For a topographic map, ask the USGS for San Francisco South.

Directions: In San Francisco, drive west on Fell Street to Lincoln Avenue where it ends at the Great Highway. Turn left and drive south on Great Highway to the exit road on the right to the primary parking lot, or continue to Skyline Boulevard. Turn right (south) and drive a short distance to the secondary parking lot (unpaved at roadside) on the right, or a little less than a mile to the park entrance (also on the right). Both parking lots are accessible only on southbound Skyline Drive.

From the Peninsula: Take I-280 north to Highway 1 in Colma. Turn west on Highway

1 and drive one mile to Highway 35/Skyline Boulevard. Turn right (north) on Highway 35 and drive about five miles to a stop sign at John Muir Drive (adjacent to Lake Merced). Make a U-turn and drive a short way to parking on the right; or continue north to stop sign. Turn left on Great Highway and make a U-turn when able to exit for the main parking area.

Contact: Fort Funston, Golden Gate National Recreation Area, 415/561-4700, www.nps.gov/goga; dog information, 415/561-4728.

69 SUMMIT LOOP TRAIL
3.1 mi/1.5 hr

in San Bruno Mountain State and County Park

Map 7.2, page 278

San Bruno Mountain rises to an elevation of 1,314 feet (it's the big mountain on the north Peninsula near the Cow Palace, west of Monster Park). For unforgettable moments, take the Summit Loop Trail. On clear days, the views are incredible—the best are of South San Francisco Bay and across the East Bay foothills to Mount Diablo. Yet that's only a start. To the north, you can also see across San Francisco, from the downtown skyline to Twin Peaks. Scan to the west and past Sweeney Ridge to the slopes of Montara Mountain. On perfect days, you can even get a glimpse of Mount Tamalpais north in Marin.

The signed trailhead for the Summit Loop is located at the south parking lot (not the main parking lot). From that lot, take the 100-yard connector spur that is routed to a three-way junction. Turn left for a short climb, and within a mile, you get sweeping views of South San Francisco Bay. Continue on the trail north (do not turn on the Dairy Ravine Trail) to the cut-off fork on the left for the lookout bench. Bring a friend, a picnic, and a camera. From your perch high atop San Bruno Mountain, you can look down on U.S. 101 in South San Francisco and easily imagine the temporary insanity that grips some drivers in their mission to reach San Francisco International Airport.

When you're ready, return to the main Summit Loop trail. The trail climbs near the antenna-spiked mountaintop for 360-degree views. To complete the trip, head downhill on paved Radio Road, cross the road, and turn left at the signed trail to the right of the gated road. Follow the Summit Loop back to the parking lot. Various routes are also easy to follow with the park map.

User Groups: Hikers and horses. No dogs or mountain bikes. No wheelchair facilities.

Permits: No permits are required. An entrance fee of $6 per vehicle is charged (self-registration, cash only).

Maps: A brochure and map are available at the entrance kiosk. For a free trail map, contact San Bruno Mountain State and County Park. For a topographic map, ask the USGS for San Francisco South.

Directions: Takes U.S. 101 to Exit 429B for Brisbane/Cow Palace. Take that exit and merge to Bayshore Boulevard and drive two miles to Guadalupe Canyon Parkway. Turn west (right) and drive 2.2 miles to the park entrance. Turn right to entrance kiosk, then continue for 0.2 mile (loop under road to south side of Guadalupe Canyon Parkway) to parking area/trailhead and Radio Road. Continue straight on Radio Road and go two miles (up hill, paved) to summit parking and trailheads for Summit Loop and Ridge Trail.

Contact: San Bruno Mountain State and County Park, 650/589-5707, or 650/573-2592 (Coyote Point); San Mateo County Department of Parks, 650/363-4020, http://parks.smcgov.org.

summit, the Ridge Trail extends along the Southeast Ridge for 2.2 miles to trail's end at a 1,000-foot perch overlooking the South Bay. On bright, crystal winter days, you can see the reflection of the domes at Lick Observatory on top of 4,209-foot Mount Hamilton east of San Jose. It's a sweeping view across the South Bay. You can often have it to yourself.

Near the parking area on top, you can see the remnants and foundation of one of the Bay Area's NIKE Missile radar sites. In addition, look for detail along the trail. More than 100 million years ago, San Bruno Mountain was the bottom of the sea. Ancient marine deposits can be found throughout the park.

User Groups: Hikers and horses. No dogs or mountain bikes. No wheelchair facilities.

Permits: No permits are required. An entrance fee of $5 per vehicle is charged (self-registration, cash only).

Maps: For a free trail map, contact San Bruno Mountain State and County Park. For a topographic map, ask the USGS for San Francisco South.

Directions: From San Francisco, take U.S. 101 south for 3.3 miles to Exit 429B for Brisbane/Cow Palace. Take that exit and merge onto Bayshore Boulevard. Drive two miles to Guadalupe Canyon Parkway. Turn west (right) and drive 2.2 miles to the park entrance. Turn right through the entrance kiosk and park in the main lot.

Contact: San Bruno Mountain State and County Park, 650/589-5707 or 650/573-2592; San Mateo County Department of Parks, 650/363-4020, http://parks.smcgov.org.

70 RIDGE TRAIL
4.4 mi/2.0 hr   🚶2 ⛰9

in San Bruno Mountain State and County Park

Map 7.2, page 278

The Ridge Trail gets overlooked by newcomers to the park (because of the landmark qualities of the Summit Loop, the previous hike). From the south end of the parking area at the

71 SWEENEY RIDGE
5.0 mi/3.0 hr   🚶2 ⛰10

in San Bruno

Map 7.2, page 278

Sweeney Ridge can be an eye-popping getaway to take in the coronation of spring. The drive up to it is within easy range of most Bay Area residents and the hits just keep on coming along the way, topped by gorgeous long-distance views.

Sweeney Ridge splits San Bruno to the east and Pacifica to the west. There are four trailheads, but the launch point with the best parking is at Skyline College at Parking Lot #2. From the trailhead to the locked gate, it is an estimated 700-foot climb (with a climb, drop, and climb again on the way in). On the ridge, you get sweeping views to your left of San Andreas Lake, the South Bay, and on the horizon, distant Mount Diablo. To your right, you can scan across the wilderness east flank of Montara Mountain, Pacifica, and the sea. You will pass a graffiti-smeared concrete shell of a building that was once a former NIKE radar station, the marker for the Portola Discovery Site, and then head beyond on the ridge to a cutoff trail on your right to South Meadow. Look for a cutoff trail to Cattle Hill on the right (it is unsigned and not on maps). Turn right, and in just five minutes, this small cutoff provides an overlook for what is known as South Meadow, an outstanding wildlife habitat with a stunning view of the ocean. On clear days, plan a picnic here, facing out to sea, and take in the view of Pacifica below, and on pristine days, across the ocean to the Farallon Islands. Wildlife includes lots of bush bunnies, decent numbers of small black-tailed deer, and if you're lucky, occasional fox or bobcat.

Sadly, access ends at the locked gate for the Crystal Springs Watershed (instead of allowing you to hike up a service road on the east flank of Montara Mountain, and then down the other side to Montara State Beach).

A favorite spot as you approach the gate is South Meadow.

User Groups: Hikers, dogs, horses, and mountain bikes. No wheelchair facilities.

Permits: No permits are required. Parking and access are free.

Maps: For a free map, contact the Golden Gate National Recreation Area. For a topographic map, ask the USGS for San Francisco South.

Directions: From San Francisco, take I-280 south to Daly City and Exit 47B for Highway 1 south toward Pacifica. Take that exit and drive 1.1 miles up the hill to the exit for Skyline Boulevard/Highway 35. Take the exit for Highway 35 south and drive south on Skyline Blvd. for 3.5 miles (past Sharp Park Drive/Westborough) to College Drive. Turn right on College Drive and go 0.4 mile to College Loop Drive. Turn left and drive a short distance to Parking Lot #2 and the trailhead on south side.

From the Peninsula: Take I-280 north to Exit 41 for Skyline Boulevard/Highway 35. Take that exit and drive 2.8 miles north to College Drive. Turn left on College Drive and go 0.4 mile to College Loop Drive. Turn left and drive a short distance to Parking Lot #2 and the trailhead at south side.

Contact: Golden Gate National Recreation Area, 415/561-4700, www.nps.gov/goga.

72 SAN ANDREAS TRAIL
6.0 mi/3.0 hr 👫1 ⛰7

on Skyline Boulevard

Map 7.2, page 278

Of the county trails along the eastern border of Crystal Springs Watershed, this one provides the best views. The San Andreas Trail overlooks Upper San Andreas Lake, winding most of its way through wooded foothills. The only downer is that much of the route runs adjacent to Highway 35/Skyline Boulevard. Regardless, it is worth the trip, because to the west you can see the untouched slopes of Montara Mountain, a game preserve, and that sparkling lake—all off-limits to the public.

The trail starts near the northern end of the lake; a signed trailhead marker is posted on Skyline Boulevard. The route runs about three miles south to the next access point, at Hillcrest Boulevard, and from there, it connects to Sawyer Camp Trail. The view of Montara Mountain to the west is particularly enchanting during the summer, when rolling fog banks crest the ridgeline: a spectacle.

User Groups: Hikers, horses, and mountain bikes. Note that the northern section is paved, but the southern section is not. There are some wheelchair-accessible facilities. No dogs.

Permits: No permits are required. Parking and access are free.

Maps: For a free trail map, contact San Mateo County Division of Parks. For a topographic map, ask the USGS for Montara Mountain.

Directions: To access the north gate: From I-280 in San Bruno, take the Westborough exit and drive west up the hill to the intersection with Highway 35/Skyline Boulevard. Turn left on Highway 35 and drive about 2.5 miles to the trailhead entrance on the right side of the road.

To access the south gate: On I-280, drive to the Millbrae Avenue exit. Take that exit and drive north on Skyline Boulevard, a frontage road on the west side of I-280, and continue to the parking area on the left.

Contact: San Mateo County Parks Department, 650/363-4020, http://parks.smc-gov.org.

73 SAWYER CAMP RECREATION TRAIL

12.0 mi/5.0 hr 👣1 ⛰8

in San Mateo County south of San Bruno

Map 7.2, page 278

The six-mile Sawyer Camp Trail is the most popular segment of the 15.3-mile Crystal Springs Regional Trail. It is routed along a pretty lake and through a forest, so you get more nature. Most visitors access at the southern trailhead located near Crystal Springs Dam. From here, you walk adjacent the northern end of Crystal Springs Reservoir. Views of the lake and beyond up Montara Mountain are beautiful. The trail runs adjacent to the lake for about three miles, then enters a gorgeous riparian area with a 600-year-old Jepson Laurel on the left. At 5.5 miles, you arrive at the dam for San Andreas Lake, and a half mile beyond, another access point and trailhead. The trail is paved and marked for two-way traffic, and even though park rangers occasionally use radar, high-end street bikes can easily cruise

faster than the 15-mph speed limit. Watch out on blind turns. Portable restrooms are available at each trailhead and at two sites along the trail. From the trailhead at Crystal Springs Dam, it is a 400-foot climb over six miles. On Saturday and Sunday mornings, it is crowded.

User Groups: Hikers, horses, and mountain bikes. There are some wheelchair-accessible facilities at the south end. No dogs.

Permits: No permits are required. Parking and access are free.

Maps: For a free trail map, contact San Mateo County Division of Parks. For a topographic map, ask the USGS for Montara Mountain.

Directions: Take I-280 to San Bruno and Exit 36 for Black Mountain Road. Take that exit a short distance to Highway 35 (frontage road west of I-280). Turn south on Highway 35 and drive 1.6 miles to parking and trailhead.

Contact: San Mateo County Parks Department, 650/363-4020, http://parks.smc-gov.org.

74 MORI POINT TRAIL

2.5 mi/1.5 hr 👣1 ⛰8

in Pacifica near Pacifica State Beach/Linda Mar

Map 7.2, page 278

At Mori Point, all you need is a clear day. Your reward is big-time coastal views, a long expanse of beach, and a pretty walk. Mori Point is a dramatic coastal outcrop in Pacifica that is sometimes overlooked. On this route, you get access to extended beach frontage, a walk that starts out dead flat, with the option to climb to hilltop lookouts and bluff-top cliffs. Nearby is the best fishing pier on the Bay Area coast, Pacifica Pier, and adjacent is the Laguna Salada, a freshwater lagoon tucked on the edge of the Sharp Park Golf Course.

On the drive in, there isn't a sign on Highway 1 that says "Mori Point," so outside of locals and overnighters at the local hotels, it can get overlooked. From the trailhead at the corner of Beach Road and Clarendon, you walk south, with a dark-sand beach on your right, the golf course on your left, for about 0.7 mile. It's flat and pretty, with beach access all the way. For many, this is plenty. For others more ambitious, continue on.

The walk then turns into a short, steep hike that climbs to a coastal ridge. A matrix of trails from other trailheads converge on top. Most venture to the edge of the oceanfront cliffs; if you have young kids, keep them on a leash. You can explore to the top of the ridge for dramatic views. You can see north past Mussel Rock and along the San Francisco coast to the Cliff House, and beyond to the curving Point Reyes waterfront.

User Groups: Hikers and dogs. No horses or mountain bikes. No wheelchair facilities.

Permits: No permits are required. Parking and access are free.

Maps: For a topographic map, ask the USGS for Montara Mountain.

Directions: From San Francisco, take I-280 South to Daly City to the exit for Highway 1/ Pacifica. Bear right at the exit from Highway 1 and drive 3.7 miles into Pacifica and to Exit 506 (toward Paloma Avenue/Francisco Boulevard). Take that exit and continue south 0.2 mile to Paloma Avenue. Turn right on Paloma and drive 0.2 mile to Beach Boulevard. Turn left on Beach and go 0.5 mile (you will pass Pacifica Pier on right) to parking on right and trailhead ahead at corner of Beach and Clarendon Road.

Access points and trailheads to the park are also available at Bradford Way, Mori Point Road, and the end of Fairway Drive.

Contact: Mori Point, Golden Gate National Recreation Area, Presidio Visitors Center, 415/561-4323, www.nps.gov/prsf; Pacifica Visitors Center, 650/355-4122, www.pacifica-chamber.com.

75 MONTARA MOUNTAIN TRAIL

7.0 mi/3.0 hr

in San Pedro Valley County Park in Pacifica

Map 7.2, page 278

Here's one of the best day hikes in the Bay Area. Just 20 minutes south of San Francisco is this sensational trail in San Pedro Valley County Park. The coastal beauty is divine, and hikers can carve out their own personal slice of heaven. The Montara Mountain Trail is the prize of the park, featuring the best viewing area for wispy Brooks Falls and great lookouts to the Pacific Coast.

From the west side of the parking lot, look for the signed trailhead for the Montara Mountain Trail. Take that uphill for 1.3 miles through the eucalyptus grove to the junction of the Brooks Creek Trail. Continue a short distance on the Montara Mountain Trail, where you will rise above tree line, to a spur that leads a short distance to a rock outcrop along San Pedro Ridge for a sensational coastal view to the north. The trail is routed uphill to a sub-ridge to a junction, inside McNee Ranch/ Montara Beach State Park, at a service road. Turn left for the final 1.1-mile push to reach the summit. You can stand atop the actual pinnacle, with a fenced antenna station off to the side a bit.

On a clear spring day, the views are absolutely stunning in all directions—highlighted by the Pacific Ocean, the Farallon Islands, and miles of the adjacent off-limits Crystal Springs Watershed. If you look down-slope to the southeast, you can glimpse a piece of gorgeous, off-limits Pilarcitos Lake.

On the way back, when you reach the forks with the Brooks Creek Trail, bear right and see if there is any water in Brooks Falls. There is a good lookout of the gorge across the canyon. Brooks Falls is connected in a series of narrow, silver-tasseled tiers in a gorge of chaparral-covered wilderness canyon. It falls 175 feet in all, from top to bottom, including breaks. At peak flow, there can be five strands. There never seems to be enough water in this waterfall, but it still is a very pretty gorge. It usually only runs in late winter and spring (best, of course, after several days of rain).

Though few take advantage of it, with a partner and a shuttle car, you could complete a great one-way hike. After you reach the top of Montara Mountain, hike 3.8 miles, where you sail down into McNee Ranch State Park above Montara and to Montara State Beach. You descend all the way, with glorious views for the entire route. So with cars parked at each end of the trail, you can hike 7.3 miles one-way from San Pedro Valley County Park, up Montara Mountain, and down to Montara State Beach.

User Groups: Hikers and horses (on designated trails only). Some trails and facilities are wheelchair-accessible. No dogs or mountain bikes.

Permits: No permits are required. An entrance fee of $6 per vehicle is charged.

Maps: For a free trail map, contact San Pedro Valley County Park. For a topographic map, ask the USGS for Montara Mountain.

Directions: From San Francisco, take Highway 1 south to Pacifica. Turn east on Linda Mar Boulevard and continue until it dead-ends, at Oddstad Boulevard. Turn right and drive to the park entrance, located about 50 yards on the left. The trailhead is on the southwest side of the parking lot.

Contact: San Pedro Valley County Park, 650/355-8289, http://parks.smcgov.org; City of Pacifica, Parks Department, 650/738-7300, www.cityofpacifica.org.

76 WEILER RANCH ROAD
1.5 mi/1.0 hr 🚶1 ⛰7

in San Pedro Valley County Park in Pacifica

Map 7.2, page 278

From parking, go to the north end and take the service road to Weiler Ranch Road, then continue for a half mile to the end of the road at the headwaters of San Pedro Creek and the foot of the hills below Sweeney Ridge and San

Francisco Fish and Wildlife Refuge. This is the best area in the park for wildlife sightings, with the best wildlife watching opportunities at dusk. Weiler Ranch Road is a service road that is routed out through the heart of a valley nestled with meadows that attract wildlife at dawn and dusk. It's common to see deer and rabbits in the meadow, and red-tailed hawks and turkey vultures overhead. If you get real lucky, you might get a glimpse of a bobcat. In fact, we've had these wildlife sightings many times, but it's always best right at dusk. Turn back when ready.

The gate to the park is often closed at the best times to see wildlife, at dawn and dusk. One tip is to park outside the park entrance, so you have access even when gated.

User Groups: Hikers and horses (on designated trails only). Some trails and facilities are wheelchair-accessible. No dogs or mountain bikes.

Permits: No permits are required. An entrance fee of $6 per vehicle is charged.

Maps: A brochure and map are available at entrance kiosk and visitors center. For a free trail map, contact San Pedro Valley County Park. For a topographic map, ask the USGS for Montara Mountain.

Directions: From San Francisco, take Highway 1 south to Pacifica. Turn east on Linda Mar Boulevard and continue until it dead-ends at Oddstad Boulevard. Turn right and drive to the park entrance, located about 50 yards ahead on the left. The trailhead is on the southwest side of the parking lot.

Contact: San Pedro Valley County Park, 650/355-8289, http://parks.smcgov.org; City of Pacifica, Parks Department, 650/738-7300, www.cityofpacifica.org.

77 SAN PEDRO MOUNTAIN
6.0 mi/2.5 hr 🚶2 ⛰7

in McNee Ranch State Park in Montara

Map 7.2, page 278

On one side is an expanse of gorgeous beach,

Montara State Beach. On the other is a 1,898-foot wilderness mountain, Montara Mountain and McNee Ranch/Montara State Beach. Together they comprise a can't-miss get-out. If you can go early enough to beat the traffic, this one can be great, start to finish.

The park spans for miles from beachfront to mountaintop. You get access at the yellow pipe gate and service road (there is parking space for only a few cars; a better idea is to park down Highway 1 a short ways on the west side, then return on foot to the gate). At the gate, turn left and hike the trail that tracks along the coastal ridgelines, an easy to moderate climb that leads to an overlook of Gray Whale Cove and the ocean. From this viewpoint, you may feel an odd sense of irony: Below is Highway 1, typically filled with a stream of slow-moving cars driven by people who want to get somewhere else; meanwhile, you are in a place of peace and serenity, happy right where you are.

Montara State Beach is a long sandy beach with pretty waves, views of passing fishing boats and ships, and surf fishing for perch. The extreme north end has a feeling of seclusion, edged by a cliff, even with Highway 1 just above. This is one of the few state beaches in California to allow dogs.

User Groups: Hikers and dogs. No horses or mountain bikes. No wheelchair facilities.

Permits: No permits are required. Parking and access are free.

Maps: For a topographic map, ask the USGS for Montara Mountain.

Directions: Take I-280 to Daly City and the split for Highway 1/Pacifica. Follow Highway 1 south for 11 miles (through Pacifica and past Devil's Slide) and emerge at Montara State Beach on your right, McNee Ranch on your left.

From East Bay and Peninsula: Take U.S. 101 or I-280 to Highway 92 in San Mateo. Follow Highway 92 west to Half Moon Bay and Highway 1. Turn right on Highway 1 and drive six miles to Moss Beach, then continue two miles to Montara. Park on the beach side of highway at the north end of Montara State Beach, or at southern end of beach adjacent to Outrigger Restaurant.

Contact: Half Moon Bay State Parks, 650/726-8820; Half Moon Bay State Ranger, 650/726-8819, www.parks.ca.gov.

78 MONTARA MOUNTAIN/ MCNEE RANCH
7.6 mi/3.75 hr

in McNee Ranch State Park in Montara

Map 7.2, page 278

Of the two major routes to the top of Montara Mountain, this is the one with two butt-kicker sections. It is well worth it. On a clear day from the top of Montara Mountain, the Farallon Islands to the northwest appear so close you may think you could reach out and pluck them from the ocean. To the east, it looks as if you could take a giant leap across the bay and land atop Mount Diablo.

Some 10 miles to the north and south, there's nothing but mountain wilderness connecting Sweeney Ridge to an off-limits state game preserve. By now you should be properly motivated for the climb. From the main access gate to the top, it's 3.8 miles, a rise of nearly 2,000 feet that includes two killer "ups."

From the pipe entrance gate, start the trip by hiking straight ahead, on the ranch-style service road. Follow this ranch road up the San Pedro Mountain ridgeline to the Montara Coastal Range. At the first fork, stay to the right on the dirt road as it climbs and turns.

Here's a secret: At the power lines, look for a deer trail on your left that is routed down through the chaparral to the west. This leads to an old concrete military army bunker. Enjoy the history, then head back up to the main road/trail.

After a 20-minute wheezer of an ascent—yes, butt-kicker level—look for a cutoff spur trail at a flat spot on the left side of the trail. This 30-yard cutoff trail leads to a perch for a dazzling view of Pacifica and northward along the Pacific Coast. After catching your breath, return to the trail and continue on, heading up, up, and up, eventually topping out at the summit. While antennas and transmitters are perched near the top, the actual summit, directly adjacent to the fenced transmitter station, is clear, so you can stand right on the tip-top. All you need for this hike is a clear day, some water, and plenty of inspiration. If you need reason to stay fit, this hike is it.

User Groups: Hikers, dogs, and mountain bikes. No horses. No wheelchair facilities.

Permits: No permits are required. Parking and access are free.

Maps: For a topographic map, ask the USGS for Montara Mountain.

Directions: Take I-280 to Daly City and the split for Highway 1/Pacifica. Follow Highway 1 south for 11 miles (through Pacifica and past Devil's Slide) and emerge at Montara State Beach on your right, McNee Ranch on your left.

From East Bay and Peninsula: Take U.S. 101 or I-280 to Highway 92 in San Mateo. Follow Highway 92 west to Half Moon Bay and Highway 1. Turn right on Highway 1 and drive six miles to Moss Beach, then continue two miles to Montara. Park on the beach side of highway at the north end of Montara State Beach, or at southern end of beach adjacent to Outrigger Restaurant.

Contact: Half Moon Bay State Parks, 650/726-8820; Half Moon Bay State Ranger, 650/726-8819, www.parks.ca.gov.

7 9 COYOTE POINT/ SHORELINE TRAIL

1.0-10.0 mi/0.5-5.0 hr 🏃1 ⛺7

in Coyote Point County Park in San Mateo

Map 7.2, page 278

Coyote Point is perched on the extended shore of the South Bay, an outstanding recreation site on the Peninsula. You get long-distance water views and a chance at many adventures. At the minimum, take the Marina Trail out to land's end at Coyote Point. You get a pretty view of the South Bay tidewaters, often with good numbers of shorebirds. It's just a start. Just east of the marina, take the gravel Shoreline Trail. These wetlands and adjacent flats attract resident ducks and geese, along with egrets, coots, sandpipers, and other migrants (avocets, for instance, arrive every March). You can take the Shoreline Trail along water's edge of the South Bay to where the trail turns north, and then heads inland. In the process, you get a cool view of jets coming in for landings.

The Bay Trail can also be linked with the Promenade Trail and Bluff Trail (flat and easy) that roughly circles the recreation area.

User Groups: Hikers, wheelchairs, and mountain bikes. No dogs or horses.

Permits: No permits are required. An entrance fee of $6 per vehicle is charged.

Maps: For a free trail map, contact Coyote Point County Park. For a topographic map, ask the USGS for San Mateo.

Directions: Take U.S. 101 to San Mateo and Exit 417 (for Poplar Avenue). Take the exit and merge onto East Poplar; drive a short distance to North Humboldt Street. Turn right and go 0.4 mile to (third right) Peninsula Avenue. Turn right and go 0.2 mile to Coyote Point Drive. Continue on Coyote Point Drive for 0.5 mile to Coyote Point Marina.

From the south, take U.S. 101 north (eight miles north of Redwood City) to Exit 417B (for Peninsula Avenue). Take that exit, keep right at the fork, and continue a short distance to Airport Boulevard. Turn right on Airport Boulevard and drive to Coyote Point Drive. Turn left and drive 0.5 mile to Coyote Point Marina.

Contact: Coyote Point County Park, San Mateo, 650/573-2592; San Mateo County Division of Parks, 650/363-4020, http://parks.smcgov.org.

80 FITZGERALD MARINE RESERVE
1.0 mi/0.5 hr   👣1 ⛰9

in Moss Beach

Map 7.2, page 278   **BEST**

The Fitzgerald Marine Reserve provides the best tidepool hopping in California. After parking, it's a short walk down to the tidepools; from here, you walk on exposed rock, watching the wonders of the tidal waters. In the tidepools, you may see hermit crabs, rock crabs, sea anemones, sculpins, starfish, sea snails, and many other animals and plants in various colors. The best bet is to pick a minus low tide and explore the tidepool world. The closer you look, the better it gets. When you go tidepool hopping, there is nothing more fascinating than discovering a variety of tiny sea creatures. The reef spans 30 acres with hundreds and hundreds of pockets, crevices, and cuts every time a minus low tide rolls back to the ocean. Be sure to wear boots that grip well, and take care not to crush any fragile sea plants as you walk. An option during low tides is to continue walking south on the beach to a beautiful cove at the foot of the Moss Beach Distillery, a popular watering hole. Note: No dogs, no beachcombing, no shell gathering. In other words, okay looky, but no touchy.

User Groups: Hikers only. No dogs, horses, or mountain bikes. No wheelchair facilities.

Permits: No permits are required. Parking and access are free.

Maps: For a topographic map, ask the USGS for Montara Mountain.

Directions: Take I-280 to Highway 1 in Daly City and drive through Pacifica, over Devil's Slide, and into Moss Beach. Turn right (west) at the signed turnoff at California Street and continue one mile to the parking area.

Contact: Fitzgerald Marine Reserve, Moss Beach, 650/728-3584; San Mateo County Parks Department, 650/363-4020 or 650/340-7598, http://parks.smcgov.org.

81 MAVERICKS BEACH
2.5 mi/1.5 hr   👣1 ⛰8

in Princeton at Half Moon Bay

Map 7.2, page 278

Mavericks is world famous for its big waves and surfing competition. But many people do not even know where it is. Even for those who know the place, it can be a stunner if you arrive at a nonpeak time: You will find a secluded stretch of beach at Pillar Point Head, hidden tidepools at low tides, and a pretty walk on a bluff that overlooks Pillar Point Harbor. When you drive Highway 1 along Half Moon Bay, you'll see a radar station that looks like a giant tennis ball at Pillar Point Head. Mavericks is located on the south side of Pillar Point Head. The parking lot is located at the foot of the road that leads to the radar station.

From the parking lot, a trail extends along a bluff perched above a beach and waterfront of Pillar Point Harbor. You get views across the water, harbor, and beyond to the coastal hills. Bird life is excellent, with grebes, gulls, and the usual suspects. I've seen otters on this side of the harbor, too. The walk leads out to the foot of the north rock jetty, which you can rock hop to fishing spots, or continue to Mavericks Beach. From the foot of the jetty, you turn right and arrive at an extended sandy beach. When seas are calm, sea lions often play peek-a-boo amid nearby kelp beds. At the end of the beach at Pillar Point, minus low tides unveil expansive rocky tide pools and crevices. If you continue exploring, during low tides you can boulder hop your way around Pillar Point Head (a gap stops you from reaching a hidden beach).

The big waves for world-class surfing arrive just offshore during periods of huge ocean swells, often 15-foot swells or bigger, and often (but not always) timed at the top of the tide.

User Groups: Hikers, dogs, and horses (not advised). No mountain bikes. No wheelchair facilities.

Permits: No permits are required. Parking and access are free.

Maps: For a topographic map, ask the USGS for Half Moon Bay.

Directions: Take I-280 to Daly City and the exit for Highway 1/Pacifica. Take that exit and drive 15.2 miles to Princeton/El Granada and a lighted intersection with Capistrano Road. Turn right on Capistrano Road and drive 0.4 mile to Prospect Way. Turn left on Prospect and drive 350 feet to Broadway. Turn left on Broadway and go 150 feet to Princeton Avenue. Turn right on Princeton and drive 0.3 mile to West Point Avenue. Turn right on West Point and go 300 feet, then turn left and drive 0.5 mile to a short, signed cutoff on left to parking lot.

From East Bay and Peninsula: From San Mateo, take Highway 92 west for 12 miles to Half Moon Bay and the junction with Highway 1. Turn right on Highway 1 and drive 3.9 miles to Princeton/El Granada and a lighted intersection with Capistrano Road. Turn left and continue to Pillar Point as above.

Contact: Pillar Point Harbor, 650/726-5727, www.smharbor.com/pillarpoint; weather recording 650/726-6070.

82 BAY RIDGE TRAIL/ CRYSTAL SPRINGS

11.0 mi one-way/ 5.0 hr   🥾 3   ⛰ 10

near Woodside

Map 7.2, page 278

The fight that took 70 years to win was resolved with one turn of a key. A locked gate at the Crystal Springs Watershed on the Peninsula was finally cracked open to the public. Access to the 23,000-acre watershed—which we once nicknamed the Forbidden Paradise—is finally possible, though by reservations only, where you join a group. Still, this is something special.

The trip is 11 miles, one-way with a shuttle, from the Quarry Gate near Highway 92 and extending on the Bay Ridge Trail to Sweeney Ridge, and then beyond to Sneath Lane Gate in San Bruno. The trip starts by passing through Quarry Gate. On a service road, climb 640 feet over the course of a mile to Cemetery Gate. This is the hardest part of the trip: a challenging climb on a bike, a steady rhythmic pull for hikers. You will pass through cypress forest

Pillar Point

© TOM STIENSTRA

and patches of chaparral, with views of Upper Crystal Springs.

Cemetery Gate to Five Points: After topping out at Cahill Ridge, enjoy an easy descent through old-growth cypress and Douglas fir, and farther north, redwoods. Keep an eye out on your left for a giant old-growth Douglas fir called "Big Doug." It's three miles to Five Points, a five-way road junction, and your link north to the Fifield Ridge Route.

Fifield Ridge to Portola Gate: This is the best part of the trip. From Five Points, you are routed up above hidden Pilarcitos Lake to Fifield Ridge, emerging in wilderness for stunning views of the wild east flank of Montara Mountain to your left. As you continue north, you then get sweeping views to your right of the South Bay. In spring, this area is loaded with wildflowers. Deer, bobcat, and fox provide occasional sightings.

Portola Gate to Sneath Lane: First pass a hidden meadow on your left with views of Pacifica and the ocean. Continue to the Bay Discovery Site, with a dramatic scope below of the Peninsula's wildlands, the lakes in the watershed, and the South Bay. The end of the trip is a downhill glide to the Sneath Lane Gate and your shuttle car.

As good as this is, it could get far better. For instance, another service road junctions with Fifield Ridge, providing a route up the little-seen eastern flank of Montara Mountain all the way to the 1,898-foot summit. Then the route goes over the top to McNee State Park and San Pedro Valley County Park. Opening that route would provide a sensational one-way hike, starting from the Sneath Lake access. You would climb to Sweeney Ridge, then into the watershed and to the summit of Montara Mountain, and then down the north side to McNee Ranch State Park in Montara.

User Groups: Hiking, biking, and horseback riding permitted, but not at the same time; volunteer trail leader required with all parties. No dogs. Limited wheelchair access from Skylawn trailhead.

Permits: Reservations are required.

Reserve online at www.sfwater.org (click on Community, Explore). Public access is restricted to groups under the supervision of a trained leader on Wednesdays, Saturdays, and Sundays.

Maps: For a free trail map, contact San Francisco Public Utilities Commission. For a topographic map, ask the USGS for San Mateo.

Directions: To Quarry Gate: From the Peninsula, take I-280 to Highway 92. Turn west on Highway 92, drive over Crystal Springs Reservoir and continue 0.5 mile to Quarry Gate on right. Turn right and go short distance to parking and trailhead.

To Sneath Lane Trailhead: To drop off the shuttle car, take I-280 to San Bruno and the exit for Sneath Lane. Take that exit, and drive west on Sneath Lane to the road's end. Leave the car near the access point for Golden Gate National Recreation Area.

Contact: San Francisco Public Utilities Commission, 650/652-3203, www.sfwater.org.

83 CRYSTAL SPRINGS TRAIL
6.4 mi/3.0 hr 🏃1 ⛰7

along Crystal Springs Reservoir near Woodside

Map 7.2, page 278

From the parking area, the Crystal Springs trail runs along the border of San Francisco watershed land, adjacent to Canada Road. Your destination is 3.2 miles away at the Pulgas Water Temple, where waters from Hetch Hetchy in Yosemite arrive via pipe and thunder into this giant, sunken bathtub-like structure surrounded by Roman pillars and a canopy. It's quite a sight. Beautiful Crystal Springs Reservoir is off to the west for most of the hike, though it occasionally disappears from view behind a hill as you continue south. Deer are commonly seen in this area—a nice bonus. The adjacent road, Canada Road, is a famous family bike trip on Bicycle Sundays, when it is closed to all vehicles.

User Groups: Hikers and mountain bikes. No dogs or horses. No wheelchair facilities.

Permits: No permits are required. Parking and access are free.

Maps: For a free trail map, contact San Mateo County Division of Parks. For a topographic map, ask the USGS for San Mateo.

Directions: From I-280 in San Mateo, take the Highway 92 exit and drive west to Canada Road/Highway 95. Turn south on Canada Road and drive 0.2 mile to the parking area, on the right.

Contact: San Mateo County Parks Department, 650/363-4020, http://parks.smc-gov.org.

84 HARKINS RIDGE LOOP FROM HALF MOON BAY
6.5 mi/3.5 hr 👥3 ⛰9

in Purisima Creek Redwoods Open Space Preserve

Map 7.2, page 278

One of our favorites. From staging area on Higgins Road south of Half Moon Bay, take the trailhead for Harkins Ridge Trail. It is routed through a redwood canyon and then rises up a sub-ridge 1,600 feet, within earshot of Skyline. Turn left on the North Ridge Trail, then left again on Whittemore Gulch Trail and sail back down to the starting spot. For much of the route, deep valleys plunge on each side.

There's one steep spot, but it's shaded for the most part, with pretty valley views. The route then turns left and climbs out of the canyon to a ridge, where a few steep spots on the way up make for dramatic drops on each side into remote valleys. At three miles, just a short distance from Skyline (close enough that you might even hear people at the parking lot), you emerge at a junction with the North Ridge Trail. Turn left on the North Ridge Trail for 0.5 mile, then take another left on Whittemore Gulch Trail for the easy 2.8 mile downhill glide back to the trailhead.

This trip can also be started from Skyline as

the Whittemore Gulch Loop, but the return trip will be up rather than down.

User Groups: Hikers. No bikes on Purisima Creek Trail or Harkins Ridge Trail. Bikes and horses often restricted on Whittemore Gulch Trail in wet weather. No dogs. No wheelchair facilities.

Permits: No permits are required. Parking and access are free.

Maps: For a free map, contact the Midpeninsula Regional Open Space District or pick one up at the trailhead. For a topographic map, ask the USGS for Woodside.

Directions: Take I-280 to Highway 92. Bear west on 92 and drive up to ridge and continue west to Half Moon Bay and lighted intersection at Main Street. Turn south (left) on Main Street and drive through town (about a mile) to Higgins-Purisima Road. Turn left on Higgins-Purisima and drive four miles (becomes curvy, watch out for bikes) to the staging area for Purisima Creek Redwoods Open Space Preserve on the left. Note: If the small parking lot is full, park on the road's shoulder ahead, on the right.

Contact: Midpeninsula Regional Open Space District, 650/691-1200, www.openspace.org.

85 WHITTEMORE GULCH LOOP FROM SKYLINE
6.5 mi/3.5 hr 👥1 ⛰9

in Purisima Creek Redwoods Open Space Preserve

Map 7.2, page 278

Purisima Creek Redwoods is a magnificent 2,633-acre preserve set on the western slopes of the Santa Cruz Mountains, from Skyline Boulevard down to Half Moon Bay. One of the best ways to explore the area is on this great loop hike. You can make it a one-way trip by having a shuttle car waiting at the trail's end at the Higgins-Purisima parking access.

This trail starts at the Skyline Access on Skyline Boulevard, located at a parking area just south of a small building (it used to be a store). From the trailhead, descend a short distance to a junction with the North Ridge Trail. Turn right and descend a further 0.5 mile to a junction with the Whittemore Gulch Trail. The trail drops quickly at first, then more gradually to the rim of the canyon.

At the canyon rim, a series of switchbacks takes you down the hill about 1,000 feet into the redwood canyon. It is well graded (about 10 percent). In all, the descent is 1,600 feet. At the bottom of the forest floor, turn left on the Harkins Ridge Trail and climb 3.3 miles back to the top.

Timing: On weekday mornings, this place can be paradise—Purisima can feel like a vast uninhabited wilderness, complete with the long-distance coastal views and a hidden redwood canyon. On Sunday afternoons, however, it's often crowded. Mountain bikers can be an issue when they ride fast downhill on Harkins Ridge Trail.

User Groups: Hikers. No bikes on Purisima Creek Trail or Harkins Ridge Trail. Bikes and horses often restricted on Whittemore Gulch Trail in wet weather. No dogs. No wheelchair facilities.

Permits: No permits are required. Parking and access are free.

Maps: For a free map, contact the Midpeninsula Regional Open Space District or pick one up at the trailhead. For a topographic map, ask the USGS for Woodside.

Directions: Take I-280 to Highway 92. Bear west on 92 and drive past Crystal Springs and up to the ridge and the junction with Highway 35/Skyline. Turn left on Skyline and drive 4.5 miles to parking area on right, signed for preserve.

Contact: Midpeninsula Regional Open Space District, 650/691-1200, www.openspace.org.

86 REDWOOD TRAIL
0.5 mi/0.5 hr

in Purisima Creek Redwoods Open Space Preserve

Map 7.2, page 278

The 0.25-mile-long Redwood Trail allows just about anybody to experience the grandeur of a redwood forest. Anybody? People with baby strollers, wheelchairs, or walkers, as well as those recovering from poor health, will be able to do this trail. It starts at an elevation 2,000 feet on Skyline Boulevard and is routed north under a canopy of giant redwoods. At the end, there are picnic tables and restrooms. And the return trip is just as easy. Most people don't really hike the trail, they just kind of mosey along, seeing how it feels to wander freely among ancient trees.

User Groups: Hikers and wheelchairs. No dogs, horses, or mountain bikes.

Permits: No permits are required. Parking and access are free.

Maps: For a free map, contact the Midpeninsula Regional Open Space District or pick one up at the trailhead. For a topographic map, ask the USGS for Woodside.

Directions: Take I-280 to Highway 92. Bear west on 92 and drive past Crystal Springs and up to the ridge and the junction with Highway 35/Skyline. Turn left on Skyline and drive 4.5 miles (past parking area on right) and continue to mile marker 16.65 to parking area on right, signed for preserve and Redwood Trail.

Contact: Midpeninsula Regional Open Space District, 650/691-1200, www.openspace.org.

87 HUDDART PARK LOOP
7.5 mi/3.5 hr

in Woodside

Map 7.2, page 278

With two slight changes (and we'll get to that) this hike could be a 9. As it is, the Huddart Park Loop is still a treasure. Huddart Park covers 1,000 acres from the foothills near Woodside on up to Skyline Boulevard. Nestled in a grassy area surrounded by woods, you can picnic, play, or head off into the wild. The best hike is a 7.5-mile loop that provides a tour through deep woods and along hidden creeks. This trek includes a 1,400-foot climb, but because trail makers kept grades at 6 percent, it's a steady, rhythmic pull to the top for hikers or runners, with all junctions signed. The woods extend up the slopes of Kings Mountain and a network of trails are routed through the redwoods, amid patches of hardwoods, and along small creeks.

Start the hike at the Zwierlein Picnic Area (set next to a small parking lot near a restroom). Be sure to grab a trail map first, though; there are dozens of loop options at virtually every trail junction. At the trailhead sign, start on the left by hiking 0.2 mile to the Dean Trail, and then continue down into the canyon to the bridge at McGarvey Gulch and the junction with the Crystal Springs Trail. Turn right, and from the start, the trail feels like a tunnel through vegetation. It then quickly drops into redwood forest and crosses two small wood bridges over a pretty creek. From here, the Crystal Springs Trail rises 3.4 miles and 1,400 feet to Skyline. The grade is perfect. From the bridge, it took us an hour and 15 minutes to reach the top (2,000 feet), always in rhythm.

Before reaching Skyline, turn left on Summit Springs Trail (a dirt road) and climb steeply for 0.4 mile to the top of the ridge and the Skyline Trail. Turn left on Skyline Trail and continue another 0.3 mile to the Chinquapin Trail on the left. The Chinquapin Trail is routed in and out of heavily wooded canyons near the headwaters of McGarvey Gulch creek, down all the way. It eventually links to the Dean Trail; turn left to be routed back to the Zwierlein trailhead and parking lot. Add variety to your hike, or make it shorter or longer, by carrying a map.

The park has applied crushed gravel on a good part of the route to stop erosion caused by horses. For many, it looks almost paved. Instead, rangers should clear some trees at Skyline to create what could be a gorgeous sweeping view of the South Bay. (Rangers cleared a wooded hilltop at China Camp State Park in San Rafael to create one of the best lookouts in the Bay Area—see the *Patrick's Point* hike in this chapter).

User Groups: Hikers and horses. Mountain bikes are permitted on paved roads only. Horses restricted when trails are wet. The Chickadee Trail at Huddart Park is wheelchair-accessible. No dogs.

Permits: No permits are required. An entrance fee of $6 per vehicle is charged.

Maps: A brochure and map are available in a box at the entrance. For a trail map, contact Huddart Park. For a topographic map, ask the USGS for Woodside.

Directions: From San Francisco, take I-280 south and drive 20 miles to Woodside and the exit for Highway 84/Woodside Road. Take that exit, turn west (right) on Woodside Road, and drive 2.8 miles to Woodside. Continue 1.7 miles to Kings Mountain Road. Turn right and drive 2.8 miles (curvy) to the park entrance on the right. Take the entrance road to the kiosk, then continue to the parking area at Zwierlein Picnic Area. The trailhead is on the far side of the parking lot (adjacent to a restroom).

Contact: Huddart Park, 650/851-0326; San Mateo County Parks Department, 650/363-4020 or 650/340-7598 (group tour reservations), http://parks.smcgov.org.

88 TAFONI MONOLITH TO VISTA POINT

6.5 mi/3.5 hr   🥾 2   ⛰ 9

El Corte de Madera Open Space Preserve

Map 7.2, page 278

This is a 6.5-mile walk with about everything you could ask for: a beautiful destination with big trees, epic views, parking, and nice folks on the trail. From the trailhead, the first leg is 0.5-mile through a mixed forest, where the trail undulates up and down in short rises and falls north (roughly along Skyline) to another access point (Gate CM02) along Skyline/Highway 35. To reach the Methuselah Tree, cross Skyline

Tafoni Monolith

here and walk a short a short distance to the monolith. The diameter of the base of the tree is 14 feet across, with a circumference of 44 feet—the biggest redwood on the north Peninsula. The park district estimates the tree is 1,800 years old.

From the Methuselah Tree, recross Skyline Boulevard and take the Sierra Morena Trail for 0.4 mile to the Fir Trail. Turn left and walk 0.6 mile to a major junction with the Tafoni Trail. From here, it's just 0.1 mile to the spur to the Tafoni, then another 0.1 mile with an easy descent to the Tafoni monolith. The trail leads a short way into a canyon and to a viewing deck perched at the base of the Tafoni, a 50-foot sandstone monolith that juts up from the wooded slope. From the deck, you get a close-up view what looks like etched fretwork in the rock. As you peer up, you can see a matrix of holes, hollows, and crevices. There's nothing else quite like it anywhere.

Return to the junction of the Tafoni Trail and Fir Trail and follow the Fir Trail to the DC-6 crash monument. A short cutoff then leads to Vista Point. You top out at a 2,200-foot sub-ridge, where a break in the forest provides a view to the west that extends to the coast and ocean.

Most call the preserve "ECM" for short. It's a big preserve and it spans a variety of landscapes with a matrix of trails and abandoned roads. ECM spans 2,817 acres with 36 miles of trails, with excellent easy hikes and outstanding mountain biking, including plenty of single track. From what I've seen on the trail here, the people riding do everything they can to slow down, smile, greet, and pass hikers with care. Maybe there is hope for the human race, after all.

User Groups: Hiking, mountain bikes, horses. No dogs. No bikes or horses on short spur to Tafoni Monolith. No wheelchair facilities.

Permits: Parking and access are free.

Maps: Obtain a free map at the trailhead or from the Midpeninsula Regional Open Space District. For a topographic map, ask the USGS for Woodside.

Directions: Take I-280 to the exit for Highway 35/Bunker Hill Road (also signed for Highway 92W). Take that exit, continue

0.2 mile to frontage road, turn left and go 1.1 miles to Highway 92 (stoplight). Turn right on Highway 92 and drive two miles up the hill to a left turn lane for Highway 35/Skyline. Turn left and drive 9.6 miles to El Corte de Madera Open Space Preserve on the right. In 2015, the Midpeninsula Open Space District opened a new parking lot with a big sign off Highway 35, with a new staging area with trail maps, trailhead, and portable restroom.

From the Peninsula: Take I-280 to Highway 84. Turn west on Highway 84 and drive about seven miles (curvy through Woodside) to Sky Londa and Highway 35 (Skyline Boulevard). Turn right (north) and go 2.8 miles to El Corte de Madera Open Space Preserve on the left.

From East Bay: Take Highway 92 west to Crystal Springs and continue to crest at Skyline. Turn left and drive 9.6 miles to parking on right.

Contact: Midpeninsula Regional Open Space District, 650/691-1200, www.openspace.org.

89 ALAMBIQUE TRAIL
4.5 mi/2.5 hr

in Wunderlich County Park near Woodside

Map 7.2, page 278

This trailhead features a 4.5-mile loop hike that drops into a remote redwood canyon with a creek, then rises back up, looping back through forest to the starting point. The only thing the trail lacks is a series of gorgeous lookouts. You want views? Not here.

The trip starts on the east side of Skyline Boulevard, where a large blue sign for the Bay Ridge Trail marks the trailhead. From Skyline, start the trip on the Alambique Trail (signed). Here you work your way down a canyon for two miles amid a second-growth redwood forest. On foggy mornings, moisture can be so heavy that it can drip from the branches of redwoods and Douglas firs like a sparse rain. Everything smells wet, dense, and old. Our personal preference is a fogbound morning, when the heavy air smothers distant sounds, creating perfect quiet.

It takes only about 40 minutes to reach a canyon bottom, where you cross a feeder stream to Alambique Creek. This watershed is home to many banana slugs and newts, and when the forest is dripping with moisture, they are often on the trail—so be careful not to accidentally squish the little fellers. Though the canyon is cool and moist, it is the kind of place you can sit for a while and enjoy a trail lunch in complete peace. For the moment, you can let the rest of the world worry about their latest problems. There's always something, right?

Shortly after a creek crossing, you will reach a four-way junction with the Skyline Trail in about two miles. To return to the starting point, take the sharpest right on the Skyline Trail and climb back out (with a few short drops) for 2.4 miles to a staging area.

If you want to extend your trip at the junction, instead turn left on the Alambique Trail. This is routed farther down into the park to an additional network of trails. The best offshoots are to The Meadows (turn left on Bear Gulch Trail for 0.3 mile) or to Alambique Flat (to the right for 0.2 mile). Amid the second-growth forest along the lower portion of the Alambique Trail, there is a single awesome redwood giant called The Methuselah Tree that still remains. Its trunk is roughly 45 feet around, with massive burls and a burned-out gap.

User Groups: Hikers and horses. No dogs or mountain bikes. No wheelchair facilities.

Permits: No permits are required. Parking and access are free.

Maps: For a trail map, contact Huddart Park. For a topographic map, ask the USGS for Woodside.

Directions: Take I-280 to Woodside and Highway 84. Turn east on Highway 84 and go to Sky Londa and Highway 35/Skyline Boulevard. Turn right (north) and go 2.5 miles to the trailhead, on the right (signed Bay Ridge Trail). Limited parking is available on the road's shoulder.

From the East Bay: Take Highway 92 west to the junction of I-280 and continue three miles to Highway 35/Skyline Boulevard. Turn left (south) and go 10 miles to the trailhead, on the left.

Contact: Wunderlich County Park, c/o Huddart Park, 650/851-1210 or 650/851-0326 (entry kiosk); San Mateo County Parks Department, 650/363-4020, www.co.sanmateo.ce.us.

90 MEADOW LOOP TRAIL

5.5 mi/3.0 hr 🚶3 ⛰️7

in Wunderlich County Park near Woodside

Map 7.2, page 278

Wunderlich County Park is one of the better spots on the Peninsula for clearing out the brain cobwebs. The network of trails here provides a variety of adventures, from short strolls to all-day treks. Take your pick. The Meadow Loop is the preferred route; it circles much of the park, first crosses through oak woodlands, then rises to open grasslands, and finally passes a second-growth redwood forest on the way back. The Alambique Trailhead spans from Wunderlich near Woodside (this hike) to Skyline and Highway 35 (the previous hike).

Make sure you have a trail map, then take this route: Near the park entrance off Woodside Road, look for the signed trailhead for Alambique Trail and hike for 0.7 mile. At the junction with Meadow Trail, turn right, hike for 0.4 mile, and then turn left on to Meadow Trail and climb up to The Meadows in 1.1 miles. This is a perfect picnic site, with rolling hills, grasslands, and great views. To complete the loop, forge onward, then turn right at Bear Gulch Trail and take it all the way back, including switchbacks, to the park entrance. This hike includes an elevation gain of nearly 1,000 feet, so come prepared for a workout.

User Groups: Hikers and horses. No dogs or mountain bikes. No wheelchair facilities.

Permits: No permits are required. A $6 fee is charged per vehicle.

Maps: For a free map, contact San Mateo County Division of Parks. For a topographic map, ask the USGS for Woodside.

Directions: From San Francisco, take I-280 south and drive 20 miles to the exit for Highway 84/Woodside Road. Take that exit to Woodside Road, turn right and drive 2.7 miles (through Woodside) to the park entrance on the right.

Contact: Wunderlich Park, c/o Huddart Park, 650/851-1210; San Mateo County Parks Department, 650/363-4020, http://parks.smcgov.org.

91 RAVENSWOOD OPEN SPACE PRESERVE

2.0 mi/0.75 hr 🚶1 ⛰️8

near Menlo Park

Map 7.2, page 278

This 370-acre parcel of land is rich in marshland habitat and is home to many types of birds. The highlights are two excellent observation decks. From the parking area at the end of Bay Road, backtrack by walking across a bridged slough to the trailhead, on the north side of the road. You will immediately come to a fork in the road. You can turn right and walk 200 feet to an observation deck with great views of the South Bay. If you go left instead, you will find a hard-surface path that heads north and hooks out toward the bay to another wood observation deck. This is the primary destination for most visitors. There always seems to be egrets and herons, but sandpipers and dozens of other species will stop here on their migratory journeys.

User Groups: Hikers, wheelchairs, and mountain bikes. No dogs or horses.

Permits: No permits are required. Parking and access are free.

Maps: For a free map, contact the Midpeninsula Regional Open Space District. For a topographic map, ask the USGS for Mountain View.

Directions: Take U.S. 101 to Palo Alto and the exit for University Avenue. Take that exit and follow the signs a short distance to University Avenue/East Palo Alto, and continue three long blocks to Bay Road. Turn right on Bay Road and drive one mile (through the gate, becomes dirt) to the end of the road and the preserve entrance and parking on the left.

Contact: Midpeninsula Regional Open Space District, 650/691-1200, www.openspace.org.

92 PALO ALTO BAYLANDS TRAIL

4.0 mi/1.5 hr 🏃1 ⛰7

in Palo Alto

Map 7.2, page 278

Of the bay's 20 richest wetlands, the Palo Alto Baylands Preserve offers some of the best access and sightings to take in the annual migrations in late fall, winter, and spring. You can sight residents year-round, as well as good opportunities for ground squirrels, rabbits, and fox. From the Nature Center, take the trail that runs out along the slough and turns left to parallel the Palo Alto Municipal Airport. It's called the San Francisquito Trail. Many enjoy watching the small planes take off and land. The trail runs north to San Francisquito Creek. Here you turn right, and venture out to where the creek, which looks more like a tidal slough most of the year, enters the South Bay. Return when you're ready.

At peak migrations, you can see ducks, curlews, killdeers, willets, avocets, stilts, coots, herons, egrets, and other waterfowl making this stop on the Pacific Flyway. As they arrive to the bay's wetlands, they join resident marsh wrens, sandpipers, song sparrows, red-tailed hawks, and other wildlife including rabbits, ground squirrels, and foxes. Ground squirrels can provide a sideshow, along with surprise jackrabbits. The rabbits can pop up literally at your feet—and take your breath away by the shock, then sprint off at warp speed.

User Groups: Hikers, wheelchairs, and mountain bikes. No dogs or horses.

Permits: No permits are required. Parking and access are free.

Maps: For a topographic map, ask the USGS for Mountain View.

Directions: Take U.S. 101 to Palo Alto and the exit for Embarcadero East. Take that exit and drive east (past the golf course and airport on left) to a stop sign. Turn left and drive past the abandoned yacht harbor until you reach a sharp right turn. Park at the lot on the right (south). The nature preserve is on the left (north).

Contact: Palo Alto Baylands Nature Center, 650/617-3156, www.cityofpaloalto.org.

93 BAY TRAIL TO CHARLESTON SLOUGH

4.0 mi/1.5 hr 🏃1 ⛰7

at Shoreline at Mountain View Park

Map 7.2, page 278

This 750-acre swath of wetlands, ponds, and levee trails is one of the Bay Area's great local parks. Plus it's free. It is located east of U.S. 101 in Mountain View near the Shoreline Amphitheater and spans to the shore of South San Francisco Bay. The park provides an array of recreation—bike, hike, and boat—plus on clear days, great long-distance views from the shore of the bay.

From the parking area at Shoreline Lake, walk north on the Bay Trail (a levee road) out past Charleston Slough (on your right). You then connect to the Adobe Creek Loop Trail (a right turn), which is routed out to the shore of the South Bay. Great views, bird-watching, and fresh air.

A great easy walk, in other words. It's also a testament to the Bay Area's 10-mile "Bubble Rule." That's where residents rarely visit local destinations that are outside a 10-mile radius of their home, and in turn, miss out on many great parks.

This trail provides access to an expanse of wetlands and marsh habitat. Within minutes, with each step you will gain access to marshland that has been preserved in its natural state. From afar, the surroundings may appear to be nothing more than pickleweed and mud, but look closer, and you will begin to see the huge diversity of birds and wildlife that thrive in this very rich ecosystem. Egrets seem particularly plentiful.

User Groups: Hikers and mountain bikes. No dogs or horses, and no dogs are permitted beyond entry kiosk. No wheelchair facilities.

Permits: No permits are required. Parking and access are free.

Maps: For a topographic map, ask the USGS for Mountain View.

Directions: From San Francisco, take U.S. 101 south for 34 miles to Mountain View and the exit for Rengstorff Avenue. Take that exit, keep right at the fork (signed for Amphitheatre Parkway) and merge onto Rengstorff Avenue, and continue 0.3 mile to Amphitheatre Parkway. Continue onto Amphitheatre Parkway and drive 0.7 mile to North Shoreline Boulevard. Turn left and drive 1.4 miles (stay right at the island/golf course on left) to entrance for Shoreline Regional Park. Continue ahead and turn left to main parking area, boat ramp, aquatic center/boathouse, and trailheads.

Contact: Shoreline at Mountain View Park, 650/903-6392, www.mountainview.gov.

94 WINDY HILL LOOP
7.5 mi/3.5 hr

in Windy Hill Open Space Preserve

Map 7.2, page 278

For most, the big thing is the view from the top. The ridge rises up above oak woodlands, and from the grasslands across the hilltops, where on clear days you have unobstructed views to the east across the South Bay, East Bay hills, and to Mount Diablo on the horizon. In winter, an inversion layer at roughly 800-1,000-foot elevation, like a lid, is common across the South Bay, and at other times, low-lying stratus. In each case, you can peer over the top like it's a foggy sea.

A 7.5-mile loop takes you around most of the park, a bottom-to-top-to-bottom route that connects several trails (be sure to have a trail map with you). From the Portola Gate, take the Spring Ridge Trail past Sausal Pond, and with a few cutoffs, to the Hamms Gulch Trail. That climbs to the top, with switchbacks to make the 600-foot climb (over 2.6 miles) less of a challenge. At the ridge, you turn right on the Lost Trail/Anniversary Trail and enjoy the views en route 1.1 mile to the Spring Ridge Trail. Turn right and sail back down.

From the 1,900-foot summit, a grass-covered hilltop, you can see San Francisco Bay on one side and the Pacific Ocean on the other. If views are all you want, just drive to the trailhead at Skyline and the 0.7-mile Anniversary Trail, which is routed from the parking area to the summit, provides them.

The park spans 1,335 acres from the foothills (elevation 600 feet) and up the slope to Skyline (1,200 feet), with staging areas located both at the foot of the preserve near Portola Valley and on top of Skyline. Its location creates a microclimate and a procession of habitats across its landscape: oak woodlands, gulches with conifers and riparian zones, wetlands and a pond, and ridge-top grasslands.

User Groups: Hikers, horses, and dogs (allowed on Hamms Gulch Trail, Eagle Trail, and Anniversary Trail; prohibited on others). No mountain bikes (except on the preserve's Spring Ridge Trail). There are wheelchair facilities in the picnic area adjacent to the parking area.

Permits: No permits are required. Parking and access are free.

Maps: A brochure and map are available at the trailhead. For a free trail map and brochure, contact the Midpeninsula Regional Open Space District. For a topographic map, ask the USGS for Mindego Hill.

Directions: Take I-280 to the exit for Sand Hill Road near Menlo Park. Turn west on Sand Hill Road. Drive 2.1 miles (becomes Portola Rd.) and continue straight for 2.5 miles to signed parking on right.

Skyline Trailhead: Take I-280 to Woodside and the exit for Woodside Road/Highway 84. Turn west and drive 6.5 miles (curvy through Woodside) to Sky Londa and Skyline

Boulevard/Highway 35. Turn left on Skyline and drive 2.3 miles to trailhead on left.

Contact: Midpeninsula Regional Open Space District, 650/691-1200, www.openspace.org.

95 SAN ANDREAS FAULT TRAIL
0.6 mi/0.5 hr 👫1 ⛰7

in Los Trancos Open Space Preserve

Map 7.2, page 278

This trail may not have heartbreaking beauty, but it is unique: the San Andreas Fault Trail. This is a self-guided tour of an earthquake trail, and it includes several examples of fault movement. The 13 numbered signposts along the way correspond with numbered explanations in the park brochure. If you don't want a geology lesson, you may be content with the good views of the Peninsula from the 2,000-foot ridgeline. Most hikers connect San Andreas Fault Trail to Lost Creek Loop Trail, a pleasant and easy bonus leg that is routed into secluded spots along a pretty creek.

The Monte Bello Open Space Preserve is located on the other side of Page Mill Road and provides a more dynamic landscape. But if you want unique, you can get it on the Fault Trail.

User Groups: Hikers only. The trail is not wheelchair-accessible, but the parking lot is and offers a nice view. No dogs, horses, or mountain bikes.

Permits: No permits are required. Parking and access are free.

Maps: A brochure and map are available at the trailhead. For a free trail map, contact the Midpeninsula Regional Open Space District. For a topographic map, ask the USGS for Mindego Hill.

Directions: From I-280 in Palo Alto, turn west on Page Mill Road and drive seven twisty miles to the signed parking area, on the right. The Monte Bello Open Space Preserve is directly across the street, on the left (south).

Contact: Midpeninsula Regional Open Space District, 650/691-1200, www.openspace.org.

96 CLOUDS REST TRAIL
4.0 mi/2.0 hr 👫1 ⛰7

in Coal Creek Open Space Preserve

Map 7.2, page 278

The Clouds Rest Trail at Coal Creek Open Space Preserve is perched on the slopes from Skyline that face the South Bay. The trailhead is at Vista Point on Skyline, so the pay-offs start before you take a step on the trail. From here, take Clouds Rest Trail to Alpine Road and back, an easy in-and-outer; dogs OK.

From the lookout, you tower over the South Bay. You get sweeping views across the foothills, the valley floor, and across the South Bay to the East Bay hills. You can point out Stanford Tower, the Dumbarton Bridge, Lick Observatory, and Mount Diablo.

The preserve spans from Skyline east across 508 acres. The park's trails, actually old ranch roads, cover only four miles as they traverse the grasslands past a classic-looking barn and down along a small creek. You can make a quick loop by following Clouds Rest Trail to Meadow Trail and returning back along Alpine Road, or hiking farther north for an out-and-back trip. On a clear day, you'll never forget the view. Most Peninsula residents have never heard of the Coal Creek Open Space Preserve—it is one of the lesser-developed parklands in the Bay Area.

User Groups: Hikers, dogs, horses, and mountain bikes. No wheelchair facilities.

Permits: No permits are required. Parking and access are free.

Maps: A brochure and map are available at the trailhead. For a free trail map, contact the Midpeninsula Regional Open Space District. For a topographic map, ask the USGS for Mindego Hill.

Directions: Take I-280 to Woodside and the exit for Woodside Road/Highway 84. Take the exit to Woodside Road, turn west and drive 6.5 miles (through Woodside, enter redwoods, becomes curvy as you climb) to Sky Londa and Skyline Boulevard/Highway 35. Turn left on

Skyline and drive six miles to Caltrans Vista Point on left.

Alternate route from South Peninsula: Coal Creek Open Space Preserve and Vista Point is located 1.2 miles north of the junction of Page Mill Road and Skyline. Page Mill out of Palo Alto is narrow, twisty, with blind turns and dangerous for cars vs. bikes.

Contact: Midpeninsula Regional Open Space District, 650/691-1200, www.openspace.org.

97 BLACK MOUNTAIN
3.5 mi/2.0 hr   🏃2 ⛰8

in Monte Bello Open Space Preserve

Map 7.2, page 278   **BEST (**

The Monte Bello Open Space Preserve encompasses more than 2,700 acres of the most natural and scenic lands on the east-facing slopes of the Peninsula foothills. It includes 2,800-foot Black Mountain, the headwaters of Stevens Creek, and this pretty trail, which is crowned by great views and offers the opportunity to camp at a little-known backpack site. For most, a map is a must.

From the parking area, start the trip by taking the Stevens Creek Nature Trail for 0.3 mile (ignore the fork) to Canyon Trail. Turn right on Canyon Trail, and go 0.25 mile to the Bella Vista Trail. Turn left and climb a mile to the ridge and the Old Ranch Trail. Turn right on Old Ranch Trail and you will arrive at the Black Mountain Campground (permit only) in about 0.5 mile. In the process, you will pass the headwaters of Stevens Creek as well as the San Andreas Fault. You'll also get long-distance views of the valley and the ridge above San Jose, and opportunities to see squirrels, hawks, rabbits, and deer. It's about a 500-foot climb from the parking area to the campground.

Then, from the campground, it's a 0.2 mile walk on Monte Bello Road to the summit of Black Mountain (some transmitters mar the perfection). On clear spring days, the views are eye-popping. For campers, bring flashlights with fresh batteries, and be sure to make the walk here in darkness for stargazing, or time the trip for a meteor shower.

From the summit, another bonus is available by continuing on Monte Bello Road for a short distance to a picnic site on the right. It is set adjacent to a sprinkling of rock crags that look like a movie set simulating another planet (great for kids). There are more stellar views of the canyon and foothills below to the east.

User Groups: Hikers, horses, and mountain bikes (restricted from some trails). This trail is not open to wheelchairs, but the parking lot and a short side trail are wheelchair-accessible and offer a good view. No dogs.

Permits: No permits are required for day-use. Campers must have reservation and permit for the backpack camp.

Maps: A brochure and map are available at the trailhead. For a free trail map, contact the Midpeninsula Regional Open Space District. For a topographic map, ask the USGS for Mindego Hill.

Directions: From I-280 in Palo Alto, turn west on Page Mill Road and drive seven twisty miles to the signed parking area for Monte Bello Open Space Preserve on the left (south). Los Trancos Open Space Preserve is directly across the street to the right (north).

Contact: Midpeninsula Regional Open Space District, 650/691-1200, www.openspace.org.

98 BOREL HILL TRAIL
1.4 mi/1.0 hr   🏃2 ⛰9

in Russian Ridge Open Space Preserve

Map 7.2, page 278

Borel Hill is one of the great lookouts on the San Francisco Peninsula. The summit tops out at 2,572 feet and is surrounded by grasslands. Hikers get unobstructed, 360-degree views. Borel Hill is a favorite destination of hikers who visit the Russian Ridge Open Space Preserve.

From the parking area, hike north on the Bay Area Ridge Trail over the course of 0.7 mile to Borel Hill. The hill is the highest spot around, bordered by grasslands and with no trees. You get gorgeous views west across coastal foothills to the azure-blue horizon of the sea. This trail connects to a network of routes that provide access to the interior of the preserve's 3,137 acres.

Russian Ridge is located just across the road from Caltrans Vista Point on the Peninsula's Skyline. You get views across the South Bay there. Then cross the road and climb Borel Hill for the coastal panorama.

User Groups: Hikers, horses, and mountain bikes. A wheelchair-accessible trail starting at the parking area leads to Alpine Pond in the Skyline Ridge Open Space Preserve. No dogs.

Permits: No permits are required. Parking and access are free.

Maps: A brochure and map are available at the trailhead. For a free trail map, contact the Midpeninsula Regional Open Space District. For a topographic map, ask the USGS for Mindego Hill.

Directions: Take I-280 to Woodside and the exit for Woodside Road/Highway 84. Take the exit to Woodside Road, turn west and drive 6.5 miles (through Woodside, enter redwoods, becomes curvy as you climb) to Sky Londa and Skyline Boulevard/Highway 35. Turn left on Skyline and drive six miles to Caltrans Vista Point on left.

Alternate route from South Peninsula: Coal Creek Open Space Preserve and Vista Point is located 1.2 miles north of the junction of Page Mill Road and Skyline. Page Mill out of Palo Alto is narrow, twisty, with blind turns and dangerous for cars vs. bikes.

Contact: Midpeninsula Regional Open Space District, 650/691-1200, www.openspace.org.

99 ALPINE POND/ SKYLINE RIDGE

3.0 mi/1.5 hr

in Skyline Ridge Open Space Preserve

Map 7.2, page 278

From the parking area, walk south through a tunnel and continue a short distance to Alpine Pond and the nature center. Gorgeous spot.

Good bird-watching. Nature trail available around the pond. No fishing permitted. Many folks can't believe how pretty little Alpine Pond is, the easiest pay-off for visitors to Skyline Ridge Open Space. From this pond, the trail then pushes into the interior of the parkland, skirting the flank of the highest mountain in park boundaries (2,493 feet), and then loops back to Skyline Boulevard. You play peek-a-boo here, heading in and out of woodlands and gaining occasional views of plunging canyons to the west. You can create a loop hike, but that requires going back on a fire road; most people return to the parking area via the same route they walked on the way in.

Note that another trailhead is located south from the junction of Skyline and Alpine Road. This leads a short distance down to pretty Horseshoe Lake.

User Groups: Hikers, horses, and mountain bikes. A wheelchair-accessible trail leads to Horseshoe Lake. No dogs.

Permits: No permits are required. Parking and access are free.

Maps: A brochure and map are available at the trailhead. For a free trail map, contact the Midpeninsula Regional Open Space District. For a topographic map, ask the USGS for Mindego Hill.

Directions: Take I-280 to Woodside and the exit for Highway 84/Woodside Road. Take that exit, turn west on Woodside Road and drive 2.8 miles. Continue on Woodside Road/Highway 84 (becomes curvy) to Sky Londa and Highway 35/Skyline Boulevard. Turn left on Skyline and drive six miles to Vista Point parking on left or continue one mile to junction with Alpine Road. Turn right on Alpine Road and immediately look for exit on right to parking for Skyline Ridge Open Space. For trailhead to Horseshoe Lake, at junction of Skyline and Alpine Road, continue short distance south to parking and staging area on right.

Options from South Bay: From Palo Alto at I-280, take Page Mill Road west about 10 miles (narrow and curvy, watch for bikes) to Skyline/Highway 35. Continue straight on Alpine Road a short distance to exit for parking lot on right for Skyline Ridge.

Contact: Midpeninsula Regional Open Space District, 650/691-1200, www.openspace.org.

100 RIDGE TRAIL LOOP

2.6 mi/1.25 hr

in Sam McDonald County Park near La Honda

Map 7.2, page 278

This loop trail provides a stellar introduction to the area and makes an excellent hike year-round. It features about a 700-foot climb, a route through deep redwood canyons, and then ridge-top views across coastal foothills. Very enjoyable.

After a quick orientation with the park map (they're self-serve at the ranger station), choose the posted four-mile Ridge Trail Loop. As you enter the parking lot, the trailhead is on the right of the restroom. The hike starts on a narrow dirt path that is carved in the side of a steep redwood canyon, where you walk north. Even on hot Bay Area days, this forest is cool and refreshing, with occasional banana slugs on the trail. The trail contours up and down, then eventually rises into hardwood forest (mainly oaks, bays, and madrones) to a sub-ridge with a partial lookout to the north across miles of pretty foothills.

The trail then curves left (west) and climbs toward Towne Ridge. You emerge at a crossing of Pescadero Road (you're now heading south). You cross the road and the trail turns from single track to a service road. The views to the west of the coastal foothills, into the Pescadero Creek Canyon, and across to Butano Rim start to open up. In March, April, and early May, there are also many blooming wildflowers, highlighted by occasional rafts of sprawling forget-me-nots. The trail/road contours up and down, generally climbing and you emerge in foothill grasslands (a ride-in horse camp is off to the left). Look to the left as well for the Towne Trail. Turn left on the Towne Trail and you descend into another deep redwood canyon. At a water tank, turn right on the Big Tree Loop, which is highlighted by a big redwood. The Big Tree Loop is routed to a crossing of Pescadero Road and the parking lot.

For a short side trip, visit the adjacent Heritage Grove, which is accessible on Alpine Road.

User Groups: Hikers only. No dogs, horses, or mountain bikes. No wheelchair facilities.

Permits: No permits are required. A parking fee of $5 is charged per vehicle.

Maps: PDF at website. For a topographic map, ask the USGS for La Honda.

Directions: From San Francisco, take I-280 south and drive 20 miles to Woodside and the exit for Highway 84/Woodside Road. Take that exit, turn west (right) on Woodside Road, and drive 2.8 miles to Woodside. Continue straight on Woodside Road/Highway 84 for 10 miles (continue straight at Sky Londa at Skyline) to La Honda and continue a short distance to Pescadero Road on left. Turn left and drive 1.1 miles to Redwood Triangle and Pescadero Creek Road. Bear right and drive 0.7 mile to park entrance and parking on right.

Heritage Grove: At Redwood Triangle, turn southeast (right if emerging from San McDonald; left if approaching Sam McDonald from La Honda) on Alpine Road and drive short distance to Heritage Grove on right.

Coastal option: From Half Moon Bay, take Highway 1 south for 10 miles to San Gregorio and Highway 84. Turn left on 84 and drive 8.3 miles to Pescadero Road. Turn right and drive 1.1 miles to Redwood Triangle and Pescadero Creek Road. Bear right and drive 0.7 mile to park entrance on right.

Contact: Sam McDonald County Park, 650/879-0238; San Mateo County Parks Department, 650/363-4020, http://parks.smc-gov.org.

101 PESCADERO MARSH
3.0 mi/1.5 hr   👫1 ⛰8

in Pescadero Marsh south of Pescadero

Map 7.2, page 278	BEST (

On one side of the road is Pescadero Marsh Natural Preserve. On the other is Pescadero State Beach. Pescadero Marsh is a 600-acre wetland and lagoon fed by Pescadero Creek that is home for blue herons, egrets, and owls, and resting habitat for many migratory shorebirds. A dirt path, the North Pond Trail, ventures into the wetlands to Audubon Marsh and the edge of the lagoon and provides a three-mile hike. Roughly 200 migratory species of shorebirds, waterfowl, and raptors have been verified here. Deer and rabbits are common. Fox, skunk, and badger occasionally sighted.

A great easy trip is a three-mile loop through the marsh. From the parking area, take the North Pond Trail to Audubon Marsh. For some this is all they need, but it gets better if you return on the Sequoia Trail. The route traces the edge of the marsh and then heads along Pescadero Creek. This dirt path ventures through the heart of the wetlands and provides a good chance to see many birds, as well as occasional deer.

Pescadero Marsh is located just east of Highway 1 along Pescadero Creek, 15 miles south of Half Moon Bay. Just across the highway from Pescadero Marsh is the parking lot and access point for Pescadero State Beach.

User Groups: Hikers only. No dogs, horses, or mountain bikes. No wheelchair facilities.

Permits: No permits are required. Parking and access are free.

Maps: A map is available from Half Moon Bay State Parks. For a topographic map, ask the USGS for San Gregorio.

Directions: From the Peninsula in San Mateo, take Highway 92 west to Half Moon Bay. Turn south on Highway 1 and drive 17 miles to Pescadero Road. Turn left and drive about 0.25 mile to the parking area and trailhead on the left.

Contact: Pescadero State Beach, 650/879-2170;

Half Moon Bay State Parks, 650/726-8820, www.parks.ca.gov.

102 MILL OX LOOP
5.0 mi/2.75 hr   👫3 ⛰8

in Butano State Park near Pescadero

Map 7.2, page 278

If you love redwoods and ferns but are also partial to sun and warm afternoons, the Mill Ox Loop at Butano State Park may be the ideal hike for you. Why? The Mill Ox Loop provides a tour through deep redwoods and amid open sun, both in good doses.

To find the Mill Ox Trailhead, drive past the entry kiosk and continue ahead into the redwoods and look for the signed trailhead on your left. You park on the road's shoulder. The trail starts where you cross a small creek in a dense redwood forest, then heads up a very steep grade on switchbacks, emerging at the top of the canyon on Butano Fire Road. Some readers emailed that they were stunned at how steep this section is, but the climb is very short and the worst of it is over quickly.

At the Butano Fire Road, turn right. You will climb gradually as you head east toward the park's interior. The fire road gets plenty of sun, and plenty of shirts come off en route to 1,138 feet. At a few spots, if you turn and look back to the west, you have views of the Pacific Ocean. Continue to a junction with Jackson Flats Trail, turn right for the return loop. Here the trail descends quite steeply over a bare rock and sandstone facing for 0.25 mile, then links to a pretty dirt path. You then drop into Butano Canyon and the surrounding redwood forest. The forest is lush and beautiful as you return to the start point, where you walk past ferns, trillium, redwoods, and plenty of wild iris. This is one of our favorites.

User Groups: Hikers only. No dogs, horses, or mountain bikes. No wheelchair facilities.

Permits: No permits are required. A state park entrance fee of $10 is charged per vehicle.

Maps: A brochure and map are available at the

entrance station. For a topographic map, ask the USGS for Franklin Point.

Directions: Take I-280 south to Daly City and the split for Highway 1/Pacifica. Follow Highway 1 south for 20 miles to Half Moon Bay. Continue south on Highway 1 for 15.2 miles to Pescadero Creek Road. Turn left and drive 2.5 miles (through Pescadero) to Cloverdale Road. Turn right and go 4.4 miles to park entrance road on left. Turn left and drive short distance to park entrance and kiosk.

From East Bay/Peninsula: From San Mateo, take Highway 92 west to Half Moon Bay and Highway 1. Turn left on Highway 1 and continue as above.

Contact: Butano State Park, 650/879-2040; Half Moon Bay State Parks, 650/726-8820, www.parks.ca.gov.

103 TRAIL CAMP
10.0 mi/2 days

in Butano State Park near Pescadero

Map 7.2, page 278

The Bay Area's most hidden and least known campground is Butano's backpack campground, Trail Camp. Seven pretty sites are set in forest just below the west-facing Butano rim at 1,550 feet. The prettiest site is No. 7, set amid towering Douglas firs. It takes a five-mile hike with a 1,500-foot climb to get here. Near the park entrance, take the Jackson Flats Trail. This is routed east uphill for 2.75 miles to the Canyon Trail. Take the left fork for the Canyon Trail, which rises steeply at times, up to the camp.

Just above the Trail Camp, you will find a route that connects to the Butano Fire Road. If you head to the left (northwest), you can find an abandoned airstrip. At the end of the old strip, there are great views to the west of the Butano Canyon and beyond to the coast.

The heart of this park is a deep redwood canyon. From here, you can launch off on adventures that explore the slopes up to the horseshoe-shaped mountain rim. On the canyon

floor, the place is cool, quiet, and lush. On the canyon rim, peer across a sea of conifers below to glimpses of the Pacific Ocean.

Note: No drinking water is available. You must pump-filter water from a creek located 0.25 mile from camp. In drought years, it can go dry.

Messing with your mind: Butano is not pronounced "Bew-TAH-no," but rather "Bute-UH-no."

User Groups: Hikers only. No dogs, horses, or mountain bikes. No wheelchair facilities.

Permits: Trail camp fee and permits are required at the entrance station or visitors center (adjacent to entrance station). A state park entrance fee of $10 is charged per vehicle. Register at entrance station; no reservations are accepted.

Maps: A brochure and map are available at the entrance station. For a topographic map, ask the USGS for Franklin Point.

Directions: Take I-280 south to Daly City and the split on right for Highway 1/Pacifica. Follow Highway 1 south for 20 miles to Half Moon Bay. Continue south on Highway 1 for 15.2 miles to Pescadero Creek Road. Turn left and drive 2.5 miles (through Pescadero) to Cloverdale Road. Turn right and go 4.4 miles to park entrance road on left. Turn left and drive short distance to park entrance and kiosk.

From East Bay and Peninsula: From San Mateo, take Highway 92 west to Half Moon Bay and Highway 1. Turn left on Highway 1 and continue as above.

Contact: Butano State Park, 650/879-2040; Half Moon Bay State Parks, 650/726-8820, www.parks.ca.gov.

104 BUTANO RIM LOOP
11.0 mi/1-2 days

in Butano State Park near Pescadero

Map 7.2, page 278

This is one of the great rides on a mountain bike or on a horse, a 10. For hiking, the first half of the route on a fire road makes it a 9. Start at the Mill Ox trailhead, at an elevation of 200 feet. Hike up the steep grade (the steepest part of the trip) for a short distance to the Butano Fire Road (700 feet). Turn right and away you go. From here, trace the rim of Butano Canyon, and enjoy views of the redwood-filled valley (below) and the Pacific Ocean (behind you and off to the west). The trail climbs steadily before reaching 1,713 feet, where it crosses a short spur to an old, abandoned, overgrown airstrip on the ridgeline (at the west end of the air strip, there's a great view to the west overlooking the Butano Canyon). Just past the airstrip, the trail enters forest. A signed cutoff on the right provides a short spur to the Butano Trail Camp (at 1,550 feet). If you were to stay overnight, this would make a first-day total of 5.5 miles.

This is the halfway point and the rest of the trip is more sheltered. Turn right on the Olmo Fire Road and then hike out to the Doe Ridge/Goat Hill Trails, which drop back down into the Butano Canyon and the starting point. Much of this second half of the route is a soft dirt trail amid redwoods, and it laterals and descends into the south side of Butano Canyon.

User Groups: Hikers, bikes, horses to Trail Camp. No bikes on single track after Trail Camp (bikes have access to China Grade and other routes). No wheelchair facilities.

Permits: For camping, trail camp permits are required at the entrance station or visitors center (adjacent to entrance station). A state park entrance fee of $10 is charged per vehicle.

Maps: A brochure and map are available at the entrance station. For a free trail map, contact Butano State Park. For a topographic map, ask the USGS for Franklin Point.

Directions: Take I-280 to Daly City and the split for Highway 1/Pacifica. Follow Highway 1 south for 20 miles to Half Moon Bay. Continue south on Highway 1 for 15.2 miles to Pescadero Creek Road. Turn left and drive 2.5 miles (through Pescadero) to Cloverdale Road. Turn right and go 4.4 miles to park entrance road on left. Turn left and drive short distance to park entrance and kiosk.

From East Bay/Peninsula: Drive to San Mateo and the junction with Highway 92. Take Highway 92 west over Crystal Springs Reservoir, and then continue eight miles to Half Moon Bay and Highway 1. Turn left on Highway 1 and continue as above.

Contact: Butano State Park, 650/879-2040; Half Moon Bay State Parks, 650/726-8820, www.parks.ca.gov.

105 AÑO NUEVO TRAIL
2.75 mi/1.5 hr

in Butano State Park near Pescadero

Map 7.2, page 278

The Año Nuevo Trail to the lookout climbs 730 feet in less than a mile. It's one of the steepest stretches of trails on the coast. On the ridge, a park bench offers a place to sit and catch your breath, as well as a glimpse of Año Nuevo Island. Continue on Año Nuevo Trail to the junction with the Goat Hill Trail. Turn left and drop down steeply back into the canyon to complete the loop. Although short, this hike provides a good climb and a chance to walk through redwoods on the return descent. It's not unusual to see pileated woodpeckers on this loop.

User Groups: Hikers only. No dogs, horses, or mountain bikes. No wheelchair facilities.

Permits: No permits are required. A day-use fee of $10 is charged per vehicle.

Maps: For a free trail map, contact Butano State Park. For a topographic map, ask the USGS for Franklin Point.

Directions: Take I-280 south to Daly City and the split on right for Highway 1/Pacifica. Follow Highway 1 south for 20 miles to Half Moon Bay. Continue south on Highway 1 for 15.2 miles to Pescadero Creek Road. Turn left and drive 2.5 miles (through Pescadero) to Cloverdale Road. Turn right and go 4.4 miles to park entrance road on left. Turn left and drive short distance to park entrance and kiosk. The trailhead is on the right (south).

From East Bay/Peninsula: Drive to San Mateo and the junction with Highway 92.

Take Highway 92 west over Crystal Springs Reservoir, and then continue eight miles to Half Moon Bay and Highway 1. Turn left on Highway 1 and continue as above.

Contact: Butano State Park, 650/879-2040; Half Moon Bay State Parks, 650/726-8820, www.parks.ca.gov.

106 PETERS CREEK GROVE
12.5 mi/1 day   🚶4 ⛰10

in Portola Redwoods State Park

Map 7.2, page 278

Portola Redwoods State Park is highlighted by a site we call "The Bay Area's Lost World," the remote Peters Creek Grove of old-growth redwoods. The grove is nestled in a distant canyon where the forest floor is covered with wall-to-wall sorrel. A few of the giants are 30-35 feet around; several are more than 200 feet tall.

The hike to the Peters Creek Grove is about a 12.5-mile round-trip with two grind-it-out climbs. From park headquarters it's a 5.5-mile trek up 1,000 feet to a ridge; you then plummet 600 feet into a deep canyon to connect to a one-mile loop trail that runs along each side of Peters Creek and amid the giant trees.

Since it is a long drive to reach Portola Redwoods, one option is to camp at a trail site (Slate Creek) 2.4 miles out from headquarters. It is located on the route out to Peters Creek Grove.

Permits: No permits are required. A state park entrance fee of $10 is charged per vehicle; pay at the visitors center.

Maps: A map/brochure is available at the visitors center. For a topographic map, ask the USGS for Mindego Hill.

Directions: From San Francisco, take I-280 south and drive 20 miles to Woodside and the exit for Highway 84/Woodside Road. Take that exit, turn west (right) on Woodside Road, and drive 2.8 miles to Woodside. Continue straight on Woodside Road/Highway 84 for 5.8 miles to Sky Londa. Continue straight for 6.7 miles to La Honda, then a short distance to Pescadero

Road on the left. Turn left and drive 1.1 miles to Redwood Triangle and Alpine Road. Turn left on Alpine Road and drive four miles (slow, narrow, twisty; 1.2 miles to Heritage Grove on right) to Portola State Park Road. Turn right (still twisty) and drive three miles to park entrance. Continue 0.5 mile to visitors center.

Contact: Portola Redwoods State Park, La Honda, 650/948-9098, www.parks.ca.gov.

107 BAY VIEW LOOP
3.0 mi/1.5 hr   🚶1 ⛰8

in Point Pinole Regional Shoreline

Map 7.3, page 279

On the Bay View Loop, you can walk several miles along the shore of San Pablo Bay, or on a wood bluff overlooking the shore, and take in a beautiful view of water, passing ships, and birds. The trip is unique from the start, where you park at the entrance station and catch a shuttle bus to the shoreline. There you will find a long, pretty, cobbled beach and beautiful views of San Pablo Bay, Marin, and Mount Tamalpais. An excellent fishing pier is also here. This is the launch point. Make sure you head out to the end of the pier to take in the water views and see if anybody has caught a sturgeon or striped bass.

Then take the Bay Trail. It is perched on a bluff above the cobbled beach. Along the way are beautiful glimpses of San Pablo Bay. The long distance views across the bay of the Marin shoreline backed by Mt. Tamalpais are exceptional. To turn this into a three-mile loop, turn back (left) on the Woods Trail. This trail is routed through a small eucalyptus forest, with occasional remnants of the dynamite era, a few small buildings, and pretty dirt roads. The trail eventually returns to the staging area.

A highlight of Point Pinole Regional Shoreline is a long, undisturbed stretch of shoreline on a cobbled beach along San Pablo Bay. The stone beach is unparalleled, as if this were the final resting place of every stone ever cast in the bay. It is a quiet place, where you can watch passing ships, go for an easy hike, take a dog for a walk, or fish from the pier. Yet the defining landscape feature of the park is the Hayward Fault—marked by the cliffs and Point Pinole itself as it goes out to sea.

In the World War II era, this was the site of the Giant Powder Company, that is, dynamite manufacturers. This was their fourth site in the Bay Area after factories blew up in San Francisco, South San Francisco, and Albany. So no one wanted to be anywhere near the place. The dynamite company built all the present trails and roads, planted eucalyptus trees, and is responsible for the basic layout of the park.

User Groups: Hikers, dogs, horses, and mountain bikes. The trail is partially wheelchair-accessible.

Permits: No permits are required. A $3 day-use fee is charged on weekends when the kiosk is attended. The shuttle costs $1 round-trip for people ages 12 through 61; it's free for seniors, and $0.50 for youngsters 6 through 11. There is a fee for dogs ($2) on weekends.

Maps: A brochure and map are available at the trailhead. For a free trail map, phone the East Bay Regional Park District toll-free at 888/327-2757, option 3, ext. 5; follow directions, leave your name and address, and ask for the Point Pinole Regional Shoreline brochure. For a topographic map, ask the USGS for Richmond.

Directions: Take I-80 to Pinole and the exit for Fitzgerald Drive to Richmond Parkway. Take that exit to Richmond Parkway and drive 1.3 miles to Atlas Road. Turn right on Atlas and drive 0.9 mile to Giant Road. Turn left on Giant and drive 0.5 mile to the park entrance on the right. Take the shuttle to the Point Pinole Pier, and trailhead.

Contact: Point Pinole Regional Park, 888/327-2757; East Bay Regional Park District, www.ebparks.org.

108 SOARING EAGLE TRAIL
4.0 mi/2.0 hr 　　　　　🥾2 ⛰️8

in Crockett Hills Regional Park near Crockett

Map 7.3, page 279

The highlights at Crockett Hills Regional Park are the ridge-top views, good prospects of seeing golden eagles, and well hidden valley. There are five foothill peaks where you get sweeping views of San Pablo Bay. From the hilltops, you can see across Carquinez Strait, the Lower Delta, and to the west, a pretty silhouette of Mount Tamalpais. There is also a pretty valley from where you can often see golden eagles fly, hover, and search for ground squirrels.

From the staging area, take the Edwards Loop Trail for a short climb to the tunnel at the Cummings Skyway. Walk through the tunnel, and on the other side, take the Soaring Eagle Trail (also signed as Bay Area Ridge Trail). It contours on the foothills and weaves its way around to valleys to the Sky Trail. Turn left on Sky Trail and return to the tunnel to complete the loop.

For a bonus, at the junction of Soaring Eagle Trail and Sky Trail, turn right and within 15 minutes, you'll reach the Big Valley Trail, on the right. This is where we've seen a mated pair of golden eagles who often hunt and hover here at midmorning as the air temperature warms.

In the remote southern section of the park, you'll notice that birds flourish here. A ravine with a small, unnamed pond edged by cattails is a sanctuary for redwing blackbirds, many small songbirds, and kestrels, the smallest bird of prey in North America. It turns out that the wildlife habitat here supports all levels of the wildlife food chain.

User Groups: Hikers, mountain bikes, horses, and dogs. No wheelchair facilities.

Permits: No permits are required. Parking and access are free.

Maps: A brochure and map are available at the trailhead. For a free trail map, phone the East Bay Regional Park District toll-free at 888/327-2757, option 3, ext. 5; follow directions, leave your name and address, and ask for the Crockett Hills brochure.

Directions: From Concord: Take Highway 4 west to the exit for Cummings Skyway/Vallejo-Crockett. Take that exit to Cummings Skyway and drive about 2.5 miles to Crockett Boulevard. Turn right and drive 0.7 mile to the staging area on the left.

From San Francisco: Take I-80 east to Crockett and Exit 27 for Port Costa/Crockett. Take that exit to Pomona Street. Turn left on Pomona and drive to Crockett Boulevard. Turn right to the staging area on the right.

Contact: Crockett Hills Regional Park, 925/228-0112 or 888/327-2757; East Bay Regional Park District, www.ebparks.org.

109 FRANKLIN RIDGE LOOP
2.0 mi/1.75 hr 🏃3 ⛰9

at Carquinez Strait Regional Shoreline near Martinez

Map 7.3, page 279

It seems that everybody starts at the Negedly Staging Area and its big parking lot and restroom. Instead, drive another 1.5 miles on Carquinez Scenic Drive. You'll see a gated trailhead/road on the left. Pullouts are available along the road to park. From here, you walk along a ranch road (a seasonal creek, often dry, is on your right) to a sharp left turn. You turn left and climb, steep but short on the Franklin Ridge Loop Trail. After about 10 minutes, you emerge over a sub-ridge and in a valley. At one spot, you can see a silhouette of the lookout bench, under an oak, on a hilltop to your left. The trail then cuts off to your left and climbs a short distance to the hilltop vista point. If you have a dog, keep them on a leash here because the trail is edged by sharp star thistles. The bench is shaded on the ridge and is a great site for a trail picnic. As you gain the hill the view over Martinez and Carquinez Strait is revealed all at once. On one side, you tower over Martinez and the Carquinez Strait, with long-distance views across Suisun Bay, the Mothball

Fleet, and beyond to the Lower Delta. On another side, you see across to Benicia and west to San Pablo Bay and beyond to Mount Burdell. To the south are pretty rolling foothills, golden brown, where you often sight black-tailed deer.

Sunsets can be absolutely spectacular here in winter, often with sunlight refracted through distant stratus and a dark silhouette of Mount Tamalpais. Even after sunset, it remains pretty as the lights of the Benicia Bridge and nearby towns take hold.

The park covers 2,795 acres, most of it foothill country, with oaks, short ridges, and ravines. It is wild enough to provide habitat for wildlife; red-tailed hawks and deer are the most common. At dusk, it's possible to see great horned owls, kestrels, and occasionally even golden eagles.

User Groups: Hikers, dogs, horses, and mountain bikes. No wheelchair facilities.

Permits: No permits are required. Parking and access are free.

Maps: A brochure and map are available at the trailhead. For a free trail map, phone the East Bay Regional Park District toll-free at 888/327-2757, option 3, extension 5; follow directions, leave your name and address, and ask for the Carquinez Strait Regional Shoreline brochure. For a topographic map, ask the USGS for Benicia.

Directions: From San Francisco, take I-80 East over Bay Bridge six miles (get in center/left lane) to split for 80-580/24. Stay left on I-80 East and drive about 15 miles to the exit for Highway 4 East. Take that exit, merge onto Highway 4 and drive 8.7 miles to the exit for Alhambra Avenue/Martinez. Take that exit to Alhambra Avenue, turn left and go 2.1 miles to Buckley Street. Turn left on Buckley and continue 0.1 mile to Talbart Street. Turn right on Talbart and go three blocks to Carquinez Scenic Drive. Turn left and go 1.2 miles to Alhambra Cemetery on right, or continue short distance to Nejedly Staging Area (signed on left), and continue another 1.5 miles to gated trailhead on left (park at dirt pullouts).

Contact: Carquinez Strait Regional Shoreline,

925/228-0112 or 888/327-2757; East Bay Regional Park District, www.ebparks.org.

110 MARTINEZ SHORELINE
2.0 mi/1.0 hr   🏃1 ⛰8

at Martinez Regional Shoreline near Martinez

Map 7.3, page 279

You can change your world in just 2.5 miles of driving, from highway to park. Some might view Martinez Regional Shoreline and the nearby marina as a destination for locals only. Wrong. It provides a surprise escape hatch from the push-push-push on I-680 or Highway 4, only minutes away.

From the parking area off North Court Street, take the Killdeer Trail 0.25 mile to the Boardwalk Trail, turn left and walk a short distance to gorgeous Arch Bridge. It crosses Alhambra Creek and provides an elevated view of the wetlands. Then continue ahead, tidal wetlands to your left, Carquinez Strait to your right, and bear right on the Pickleweed Trail. The trail leads out to water's edge, 1.4 miles round-trip. You can extend another quarter mile on the Pickleweed Trail (it jogs left for a short distance) to a waterfront picnic site; two miles round-trip. The rewards are beautiful shoreline trails with water views, wildlife preserves for waterfowl, marine birds and songbirds, and a fishing pier set in the path of migratory striped bass and resident flounder. For those rushing to get in or out of the Bay Area, stop the clock and enjoy this trip.

Martinez Regional Shoreline and adjacent Waterfront Park are located on the banks of Carquinez Strait near downtown Martinez, just west of the Carquinez Bridge. While the parks are popular among locals for picnics, bocce ball, soccer, and softball, it shines best as a wetland preserve with several pretty trails with waterfront views.

Side trip: If you continue on North Court Street (past the entrance to Martinez Regional Shoreline), it leads to parking for the duck pond (on left) and the fishing pier (straight ahead).

If you turn right on Tarantino Drive, it leads to access for the ball fields (on right) and dead-ends at a short trail to an observation platform for bird-watching.

User Groups: Hikers and mountain bikes. No horses or dogs. The restrooms are wheelchair-accessible, but the trail is not.

Permits: No permits are required. Parking and access are free.

Maps: A brochure and map are available at the trailhead. For a free trail map, call the East Bay Regional Park District (888/327-2757, option 3, extension 5; follow directions, leave your name and address, and ask for the Martinez Regional Shoreline brochure). For a topographic map, ask the USGS for Benicia.

Directions: Take I-80 to Exit 23 for Highway 4. Take that exit to Highway 4 and drive 8.7 miles to Exit 9 for Alhambra Avenue toward Martinez. Take that exit, turn left on Alhambra and go 2.1 miles to Marina Vista Avenue. Turn right on Marina Vista and go a short distance to Ferry Street. Turn left on Ferry Street and go a short distance to Joe DiMaggio Drive. Turn right and go a short distance to North Court Street. Turn left and drive to end: parking and Martinez Regional Shoreline is on left, fishing pier is ahead, marina is on right, Martinez Waterfront Park is on right.

Contact: Martinez Regional Shoreline, 888/327-2757; East Bay Regional Park District, www.ebparks.org.

111 FALSE GUN VISTA POINT
1.0 mi/0.75 hr   🏃1 ⛰8

in Miller-Knox Regional Shoreline west of Richmond

Map 7.3, page 279

A little-known lookout over San Francisco Bay is the highlight of Miller-Knox Regional Shoreline, and getting to it requires only a short hike and climb. This parkland covers 260 acres of hill and shoreline property at Point Richmond, where strong afternoon winds in the summer create excellent conditions for kite flying. Whereas most people just make the short stroll along Keller Beach, this hike is preferred for the view. From the parking area, it leads about 0.5 mile up Old Country Road and Marine View Trail, making a right turn on Crest Trail to reach the False Gun Vista Point. In the process, the trail climbs 300 feet to the lookout, at 322 feet. On clear days, you get picture-perfect views of San Francisco Bay and its many surrounding landmarks. Most people enjoy a landscaped picnic area with pretty views of the North Bay. Take it the extra mile, literally.

User Groups: Hikers and dogs. No horses or mountain bikes. No wheelchair facilities.

Permits: No permits are required. Parking and access are free.

Maps: A brochure and map are available at the trailhead. For a free trail map, phone the East Bay Regional Park District toll-free at 888/327-2757, option 3, extension 5; follow directions, leave your name and address, and ask for the Miller-Knox Regional Shoreline brochure. For a topographic map, ask the USGS for San Quentin.

Directions: From Berkeley: Drive north on I-80 to the exit for I-580 west. Take the exit for I-580 west to Canal Boulevard (lighted). Turn left on Canal Boulevard and drive 0.75 mile to Seacliff Drive. Turn right on Seacliff and drive 1.5 miles (Seacliff Drive becomes Brickyard Cove Road) to Dornan Drive. Turn right on Dornan and drive 0.5 mile to the parking entrance on the left.

Contact: Miller-Knox Regional Shoreline, 888/327-2757; East Bay Regional Park District, www.ebparks.org.

112 POINT ISABEL SHORELINE

1.0 mi/0.75 hr

at Point Isabel Regional Shoreline near Berkeley

Map 7.3, page 279

When it comes to California bests, Point Isabel ranks right at the top for best parks to bring a doggy. Half a million dogs a year visit Point Isabel Shoreline, the ultimate dog park in California, complete with showers, tennis balls, and treats. It's good for people, too. Beautiful bay-front views of San Francisco and the Golden Gate—plus the fact that it's a popular place to walk dogs—attract visitors to this stretch of shore. From the parking area, the trail extends northward along the shore of the bay, then east along Hoffman Channel, where it meets the Bay Trail, and offers great views of Hoffman Marsh. The best time to see birds here is in the fall, when year-round residents are joined by migratory species. Point Isabel extends into San Francisco Bay just north of Golden Gate Fields Racetrack, and the 21-acre park provides an easy shoreline walk, rich bird-watching opportunities, and those great views.

User Groups: Hikers and dogs. No horses or mountain bikes. The restrooms and trail are wheelchair-accessible.

Permits: No permits are required. Parking and access are free.

Maps: A brochure and map are available at the trailhead. For a free trail map, phone the East Bay Regional Park District toll-free at 888/327-2757, option 3, extension 5; follow directions, leave your name and address, and ask for the Point Isabel Regional Shoreline brochure. For a topographic map, ask the USGS for Richmond.

Directions: From I-80 in south Richmond, take the Central Avenue exit and drive west to Isabel Street. Turn right and drive to the parking area, at the end of the road.

Contact: Point Isabel Regional Shoreline, 888/327-2757; East Bay Regional Park District, www.ebparks.org.

113 SAN PABLO RIDGE LOOP

6.2 mi/3.5 hr   3   10

in Wildcat Canyon Regional Park

Map 7.3, page 279

Of all the views of San Francisco Bay, this is certainly one of the best. From San Pablo Ridge, you get an eye-popping view of San Francisco Bay, Alcatraz, and across to the Golden Gate Bridge. Up on top, you can see south to Rocky Ridge as Las Tampas Regional Wilderness, and northwest across San Pablo Bay to a silhouette of Mount Tamalpais. From the parking area, start the trip by hiking up the Belgum Trail. Turn right at San Pablo Ridge and climb about 750 feet over the course of 2.5 miles. Once on top, slow down and enjoy the cruise. You will find a series of hilltops to climb for 360-degreee panoramas. Make sure you do this. To loop around, head back on Mezue Trail, then right again on Wildcat Creek Trail, and walk back to the parking area.

It takes a short grunt of a hike to get to the top, but you'll find it well worth the grunting. These hilltops offer gorgeous views and can also be accessed out of Tilden Regional Park from Inspiration Point on Nimitz Way.

User Groups: Hikers, dogs, horses, and mountain bikes. No wheelchair facilities.

Permits: No permits are required. Parking and access are free.

Maps: A brochure and map are available at the trailhead. For a free trail map, phone the East Bay Regional Park District toll-free at 888/327-2757, option 3, extension 5; follow directions, leave your name and address, and ask for the Wildcat Canyon Regional Park brochure. For a topographic map, ask the USGS for Richmond.

Directions: Take I-80 to Richmond and the exit to Solano Avenue. Take that exit a short distance to fork, keep left at fork (signed for Solano) and merge onto Amador Street. Continue on Amador for 0.4 mile (second stop sign) to McBryde Avenue. Turn right and drive 0.3 mile to parking (signed) on left.

Contact: Wildcat Canyon Regional Park, 510/544-3092 or 888/327-2757; East Bay Regional Park District, www.ebparks.org.

114 LAUREL LOOP TRAIL
0.7 mi/0.5 hr

in the Kennedy Grove Regional Recreation Area

Map 7.3, page 279

Kennedy Grove is set at the base of San Pablo Dam, where visitors will discover a rich grove of eucalyptus adjacent to a large lawn/meadow. This loop hike takes hikers through the eucalyptus and then back, skirting the lawn areas. It is best hiked in a clockwise direction, departing from the trailhead at the gate in the northeast corner of the parking area. This is the kind of park where people toss Frisbees, pass footballs, or play low-key games of softball.

User Groups: Hikers, dogs, and horses. No mountain bikes on the Seafoam Trail. Restrooms and a short walking path at park's main lawn area are wheelchair-accessible.

Permits: No permits are required. An entrance fee of $5 per vehicle is charged when the kiosk is attended; $2 for dogs.

Maps: A brochure and map are available at the trailhead. For a free trail map, phone the East Bay Regional Park District toll-free at 888/327-2757, option 3, ext. 5; follow directions, leave your name and address, and ask for the Kennedy Grove Regional Recreation Area brochure. For a topographic map, ask the USGS for Richmond.

Directions: From I-80 in Richmond, take the San Pablo Dam Road exit. Turn east and drive through El Sobrante for 3.5 miles to the park entrance (0.25 mile south of intersection of Castro Ranch Road), on the left. Follow the pavement to the northwestern parking lot.

From Highway 24 in Orinda, turn north on Camino Pablo and drive north along San Pablo Reservoir to the park entrance (one mile past main entrance to San Pablo Recreation Area), on the right.

Contact: Kennedy Grove Regional Park, 888/327-2757; East Bay Regional Park District, www.ebparks.org.

115 SOBRANTE RIDGE TRAIL

1.6 mi/1.0 hr 🏃1 ⛰8

in the Sobrante Ridge Regional Preserve

Map 7.3, page 279

Sobrante Ridge Park covers 277 acres of a former ranch that spans across rolling hills, open ridgeline, and wooded ravines. This hike accesses the best of it. From the trailhead at Coach Drive, take Sobrante Ridge Trail, which rises in an elliptical half loop to the left. After 0.7 mile, you will come to the junction with Broken Oaks Trail. Turn left here and make the short loop (less than 0.25 mile long), and then retrace your steps on Sobrante Ridge Trail. The best of it is on top of the ridge. You get a pretty view of San Pablo Bay across to Mount Tamalpais. This walk provides an easy yet intimate look at one of the Bay Area's key parklands, a link to open space.

User Groups: Hikers, dogs, horses, and mountain bikes. No wheelchair facilities.

Permits: No permits are required. Parking and access are free.

Maps: A brochure and map are available at the trailhead. For a free trail map, phone the East Bay Regional Park District toll-free at 888/327-2757, option 3, extension 5; follow directions, leave your name and address, and ask for the Sobrante Ridge Regional Preserve brochure. For a topographic map, ask the USGS for Briones Valley.

Directions: Take I-80 to Richmond and the exit for San Pablo Dam Road. Take that exit to San Pablo Dam and drive south for three miles (through El Sobrante) to Castro Ranch Road. Turn left on Castro Ranch Road and drive about two miles to Conestoga Way. Turn left on Conestoga and drive to Carriage Drive. Turn left on Carriage and go two blocks to Coach Way. Turn right and proceed to the park entrance and parking area, at the end of the road.

Contact: Sobrante Ridge Regional Preserve, 888/327-2757; East Bay Regional Park District, www.ebparks.org.

116 BRIONES PEAK LOOP

5.6 mi/3.25 hr 🏃3 ⛰8

in Briones Regional Park north of Lafayette

Map 7.3, page 279

Briones Regional Park is a vast wildland with a mosaic of trails for short walks, ambitious treks, mountain biking, and horseback riding. It is crowned by 1,483-foot Briones Peak and its great views. In spring, the hills practically glow, alive with wildflowers, one of the best parks in Northern California. From parking, start on the Alhambra Creek Trail and Spengler Trail (turn right) to Old Briones Road Trail. Turn left and hike a half mile to Briones Crest Trail. Turn left again and you will rise to Briones Peak in less than a mile. To complete the loop, turn left on the Spengler Trail (it bends to the left), then right on Diablo View Trail, 1.1 miles back to parking.

From 1,483-foot Briones Peak, you get a rare panorama of miles of rolling foothills that extends far beyond to Mount Diablo, the west Delta, and Suisun Bay. At the end of the loop, on the Diablo View Trail, you get a southeast-facing lookout that spans across the I-680 corridor, past Shell Ridge, and across the northwest slopes of Mount Diablo.

Briones is an island wilderness, bordered to the north by Martinez and the Highway 4 corridor, east by Walnut Creek and I-680, and south by Lafayette and Highway 24. The park spans 6,255 acres that stretch west past Briones Reservoir and beyond to San Pablo Reservoir.

User Groups: Hikers, dogs, and horses. Mountain bikes are allowed on all but the last mile of the loop. No wheelchair facilities.

Permits: No permits are required. An entrance fee of $3 per vehicle is charged when the kiosk is attended (there are five entrances at Briones, and only two have kiosks); $2 for dogs.

Maps: A brochure and map are available at the trailhead. For a free trail map, phone the East Bay Regional Park District toll-free at 888/327-2757, option 3, extension 5; follow directions, leave your name and address, and ask for the Briones Regional Park brochure. For a topographic map, ask the USGS for Briones Valley.

Directions: From I-680 north of Pleasant Hill, take Highway 4 west for three miles to the Alhambra Avenue exit. Turn south on Alhambra Avenue, drive for 0.5 mile, and bear right onto Alhambra Valley Road. Drive another mile to Reliez Valley Road. Turn left and follow Reliez Valley Road 0.5 mile to the park entrance. Turn right and drive 0.5 mile to the parking area. Look for the trailhead indicating Alhambra Creek Trail.

From San Francisco, take the Bay Bridge east 6.4 miles (stay to the far right) to the split and I-580. Bear right on I-580 (stay to the far right) and go 1.6 miles to the exit for Highway 24. Take Highway 24 east, drive 0.9 mile to merge with Highway 24, and then continue 11.2 miles to the exit for Pleasant Hill Road. Take that exit 0.1 mile, keep left and continue 0.2 mile to fork, and then bear right, merge onto Pleasant Hill Road and drive two miles to Taylor Boulevard (stay left). Keep left on Taylor and drive 2.1 miles to Grayson Road. Turn left on Grayson and drive 0.5 mile to Reliez Valley Road. Turn right and drive 1.6 miles to park entrance road (Brookwood Drive) on left. Turn left and drive 0.5 mile to park, trailhead for Alhambra Creek Trail.

Contact: Briones Regional Park, 888/327-2757; East Bay Regional Park District, www.ebparks.org.

117 NIMITZ WAY

10.0 mi/4.0 hr

in Tilden Regional Park in the Berkeley hills

Map 7.3, page 279

You are rewarded whether you walk (or ride) five minutes or five hours, or whether you are making your first visit or your 100th. In the first five minutes, you will reach a bench with a gorgeous view to the west over Meadows Canyon and beyond across the hills to the bay. The trail is paved for 4.1 miles and then turns to dirt and arrives at a gate. Continue through

the gate; ahead of you, you'll see a towering hilltop. Walk to the top of that. You get a fantastic panorama of San Pablo Bay, San Francisco Bay, and silhouettes of distant peaks and landmarks across to San Francisco.

Nimitz Way is paved with a center divider, with space on the shoulder, to accommodate all users. Mile markers are posted for joggers. What I do is ride a mountain bike past the gate and into Wildcat Regional Park (five miles), then drop the bike and hike to a hilltop for a view. This is one of the best bike-and-hikes in the Bay Area.

When you depart from Inspiration Point, look for the small grove of conifers on the left. Then look closer. Yep, they are giant sequoia redwoods.

User Groups: Hikers, dogs, horses, and mountain bikes. The trail is partially wheelchair-accessible.

Permits: No permits are required. Parking and access are free.

Maps: A brochure and map are available at the trailhead. For a free trail map, phone the East Bay Regional Park District toll-free at 888/327-2757, option 3, extension 5; follow directions, leave your name and address, and ask for the Tilden Regional Park brochure. For a topographic map, ask the USGS for Briones Valley.

Directions: From San Francisco, take the Bay Bridge east for 6.4 miles (stay far right) to the split and I-580. Bear right on 580 (stay far right) and go 1.5 miles to exit for Highway 24. Take Highway 24 and go seven miles (through tunnel) to Orinda and Exit 9/Moraga. Take that exit to stoplight at Camino Pablo. Turn left on Camino Pablo and go 2.3 miles to Wildcat Canyon Road. Turn left and go 2.4 miles to Inspiration Point and parking on the right. The parking lot often fills on weekends and afternoons, but turnover is high and spots often become quickly available.

From Walnut Creek, take Highway 24 east for 8.1 miles to Orinda and the exit for Camino Pablo Road. Take that exit, merge north on Camino Pablo Road and drive two miles to Wildcat Canyon Road. Turn left and drive 2.4

miles to Inspiration Point and parking on the right.

Contact: Tilden Regional Park, 888/327-2757; East Bay Regional Park District, www.ebparks. org.

118 BOTANIC GARDEN LOOP
0.4 mile/1.0 hr

in Tilden Regional Park in Berkeley hills

Map 7.3, page 279

If you have ever seen a flower, plant, or tree and wondered what the heck it was, you can get the answers on this walk. The Regional Parks District has carved out a 10-acre parcel at Tilden in the Berkeley Hills, creating areas that represent 10 distinctive California landscapes and their respective flora. So what you get is a capsule look at the state's 160,000 square miles over the course of a walk that takes 1-2 hours—and the answer to your question.

Start at the visitors center, then plan a counterclockwise route. From the visitors center, turn left and then turn in a right-bending horseshoe—you'll end up in a landscape that resembles the high Sierra. As you walk over a creek on a wood bridge, bear right through some hardwoods, emerging at what looks exactly like a Sierra meadow at 10,000 feet near Bishop Pass—complete with aspens, fir, meadow, and what could be an old miner's cabin. The adventure provides a series of such discoveries. The landscape's captures include Pacific Rain Forest, Southern California Desert, Sea Bluff, Shasta-Klamath, and Valley-Foothills.

The site has 1,500 plant, tree, and wildflower species, including 300 endangered species, including virtually all of the state's oaks, conifers, ceanothus, and manzanita species. One phenomenon of creating a mini-California is that, just like in the great outdoors across the state, there are blooming wildflowers over a seven-month period, depending on landscape. Typical blooms in April, for instance, are Douglas iris, ceanothus, monkeyflower, poppy,

and blue dicks. In May and June, mariposa tulips, western azalea, fireweed, and columbines, among many others, are at peak blooms.

User Groups: Hikers only. No dogs, horses, and mountain bikes. The trail is partially wheelchair-accessible.

Permits: No permits are required. Parking and access are free.

Maps: A brochure and map are available at the visitors center. For a free trail map, phone the East Bay Regional Park District toll-free at 888/327-2757, option 3, extension 5; follow directions, leave your name and address, and ask for the Tilden Regional Park brochure.

Directions: Take Highway 24 to Orinda and the exit for Camino Pablo. Take that exit to Camino Pablo, turn north (left if coming from Berkeley, right if coming from Walnut Creek) and drive two miles to Wildcat Canyon Road. Turn left and go 3.7 miles to a junction with South Park Drive. Bear right for 20 yards to a parking lot across the road to the botanic gardens. Walk across the road to the signed entrance.

Contact: Regional Parks Botanic Garden, 510/544-3169 or 888/327-2757; East Bay Regional Park District, www.ebparks.org.

119 ABRIGO FALLS
2.7 mi/1.5 hr

in Briones Regional Park north of Orinda

Map 7.3, page 279

Little Abrigo Falls, the Bay Area's smallest waterfall (anything smaller is not a waterfall) and often one of the most elusive (and for some, most disappointing), can be the missing piece in a hiker's waterfall list. It goes dry in summer and fall, but it is a pretty little chute after heavy rains in winter. Start your hike at the Oak Grove picnic area at the trailhead for Abrigo Valley Trailhead. Continue past the Maud Whalen campsite 0.9 mile to the Wee-Ta-Chi campsite, and then continue 0.4 mile to the cutoff spur on the right to Abrigo Falls

You'll hike amid grasslands, oaks, and bays,

and along canyons and creeks with riparian habitat. Watch for deer, red-tailed hawks, and golden eagles. Coyotes, foxes, bobcats, and mountain lions are seen occasionally, usually at dusk. A picnic area is available near the trailhead.

User Groups: Hikers, dogs, and horses. No wheelchair facilities.

Permits: No permits are required. An entrance fee of $3 per vehicle is charged when the kiosk is attended (there are five entrances at Briones, and only two have kiosks); there is a $2 fee for dogs.

Maps: A brochure and map are available at the trailhead. For a free trail map, phone the East Bay Regional Park District toll-free at 888/327-2757, option 3, extension 5; follow directions, leave your name and address, and ask for the Briones Regional Park brochure. For a topographic map, ask the USGS for Briones Valley.

Directions: Take Highway 24 for 7.5 miles to Orinda and the exit for Camino Pablo North. Take Camino Pablo North for 2.2 miles to Bear Creek Road on right. Turn right on Bear Creek Road and drive to the signed turnoff on right for Bear Creek Staging Area (if you reach Alhambra Valley Road, you have gone too far). Turn right and drive past the Bear Creek Staging Area to the Oak Grove Picnic Area and trailhead.

Contact: Briones Regional Park, 888/327-2757 or 925/370-3020; East Bay Regional Park District, 888/327-2757, www.ebparks.org.

120 ROUND TOP LOOP TRAIL

3.0 mi/1.5 hr 🏃1 ⛰8

in Sibley Volcanic Regional Preserve

Map 7.3, page 279

A trek through a volcanic complex that dates 10.2 million years old is the pay-off on this adventure. Your destination is Sibley Volcanic Regional Preserve, the Bay Area's best example of ancient volcanic geology. To see it, hike the Round Top Trail to the Volcanic Trail for a loop hike through the volcanic center of the park. For much of the trek, you walk amid prehistoric lava rock. Yet the park is easy to reach and within close range of many on both sides of the bay and along the Highway 24 corridor.

There are some side-trip options as well. Hike up the short, paved cutoff road to the water tank (signed on the map) for a sweeping view of a series of volcanic formations and your destinations on the Volcanic Trail. Few take advantage of this. You can also take a self-guided volcanic tour at the park, a 1.8-mile volcanic interpretive loop with numbered signposts, and many short cutoff trails. Mount Round Top, you can learn, was an infilling of a great crater and was tilted to the side by strains on the Hayward and Moraga fault systems.

In addition, the drive up features a series of pullouts along the west side of Grizzly Peak Boulevard for sensational lookouts below of the Bay Bridge, San Francisco Bay, and dozens of landmarks. These roadside vistas are among the best places in California to see a sunset.

The big dud is 1,763-foot Round Top Peak, the highest point in the park. It's a short, steep walk on a paved road to the top. Your "reward" is a series of transmitter stations and antennas, and views blocked by trees.

User Groups: Hikers and dogs. Partially accessible for wheelchairs, horses, and mountain bikes. Mountain bikes OK on Skyline Trail between parking and Old Tunnel Road, paved roads, and fire trails. No bikes permitted on Round Top Road above cutoff on Skyline Trail, or Skyline Trail heading south, and Volcanic Loop (rules signed).

Permits: No permits are required. Parking and access are free.

Maps: A brochure and map are available at the trailhead. For a free trail map, phone the East Bay Regional Park District toll-free at 888/327-2757, option 3, extension 5; follow directions, leave your name and address, and ask for the Sibley Volcanic Regional Preserve brochure. For a topographic map, ask the USGS for Briones Valley.

Directions: From the East Bay, take Highway 24 east for 5.3 miles (get in right lane) through tunnel to the exit for Fish Ranch Road. Take that exit, merge onto Old Tunnel Road and continue 0.2 mile to Fish Ranch Road. Turn right at Fish Ranch Road and go 0.8 mile to Grizzly Peak Boulevard. Turn left on Grizzly Peak Boulevard and drive 2.4 miles to Skyline Boulevard. Turn left on Skyline and drive short distance to park entrance and parking on left.

Contact: Robert Sibley Volcanic Regional Preserve, 888/327-2757; East Bay Regional Park District, www.ebparks.org.

121 HUCKLEBERRY LOOP PATH

1.7 mi/1.0 hr

in Huckleberry Botanic Regional Preserve

Map 7.3, page 279

If you know what you're looking for, this is a trip into an ecological wonderland. If you don't, well, it's still a rewarding, tranquil venture. That is because the Huckleberry Loop is routed through a remarkable variety of rare and beautiful plants. Pick up a brochure at the trailhead and follow the self-guided tour that points out the plants and points of interest specific to this area.

The Huckleberry Path starts at the staging area off of Skyline Boulevard. From the parking area, follow the path to the left fork. At the first junction in 0.5 mile, turn left and descend steeply through a mature bay forest. Follow the lower Huckleberry Path for 0.3 mile and experience the succession of forest, dense ferns, and huckleberries. At the junction with the Skyline National Trail and the Bay Area Ridge Trail, stay right. Continue on the Bay Area Ridge Trail for 0.5 mile until it again junctions with the Huckleberry Path on the right. After a steep stair climb, the Huckleberry Path resumes its loop back to the trailhead in a little over a mile. Along the way, explore the dead-end spur trails that branch off the upper Huckleberry Path on the right. The first trail spur shows off spectacular pallid manzanita specimens and provides a great viewpoint. The second spur provides

another great view and several plants of interest including the Western Leatherwood.

User Groups: Hikers only on Huckleberry Path; no dogs, horses, or mountain bikes. Horses are allowed on the Skyline National Trail and the Bay Area Ridge Trail. No wheelchair facilities.

Permits: No permits are required. Parking and access are free.

Maps: A brochure and map are available at the trailhead. For a free trail map, phone the East Bay Regional Park District toll-free at 888/327-2757, option 3, extension 5; follow directions, leave your name and address, and ask for the Huckleberry Botanic Regional Preserve brochure. For a topographic map, ask the USGS for Oakland East.

Directions: From the East Bay, take Highway 24 east for 5.3 miles (get in right lane) through tunnel to the exit for Fish Ranch Road. Take that exit, merge onto Old Tunnel Road and continue 0.2 mile to Fish Ranch Road. Turn right at Fish Ranch Road and go 0.8 mile to Grizzly Peak Boulevard. Turn left on Grizzly Peak Boulevard and drive 2.4 miles to Skyline Boulevard. Turn left on Skyline and drive a short distance past Robert Sibley Volcanic Regional Preserve to the park entrance and parking lot, on the left.

Contact: Huckleberry Botanic Regional Preserve, 888/327-2757; East Bay Regional Park District, www.ebparks.org.

122 LAFAYETTE-MORAGA TRAIL

7.75 mi one-way/4.0 hr

north of the San Leandro Reservoir

Map 7.3, page 279

This trail is a hit with locals who use it for exercise, dog walks, jogs, even stroller walks. For nonlocals, not so much. The Lafayette-Moraga Trail is a 7.75-mile linear park. In other words, the trail is a park that forms a line from Lafayette to Moraga. All of it is paved. The trail starts at the Olympic Staging Area in Lafayette and curls to the left for the first 3.5 miles. It eventually heads south along Las Trampas Creek to Bollinger Canyon. It then passes through downtown Moraga to the Valle Vista Staging Area on Canyon Road.

User Groups: Hikers, wheelchairs, dogs, horses, and mountain bikes.

Permits: No permits are required except on EBMUD lands. Parking and access are free.

Maps: A brochure and map are available at the trailhead under the information panel. For a free trail map, phone the East Bay Regional Park District toll-free at 888/327-2757, option 3, extension 5; follow directions, leave your name and address, and ask for the Lafayette-Moraga Regional Trail brochure. For topographic maps, ask the USGS for Walnut Creek and Las Trampas Ridge.

Directions: From Highway 24 near Lafayette, take the Pleasant Hill Road exit south. Drive one mile to Olympic Boulevard. Turn right and drive 0.1 mile to the Olympic Staging Area.

Contact: Contra Costa Trails Office, 510/544-3028; Lafayette-Moraga Linear Park, 888/327-2757; East Bay Regional Park District, www.ebparks.org.

123 SHORELINE TRAIL
5.0 mi/2.25 hr

at Crown Memorial State Beach in Alameda

Map 7.3, page 279

The revival of Crown Memorial State Beach is complete on the shore of San Francisco Bay in Alameda. A $5.7 million project restored the beach and dune system. The beach spans 2.5 miles, and on its north end, extends in a half-moon curve to Ballena Bay. The Shoreline Trail is paved and starts near the visitors center. Dunes adjoin the trail for a portion of the walk. You get sweeping views across South San Francisco Bay, best from the beach and bike trail along the southeast portions of the shoreline. There is also an overlook of the Elsie Roemer Bird Sanctuary. A series of eight picnic sites are located from the Crab Cove Visitors Center at the northwest end of the beach on past Freshwater Lagoon and the dunes. The best for a lookout of the bay is City View, located near the rental shop for windsurfing.

The tide book is your bible at Crown Memorial State Beach. High tide is the best time to observe seabirds such as loons, grebes, and ducks. Low tide, however, is the best time to watch shorebirds such as sandpipers poking around the exposed mudflats.

User Groups: Hikers, wheelchairs, dogs (on the paved trail only, not the beach), and mountain bikes. No horses.

Permits: No permits are required. An entrance fee of $5 per vehicle is charged when kiosk is attended; $2 for dogs.

Maps: A brochure and map are available at the trailhead. For a free trail map, phone the East Bay Regional Park District toll-free at 888/327-2757, option 3, extension 5; follow directions, leave your name and address, and ask for the Crown Memorial State Beach brochure. For a topographic map, ask the USGS for Oakland West.

Directions: From San Francisco, take the Bay Bridge east for 5.2 miles (and stay to the right) to the split with I-80/580/880. Take the exit for I-880 South (signed for airport), go 1.6 miles and merge onto I-880 South and continue 1.2 miles to the exit for Broadway/Alameda. Take that exit and go 0.4 mile to 5th Street. Turn right on 5th Street, go 0.2 mile, stay right to stay on 5th Street and continue 0.7 mile (stay left) to merge with CA-260/Webster Street Tube. Turn left to merge with CA-260 and go one mile (when in the tube, get to the left) to Constitution Way (also signed by Marina Village Parkway) on left. Bear left toward Constitution Way for 0.3 mile, then continue on Constitution Way for 0.5 mile to 8th Street, and continue ahead on 8th Street for 0.6 mile to Otis Drive. Turn right on Otis Drive and go 0.1 mile to park entrance.

Contact: Crown Memorial State Beach, Crab Cove Visitors Center, 888/327-2757; East Bay Regional Park District, www.ebparks.org.

124 ARROWHEAD MARSH
2.0 mi/1.0 hr 🏃1 ⛰8

at Martin Luther King Regional Shoreline near Oakland

Map 7.3, page 279 BEST (

Martin Luther King Jr. Regional Shoreline is located on southern edge of San Leandro Bay, just east of the Oakland International Airport. The access road and a nearby trail are routed between Arrowhead Marsh and New Marsh. The San Leandro Creek channel is on one side, Airport channel is on the other, both of which feed into San Leandro Bay. From the main parking area, you can walk or ride a bike on the Arrowhead Marsh Trail along the Airport Channel for a mile to its back cove, or along the San Leandro Creek channel for a mile to Hegenberger. Arrowhead Marsh is a 50-acre tidal marsh (shaped like an arrowhead) located on the edge of San Leandro Bay, a short walk from the primary parking area. Though this wetland is small, a huge variety of migratory birds on the Pacific Flyway use this marsh as a resting spot in winter. Bring your picnic, binoculars, bike, or kayak, and then get ready to launch, no matter what your preference. A series of four picnic areas with water views are located along the park entry road. Note: As we went to press in 2016, the boardwalk that extends over Arrowhead Marsh to a viewing platform on the edge of San Leandro Bay was still closed due to structural damage in 2013, with no date for repair.

User Groups: Hikers, leashed dogs, wheelchairs, and mountain bikes. No horses.

Permits: No permits are required. Parking and access are free.

Maps: A brochure and map are available at the trailhead. For a free trail map, phone the East Bay Regional Park District toll-free at 888/327-2757, option 3, extension 5; follow directions, leave your name and address, and ask for the Martin Luther King Regional Shoreline brochure. For a topographic map, ask the USGS for San Leandro.

Directions: From San Francisco, take Bay Bridge east for six miles (do not get in left lane) and continue to the split with I-80/880/580. At the split, take I-880 South for 0.5 mile, then bear left to continue on I-880 South and continue 8.3 miles to the exit for Hegenberger Road. Take that exit for 0.3 mile to Hegenberger Road. Turn right on Hegenberger and drive 0.7 mile to Pardee Drive. Turn right and go 0.3 mile to Swan Way. Turn left and go 0.2 mile to park entrance road on right. Turn right and drive 0.8 mile to main parking area at end of road.

Contact: Martin Luther King Regional Shoreline, 888/327-2757 or 510/562-1373; East Bay Regional Park District, 888/327-2757, www. ebparks.org.

125 GRAHAM TRAIL LOOP
0.75 mi/0.5 hr 🏃1 ⛰6

in Roberts Regional Recreation Area

Map 7.3, page 279

A rare grove of redwood trees lines the entrance of Roberts Regional Recreation Area. That makes it popular for short visits and picnics. If you want to enter a redwood forest in the East Bay without having to walk far, this is the best bet. From the entrance of the parking area, near the swimming pool, take the short trail that is linked to Graham Trail. Turn right, and you will be routed in a short circle past a restroom to Diablo Vista; then turn right and head back to the parking area. The walk is short and sweet, just right for those on a picnic who do not wish for a challenging encounter.

User Groups: Hikers and dogs. No horses or mountain bikes. The restroom is wheelchair-accessible, but the trail is not.

Permits: No permits are required. An entrance fee of $5 per vehicle is charged; $2 for dogs. A fee is charged for access to the swimming pool (wheelchair-accessible).

Maps: A brochure and map are available at the trailhead. For a free trail map, phone the East Bay Regional Park District toll-free at 888/327-2757, option 3, extension 5; follow directions, leave your name and address, and ask for the Roberts Regional Recreation Area and Redwood Regional Park brochures. For a topographic map, ask the USGS for Oakland East.

Directions: From Highway 24 in the East Bay, drive to Highway 13 in Oakland. Turn south on Highway 13 and drive three miles to the exit for Joaquin Miller Road/Lincoln Avenue. Take that exit and continue to Monterey Boulevard. Turn on Monterey and go to Joaquin Miller Road. Turn left and drive one mile (up the hill) to Skyline Boulevard. Turn left on Skyline Boulevard and drive about one mile (keep to the right) to the park entrance, on the right.

Contact: Roberts Regional Recreation Area, 888/327-2757; East Bay Regional Park District, www.ebparks.org.

126 STREAM TRAIL LOOP
4.5 mi/2.5 hr   👫2 ⛰8

in Redwood Regional Park

Map 7.3, page 279

The surprise redwoods in the Oakland hills makes Redwood Regional Park one of the Bay Area's better finds. Pretty Redwood Creek, recharged each winter by rain, runs down its center. When you drive in, from the main park entrance at Redwood Gate, take the park road to its end at the Canyon Meadow Staging Area. A trailhead here provides access to the Stream Trail. It is routed a quarter mile upstream to a bridge over the creek, then another 1.2 miles to another bridge crossing. The route goes another 0.8 mile up to a third bridge. Most turn around here. It's 4.5 miles round-trip, pretty and easy.

Just beyond the entry kiosk at Redwood Gate, a fish ladder is located a short distance ahead to your left. After February rains, a strain of wild trout found nowhere else swim up from Upper San Leandro Reservoir, jump the ladder and spawn in the stream. A rarity to see. Fishing is not permitted in Redwood Creek and no access is allowed downstream at Upper San Leandro Reservoir.

User Groups: Hikers, wheelchairs, dogs, and horses. No mountain bikes.

Permits: No permits are required. An entrance fee of $5 per vehicle is charged when the kiosk is attended; $2 for dogs.

Maps: A brochure and map are available at the trailhead. For a free trail map, phone the East Bay Regional Park District toll-free at 888/327-2757, option 3, extension 5; follow directions, leave your name and address, and ask for the Redwood Regional Park brochure. For a topographic map, ask the USGS for Oakland East.

Directions: From San Francisco, take the Bay Bridge east for 6.4 miles (stay far right) to the split and I-580. Bear right on I-580 (stay far right) and go 6.2 miles to Exit 24 for 35th Avenue. Take that exit to the stop sign at 35th Avenue; turn left and drive 0.2 mile up hill (becomes Redwood Road) and continue straight for 2.3 miles to Redwood Regional Park on the left. Turn left and continue past the kiosk to the end of the road to parking for the Canyon Meadow Staging Area and trailheads for the Stream Trail (walks, hikes) and Canyon Trail (bikes).

From Highway 24: Take Highway 24 to the exit for Highway 13. Take that exit to Highway 13 South and drive to Redwood Road. Turn left on Redwood Road and drive two miles past Skyline Boulevard to the park entrance, on the left. Turn left and park at the Canyon Meadow Staging Area, at the end of the road.

Contact: Redwood Regional Park, 888/327-2757; East Bay Regional Park District, www.ebparks.org.

127 EAST RIDGE LOOP
4.0 mi/2.5 hr   👫3 ⛰7

in Redwood Regional Park

Map 7.3, page 279

The number one hike at Redwood Regional Park, the Stream Trail, is pretty and easy. This trip is for hikers and mountain bikers with a little more ambition. From the parking area, turn right on Canyon Trail, climbing up to the

East Ridge in 0.3 mile. Turn left onto the East Ridge Trail and make a loop by hiking out on the ridge, climbing much of the way. You climb roughly 900 feet. From atop the East Ridge, at 1,100 feet, you can look down into a canyon that appears to be a sea of redwoods. Another reward comes when you turn left and loop down into that canyon, where Redwood Creek awaits under the cool canopy of a lush forest. To do this, turn left again on Prince Trail, and another left on Stream Trail. Follow Stream Trail back to the Canyon Meadow Staging Area.

User Groups: Hikers, dogs, and horses. Mountain bikes and wheelchairs permitted on the paved part of the trail.

Permits: No permits are required. An entrance fee of $5 per vehicle is charged when the kiosk is attended; $2 for dogs.

Maps: A brochure and map are available at the trailhead. For a free trail map, phone the East Bay Regional Park District toll-free at 888/327-2757, option 3, extension 5; follow directions, leave your name and address, and ask for the Redwood Regional Park brochure. For a topographic map, ask the USGS for Oakland East.

Directions: From San Francisco, take the Bay Bridge east for 6.4 miles (stay far right) to the split and I-580. Bear right on I-580 (stay far right) and go 6.2 miles to Exit 24 for 35th Avenue. Take that exit to the stop sign at 35th Avenue, turn left, and drive 0.2 mile up hill (becomes Redwood Road). Continue straight for 2.3 miles to Redwood Regional Park on the left. Turn left, continue past the kiosk to the end of the road to parking for the Canyon Meadow Staging Area at the end of the road.

From Highway 24: Take Highway 24 to the exit for Highway 13. Take that exit to Highway 13 South and drive to Redwood Road. Turn left on Redwood Road and drive two miles past Skyline Boulevard to the park entrance, on the left. Turn left and park at the Canyon Meadow Staging Area, at the end of the road.

Contact: Redwood Regional Park, 888/327-2757; East Bay Regional Park District, www.ebparks.org.

128 GRASS VALLEY LOOP

2.8 mi/1.5 hr   👥2 △8

in Anthony Chabot Regional Park

Map 7.3, page 279   **BEST (**

Grass Valley provides a simple paradise nestled in the East Bay hills. This meadow lines more than a mile of a valley floor that is framed on each side by the crowned rims of foothills. From late March through mid-April, you can find a quiet valley that glows in shades of greens from wild grass and sparkles with the blooms of golden poppies and tiny blue-eyed grass and wild radish. The scene is quiet and beautiful, and the Grass Valley Trail provides a route to this tranquility. Start at the Bort Meadow Staging Area (at the MacDonald Trailhead for the East Bay Skyline National Trail) and hike downhill to the Bort Meadow Picnic Area. At the bottom of the valley, it feels secluded, quiet, and beautiful. Picnic tables are located in the shade of oaks, at the head of Grass Valley. Near the picnic area, head south on Grass Valley Trail for 1.5 miles. Take your time and enjoy it. At Stonebridge and the junction with the Brandon Trail, turn right on the Brandon Trail, which runs north along the west side of Grass Valley, and return to the picnic area. To crown a perfect day, end the hike with lunch at Bort Meadow.

User Groups: Hikers, dogs, horses, and mountain bikes. No wheelchair facilities.

Permits: No permits are required. Parking and access are free.

Maps: A brochure and map are available at the trailhead. For a free trail map, phone the East Bay Regional Park District toll-free at 888/327-2757, option 3, extension 5; follow directions, leave your name and address, and ask for the Anthony Chabot Regional Park brochure. For a topographic map, ask the USGS for Las Trampas Ridge.

Directions: From I-580 in Oakland, take the 35th Avenue exit and drive east (35th Avenue becomes Redwood Road). Follow Redwood Road past Skyline Boulevard and continue for

4.3 miles to the Bort Meadow Staging Area, on the right.

Contact: Anthony Chabot Regional Park, 888/327-2757; East Bay Regional Park District, www.ebparks.org.

129 MACDONALD TRAIL
5.4 mi/3.25 hr   🚶1 ⛰7

in Anthony Chabot Regional Park

Map 7.3, page 279

Start at the Bort Meadow Staging Area. From the north end of the parking lot, head north on the old ranch road, which is called the MacDonald Trail, and is part of the East Bay National Skyline Trail. Head out north (to the right), where the trail meanders along an old ranch road, climbing only slightly above Bort Meadow and Grass Valley. At the ridge, turn and look south for a great view of Grass Valley—a divine sight in the springtime. From the ridge, the trail/road proceeds north, with valley and hilltop views along the way. Watch closely for the hidden bench on the right side of the trail. You can sit here and look out over the remote foothill country to the east. After enjoying the views, return the way you came. The trail eventually drops steeply and connects to Redwood Regional Park, but most people turn around and return when they reach the drop in the trail.

User Groups: Hikers, dogs, horses, and mountain bikes. No wheelchair facilities.

Permits: No permits are required. Parking and access are free.

Maps: A brochure and map are available at the trailhead. For a free trail map, phone the East Bay Regional Park District toll-free at 888/327-2757, option 3, extension 5; follow directions, leave your name and address, and ask for the Anthony Chabot Regional Park brochure. For a topographic map, ask the USGS for Las Trampas Ridge.

Directions: From I-580 in Oakland, take the 35th Avenue exit and drive east (35th Avenue becomes Redwood Road). Follow Redwood Road past Skyline Boulevard and drive 4.3 miles to the Bort Meadow Staging Area, on the right.

Contact: Anthony Chabot Regional Park, 888/327-2757; East Bay Regional Park District, www.ebparks.org.

130 ROCKY RIDGE LOOP
4.4 mi/2.5 hr   🚶3 ⛰10

in Las Trampas Regional Wilderness south of Moraga

Map 7.3, page 279

Rocky Ridge provides the biggest bay view that is seen by the least. It's a ridge-top perch near San Ramon, just west of I-680. When you top the ridge, the view to the west emerges all at once, where you tower 2,000 feet over the South Bay. With the recent eye-popping air clarity, you can spot hundreds of landmarks in all directions. From the parking lot at 1,080 feet, the Rocky Ridge View Trail starts out as a service road and climbs 800 feet in 1.5 miles to a ridge trail. You continue—you can see the top all the way—and climb another 200 feet over the course of 0.7 mile as the views emerge over the bay. A spot called "Rock 2," at an elevation of 2,024 feet, is the prime pay-off. With one sweep of the eye across the bay, you can scan from the high-risers of downtown San Francisco on south past the Bay Bridge, San Mateo Bridge, Dumbarton Bridge, and across to Skyline and Mount Umunhum on the far horizon. Mount Hamilton rises to the south. Then in a turn to the east, you can scan across Mount Rose and the Sunol-Ohlone Wilderness, Livermore Valley, and Mount Diablo.

On the west bay-facing flank of the ridge, those who love to find and explore unique geologic formations can find them in the hollowed-out sandstone at the wind caves and Devil's Hole. To get there, follow the Rocky Ridge View Trail (map in hand) to its junction with Sycamore Trail. Turn right on Sycamore Trail and tromp a little more than 0.25 mile down to the caves. This is a fairly steep, though short, descent. This area also has many raptors. In the spring, the wind out of the northwest will hit the ridge and get pushed straight up, which creates a lifting effect that the raptors can glide on and hunt for hours. Like many parks in the East Bay hills, the landscape is loaded with rabbits, and to a lesser extent, ground squirrels. With so much prey, many see bobcats on the hunt, as well as raptors, including golden eagles, several species of falcons, and red-tailed hawks.

User Groups: Hikers, dogs, and horses. No mountain bikes (but permitted on the park's service roads). No wheelchair facilities.

Permits: No permits are required. Parking and access are free. A permit is required to access and hike on adjoining EBMUD lands.

Maps: A brochure and map are available at the trailhead. For a free trail map, phone the East Bay Regional Park District toll-free at 888/327-2757, option 3, extension 5; follow directions, leave your name and address, and ask for the Las Trampas Regional Wilderness brochure. For a topographic map, ask the USGS for Las Trampas Ridge.

Directions: From San Francisco, take I-80 east over the Bay Bridge for 5.8 miles (get in right lane) to the I-580 split. Bear right on I-580 east (get in right lane) and go 1.5 miles to exit for Highway 24. Take Highway 24 east (toward Walnut Creek) for 13.3 miles to the exit for I-680 south. Take that exit to I-680 south and drive 10.4 miles to Exit 36 for Crow Canyon Road. Take that exit and continue 0.4 mile to Crow Canyon Road. Turn right on Crow Canyon and go 1.1 miles to Bollinger Canyon Road. Turn right and drive four miles to end of road, parking, and trailheads.

Contact: Las Trampas Regional Wilderness, 888/327-2757 or 510/544-3276; East Bay Regional Park District, www.ebparks.org.

131 IRON HORSE REGIONAL TRAIL

1.0-28.0 mi one-way/1-3 days

🏃1 ⛰️4

in the San Ramon Valley

Map 7.3, page 279

The Iron Horse Regional Trail is a focal point of the national Rails to Trails program, which converts abandoned rail lines into hiking trails. The continuous trail runs 28 miles from Dublin north to Concord and Highway 4. The completed south portion starts at the Dublin-Pleasanton BART and goes north from there to Highway 4. This has become a prominent destination for locals out jogging, biking, and walking. The trail is a 10-foot wide asphalt strip, but the trail corridor ranges from 200 feet to as little as 12 feet in some areas of Walnut Creek. It is often hot and dry out here, with a few drinking fountains sprinkled along the way. Shade trees have been planted, affirmation of the sense of long-range vision.

The rail route that it follows was established in 1890 and was abandoned officially in 1976. It took only two years to remove all the tracks, but the trail conversion is requiring quite a bit more time. The plan is to extend the Iron Horse Regional Trail into Livermore on the south end, and to Carquinez Strait on the north.

User Groups: Hikers, wheelchairs, dogs, horses, and mountain bikes.

Permits: No permits are required. Parking and access are free.

Maps: A brochure and map are available at the trailheads. For a free trail map, phone the East Bay Regional Park District toll-free at 888/327-2757, option 3, extension 5; follow directions, leave your name and address, and ask for the Iron Horse Regional Trail brochure. For a topographic map, ask the USGS for Las Trampas Ridge.

Directions: South trailhead: Take I-580 east to the Dublin-Pleasanton BART station and park. The trailhead begins on Santa Rita Road.

North trailhead: From I-680 in Walnut Creek, take the Rudgear Road exit. Turn east and park at either the park-and-ride lot (on the east side of the freeway) or the staging area (south side).

Contact: Iron Horse Regional Trail, 888/327-2757; East Bay Regional Park District, www.ebparks.org.

132 CASTLE ROCK TRAIL
3.9 mi/2.0 hr

in Diablo Foothills Regional Park on Mount Diablo

Map 7.3, page 279

The views of Castle Rock, towering Mount Diablo, and access to a shady ravine make a visit to Diablo Foothills Regional Park very special. The Castle Rocks are a series of sandstone crags that form pieces of wall in the foothills of Diablo. Thousands make the long drive to the top of Mount Diablo; this trip can be more memorable.

From the Orchard Staging Area, follow Castle Rock Trail south to Stage Road Trail. This pretty, shaded riparian zone runs along Pine Creek and the border of Mount Diablo State Park. To the east are Castle Rock's monolithic sandstone structures, gorgeous when the sun is low in the sky at dawn and dusk. At the junction with Buckeye Ravine Trail, turn right (west) to complete the loop along a short section of the Briones-to-Mount Diablo Regional Trail, with photo-quality views of Castle Rock and the silhouette of Mount Diablo. Buckeye Ravine Trail picks up again to the right and connects with Shell Ridge Loop Trail for pretty, long-distance views on the way back to Castle Rock Trail.

Diablo Foothills encompasses more than 1,000 acres and is linked to Shell Ridge Open Space on one side, and Castle Rock Regional Recreation Area and Mount Diablo State Park on the other. There are several staging areas and a network of trails link to the surrounding parks. The busy Walnut Creek/Concord corridor can cause many to overlook the nearby foothills of giant Diablo. Once you depart I-680, the procession to the park moves quickly from highway traffic, past city and suburbia, to rural landscapes and some of Diablo's wildest lands, prettiest trails, and striking geologic formations.

User Groups: Hikers, dogs, horses, and mountain bikes, partially wheelchair-accessible.

Permits: No permits are required. Parking and access are free.

Maps: A brochure and map are available at the trailhead. For a free trail map, phone the East Bay Regional Park District toll-free at 888/327-2757, option 3, extension 5; follow directions, leave your name and address, and ask for the Diablo Foothills Regional Park brochure. For a topographic map, ask the USGS for Diablo.

Directions: From the Bay Bridge, bear right on I-580 (stay far right) and go 1.5 miles to exit for Highway 24. Take Highway 24 and drive 13.4 miles (through the tunnel) to Walnut Creek and I-680 (stay left). Continue on I-680 for 0.4 mile to exit for Ygnacio Valley Road. At bottom of the ramp, turn right on Ygnacio Valley Road and continue 2.2 miles to Walnut Avenue. Turn right onto Walnut Avenue and go 1.6 miles to a roundabout. Exit the roundabout to the right onto Castle Rock Road. Continue 1.5 miles to the Orchard Staging Area.

Contact: Diablo Foothills Regional Park, 888/327-2757; East Bay Regional Park District, www.ebparks.org.

133 LITTLE GIANT LOOP
8.1 mi/4.5 hr

at Mitchell Canyon in Mount Diablo State Park

Map 7.3, page 279

High on the north flank of Mount Diablo, the world seems simple and clean, with a view that never ends. From Deer Flat and Meridian Ridge, you can peer down Mitchell Canyon, across the Carquinez Strait and San Joaquin Delta, and across miles of greenbelt to the silhouette of Mount St. Helena, north of Calistoga. At Mount Diablo, the best way to

© TOM STIENSTRA

Little Giant Loop on the flank of Mount Diablo

commemorate the annual coronation of spring is from the Mitchell Canyon trailhead.

Our favorite trip here is an 8.1-mile loop, named the Little Giant Loop, and it takes most hikers about four hours to complete. It features an elevation gain of about 1,600 feet, a great picnic site with sensational views, and the option to fork off and create more ambitious trips.

The trip starts at the Mitchell Canyon trailhead (elevation 600 feet), located just outside of Clayton. This provides access to Mount Diablo's prettiest regions in spring.

In the first two miles, the climb is steady, and you can establish a good rhythm as you open the day and gain entry to Mitchell Canyon. You will pass amid grasslands, chaparral, and the first wildflowers of the year. In late March and April, this area features rafts of a purple bloom on a long stalk (linathus), along with dozens of other species. In April and early May, there can also be hummingbirds, butterflies, and ladybugs galore (don't laugh—on one trip we saw maybe 50,000 ladybugs in a 100-yard radius).

Then it gets steep, climbing about 1,000 feet in a mile, but it's graded with switchbacks,

making for a strong aerobic rhythm for hikers—but it's butt-kicker level for bikers. You will top out at Deer Flat and reach a fork in the trail. Everybody stops here, turns, and takes in the long-distance views, often enjoying a drink and maybe a trail snack at the picnic table. Deer Flat is primarily grasslands and chaparral, sprinkled with some small pines. The lookout points here tower over Mitchell Canyon and beyond to the valley flatlands to the north.

To complete the loop, turn left at Deer Flat to the Meridian Ridge Fire Road (more great views) and continue to Murchio Gap at a major junction. The best route is to continue straight for a short distance to the Back Trail, turn left, and enjoy the saunter downhill into a canyon setting. At the Coulter Pine Trail (single track, no bikes), turn left, which is routed back to the Mitchell Canyon trailhead and parking area.

Mount Diablo is beautiful in the spring. Sometimes we wish the experience could be captured in a bottle, and then taken in little doses when needed for the rest of the year.

User Groups: Hikers and horses. Mountain

bikes are allowed on a portion of this route. No dogs. No wheelchair facilities.

Permits: No permits are required. A state park entrance fee of $10 is charged for each vehicle.

Maps: A trail map is available from Mount Diablo State Park for a fee. For a topographic map, ask the USGS for Diablo.

Directions: From the Bay Bridge, bear right on I-580 and continue 1.6 miles (stay to the right) to Highway 24. Take Highway 24 east for 13.2 miles to Walnut Creek and I-680. Take I-680 north and go 0.4 mile to the exit for Ygnacio Valley Road. Take that exit, turn right, and drive 10 miles to Clayton and Clayton Avenue. Turn right on Clayton and drive one mile to Mitchell Canyon Road. Turn right and drive to the trailhead at the end of the road.

Contact: Mount Diablo State Park, 925/837-2525 or 925/838-9225 (weather); Summit Visitors Center, 925/837-6119; www.parks.ca.gov or www.mdia.org.

134 DONNER FALLS
6.5 mi/2.5 hr

🏃2 ⛰9

in Mount Diablo State Park near Danville

Map 7.3, page 279

In wet years, this hike is a 10. In dry years, a 6. In the spring, always an 8. Time it right and the world is yours. At Mount Diablo, the Bay Area's grand old mountain rising above the East Bay hills, there is a series of hidden waterfalls that can be as pretty as anything in the East Bay hills after a heavy rain. Reaching them requires a 6.5-mile hike, a good climb, and something of a fortune hunt.

The trailhead for Donner Creek Falls is at the end of Regency Drive, which is located off Clayton Road (and becomes Marsh Creek Road) out of Clayton. From here, turn left on an old ranch road and walk alongside a pretty creek set amid rolling hills peppered with oaks. At Cardinet Junction, turn left, and after a short time, cross the creek. Then it's a 600-foot climb in five switchbacks before you reach the signed turnoff for the falls trail. As you go,

rewards feature views to the north of Clayton, Suisun Bay, and the Mothball Fleet, as well as a good chance of seeing rabbits, deer, and hawks.

From here, the trail turns to single track and laterals the left side of a canyon. In wet years, one by one, the falls start to come in view. The first is a 20-foot cascade across the other side of the canyon. Then, moments later, there's another fall, straight ahead, that's more of a chute. As you continue up the trail, two more come into view, including one short but pretty free fall. Continuing straight, the trail will guide you right across two streams, the source of the falls. Most stop to enjoy the treat. If you can time your trip for peak flow, it's a stunner.

When you're ready to head back: The trail loops back to Cardinet Junction, and from there it's an easy (but often muddy in winter) traipse downhill back to the trailhead. It's hard to imagine Diablo any prettier than on this hike.

User Groups: Hikers and horses. No dogs. Mountain bikes permitted on the service road, but not the single-track trail that provides access to the waterfalls. The first half of the trail is designed for wheelchair use.

Permits: No permits are required. Parking and access are free.

Maps: A trail map is available from Mount Diablo State Park for a fee. For a topographic map, ask the USGS for Diablo.

Directions: From the Bay Bridge, bear right on I-580 and continue 1.6 miles (stay to the right) to Highway 24. Take Highway 24 east for 13.2 miles to Walnut Creek and I-680. Take I-680 north and go 0.4 mile to the exit for Ygnacio Valley Road. Take that exit, turn right, and drive 10 miles to Clayton and Clayton Avenue. Turn right (becomes Marsh Creek Road) and go three miles to Regency Drive. Turn right on Regency Drive and drive 0.5 mile to the end of the road and the trailhead.

Contact: Mount Diablo State Park, 925/837-2525; summit weather, 925/838-9225; Summit Visitors Center, 925/837-6119; www.parks.ca.gov or www.mdia.org.

135 DEVIL'S ELBOW/ NORTH PEAK

4.0 mi/2.5 hr   🏃3   ⛰10

in Mount Diablo State Park near Danville

Map 7.3, page 279

According to Native American legend, at the dawn of time, Tuyshtak was the sacred birthplace of the world. Supernatural beings, the First People, lived here in the Bay Area. Tuyshtak, you see, is Mount Diablo, the old mountain that towers over the East Bay hills and San Joaquin Delta. It is still one of the best places anywhere in the spring to visit, explore, and take in the views.

The trail does not start at the summit. As you drive up and near the summit, look for the signed trailhead on the right. It is 0.7 mile from the overflow parking lot on top; you can usually park along the road's shoulder near the trailhead, signed Devil's Elbow/North Peak Trail. The hike starts easy, a downhill romp to Prospector's Gap. You then turn right toward the North Summit and start a rhythmic climb for about a mile, before facing a butt-kicker: a seemingly straight-up section of about 150 yards. This is one of the steepest sections of trail anywhere, but it's short. Once near the top, hike over to the crag to the east and scramble to the top. This is a sensational spot with a lookout view that towers over Brentwood and the Delta. This is a four-mile round-trip hike, but it feels longer and takes 2.5 hours.

Note: Mount Diablo is a "dry park." No beer, wine, or alcohol of any kind is permitted.

User Groups: Hikers only. No mountain bikes, dogs or horses. No wheelchair access.

Permits: No permits are required. A state park entrance fee of $10 is charged for each vehicle.

Maps: A trail map is available from Mount Diablo State Park for a fee. For a topographic map, ask the USGS for Diablo.

Directions: North Gate: From San Francisco, take the Bay Bridge to the split and I-580. Bear right on I-580 and continue 1.6 miles (stay to the right) to Highway 24. Take 24 east for 13.2 miles to Walnut Creek. Take I-680 north and go 0.4 mile to the exit for Ygnacio Valley Road. Turn right on Ygnacio Valley Road and go 2.2 miles to Walnut Avenue. Bear right and go 1.5 miles to Oak Grove Road, then continue a short distance to North Gate Road. Turn left and go 1.4 miles to park entrance and kiosk. Continue 17 miles to upper summit parking lot.

South Gate: Take Highway 24 to Walnut Creek (stay right) and I-680 south. Go south on I-680 and drive 7.2 miles to Danville and the exit for Diablo Road. Take Diablo Road east for 2.9 miles (at 0.7 mile, you jog right to stay on Diablo Road) to Mount Diablo Scenic Boulevard. Turn left and go 3.8 miles (becomes South Gate Road) to the kiosk at the park entrance. Continue 0.8 mile to Live Oak Campground and park at the adjacent picnic area. Trailhead is behind site 20. Parking at Live Oak, continue on South Gate Road to Summit Road. Turn right and drive to summit parking area, visitors center, and lookout.

Contact: Mount Diablo State Park, 925/837-2525; summit weather, 925/838-9225; Summit Visitors Center, 925/837-6119; www.parks.ca.gov or www.mdia.org.

136 MARY BOWERMAN TRAIL

1.0 mi/0.5 hr   🏃1   ⛰10

in Mount Diablo State Park near Danville

Map 7.3, page 279

From the parking lot at the summit, start your visit to the summit by making the short walk to the old lookout station. Head up the stairs to the lookout perch that towers over the San Joaquin Delta and Sacramento Valley. From each side of the lookout, you get a chance to see long distances that encompass a huge landscape.

As you face the visitors center, the trailhead for the Mary Bowerman Trail is on your left. The trail runs on the shoulder of the summit in a counter-clockwise route. It offers a variety of views every step of the way. You will see some fire damage, both on the south flank and into the valley below as well. It takes about a half hour, out and back.

The best time of year for this hike is in late March and April, when the hills glow neon green and the skies often clear. Those familiar with the old mountain know this as the former Fire Interpretive Trail, a rim trail that rings the Diablo summit with fantastic views. Mary Bowerman, in case you don't recognize the name, was an esteemed Diablo botanist.

Note: Mount Diablo is a "dry park." No beer, wine, or alcohol of any kind is permitted.

User Groups: Hikers and wheelchairs. No mountain bikes, dogs, or horses.

Permits: No permits are required. A state park entrance fee of $10 is charged for each vehicle.

Maps: A trail map is available from Mount Diablo State Park for a fee. For a topographic map, ask the USGS for Diablo.

Directions: North Gate: From San Francisco, take the Bay Bridge to the split and I-580. Bear right on I-580 and continue 1.6 miles (stay to the right) to Highway 24. Take 24 east for 13.2 miles to Walnut Creek. Take I-680 north and go 0.4 mile to the exit for Ygnacio Valley Road. Turn right on Ygnacio Valley and go 2.2 miles to Walnut Avenue. Bear right and go 1.5 miles to Oak Grove Road, then continue a short distance to North Gate Road. Turn left and go 1.4 miles to park entrance and kiosk. Continue 17 miles to upper summit parking lot.

South Gate: Take Highway 24 to Walnut Creek (stay right) and I-680 south. Go south on I-680 and drive 7.2 miles to Danville and the exit for Diablo Road. Take Diablo Road east for 2.9 miles (at 0.7 mile, you jog right to stay on Diablo Road) to Mount Diablo Scenic Boulevard. Turn left and go 3.8 miles (becomes South Gate Road) to the kiosk at the park entrance. Continue 0.8 mile to Live Oak Campground and park at the adjacent picnic area. Trailhead is behind campsite 20. From parking at Live Oak, continue on South Gate Road to Summit Road. Turn right and drive to summit parking area, visitors center, and lookout.

Contact: Mount Diablo State Park,

925/837-2525; summit weather, 925/838-9225; Summit Visitors Center, 925/837-6119; www.parks.ca.gov or www.mdia.org.

137 SENTINEL ROCK/ ROCK CITY
1.0 mi/2.0 hr 👣1 ⛰10

in Mount Diablo State Park near Danville

Map 7.3, page 279

Sentinel Rock at Mount Diablo's Rock City is a stunner. You will be forever imprinted by the sight of this series of sandstone monoliths and the adventures that await. You can explore for hours.

The most popular trailhead is near site 20 at the Live Oak campground. It's about 0.25 mile to Sentinel Rock, a massive crag of sandstone with hollows like Swiss cheese. At the base of Sentinel Rock, on the east side, you'll find a carved staircase that signals the trek to the top (cables are set up for safety). There is a mosaic of unsigned trails in the area, and it can be confusing for first-timers. The best suggestion is to follow Wall Point Road to a spur trail (CCC Trail) south to Sentinel Rock. Soak in the views, then return on the spur trail to Wall Point Road and continue following that northwest to other sandstone structures: the Wind Caves, Wall Point, Lower Rock City, and Gibraltar Rock. Below Lower Rock City, Gibraltar Rock is the big attraction. On its backside, it's an easy scramble to the top and you can often see rock climbers rappelling down the face.

Note: Mount Diablo is a "dry park." No beer, wine, or alcohol of any kind is permitted.

User Groups: Hikers. No mountain bikes, dogs, horses, or wheelchair access on trail. Some wheelchair facilities at a picnic area.

Permits: No permits are required. A state park entrance fee of $10 is charged for each vehicle.

Maps: A trail map is available from Mount Diablo State Park for a fee. For a topographic map, ask the USGS for Diablo.

Directions: From San Francisco, take the Bay Bridge east for 6.4 miles (stay far right) to the split and I-580. Bear right on I-580 (stay far right) and go 1.5 miles to exit for Highway 24. Take Highway 24 and go 13.4 miles (through the tunnel) to Walnut Creek (stay right) and I-680 south. Take the exit to I-680 south and drive 7.2 miles to Danville and the exit for Diablo Road. Take Diablo Road east for 2.9 miles (at 0.7 mile, you jog right to stay on Diablo Road) to Mount Diablo Scenic Boulevard. Turn left and go 3.8 miles (becomes South Gate Road) to the kiosk at the park entrance. Continue 0.8 mile to Live Oak Campground and park at the adjacent picnic area. Trailhead is behind site 20.

Contact: Mount Diablo State Park, 925/837-2525; summit weather, 925/ 838-9225; Summit Visitors Center, 925/837-6119; www.parks.ca.gov or www.mdia.org.

138 HAZEL-ATLAS MINE
1.0-3.0 mi/1.5 hr   🏃2 ⛰️8

in Black Diamond Mines Regional Preserve near Antioch

Map 7.3, page 279

Here's a chance to combine a hike through pretty foothill country with an underground tour into the Bay Area's landmark coal and silica mines. Black Diamond Mines spans more than 7,500 acres, with 5,315 acres open to the public and a variety of routes amid 57 miles of trails for hiking (dogs permitted), biking, and horseback riding. The trails include valley walks and climbs to ridges for sweeping foothill views, and a 3.2-mile hike with a moderate climb to a backpack-style primitive campground. Plan your trip for the Hazel-Atlas Mine Tour (noon and 3pm Sat.-Sun. Mar.-Nov.).

After passing the park's entrance kiosk (usually staffed only on weekends), drive straight past the first parking area on the left and continue about one mile to the end of the road. A parking area, picnic area, and several trailheads are located here. From this point, take the signed Hazel-Atlas Mine Trail for a short walk up the hill to the mine entrance on the left. (Remember: Access to the mines is permitted by guided tour only.) As you near the mine entrance, on hot days you can feel the rush of cool air emerging from deep below the surface. A few dozen hard hats are provided for public use (mandatory); choose from a wooden box set just inside the mine entrance. In the first 400 feet, you follow a rail line to the underground office of the sand mine boss on the left. Peering through the office door, you see an old desk, a variety of old glass bottles, and other vintage accessories. Outside is the switchback for the rail cars.

The tunnel starts out small, and then opens with a series of cavernous chutes above and below you. Lighted stairways provide access to multiple chambers. Some spurs seem dark, deep, and endless, and are walled off by jail cell-like grates. There are multiple levels, and eventually they lead down into the coal mine chambers.

In the spring, this is one of the best of the 150 parks in the Bay Area for wildflower blooms. Deer, squirrels, foxes, hawks, and owls are common sightings.

Stewartville Backpack Camp: This public campground requires a 3.2-mile hike with a moderate climb. There is room for 20 people, with picnic tables and a pit toilet available. There is no drinking water (bring your own) and you must pack out all trash. Reservations required.

User Groups: Hikers, dogs, horses, and mountain bikes. The underground tours are accessible for hikers only. Limited wheelchair facilities.

Permits: No permits are required. A parking fee of $5 per vehicle is charged when the kiosk is attended; $2 per dog. Guided tours of the underground mining museum cost $5 per person; tickets can be purchased at the Sidney Flat Visitors Center. Reservations are required for Stewartville Backpack Camp (510/636-1684, $5 per person per night).

Maps: A brochure and map are available at the trailhead. For a free trail map, phone the East Bay Regional Park District toll-free at 888/327-2757, option 3, extension 5; follow directions, leave your name and address, and ask for the Black Diamond Mines Regional Preserve brochure. For a topographic map, ask the USGS for Antioch South.

Directions: From the Bay Bridge, take I-80 northeast for 22 miles to the exit for Highway 4/Martinez. Take that exit and continue east on Highway 4 for 25 miles to Exit 26A for Somersville Road. Take that exit, turn right on Auto Center Road/Somersville Road, and continue three miles to the park entrance. Continue straight 0.7 mile to the parking lot and trailhead.

Contact: Black Diamond Mines Regional Preserve, 510/544-2750 or 888/327-2757; East Bay Regional Park District, www.ebparks.org.

139 CONTRA LOMA LOOP
1.6 mi/1.0 hr   🚶1 ⛰7

in Contra Loma Regional Park near Antioch

Map 7.3, page 279

Most people go to Contra Loma Regional Park to fish, swim, sunbathe, or picnic at Contra Loma Lake. This short loop trail provides an alternative to those activities, tracing along the northwest shore of the lake, then climbing up and over a short hill and looping back to the starting point. From the parking area, head out on the trail to the Cattail Cove Picnic Area. Just after that, the trail turns right, and you'll follow the shore of the lake, pass a fishing pier, and then start a 10-minute climb up a small hill. To close out the loop, glide down the hill. The trail turns left and a mile later returns to the Cattail Cove Picnic Area. A great, easy romp, this hike is best done in spring.

User Groups: Hikers, wheelchairs, dogs, horses, and mountain bikes.

Permits: No permits are required. A parking fee of $5 per vehicle is charged; $2 for dogs. An additional fee is charged for access to the swim lagoon.

Maps: A brochure and map are available at the trailhead. For a free trail map, phone the East Bay Regional Park District toll-free at

888/327-2757, option 3, extension 5; follow directions, leave your name and address, and ask for the Contra Loma Regional Park brochure. For a topographic map, ask the USGS for Antioch South.

Directions: Take Highway 4 to Antioch and the exit for Lone Tree Way. Take that exit to Lone Tree Way and drive south to Golf Course Road. Turn right on Golf Course Road and drive to Frederickson Lane. Bear right on Frederickson and drive to the entry gate. Pass the kiosk, bear left, and continue to the parking lot by the beach.

Contact: Contra Loma Regional Park, 888/327-2757; East Bay Regional Park District, www.ebparks.org.

140 VOLVON LOOP TRAIL/ BOB WALKER RIDGE
5.7 mi/3.0 hr   🚶3 ⛰9

in Morgan Territory Regional Preserve north of Livermore

Map 7.3, page 279

Morgan Territory Regional Preserve is located within the traditional homeland of the Volvon, one of five historical Indian nations in the Mount Diablo area. This trail, named after the first people to live here, is the preserve's featured hike. You can create an easy 5.7-mile loop where you trace along a ridge as it rises along sandstone hills. You reach a ridgeline with terrific views toward Los Vaqueros Reservoir below.

The staging area is set near the ridge at 1,900 feet. Start the trip by heading up the short hill (a 100-foot climb) on the Volvon Trail and then continue over the other side a short distance to the T (about 0.5 mile from the trailhead) at the intersection of the Blue Oak Trail. At the T intersection, scan across the meadow ahead and to your right and look for the sandstone rocks on the edge of the meadow. You can find a series of bowls in the rock that the Ohlone Indians used for grinding the seeds of acorn into paste and leeching out (with water) the bitter taste.

Then it's on to Bob Walker Ridge. Head back and out north on the Blue Oak Trail and hike 1.3 miles to the Valley View Trail; a portable toilet is located here and you will pass a few other signed trail junctions. The trail meanders in and out of sub-ridge valleys, green and sprinkled with a few wildflowers in the spring, and is easy all the way. Continue right on the Valley View Trail and continue to Bob Walker Ridge. Here the trail is routed northward on a ranch road to a rounded mountain peak. There are beautiful views of Los Vaqueros Reservoir, as well as below to Round Valley, to the San Joaquin Valley to the east and Mount Diablo to the north.

The Loop Trail circles Bob Walker Ridge in a left-turning horseshoe and then links up again with the Volvon Trail. From here the Volvon Trail runs all the way back to the trailhead. As you near the parking lot, you can take a shortcut by turning right on the Concor Trail and then coasting downhill to the staging area. You can also extend the trip a mile by returning on the Corral Trail/Coyote Trail (hikers only, a good choice on weekends when the bikes are out).

The ridge was named in the 1990s for Bob Walker, a landscape photographer and open-space advocate who helped ensure that Morgan Territory was added to the East Bay Regional Park District. This parkland is most beautiful in the spring, and not just because the hills are greened up; one of the best wildflower displays in the Bay Area occurs here at that time. The one downer: too many cows.

User Groups: The first half of the loop is accessible to hikers, dogs, horses, and mountain bikes. The second half is for hikers and dogs only. No wheelchair facilities.

Permits: No permits are required. Parking and access are free.

Maps: A brochure and map are available at the trailhead. For a free trail map, phone the East Bay Regional Park District toll-free at 888/327-2757, option 3, extension 5; follow directions, leave your name and address, and ask for the Morgan Territory Regional Preserve brochure. For a topographic map, ask the USGS for Tassajara.

Directions: From I-580 in Livermore, take the N. Livermore Avenue exit and turn north. Drive to the junction of Morgan Territory Road and turn right. Drive 10.7 miles (narrow, drive slow) to the staging area on the right side of the road.

From I-680 in Concord, take the Clayton Road exit and head east. Clayton Road becomes Marsh Creek Road. Continue to Morgan Territory Road. Turn right and drive 9.4 miles (narrow, drive slow) to the staging area on the left side of the road.

Contact: Morgan Territory Regional Preserve, 510/544-3060 or 888/327-2757; East Bay Regional Park District, www.ebparks.org.

141 ROUND VALLEY LOOP
6.0 mi/3.0 hr

in Round Valley Regional Preserve

Map 7.3, page 279

Round Valley Regional Preserve sits in a beautiful pocket below the ridgeline that extends from the southeast flank of Mount Diablo, located off Marsh Creek Road. This park is a great back-road discovery and the pay-off on this nearly flat hike is seeing the bedrock mortars used for acorn grinding.

The trip starts with a pretty drive into the foothills of Contra Costa County. The park entrance is actually a staging area—a gravel parking lot with chemical toilets. This is the gateway to the 2,024-acre preserve. After parking, begin the trek by crossing a bridge. You then bear right on a service road that runs along Round Valley Creek and continues west to gain entry into Round Valley. The route extends 2.82 miles (as measured by an odometer wheel) to a junction with the Murphy's Meadow Trail. At Murphy's Meadow Trail, look to the left for a nearby grove of oaks. Hidden beneath them is a series of 10 bowl-like mortars in the rock, where Native Americans once met to grind acorns, leech out the bitter taste with water, and turn it into flour.

As you hike amid this riparian-oak woodland habitat, keep a lookout on the valley floor for wildlife, and to the air for raptors. This area is loaded with ground squirrels, and they can pop up and down like a game of pop-goes-the-weasel. Because of the high squirrel population, there are an equally high numbers of raptors that feed on them, with lots of red-tailed hawks, but also golden eagles, prairie falcons, owls, and turkey vultures.

User Groups: Hikers, dogs, horses, and mountain bikes. No wheelchair facilities. Dogs are not permitted in the adjoining Los Vaqueros Watershed to the south.

Permits: No permits are required. Parking and access are free.

Maps: A brochure and map are available at the trailhead. For a free trail map, phone the East Bay Regional Park District toll-free at 888/327-2757, option 3, extension 5; follow directions, leave your name and address, and ask for the Round Valley Regional Park brochure. For a topographic map, ask the USGS for Diablo.

Directions: From San Francisco, take the Bay Bridge east for 6.4 miles (stay far right) to the split and I-580. Bear right on I-580 (stay far right) and go 1.5 miles to exit for Highway 24. Take Highway 24 and go 13.4 miles (through the tunnel) to Walnut Creek (stay left) and I-680 North. Continue on I-680 North for 0.4 mile to exit for Ygnacio Valley Road. At bottom of ramp turn right on Ygnacio Valley Road and drive 7.5 miles to Clayton Road. Turn right and go 2.5 miles (it becomes Marsh Creek Road) and then continue 12 miles (past Morgan Territory Road on right, Deer Valley Road on left) to entrance on right (signed) to Round Valley Regional Preserve (parking and trailhead visible from Marsh Creek Road).

Alternate route from Livermore: Take I-580 east to the exit for Vasco Avenue. Take that exit, turn north on Vasco and go 12 miles to Camino Diablo Road. Turn left and go to junction with Marsh Creek Road and continue north 1.5 miles to the staging area on left.

Contact: Round Valley Regional Preserve, 888/327-2757; East Bay Regional Park District, www.ebparks.org.

142 COGSWELL MARSH LOOP

2.9 mi/1.5 hr

at Hayward Regional Shoreline in Hayward

Map 7.3, page 279

Cogswell Marsh, a 250-acre tidal wetland, is the heart of the 1,713-acre Hayward Regional Shoreline. It is located just north of Highway 92 and the San Mateo Bridge. It is so close to so many who drive right by, yet once afoot, has a feel of a world apart with big-time views and bird sightings. From the Peninsula, it's a quick shot over the bridge, yet few take that shot.

Cogswell Marsh Loop: From West Winton, hike south for 0.4 mile and then pick up the Bay Trail and continue south on the levee through Cogswell Marsh to Johnson's Landing. Turn right to route along the bay's shore and complete loop.

Longer trips can be crafted to the Oro Loma Marsh or beyond to the north on the Bay Trail. From West Winton, hike west for 0.3 mile to Hayward Landing. Turn right on the Bay Trail and head north, with the shore of the South Bay on your left, the 364-acre Oro Loma Marsh (constructed in 1997) on your right, to Bockman Channel, four miles round-trip. The ambitious can continue north, another half mile one-way over the San Lorenzo Creek and another 2.3 miles to San Leandro Marina.

User Groups: Hikers and mountain bikes. No dogs (south of flood control channel) or horses. No wheelchair facilities.

Permits: No permits are required. Parking and access are free.

Maps: A brochure and map are available at the trailhead. For a free trail map, phone the East Bay Regional Park District toll-free at 888/327-2757, option 3, extension 5; follow directions, leave your name and address, and ask for the Hayward Regional Shoreline brochure. For a topographic map, ask the USGS for San Leandro.

Directions: From San Francisco, take the Bay Bridge (get in right lane) to the split and Exit 8A and I-880. Merge right on I-880 south and drive 18 miles to Exit 28 for Winton Avenue. Take that exit, keep right at a fork, and merge onto West Winton Avenue. Drive 2.5 miles to the park office and continue a short distance to the parking area and trailhead.

From the Peninsula: Take U.S. 101 to exit for Highway 92 east. Take Highway 92 and drive 11 miles (over San Mateo Bridge) to Exit 24 for Clawiter Road/Eden Landing Road. Take that exit 0.2 mile to Clawiter Road, turn left, and go one mile to Depot Road. Turn left on Depot Road and go 0.7 mile to Cabot Boulevard. Turn right and go 1.1 miles to West Winton Avenue (second left). Turn left and drive 0.4 mile to park office; continue a short distance to the parking area and trailhead.

Contact: Hayward Regional Shoreline, 888/327-2757; East Bay Regional Park District, www.ebparks.org.

143 EAST BAY SKYLINE NATIONAL TRAIL

31.0 mi one-way/2-4 days

from Anthony Chabot to Wildcat Canyon Regional Park

Map 7.3, page 279

A 31-mile trail along the East Bay's skyline offers an opportunity for a long-distance hike that can be chopped into many short segments over the course of days or even weeks. The trail spans from the Castro Valley foothills northward to the ridgeline behind Richmond, crossing six regional parks for a view into the area's prettiest and wildest lands. The East Bay Skyline National Trail can be hiked from south to north in two days, but it can also be divided into seven sections from the different access points at the parking areas. Bicycles and horses

are permitted on 65 percent of the trail, where it is wide enough to accommodate them.

It is a great trip, whether you do it all in one weekend or cover a bit at a time over several weeks. No permits are needed, leashed dogs are allowed in undeveloped areas or as posted, and access is free. There are no campgrounds directly along the way, but you can use a shuttle car and come back to do a different section each day. The marked absence of drinking water along much of the route is another drawback. Water is available at only four points over the 31 miles, at Lomas Cantadas, Sibley Preserve, Skyline Gate, and Bort Meadow. So come prepared with two full canteens per person, along with a hat and sunscreen. Following are detailed descriptions of the trail from south to north.

Proctor Gate to Bort Meadow, Lake Chabot, and Anthony Chabot Regional Park: The Brandon Trail starts adjacent to Willow Park Public Golf Course and is routed up a ridge. It then meanders on a ranch road in Anthony Chabot Regional Park. At Stonebridge (don't turn left at the trail junction!), the trail leads into Grass Valley and on to Bort Meadow. The trail climbs 600 feet, then drops 320 feet, all over 6.5 miles.

Directions: From I-580 in Oakland, take the 35th Avenue exit and drive east (35th Avenue becomes Redwood Road). Drive on Redwood Road to the Proctor Gate Staging Area, located on the east border of the park, next to Willow Park Public Golf Course.

Bort Meadow to MacDonald Gate, Anthony Chabot Regional Park: If you are hiking the entire East Bay National Skyline Trail, the trail climbs steeply out of Bort Meadow. If you are starting at the parking area, however, no such climb is needed. The trail becomes a service road, from which you can turn and look south for the great view of Grass Valley. Hikers are completely exposed on the ascent; it's hot and dry in the afternoon, so it's best to go early in the morning. Once on top, it's an easy hike, with many wildflowers in spring. It then descends into a canyon, and drops you

© TOM STIENSTRA

Bort Meadow

into MacDonald Staging Area. Continue on MacDonald Trail a very short distance to Big Bear Staging Area (hikers only, no bicycles). You will cross Redwood Road, putting you at the entrance to Redwood Regional Park. Bikers can exit on to Redwood Road, but should use caution. Distance: 2.7 miles; climbs 300 feet, then drops 500 feet.

Directions: From I-580 in Oakland, take the 35th Avenue exit and drive east (35th Avenue becomes Redwood Road). Drive on Redwood Road three miles past Skyline Boulevard to the Bort Meadow Staging Area, on the right.

MacDonald Gate to Skyline Gate, Redwood Regional Park: Hikers have two options here, and the suggested route is to split off at French Trail to hike up the canyon bottom on Stream Trail, enveloped by redwoods. Note that bikes are banned from this section. The alternative, a must-do for bikers, is to take West Ridge Trail for a steep climb to the canyon rim, then drop to the junction at Skyline Gate. Distance: five miles; French Trail drops 200 feet, then climbs 400 feet; West Ridge Trail climbs 900 feet, then drops 200 feet.

Directions: From I-580 to the west or I-680 to the east, take Highway 24 to Highway 13 and go south. Drive to Redwood Road and turn left. Go straight at the stop sign, then turn right onto Redwood Road at the light. Continue driving east on Redwood Road for 1.7 miles from the intersection of Skyline and turn right into the MacDonald Gate Staging Area.

Skyline Gate through Huckleberry Preserve to Sibley Preserve: This section of trail is a choice hike for nature lovers, who will see an abundance of birdlife and other animals, especially in the early morning and late evening. The trail passes through a deciduous woodland habitat, with a short but quite steep climb after entering Huckleberry Preserve. Distance: three miles; drops 200 feet, then climbs 480 feet.

Directions: From Highway 24 in Oakland, drive east to Highway 13. Go south and drive to Joaquin Miller Road, then head east until you hit Skyline Boulevard. Turn left on Skyline Boulevard and drive to the Skyline Gate Staging Area.

Sibley Preserve to Lomas Cantadas,

Tilden Regional Park: A unique section of trail, this part crosses over the Caldecott Tunnel in a relatively unpeopled area. Many hawks are seen here, a nice bonus. Sibley is best known for its volcanic past, and hikers can take a side trip to Round Top Peak (see the *Round Top Loop Trail* listing in this chapter). This area was a volcanic region 10 million years ago, when the Hayward and Moraga fault systems greatly uplifted this land. Bicycles are permitted on the section of the Skyline Trail between Sibley Staging Area (6800 Skyline Blvd.) to Old Tunnel Staging Area. Distance: 3.4 miles; drops 300 feet, then climbs 600 feet.

Directions: From I-580 to the west or I-680 to the east, drive to Highway 24. Continue to just east of the Caldecott Tunnel and take the Fish Ranch Road exit northwest to Grizzly Peak Boulevard. Turn left and drive to Skyline Boulevard. The park entrance and parking area are on the left.

Lomas Cantadas to Inspiration Point, Tilden Regional Park: This section of trail starts at a major access area off Grizzly Peak Boulevard. Also possible is an adjacent side trip to Vollmer Peak, the highest point on East Bay Skyline National Trail. The trail is then routed north to Inspiration Point at Wildcat Canyon Road, another well-known access point, losing elevation most of the way. Many sweeping views of the East Bay's untouched foothills are found on this hike. Distance: three miles; drops 860 feet.

Directions: From I-580 to the west or I-680 to the east, drive to Highway 24. Continue to just east of the Caldecott Tunnel and take the Fish Ranch Road exit to Grizzly Peak Boulevard. At the stop sign, turn right and drive on Grizzly Peak Boulevard to Lomas Cantadas Road. Turn right, then immediately turn left, following the signs for the Steam Train to the parking area.

Inspiration Point (Tilden Regional Park) to Wildcat Canyon Regional Park: The last stretch starts at the most heavily used section of the entire route, then crosses its most dramatic and unpeopled terrain. From Inspiration Point, the trail is actually paved for four miles—ideal for bicycles and wheelchairs. Beyond that, the trail turns to dirt and traces San Pablo Ridge, with inspiring views in all directions before dropping steeply into Wildcat Canyon Regional Park in the Richmond foothills. Distance: 7.2 miles; drops 800 feet.

Directions: From I-580 to the west or I-680 to the east, drive to Highway 24. Continue to just east of the Caldecott Tunnel and take the Fish Ranch Road exit northwest to Grizzly Peak Boulevard. Turn right, drive up the hill, and turn right on South Park Drive. Drive one mile to Wildcat Canyon Road, bear right, and drive to the parking area at Inspiration Point, on the left.

Alternate Route: To avoid South Park Drive, which is sometimes closed in the winter due to newt migrations, from Highway 24 go through the Caldecott Tunnel and exit at Orinda. Turn left on Camino Pablo. Drive north for about two miles, then turn left on Wildcat Canyon Road. Follow the road to Inspiration Point on the right.

User Groups: Hikers, dogs, horses, and mountain bikes. Horses and mountain bikes are restricted in some sections. Also see individual trailhead listings.

Permits: No permits are required. Access is free, but a parking fee may be charged at some trailheads.

Maps: For a map of the East Bay Skyline National Trail, contact the East Bay Regional Park District and request the individual regional parks map brochures.

Directions: See individual trailhead listings for specific directions.

Contact: East Bay Regional Park District, 888/327-2757, www.ebparks.org.

144 DON CASTRO LAKE LOOP

1.7 mi/1.0 hr   🥾1 ⛰6

in Don Castro Regional Recreation Area

Map 7.3, page 279

Don Castro is a small (23 acres) but pretty lake

that attracts swimmers to its lagoon and its clear, warm, blue waters. Take the Shoreline Trail along the north side of the lake. It leads to the upper end of the lake and a bridged crossing on your right and the Whispering Creek Trail. That runs the length of the more remote far side of the lake. Easy, pretty, with good bird sightings. The trail (actually, it's a road) is routed around the lake for an easy walk or jog in a nice setting. The lake has a fishing pier, swimming lagoon, and is fed by the headwaters of the lake at San Lorenzo Creek.

User Groups: Hikers and dogs. Portions of the trail are paved for bicycle and wheelchair use. No horses.

Permits: No permits are required. An entrance fee of $5 per vehicle is charged when the kiosk is attended; $2 for dogs. A swimming fee is extra.

Maps: A brochure and map are available at the trailhead. For a free trail map, phone the East Bay Regional Park District toll-free at 888/327-2757, option 3, extension 5; follow directions, leave your name and address, and ask for the Don Castro Regional Recreation Area brochure. For a topographic map, ask the USGS for Hayward.

Directions: Take I-580 east to Castro Valley and the exit for Grove Way. Take the exit for Grove Way (toward Crow Canyon Road) for 0.2 mile to Grove Way. Turn right and go 0.2 mile, bear slight left onto Center Street and continue 0.5 mile to Kelly Street. Turn left on Kelly and go 0.5 mile to Woodroe Avenue. Turn left on Woodroe and drive 0.5 mile to park entrance on the right.

From westbound I-580, take the exit for Castro Valley/E. Castro Valley Boulevard and drive west on E. Castro Valley Boulevard to Grove Street. Turn left on Grove and continue to Center Street. Bear slight left onto Center Street and continue 0.5 mile to Kelly Street. Turn left on Kelly and go 0.5 mile to Woodroe Avenue. Turn left on Woodroe and drive 0.5 mile to park entrance on the right.

Contact: Don Castro Regional Recreation Area, 510/544-3073 or 888/327-2757; East Bay Regional Park District, www.ebparks.org.

145 CREST TRAIL/ VISTA GRANDE

at North Gate, Los Vaqueros Reservoir near Brentwood

Map 7.3, page 279

From near the John Muir Interpretive Center, take the Crest Trail up to the ridge, where you emerge on the Vista Grande Trail. Turn left and walk toward the dam. You get sweeping views across Los Vaqueros Reservoir to the foothills of Morgan Territory and beyond to Mount Diablo. The trail then descends past the dam and back to the interpretive center.

The Los Vaqueros Watershed spans nearly 20,000 acres across deep valleys and foothills roughly between Livermore and Brentwood in remote Contra Costa County. It's the Bay Area's biggest lake. The adjoining foothills provide habitat for an abundance of ground squirrels. That furnishes a perpetual food source for the highest numbers of golden eagles (tops in winter when migrants arrive) and bobcat in the region. Other raptors are common.

User Groups: Hikers only; youth ages 12-17 must not hike alone; those under 12 years old must hike with an adult. No mountain bikes, dogs, or horses. Limited wheelchair facilities. Mountain bikes permitted on ranch-style roads elsewhere in watershed.

Permits: No permits are required. A fee of $6 per car is charged. No alcohol is allowed. Helmets are required for all bike riders. No privately owned boats permitted.

Maps: A brochure and map are available online and at the Interpretive Center.

Directions: In Contra Costa County, take Highway 4 east through Antioch past Hillcrest and merge left onto the Brentwood Bypass. Continue on the Bypass (past Oakley and Brentwood) to Walnut Boulevard. Turn right on Walnut and drive one mile to the entrance gate and parking at the John Muir Interpretive Center.

Contact: Los Vaqueros Marina, 925/371-2628, www.ccwater.com/losvaqueros.

146 VISTA LOOP

3.3 mi/2.0 hr

in Garin Regional Park in the Hayward foothills

Map 7.3, page 279

Garin spans a vast swath of greenbelt above Hayward, with foothills, canyons, creeks, and ponds. Garin Regional Park and adjoining Dry Creek Pioneer Regional Park encompass nearly 4,800 acres of wildlands. A 3.3-mile round-trip with a 550-foot climb tops out at 934-foot Vista Peak (and nearby 948-foot Garin Peak). From the parking area, walk 0.25 mile to Arroyo Flats and a trail junction. Turn left to connect with Vista Peak Loop Trail. On a clear day after a rain, you get a gorgeous view of the South Bay. Take your time and enjoy the views.

For family-style trips, a short walk leads to Jordan Pond and its ranch-style bass fishing, bird watching, a picnic area, and kite field. A trail circles the pond. A 20-mile network of ranch roads provides a matrix of routes for excellent mountain biking and horseback riding.

User Groups: Hikers, dogs, horses, and mountain bikes. No wheelchair facilities.

Permits: No permits are required. An entrance fee of $5 per vehicle is charged when the kiosk is attended; $2 for dogs.

Maps: A brochure and map are available at the trailhead. For a free trail map, phone the East Bay Regional Park District toll-free at 888/327-2757, option 3, extension 5; follow directions, leave your name and address, and ask for the Garin and Dry Creek Pioneer Regional Parks brochure. For a topographic map, ask the USGS for Hayward.

Directions: From San Francisco, take I-80 east over the Bay Bridge (get in right lane) to the split with I-580/I-880. Take the fork for I-880 South, merge onto I-880 and drive 20 miles to Hayward and Exit 25 for Industrial Parkway. Take that exit to Industrial Parkway, turn left and drive 1.9 miles; continue a short distance on Alquire Parkway to Vanderbilt Street. Turn right on Vanderbilt and go 0.3 mile to Garin Avenue. Turn left on Garin and drive 0.8 mile to park entrance and parking.

Contact: Garin Regional Park, 888/327-2757; East Bay Regional Park District, www.ebparks.org.

147 BAYVIEW TRAIL

3.0 mi/1.5 hr

in Coyote Hills Regional Park near Fremont

Map 7.3, page 279

Coyote Hills is a special park with a rare blend of views, birds, walking trails, a bike route, and an Ohlone history that can make every trip special. Most first-time visitors take the paved Bay View Trail or climb to a hilltop for sweeping views across South San Francisco Bay and the East Bay foothills. But you'll likely return for a walk on the wood boardwalk amid a bird-filled marsh, or take a guided tour of an Ohlone shellmound.

The Bay View Trail is an easy, paved 3.5-mile walk that is routed around much of the park, including more than a mile of bay frontage. You can detour on a wood boardwalk through the North Marsh.

Coyote Hills has four shellmounds, that is, piles of accumulated debris from historic Ohlone that lived in the area. Interpretive walks are available most weekends. Coyote Hills is located along the eastern shore of South San Francisco, bordered to the north by Alameda Creek and the Hayward Regional Shoreline. To the south is the Dumbarton Bridge and beyond to the Don Edward San Francisco Bay National Wildlife Refuge.

User Groups: Hikers, dogs, horses, and mountain bikes. The trail is paved and is technically wheelchair-accessible but is quite steep in some sections.

Permits: No permits are required. An entrance fee of $5 per vehicle is charged when the kiosk is attended; $2 for dogs.

Maps: A brochure and map are available at the trailhead. For a free trail map, phone the East Bay Regional Park District toll-free at 888/327-2757, option 3, extension 5; follow directions, leave your name and address, and ask for the

Coyote Hills Regional Park brochure. For a topographic map, ask the USGS for Newark.

Directions: Take I-880 south from Oakland for 23.5 miles to the exit for Dumbarton Bridge/Highway 84. Take that exit, continue 0.4 mile, merge with Highway 84 West, and drive 0.5 mile to the exit for Ardenwood Boulevard (toward Newark Boulevard). Take that exit for 0.4 mile to Ardenwood. Turn right on Ardenwood and drive 0.6 mile to Commerce Drive. Turn left and go 0.3 mile (when you cross Paseo Parkway, becomes Patterson Ranch Road) and continue 1.5 miles to park, 35 miles from San Francisco.

From the Peninsula: Take U.S. 101 to the South Peninsula (south of Redwood City, 27 miles south of San Francisco) and the exit for Highway 84 East/Marsh Road. Take that exit and go 0.2 mile to Highway 84/Marsh Road. Turn left and go 0.3 mile to Bayfront Expressway. Turn right and drive three miles (becomes Highway 84). Continue 4.6 miles (over Dumbarton Bridge) to the exit for Thornton Avenue (toward Paseo Padre Parkway). Take that exit for 0.2 mile and continue on Paseo Padre Parkway and drive one mile to Patterson Ranch Road. Turn left and drive 1.5 miles to park.

Contact: Coyote Hills Regional Park, visitors center, 888/327-2757 or 510/795-9385; East Bay Regional Park District, www.ebparks.org.

148 RIDGELINE TRAIL
7.0 mi/4.0 hr   🏃3 ⛰8

in Pleasanton Ridge Regional Park west of Pleasanton

Map 7.3, page 279

Pleasanton Ridge Regional Park is a huge swath of foothills and ridges that spans 5,271 acres. The Ridgeline Trail climbs to elevations of 1,600 feet, with the northern sections giving way to sweeping views featuring miles of rolling foothills and valleys at the threshold of Mount Diablo. From the parking area, elevation 300 feet, start hiking on Oak Tree Trail.

The Oak Tree Trail is routed 1.4 miles up to Ridgeline Trail, and in the process, you climb 750 feet. Turn right on the Ridgeline Trail and hike two miles along the ridge. You can return on a loop route by the Thermalito Trail. You get excellent views across the Livermore Valley. Development in and around the park has been limited. The surroundings retain a wild feel.

User Groups: Hikers, dogs, horses, and mountain bikes. No wheelchair facilities.

Permits: No permits are required. Parking and access are free.

Maps: A brochure and map are available at the trailhead. For a free trail map, phone the East Bay Regional Park District toll-free at 888/327-2757, option 3, extension 5; follow directions, leave your name and address, and ask for the Pleasanton Ridge Regional Park brochure. For a topographic map, ask the USGS for Dublin.

Directions: Take I-680 to Pleasanton and the exit for Castlewood Drive. Take that exit to Castlewood, turn west and drive to Foothill Road. Turn left (south) on Foothill and drive to the staging area (about two miles from Castlewood Drive).

Contact: Pleasanton Ridge Regional Park, 510/544-3030; East Bay Regional Park District, 888/327-2757, www.ebparks.org.

149 NORTH ARROYO TRAIL
1.3 mi/0.75 hr   🏃1 ⛰6

in Shadow Cliffs Regional Recreation Area in Pleasanton

Map 7.3, page 279

The centerpiece at Shadow Cliffs is a pretty 80-acre lake on the outskirts of Pleasanton. It has one of the best swimming beaches at any lake in the Bay Area. It also provides fishing for trout and catfish, and a spot for kayaking and other low-speed boating. Though you can't walk all the way around Shadow Cliffs Lake, you can explore a series of smaller ponds in the Arroyo area. From the back of the first parking area, take a trail over the top of a levee and down to the shore of the first pond. Then just follow North Arroyo Trail along the shores of several ponds for about 0.5 mile. For a view of the ponds, make the short climb up the adjacent levee. These ponds are water holes left over from a gravel quarry.

Shadow Cliffs Lake, the biggest pond covering some 80 acres, has been stocked with trout and catfish and can be one of the better fishing spots in the East Bay. It is also a good place to swim. In winter during heavy rains, the lake often has better clarity than any other lake in the Bay Area.

User Groups: Hikers and dogs. Portions of the trail are accessible to horses and mountain bikes, and wheelchair facilities are available.

Permits: No permits are required. A fee of $6 per vehicle is charged for parking; $2 for dogs.

Maps: A brochure and map are available at the trailhead. For a free trail map, phone the East Bay Regional Park District toll-free at 888/327-2757, option 3, extension 5; follow directions, leave your name and address, and ask for the Shadow Cliffs Regional Recreation Area brochure. For a topographic map, ask the USGS for Livermore.

Directions: From San Francisco, take the Bay Bridge east 6.4 miles (stay to the far right) to the split and I-580. Bear right on I-580 (stay to the far right), merge with I-580 and drive 28 miles (continue east of I-580 at interchange with I-680) to Pleasanton and the exit for Santa Rita Road (toward Tassajara Road). Take that exit for 0.2 mile, keep right at fork (signed for downtown), merge with Santa Rita Road, and drive 1.7 miles to Valley Avenue. Turn left and drive 1.1 miles to Stanley Boulevard. Turn left on Stanley and go 0.7 mile to park entrance on the right.

Contact: Shadow Cliffs Regional Recreation Area, 510/544-3230 or 888/327-2757; East Bay Regional Park District, www.ebparks.org.

150 TIDELANDS TRAIL
2.5 mi/1.5 hr   🚶1 △7

in San Francisco Bay National Wildlife Refuge

Map 7.3, page 279

Roughly 1.5 million migratory waterfowl spend the winter on bay wetlands. Hundreds of thousands will arrive at the Don Edwards San Francisco Bay National Wildlife Refuge. As you arrive, a 30,000-acre expanse of salt marshes, tidal flats, and beyond to the South Bay is unveiled to you. The visitors center at the refuge is perched on a hilltop with an observation deck for views of the marsh. Tidelands Trail and Newark Slough Trail provide easy walks with good bird-watching and bay views. This is actually a wide dirt pathway on a levee routed amid salt marsh and bay tidewaters. At first arrival, it does not appear very pretty, but it gets better. The views of the South Bay and (on clear days) the surrounding foothills are a panoramic urban backdrop. More than 250 species in a given year use this habitat for food, resting space, and nesting sites. It is not unusual to see a half-dozen species of ducks, an egret, a sandpiper, a willet, and herons in just 15 or 20 minutes.

This refuge not only has the longest name of any place around, but great views, bike rides, walks, fishing, and kayaking, and one of the better visitors centers available for free. Group nature tours on this trail are offered regularly on weekends.

User Groups: Hikers, dogs, and mountain bikes. There are no wheelchair facilities, but the trail can be navigated by most wheelchair users. No horses.

Permits: No permits are required. Parking and access are free.

Maps: For a free brochure, contact the refuge. For a topographic map, ask the USGS for Newark.

Directions: From San Francisco and the Peninsula: Take U.S. 101 to Menlo Park (27 miles south of San Francisco) and Exit 406 for Highway 84/East Marsh Road-Dumbarton Bridge. Take that exit and continue to Highway

84 East/Marsh Road and drive 7.6 miles (over Dumbarton Bridge) to Exit 36 for Thornton Avenue (toward Paseo Padre Parkway). Take Exit 36 to Thornton, turn right and go 0.6 mile to Marshlands Road. Turn right and go 0.5 mile to parking.

From East Bay counties: Take I-880 to Fremont (about 20 miles south of Oakland) and Exit 21 for Highway 84/Dumbarton Bridge. Take that exit and continue 0.4 mile toward Dumbarton Bridge, merge with Highway 84 and drive 1.8 miles to Exit 36 for Paso Padre Parkway/Thornton Avenue. Take that exit to Thornton, turn left, and go 0.6 mile to Marshlands Road. Turn right and go 0.5 mile to parking.

Contact: Don Edwards San Francisco Bay National Wildlife Refuge, 510/792-0222, www.fws.gov/refuge.

151 ALAMEDA CREEK REGIONAL TRAIL
1-12.0 mi one-way/0.5 hr.-1 day
🏃1 ⛺8

on Alameda Creek from Niles to the South Bay

Map 7.3, page 279

By bike or on foot, the Alameda Creek Regional Trail provides a series of portals for entry to an extended tour of adventure. From Niles to San Francisco Bay at Coyote Hills, this trip is a can't-miss for fun, wildlife, and bay views. Unlike other regional trails, there are actually two routes; an unpaved route for walking, hiking, and horseback riding on the north side of Alameda Creek, and a paved pathway for biking and jogging on the south side of the creek.

The route, north side: Start to finish, the unpaved north side is 12.4 miles, one-way, and spans from Niles past Shinn Pond, Quarry Lakes, and extends the final four miles out to remote bay wetlands and where Alameda Creek enters the South Bay.

The route, south side: The paved route, a great bike trip, is 12 miles and passes the Kaiser water pits, has bridged access to Quarry Lakes,

and extends west to Coyote Hills Regional Park and the shore of the South Bay.

Six parking areas are available with trailheads, with many other access points. If you do not want to do the entire round-trip (24-25 miles), enter the trail instead at Coyote Hills, Quarry Lakes or Shinn Pond. North side/distances: Unpaved for walking, hiking, horseback riding. From Old Canyon Road/Niles Staging Area: Concrete Bridge/Thornton (2.3 miles one-way), Isherwood/Quarry Lakes (3.1) Alvarado Niles (5.3), Union City Blvd. (8.2), San Francisco Bay (12.4). South side/distances: Paved for bicycling, jogging. From Old Canyon Road/Niles Staging Area: Kaiser Ponds (1.4 miles one-way), Isherwood/Quarry Lakes (3.5), Alvarado (6.4), Coyote Hills (9.7), San Francisco Bay (12). As part of an Eagle Scout project, mileage markers are set along the routes.

At trail's end, on the paved southern trail, the official regional trail ends at the shore of the South Bay, directly adjacent to the Don Edwards San Francisco Bay National Wildlife Refuge to the south. It connects with the Shoreline Trail (dirt, no bikes) on a land spit that extends south for bird-watching on tidal flats and bay views.

User Groups: South Trail: Hikers, dogs, and mountain bikes. North Trail: Hikers, dogs, and horses. No wheelchair facilities.

Permits: No permits are required. Parking and access are free.

Maps: A brochure and map are available at the trailhead. For a free trail map, phone the East Bay Regional Park District toll-free at 888/327-2757, option 3, extension 5; follow directions, leave your name and address, and ask for the Alameda Creek Regional Trail brochure. For a topographic map, ask the USGS for Niles.

Directions: From San Francisco, take the Bay Bridge east for 6.4 miles to the split and I-880. Bear right, continue 1.6 miles to the merge with I-880, then drive 20.8 miles to the exit for Alvarado-Niles Road. Take that exit 0.2 mile to Alvarado-Niles Road. Turn left and drive 3.5 miles, continue ahead on Niles Boulevard for

0.7 mile to Nursery Avenue. Turn left and drive 100 yards to Mission Boulevard. Turn right and go 1.1 miles to Niles Canyon Road. Turn left, go 0.1 mile (second right) to Old Canyon Road. Go short distance, then turn left to stay on Old Canyon Road (drive over bridge at Alameda Creek; access to trailhead for unpaved Alameda Creek Trail located on right near bridge before crossing), and continue to park entrance on left for Niles Staging Area (direct access to trailhead to paved trail on south side of Alameda Creek).

Contact: Alameda Creek Regional Trail, 510/544-3137 or 888/327-2757; East Bay Regional Park District, www.ebparks.org.

152 MISSION PEAK TRAIL
7.0 mi/5.0 hr ♨️4 ⛰️10

in Mission Peak Regional Preserve near Fremont

Map 7.3, page 279

Climbing 2,517-foot Mission Peak and touching the Summit Post has become a rite of passage. The mountain rises up above Fremont to tower over the South Bay and provides a panorama east over miles of East Bay hills topped by Mount Hamilton, Rose Peak, and Mount Diablo. The Summit Post is set in the summit crag, with pipes affixed to it where you can peer through each pipe to ID sites around the Bay Area.

The best trailhead is at the end of Stanford Avenue for the Ohlone Wilderness Trail. Problem is, it fills up with cars on weekends. (A 9pm park curfew and $300 fine is often enacted.) From the Stanford Avenue Trailhead, take the Ohlone Wilderness Trail for 2.6 miles, with a climb of about 1,500 feet, to the junction of the Peak Trail (elevation 2,000 feet). Turn right and it's another 0.5 mile with a 500-foot climb to the top; 6.2 miles round-trip.

Or, from the Ohlone College Trailhead, take the Peak Trail, also signed Bay Area Ridge Trail. Hike about three miles up to the junction

with the Peak Trail. Turn right for the 0.5 mile; 7 miles round-trip.

Do not head up Mission Peak if you are out of shape. For some, it can turn into what we call "kill me, eat me." Pan about five hours for the round-trip, including a trail lunch on top. The routes are former ranch roads; erosion is severe and cutting across switchbacks results in a loss of vegetation.

User Groups: Hikers, dogs, and horses. No mountain bikes. No wheelchair facilities.

Permits: No permits are required. Parking is free.

Maps: A brochure and map are available at the trailhead. For a free trail map, phone the East Bay Park District toll-free at 888/327-2757, option 3, extension 5; follow directions, leave your name and address, and ask for the Mission Peak Regional Preserve brochure. For a topographic map, ask the USGS for Niles.

Directions: From San Francisco, take the Bay Bridge east for 6.4 miles to the split and I-880. Bear right, continue 1.6 miles to the merge with I-880, then drive 39 miles to Mission Boulevard in Fremont. Take that exit and continue 1.8 miles, merge with Mission Boulevard and continue 1.4 miles to Stanford Avenue. Turn right and drive to trailhead at end of road. Overflow parking is available at Ohlone College; from Stanford Avenue, continue north on Mission Boulevard.

Contact: Mission Peak Regional Preserve, 510/544-3246 or 888/327-2757; East Bay Regional Park District, www.ebparks.org.

153 LITTLE YOSEMITE
1.8 mi/1.5 hr 🥾3 ⛰️8

in Sunol Regional Wilderness near Sunol

Map 7.3, page 279

Little Yosemite is a miniature canyon with a pretty stream (Alameda Creek) with little pool-and-drop waterfalls at high flow in late winter. To see it, don't park near the visitors center, but instead drive a short distance east to the parking area next to the corral. You'll see a gated ranch road, Camp Ohlone Road. That's where you start. It's less than a mile to Little Yosemite. The ranch road runs adjacent to Alameda Creek, over a bridge, easy and near flat, then over a short hill and down to the falls. At peak flow, it is always a surprise how beautiful the pool-and-drops can be. Bring a tripod for time-lapse photography to capture the flush of movement.

You can extend this trip by heading into the hills above the canyon. The Canyon View Trail, Cave Rock, and Cerro Este (1,720 feet) are all good treks.

User Groups: Hikers, dogs, horses, and mountain bikes. The Indian Joe Creek section of the loop is limited to hikers. Canyon View Trail is limited to hikers on the eastern half, and hikers and horses on the western half. The trail to Little Yosemite is wheelchair-accessible.

Permits: No permits are required for day use. A fee of $5 per vehicle is charged; $2 for dogs. A wilderness permit and a camping reservation are required for overnight backpackers.

Maps: A brochure and map are available at the trailhead. For a free trail map, phone the East Bay Regional Park District toll-free at 888/327-2757, option 3, extension 5; follow directions, leave your name and address, and ask for the Sunol-Ohlone Regional Wilderness brochure. For a topographic map, ask the USGS for La Costa Valley.

Directions: From San Francisco, take the Bay Bridge east for 6.4 miles (stay far right) to the split and I-580. Bear right on I-580 east and drive 26 miles to I-680 south. Take exit to I-680 south and go 8.2 miles to exit for Calaveras Road/Highway 84. Take exit and go 0.4 mile to fork, stay left, and go short distance to Highway 84-Paloma Road. Turn left at Highway 84/Paloma and drive under the freeway; continue 4.3 miles (becomes Calaveras Road) to Geary Road. Turn left at Geary and drive 2.3 miles to park entrance and continue to parking at corral at end of road.

Contact: Sunol Regional Wilderness, 510/544-3249 or 888/327-2757; East Bay Regional Park District, www.ebparks.org.

154 FLAG ROCK

4.2 mi/3.0 hr 🥾3 ⛰8

in Sunol Regional Wilderness near Sunol

Map 7.3, page 279

You get a perch that towers over the Alameda Creek Valley and beyond, with a birds-eye view of hovering falcons, eagles, and hawks. Look close in the rock and you can find sea fossils embedded in the sandstone. This is a great tromp, but with a rough climb for those who are not fit. Flag Hill is a prominent rock outcropping that overlooks the valley floor in Sunol Regional Wilderness. The common route up is on Hayfield Road (2.13 miles one-way, with an 800-foot climb). This trail is actually a ranch-style road, which means you and your hiking buddy can walk side-by-side—a plus for some, but it can be steep, hot, and hard. Another route, the narrow Flag Hill Trail, is also quite steep (1.26 miles one-way, 800-foot climb).

But the views are gorgeous. At the top of Flag Hill, golden eagles, prairie falcons, turkey vultures, and red-tailed hawks take turns patrolling the skies along the canyon rim, you are often at eye-level with hawks gliding in the rising thermals. Lots of ground squirrels for food mean lots of raptors. Directly below is Alameda Creek and valley. Always examine the rock outcrops at this park for sea fossils and bedrock mortars. You will find fossilized shells in the rock at the summit that show that this region was once the bottom of an inland sea.

Sunol Regional Wilderness is a big park, spanning 6,859 acres. It is connected to the 9,736-acre Ohlone Wilderness, 4,395-acre Del Valle Regional Park, and the 20,000-acre Alameda Creek/San Antonio/Calaveras watersheds.

User Groups: Hikers, dogs, horses, and mountain bikes.

Permits: No permits are required for day use. A fee of $5 per vehicle is charged; $2 for dogs. A wilderness permit and a camping reservation are required for overnight backpackers.

Maps: A brochure and map are available at the trailhead. For a free trail map, phone the East

Bay Regional Park District toll-free at 888/327-2757, option 3, extension 5; follow directions, leave your name and address, and ask for the Sunol-Ohlone Regional Wilderness brochure. For a topographic map, ask the USGS for La Costa Valley. A topographic map/Wilderness Permit is also available for $2 from the Sunol Visitors Center.

Directions: From San Francisco, take the Bay Bridge east for 6.4 miles (stay far right) to the split and I-580. Bear right on I-580 east and drive 26 miles to I-680 south. Take exit to I-680 south and go 8.2 miles to exit for Calaveras Road/Highway 84. Take exit and go 0.4 mile to fork, stay left, and go short distance to Highway 84-Paloma Road. Turn left at 84/Paloma and drive under freeway and continue 4.3 miles (becomes Calaveras Road) to Geary Road. Turn left at Geary and drive 2.3 miles to park entrance and continue to parking at corral at end of road.

Contact: Sunol Regional Wilderness, 510/544-3249 or 888/327-2757; East Bay Regional Park District, www.ebparks.org.

155 OHLONE WILDERNESS TRAIL
2.5-27.0 mi one-way/1-3 days

in Sunol-Ohlone Regional Wilderness

Map 7.3, page 279

Hikers can traverse the East Bay's most unspoiled backcountry via the spectacular 28-mile Ohlone Wilderness Trail. The route crosses wildlands from start to finish. Always start south of Livermore at Del Valle Regional Park. The trail rises through fields of wildflowers, grasslands, and oaks. It also climbs three major summits, Rocky Ridge, Rose Peak (elevation 3,817 feet), and Mission Peak (elevation 2,517 feet). It is best hiked as a three-day backpacking venture. You can set up trail camps at designated wilderness sites. You can also do the first section as a day hike.

The trailhead is located on the southwest side of Del Valle Reservoir at the Lichen Bark Picnic Area. Shortly after you start the trek, you will reach a box on the right with a sign-in sheet. After the sign-in, the route starts to climb, easy at first, and then quickly rises more steeply. The trail weaves in a canyon and then up to a sub-ridge. In about 1.25 miles from the trailhead (quarter mile past the sign-in box), you will reach a clearing where you can turn and get a pretty view of Del Valle Reservoir.

On to Rocky Ridge: From the trailhead, it's 2.4 miles and a 1,700-foot climb to Rocky Ridge (2,426 feet). The trail turns west and cuts up the far side of a deep canyon, and then rises very steeply to crest Rocky Ridge. Here's the catch: 1,600 feet of the climb is in 1.5 miles, one of the steepest sections of trail in the Bay Area. The payoff is a spectacular perch overlooking the Del Valle canyon to the east and beyond to 3,675-foot Cedar Mountain and the southern Diablo Range. Yet you can turn toward Rose Peak and take in a near-equal scope of wild landscape to the west. Wildflower blooms can be among the best in California near Rocky Ridge. An excellent side trip in late winter and early spring from here is to Murietta Falls; see next listed hike.

On to the trail camp: The trail drops 500 feet, then rises up 1,200 feet toward Wauhab Ridge. A short distance after a cow pond, you'll reach the signed Springboard Trail/Murietta Falls. Stewart's Camp, a wilderness-style camp for backpackers is located about 0.5 mile from Murietta Falls. Drinking water and a restroom are available. Reservations required.

Trailhead to Rose Peak: From the trailhead, it's a round-trip of 19.5 miles to Rose Peak (which is why this is a favorite run of ambitious ultra runners). However, it can be a stunning disappointment. After all, at 3,817 feet, Rose Peak is the Bay Area's highest wilderness-style peak. But it is not a conical-shaped summit, so first-timers can get a letdown ("What, this is it?"). But since it is the heart of the Ohlone Wilderness, the 360-degree views from the top provide a fantastic panorama of oak/foothill wildlands, ridges, and canyons.

All the way: To complete the entire 27-mile trek, wilderness camps are set up at the 12- and 16-mile marks. Hiking the trail east to west is the only way to fly. This way you'll face the steepest ascent right at the beginning, when you are still fresh, and end with sweeping views of the South Bay. As you crest the final ridge, Mission Peak, you'll face a moment of truth: You can actually see your car waiting at the parking lot—even though it's still more than an hour away. This last stretch drops 2,100 feet in 3.5 miles, a terrible toe-jammer that will have your knees and thighs screaming for mercy. Weeks later, though, when you replay this adventure in your memory banks, the hike will suddenly seem like "fun."

Most backpackers will cover about 12 miles the first day, followed by two days at about eight miles each. Many even make it a weekend trip, camping 12 miles in on Saturday night, then completing the final 16 miles on Sunday. And it's not unusual for cross-country runners to run the entire route in a single day; an organized race is held here every year.

Note: It is absolutely essential to have your itinerary and water supply timed for the trail camps. This isn't difficult, but those who don't do this may have to be carried out by a camel. You might even encounter a moment of irony as you begin to feel a strange sense of solitude, yet know that just over the final ridge to the west is a pit with 6.8 million people.

User Groups: Hikers, dogs (daytime only, not permitted on overnight trips), and horses. No mountain bikes. No wheelchair facilities.

Permits: A trail permit/map for the Ohlone Wilderness Trail is required; $6 per vehicle at entrance station, $4 trail permit/map per person (includes mailing fee); $2 for dogs (no dogs permitted overnight); $5 per person, per night fee for wilderness camping.

Maps: You will receive a trail map when you purchase your permit. For a topographic map, ask the USGS for Mendenhall Springs.

Directions: From San Francisco, take I-80 east over the Bay Bridge (get in right lane) to the split with I-580. Bear right on I-580 east and drive 34 miles to Livermore and Exit 52A for Portola Avenue/North Livermore Avenue. Take that exit and go a short distance to Portola. Turn left and drive 0.8 mile to North Livermore Avenue. Turn right and drive 2.5 miles (through Livermore) and continue (the road becomes Tesla Avenue) 0.5 mile to Mines Road. Turn right and drive 3.5 miles to Del Valle Road. Continue straight (Mines Road turns left) on Del Valle Road and drive 3.1 miles to park entrance. Pay entrance fees and continue ahead to a fork. Turn left at the fork, drive less than a mile to the bridge at Del Valle Reservoir, cross it, then turn right and drive 0.5 mile to the Lichen Bark Picnic Area. Park and walk a short distance to the trailhead for the Ohlone Trail.

To reach the west trailhead/Mission Peak: From San Francisco, take the Bay Bridge east for 6.4 miles to the split and I-880. Bear right, continue 1.6 miles to the merge with I-880, then drive 39 miles to Mission Boulevard in Fremont. Take that exit and continue 1.8 miles, merge with Mission Boulevard, and continue 1.4 miles to Stanford Avenue. Turn right and drive to trailhead at end of road.

Contact: Del Valle Regional Park, 888/327-2757; Sunol Regional Wilderness, 510/544-3249; East Bay Regional Park District, www.ebparks.org.

156 MURIETTA FALLS TRAIL
12.25 mi/1 day   🥾5 ⛺8

in Sunol-Ohlone Regional Wilderness

Map 7.3, page 279

The Bay Area's most mercurial destination is 100-foot Murietta Falls. It can feel like an endless trek to the mythical end of the rainbow; there is no guarantee of a pot of gold here either. The hike to Murietta Falls is a grueling round-trip hike of 12.25 miles, with a cumulative elevation gain of 4,000 feet. There's one steep spot up to Rocky Ridge that qualifies as a "kill-me, eat-me" kind of climb. When the hills are saturated and the aquifer is pumping, the gorge is transformed into this huge fountain of whitewater that pounds over the top and down the gorge in magical froth. This waterfall is a 100-foot cataract that tumbles down a rocky gorge, a beautiful mix of short freefalls, horsetails, cascades, and chutes—not a freefall. In most years, it is only a trickle, and outside of winter, it goes dry. For those who want the big-time pay-off to complete such a challenging trek, that is a colossal disappointment.

The trailhead for Murietta Falls is the Ohlone Wilderness Trail out of the southern end of Del Valle Regional Park.

You'll know within the first hour if you made a mistake. The hike starts with a 1,700-foot gain to Rocky Ridge (2.4 miles), with a pretty view to the north of Del Valle Reservoir and beyond, and then drops 500 feet in 0.5 mile to the bottom of a canyon. This is just the start. You then climb out of the canyon, gutting it out up 1,200 feet as you rise toward Wauhab Ridge, where you get more pretty long-distance foothill views. You will pass a series of impressive rock outcrops and then reach a little watering hole for cows (mapped as Johnny's Pond). From the pond, continue a short distance to the junction with the Springboard Trail, signed Murietta Falls, signpost 35.

Turn on this trail and walk about 0.25 mile (to a sharp turn in the trail)—then be sharp-eyed for the footpath on your left, along a small creek. Take this path to the brink of the falls. Alas, the view is lousy. No problem. From here, there is a well-worn route that everybody takes that leads down to the plunge pool of the falls. Here you get a picture-perfect view of the gorge and can enjoy a long picnic.

Some choose to extend the trip to two days by camping at a trail site called Stewart's Camp, located about 0.5 mile from the base of the falls. Although this splits the hiking distance into two days, it also means you must carry all your backpacking gear in and out, a heavy price.

Murietta Falls is named after Joaquin Murietta, of course, the legendary outlaw of the 1800s. If you hit it right, when the waterfall is gushing, you might wonder why such a beautiful place was named after a notorious killer. If you hit it wrong, however, you will understand. It is his final curse.

User Groups: Hikers, dogs (daytime only, not permitted on overnight trips), and horses. No mountain bikes. No wheelchair facilities.

Permits: A trail permit/map for the Ohlone Wilderness Trail is required; $6 per vehicle at entrance station; $4 trail permit/map per person (includes mailing fee); $2 for dogs (no dogs permitted overnight); $5 per person, per night fee for wilderness camping.

Maps: You will receive a trail map when you purchase your permit. For a topographic map, ask the USGS for Mendenhall Springs.

Directions: From San Francisco, take I-80 east over the Bay Bridge (get in right lane) to the split with I-580. Bear right on I-580 east and drive 34 miles to Livermore and Exit 52A for Portola Avenue/North Livermore Avenue. Take that exit and go a short distance to Portola. Turn left and drive 0.8 mile to North Livermore Avenue. Turn right and drive 2.5 miles (through Livermore) and continue (the road becomes Tesla Avenue) 0.5 mile to Mines Road. Turn right and drive 3.5 miles to Del Valle Road. Continue straight (Mines Road turns left) on Del Valle Road and drive 3.1 miles to park entrance. Pay entrance fees and continue ahead to a fork. Turn left at the fork, drive less than a mile to the bridge at Del Valle Reservoir, cross it, then turn right and drive 0.5 mile to the Lichen Bark Picnic Area. Park and walk a short distance to the trailhead for the Ohlone Trail.

Contact: Del Valle Regional Park, 888/327-2757; East Bay Regional Park District, www.ebparks.org.

157 SOUTH BAY NATURE TRAIL

2.0 mi/1.0 hr 🥾1 ⛰7

in San Francisco Bay National Wildlife Refuge near Alviso

Map 7.4, page 280

This portion of the San Francisco Bay National Wildlife Refuge is set deep in the South Bay marsh near Alviso, where it receives scant attention compared to its big brother to the north at the Dumbarton Bridge.

The trailhead is at the Environmental Education Center. From here, you walk on a dirt path along a wild tidal marshland. You head north on a levee along Coyote Creek, which often looks more like a slough, in its course to entering the South Bay. As you stroll northward, you will delve into wilder and wilder habitat, and in the process have a chance at seeing a dozen species of birds in a matter of minutes. The endangered harvest salt mouse lives in this habitat. Guided nature walks are held regularly on weekend mornings. The sloughs and quiet waters here also make for a unique opportunity for saltwater canoeing and kayaking during high tides.

User Groups: Hikers and mountain bikes. No dogs or horses. No wheelchair facilities.

Permits: No permits are required. Parking and access are free.

Maps: A brochure and map are available at the trailhead. For a topographic map, ask the USGS for Mountain View.

Directions: Take U.S. 101 to Santa Clara and the exit for Montague Expressway. Take the exit 0.4 mile for Montague Expressway (north) and drive 2.3 miles (get in left two lanes) to Zanker Road. Turn left on Zanker and drive 2.1 miles (toward Alicante Drive/De Soto) to Los Esteros Road, and continue on Los Esteroa Road for 1.4 miles to Grand Boulevard. Turn right on Grand Boulevard and drive 0.8 mile to parking and visitors center on the left.

Contact: Environmental Education Center, 408/262-5513; Don Edwards San Francisco Bay National Wildlife Refuge, 510/792-0222, www.fws.gov/refuge.

158 SUNNYVALE BAYLANDS

2.0 mi/1.0 hr 🥾1 ⛰6

in Sunnyvale

Map 7.4, page 280

Sunnyvale Baylands County Park really isn't much of a park at all, but rather a wildlife preserve surrounded by a levee that makes a trail for hiking and jogging. It covers 177 acres of South Bay marshland, home to blue herons, great egrets, avocets, black-necked stilts, mallards, pintails, and burrowing owls.

From the parking area adjacent to Highway 237, hike along the levee. You will turn left as it parallels Calabazas Creek. To your left is a seasonal wetlands preserve. The trail continues along the creek, then turns left again and runs alongside Guadalupe Slough. The open-water bird preserve will be just off to your left. One downer is the adjacent proximity of the highway, which is why it does not merit a higher rating, and yet it deserves entry as an urban wildlife area.

On nearly every trip, you will see a jackrabbit or two. In fact, these rabbits have a way of scaring the bejesus out of hikers. They hide in the weeds until you get close, then suddenly pop up and take off at warp speed, shocking you every time.

User Groups: Hikers only. No dogs, horses, or mountain bikes. No wheelchair facilities.

Permits: No permits are required. An entrance fee of $5 per vehicle is charged from May to October (season pass available), with no parking fee from November to April. No fees for walk-in or bike-in traffic.

Maps: For a free map, write to Sunnyvale Baylands County Park. For a topographic map, ask the USGS for Mountain View.

Directions: Take Highway 237 to the exit for Lawrence Expressway/Caribbean exit. Take that exit and go 0.1 mile to Caribbean Drive North and drive 0.3 mile to park entrance on the right (if you arrive at the entrance for the Twin Creeks softball complex, you have gone a short distance too far).

Contact: Sunnyvale Baylands County Park, Sunnyvale, 408/730-7751, www.sccgov.org.

159 MONUMENT PEAK TRAIL
7.5 mi/4.0 hr   👫3 ⛰8

in Ed R. Levin County Park

Map 7.4, page 280

The best view in the Bay Area that is missed the most is from 2,594-foot Monument Peak. It towers over the South Bay and Santa Clara Valley on one side, with miles of wilderness across remote Alameda and Santa Clara counties on the other. You also get views of two hidden lakes, Calaveras and San Antonio reservoirs.

The trailhead is at 300 feet at Sandy Wool Lake, which makes it a 2,300-foot climb over the course of about 3.75 miles. To start, take the Tularcitos Trail a short distance to the Agua Caliente Trail (you'll see the gate, signed). It starts out as an easy walk. After you pass Launch Site Road (hang gliding is popular in spring and early summer), the climb becomes steeper, and after a climb of 900 feet, you reach the junction of the Monument Peak Trail (actually an old road). Turn right, and it's about another hour to the top. Near the top, a jog on Monument Peak Road will get you near the summit, where a short cutoff will take you to the peak.

Monument Peak Road, a service road, and Monument Peak Trail, a dirt road, are two different routes.

User Groups: Hikers and horses. Leashed dogs permitted only on Calera Creek Trail and Agua Caliente Trail, a service road. No mountain bikes. No wheelchair facilities.

Permits: No permits are required. A day-use fee of $6 per vehicle is charged. Hikers are encouraged to wait two days after a rain before hiking in order to prevent trail damage.

Maps: For a free trail map, contact Ed R. Levin

County Park. For topographic maps, ask the USGS for Milpitas and Calaveras Reservoir.

Directions: U.S 101 south to Mountain View (about 35 miles south of San Francisco) and the exit for Highway 237. Take that exit, merge onto 237 east and drive 6.5 miles, and then continue on Highway 237 (under I-880) ahead (signed for Calaveras Boulevard) for 2.5 miles to Calaveras Boulevard. Continue onto East Calaveras Boulevard and go 0.8 mile to Evans Road. Turn left and go 0.4 mile to Old Calaveras Road. Turn right and go 1.3 miles to Downing Road. Turn right on Downing Road and go short distance to park entrance. Proceed to the parking area near Sandy Wool Lake.

From the East Bay: From Dublin at junction of I-580 and I-680, take I-680 south and drive 20 miles to exit for Jacklin Road. Take that exit to stop sign, turn left on Jacklin Road, drive 0.3 mile and continue straight on Evans Road for 0.6 mile to Old Calaveras Road. Turn left and go 1.3 miles to Downing Road. Turn left on Downing Road and go 0.2 mile to park entrance. Proceed to the parking area near Sandy Wool Lake.

Contact: Ed R. Levin County Park, 408/262-6980, www.sccgov.org.

160 OHLONE RIDGE TRAIL
1.5 mi/1.0 hr   👫1 ⛰8

at Costanoa near Año Nuevo State Reserve

Map 7.4, page 280

From Ohlone Ridge, you can face west and take in the scope of the Pacific Ocean, Año Nuevo, and miles of wild coast. Every care, stress, and worry will slip away like the outgoing tide. Ohlone Ridge is the easy must-do loop hike for every visitor to Costanoa, the coastal lodge, camp, and recreation getaway that provides a vacation destination. Day use is free.

Costanoa is located on hillside bluffs overlooking the ocean, just east of Highway 1 near Año Nuevo State Reserve and the San Mateo and Santa Cruz County line. From the lodge headquarters, walk a short distance on the entrance road to the trail on the left. From here, the route passes Whitehouse Creek and rises through a meadow, then climbs into the foot-hill to a sub-ridge and lookout with a bench. The views of the local coast out toward Año Nuevo are sensational.

If you want more after this taste, or are spending the night here: On the west side of the highway, the Atkinson Bluff Trail extends on the cliff-edge overlooking the beach and is routed in a loop out to Franklin Point and past a secluded beach and tidepools.

What makes Costanoa work as a vacation getaway is the overnight accommodations. They feature 89 canvas bungalows with ocean views, deluxe-style lodge rooms and suites, and campsites for tents and RVs with hookups. Everything is deluxe, including the on-site store and restaurant.

User Groups: Hikers, mountain bikes, and horses. Mountain bike rentals and guided horseback riding trips are available. No dogs. Headquarters is wheelchair-accessible.

Permits: No permits are required. Day use and parking are free. Overnight camping and lodging are available.

Maps: A brochure and map are available at the check-in desk. For a topographic map, ask the USGS for Franklin Point.

Directions: From Half Moon Bay, take Highway 1 south and drive 26 miles (nine miles past the turnoff for Pescadero Road) to Rossi Road. Turn left and go 0.5 mile to parking.

Contact: Costanoa Lodge, 877/262-7848, www.costanoa.com.

161 AÑO NUEVO TRAIL
3.0 mi/2.0 hr

in Año Nuevo State Reserve south of Pescadero

Map 7.4, page 280   **BEST (**

Año Nuevo State Reserve is home to the largest breeding colony of northern elephant seals. Yep, this is the place where these giant creatures fight, mate, give birth, sunbathe, and make funny noises. So many people want to watch them that you must make reservations and join a tour group (Dec. 15-Mar. 31).

The rest of the year you are free to hike on your own. But note that the elephant seal population has increased to the point that there are now year-round residents on the beach here. So this has become one of the few sure spottings in the Bay Area.

After parking, start by hiking the well-signed trail through a series of sandy mounds and flats en route to the beach. During the tour-only season, you must be part of a tour group, and you will walk along roped-off trails, where you wind your way amid the animals. In the off-season, at times rangers will post the beach and nearby routes to it as off limits.

Elephant seals look like giant slugs, often weighing 2,000-3,000 pounds—even the new-borns weigh 75 pounds. The old boars reach nearly 20 feet in length and weigh as much as 5,000 pounds. With a 200mm camera lens, you can get excellent pictures. The best times to visit are in mid-December, when the males battle for harems, and in late January, when hundreds of pups are born. The rest of the year, this is a nice place to enjoy a quiet beach walk, with decent numbers of the giant slothlike mammals available for photos.

User Groups: Hikers only. No dogs, horses, or mountain bikes. No wheelchair facilities.

Permits: A year-round parking fee of $10 is charged per vehicle. From mid-December through March, access to the park is available only by accompanying a ranger on a scheduled walk; $7 per person. To make a reservation, call 800/444-7275 or at www.anonuevo.reserveamerica.com.

Maps: A map is available at the entrance station for a fee. For a topographic map, ask the USGS for Franklin Point.

Directions: From I-280 in San Mateo, turn west on Highway 92 and drive to Half Moon Bay and Highway 1. Turn left (south) on Highway 1 and drive 27 miles (6.5 miles south of turnoff for Pigeon Point Lighthouse) to the reserve entrance on the right (well signed).

Contact: Año Nuevo State Reserve, Pescadero, 650/879-0227 or 650/879-2025, www.parks.ca.gov.

162 BYPASS TRAIL

13.6 mi/7.0 hr 👣3 ⛰9

at Rancho del Oso south of Año Nuevo

Map 7.4, page 280

Thousands walk by the cut-off to this trail every year. We tried it and found it an excellent route, best in spring when there are lots of forget-me-nots and many other wildflowers.

From the parking area, walk a short distance past the gate; at 0.2 mile, look for the cutoff on the left to the Skyline-to-the-Sea Bypass Trail. Turn left and you are on your way. (Mountain bike traffic is heavy at Rancho del Oso, but you'll find no bikes on this trail.) The trail climbs up a short ridge, then laterals along the mountain east about 1.5 miles and descends back down to the valley floor. In the process you get occasional peek-a-boo valley views off the Waddell Creek Valley. The trail junctions with the service road, the Skyline-to-the-Sea Trail. Turn right for the easy flat walk back to headquarters.

If you want more, visit the Nature and History Center on your way back and take the marsh trail to a pretty wetland and lagoon.

User Groups: Hikers only. No horses, mountain bikes, or dogs. No wheelchair facilities.

Permits: No permits are required. A parking/access fee of $10 is charged per vehicle. Permits required for overnight use.

Maps: A trail map is available on weekends at the ranger station for a fee. It can be also obtained by mail by calling Mountain Parks Foundation, 831/335-3174; credit cards accepted. For a topographic map, ask the USGS for Franklin Point.

Directions: From I-280 in San Mateo, turn west onto Highway 92 and drive to Half Moon Bay. Turn left (south) onto Highway 1 and drive 30.3 miles (past San Mateo/Santa Cruz county line) to park entrance on left (19 miles from Santa Cruz). Turn and park at Rancho del Oso.

Contact: Rancho del Oso Nature and History Center, 831/427-2288, http://ranchodeloso.org; Big Basin Redwoods State Park, 831/338-8860, www.parks.ca.gov.

163 REDWOOD LOOP NATURE TRAIL

0.6 mi/0.5 hr 👣1 ⛰9

in Big Basin Redwoods State Park

Map 7.4, page 280

At the foot of a giant redwood tree in Big Basin Redwoods State Park, it can feel like you are taking in immortality. Near park headquarters on the Redwood Trail, you'll find that tree, which is about 280 feet tall. It's still a behemoth even though the top 50 feet snapped off in a storm a few years ago (and a park sign credits it as 329 feet tall). For a first visit, walk the Redwood Loop Nature Trail, located just beyond the primary parking area. A flat, 0.6-mile loop meanders among groves of cathedral redwoods as well as the forest goliaths. Highlights include the base of a giant redwood with so many burls that it looks like a mutated, amorphous blob, the Mother of the Forest, Father of the Forest, and moments where cathedral-like filtered sunlight refracts through the high limbs of the forest canopy. The Mother of the Forest has a 70-foot circumference, Father of the Forest is 250 feet high, and the Santa Clara Tree is 17 feet in diameter.

User Groups: Hikers only. Wheelchair-accessible. No dogs, horses, or mountain bikes.

Permits: No permits are required. A state park entrance fee of $10 per vehicle is charged. For backpack campsites, reservations are required at 831/338-8861.

Maps: Detailed trail maps of Big Basin Redwoods State Park are available for a fee from Mountain Parks Foundation, 525 N. Big Trees Road, Felton, CA 95018, 831/335-3174. For topographic maps, ask the USGS for Castle Rock Ridge and Big Basin.

Directions: From San Francisco, take I-280 for 10 miles to Daly City and the exit for Highway 1. Bear right at that exit and take Highway 1 for 20 miles to Half Moon Bay and continue south for 50 miles into Santa Cruz and to a stoplight junction with Highway 9/River Street. Turn left on Highway 9 and drive 12 miles to Boulder Creek and lighted intersection with Highway 236/Big Basin Way. Turn left and go 6.4 miles to Little Basin Road (turn left for Little Basin) and continue 3.5 miles to Big Basin Redwoods (parking on left, pay fee, get brochure/map on right).

Alternate route: From San Francisco, take I-280 south to Cupertino and the exit for Highway 85. Take 85 South and drive to the exit for Sunnyvale-Saratoga Road. Take that exit, turn right (south) and drive into Saratoga to Big Basin Way/Highway 9. Turn right, drive short distance through town and continue up hill (becomes curvy) to Skyline/Highway 35, and continue straight 13 miles to Boulder Creek and Big Basin Way. Turn right and go 10 miles to park headquarters.

Contact: Big Basin Redwoods State Park, 831/338-8860, www.parks.ca.gov; district headquarters, 831/429-2851.

164 BERRY CREEK FALLS
12.0 mi/6.0 hr   🏃4 ⛺10

in Big Basin Redwoods State Park

Map 7.4, page 280

The Berry Creek Canyon and its succession of waterfalls is one of the prettiest spots in California. Our favorite spot here is just above the brink of Silver Falls, where you can reach out and touch the water, then take a few steps upstream and admire the lower chute of the Golden Cascade. Yet just above is a fall my brother Rambob named Aztec Falls, where clear water rushes over what looks like a golden sandstone temple. Downstream one mile is the famous Berry Creek Falls, a 70-foot waterfall framed by a canyon and complete with ferns, redwoods, and the sound of rushing water.

Start at park headquarters and take the Skyline-to-the-Sea Trail amid the giant redwoods up to the Big Basin rim; then head down the other side, hiking west toward the coast. After topping the rim at 1,200 feet, the hike descends 600 feet over the course of about four miles to Berry Creek Falls (4.7 miles from the trailhead). You round a bend and suddenly, there it is, a divine waterfall. A small bench is perfectly situated for viewing the scene while eating a picnic lunch. At a steady pace, it takes one hour, 50 minutes. So despite the warning sign you will pass, it's a four-hour round-trip if you make it an in-and-outer. The best suggestion is to head beyond, up the canyon.

Go the long way—up the staircase, past the Cascade Falls (Silver Falls and Golden Falls), and return on Sunset Trail. At Silver Falls, it is possible to dunk your head into the streaming water without getting the rest of your body wet—a real thrill. At the brink, the trail is rock steps cut into the canyon, with a woven wire safety rail to keep you from falling off the cliff. Just upstream past the brink, Golden Falls is a beautiful cascade of water over golden sandstone, like a giant water slide. One of the golden cascades looks like a miniature Aztec Temple.

Once you pass Golden Falls, the trail climbs out to a service road near Sunset Camp. Do not miss the right turn off the service road to Sunset Trail. From here, Sunset Trail meanders through the most remote sections of the park, in and out of chaparral and forest, then loops back into redwoods, and leads back to park headquarters. Though you can trim the hiking time down if you double back on the same trail you came in on, why cut the experience short? Getting an early start helps to ensure a carefree trip with no pressure to complete the loop by a certain time.

User Groups: Hikers only. No dogs, horses, or mountain bikes. No wheelchair facilities.

Permits: No permits are required. A state park entrance fee of $10 per vehicle is charged. For backpack campsites, reservations are required at 831/338-8861, $15 per person per night.

Maps: Detailed trail maps of Big Basin

Redwoods State Park are available for a fee from Mountain Parks Foundation in Felton (831/335-3174). For topographic maps, ask the USGS for Castle Rock Ridge and Big Basin.

Directions: From San Francisco, take I-280 for 10 miles to Daly City and the exit for Highway 1. Bear right at that exit and take Highway 1 for 20 miles to Half Moon Bay and continue south for 50 miles into Santa Cruz and to a stoplight junction with Highway 9/River Street. Turn left on Highway 9 and drive 12 miles to Boulder Creek and lighted intersection with Highway 236/Big Basin Way. Turn left and go 6.4 miles to Little Basin Road (turn left for Little Basin) and continue 3.5 miles to Big Basin Redwoods (parking on left, pay fee, get brochure/map on right).

Alternate route: From San Francisco, take I-280 south to Cupertino and the exit for Highway 85. Take 85 South and drive to the exit for Sunnyvale-Saratoga Road. Take that exit, turn right (south) and drive into Saratoga to Big Basin Way/Highway 9. Turn right, drive short distance through town and continue up hill (becomes curvy) to Skyline/Highway 35, and continue straight 13 miles to Boulder Creek and Big Basin Way. Turn right and go 10 miles to park headquarters.

Contact: Big Basin Redwoods State Park, 831/338-8860, www.parks.ca.gov; Santa Cruz District, 831/429-2850; camping reservations, 800/444-7275; backpacking reservations, 831/338-8861; tent cabins, www.bigbasintent-cabins.com, reserve at www.reserveamerica.com.

165 METEOR TRAIL

5.2 mi/2.5 hr

in Big Basin Redwoods State Park

Map 7.4, page 280

Under the heavy redwood canopy of Big Basin, most hikers don't worry about whether or not it's foggy on the coast. But with the park's best coastal lookout at trail's end, you don't want fog on this hike. The Meteor Trail starts at the parking area across the lot from park headquarters on the Skyline-to-the-Sea Trail. Walk over the wood bridge at Opal Creek and turn right. If you turn left and see a sign for Berry Creek Falls, you're going in the wrong direction.

For much of the route, you hike along Opal Creek, a pretty stream in the spring, surrounded by redwoods. Two miles out, you will arrive at the intersection with Meteor Trail. This is where you turn left and then climb 400 feet over the space of a mile to the Middle Ridge Fire Road. The Ocean View Summit (1,600 feet) is only a couple hundred yards off, featuring a glimpse to the west of the Waddell Creek watershed and the Pacific Coast. Return by doubling back the way you came. If you visit Big Basin and don't have time for the Berry Creek Falls hike, this is the next best option.

The view from the summit had been eclipsed by trees in recent years, but has broken spots now, thanks to a prescribed burn over a few hundred acres along the summit ridge.

The biggest of the park's redwoods is off the Meteor Trail, though not marked for easy sighting. Steve Sillett, a world-renowned scientist with a specialty on the ecology of tall trees, hiked out the Meteor Trail, and with Jim Speckler, verified its height of 328.12 feet by direct tape drop. According to the Native Tree Society, that could make it the tallest tree in the world south of 38 degrees latitude.

User Groups: Hikers only. No dogs, horses, or mountain bikes. No wheelchair facilities.

Permits: No permits are required. A state park entrance fee of $10 per vehicle is charged.

Maps: Detailed trail maps of Big Basin Redwoods State Park are available for a fee from Mountain Parks Foundation, Felton, 831/335-3174. For topographic maps, ask the USGS for Castle Rock Ridge and Big Basin.

Directions: From San Francisco, take I-280 for 10 miles to Daly City and the exit for Highway 1. Bear right at that exit and take Highway 1 for 20 miles to Half Moon Bay and continue south for 50 miles into Santa Cruz and to a stoplight junction with Highway 9/River Street. Turn left on Highway 9 and drive 12 miles to Boulder

Creek and lighted intersection with Highway 236/Big Basin Way. Turn left and go 6.4 miles to Little Basin Road (turn left for Little Basin) and continue 3.5 miles to Big Basin Redwoods (parking on left, pay fee, get brochure/map on right).

Alternate route: From San Francisco, take I-280 south to Cupertino and the exit for Highway 85. Take 85 South and drive to the exit for Sunnyvale-Saratoga Road. Take that exit, turn right (south) and drive into Saratoga to Big Basin Way/Highway 9. Turn right, drive short distance through town and continue up hill (becomes curvy) to Skyline/Highway 35, and continue straight 13 miles to Boulder Creek and Big Basin Way. Turn right and go 10 miles to park headquarters.

Contact: Big Basin Redwoods State Park, 831/338-8860, www.parks.ca.gov; Santa Cruz District, 831/429-2850; camping reservations, 800/444-7275; backpacking reservations, 831/338-8861; tent cabins, www.bigbasintent-cabins.com, reserve at www.reserveamerica.com.

166 LONG RIDGE LOOP
4.6 mi/2.5 hr

in Long Ridge Open Space Preserve

Map 7.4, page 280

This is one of the best day hikes on the Peninsula, a place to recharge your senses in a few hours. After parking, get the brochure/trail map from the box near the trailhead and orient yourself. This adventure starts by heading west down into the adjacent valley and past the intersection with the Bay Ridge Trail at 0.4 mile, then reaches the junction with the Long Ridge Trail and Peters Creek Trail (at 0.5 mile). Here you turn right and make a climb through oak woodlands, including one short, steep spot, where the trail horseshoes its way eventually to the south up to Long Ridge Road (at 1.2 miles; a dirt service road). You then arrive at the Wallace Stegner Bench. This is a great coastal lookout, one of the best on the

Peninsula. Everybody takes at least five minutes to enjoy it, and some even have a picnic.

From here, the going is easy to Four Corners, heading south on Long Ridge, with a slight elevation gain, rewarded by gorgeous views off to the west. On clear days, you get long-distance views of the ocean, and as you continue south, across miles of foothills and forested valleys. The highest point in San Mateo County, 2,600 feet, is just off the trail here, but it is hardly a prominent point in the landscape.

At Four Corners (2.5 miles), you turn left, encounter a series of switchbacks as you descend into a heavily wooded canyon, extremely lush in late winter and spring. The surprise of the trip is just ahead: You will pass a surprise and secret pond (3.0 miles), ringed by tules and quite pretty. To complete the loop hike, continue on the Peters Creek Trail, a rich riparian zone, back to the junction with Long Ridge Trail (4.1 miles). Turn right and hike back to the parking area (4.6 miles).

Trails are routed through a variety of beautiful landscapes, including sheltered canyons, creeks, meadows, and oak woodlands, past a beautiful hidden pond, and up on Long Ridge itself for great open views to the west of the Butano Rim and Pacific Ocean. And you can get this with one 4.6-mile loop trip, including only about a 400-foot climb. There is also a good chance of spotting wild turkeys, rabbits, deer, raptors, and songbirds.

User Groups: Hikers, horses, and mountain bikes (restricted from some trails, signed). No dogs. No wheelchair facilities.

Permits: No permits are required. Parking and access are free.

Maps: A brochure and map are available at the trailhead. For a free trail map, contact the Midpeninsula Regional Open Space District. For a topographic map, ask the USGS for Mindego Hill.

Directions: From San Francisco, take I-280 south and drive 20 miles to Woodside and the exit for Highway 84/Woodside Road. Take that exit, turn west (right) on Woodside Road, and drive 2.8 miles to Woodside. Continue straight on Woodside Road/Highway 84 (becomes curvy) to Sky Londa and Highway 35/Skyline Boulevard. Turn left on Skyline and drive 7.2 miles to Page Mill Road, then continue straight on Skyline for 3.3 miles (a short distance past Portola Heights Road) to pullouts along Skyline for parking. The preserve entrance and trailhead are on the right.

From the South Bay: From Palo Alto at I-280, take Page Mill Road west about 10 miles (becomes curvy, watch out for bikes) to Skyline Boulevard. Turn left and drive 3.3 miles to the preserve entrance on the right.

From Saratoga: Take Big Basin Way/Highway 9 for about seven miles to Skyline Boulevard. Turn right and drive 3.6 miles to the preserve entrance on the left (parking is also available on the right shoulder).

Contact: Midpeninsula Regional Open Space District, 650/691-1200, www.openspace.org.

167 SARATOGA GAP LOOP

8.8 mi/5.0 hr   🏃2   ⛰8

in Saratoga Gap and Long Ridge Open Space Preserves

Map 7.4, page 280

Here's a first-class hike that you can chop short if necessary because of weather or time. With the trail network here linked to five other nearby major parks, you can create a trip of nearly any length, short or long.

After parking, cross Highway 9 to the northeast corner of this junction for the trailhead, signed Saratoga Gap Trail/Bay Area Ridge Trail. This is the starting point: The trail heads north for the first 1.7 miles, adjacent to the road, meandering along Skyline. The landscape is a mix of hardwoods and Douglas fir, with occasional peek-a-boo views to the east. You then enter Upper Stevens Creek County Park and arrive at the junction with Charcoal Road. Continue on the Bay Ridge Trail (it jogs left) for 0.3 mile back to Skyline Boulevard.

At Skyline, cross the road, arriving at Long Ridge Open Space Preserve, and connect to Long Ridge Road/Hickory Oaks Trail. This is routed northwest into the foothills toward Long Ridge. The climb is mostly gentle here, where it rises over the course of 1.1 miles to a junction with Ward Road.

Continue straight (north) on Long Ridge Road for 1.3 miles, where you hike up and down a few hills and with a mostly gentle rise, to arrive at your pay-off: a perfectly situated bench on the west-facing ridge for a lookout of the Santa Cruz Mountains and Pacific Ocean. To finish the trek, head north for the final 4.4-mile leg.

The pay-offs are a changing panorama of views across foothill woodlands and canyons on the east side of Skyline Ridge, and the Santa Cruz Mountains, a sea of conifers, and the Pacific Ocean on the west side. It's an example of how contiguous parklands can be networked to create a special trek.

User Groups: Hikers, horses, and mountain bikes. No dogs. No wheelchair facilities.

Permits: No permits are required. Parking and access are free.

Maps: A brochure and map are available at the trailhead. For a free trail map, contact the Midpeninsula Regional Open Space District. For topographic maps, ask the USGS for Mindego Hill and Cupertino.

Directions: From San Francisco, take I-280 south and drive about 30 miles to Woodside and Exit 25 for Highway 84/Woodside Road. Take that exit, turn west (right) on Woodside Road, and drive one mile to Woodside. Continue straight on Woodside Road/Highway 84 and drive six miles (curvy) to Sky Londa and Highway 35/Skyline Boulevard. Turn left on Skyline and drive 14.3 miles to junction with Highway 9. At the junction, look for the CalTrans parking area on the left (southeast) corner. Park there. The preserve is on the northeast corner of this junction, across the road from the parking lot.

From South Bay: Take Highway 85 South toward Santa Cruz/Cupertino to Exit 14 for Saratoga Avenue. Take that exit to Saratoga Avenue. Turn right and drive 1.8 miles to

Big Basin Way/Highway 9, and continue on Highway 9 for 2.5 miles into Los Gatos. Turn right (Big Basin Way/Highway 9, signed) and drive 4.8 miles up hill (curvy) to junction and stop sign with Highway 35/Skyline. At the junction, look for the CalTrans parking area on the left (southeast) corner. Park there. The preserve is on the northeast corner of this junction, across the road from the parking lot.

Contact: Midpeninsula Regional Open Space District, 650/691-1200, www.openspace.org.

168 TRAIL CAMP LOOP
5.3 mi/2.5 hr   👣2   ⛰10

in Castle Rock State Park

Map 7.4, page 280

Here you can discover a great and easy 5.3-mile walk that takes about 2.5 hours. It is highlighted by a surprise waterfall with a viewing deck, honeycombed sandstone formations, sweeping views of the Santa Cruz Mountains and Monterey Bay to the west, and then a top-of-the-world perch atop Goat Rock.

Begin on Saratoga Gap Trail. In the first few minutes, the trail descends into a lush riparian canyon. Within 0.5 mile, you arrive at the cutoff on your left for the viewing deck. This puts you at the brink of a canyon and adjacent to the waterfall, best after recent rainfall, of course. Back on the main trail, the route breaks out from forest and into the open along a rock facing. On stellar days, those with sharp vision can see the white foam of the breakers on the beaches of Monterey Bay to the west. As you head on, you will pass a series of sandstone formations to your right, where material has eroded over time to create a series of holes and cavities. The most dramatic of these is at Goat Rock, where the trail runs right past its base. At this spot there is a permanent climbing cable, and on weekends, climbers practice technical skills here.

The trail continues to a junction with Ridge Trail, a distance of 2.6 miles from the parking lot. At this junction, turn right and start the loop back to the parking area. The return loop features a gentle climb, primarily amid chaparral and woodlands. Watch for a cutoff trail on the right to Goat Rock Lookout. Don't miss this side trip; walk a short distance to the top of Goat Rock. You get sweeping, long-distance views across a sea of conifers and beyond to the ocean. Perches and scoops atop Goat Rock provide excellent picnic sites.

There are 32 miles of hiking trails in 3,600 acres of semi-wilderness land at this park, so you can extend your adventure.

User Groups: Hikers and horses. No dogs or mountain bikes. No wheelchair facilities.

Permits: No permits are required, but you must self-register at the park entrance. A day-use fee of $10 per vehicle is charged.

Maps: A brochure and map are available at the trailhead. A trail map of Castle Rock State Park is available for a fee from Mountain Parks Foundation in Felton (831/335-3174). For a topographic map, ask the USGS for Castle Rock Ridge.

Directions: From San Francisco, take I-280 south and drive about 30 miles to Woodside and Exit 25 for Highway 84/Woodside Road. Take that exit, turn west (right) on Woodside Road, and drive one mile to Woodside. Continue straight on Woodside Road/Highway 84 and drive six miles (curvy) to Sky Londa and Highway 35/Skyline Boulevard. Turn left on Skyline and drive 14.3 miles (at junction with Highway 9, continue straight ahead 2.5 miles) to Castle Rock State Park on right.

From South Bay: Take Highway 85 South toward Santa Cruz/Cupertino to Exit 14 for Saratoga Avenue. Take that exit to Saratoga Avenue. Turn right and drive 1.8 miles to Big Basin Way/Highway 9, and continue on Highway 9 for 2.5 miles into Los Gatos. Turn right (still Big Basin Way/Highway 9, signed) and drive 4.8 miles up hill (becomes curvy) to junction and stop sign with Highway 35/Skyline. Turn left and drive 2.5 miles to park on right.

Contact: Castle Rock State Park, 408/867-2952;

California State Parks, Santa Cruz District, 831/429-2850, www.parks.ca.gov.

169 SKYLINE-TO-THE-SEA TRAIL

34.0 mi one-way/2.5 days

👥3 ⛰10

in Castle Rock State Park

Map 7.4, page 280

This is one of the most worshipped trails in the Bay Area. The workings of this trail started with a vision to create a route that connected Castle Rock State Park on Skyline Ridge to Big Basin and then to Waddell Creek on the coast. The result, much of it built by volunteers, is this 34-mile backpack route, complete with primitive trail camps. It is ideal in many ways, including the fact that the hike is generally downhill, starting at 3,000 feet at Castle Rock and dropping all the way down to sea level. You get fantastic views, redwood forests, waterfalls, and backpack camps. Most hike the trail in three days, camping at Waterman Gap and at Big Basin headquarters, with a shuttle car waiting at the end of the trail at Waddell Creek on Highway 1.

From the trailhead at Castle Rock State Park, take the Saratoga Gap Trail, where your destination is Waterman Gap trail camp (water is available), for a first-day hike of 9.6 miles. In the first two miles, you will cross an open rock facing the leads past the foot of Goat Rock. As the landscape opens up, you get fantastic views of Big Basin and the Pacific Coast to the west. This will help you envision the upcoming route. You then drop down into the headwaters of the San Lorenzo River, pass an old homestead, and through mixed forest.

The logical plan for the second day is to hike from Waterman Gap 9.5 miles to Jay Camp at Big Basin headquarters. Once you cross Highway 9, you will enter the state park. For a few miles the route roughly parallels the park's access road. Then it breaks off, passes an open sandstone face with great westerly views, traces a narrow ridge, and drops down into a lush redwood canyon with a stream. Only Skyline-to-the-Sea hikers typically travel this area, so by seeing this landscape you join a select club. Eventually the trail emerges at the bottom of Big Basin, and you camp relatively near park headquarters. Although this camp is not a backcountry experience, the convenience of restrooms, coin showers, drinking water, and a small store are usually well received.

On the last day, from park headquarters, you face hiking 12.5 miles out to the finish. It starts by heading through giant redwoods, up and over the Big Basin rim, then down a wooded canyon. You will see beautiful 70-foot Berry Creek Falls, a free-fall at high water, and moss-lined water mosaic in low flows. At Berry Creek Falls, be sure to hike up the stairs to the brink of the waterfall, then head up the canyon to see Silver Falls (a gorgeous free-fall, perfect for photographs), and then above that, Golden Falls, where clear water cascades over golden sandstone like a gigantic water slide. After that side-trip adventure, return to the main trail, turn west (right), and cross Waddell Creek.

From Berry Creek Falls to the coast is a breeze, crossing over the stream with a make-shift bridge, then making the sea-level walk to Rancho del Oso and the parking area. It's a shortcut to hike out on the service road and bike path, but in the spring, take the longer, official route that loops around the valley hills (to the north) and down to the parking area to see 20 or 30 species of wildflowers, including occasional rafts of forget-me-nots. Finish up at the coast, and experience a moment of exultation when you arrive at your vehicle.

User Groups: Hikers and horses. No dogs or mountain bikes. No wheelchair facilities.

Permits: Trail camp reservations are required with a reservation fee, plus a camping fee per night, and a $10 parking fee per extra vehicle at the trailheads. Call 831/338-8861.

Maps: Detailed trail maps of Castle Rock State Park and Big Basin Redwoods State Park are available for a fee from Mountain Parks Foundation in Felton (831/335-3174). A free information sheet and a mileage chart between trail camps are available from Big Basin Redwoods State Park (831/338-8861). For topographic maps, ask the USGS for Castle Rock Ridge and Big Basin.

Directions: From San Francisco, take I-280 south and drive about 30 miles (depending on starting point) to Woodside and Exit 25 for Highway 84/Woodside Road. Take that exit, turn west (right) on Woodside Road, and drive one mile to Woodside. Continue straight on Woodside Road/Highway 84 and drive six miles (becomes curvy) to Sky Londa and Highway 35/Skyline Boulevard. Turn left on Skyline and drive 14.3 miles (at junction with Highway 9, continue straight ahead 2.5 miles) to Castle Rock State Park on the right.

From South Bay: Take Highway 85 South toward Santa Cruz/Cupertino to Exit 14 for Saratoga Avenue. Take that exit to Saratoga Avenue. Turn right and drive 1.8 miles to Big Basin Way/Highway 9, and continue on Highway 9 for 2.5 miles into Los Gatos. Turn right (still Big Basin Way/Highway 9, signed) and drive 4.8 miles up hill (becomes curvy) to junction and stop sign with Highway 35/Skyline. Turn left and drive 2.5 miles to park on right.

To Rancho del Oso: From I-280 in San Mateo, turn west onto Highway 92 and drive to Half Moon Bay. Turn left (south) onto Highway 1 and drive 30 miles (past San Mateo/Santa Cruz county line) to park entrance on left (19 miles from Santa Cruz). Turn left and park at Rancho del Oso. (Your vehicle must be registered in advance with park rangers.)

Contact: Big Basin Redwoods State Park, 831/338-8860; Castle Rock State Park, 408/867-2952; trail camp reservations, 831/338-8861; www.parks.ca.gov.

170 SUMMIT ROCK LOOP
2.0 mi/1.0 hr   👫1 ⛺8

in Sanborn-Skyline County Park

Map 7.4, page 280

The lookout point at Summit Rock is perched just east of the Skyline Ridge. You tower over the Santa Clara Valley just below. From the trailhead across Highway 35 from Castle Rock State Park, hikers start on the Skyline Trail and head north, adjacent to the road. The Skyline Trail leads right into the Summit Rock Loop, providing easy access to this great lookout. For people who like their views to come even easier, a popular option at the Skyline trailhead is the 0.25-mile hike that leads to Indian Rock.

The park is named Sanborn-Skyline because it connects Sanborn Creek with the Skyline Ridge, and covers some 2,850 acres of mountain terrain in between. Some people get thrown off because this park is technically in Sanborn-Skyline County Park, yet the trailhead is nowhere near the park headquarters, but rather off Sanborn Road where full facilities, a campground, and other trails are available. So when you drive up Highway 9, ignore the signs for the park entrance.

User Groups: Hikers and horses. No dogs (otherwise permitted on most trails in Sanborn-Skyline; watch for signs at trailheads) or mountain bikes. No wheelchair facilities.

Permits: No permits are required. A day-use fee of $6 is charged per vehicle.

Maps: For a free trail map, contact Sanborn-Skyline County Park. For a topographic map, ask the USGS for Castle Rock Ridge.

Directions: From San Francisco, take I-280 south and drive about 30 miles (depending on starting point) to Woodside and Exit 25 for Highway 84/Woodside Road. Take that exit, turn west (right) on Woodside Road, and drive one mile to Woodside. Continue straight on Woodside Road/Highway 84 and drive six miles (becomes curvy) to Sky Londa and Highway 35/Skyline Boulevard. Turn left on Skyline and drive 14.3 miles (at junction with Highway 9, continue straight ahead 2.5 miles) to Castle Rock State Park on left. The trailhead is located roughly across from Castle Rock State Park.

From South Bay: Take Highway 85 South toward Santa Cruz/Cupertino to Exit 14 for Saratoga Avenue. Take that exit to Saratoga Avenue. Turn right and drive 1.8 miles to Big Basin Way/Highway 9, and continue on Highway 9 for 2.5 miles into Los Gatos. Turn right (still Big Basin Way/Highway 9, signed) and drive 4.8 miles up hill (becomes curvy) to junction and stop sign with Highway 35/Skyline. Turn left and drive 2.5 miles to park on left. The trailhead is located roughly across from Castle Rock State Park.

Contact: Sanborn-Skyline/Upper Stevens Creek County Park, Saratoga, 408/867-9959; Santa Clara County Parks and Recreation, 408/355-2201, www.sccgov.org/sites/parks.

171 EAGLE ROCK OVERLOOK LOOP
2.2 mi/1.0 hr 🏃2 ⛰6

in Alum Rock City Park

Map 7.4, page 280

Eagle Rock is pretty short as far as mountains go, only 795 feet. But at Alum Rock City Park, it's the best perch in the vicinity for a picnic site and a view. When you drive into the park, after passing through the kiosk, continue to road's end at the east end of the park and the trailhead for the North Rim Trail near the bridge at Penitencia Creek. Take the North Rim Trail. It is routed on the north side of the valley for 0.9 mile and rises about 300 feet to a fork with the Eagle Rock Trail. Turn right and hike 0.2 mile to the Eagle Rock Lookout.

To turn this hike into a loop, from Eagle Rock, return to the North Rim. Turn right and descend 0.22 mile to a junction, and turn left to complete the descent to the Penitencia Creek Trail (more like a road). Turn left. It is routed back along the creek (with one bridge crossing) back past the playground and picnic area to the parking area. In the winter, after rain

has cleared the air, it becomes a choice spot. Thirteen miles of trails provide access to the park's 700 acres, but this hike is our favorite.

Note: Some unsavory characters are known to occasionally frequent this park. Women are advised to avoid hiking solo.

User Groups: Hikers, horses, and mountain bikes. No dogs. No wheelchair facilities.

Permits: No permits are required. An entrance fee of $6 is charged on weekends and holidays; $10 per vehicle on high-use holidays.

Maps: A brochure and map are available at the trailhead. For a free trail map, contact Alum Rock City Park. For a topographic map, ask the USGS for Calaveras Reservoir.

Directions: From I-680 in San Jose, drive to the exit for McKee Road. Take that exit 0.1 mile, keep right at the fork, merge onto McKee Road and drive 0.8 mile to North White Road. Turn left on North White and drive 1.2 miles to Penitencia Creek Road. Turn right and drive 1.1 miles to the park entrance. From the park kiosk, continue east to the end of the road and trailhead.

Contact: Alum Rock City Park, San Jose, 408/277-4539 or 408/259-5477, www.sanjoseca.gov.

172 HALLS VALLEY LOOP
5.5 mi/3.0 hr 🏃2 ⛰8

in Joseph D. Grant County Park

Map 7.4, page 280

Halls Valley Loop provides the best introduction to Grant County Park. As you drive in, park at the Grant Lake Parking Area along Mount Hamilton Road (on the left as you drive in from San Jose), and not at the headquarters, such as for camping, on the right. From the trailhead take the main trail/road that is routed out past Grant Lake to a junction with the Halls Valley Trail. Bear left at the junction. This route skirts Halls Valley to the left, an open landscape of foothills and grasslands sprinkled with oaks, a quiet and pretty scene. The trail then heads out 2.5 miles, climbing east toward Mount Hamilton until it meets the Canada de Pala Trail. Turn right, hike up 0.4 mile, and turn right again on Los Huecos Trail to complete the loop. From here, it's a 1.8-mile trip back to the parking area. You will descend steeply on the way back to your car.

There are many great side trips on this route. Here are the best two: 1) After heavy rains, search out the little creek at the bottom of Halls Valley, then follow it upstream to discover a procession of little waterfalls (this is an off-trail trek); 2) For the ambitious, climb 2.2 miles and 500 feet up the ridge on Pala Seca Trail above Halls Valley to the park's highest point—from Antler Point at 2,999 feet, you can look out over the Santa Clara Valley.

This park covers 9,553 acres in the foothills of Mount Hamilton and can be the perfect setting for hiking and mountain biking. There is plenty of room for both endeavors, with 40 miles of trails, a combination of single track and ranch roads.

User Groups: Hikers, horses, and mountain bikes. No dogs. No wheelchair facilities (wheelchair-accessible facilities available at headquarters).

Permits: No permits are required. An entrance fee of $6 per vehicle is charged (pay at the entrance across the street from the trailhead).

Maps: For a free trail map, contact Joseph D. Grant County Park. For a topographic map, ask the USGS for Lick Observatory.

Directions: Take U.S. 101 to San Jose and to exit 382 for Capitola Expressway/Yerba Buena Road. Use one of the two right lanes for that exit and go 0.3 mile (then use one of left three lanes) to E. Capitol Expressway and continue 1.7 miles to Quimby Road. Turn right on Quimby Road and drive 6.8 miles to Highway 130/Mount Hamilton Road. Turn right and go 0.4 mile. Park along the road on the left at the trailhead to the right side of Grant Lake.

Contact: Joseph D. Grant County Park, San Jose, 408/274-6121; Santa Clara County Parks and Recreation, 408/355-2201, www.sccgov.org/sites/parks.

173 HOTEL TRAIL

7.0 mi/3.25 hr

in Joseph D. Grant County Park

Map 7.4, page 280

The landscape around Eagle Lake in Grant County Park provides visitors with precious tranquility as well as good chances of seeing wildlife. Eagle Lake, set in the southernmost reaches of the park's 9,553 acres, is the prime destination of Hotel Trail. Park along Mount Hamilton Road, then cross the road and look for the trailhead for the Hotel Trail on the south side. You start the trek where you hike southeast on the ranch road (Hotel Trail). Scan your surroundings for the wild turkeys that are commonly seen in this area. As you head deeper into the interior, you will be hiking through foothill country; cows are often encountered (keep your distance, of course). The route to Eagle Lake is a direct route of 3.5 miles where you climb a few hundred feet in the process. There are several options for side trips along the way: the best is to turn right on Canada de Pala Trail and drop down about 0.5 mile to San Felipe Creek.

User Groups: Hikers, horses, and mountain bikes. No dogs. No wheelchair facilities.

Permits: No permits are required. An entrance fee of $6 per vehicle is charged.

Maps: For a free trail map, contact Joseph D. Grant County Park. For a topographic map, ask the USGS for Lick Observatory.

Directions: Take U.S. 101 to San Jose and to exit 382 for Capitola Expressway/Yerba Buena Road. Use one of the two right lanes for that exit and go 0.3 mile (then use one of left three lanes) to E. Capitol Expressway and continue 1.7 miles to Quimby Road. Turn right on Quimby Road and drive 6.8 miles to Highway 130/Mount Hamilton Road. Turn right and go 0.4 mile. The Hotel Trail starts on the south side of the road, across the road from the parking area.

Contact: Joseph D. Grant County Park, San Jose, 408/274-6121; Santa Clara County Parks and Recreation, 408/355-2201, www.sccgov.org/sites/parks.

174 AQUINAS/ SERENITY TRAIL
6.0 mi/2.75 hr   🚶2 ⛰8

in El Sereno Open Space Preserve

Map 7.4, page 280

El Sereno Open Space is one of the lesser-used parklands in the Bay Area. Why? Not only is it remote, but there's room at the trailhead for only six vehicles to park. The parking spaces are available by permit (free) only. What you have is a pullout along the end of Montevina Road, set near redwoods, and then a trailhead for what looks like a gated jeep trail. This is it, elevation 2,400 feet. Start by heading out 0.2 mile to a fork. Turn right on the Aquinas Trail. It bears east and contours in and out of the canyonlands for 2.7 miles to a junction on the left (with the Loma Vista Trail), 1,800 feet. Bear right (still Aquinas Trail) and walk 0.5 mile to the junction with the Serenity Trail. Turn right and walk out 1.3 miles, a gentle descent to the end of the trail at the park boundary, 1,400 feet. You have occasional views south of Lexington Reservoir and the 17 corridor below.

User Groups: Hikers, horses, and mountain bikes. No dogs. No wheelchair facilities.

Permits: No permits are required. Parking and access are free.

Maps: A brochure and map are available at the trailhead. For a free trail map, contact the Midpeninsula Regional Open Space District. For a topographic map, ask the USGS for Castle Rock Ridge.

Directions: From the intersection of I-280 and Highway 17 in San Jose, turn south on Highway 17 and drive about eight miles to Los Gatos and continue to the exit for Bear Creek Road/Montevina Road. Take that exit to Montevina Road and continue three miles to the end of the road and trailhead. You must have a parking permit.

Contact: Midpeninsula Regional Open Space District, 650/691-1200, www.openspace.org.

175 MOUNT EL SOMBROSO
12.2 mi/1 day   🚶5 ⛰9

in Sierra Azul Open Space Preserve

Map 7.4, page 280

You get a little bit of hell on this trail to gain entry to a whole lot of heaven. It's a 5.9-mile hike with a climb of 2,100 feet to the top of 2,999-foot Mount El Sombroso. You get a panoramic view of the Santa Clara Valley, and also to Mount Umunhum, which looks like a Borg spaceship out of Star Trek is perched atop it. Start at Lexington Reservoir County Park at the gated trailhead (SA22) for the Limekiln Trail. The trail rises up 5.1 miles to Woods Trail (no dogs past this junction), with Soda Springs Canyon falling off deep to your right. At times, it is a kill-me, eat-me hike, with no shade, very steep, and only the water you choose to bring. The final mile skirts the summit of Mount El Sombroso. Up on top, you will get the sense of a paradox, that landscape this wild could exist so close to so many people who will never set foot here.

User Groups: Hikers, horses, and mountain bikes. No dogs. No wheelchair facilities.

Permits: No permits are required. A parking fee of $6 is charged at Lexington Reservoir County Park.

Maps: A brochure and map are available at the trailhead. For a free trail map, contact the Midpeninsula Regional Open Space District. For a topographic map, ask the USGS for Santa Teresa Hills.

Directions: From Los Gatos, drive south on Highway 17 for about four miles to the exit for Bear Creek Road. Take that exit, cross over the highway, enter Highway 17 north and drive 0.4 mile to Alma Bridge Road. Take Alma Bridge Road for 1.5 miles across the dam and park at Lexington Reservoir County Park. After parking, continue a short distance on Alma Bridge

Road to the Limekiln Trailhead at Gate SA22 on the left.

Contact: Midpeninsula Regional Open Space District, 650/691-1200, www.openspace.org; Lexington Reservoir County Park, 408/356-2729, www.sccgov.org/sites/parks.

176 LEXINGTON DAM TRAIL
1.0 mi/0.5 hr

🏃1 ⛰6

in Lexington Reservoir County Park

Map 7.4, page 280

Lexington Reservoir can be one of the prettiest places in Santa Clara County. When the lake is full and spilling in late winter and early spring, some people show up just to stare at all the water. Take it the extra mile for a nice bonus. Park at the lot just east of the dam, then walk across the dam and turn right on the "Pedway." That's as far as many people get, as most come for the view of the lake from the dam. Keep walking, though, and you will be surprised, as the trail drops down along Los Gatos Creek. After 1.5 miles, it links up with Los Gatos Creek Trail. This trail is routed all the way into town and it's also a great bike route.

User Groups: Hikers and mountain bikes. No dogs or horses. No wheelchair facilities.

Permits: No permits are required. A day-use fee of $6 per vehicle is charged.

Maps: For a free trail map, contact Lexington Reservoir County Park. For a topographic map, ask the USGS for Los Gatos.

Directions: From Los Gatos, drive south on Highway 17 for about four miles to the exit for Bear Creek Road. Take that exit, cross over the highway, enter Highway 17 north and drive 0.4 mile to Alma Bridge Road. Take Alma Bridge Road for 1.5 miles across the dam and park at Lexington Reservoir County Park. After parking, continue a short distance on Alma Bridge Road to the Limekiln Trailhead at Gate SA22 on the left.

Contact: Midpeninsula Regional Open Space District, 650/691-1200, www.openspace.org;

Lexington Reservoir County Park, 408/356-2729, www.sccgov.org/sites/parks.

177 BALD MOUNTAIN TRAIL
1.0 mi/0.5 hr

🏃1 ⛰9

in Sierra Azul Open Space Preserve south of Los Gatos

Map 7.4, page 280

The trailhead for Bald Mountain is along Mount Umunhum Road and leads 0.5 mile to 2,387-foot Bald Mountain and sweeping views across Santa Clara Valley and up to 3,486-foot Mount Umunhum. In an Ohlone language, Umunhum means "resting place of the hummingbird." It's the mountain that crowns the ridge to the west above Santa Clara Valley, of course. Nearby Bald Mountain and Mount El Sobroso both provide hiking access. From Blossom Hill near Los Gatos, the drive rises up from the valley floor, winds its way up through the pretty oak woodlands and foothills, and emerges high in the Sierra Azul Range. The views are sensational across the valley to Mount Hamilton and to the South Bay. On perfect fall days, you can see miles south to the ridge tops above the Hollister valley. This view is a highlight for the 18,000-acre Sierra Azul Open Space Preserve.

Note: The weird, square building on top of Mount Umunhum looks like a Borg spacecraft out of a Star Trek episode. It's a radar tower that was part of a former Air Force base from the Cold War era.

User Groups: Hikers, horses, and mountain bikes. No dogs. No wheelchair facilities.

Permits: No permits required. Parking and access are free.

Maps: A brochure and map are available at the trailhead. For a free trail map, contact the Midpeninsula Regional Open Space District. For a topographic map, ask the USGS for Santa Teresa Hills.

Directions: From the Peninsula, take U.S. 101 south to Highway 85. Merge right on 85 and drive 16 miles to the exit for Camden Avenue.

Take that exit to Camden, turn left and drive 1.7 miles to Hicks Road. Turn right on Hicks, go 0.2 mile, turn left to stay on Hicks, and drive 6.1 miles (past Guadalupe Reservoir) up the mountain to Mt. Umunhum Road. Turn right and drive up Mt. Umunhum Road for 1.6 miles to closed gate (No. SA08). Park on road's shoulder on right side of road (space for three cars). Trailhead is just across road (on left side of road).

Contact: Midpeninsula Regional Open Space District, 650/691-1200, www.openspace.org.

178 MINE HILL TRAIL LOOP

3.4/2 hr   🏃2   ⛰7

in Almaden Quicksilver County Park

Map 7.4, page 280

The Mine Hill Trail is the most unusual of the dozen trails that cover 34 miles across 4,152 acres at Almaden Quicksilver County Park. Almaden Quicksilver covers a vast terrain and has two reservoirs (Almaden and Guadalupe; don't eat the fish). It is the evidence of historical mining operations that makes it fascinating.

The Mine Hill Trail starts just inside the park entrance off of Almaden Road (Hacienda entrance). From here, Mine Hill Trail is routed out 1.1 miles to a junction (with the Randol Trail). Turn left (still on Mine Hill Trail) and go 0.7 mile (you will pass a cutoff for the Day Tunnel Trail) to another junction (still Day Tunnel Trail). Turn left and go 0.1 mile to English Camp and the junction with the English Camp Trail/Deep Gulch Trail. Turn left here and go 0.4 mile to a junction; stay right on the Deep Gulch for the final 1.2 miles back to parking.

In the spring, wildflower blooms are good. With a network of trails here, many routes and long trips are possible. Almaden was the site of the first "quicksilver" mine in North America. Mining began in 1845 and continued until 1975. There are still burnt ore dumps along the trail. Wallace Stegner set part of his novel *Angle of Repose* in the area now within the park.

User Groups: Hikers, mountain bikes (Hacienda/Wood/Mockingbird entrances only), and horses. Leashed dogs are permitted. No wheelchair trail access.

Permits: No permits are required. Park entrance is free.

Maps: A trail map is also available at the trailhead. For a topographic map, ask the USGS for Santa Teresa Hills.

Directions: Take Highway 82 to the exit for Almaden Expressway. Take that exit and drive south on Almaden Expressway to Almaden Road. Turn right on Almaden Road and drive three miles through New Almaden to the Hacienda park entrance and unpaved staging area on the right. (Note that there are four major access points to the park.)

Contact: Almaden Quicksilver County Park, San Jose, 408/268-3883; Santa Clara County Parks and Recreation, 408/355-2201, www.sccgov.org/sites/parks.

179 COYOTE PEAK LOOP

2.9 mi/2.0 hr   🏃2   ⛰7

in Santa Teresa County Park south of San Jose

Map 7.4, page 280

The most notable hike at Santa Teresa County Park is the tromp up to Coyote Peak. This feature destination provides a good loop hike and a lookout to the southern Santa Clara Valley. At the Pueblo day use and picnic area, start the trip on Hidden Springs Trail (trailhead located just east of the picnic area and parking), elevation 600 feet. Take the Hidden Springs Trail 0.6 mile to a junction with the Coyote Peak Trail. Turn right and climb 0.4 mile to the spur on the left that loops around Coyote Peak, 1,155 feet. That is a climb of 555 feet in one mile. After you enjoy the summit, return a short distance to the main trail. Turn left at the junction, the Boundary Trail, and hike 0.8 feet in a half-moon arcing curve to the left around the flank of Coyote Peak to a junction with the Hidden Springs Trail. Turn left and sail 0.9 mile back to the trailhead.

User Groups: Hikers, mountain bikers, leashed dogs, and horses. No mountain bikes, except on Ohlone Trail. No wheelchair facilities.

Permits: No permits are required. A $6 park entrance fee is charged per vehicle.

Maps: A brochure and map are available at the trailhead. For a free trail map, contact Santa Teresa County Park. For a topographic map, ask the USGS for Santa Teresa Hills.

Directions: From San Jose, take U.S. 101 south to the exit for Bernal Road. Take that exit to Bernal, turn west on Bernal Road and drive 1.3 miles (across Santa Teresa Boulevard, past the golf course) to the Pueblo Day Use area.

Contact: Santa Teresa County Park, 408/225-0025; Santa Clara County Parks and Recreation, 408/355-2201, www.sccgov.org/sites/parks.

180 LOS CERRITOS TRAIL/ CALERO RESERVOIR
3.2 mi/2.0 hr   🏃1 ⛰7

in Calero County Park southeast of San Jose

Map 7.4, page 280

The pay-off for this hike is a view of Calero Reservoir to the north. Start near the entrance gate and take the Los Cerritos Trail to the right (west). The trail bears right, toward Calero Reservoir, and then runs along the southern shoreline of the reservoir before it makes a 180-degree looping left turn (if you don't want to climb, turn around and go back at this point). The trail climbs a few hundred feet to a sub-ridge. There it junctions with the Pena Trail. To complete the loop, turn left on the Pena Trail and make the descent back to parking near.

At the junction with the Pena Trail, an option is to instead turn right on the Los Vallecitos Trail, and then turn left on Figueroa Trail. It is prettiest and add adds two miles to the trip.

User Groups: Hikers and horses. No dogs or mountain bikes. No wheelchair facilities.

Permits: No permits are required. Park

entrance is free at this access point for hiking, but a fee is charged at the boat ramp at Calero.

Maps: A brochure and map are available at the trailhead. For a topographic map, ask the USGS for Santa Teresa Hills.

Directions: From San Jose, take U.S. 101 south to the exit for Bailey Avenue. Take that exit, turn right onto Bailey Avenue and drive three miles to McKean Road. Turn left on McKean Road for 0.5 mile to the park entrance on the right. Drive to the sign for the park office and park adjacent to the ranger office.

Contact: Calero County Park, 408/268-3883; Santa Clara County Parks and Recreation, 408/355-2201, www.sccgov.org/sites/parks.

181 LOCH LOMOND LOOP
5.0 mi/3.25 hr   🏃2 ⛰8

in Loch Lomond Recreation Area near Ben Lomond

Map 7.4, page 280

Loch Lomond Reservoir is a jewel set in the Santa Cruz Mountains. There is no prettier lake in the greater Bay Area than this, complete with an island and with shores lined by conifers. Of the 12 miles of trails here, the best hike is the Loch Lomond Loop. From the parking area, take the Loch Trail, a level path that extends northward along the lakeshore for 1.5 miles out to Deer Flat. There you turn uphill on Highland Trail, where you climb, at a moderate ascent, and work your way to the east up the ridge. It peaks out at a weather station where you get a sweeping view of the lake below and the surrounding forested mountains.

To complete the loop, continue southward along the ridge down to the Glen Corrie Picnic Area (or you can take the paved road back to the starting point). Great lake, great views, great hike.

This park closes from mid-September through February.

User Groups: Hikers and dogs. No horses or mountain bikes. No wheelchair facilities.

Permits: No permits are required. A day-use

fee of $4 per vehicle is charged; $1 for dogs. The Loch Lomond Recreation Area is open only from March 1 through September 15. Rangers are on duty during the winter and will cite trespassers.

Maps: For a free trail map, contact Loch Lomond Recreation Area. For a topographic map, ask the USGS for Felton.

Directions: From San Francisco, take I-280 to Daly City and the exit for Highway 1. Bear right at that exit and take Highway 1 to Half Moon Bay and continue south into Santa Cruz and Exit 442 for Ocean Street. Turn left on Ocean Street and drive 0.3 mile to Graham Hill Road. Continue on Graham Hill Road for 5.3 miles to East Zayante Road. Turn right on East Zayante Road and go 2.6 miles to Lompico Road. Turn left and go 1.7 miles to West Drive. Turn left and drive 0.5 mile (it jogs twice on Trinkling Creek Lane) to Sequoia Drive. Turn right on Sequoia and go 0.2 mile (it jogs left); it then becomes Loch Lomond Way. Continue to the entrance station.

Alternate route: From San Francisco, take I-280 south to Cupertino and the exit for Highway 82. Take Highway 82 south to the exit for Sunnyvale-Saratoga Road. Take that exit, turn right (south), and drive into Saratoga to Big Basin Way/Highway 9. Turn right, drive a short distance through town, and continue up the hill (curvy) to Skyline/Highway 35. Drive straight through the intersection and continue (curvy and fun) to Felton and Graham Hill Road. Turn left on Graham Hill Road and after two stoplights reach East Zayante Road. Turn left on East Zayante and continue as above. The trailhead is located adjacent to the boat ramp.

Contact: Loch Lomond Recreation Area, Felton, 831/420-5320; marina 831/335-7424, www.cityofsantacruz.com.

182 BIG TREES NATURE TRAIL

1.0 mi/0.5 hr

in Loch Lomond Recreation Area near Ben Lomond

Map 7.4, page 280

This short trail starts at the Glen Corrie Picnic Area and provides a reminder of the power of nature. First, pick up a free trail guide at the park store. As the trail ascends, numbered signs note many natural features and plants of the redwood forest. The only remaining old-growth redwoods in this watershed are located near the ridge. These massive, 500- to 1,000-year-old trees offer a glimpse into the area's old-growth magnificence before it was logged. Just around the bend from the giant trees is a highly disturbed area that suffered major storm damage during the 1970s and 1980s from high winds, snowfall, and heavy rainfall. The biggest hit came from a January 1982 storm in which 15 inches of rain fell in a 24-hour period, causing major debris flows (mud slides). As the trail descends through this still-recovering area, you'll notice many trees that had their tops knocked off. The debris flows clogged existing drainage channels and created several massive logjams. Remnants of early-20th-century logging activities can also be seen along this short, fascinating trail.

This park closes from mid-September through February.

User Groups: Hikers and dogs. No horses or mountain bikes. No wheelchair facilities.

Permits: No permits are required. A day-use fee of $4 per vehicle is charged; there is also a fee for dogs. The Loch Lomond Recreation Area is open only March 1-September 15. Rangers are on duty during the winter and will cite trespassers.

Maps: For a free trail map, contact Loch Lomond Recreation Area. For a topographic map, ask the USGS for Felton.

Directions: From San Francisco, take I-280 to Daly City and the exit for Highway 1. Bear right at that exit and take Highway 1 to Half

Moon Bay. Continue south into Santa Cruz and Exit 442 for Ocean Street. Turn left on Ocean Street and go 0.3 mile to Graham Hill Road. Continue on Graham Hill Road for 5.3 miles to East Zayante Road. Turn right on East Zayante Road and go 2.6 miles to Lompico Road. Turn left and drive 1.7 miles to West Drive. Turn left and go 0.5 mile (it jogs twice on Trinkling Creek Lane) to Sequoia Drive. Turn right on Sequoia and drive 0.2 mile (it jogs left); it then becomes Loch Lomond Way. Continue to entrance station.

Alternate route: From San Francisco, take I-280 south to Cupertino and the exit for Highway 82. Take Highway 82 south and the exit for Sunnyvale-Saratoga Road. Take that exit, turn right (south), and drive into Saratoga to Big Basin Way/Highway 9. Turn right, drive a short distance through town, and continue up the hill (curvy) to Skyline/Highway 35. Continue straight through the intersection and on to Felton and Graham Hill Road (curvy and fun). Turn left on Graham Hill Road and drive past stoplights to East Zayante Road. Turn left on East Zayante and continue as above.

Contact: Loch Lomond Recreation Area, Felton, 831/420-5320, www.cityofsantacruz.com.

183 REDWOOD GROVE LOOP TRAIL

0.8 mi/0.5 hr   🚶1   ⛰9

in Henry Cowell Redwoods State Park near Santa Cruz

Map 7.4, page 280

A 40-acre grove of old-growth redwoods is the crown jewel of Henry Cowell Redwoods. This is a short, flat (and wide) trail that loops through the best of it. The trailhead is located at a parking area just south of the park office and entrance. The trail ventures a short distance to a junction. Either way you turn, it meanders through the old-growth for about a 10-minute walk and returns in the loop back to this junction. In addition to the old-growth redwoods,

there are also some large Douglas firs and California bays. What is most striking is the burl on some of the old-growth giants, where they look like something out of a science fiction film. There are numbered sites along the trail that correspond to a brochure interpretive guide. Only one problem, or for some, maybe not: You can occasionally hear the Roaring Camp Railroad rumbling past nearby, with occasional blasts of its whistle.

User Groups: Hikers and horses. No dogs or mountain bikes. No wheelchair facilities.

Permits: No permits are required. A fee of $10 is charged per vehicle.

Maps: Park maps are available at the visitors center at the main unit of Henry Cowell State Park on Highway 9. For a topographic map, ask the USGS for Felton.

Directions: Take I-280 to Cupertino and the junction with Highway 85. Bear south on Highway 85 and drive seven miles to the exit for Highway 17 south. Take that exit (signed toward Santa Cruz) and drive 18.7 miles to the exit for Mount Hermon Road (signed for Felton/Big Basin). Take that exit to Mount Hermon Road. Turn right and drive 3.5 miles to Graham Hill Road. Turn right and go 0.2 mile to Highway 9. Turn left on Highway 9 and go 0.6 mile to N. Big Trees Park Road. Turn left and drive 0.5 mile to the park entrance and continue a short distance to parking on right (directly across from Roaring Camp Big Trees Railroad).

Alternate route: From Half Moon Bay, take Highway 1 south for 48 miles into Santa Cruz and the signed turnoff for Highway 1 (get in left lane). Turn left on Highway 1 and drive 11.7 miles to signed turn for Highway 9 (get in left lane). Turn left and drive 5.8 miles to N. Big Trees Park Road (signed for park). Turn right and drive 0.5 mile to park entrance and continue short distance to parking on right (directly across from Roaring Camp Big Trees Railroad).

Contact: Henry Cowell Redwoods State Park, 831/335-4598; nature center, 831/335-7077, www.parks.ca.gov.

184 EAGLE CREEK TRAIL
3.0 mi/1.5 hr

in Henry Cowell Redwoods State Park near Santa Cruz

Map 7.4, page 280

There are three places you don't want to miss on a visit to Henry Cowell Redwoods State Park. The first one is Eagle Creek Trail, the most direct hiking route to River Trail and the San Lorenzo River. Another is the park's observation deck, offering first-class views on clear days. And, of course, the 40-acre old-growth grove of redwoods, detailed in the previous hike.

The Eagle Creek Trail starts between campsite Nos. 82 and 84, crosses Eagle Creek, and continues adjacent to the stream as it heads out toward the San Lorenzo River. As you hike this portion of the trail, you are surrounded by redwoods. The trail then crosses Pipeline Road and junctions with the River Trail. Many people turn around and head back at this point. A great way to extend your hike is to head north on the River Trail alongside the river and add an extra three miles to the trip.

A good side trip at Henry Cowell is the observation deck, the highest point in the park. It's only a 0.3-mile hike from the campground via Pine Trail, which starts near site 49. Right alongside the observation deck are a few ponderosa pine trees, growing far from their normal range in the Sierra Nevada. You'll recognize them by their distinctive jigsaw-puzzle bark. Except on foggy days, you get a panorama of the local coast.

User Groups: Hikers and horses. No dogs or mountain bikes. No wheelchair facilities.

Permits: No permits are required. A day-use fee of $10 is charged per vehicle.

Maps: Park maps are available at the campground entrance station or at the park visitors center off Highway 9. For a topographic map, ask the USGS for Felton.

Directions: From San Jose, drive south on Highway 17 for 24 miles to Scotts Valley. Take the Mount Hermon Road exit, turn right, and drive toward Felton for about one mile to Lockewood Lane. Turn left on Lockewood Lane and drive one mile to Graham Hill Road. Turn left on Graham Hill Road and drive 0.5 mile to the campground entrance on the right. The trailhead is located between campsite Nos. 82 and 84.

Contact: Henry Cowell Redwoods State Park, 831/335-4598; nature center, 831/335-7077; www.parks.ca.gov.

185 BAYVIEW LOOP
1.0 mi/0.5 hr

in Mount Madonna County Park west of Gilroy

Map 7.4, page 280

Note: The Blackhawk Trail was closed in 2015 due to erosion and is not expected to open until 2017.

On perfect days, you get views of Monterey Bay. The trailhead for the Bayview Trail is located near the park entrance station (and nearby campground, restrooms, and yurts), at 1,270 feet. A short ways past the entrance station, look for the trail on the left (west side of the road). Turn left and walk 0.3 mile to a junction. Turn right on a nice footpath (still Bayview Trail) and hike 0.5 mile to the Sprig Trail. Turn right, then return 0.2 mile to the starting point. An easy walk with a pay-off, and a pretty introduction to a great park.

Mount Madonna County Park provides great scenic beauty, good hiking, camping, and horseback riding. The park is set around the highest peak, Mount Madonna, in the southern range of the Santa Cruz Mountains. With a network of 18 miles of hiking trails, the best routes are combinations of different trails. By linking them, you can make your adventure as short or as long as desired.

User Groups: Hikers, horses, and dogs. No mountain bikes. No wheelchair facilities.

Permits: No permits are required. A day-use fee of $6 is charged per vehicle.

Maps: A free trail map is available at the park

entrance station. For a topographic map, ask the USGS for Mount Madonna.

Directions: From San Jose, drive south on U.S. 101 to Morgan Hill and Exit 365 for Tennant Avenue. Take that exit and drive 0.4 mile to Tennant Avenue. Turn right on Tennant Avenue and go 0.9 mile to Monterey Avenue. Turn left on Monterey and go a short distance to Watsonville Road/County Road G8. Turn right and drive 7.4 miles to Highway 152. Turn right and drive 5.1 miles to Pole Line Road. Turn right and drive 1.5 miles to park entrance.

Contact: Mount Madonna County Park, 408/842-2341; Santa Clara County Parks and Recreation, 408/355-2201, www.sccgov.org/sites/parks.

186 UVAS PARK WATERFALL LOOP

3.0 mi/2.0 hr 　　　　　🥾2 ⛰️9

in Uvas Canyon County Park near Morgan Hill

Map 7.4, page 280

Uvas Canyon County Park is a little slice of waterfall heaven on the east side of the Santa Cruz Mountains. The best advice is to visit during the rainy season, preferably just after a good downpour when the waterfalls are at peak flows. The trailhead is at the Black Rock Picnic Area and is routed up Swanson Creek. You'll pass Black Rock Falls (a 30-foot cascade, clear water over black rock), then Basin Falls (where a 20-foot stream flows into a hollowed-out rock that looks like a big tub if you get the right angle), and then a short ways beyond to Upper Falls. That's just 0.7 mile, or 1.5-mile round-trip. Note there is also a service road that is routed up the canyon that some take by accident as the hike. At high flows, Black Rock Falls is often the prettiest. At low flows, Upper Falls is still very pretty.

From Upper Falls, continue to hike up Swanson Creek, a bit of a climb. You will then cross Swanson Creek to the left (do not take what looks like a faint trail farther up the canyon). Take the Contour Trail, which is routed in

and out of several ravines, to the Alec Canyon Trail (a service road). Turn left and sail downhill. A pretty lookout east over the canyon toward the Santa Clara Valley is available here. It's a final 0.5 mile back to the starting point.

Ambitious side trip: At the junction of the Contour Trail and the Alec Canyon trail, instead of turning left and heading back to the trailhead, you can instead go the extra mile. Turn right and hike up a half mile, the steepest trail section in the park, past Manzanita Point to a spur (0.2 mile) on the right to 40-foot Triple Falls. That adds 1.4 miles to the trip and makes it a 4.5-mile hike. In rainy season, the climb is well worth it. In summer, well, it's not.

User Groups: Hikers and dogs. No horses or mountain bikes. No wheelchair facilities.

Permits: No permits are required. A day-use fee of $6 is charged per vehicle.

Maps: A brochure and map are available at the trailhead. For a topographic map, ask the USGS for Loma Prieta.

Directions: Take U.S. 101 south of San Jose to Coyote and the exit for Bailey Avenue. Take that exit, turn right on Bailey Avenue and drive 3.2 miles to McKean Road. Turn left on McKean Road and drive 6.1 miles (at 2.4 miles, it becomes Uvas Road) to Croy Road. Turn right on Croy Road and drive 4.4 miles (go slow, passes through Sveadal) to park entrance.

Contact: Uvas Canyon County Park, 408/779-9232; Santa Clara County Parks and Recreation, 408/355-2201, www.sccgov.org/sites/parks.

187 SYCAMORE NATURE TRAIL

1.2 mi/0.5 hr 　　　　　🥾1 ⛰️7

along Coyote Creek south of San Jose

Map 7.4, page 280

From the Walnut Rest Area, this is a pretty, easy nature walk along Coyote Creek. The setting is pretty and peaceful, the kind of place you enjoy in the moment, not a trek with a distant payoff. The trail starts where you walk on a path with Coyote Creek on your right. You head downstream for a short stretch, then cross a bridge and walk along the far side of the creek to a picnic site. Easy, simple, with a nice pay-off.

User Groups: Hikers only. An equestrian trail is available nearby for horses. The Coyote Creek Parkways is available nearby for mountain bikes, leashed dogs, wheelchairs.

Permits: No permits are required. Parking and access is free. A day-use fee of $6 is charged per vehicle if parking at nearby Anderson Lake County Park or Hellyer County Park.

Maps: A brochure and map are available at the trailhead. For a free map, contact Coyote-Hellyer County Park. For a topographic map, ask the USGS for Morgan Hill.

Directions: From San Jose, take U.S. 101 south for six miles to Coyote and the exit for Cochran Road. Take that exit to Cochran Road, turn east and drive (toward the base of Anderson Dam) to the parking area for Walnut Rest Area on the left (right is signed for Anderson Lake).

Contact: Coyote Creek Parkway County Park, 408/629-9111; Santa Clara County Parks and Recreation, 408/355-2201, www.sccgov.org/sites/parks.

188 FROG POND LOOP
4.7 mi/3.0 hr 🏃2 ⛰️7

in Henry W. Coe State Park east of Morgan Hill

Map 7.4, page 280

From headquarters, the Frog Pond Loop is a day hike that provides a glimpse of the park's primitive charms, along with a sampling of a few of the ups and downs. Think of it as a test case: If you like this, then load your backpack for an overnighter and launch off on one of the butt-kickers from here or the Hunting Hollow Trailhead.

Start this trip from park headquarters at Monument Trail (elevation 2,500 feet), located about 100 yards from the visitors center. The trip starts by hiking 0.5 mile to Hobbs Road, climbing to nearly 3,000 feet. At Hobbs Road, turn left and tromp down for 0.8 mile into Little Fork Coyote Creek (2,400 feet). This stream is

very pretty in the spring, and though you must then walk out of the canyon, it is a tranquil and memorable setting. Then make the short 0.25-mile rise from the creek up to Frog Pond. This first leg is about 1.6 miles. Frog Pond is a pretty little spot, complete with fishing line hanging from tree limbs (this lake is fished often and the catch rates are low). Many people then simply return the way they came.

Henry W. Coe State Park is the Bay Area's backyard wilderness. This wildland is located south of Mount Hamilton and covers 87,000 acres and 134 square miles, the largest state park in Northern California. A trip to headquarters provides a visitors center and access to a drive-in campground with excellent stargazing. The best trailheads are not at headquarters, but at Hunting Hollow. From headquarters, the trips into the park's interior are very long and difficult.

User Groups: Hikers, horses, and mountain bikes. No dogs. No wheelchair facilities. After 0.5 inch of rain or more, bikes are prohibited from single-track trails for 48 hours.

Permits: A state park day-use fee of $8 per vehicle is charged. No permits are required unless you plan to camp in the backcountry.

Maps: A brochure and map are available at the visitors center. For a detailed topographic map, contact Pine Ridge Association (Morgan Hill, 408/779-2728, www.coepark.org). For a topographic map, ask the USGS for Mount Sizer.

Directions: Take U.S. 101 south of San Jose to Morgan Hill and the exit for East Dunne Avenue. Take that exit, turn east on East Dunne Avenue and drive (over the bridge at the head of Lake Anderson) for 13 miles (slow and twisty) to the park headquarters and visitors center.

Contact: Henry W. Coe State Park, 408/779-2728, www.parks.ca.gov.

189 MISSISSIPPI LAKE TRAIL

27.0 mi/3 days 🥾5 ⛰8

in Henry W. Coe State Park east of Morgan Hill

Map 7.4, page 280

Mississippi Lake is the marquee destination at Henry W. Coe State Park, a small lake edged by tules that provides a wilderness-style pond for bass fishing and nearby trail campsites. It is set in the virtual center of this huge park, and reaching Mississippi Lake requires an extended endurance test.

An early start is paramount. From park headquarters, begin this expedition by hiking out on Corral Trail for 1.9 miles to its junction with Manzanita Point Road. Turn right and hike 1.5 miles, past the group campgrounds, to China Hole Trail on the left. This can seem like a launch point off the edge of the earth: The China Hole Trail drops from 2,320 feet elevation to 1,150 feet in the course of 2.6 miles. Switchbacks have improved the trail gradient to about 10 percent.

At China Hole, you'll reach the East Fork of Coyote Creek, a beautiful stream that is cool, fresh, and full of water in late winter and early spring. Then you'll hike through The Narrows en route to Los Cruzeros, amd in the process, add 1.1 miles to the day. Los Cruzeros is one of the park's prettiest spots, a junction of canyons and streams. A trail camp is available at Los Cruzeros. Before you leave the stream, make sure you pump two canteens full of water.

From here, you start to climb. You hike out on Willow Ridge Trail for 1.6 miles with an elevation gain of 1,350 feet to Willow Ridge Road. Turn left on Willow Ridge Road for a series of foothill-like climbs and drops as the trip extends 3.8 miles to the southern edge (and earth dam) at Mississippi Lake. The nearest trail camp, Mississippi Creek Horse Camp, is one mile south of the lake. That makes the trip a one-way excursion of 13.5 miles. It's a long and challenging day, especially if temperatures are hot.

This is a grueling hike from headquarters. Many unprepared hikers have suffered from dehydration and had to be rescued by park staff. Some hikers will try to shortcut the trip by bringing a mountain bike, but find themselves pushing the bike uphill, then speeding fast on downhill portions. Many can accomplish the hike in two days, but after the workout, you'll most likely want to relax on day two and head back to your car on day three.

It is Coe's preeminent destination. The lake borders the 23,000-acre Orestimba Wilderness to the east; fishing for bass, swimming in cool waters in early summer, and viewing wildflower blooms in spring are exceptional. If you catch it just right, the color of the lake seems almost tourmaline, a beautiful sight in this foothill wildland.

Even though Henry W. Coe State Park has been open to the public only since 1981, a few legends have already developed, and the most mysterious involves Mississippi Lake. The lake once had a one-of-a-kind ability to create huge trout. The first time I visited, scientists had documented 26-inch wild trout that were only 18 months old. The trout are long gone now, as low water in the feeder creek prevented spawning in droughts; any trout you catch should be released immediately. Still, the legendary huge trout of Mississippi Lake have inspired many to make the trip out, often out of curiosity, to see such a unique habitat. Bass were planted in 1991 and have taken over the lake and provide good fishing.

User Groups: Hikers, horses, and mountain bikes. No dogs. No wheelchair facilities. After 0.5 inch of rain, bikes are prohibited from single-track trails for 48 hours.

Permits: A trail map and camp permit are required. A state park day-use fee of $8 per vehicle is charged.

Maps: A brochure and map are available at park headquarters. For a detailed topographic map, contact Pine Ridge Association (Morgan Hill, 408/779-2728, www.coepark.org). For topographic maps, ask the USGS for Mount Sizer and Mississippi Creek.

Directions: Take U.S. 101 south of San Jose to Morgan Hill and the exit for East Dunne

Avenue. Take that exit, turn east on East Dunne Avenue and drive (over the bridge at the head of Lake Anderson) for 13 miles (slow and twisty) to the park headquarters and visitors center.
Contact: Henry W. Coe State Park, 408/779-2728, www.parks.ca.gov.

190 COIT LAKE

11.6 mi/2 days

in Henry W. Coe State Park east of Morgan Hill

Map 7.4, page 280

The Hunting Hollow Trailhead near Coyote Lake east of Gilroy is a great launch point for Kelly Lake and Coit Lake. Start by parking at Hunting Hollow, or along the shoulder of the road at the Coyote Creek Gate. From the Coyote Creek Gate, walk a short distance (about 0.1 mile) and look for Grizzly Gulch Trail off to the right. Take Grizzly Gulch Trail. After just five minutes (0.2 mile) you will reach a fork. Take the left fork to stay on Grizzly Gulch Trail, where you will start a climb through oak woodlands, ridges, and canyons. This extends for 1.2 miles to another fork, with the elevation nearly 1,900 feet. Bear right, staying on Grizzly Gulch Trail, and head out for one mile on the road to a fork with Dexter Trail (2,000 feet). Bear to the left on Dexter Trail, and continue the climb for another 0.6 mile (topping out at 2,400 feet) before finally reaching Wasano Ridge and Wasano Ridge Road. Turn left and hike 0.2 mile on the road to Kelly Lake Trail. Turn right and enjoy the one-mile descent to Kelly Lake. So far you have invested 4.3 miles with a 1,500-foot climb and 300-foot descent. Much of the route feels like foothill wilderness, and with mountain bikers on ambitious treks on the park's ranch-style roads, you'll have it to yourself.

After enjoying pretty Kelly Lake, you are ready to top off the trip by heading 1.5 miles to Coit Lake and the campground that is available there. Most of this is a climb. From below the earth dam at Kelly Lake, take the right fork on Coit Road and climb out 0.8 mile to the junction with Willow Road (2,386 feet).

Simply continue straight for 0.3 mile and you will reach the inlet to Coit Lake. A well-worn trail circles the lake. From the Coyote Creek Gate trailhead to Coit Lake with this route will make for a 5.8-mile hike for the day, one-way.

This is a great trip at the peak of spring, with 400 species of wildflowers documented, as well as deer, coyote, bobcat, fox, wild turkey, hawks, owls, eagles, and, of course, pigs.

Overnight users are required to obtain a camping/wilderness permit. Hikers who choose to enter by the Coyote Creek access point must have a trail map. And if the limited parking along the road's shoulder at the Coyote Creek Gate is full, you must instead park at the Hunting Hollow parking area (along Gilroy Springs Road, the access road you drove in on), which will add two miles to this route.

User Groups: Hikers, horses, and mountain bikes. No dogs. No wheelchair facilities.

Permits: A trail map and camp permit are required. A self-registration area is available at the Hunting Hollow parking area, located just off the trailhead access road. A state park day-use fee of $8 per vehicle is charged. After 0.5 inch of rain or more, bikes are prohibited from single-track trails for 48 hours.

Maps: A brochure and map are available at the trailhead. For a detailed topographic map, contact Pine Ridge Association (Morgan Hill, 408/779-2728, www.coepark.org). For topographic maps, ask the USGS for Gilroy Hot Springs and Mississippi Creek.

Directions: Take U.S. 101 south (30 miles south of San Jose) to Gilroy and Exit 357 for Leavesley Road/Highway 152. Take that exit to Leavesley, turn left and go 1.8 miles to New Avenue. Turn left and go 0.6 mile to Roop Road. Turn right and go 1.9 miles, turn left to stay on Roop (well signed) and continue 3.3 miles (becomes Gilroy Hot Springs Road) to Hunting Hollow Parking on right (nine miles from U.S. 101) or continue 1.8 miles to Coyote Gate.

Contact: Henry W. Coe State Park, 408/779-2728, www.parks.ca.gov.

191 ROOSTER COMB LOOP (LONG VERSION)

60.0 mi/6 days 🚶5 ⛰7

in Henry W. Coe State southeast of San Jose

Map 7.4, page 280 **BEST (**

No trail on public land in the Bay Area provides access to more remote wildlands. A series of short cutoff trips can take you to the park's best fishing spots and little-seen gems: Mississippi Lake, Mustang Pond, Jackrabbit Lake, Paradise Lake, and all the way out to Orestimba Creek. You also climb the Rooster Comb, a rock formation that looks something like a miniature stegosaurus-back rim.

There is no metropolitan area in the world with such a remote area, but you have to pay dearly for your pleasures. Either that or border on insanity. To some, Paradise Lake will seem like a mirage after you've walked 33 miles.

For this 60-mile loop, start at the Coyote Creek entrance gate, or the nearby (two miles) Hunting Hollow parking area. From the gate, it's a 5.8-mile trip to Coit Lake (see listing in this chapter).

From Coit Lake, take Coit Road out 4.2 miles to Pacheco Junction, then continue on Coit Road another 1.8 miles to a major fork. This fork marks the beginning and the end of the Rooster Comb Loop. At this point, you have traveled 15.8 miles.

Turn left at this fork, taking County Line Road, to start the Rooster Comb Loop and a route, in a clockwise manner, through the Orestimba Wilderness Zone. From the fork, it is 2.7 miles to the short cutoff to Mississippi Lake. Stop, rest up, tank up, fuel up, and get your thoughts straight before heading out. That is because from Mississippi Lake, the trip heads off into a land that seems to have no end. Take County Line Road to a short cutoff, Chaparral Trail, and then link that to Red Creek Road. Turn right, and it is 6.1 miles to Robinson Creek Trail. Turn left and hike along Robinson Creek, a remote canyon with a sliver of water, for 5.6 miles to Orestimba Creek Road.

Turn right on Orestimba Creek Road and you start your return, though it won't seem like it, from the depths of the wilderness. The route heads 3.2 miles to a cutoff trail on the right for Rooster Comb Summit Trail. This is a must-do, if you've come this far, a 1.4-mile hike with a 600-foot climb (2.8 miles round-trip) up the north flank of the Rooster Comb, where you top out at 1,836 feet.

From here you head back, heading south on Orestimba Creek Road. You'll pass short cutoff trails for Paradise Lake, Mustang Pond, and Kingbird Pond, a distance of 8.7 miles back to the fork with Coit Road. This area is so far away from anything that it can feel unbelievable to be here. It is also typically dry and hot most of the year, and in 2015, drought hit the ponds hard. I have flown it, driven it with rangers, and hiked it, and the remoteness you will feel at one of the ponds, where you camp, swim, or fish, is amazing for a destination in the greater Bay Area.

When you reach the junction with Coit Road, you have completed the loop, a distance of 36.9 miles (including the Rooster Comb Summit trail). Turn left and return the final 11.6 miles back to the Coyote Creek entrance station. With this route, in all, you have completed 60.1 miles, not including side-trip cutoff trails to several lakes, which can typically add another 10 miles to the trip.

So there you have it: 60 miles, best done in five or six days, exploring a land that few have seen, and fewer yet have experienced.

Several trail camps are situated along the way, and camping is permitted throughout the wilderness area. If the weather turns hot, physically unprepared hikers can find themselves in real danger. Let me say that again before you head off full of excitement and a limited amount of logic: unprepared hikers can find themselves in real danger. OK? Got it? Very few do this trip. Be sure to purchase added life insurance before embarking. Not only is it just plain long, but it includes seven climbs that'll have you cussing, and yet explores the park's most remote wildlands. It's like nothing else.

User Groups: Hikers, horses, and mountain bikes. No dogs. No wheelchair facilities. After

0.5 inch of rain, bikes are prohibited from single-track trails for 48 hours.

Permits: A trail map and camp permit are required. A self-registration area is available at the Hunting Hollow parking area, located just off the trailhead access road. A state park day-use fee of $8 per vehicle is charged.

Maps: A brochure and map are available at park headquarters. For a detailed topographic map for a fee, contact Pine Ridge Association (Morgan Hill, 408/779-2728, www.coepark. org). For topographic maps, ask the USGS for Gilroy Hot Springs and Mississippi Creek.

Directions: Take U.S. 101 south (30 miles south of San Jose) to Gilroy and Exit 357 for Leavesley Road/Highway 152. Take that exit to Leavesley, turn left and go 1.8 miles to New Avenue. Turn left and go 0.6 mile to Roop Road. Turn right and go 1.9 miles, turn left to stay on Roop (well signed) and continue 3.3 miles (becomes Gilroy Hot Springs Road) to Hunting Hollow Parking on right (nine miles from U.S. 101) or continue 1.8 miles to Coyote Gate.

Contact: Henry W. Coe State Park, 408/779-2728, www.parks.ca.gov.

192 DOWDY RANCH/ ROOSTER COMB LOOP

27.5 mi/3 days   🏃4 ⛰9

in Orestimba Wilderness at Henry W. Coe State Park

Map 7.4, page 280

You have to wonder if the trailhead out of Bell Station along Highway 152 to Dowdy Ranch will ever open again. At best, it was open on an extremely limited basis, some years just a few days. If such an opportunity occurs again, this is how you take advantage of it. The trailhead at Dowdy Ranch/Bell Station provides nearby access (when open) to the Orestima Wilderness, including bass fishing at Jackrabbit Lake and a great campsite at the foot of the Rooster Comb.

This is how it works from the Dowdy Ranch Trailhead:

Hole in the Rock, 1.9 miles: Your destination is a fantastic swimming hole on Pacheco Creek. To get there from the new trailhead, take the main Kaiser-Etna Road (1.9 miles) or the North Fork Trail (2.7 miles). When you reach the creek, walk upstream a few hundred yards to find Hole in the Rock. Another decent swimming hole is located if you head downstream instead.

Kingbird Pond, 7.9 miles: Little Kingbird Pond provides bass fishing and is the first fishing spot out of Bell Station. To reach it, take Kaiser-Etna Road five miles to a four-way junction. Go straight (north) on Orestimba Creek Road for 2.4 miles to the Kingbird Pond Trail. Turn right and go 0.5 mile to the pond. Note: Once you get to Orestimba Corral, about six miles in, the route is pretty flat, with just gentle hills.

Mustang Pond, 11.1 miles: This little lake is only 3.2 miles from Kingbird Pond, but there are several creek crossings on this route. At high water you might get wet, but it's a lot of fun. From Kingbird Pond, head 0.5 mile back to the Orestimba Creek Road. Turn right (so you're going north) and head 2.2 miles to the Mustang Pond Trail on the right. It's 0.5 mile to this pond.

Jackrabbit Lake, 13.9 miles: This lake is about twice the size of Kingbird and Mustang, and provides what is probably the best bass fishing in the park. It is only 2.8 miles from Mustang Pond. To get there, from Mustang Pond continue on the Mustang Pond Trail (it horseshoes) northwest to Orestimba Creek Road. Turn right, heading north again, and go 0.75 mile to a spur junction with Long Ridge Road. Turn right and go 1.2 miles, a bit of a climb, to an unsigned spur junction on the left that we call Jackrabbit Lake Road. Turn left and push out a short climb and drop of 0.4 mile to the lake.

Base of Rooster Comb, 16.5 miles: The Rooster Comb is a large, rocky exposed ridge formation that rises up 500 feet from the valley floor to an elevation of 1,836 feet. Below, Orestimba Creek Flat is a good area to camp. To get here from Jackrabbit Lake, it's a 2.6-mile ride: Backtrack on Jackrabbit Lake Trail to Long Ridge Road. Turn right and return to Orestimba Creek Road. Turn north (right) and go one mile to the base of the Rooster Comb.

Return to park entrance: From the Rooster Comb, it's 11 miles back to the park access at Dowdy Ranch. This makes for a fantastic 27.5-mile loop, with three lakes and plenty of places to camp.

With April showers and a warm May, the valley flats below Rooster Comb can yield tremendous wildflower blooms: owl clover, California poppy, shooting stars, butter and eggs, and rafts of smooth layia. The layia is found almost only in undeveloped grasslands and is an awesome bloom—kind of like a daisy, yet with yellow petals tipped in white, in spectacular clusters.

Since Henry W. Coe State Park opened in 1959, this area has been out of reach for almost all that time. It took a 56-mile round-trip with about a 15,000-foot aggregate vertical climb to reach Jackrabbit Lake. You can add a lot of miles if you visit the Rooster Comb and the best small lakes for fishing—Jackrabbit Lake, Mustang Pond, Kingbird Pond, and several others. In the process, you will explore the matrixes of valleys, creeks, and foothill grasslands for wildflowers and wildlife. From park headquarters or Hunting Hollow, the route is so long and grueling that almost nobody tries it. We've been back in this wild country on perfect spring days and the fishing, wildlife, wildflowers, and campsites can be spectacular.

User Groups: Hikers, horses, and mountain bikes. No dogs. No wheelchair facilities.

Permits: A trail map and camp permit are required. A state park day-use fee of $8 per vehicle is charged. After 0.5 inch of rain or more, bikes are prohibited from single-track trails for 48 hours.

Maps: A brochure and map are available at Dowdy Visitors Center. For a detailed topographic map, contact Pine Ridge Association (Morgan Hill, 408/779-2728, www.coepark. org). For topographic maps, contact the Pine Ridge Association.

Directions: Take U.S. 101 south (30 miles south of San Jose) to Gilroy and Exit 357 for Leavesley Road/Highway 152. Take that exit to Leavesley, turn left and go 1.8 miles to New Avenue. Turn left and go 0.6 mile to Roop Road. Turn right and go 1.9 miles, turn left to stay on Roop (well signed) and continue 3.3 miles (becomes Gilroy Hot Springs Road) to Hunting Hollow Parking on right (nine miles from U.S. 101) or continue 1.8 miles to Coyote Gate.

Contact: Henry W. Coe State Park, 408/779-2728, www.parks.ca.gov.

193 HARVEY BEAR/ BAY RIDGE TRAIL
6.0 mi/3.0 hr   👟2 ⛰8

in Coyote Lake-Harvey Bear County Park near Coyote Reservoir

Map 7.4, page 280

You get spectacular views on this, where you scan across southern Santa Clara Valley and beyond across the Santa Cruz Mountains. To the east, you take in gorgeous Coyote Lake backed by a wilderness ridge to the east. Yet with Coyote Reservoir and Henry W. Coe State Park so nearby, many still overlook this trip.

Start at the parking area for Harvey Bear—a park, not a cousin of Yogi's, actually named after the landowner whose family made the park possible. From there, head off on the 4.5-mile trail, dedicated as a section of the perpetual work-in-progress, the 500-mile Bay Ridge Trail. The landscape consists of rolling hills with oaks and buckeyes and lots of wild turkey, deer, squirrels, red-tailed hawks, and turkey vultures. On summer mornings, it seems spotting wild turkey is a sure thing. You can get in a nice rhythm for easy climbs that average only 200 feet, and then take in the dramatic views of the lower Santa Clara Valley off to the west and gorgeous Coyote Lake backed by a wilderness ridge to the east. Return when ready. The parkland adjoins Coyote Lake, creating a continuous swath of 4,595 acres of public land.

An option is a fairly new loop route, Rancho La Polka.

User Groups: Hikers, mountain bikes, horses, and dogs on leash. No wheelchair facilities.

Permits: A parking and access fee of $6 per vehicle is charged. No permit required.

Maps: A brochure and map are available at the trailhead.

Directions: Take U.S. 101 south to Gilroy and the exit for Leavesley Road. Take that exit, turn east and drive two miles to New Avenue. Turn left and go 0.5 mile to Roop Road. Turn right and go three miles (it becomes Gilroy Hot Springs Road) to the park entrance and staging area on the left.

Contact: Coyote Lake Harvey Bear County Park, 408/842-7800; Santa Clara County Parks and Recreation, 408/355-2201, www.sccgov.org/sites/parks.

MONTEREY AND BIG SUR

© ANN MARIE BROWN

This visually stunning coast contains 130 miles of oceanfront drama that runs from Davenport to San Simeon. Largely undeveloped, this region offers rugged cliffs, redwood forests, rock-strewn beaches, and waterfalls.

South of Carmel, services are clustered in Big Sur, Lucia, and Gorda. In between, a string of state parks provide a bounty of trails: Point Lobos State Reserve, Garrapata State Park, Andrew Molera State Park, Julia Pfeiffer Burns State Park, Pfeiffer Big Sur State Park, and Limekiln State Park. As you hike these parks' trails, you have a near guarantee of spotting migrating gray whales or fuzzy sea otters. For a more remote adventure, head to the Ventana Wilderness or Silver Peak Wilderness. Or head inland to Pinnacles National Park, where trails tunnel through volcanic caves and travel over and around craggy rock formations.

MONTEREY AND BIG SUR

see San Francisco
Bay Area
page 276

Mountain View

Los Gatos

Santa Cruz Mtns

Santa Cruz

Monterey Bay

Monterey

Carmel

PACIFIC

Big Sur

Julia Pfeiffer
Burns State Park

Limekiln Creek
State Park

Lucia

OCEAN

Gorda

SAN JOSE

Henry W Coe
State Park

Mt Madonna
County Park

Pinto Lake

Hollister

San Juan Bautista

Salinas

Carmel R

Los Padres

Ventana Wilderness

National

Forest

San Luis Reservoir

Los Baños

Diablo

see
San Joaquin Valley
page 452

MAP 8.1
page 425

Pinnacles
National
Park

Salinas

Range

King City

FORT HUNTER
LIGGETT
MILITARY
RESERVATION

Lake San Antonio

CAMP
ROBERTS
MILITARY
RES

Lake Nacimiento

Paso Robles

Hearst San Simeon
State Historical
Monument

San Simeon

San Joaquin Valley

Atwater

Los Baños

River

Santa Lucia Range

0   10 mi
0   10 km

©AVALON TRAVEL

Map 8.1

Sites 1-36
Pages 426-450

1 OLD LANDING COVE TRAIL
2.5 mi/1.5 hr   🥾1 ⛰10

in Wilder Ranch State Park north of Santa Cruz

Map 8.1, page 425   **BEST (**

When you visit Wilder Ranch, you may notice that on some maps and park signs this trail is called Old Cove Landing, while on others it's called Old Landing Cove. Take your pick. The Old Landing Cove Trail is a gem of a coastal hike that offers a look at a seal rookery, some spectacular pocket beaches, and a hidden fern cave. Although the trail is open to both hikers and mountain bikers, everybody seems to mind their manners and get along fine.

The trail leads past brussels sprouts fields to the coast. An odd but interesting fact is that 12 percent of our nation's brussels sprouts production happens right here in this park. The trail leads from the main parking lot toward the ocean, then traces along the coastal bluff tops, with farm fields on your right and the dramatic coastline on your left. In short order you reach the trail's namesake, Old Landing Cove, where small schooners loaded lumber in the late 19th century. A little more walking brings you to the bluffs above the seal rookery, where you look down on huge flat rocks covered with wall-to-wall seals. Finally, near post No. 8, a spur trail leads down to a small beach cove. Follow the spur and you will find on the inland side of the cove a shallow cave filled with ferns from floor to ceiling. A quarter mile past the fern-cave beach is another excellent pocket beach, perfect for picnicking or lying around. Although this is a fine destination for most visitors, you can keep hiking along the bluffs beyond this beach to several more beaches in the next few miles. (The trail's name changes from Old Landing Cove Trail to Ohlone Bluff Trail.) If you decide to keep going, be forewarned that you might get an anatomy lesson along the way: Both Three-Mile and Four-Mile Beaches often attract nude sunbathers.

User Groups: Hikers and mountain bikes. No horses or dogs. No wheelchair facilities.

Permits: No permits are required. A $10 day-use fee is charged per vehicle.

Maps: A free map of Wilder Ranch is available at the entrance station or by free download at www.parks.ca.gov. A more detailed map is available from Pease Press (www.peasepress. com). For a topographic map, go to the USGS website to download Santa Cruz.

Directions: From Santa Cruz, drive north on Highway 1 for four miles. Turn left into the entrance for Wilder Ranch State Park and follow the park road to its end, at the main parking area. Take the signed trail from the southwest side of the parking lot.

Contact: Wilder Ranch State Park, Santa Cruz, 831/423-9703, www.parks.ca.gov or www. santacruzstateparks.org.

2 WILDER RIDGE AND ZANE GREY TRAILS
6.0 mi/3.0 hr   🥾3 ⛰9

in Wilder Ranch State Park north of Santa Cruz

Map 8.1, page 425

Once you find your way to the hiker/biker tunnel underneath Highway 1 near the farm buildings at Wilder Ranch, you're on your way to a great six-mile hike with just enough of a climb to give you a workout and a spectacular vista of Monterey Bay. Keep in mind that this side of the park is the domain of mountain bikers—hundreds of them on weekends—but the trails are wide, and there's plenty of room for everybody. The Wilder Ridge Trail features a 500-foot climb to a coastal overlook. You reach it by exiting the tunnel and heading straight and then uphill on Wilder Ridge, then bearing right on the Wilder Ridge Loop. At about 2.5 miles out, shortly after Twin Oaks Trail forks right, you come to an obvious grassy overlook at the top of the ridge—about 40 feet off the main trail. Enjoy the wide vista, then continue hiking along the ridge top on Wilder Ridge Loop. For an interesting loop, take the Zane Grey cutoff on the left (it's single track) and then go left again on the other side of the Wilder Ridge Loop.

User Groups: Hikers, horses, and mountain bikes. No dogs. No wheelchair facilities.

Permits: No permits are required. A $10 day-use fee is charged per vehicle.

Maps: A free map of Wilder Ranch State Park is available at the entrance station or by free download at www.parks.ca.gov. A more detailed map is available from Pease Press (www.peasepress.com). For a topographic map, go to the USGS website to download Santa Cruz.

Directions: From Santa Cruz, drive north on Highway 1 for four miles. Turn left into the entrance for Wilder Ranch State Park and follow the park road to its end, at the main parking area. Take the trail signed Nature Trail from the southwest side of the parking lot. Walk down the park road to the Wilder Ranch and Cultural Preserve, then through the cultural preserve to the picnic area and chicken coops, to reach the tunnel that leads underneath Highway 1.

Contact: Wilder Ranch State Park, Santa Cruz, 831/423-9703, www.parks.ca.gov or www.santacruzstateparks.org.

3 MAPLE FALLS
7.0-9.0 mi/4.5 hr

in The Forest of Nisene Marks State Park near Aptos

Map 8.1, page 425

It's either a seven- or nine-mile round-trip hike to Maple Falls, and it all depends on whether the park road is gated at Porter Picnic Area, the main trailhead. In winter and spring, the road is usually closed, which means you need to walk an extra mile in each direction in order to see the falls. Winter and spring are the best seasons to go, of course, because that's when Maple Falls is flowing at its fullest. The trip starts out with an easy walk on Aptos Creek Fire Road, which you'll share with mountain bikers. Follow it 0.25 mile past Porter Picnic Area, where you turn left on Loma Prieta

Grade Trail. The second-growth redwood and Douglas fir forest just keeps getting thicker, greener, and prettier, and the trail turns to sweet single track. Where Loma Prieta Grade splits, stay to the right, heading toward Bridge Creek Historic Site, for the shortest route to the falls. You can take the other side of the Loma Prieta Grade loop on your way back if you still have the energy. When you reach Bridge Creek Historic Site, the site of a former logging camp, the maintained trail ends, and you begin a fun 0.5-mile stream scramble to Maple Falls, following the course of Bridge Creek. The canyon narrows as you travel through a dense green world of ferns, moss, foliage, and water, and at last you reach the back of the canyon, where 30-foot Maple Falls spills over the wall.

User Groups: Hikers only. No dogs or horses. Mountain bikes allowed only on fire roads. No wheelchair facilities.

Permits: No permits are required. An $8 day-use fee is charged per vehicle.

Maps: A free map of The Forest of Nisene Marks is available at the entrance kiosk or by free download at www.parks.ca.gov. A more detailed map is available from Pease Press (www.peasepress.com). For topographic maps, go to the USGS website to download Laurel, Soquel, and Loma Prieta.

Directions: From Santa Cruz, drive south on Highway 1 for six miles to the Aptos/State Park Drive exit. Bear left at the exit, cross over the highway, then turn right on Soquel Drive and drive 0.5 mile. Turn left on Aptos Creek Road. Stop at the entrance kiosk, then continue up the park road and park at Porter Picnic Area. In the winter months, you must park at George's Picnic Area, a mile before Porter Picnic Area, because the park road is gated off at that point.

Contact: The Forest of Nisene Marks State Park, Watsonville, 831/763-7063 or 831/429-2850, www.parks.ca.gov or www.santacruzstateparks.org.

4 LOMA PRIETA EARTHQUAKE EPICENTER
4.0 mi/2.0 hr 👣2 ⛰8

in The Forest of Nisene Marks State Park near Aptos

Map 8.1, page 425

The destination on this trail is the epicenter of the 1989 Loma Prieta earthquake, but the pleasure of the trip has little to do with its interesting geological history. Instead, the joy is in the scenery, a lush second-growth redwood forest that regenerated after a clear-cut operation at the end of the 19th century. The hike follows Aptos Creek Fire Road, which leads gently uphill (expect plenty of mountain bikers and joggers on the weekends). At 1.5 miles from the Porter Picnic Area, cross a footbridge and descend a bit on the trail until you come to the spot where a large sign proclaims the proximity of the earthquake epicenter. There's a small bike rack. Cross the creek and continue up the single-track Aptos Creek Trail for 0.5 mile to the actual epicenter, where you will see surprisingly little evidence of anything earthshaking,

but rather a lovely and peaceful redwood forest. Turn around here for a four-mile round-trip (or six miles if you had to start from George's Picnic Area instead of Porter Picnic Area).

It's possible, although quite challenging, to hike Five Finger Falls from the epicenter by following Aptos Creek Trail for 4.5 additional miles. This epic hike has long been a favorite of intrepid waterfall lovers, who revel in the chance to see one of the least visited waterfalls in the Santa Cruz mountains. However, almost every winter, this trail is subject to weather-related damage, including landslides and flood-level waters in Aptos Creek. During the rainy months, plan on getting wet feet, as you must walk in the creek where the trail peters out. There is never any guarantee that you will reach your destination when you set out for Five Finger Falls, but nonetheless, this hike remains a beloved challenge for waterfall aficionados.

User Groups: Hikers and mountain bikes (bikers must stay on the fire roads). No dogs or horses. No wheelchair facilities.

Forest of Nisene Marks State Park

© ANN MARIE BROWN

Permits: No permits are required. An $8 day-use fee is charged per vehicle.

Maps: A free map of the The Forest of Nisene Marks State Park is available at the entrance kiosk or by free download at www.parks.ca.gov. A more detailed map is available from Pease Press (www.peasepress.com). For topographic maps, go to the USGS website to download Laurel, Soquel, and Loma Prieta.

Directions: From Santa Cruz, drive south on Highway 1 for six miles to the Aptos/State Park Drive exit. Bear left at the exit, cross over the highway, then turn right on Soquel Drive and drive 0.5 mile. Turn left on Aptos Creek Road. Stop at the entrance kiosk, then continue up the park road and park at Porter Picnic Area. In the winter months, you must park at George's Picnic Area, a mile before Porter Picnic Area, because the park road is gated off at that point.

Contact: The Forest of Nisene Marks State Park, Watsonville, 831/763-7063 or 831/429-2850, www.parks.ca.gov or www.santacruz-stateparks.org.

5 WEST RIDGE AND APTOS CREEK LOOP

12.5 mi/7.0 hr or 2 days

in The Forest of Nisene Marks State Park near Aptos

Map 8.1, page 425

The West Ridge and Aptos Creek Loop is the grand tour of the Forest of Nisene Marks State Park, suitable only for hikers in good condition and with a lot of time on their hands. An option is to get reservations for West Ridge Trail Camp and turn this into an overnight trip; the camp is situated conveniently near Sand Point Overlook—a great spot for sunsets. (Backpacking stoves are necessary; no campfires are allowed.) From George's Picnic Area, walk up Aptos Creek Road for 0.25 mile to the left cutoff for West Ridge Trail, and start climbing uphill along the west ridge of Aptos Canyon. (You can also take Loma Prieta Grade Trail if you prefer. Follow the left side

of its loop, then take the connector trail to West Ridge Trail.) Finally you ascend all the way to Hinckley Ridge (at 1,300 feet) and meet up with the fire road that leads to West Ridge Trail Camp and Sand Point Overlook. From the overlook at 1,500 feet, you can see down into the densely forested Bridge Creek drainage and far off across sky-blue Monterey Bay. Finish out the loop with a long downhill walk on Aptos Creek Fire Road, a wide path through dense redwoods and Douglas firs.

User Groups: Hikers and mountain bikes. No dogs or horses. No wheelchair facilities.

Permits: No permits are required. An $8 day-use fee is charged per vehicle. An advance reservation is necessary to stay overnight at West Ridge Trail Camp; call the park for reservations.

Maps: A free map of The Forest of Nisene Marks State Park is available at the entrance kiosk or by free download at www.parks.ca.gov. A more detailed map is available from Pease Press (www.peasepress.com). For topographic maps, go to the USGS website to download Laurel, Soquel, and Loma Prieta.

Directions: From Santa Cruz, drive south on Highway 1 for six miles to the Aptos/State Park Drive exit. Bear left at the exit, cross over the highway, then turn right on Soquel Drive and drive 0.5 mile. Turn left on Aptos Creek Road. Stop at the entrance kiosk, then continue up the park road and park at George's Picnic Area.

Contact: The Forest of Nisene Marks State Park, Watsonville, 831/763-7063 or 831/429-2850, www.parks.ca.gov or www.santacruz-stateparks.org.

6 ELKHORN SLOUGH SOUTH MARSH LOOP

2.5 mi/1.5 hr

near Moss Landing

Map 8.1, page 425   BEST (

Elkhorn Slough is 1,400 acres of marsh and tidal flats, the precious borderline between sea and land that is home to thousands of species of birds, fish, and invertebrates. It's the second-largest salt marsh in California, where birds numbering in the thousands can be seen. Hikers with binoculars (and sometimes with just their own eyes) may spot a long list of species that includes peregrine falcons, American white pelicans, and thousands of shore birds. The South Marsh Loop Trail is a 2.5-mile walking tour of this salty, marshy, bird-filled land, crossing footbridges over the slough and staying close to mudflats and the water's edge. Make sure you take all the spurs off the loop, including the short walk to Hummingbird Island, which sits right on the edge of the main channel of the Slough.

Note: The reserve is open Wednesday through Sunday from 9am-5pm. Guided tours are available on Saturday and Sunday.

User Groups: Hikers only. No dogs, horses, or mountain bikes. Several boardwalks and overlook areas are wheelchair accessible.

Permits: No permits are required. A $4 entrance fee is charged per adult. Children under 16 and anyone in possession of a California fishing or hunting license may enter free.

Maps: A map of Elkhorn Slough is available at the visitors center and online. For a topographic map, go to the USGS website to download Moss Landing.

Directions: From Highway 1 at Moss Landing, turn east on Dolan Road by the PG&E power station. Drive three miles to Elkhorn Road, turn left (north), and drive two miles to the reserve entrance. The trail begins by the visitors center.

Contact: Elkhorn Slough National Estuarine Research Reserve, Watsonville, 831/728-2822, www.elkhornslough.org.

7 FREMONT PEAK TRAIL
0.6 mi/0.5 hr   🚶1 ⛰️10

in Fremont Peak State Park near San Juan Bautista

Map 8.1, page 425

Fremont Peak State Park is a small park with a big view. There are only five miles of hiking trails here, including the most popular 0.6-mile trail to the summit of Fremont Peak (elevation 3,169 feet). But that one little trip packs one heck of a punch. Pick a clear day in winter or spring (summer gets brutally hot, and the visibility can be worse) to make the narrow and winding drive from San Juan Bautista, and prepare to witness a panorama of Monterey Bay, Santa Cruz, Salinas, Watsonville, Hollister, and the Santa Lucia Mountains. From the southwest parking area, walk up the gated, paved service road for several yards, and then cut off to the right on the signed Peak Trail, which winds its way up the mountain. The last 50 yards is very rocky, and the final summit climb is a bit of a scramble. Ignore the close-by radio transmitters, and check out the far-off views.

Another popular activity at the park is stargazing. Fremont Peak Observatory is open to the public on Saturday nights from April to October when there is no moon, and observatory members hold astronomy programs here. Visit the FPOA website for a program schedule, www.fpoa.net.

User Groups: Hikers only. No dogs, horses, or mountain bikes. No wheelchair facilities.

Permits: No permits are required. A $6 day-use fee is charged per vehicle.

Maps: A map of Fremont Peak State Park is available at the entrance kiosk. For a topographic map, go to the USGS website to download San Juan Bautista.

Directions: From Gilroy, drive south on U.S. 101 for 11 miles to the Highway 156 East/San Juan Bautista exit. Turn east on Highway 156 and drive three miles to San Juan Bautista. Then turn right (south) on the Alameda and then right on San Juan Canyon Road. (It's signed for the state park.) Follow it 11 miles to its end in Fremont Peak State Park. Park in the southwest parking area.

Contact: Fremont Peak State Park, San Juan Bautista, 831/623-4255, www.parks.ca.gov; Fremont Peak Observatory, 831/623-2465, www.fpoa.net.

8 ASILOMAR COAST TRAIL
2.4 mi/1.5 hr

in Pacific Grove

Map 8.1, page 425

Even if you aren't lucky enough to attend a conference at the historic Asilomar Conference Center, you can still walk its adjoining Asilomar Coast Trail, a spectacular 1.2-mile trail along coastal bluffs above rugged, windswept Asilomar Beach. There's plenty to look at and many side trails to explore. You'll see waves crashing against jagged rocks, plentiful tidepools, tiny pocket beaches, wide sandy stretches with big white dunes, and much sea life. Be sure to take the separate boardwalk trail (on the west side of the conference center) that leads across the dunes. Kite flying is also popular along some stretches of Asilomar Beach.

User Groups: Hikers and dogs. No horses or mountain bikes. Portions of the trail are wheelchair-accessible.

Permits: No permits are required. Parking and access are free.

Maps: For a topographic map, go to the USGS website to download Monterey.

Directions: From Salinas on U.S. 101, take the Highway 68/Monterey exit and drive 15 miles into Monterey. Continue into Pacific Grove, where Highway 68 becomes Sunset Drive. Continue to Asilomar State Beach. Park alongside Sunset Drive; the trail begins opposite the conference center.

Contact: Asilomar State Beach, Pacific Grove, 831/646-6440, www.parks.ca.gov.

9 SKYLINE NATURE AND JACKS PEAK TRAILS
1.2 mi/0.5 hr

in Jacks Peak County Park near Monterey

Map 8.1, page 425

At 1,068 feet, Jacks Peak is the highest point on the Monterey Peninsula. Hey, it's not the High Sierra, but this summit is still worthy of a hike. The peak and its surrounding park are named after David Jacks, the guy who got his name on Monterey Jack cheese. The Skyline Nature Trail is an easy loop walk around the summit of Jacks Peak, set amid a dense forest of Monterey pines. The Jacks Peak Trail is a smaller loop inside Skyline Nature Trail loop, and you can easily branch off the latter to join the former for a half-hour walk that provides unparalleled views of Carmel Valley, the Monterey Peninsula, Point Lobos, the Santa Lucia Mountains, and the Pacific Ocean. That's on a clear day, of course, which is not every day in Monterey. Even though the view is about the same on both trail loops, make sure you walk a leg of Jacks Peak Trail to the top of Jacks Peak, where you can sit on a bench and pull out a picnic of Jack cheese sandwiches. Don't plan on watching the sun set from here, though; unfortunately the park closes before then.

User Groups: Hikers and dogs. No horses or mountain bikes. No wheelchair facilities.

Permits: No permits are required. A $5 entrance fee is charged per vehicle.

Maps: A free map of Jacks Peak County Park is available at the entrance station. For a topographic map, go to the USGS website to download Seaside.

Directions: From Monterey, take Highway 68 east from Highway 1 for 1.7 miles to Olmsted Road. Turn right on Olmsted Road and drive 1.5 miles to Jacks Peak Drive, then follow Jacks Peak Drive to the park entrance. After passing through the entrance kiosk, turn right and drive to the parking area for Jacks Peak.

Contact: Jacks Peak County Park, Monterey, 888/588-2267, www.co.monterey.ca.us/parks.

10 OLLASON PEAK
7.5 mi/3.5 hr

in Toro County Park near Monterey

Map 8.1, page 425

Pick a cool day in spring to take this inspiring jaunt to the top of Ollason Peak, elevation 1,800 feet, high up and far away from the madding crowds of popular Toro County Park.

Even with a cool breeze, Ollason Trail can be a butt-kicker, with many steep sections over a less-than-smooth route. It leads from the Quail Meadow Group Picnic Area and climbs through wide grasslands and occasional oak groves, most of the time on a wide double-track trail. Increasingly wide views and an excellent variety of grassland wildflowers are your reward for the work. After a long stint heading southwest, the trail suddenly veers east, then resumes its southern course for the final climb to Ollason Peak, four miles from the trailhead. You get lovely views toward Monterey Bay and the Central Valley from the summit, plus a set of rugged-looking peaks to the east. Retrace your steps from there or continue a little farther to Coyote Spring Trail, bearing left for a 7.5-mile loop. If you're making the loop, be sure to watch for the left turnoff on Cougar Ridge from Coyote Spring, which returns you to a connector trail back to Quail Meadow.

User Groups: Hikers and dogs. Mountain bikes and horses allowed on only a portion of the trail. No wheelchair facilities.

Permits: No permits are required. An $8 entrance fee is charged per vehicle ($10 on holidays).

Maps: A free map of Toro County Park is available at the entrance station. For a topographic map, go to the USGS website to download Spreckels.

Directions: From Monterey, take Highway 68 east from Highway 1 for 13 miles to the Portola Drive exit. Turn right into the Toro County Park entrance road. Drive 0.5 mile past the entrance kiosk to the parking area by Quail Meadow Group Picnic Area.

Contact: Toro County Park, Salinas, 831/484-1108, www.co.monterey.ca.us/parks.

11 LACE LICHEN TRAIL TO SEA LION POINT

2.0 mi/1.0 hr

in Point Lobos State Reserve near Carmel

Map 8.1, page 425

On summer weekends, the cars are parked in a long line along the road outside Point Lobos State Reserve, one of the crown jewels of the state park system, which sees more than 550,000 visitors each year. Even on weekdays, the parking lots are often full, but the reserve's stunning coastal beauty and plentiful wildlife explain why. Point Lobos also holds a claim to literary fame—Robert Louis Stevenson used this rocky coast as the inspiration for his novel *Treasure Island.*

One of the best destinations at Point Lobos is Sea Lion Point, where you can look for cute little sea otters floating on their backs in the kelp beds and chubby harbor seals and sea lions hauling out on the rocks. The best way to reach the point is by hiking the Lace Lichen Trail from the park entrance kiosk, which roughly parallels the park road. Extended and improved in 2015, this wheelchair-accessible trail saves you the hassle of driving through the reserve and fighting for a parking spot. The trail is named for the gray-green lichen that many call "old man's beard," which hangs from the branches of Monterey pines and coast live oaks. The lace lichen is not a parasite and does not harm the trees; in fact, it helps the trees to retain moisture. You'll see plenty of it as you head toward Sea Lion Point. Once you arrive, you'll be caught up in the spectacle of hundreds of blubbery pinnipeds hauled out on the rocks and on the beaches. In the last few years, the stairs to the lower point have been closed because the seals and sea lions have been coming to shore in such large numbers that they are now using every inch of available real estate. Some biologists believe that the pinnipeds are establishing a permanent colony here, much like they have at Año Nuevo and San Simeon.

User Groups: Hikers only. No dogs, horses,

or mountain bikes. Part of the trail is wheelchair-accessible.

Permits: No permits are required. A $10 day-use fee is charged per vehicle.

Maps: A map of Point Lobos State Reserve is available at the entrance station or by free download at www.parks.ca.gov. For a topographic map, go to the USGS website to download Monterey.

Directions: From Carmel at Rio Road, drive south on Highway 1 for three miles to the entrance to Point Lobos State Reserve, on the right. Turn right and drive through the entrance kiosk, and continue straight to the information station and Sea Lion Point parking area.

Contact: Point Lobos State Reserve, Carmel, 831/624-4909, www.pointlobos.org.

12 WHALER'S KNOLL AND CYPRESS GROVE

3.0 mi/2.0 hr

in Point Lobos State Reserve near Carmel

Map 8.1, page 425

Two excellent trails lead from the north side of the Sea Lion Point parking area near the information station at Point Lobos, and you can connect them to make a stellar three-mile round-trip. Start by hiking on Cypress Grove Trail, which shows off the park's Monterey cypress trees, one of only two remaining native Monterey cypress groves on earth. (The other grove is across Carmel Bay at Cypress Point.) In addition to getting a look at these gnarled, windswept trees, you also walk through coastal scrub to rocky cliffs with picture-perfect ocean views. The trail loops around and heads back toward the parking area, but just before you reach it, you can turn left on North Shore Trail and climb a bit to the right turnoff for Whaler's Knoll Trail. Whaler's Knoll Trail makes loose switchbacks uphill to the top of Whaler's Knoll, a bluff top that provides the best view in the park. Early twentieth-century whale spotters used this high knoll to scan the seas for the spouts of whales. When they spotted them, they

would hang a signal flag, alerting the whaling boats to head out to sea. From Whaler's Knoll, head downhill and make a loop along the coast on North Shore Trail.

User Groups: Hikers only. No dogs, horses, or mountain bikes. No wheelchair facilities.

Permits: No permits are required. A $10 day-use fee is charged per vehicle.

Maps: A map of Point Lobos State Reserve is available at the entrance station or by free download at www.parks.ca.gov. For a topographic map, go to the USGS website to download Monterey.

Directions: From Carmel at Rio Road, drive south on Highway 1 for three miles to the entrance to Point Lobos State Reserve on the right. Turn right and drive through the entrance kiosk and continue straight to the information station and Sea Lion Point parking area.

Contact: Point Lobos State Reserve, Carmel, 831/624-4909, www.pointlobos.org.

13 POINT LOBOS PERIMETER

6.0 mi/3.0 hr

in Point Lobos State Reserve near Carmel

Map 8.1, page 425   **BEST (**

The perimeter hike at Point Lobos connects a number of trails to view some of the park's best highlights. Make sure you get a map at the entrance station so you can scope out the many side-trip options that are possible (and the many shortcuts if you're getting tired). Starting from the Sea Lion Point parking area, make your first destination Sea Lion Point. Then bear left on Sand Hill Trail and connect to South Shore Trail. The latter leads along the quieter, south part of the park, past numerous spectacular beaches and coves, to the wheelchair-accessible Bird Island Trail. Make sure you take the short side path to Bird Island Overlook, then walk the stairs down to Gibson Beach. (You may be tempted to visit emerald-green China Cove, which is arguably one of the most beautiful beaches on the California Coast, but it has been closed to the public since 2014 due to concerns about wildlife protection, and is unlikely to reopen any time soon. Please obey all posted signs.) From Bird Island Trail, connect with South Plateau Trail, follow it northward, cross the park road to follow Carmelo Meadow Trail, and bear right for a side trip to Granite Point. Don't miss this; it's a rocky outcrop on a short loop trail with great views toward Carmel to the north. Then retrace your steps along Granite Point Trail and finish out your loop by walking along the park's northern shoreline, following Granite Point Trail to Cabin Trail to North Shore Trail. Other possible side trips include the Whaler's Cabin cultural history museum (the cabin was built by Chinese fishermen and its foundation is made of whale bones), a lookout of Guillemot Island and its millions of birds (from a spur trail), or Whaler's Knoll and Cypress Grove. If you take all of the possible side trips along the route, this hike will take you almost all day—and what a fine day it will be.

User Groups: Hikers only. No dogs, horses, or mountain bikes. Wheelchair users can travel on the Bird Island Trail.

Permits: No permits are required. A $10 day-use fee is charged per vehicle.

Maps: A map of Point Lobos State Reserve is available at the entrance station or by free download at www.parks.ca.gov. For a topographic map, go to the USGS website to download Monterey.

Directions: From Carmel at Rio Road, drive south on Highway 1 for three miles to the entrance to Point Lobos State Reserve on the right. Turn right and drive through the entrance kiosk; continue straight to the information station and Sea Lion Point parking area.

Contact: Point Lobos State Reserve, Carmel, 831/624-4909, www.pointlobos.org.

14 ROCKY RIDGE AND SOBERANES CANYON LOOP

7.0 mi/3.5 hr   🏃3 ⛰10

in Garrapata State Park south of Carmel

Map 8.1, page 425   **BEST (**

Garrapata State Park is situated on both sides of Highway 1, with some trails leading to the ocean and others leading up inland canyons and hillsides. Hikers looking for a long, heart-pumping walk will enjoy this loop trip on the inland side of the park, which travels through a remarkable variety of terrain. In spring, the wildflower display along these coastal hills will blow you away. Both the number and variety of species is truly remarkable.

Begin hiking on Soberanes Canyon Trail. What starts out as a ranch road through cactus- and chaparral-covered hillsides quickly becomes single-track trail through an increasingly narrow and wet canyon. The big surprise is a gorgeous stand of redwoods along Soberanes Creek, an extreme contrast to the chaparral and cacti at the start of the trail. The grove is a good turnaround spot for those looking for a short, easy trip. If you continue on, the trail begins a substantial ascent with not nearly enough switchbacks; after the initial easy grade of this trail, this stretch comes as a major surprise for many hikers. The trail then travels north to meet up with Peak Trail heading right, which leads to 1,977-foot Doud Peak, and Rocky Ridge Trail heading left. In case you are wondering why you are so out of breath, you've just climbed 1,850 feet in just under three miles. Unless you are feeling an irresistible urge to bag Doud Peak, turn left and finish out your loop on Rocky Ridge Trail, where on a clear day you can look out over the ocean for miles. The trail then winds back down the hillsides and deposits you back at your car on Highway 1.

User Groups: Hikers only. No dogs, horses, or mountain bikes. No wheelchair facilities.

Permits: No permits are required. Parking and access are free.

Maps: A map of Garrapata State Park is available for free download at www.parks.ca.gov. For a topographic map, go to the USGS website to download Soberanes Point.

Directions: From Carmel at Rio Road, drive south on Highway 1 for seven miles to mile marker 13 and the dirt pullouts along the highway at Garrapata State Park. It's four miles south of Point Lobos State Park and easy to miss; go slowly and watch for cars parked alongside the road. The Soberanes Canyon Trail begins on the east side of the road.

Contact: Garrapata State Park, Big Sur, 831/667-2315 or 831/649-2836, www.parks.ca.gov.

15 SOBERANES POINT TRAIL
2.0 mi/1.0 hr 🏃2 ⛰9

in Garrapata State Park south of Carmel

Map 8.1, page 425

You can access Soberanes Point Trail from three different gates along Highway 1, so if you miss mile marker 13, you can always stop at markers 15 or 16. Wherever you begin, you'll end up on a spectacular and easy set of trails that joins in a series of loops around Soberanes Point, all basically around Whale Peak. If you time your trip at low tide, you'll have access to some excellent tidepools, and even if not, you have views of rocky shoreline bluffs and plenty of birdlife and other animals. Many anglers try their luck rock fishing here at the point, and it's also a popular spot for whale-watching from November to January. Note that if you start from mile marker 13, you can hike a short loop to your right and then a much larger loop to your left. If you start from mile marker 15, you're at the middle of the larger loop, so you can start hiking either right or left. Just wander as you please; the coastline and the perimeter of the point make it impossible to get lost.

User Groups: Hikers only. No dogs, horses, or mountain bikes. No wheelchair facilities.

Permits: A map of Garrapata State Park is available for free download at www.parks.

ca.gov. No permits are required. Parking and access are free.

Maps: For a topographic map, go to the USGS website to download Soberanes Point.

Directions: From Carmel at Rio Road, drive south on Highway 1 for seven miles to mile marker 13 and the dirt pullouts along the highway at Garrapata State Park. It's four miles south of Point Lobos State Park and easy to miss; go slowly and watch for cars parked alongside the road. The Soberanes Point Trail begins on the east side of the road.

Contact: Garrapata State Park, Big Sur, 831/667-2315 or 831/649-2836, www.parks.ca.gov.

16 LUPINE, WATERFALL, AND MESA LOOP
3.2 mi/1.5 hr 🏃2 ⛰8

in Garland Ranch Regional Park near Carmel

Map 8.1, page 425

Garland Ranch's excellent visitors center is the perfect place to begin your trip to this 4,500-acre park. Take a look inside, get a trail map, and learn a few things about the area's animals, trees, and wildflowers. The center is also the trailhead for this combined loop on Lupine, Waterfall, and Mesa Trails. Although the park's waterfall flows only during the wettest of rainy seasons, its well maintained trails are good to walk year-round. Begin by heading to the left (southeast) from the visitors center on Lupine Loop, which travels along the open, flat floodplains of the Carmel River. In 0.5 mile, leave the loop and continue straight on the Waterfall Trail, then climb through a more shady area to the rocky cliff where the waterfall sometimes falls. Beyond it, you'll ascend more seriously to the mesa, a large high meadow with views of Carmel Valley and beyond. Continuing uphill, 300 feet to the south lies Mesa Pond, which offers year-round fishing for smallmouth bass and bluegill (catch and release only, no fishing license required). Two benches are situated at the pond's eastern edge. Follow Mesa Trail back downhill to the other side of Lupine Loop and follow Lupine Loop back to the visitors center. In springtime, expect to be wowed by the wildflower show. They don't call this "Lupine Loop" for nothing.

User Groups: Hikers, dogs, and horses. No mountain bikes. No wheelchair facilities.

Permits: No permits are required. Parking and access are free.

Maps: A free map of Garland Ranch Regional Park is available by download at www.mprpd. org. For topographic maps, go to the USGS website to download Mount Carmel and Carmel Valley.

Directions: From Highway 1 at Carmel, turn east on Carmel Valley Road. Drive 8.6 miles on Carmel Valley Road to the Garland Ranch parking area, on the right side of the road. From late spring to fall, you can walk across the river bridge from the parking lot to access the trails. In the winter months when the bridge is removed, walk 300 feet west of the parking lot and cross the vehicle bridge.

Contact: Garland Ranch Regional Park Visitor Center, 831/659-6065; Monterey Peninsula Regional Park District, Monterey, 831/659-4488 (ranger station) or 831/372-3196 (administrative office), www.mprpd.org.

17 SNIVLEY'S RIDGE TRAIL
5.6 mi/3.0 hr 🥾3 ⛰️8

in Garland Ranch Regional Park near Carmel

Map 8.1, page 425

If it's winter or spring, a trip to the top of Snivley's Ridge could be just what you need to keep your hiking legs in shape. It's a healthy, 1,600-foot climb up to the ridge, plus a 250-foot climb to get to the ridge's highest point, so be prepared to pant a little. Much of the walk is exposed; be sure to bring water, and pick a cool day to hike the trail. From the visitors center, set out on either side of Lupine Loop (heading left is a little shorter), and continue uphill on Mesa Trail to its junction with Fern Trail. This stretch is moist and shady, so enjoy it

while you can. Follow Fern Trail as it steeply ascends, turn left on Sage Trail and then right on Sky Trail, and continue to climb. Well-graded switchbacks make it easier. Many people stop where Sky Trail meets Snivley's Ridge Trail, at a bench with a panoramic view of Carmel Valley, the forested Santa Lucia Mountains, and the ocean. But those determined to go as high as possible should turn right on Snivley's Ridge Trail and walk another 0.75 mile west to the ridge with its spectacular views of Carmel Bay and the Monterey Peninsula. Turn left on the trail that leads to the park's highest point at 2,038 feet. Note that if you want to get to this high point via a slightly longer but less steep route, you can follow Mesa Trail all the way to Sky Trail and bypass the steep Fern Trail.

User Groups: Hikers, dogs, and horses. No mountain bikes. No wheelchair facilities.

Permits: No permits are required. Parking and access are free.

Maps: A free map of Garland Ranch Regional Park is available by download at www.mprpd. org. For topographic maps, go to the USGS website to download Mount Carmel and Carmel Valley.

Directions: From Highway 1 at Carmel, turn east on Carmel Valley Road. Drive 8.6 miles on Carmel Valley Road to the Garland Ranch parking area, on the right side of the road. From late spring to fall, you can walk across the river bridge from the parking lot to access the trails. In the winter months when the bridge is removed, walk 300 feet west of the parking lot and cross the vehicle bridge.

Contact: Garland Ranch Regional Park Visitor Center, 831/659-6065; Monterey Peninsula Regional Park District, Monterey, 831/659-4488 (ranger station) or 831/372-3196 (administrative office), www.mprpd.org.

18 CONDOR GULCH AND HIGH PEAKS LOOP

5.3 mi/3.0-5.0 hr   🚶3 ⛰9

in Pinnacles National Park near Soledad

Map 8.1, page 425

The Condor Gulch Trail begins across the road from the Bear Gulch Nature Center, and it's a good 30-minute climb up the hill on a smooth, winding trail to an overlook of High Peaks. Starting early is recommended, especially in warmer temperatures, since this trail is exposed and can get extremely hot in the afternoons. The scent of wild black sage is enticingly aromatic along the route, and your eyes are continually drawn to the colorful lichens growing on equally colorful rocks. The overlook is a piped railing on a high ledge, and it's a good spot to look out over the canyon you just climbed. It's also a good turnaround spot if you don't want to go farther. If you do, continue uphill for 0.7 mile to a junction with High Peaks Trail and turn left. In just over a half mile, you'll reach a split in the trail. One path heads toward the steep and narrow section of the High Peaks Trail; the other toward the Tunnel Trail. Here, people who are afraid of heights should consider taking Tunnel Trail downhill. They can then turn left on the Juniper Canyon Trail to meet up with their fellow hikers at a bench and an overlook area at the junction of Juniper Canyon Trail and High Peaks Trail. This adds about one mile to the total mileage of this hike. Those willing to have an adventure should continue on the High Peaks Trail through narrow passageways and over and under the steep rock formations of the High Peaks.

In many places, the trail is a series of steps and handrails that have been carved into the rock. The near-vertical drop-offs appear daunting, but this trail gives an amazing up-close view of the rock formations in addition to chances of seeing falcons or California condors. After 0.7 mile, you'll reach Scout Peak, where there is a bench, a fine view to the west, and a restroom. Take advantage of any or all of these, then turn left to stay on the High Peaks

Trail and head back to Bear Gulch. You'll have to walk down Moses Spring Trail a short distance to get back to your car. There is an option to add about a mile to this hike by visiting the reservoir and Bear Gulch Cave. That detour takes a right turn at the Rim Trail about 1.5 miles below Scout Peak.

User Groups: Hikers only. No dogs, horses, or mountain bikes. No wheelchair facilities.

Permits: No permits are required. There is a $15 per vehicle entrance fee, good for seven days, at Pinnacles National Park.

Maps: A free map of Pinnacles National Park is available at the visitors center or by download at www.nps.gov/pinn. For topographic maps, go to the USGS website to download Bickmore Canyon and North Chalone Peak.

Directions: From King City on U.S. 101, take the First Street exit and head east. First Street turns into Highway G13/Bitterwater Road. Follow it for 15 miles to Highway 25, where you turn left (north). Follow Highway 25 for 14 miles to Highway 146. Turn left on Highway 146 and drive 1.9 miles to Pinnacles Visitors Center, then continue another three miles to Bear Gulch Nature Center. The trailhead for the Condor Gulch Trail is across the road from Bear Gulch Nature Center.

Alternatively, from Gilroy, drive south on U.S. 101 for two miles and take the Highway 25 exit. Drive south on Highway 25 for 43 miles to Highway 146. Turn right on Highway 146 and drive 1.9 miles to Pinnacles Visitors Center, then continue another three miles to Bear Gulch Nature Center. The trailhead for the Condor Gulch Trail is across the road from Bear Gulch Nature Center.

Contact: Pinnacles National Park, Paicines, 831/389-4485, www.nps.gov/pinn.

19 BEAR GULCH CAVE

2.2 mi/1.5 hr   🚶2 ⛰9

in Pinnacles National Park near Soledad

Map 8.1, page 425

Pinnacles National Park is well loved for its

© ANN MARIE BROWN

Pinnacles National Park

craggy volcanic formations, abundant hiking trails, and challenging rock climbing. But what many visitors come to see is Bear Gulch Cave, a tunnel-like jumble of boulders formed by thousands of years of water erosion. Bear Gulch Cave was closed in 1998 in order to protect its local residents—a colony of Townsend's big-eared bats. In 2004, the Park Service installed a system of gates to protect the roosting bats and allow visitors access to the lower part of the cave for 10 months of the year (mid-July–mid-May). During short periods in October and March when the bats leave their home, the entire cave is open to visitors, and this is the best time to come. (Phone the park before making the long drive to confirm the current status of Bear Gulch Cave; the bats don't conform to an exact timetable, and occasionally the entire cave is closed for safety due to flooding.) Be sure to come prepared for this adventure. Bring a flashlight and good walking shoes, and be mentally prepared to wedge through clefts in the rock, duck your head under ledges, and squint in the darkness to locate painted arrows pointing the way through the maze. The

adventure is easy enough for children to accomplish, but equally fun for visitors of all ages.
User Groups: Hikers only. No dogs, horses, or mountain bikes. No wheelchair facilities.
Permits: No permits are required. There is a $15 per vehicle entrance fee, good for seven days, at Pinnacles National Park.
Maps: A free map of Pinnacles National Park is available at the visitors center or by download at www.nps.gov/pinn. For topographic maps, go to the USGS website to download Bickmore Canyon and North Chalone Peak.
Directions: From King City on U.S. 101, take the First Street exit and head east. First Street turns into Highway G13/Bitterwater Road. Follow it for 15 miles to Highway 25, where you turn left (north). Follow Highway 25 for 14 miles to Highway 146. Turn left on Highway 146 and drive 1.9 miles to Pinnacles Visitors Center, then continue another three miles to Bear Gulch Nature Center and the Bear Gulch Cave trailhead.

Alternatively, from Gilroy, drive south on U.S. 101 for two miles and take the Highway 25 exit. Drive south on Highway 25 for 43 miles to Highway 146. Turn right on Highway 146 and drive 1.9 miles to Pinnacles Visitors Center, then continue another three miles to Bear Gulch Nature Center and the Bear Gulch Cave trailhead.
Contact: Pinnacles National Park, Paicines, 831/389-4485, www.nps.gov/pinn.

20 NORTH CHALONE PEAK
9.0 mi/3.0-5.0 hr 🏃4 ⛰9

in Pinnacles National Park near Soledad

Map 8.1, page 425

Sure, the High Peaks at Pinnacles National Park are high—about 2,700 feet. But if you want to go higher and get a better look around, take this hike to North Chalone Peak. Located in the western area of the park at 3,304 feet in elevation, North Chalone Peak has a decommissioned fire lookout tower on its summit. It's a great place to take in the view and enjoy some peace and quiet. This trail is much less traveled than the popular High Peaks Loop.

Take Moses Spring Trail from the Bear Gulch Nature Center parking lot, and then climb the stairs up to Bear Gulch Reservoir. Continue over the dam and along the left side of the reservoir until you meet the signed trail for North Chalone Peak. You are likely to see a posse of rock climbers who are busy doing their thing on the cliff faces around the reservoir. As you start along the North Chalone Peak Trail, you are only one mile from the nature center, but you've left the vast majority of people behind. Enjoy the fascinating volcanic rock formations and spring wildflowers on the next stretch of trail. At 3.5 miles, you'll climb a stile to cross the park's pig-proof fence, then follow the trail until it meets up with a fire road. This road will lead you to another stile over the pig fence. After crossing this fence, the summit is a short distance ahead. The final 0.75 mile is the steepest stretch of the whole trip, but the reward at the top is a fine view of the Salinas River curving through its valley, the Santa Lucia Mountains, and all of Pinnacles. During winter the Santa Lucias may be snow dusted, and on very rare, crystal-clear days, you can see all the way to the Pacific Ocean.

User Groups: Hikers only. No dogs, horses, or mountain bikes. No wheelchair facilities.

Permits: No permits are required. There is a $15 per vehicle entrance fee at Pinnacles National Park, good for seven days.

Maps: A free map of Pinnacles National Park is available at the visitors center or by download at www.nps.gov/pinn. For topographic maps, go to the USGS website to download Bickmore Canyon and North Chalone Peak.

Directions: From King City on U.S. 101, take the First Street exit and head east. First Street turns into Highway G13/Bitterwater Road. Follow it for 15 miles to Highway 25, where you turn left (north). Follow Highway 25 for 14 miles to Highway 146. Turn left on Highway 146 and drive 1.9 miles to Pinnacles Visitors Center, then continue another three miles to Bear Gulch Nature Center and the trailhead.

Alternatively, from Gilroy, drive south on U.S. 101 for two miles and take the Highway 25 exit. Drive south on Highway 25 for 43 miles to Highway 146. Turn right on Highway 146 and drive 1.9 miles to Pinnacles Visitors Center, then continue another three miles to Bear Gulch Nature Center and the trailhead.

Contact: Pinnacles National Park, Paicines, 831/389-4485, www.nps.gov/pinn.

21 BALCONIES CAVE
2.4 mi/1.5 hr   🏃‍♀️2 ⛰️10

in Pinnacles National Park near Soledad

Map 8.1, page 425

Pinnacles National Park has two famous sets of caves: Bear Gulch Cave, on the east side of the park; and Balconies Cave, on the west. Access to Bear Gulch Cave is often partially restricted in order to protect the resident bats, but Balconies Cave is open almost year-round (except immediately after the heaviest rains when the water can be dangerously high). Got your flashlight and sturdy footwear? Then get ready for tons of fun. Set off on the Balconies Trail, following the often dry west fork of Chalone Creek toward the narrow canyon between Machete Ridge and the Balconies. A mere 0.6 mile brings you to some huge, colorful, lichen-covered volcanic rocks. The sounds of the wind in the gray pines and the scurrying of squirrels keep you company. At the junction with the Balconies Cliffs Trail, you have a choice: go left over the cliffs and then loop back through the cave, or go right to enter the cave immediately. If you go right, you face a steep downhill scramble that some less agile hikers find difficult. (It's much easier to climb up this than down it.) Either way, you'll eventually find yourself in the cave. Turn on your flashlight and proceed through a narrow slotlike canyon, squeezing through clefts in the rock, ducking under boulders, and climbing down rocky staircases. Note that if you drove all the way to the east side of the park but you want to visit Balconies Cave, you don't have to drive 1.5 hours around the park's perimeter to get to this trailhead. Balconies Cave can also be reached from the east side via a much longer hike on the Old Pinnacles Trail.

User Groups: Hikers only. No dogs, horses, or mountain bikes. No wheelchair facilities.

Permits: No permits are required. There is a $15 per vehicle entrance fee at Pinnacles National Park, good for seven days.

Maps: A free map of Pinnacles National Park is available at the ranger station or by download at www.nps.gov/pinn. For topographic maps, go to the USGS website to download Bickmore Canyon and North Chalone Peak.

Directions: From Salinas, drive south on U.S. 101 for 22 miles to Soledad, and take the Soledad/Highway 146 exit. Drive east on Highway 146 for 10 miles to the West Side Visitors Contact Station. (The road is signed for West Pinnacles.) Then continue another two miles to the road's end at the trailhead parking lot. (Note that you can also hike to Balconies Cave from the east side of the park via the Old Pinnacles Trail.)

Contact: Pinnacles National Park, Paicines, 831/389-4485, www.nps.gov/pinn.

22 JUNIPER CANYON AND HIGH PEAKS LOOP

8.4 mi/5.0 hr

in Pinnacles National Park near Soledad

Map 8.1, page 425

Pinnacles National Park is a hiker's park. The first clue you get is that no road connects the east and west sides of the park, so the only way to get from one side to the other is to walk. And that's just fine, especially since the park's first-rate trail system makes it possible to string together a loop tour around the park on the Juniper Canyon Trail, High Peaks Trail (the part known as the Steep and Narrow Section), Old Pinnacles Trail, and Balconies Trail. If you follow the trails in this order, you get almost all your climbing done in the first half of the trip and then have a fairly easy and flat home stretch.

Begin hiking from the right side of the large parking lot at the end of Highway 146, following Juniper Canyon Trail from grasslands into the rocky hills. The trail gets steeper as you go, but it's well built and has many switchbacks. Ignore the Tunnel Trail turnoff at 1.2 miles, and keep climbing to the junction with High Peaks Trail, at 1.8 miles. Here, at a saddle, are fine views to the west and east, as well as a bench and restroom. The High Peaks Trail goes both north and southeast. Turn north (left) and prepare yourself for the most thrilling part of the trip: a narrow and exciting stretch of trail with many handrails and footholds carved into the rock. Continue on the High Peaks Trail for 3.3 miles until it ends at the Bench Trail. Make a left onto the Bench Trail and soon it becomes the Old Pinnacles Trail, a pleasant route that meanders along the west fork of Chalone Creek. In winter, the creek runs with water, and spring wildflowers are tremendous. In 2.3 miles, you'll go through six unbridged creek crossings and reach a fork for the Balconies Trail. If you've never been to Balconies Cave, take the left fork, which leads you through it. (The right fork climbs above the cave and offers some excellent views.) After ducking your head and bending your knees a lot as you wander through the cave, you'll come out to an easy and flat section of the Balconies Trail, which brings you back to the trailhead parking lot. If you pick a cool day and carry plenty of water, this is a stellar half-day hike at Pinnacles.

User Groups: Hikers only. No dogs, horses, or mountain bikes. No wheelchair facilities.

Permits: No permits are required. There is a $15 per vehicle entrance fee at Pinnacles National Park, good for seven days.

Maps: A free map of Pinnacles National Park is available at the ranger station or by download at www.nps.gov/pinn. For topographic maps, go to the USGS website to download Bickmore Canyon and North Chalone Peak.

Directions: From Salinas, drive south on U.S. 101 for 22 miles to Soledad, and take the Soledad/Highway 146 exit. Drive east on Highway 146 for 10 miles to the West Side

Visitors Contact Station. (The road is signed for West Pinnacles.) Then continue another two miles to the road's end at the trailhead parking lot.

Contact: Pinnacles National Park, Paicines, 831/389-4485, www.nps.gov/pinn.

23 MILL CREEK TRAIL
5.4 mi/2.5 hr   🚶2 ⛰9

in Mill Creek Redwood Preserve

Map 8.1, page 425

Mill Creek Redwood Preserve is a special place on the Big Sur Coast. In fact, it's so special that you have to obtain a permit in order to hike there. Only eight permits per day are given out for this trail, with a maximum of five people allowed per permit. And that's how it should be, because this redwood grove has the sanctity of a holy cathedral. Although Mill Creek canyon was logged to some extent in the early 20th century, some of the redwoods here are still old-growth, and huge in size. The preserve is home to many special creatures, including a few magnificent owl species: great horned, northern saw-whet, and spotted. The Mill Creek Trail, built in 2006, laterals across Mill Creek's canyon, traveling under a dense canopy of tanoaks, madrones, and redwoods, and crossing over cascading streams on sturdy footbridges. In the wettest months of the year, these small streams produce lovely waterfalls. The trail very gradually gains 250 feet in elevation until it tops out at a high viewpoint that overlooks the Santa Lucia Mountains and the coast. A few wooden benches invite hikers to linger a while over the view, which overlooks the Santa Lucia Mountains and the coast.

User Groups: Hikers only. No dogs, horses, or mountain bikes. No wheelchair facilities.

Permits: A free permit is required to enter the preserve; go to www.mprpd.org to reserve a permit at least 48 hours in advance of your hike. Permits are processed only on weekdays. Parking and access are free.

Maps: For topographic maps, go to the USGS

website to download Mount Carmel and Big Sur.

Directions: From Carmel, drive south on Highway 1 for 12 miles, past Garrapata State Park, to the left (east) turnoff for Palo Colorado Road, about 0.25 mile south of Rocky Point Restaurant. Turn left and drive east 6.8 miles to the trailhead. Park alongside the road.

Contact: Monterey Peninsula Regional Park District, Monterey, 831/659-4488 or 831/372-3196, www.mprpd.org.

24 SKINNER RIDGE TRAIL TO DEVIL'S PEAK
7.6 mi/3.5 hr or 2 days   🚶3 ⛰8

in the Ventana Wilderness near Carmel Valley

Map 8.1, page 425

What's the best thing about this trip? The far-off ocean views in the first mile of the climb? The white marble of giant Pico Blanco to the southwest? The colors of the oak leaves in autumn? The huge old madrone trees that pepper Skinner Ridge? It's hard to decide; you'd better go see for yourself. Pick a cool and clear day to make the trip, preferably in autumn, or arm yourself with a ton of sunscreen and water in summer. The trailhead is at 2,000 feet in an area that was severely burned in the wildfires of 2008, but the trail has been carefully rebuilt and is in better shape now than it was before the fire. It begins with an ascent through chaparral, offering many wide views. Then the trail enters the trees (madrones and oaks) and twists its way to a short, steep ascent to the top of Skinner Ridge, at 3,450 feet and 2.1 miles out. A wide bulldozer line runs up the ridge, left from the huge Marble Cone fire of the 1970s. From the ridge, backpackers usually continue down the other side for 0.75 mile to a trail junction for Turner Creek. Apple Tree Camp is a left turn and one mile away—a good place for an overnight. Day hikers should proceed straight ahead at that junction for the climb to Devil's Peak, elevation 4,158 feet, and one mile farther.

That final mile will get you huffing and puffing for sure, but hey, exercise is good for you, right?

User Groups: Hikers, dogs, and horses. No mountain bikes. No wheelchair facilities.

Permits: No day hiking permits are required. A parking fee of $5 per vehicle is charged.

Maps: A Ventana Wilderness or Los Padres National Forest map is available from the U.S. Forest Service. For topographic maps, go to the USGS website to download Mount Carmel and Big Sur.

Directions: From Carmel, drive south on Highway 1 for 12 miles, past Garrapata State Park, to the left (east) turnoff for Palo Colorado Road, south of Rocky Point Restaurant. Turn left and drive eight miles to Bottcher's Gap Campground. The Skinner Ridge Trail begins at the edge of the parking lot.

Contact: Big Sur Station, Highway 1, Big Sur, 831/667-2315; Los Padres National Forest, Monterey Ranger District, King City, 831/385-5434, www.fs.usda.gov/lpnf.

25 MOLERA POINT TRAIL
2.5 mi/1.5 hr 🥾1 ⛰9

in Andrew Molera State Park north of Big Sur

Map 8.1, page 425

Andrew Molera is a low-key state park without all the development and fanfare that often come with state park status. But the park has plenty to offer for hikers and coast lovers. An easy trail leads from the park's main parking lot to Molera Point, where you can look down on spectacular Molera Beach and count the sea lions lying on the rocks. To reach the point, take the trail from the right side of the main parking lot, signed for the campground (not the main trail to the beach, which starts with a bridge crossing). The Molera Point Trail stays on the north side of the Big Sur River and winds past the park's walk-in camp, set in a wide meadow, and historic Cooper Cabin, which was built in 1861 and is the oldest structure on the Big Sur coast. At the river's mouth, the trail forks to the right, heading out to Molera Point. Check out

the view from this often windswept promontory; then if the tide is low, go play on the beach at the river's edge before heading back.

User Groups: Hikers and horses. No dogs or mountain bikes. No wheelchair facilities.

Permits: No permits are required. A $10 day-use fee is charged per vehicle.

Maps: A map of Andrew Molera State Park is available at the entrance station or by free download at www.parks.ca.gov. For a topographic map, go to the USGS website to download Big Sur.

Directions: From Carmel, drive 22 miles south on Highway 1 to Andrew Molera State Park's main entrance, on the west side of the highway. Trails begin at the parking lot. The park is two miles north of Big Sur.

Contact: Andrew Molera State Park, Big Sur, 831/667-2315 or 831/649-2836, www.parks.ca.gov.

26 MOLERA STATE PARK LOOP
8.0 mi/4.0 hr 🥾3 ⛰10

in Andrew Molera State Park north of Big Sur

Map 8.1, page 425

This big loop around the western side of Andrew Molera State Park is easiest in summer, when the footbridge is in place over the Big Sur River. If the bridge isn't there, you must take off your shoes and socks and suffer through a very cold ford over smooth, rounded rocks. But this trail is worth the effort. It offers several miles of lovely ocean vistas, plus a visit to a remote beach. Start by taking the path from the west side of the parking lot and immediately crossing the river. In a few minutes of walking, you'll leave the crowds behind as you turn left (south) on the River Trail, then in less than a mile, turn right on the single-track Hidden Trail. Enjoy a heart-pumping climb through forest and meadows up to the Ridge Trail, where you turn left and hike southward, paralleling the ocean. The Ridge Trail is a wide fire road and rolls gently, still heading generally uphill. In addition to the ocean vistas to the west, you also have fine views inland of Big Sur's rugged peaks, and you pass through a small, surprising grove of redwood trees.

At 3.5 miles, the Ridge Trail meets the Panorama Trail at a bench and overlook point. Turn right and start to switchback steeply downhill toward the ocean, enjoying more wide views all the way. Spring wildflowers are lovely along the open hillsides. As you near the coast, you'll reach a junction with the Spring Trail. Turn left for a few hundred feet to a lovely, driftwood-laden beach. This makes a perfect lunch stop, provided the wind isn't howling. A fascinating log jam at the beach's entrance makes for great photographs. For your return, follow the Bluffs Trail 2.5 miles back to Molera Beach. This is the loveliest stretch of the entire loop, offering long and beautiful looks at Molera Point and beach and Point Sur Light Station. Finally, take the trail from Molera Beach back to the parking lot. Wow, what a perfect Big Sur day.

User Groups: Hikers and horses. No dogs. Mountain bikes are allowed on Ridge Trail and part of Bluffs Trail only. No wheelchair facilities.

Permits: No permits are required. A $10 day-use fee is charged per vehicle.

Maps: A map of Andrew Molera State Park is available at the entrance station or by free download at www.parks.ca.gov. For a topographic map, go to the USGS website to download Big Sur.

Directions: From Carmel, drive 22 miles south on Highway 1 to Andrew Molera State Park's main entrance, on the west side of the highway. Trails begin at the parking lot. (The park is two miles north of Big Sur.)

Contact: Andrew Molera State Park, Big Sur, 831/667-2315 or 831/649-2836, www.parks. ca.gov.

© ANN MARIE BROWN

Andrew Molera State Park

27 VALLEY VIEW AND PFEIFFER FALLS

3.0 mi/1.0 hr

in Pfeiffer Big Sur State Park near Big Sur

Map 8.1, page 425

The Pfeiffer Falls Trail section of this popular hiking loop suffered serious damage in the 2008 Basin Fire and will be closed from June 2016 to January 2018 for reconstruction, but you can still hike the Valley View Trail to see Pfeiffer Falls, a 60-foot waterfall that streams down a vertical rock face. By sticking with Valley View Trail, you'll also gain a great view of the Big Sur Valley. Start at the Ernst Ewoldsen Memorial Nature Center at Pfeiffer Big Sur State Park. Follow Valley View Trail uphill through the redwoods for about a mile to a trail fork. If the right-hand trail to Pfeiffer Falls is open, switchback downhill for 0.2 mile to a bridge over Pfeiffer Creek located near the base of the falls. Enjoy the watery splendor, then backtrack and continue uphill beyond the junction to the high point of Valley View Trail, where the shady redwoods are replaced by sun-loving oaks. Brilliant blooms of Douglas iris color the ground in the spring. The path tops out at an overlook of the Big Sur River Valley looking northwest to Point Sur. The sight of tiny cars on Highway 1 somewhat diminishes the effect, but it's still a worthy view. Until the Pfeiffer Falls Trail reopens, your return trip is a simple backtrack on Valley View Trail back to the nature center.

User Groups: Hikers only. No dogs, horses, or mountain bikes. No wheelchair facilities.

Permits: No permits are required. A $10 day-use fee is charged per vehicle.

Maps: A map of Pfeiffer Big Sur State Park is available at the entrance station or by free download at www.parks.ca.gov. For a topographic map, go to the USGS website to download Big Sur.

Directions: From Carmel, drive 26 miles south on Highway 1 to Pfeiffer Big Sur State Park, on the east side of the highway. It's two miles south of Big Sur. Drive through the entrance kiosk, turn left at the lodge, and then turn right, following the signs to the Pfeiffer Falls trailhead and the nature center. Park just beyond the nature center. The trail is on the left side of the lot, signed as Oak Grove Trail, Valley View Trail, and Pfeiffer Falls Trail. If the small parking lot is full, you may have to park by the lodge and walk to the trailhead.

Contact: Pfeiffer Big Sur State Park, Big Sur, 831/667-2315 or 831/649-2836, www.parks.ca.gov.

28 MOUNT MANUEL

9.0 mi/5.0 hr

on the southern edge of the Ventana Wilderness near Big Sur

Map 8.1, page 425

This trail leads to one of the best vantage points in the Ventana Wilderness, the summit of Mount Manuel, where all of Big Sur, the Santa Lucia Mountains, and the Pacific Ocean are spread out before you. Odd as it seems, the trail starts out by the softball fields and picnic areas at Pfeiffer Big Sur State Park. Over the course of the trail's 4.5-mile length, you'll climb 3,100 feet to Mount Manuel's summit at 3,379 feet in elevation, so make sure you have fresh soles on your boots and plenty of water. Pick a cool day to make the climb, because although the trail starts in the trees, the vast majority of the route is completely exposed. Winter and spring are usually the best seasons to head for the summit, both for the clarity of the view (less chance of fog) and for cool temperatures.

Negotiate your way through a half-mile series of signed state park trails to access the official start of the Mount Manuel Trail. You'll enter Los Padres National Forest and begin a long series of switchbacks over chaparral-covered slopes. As you climb, you gain views of the Big Sur River canyon and the coast. About three miles from the start, the trail enters a forest of tanoaks, bay laurels, and redwoods, then exits it again, returning to the chaparral. Finally you near the summit, or rather, a series of summits. Head for the obvious highest point, where the view of the vast Pacific Ocean and the beauty of the Santa Lucia Mountains will blow you away.

User Groups: Hikers only. No dogs, horses, or mountain bikes. No wheelchair facilities.

Permits: No day hiking permits are required. A $10 day-use fee is charged per vehicle.

Maps: A Ventana Wilderness or Los Padres National Forest map is available from the U.S. Forest Service. For topographic maps, go to the USGS website to download Pfeiffer Point and Big Sur.

Directions: From Carmel, drive 26 miles south on Highway 1 to Pfeiffer Big Sur State Park, on the east side of the highway. It's two miles south of Big Sur. Drive through the entrance kiosk and continue straight past the campfire center to the parking lot near the picnic areas and softball field. The trailhead is signed for Oak Grove Trail and Mount Manuel.

Contact: Big Sur Station, Highway 1, Big Sur, 831/667-2315 or 831/649-2836, www.parks.ca.gov; Los Padres National Forest, Monterey Ranger District, King City, 831/385-5434, www.fs.usda.gov/lpnf.

29 BUZZARDS ROOST OVERLOOK
4.0 mi/2.0 hr   🏃3 ⛰9

in Pfeiffer Big Sur State Park near Big Sur

Map 8.1, page 425

Hikers looking for a bit of a challenge in Pfeiffer Big Sur State Park will want to try out this trail to the Buzzards Roost Overlook. Compared to other trails in the park, this trail gets surprisingly little traffic unless there are large groups camping at the nearby group campground. The trail leads along the Big Sur River through a forest of many splendid redwoods, switches back uphill onto slopes filled with oaks and bays, and finally climbs into chaparral country. You get to walk in every kind of Big Sur terrain. High up on Pfeiffer Ridge, there's a 360-degree view of the Pacific Ocean, the Big Sur River

gorge, and the Santa Lucia Mountains, providing a fine reward for your effort in climbing here. The trailhead is at 200 feet in elevation, and the overlook is at nearly 1,000 feet.

User Groups: Hikers only. No dogs, horses, or mountain bikes. No wheelchair facilities.

Permits: No permits are required. A $10 day-use fee is charged per vehicle.

Maps: A map of Pfeiffer Big Sur State Park is available at the entrance station or by free download at www.parks.ca.gov. For topographic maps, go to the USGS website to download Big Sur and Pfeiffer Point.

Directions: From Carmel, drive 26 miles south on Highway 1 to Pfeiffer Big Sur State Park, on the east side of the highway. It's two miles south of Big Sur. Drive through the entrance kiosk, go past the lodge, and turn right to cross the bridge over the Big Sur River. A parking area is on the left side of the road. The Buzzards Roost trailhead is signed.

Contact: Pfeiffer Big Sur State Park, Big Sur, 831/667-2315 or 831/649-2836, www.parks.ca.gov.

30 SYKES HOT SPRINGS
20.0 mi/2 days   🏃3 ⛰9

in the Ventana Wilderness near Big Sur

Map 8.1, page 425

The trip to Sykes Hot Springs is one that just about every California backpacker takes at one time or another. This is a quintessential Big Sur/Ventana Wilderness trip, with deep swimming holes, three hot springs pools, and plenty of coastal mountain scenery. Although much of the land surrounding the Pine Ridge Trail to the springs was badly burned in 2008 wildfires, the trail has been thoroughly cleared and maintained and this trip remains as popular as ever, so plan your trip for the off-season if possible. Fall and winter are the best times to visit, and if you go on a weekday, you might just get the hot springs all to yourself. The first four miles of Pine Ridge Trail will have you huffing and puffing through shadeless switchbacks, with only occasional breaks as the path travels through small redwood groves. The route eventually levels and gets much easier. At a junction just past the four-mile mark, the left trail leads to Ventana Camp, one mile farther. This camp near Ventana Creek makes a great overnight for people who have gotten a late start; it even has a "wilderness toilet." At 5.4 miles, the trail reaches Terrace Creek Camp, another option for spending the night. At 7.0 miles, you reach the Big Sur River for the first time, and another camp at Barlow Flat. You'll cross the river at 9.7 miles and head for Sykes Camp and the hot springs. Note that after a period of rain, this can be a difficult or even impossible ford, so if you plan to hike in the wet season, check on conditions before setting out. The hot springs are less than a quarter mile from the camp. Depending on current conditions, two or three pools are terraced along the Big Sur River. The largest of the group is 10 feet long and gracefully sheltered by a large boulder. It averages 100 degrees; the other pools are slightly cooler.

User Groups: Hikers, dogs, and horses. No mountain bikes. No wheelchair facilities.

Permits: A California campfire permit is required year-round for overnight stays whether you are using a camp stove or building a fire; permits are free and available online at fs.usda.gov/lpnf or in person at the Big Sur Visitors Center. An $8 parking fee is charged per vehicle.

Maps: A Ventana Wilderness or Los Padres National Forest map is available from the U.S. Forest Service. For topographic maps, go to the USGS website to download Pfeiffer Point, Partington Ridge, and Ventana Cones.

Directions: From Carmel, drive 30 miles south on Highway 1 to Big Sur Station, on the east side of the highway. It's three miles south of Big Sur. The Pine Ridge Trail begins behind the ranger station at the backpacker's parking lot.

Contact: Big Sur Station, Highway 1, Big Sur, 831/667-2315 or 831/649-2836; Los Padres National Forest, Monterey Ranger District, King City, 831/385-5434, www.fs.usda.gov/lpnf.

31 PARTINGTON POINT AND TANBARK TRAILS

4.0 mi/2.0 hr   🚶2 ⛰9

in Julia Pfeiffer Burns State Park south of Big Sur

Map 8.1, page 425

If you want to hike at Julia Pfeiffer Burns State Park without the crowds, a combined out-and-back trip on Partington Point and Tanbark Trails could be just your cup of tea. The two trails are about as different as any trails could be, except that they both start from the same point along Highway 1. The Partington Point Trail is a dirt road that leads westward and steeply downhill to an obvious fork at 0.5 mile. The right fork leads a few hundred feet to a tiny rock-strewn beach at Partington Creek's mouth. The left fork leads into the redwoods, across a wooden footbridge, and through a rock tunnel built in the 1880s by pioneer John Partington. On the tunnel's far side is the remains of a narrow dog-hole port at Partington Cove, where lumber was loaded onto seagoing freighters. Partington Point is home to the park's underwater playground of caves and natural bridges, but unless you're a scuba diver, you won't be able to see them. Instead, you can have a seat on a rock and look for sea otters, sea lions, and pelicans. Also keep your eyes peeled for spouting whales.

After visiting Partington Cove, hike back uphill and cross the highway to the start of Tanbark Trail, which leads along Partington Creek, heading inland. Much of this inland area was burned in the wildfires of 2008, but the forest is recovering quickly. You can walk a short half-mile loop on the trail (a bridge carries you across Partington Creek and then back down the other side), or you can continue farther, climbing steeply uphill for 1.5 miles to a confluence of streams at a spot known as Swiss Camp. A half-mile beyond Swiss Camp, your trail junctions with a fire road, which leads to the historic Tin House (it was constructed by Lathrop Brown in 1944 out of tin from two old gas stations), a total of 3.2 miles from the trailhead. Follow the fire road steeply downhill, enjoying fantastic coastal views all the way (hiking poles are handy for this steep descent). The dirt road ends at Highway 1, and you'll need to walk alongside the highway for a mile to get back to your car (head north, or to your right). Or, if you have arranged a car shuttle in advance, you can follow a new trail, built in 2013, that connects to the Ewoldsen Trail, a distance of about one mile.

User Groups: Hikers only. No dogs, horses, or mountain bikes. No wheelchair facilities.

Permits: No permits are required. Parking and access are free.

Maps: A map of Julia Pfeiffer Burns State Park is available at the entrance kiosk (2.2 miles south of this trailhead) or by free download at www.parks.ca.gov. For a topographic map, go to the USGS website to download Partington Ridge.

Directions: From Carmel, drive 34 miles south on Highway 1 to a dirt pullout along the highway and the trailheads for the Partington Point and Tanbark Trails. The trailheads are 10.5 miles south of Big Sur and 2.2 miles north of the main entrance to Julia Pfeiffer Burns State Park. Partington Point Trail is on the west side of the highway; Tanbark Trail is on the east side.

Contact: Julia Pfeiffer Burns State Park, Big Sur, 831/667-2315 or 831/649-2836, www.parks.ca.gov.

32 MCWAY FALLS OVERLOOK
0.5 mi/0.5 hr   🚶1 ⛰9

in Julia Pfeiffer Burns State Park south of Big Sur

Map 8.1, page 425   **BEST (**

After Yosemite Falls and Bridalveil Fall, McWay Falls is probably the waterfall that appears most often on family snapshots of California vacations. Although few know its name, its image is unforgettable: an 80-foot waterfall leaping off a rugged ocean bluff and pouring gracefully into the Pacific. The walk to the waterfall's overlook is on a paved trail that leads through a tunnel underneath Highway 1 and comes out to a spectacular overlook of McWay Cove. A bench is placed along the trail, and you can sit there and admire the action—and maybe even catch sight of a passing gray whale. You can continue a few hundred feet beyond the bench, where the trail ends at the ruins of Waterfall House, the home of Lathrop and Helen Hooper Brown in the 1940s. There's not much left of it now, but at one time, it was quite a place.

User Groups: Hikers only. No dogs, horses, or mountain bikes. The McWay Falls Overlook Trail is wheelchair-accessible via a special bridge that bypasses the stairs from the parking lot.

Permits: No permits are required. A $10 day-use fee is charged per vehicle.

Maps: A map of Julia Pfeiffer Burns State Park is available at the entrance kiosk or by free download at www.parks.ca.gov. For a topographic map, go to the USGS website to download Partington Ridge.

Directions: From Carmel, drive 37 miles south on Highway 1 to Julia Pfeiffer Burns State Park, located on the east side of the highway, 13 miles south of Big Sur. Drive through the entrance kiosk and park near the restrooms. The Overlook Trail starts on a series of wooden stairs across the pavement from the restrooms.

Contact: Julia Pfeiffer Burns State Park, Big Sur, 831/667-2315 or 831/649-2836, www.parks.ca.gov.

33 EWOLDSEN LOOP TRAIL
5.3 mi/2.5 hr   🚶3 ⛰5

in Julia Pfeiffer Burns State Park south of Big Sur

Map 8.1, page 425

The Ewoldsen Trail, one of the best day-hiking trails in all of Big Sur, was closed for several years after the 2008 Basin Fire, but is now open again and as spectacular as ever. The trail begins with an easy saunter along McWay Creek and its spectacular redwood forest, passing within a few yards of the second-largest redwood tree in Monterey County (there's no sign; you have to guess which one it is). Soon the trail splits, with Canyon Trail to the left and Ewoldsen Trail switchbacking uphill. Take the short Canyon Trail spur to its end, 0.25 mile away, and visit McWay Canyon's sweet little waterfall. Then retrace your steps to the junction and head uphill on Ewoldsen Trail, which climbs steadily above the tops of the tall redwood trees below. The next fork, about 1.5 miles in, is the beginning of the loop. Hike the right side first. You'll alternate between dense redwood forest and more sparse oak woodland until at 2.6 miles you'll see a spur trail signed as Overlook/Lookout. Take it and climb very steeply uphill for 0.25 mile until you come out to a wide, grassy ridgetop with stunning views over McWay Canyon and out to the ocean. After all your time in the forest, this bald, grassy viewpoint comes as quite a surprise. A bench and never-ending Pacific Views are yours for the taking, so pull out your lunch and your camera. California condors like this spot, too, so keep your eyes on the skies for these massive creatures. After a rest, retrace your steps to the junction, bear right, and take the downhill side of the loop. You'll notice a lot of recent trail work here as the park tried to slow the massive erosion that occurred after the Basin Fire. The steep dropoffs offer more fine views of the ocean before you drop back into redwood forest. The total elevation gain along the trail is 1,600 feet. Note that if you want to hike a bit farther, it's now possible to hike a connector trail from this trail to the Tanbark Trail and the Tin House, a distance of about one mile (see Tanbark Trail in this chapter).

User Groups: Hikers only. No dogs, horses, or mountain bikes. No wheelchair facilities.

Permits: No permits are required. A $10 day-use fee is charged per vehicle.

Maps: A map of Julia Pfeiffer Burns State Park is available at the entrance kiosk or by free download at www.parks.ca.gov. For a topographic map, go to the USGS website to download Partington Ridge.

Directions: From Carmel, drive 37 miles south on Highway 1 to Julia Pfeiffer Burns State Park, on the east side of the highway. It's 13 miles south of Big Sur. Drive through the entrance kiosk, and park near the restrooms. The Ewoldsen Trail starts near the picnic areas on the inland side of the parking area.

Contact: Julia Pfeiffer Burns State Park, Big Sur, 831/667-2315 or 831/649-2836, www.parks.ca.gov.

34 PINE VALLEY
10.6–13.0 mi/6.0 hr or 2 days
🥾 3 ⛺ 10

in the Ventana Wilderness near Carmel Valley

Map 8.1, page 425

The Pine Valley hike is a great one-night backpacking trip or long day hike into the Ventana Wilderness and can easily be extended into a 13-mile loop. The hike begins on the northern end of Pine Ridge Trail at China Campground, following an up-and-down course that soon becomes more down than up. At 3.5 miles, you turn right on Carmel River Trail and descend some more to the headwaters of the Carmel River and the beginning of a fir and ponderosa pine forest. Pine Valley Camp is 5.3 miles from the trailhead, set in lush Pine Valley, a spacious high meadow lined with ferns, ponderosa pines, and rocky sandstone formations. A short side trip to Pine Falls is possible from the camp; follow a well-worn route downstream along the river for 0.5 mile to the waterfall. From there, you can retrace your steps to the trailhead for a 10.6-mile round-trip, or make camp at Pine Valley, or take the trail from the upper end of camp, which meets up with Pine Ridge Trail. Turn left on Pine Ridge Trail and hike back to the trailhead to complete a 13-mile loop.

User Groups: Hikers, dogs, and horses. No mountain bikes. No wheelchair facilities.

Permits: A California campfire permit is required year-round for overnight stays whether you are using a camp stove or building a fire; permits are free and available online at fs.usda gov/lpnf or in person at the King City Forest Service office or the Big Sur Visitors Center.

Maps: A Ventana Wilderness or Los Padres National Forest map is available from the U.S. Forest Service. For a topographic map, go to the USGS website to download Chews Ridge.

Directions: From Greenfield on U.S. 101, take the G-16/Monterey County Road exit and drive west for 29 miles. Turn south on Tassajara Road and drive 1.3 miles to Cachagua Road. Turn left and drive nine miles to the trailhead, located just past the turnoff for China Campground. High-clearance vehicles are recommended. The county sometimes closes the road during bad weather; call the Monterey Ranger District before traveling.

Contact: Los Padres National Forest, Monterey Ranger District, King City, 831/385-5434, www.fs.usda.gov/lpnf.

35 LIMEKILN TRAIL AND LIMEKILN FALLS

1.8 mi/1.0 hr   🏃2   ⛰10

in Limekiln State Park south of Big Sur

Map 8.1, page 425

What's Big Sur's best-kept secret? That's easy—the hiking trail at Limekiln State Park. The state park is so far south of Big Sur that it doesn't get inundated by visitors, as does Pfeiffer Big Sur and Julia Pfeiffer Burns State Parks. The Limekiln Trail leads from the inland campground into a gorgeous redwood forest. It follows Limekiln Creek for a half mile to the park's namesake limekilns, which were used to make limestone bricks and cement in the 1880s. The four kilns look like giant smokestacks with mossy, brick bottoms; they're interesting to see and photograph, but in the wet season, they are not the biggest attraction on this trail. What is? A fork off the main trail leads to Limekiln Falls, a spectacular 100-foot waterfall that drops over a limestone face. When the water is running with vigor, you'll probably end up with wet feet as you boulder-hop your way to its base, but it's worth it. This waterfall is a beauty.

If you find yourself enchanted by the lands of this state park and want to hike farther, consider following the Alvin Trail to Twitchell Flats, a fork off the Limekiln Trail. This trail quickly leaves the redwoods behind and travels uphill through coastal grasslands, finally reaching the Twitchell jeep trail and an 1880s homestead site where you can see the remains of a foundation, hearth, and cistern. The ocean views on this trail make all the climbing worth it. Some hikers use this trail to access Stony Ridge and the summit of Cone Peak—an arduous trek but worth it for the views.

User Groups: Hikers only. No dogs, horses, or mountain bikes. No wheelchair facilities.

Permits: No permits are required. An $8 day-use fee is charged per vehicle.

Maps: A map of Limekiln State Park is available at the entrance kiosk or by free download at www.parks.ca.gov. For a topographic map, go to the USGS website to download Lopez Point.

Directions: From Carmel, drive 52 miles south on Highway 1 to Limekiln State Park, on the east side of the highway. It's 2.5 miles south of Lucia and 14.8 miles south of Julia Pfeiffer Burns State Park. The trailhead is at the far side of the inland campground.

Contact: Limekiln State Park, Big Sur, 831/667-2315 or 831/667-2403, www.parks.ca.gov.

36 CONE PEAK LOOKOUT TRAIL

4.8 mi/2.5 hr   🏃3   ⛰10

in the Ventana Wilderness north of Lucia

Map 8.1, page 425

The 2.4-mile climb to Cone Peak is a classic Ventana Wilderness adventure, and the fun begins with the drive to the trailhead. After leaving Highway 1, first you get wide coastal views and then views of the inland mountain ranges as your car chugs its way uphill. But those are nothing compared to the views you get at the fire lookout on Cone Peak's summit, at 5,155 feet above sea level. This is the second highest mountain in the Santa Lucia Range (after

5,862-foot Junipero Serra Peak, also known as "Pinkolam" and much harder to hike to), but what makes this summit really special is the fact that it is only three miles from the ocean. The average gradient from sea level to the summit is about 30 percent, which creates an extremely dramatic, high-contrast view. The short hike from the trailhead to the summit is a steep climb, and the last mile feels like it goes straight up (total elevation gain is 1,400 feet). Make sure you have plenty of water with you, and in the spring months, bring along a wildflower identification book. These slopes are littered with penstemon, poppies, sticky monkeyflower, paintbrush, and many other colorful blooms. After zig-zagging upward through a mix of low chapparal, hardwoods, and then conifers (mostly Coulter pines), you reach a trail junction at 1.9 miles. Go east (right) and walk the final half mile to the fire lookout. In this last stretch, the trail is literally cut into the rock. At the top you'll find the historic lookout tower, built in 1923, as well as an eye-popping vista. You can see as far as 100 miles on clear days, and if the fog has burned off, you can look down the west side of Cone Peak for almost a vertical mile to the ocean. Be sure to pack along a good map, so you can name all the peaks and valleys in the 360-degree panorama that surrounds you.

User Groups: Hikers, dogs, and horses. No mountain bikes. No wheelchair facilities.

Permits: No permits are required. Parking and access are free.

Maps: A Ventana Wilderness or Los Padres National Forest map is available from the U.S. Forest Service. For a topographic map, go to the USGS website to download Cone Peak.

Directions: From Big Sur, drive 27 miles south on Highway 1 to Kirk Creek Campground, on the west side of the highway, and the left turn-off for Nacimiento-Fergusson Road, on the east side of the highway. Turn left and drive 7.2 miles, then turn left on the dirt Coast Ridge Road (sometimes called Cone Peak Road) and drive 5.5 miles to the trailhead on the left (do not follow the road to its end). Park off the road; there is space for about six cars. A high-clearance vehicle is recommended, although not always necessary.

Note: Coast Ridge Road/Cone Peak Road is usually closed during the rainy season (Nov.-Mar.).

Contact: Los Padres National Forest, Monterey Ranger District, King City, 831/385-5434, www.fs.usda.gov/lpnf.

SAN JOAQUIN VALLEY

The San Joaquin Valley is best known for its agricultural bounty, not its wilderness. But the region's few untouched natural areas offer a unique look into the Golden State's past, when open plains and untamed waterways once comprised a huge part of central California. An extensive wetland ecosystem is preserved at Los Banos Wildlife Area and the San Luis National Wildlife Refuge complex, creating a paradise for birdwatchers. Carrizo Plain, declared a national monument in 2000, is considered California's largest nature preserve, containing thousands of acres of grassland prairie. Wildflowers carpet the grasslands in early spring, and thousands of sandhill cranes visit in the winter. Pronghorn antelope and tule elk roam year-round. In the San Joaquin Valley, a pair of binoculars and a sense of wonder are as necessary as hiking boots.

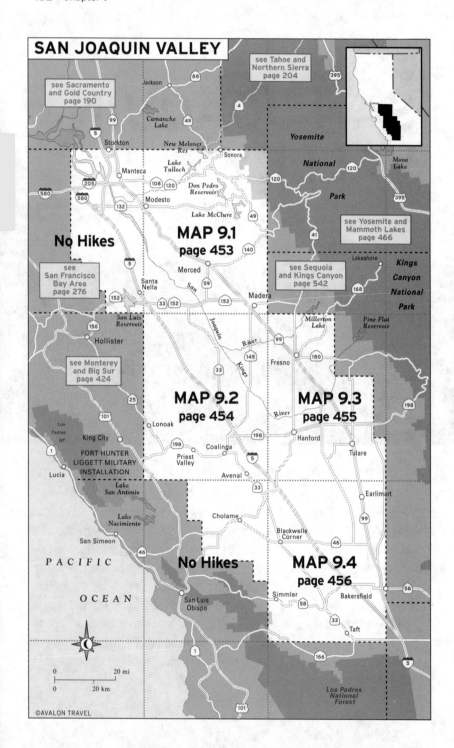

SAN JOAQUIN VALLEY

see Sacramento
and Gold Country
page 190

see Tahoe and
Northern Sierra
page 204

No Hikes

see
San Francisco
Bay Area
page 276

MAP 9.1
page 453

see Yosemite and
Mammoth Lakes
page 466

see Sequoia
and Kings Canyon
page 542

see Monterey
and Big Sur
page 424

MAP 9.2
page 454

MAP 9.3
page 455

FORT HUNTER
LIGGETT MILITARY
INSTALLATION

No Hikes

MAP 9.4
page 456

PACIFIC

OCEAN

Yosemite

National

Park

Kings

Canyon

National

Park

| 0 | 20 mi |
| 0 | 20 km |

©AVALON TRAVEL

Map 9.1

Sites 1-7
Pages 457-460

9.2

Map 9.2
Sites 8-9
Pages 461-462

Map 9.3

Sites 10-11
Pages 462-463

Map 9.4
Sites 12-13
Pages 463-464

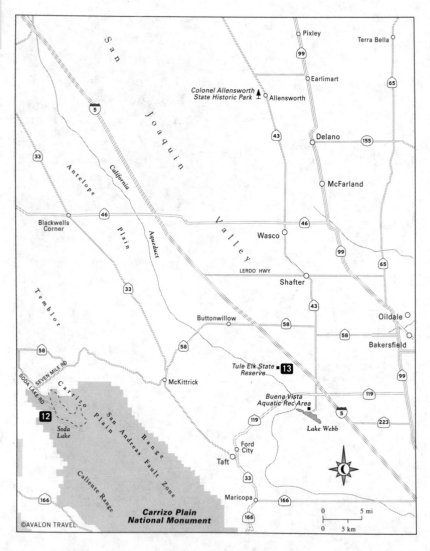

1 NATURAL BRIDGES
1.4 mi/1.0 hr

at New Melones Reservoir near Sonora

Map 9.1, page 453

This short, easy trail leads from Parrotts Ferry Road to Natural Bridges, a unique series of limestone caves with Coyote Creek running through them. This geologic wonder is only a short drive from downtown Sonora, but it's like nothing else around this Gold Rush town. The upper Natural Bridge is 270 feet high, and the clear water underneath it creates a popular locals' swimming hole. Because Coyote Creek is spring-fed, the water is cool year-round. Most swimmers bring inner tubes with them so they can float through the cave. The rocky trail that accesses the upper bridge has a 300-foot elevation gain, but is easily accomplished by children and adults alike. Because it takes thousands of years to create the cave's fragile formations, visitors are asked not to touch them. The oil on human hands can stop the formations from growing. A second bridge lies downstream from the upper bridge, accessible by a rough, unmaintained trail. If you are willing to walk the extra 0.5 mile to the lower bridge, you have a greater chance of solitude.

User Groups: Hikers only. No dogs, horses, or mountain bikes. No wheelchair facilities.

Permits: No permits are required. Parking and access are free.

Maps: A free map is available at the New Melones Visitors Center or by download at www.usbr.gov. For a topographic map, go to the USGS website to download Sonora.

Directions: From Highway 49 in Sonora, take the turnoff for Parrotts Ferry Road (signed for Columbia State Historic Park). Drive north on Parrotts Ferry Road for about seven miles, crossing the bridge over New Melones Reservoir, to the trailhead on the left side of the road (1.2 miles north of the highway bridge and four miles south of the Hwy. 4 junction).

Contact: New Melones Reservoir Visitors Center, Sonora, 209/536-9543 or 209/536-9094, www.usbr.gov.

2 TABLE MOUNTAIN
3.0 mi/1.5 hr

at New Melones Reservoir near Jamestown

Map 9.1, page 453

Wildflower lovers, this is your trail. The only trick is timing your visit for the exact period when Table Mountain is at its most colorful splendor. Of course, the timing of the bloom varies from year to year, so your best bet is to call the New Melones Visitors Center starting in late February to see how the flowers are coming along. When they say "go time," don't wait too long. Some years the bloom is all over by late April, although Table Mountain's high vistas are there for the taking at any time of year. From the pavement's end at the yellow gate, the trail crosses through a grassy oak woodland dotted with basalt (volcanic) rocks. Straight ahead is Table Mountain, a 2,200-foot-high, 1,200-foot-wide, flat-topped plateau that juts upward from the surrounding lowlands. The plateau was formed by a lava flow about 10 million years ago, when a volcano erupted east of Sonora Pass. Its volcanic soil creates ideal conditions for vernal pools in February and March (look for fairy shrimp in the pools) and a colorful array of grassland wildflowers in April and May, including lupine, Indian paintbrush, blue dicks, and goldfields. Although this trail's distance is short, the last 0.5 mile is slow-going because it requires a modicum of scrambling over rough volcanic rock. Be sure to wear sturdy boots or shoes.

User Groups: Hikers, dogs, horses, and mountain bikes. No wheelchair facilities.

Permits: No permits are required. Parking and access are free.

Maps: A free map is available at the New Melones Visitors Center or by download at www.usbr.gov. For a topographic map, go to the USGS website to download Sonora.

Directions: From Highway 49 in Sonora, drive south for three miles to Jamestown, then turn right (north) on Rawhide Road. Drive two miles and turn left on Shell Road; follow Shell Road 1.8 miles (take the left fork) to the pavement's end at a yellow gate across the road. The trail begins to the right of the gate. (You can choose to continue driving past the yellow gate for another mile on a dirt road, but a high-clearance vehicle may be necessary. This will shorten your hike considerably.)

Contact: New Melones Reservoir Visitors Center, Sonora, 209/536-9543 or 209/536-9094, www.usbr.gov.

3 RED HILLS

5.0 mi/2.5 hr

near Chinese Camp and La Grange

Map 9.1, page 453

Flower aficionados, check your calendar. Is it late March to early May? Then head for the Red Hills Area of Critical Environmental Concern, the very long name for 11 square miles of gray-pine-studded Bureau of Land Management (BLM) land in the Sierra foothills. This is not a place you would ever want to visit in the heat of summer, but in early spring, the rocky landscape comes alive with color from coreopsis, five-spots, bird's-eye gilia, fiddlenecks, goldfields, poppies, and other native wildflowers. The serpentine soil here supports a wide variety of plants, including seven that are rare and/or endangered. Keep an eye out for California verbena, which grows here and nowhere else in the world. It can be found near the stream that parallels Red Hills Road. Numerous loop hikes are possible in the preserve; a good starter hike is to set off on Soaproot Ridge Trail, then bear left and walk Overlook Loop to Verbena Loop. From there you can walk back to your car on Red Hills Road, or cross the road and walk back most of the way on Red Hills Trail, which parallels the road. As you hike, keep scanning the sky for bald eagles, which are fond of this area because of its proximity to huge Don Pedro Reservoir.

User Groups: Hikers, dogs, horses, and mountain bikes. No wheelchair facilities.

Permits: No permits are required. Parking and access are free.

Maps: A free trail map can be downloaded at www.blm.gov/ca. For a topographic map, go to the USGS website to download Chinese Camp.

Directions: From Sonora, take Highway 49 south for 15 miles to Chinese Camp. Turn right (south) on Red Hills Road and drive one mile to the trailhead parking on the left.

Or, from Oakdale, drive east on Highway 108/120 for about 20 miles. Turn right on La Grange Road. Drive 1.5 miles and turn left on Red Hills Road. Drive 0.75 mile to the trailhead parking lot on the right side of the road.

Contact: Bureau of Land Management Mother Lode Field Office, El Dorado Hills, 916/941-3101, www.blm.gov/ca.

4 RAINBOW POOL AND CONFLUENCE TRAIL

2.5 mi/1.5 hr

in Stanislaus National Forest near Groveland

Map 9.1, page 453

While everybody else is hanging out at Rainbow Pool, a popular swimming hole and waterfall right off Highway 120, you can leave the thronging crowds behind by taking this short but steep hike to the confluence of the South Fork and Middle Fork of the Tuolumne River. Rainbow Pool is located on the south side of Highway 120, but you'll park your car and start hiking on the north side, heading steeply downhill on an old dirt road known as the Confluence Trail, which parallels the cascading South Fork as it tumbles down a dramatic, rocky gorge. In the springtime, when the powerful Tuolumne is frothing with excess snowmelt, this canyon can really roar with noise. The watery extravaganza reaches a deafening crescendo at the canyon bottom, where the two forks of the river merge. This was once the site of the South Fork Tunnel Camp, one of the major construction sites for the Hetch Hetchy Reservoir system. The old road you are walking on was used to haul men and building materials back and forth to the camp. Where the road ends at a particularly scenic point in the narrow gorge, just retrace your steps back up-hill. After a hot, sweaty ascent back to your car, you might just want to walk (or drive) over to Rainbow Pool and take a dip in its always re-freshing waters.

User Groups: Hikers, dogs, horses, and moun-tain bikes. No wheelchair facilities.

Permits: No permits are required. Parking and access are free.

Maps: A Stanislaus National Forest map is available from the U.S. Forest Service. For a topographic map, go to the USGS website to download Jawbone Ridge.

Directions: From Groveland, drive east on Highway 120 for 14 miles to the left turnoff for Cherry Lake Road. Turn left and then left again immediately. Drive about 100 yards and park in the dirt pullout just before the gate across the road. Walk past the gate and then turn right and follow the unsigned dirt road head-ing downhill.

Contact: Groveland Ranger District, Stanislaus National Forest, Groveland, 209/962-7825, www.fs.usda.gov/stanislaus.

5 DIANA FALLS AND POOLS
1.5 mi/0.5 hr   👥1 ⛰8

in Stanislaus National Forest near Greeley Hill

Map 9.1, page 453

You could think of it as a neighborhood back-yard swimming hole, except there's no neigh-borhood anywhere nearby. Diana Falls is located not far from the towns of Groveland and Coulterville and within an hour's drive of Yosemite National Park. But it's not on the road to any of those places, so you won't come across it by accident. It's an out-of-the-way waterfall on Bean Creek, near its confluence with the North Fork Merced River. From the trailhead, hike along the west side of the river, following an old dirt road for 0.5 mile. Here the Merced River is a small, tame stream, with bunches of Indian rhubarb growing along its banks. The dirt road gets narrower as you walk. At a fork in the trail, bear right. You'll leave the river and

hike along the Bean Creek canyon. In just a few minutes, or about 250 yards, you'll reach the brink of 20-foot-tall Diana Falls. Several spurs descend the slope to its base and to the many cool swimming holes that locals call Diana Pools. There may be no better place to spend a hot summer afternoon.

User Groups: Hikers, dogs, horses, and moun-tain bikes. No wheelchair facilities.

Permits: No permits are required. Parking and access are free.

Maps: A Stanislaus National Forest map is available from the U.S. Forest Service. For a topographic map, go to the USGS website to download Groveland.

Directions: From Groveland, drive east on Highway 120 for seven miles to the right turn-off for Smith Station Road (also signed as County Road J132 to Coulterville). Turn right and drive 5.7 miles, then turn sharply left on Greeley Hill Road. Drive 4.2 miles to the trail-head, just before a one-lane bridge. The trail begins on the right at the gated dirt road signed as "Road Closed."

Contact: Groveland Ranger District, Stanislaus National Forest, Groveland, 209/962-7825, www.fs.usda.gov/stanislaus.

6 CHESTER, SOUSA, AND WINTON MARSH TRAILS
4.0 mi/2.0 hr   👥1 ⛰8

in the San Luis National Wildlife Refuge north of Los Banos

Map 9.1, page 453   **BEST (**

The San Luis National Wildlife Refuge offers two main driving tours: the Tule Elk Auto Tour Loop and the Waterfowl Auto Tour Loop, and both are great opportunities for visitors to see wildlife. But if you want to get out of your car and on to your feet for a while, check out the three short hiking trails located off the 8.5-mile Waterfowl Auto Tour Loop. Walk all three, and you can easily chalk up about four miles of ex-ercise. The trails lead to three different marsh areas, each with its own character.

As you drive the auto route, the first trail-head you reach is for the Chester Marsh Trail. It's open for hiking only from February to September; from October to January, it is part of the refuge's hunting area. It's a one-mile loop, and you can pick up an interpretive brochure at the trailhead. After your walk, get back in your car and continue driving along the Waterfowl Auto Tour Route until you reach the trailhead for the Sousa Marsh. This area consists of an inner and outer loop trail through a canopy of riparian trees. The longest trail (1.2 miles) goes to the Sousa observation platform, with its telescope and benches. The 0.7-mile Winton Marsh Trail, located just beyond the Sousa Marsh parking lot, also leads to an observation platform and several benches situated slightly above the marsh, so you can pull out your binoculars and peer at the feathered fowl below. What will you see? The usual cabal: ducks, geese, moorhens, coots, pheasants, snipe, hawks, owls, egrets, herons, and even some rare types, like the endangered tricolored blackbird. In case you haven't gotten the idea yet, this place is crawling with wildlife. Even while just driving around, we saw a coyote and about a zillion bunnies, in addition to numerous Swainson's hawks.

User Groups: Hikers and dogs. No horses or mountain bikes. No wheelchair facilities.

Permits: No permits are required. Parking and access are free.

Maps: A free map is available at the refuge visitors center. For a topographic map, go to the USGS website to download Los Banos.

Directions: From Los Banos on Highway 152/33, drive north on Highway 165 (Mercey Springs Road) for 6.4 miles to Wolfsen Road. Bear right and follow Wolfsen Road for 2.5 miles into the National Wildlife Refuge. Follow the signs for the Waterfowl Auto Tour Loop.

Contact: San Luis National Wildlife Refuge, Los Banos, 209/826-3508, www.fws.gov/refuge/san_luis.

7 MEADOWLARK TRAIL
1.5 mi/1.0 hr

in the Merced National Wildlife Refuge southwest of Merced

Map 9.1, page 453

It doesn't seem like a 1.5-mile loop trail could offer much in the way of a pay-off, but you may be surprised by the rewards on the Meadowlark Trail. First off, it's one of only two places in the Merced National Wildlife Refuge where you're allowed to get out of your car and walk. Walking is prohibited in most of the preserve in order to reduce the disturbance to the thousands of geese and cranes that winter here. Driving your car along the Auto Tour Route is okay, though; it turns out that birds aren't bothered much by cars. The Meadowlark Trail gives you a chance to stretch your legs within the wildlife refuge, which serves as a precious island of wildlife habitat in the midst of Merced's vast agricultural fields. A thicket of tules, cattails, and willows in the refuge provides heavy cover for birds—particularly raptors, wintering shorebirds, and waterfowl. Because morning fog is common here in the winter months, bird-watching is often better at midday, when you may see concentrations of snow geese and Ross's geese. Magnificent sandhill cranes also make an appearance in winter. The rest of the year, you're more likely to see a variety of raptors. Barn owls are particularly common—one visitor saw 14 of them while walking this short loop. Great horned owls and a variety of hawks are also frequently sighted.

User Groups: Hikers and dogs. No horses or mountain bikes. No wheelchair facilities.

Permits: No permits are required. Parking and access are free.

Maps: A free map is available at the San Luis National Wildlife Refuge headquarters. For a topographic map, go to the USGS website to download Los Banos.

Directions: From Merced, take Highway 59 south for eight miles. Turn west on Sandy Mush Road and drive eight miles to the refuge entrance.

Contact: San Luis National Wildlife Refuge, Los Banos, 209/826-3508, www.fws.gov/refuge/merced.

8 PATH OF THE PADRES
5.0 mi/8.0 hr 🥾2 ⛰️8

on Los Banos Creek, in San Luis Reservoir State Recreation Area

Map 9.2, page 454   **BEST ☾**

You have to plan way in advance to take this unusual hike at Los Banos Creek Reservoir. That's because the only way to go is in the company of a guide and via boat to the trailhead, and guided trips are offered only on weekends in February, March, and sometimes April. The trip has become so popular that it usually sells out as soon as reservations are available, which is typically January 2 each year. Don't procrastinate on making your call for reservations. Although the hike itself is only five miles, the trip is an all-day affair, so don't forget to bring plenty of water, snacks, and lunch. It begins at 8am with a boat ride down the long and narrow reservoir, which is set in a steep-walled canyon and is popular for fishing. At the reservoir's far end, everyone gets off the boat and hikes 2.5 miles up the narrow canyon of Los Banos Creek, where old-growth sycamore groves and a cornucopia of spring wildflowers may be seen. Sturdy shoes are a must as the trail is rocky in places. As you walk, your guide will teach you about how the native Yokut Indians used the plants in this area, and you'll see bedrock mortars that they used for pounding acorns and natural medicines. Bird-watchers may thrill to see a peregrine falcon or other cliff-dwelling species. If the conditions are right, the hike may include an optional climb to the top of a knoll that offers panoramic views of the surrounding valleys and the Coast Range. So why is this trail called the Path of the Padres? Because the fathers at Mission San Juan Bautista traveled along the creek in the early 19th century to evangelize the Yokut Indians of the Central Valley. Along the way, they often bathed in the creek, which is why the nearby town is named "Los Banos."

User Groups: Hikers only. No dogs, horses, or mountain bikes. No wheelchair facilities.

Permits: Reservations are required; call to reserve a space starting February 1. A $12 fee is charged for the reservation and guided tour (children must be at least 6 years old). An additional $8 day-use fee is charged per vehicle.

Maps: For a topographic map, go to the USGS website to download Los Banos Valley.

Directions: From I-5 at the junction with Highway 152 (south of Santa Nella), turn east on Highway 152 and drive 2.5 miles. Turn right (south) on Volta Road and drive one mile. Turn left (east) on Pioneer Road and drive 0.8 mile, then turn right on Canyon Road. Drive south on Canyon Road for five miles to Los Banos Creek Reservoir. (You will cross back to the west side of I-5.) Park near the boat ramp.

Contact: San Luis Reservoir State Recreation Area, Four Rivers Sector, Gustine, 209/826-1197, www.parks.ca.gov.

9 COALINGA MINERAL SPRINGS NATIONAL RECREATION TRAIL
4.8 mi/2.5 hr 🥾2 ⛰️8

northwest of Coalinga

Map 9.2, page 454

Most people don't realize that there's a National Recreation Trail out here near Coalinga, the town that was made famous by an earthquake, but it's true. In winter and spring, this is a first-class hike to the summit of Kreyenhagen Peak (elevation 3,558 feet), climbing through chaparral-covered hillsides. The trail begins at the far end of the picnic area and crosses a dry streambed, then begins to ascend. It's well graded all the way, with the second mile slightly steeper than the first. Plenty of switchbacks ease you through it. Views are good all the way up this 2.4-mile trail, but the impressive vista from the summit ridge includes the Diablo Range, the San Joaquin Valley, and miles of surrounding

Bureau of Land Management (BLM) land. Considering how little effort is required to get here, it's quite a view. Have a seat on one of the rock outcrops and take it all in.

User Groups: Hikers, dogs, horses, and mountain bikes. No wheelchair facilities.

Permits: No permits are required. A $3 day-use fee is charged per vehicle.

Maps: Free trail maps are available at the trailhead. For a topographic map, go to the USGS website to download Curry Mountain.

Directions: From Coalinga, drive 20 miles west on Highway 198 to the Coalinga Mineral Springs County Park exit. Turn right (north) and drive four miles to Coalinga Mineral Springs County Park. Park in the main lot and walk to the far end of the park. The trail begins across the creek bed.

Contact: Bureau of Land Management, Hollister Field Office, Hollister, 831/630-5000, www.ca.blm.gov/hollister.

10 LEWIS S. EATON TRAIL
1.0-12.0 mi/0.5-5.5 hr 🏃🏽1 ⛰️7

on the San Joaquin River near Fresno

Map 9.3, page 455

Woodward Park is the kind of city park that has a par course, children's playgrounds, and barbecue areas. But it's also a convenient access point for the San Joaquin River Parkway, also called the Lewis S. Eaton Trail. When completed, the multiuse parkway will cover a 22-mile distance between Highway 99 and Friant Dam in Millerton Lake State Park. Currently six miles are finished, which means you can walk, jog, rollerblade, bike, or cruise in a wheelchair up to 12 miles round-trip on a paved trail that parallels the river and Friant Road for its entire distance. The good folks at the San Joaquin River Parkway and Conservation Trust are working hard to add to the current trail system; various loops and extensions from the paved trail are in the works. If you want to explore some of them, start with the River Access Trail, which branches off the Lewis S. Eaton

Trail on the north side of Woodward Park. The trail meanders down to the riverbanks at the Jensen River Ranch, a small park that is under restoration by the conservancy.

User Groups: Hikers, dogs, horses, mountain bikes, and wheelchairs.

Permits: No permits are required. A $5 fee is charged per vehicle.

Maps: A park map is available at the entrance kiosk. For a topographic map, go to the USGS website to download Fresno North.

Directions: From Highway 41 heading north in Fresno, take the Friant Road exit. Turn left on Audubon Avenue and then turn right into Woodward Park.

Contact: Woodward Regional Park, Fresno, 559/621-2900; San Joaquin River Parkway and Conservation Trust, Fresno, 559/248-8480, www.riverparkway.org.

11 KAWEAH OAKS PRESERVE
2.0 mi/1.0 hr 🏃🏽1 ⛰️7

east of Visalia

Map 9.3, page 455

The Kaweah Oaks Preserve is Tulare County's premier private nature preserve, a small remnant of what was once a vast valley oak forest. Groves of majestic oaks still stand, as well as wild grapevines growing as high as 30 feet. Four easy hiking trails take you through a vast alkali meadow, valley oak riparian forests, sycamore woodlands, wild roses, valley elderberries, and swamp habitat. From the parking area, enter through the obvious gateway, which features maps and interpretive signage, and pick up a trail guide. Head west down the old ranch road to the picnic area on the left (less than a quarter mile). Follow the ranch road west or north to hike the self-guided interpretive trails. Because this is a grazing area, leave all cattle gates the way you found them, whether open or closed, and keep Fido on his leash. As you stroll, listen for sounds of birdlife, and watch for herons, hawks, and owls, as well as the preserve's five species of woodpeckers. In addition to the diverse birdlife, you'll enjoy abundant native flora, including valley oak, California sycamores, cottonwoods, and willows growing near the streams. This is a good walk for late winter, spring, or fall. In the heat of summer, confine your visits to the early morning, when the valley is at its coolest. The preserve closes at dusk, so evening walks are not an option.

User Groups: Hikers and dogs. No horses or mountain bikes. No wheelchair facilities.

Permits: No permits are required. Parking and access are free.

Maps: For a topographic map, go to the USGS website to download Visalia. Trail guides are available at the trailhead for a $3 donation.

Directions: From Tulare on Highway 99, drive north for 10 miles and turn east on Highway 198. Drive 13 miles on Highway 198, passing through Visalia, and take the left turnoff for Road 182. Drive 0.5 mile north on Road 182 to the trailhead parking area on the left.

Contact: Sequoia Riverlands Trust, Visalia, 559/738-0211, www.sequoiariverlands.org.

12 CARRIZO PLAIN AND PAINTED ROCK

1.5 mi/1.0 hr   🏃1 ⛰9

in Carrizo Plains National Monument, eastern San Luis Obispo County

Map 9.4, page 456   **BEST (**

Carrizo Plain was designated a national monument in 2001 and is considered to be one of California's largest grassland ecosystems. It's best known for its abundant wildlife, spring wildflowers, and peace and quiet. Located at the north end of the monument is Soda Lake, a 3,000-acre expanse that comprises one of the largest remaining alkaline wetlands left in California. It's dry for most of the year, but during the wet season, it attracts migrating birds. Tule elk, pronghorn, coyotes, and other wildlife can also be seen in various areas of the monument. In early spring, when conditions are right, wildflowers can fill the valley and cover

the mountains, attracting photographers and visitors from all over the country.

Soda Lake and the surrounding grasslands are spectacular enough, especially when the spring wildflower bloom is on, but if you've driven all the way out here, you don't want to miss a visit to Painted Rock. However, you need to obtain a permit in advance or be part of a docent-led tour to hike the easy Painted Rock Interpretive Trail, which leads to the 55-foot-high formation. The interior of this rounded sandstone amphitheater has some of the most significant Native American pictographs in the country. Although many have been vandalized, Painted Rock is still considered a very sacred place by Native Americans. While visiting, please respect the site by not touching the paintings or rock.

User Groups: Hikers only. No dogs, horses, or mountain bikes. No wheelchair facilities.

Permits: While the monument is open year-round, Painted Rock is closed March 1-July 15 to protect nesting birds. You can still sign up for a guided hike to Painted Rock on Saturdays in March, April, and May. The rest of the year, you can visit Painted Rock on your own, but you must obtain a "self-guided tour" permit in advance. Permits and tour reservations can be obtained at www.recreation.gov or by phoning 877/444-6777 ($1.50 fee). Parking and access are free.

Maps: A brochure on Carrizo Plain National Monument is available from the Bureau of Land Management (BLM). For a topographic map, go to the USGS website to download Painted Rock.

Directions: From San Luis Obispo on US 101, drive north for 10 miles and take the Santa Margarita/Highway 58 exit. Drive east on Highway 58 for 50 miles to the Soda Lake Road turnoff. Turn right (south) and drive 13.5 miles to the Painted Rock Trail and Goodwin Education Center turnoff. Turn right and drive to the visitors center, then turn left and drive two miles to the Painted Rock trailhead.

Contact: Bureau of Land Management, Bakersfield Field Office, Bakersfield,

661/391-6000; Goodwin Education Center at Carrizo Plain (open Thurs.-Sun. Dec.-May, 9 am-4 pm), 805/475-2131, wwww.blm.gov.

13 TULE ELK STATE NATURAL RESERVE

0.25 mi/0.25 hr 👥1 ⛰8

off I-5 west of Bakersfield

Map 9.4, page 456 **BEST (**

Most people just don't know that there's a herd of magnificent tule elk wandering around a few miles from I-5. If you didn't know, better pull off the highway and get yourself to the Tule Elk State Natural Reserve near Tupman. There aren't a lot of trails to choose from, and you won't do much that resembles true hiking here, but if you've been driving on I-5 long enough, just getting out of the car and stretching your legs is a big deal. The animals are most active in the late summer, when their rutting season begins. Bring binoculars for your best chance at a good view, or take a stroll to the walk-up platform, where you can look through a spotting scope at the elk. Make sure you stop in at the visitors center and check out the interesting displays on the elk and the history of the Central Valley.

User Groups: Hikers and dogs. No horses or mountain bikes. Some facilities are wheelchair-accessible.

Permits: No permits are required. An $8 day-use fee is charged per vehicle.

Maps: For a topographic map, go to the USGS website to download Tupman.

Directions: From the junction of I-5 and Highway 99 north of the Grapevine, drive north on I-5 for 33 miles to the Stockdale Highway exit. Drive west for 1.2 miles and turn left (south) on Morris Road. Drive 1.6 miles on Morris Road. The road turns right at Station Road. After 0.25 mile, turn left into the Tule Elk State Natural Reserve. The route is well signed.

Contact: Tule Elk State Natural Reserve, Buttonwillow, 661/764-6881, www.parks. ca.gov.

YOSEMITE AND MAMMOTH LAKES

Plunging waterfalls, stark granite, alpine lakes, pristine meadows, giant sequoias, and raging rivers—you'll find them all in this region, which encompasses not only Yosemite National Park but also Mammoth Lakes and the Eastern Sierra.

The centerpiece is Yosemite National Park, a must-see on every hiker's itinerary. Just beyond the park boundaries lie the Hoover, Ansel Adams, and John Muir wilderness areas. To the east of Yosemite, Mammoth Lakes and June Lake offer unusual diversity—volcanic craters, hot springs, lava flows, the saline waters of Mono Lake, and the geologic wonders of Devils Postpile National Monument.

The prime season here is April through October, but the higher elevations are often accessible only from June to September. To avoid the crowds in hot spots like Yosemite Valley, travel in the offseason or on weekdays.

YOSEMITE AND MAMMOTH LAKES

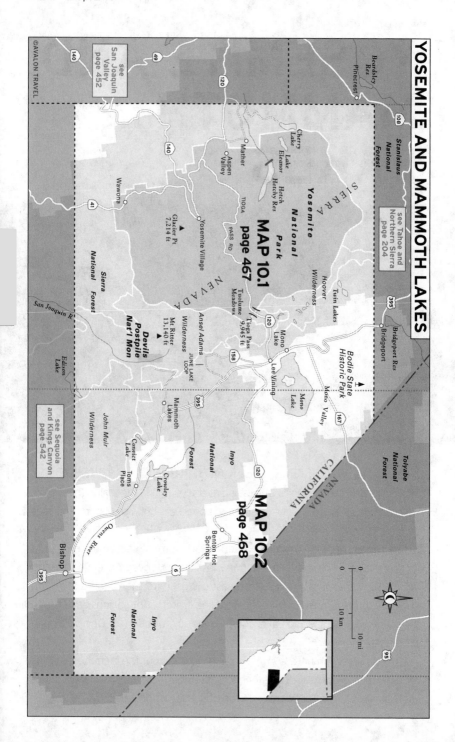

Map 10.1

Sites 1-92
Pages 469-533

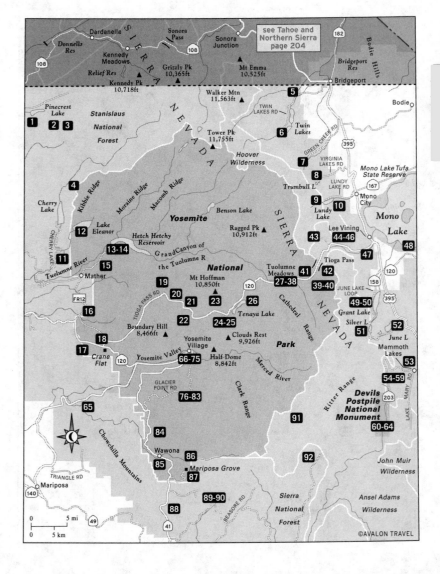

Map 10.2
Sites 93-100
Pages 533-538

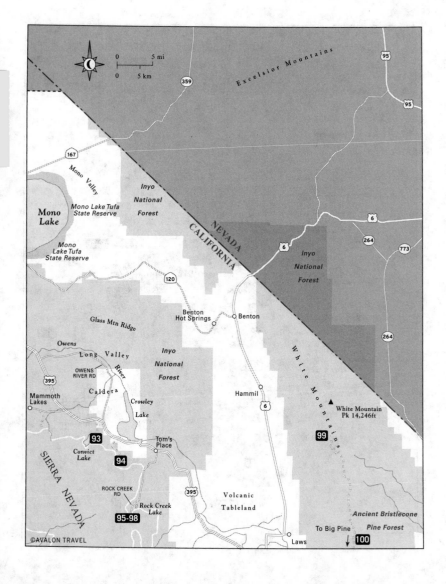

©AVALON TRAVEL

1 PINECREST LAKE NATIONAL RECREATION TRAIL

4.2 mi / 2.0 hr 🏃1 ⛺7

on Pinecrest Lake near Strawberry in Stanislaus National Forest

Map 10.1, page 467 **BEST (**

Pinecrest Lake is a tremendously popular family vacation resort just off Highway 108, the kind of place that people go year after year for a week of boating, camping, and fishing. Many own or rent cabins and stay all summer. The trail that circles its shoreline is a lot like the lake itself—it's pretty and extremely popular. The four-mile loop makes a pleasant early morning walk or run, provided you're up and at it before the crowds get out of bed. In the afternoons, you can hike to the east side of the lake and follow a spur trail along the South Fork Stanislaus River to some excellent swimming holes known as Cleo's Bath. This trail is by no means a wilderness experience, but it's a pleasant walk. If you're looking for solitude, try it on an autumn weekday.

User Groups: Hikers and dogs. No horses or mountain bikes. Part of this trail is wheelchair-accessible.

Permits: No permits are required. Parking and access are free.

Maps: An Emigrant Wilderness map is available from Tom Harrison Maps or Stanislaus National Forest. For a topographic map, go to the USGS website to download Pinecrest.

Directions: From Sonora, drive east on Highway 108 for 31 miles to the Pinecrest turnoff. Turn right on Pinecrest Lake Road and continue for another mile to the day-use parking area, on the south side of the lake. Park as close to the end of the road as possible.

Contact: Stanislaus National Forest, Summit Ranger District, Pinecrest, 209/965-3434, www.fs.usda.gov/stanislaus.

2 CAMP AND BEAR LAKES

8.0 mi / 4.0 hr 🏃2 ⛺9

in the Emigrant Wilderness near Pinecrest Lake

Map 10.1, page 467

The Crabtree trailhead, at elevation 7,180 feet, is the trailhead of choice for most casual hikers and backpackers entering the Emigrant Wilderness. It's easy to reach and allows access to many excellent destinations with a relatively short walk. From Crabtree, it's a moderate 2.6-mile hike to Camp Lake, which is just inside the Emigrant Wilderness boundary. This lake is best as a day-hiking destination, but some backpackers opt to spend the night here (there is a one-night limit). A better choice is to continue another 1.5 miles to Bear Lake, accessible via a one-mile left spur trail. Both lakes offer stellar granite-country scenery, good (but icy) swimming, decent rainbow trout fishing, and the chance to see plenty of early summer wildflowers. You, too, can be wowed by the wandering daisies and blue lupine. You'll face only one sustained hill climb along the route; most of the trail gently undulates. Watch for beaver evidence at Bear Lake.

User Groups: Hikers, dogs, and horses. No mountain bikes. No wheelchair facilities.

Permits: A free wilderness permit is required for overnight stays and is available from the Summit Ranger Station. There is a one-night stay limit at Camp Lake. Parking and access are free.

Maps: An Emigrant Wilderness map is available from Tom Harrison Maps or Stanislaus National Forest. For a topographic map, go to the USGS website to download Pinecrest.

Directions: From Sonora, drive east on Highway 108 for 31 miles to the Pinecrest turnoff. Turn right on Pinecrest Lake Road and continue 0.5 mile to the right fork for Dodge Ridge Ski Area. Bear right and drive 2.9 miles, then turn right at the sign for Aspen Meadow and Gianelli trailhead. Drive 0.5 mile, turn left, and drive four miles to the turnoff for the Crabtree trailhead (follow the signs). Turn right and drive 0.25 mile.

Contact: Stanislaus National Forest, Summit Ranger District, Pinecrest, 209/965-3434, www.fs.usda.gov/stanislaus.

❸ BURST ROCK/ POWELL LAKE

4.6 mi / 2.5 hr

in the Emigrant Wilderness near Pinecrest Lake

Map 10.1, page 467

Both Burst Rock and Powell Lake are supreme day-hike destinations, but they present a problem for first-time visitors: Neither one is located right along the trail and neither one is signed. This results in a lot of people wandering around asking, "So which rock is Burst Rock?" The answer: it's the entire plateau above the plaque commemorating the Clark-Skidmore Emigrant Party of 1852. You'll see it after hiking gently but steadily uphill for 1.3 miles. At the wilderness boundary sign, cut off to your left for about 50 yards and you'll witness an incredible vista looking out over the valley below. Retrace your steps and continue another mile until you reach a fork. Go left for less than 0.25 mile to Powell Lake, a favorite spot of young anglers. If you miss the fork, shortly you'll catch sight of the lake, off to your left. The peninsula of rocks that juts out into the water is the perfect place for afternoon sunning and swimming. If you choose to camp at Powell Lake, note that there is a one-night stay limit.

User Groups: Hikers, dogs, and horses. No mountain bikes. No wheelchair facilities.

Permits: A free wilderness permit is required for overnight stays and is available from the Summit Ranger Station. There is a one-night stay limit at Powell Lake. Parking and access are free.

Maps: An Emigrant Wilderness map is available from Tom Harrison Maps or Stanislaus National Forest. For a topographic map, go to the USGS website to download Pinecrest.

Directions: From Sonora, drive east on Highway 108 for 31 miles to the Pinecrest turn-off. Turn right on Pinecrest Lake Road and continue for 0.5 mile to the right fork for Dodge Ridge Ski Area. Bear right, drive 2.9 miles, and turn right at the sign for Aspen Meadow and Gianelli trailhead. Drive 0.5 mile, turn left, and drive 8.3 miles to the trailhead parking area. The route is well signed.

Contact: Stanislaus National Forest, Summit Ranger District, Pinecrest, 209/965-3434, www.fs.usda.gov/stanislaus.

❹ KIBBIE LAKE

8.4 mi / 1-2 days

in northwest Yosemite National Park

Map 10.1, page 467

This day hike or easy backpacking trip starts near Cherry Lake in Stanislaus National Forest and heads into the Hetch Hetchy region of Yosemite. Yes, much of this area was severely burned in the massive Rim Fire of 2013, but that just makes this trip all the more interesting—especially the long drive to Cherry Lake, which offers many views of the fire's devastation. In the spring, you can see thousands of colorful lupines blooming amid the blackened soil. Kibbie Lake is a rewarding weekend trip for all levels of backpackers since the one-way distance is only 4.2 miles. From the trailhead, follow the Kibbie Ridge Trail 1.2 miles to the Kibbie Lake Trail, then go right and head for the lake in another three miles. Near this main junction you leave Stanislaus National Forest and enter Yosemite National Park, so dogs are not allowed past this point. The trail deposits you at the southern tip of the granite-bound lake, elevation 6,513 feet. Although quite large (more than 100 surface acres), Kibbie Lake is fairly shallow and supports a good population of rainbow trout. The long and narrow body of water has high rocky cliffs on some of its shoreline, so not all of it is easily accessible. On summer weekends, the lake gets visited fairly heavily, but on weekdays, you are likely to be the only soul around.

Note: Check your calendar before you go. The gate at Cherry Lake is closed every year one week before deer season, which is usually sometime in September, and doesn't reopen until spring. Most years, the road is open from May 1 to September 15.

User Groups: Hikers and horses. No dogs or mountain bikes. No wheelchair facilities.

Permits: There is a $30 entrance fee per vehicle at Yosemite National Park ($25 Nov.-Mar.), good for seven days. Free wilderness permits are required for overnight stays. They are available on a first-come, first-served basis up to one day in advance at the Yosemite Wilderness kiosk near your chosen trailhead, or further in advance by mail, phone, or online for a $5 reservation fee per person.

Maps: A Hetch Hetchy map is available from Tom Harrison Maps. For topographic maps, go to the USGS website to download Kibbie Lake and Hetch Hetchy Reservoir.

Directions: From Groveland, drive east on Highway 120 for 14 miles toward Yosemite National Park. Turn left on Cherry Lake Road and drive 24 miles to Cherry Lake's dam, then cross it. On the far side of the dam, bear right and drive 0.4 mile, then turn left on Road 1N45Y and follow it for 4.5 miles to its end at the Kibbie Ridge trailhead.

Contact: Yosemite National Park, Yosemite, 209/372-0200 or 209/372-0740 (permit reservations), www.nps.gov/yose or www.nps.gov/yose/wilderness (permit reservations).

5 BUCKEYE CREEK TRAIL
5.0 mi / 2.5 hr   🏃1 ⛺8

in Humboldt-Toiyabe National Forest west of Bridgeport and Highway 395

Map 10.1, page 467

You can hike up to eight miles one-way along Buckeye Creek to the Hoover Wilderness boundary below the Buckeye Roughs. But most hikers do less than that; they just take off from

Buckeye Campground (7,000 feet), maybe pack along their fishing rods, and walk a couple of miles each way up and down the stream. Brook trout are planted close to the campground all summer. It's rare to hike far in the Eastern Sierra without having to climb, but that's what you get here at the base of Buckeye Canyon. If you don't like to fish, there's plenty of other stuff to do, like admire the wildflowers in the meadows or gape at the impressive walls of glacial summits and ridges that surround you. A popular hot spring is found in Buckeye Creek less than a mile from the campground, but be forewarned: You might get an anatomy lesson there. Occasional Buckeye Creek bathers have been spotted wearing only birthday suits. Note that the lower portions of the Buckeye Creek Trail can be difficult to follow. Cattle graze this area in the summer and create their own trail system.

User Groups: Hikers, dogs, and horses. No mountain bikes. No wheelchair facilities.

Permits: No day-hiking permits are required. Parking and access are free.

Maps: A Hoover Wilderness map is available from Tom Harrison Maps or the U.S. Forest Service. For a topographic map, go to the USGS website to download Twin Lakes.

Directions: From Bridgeport on U.S. 395, drive west on Twin Lakes Road for seven miles to the Buckeye Road turnoff. Turn right on Buckeye Road and drive 3.5 miles to the Buckeye Campground and trailhead. (Buckeye Road turns to dirt at Doc and Al's Resort.)

Contact: Humboldt-Toiyabe National Forest, Bridgeport Ranger District, HC Bridgeport, 760/932-7070, www.fs.usada.gov/htnf.

6 BARNEY LAKE TRAIL
7.8 mi / 5.0 hr   🏃2 ⛺8

in the Hoover Wilderness west of Bridgeport

Map 10.1, page 467

Some call it Barney Lake Trail and others call it Robinson Creek Trail. Whatever you call it, you should know that this is the busiest trail into the Hoover Wilderness. Why? It's downright easy, gaining only 1,000 feet along its four-mile length. The remedy for the crowds? Start hiking very early in the day, before the hundreds of campers in the Twin Lakes area have risen from their sleeping bags. You must park outside Mono Village Campground and then walk due east through it to reach the trailhead, which is signed for Barney Lake. (The attendant in the camp entrance kiosk can point you to the trailhead. Day hikers can park for free but backpackers must pay a parking fee.) The trail roughly parallels Robinson Creek, first in a pine forest and then skirting big meadows highlighted by vast stands of aspen trees. While in the wide open meadows, you are rewarded with impressive views of the jagged Sawtooth Range. The path passes a Hoover Wilderness sign at 1.5 miles, then climbs a bit more steeply and reaches the lake at 3.9 miles. If you get there before everyone else, you are one lucky hiker. Ambitious day hikers and backpackers can continue another 3.5 miles to larger Peeler Lake. Because of the amount of aspens seen along this trail, it's a real treat to hike here from late September to mid-October when the color show happens.

User Groups: Hikers, dogs, and horses. No mountain bikes. No wheelchair facilities.

Permits: A free wilderness permit is required for overnight stays and is available from the Bridgeport Ranger Station. Quotas are in effect from the end of June to mid-September; permits are available in advance by mail for this period for a $3 fee per person.

Maps: A Hoover Wilderness map is available from Tom Harrison Maps or the U.S. Forest Service. For a topographic map, go to the USGS website to download Twin Lakes.

Directions: From Bridgeport on U.S. 395, drive west on Twin Lakes Road for 13.2 miles to the signed parking area, on the west end of the lakes, near Mono Village Campground.

Contact: Humboldt-Toiyabe National Forest, Bridgeport Ranger District, Bridgeport, 760/932-7070, www.fs.usada.gov/htnf.

◪ GREEN, EAST, AND WEST LAKES
8.6-11.6 mi / 5.0 hr

in the Hoover Wilderness west of Bridgeport

Map 10.1, page 467

Three beautiful lakes—Green, East, and West—are situated right around 9,000 feet in elevation in the spectacular Hoover Wilderness. They offer fair trout fishing and are accessible via Green Creek Trail (sometimes called Green Lake Trail). It's only 4.6 miles round-trip to Green Lake, but you can go two miles farther for an 8.6-mile round-trip that includes East Lake as well. Or, you can take a 1.5-mile spur off the main trail for a much steeper (but well worth it) jaunt to stark, rockbound West Lake. Some people make a short backpacking trip out of it and see all three lakes. If you do, note that Green Lake is the only one of the three that is just below 9,000 feet in elevation, which means it is the only one where campfires are permitted. (You must use the established campfire rings.) At the other, higher lakes, only backpacking stoves are allowed. The fishing is generally better at East and West Lakes than at Green Lake, although it's nothing to write home about. The high mountain scenery, on the other hand, will knock your socks off.

The Green Creek Trail climbs, of course—but not so much that you'll be worn out when you reach Green Lake; just enough to provide you with expansive valley views most of the way. The path closely parallels the tumbling cascades of the main fork of Green Creek, and the July wildflower show is outstanding here. (The autumn aspen show is also noteworthy.) The turnoff for West Lake is on the right at 2.2 miles. This trail makes a memorably steep 1,000-foot ascent over 1.5 miles, climbing high above Green Lake. After the easy grade of the first two miles of trail, this last stretch can really take you by surprise. For solitude lovers, West Lake is your best bet. The main trail reaches the shore of Green Lake 200 yards past the West Lake turnoff. East Lake can be reached by following the main trail (go left at the fork) and gaining another 500 feet in elevation over two miles. All three lakes are sparkling, rock-bound gems, so you can't go wrong here no matter which one you choose to visit.

User Groups: Hikers, dogs, and horses. No mountain bikes. No wheelchair facilities.

Permits: A free wilderness permit is required for overnight stays and is available from the Bridgeport Ranger Station. Quotas are in effect from the end of June to mid-September; permits are available in advance by mail for this period for a $3 fee per person.

Maps: A Hoover Wilderness map is available from Tom Harrison Maps or the U.S. Forest Service. For a topographic map, go to the USGS website to download Twin Lakes.

Directions: From Bridgeport, drive south on U.S. 395 for 4.5 miles to Green Creek Road (dirt). Turn west and drive 8.2 miles to the signed trailhead parking area, shortly before Green Creek Campground.

Contact: Humboldt-Toiyabe National Forest, Bridgeport Ranger District, Bridgeport, 760/932-7070, www.fs.usada.gov/htnf.

8 VIRGINIA LAKES TRAIL
6.2-10.2 mi / 3.0 hr-2 days 🏃3 ⛰9

in the Hoover Wilderness south of Bridgeport

Map 10.1, page 467

Virginia Lakes form the gateway to a beautiful high-mountain basin that contains eight small alpine lakes within a two-mile radius. The trailhead is at the Big Virginia Lake day-use area, set at 9,500 feet between mountain peaks that jut 12,000 feet into the sky. From here, you hike west past Blue Lake to Cooney Lake and on to Frog Lakes (a very easy 1.4 miles), then start climbing seriously, continuing 1.8 more miles to 11,100-foot Summit Pass. The landscape here is windswept, barren, and beautiful—a mix of rock, occasional whitebark pines, and high alpine wildflowers. Many hikers take a look at the scene from the pass, then retreat to one of the aforementioned lakes to spend the afternoon, making a 6.2-mile day. If you

continue beyond the pass, you curve downhill through dozens of switchbacks for 1.4 miles, then climb gently 0.5 mile west to Summit Lake (at 10,203 feet), on the northeast boundary of Yosemite National Park. Summit Lake is set between Camiaca Peak (11,739 feet) to the north and Excelsior Mountain (12,446 feet) to the south. This is the logical place for backpackers to make camp, and for day-trippers to turn around for a 10.2-mile day. If you want to take a longer trip into even wilder country, you can do so from this point. The trail skirts Summit Lake's north side, then enters Yosemite National Park in Virginia Canyon, one of the least-visited areas of the park. Another option is to take the fork right before Summit Lake that leads east (right) to the double Hoover Lakes, connecting with the Green Creek Trail. Some backpackers and day hikers make a one-way hike of about 11 miles out of this trip by arranging to have a shuttle car waiting for them at the Green Creek trailhead (see listing in this chapter).

User Groups: Hikers, dogs, and horses. No dogs on trail in the Yosemite National Park portion. No mountain bikes. No wheelchair facilities.

Permits: A free wilderness permit is required for overnight stays and is available from the Bridgeport Ranger Station. Quotas are in effect from the end of June to mid-September; permits are available in advance by mail for this period for a $3 fee per person.

Maps: A Hoover Wilderness map is available from Tom Harrison Maps or the U.S. Forest Service. For a topographic map, go to the USGS website to download Dunderberg Peak.

Directions: From Bridgeport, drive 13.5 miles south on U.S. 395 (or from Lee Vining, drive 12 miles north on U.S. 395) to Conway Summit. Turn west on Virginia Lakes Road and drive 6.5 miles to the trailhead, at the Big Virginia Lake day-use area.

Contact: Humboldt-Toiyabe National Forest, Bridgeport Ranger District, Bridgeport, 760/932-7070, www.fs.usada.gov/htnf.

9 LUNDY CANYON TRAIL
4.4-10.0 mi / 2.0 hr-2 days 🏃3 ⛰9

north of Lee Vining in the Hoover Wilderness

Map 10.1, page 467   **BEST (**

The Lundy Canyon Trail is the back door into the 20 Lakes Basin, a well-traveled area of the Hoover Wilderness that is most commonly accessed from Saddlebag Lake off Highway 120. The trailhead lies about two miles past Lundy Lake, a long, narrow pool set at 7,800 feet. From here, the trail rises along Mill Creek, passing several beaver ponds, a dilapidated trapper's cabin, and two small but boisterous waterfalls (Lower and Upper Lundy Falls, also called Mill Creek Falls) as it heads into the Hoover Wilderness. Most visitors hike to the first or second falls, enjoying the gorgeous Eastern Sierra scenery with a relatively mellow walk, then hike back out. Those who continue find that the trail, which climbed gently but steadily for the first 2.2 miles, suddenly reaches what appears to be the back of the canyon. But look straight up the canyon wall to your left—that's where the path continues, although it isn't much of a path. An unmaintained, marginally switchbacked route leads 0.8 mile upward through a frighteningly steep wall of shale, and the difficulty rating for this trail changes abruptly from a 3 to a 4 (and maybe a 5 on the way back downhill). Use great caution here; one slip and you could take a nasty fall. You don't want to be carrying a pack that is too heavy or unbalanced on this stretch.

When you finally make it to the top of the canyon wall, you come out to a beautiful high mountain meadow and a junction near the austere shores of Lake Helen, elevation 10,100 feet (3.3 miles from your start). By going right, you can follow the trail to Shamrock and Steelhead Lakes. Shamrock is 0.3 mile farther and dotted with many islands; Steelhead is another 0.5 mile beyond and is framed by 12,242-foot North Peak, towering above. The opposite trail goes left to Odell Lake (3.6 miles from your start). From Odell Lake, you could continue on to Hummingbird Lake, then to the north shore of Saddlebag Lake. If you can arrange a car shuttle at Saddlebag Lake, you can extend your trip into a one-way hike of seven miles, and that would save you the harrowing trip back down that shale-covered slope.

Note that one of the best times to visit here is in October, when Lundy Canyon's stands of quaking aspen turn bright gold and seem to dance in the breeze. This is one of the best places to admire fall colors in the Eastern Sierra. July is another first-rate time to visit; the canyon's wildflower displays are remarkable.

User Groups: Hikers, horses, and dogs. No mountain bikes. No wheelchair facilities.

Permits: A free wilderness permit is required for overnight stays and is available from the Mono Basin Scenic Area Visitors Center. There are no quotas on this trail, so advance reservations are not required.

Maps: A Hoover Wilderness map is available from Tom Harrison Maps or the U.S. Forest Service. For topographic maps, go to the USGS website to download Lundy and Dunderberg Peak.

Directions: From Lee Vining, drive north on U.S. 395 for seven miles to Lundy Lake Road. Turn west on Lundy Lake Road and drive five miles to Lundy Lake. Continue beyond the lake and Lundy Lake Resort, driving two miles farther on a dirt road that ends at the trailhead.

Contact: Inyo National Forest, Mono Basin Scenic Area Visitors Center, Lee Vining, 760/647-3044, www.fs.usda.gov/inyo.

10 LAKE CANYON AND MAY LUNDY MINE
7.0 mi / 3.5 hr or 2 days 🏃3 ⛰9

north of Lee Vining in the Hoover Wilderness

Map 10.1, page 467

The Lundy Lake area is blessed with two first-rate day-hiking trails that lead into two separate and distinct canyons: Lundy Canyon (see listing in this chapter) and Lake Canyon. Both paths offer so many rewards that when you drive up to Lundy Lake, it's hard to decide which one to take. History buffs and fishing-minded hikers would do well to take this trip from Lundy's dam into Lake Canyon, where they can see the remains of the May Lundy Mine. The mine was worked continuously for two decades starting in 1878, producing a total of about $2 million in gold. As a result, the surrounding community of Lundy grew to support 500 people, despite severe winters and deadly avalanches. Besides mining, a primary activity here was the operation of three sawmills along Lundy Creek, used to supply timber to the nearby bustling gold rush town of Bodie.

The hike to the May Lundy Mine is a fairly steep 3.5 miles one-way, climbing above Lundy Lake on the old mine road that was built in 1881. You can see the trail plain as day from the trailhead on the east side of Lundy Lake. The road/trail passes Blue Lake and Crystal Lake, where mining relics can be found. (Crystal Lake is 0.3 mile off the trail via a left fork.) Continue on the main trail, and you'll see the mine remains—old railcar tracks, tailings, and a closed-off mine shaft. Just beyond is Oneida Lake, whose waters were used to run the stamp mill for the mine. Even without the fascinating traces of history, this is an extraordinarily beautiful place. You'll want to linger awhile at sparkling Oneida Lake. Both the scenery and the fishing are quite rewarding.

User Groups: Hikers, horses, and dogs. No mountain bikes. No wheelchair facilities.

Permits: A free wilderness permit is required for overnight stays and is available from the Mono Basin Scenic Area Visitors Center. There are no quotas on this trail, so advance reservations are not required.

Maps: A Mono Lake map is available from Tom Harrison Maps. An Inyo National Forest map is available from the U.S. Forest Service. For a topographic map, go to the USGS website to download Lundy.

Directions: From Lee Vining, drive north on U.S. 395 for seven miles to Lundy Lake Road. Turn west on Lundy Lake Road and drive five miles to Lundy Lake's dam, on the east side

of the lake. Turn left and drive 0.25 mile to a locked gate and trailhead.

Contact: Inyo National Forest, Mono Basin Scenic Area Visitors Center, Lee Vining, 760/647-3044, www.fs.usda.gov/inyo.

11 PRESTON FLAT TRAIL
8.8 mi / 4.0 hr or 2 days

in Stanislaus National Forest

Map 10.1, page 467

Although some day hikers choose to suffer through the nearly intolerable grade of the Poopenaut Valley Trail to reach the swimming holes and fishing spots on the Tuolumne River's free-flowing stretch west of Hetch Hetchy Dam, a much more pleasant approach is on the Preston Flat Trail. The trailhead is off Cherry Lake Road in Stanislaus National Forest, near the epicenter of the 2013 Rim Fire, the third largest wildfire in California's history. But this foothill ecosystem is well adapted to fire, and the Preston Flat Trail shows plenty of regrowth already. A walk here is a fascinating study in wildfire ecology and recovery. The path travels 4.4 miles up the north side of the Tuolumne River Canyon on a gently undulating grade. Shortly before the trail's end is a rock chimney and a few other remains of an old cabin that was built here by a homesteader named Preston. A few hundred yards farther is a photogenic vista of Preston Falls, a cascade formed where the Tuolumne River drops 15 feet over a granite ledge into a wide, clear pool. The cataract is just a half-mile downstream of Yosemite's boundary line. If you want to stay overnight, you can. Several good campsites are found along the trail, which sticks closely to the river for most of its length.

Compared to the Poopenaut Valley Trail, the Preston Flat Trail is by far the better choice for hikers who wish to reach the river. Hike it in early spring, when the raging Tuolumne River provides the most exciting viewing. Those who wish to fish or swim should wait to visit until late spring or early summer, when the river quiets down. Winter is also a great option; the elevation is low enough that the trail is always snow-free.

User Groups: Hikers, horses, dogs, and mountain bikes. No wheelchair facilities.

Permits: A free campfire permit is required for overnight stays and is available from the Groveland Ranger Station. Parking and access are free.

Maps: A Stanislaus National Forest map is available from the U.S. Forest Service. For a topographic map, go to the USGS website to download Cherry Lake South.

Directions: From Groveland drive east on Highway 120 for 14 miles toward Yosemite. Turn left on Cherry Lake Road and drive 8.5 miles to Early Intake, where you cross a bridge over the Tuolumne River. Turn right on the far side of the bridge and drive 0.8 mile to the trailhead parking area at the end of the road, just beyond Kirkwood Powerhouse.

Contact: Stanislaus National Forest, Groveland Ranger District, Groveland, 209/962-7825, www.fs.usda.gov/stanislaus.

12 LAKE ELEANOR
3.0 mi / 1.5 hr

🏃1 ⛰️8

in northwest Yosemite National Park

Map 10.1, page 467

Lake Eleanor is a reservoir in the Hetch Hetchy region of Yosemite—not as famous or as large as Hetch Hetchy itself, but still having an important role in the San Francisco water storage system. The forest surrounding the lake was obliterated in the 2013 Rim Fire, and the Forest Service closed off access to Lake Eleanor and nearby Cherry Lake for nearly two years. It's open now, and it's incredible to see how much foliage is regenerating in this scorched landscape. Eleanor is no longer the beautiful Sierra gem that it once was, but it's still worth a visit and a short walk, if only to witness the fascinating process of fire regrowth.

Originally a naturally shallow glacial lake, Lake Eleanor was "improved" by the city of San Francisco by damming Eleanor Creek in 1928, five years before O'Shaughnessy Dam at Hetch Hetchy was completed. The dam raised the lake's water level 40 feet. Today it is the second largest lake in Yosemite after Hetch Hetchy. Its waters are not used by San Francisco as a drinking supply but rather to generate power. Set at an elevation of 4,657 feet, Lake Eleanor is popular with anglers who tote along a fishing rod while traversing the trail around the three-mile-long lake's edge. The access road to Lake Eleanor ends at a gate 0.25 mile before the lake, so start your hike there, then take a mellow walk along the lake's south and west shores. Much of Lake Eleanor's western side is dotted with islands.

It takes more than an hour's drive from Highway 120 to access Lake Eleanor, so people who come here to hike or fish often plan on spending the night. A first-come, first-served campground is located at nearby Cherry Lake, and several backpacking campsites are located on the northwest edge of Lake Eleanor (a wilderness permit is required). Note that the road to Lake Eleanor is open only May 1 to September 15 each year (the road is usually closed beyond Cherry Lake's dam).

User Groups: Hikers and horses. No dogs or mountain bikes. No wheelchair facilities.

Permits: No permits are required for day hiking. Parking and access are free (the trailhead is outside Yosemite National Park).

Maps: A Hetch Hetchy map is available from Tom Harrison Maps. For a topographic map, go to the USGS website to download Lake Eleanor.

Directions: From Groveland, drive east on Highway 120 for 14 miles toward Yosemite National Park. Turn left on Cherry Lake Road and drive 24 miles to Cherry Lake's dam, then across it. On the far side of the dam, bear right and drive 0.4 mile, then turn right on the dirt road that is signed for Lake Eleanor. Follow this road four miles to its end, at the gated Yosemite National Park boundary, 0.25 mile south of the lake.

Contact: Yosemite National Park, Yosemite, 209/372-0200, www.nps.gov/yose.

13 WAPAMA FALL
4.8 mi / 2.5 hr

in northwest Yosemite National Park

Map 10.1, page 467

The trail to this spectacular early-season waterfall starts by crossing the giant O'Shaughnessy Dam, where you may pause to curse (or admire, depending on your sensibilities) the San Francisco politicians who in 1908 believed that flooding Hetch Hetchy Valley was a good idea. In terms of geology and natural features, Hetch Hetchy is a near twin to Yosemite Valley, although somewhat smaller in scale. The valley today is filled by an immense reservoir that supplies water and power to the city of San Francisco and environs. After walking across its impressive dam and passing through a dimly lit, 500-foot-long tunnel, the trail opens out to a mixed forest along the edge of the deep blue lake. Here you will start to see a fair amount of burned trees and other evidence of the 2013 Rim Fire. But that also means that the spring wildflower displays at Hetch Hetchy are better than ever. In 1.5 miles you reach Tueeulala Fall, a delicate wisp of a freefall that only runs during peak snowmelt, and is often dry by late May. Less than a mile farther you reach powerful Wapama Fall on Falls Creek, a Bridalveil-like plume of white water that makes a dramatic plunge into the reservoir. Depending on how early in the year you visit, you may get soaking wet standing on the sturdy steel bridges that cross over Wapama Fall's coursing flow. In early spring, Wapama Falls sometimes flows so furiously that the park rangers have to close this trail. In late spring and early summer, the temperature can get hot out at Hetch Hetchy, so this spray of water can be very refreshing. If this is your first trip to this part of Yosemite, be sure to stop and read the interpretive plaques at the dam that explain about the building of Hetch Hetchy Reservoir and its service to the city of San Francisco. Whatever else you may think about it, it's a fascinating story.

User Groups: Hikers only. No dogs, horses, or mountain bikes. No wheelchair facilities.

Permits: No permits are required. There is a $30 entrance fee per vehicle at Yosemite National Park ($25 Nov.-Mar.), good for seven days.

Maps: A Hetch Hetchy map is available from Tom Harrison Maps. For topographic maps, go to the USGS website to download Lake Eleanor and Hetch Hetchy Reservoir.

Directions: From Groveland, drive east on Highway 120 for 22.5 miles to the Evergreen Road turnoff signed for Hetch Hetchy Reservoir on the left, a mile west of the Big Oak Flat entrance to Yosemite. Drive north on Evergreen Road for 7.4 miles and turn right on Hetch Hetchy Road. Drive nine miles to the dam and trailhead.

Contact: Yosemite National Park, Yosemite, 209/372-0200 or 209/372-0740 (permit reservations), www.nps.gov/yose or www.nps.gov/yose/wilderness (permit reservations).

14 RANCHERIA FALLS
13.0 mi / 1 or 2 days

in northwest Yosemite National Park

Map 10.1, page 467

It's spring and you are hungering for a Yosemite backpacking trip, but Tuolumne Meadows is knee-deep in melting snow. This is a good time to hike the northern edge of Hetch Hetchy Reservoir (elevation 3,796 feet), admiring three stunning waterfalls along the way: Tueeulala, Wapama, and Rancheria. This easy backpacking trip (or long day hike, if you prefer) travels along the length of the reservoir to its far eastern edge, where the bears are some of the boldest in all of Yosemite. (Bear canisters are required for backpackers.) Whereas Tueeulala and Wapama Falls are both freefalling cataracts, Rancheria Falls is a series of rolling cascades pouring over polished granite.

To make the trip, follow the trail notes for Wapama Falls (see listing in this chapter), then continue onward, following the trail as it contours along the reservoir's edge. Yes, there is some burn evidence here from the 2013 Rim Fire, and it's fascinating to notice how some trees were scorched while their neighbors were not. For much of the walk you are high above the water, which allows fine views of Kolana Rock and its neighboring granite formations across the reservoir. The trail follows a gentle grade with many small ups and downs, gaining only 1,300 feet along its entire length. This trip is manageable even for beginning backpackers. Shoreline trout fishing in the reservoir can be good in spring and fall. And remember: Swimming in Hetch Hetchy is not allowed.

User Groups: Hikers and horses. No dogs or mountain bikes. No wheelchair facilities.

Permits: There is a $30 entrance fee per vehicle at Yosemite National Park, ($25 Nov.-Mar.), good for seven days. Free wilderness permits are required for overnight stays. They are available on a first-come, first-served basis up to one day in advance at the Yosemite Wilderness kiosk near your chosen trailhead, or further in advance by mail, phone, or online for a $5 reservation fee per person.

Maps: A Hetch Hetchy map is available from Tom Harrison Maps. For topographic maps, go to the USGS website to download Lake Eleanor and Hetch Hetchy Reservoir.

Directions: From Groveland, drive east on Highway 120 for 22.5 miles to the Evergreen Road turnoff signed for Hetch Hetchy Reservoir on the left, a mile west of the Big Oak Flat entrance to Yosemite. Drive north on Evergreen Road for 7.4 miles and turn right on Hetch Hetchy Road. Drive nine miles to the dam and trailhead.

Contact: Yosemite National Park, Yosemite, 209/372-0200 or 209/372-0740 (permit reservations), www.nps.gov/yose or www.nps.gov/yose/wilderness (permit reservations).

15 SMITH PEAK

15.0 mi / 1 or 2 days

in northwest Yosemite National Park

Map 10.1, page 467

Smith Peak and its environs were severely burned in the 2013 Rim Fire, but the Park Service reopened the trail to the peak quickly. This is a different hike than it used to be (there are a lot less trees!), but the view from the top (7,751 feet) is still worth the effort. The route begins by the Mather Ranger Station. Follow the Lookout Point Trail for 1.2 miles, then turn right on the trail signed for Smith Meadow. You'll travel through a fire-scarred forest, then climb up a ridge to meet up with Cottonwood Creek at Lower Cottonwood Meadow, shortly followed by Upper Cottonwood Meadow. Smith Meadow lies another two miles farther, and just beyond it you'll find a junction of trails. The path on the right is another popular route to Smith Peak leading from White Wolf Campground off Tioga Road. Campsites are found a short distance to the west at this junction. Get a good night's rest before bagging Smith Peak the next morning. (You've hiked six miles thus far; it's only 1.5 more to the summit.) The peak, like the nearby meadows, was named after a 1920s sheep rancher. Many people day hike this trail, but it's possible to camp very near the summit, and if you do, you'll be treated to a memorable sunset and sunrise, plus a panoramic view of the Grand Canyon of the Tuolumne River, situated 4,000 dramatic feet below you. To the east, Yosemite's high country peaks are prominent, among them distinctive Mount Conness, Matterhorn Peak, and Mount Hoffman. Total elevation gain on this trip is 2,900 feet.

User Groups: Hikers only. No dogs, horses, or mountain bikes. No wheelchair facilities.

Permits: There is a $30 entrance fee per vehicle at Yosemite National Park, ($25 Nov.-Mar.), good for seven days. Free wilderness permits are required for overnight stays. They are available on a first-come, first-served basis up to one day in advance at the Yosemite Wilderness kiosk near your chosen trailhead, or further in advance by mail, phone, or online for a $5 reservation fee per person.

Maps: A Hetch Hetchy map is available from Tom Harrison Maps. For topographic maps, go to the USGS website to download Hetch Hetchy Reservoir.

Directions: From Groveland, drive east on Highway 120 for 22.5 miles to the Evergreen Road turnoff (on the left), signed for Hetch Hetchy Reservoir (it's a mile west of the Big Oak Flat entrance to Yosemite). Drive north on Evergreen Road for 7.4 miles, then turn right on Hetch Hetchy Road. Drive 1.6 miles to the entrance kiosk by the Mather Ranger Station; the trail begins 100 yards past the entrance kiosk, just beyond the ranger station, on the right.

Contact: Yosemite National Park, Yosemite, 209/372-0200 or 209/372-0740 (permit reservations), www.nps.gov/yose or www.nps.gov/yose/wilderness (permit reservations).

16 CARLON FALLS
3.8 mi / 2.5 hr

on the border of Stanislaus National Forest and northwest Yosemite National Park

Map 10.1, page 467

Carlon Falls is a pretty cascade on the South Fork Tuolumne River in the far western region of Yosemite. It is so far west that the trailhead is actually in Stanislaus National Forest, outside the park border, in a region that is well known as the heart of the 2013 Rim Fire. It was the third largest wildfire in California history, and you'll see much evidence of it as you drive through this region. But the trail to Carlon Falls was spared, and this short, easy hike remains one of the most popular on the west side of the park. The trailhead is across the river from Carlon Day-Use Area, a popular picnicking and fishing spot on the Tuolumne River. Follow the trail for a mere 50 feet and you enter Yosemite National Park, but with no park entrance fee and no waiting in line at the entrance kiosk. The path skirts along the river's northern

bank to reach the falls in just under two miles. It's almost completely shaded, mostly level (except for one brief steep climb that skirts a landslide area), and fairly easy to follow, although it does require clambering over a few fallen trees. The waterfall drops in two tiers over wide granite ledges, and the riverbanks surrounding it are covered with big conifers and dense foliage. A bonus is that unlike most Yosemite waterfalls, Carlon Falls runs year-round. The waterfall's namesakes are Dan and Donna Carlon, who operated the popular Carl Inn from 1916 to 1930 near what is now the Carlon Day-Use Area. This trail is popular with swimmers and anglers in summer, but mostly deserted the rest of the year.

User Groups: Hikers only. No dogs, horses, or mountain bikes. No wheelchair facilities.

Permits: No permits are required. Parking and access are free.

Maps: For a topographic map, go to the USGS website to download Ackerson Mountain.

Directions: From Groveland, drive east on Highway 120 for 22.5 miles to the Evergreen Road turnoff, signed for Hetch Hetchy Reservoir, one mile west of the Big Oak Flat entrance to Yosemite. Follow Evergreen Road north for one mile to the far side of the bridge just past Carlon Day-Use Area. Park on the right at the closed-off dirt road on the north side of the bridge, signed only as No Camping. There is room for about five cars. Begin hiking on the closed road, heading upstream. The road narrows to single track after about 100 yards.

Contact: Yosemite National Park, Yosemite, 209/372-0200, www.nps.gov/yose.

17 MERCED GROVE
3.0 mi / 1.5 hr

in western Yosemite National Park

Map 10.1, page 467

There are three giant sequoia groves in Yosemite National Park—Merced, Tuolumne, and Mariposa. Because the Merced Grove is the smallest of the three groves and requires the longest walk to reach it, it is the least visited. Generally it only gets traffic from people who enter Yosemite at the Big Oak Flat entrance and drive by it on their way to Yosemite Valley. The hiking is on a closed-off dirt road that is ideal for snowshoeing in winter. The trail cuts a level course through a mixed conifer forest for the first 0.5 mile. Bear left at the only junction and head downhill through a canopy of white firs, incense cedars, ponderosa pines, and sugar pines. You reach the small sequoia grove at 1.5 miles; the first group of six trees will take your breath away. Continue another 100 yards past these beauties; the two largest sequoias of the Merced Grove are directly across from a handsome old log cabin. It was originally built as a retreat for the park superintendent but is no longer used. Retrace your steps from the cabin, hiking uphill for your return.

User Groups: Hikers only. No dogs, horses, or mountain bikes. No wheelchair facilities.

Permits: No permits are required. There is a $30 entrance fee per vehicle at Yosemite National Park ($25 Nov.-Mar.), good for seven days.

Maps: A Yosemite National Park map is available from Tom Harrison Maps. For a topographic map, go to the USGS website to download Ackerson Mountain.

Directions: From Merced, drive 70 miles northeast on Highway 140 to Yosemite National Park. Follow the signs toward Yosemite Valley, entering through the Arch Rock entrance station. Continue 4.5 miles to the left turnoff for Highway 120, looping back out of the valley on Big Oak Flat Road. Continue straight on Big Oak Flat Road for 13.5 miles (past the Tioga Pass Road turnoff) to the Merced Grove parking area, on the left. If you enter Yosemite at the Big Oak Flat entrance station on Highway 120, drive 4.3 miles southeast to reach the trailhead, on your right.

Contact: Yosemite National Park, Yosemite, 209/372-0200, www.nps.gov/yose.

18 TUOLUMNE GROVE
2.5 mi / 1.5 hr   🥾2 ⛺8

in western Yosemite National Park

Map 10.1, page 467

Up until 1993 you could drive right in to the Tuolumne Grove of Giant Sequoias, but now the road is closed off and visitors have to hike in. The grove is found on the old Big Oak Flat Road, a paved, six-mile historic road/trail that is open to bikes and hikers (although bikes are a rarity here). This is a popular destination, so arrive early in the morning to have the best chance at solitude. Leave your car at the parking lot near Crane Flat and hike downhill into the big trees. It's one mile to the first sequoias. The Tuolumne Grove's claim to fame is that it has one of the two remaining walk-through trees in Yosemite; this one is called the Dead Giant. It's a tall stump that was tunneled in 1878. Go ahead, walk through it—everybody does. At a small picnic area, a half-mile trail loops around the forest. Make sure you save some energy for the trip back uphill to the parking lot; the moderate grade ascends 550 feet. The old paved road continues downhill beyond the grove all the way to Hodgdon Meadow Campground. Some people hike the entire six-mile distance, then have someone pick them up at Hodgdon Meadow.

User Groups: Hikers and mountain bikes. No dogs or horses. No wheelchair facilities.

Permits: No permits are required. There is a $30 entrance fee per vehicle at Yosemite National Park ($25 Nov.-Mar.), good for seven days.

Maps: A Yosemite National Park map is available from Tom Harrison Maps. For a topographic map, go to the USGS website to download Ackerson Mountain.

Directions: From Merced, drive 70 miles northeast on Highway 140 to Yosemite National Park. Follow the signs toward Yosemite Valley, entering through the Arch Rock entrance station. Continue 4.5 miles to the left turnoff for Highway 120, looping back out of the valley on Big Oak Flat Road. In 9.3 miles at Crane Flat, turn right on Tioga Pass Road, then drive 0.5 mile to the Tuolumne Grove parking lot, on the left, near Crane Flat. If you enter Yosemite at the Big Oak Flat entrance station on Highway 120, drive 7.7 miles southeast to the Crane Flat/Highway 120 East turnoff. Turn left and drive 0.5 mile to the Tuolumne Grove trailhead.

Contact: Yosemite National Park, Yosemite, 209/372-0200, www.nps.gov/yose.

19 HARDEN LAKE

5.6 mi / 3.0 hr

off Tioga Pass Road in Yosemite National Park

Map 10.1, page 467

Harden Lake itself isn't a scene stealer—by late summer, it's not much more than a large pond, framed by a few stands of aspen trees on its northeast shore. But many people come here for another reason, and that's to see the wildflowers that bloom in a region known informally as Harden's Gardens, about a quarter-mile beyond the lake. July is the most dependable month for the wildflower bloom. Plus there are other rewards, including fine views of the Grand Canyon of the Tuolumne River just a half-mile north of the lake. Also, because of the small size of Harden Lake, it is dependably warm for swimming by midsummer. The hike is simple enough. The trail follows White Wolf's gravel service road (a stretch of the original Tioga Road) past the campground entrance and across the Tuolumne River. Follow the obvious signs that point you through a few junctions to a blossom-filled marshy area. A few more steps and you're at the lake. If you haven't yet gotten your fill of the flower show, proceed a short distance farther and feast your eyes on Harden's Gardens.

User Groups: Hikers only. No dogs, horses, or mountain bikes. No wheelchair facilities.

Permits: No permits are required. There is a $30 entrance fee per vehicle at Yosemite National Park ($25 Nov.-Mar.), good for seven days.

Maps: A Yosemite National Park map is available from Tom Harrison Maps. For a topographic map, go to the USGS website to download Tamarack Flat.

Directions: From Merced, drive 70 miles northeast on Highway 140 to Yosemite National Park. Follow the signs to Yosemite Valley, entering through the Arch Rock entrance station. Continue 4.5 miles to the left turnoff for Highway 120, looping back out of the valley on Big Oak Flat Road. In 9.3 miles at Crane Flat, turn right on Tioga Pass Road and drive 14 miles to the left turnoff for White Wolf. Turn left and drive one mile to the lodge and trailhead.

Contact: Yosemite National Park, Yosemite, 209/372-0200, www.nps.gov/yose.

20 LUKENS LAKE

1.5-4.6 mi / 1.0-2.0 hr

off Tioga Pass Road in Yosemite National Park

Map 10.1, page 467

The Lukens Lake Trail is the perfect introductory lake hike for families in Yosemite National Park. A six-year-old could make the trip easily. A bonus is that the trailhead is on the western end of Tioga Road, so it's quickly reached from points in Yosemite Valley. The trail is 0.75 mile long and leads from Tioga Road up to a saddle, then drops down to a meadow on the lake's eastern edge. The path winds through a dense red fir forest, filled with mammoth trees, then skirts alongside a corn lily-filled meadow to the southern edge of the shallow, spring-fed lake (the trail used to travel on the lake's north side, but it was rerouted). If you time it right—usually late July—you may see a spectacular wildflower show featuring thousands of pink shooting stars. Swimming in Lukens Lake is highly recommended; by midsummer, this is one of the warmest lakes in the park. If you want to take a longer trail to Lukens Lake, you can start from the trailhead at White Wolf Lodge and make a 4.6-mile round-trip.

User Groups: Hikers only. No dogs, horses, or mountain bikes. No wheelchair facilities.

Permits: No permits are required. There is a $30 entrance fee per vehicle at Yosemite National Park ($25 Nov.-Mar.), good for seven days.

Maps: A Yosemite National Park map is available from Tom Harrison Maps. For a topographic map, go to the USGS website to download Tamarack Flat.

Directions: From Merced, drive 70 miles northeast on Highway 140 to Yosemite National Park. Follow the signs to Yosemite Valley, entering through the Arch Rock entrance station. Continue 4.5 miles to the left turnoff for Highway 120, looping back out of the valley on Big Oak Flat Road. In 9.3 miles at Crane Flat, turn right on Tioga Pass Road and drive 16.2 miles to the Lukens Lake trailhead parking area, on the south side of the road. The trail begins across the road.

Contact: Yosemite National Park, Yosemite, 209/372-0200, www.nps.gov/yose.

21 TEN LAKES / GRANT LAKES

12.8 mi / 1 or 2 days 3 ▲ 10

off Tioga Pass Road in Yosemite National Park

Map 10.1, page 467

The Ten Lakes area is incredibly popular with backpackers, so get your wilderness permit early. Or get an early-morning start and make this trip as a day hike; just be prepared for some serious climbing and long miles. From the Ten Lakes trailhead at Tioga Pass Road (elevation 7,500 feet), the path climbs steadily for the first four miles. There's only one brutally steep stretch, which comes between miles four and five, after a pretty stroll around Half Moon Meadow. A series of tight switchbacks pulls you through a nasty 800-foot elevation gain to the top of a ridge and the Ten Lakes/Grant Lakes junction. From there, you make a choice. Turn right to reach Grant Lakes and head mostly downhill for a mile; or, to reach Ten Lakes, continue straight, soon heading steeply downhill for 1.4 miles. The Grant Lakes offer a little more

solitude (good for day hikers), while the two larger of the Ten Lakes have the best campsites, with many trees along their shorelines offering protection from the wind. All of the lakes are sparkling, rockbound beauties. Whether you go to Ten Lakes or Grant Lakes, don't miss taking a side trip to the rocky overlook above the Ten Lakes Basin. It's only 0.5 mile from the Ten Lakes/Grant Lakes junction (continue straight for Ten Lakes, then take the unsigned trail to the left of the main trail and head for the highest point). Four of the Ten Lakes are visible from this promontory, as well as a section of the Grand Canyon of the Tuolumne.

User Groups: Hikers only. No dogs, horses, or mountain bikes. No wheelchair facilities.

Permits: There is a $30 entrance fee per vehicle at Yosemite National Park, good for seven days. Free wilderness permits are required for overnight stays. They are available on a first-come, first-served basis up to one day in advance at the Yosemite Wilderness kiosk near your chosen trailhead or further in advance by mail, phone, or online for a $5 reservation fee per person.

Maps: A Yosemite National Park map is available from Tom Harrison Maps. For topographic maps, go to the USGS website to download Yosemite Falls and Ten Lakes.

Directions: From Merced, drive 70 miles northeast on Highway 140 to Yosemite National Park. Follow the signs toward Yosemite Valley, entering through the Arch Rock entrance station. Continue 4.5 miles to the left turnoff for Highway 120, looping back out of the valley on Big Oak Flat Road. In 9.3 miles at Crane Flat, turn right on Tioga Pass Road and drive 19.4 miles to the Yosemite Creek and Ten Lakes trailhead parking area, which is on the south side of the road. The trail begins on the north side of the road.

Contact: Yosemite National Park, Yosemite, 209/372-0200 or 209/372-0740 (permit reservations), www.nps.gov/yose or www.nps.gov/yose/wilderness (permit reservations).

22 NORTH DOME
9.0 mi / 5.0 hr   🏃3 ⛰9

off Tioga Pass Road in Yosemite National Park

Map 10.1, page 467

There are those who say that climbing Half Dome is a bit of a disappointment, and not just because of the crowds. When you reach the top and check out the commanding view, the panorama of granite is not quite as awesome as you might expect, and that's because you can't see Half Dome—you're standing on it.

That's a dilemma that's easy to fix. If Half Dome is an absolute necessity in your view of Yosemite, climb North Dome instead, which offers a heart-stopping view of that big piece of granite. The route is not for the faint of heart, but when you are way up high looking down at Tenaya Canyon and across at Half Dome and Clouds Rest—well, you'll know why you came. The preferred route to North Dome begins at the Porcupine Creek trailhead on Tioga Pass Road, and has only a 1,500-foot gain to the summit. A dirt access road quickly brings you to a proper trail, signed as Porcupine Creek. Continue straight at two possible junctions near the 2.5-mile mark, heading due south for North Dome. After the third mile, your views begin to open up, providing fine vistas of North Dome and Half Dome and increasing your anticipation. At the trail junction at 4.5 miles, take the left spur for the final hike to North Dome's summit. Surprise—it's a downhill grade to reach it. Hope you brought a full supply of film or memory cards with you; the view from the top is sublime. Half Dome, just across the canyon, appears close enough to touch. Clouds Rest is a dramatic sight to the northeast. To the southwest, you can see cars crawling along the Yosemite Valley floor. On your return trip, consider taking the unsigned spur trail two miles from North Dome, at an obvious saddle. The spur leads a steep 0.25 mile to Indian Rock, the only natural arch on land in Yosemite. It's great fun to climb around on.

User Groups: Hikers only. No dogs, horses, or mountain bikes. No wheelchair facilities.

Permits: There is a $30 entrance fee per vehicle at Yosemite National Park ($25 Nov.-Mar.), good for seven days. Free wilderness permits are required for overnight stays. They are available on a first-come, first-served basis up to one day in advance at the Yosemite Wilderness kiosk near your chosen trailhead or further in advance by mail, phone, or online for a $5 reservation fee per person.

Maps: A Half Dome or Yosemite National Park map is available from Tom Harrison Maps. For a topographic map, go to the USGS website to download Yosemite Falls.

Directions: From Merced, drive 70 miles northeast on Highway 140 to Yosemite National Park. Follow the signs toward Yosemite Valley, entering through the Arch Rock entrance station. Continue 4.5 miles to the left turnoff for Highway 120, looping back out of the valley on Big Oak Flat Road. In 9.3 miles at Crane Flat, turn right on Tioga Pass Road and drive 24.5 miles to the Porcupine Creek trailhead parking area, on the right, a mile past Porcupine Flat Campground.

Contact: Yosemite National Park, Yosemite, 209/372-0200 or 209/372-0740 (permit reservations), www.nps.gov/yose or www.nps.gov/yose/wilderness (permit reservations).

23 MAY LAKE AND MOUNT HOFFMAN
2.4-6.0 mi / 2.0-4.0 hr   🏃1 ⛰9

off Tioga Pass Road in Yosemite National Park

Map 10.1, page 467

Here's a hike that you can take the kids on—well, the first part, anyway. It's an easy 1.2 miles to May Lake, tucked in below 10,850-foot Mount Hoffman. The trail to the lake has a total elevation gain of only 400 feet, and better yet, it's downhill all the way home. Attaining the summit of Mount Hoffman, on the other hand, requires a challenging ascent, and is best left to more seasoned hikers. (Leave the kids at home if you are going to continue from the shores of May Lake to the top of Mount

Hoffman.) The trail to both destinations begins at the Snow Flat trailhead (two miles off Tioga Pass Road), passes through a lodgepole pine forest, climbs up a granite-lined slope, then drops down to May Lake's southern shore. A High Sierra Camp is located here. Wandering along the scenic, granite-ringed shoreline is a pleasant way to spend the afternoon.

To turn this easy walk into a moderate butt-kicker, follow the obvious use trail to the west, which leads around to the north side of May Lake. From the northwest shore, a fairly distinct use trail leads to Hoffman's summit. This is not an official park trail, and it requires scrambling skills and sure footing, especially as you near the top. It also requires good lungs and legs: You have to gain another 1,500 feet in about two miles. So why do it? The view from Mount Hoffman's ridgeline is first-class, with Half Dome, Clouds Rest, Tenaya Lake, and May Lake all in sight. Mount Hoffman is the exact geographical center of Yosemite National Park. The peak has two main summits; the one with the weather station on top is the highest. Explore the entire ridgeline, and visit both summits if you have the time; the view is surprisingly different.

User Groups: Hikers and horses. No dogs or mountain bikes. No wheelchair facilities.

Permits: No permits are required. There is a $30 entrance fee per vehicle at Yosemite National Park ($25 Nov.-Mar.), good for seven days.

Maps: A Tuolumne Meadows or Yosemite National Park map is available from Tom Harrison Maps. For a topographic map, go to the USGS website to download Tenaya Lake.

Directions: From Merced, drive 70 miles northeast on Highway 140 to Yosemite National Park. Follow the signs toward Yosemite Valley, entering through the Arch Rock entrance station. Continue 4.5 miles to the left turnoff for Highway 120, looping back out of the valley on Big Oak Flat Road. In 9.3 miles at Crane Flat, turn right on Tioga Pass Road and drive 26.6 miles to the May Lake Road turnoff, on the left

(near road marker T-21). Drive two miles to the trailhead parking lot.

Contact: Yosemite National Park, Yosemite, 209/372-0200, www.nps.gov/yose.

24 CLOUDS REST

14.0 mi / 8.0 hr   🥾3   ⛰10

off Tioga Pass Road in Yosemite National Park

Map 10.1, page 467   BEST (

Hiking to Clouds Rest is a trip that's as epic as climbing Half Dome, but with far fewer people elbowing you along the way. With a 2,300-foot climb and 14 miles to cover, it's not for those who are out of shape. The trail ascends steadily for the first four miles, descends steeply for 0.5 mile, then climbs again more moderately. Keep the faith—the first 2.5 miles from the trailhead are the toughest. The final summit ascent is a little dicey because of the terrifying dropoffs, but as with other Yosemite peaks, watch your footing on the granite slabs, and you'll be fine. Overall, the route is much safer than climbing Half Dome, because the final ascent is far more gradual, and there are no cables to maneuver. The view from the top of Clouds Rest— of Tenaya Canyon, Half Dome, Yosemite Valley, Tenaya Lake, the Clark Range, and various peaks and ridges—will knock your socks off (hope you brought along an extra pair). Note that if this long hike has made you hot and sweaty, you can stop at the Sunrise Lakes for a swim on the way back—the first lake is only 0.25 mile from the Clouds Rest/Sunrise Trail junction.

User Groups: Hikers only. No dogs, horses, or mountain bikes. No wheelchair facilities.

Permits: No permits are required. There is a $30 entrance fee per vehicle at Yosemite National Park ($25 Nov.-Mar.), good for seven days.

Maps: A Tuolumne Meadows or Yosemite National Park map is available from Tom Harrison Maps. For a topographic map, go to the USGS website to download Tenaya Lake.

Directions: From Merced, drive 70 miles

northeast on Highway 140 to Yosemite National Park. Follow the signs toward Yosemite Valley, entering through the Arch Rock entrance station. Continue 4.5 miles to the left turnoff for Highway 120, looping back out of the valley on Big Oak Flat Road. In 9.3 miles at Crane Flat, turn right on Tioga Pass Road and drive 30.3 miles to the Sunrise Lakes trailhead, on the south side of the highway just west of Tenaya Lake.

Contact: Yosemite National Park, Yosemite, 209/372-0200, www.nps.gov/yose.

25 SUNRISE LAKES

7.5 mi / 4.5 hr or 2 days

off Tioga Pass Road in Yosemite National Park

Map 10.1, page 467

With all the people hiking to Clouds Rest, combined with all the people hiking to the Sunrise Lakes, the Sunrise trailhead can look like a mall parking lot on a Saturday. But don't be scared off; the hike to Sunrise Lakes is a great day hike or easy backpacking trip, especially during the week or off-season, with only a 1,000-foot elevation gain and a ton of stellar scenery, including great views of Clouds Rest at your back as you hike the final stretch to the lakes. You follow the trail as it climbs steeply above the edge of Tenaya Canyon. At 2.5 miles, turn left at the sign for the Sunrise High Sierra Camp. In about 10 minutes of easy walking, Lower Sunrise Lake shows up on the right, and the other lakes are shortly after it, on the left. The upper lake is the largest and by far the most popular; lots of folks like to swim and picnic there on warm summer days. Backpackers can pick a site here or continue onward for two more miles to the backpackers' camp or the High Sierra Camp, depending on where they've made their plans.

User Groups: Hikers only. No dogs, horses, or mountain bikes. No wheelchair facilities.

Permits: There is a $30 entrance fee per vehicle at Yosemite National Park ($25 Nov.-Mar.), good for seven days. Free wilderness permits are required for overnight stays. They are available on a first-come, first-served basis up to one day in advance at the Yosemite Wilderness kiosk near your chosen trailhead or further in advance by mail, phone, or online for a $5 reservation fee per person.

Maps: A Tuolumne Meadows or Yosemite National Park map is available from Tom Harrison Maps. For a topographic map, go to the USGS website to download Tenaya Lake.

Directions: From Merced, drive 70 miles northeast on Highway 140 to Yosemite National Park. Follow the signs toward Yosemite Valley, entering through the Arch Rock entrance station. Continue 4.5 miles to the left turnoff for Highway 120, looping back out of the valley on Big Oak Flat Road. In 9.3 miles at Crane Flat, turn right on Tioga Pass Road and drive 30.3 miles to the Sunrise Lakes trailhead, on the south side of the highway just west of Tenaya Lake.

Contact: Yosemite National Park, Yosemite, 209/372-0200 or 209/372-0740 (permit reservations), www.nps.gov/yose or www.nps.gov/yose/wilderness (permit reservations).

26 TENAYA LAKE

2.0 mi / 1.0 hr

off Tioga Pass Road in Yosemite National Park

Map 10.1, page 467

Lots of people drive east down Tioga Pass Road in a big rush to get to Tuolumne Meadows, but when they see giant Tenaya Lake right along the road, they stop short in their tire tracks. Luckily the 150-acre, sapphire-blue lake has a parking lot and picnic area at its east end, where you can leave your car and take a stroll down to the lake's edge. Although most people stop at the white-sand beach and picnic tables to watch the rock climbers on nearby Polly Dome, you can leave the crowds behind by strolling to the south side of the beach and joining the newly restored trail built by the Yosemite Conservancy in 2015. The path leads along the back side of Tenaya Lake, far from the road on the north side. When you get to the lake's west end, where the trail continues but the water views end, just turn around and walk back. It's a perfect, easy hike alongside one of the most beautiful lakes in Yosemite. The Yosemite Conservancy plans to continue trail work here in 2016, eventually completing a loop trail around the lake.

User Groups: Hikers only. No dogs, horses, or mountain bikes. No wheelchair facilities.

Permits: No permits are required. There is a $30 entrance fee per vehicle at Yosemite National Park ($25 Nov.-Mar.), good for seven days.

Maps: A Tuolumne Meadows or Yosemite National Park map is available from Tom Harrison Maps. For a topographic map, go to the USGS website to download Tenaya Lake.

Directions: From Merced, drive 70 miles northeast on Highway 140 to Yosemite National Park. Follow the signs toward Yosemite Valley, entering through the Arch Rock entrance station. Continue 4.5 miles to the left turnoff for Highway 120, looping back out of the valley on Big Oak Flat Road. In 9.3 miles at Crane Flat, turn right on Tioga Pass Road and drive 31.7 miles to the eastern Tenaya Lake Picnic Area (another Tenaya Lake picnic area lies 0.5 mile west). The trail leads from the parking lot.

Contact: Yosemite National Park, Yosemite, 209/372-0200, www.nps.gov/yose.

27 CATHEDRAL LAKES
7.4 mi / 4.0 hr or 2 days   🏃3   ⛰10

near Tuolumne Meadows in Yosemite National Park

Map 10.1, page 467

The Cathedral Lakes are a tremendously popular easy backpacking destination in Yosemite, but it's such a short hike to reach them that they also make a great day trip. Located on a 0.5-mile spur off John Muir Trail, the lakes are within a classic glacial cirque, tucked in below 10,840-foot Cathedral Peak. It's as scenic a spot as you'll find anywhere in Yosemite. Campsites are found close to the lakes, but you will need to secure your wilderness permit way in advance in order to spend the night. From the trail's start at Tioga Pass Road, you hike 3.2 miles on the John Muir Trail, with a 1,000-foot elevation gain. Much of the trail is shaded by lodgepole pines, but when the path breaks out of the trees, views of surrounding peaks (especially distinctive Cathedral Peak, which looks remarkably different from every angle) keep you oohing and ahhing the whole way. At 3.2 miles, turn right on the Cathedral Lake spur to reach the lower, larger lake in 0.5 mile. You'll follow the lake's inlet stream through a gorgeous meadow to the water's edge—then start snapping photographs like crazy. Many hikers stop here and go no farther, but it's a pity not to see Upper Cathedral Lake as well. To reach the upper lake, retrace your steps to John Muir Trail and continue another 0.5 mile. Fishing is often better in the upper lake, and the scenery is even more sublime.

User Groups: Hikers and horses. No dogs or mountain bikes. No wheelchair facilities.

Permits: There is a $30 entrance fee per vehicle at Yosemite National Park ($25 Nov.-Mar.), good for seven days. Free wilderness permits are required for overnight stays. They are available on a first-come, first-served basis up to one day in advance at the Yosemite Wilderness kiosk near your chosen trailhead or farther in advance by mail, phone, or online for a $5 reservation fee per person.

Maps: A Tuolumne Meadows or Yosemite National Park map is available from Tom Harrison Maps. For a topographic map, go to the USGS website to download Tenaya Lake.

Directions: From Merced, drive 70 miles northeast on Highway 140 to Yosemite National Park. Follow the signs toward Yosemite Valley, entering through the Arch Rock entrance station. Continue 4.5 miles to the left turnoff for Highway 120, looping back out of the valley on Big Oak Flat Road. In 9.3 miles at Crane Flat, turn right on Tioga Pass Road and drive 37.4 miles to the Cathedral Lakes trailhead, on the right, by Tuolumne Meadows. Park your car in the pullouts on either side of Tioga Pass Road near the trailhead; there is no formal parking lot.

Contact: Yosemite National Park, Yosemite, 209/372-0200 or 209/372-0740 (permit reservations), www.nps.gov/yose or www.nps.gov/yose/wilderness (permit reservations).

28 VOGELSANG LOOP
19.0 mi / 3 or 4 days

near Tuolumne Meadows in Yosemite National Park

Map 10.1, page 467

Although this loop is popular with hikers staying at the Vogelsang High Sierra Camp, backpackers who plan early can get a wilderness permit for their own self-designed trip. The traditional route is to head out on the western side of the loop along Rafferty Creek, then take a short spur and spend the night at Vogelsang Lake, which is without question the most visually dramatic spot seen on this trip. It's flanked by Fletcher Peak, a steep and rugged wall of glacier-carved granite. Few trees can grow in this sparse, high-alpine environment. The next day, you rejoin the loop and continue eastward to Evelyn Lake, another favorite camping spot. When it's time to return, you hike down to Lyell Fork, a 2,000-foot descent that takes a few hours, then meet up with John Muir Trail and follow it north through lush green and gorgeous Lyell Canyon, back to the trailhead at Tuolumne Meadows. The trailhead is at 8,600 feet—plenty high to start—and for the most part, the trail undulates along, never gaining or losing more than 2,000 feet.

User Groups: Hikers and horses. No dogs or mountain bikes. No wheelchair facilities.

Permits: There is a $30 entrance fee per vehicle at Yosemite National Park ($25 Nov.-Mar.), good for seven days. Free wilderness permits are required for overnight stays. They are available on a first-come, first-served basis up to one day in advance at the Yosemite Wilderness kiosk near your chosen trailhead or farther in advance by mail, phone, or online for a $5 reservation fee per person.

Maps: A Tuolumne Meadows or Yosemite National Park map is available from Tom Harrison Maps. For a topographic map, go to the USGS website to download Vogelsang Peak.

Directions: From Merced, drive 70 miles northeast on Highway 140 to Yosemite National Park. Follow the signs toward Yosemite Valley, entering through the Arch Rock entrance station. Continue 4.5 miles to the left turnoff for Highway 120, looping back out of the valley on Big Oak Flat Road. In 9.3 miles at Crane Flat, turn right on Tioga Pass Road and drive 39.5 miles to the Tuolumne Lodge and Wilderness Permits turnoff, on the right. Turn right and drive 0.4 mile toward Tuolumne Lodge. Park in the lot on the left signed for Dog Lake and John Muir Trail. The trail begins across the road from the parking lot. Additional parking is available in the Wilderness Permit parking lot, at the turnoff from Tioga Pass Road.

Contact: Yosemite National Park, Yosemite, 209/372-0200 or 209/372-0740 (permit reservations), www.nps.gov/yose or www.nps.gov/yose/wilderness (permit reservations).

29 LOWER GAYLOR LAKE
8.0 mi / 4.0 hr

near Tioga Pass in Yosemite National Park

Map 10.1, page 467

This mellow, pretty hike starts on John Muir Trail near Tuolumne Lodge, then heads east along the south side of the Dana Fork of the Tuolumne River. After two miles, the trail crosses the river and Tioga Pass Road, and heads uphill through a dense lodgepole pine forest to Lower Gaylor Lake, elevation 10,049 feet. The shallow lake is a deep turquoise color and is surrounded by a grassy alpine meadow. From its edge, you gain wide vistas of the peaks in the Tuolumne Meadows area. This is classic high-country beauty at its finest. Note that if you wish to get to the Middle and Upper Gaylor Lakes from the lower lake, you have to go cross-country. An easier way is to drive to the Tioga Pass trailhead and follow the trail notes in this chapter for the *Middle and Upper Gaylor Lakes* hike. Elevation at this trailhead is 9,250 feet; the total gain is about 800 feet to Lower Gaylor Lake, a gentle climb the whole way.

User Groups: Hikers only. No dogs, horses, or mountain bikes. No wheelchair facilities.

Permits: No permits are required. There is a $30 entrance fee per vehicle at Yosemite National Park ($25 Nov.-Mar.), good for seven days.

Maps: A Tuolumne Meadows or Yosemite National Park map is available from Tom Harrison Maps. For topographic maps, go to the USGS website to download Vogelsang Peak and Tioga Pass.

Directions: From Merced, drive 70 miles northeast on Highway 140 to Yosemite National Park. Follow the signs toward Yosemite Valley, entering through the Arch Rock entrance station. Continue 4.5 miles to the left turnoff for Highway 120, looping back out of the valley on Big Oak Flat Road. In 9.3 miles at Crane Flat, turn right on Tioga Pass Road and drive 39.5 miles to the Tuolumne Lodge and Wilderness Permits turnoff, on the right. Turn right and drive 0.4 mile toward Tuolumne Lodge, then park in the lot on the left signed for Dog Lake and John Muir Trail. The trail begins across the road from the parking lot. Additional parking is available in the Wilderness Permit parking lot, at the turnoff from Tioga Pass Road.

Contact: Yosemite National Park, Yosemite, 209/372-0200, www.nps.gov/yose.

30 ELIZABETH LAKE

4.5 mi / 2.5 hr

near Tuolumne Meadows in Yosemite National Park

Map 10.1, page 467

Starting at the trailhead elevation of 8,600 feet, you have a mere 850-foot elevation gain over 2.25 miles to get to lovely Elizabeth Lake, set in a basin at the foot of distinctive Unicorn Peak. It's a day hike that is attainable for almost anybody, and you can bet that every camper at Tuolumne Meadows Campground makes

Cathedral Peak towers over Cathedral Lakes

the trip at some point during their vacation. For noncampers, the trailhead is a bit tricky to find—it's tucked into the back of Tuolumne Meadows Campground, across from the group camp restrooms. Once you locate it, be prepared to climb steeply for the first mile, then breathe easier when the trail levels out. Fortunately the route is mostly shaded by a dense grove of lodgepole pines. Upon reaching its shore, you'll see that Elizabeth Lake is a gorgeous body of alpine water. Some visitors swim or fish here; others try to climb Unicorn Peak (10,900 feet); most are happy to sit near the lake's edge and admire the views of the sculpted peak and its neighbors in the Cathedral Range.

User Groups: Hikers only. No dogs, horses, or mountain bikes. No wheelchair facilities.

Permits: No permits are required. There is a $30 entrance fee per vehicle at Yosemite National Park ($25 Nov.-Mar.), good for seven days.

Maps: A Tuolumne Meadows or Yosemite National Park map is available from Tom Harrison Maps. For a topographic map, go to the USGS website to download Vogelsang Peak.

Directions: From Merced, drive 70 miles northeast on Highway 140 to Yosemite National Park. Follow the signs toward Yosemite Valley, entering through the Arch Rock entrance station. Continue 4.5 miles to the left turnoff for Highway 120, looping back out of the valley on Big Oak Flat Road. In 9.3 miles at Crane Flat, turn right on Tioga Pass Road and drive 39 miles to the Tuolumne Meadows Campground. Turn right and follow the signs through the main camp to the group camp. The trail begins across from the group camp restrooms, near group site No. B49.

Contact: Yosemite National Park, Yosemite, 209/372-0200, www.nps.gov/yose.

31 LYELL CANYON
6.0 mi / 3.0 hr

near Tuolumne Meadows in Yosemite National Park

Map 10.1, page 467

This hike is one of the easiest in the Yosemite high country, and since it starts out beautiful and stays that way, you can hike it as long or as short as you like. The total trail length is six miles one-way, paralleling the Lyell Fork of the Tuolumne River on the Pacific Crest Trail/John Muir Trail. But most people just head out for two or three miles, carrying their fishing rods, and then turn back. To reach the Lyell Fork, you must first cross the Dana Fork on a footbridge less than 0.5 mile from the parking lot. Then after 0.5 mile, you cross the Lyell Fork on a second footbridge, and head left along the river's south side. A third bridge takes you across Rafferty Creek and into Lyell Canyon. If you like looking at gorgeous meadows and a meandering river, this is your hike. Small trout are plentiful. A bonus is that backpacking sites are located three to four miles out on the trail, so if you get a wilderness permit, you can linger for a few days in paradise.

User Groups: Hikers and horses. No dogs or mountain bikes. No wheelchair facilities.

Permits: No permits are required. There is a $30 entrance fee per vehicle at Yosemite National Park ($25 Nov.-Mar.), good for seven days.

Maps: A Tuolumne Meadows or Yosemite National Park map is available from Tom Harrison Maps. For a topographic map, go to the USGS website to download Vogelsang Peak.

Directions: From Merced, drive 70 miles northeast on Highway 140 to Yosemite National Park. Follow the signs toward Yosemite Valley, entering through the Arch Rock entrance station. Continue 4.5 miles to the left turnoff for Highway 120, looping back out of the valley on Big Oak Flat Road. In 9.3 miles at Crane Flat, turn right on Tioga Pass Road and drive 39.5 miles to the Tuolumne Lodge and Wilderness Permits turnoff, on the right. Turn right and drive 0.4 mile toward Tuolumne Lodge; park in the lot on the left signed for Dog Lake and John Muir Trail. The John Muir Trail begins across the road from the parking lot. Additional parking is available in the Wilderness Permit parking lot, at the turnoff from Tioga Pass Road.

Contact: Yosemite National Park, Yosemite, 209/372-0200, www.nps.gov/yose.

32 YOUNG LAKES LOOP
14.6 mi / 1 or 2 days 　　　👣 3 　⛰10

near Tuolumne Meadows in Yosemite National Park

Map 10.1, page 467

Starting from the Lembert Dome parking lot at 8,600 feet in elevation, the Young Lakes Loop is a classic Yosemite trip that works equally well as a short backpacking trip or a long day hike. The destination is a series of lakes set in a deep and wide glacial cirque—the kind of awesome scenery that sticks in your mind months later, when you're sitting at a desk somewhere staring at your computer screen. The trip starts with a walk down the wide dirt road that leads to Soda Spring. Pick up the trail near Parson's Lodge that leads to Glen Aulin, and follow it through lodgepole pines for 1.8 miles until you see the right turnoff for Young Lakes. Follow Young Lakes Trail for 3.5 more miles, climbing steadily. At 5.5 miles out, you'll see the return leg of your loop leading off to the right (signed for Dog Lake). You'll continue straight for another 1.5 miles to Lower Young Lake and a stunning view of Ragged Peak, Mount Conness, and White Mountain. Two more lakes are accessible within a mile to the east. If you have the energy, don't miss the third, upper lake, the most visually stunning of them all, perched in a high meadow at 10,218 feet in elevation. When you're ready to head home, retrace your steps to the junction, and take the eastern (left) fork, returning via Dog Lake and Lembert Dome. Be forewarned: If you loop back this way, it won't be an all-downhill cruise, but the scenery makes the additional climbing

worthwhile. If you're exhausted from your trip to the lakes, skip the loop and return the way you came—it's downhill all the way.

User Groups: Hikers and horses. No dogs or mountain bikes. No wheelchair facilities.

Permits: There is a $30 entrance fee per vehicle at Yosemite National Park ($25 Nov.-Mar.), good for seven days. Free wilderness permits are required for overnight stays. They are available on a first-come, first-served basis up to one day in advance at the Yosemite Wilderness kiosk near your chosen trailhead or farther in advance by mail, phone, or online for a $5 reservation fee per person.

Maps: A Yosemite National Park map is available from Tom Harrison Maps. For topographic maps, go to the USGS website to download Tioga Pass and Falls Ridge.

Directions: From Merced, drive 70 miles northeast on Highway 140 to Yosemite National Park. Follow the signs toward Yosemite Valley, entering through the Arch Rock entrance station. Continue 4.5 miles to the left turnoff for Highway 120, looping back out of the valley on Big Oak Flat Road. In 9.3 miles at Crane Flat, turn right on Tioga Pass Road and drive 39 miles to the Lembert Dome/Soda Spring/Dog Lake/Glen Aulin trailhead parking, on the left. Begin hiking on the western edge of the parking lot, where there is a gated dirt road signed for Soda Spring.

Contact: Yosemite National Park, Yosemite, 209/372-0200 or 209/372-0740 (permit reservations), www.nps.gov/yose or www.nps.gov/yose/wilderness (permit reservations).

33 WATERWHEEL FALLS
16.0 mi / 1 or 2 days 　　　👣 3 　⛰10

near Tuolumne Meadows in Yosemite National Park

Map 10.1, page 467 　　　　　**BEST (**

This hike could be called the Epic Waterfall Trip. If you hike the entire route, you'll see so many waterfalls and so much water along the way that you'll have enough memories to get you through a 10-year drought. Arrange for a wilderness permit in advance, or reserve a stay at the Glen Aulin High Sierra Camp, so that you can divide the 16 miles over two or more days. If you're in good enough shape, you can do the trip in one day, because the trail is nearly level for the first four miles (a 400-foot elevation loss), then descends more steeply over the next four miles (a 1,500-foot elevation loss). Unfortunately, all the climbing must be done on the way home, so you must reserve your energy and have plenty of food and water (or at least a purifying device so you can filter water from the river).

Follow the trail notes for Glen Aulin and Tuolumne Falls (see listing in this chapter) for the first four miles of trail; then continue downstream past Glen Aulin Camp, alternating between stretches of stunning flower- and aspen-lined meadows and stark granite slabs. Waterwheel Falls is only three miles from the camp, and two other major cascades, California and LeConte, are along the way. To see all three falls, make sure you take each spur trail you see that leads to the river; none of the waterfalls is apparent from the main trail. Other hikers will stop you on the trail to ask if you know where the waterfalls are. Whereas all three falls are long white-water cascades, Waterwheel is considered Yosemite's most unusual-looking waterfall because it has sections of churning water that dip into deep holes in the granite, then shoot out with such velocity that they double back on themselves. When the river level is high, they actually appear to circle around like waterwheels.

User Groups: Hikers and horses. No dogs or mountain bikes. No wheelchair facilities.

Permits: There is a $30 entrance fee per vehicle at Yosemite National Park ($25 Nov.-Mar.), good for seven days. Free wilderness permits are required for overnight stays. They are available on a first-come, first-served basis up to one day in advance at the Yosemite Wilderness kiosk near your chosen trailhead or farther in advance by mail, phone, or online for a $5 reservation fee per person.

Maps: A Tuolumne Meadows or Yosemite National Park map is available from Tom Harrison Maps. For topographic maps, go to the USGS website to download Tioga Pass and Falls Ridge.

Directions: From Merced, drive 70 miles northeast on Highway 140 to Yosemite National Park. Follow the signs toward Yosemite Valley, entering through the Arch Rock entrance station. Continue 4.5 miles to the left turnoff for Highway 120, looping back out of the valley on Big Oak Flat Road. In 9.3 miles at Crane Flat, turn right on Tioga Pass Road and drive 39 miles to the Lembert Dome/Soda Spring/Dog Lake/Glen Aulin trailhead parking, on the left. Begin hiking on the western edge of the parking lot, where there is a gated dirt road signed for Soda Spring.

Contact: Yosemite National Park, Yosemite, 209/372-0200 or 209/372-0740 (permit reservations), www.nps.gov/yose or www.nps.gov/yose/wilderness (permit reservations).

34 GLEN AULIN AND TUOLUMNE FALLS

9.0 mi / 5.0 hr   👣2 ⛰9

near Tuolumne Meadows in Yosemite National Park

Map 10.1, page 467   **BEST (**

Those who aren't up for the Epic Waterfall Trip to Waterwheel Falls (see listing in this chapter) can take this trip instead and maybe even sneak in a good meal at the Glen Aulin High Sierra Camp. To stay in the camp, you must reserve a spot far in advance, but you can often purchase a hot meal just by showing up. Tuolumne Falls drop right by the High Sierra Camp, and reaching the waterfall requires only a 4.5-mile walk with a 400-foot elevation loss. The return climb is easy, with most of the ascent being in the first mile as you head up and over the various cascades of Tuolumne Falls on granite stairs. Follow the dirt road from the Lembert Dome parking lot toward Soda Spring. When you near Parson's Lodge, veer right on the signed trail to Glen Aulin. You'll walk through lodgepole pine forest, then move closer to the Tuolumne River and get incredible views of Cathedral and Unicorn Peaks, as well as Fairview Dome. After three miles, you'll cross the Tuolumne on a footbridge, and in another 0.25 mile, you'll reach the first stunning drop of Tuolumne Falls, a 100-foot, churning freefall. Keep descending past more cascades to the base of the falls, where another footbridge leads back across the river and to Glen Aulin. Pick a spot downstream beside a river pool or near the bridge at the base of the waterfall, have a seat, and ponder the exquisite beauty of this place.

User Groups: Hikers and horses. No dogs or mountain bikes. No wheelchair facilities.

Permits: No permits are required. There is a $30 entrance fee per vehicle at Yosemite National Park ($25 Nov.-Mar.), good for seven days.

Maps: A Tuolumne Meadows or Yosemite National Park map is available from Tom Harrison Maps. For topographic maps, go to the USGS website to download Tioga Pass and Falls Ridge.

Directions: From Merced, drive 70 miles northeast on Highway 140 to Yosemite National Park. Follow the signs toward Yosemite Valley, entering through the Arch Rock entrance station. Continue 4.5 miles to the left turnoff for Highway 120, looping back out of the valley on Big Oak Flat Road. In 9.3 miles at Crane Flat, turn right on Tioga Pass Road and drive 39 miles to the Lembert Dome/Soda Spring/Dog Lake/Glen Aulin trailhead parking, on the left. Begin hiking on the western edge of the parking lot, where there is a gated dirt road signed for Soda Spring.

Contact: Yosemite National Park, Yosemite, 209/372-0200, www.nps.gov/yose.

35 LEMBERT DOME

2.8 mi / 1.5 hr   🏃3   ⛰10

near Tuolumne Meadows in Yosemite National Park

Map 10.1, page 467

Lembert Dome is a *roche moutonné* (a French geologic term that means it looks something like a sheep). We never see the resemblance, but we did feel like a couple of mountain goats when we climbed Lembert Dome, elevation 9,450 feet. From the parking area at the base, you can see rock climbers practicing their stuff on the steep side of the dome, but luckily the hiker's trail heads around to the more-sloped back side. You can walk right up the granite—no ropes necessary. The Dog Lake and Lembert Dome Trail winds its way steeply around to the dome's north side (see listing in this chapter); from there, pick any route along the granite that looks manageable. When you reach the top of the dome, you know that you've accomplished something. The view from its highest point—of Tuolumne Meadows and surrounding peaks and domes—is more than worth the effort.

User Groups: Hikers only. No dogs, horses, or mountain bikes. No wheelchair facilities.

Permits: No permits are required. There is a $30 entrance fee per vehicle at Yosemite National Park ($25 Nov.-Mar.), good for seven days.

Maps: A Tuolumne Meadows or Yosemite National Park map is available from Tom Harrison Maps. For a topographic map, go to the USGS website to download Tioga Pass.

Directions: From Merced, drive 70 miles northeast on Highway 140 to Yosemite National Park. Follow the signs toward Yosemite Valley, entering through the Arch Rock entrance station. Continue 4.5 miles to the left turnoff for Highway 120, looping back out of the valley on Big Oak Flat Road. In 9.3 miles at Crane Flat, turn right on Tioga Pass Road and drive 39 miles to the Lembert Dome/Soda Spring/Dog Lake/Glen Aulin trailhead parking, on the left. Begin hiking on the trail near the restrooms.

Contact: Yosemite National Park, Yosemite, 209/372-0200, www.nps.gov/yose.

36 DOG LAKE
3.4 mi / 2.0 hr

near Tuolumne Meadows in Yosemite National Park

Map 10.1, page 467

Dog Lake is an easy-to-reach destination from Tuolumne Meadows, a perfect place for a family to spend an afternoon in the high country. The hike begins near the base of Lembert Dome, then heads through a gorgeous meadow that offers views of snowy Cathedral and Unicorn Peaks. The trail traverses a granite slab, then splits off from the path to Lembert Dome and starts to climb quite steeply through a lodgepole pine and fir forest. When you reach an intersection with Young Lakes Trail, you're only 0.25 mile from Dog Lake. The lake is a delight, although with its grassy shoreline, it is often plagued with mosquitoes (don't forget the bug spray). Set at 9,170 feet in elevation, it is wide, shallow, and deep blue. The colorful peaks to the east are Mount Dana and Mount Gibbs. You can hike around Dog Lake's perimeter if you please, take a swim in late summer, or just sit by the peaceful shoreline and relax.

User Groups: Hikers and horses. No dogs or mountain bikes. No wheelchair facilities.

Permits: No permits are required. There is a $30 entrance fee per vehicle at Yosemite National Park ($25 Nov.-Mar.), good for seven days.

Maps: A Tuolumne Meadows or Yosemite National Park map is available from Tom Harrison Maps. For a topographic map, go to the USGS website to download Tioga Pass.

Directions: From Merced, drive 70 miles northeast on Highway 140 to Yosemite National Park. Follow the signs toward Yosemite Valley, entering through the Arch Rock entrance station. Continue 4.5 miles to the left turnoff for Highway 120, looping back out of the valley on Big Oak Flat Road. In 9.3 miles at Crane Flat,

turn right on Tioga Pass Road and drive 39 miles to the Lembert Dome/Soda Spring/Dog Lake/Glen Aulin trailhead parking, on the left. Begin hiking on the trail near the restrooms.

Contact: Yosemite National Park, Yosemite, 209/372-0200, www.nps.gov/yose.

37 TUOLUMNE MEADOWS TO SONORA PASS (PCT)
77.0 mi one-way / 8 days

from Tuolumne Meadows on Highway 120 north to Sonora Pass on Highway 108

Map 10.1, page 467

This is a spectacular week-plus backpack trip that follows a section of the Pacific Crest Trail (PCT). The beauty of this region's deep canyons, glacial-cut peaks, verdant meadows, and abundant wildlife makes it a hiker's paradise.

From Tuolumne Meadows, the trail starts out deceptively easy as it follows the Tuolumne River toward the Grand Canyon of the Tuolumne River. It heads gently downhill to Glen Aulin, where you get a great view of Tuolumne Falls. When you cross the bridge at the base of the falls and head up-canyon, you'll leave the day hikers behind. In the next three days, you'll go up one canyon and down the next, one after another, with breathtaking views and long, demanding climbs. Highlights include Matterhorn Canyon (many deer, trout, and views), Benson Lake (the largest white-sand beach in the Sierra Nevada), Dorothy Lake (panoramic views to the north), and many pristine, high-country meadows. The incredible clouds of mosquitoes at the Wilmer Lake area during early summer can be a major annoyance.

When you leave Yosemite and enter Humboldt-Toiyabe National Forest, the landscape changes quickly from glacial-cut granite to volcanic rock. The trail drops past several pretty lakes and into a river drainage, and at points can be difficult to follow. In a few areas, you may be surprised to meet up with grazing cows, especially from midsummer onward.

You'll make a long, slow, climb up toward Leavitt Pass, set just below 10,800-foot Leavitt Peak. This landscape is entirely above tree line, in gray, stark country. At Leavitt Pass, the wind whistles by at high speed almost year-round. The final drop down to Sonora Pass is a one-hour descent that seems to wind all over the mountain. When you reach Highway 108, cross the road and walk about 100 yards west to a large day-use parking area. That's where your car shuttle should be waiting for you.

User Groups: Hikers and horses. No dogs or mountain bikes. No wheelchair facilities.

Permits: A wilderness permit is required for traveling through various wilderness and special-use areas the trail traverses. Contact either the Wilderness Office of the National Park Service or the Stanislaus National Forest for a permit that is good for the length of your trip. There is a $30 entrance fee per vehicle at Yosemite National Park ($25 Nov.-Mar.), good for seven days.

Maps: For topographic maps, go to the USGS website to download Pickel Meadow, Tower Peak, Piute Mountain, Matterhorn Peak, Dunderberg Peak, Vogelsang Peak, Tioga Pass, Falls Ridge, Buckeye Ridge, and Sonora Pass.

Directions: From Merced, drive 70 miles northeast on Highway 140 to Yosemite National Park. Follow the signs toward Yosemite Valley, entering through the Arch Rock entrance station. Continue 4.5 miles to the left turnoff for Highway 120, looping back out of the valley on Big Oak Flat Road. In 9.3 miles at Crane Flat, turn right on Tioga Pass Road and drive 39 miles to the Lembert Dome/Soda Spring/Dog Lake/Glen Aulin trailhead parking, on the left. Begin hiking on the western edge of the parking lot, where there is a gated dirt road signed for Soda Spring.

Contact: Yosemite National Park, Yosemite, 209/372-0200, www.nps.gov/yose; Stanislaus National Forest, Calaveras Ranger Station, Hathaway Pines, 209/795-1381, www.fs.usda.gov/stanislaus.

38 TUOLUMNE MEADOWS TO YOSEMITE VALLEY (JMT)

22.0 mi one-way / 2 days 🏃5 ⛰10

near Tuolumne Meadows in Yosemite National Park

Map 10.1, page 467

The first glimpses of Yosemite Valley will seem like a privileged view into heaven after having hiked the entire John Muir Trail (JMT) from Mount Whitney. For hikers making only this 22-mile section, the rewards can seem just as profound. The trip starts at Tuolumne Meadows, where backpackers can buy a good cheap breakfast, obtain wilderness permits, and camp in a special area set aside for JMT hikers. When you take your first steps away from Tuolumne Meadows, resist the urge to rush to the finish line in order to close out a historic expedition. Instead, relax and enjoy the downhill glide, always remembering that you are in sacred land. Compared to the rest of the JMT, this leg will come with far less strain, starting with a 3.1-mile tromp past Cathedral Lakes and requiring a 0.5-mile walk on a signed cutoff trail. If you can time it right, this area can make a great layover camp, with deep, emerald-green water and Cathedral Peak in the background. Beyond Cathedral Lakes, the trail makes a relatively short 500-foot climb over Cathedral Pass, skirts Tresidder Peak, and then descends through pristine Long Meadow. After passing Sunrise Trail Camp, a decent layover, the trail picks up little Sunrise Creek and follows it all the way down to Little Yosemite Valley, a popular trail camp. From Cathedral Lakes, it's 14.5 miles to the junction of Half Dome Trail, and another 2.2 miles to Little Yosemite.

For JMT hikers, making the climb to the top of Half Dome is a must, even though it often means putting up with a parade of people and even delays waiting for the line to move at the climbing cable. The Half Dome climb starts with a steep hike for the first mile, followed by steep switchbacks across granite on good trail to the foot of Half Dome's back wall. Here you'll find climbing cables to aid your final 300-foot ascent, and as you go, you'll discover breathtaking views of Tenaya Canyon. This is considered one of the world's glamour hikes, and while it turns hiking into an act of faith, we have seen eight-year-olds and 70-year-olds make the cable climb. By the way, if you take on Half Dome, be certain to have two canteens of water per person. Adding the Half Dome side trip to the rest of the JMT leg will add a round-trip of 5.2 miles to your hike. Because of its proximity to Half Dome, the Little Yosemite Valley Trail Camp is often crowded. From here, though, it's an easy five-mile hike downhill to Yosemite Valley. Again, try not to speed through to the end, even though it's an easy tromp downhill all the way. The magic is in the moment.

From Little Yosemite, the JMT is routed along the Merced River. In a mile, you'll reach Liberty Cap, and shortly later, Nevada Fall. Then down, down you go, with the trail often turning to giant granite steps, down past Emerald Pool and then to Vernal Fall, another spectacular waterfall. Since Vernal Fall is just 1.7 miles from the end of the trail, you'll start meeting lots of day hikers coming from the other direction, many gasping for breath as they make the uphill climb out of Yosemite Valley. Many will ask how far you've hiked; some may even want to take your photograph. It may feel a bit inane, but, hey, enjoy it. After all, you just finished John Muir Trail, the greatest hiking trail in the world.

User Groups: Hikers and horses. No dogs or mountain bikes. No wheelchair facilities.

Permits: A wilderness permit is required for traveling through various wilderness and special-use areas that the trail traverses. Contact the Wilderness Office of the National Park Service for a permit that is good for the length of your trip. There is a $30 entrance fee per vehicle at Yosemite National Park ($25 Nov.-Mar.), good for seven days.

Maps: A John Muir Trail Map Pack is available from Tom Harrison Maps. For topographic maps, go to the USGS website to download Vogelsang Peak, Half Dome, Yosemite Falls, and Tenaya Peak.

Directions: From Merced, drive 70 miles northeast on Highway 140 to Yosemite National Park. Follow the signs toward Yosemite Valley, entering through the Arch Rock entrance station. Continue 4.5 miles to the left turnoff for Highway 120, looping back out of the valley on Big Oak Flat Road. In 9.3 miles at Crane Flat, turn right on Tioga Pass Road and drive 39.5 miles to the Tuolumne Lodge and Wilderness Permits turnoff, on the right. Turn right and drive 0.4 mile toward Tuolumne Lodge; park in the lot on the left signed for Dog Lake and John Muir Trail. The John Muir Trail begins across the road from the parking lot. Additional parking is available in the Wilderness Permit parking lot, at the turnoff from Tioga Road.

Contact: Yosemite National Park, Yosemite, 209/372-0200 or 209/372-0740 (permit reservations), www.nps.gov/yose or www.nps.gov/yose/wilderness (permit reservations).

39 MONO PASS
8.4 mi / 4.5 hr   2   9

near Tioga Pass in Yosemite National Park

Map 10.1, page 467

With an elevation gain of only 900 feet spread out over four miles, you'll hardly even notice you're climbing on the route to Mono Pass. That's if you're acclimated, of course, because you start out at 9,700 feet, where the air is mighty thin. The Mono Pass Trail begins in a mix of lodgepole pines and grassy meadows, then crosses the Dana Fork of the Tuolumne River, which is an easy boulder-hop by midsummer. (Earlier in the season you may need to find a log to cross.) The trail soon meets up with Parker Pass Creek and parallels it for most of the trip. As you proceed, you'll gain great views of Mount Gibbs, Mount Dana, and the Kuna Crest. At a trail junction at 2.0 miles, bear left and start to climb more noticeably. When you reach the Mono Pass sign at 3.8 miles, take the right spur trail (unsigned). It leads 0.3 mile to a cluster of four 19th-century mining cabins, which have been beautifully restored. It's fascinating to explore the small cabins and surrounding mine ruins and consider the hard life of those who lived and worked here. Then, heading back to the main trail, continue another 0.5 mile beyond the sign marking Mono Pass for the best views of the trip. From a granite promontory above a water-filled tarn, you can see far down Bloody Canyon to Mono Lake and the surrounding desert.

User Groups: Hikers and horses. No dogs or mountain bikes. No wheelchair facilities.

Permits: No permits are required. There is a $30 entrance fee per vehicle at Yosemite National Park ($25 Nov.-Mar.), good for seven days.

Maps: A Yosemite High Country map is available from Tom Harrison Maps. For a topographic map, go to the USGS website to download Tioga Pass.

Directions: From Merced, drive 70 miles northeast on Highway 140 to Yosemite National Park. Follow the signs toward Yosemite Valley, entering through the Arch Rock entrance station. Continue 4.5 miles to the left turnoff for Highway 120, looping back out of the valley on Big Oak Flat Road. In 9.3 miles at Crane Flat, turn right on Tioga Pass Road and drive 44.5 miles to the Mono Pass trailhead on the right, 1.5 miles west of Tioga Pass.

Contact: Yosemite National Park, Yosemite, 209/372-0200, www.nps.gov/yose.

40 SPILLWAY AND HELEN LAKES
9.0 mi / 5.0 hr   🏃3 ⛰9

near Tioga Pass in Yosemite National Park

Map 10.1, page 467

Another option on the Mono Pass Trail (see trail notes for previous hike) is to take the right fork at 2.0 miles and head for Spillway Lake, a wide, shallow lake that is only 1.6 miles from this junction, and then large Helen Lake, which is reached by some easy cross-country travel. It seems like a completely different trip than the aforementioned hike to Mono Pass.

The highlights here are two high alpine lakes that epitomize the beauty of the Yosemite high country. Backpackers rarely travel to these lakes, so day hikers are likely to have more solitude here. The views of the Kuna Crest and the high alpine meadow surrounding the upper reaches of Parker Pass Creek will take your breath away. A maintained trail travels to Spillway Lake, and from its southeast edge you simply follow Helen Lake's outlet creek uphill to the shores of Helen Lake. Helen Lake is set at 11,000 feet in elevation, and it's as lovely as any high mountain lake can be. Total elevation gain to see both lakes is only 1,300 feet.

User Groups: Hikers only. No dogs, horses, or mountain bikes. No wheelchair facilities.

Permits: No permits are required. There is a $30 entrance fee per vehicle at Yosemite National Park ($25 Nov.-Mar.), good for seven days.

Maps: A Yosemite High Country map is available from Tom Harrison Maps. For a topographic map, go to the USGS website to download Tioga Pass.

Directions: From Merced, drive 70 miles northeast on Highway 140 to Yosemite National Park. Follow the signs toward Yosemite Valley, entering through the Arch Rock entrance station. Continue 4.5 miles to the left turnoff for Highway 120, looping back out of the valley on Big Oak Flat Road. In 9.3 miles at Crane Flat, turn right on Tioga Pass Road and drive 44.5 miles to the Mono Pass trailhead on the right, 1.5 miles west of Tioga Pass.

Contact: Yosemite National Park, Yosemite, 209/372-0200, www.nps.gov/yose.

41 MIDDLE AND UPPER GAYLOR LAKES
4.0 mi / 2.5 hr   🏃3 ⛰9

near Tioga Pass in Yosemite National Park

Map 10.1, page 467

Middle and Upper Gaylor Lakes are deservedly popular destinations, because of the short distance required to reach them and their great opportunities for trout fishing. Oh yeah, and then there is the amazing high-alpine scenery. Starting near Tioga Pass (at nearly 10,000 feet), the trail climbs a steep ridge and then drops down to Middle Gaylor Lake. Although it's only one mile of ascent, it's a high-elevation butt-kicker that causes many to beg for mercy. From the middle lake, you can follow the creek gently uphill to the east for another mile to reach smaller Upper Gaylor Lake. Be sure to take the trail around its north side and uphill for a few hundred yards to the site of the Great Sierra Mine and the remains of an old stone cabin. The Great Sierra Mine turned out to be not so great—no silver ore was ever refined, and the mine was eventually abandoned. The hauntingly beautiful glacial scenery is what remains. Total elevation gain on the hike to Upper Gaylor Lake is about 1,000 feet, and it's worth every step. If you want to see more of this sublime lake basin, the twin Granite Lakes lie about 0.75 mile northwest of Middle Gaylor Lake. Although there is no formal trail, it's an easy cross-country ramble to see the Granite Lakes as well, which are tucked in below a massive granite cirque.

User Groups: Hikers only. No dogs, horses, or mountain bikes. No wheelchair facilities.

Permits: No permits are required. There is a $30 entrance fee per vehicle at Yosemite National Park ($25 Nov.-Mar.), good for seven days.

Maps: A Yosemite High Country map is available from Tom Harrison Maps. For a topographic map, go to the USGS website to download Tioga Pass.

Directions: From Merced, drive 70 miles northeast on Highway 140 to Yosemite National Park. Follow the signs toward Yosemite Valley, entering through the Arch Rock entrance station. Continue 4.5 miles to the left turnoff for Highway 120, looping back out of the valley on Big Oak Flat Road. In 9.3 miles at Crane Flat, turn right on Tioga Pass Road and drive 46 miles to the parking lot just west of the Tioga Pass entrance station, on the north side of Tioga Pass Road.

Contact: Yosemite National Park, Yosemite, 209/372-0200, www.nps.gov/yose.

42 MOUNT DANA

6.0 mi / 4.0 hr

near Tioga Pass in Yosemite National Park

Map 10.1, page 467   **BEST (**

Mount Dana is a grueling hike. Yet many hikers make the trip every summer, perhaps as some sort of rite of passage to affirm that the long winter has truly ended in the high country. The path to the 13,053-foot summit requires a 3,100-foot elevation gain condensed into a mere three miles. To make matters more difficult, there is no maintained trail, only a series of informal "use" trails created by generations of hearty Yosemite hikers who have traveled the route. To join their ranks, leave your car at the Gaylor Lakes trailhead by the Tioga Pass entrance station, then cross the road and hike southeast on the unsigned but obvious trail that begins just a few feet from the park entrance kiosk. The path starts with a pleasant ramble through Dana Meadows, then enters a dense lodgepole pine forest. Soon the grade becomes more intense, but this first stretch of climbing is highlighted by a spectacular wildflower show that usually peaks in late July. Lupine, larkspur, Indian paintbrush, senecia—they're all here, in all their glory. The climbing gets tougher on the second mile of the hike, but stick with it and soon you've climbed above 11,000 feet, and now you're above tree line. The path keeps ascending to the 11,600-foot mark, where a giant trail cairn marks a large, rock-covered plateau. This is a good place to rest and do a check on your physical and mental state. Although the summit may look close from here, you still have a long, hard way to go. Two fairly obvious paths head uphill from this point; if you're feeling comfortable with the altitude, pick either one and continue onward, zigzagging your way up the shale-covered slope. In the final mile you must gain 1,500 feet, and to say it is slow going would be a major understatement. There's no shade, often a fierce wind, plenty of loose rock underfoot, and the breathtakingly thin air of high altitude. With what may seem like your last breath, you finally reach the summit, where you are witness to one of the finest views in the Sierra. Your field of vision encompasses Mono Lake, Ellery and Saddlebag Lakes, Glacier Canyon, Tuolumne Meadows, Lembert Dome, and an untold wealth of high peaks. Bring a map and identify all you can survey, or forget the map and just take in the majesty of it all.

A few tips for making the ascent safely: First, wait until mid-July or later to make the trip, as Mount Dana can be snow-covered long into the summer. Second, get an early start in the morning so you have no chance of encountering afternoon thunderstorms. Third, carry (and drink) as much water as you can. Fourth, wear good sunglasses and sun protection at this high elevation. And lastly, pace yourself to give your body a chance to adjust to the 13,000-foot altitude.

User Groups: Hikers only. No dogs, horses, or mountain bikes. No wheelchair facilities.

Permits: No permits are required. There is a $30 entrance fee per vehicle at Yosemite National Park ($25 Nov.-Mar.), good for seven days.

Maps: A Yosemite High Country map is available from Tom Harrison Maps. For a topographic map, go to the USGS website to download Tioga Pass.

Directions: From Merced, drive 70 miles northeast on Highway 140 to Yosemite National Park. Follow the signs toward Yosemite Valley, entering through the Arch Rock entrance station. Continue 4.5 miles to the left turnoff for Highway 120, looping back out of the valley on Big Oak Flat Road. In 9.3 miles at Crane Flat, turn right on Tioga Pass Road and drive 46 miles to the parking lot just west of the Tioga Pass entrance station, on the north side of Tioga Pass Road. The trail begins on the south side of Tioga Pass Road; begin hiking on the unsigned trail across from the park entrance kiosk.

Contact: Yosemite National Park, Yosemite, 209/372-0200, www.nps.gov/yose.

43 BENNETTVILLE
2.6 mi / 2.0 hr   🥾2   ⛺10

in Inyo National Forest just east of Tioga Pass

Map 10.1, page 467

This first-class high-country hike is suitable for even the most novice hikers, and is sure to spark your imagination. The remote high-country region of Bennettville was the site of a 19th-century silver mining community. Although the town thrived only from 1882 to 1884, it was the primary reason for the construction of the Tioga Pass Road from the west. The original road, called the Great Sierra Wagon Road, was built by the Great Sierra Consolidated Silver Company in anticipation of the riches they would make from the mines at Bennettville and nearby. Ultimately, no valuable minerals were ever extracted, and the company went broke in record time. A mostly level trail leads to the two buildings that remain from Bennettville's heyday: the assay office and barn/bunkhouse. An open mine tunnel lined with railcar tracks can also be seen, as well as some rusting mining equipment. Much of the machinery and supplies for this mine was hauled here from the May Lundy Mine over Dore Pass. Men and animals carried several tons of equipment on their backs and on sleds, sometimes through driving snowstorms in the middle of winter at this 10,000-foot elevation.

You can extend this hike by following the trail alongside Mine Creek 0.5 mile uphill from the mine buildings to small Shell Lake, followed by three more shallow lakes in the next mile or so: Mine, Fantail, and finally Spuller. More mine sites can be seen along the way. The high-country landscape here is a mix of open meadows, delicate high-alpine wildflowers, and wind-sculpted whitebark pines. The scenery is as good as you'll find anywhere, and you'll want to return to this area again and again.

User Groups: Hikers, horses, and dogs. No mountain bikes past Shell Lake (wilderness boundary). No wheelchair facilities.

Permits: No permits are required. Parking and access are free.

Maps: A Yosemite High Country map is available from Tom Harrison Maps. An Inyo National Forest map is available from the U.S. Forest Service. For a topographic map, go to the USGS website to download Tioga Pass.

Directions: From Merced, drive 70 miles northeast on Highway 140 to Yosemite National Park. Follow the signs toward Yosemite Valley, entering through the Arch Rock entrance station. Continue 4.5 miles to the left turnoff for Highway 120, looping back out of the valley on Big Oak Flat Road. In 9.3 miles at Crane Flat, turn right on Tioga Pass Road and drive 48 miles (you'll exit the park) to the Saddlebag Lake turnoff, on the left, two miles east of Tioga Pass. Turn left, and then left again immediately, to enter Junction Campground. The trail begins at the campground entrance.

Contact: Inyo National Forest, Mono Basin Scenic Area Visitors Center, Lee Vining, 760/647-3044, www.fs.usda.gov/inyo.

44 GARDISKY LAKE

2.0 mi / 2.0 hr

in Hoover Wilderness just east of Tioga Pass

Map 10.1, page 467

How can a two-mile round-trip hike be rated a 3 for difficulty? It can because it goes straight up, gaining 700 feet in just one mile, with not nearly enough switchbacks. Although the trail distance is short, the trailhead is set at 9,800 feet, which means you need to be well acclimated to pant your way through that steep of a grade. The trip offers many rewards, though, including many fewer people than at nearby Saddlebag Lake and a stellar high-alpine setting. Once you huff and puff your way to the ridge top, you have a nearly level 0.25-mile stroll through a fragile alpine meadow to reach the lake, a shallow body of water surrounded by high-alpine meadows. That 11,513-foot mountain you see as you climb (ahead and to your right) is Tioga Peak; from the southwest edge of Gardisky Lake it's a short but steep tromp to its windy summit (this will add a couple extra

miles and 1,000 feet of extra elevation gain to your day). White Mountain and Mount Conness are also prominent, both over 12,000 feet.

User Groups: Hikers, horses, and dogs. No mountain bikes. No wheelchair facilities.

Permits: No permits are required for day-use; an overnight permit is required for backpacking. Parking and access are free.

Maps: A Yosemite High Country map is available from Tom Harrison Maps. An Inyo National Forest map is available from the U.S. Forest Service. For a topographic map, go to the USGS website to download Tioga Pass.

Directions: From Merced, drive 70 miles northeast on Highway 140 to Yosemite National Park. Follow the signs toward Yosemite Valley, entering through the Arch Rock entrance station. Continue 4.5 miles to the left turnoff for Highway 120, looping back out of the valley on Big Oak Flat Road. In 9.3 miles at Crane Flat, turn right on Tioga Pass Road and drive 48 miles (you'll exit the park) to the Saddlebag Lake turnoff, on the left, two miles east of Tioga Pass. Turn left and go 1.3 miles to the trailhead parking area, on the west side of the road before you reach Saddlebag Lake. The trail begins across the road.

Contact: Inyo National Forest, Mono Basin Scenic Area Visitors Center, Lee Vining, 760/647-3044, www.fs.usda.gov/inyo.

45 SLATE CREEK TRAIL TO GREEN TREBLE LAKE

4.5 mi / 2.0 hr

in Hoover Wilderness just east of Tioga Pass

Map 10.1, page 467

One of the most beautiful and serene campgrounds in the High Sierra, Sawmill Walk-In Camp is accessed by a quarter-mile walk from its parking area. A wide trail continues through and past the campsites into Hall Research Natural Area, a specially protected region of Inyo National Forest that is open to day hikers only (no backpacking). The trail leads one mile to Timberline Station, an old research station built in 1929. From here you can cross Slate Creek and hike another mile to Green Treble Lake at the headwaters of Slate Creek. Where two forks of the creek join, about 0.5 mile beyond Timberline Station, follow the south fork (left) another 0.5 mile to Green Treble Lake. This is a remarkably level hike at 10,000-plus feet in elevation—pristine high country that is only accessible a few months each year. You know you are in a special place when you are here.

User Groups: Hikers, horses, and dogs. No mountain bikes. No wheelchair facilities.

Permits: No permits are required. Parking and access are free.

Maps: A Yosemite High Country map is available from Tom Harrison Maps. An Inyo National Forest map is available from the U.S. Forest Service. For a topographic map, go to the USGS website to download Tioga Pass.

Directions: From Merced, drive 70 miles northeast on Highway 140 to Yosemite National Park. Follow the signs toward Yosemite Valley, entering through the Arch Rock entrance station. Continue 4.5 miles to the left turn-off for Highway 120, looping back out of the valley on Big Oak Flat Road. In 9.3 miles at Crane Flat, turn right on Tioga Pass Road and drive 48 miles (you'll exit the park) to the Saddlebag Lake turnoff, on the left, two miles east of Tioga Pass. Turn left and drive 1.5 miles north on Saddlebag Lake Road to Sawmill Campground's parking area on the left.

Contact: Inyo National Forest, Mono Basin Scenic Area Visitors Center, Lee Vining, 760/647-3044, www.fs.usda.gov/inyo.

46 SADDLEBAG LAKE LOOP
3.6-8.4 mi / 2.0-4.0 hr 👥2 ⛰9

in Inyo National Forest just east of Tioga Pass

Map 10.1, page 467

Starting from the resort buildings at the south end of 10,087-foot Saddlebag Lake, you can design a wonderfully scenic hiking trip into the 20 Lakes Basin of any length that suits your time and energy. A benefit of hiking here is that you can cut off some miles by taking the boat taxi across the lake, rather than hiking along its lakeshore. A one-way ride on the boat taxi will cut 1.5 miles off your mileage; a round-trip cuts off three miles. Unfortunately, this high-country region is so beautiful, so easy to access, and so close to Yosemite that on summer weekends, it can be as crowded as the most popular trails in the park. A great time to hike here is a few weeks after Labor Day, when the vacation crowds have dispersed.

To hike alongside Saddlebag Lake instead of riding in the boat taxi, follow the trail on either the lake's east or west side. The east side trail is more scenic; the west side trail is shorter. If you just want to make a short 3.6-mile loop, hike out on one trail and back on the other, but be sure to take the short left spur at Saddlebag's northwest edge to Greenstone Lake, which is backed by photogenic North Peak. If you want to hike farther, you can continue past Greenstone Lake to Wasco Lake and then on to deep, stark Steelhead Lake (three miles out if you start on the west side trail). Several more lakes lie beyond, including Shamrock, Helen, and Odell. If you hike the entire loop and visit all six lakes that lie immediately beyond Saddlebag, you'll have an 8.4-mile day (or a 5.4-mile day, if you take the boat taxi round-trip). No matter how far you go, you'll be awed by the incredible high-country scenery—a blend of blue sky, granite, water, and hardy white-bark pines.

User Groups: Hikers and dogs. No horses or mountain bikes. No wheelchair facilities.

Permits: No permits are required. Parking and access are free.

Maps: A Yosemite High Country map is available from Tom Harrison Maps. An Inyo National Forest map is available from the U.S. Forest Service. For a topographic map, go to the USGS website to download Tioga Pass.

Directions: From Merced, drive 70 miles northeast on Highway 140 to Yosemite National Park. Follow the signs toward Yosemite Valley, entering through the Arch Rock entrance station. Continue 4.5 miles to the left turnoff for Highway 120, looping back out of the valley on Big Oak Flat Road. In 9.3 miles at Crane Flat, turn right on Tioga Pass Road and drive 48 miles (you'll exit the park) to the Saddlebag Lake turnoff, on the left, two miles east of Tioga Pass. Turn left and drive another 2.7 miles to the trailhead parking area.

Contact: Inyo National Forest, Mono Basin Scenic Area Visitors Center, Lee Vining, 760/647-3044, www.fs.usda.gov/inyo.

47 GIBBS LAKE

5.4 mi / 2.5 hr or 2 days

west of Lee Vining on the northern boundary of the Ansel Adams Wilderness

Map 10.1, page 467

The 2.7-mile hike from Upper Horse Meadow to Gibbs Lake is a great day hike that sees surprisingly few people. Since the trailhead isn't located at a lake or some other attractive setting, nobody gets here by accident. The trail starts at Upper Horse Meadow (elevation 8,000 feet), and climbs up Gibbs Canyon to Gibbs Lake, at 9,530 feet. That's about a 1,500-foot climb, but unfortunately the first stretch goes straight uphill on an old dirt road with nary a switchback. Once you get through that grunt of an ascent, the rest of the route is on a much mellower grade as it travels alongside Gibbs Creek. The trail ends at Gibbs Lake, a lovely glacial cirque that is backed by bare granite and fronted by conifers. Are you feeling ambitious? If you study the lake's back wall for a few minutes, it will soon become obvious that there is another, higher lake in this drainage. If you are sure-footed and have plenty of energy, you can pick out your route and go take a look at that lake. Although Gibbs Lake is pretty, the higher Kidney Lake (10,388 feet) is a stunner. It will take you about 40 minutes of challenging cross-country scrambling to get from Gibbs to Kidney; you'll gain almost 900 feet in less than a mile. Just pick your route carefully

and go slow. Kidney Lake is indeed kidney-shaped, and it is flanked by the Dana Plateau on one side and Mount Gibbs (12,773 feet) on the other.

Note: While not required, high-clearance vehicles are a good idea on Forest Road 1N16.

User Groups: Hikers, horses, and dogs. No mountain bikes beyond the wilderness boundary. No wheelchair facilities.

Permits: A free wilderness permit is required for overnight stays and is available from the Mono Basin Scenic Area Visitors Center. Quotas are in effect from May 1 to November 1; for this period, permits are available in advance for a $5 reservation fee per person.

Maps: Mono Lake and Mammoth High Country maps are available from Tom Harrison Maps. An Inyo National Forest or Ansel Adams Wilderness map is available from the U.S. Forest Service. For a topographic map, go to the USGS website to download Lee Vining.

Directions: From Lee Vining, drive 1.3 miles south on U.S. 395 and turn west on unsigned Forest Road 1N16 (look for the sign indicating Horse Meadow). Drive 3.4 miles past Upper Horse Meadow to the trailhead at the end of the road. A high-clearance vehicle is recommended.

Contact: Inyo National Forest, Mono Basin Scenic Area Visitors Center, Lee Vining, 760/647-3044, www.fs.usda.gov/inyo.

48 MONO LAKE SOUTH TUFA TRAIL

1.0 mi / 0.5 hr

at the southern end of Mono Lake in Mono Lake Tufa State Reserve

Map 10.1, page 467   **BEST (**

The strange and remarkable tufa towers at Mono Lake create one of the most extraordinary landscapes in California. The terrain resembles a moonscape, but a strangely beautiful one. The area is extremely popular with photographers, especially at sunset. This short loop trail is the best way to get a good look at the tufa formations, which are formed when calcium-rich underwater springs are released from the lake bottom and then combine with Mono Lake's saline water, forming calcium carbonate. The trail leads through sagebrush plains to the southern shore of the lake, where the tufas rest like old, untouched earth castles. Some of them poke out of the lake surface; others are high and dry on land. Mono Lake itself is vast (covering 60 square miles) and is estimated to be more than 700,000 years old, making it one of the oldest lakes in North America. The lake's basin has become one of the world's most prolific stopover points for gulls, grebes, plovers, and phalaropes during their annual southbound flights. That's because the alkaline properties of the water create prime habitat for brine shrimp (an ideal food for these birds), and the lake's two large islands provide isolation from predators. Eighty-five percent of the California gull population was born at Mono Lake.

User Groups: Hikers, horses, dogs, and wheelchairs. No mountain bikes.

Permits: No permits are required. A $3 entrance fee is charged per adult. Youth ages 17 and under are free.

Maps: A Mono Lake map is available from Tom Harrison Maps. For topographic maps, go to the USGS website to download Lee Vining and Mono Mills.

Directions: From Lee Vining, drive five miles south on U.S. 395 and turn east on Highway 120 (signed for Mono Lake South Tufa). Drive 4.7 miles, then turn left and drive one mile on a dirt road to the parking area.

Contact: Mono Lake Tufa State Reserve, 760/647-6331, www.parks.ca.gov; Inyo National Forest, Mono Basin Scenic Area Visitors Center, Lee Vining, 760/647-3044, www.fs.usda.gov/inyo.

49 BLOODY CANYON TRAIL

8.2 mi / 5.0 hr 🏃4 ⛰9

southwest of Lee Vining at the northeastern boundary of the Ansel Adams Wilderness

Map 10.1, page 467

Lower Sardine Lake is a jewel cradled in a high glacial cirque at 9,888 feet, the kind of lake that makes the Ansel Adams Wilderness one of the most treasured places in the world. Beyond the first easy mile, this hike is tough and steep. Much of the trail is a historic Native American trading route, used by the Indians of the Mono Basin to visit the Indians of the Yosemite high country. The first mile to Walker Lake is an easy downhill cruise, dropping 600 feet in elevation. Walker Lake is a popular destination for anglers and has a small private resort on its eastern shore. From the aspen-lined western edge of the lake, you head up Bloody Canyon, climbing nearly 2,000 feet in about three miles. The hike parallels Walker Creek, requiring two stream crossings on the way up to Lower Sardine Lake. For anyone who is either out of shape or not acclimated to the altitude, the climb can be rough going. As you near Lower Sardine Lake, the sight of a beautiful waterfall (the lake's outlet stream) will help to spur you on. When you reach the lake at elevation 9,888 feet, you'll find it is surrounded by rocky cliffs on three sides and provides great views of the Mono Basin to the east. Backpackers can continue hiking up and over Mono Pass and into Yosemite National Park's backcountry, but to do so, they face still more of a climb. Remember that if you are entering the national park, dogs are not allowed.

User Groups: Hikers, horses, and dogs. No mountain bikes beyond the wilderness boundary. No wheelchair facilities.

Permits: A free wilderness permit is required for overnight stays and is available from the Mono Basin Scenic Area Visitors Center. Quotas are in effect from May 1 to November 1; for this period, permits are available in advance for a $5 reservation fee per person.

Maps: Yosemite High Country and Mammoth

High Country maps are available from Tom Harrison Maps. An Inyo National Forest or Ansel Adams Wilderness map is available from the U.S. Forest Service. For topographic maps, go to the USGS website to download Mount Dana and Koip Peak.

Directions: From Lee Vining, drive five miles south on U.S. 395 to the north end of the June Lake Loop (Highway 158). Turn right and drive 1.3 miles on Highway 158, then turn right on a dirt road signed for Parker and Walker Lakes. Drive 0.5 mile to a junction, turn right, then drive 0.3 mile and turn right again, following the signs for Walker Lake. Drive 0.5 mile and turn left on Forest Road 1S23. Drive 2.7 miles to the Walker Lake trailhead.

Contact: Inyo National Forest, Mono Basin Scenic Area Visitors Center, Lee Vining, 760/647-3044, www.fs.usda.gov/inyo.

50 PARKER LAKE TRAIL
3.8 mi / 2.0 hr 🏃2 ⛰8

in the Ansel Adams Wilderness west of Grant Lake

Map 10.1, page 467	BEST (

This short trail has a whole lot going for it. The beauty of Parker Lake and towering Parker Peak just might knock your boots off—or at least your socks. Although the nearby June Lake Loop gets a lot of vacation traffic, this trailhead is obscure enough that most visitors pass it by. And get this: The 1.9-mile-long trail has an elevation gain of only a little more than 300 feet. Beginning at an elevation of 8,000 feet above Parker Creek, the trail follows the creek upstream on a fairly mellow grade before arriving at Parker Lake, at 8,318 feet. As you ascend, the landscape transitions from sagebrush plains into a mixed forest alongside Parker Creek, complete with quaking aspens and mammoth-sized Jeffrey pines. Look behind you once in a while, and you'll catch great views of Mono Lake. In short order, you will suddenly emerge from the forest onto the lake's

© ANN MARIE BROWN

Mono Lake South Tufa Trail

shore. Parker Lake is a deep blue beauty backed by 12,861-foot Parker Peak—a great place to have a picnic or just sit and enjoy the scenery. The only downer on this trip is that many of the largest aspen trees have had their trunks carved with initials by idiots. Let's hope they didn't know any better. Please teach your children never, ever to carve into trees.

User Groups: Hikers, dogs, and horses. No mountain bikes. No wheelchair facilities.

Permits: A free wilderness permit is required for overnight stays and is available from the Mono Basin Scenic Area Visitors Center. Quotas are in effect from May 1 to November 1; for this period, permits are available in advance for a $5 reservation fee per person.

Maps: A Mammoth High Country map is available from Tom Harrison Maps. An Inyo National Forest or Ansel Adams Wilderness map is available from the U.S. Forest Service. For topographic maps, go to the USGS website to download Mount Dana and Koip Peak.

Directions: From Lee Vining, drive five miles south on U.S. 395 to the north end of the June Lake Loop (Highway 158). Turn right and drive 1.3 miles on Highway 158, then turn right on a dirt road signed for Parker and Walker Lakes. Drive 2.4 miles to the Parker Lake trailhead, at the end of the road.

Contact: Inyo National Forest, Mono Basin Scenic Area Visitors Center, Lee Vining, 760/647-3044, www.fs.usda.gov/inyo.

51 RUSH CREEK TRAIL

19.2 mi / 3 days 4 ▲ 10

on the eastern boundary of the Ansel Adams Wilderness west of June Lake

Map 10.1, page 467

Some places will never change, and people are drawn to them because they provide a sense of permanence that can't be found anywhere else. That is how it is at the Rush Creek headwaters. Created from drops of melting snow near the Sierra crest (at 10,500 feet), this stream runs downhill for miles, rolling into the forest like a swirling, emerald-green fountain. Even a short visit requires a long drive to the trailhead, followed by a demanding backpacking trek. In the process, hikers contend with a 10-mile climb out, ice-cold stream crossings, and the possibility of afternoon thunderstorms, in which lightning bolts and thunderclaps rattle off the canyon rims.

The trailhead lies near the pack station at Silver Lake (elevation 7,215 feet). After departing Silver Lake, follow the trail as it climbs above the June Lake Loop and soon starts to parallel Lower Rush Creek. You'll cross over an old tramway system that was used for the hydroelectric projects found in this watershed. Near the dam at Agnew Lake, you reach a trail junction, 2.2 miles from your start. The left fork heads up to Agnew Pass, but continue straight and in one more mile you arrive at beautiful Gem Lake (9,058 feet) and then Waugh Lake (9,442 feet), at the seven-mile point. Many visitors never venture farther than these lakes, simply stopping to camp, swim, or fish. But upstream of Waugh Lake is where you find the Rush Creek headwaters, along with the flawless symmetry of the untouched high country. Getting there requires a total climb of 3,300 feet over the course of 9.6 miles, but it is one of the prettiest streams anywhere and is well worth the effort.

Note that because this trail begins near the Silver Lake pack station, it is heavily used by horses. On some days, the amount of horse "evidence" on this trail can be a real downer, especially in the first few miles.

User Groups: Hikers, dogs, and horses. No mountain bikes. No wheelchair facilities.

Permits: A free wilderness permit is required for overnight stays and is available from the Mono Basin Scenic Area Visitors Center. Quotas are in effect from May 1 to November 1; for this period, permits are available in advance for a $5 reservation fee per person.

Maps: A Mammoth High Country map is available from Tom Harrison Maps. An Inyo National Forest or Ansel Adams Wilderness map is available from the U.S. Forest Service.

For topographic maps, go to the USGS website to download June Lake and Koip Peak.

Directions: From Lee Vining, drive about 11 miles south on U.S. 395 to June Lake Junction. Turn right on Highway 158/June Lake Road and drive 7.2 miles to the Rush Creek trailhead, between Silver Lake Resort and the pack station.

Contact: Inyo National Forest, Mono Basin Scenic Area Visitors Center, Lee Vining, 760/647-3044, www.fs.usda.gov/inyo.

52 YOST LAKE

4.8-9.4 mi / 2.5 hr-1 day

in Hoover Wilderness near June Lake

Map 10.1, page 467

Yost Lake is a small glacial lake hidden at 9,000 feet on the June Mountain slopes. Many people visit the June Lake area for years without even knowing Yost exists. But it is up here, tucked away and accessible only to those willing to hike. From the trailhead (7,800 feet) at June Lake, Yost Meadows Trail rises very steeply in the first mile, climbing 800 feet—a real buttkicker for many. That discourages many from going farther—after all, it is 4.7 miles to the lake. But after that first grunt of a climb, the trail gets much easier, contouring across the mountain slopes. It rises gradually to the headwaters of Yost Creek and then drops into the small basin that guards the lake.

A shorter option is to begin at the Yost Creek/Fern Lake trailhead, making it a much shorter, 4.8-mile round-trip. It is just as pretty, but it has a more difficult grade and can be slippery for those not wearing heavy, firm-gripping hiking boots. The trailhead is located three miles west of the town of June Lake, on the west (left) side of June Lake Road, past the ski resort.

User Groups: Hikers, horses, and dogs. No mountain bikes. No wheelchair facilities.

Permits: No permits are required for day-use; an overnight permit is required for backpacking. Parking and access are free.

Maps: A Mammoth High Country map is

available from Tom Harrison Maps. An Inyo National Forest or Ansel Adams Wilderness map is available from the U.S. Forest Service. For topographic maps, go to the USGS website to download June Lake and Mammoth Mountain.

Directions: From Lee Vining, drive about 11 miles south on U.S. 395 to June Lake Junction. Go right on Highway 158/June Lake Road and drive two miles to the town of June Lake. The trailhead is on the west (left), across the road from the fire station.

Contact: Inyo National Forest, Mono Basin Scenic Area Visitors Center, Lee Vining, 760/647-3044, www.fs.usda.gov/inyo.

53 INYO CRATERS

0.5 mi / 0.5 hr

in Inyo National Forest north of Mammoth Lakes

Map 10.1, page 467

A geologic phenomenon, the Inyo Craters make a great destination for an easy day hike in the Mammoth Lakes area. They are part of a chain of craters and other volcanic formations that reaches from Mammoth Lake to Mono Lake. The craters—evidence of Mammoth's fiery past—are the remains of a volcanic explosion of steam that occurred a mere 600 years ago. At that time, the mountain was a smoldering volcano. Magma pushed up into the water table, heated the water, and kaboom! The result was a phreatic blast that created these craters. The hike to see them is a short, gentle climb, but the elevation sucks the air out of many visitors who have just arrived in Mammoth. The trail leads through a lovely open forest of red fir and Jeffrey pine. In each of the two Inyo Craters a small pond fills with melted snow each spring, and at least some water remains throughout the summer.

User Groups: Hikers, horses, and dogs. No mountain bikes. No wheelchair facilities.

Permits: No permits are required. Parking and access are free.

Maps: A Mammoth High Country map is available from Tom Harrison Maps. An Inyo National Forest map is available from the U.S. Forest Service. For a topographic map, go to the USGS website to download Mammoth Mountain.

Directions: From the Mammoth Lakes junction on U.S. 395, turn west on Highway 203 and drive four miles through the town of Mammoth Lakes to the junction of Minaret Road/Highway 203 and Lake Mary Road. Turn right on Minaret Road and drive one mile. At the sign for Mammoth Lakes Scenic Loop, turn right and drive 2.7 miles. Turn left at the sign for Inyo Craters (the road turns to dirt) and drive 1.3 more miles to the Inyo Craters parking lot.

Contact: Inyo National Forest, Mammoth Lakes Welcome Center, Mammoth Lakes, 760/924-5500, www.fs.usda.gov/inyo.

Permits: No permits are required. Parking and access are free.

Maps: A Mammoth High Country map is available from Tom Harrison Maps. An Inyo National Forest map is available from the U.S. Forest Service. For a topographic map, go to the USGS website to download Crystal Crag.

Directions: From the Mammoth Lakes junction on U.S. 395, turn west on Highway 203 and drive four miles through the town of Mammoth Lakes to the junction of Minaret Road/Highway 203 and Lake Mary Road. Continue straight on Lake Mary Road and drive four miles to a junction for Lake George. Turn left here, drive 0.3 mile, then turn right and drive another 0.4 mile to Lake George. The trailhead is located near the campground.

Contact: Inyo National Forest, Mammoth Lakes Welcome Center, Mammoth Lakes, 760/924-5500, www.fs.usda.gov/inyo.

54 BARRETT AND TJ LAKES
1.0 mi / 0.5 hr   🥾1 ⛰8

at Lake George in Mammoth Lakes

Map 10.1, page 467

Campers at Lake George and Mammoth Lakes visitors who just want a short and easy day hike will be pleased to find that this no-sweat trail provides access to hidden Barrett and TJ Lakes. The trail starts on the northeast shore of Lake George (which in itself is a gorgeous spot), follows the lakeshore for about 100 yards, then climbs alongside a small stream to little Barrett Lake. The tiny lake is framed by Red Mountain in the background. Hey, this was so easy, you might as well continue another 0.25 mile to TJ Lake, the more scenic of the two lakes. The distinctive granite fin of Crystal Crag (10,377 feet) towers above TJ Lake's basin, adding drama to the scene. In addition to the pretty but popular lakes, this trail shows off some lovely mountain meadows, gilded with colorful penstemon, shooting stars, and paintbrush in midsummer.

User Groups: Hikers and horses. No mountain bikes. No wheelchair facilities.

55 CRYSTAL LAKE
3.2 mi / 2.0 hr   🥾2 ⛰9

at Lake George in Mammoth Lakes

Map 10.1, page 467

If you think Lake George is gorgeous, wait until you see Crystal Lake, located southwest of Lake George in a bowl scoured by glaciers and tucked into a hollow below 10,377-foot Crystal Crag. The trail to reach it has a 700-foot elevation gain and is pleasantly shaded by a hearty hemlock, pine, and fir forest. The path begins near the cabins at Woods Lodge but rises quickly above them. Many hikers huff and puff as they climb this ridge, but the view of the Mammoth Lakes Basin makes it all worthwhile. This high ridge gives you a bird's-eye look at the basin's four major lakes: George, Mary, Mamie, and Twin. At a junction at 1.3 miles, go left and you'll descend 0.3 mile to the outlet of Crystal Lake. The lake is a true jewel, highlighted by permanent snowfields that line its granite backdrop. You aren't likely to find much solitude here, since the lake is so easy to reach, but the scenery more than makes up for it.

If you want to turn this into a longer hike, you can take the other trail at the fork and head for Mammoth Crest, two miles farther and at 10,400 feet. The trail gains another 700 feet as it leaves the forest and enters a stark, volcanic landscape peppered with whitebark pines. The expansive view from the high point on the crest includes the Mammoth Lakes Basin, the San Joaquin River, the Minarets and the Ritter Range, and Mammoth Mountain. If this hike hasn't taken your breath away, the vista will.

User Groups: Hikers, horses, and dogs. Mountain bikes are not advised. No wheelchair facilities.

Permits: No permits are required. Parking and access are free.

Maps: A Mammoth High Country map is available from Tom Harrison Maps. An Inyo National Forest map is available from the U.S. Forest Service. For a topographic map, go to the USGS website to download Crystal Crag.

Directions: From the Mammoth Lakes junction on U.S. 395, turn west on Highway 203 and drive four miles through the town of Mammoth Lakes to the junction of Minaret Road/Highway 203 and Lake Mary Road. Continue straight on Lake Mary Road and drive four miles to a junction for Lake George. Turn left, drive 0.3 mile, then turn right and drive another 0.4 mile to Lake George. The trailhead is on the right, near some cabins.

Contact: Inyo National Forest, Mammoth Lakes Welcome Center, Mammoth Lakes, 760/924-5500, www.fs.usda.gov/inyo.

56 EMERALD LAKE AND SKY MEADOWS

4.0 mi / 2.0 hr

at Lake Mary in Mammoth Lakes

Map 10.1, page 467

This is one of the Eastern Sierra's premier wildflower trails, and it's easy enough for children to hike. The trail starts just south of Lake Mary, at the end of the Coldwater Campground road. The hike is short and direct, climbing straight to Emerald Lake on a wide, well-used path. A trail branches off to the right to Barrett and TJ Lakes, but just keep heading straight uphill to reach Emerald Lake. Picnickers are often found seated among the rocks by the water's edge, although by midsummer, the lake dwindles to something that more closely resembles a pond. No matter, the lake is just one small part of this trail's beauty. The trail skirts the east shore of Emerald Lake and continues along its inlet stream, where wildflowers grow in profusion. Among the wide variety of species to be seen and admired, one standout is the tall orange tiger lilies, a flower that is showy enough to be in a florist's shop. It has a scent that will knock your socks off. From here, the trail climbs more gradually as it leads you past Gentian Meadow (you may hear the voices of rock climbers as they climb the cliffs beyond the meadow) to the southeast edge of Sky Meadows. Beyond the meadows, permanent snowfields decorate the granite cliffs of Mammoth Crest.

User Groups: Hikers, dogs, and horses. No mountain bikes allowed past the wilderness boundary. No wheelchair facilities.

Permits: No day permits are required. Parking and access are free.

Maps: A Mammoth High Country map is available from Tom Harrison Maps. An Inyo National Forest map is available from the U.S. Forest Service. For a topographic map, go to the USGS website to download Crystal Crag.

Directions: From the Mammoth Lakes junction on U.S. 395, turn west on Highway 203 and drive four miles through the town of Mammoth Lakes to the junction of Minaret Road/Highway 203 and Lake Mary Road. Continue straight on Lake Mary Road and drive 3.5 miles to a fork just before Lake Mary; turn left and drive 0.6 mile to the Coldwater Campground turnoff, on the left. Turn left and drive 0.5 mile through the camp to the trailhead, at the first parking lot.

Contact: Inyo National Forest, Mammoth Lakes Welcome Center, Mammoth Lakes, 760/924-5500, www.fs.usda.gov/inyo.

57 DUCK LAKE

10.0 mi / 6.0 hr or 2 days 🥾3 ⛰9

in the John Muir Wilderness near Mammoth Lakes

Map 10.1, page 467

How far you hike on Duck Pass Trail is up to you, but if it were up to us, we'd hike at least as far as five miles to Duck Lake, elevation 10,450 feet. Sure, lots of people stop at the other lakes this trail passes along the way—Arrowhead Lake at 1.3 miles out, Skelton Lake at two miles, or Barney Lake at three miles—and these make fine destinations. But you might as well see them all and then keep climbing through Duck Pass to much larger Duck Lake, at five miles. The pass is only a 1,600-foot climb from the trailhead at Coldwater Campground, with plenty of well-graded switchbacks. Just beyond the pass, the trail drops 300 feet to reach Duck Lake, one of the largest natural lakes in the Eastern Sierra. Your first glimpse of its size will blow your mind. Most of the climbing is in the stretch from Barney Lake to the pass, as the trail switchbacks up a talus-covered slope. Day hikers can make their way from Duck Lake on a faint path to Pika Lake, which is visible in the distance about a half-mile away. Backpackers can continue on to Purple Lake (at 7.5 miles) and Lake Virginia (at nine miles). There are usually tons of people on this trail, but with this kind of scenery, everybody is in a good mood.

User Groups: Hikers, dogs, and horses. No mountain bikes allowed past the wilderness boundary. No wheelchair facilities.

Permits: A free wilderness permit is required for overnight stays and is available from the Mammoth Lakes Welcome Center. Quotas are in effect from May 1 to November 1; for this period, permits are available in advance for a $5 reservation fee per person.

Maps: A Mammoth High Country map is available from Tom Harrison Maps. An Inyo National Forest or John Muir Wilderness map is available from the U.S. Forest Service. For a topographic map, go to the USGS website to download Crystal Crag.

Directions: From the Mammoth Lakes junction on U.S. 395, turn west on Highway 203 and drive four miles, through the town of Mammoth Lakes, to the junction of Minaret Road/Highway 203 and Lake Mary Road. Continue straight on Lake Mary Road and drive 3.5 miles to a fork just before Lake Mary; turn left and drive 0.6 mile to the Coldwater Campground turnoff, on the left. Turn left and drive 0.8 mile through the camp to the Duck Pass trailhead at the farthest parking lot.

Contact: Inyo National Forest, Mammoth Lakes Welcome Center, Mammoth Lakes, 760/924-5500, www.fs.usda.gov/inyo.

58 VALENTINE LAKE TRAIL

11.2 mi / 6.0 hr or 2 days 🥾3 ⛰9

in the John Muir Wilderness south of Mammoth Lakes

Map 10.1, page 467

The Mammoth Lakes area is one of the Eastern Sierra's star attractions, yet nearby Valentine Lake is perhaps overlooked because the trailhead (at 7,600 feet) is not found at one of the lakes in the Mammoth Lakes Basin. Or perhaps it's because the climb required to get there is so steep. Regardless of the reason, a morning's hike—rising some 1,900 feet over 5.6 miles, but with most of the climb compressed in the first two miles to Sherwin Lake—gets you to Valentine Lake, which sits at 9,698 feet.

Some say the lake is shaped like a teardrop, but we think it looks more like a drop of sweat. The hike starts out with a very steep climb (including 0.5 mile of sandy switchbacks in a dry pine forest) and doesn't level out for the first two miles. You'll pass a side trail to the Sherwin Lakes at 2.9 miles (a fine destination for those who have had enough, or those who just want to catch fish). From the Sherwin Lakes junction, the grade lessens dramatically, gently climbing and finally meeting up with Valentine Lake's outlet stream. Valentine Lake has rocky cliffs ringing its edges, making it difficult to explore its shoreline. Pick a spot and toss in a line; the lake has plentiful brook trout.

User Groups: Hikers, dogs, and horses. No mountain bikes. No wheelchair facilities.

Permits: A free wilderness permit is required for overnight stays and is available from the Mammoth Lakes Welcome Center. Quotas are in effect from May 1 to November 1; for this period, permits are available in advance for a $5 reservation fee per person.

Maps: A Mammoth High Country map is available from Tom Harrison Maps. An Inyo National Forest or John Muir Wilderness map is available from the U.S. Forest Service. For a topographic map, go to the USGS website to download Crystal Crag.

Directions: From the Mammoth Lakes junction on U.S. 395, turn west on Highway 203 and drive 2.6 miles to Old Mammoth Road. Turn left and drive 0.8 mile to Sherwin Creek Road. Turn left and drive 2.9 miles to the signed trailhead on the right for Valentine Lake (past the Sherwin Creek Campground and YMCA camp).

Contact: Inyo National Forest, Mammoth Lakes Welcome Center, Mammoth Lakes, 760/924-5500, www.fs.usda.gov/inyo.

59 RED CONES LOOP
6.7 mi / 4.0 hr   3   7

at Horseshoe Lake in Mammoth Lakes

Map 10.1, page 467

Horseshoe Lake, elevation 8,900 feet, lies at the end of the Mammoth Lakes road and has an excellent trailhead that makes for a great day hike. Don't be put off by the dead trees and the barren look of the place. A relatively small area by the lake has been affected by carbon-dioxide gas venting up through the soil—the result of seismic activity. You get away from this strange-looking forest quickly. Set out from the northwest side of the lake, ascend the slope, and take the left fork for McLeod Lake. In just under two miles, you'll reach the start of the loop. Go right to reach Crater Meadow, a beautiful little

spot set just below Red Cones, and then circle around to Upper Crater Meadow. Either meadow is a fine destination for a picnic lunch in peace. The contrast is striking: Just a short distance below, there are typically many people at Twin Lakes, Lake Mary, Lake Mamie, and Lake George, yet you are separated from them by Mammoth Pass. You will be surprised at how relatively few people take this loop hike, and glad that you made the choice to do so.

User Groups: Hikers, dogs, and horses. No mountain bikes. No wheelchair facilities.

Permits: No permits are required. Parking and access are free.

Maps: A Mammoth High Country map is available from Tom Harrison Maps. An Inyo National Forest map is available from the U.S. Forest Service. For a topographic map, go to the USGS website to download Crystal Crag.

Directions: From the Mammoth Lakes junction on U.S. 395, turn west on Highway 203 and drive four miles through the town of Mammoth Lakes to the junction of Minaret Road/Highway 203 and Lake Mary Road. Continue straight on Lake Mary Road and drive 4.8 miles to the road's end, at Horseshoe Lake. The trailhead is on the northwest side of the lake, signed for Mammoth Pass.

Contact: Inyo National Forest, Mammoth Lakes Welcome Center, Mammoth Lakes, 760/924-5500, www.fs.usda.gov/inyo.

60 DEVILS POSTPILE AND RAINBOW FALLS
2.0-5.0 mi / 1.0-2.0 hr   2   10

in Devils Postpile National Monument west of Mammoth Lakes

Map 10.1, page 467   **BEST**

The first time you lay eyes on 101-foot Rainbow Falls, the tall, wide, and forceful waterfall comes as an awesome surprise. Most first-time visitors see it before or after a trip to the Devils Postpile, a fascinating collection of volcanic rock columns and rubble left from a lava flow nearly 100,000 years ago. It's like nothing you've seen anywhere else. You can hike to Rainbow Falls two ways, either from the ranger station at Devils Postpile National Monument or from the Rainbow Falls trailhead, near Reds Meadow Resort. Either way, this is one of the best short hikes in California.

Your best bet is to start at the ranger station, then pass by the Devils Postpile lava columns in only 0.5 mile. Stop and gape at this geologic wonder, and perhaps take the short but steep side trip to the top of the columns, then continue downhill to Rainbow Falls, at 2.5 miles. (If you start at the trailhead by Reds Meadow, your trip to Rainbow Falls is only one mile, but you'll miss out on the Postpile.)

In order to see the rainbow that gives the waterfall its name, you must show up in late morning or at midday. The rainbow is the result of a prism effect from sun's rays refracting through the falling water. Two overlook areas across from the waterfall's brink give you an excellent view, but you can hike down a series of stairs to the falls' base for an even better vantage point. If you're inspired, you can travel another 0.5 mile on the trail to find a smaller waterfall on the San Joaquin River, called Lower Falls.

User Groups: Hikers and horses. No mountain bikes. Dogs must be leashed in the national monument. No wheelchair facilities.

Permits: Each person entering the Devils Postpile/Reds Meadow area must purchase an access pass. (See *Access Note,* below.) The fee is $7 per adult and $4 for children ages 3-15. Children ages 2 and under are free. Passes may be purchased at the Mammoth Mountain Adventure Center at Mammoth Ski Area.

Maps: A Devils Postpile map is available from Tom Harrison Maps. An Inyo National Forest map is available from the U.S. Forest Service. For a topographic map, go to the USGS website to download Mammoth Mountain.

Directions: From the Mammoth Lakes junction on U.S. 395, turn west on Highway 203 and drive four miles through the town of Mammoth Lakes to Minaret Road (still Highway 203). Turn right and drive 4.5 miles to the shuttle bus terminal (adjacent to the Mammoth Mountain Ski Area). Purchase an access pass and board a shuttle bus here. Disembark at the Devils Postpile Ranger Station or Rainbow Falls trailhead, which is just before Reds Meadow Resort.

Access Note: Visitors arriving between 7am and 7pm are required to ride a shuttle bus (free with purchase of an access pass) from Mammoth Mountain Ski Area. If you are camping in the Devils Postpile area, or if you arrive before 7am, you are permitted to drive your own car instead of taking the shuttle, but you must pay an entrance fee of $10 per vehicle.

Contact: Inyo National Forest, Mammoth Lakes Welcome Center, Mammoth Lakes, 760/924-5500, www.fs.usda.gov/inyo; Devils Postpile National Monument, Mammoth Lakes, 760/934-2289 (summer only), www.nps.gov/depo.

61 MINARET LAKE
16.0 mi / 2 days
3 / 9

in the Ansel Adams Wilderness west of Mammoth Lakes

Map 10.1, page 467

Minaret Lake is a real prize, set just below the awesome glacial-carved Ritter Range, at 9,793 feet. Reaching it requires an eight-mile hike with a 2,400-foot elevation gain, and every step is completely worth it. From the trailhead at Devils Postpile Ranger Station, you hike south to access a bridge across the San Joaquin River, then head northward two miles on John Muir Trail. (You can also start from Upper Soda Spring Campground and hike south on the Pacific Crest Trail, then turn north on the John Muir Trail. The distance is about the same.) After passing tiny Johnston Lake, you reach the junction with Minaret Lake Trail. Turn left and follow Minaret Creek. The trail rises with the creek and in the last mile climbs steeply above tree line before skirting the Minaret Lake outlet and tracing the line of the north shore. The granite peaks that form the lake's backdrop are Clyde and Ken Minaret. Good campsites are found near Minaret Lake's rocky shore. If you want to do some exploring, Cecile Lake (at 10,239 feet) can be reached via a cross-country route to the northwest of the lake.

User Groups: Hikers, dogs, and horses. Dogs must be leashed in national monument. No mountain bikes. No wheelchair facilities.

Permits: Each person entering the Devils Postpile/Reds Meadow area must purchase an access pass. (See *Access Note,* below.) The fee is $7 per adult and $4 for children ages 3-15. Children ages 2 and under are free. Passes may be purchased at the Mammoth Mountain Adventure Center at Mammoth Ski Area.

A free wilderness permit is required for overnight stays and is available from the Mammoth Lakes Welcome Center. Quotas are in effect from May 1 to November 1; for this period, permits are available in advance for a $5 reservation fee per person.

Maps: A Devils Postpile map is available from Tom Harrison Maps. An Inyo National Forest or Ansel Adams Wilderness map is available from the U.S. Forest Service. For topographic maps, go to the USGS website to download Mammoth Mountain and Mount Ritter.

Directions: From the Mammoth Lakes junction on U.S. 395, turn west on Highway 203 and drive four miles through the town of Mammoth Lakes to Minaret Road (still Highway 203). Turn right and drive 4.5 miles to the shuttle bus terminal (adjacent to the Mammoth Mountain Ski Area). Purchase an access pass and board a shuttle bus here. Disembark at the Devils Postpile Ranger Station.

Note: Visitors arriving between 7am and 7pm are required to ride a shuttle bus (free with purchase of an access pass) from Mammoth Mountain Ski Area. If you are camping in the Devils Postpile area, or if you arrive before 7am, you are permitted to drive your own car instead of taking the shuttle, but you must pay an entrance fee of $10 per vehicle.

Contact: Inyo National Forest, Mammoth Lakes Welcome Center, Mammoth Lakes, 760/924-5500, www.fs.usda.gov/inyo; Devils Postpile National Monument, Mammoth Lakes, 760/934-2289 (summer only), www.nps.gov/depo.

62 FERN LAKE LOOP
10.0-16.0 mi / 1-2 days

in the Ansel Adams Wilderness west of Mammoth Lakes

Map 10.1, page 467

Fern Lake can be the destination on an ambitious day hike from Devils Postpile, or the start of a great 15-mile backpacking loop. Either way, this is an excellent hike that has become very popular. Starting from the ranger station at Devils Postpile, you head south to access the bridge across the San Joaquin River, then follow the King Creek Trail. About two miles in, you face a crossing of King Creek that can be tricky early in the summer. Exercise some caution. Then climb through the pine forest to reach a junction, at 4.9 miles. Follow the spur to Fern Lake, elevation 8,800 feet, where many good campsites are found. The lake is set in a small rock bowl at tree line, below Iron Mountain, in the Minarets. Day hikers will often while away a few hours here and then retrace their steps for a 10-mile round-trip.

Those continuing onward will find the trail pokes in and out of sparse forest for the next two miles to Becks Cabin. From here, a one-mile side trip leads to Superior Lake (7.5 miles from your start, and at 9,400 feet), another excellent spot for an overnight. A faint path leads 0.7 mile from Superior Lake to the two Beck Lakes (at 9,800 feet), which are surrounded by high granite ridges. A visit to Beck Lakes—set in a glacial-formed pocket below the Minarets and amid celestial mountain scenery—is highly recommended. When you return to the loop at Becks Cabin, you have a 4.8-mile descent to reach John Muir Trail, where you turn right and head back to the bridge and the ranger station.

User Groups: Hikers, dogs, and horses. Dogs must be leashed in national monument. No mountain bikes. No wheelchair facilities.

Permits: Each person entering the Devils Postpile/Reds Meadow area must purchase an access pass. (See *Access Note,* below.) The fee is $7 per adult and $4 for children ages 3-15. Children ages 2 and under are free. Passes may be purchased at the Mammoth Mountain Adventure Center at Mammoth Ski Area.

A free wilderness permit is required for overnight stays and is available from the Mammoth Lakes Welcome Center. Quotas are in effect from May 1 to November 1; for this period, permits are available in advance for a $5 reservation fee per person.

Maps: A Devils Postpile map is available from Tom Harrison Maps. An Inyo National Forest or Ansel Adams Wilderness map is available from the U.S. Forest Service. For topographic maps, go to the USGS website to download Mammoth Mountain and Mount Ritter.

Directions: From the Mammoth Lakes junction on U.S. 395, turn west on Highway 203 and drive four miles through the town of Mammoth Lakes to Minaret Road (still Highway 203). Turn right and drive 4.5 miles to the shuttle bus terminal (adjacent to the Mammoth Mountain Ski Area). Purchase an access pass and board a shuttle bus here. Disembark at the Devils Postpile Ranger Station.

Note: Visitors arriving between 7am and 7pm are required to ride a shuttle bus (free with purchase of an access pass) from Mammoth Mountain Ski Area. If you are camping in the Devils Postpile area, or if you arrive before 7am, you are permitted to drive your own car instead of taking the shuttle, but you must pay an entrance fee of $10 per vehicle.

Contact: Inyo National Forest, Mammoth Lakes Welcome Center, Mammoth Lakes, 760/924-5500, www.fs.usda.gov/inyo; Devils Postpile National Monument, Mammoth Lakes, 760/934-2289 (summer only), www.nps.gov/depo.

63 SHADOW LAKE
7.6 mi / 4.0 hr or 2 days

in the Ansel Adams Wilderness west of Mammoth Lakes

Map 10.1, page 467

Shadow Lake is one of the most popular destinations in the Devils Postpile region simply because of its sheer beauty. The only unpleasant part of this hike is making your way through the busy trailhead parking lots at Agnew Meadows. Once that's accomplished and you're on the trail, all is bliss, as long as you're in good condition and ready for a sustained climb. (Campers at Agnew Meadows can cut a half mile off this trip each way by starting from the trail at camp, not from the trailhead parking lot.) The route starts out quite mellow as it wanders through the wildflowers at Agnew Meadows. It then follows the River Trail along the middle fork of the San Joaquin River. Just beyond shallow Olaine Lake (at two miles) lies a junction, where you go left for Shadow Lake. Cross a bridge and prepare to climb. A long series of steep, shadeless switchbacks ensues as you climb alongside a narrow creek gorge. Fortunately the view looking down the San Joaquin River Canyon becomes ever more grand as you rise upward. At last you reach the waterfall on Shadow Lake's outlet stream and then climb the final stretch to the lake. Its backdrop is like something you've seen on a million Sierra postcards, with the Minarets and Mounts Ritter and Banner towering above the lake. Day hikers have the best deal here; they can just pick a spot along the 8,737-foot lakeshore and drink in the view. Camping is not permitted at Shadow Lake, so backpackers must continue on to smaller Rosalie Lake (much more climbing over the next two miles). Ediza Lake is also a popular overnight option, 2.5 miles from Shadow Lake.

User Groups: Hikers, dogs, and horses. No mountain bikes. No wheelchair facilities.

Permits: Each person entering the Devils Postpile/Reds Meadow area must purchase an access pass. (See *Access Note,* below.) The fee is $7 per adult and $4 for children ages 3-15. Children ages 2 and under are free. Passes may be purchased at the Mammoth Mountain Adventure Center at Mammoth Ski Area.

A free wilderness permit is required for overnight stays and is available from the Mammoth Lakes Welcome Center. Quotas are in effect from May 1 to November 1; for this period, permits are available in advance for a $5 reservation fee per person.

Maps: A Devils Postpile map is available from Tom Harrison Maps. An Inyo National Forest or Ansel Adams Wilderness map is available from the U.S. Forest Service. For topographic maps, go to the USGS website to download Crystal Crag and Cattle Mountain.

Directions: From the Mammoth Lakes junction on U.S. 395, turn west on Highway 203 and drive four miles through the town of Mammoth Lakes to Minaret Road (still Highway 203). Turn right and drive 4.5 miles to the shuttle bus terminal (adjacent to the Mammoth Mountain Ski Area). Purchase an access pass and board a shuttle bus here. Disembark at the Agnew Meadows Campground. Walk through the trailhead parking lots to the Shadow Lake trailhead.

Note: Visitors arriving between 7am and 7pm are required to ride a shuttle bus (free with purchase of an access pass) from Mammoth Mountain Ski Area. If you are camping in the Devils Postpile area, or if you arrive before 7am, you are permitted to drive your own car instead of taking the shuttle, but you must pay an entrance fee of $10 per vehicle.

Contact: Inyo National Forest, Mammoth Lakes Welcome Center, Mammoth Lakes, 760/924-5500, www.fs.usda.gov/inyo; Devils Postpile National Monument, Mammoth Lakes, 760/934-2289 (summer only), www.nps.gov/depo.

64 AGNEW MEADOWS TO TUOLUMNE MEADOWS (JMT/PCT)

28.0 mi one-way / 3 days 🏃5 ⛰10

from the Agnew Meadows trailhead north to the trailhead parking area at Tuolumne Meadows on Highway 120

Map 10.1, page 467

This section of the JMT/PCT features breathtaking views of the Minarets, many glacial-cut lakes, and the wondrous descent into Yosemite. The PCT starts here by leaving Reds Meadow, an excellent place to arrange a food drop and a chance to eat your first cheeseburger in weeks. The trail heads out into the most beautiful section of Inyo National Forest and the Ansel Adams Wilderness. All in a row, the PCT passes Rosalie, Shadow, Garnet, and Thousand Island Lakes. If they look like Ansel Adams's pictures in real life, it's because they are. The background setting of Banner and Ritter Peaks is among the most spectacular anywhere. From Thousand Island Lake, the PCT makes a fair climb over Island Pass (10,200 feet), then drops down into the headwaters of Rush Creek, where emerald green flows swirl over boulders, pouring like a wilderness fountain. From here, it's a decent, steady ascent back above tree line to Donohue Pass (11,056 feet), the southern wilderness border of Yosemite National Park. It was here, while munching a trail lunch, that we saw a huge landslide on the westward canyon wall. A massive amount of rock material fell in just a few seconds—an unforgettable show of natural forces. The trail becomes quite blocky at Donohue Pass, and you rock hop your way down to the headwaters of Lyell Fork, a pretzel-like stream that meanders through the meadows. It pours all the way to Tuolumne Meadows, and following it, the trail is nearly flat for more than four miles. At Tuolumne Meadows you can resupply—and get another cheeseburger.

To continue north on the JMT, see the *Tuolumne Meadows to Yosemite Valley (JMT)* hike in this chapter. If you are walking this trail in reverse, see the *Lake Thomas Edison to Agnew Meadows (JMT/PCT)* hike in the *Sequoia and Kings Canyon* chapter.

User Groups: Hikers and horses. No dogs or mountain bikes. No wheelchair facilities.

Permits: A wilderness permit is required for traveling through various wilderness and special-use areas the trail traverses. Contact either the Inyo National Forest or Yosemite National Park for a permit that is good for the length of your trip.

Maps: A John Muir Trail Map Pack is available from Tom Harrison Maps. An Inyo National Forest map is available from the U.S. Forest Service. For topographic maps, go to the USGS website to download Vogelsang Peak, Mount Ritter, Koip Peak, and Mammoth Mountain.

Directions: From Lee Vining, drive 26 miles south on Highway 395 to Mammoth Junction. Turn west on Highway 203/Minaret Summit Road to the town of Mammoth Lakes and drive 14 miles to the Agnew Meadows Campground and the trailhead parking area.

Contact: Yosemite National Park, Yosemite, 209/372-0200, www.nps.gov/yose; Inyo National Forest, Mono Basin Scenic Area Visitors Center, Lee Vining, 760/647-3044, www.fs.usda.gov/inyo.

65 HITE COVE TRAIL
9.0 mi / 5.0 hr 🥾2 ⛰10

on the South Fork Merced River in Sierra National Forest

Map 10.1, page 467   **BEST (**

Considered by many to be the premier Sierra spring wildflower trail, Hite Cove Trail offers hikers a look at 60 flower varieties, including goldfields, lupine, poppies, brodaiea, monkeyflower, shooting stars, fiesta flowers, fairy lanterns, baby blue eyes, and Indian pinks. To see them, visit from late February to early May, before the show is over. Conveniently, this is usually the only time of the year when the trail is open, because the first 0.75 mile of trail is on private property, and access is restricted during fire season.

You start hiking on a paved driveway, but the asphalt only lasts for a few yards, then the trail transitions to a narrow single track that hugs the side of the steep canyon wall, high above the South Fork Merced River. Even if you aren't terribly interested in wildflowers, the river and canyon views are tremendous. About one mile out is an obvious rock outcrop, a few feet off the trail, where you can sit and enjoy the rushing river below. Another 0.5 mile farther, the trail drops down right alongside the river, and where the current mellows out, there are many tempting swimming holes. Those wishing to turn this hike into an overnight trip can camp at Hite Cove, the site of the 1879 Hite Cove Hotel. A campfire permit is required for overnight stays. From there, you can continue hiking to Devils Gulch, 2.5 miles farther. To do so, however, requires crossing the South Fork Merced River at Hite Cove, a difficult feat early in the year.

Note: Call the Bass Lake Ranger Station or visit the Sierra National Forest website to make sure this trail is open before planning your trip. Access to the trail is restricted during fire season.

User Groups: Hikers, dogs, and horses. No mountain bikes. No wheelchair facilities.

Permits: No permits are required. Parking and access are free.

Maps: A Sierra National Forest map is available from the U.S. Forest Service. For a topographic map, go to the USGS website to download El Portal.

Directions: From Mariposa, drive 22 miles east on Highway 140 to Savage's Trading Post. The parking area is on the north side of the road, but the trail begins on the south side, near Savage's Trading Post.

Contact: Sierra National Forest, Bass Lake Ranger Station, North Fork, 559/877-2218, www.fs.usda.gov/sierra.

66 UPPER YOSEMITE FALL
7.4 mi / 5.0 hr 👣4 ⛰10

in Yosemite Valley

Map 10.1, page 467   **BEST (**

At 2,425 feet, Yosemite Falls is the highest waterfall in North America. That's why hundreds of park visitors hike this strenuous trail every day in the spring and summer. There's no feeling quite like standing at the waterfall's brink and realizing you've conquered a landmark of this magnitude.

Still, if you tucker out on this demanding climb to Upper Yosemite Fall, just remember that you always have a fallback position: you can hike only 1.2 miles one-way to the Columbia Point overlook, which is reached via more than 100 switchbacks and a total gain of 1,200 feet, then call it a day. The view of Yosemite Valley from Columbia Point is a stunner, and plenty of people who planned on hiking to Upper Yosemite Fall turn around here and still leave satisfied.

Those who push on are also rewarded. After a level section and then a short, surprising descent, you get your first full-impact view of horsetail-shaped Upper Yosemite Fall. In the spring and early summer months, this view will blow you away. The trail then switchbacks upward, more steeply now, through a canyon to the west of the fall, which allows passage to the top of the north rim of Yosemite Valley. At this point, you've gained 2,700 feet and hiked 3.5 miles; it's only another 0.2 mile to the brink of Upper Yosemite Fall. (Make sure you take the spur trail signed as Overlook.) From the metal fence above the fall's lip, you gain an incredible perspective on the waterfall's drop and the valley floor far below.

If this trip hasn't provided you with enough exertion, continue another 0.75 mile, crossing the bridge above the falls, to Yosemite Point at 6,936 feet in elevation, where you get a stunning view of the south rim of the Valley, Half Dome, and North Dome, and a look at the top of Lost Arrow Spire, a single shaft of granite jutting into the sky.

User Groups: Hikers only. No dogs, horses, or mountain bikes. No wheelchair facilities.

Permits: No permits are required. There is a $30 entrance fee per vehicle at Yosemite National Park ($25 Nov.-Mar.), good for seven days.

Maps: A Half Dome or Yosemite National Park map is available from Tom Harrison Maps. For a topographic map, go to the USGS website to download Yosemite Falls.

Directions: From Merced, drive 70 miles northeast on Highway 140 to Yosemite National Park. Follow the signs toward Yosemite Valley, entering through the Arch Rock entrance station. Continue on Highway 140/El Portal Road, which becomes Southside Drive, for 10.5 miles. Just beyond the Yosemite Chapel, bear left at the fork and head toward Yosemite Village and the visitors center, then turn left and drive west on Northside Drive 0.75 mile to the parking lot. Park in the lot (do not park in the spaces marked Permit Parking Only), then walk to Camp 4, which is across Northside Drive and 0.25 mile west of Yosemite Lodge (aka Yosemite Valley Lodge). You may not park in the Camp 4 lot unless you are camping there. If you are riding the free Yosemite Valley shuttle bus, disembark at Camp 4 or Yosemite Lodge (aka Yosemite Valley Lodge).

Contact: Yosemite National Park, Yosemite, 209/372-0200, www.nps.gov/yose.

67 EAGLE PEAK
13.5 mi / 1 or 2 days 👣4 ⛰10

in Yosemite Valley

Map 10.1, page 467

If you seek more of a challenge than the day hike to Upper Yosemite Fall, the trail to Eagle Peak delivers the stunning destinations of the shorter trip (Columbia Point and Upper Yosemite Fall) plus an additional three miles one-way to a lookout atop the highest rock of the Three Brothers formation. Here, the vista is sublime. All of Yosemite Valley comes into view from the top of Eagle Peak, including an interesting perspective on North Dome, Clouds Rest, and Half Dome. On rare, extremely clear days you can also see the mountains and foothills of the Coast Range, 100 miles to the west.

Follow the trail notes for the hike to Upper Yosemite Fall (see listing in this chapter), then after taking the spur trail to the fall's brink, backtrack 0.25 mile to the trail junction for Eagle Peak Trail. Follow Eagle Peak Trail northwest for 1.5 miles, enjoying plentiful shade from Jeffrey pines and white firs, then hike south for one mile through Eagle Peak Meadows (prepare to get your feet wet here unless it is very late in summer). At a trail junction with El Capitan Trail, bear left for a 0.6-mile ascent to your final destination—the summit of Eagle Peak, elevation 7,779 feet. After completing this trip, you'll never view the Three Brothers from the valley floor the same way again.

User Groups: Hikers only. No dogs, horses, or mountain bikes. No wheelchair facilities.

Permits: There is a $30 entrance fee per vehicle at Yosemite National Park ($25 Nov.-Mar.), good for seven days. Free wilderness permits are required for overnight stays. They are available on a first-come, first-served basis up to one day in advance at the Yosemite Wilderness kiosk near your chosen trailhead or farther in advance by mail, phone, or online for a $5 reservation fee per person.

Maps: A Half Dome or Yosemite National Park map is available from Tom Harrison Maps. For a topographic map, go to the USGS website to download Yosemite Falls.

Directions: From Merced, drive 70 miles northeast on Highway 140 to Yosemite National Park. Follow the signs toward Yosemite Valley and enter through the Arch Rock entrance station. Continue on Highway 140/El Portal Road, which becomes Southside Drive, for 10.5 miles. Just beyond the Yosemite Chapel, bear left at the fork and head toward Yosemite Village and the visitors center, then turn left and drive west on Northside Drive 0.75 mile to the parking lot. Park in the lot (do not park in the spaces marked Permit Parking Only), then walk to

Camp 4, which is across Northside Drive and 0.25 mile west of Yosemite Lodge (aka Yosemite Valley Lodge). You may not park in the Camp 4 lot unless you are camping there. If you are riding the free Yosemite Valley shuttle bus, disembark at Camp 4 or Yosemite Lodge (aka Yosemite Valley Lodge).

Contact: Yosemite National Park, Yosemite, 209/372-0200 or 209/372-0740 (permit reservations), www.nps.gov/yose or www.nps.gov/yose/wilderness (permit reservations).

68 LOWER YOSEMITE FALL

1.1 mi / 0.5 hr

in Yosemite Valley

Map 10.1, page 467   BEST

It's so short you can hardly call it a hike, and the route is perpetually crawling with people. Still, the trail to Lower Yosemite Fall is an absolute must for visitors to Yosemite Valley. When the falls are roaring with snowmelt in the spring and early summer, they never disappoint even the most seasoned hiker.

The only problem is that many visitors can't figure out where to leave their car and start the hike. Your best bet is to ride the shuttle bus from other points in the Valley, which deposits you at the "new" Yosemite Fall Trailhead, an attractive log structure positioned alongside Northside Drive. You can also park your car alongside the road near the shuttle bus stop, but good luck finding a space in the summer months. Either way, once you get started, the trail is simple enough to follow. Within about 10 minutes of walking, you are standing at the footbridge below the falls, and in the spring you can get soaking wet from the incredible mist and spray. By late summer, on the other hand, the fall often dries up completely. Be sure to walk the entire loop instead of just heading out-and-back to the falls; there is much to see along the way. And most important of all: if you really want to see the waterfall at its most magnificent, plan your trip for some time between April and June, during peak snowmelt.

Seasoned waterfall lovers should also plan to visit on full moon nights in spring; if conditions are just right, a "moonbow" will appear surrounding the lower fall.

User Groups: Hikers and wheelchairs. No dogs, horses, or mountain bikes.

Permits: No permits are required. There is a $30 entrance fee per vehicle at Yosemite National Park ($25 Nov.-Mar.), good for seven days.

Maps: A Half Dome or Yosemite National Park map is available from Tom Harrison Maps. For a topographic map, go to the USGS website to download Half Dome.

Directions: From Merced, drive 70 miles northeast on Highway 140 to Yosemite National Park. Follow the signs to Yosemite Valley, entering through the Arch Rock entrance station. Continue on Highway 140/El Portal Road, which becomes Southside Drive, for 10.5 miles. Just beyond the Yosemite Chapel, bear left at the fork and head toward Yosemite Village and the visitors center, then turn left and drive west on Northside Drive 0.75 mile to the parking lot. Park in the lot (do not park in the spaces marked Permit Parking Only). The trail begins across Northside Drive from Yosemite Lodge (aka Yosemite Valley Lodge). You can also park on either side of Northside Drive near the Lower Yosemite Fall bus shuttle stop and walk from there.

Contact: Yosemite National Park, Yosemite, 209/372-0200, www.nps.gov/yose.

69 MIST TRAIL TO VERNAL FALL

3.0 mi / 2.0 hr

in Yosemite Valley

Map 10.1, page 467

This is a hike that every visitor to the Valley should take, even if it's the only trail they walk all year. Despite how crowded the trail inevitably is, this is a world-class hike to one of the most photographed waterfalls in the world. Make your trip more enjoyable by starting as

early in the morning as possible, before the hordes are out in full force.

Start by taking the free Yosemite shuttle bus to the trailhead at Happy Isles. (Or you can add on an extra mile each way by hiking from the day-use parking area in Curry Village/Half Dome Village to Happy Isles.) The partially paved route is a moderate 500-foot climb to the Vernal Fall footbridge, then a very steep tromp up the seemingly endless granite staircase to the top of the fall. Although many people hike only to the footbridge, 0.8 mile from Happy Isles, it's definitely worth the extra effort to push on another 0.5 mile to reach the top of Vernal Fall.

Doing so means ascending another 500 feet on the Mist Trail's famous granite stairway, which frames the edge of Vernal Fall. You will come so close to the plunging spray that you may feel as if you are part of it. Sometimes you are—during peak snowmelt in spring, hikers are frequently drenched in spray and mist. Remember to bring a rain poncho if you don't like getting wet.

When you reach the 317-foot-high fall's brink, you can stand at the railing and watch the dizzying flow of rushing whitewater as it tumbles downward. This is a trip you have to do at least once in your life.

Warning: Do not cross or wade the Merced River at the top of Vernal Falls, and do not under any circumstances climb over the railing, especially during peak flows. Fatalities do occur here; don't be one of them.

User Groups: Hikers only. No dogs, horses, or mountain bikes. No wheelchair facilities.

Permits: No permits are required. There is a $30 entrance fee per vehicle at Yosemite National Park ($25 Nov.-Mar.), good for seven days.

Maps: A Half Dome or Yosemite National Park map is available from Tom Harrison Maps. For a topographic map, go to the USGS website to download Half Dome.

Directions: From Merced, drive 70 miles northeast on Highway 140 to Yosemite National Park. Follow the signs toward Yosemite Valley, entering through the Arch Rock entrance station. Continue on Highway 140/El Portal Road, which becomes Southside Drive, for 11.6 miles to the day-use parking lot at Curry Village (aka Half Dome Village). Then ride the free Yosemite Valley shuttle bus to Happy Isles. In winter, when the shuttle does not run, you must hike from the day-use parking lot in Curry Village (aka Half Dome Village), adding two miles to your round-trip. The Mist Trail may be closed in winter; call to check on weather conditions.

Contact: Yosemite National Park, Yosemite, 209/372-0200, www.nps.gov/yose.

70 MIST TRAIL AND JOHN MUIR LOOP TO NEVADA FALL

6.8 mi / 4.0 hr   🥾3 ⛰10

in Yosemite Valley

Map 10.1, page 467   **BEST (**

You can hike either the John Muir Trail or Mist Trail to reach Yosemite's classic Nevada Fall, but the best choice is to make a loop out of it by hiking up on the Mist Trail, then down partway or all the way on the John Muir Trail. Both trails join above and below Nevada Fall, so you have some options. By hiking uphill rather than downhill on the Mist Trail's treacherous granite staircase, you can look around at the gorgeous scenery every time you stop to catch your breath. The John Muir Trail is somewhat less scenic, especially in its lower reaches, so save it for the way back downhill.

Start at Happy Isles and follow the signed trail to the footbridge over the Merced River, below Vernal Fall. After crossing the bridge, stay close along the river's edge on the Mist Trail for 1.2 miles to the top of Vernal Fall. If it's springtime, make sure you bring your rain gear for this stretch, or you will be drenched in spray. After a brief rest at the waterfall overlook, continue along the river's edge, passing a gorgeous stretch of stream known as the Emerald Pool, still following the Mist Trail. In 0.5 mile,

the path crosses the river again, then climbs another mile to the brink of Nevada Fall. Total elevation gain to the top of the 594-foot falls is 2,600 feet, a healthy ascent. But when you get to walk this close to two world-class waterfalls, who's complaining? For your return trip, cross the footbridge above Nevada Fall and follow John Muir Trail to loop back. As you descend, check out the great view of Nevada Fall with Liberty Cap in the background. This is one of the most memorable scenes in Yosemite Valley.

Note that you can cut back over to the Mist Trail at Clark Point, just above Vernal Fall, if you so desire. That way, you get a second chance to see Vernal Fall and hike the Mist Trail's granite staircase. But let your knees decide—plenty of hikers don't want to face those stairs a second time, especially in the downhill direction.

User Groups: Hikers only. No dogs or mountain bikes. Horses are allowed only on John Muir Trail. No wheelchair facilities.

Permits: No permits are required. There is a $30 entrance fee per vehicle at Yosemite National Park ($25 Nov.-Mar.), good for seven days.

Maps: A Half Dome or Yosemite National Park map is available from Tom Harrison Maps. For a topographic map, go to the USGS website to download Half Dome.

Directions: From Merced, drive 70 miles northeast on Highway 140 to Yosemite National Park. Follow the signs toward Yosemite Valley, entering through the Arch Rock entrance station. Continue on Highway 140/El Portal Road, which becomes Southside Drive, for 11.6 miles to the day-use parking lot at Curry Village (aka Half Dome Village). Then ride the free Yosemite Valley shuttle bus to Happy Isles, stop No. 16. In winter, when the shuttle does not run, you must hike from the day-use parking lot in Curry Village (aka Half Dome Village), adding two miles to your round-trip. Trails may be closed in winter; call to check on weather conditions.

Contact: Yosemite National Park, Yosemite, 209/372-0200, www.nps.gov/yose.

71 MIRROR LAKE LOOP

4.6 mi / 2.0 hr

in Yosemite Valley

Map 10.1, page 467

Thousands of Yosemite visitors walk to Mirror Lake every day in summer, but the vast majority of them miss the best part of this hike. The first thing you need to know: Mirror Lake is not really a lake; it's a large, shallow pool in Tenaya Creek. The pool is undergoing the process of sedimentation (filling with sand and gravel from Tenaya Creek), so every year it shrinks a little more. Many visitors walk up and down this canyon, shake their heads, and ask each other "Where's Mirror Lake?" If you know what you are looking for, the shallow pool is interesting to see, especially when its still waters produce a lovely reflective image of the granite domes above. But if you leave Mirror Lake behind and head back a mile or more into Tenaya Canyon, you will get the most out of this hike, and perhaps find the kind of quiet nature experience that most visitors seek in Yosemite.

Start by riding the free shuttle from Curry Village (aka Half Dome Village) parking lot to Mirror Lake Junction. (Or walk there, if you wish, adding 1.5 miles round-trip to your hike.) From the bus stop, walk 0.5 mile on pavement to Mirror Lake and check out the interpretive signs at its edges. Then follow the foot trail up Tenaya Creek for 1.5 miles, passing the left turnoff for Snow Creek Trail. When you reach a footbridge across Tenaya Creek, cross it and loop back on the other side. Views of Half Dome, Mount Watkins, and neighboring granite walls are spectacular, and the forested creek canyon presents an intimate amphitheater in which to view them. Find a boulder somewhere, have a seat, and take in the show. This loop trail is nearly level the whole way, and once you go beyond Mirror Lake and into the lower Tenaya Creek Canyon, you are likely to find a little solitude.

User Groups: Hikers only. No dogs, horses, or mountain bikes. No wheelchair facilities.

Permits: No permits are required. There is a $30 entrance fee per vehicle at Yosemite National Park ($25 Nov.-Mar.), good for seven days.

Mist Trail and John Muir Loop to Nevada Fall

Maps: A Half Dome or Yosemite National Park map is available from Tom Harrison Maps. For a topographic map, go to the USGS website to download Half Dome.

Directions: From Merced, drive 70 miles northeast on Highway 140 to Yosemite National Park. Follow the signs toward Yosemite Valley, entering through the Arch Rock entrance station. Continue on Highway 140/El Portal Road, which becomes Southside Drive, for 11.6 miles to the day-use parking lot at Curry Village (aka Half Dome Village). Then ride the free Yosemite Valley shuttle bus to Mirror Lake Junction.

Contact: Yosemite National Park, Yosemite, 209/372-0200, www.nps.gov/yose.

72 HALF DOME
17.0 mi / 1 or 2 days 🥾5 △9

in Yosemite Valley

Map 10.1, page 467   **BEST (**

No argument about it, Half Dome is one of those once-in-your-life-you-gotta-do-it hikes. Just be sure you know what you're in for before you set out on this epic trail.

The season is fairly short: if the weather cooperates, the Half Dome cables are usually in place from the weekend before Memorial Day in May through Columbus Day in early October. If the cables aren't up and signs state that Half Dome is closed to hikers, *turn around*. You're in for 17 miles round-trip and a 4,800-foot elevation gain—a demanding hike by any standards. You'll have an unbelievable amount of company. During the summer about 400 people a day make the trek to Half Dome's summit.

The vast majority of people make the trek as a day hike, and that's why a permit system was put in place to manage traffic and help keep hikers safe on the Half Dome Trail. Now backpackers *and* day hikers need a permit to hike Half Dome. Permits are available up to four months in advance through the National Recreation Reservation Service (www.

recreation.gov, 518/885-3639 or 877/444-6777 from outside the U.S. and Canada) for a service fee of $1.50 per permit. Up to four permits are available per web session or phone call, and permits for the peak summer months sell out quickly. Permits are not available in the park, so the only way to get one is in advance through the reservation service. The good news is that even though permits may be sold out for the day you want to hike, you can keep calling back (or checking the website) right up until midnight before your chosen day. Last-minute cancellations often become available.

Got your permit? Okay, now check the contents of your backpack. All day hikers should be sure to bring a load of water and food with them. You'll be handing it out to others who are not so well prepared, as well as gulping it down yourself. To begin the trip, follow either the John Muir Trail or the Mist Trail from Happy Isles to the top of Nevada Fall (the Mist Trail is 0.6 mile shorter), then go left and enter Little Yosemite Valley, where backpackers make camp. At 6.2 miles the John Muir Trail splits off from the Half Dome Trail and you head left for Half Dome. Just under two miles later you approach Half Dome's shoulder, which is a massive hump that is informally called Sub Dome. This is where a ranger is usually stationed to check to make sure that you have a permit (people without permits will not be allowed beyond the base of Sub Dome). A granite stairway, consisting of about 600 steps, leads you up the dauntingly steep face of Sub Dome. Then the trail descends a bit, and you reach the steel cables that run 200 yards up the back of Half Dome. Here, many people start praying a lot and wishing there weren't so many other hikers on the cables at the same time. Do some soul-searching before you begin the cable ascent; turning around is not an option once you're halfway up. Pick up a pair of old work gloves from the pile at the base of the cable route; you'll need them to protect your hands as you pull yourself up the cables. It takes both hands and feet to haul yourself up 440 feet of nearly vertical granite. Unless you somehow managed to get here before the rest of the Half Dome hopefuls, the going will be slow as you wait for the masses ahead to make the ascent. When you reach the top, the views are so incredible that you forget all about your tired arms and feet. There's plenty of room for everyone on top of Half Dome; its vast, mostly flat surface covers about 13 acres.

To make the trip easier, you can choose to split the hike into two days by camping at Little Yosemite Valley, 4.7 miles in (a wilderness permit is required, and on weekday nights these are often easier to obtain than Half Dome day-hiking permits). This lets you save the final ascent for the next day. Don't plan on sleeping much, though. Little Yosemite Valley is one zoo of a backpacking camp.

User Groups: Hikers only. No dogs, horses, or mountain bikes. No wheelchair facilities.

Permits: There is a $30 entrance fee per vehicle at Yosemite National Park ($25 Nov.-Mar.), good for seven days. Day hikers need a permit to hike Half Dome. Permits are available up to four months in advance through the National Recreation Reservation Service (www.recreation.gov, 518/885-3639 or 877/444-6777 from outside the U.S. and Canada) for a service fee of $1.50 per permit. Free wilderness permits are required for overnight stays; these are available on a first-come, first-served basis up to one day in advance at the Yosemite Wilderness kiosk near your chosen trailhead (or farther in advance by mail, phone, or online for a $5 reservation fee per person).

Maps: A Half Dome or Yosemite National Park map is available from Tom Harrison Maps. For a topographic map, go to the USGS website to download Half Dome.

Directions: From Merced, drive 70 miles northeast on Highway 140 to Yosemite National Park. Follow the signs toward Yosemite Valley, entering through the Arch Rock entrance station. Continue on Highway 140/El Portal Road, which becomes Southside Drive, for 11.6 miles to the day-use parking lot at Curry Village (aka Half Dome Village). Then ride the free Yosemite Valley shuttle bus to Happy Isles.

Half Dome

Contact: Yosemite National Park, Yosemite, 209/372-0200 or 209/372-0740 (permit reservations), www.nps.gov/yose or www.nps.gov/yose/wilderness (permit reservations).

7.3 INSPIRATION AND STANFORD POINTS

7.6 mi / 4.0 hr

in Yosemite Valley near the Wawona Tunnel

Map 10.1, page 467

Many consider the view from Inspiration Point at the entrance to the Wawona Tunnel to be one of the finest scenes in Yosemite—a wide panorama of Yosemite Valley, El Capitan, Half Dome, and Bridalveil Fall. If you like this view, you might want to see more of it by taking this hike from the trailhead at the vista point parking lot. The Pohono Trail leads uphill on a moderately steep grade until at 1.3 miles it reaches the "old" Inspiration Point. This is where the road to Yosemite Valley went through in the days before the Wawona Tunnel, and the view is now largely obscured by trees.

© ANN MARIE BROWN

Keep climbing, however, because with another 1,000 feet of elevation gain, you will cross Meadow Brook and reach the left cutoff trail for Stanford Point. You're 3.8 miles from the trailhead and you've climbed 2,200 feet, but your reward is an eagle's-eye view of the valley floor, 3,000 feet below, and a vista to the east of Half Dome and all its granite cousins. This stretch of the Pohono Trail is a dependable workout and the trail is never crowded with hikers.

User Groups: Hikers only. No dogs, horses, or mountain bikes. No wheelchair facilities.

Permits: No permits are required. There is a $30 entrance fee per vehicle at Yosemite National Park ($25 Nov.-Mar.), good for seven days.

Maps: A Yosemite National Park map is available from Tom Harrison Maps. For a topographic map, go to the USGS website to download El Capitan.

Directions: From Merced, drive 70 miles northeast on Highway 140 to Yosemite National Park. Follow the signs to Yosemite Valley, entering through the Arch Rock entrance station. Continue 6.3 miles on Highway 140/El Portal Road, which becomes Southside Drive, and turn right at the fork for Highway 41/Wawona/Fresno. Continue 1.5 miles to the parking lots on either side of the road just before you enter the Wawona Tunnel. The trailhead is at the parking lot on the left (south) side of the road.

Contact: Yosemite National Park, Yosemite, 209/372-0200, www.nps.gov/yose.

74 BRIDALVEIL FALL
0.5 mi / 0.5 hr   🏃1 ⛰9

in Yosemite Valley

Map 10.1, page 467   BEST (

Bridalveil Fall is right up there with Lower Yosemite Fall as a must-do walk for visitors (including nonhikers) to Yosemite Valley. Like that other famous waterfall walk, the path to Bridalveil Fall is paved with people. But the best thing about this waterfall is that unlike other falls in Yosemite Valley, Bridalveil runs year-round. It never dries up and disappoints visitors. The walk to its overlook is short and nearly level; the trail delivers you to a small viewing area about 70 yards from the fall. You can look straight up and see Bridalveil Creek plunging 620 feet off the edge of the south canyon wall. In high wind the fall billows and sways; if you are lucky you might see rainbows dancing in its mist. Another bonus is that your position at the Bridalveil overlook is such that if you do an about-face, you have an excellent view of Ribbon Fall flowing off the northern Yosemite Valley rim. Ribbon Fall is the highest single drop in the park at 1,612 feet, but it only flows in the earliest months of spring.

User Groups: Hikers and wheelchairs. No dogs, horses, or mountain bikes.

Permits: No permits are required. There is a $30 entrance fee per vehicle at Yosemite National Park ($25 Nov.-Mar.), good for seven days.

Maps: A Yosemite National Park map is available from Tom Harrison Maps. For a topographic map, go to the USGS website to download El Capitan.

Directions: From Merced, drive 70 miles northeast on Highway 140 to Yosemite National Park. Follow the signs toward Yosemite Valley, entering through the Arch Rock entrance station. Continue for 6.3 miles on Highway 140/El Portal Road, which becomes Southside Drive, and turn right at the fork for Highway 41/Wawona/Fresno. Turn left almost immediately into the Bridalveil Fall parking lot. The trail begins at the far end of the parking lot. If you are driving into Yosemite Valley on Highway 41 from the south, watch for the Bridalveil Fall turnoff on your right about one mile after you exit the Wawona Tunnel.

Contact: Yosemite National Park, Yosemite, 209/372-0200, www.nps.gov/yose.

75 FOUR-MILE TRAIL
9.6 mi / 6.0 hr   🏃3 ⛰️8

in Yosemite Valley

Map 10.1, page 467

Many years ago, we hiked this trail on our first-ever visit to Yosemite and were shocked when we got to the top and found a giant parking lot and refreshment stand located there. What, you mean we could have driven to the high point on this trail? It's true, but your arrival at dramatic Glacier Point is somehow made all the more meaningful if you get there the hard way, which means hiking Four-Mile Trail all the way up from the valley floor, gaining 3,220 feet in 4.8 miles (not 4.0 miles, as the name implies). The trail is partially shaded and makes for a terrific day hike with an early morning start. Then you can have a leisurely brunch or lunch from your bird's-eye perch on Glacier Point. Don't like what you brought in your daypack? No problem. A snack shop sells hot dogs and the like all summer. From Glacier Point, you have unobstructed views of just about every major landmark in Yosemite Valley—most notably Half Dome, Basket Dome, Yosemite Falls, Vernal and Nevada Falls, and the valley floor far, far below you.

User Groups: Hikers only. No dogs, horses, or mountain bikes. No wheelchair facilities.

Permits: No permits are required. There is a $30 entrance fee per vehicle at Yosemite National Park ($25 Nov.-Mar.), good for seven days.

Maps: A Half Dome or Yosemite National Park map is available from Tom Harrison Maps. For a topographic map, go to the USGS website to download Half Dome.

Directions: From Merced, drive 70 miles northeast on Highway 140 to Yosemite National Park. Follow the signs to Yosemite Valley, entering through the Arch Rock entrance station. Continue on Highway 140/El Portal Road, which becomes Southside Drive, for 9.5 miles. The trailhead is located next to mile marker V18 on the right side of Southside Drive. Park in the pullouts along the road.

Contact: Yosemite National Park, Yosemite, 209/372-0200, www.nps.gov/yose.

76 MCGURK MEADOW AND DEWEY POINT
2.0-7.0 mi / 1.0-4.0 hr   🏃2 ⛰️8

off Glacier Point Road in Yosemite National Park

Map 10.1, page 467

Some trails seem to capture the essence of Yosemite, and the McGurk Meadow Trail is one of those. The trailhead is the first one you reach as you wind along Glacier Point Road to spectacular Glacier Point. It's worth a stop to take the short walk through a fir and pine forest to pristine McGurk Meadow, a mile-long meadow crossed by a footbridge over a small feeder creek. A quarter-mile before the meadow the trail passes an old pioneer cabin, still standing in half-decent repair.

You can turn around at the meadow for a short and easy trip, or you can follow the trail until it connects to the Pohono Trail, which traverses Yosemite's south rim. An ideal destination is Dewey Point, a spectacular promontory with an unforgettable view of Yosemite Valley, located just off the Pohono Trail. That option turns this hike into a seven-mile round-trip.

User Groups: Hikers only. No dogs, horses, or mountain bikes. No wheelchair facilities.

Permits: No permits are required. There is a $30 entrance fee per vehicle at Yosemite National Park ($25 Nov.-Mar.), good for seven days.

Maps: A Yosemite National Park map is available from Tom Harrison Maps. For a topographic map, go to the USGS website to download El Capitan.

Directions: From Merced, drive 70 miles northeast on Highway 140 to Yosemite National Park. Follow the signs toward Yosemite Valley, entering through the Arch Rock entrance station. Continue 6.3 miles on Highway 140/El Portal Road, which becomes Southside Drive, and turn right at the fork for Highway 41/

Wawona/Fresno. Continue for 9.2 miles, turn left on Glacier Point Road, and drive 7.5 miles to the McGurk Meadow trailhead, on the left. Park in the pullout about 75 yards farther up the road.

Contact: Yosemite National Park, Yosemite, 209/372-0200, www.nps.gov/yose.

77 BRIDALVEIL CREEK
3.2 mi / 1.5 hr   🥾1   ⛰7

off Glacier Point Road in Yosemite National Park

Map 10.1, page 467

Perhaps the best time to take this hike to Bridalveil Creek is immediately after visiting Bridalveil Fall. After a short walk from Glacier Point Road through a forested area, you wind up at the edge of Bridalveil Creek, a babbling brook that seems far too tame to produce the giant waterfall downstream. To make the trip, follow Ostrander Lake Trail from Glacier Point Road for 1.4 miles. This stretch is almost completely level and is framed by colorful bunches of lupine in midsummer. When the trail splits, take the right fork toward Bridalveil Creek. The stream is so tame here that there is no bridge to cross—it's an easy rock hop by midsummer, although it can be a dangerous crossing in late spring. Pick a spot along its banks, and spend some time counting the wildflowers or the small, darting trout. If you are camping at Bridalveil Creek Campground or just heading up the road to visit Glacier Point, this easy walk is a pleasant leg-stretcher that will take you away from the crowds that throng so many of Yosemite's famous destinations.

User Groups: Hikers only. No dogs, horses, or mountain bikes. No wheelchair facilities.

Permits: No permits are required. There is a $30 entrance fee per vehicle at Yosemite National Park ($25 Nov.-Mar.), good for seven days.

Maps: A Yosemite National Park map is available from Tom Harrison Maps. For a

topographic map, go to the USGS website to download Half Dome.

Directions: From Merced, drive 70 miles northeast on Highway 140 to Yosemite National Park. Follow the signs toward Yosemite Valley, entering through the Arch Rock entrance station. Continue for 6.3 miles on Highway 140/El Portal Road, which becomes Southside Drive, and turn right at the fork for Highway 41/Wawona/Fresno. Continue for 9.2 miles, turn left on Glacier Point Road, and drive another 8.9 miles to the Ostrander Lake trailhead, on the right.

Contact: Yosemite National Park, Yosemite, 209/372-0200, www.nps.gov/yose.

78 OSTRANDER LAKE
12.5 mi / 1 or 2 days   🥾2   ⛰8

off Glacier Point Road in Yosemite National Park

Map 10.1, page 467

While many people take short day hikes from Glacier Point Road, a longer 12.5-mile trip to Ostrander Lake may better suit your taste. The trail is surprisingly easy, considering the long miles, and the first half is quite level. You can hike out and back in a day, or get a wilderness permit and camp near the lake's shores. The wide blue lake, set at 8,580 feet, is a popular destination for cross-country skiers in the winter, as is evidenced by the stone Ostrander Ski Hut and the ski markers tacked high up on trees along the route. Although the trail (really an old road) begins in a regenerated forest fire area, it traverses a typical high-country landscape of firs, pines, and, as you ascend, granite. You have to gain 1,600 feet along the way, most of it in the final three miles to the lake. The culmination of the climb occurs at nearly six miles out, as you reach the trail's highest point, a saddle on top of 8,700-foot Horizon Ridge. Here you are rewarded with excellent views of Half Dome, North Dome, Basket Dome, and Liberty Cap. This is a fine place to catch your breath. From here, the lake is less than 0.5 mile farther. On summer days, bring your swimsuit and a book, and plan to spend a few hours on Ostrander's sand- and boulder-lined shoreline.

User Groups: Hikers only. No dogs, horses, or mountain bikes. No wheelchair facilities.

Permits: There is a $30 entrance fee per vehicle at Yosemite National Park ($25 Nov.-Mar.), good for seven days. Free wilderness permits are required for overnight stays. They are available on a first-come, first-served basis up to one day in advance at the Yosemite Wilderness kiosk near your chosen trailhead or farther in advance by mail, phone, or online for a $5 reservation fee per person.

Maps: A Yosemite National Park map is available from Tom Harrison Maps. For topographic maps, go to the USGS website to download Half Dome and Mariposa Grove.

Directions: From Merced, drive 70 miles northeast on Highway 140 to Yosemite National Park. Follow the signs toward Yosemite Valley, entering through the Arch Rock entrance station. Continue for 6.3 miles on Highway 140/El Portal Road, which becomes Southside Drive, and turn right at the fork for Highway 41/Wawona/Fresno. Continue for 9.2 miles, turn left on Glacier Point Road, and drive 8.9 miles to the Ostrander Lake trailhead, on the right.

Contact: Yosemite National Park, Yosemite, 209/372-0200 or 209/372-0740 (permit reservations), www.nps.gov/yose or www.nps.gov/yose/wilderness (permit reservations).

79 SENTINEL DOME
2.2 mi / 1.0 hr

off Glacier Point Road in Yosemite National Park

| Map 10.1, page 467 | BEST (|

It's hard to believe you can get so much for so little, but on Sentinel Dome Trail, you can. The granite dome is located about a mile before Glacier Point on Glacier Point Road, and its elevation is 1,000 feet higher than the point's. Views from the dome's summit extend a full 360 degrees. A short and nearly level walk leads

you to the base of the dome, and a 100-yard climb up its smooth granite back side brings you to its summit. There you are greeted by stunning vistas in all directions, including an unusual perspective on Upper and Lower Yosemite Falls. This is one of the best places in Yosemite to watch the sun set. To make a longer excursion, you can easily combine this hike with the hike to Taft Point and the Fissures (see listing in this chapter), which starts from the same trailhead but heads in the opposite direction.

User Groups: Hikers only. No dogs, horses, or mountain bikes. No wheelchair facilities.

Permits: No permits are required. There is a $30 entrance fee per vehicle at Yosemite National Park ($25 Nov.-Mar.), good for seven days.

Maps: A Half Dome or Yosemite National Park map is available from Tom Harrison Maps. For a topographic map, go to the USGS website to download Half Dome.

Directions: From Merced, drive 70 miles northeast on Highway 140 to Yosemite National Park. Follow the signs to Yosemite Valley, entering through the Arch Rock entrance station. Continue 6.3 miles on Highway 140/El Portal Road, which becomes Southside Drive, and turn right at the fork for Highway 41/Wawona/Fresno. Continue for 9.2 miles, turn left on Glacier Point Road, and drive 13.2 miles to the Taft Point/Sentinel Dome trailhead parking lot, on the left side of the road.

Contact: Yosemite National Park, Yosemite, 209/372-0200, www.nps.gov/yose.

80 TAFT POINT AND THE FISSURES
2.2 mi / 1.0 hr

off Glacier Point Road in Yosemite National Park

| Map 10.1, page 467 |

It's not so much the sweeping vista from Taft Point that you remember (although certainly you could say that the views of Yosemite's north rim and the valley floor are stunning). What you remember is the incredible sense of awe that you feel, perhaps mixed with a little fear and a lot of respect, as you peer down into the fissures in Taft Point's granite—huge cracks in the rock that plunge hundreds of feet down toward the valley. One of the fissures has a couple of large boulders captured in its jaws; they're stuck there, waiting for the next big earthquake or ice age to set them free. Be sure to walk to the metal railing along the edge of Taft Point's cliff, where you can hold on tight and peer down at the valley far, far below. If you have kids with you or anyone who is afraid of heights, be sure to keep a tight handhold on them.

User Groups: Hikers only. No dogs, horses, or mountain bikes. No wheelchair facilities.

Permits: No permits are required. There is a $30 entrance fee per vehicle at Yosemite National Park ($25 Nov.-Mar.), good for seven days.

Maps: A Half Dome or Yosemite National Park map is available from Tom Harrison Maps. For a topographic map, go to the USGS website to download Half Dome.

Directions: From Merced, drive 70 miles northeast on Highway 140 to Yosemite National Park. Follow the signs to Yosemite Valley, entering through the Arch Rock entrance station. Continue for 6.3 miles on Highway 140/El Portal Road, which becomes Southside Drive, and turn right at the fork for Highway 41/Wawona/Fresno. Continue for 9.2 miles, turn left on Glacier Point Road, and drive 13.2 miles to the Taft Point/Sentinel Dome trailhead parking lot, on the left side of the road.

Contact: Yosemite National Park, Yosemite, 209/372-0200, www.nps.gov/yose.

81 POHONO TRAIL

13.0 mi one-way / 7.0 hr

off Glacier Point Road in Yosemite National Park

Map 10.1, page 467

If you can arrange a shuttle trip, Pohono Trail from Glacier Point downhill to its end at Wawona Tunnel is worth every step of its 13 miles. The two ends of the trail have the best drive-to viewpoints in all of Yosemite, and in between, you are treated to dozens of other scenic spots (including Sentinel Dome, at 1.5 miles, and Taft Point, at 3.8 miles), as well as four bird's-eye lookouts over the valley floor: Inspiration, Stanford, Dewey, and Crocker Points. Starting at Glacier Point and ending at Wawona Tunnel, you'll cover a 2,800-foot descent, but there are some "ups" along the way, too—like at the very beginning (from Glacier Point to Sentinel Dome), and between Bridalveil Creek and Dewey Point. The trail stays on or near Yosemite Valley's southern rim the entire way except for one major detour into the woods to access the bridge crossing of Bridalveil Creek. Remember to bring along a good map, because many of the trail's best offerings are just off the main path. If you don't take the short spur routes to reach them, you'll miss out on some spectacular scenery.

The view of Yosemite Falls from Pohono Trail in front of Sentinel Dome is the best in all of Yosemite. For the best overall vista along the trail, it's a toss-up between Glacier Point, Taft Point, and Dewey Point.

User Groups: Hikers only. No dogs, horses, or mountain bikes. No wheelchair facilities.

Permits: There is a $30 entrance fee per vehicle at Yosemite National Park ($25 Nov.-Mar.), good for seven days. Free wilderness permits are required for overnight stays. They are available on a first-come, first-served basis up to one day in advance at the Yosemite Wilderness kiosk near your chosen trailhead, or farther in advance by mail, phone, or online for a $5 reservation fee per person.

Maps: A Yosemite National Park map is available from Tom Harrison Maps. For topographic maps, go to the USGS website to download Half Dome and El Capitan.

Directions: From Merced, drive 70 miles northeast on Highway 140 to Yosemite National Park. Follow the signs to Yosemite Valley, entering through the Arch Rock entrance station. Continue for 6.3 miles on Highway 140/El Portal Road, which becomes Southside Drive, and turn right at the fork for Highway 41/Wawona/Fresno. Continue for 9.2 miles, turn left on Glacier Point Road, and drive 15.7 miles to Glacier Point. Park and walk toward the main viewing area across from the café and gift shop. Look for the Pohono Trail sign about 150 feet southeast of the café building, on your right.

Contact: Yosemite National Park, Yosemite, 209/372-0200 or 209/372-0740 (permit reservations), www.nps.gov/yose or www.nps.gov/yose/wilderness (permit reservations).

82 PANORAMA TRAIL

8.5 mi one-way / 5.0 hr 🏃3 ⛰10

off Glacier Point Road in Yosemite National Park

Map 10.1, page 467   **BEST ☾**

The Panorama Trail follows a spectacular route from Glacier Point to Yosemite Valley, heading downhill most of the way, but you must have a shuttle car waiting at the end or it's one heck of a long climb back up. A great option is to take the Yosemite Lodge (aka Yosemite Valley Lodge) tour bus for one leg of the trip; call 209/372-1240 to reserve a seat (fee required).

The aptly named Panorama Trail begins at Glacier Point, elevation 7,214 feet. You switchback downhill, accompanied by ever-changing perspectives on Half Dome, Basket Dome, North Dome, Liberty Cap, and, in the distance, Vernal and Nevada Falls. You will gape a lot. After passing Illilouette Fall and ascending a bit for the first time on the trip, continue eastward to the Panorama Trail's end near the top of Nevada Fall. Turn right to reach the top of the fall and have a rest at the overlook, then continue downhill on the Mist Trail on the north side of the river. After a view-filled descent along the north side of Nevada Fall, you'll cross the river in 1.4 miles and walk alongside lovely Emerald Pool on your way to the top of Vernal Fall. Enjoy the show here, then tromp

down the granite staircase on the busy trail back to Happy Isles. From there you can take the free valley shuttle bus back to your car, parked somewhere in Yosemite Valley.

Note that the route has a 3,200-foot elevation loss over its course, but there is also a 760-foot climb after you cross Illilouette Creek. Also be forewarned that while the starting miles of the trip are quite tranquil, the final two miles by Vernal Fall are usually a parade of people.

User Groups: Hikers only. No dogs, horses, or mountain bikes. No wheelchair facilities.

Permits: No permits are required. There is a $30 entrance fee per vehicle at Yosemite National Park ($25 Nov.-Mar.), good for seven days.

Maps: A Half Dome or Yosemite National Park map is available from Tom Harrison Maps. For a topographic map, go to the USGS website to download Half Dome.

Directions: From Merced, drive 70 miles northeast on Highway 140 to Yosemite National Park. Follow the signs to Yosemite Valley, entering through the Arch Rock entrance station. Continue for 6.3 miles on Highway 140/El Portal Road, which becomes Southside Drive, and turn right at the fork for Highway 41/Wawona/Fresno. Continue for 9.2 miles, turn left on Glacier Point Road, and drive 15.7 miles to Glacier Point. Park and walk toward the main viewing area, across from the café and gift shop. Look for the Panorama Trail sign about 150 feet southeast of the café building, on your right.

Contact: Yosemite National Park, Yosemite, 209/372-0200, www.nps.gov/yose; lodge tour buses, 209/372-1240.

83 ILLILOUETTE FALL

4.0 mi / 2.5 hr 🏃2 ⛰10

off Glacier Point Road in Yosemite National Park

Map 10.1, page 467

Those who can't afford the time or make the car shuttle arrangements necessary to hike the entire Panorama Trail should at least take this incredible out-and-back trip on the top portion of the route. Glacier Point is your starting point, and the bridge above Illilouette Fall becomes your destination, but what happens in between is sheer magic. Some say that hiking Panorama Trail is like staring at a life-size Yosemite postcard, but we say it's more like being in the postcard. As you walk, you feel as if you've become one with the magnificent panorama of Half Dome, Basket Dome, North Dome, Liberty Cap, and far-off Vernal and Nevada Falls. The trail is downhill all the way to Illilouette Fall in two miles, which means you have a 1,200-foot elevation gain on the return trip. The path is extremely well graded, so even children can make the climb. After viewing the waterfall from a trailside overlook, walk another 0.25 mile and stand on the bridge that is perched just above the 370-foot drop. For obvious reasons, don't think about swimming here.

User Groups: Hikers only. No dogs, horses, or mountain bikes. No wheelchair facilities.

Permits: No permits are required. There is a $30 entrance fee per vehicle at Yosemite National Park ($25 Nov.-Mar.), good for seven days.

Maps: A Half Dome or Yosemite National Park map is available from Tom Harrison Maps. For a topographic map, go to the USGS website to download Half Dome.

Directions: From Merced, drive 70 miles northeast on Highway 140 to Yosemite National Park. Follow the signs to Yosemite Valley, entering through the Arch Rock entrance station. Continue for 6.3 miles on Highway 140/El Portal Road, which becomes Southside Drive, and turn right at the fork for Highway 41/Wawona/Fresno. Continue for 9.2 miles, turn left on Glacier Point Road, and drive 15.7 miles to Glacier Point. Park and walk toward the main viewing area, across from the café and gift shop. Look for the Panorama Trail sign on your right, about 150 feet southeast of the café building.

Contact: Yosemite National Park, Yosemite, 209/372-0200, www.nps.gov/yose.

84 ALDER CREEK FALLS
8.2 mi / 5.0 hr　　🥾 3　⛰ 9

off Highway 41 near Wawona in Yosemite National Park

Map 10.1, page 467

Maybe the best thing about Alder Creek Falls is that with all the world-famous waterfalls in Yosemite, this one just plain gets overlooked. Or maybe the best thing is the fun hike to reach it, starting with the challenge of locating the hidden trailhead along Highway 41. After you accomplish this feat, you begin with a one-mile beeline hike straight uphill through the forest, which will surely get your heart pumping. At the top of the ridge and a trail junction, turn left and hike through the trees for two more miles, still heading uphill but now more gently. Three miles from the trailhead, the route suddenly goes level as it joins an old railroad grade, and then it's a one-mile easy stroll to the spot where Alder Creek takes the plunge off a granite lip. The waterfall is about 250 feet tall, and the best view of it is from the trail, about 100 yards away from it. If you choose to keep hiking beyond the falls, you'll find many fine picnic spots among meadows filled with wildflowers.

User Groups: Hikers and horses. No dogs or mountain bikes. No wheelchair facilities.

Permits: There is a $30 entrance fee per vehicle at Yosemite National Park ($25 Nov.-Mar.), good for seven days. Free wilderness permits are required for overnight stays. They are available on a first-come, first-served basis up to one day in advance at the Yosemite Wilderness kiosk near your chosen trailhead, or farther in advance by mail, phone, or online for a $5 reservation fee per person.

Maps: A Yosemite National Park map is available from Tom Harrison Maps. For a topographic map, go to the USGS website to download Wawona.

Directions: From Merced, drive 55 miles

northeast on Highway 140 to Yosemite National Park. Follow the signs to Yosemite Valley, entering through the Arch Rock entrance station. Continue for 6.3 miles on Highway 140/El Portal Road, which becomes Southside Drive, and turn right at the fork for Highway 41/Wawona/Fresno. Drive south on Highway 41 for 21 miles to a hairpin turn in the road (if you are coming from the south, it is exactly 4.2 miles north of Chilnualna Falls Road in Wawona). Park in the large dirt pullout on the west side of the road; the trailhead is on the east side of Highway 41. There is no marker except for a Yosemite Wilderness sign.

Contact: Yosemite National Park, Yosemite, 209/372-0200 or 209/372-0740 (permit reservations), www.nps.gov/yose or www.nps.gov/yose/wilderness (permit reservations).

Permits: No permits are required. There is a $30 entrance fee per vehicle at Yosemite National Park ($25 Nov.-Mar.), good for seven days.

Maps: A Yosemite National Park map is available from Tom Harrison Maps. For a topographic map, go to the USGS website to download Wawona.

Directions: From Merced, drive 70 miles northeast on Highway 140 to Yosemite National Park. Follow the signs toward Yosemite Valley, entering through the Arch Rock entrance station. Continue for 6.3 miles on Highway 140/El Portal Road, which becomes Southside Drive, and turn right at the fork for Highway 41/Wawona/Fresno. Drive 27 miles to the trailhead, which is just south of the golf course and across the road from the Wawona Hotel (aka Big Trees Lodge).

Contact: Yosemite National Park, Yosemite, 209/372-0200, www.nps.gov/yose.

85 WAWONA MEADOW LOOP
3.2 mi / 1.25 hr   🥾1   ⛰7

off Highway 41 near Wawona in Yosemite National Park

Map 10.1, page 467

Sometimes you just want to take a stroll in the park, and the Wawona Meadow Loop is exactly that. Many hikers ignore this trail because of its proximity to the Wawona Golf Course, but they are missing out on an easy, pleasant meander. On this level trail (a former stage road), you can see terrific wildflowers in early summer and enjoy the good company of butterflies as you take a lazy stroll. From the signed trailhead across the road from the Wawona Hotel (aka Big Trees Lodge), hike to your left on the dirt road, following the split rail fence. At the end of the meadow the old road crosses the stream and returns to the hotel on the north side of the golf course. If you wish, you can even bring your dog or ride your bike on this trail. If you're staying at the Wawona Hotel (aka Big Trees Lodge), you can hike from there, crossing the Wawona Road on your way out and back.

User Groups: Hikers, dogs, and mountain bikes. No horses. No wheelchair facilities.

86 CHILNUALNA FALL
8.2 mi / 5.0 hr   🥾3   ⛰9

off Highway 41 near Wawona in Yosemite National Park

Map 10.1, page 467

Are you ready to climb? It's good to be mentally prepared for this hike, which includes a steady four-mile uphill, gaining 2,400 feet to reach the top of Chilnualna Fall. Pick a nice, cool day because this trail is in the lower-elevation part of Yosemite. Your nose will be continually assaulted with the intoxicating smell of bear clover, which together with manzanita and oaks makes up the majority of the vegetation along the route. Halfway up you get a great view of Wawona Dome (elevation 6,897 feet) from a granite overlook. This is a great place to take a break and stretch your hamstrings. Shortly thereafter you glimpse a section of Chilnualna Falls high up on a cliff wall, still far ahead. The trail leads above the brink of the fall's lower drop to a series of higher cascades. Keep hiking until you reach the uppermost cascade, which consists of five pool-and-drop tiers just 100 yards off the granite-lined trail. You'll want to spread out a picnic here before you begin the long descent back to the trailhead.

User Groups: Hikers and horses. No dogs or mountain bikes. No wheelchair facilities.

Permits: There is a $30 entrance fee per vehicle at Yosemite National Park ($25 Nov.-Mar.), good for seven days. Free wilderness permits are required for overnight stays. They are available on a first-come, first-served basis up to one day in advance at the Yosemite Wilderness kiosk near your chosen trailhead, or farther in advance by mail, phone, or online for a $5 reservation fee per person.

Maps: A Yosemite National Park map is available from Tom Harrison Maps. For topographic maps, go to the USGS website to download Wawona and Mariposa Grove.

Directions: From Merced, drive 55 miles northeast on Highway 140 to Yosemite National Park. Follow the signs to Yosemite Valley, entering through the Arch Rock entrance station. Continue for 6.3 miles on Highway 140/ El Portal Road, which becomes Southside Drive, and turn right at the fork for Highway 41/Wawona/Fresno. Drive south on Highway 41 for 25 miles to Wawona, and turn left on Chilnualna Falls Road. Drive 1.7 miles east and park in the lot on the right side of the road. Walk back to Chilnualna Falls Road and pick up the single-track trail across the pavement.

Contact: Yosemite National Park, Yosemite, 209/372-0200 or 209/372-0740 (permit reservations), www.nps.gov/yose or www.nps.gov/ yose/wilderness (permit reservations).

87 MARIPOSA GROVE
2.0-6.4 mi / 1.0-3.0 hr

off Highway 41 near Wawona in Yosemite National Park

Map 10.1, page 467

Note: The Mariposa Grove is closed for restoration until the spring of 2017. When the grove reopens, a new parking area will be located near the south entrance, and a free shuttle system will take visitors from the parking area to the grove.

The Mariposa Grove is the largest of the three groves of giant sequoias in Yosemite National Park. The star tree in the Mariposa Grove is the Grizzly Giant, with a circumference of more than 100 feet. At approximately 2,700 years old, it's one of the oldest known giant sequoias. If you want to see only the most famous trees in the grove, including the Grizzly Giant, take the well-signed two-mile hike through the lower grove and turn around at the signs pointing to the upper grove. If you hike the entire lower and upper grove, you will cover 6.4 miles of trail. For the best chance of avoiding the summer crowds, time your visit for early in the morning or just before sunset.

User Groups: Hikers only. No dogs, horses, or mountain bikes. No wheelchair facilities.

Permits: No permits are required. There is a $30 entrance fee per vehicle at Yosemite National Park ($25 Nov.-Mar.), good for seven days.

Maps: A brochure and trail map are available at the trailhead. A Yosemite National Park map is available from Tom Harrison Maps. For a topographic map, go to the USGS website to download Mariposa Grove.

Directions: From Merced, drive 70 miles northeast on Highway 140 to Yosemite National Park. Follow the signs toward Yosemite Valley, entering through the Arch Rock entrance station. Continue for 6.3 miles on Highway 140/ El Portal Road, which becomes Southside Drive, and turn right at the fork for Highway 41/Wawona/Fresno. Drive 32 miles to the Mariposa Grove parking area by Yosemite's south entrance, then ride the shuttle bus to the grove's trailhead. (If you enter the park on Highway 41 from the south, the parking area will be just after you pass through the entrance station.)

Contact: Yosemite National Park, Yosemite, 209/372-0200, www.nps.gov/yose.

88 LEWIS CREEK NATIONAL RECREATION TRAIL

4.0 mi / 2.0 hr   👫₁ ⛰₈

off Highway 41 north of Oakhurst

Map 10.1, page 467

Three separate trailheads access the Lewis Creek National Recreation Trail, but unless you want to hike its entire 3.7-mile one-way distance, the best place to start is at the trail's midpoint, just off Highway 41. From this roadside trailhead, you can take a 10-minute walk south to Corlieu Falls and/or walk 1.8 miles north to see Red Rock Falls. Neither waterfall is a showstopper, although both are pretty. Instead, the highlight of the trip is the hike itself, a gorgeous walk along flower-lined Lewis Creek, following the route of the historic Madera Sugar Pine lumber flume. Sugar Pine Lumber Company used the flume (an artificial river in a huge wooden trough) to float lumber over 50 miles to the town of Madera. You'll pass many anglers along the hike; Lewis Creek is stocked with catchable trout. Fishing is best below Corlieu Falls. In addition, the white western azaleas along the stream bloom in profusion in early summer, shaded by a thick canopy of dogwoods, oaks, ponderosa pines, and incense cedars.

User Groups: Hikers and dogs. No horses or mountain bikes. No wheelchair facilities.

Permits: No permits are required. Parking and access are free.

Maps: A Sierra National Forest map is available from the U.S. Forest Service. For a topographic map, go to the USGS website to download Ahwahnee.

Directions: From Oakhurst, drive north on Highway 41 for eight miles to the signed trailhead for Lewis Creek Trail, on the east side of the highway. The trailhead is four miles south of Westfall Picnic Area.

Contact: Sierra National Forest, Bass Lake Ranger Station, North Fork, 559/877-2218, www.fs.usda.gov/sierra.

89 SHADOW OF THE GIANTS

1.2 mi / 0.5 hr   👫₁ ⛰₉

off Highway 41 south of Yosemite National Park and north of Oakhurst in Sierra National Forest

Map 10.1, page 467   **BEST (**

Shadow of the Giants is a National Recreation Trail that is located within the Nelder Grove of Giant Sequoias. For the sheer numbers of sequoias and the blissful peace and quiet, it beats the heck out of the sequoia groves a few miles north, in Yosemite National Park. On a Saturday afternoon in June, it's not impossible to walk the one-mile interpretive trail all by yourself. The self-guided signs along the trail are interesting and informative, and the babble of Nelder Creek is a perfect accompaniment to the huge, majestic trees. In addition to the sequoias, the forest is filled with western azaleas, dogwoods, incense cedars, wild rose, sugar pines, and white firs. What's the best thing we learned on the trail? The bark of mature sequoias is so soft that squirrels use it to line their nests. The trail makes an easy loop

© ANN MARIE BROWN

Chilnualna Falls

and is set at 5,000 feet in elevation. The best sequoias are at the far end of the loop, so make sure you walk all the way.

User Groups: Hikers and dogs. No horses or mountain bikes. No wheelchair facilities.

Permits: No permits are required. Parking and access are free.

Maps: A Sierra National Forest map is available from the U.S. Forest Service. For a topographic map, go to the USGS website to download Bass Lake.

Directions: From Oakhurst, drive north on Highway 41 for five miles to Sky Ranch Road/Road 632. Turn east on Sky Ranch Road and drive six miles to the turnoff for Nelder Grove. Turn left, drive 1.5 miles, and take the left fork, signed for Shadow of the Giants. (The right fork takes you to an interpretive site and additional trails). Drive 0.5 mile to the trailhead.

Contact: Sierra National Forest, Bass Lake Ranger Station, North Fork, 559/877-2218, www.fs.usda.gov/sierra.

90 FRESNO DOME
2.0 mi / 1.0 hr

off Highway 41 south of Yosemite National Park and north of Oakhurst

Map 10.1, page 467

It's best to plan one hour of time for this trip, but you might want to leave room for more, because once you reach the top of Fresno Dome, you won't want to leave. The trailhead elevation is 8,000 feet, and the trail is beautiful right from the start. It traverses a verdant meadow filled with corn lilies, quaking aspens, and lavender shooting stars. The first 0.5 mile is completely flat; in the second 0.5 mile, you climb up the sloped back side of Fresno Dome. After a moderate ascent (manageable by almost anybody), you're rewarded with 360-degree views, mostly of conifer-filled valleys. You can just make out a corner of Bass Lake, the town of Oakhurst, and the far-off snowy peaks of the Ansel Adams Wilderness. From up on top of Fresno Dome, it all looks like heaven.

User Groups: Hikers and dogs. No horses or mountain bikes. No wheelchair facilities.

Permits: No permits are required. Parking and access are free.

Maps: A Sierra National Forest map is available from the U.S. Forest Service. For a topographic map, go to the USGS website to download Bass Lake.

Directions: From Oakhurst, drive north on Highway 41 for five miles to Sky Ranch Road/Road 632. Turn east on Sky Ranch Road, drive approximately 12 miles, and bear left at the sign for Fresno Dome Campground. Drive 4.8 miles to the trailhead (two miles past the camp).

Contact: Sierra National Forest, Bass Lake Ranger Station, North Fork, 559/877-2218, www.fs.usda.gov/sierra/.

91 THE NICHE AND CORA LAKES
8.6 mi / 4.0 hr-2 days

in the Ansel Adams Wilderness southeast of Yosemite National Park

Map 10.1, page 467

Reaching the trailhead for The Niche and Cora Lakes requires a long drive on the Sierra Vista National Scenic Byway, the showpiece road of the North Fork area. If you have the time for it, it's a great trip. The best approach is to drive out and spend the night at Granite Creek Campground or nearby Clover Meadow Campground, then start hiking the next day. The trip starts with a 3.1-mile gentle ascent through red firs and lodgepole pines to The Niche (at 8,000 feet), where you enter the Ansel Adams Wilderness boundary. Bear left and follow the signs to Cora Lakes, at 4.3 miles. Only one of the Cora Lakes is of substantial size; that's the lower lake, the first one you come to, on the left. The lake is partly forested and has dependable trout fishing. Because the total ascent to Cora Lakes is only 1,200 feet, you may have some energy left to burn. Backpackers should consider adding on a jaunt to Joe Crane Lake, another four miles to the north. The lake has a long and lovely sandy beach, good fishing, and even better swimming than at Cora Lakes.

User Groups: Hikers, dogs, and horses. No mountain bikes. No wheelchair facilities.

Permits: A free wilderness permit is required for overnight stays and is available from the Bass Lake Ranger Station. Quotas are in effect year-round; permits can be reserved in advance for a $5 reservation fee per person.

Maps: A Sierra National Forest or Ansel Adams Wilderness map is available from the U.S. Forest Service. For a topographic map, go to the USGS website to download Timber Knob.

Directions: From the town of North Fork south of Bass Lake, drive southeast on Road 225 to Minarets Road. Turn left (north) on Minarets Road/Road 81 and follow it for approximately 50 winding miles to the Clover Meadow Ranger Station/Granite Creek turnoff, on the right. Drive 4.5 miles to the Isberg trailhead, just beyond Granite Creek Campground.

Contact: Sierra National Forest, Bass Lake Ranger Station, North Fork, 559/877-2218, www.fs.usda.gov/sierra.

92 JACKASS LAKES

7.2 mi / 4.0 hr or 2 days

in the Ansel Adams Wilderness southeast of Yosemite National Park

Map 10.1, page 467

Campers in the Clover Meadow and Upper Chiquito campground areas have this pleasant day hike to look forward to. The trailhead is an easy reach (right off of Beasore Road), and in about two hours of hiking, you can be cooling your toes in the crystal-blue waters of Lower Jackass Lake. The trail climbs immediately from the road, then enters the Ansel Adams Wilderness boundary in one mile. This first mile can be hot and steep, but it's over with quickly. At the boundary, the grade mellows out, and you reach a junction just before the lakes, at 3.4 miles. The right fork goes to Lower Jackass Lake (the largest of three choices) in 0.2 mile, and the left fork goes to the tiny upper

lake. A third lake lies in the basin above the upper lake. Many people just bear right at the junction and visit Lower Jackass Lake, which at 8,600 feet is backed by granite cliffs and offers good swimming and fishing prospects. No, this isn't the most beautiful lake in the Sierra, but if you just want to visit a pretty spot without a whole lot of effort, this trip fits the bill.

User Groups: Hikers, dogs, and horses. No mountain bikes. No wheelchair facilities.

Permits: A free wilderness permit is required for overnight stays and is available from the Bass Lake Ranger Station. Quotas are in effect year-round; permits can be reserved in advance for a $5 reservation fee per person.

Maps: A Sierra National Forest or Ansel Adams Wilderness map is available from the U.S. Forest Service. For a topographic map, go to the USGS website to download Timber Knob.

Directions: From Oakhurst, drive north on Highway 41 for four miles, then turn right on Road 222 toward Bass Lake. In four miles, bear left on Road 274. Drive two miles and turn left on Beasore Road (gravel). Drive 29 miles to a turnoff for the Norris Trailhead. Bear left and drive two miles to the trailhead parking area.

Contact: Sierra National Forest, Bass Lake Ranger Station, North Fork, 559/877-2218, www.fs.usda.gov/sierra.

93 CONVICT CANYON TO LAKE DOROTHY

15.0 mi / 2 days

in the John Muir Wilderness south of Mammoth Lakes

Map 10.2, page 468   BEST (

Framed by a back wall of bare granite peaks, Convict Lake is a mountain shrine, and the trail that leads from here into the backcountry wilderness makes hikers feel as if they're ascending into heaven. But this is no easy trip. Not only is there a 2,700-foot climb, but a tricky and sometimes dangerous stream crossing is involved. To complicate matters, much of the trail into Convict Canyon has been washed out by frequent landslides, and the Forest Service has given up on trail maintenance. Still, this canyon is worth seeing—just be prepared for a serious hike.

Begin your trek at Convict Lake (7,621 feet). A trail circles the lake, and it doesn't matter whether you follow the north shore trail or the south shore trail. Either way you'll have plenty of company until you reach the far (west) side of the lake, where the Convict Canyon Trail takes off. You'll start to climb right away, and this section can be steep and hot, but it's fairly easy to follow except for a few washed-out sections. Occasional stands of aspen provide welcome shade. At about three miles, you must ford Convict Creek, which can be dangerous in the early summer because of high snowmelt. (By autumn, it may be a simple rock-hop.) Several attempts to bridge this crossing have failed, as the bridge always gets washed out by high flows in early summer.

Beyond the crossing, the trail gets sketchier, and the drop-offs get steeper. You'll climb high above the creek, becoming more intimate with the magnificent, colorful walls of Convict Canyon. This place is a geologist's dream. Finally you'll climb high enough to enter the high country above tree line at 10,000 feet. Only scattered stands of whitebark pines grow on the edge of Mildred Lake (4.9 miles out), a great place for day hikers to call it a day. A sketchy use trail switchbacks from the back side of Mildred up to Lake Dorothy at 6.2 miles (10,275 feet), Lake Genevieve at 7.2 miles (10,000 feet), and beyond them, Bighorn, Edith, and Cloverleaf Lakes. Backpackers can take their pick. Lake Dorothy is by far the largest of the lot and is well known for its white sand beaches. You can spend days exploring this high-mountain paradise—but it comes with a price.

Note: The crossing of Convict Creek is considered to be one of the most treacherous in the Sierra Nevada. This trail should only be hiked late in the season, when the stream flow has dropped. Check with the Mammoth Lakes Welcome Center for current conditions before planning a trip.

User Groups: Hikers, dogs, and horses. No mountain bikes. No wheelchair facilities.

Permits: A free wilderness permit is required for overnight stays and is available from the Mammoth Lakes Welcome Center. Quotas are in effect from May 1 to November 1; for this period, permits are available in advance for a $5 reservation fee per person.

Maps: A Mammoth High Country map is available from Tom Harrison Maps. An Inyo National Forest or John Muir Wilderness map is available from the U.S. Forest Service. For a topographic map, go to the USGS website to download Bloody Mountain.

Directions: From U.S. 395 at the Mammoth Lakes junction, drive south for six miles to Convict Lake Road. Turn west and drive 1.8 miles to a spur road on the right as you near the lake. Turn right and drive 0.25 mile to the parking area for the trailhead.

Contact: Inyo National Forest, Mammoth Lakes Welcome Center, Mammoth Lakes, 760/924-5500, www.fs.usda.gov/inyo.

94 MCGEE CREEK TO STEELHEAD LAKE

11.4 mi / 6.0 hr or 2 days 🏃3 ⛰9

in the John Muir Wilderness

Map 10.2, page 468   **BEST (**

Unlike many trails leading into the John Muir Wilderness, the McGee Creek Trail has the benefit of starting out with a fairly gentle grade. It follows the remains of an old mining road (now just a narrow trail), and it gives your legs and lungs the opportunity to warm up before climbing more seriously. Get an early start, though, because in the first two miles, you pass through sun-baked plains of sage and rabbit brush. There is very little shade, but you are heading toward a colorful and dramatic mountain backdrop: Mount Baldwin on the right, Mount Crocker on the left, and Red and White Mountain straight ahead—all at over

12,000 feet in elevation. To your left, along McGee Creek, grows a lush garden of aspens and cottonwoods. You'll pass Horsetail Falls on the right at two miles out, and soon the trail enters a lodgepole pine forest. The climb steepens, and at 4.5 miles, you reach a junction with Steelhead Lake Trail heading left (east). Switchbacks carry you to a short spur to tiny Grass Lake, then to much larger Steelhead Lake (10,350 feet). The total climb is 2,300 feet over 5.7 miles, but most of the work is in the last 1.2 miles.

User Groups: Hikers, dogs, and horses. No mountain bikes. No wheelchair facilities.

Permits: A free wilderness permit is required for overnight stays and is available from the Bishop/White Mountain Ranger Station. Quotas are in effect from May 1 to November 1; for this period, permits are available in advance for a $5 reservation fee per person.

Maps: A Mammoth High Country map is available from Tom Harrison Maps. An Inyo National Forest or John Muir Wilderness map is available from the U.S. Forest Service. For a topographic map, go to the USGS website to download Convict Lake.

Directions: From U.S. 395 at the Mammoth Lakes junction, drive south eight miles to the McGee Creek Road turnoff on the right (30 miles north of Bishop). Drive three miles southwest on McGee Creek Road (past the pack station) to the trailhead.

Contact: Inyo National Forest, White Mountain Ranger District, Bishop, 760/873-2500, www.fs.usda.gov/inyo.

95 MONO PASS

7.4 mi / 4.0 hr 👥4 ⛰10

in the John Muir Wilderness

Map 10.2, page 468

Since wilderness permits are hard to come by for this trail, your best bet is a day hike up to scenic, austere Mono Pass, where William Brewer and his party crossed the Sierra in 1864. Trailhead elevation is 10,300 feet, and the pass is at 12,600 feet, so get ready to climb in thin air (gasp). Also, expect it to be cold and windy at the pass, no matter how warm it is at the trailhead. Start your trip by following the trail alongside Rock Creek, with a wall of mammoth mountain peaks surrounding you. A half mile in, leave most of the crowds behind as you bear right for Mono Pass, switchbacking uphill. As you climb, you gain a view of Little Lakes Valley below, as well as continual eyefuls of classic Sierra scenery—clear blue sky, jagged mountain backdrops, and plenty of rock. Pass the side trail to Ruby Lake at two miles out (save this 0.25-mile spur for your return trip). Continue on the rocky, treeless trail until at last you reach the summit, where you get a full panoramic view, which is probably hardly different from when Brewer saw it more than a century ago. That peak just to the east of you is Mount Starr, elevation 12,835 feet. To the south, the 13,000-foot-plus peaks reign: Mount Abbot and Mount Mills. Mono Rock and the Mono Recesses lie to the west, and the blue lakes of the Pioneer Basin are to the north.

User Groups: Hikers, dogs, and horses. No mountain bikes. No wheelchair facilities.

Permits: No permits are required for day-use. A free wilderness permit is required for overnight stays and is available from the Bishop/White Mountain Ranger Station. Quotas are in effect from May 1 to November 1; permits are available in advance for a $5 reservation fee per person. Parking and access are free.

Maps: A Mono Divide High Country map is available from Tom Harrison Maps. A John Muir Wilderness map is available from the U.S. Forest Service. For topographic maps, go to the USGS website to download Mount Morgan and Mount Abbot.

Directions: From U.S. 395 at the Mammoth Lakes junction, drive south 15 miles to Tom's Place and the Rock Creek Road turnoff, on the right (24 miles north of Bishop). Follow Rock Creek Road southwest for 10.5 miles to its end, at the Mosquito Flat parking area.

Contact: Inyo National Forest, White

Mountain Ranger District, Bishop, 760/873-2500, www.fs.usda.gov/inyo.

96 LITTLE LAKES VALLEY
3.0-9.0 mi / 2.0-5.0 hr 👫2 ⛰10

in the John Muir Wilderness

Map 10.2, page 468

If the mileage shown above reflects some indecision, that's because the Little Lakes Valley makes it hard to decide which lake to visit or how far to hike. It's best to decide as you go, depending on how busy the trail is and how your energy is holding up. The Little Lakes Valley is a spectacularly beautiful, glacially carved area that is littered with lakes both large and small, and is surrounded by 13,000-foot peaks. What makes it even more special is that its trailhead is at 10,300 feet, so your car does most of the climbing, instead of your feet. For this reason, the trail is extremely popular, especially with beginning backpackers, day hikers, and dog walkers.

The trail leads past Mack Lake and shallow Marsh Lake to Heart Lake, 1.5 miles in. Box Lake is 0.25 mile farther, and then another 0.25 mile farther is the still larger Long Lake, both popular destinations right along the trail. Those with more stamina can continue to Chickenfoot Lake, at 3.0 miles out, or the Gem Lakes, at 3.5 miles. Most people consider the Gem Lakes to be the most gorgeous of the lot, but frankly, it's pretty hard to choose. Those who are willing and able continue upward through 11,100-foot Morgan Pass and descend a couple hundred feet to Upper and Lower Morgan Lakes, at 4 and 4.5 miles out, respectively. There are enough hiking options along this one trail to keep most lake-lovers busy for a week.

User Groups: Hikers, dogs, and horses. No mountain bikes. No wheelchair facilities.

Permits: A free wilderness permit is required for overnight stays and is available from the Bishop/White Mountain Ranger Station. Quotas are in effect from May 1 to November 1; for this period, permits are available in advance for a $5 reservation fee per person.

Maps: A Mono Divide High Country map is available from Tom Harrison Maps. A John Muir Wilderness map is available from the U.S. Forest Service. For topographic maps, go to the USGS website to download Mount Morgan and Mount Abbot.

Directions: From U.S. 395 at the Mammoth Lakes junction, drive south 15 miles to Tom's Place and the Rock Creek Road turnoff, on the right (24 miles north of Bishop). Follow Rock Creek Road southwest for 10.5 miles to its end, at the Mosquito Flat parking area.

Contact: Inyo National Forest, White Mountain Ranger District, Bishop, 760/873-2500, www.fs.usda.gov/inyo.

97 TAMARACK LAKES
9.4 mi / 6.0 hr or 2 days 👫3 ⛰10

in the John Muir Wilderness

Map 10.2, page 468

This fantastic Eastern Sierra hike offers a great deal of variety in terrain, a couple of gorgeous lakes with good fishing prospects, and the chance of seeing bighorn sheep. Perhaps best of all, this trail sees a lot less foot traffic than the other pathways in the popular Rock Creek area. The trailhead elevation at Rock Creek Lake is 9,700 feet, so the first stretch of this trail can be a bit breathtaking as you climb steadily for a mile on a brushy slope. Soon the trail levels out and follows an old dirt road for a while, which connects to a mountain-biking route in Sand Canyon. The terrain you are walking through is dry and sandy, with only a few pines to create some sparse shade, and it gives little indication of the dramatic high-country scenery that lies ahead. You'll pass a turnoff for Francis Lake on the right (0.7 mile distant), and shortly thereafter, Kenneth Lake on the left (0.1 mile distant). Kenneth Lake is really just a muddy pond, which usually dries up by late summer, but its surrounding meadow is filled with blooming gentian in late summer.

Stay on the path to Tamarack Lakes, and you'll find that the climbing you will face will result in a dramatic change of landscape. The trail ascends over a series of glacial moraines, and you soon find yourself in a high-alpine area, where bighorn sheep are sometimes seen grazing on the fragile grasses. You'll pass the left turnoff for Dorothy Lake (there are good camping spots here, but fishing is usually poor), but stay right, and in another mile, you will begin to follow the outlet stream from the Tamarack Lakes. Now the real work begins, as you must gain 800 more feet to climb into the high basin where the Tamarack Lakes lie. The trail ends at a small tarn just before the largest Tamarack Lake. Just beyond the big Tamarack Lake is Buck Lake, which most people assume is just another of the Tamarack Lakes. The lakes are set in a steeply sloped rocky bowl and have that barren, austere look that is common to lakes above 11,000 feet. You won't find much in the way of flat, soft spots to put your tent, but the scenery more than makes up for it. The largest Tamarack Lake has good fishing for golden trout. The total elevation gain on this hike is 2,000 feet, and it is worth every bit of it.

User Groups: Hikers, dogs, and horses. No mountain bikes. No wheelchair facilities.

Permits: A free wilderness permit is required for overnight stays and is available from the Bishop/White Mountain Ranger Station. Quotas are in effect from May 1 to November 1; for this period, permits are available in advance for a $5 reservation fee per person.

Maps: A Mono Divide High Country map is available from Tom Harrison Maps. A John Muir Wilderness map is available from the U.S. Forest Service. For a topographic map, go to the USGS website to download Mount Morgan.

Directions: From U.S. 395 at the Mammoth Lakes junction, drive south 15 miles to Tom's Place and the Rock Creek Road turnoff, on the right (24 miles north of Bishop). Follow Rock Creek Road southwest for 8.5 miles to the left turnoff for Rock Creek Lakes campground. Turn left and drive 0.4 mile to the trailhead.

Contact: Inyo National Forest, White Mountain Ranger District, Bishop, 760/873-2500, www.fs.usda.gov/inyo.

98 RUBY LAKE

4.5 mi / 2.5 hr

in the John Muir Wilderness

Map 10.2, page 468

For both day hikers and backpackers, the Little Lakes Valley is the premier destination from the Rock Creek Canyon trailhead. The only problem is the crowds, especially on the weekends, which can turn a supposedly peaceful wilderness experience into a large group encounter. A visit to Ruby Lake is a possible solution, because it's off the main trail that leads into the Little Lakes Valley, situated instead on the right fork that leads to Mono Pass. Since most trail users on this fork are backpackers heading to Mono Pass and the Pioneer Basin beyond, few take the time to stop at Ruby Lake, 0.25 mile off the main trail. From the trailhead, hike 0.5 mile, and bear right at the junction for Mono Pass. Grunt it out through the switchbacks as you enjoy a series of stunning vistas of the Little Lakes Valley. You'll reach the Ruby Lake spur trail at two miles out, on the left. A 0.25-mile walk brings you to cliffbound Ruby Lake, which is much larger than you'd expect and perfectly ringed by granite. The fishing is not great, but the picnicking is highly recommended. The lake's elevation is 11,121 feet.

User Groups: Hikers, dogs, and horses. No mountain bikes. No wheelchair facilities.

Permits: No permits are required for day-use. A free wilderness permit is required for overnight stays and is available from the Bishop/White Mountain Ranger Station. Quotas are in effect from May 1 to November 1; permits are available in advance for a $5 reservation fee per person. Parking and access are free.

Maps: A Mono Divide High Country map is available from Tom Harrison Maps. A John Muir Wilderness map is available from the U.S. Forest Service. For topographic maps, go to the

USGS website to download Mount Abbot and Mount Morgan.

Directions: From U.S. 395 at the Mammoth Lakes junction, drive south 15 miles to Tom's Place and the Rock Creek Road turnoff, on the right (24 miles north of Bishop). Follow Rock Creek Road southwest for 10.5 miles to its end, at the Mosquito Flat parking area.

Contact: Inyo National Forest, White Mountain Ranger District, Bishop, 760/873-2500, www.fs.usda.gov/inyo.

99 WHITE MOUNTAIN PEAK TRAIL

14.4 mi / 8.0 hr   👥5 ⛰10

in Inyo National Forest northeast of Bishop

Map 10.2, page 468   BEST (

White Mountain Peak is the third-tallest peak in California, only 259 feet lower than the highest, Mount Whitney (Mount Williamson is second in line), yet it is little known to hikers outside of the area. In contrast to Whitney, this 14,246-foot summit is not reached by a narrow foot trail, but instead via an old Navy-built road that climbs 2,600 feet in 7.2 miles. The trail starts at a locked gate at 11,630 feet in elevation and then leads past Mount Barcroft (13,040 feet) on a long grind. The road/trail is completely above tree line, so it's exposed and often windswept. Sunscreen alone won't suffice here; wear a hat to give yourself a break from the sun. If you aren't acclimated, the high altitude will make the trip very difficult. The summit constitutes an impressive granite massif with grand views. To the east, you can see 200 miles into Nevada; to the west, the Owens Valley and Volcanic Tableland, plus a wide panorama of the Sierra Nevada. Some hikers choose to pack along their headlamps and do all or part of the trip by moonlight. The road/trail is simple to navigate, so this is easily accomplished. Forget turning this into a backpack trip: The area is so exposed that you won't find a suitable place to camp. Also, if you are planning an early summer visit, call the White

Mountain Ranger Station to be sure the dirt road to the trailhead is open. The road is frequently snowed in at the higher elevations until mid-June or later.

User Groups: Hikers only. Dogs, horses, and mountain bikes permitted, but not advised due to extremely high altitudes. No wheelchair facilities.

Permits: No permits are required. Parking and access are free.

Maps: An Inyo National Forest map is available from the U.S. Forest Service. For a topographic map, go to the USGS website to download White Mountain Peak.

Directions: From U.S. 395 at Big Pine, take Highway 168 east for 13 miles to White Mountain Road. Turn left on White Mountain Road and drive north for 10.5 miles to Schulman Grove. Continue on White Mountain Road (it becomes unpaved just past the Schulman Grove turnoff) for 16 miles to the locked gate and trailhead, at the road's end.

Contact: Inyo National Forest, White Mountain Ranger Station, Bishop, 760/873-2500, www.fs.usda.gov/inyo.

100 METHUSELAH TRAIL

4.2 mi / 2.5 hr   👥2 ⛰8

in Inyo National Forest northeast of Bishop

Map 10.2, page 468   BEST (

The Methuselah Tree is the prize of the Ancient Bristlecone Pine Forest. Here for more than 4,000 years, it's the oldest documented living tree in the world. But forest rangers won't tell you which one it is, out of fear that some dimwit will cut it down. So you have to be satisfied just knowing you have walked among the ancients, rather than actually seeing the grandfather of all trees. No matter; each one of the thousands of trees here will impress you with its beautifully sculpted form. Amateur photographers have a field day along this trail. The path starts at the patio of the Schulman Grove Visitors Center (elevation 10,000 feet) and follows a meandering route through a forest of ancient and younger bristlecone pines, plus a few limber pines and pinyon pines. The first half of the loop drops 800 feet, which of course must be regained on your return, but the climb is nicely spread out. Still, if you're not acclimated, the high elevation will leave you huffing and puffing. Plan on bringing a picnic with you (you're a long way from the nearest convenience store), and make sure you spend some time at the excellent visitors center, which is open daily. If you want to hike a bit more, try the one-mile Discovery Trail loop (more bristlecone pines) or the one-mile Bristlecone Cabin Trail, which leads to an old Mexican mine site. If you're accustomed to modern conveniences, it's worth noting that cell phone service is limited in the area and water is not available at the trailhead or visitors center. Make sure your vehicle is well stocked for the trip.

User Groups: Hikers and leashed dogs. No horses or mountain bikes. No wheelchair facilities.

Permits: No permits are required. There is a $3 fee per adult with a maximum of $6 per vehicle.

Maps: Brochures and trail maps are available at the trailhead. An Inyo National Forest map is available from the U.S. Forest Service. For a topographic map, go to the USGS website to download Westgard Pass.

Directions: From U.S. 395 at Big Pine, take Highway 168 east for 13 miles to White Mountain Road. Turn left on White Mountain Road and drive north for 10.5 miles to Schulman Grove, on the right.

Contact: Inyo National Forest, White Mountain Ranger Station, Bishop, 760/873-2500, www.fs.usda.gov/inyo.

SEQUOIA AND KINGS CANYON

© ANN MARIE BROWN

Sequoia and Kings Canyon National Parks are famous for their giant sequoia groves, tall mountains, deep canyons, roaring rivers, and spectacular hiking trails with views of the Great Western Divide's jagged peaks. These two side-by-side national parks offer classic Sierra scenery without the infamous overcrowding that plagues Yosemite, their neighbor to the north. Tacked on to the border of Sequoia and Kings Canyon is Giant Sequoia National Monument, designated to increase protection for the last remaining giant sequoia groves in the world. On the east side of these parks, a bounty of trailheads lie at the end of almost every road leading west off U.S. 395. From Bishop to Big Pine to Independence to Lone Pine, each canyon road leads to a wilderness trailhead and a wealth of hiking opportunities.

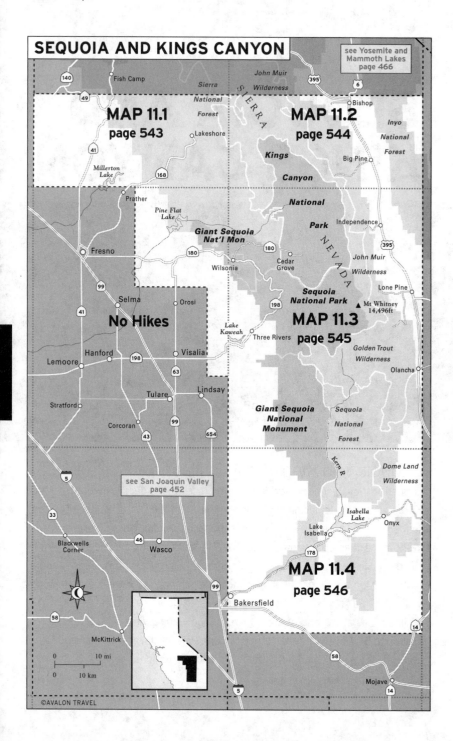

SEQUOIA AND KINGS CANYON

see Yosemite and Mammoth Lakes page 466

MAP 11.1
page 543

MAP 11.2
page 544

MAP 11.3
page 545

MAP 11.4
page 546

No Hikes

see San Joaquin Valley page 452

Fish Camp

Lakeshore

Millerton Lake

Prather

Pine Flat Lake

Fresno

Selma

Orosi

Hanford

Lemoore

Stratford

Corcoran

Tulare

Visalia

Lindsay

Blackwells Corner

Wasco

McKittrick

John Muir Wilderness

Sierra National Forest

Bishop

Big Pine

Independence

Lone Pine

Olancha

Onyx

Mojave

Kings Canyon National Park

Giant Sequoia Nat'l Mon

Wilsonia

Cedar Grove

John Muir Wilderness

Sequoia National Park

Mt Whitney 14,496ft

Golden Trout Wilderness

Giant Sequoia National Monument

Sequoia National Forest

Dome Land Wilderness

Isabella Lake

Lake Isabella

Bakersfield

Inyo National Forest

Lake Kaweah

Three Rivers

Kern R

SIERRA

NEVADA

0   10 mi

0   10 km

©AVALON TRAVEL

Map 11.1

Sites 1-10
Pages 547-551

11.2

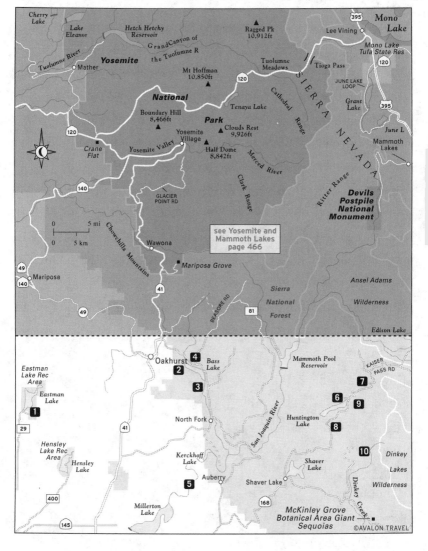

Map 11.2

**Sites 11-20
Pages 552-558**

Map 11.3

Sites 21-105
Pages 559-613

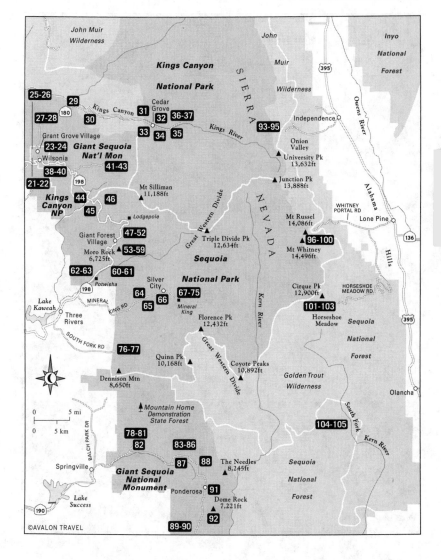

Map 11.4

Sites 106-119
Pages 614-621

1 LAKEVIEW TRAIL
4.2 mi one-way/2.0 hr

on the southeast shore of Eastman Lake east
of Chowchilla

Map 11.1, page 543

Let's get one thing straight: You don't want to
hike here at midday in July. Got it? Good. But
if it's spring and the wildflowers are in bloom,
you'd be wise to head out here to Eastman Lake,
then hike the Lakeview Trail that leads along its
south and east sides. Sure, a reservoir is a reservoir, but when the water level is high, the grasslands are green, and the flowers are blooming,
this reservoir can seem like a little slice of paradise in the Central Valley. The Lakeview Trail
leads a total of 4.2 miles one-way from the trailhead at the group campground to Raymond
Bridge. Hike as little or as much of it as you
please, watching for birds and identifying the
wildflowers as you go. Bald eagle sightings are
not uncommon. You probably won't have a lot
of human company on this trail; after all, most
people come to Eastman Lake to fish, not hike.
In addition to its trophy bass fishery, the lake
also boasts populations of crappie, bluegill, and
catfish. They even stock rainbow trout here in
the winter when the temperature cools down.
User Groups: Hikers, dogs, horses, and mountain bikes. No wheelchair facilities.
Permits: No permits are required. A $5 day-
use fee is charged.
Maps: A free map of Eastman Lake is available
at the visitors center. For a topographic map, go
to the USGS website to download Raymond.
Directions: From Merced, drive south on
Highway 99 for 20 miles to Chowchilla. Take
the Avenue 26 exit and head east for 17 miles.
Turn north on County Road 29 and drive eight
miles to the lake entrance. Turn right and
drive to the parking area by Cordorniz Group
Campground.
Contact: U.S. Army Corps of Engineers,
Eastman Lake, Raymond, 559/689-3255.

2 WAY OF THE MONO
0.5 mi/0.5 hr

on the northwest end of Bass Lake near
Oakhurst

Map 11.1, page 543

The Way of the Mono is an educational trail
that teaches about the Mono Indians, who were
the first people to live in the Bass Lake area.
They inhabited the area for more than 1,000
years. The interpretive displays along the trail
point out grinding holes in the rocks, where the
Mono people pounded acorns into meal, and
describe different methods they used to live
through the area's seasonal changes. In addition to a cultural history lesson, the trail also
offers beautiful vistas of Bass Lake and its surroundings. Check out the view from the large
granite outcrop of Bass Lake and surrounding
peaks. This great loop hike takes only about 20
minutes to walk, but leaves you with a much
greater understanding of the Bass Lake area.
User Groups: Hikers and dogs. No horses or
mountain bikes. No wheelchair facilities.
Permits: No permits are required. Parking and
access are free at the trailhead; parking in the
day-use area is $3.
Maps: A Sierra National Forest map is available
from the U.S. Forest Service. For a topographic
map, go to the USGS website to download Bass
Lake.
Directions: From Oakhurst, drive north on
Highway 41 for four miles and then turn right
on Road 222. Drive four miles and bear right to
stay on Road 222. The signed trailhead parking
area is across from Little Denver Church Day
Use Area, between the Forks Resort and the
California Land Management Office.
Contact: Sierra National Forest, Bass Lake
Ranger District, North Fork, 559/877-2218,
www.fs.usda.gov/sierra.

3 GOAT MOUNTAIN FIRE LOOKOUT

8.0 mi/4.0 hr   🥾3 ⛰️8

on the south end of Bass Lake near Oakhurst

Map 11.1, page 543

The route to Goat Mountain Fire Lookout can be hiked from trailheads at either Forks Campground or Spring Cove Campground. This is a must-do hike for the legions of campers who spend their summer vacations at Bass Lake. Both trails intersect in about two miles, then join and form one path for the last two miles to the lookout. No matter how you do it, the grade is memorably steep, but also rewarding. As you climb up the trail, you have nearly nonstop views of Bass Lake and the forested valleys surrounding it. You'll also be breathing hard. If you can talk someone into driving a second car to the other trailhead and campground, you can turn this into a pleasant semi-loop trip by hiking up one trail and down the other. Note that this trail has become increasingly popular with mountain bikers in the last few years. If you don't like sharing the trail with them, plan your hike for a weekday, when you're more likely to be out here by yourself. The fire lookout is perched at 4,675 feet in elevation, set on top of a 20-foot steel tower, and offers a 360-degree view.

User Groups: Hikers, dogs, horses, and mountain bikes. No wheelchair facilities.

Permits: No permits are required. Parking and access are free in the campgrounds, but $3 if you park in the day-use area.

Maps: A Sierra National Forest map is available from the U.S. Forest Service. For a topographic map, go to the USGS website to download Bass Lake.

Directions: From Oakhurst, drive north on Highway 41 for four miles and turn right on Road 222. Drive four miles and bear right to stay on Road 222. Continue along the western shore of Bass Lake for about five miles to Spring Cove Campground. The Spring Cove Trail begins on the east side of the campground entrance. If there is no parking there, you can park at Rocky Point Picnic Area ($3 fee). You can also hike to Goat Mountain Fire Lookout from Forks Campground, three miles north on Road 222.

Contact: Sierra National Forest, Bass Lake Ranger District, North Fork, 559/877-2218, www.fs.usda.gov/sierra.

4 WILLOW CREEK

4.8 mi/2.5 hr   🥾2 ⛰️8

on the northeast end of Bass Lake near Oakhurst

Map 11.1, page 543

Most people hike Willow Creek Trail with one of two things in mind: fishing or swimming. You can't blame them, since the moderately steep trail runs alongside Willow Creek and offers myriad quiet pools and fast, granite-lined cascades. The Forest Service requests that visitors don't swim upstream of Angel Falls, a wide cascade that looks like angel wings, because the creek is used as a domestic water supply. Downstream swimming is allowed, but be wary of the slippery granite. At 2.4 miles from the trailhead, be sure to take the left spur for Devils Slide, at a junction where the main trail continues to its end (0.4 mile farther) at McLeod Flat Road. Devils Slide is a remarkable granite water slide, with large rounded indentations in the rock. A chain-link fence keeps hikers off the dangerously slick granite. From Devils Slide, head back to the main trail and retrace your steps downhill. Expect to see some great views of bright-blue Bass Lake on the return trip.

User Groups: Hikers and dogs. No horses or mountain bikes. No wheelchair facilities.

Permits: No permits are required. Parking and access are free.

Maps: A Sierra National Forest map is available from the U.S. Forest Service. For a topographic map, go to the USGS website to download Bass Lake.

Directions: From Oakhurst, drive north on Highway 41 for four miles and turn right on Road 222. Drive four miles and bear left on

Road 274. Drive one mile to the trailhead parking area, on the left side of the road, on the west side of the highway bridge over Willow Creek. Alternatively, you can park near Falls Beach Picnic Area on Road 222 by Bass Lake's dam and access the trail via a connector route alongside Willow Creek.

Contact: Sierra National Forest, Bass Lake Ranger District, North Fork, 559/877-2218, www.fs.usda.gov/sierra.

5 SQUAW LEAP LOOP
7.8 mi/4.0 hr

near Millerton Lake

Map 11.1, page 543

The Squaw Leap area, managed by the Bureau of Land Management, straddles the San Joaquin River upstream of Millerton Lake State Park. This pretty foothill country is best visited in winter or spring, primarily due to the cooler temperatures but also for a chance to see wildflowers. The well-built Six-Mile Loop Trail, which is actually 7.8 miles as described here, rolls through chaparral country. Ceanothus and manzanita line the hillsides; gray pines and blue oaks dot the landscape. The trail begins with a one-mile stretch that leads you down to the river and the start of the loop. A surprisingly well-built footbridge takes you across the river canyon, where you have fine views of whitewater cascades, both upstream and down. On the far side of the bridge, go left on River Trail for 0.7 mile, then bear right on Ridge Trail. At mileage marker 3, you have a fine view of the river canyon; this is the best place to stop for a snack. Ridge Trail brings you right back downhill to the bridge you crossed earlier; cross it again and head back to your car to finish out the trip.

User Groups: Hikers, dogs, horses, and mountain bikes. No wheelchair facilities.

Permits: No permits are required. Parking and access are free.

Maps: For a topographic map, go to the USGS website to download Millerton Lake East.

Directions: From Fresno, drive 37 miles east on Highway 168 and turn left on Auberry Road. Drive through Auberry and turn left on Powerhouse Road. Drive 1.9 miles and turn left on Smalley Road at the sign for Squaw Leap Management Area. Park by the campground and signed trailhead.

Contact: Bureau of Land Management, Bakersfield Field Office, Bakersfield, 661/391-6000, www.ca.blm.gov/bakersfield.

6 KAISER PEAK
10.6 mi/6.0 hr or 2 days

in the Kaiser Wilderness north of Huntington Lake near Lakeshore

Map 11.1, page 543

While many visitors to Huntington Lake take the short strolls to Rancheria Falls or the Indian Pools on Big Creek, far fewer attempt the ascent of Kaiser Peak. Why? Because it's a butt-kicking, 5.3-mile climb to the top, gaining 3,000 feet of elevation on the way to the 10,320-foot peak. Luckily, you get many excellent views of Huntington Lake on the way up, and at the halfway point, you can scramble up for a view and a rest on huge College Rock. Then it's up, up, and up some more, for what seems like an eternity. Finally, you gain the rocky summit, and at last you know why you came. You're wowed by incredible 360-degree views, which take in Mammoth Pool Reservoir, Huntington Lake, Shaver Lake, Mount Ritter, and Mount Goddard. Wow. Backpackers looking for more mileage can turn the hike into a 14-mile loop trip.

User Groups: Hikers, dogs, and horses. No mountain bikes. No wheelchair facilities.

Permits: A free wilderness permit is required for overnight stays and is available from the High Sierra/Prather Ranger Station. Quotas are in effect year-round; permits are available in advance for a $5 reservation fee per person.

Maps: A Sierra National Forest or Kaiser Wilderness map is available from the U.S.

Forest Service. For a topographic map, go to the USGS website to download Kaiser Peak.

Directions: From Fresno, drive northeast on Highway 168 through Clovis for 70 miles to Huntington Lake, turn left on Huntington Lake Road, and drive one mile. Look for the large sign for the horse stables and pack station, and turn right. Follow the pack station road (Deer Creek Road) for 0.5 mile to the hikers' parking area. The trailhead is signed Kaiser Loop Trail.

Contact: Sierra National Forest, High Sierra Ranger District, Prather, 559/855-5360, www.fs.usda.gov/sierra.

7 TWIN LAKES AND GEORGE LAKE
8.0-9.8 mi/6.0-7.0 hr or 2 days
🏃3 ⛰9

in the Kaiser Wilderness north of Huntington Lake near Lakeshore

Map 11.1, page 543

Trails into the Kaiser Wilderness always seem to come with a climb, and the route to Twin Lakes and George Lake is no exception. But if you're willing to work your heart and lungs, your reward is a spectacular day hike or backpacking trip to three scenic alpine lakes. Along the way, you must ascend to Kaiser Ridge and cross over it through Potter Pass. You're witness to wildflower-filled meadows, dense conifer forests, and a classic Sierra view from the pass. You can easily make out the jagged outline of the Minarets. It's a great spot to stop and catch your breath. Then it's downhill from the pass to the granite-lined Twin Lakes, at three miles out. Many people make this their destination, then turn around for a six-mile round-trip. If you do, make sure you visit the second Twin Lake, which is much prettier than the first. For those continuing onward, it's uphill again to George Lake, 1.3 miles from Upper Twin Lake. The final push is definitely worth it. Trailhead elevation is 8,200 feet, Twin Lakes are at 8,800 feet, and George Lake is at 9,300 feet. Another

good route to these lakes is from the trailhead near Sample Meadow Campground, farther north on Kaiser Pass Road. If you're willing to drive farther, this trail has less of a climb.

User Groups: Hikers, dogs, and horses. No mountain bikes. No wheelchair facilities.

Permits: A free wilderness permit is required for overnight stays and is available from the High Sierra/Prather Ranger Station. Quotas are in effect year-round; permits are available in advance for a $5 reservation fee per person.

Maps: A Sierra National Forest or Kaiser Wilderness map is available from the U.S. Forest Service. For a topographic map, go to the USGS website to download Kaiser Peak.

Directions: From Fresno, drive northeast on Highway 168 through Clovis for 70 miles to Huntington Lake; turn right on Kaiser Pass Road and drive 4.8 miles to a large parking area on the south side of the road. The trail begins across the road from the parking area. Look for a trail sign for Trail 24E03, Twin Lakes and Potter Pass. Park on the south side of the road; the trail begins on the north side of the road.

Contact: Sierra National Forest, High Sierra Ranger District, Prather, 559/855-5360, www.fs.usda.gov/sierra.

8 INDIAN POOLS
1.5 mi/1.0 hr
🏃1 ⛰8

off Highway 168 near Huntington Lake

Map 11.1, page 543

When campers at Huntington Lake's many campgrounds are looking for a place to cool off in the afternoon, Indian Pools is where they go. The hike is really a walk, suitable for all ages and abilities. You can stop almost anywhere you like along Big Creek, pick a pool, and wade in. The trailhead is a bit tricky to find; it's all the way at the far end of the Sierra Summit Ski Area parking lot, near some mobile homes and trailers. Ignore the wide dirt road and instead look for the single-track trail signed for Indian Pools. It's a smooth, dirt path that quickly meets up with Big Creek. Flowers bloom in profusion along the stream and the rocky areas of the trail. The official path ends 0.7 mile east of the trailhead, at a huge, clear pool that is big enough to jump into and swim across. A use trail continues farther upstream, marked by trail cairns. If you follow it, you can reach quieter, more private pools.

User Groups: Hikers and dogs. No horses or mountain bikes. No wheelchair facilities.

Permits: No permits are required. Parking and access are free.

Maps: A Sierra National Forest map is available from the U.S. Forest Service. For a topographic map, go to the USGS website to download Huntington Lake.

Directions: From Fresno, drive northeast on Highway 168 through Clovis for 70 miles, past Shaver Lake. One mile before reaching Huntington Lake, turn right at the signed Sierra Summit Ski Area. Drive 0.5 mile to the far end of the ski area parking lot and look for the signed trailhead for Indian Pools. Occasionally the Sierra Summit parking lot is closed, and you must park on Highway 168 and walk the short distance into the ski area.

Contact: Sierra National Forest, High Sierra Ranger District, Prather, 559/855-5360, www. fs.usda.gov/sierra.

9 RANCHERIA FALLS
2.0 mi/1.0 hr

off Highway 168 near Huntington Lake

Map 11.1, page 543

At 7,760 feet in elevation in Sierra National Forest, the air is clean and fresh, butterflies flutter amid the wildflowers, and a 150-foot waterfall sparkles in the sunlight. Wanna go? It's an easy trip, with the trailhead located close to popular Huntington Lake. The hike to Rancheria Falls is a well-graded one mile on a National Recreation Trail, suitable for hikers of all levels. The route leads through a fir forest with an understory of wildflowers and gooseberry, and it delivers you at Rancheria Falls' base, where you watch the creek tumble over a

50-foot-wide rock ledge. On weekends the destination can be a little crowded, but you can pick a boulder downstream from the falls and call it your own. Then have a seat and watch the watery spectacle unfold.

User Groups: Hikers, dogs, horses, and mountain bikes. No wheelchair facilities.

Permits: No permits are required. Parking and access are free.

Maps: A Sierra National Forest map is available from the U.S. Forest Service. For a topographic map, go to the USGS website to download Huntington Lake.

Directions: From Fresno, drive northeast on Highway 168 through Clovis for 70 miles, past Shaver Lake. A half mile before reaching Huntington Lake, take the right turnoff signed for Rancheria Falls (Road 8S31). Follow the dirt road for 1.3 miles to the signed trailhead, at a sharp curve in the road. Park off the road.

Contact: Sierra National Forest, High Sierra Ranger District, Prather, 559/855-5360, www. fs.usda.gov/sierra.

10 DINKEY LAKES
7.0 mi/4.0 hr or 2 days

in Dinkey Lakes Wilderness off Highway 168 near Shaver Lake

Map 11.1, page 543

We've never met anybody who doesn't love the Dinkey Lakes. What's not to love? The small wilderness area has dozens of lakes, and most are so easily accessible that you can see them in a day hike rather than packing along all your gear for an overnight stay. The trip begins with a stream crossing over Dinkey Creek, where you are immediately awed by the incredible array of colors in the rock streambed. Walk on level trail through a flower-filled forest, recross the creek, and start to climb. At 1.3 miles, you reach the junction for the start of the loop. Go right and meet Mystery Lake at 1.6 miles, Swede Lake at 2.3 miles, South Lake at 3.2 miles, and finally First Dinkey Lake at 3.8 miles. First Dinkey Lake is the most beautiful of them all. After taking in the scenery, continue on the loop, now heading westward back to the parking lot. One caveat: Don't expect much solitude. The easy hiking here makes this area extremely popular. Note that the loop described here works as either a day hike or backpacking trip, but if you choose to backpack, you can explore much farther, taking the spurs off the end of the main loop, between South Lake and First Dinkey Lake, to Second Dinkey Lake, Island Lake, Rock Lake, and so on.

User Groups: Hikers, dogs, and horses. No mountain bikes. No wheelchair facilities.

Permits: A wilderness permit is required for overnight stays and is available from the High Sierra/Prather Ranger Station. Quotas are in effect year-round; permits are available in advance for a $5 reservation fee per person.

Maps: A Dinkey Lakes Wilderness map is available from Tom Harrison Maps or the U.S. Forest Service. For topographic maps, go to the USGS website to download Huntington Lake and Dogtooth Peak.

Directions: From Fresno, drive northeast on Highway 168 through Clovis for 50 miles to the town of Shaver Lake. Turn right on Dinkey Creek Road and drive nine miles. Turn left on Rock Creek Road/9S09, drive six miles, turn right on 9S10, and drive 4.7 miles. Turn right at the sign for Dinkey Lakes, on Road 9S62, and drive 2.2 miles to the trailhead. These last two miles are very rough road. Stay left at the fork to bypass the four-wheel-drive area and go straight to the trailhead.

Contact: Sierra National Forest, High Sierra Ranger District, Prather, 559/855-5360, www.fs.usda.gov/sierra.

11 LAKE THOMAS EDISON TO AGNEW MEADOWS (JMT /PCT)

38.0 mi one-way/3 days 4 ▲10

from Lake Thomas Edison north to Agnew Meadows

Map 11.2, page 544

The world is not perfect, but the scene from Silver Pass comes close. At 10,900 feet, you scan a bare, high-granite landscape sprinkled with alpine lakes. Just north of the pass are five small lakes: Chief, Papoose, Warrior, Squaw, and Lake of the Lone Indian. This is the highlight on this 38-mile section of the Pacific Crest Trail. The trip starts at Mono Creek, with a good resupply point at Edison Lake (7,650 feet), just two miles away. From the Mono Creek junction, you head north toward Silver Pass, climbing along Silver Pass Creek much of the way. Before you get to Silver Pass, there's a stream crossing that can be dangerous in high-runoff conditions. Top Silver Pass at 10,900 feet, and enjoy a five-mile descent and then a quick ascent to Tully Hole (9,250 feet). Climbing north, you pass Deer Creek, Purple Lake, and Lake Virginia. You head up to Red Cones and then make a steady descent toward Devils Postpile National Monument. A good resupply point is at nearby Reds Meadows Pack Station.

To continue north on the John Muir Trail/Pacific Crest Trail (JMT/PCT), see the *Agnew Meadows to Tuolumne Meadows (JMT/PCT)* hike in the *Yosemite and Mammoth Lakes* chapter. If you are walking this trail in reverse, see the *Whitney Portal to Lake Thomas Edison (JMT/PCT)* hike in this chapter.

Note: For food drop information, call the Vermillion Valley Resort. It is open only in summer and fall.

User Groups: Hikers, dogs, and horses. No mountain bikes. No wheelchair facilities.

Permits: A wilderness permit is required for traveling through various wilderness and special-use areas the trail traverses. Contact the Inyo National Forest or Sierra National Forest at the addresses below.

Maps: A John Muir Trail Map Pack is available from Tom Harrison Maps. For topographic maps, go to the USGS website to download Mammoth Mountain, Crystal Crag, Bloody Mountain, Graveyard Peak, Mount Ritter, and Coip Peak.

Directions: From Fresno, drive northeast on Highway 168 for about 68 miles to the

Lakeshore Resort Area, at Huntington Lake. Turn northeast onto Kaiser Pass Road/Forest Service 4S01. Kaiser Pass Road becomes Edison Lake Road at Mono Hot Springs. Drive another five miles north, past the Vermillion Resort and Campground, and beyond to the parking area for backcountry hikers. The trail begins near the west end of the lake.

Contact: Inyo National Forest, Mammoth Ranger Station, Mammoth Lakes, 760/924-5500 or 760/873-2400 (permits), www.fs.usda.gov/inyo; Sierra National Forest, High Sierra Ranger District, Prather, 559/855-5360, www.fs.usda.gov/sierra; Vermillion Valley Resort, 559/855-6558 (food drop).

12 HONEYMOON LAKE
12.4 mi/1-2 days 👣3 ⛰8

in the John Muir Wilderness

Map 11.2, page 544

Since the trailhead elevation in Pine Creek Canyon is only 7,400 feet, the best destinations must be gained with a serious climb. That includes Honeymoon Lake, 6.2 miles and a 3,200-foot ascent away. Luckily, you pass Upper and Lower Pine Lake along the route, and there's enough spectacular scenery to keep you motivated as you huff and puff. An early morning start is highly recommended; this trail is exposed and usually very hot, especially in its lower reaches. The route begins by the pack station in the trees along Pine Creek, then joins a mining road that leads to the Brownstone Mine. The huge tungsten mine at 8,000 feet was active from 1918 until 1999, and many of the buildings remain. As you switchback up and out of the trees, you gain views of the Owens River Valley and the desertlike White Mountains. Above the mine, the road becomes an extremely rocky trail as it ascends more switchbacks to meet first Lower and then Upper Pine Lake, at 4.0 and 5.0 miles. The upper lake at 10,400 feet is reached by following the trail along the lower lake's northwest shore. Less than a mile past the upper lake, leave the main trail that continues to Pine Creek Pass and take the right fork toward Granite Park and Italy Pass. Granite-bound Honeymoon Lake lies about 200 yards from the junction, set at 10,600 feet. This spot makes a great base camp for exploring the rocky wonderland of Granite Park.

User Groups: Hikers, dogs, and horses. No mountain bikes. No wheelchair facilities.

Permits: A free wilderness permit is required year-round for overnight stays and is available from the Bishop/White Mountain Ranger Station. Quotas are in effect from May 1 to November 1; permits are available in advance for a $5 reservation fee per person.

Maps: A John Muir Wilderness map is available from the U.S. Forest Service. A map of the Mono Divide High County is available from Tom Harrison Maps. For topographic maps, go to the USGS website to download Bishop and Tungsten Hills.

Directions: From Bishop, drive north on U.S. 395 for seven miles and turn left (west) on Pine Creek Road. Drive 9.5 miles to the trailhead parking area, near the pack station, on the left side of the road.

Contact: Inyo National Forest, White Mountain Ranger Station, Bishop, 760/873-2500, www.fs.usda.gov/inyo.

13 BLUE LAKE
6.0 mi/3.0 hr or 2 days 👣3 ⛰10

in the John Muir Wilderness

Map 11.2, page 544   **BEST (**

The Sabrina Basin Trail leads to a series of gorgeous alpine lakes set below lofty, 13,000-foot granite peaks. Of these, one of the most popular and easiest to reach is scenic Blue Lake, a popular spot for photographers, trout anglers, and cold-water swimmers. If you catch the light just right, you can take pictures of Blue Lake with towering Mount Thompson and the Thompson Ridge mirrored on its surface. It's a 1,250-foot climb to the lake (at 10,400 feet), but it's spread out very moderately over three miles.

Mule packers frequently utilize this trail; if you see them, be sure to get out of their way. Start by hiking along the shore of Lake Sabrina, heading in and out of the shade of aspen trees, then switchback your way uphill to Blue Lake. You'll want solid shoes for this rock-lined trail. If you get inspired to see more of this high-alpine scenery, you can bear left from Blue Lake to Donkey Lake and the Baboon Lakes (1.5 miles farther), both much smaller and more intimate than Blue Lake, or bear right and hike eastward to the Emerald Lakes and Dingleberry Lake (1.8 miles farther). Any of these are likely to have fewer visitors than Blue Lake.

User Groups: Hikers, dogs, and horses. No mountain bikes. No wheelchair facilities.

Permits: A free wilderness permit is required year-round for overnight stays and is available from the Bishop/White Mountain Ranger Station. Quotas are in effect from May 1 to November 1; permits are available in advance for a $5 reservation fee per person.

Maps: A John Muir Wilderness map is available from the U.S. Forest Service. A Bishop Pass map is available from Tom Harrison Maps. For topographic maps, go to the USGS website to download Mount Thompson and Mount Darwin.

Directions: From Bishop on U.S. 395, turn west on Line Street/Highway 168 and drive 18.5 miles to Lake Sabrina. Day-use parking is located near the end of the road, just before the boat launch area. Backpackers' parking is located at a turnout near the road to North Lake, 0.5 mile before the end of the road.

Contact: Inyo National Forest, White Mountain Ranger Station, Bishop, 760/873-2500, www.fs.usda.gov/inyo.

14 LAMARCK LAKES
6.0 mi/3.0 hr or 2 days

in the John Muir Wilderness

Map 11.2, page 544

The only downer on the Lamarck Lakes Trail is that from the trailhead parking lot, you must walk 0.5 mile down a dirt road to get to the actual trailhead, which is located in North Lake Campground. Skirt the problem by camping at this pretty little campground, one of the best in the Bishop Creek canyon, then start walking right from your tent. The trailhead is found at the signboard near the walk-in campsites, and the path heads through the aspens and crosses Bishop Creek on a footbridge. You'll climb steadily for one mile through a lodgepole pine forest, gaining 600 feet to the left fork for Grass Lake, a small and shallow lake in a wide meadow. Grass Lake is worth a brief glance, but it doesn't hold a candle to the Lamarck Lakes, so you might want to save your energy. Staying on the main trail, you leave the trees behind and begin a much more brutal ascent, marked by very short switchbacks and thigh-pumping stair-steps. In another mile and 700 feet of gain, you'll reach the Lower Lamarck Lake, set in a rock-lined granite basin. Look for Mount Emerson, Mount Lamarck, and the red-colored Piute Crags in the background. Many people make this lake their destination for the day, but it's worth the extra effort to hike the final mile to Upper Lamarck Lake, which is more than double the size of the lower lake and a deep cobalt blue. (Follow the trail alongside the creek to get there.) Upper Lamarck Lake is known for its large trout, so pack along a rod and a fishing license. Those looking for an adventure can make their way from the Lower Lamarck Lake to the Wonder Lakes, set in the basin northwest of Lower Lamarck. Trailhead elevation for this hike is 9,300 feet, the lower lake is at 10,662 feet, and the upper lake is at 10,918 feet.

User Groups: Hikers, dogs, and horses. No mountain bikes. No wheelchair facilities.

Permits: A free wilderness permit is required year-round for overnight stays and is available from the Bishop/White Mountain Ranger Station. Quotas are in effect from May 1 to November 1; permits are available in advance for a $5 reservation fee per person.

Maps: A John Muir Wilderness map is available from the U.S. Forest Service. A Bishop Pass map is available from Tom Harrison Maps.

For topographic maps, go to the USGS website to download Mount Thompson and Mount Darwin.

Directions: From Bishop on U.S. 395, turn west on Line Street/Highway 168 and drive 18 miles toward Lake Sabrina. Just before reaching the lake, turn right at the turnoff for North Lake. Drive 1.5 miles and turn right to park in the hiker parking lot by North Lake, near the pack station. Then walk 0.5 mile down the road to the trailhead, at the edge of North Lake Campground.

Contact: Inyo National Forest, White Mountain Ranger Station, Bishop, 760/873-2500, www.fs.usda.gov/inyo.

15 PIUTE LAKE & PIUTE PASS
10.4 mi/5.0 hr

in the John Muir Wilderness

Map 11.2, page 544

The well graded trail to Piute Pass offers hikers and backpackers relatively easy access to the high country, plus the chance to stop at several lakes along the way to the 11,423-foot pass. Start by walking 0.5 mile from the trailhead parking area to North Lake Campground, then follow the trail by the walk-in sites marked for Piute Pass. A steep climb in the first mile will leave you panting. Fortunately, the route is shaded by lodgepole pines, and at the point where you leave the forest, the grade lessens. As you curve your way up the ridge, be sure to stop occasionally and look back at the incredibly deep valley below and the rust-colored Piute Crags towering above. You're likely to say "wow" a bunch of times. A series of switchbacks take you to the spot where Loch Leven Lake is nestled in a rocky glacial bowl at 10,743 feet, set right alongside the trail. The trail continues another 1.2 miles to Piute Lake, now on an even easier grade. Anglers fish for brown and rainbow trout in the deep blue lake, set in grassy green tundra and surrounded by lingering patches of snow. The elevation is just

shy of 11,000 feet, and on the far side of the lake you'll notice a sturdy stone cabin, which is used for snow surveys in the winter. You now have only one mile and a couple hundred feet to go to reach the top of Piute Pass, so you might as well continue. At the top, look down on Summit Lake and start daydreaming about a future backpacking trip: The trail continues downhill into Humphreys Basin. Total elevation gain to the pass is 2,100 feet.

User Groups: Hikers, dogs, and horses. No mountain bikes. No wheelchair facilities.

Permits: No permits are required for day use. A free wilderness permit is required for overnight stays and is available from the Bishop/White Mountain Ranger Station. Quotas are in effect from May 1 to November 1; permits are available in advance for a $5 reservation fee per person. Parking and access are free.

Maps: A John Muir Wilderness map is available from the U.S. Forest Service. A Bishop Pass map is available from Tom Harrison Maps. For topographic maps, go to the USGS website to download Mount Thompson and Mount Darwin.

Directions: From Bishop on U.S. 395, turn west on Line Street/Highway 168 and drive 18 miles toward Lake Sabrina. Just before reaching the lake, turn right at the turnoff for North Lake. Drive 1.5 miles and turn right to park in the hiker parking lot by North Lake, near the pack station. Walk 0.5 mile down the road to the trailhead, at the edge of North Lake Campground.

Contact: Inyo National Forest, White Mountain Ranger Station, Bishop, 760/873-2500, www.fs.usda.gov/inyo.

16 TYEE LAKES
7.0 mi/4.0 hr or 2 days

in the John Muir Wilderness

Map 11.2, page 544

There's so much excellent hiking in the South Fork Bishop Creek Canyon, it's hard to choose where to go. Since so many backpackers opt for

Bishop Pass Trail and its many lakes (see listing in this chapter), day hikers might do well to choose this trail to the Tyee Lakes instead. Just make sure that you are in the mood for hiking up, because you'll do plenty of that, with a total 2,000-foot elevation gain to the highest lakes. From the bridge over Bishop Creek, your climb begins immediately as you tromp up a hillside covered with sagebrush and aspens, gradually making your way through a few dozen switchbacks. You get great views of the Bishop Creek Canyon as you climb, which is an especially beautiful sight when the aspens are putting on their autumn color show. Finally you enter a lodgepole pine forest, and after two miles of climbing, the grade eases up. You reach one of the smaller, lower Tyee Lakes at 2.3 miles. Another 0.5 mile of climbing brings you to the next small lake (called Tyee Lake number two). These first two lakes are small and pondlike, edged with grass, and not worth much more than a second glance. But keep pushing onward, and in another 0.5 mile, you reach one of the larger Tyee Lakes (number three). The fourth and fifth lakes are only 0.25 mile farther and are separated by a small boulder field. The fifth lake is very small, but the fourth lake (elevation 11,015 feet) is large and beautiful. Backpackers usually set up their tent at the third lake and then day hike to the fourth and fifth lakes. Named for a brand of salmon eggs, the Tyee Lakes offer dependably good trout fishing and the chance to enjoy plenty of classic high Sierra scenery. Backpackers looking to make a semi-loop can arrange to have a car waiting at Lake Sabrina in Bishop Creek Canyon, then continue from the Tyee Lakes to George Lake and then Lake Sabrina.

User Groups: Hikers, dogs, and horses. No mountain bikes. No wheelchair facilities.

Permits: A free wilderness permit is required year-round for overnight stays and is available from the Bishop/White Mountain Ranger Station. Quotas are in effect from May 1 to November 1; permits are available in advance for a $5 reservation fee per person.

Maps: A John Muir Wilderness map is available from the U.S. Forest Service. A Bishop Pass map is available from Tom Harrison Maps. For a topographic map, go to the USGS website to download Mount Thompson.

Directions: From Bishop on U.S. 395, turn west on Line Street/Highway 168 and drive 14 miles to the junction for South Lake. Go left and drive 4.5 miles on South Lake Road to the footbridge that crosses Bishop Creek. It is on the right, just before Willow Campground, and it is signed as Tyee Lakes and George Lake trailhead. Park alongside the road.

Contact: Inyo National Forest, White Mountain Ranger Station, Bishop, 760/873-2500, www.fs.usda.gov/inyo.

17 GREEN AND BROWN LAKES

6.6 mi/3.0 hr   🏃3 ⛰9

in the John Muir Wilderness

Map 11.2, page 544

Brown Lake and Green Lake are two excellent day-hiking destinations from the South Lake trailhead in Bishop Creek's South Fork Canyon. With only a 1,500-foot climb, you can visit both lakes, maybe do a little fishing for rainbow trout, and be home in time for supper. Access the trail from the pack station trailhead, and follow a stock trail as it climbs along Bishop Creek through a conifer forest and joins the main Green Lake Trail at one mile. Bear left and level out to an alpine meadow at two miles, where you have a spectacular view of Mount Tom behind you. Soon you'll meet Brown Lake's outlet stream and the little lake itself (really a pond), at 2.5 miles and 10,750 feet. Pay a brief visit, then continue another 0.5 mile to much larger and prettier Green Lake, at 11,050 feet, surrounded by wildflowers and ancient-looking whitebark pines. Both lakes host an abundance of rainbow trout, who might just invite themselves to dinner.

User Groups: Hikers, dogs, and horses. No mountain bikes. No wheelchair facilities.

Permits: No permits are required. Parking and access are free.

Maps: A John Muir Wilderness map is available from the U.S. Forest Service. A Bishop Pass map is available from Tom Harrison Maps. For a topographic map, go to the USGS website to download Mount Thompson.

Directions: From Bishop on U.S. 395, turn west on Line Street/Highway 168 and drive 14 miles to the junction for South Lake. Go left and drive six miles on South Lake Road to Parchers Resort and pack station, on the left side of the road, just beyond Willow Campground.

Contact: Inyo National Forest, White Mountain Ranger Station, Bishop, 760/873-2500, www.fs.usda.gov/inyo.

18 RUWAU AND CHOCOLATE LAKES LOOP

6.6 mi/3.5 hr or 2 days   👥3   ⛰10

in the John Muir Wilderness

Map 11.2, page 544

Lakes, lakes, lakes everywhere. That's how it is on Bishop Pass Trail, where in the space of only five miles you can access Long Lake, Spearhead Lake, Saddlerock Lake, Bishop Lake, and so on. But if you prefer a loop trip to an out-and-back hike, Bishop Pass Trail provides another lake-filled option: a two-mile hike to Long Lake, then a circular route to Ruwau Lake, the Chocolate Lakes, and Bull Lake. It's the kind of trip that fills your mind with precious memories of blue-sky Sierra scenery and gemlike, rock-lined lakes. Still, the trip is not for everyone; some of the trail is an indistinct route with steep, rocky sections that are not an official trail. Bring a good map with you.

The trail begins on the south side of the parking lot, and you head uphill along the eastern shore of South Lake. The views begin almost immediately, particularly of South Lake, Mount Thompson, and Mount Goode. Take the left fork at 0.75 mile, heading for Long Lake and Bishop Pass. Continue straight, ignoring all turnoffs as you hike up around the spectacular western shore of Long Lake, popular with anglers and backpackers. At 2.5 miles (before you reach the lake's far end), instead of continuing straight to Saddlerock Lake and Bishop Pass, take the left fork for Ruwau Lake, a steep but short 0.5 mile away. Skirt the edge of Ruwau Lake for about 75 yards, then look for a use trail leading uphill to your left. Make a steep uphill climb for 0.5 mile to the ridgetop, where you'll look down and see the Chocolate Lakes, set below Chocolate Peak. Make the steep descent to the lakes, picking your way along the rocky slope. Once you're there, the hard part is over. You'll find an easy-to-follow trail at the Chocolate Lakes, and then you'll walk downhill for 0.5 mile to Bull Lake, which is big, round, and beautiful. From Bull Lake, you keep on hiking, and in less than 0.25 mile, you rejoin Bishop Pass Trail. Turn right and walk just under two miles back to the parking lot. Wow, what a day.

User Groups: Hikers, dogs, and horses. No mountain bikes. No wheelchair facilities.

Permits: A free wilderness permit is required year-round for overnight stays and is available from the Bishop/White Mountain Ranger Station. Quotas are in effect from May 1 to November 1; permits are available in advance for a $5 reservation fee per person.

Maps: A John Muir Wilderness map is available from the U.S. Forest Service. A Bishop Pass map is available from Tom Harrison Maps. For a topographic map, go to the USGS website to download Mount Thompson.

Directions: From Bishop on U.S. 395, turn west on Line Street/Highway 168 and drive 14 miles to the junction for South Lake. Go left and drive 7.5 miles on South Lake Road to the end of the road and the trailhead parking area. This parking is for day-use only. If you are backpacking, you must park 1.5 miles from the trailhead, east of Parchers Resort.

Contact: Inyo National Forest, White Mountain Ranger Station, Bishop, 760/873-2500, www.fs.usda.gov/inyo.

19 FIRST AND SECOND FALLS

3.0 mi/1.5 hr   🚶2 ⛰9

in the John Muir Wilderness

Map 11.2, page 544

If you're camping or fishing in Big Pine Canyon, or maybe just wandering around exploring the area, there's a great walk to take starting from the end of the road near Glacier Lodge. Since it's just a day hike, you can park in the parking area right by the lodge and save yourself the long walk from the backpackers' parking lot.

Head west from the trailhead on the wide road, passing some private cabins, and in seconds you cross a bridge over First Falls, a noisy, 200-foot-long whitewater cascade. Bear right onto a narrower trail and start switchbacking uphill, paralleling the cascade. As you climb, you get awesome views into Big Pine Canyon's South Fork. At the top of the falls, cross another bridge over the creek and take a hard left onto a dirt road, staying along the creek. Now it's a flat stroll into the north fork of Big Pine Canyon. Your goal is Second Falls, a larger, more impressive cascade than First Falls; it's less than a mile away and clearly visible from the trail. Since the route is set along the canyon bottom, you get many interesting vistas along the way, from the tall surrounding canyon walls to occasional lodgepole pines and many mountain wildflowers. When the trail starts to climb out of the canyon, take the left spur cutoff to head closer to the waterfall, or just pick a big rock to sit on and admire the scenery.

User Groups: Hikers, dogs, and horses. No mountain bikes. No wheelchair facilities.

Permits: No permits are required for day use. Parking and access are free.

Maps: A John Muir Wilderness map is available from the U.S. Forest Service. A Palisades map is available from Tom Harrison Maps. For a topographic map, go to the USGS website to download Coyote Flat.

Directions: From Bishop, drive 15 miles south on U.S. 395 to Big Pine. Turn right (west) on Crocker Street, which becomes Glacier Lodge Road, and drive 10.5 miles to Glacier Lodge and the Big Pine Canyon trailhead, at the end of the road. Day hikers may park in the day-use area near the lodge, but backpackers must park 0.5 mile east, on Glacier Lodge Road, in the backpackers' parking lot.

Contact: Inyo National Forest, White Mountain Ranger Station, Bishop, 760/873-2500, www.fs.usda.gov/inyo.

20 FIRST AND SECOND LAKES

9.6 mi/6.0 hr or 2 days   🚶3 ⛰9

in the John Muir Wilderness

Map 11.2, page 544

The trail to First and Second Lakes in Big Pine Canyon follows the same route as the trail to First and Second Falls, above, but then continues onward, climbing up and over Second Falls on the well-graded trail to Cienaga Mirth, at three miles out. Off to the left of the trail you'll see a magnificent stone cabin (now sometimes used as a backcountry ranger residence) built by movie star Lon Chaney. Wildflowers are excellent at the swampy, spring-fed mirth. You reach First Lake at 4.5 miles, and Second Lake is just a few hundred yards farther. By Second Lake, you've climbed to over 10,000 feet, and the lake water is a stunning glacial blue-green. Those who wish to see more lakes can continue on a loop past Second Lake to Third, Fourth, Fifth, and Black Lakes, making a long, 14-mile day. Fifth Lake, just off the loop by a third of a mile, is the most scenic. You'll see hardy mountaineer-types with climbing equipment turning left beyond Third Lake. They're hiking a full nine miles one-way to the edge of Palisade Glacier, the southernmost glacier in the Sierra. Considering it has a 5,000-foot elevation gain, the route to the glacier is not for everybody.

User Groups: Hikers, dogs, and horses. No mountain bikes. No wheelchair facilities.

Permits: A free wilderness permit is required year-round for overnight stays and is available from the Bishop/White Mountain Ranger

Station. Quotas are in effect from May 1 to November 1; permits are available in advance for a $5 reservation fee per person.

Maps: A John Muir Wilderness map is available from the U.S. Forest Service. A Palisades map is available from Tom Harrison Maps. For topographic maps, go to the USGS website to download Coyote Flat and Split Mountain.

Directions: From Bishop, drive 15 miles south on U.S. 395 to Big Pine. Turn right (west) on Crocker Street, which becomes Glacier Lodge Road, and drive 10.5 miles to Glacier Lodge and the Big Pine Canyon trailhead, at the end of the road. Day hikers may park in the day-use area near the lodge, but backpackers must park 0.5 mile east, on Glacier Lodge Road, in the backpackers' parking lot.

Contact: Inyo National Forest, White Mountain Ranger Station, Bishop, 760/873-2500, www.fs.usda.gov/inyo.

belonged to a 26-foot-wide tree that took two men 13 days to cut down.

User Groups: Hikers only. No dogs, horses, or mountain bikes. No wheelchair facilities.

Permits: No permits are required. There is a $20 entrance fee per vehicle at Sequoia and Kings Canyon National Parks, good for seven days.

Maps: A Sequoia and Kings Canyon map is available from Tom Harrison Maps. For a topographic map, go to the USGS website to download Hume.

Directions: From Fresno, drive east on Highway 180 for 55 miles to the Big Stump Entrance at Kings Canyon National Park. The trail begins 0.5 mile past the entrance station, at the Big Stump Picnic Area.

Contact: Sequoia and Kings Canyon National Parks, Three Rivers, 559/565-3341 or 559/565-4307, www.nps.gov/seki.

21 BIG STUMP TRAIL
1.0 mi/0.5 hr

in the Grant Grove area of Kings Canyon National Park

Map 11.3, page 545

Normally it would be hard for us to get excited about a trail called the Big Stump Trail. In fact, this sort of thing could be quite depressing. But Big Stump Trail, at the entrance to Kings Canyon National Park, is a pleasant nature walk and provides an excellent history lesson as well. The size of the mammoth trees—oops, make that stumps—just blows you away. Most of the big trees were cut for timber in the 1880s, and you'll see the remains of logging activities. Be sure to pick up an interpretive brochure at the Kings Canyon Visitors Center or at the trailhead. The trail is a short loop that circles a meadow. A few mature sequoias still thrive along the route, including one in the first 50 feet from the parking lot. The path's highlights include the Burnt Monarch, a shell of a giant sequoia that has been ravaged by fire but still stands, and the Mark Twain Stump. The latter

22 SUNSET TRAIL
5.0 mi/2.5 hr

in the Grant Grove area of Kings Canyon National Park

Map 11.3, page 545

The Sunset Trail leaves Sunset Campground (elevation 6,590 feet) and heads gently downhill for 2.25 miles to Ella Falls, a pretty 40-foot cascade on Sequoia Creek. At 1.5 miles down the trail, you reach a junction with South Boundary Trail and can take a short side trip to the left to Viola Falls, which isn't much of a waterfall but is a memorably scenic spot on granite-sculpted Sequoia Creek. Most people just mosey down the trail, enjoying the big pines and firs and the flowering western azaleas, and maybe stealing a kiss on one of the wooden footbridges. If you like, you can follow the trail for its entire 2.5-mile length to Sequoia Lake. Although the lake is privately owned, hikers are allowed to walk along its edge. While you're enjoying the lake, don't forget that the return trip is all uphill with a 1,300-foot elevation gain, so save some water and energy.

User Groups: Hikers only. No dogs, horses, or mountain bikes. No wheelchair facilities.

Permits: No permits are required. There is a $20 entrance fee per vehicle at Sequoia and Kings Canyon National Parks, good for seven days.

Maps: A Sequoia and Kings Canyon map is available from Tom Harrison Maps. For topographic maps, go to the USGS website to download Hume and General Grant Grove.

Directions: From Fresno, drive east on Highway 180 for 55 miles to the Big Stump Entrance at Kings Canyon National Park. Continue 1.5 miles and turn left, following signs for Kings Canyon. Drive 1.5 miles to Grant Grove Village, and park in the large parking lot near the visitors center. Cross the road and walk on the paved trail toward Sunset Campground's amphitheater. Continue heading left through the camp to site No. 118, where the trail begins.

Contact: Sequoia and Kings Canyon National Parks, Three Rivers, 559/565-3341 or 559/565-4307, www.nps.gov/seki.

community within the national park, so just retrace your steps to return back to your car.

User Groups: Hikers only. No dogs, horses, or mountain bikes. No wheelchair facilities.

Permits: No permits are required. There is a $20 entrance fee per vehicle at Sequoia and Kings Canyon National Parks, good for seven days.

Maps: A Sequoia and Kings Canyon map is available from Tom Harrison Maps. For a topographic map, go to the USGS website to download Hume.

Directions: From Fresno, drive east on Highway 180 for 55 miles to the Big Stump Entrance at Kings Canyon National Park. Continue 1.5 miles and turn left, following signs for Kings Canyon. Drive 1.5 miles to Grant Grove Village and park in the large parking lot near the visitors center. Walk on the service road near the tent cabins to reach the start of the Manzanita Trail.

Contact: Sequoia and Kings Canyon National Parks, Three Rivers, 559/565-3341 or 559/565-4307, www.nps.gov/seki.

23 MANZANITA AND AZALEA TRAILS

3.3 mi/2.0 hr 　　　　🥾2 ⛰7

in the Grant Grove area of Kings Canyon National Park

Map 11.3, page 545

This hike is a good exercise route for vacationers staying in Grant Grove Village or in the nearby campgrounds. It climbs 800 feet, which gives your heart and lungs a workout, and it's pretty every step of the way. From the edge of the dirt service road by the tent cabins, Manzanita Trail climbs a dry slope uphill to Park Ridge. Near the top, you'll parallel the dirt road that leads to the Park Ridge Fire Lookout. Then Manzanita Trail meets up with Azalea Trail, and you'll descend on a much shadier, moister slope. The azaleas bloom bright white with prolific, showy blossoms in June and July. Azalea Trail ends at Wilsonia, a private

24 PANORAMIC POINT AND PARK RIDGE LOOKOUT

4.7 mi/3.0 hr 　　　　🥾2 ⛰9

in the Grant Grove area of Kings Canyon National Park

Map 11.3, page 545

Start your trip by taking the 300-yard paved walk from the parking area to Panoramic Point, which delivers what its name implies. An interpretive display names the many peaks and valleys you can see, including the big pointy one, which is Mount Goddard at 13,560 feet. From Panoramic Point, take the dirt Park Ridge Trail that leads to the right along the ridge. Your views continue as you contour along the ridgeline, climbing gently uphill. The trail intersects a dirt road, which you follow for about 50 yards; then bear left onto the trail again. You'll intersect this dirt road once more about 100 yards before the Park Ridge Fire Lookout. Follow the road to the lookout tower, and check out the nifty outdoor shower at its base. If someone is stationed in the tower and gives you permission to come up, do so and sign the visitors register. (The lookout person rarely gets visitors on cloudy days, but he or she gets a good number of them when it's sunny, and you can see for miles around.) The lookout is operated by volunteers during the fire season, which is usually May to October. For your return trip, you can walk down the trail back to Panoramic Point or take the shorter fire road, which also leads back to the parking lot. Views are far better along the trail than on the fire road.

User Groups: Hikers only. No dogs, horses, or mountain bikes. No wheelchair facilities.

Permits: No permits are required. There is a $20 entrance fee per vehicle at Sequoia and Kings Canyon National Parks, good for seven days.

Maps: A Sequoia and Kings Canyon map is available from Tom Harrison Maps. For a topographic map, go to the USGS website to download Hume.

Directions: From Fresno, drive east on Highway 180 for 55 miles to the Big Stump Entrance at Kings Canyon National Park. Continue 1.5 miles and turn left, following signs for Kings Canyon. Drive 1.5 miles to Grant Grove Village and turn right by the visitors center and store. Follow the road past the cabins, and just before the John Muir Lodge, turn right on the road signed for Panoramic Point. It's 2.3 miles from the visitors center to Panoramic Point.

Contact: Sequoia and Kings Canyon National Parks, Three Rivers, 559/565-3341 or 559/565-4307, www.nps.gov/seki.

25 GENERAL GRANT TREE TRAIL

0.6 mi/0.5 hr   🚶1 ⛰8

in the Grant Grove area of Kings Canyon National Park

Map 11.3, page 545   **BEST (**

This paved loop through a giant sequoia grove allows visitors a look at the General Grant Tree, the second-largest tree in the world. Estimated to be 1,800 to 2,000 years old, the General Grant is 267 feet tall and 107 feet in circumference at its base. Every year since 1926, the City of Sanger has held a Christmas celebration around its base, and so the tree is known as "the Nation's Christmas Tree." Its neighbors include the Fallen Monarch, a hollow downed tree that is so wide, it was once used as a park employee camp. Also nearby is a group of big sequoias named after various U.S. states. It may seem a little campy, but there are many excellent photo opportunities in the grove. A bonus: Most, but not all, of this trail is accessible to wheelchair users.

User Groups: Hikers. No dogs, horses, or mountain bikes. Partial wheelchair accessibility.

Permits: No permits are required. There is a $20 entrance fee per vehicle at Sequoia and Kings Canyon National Parks, good for seven days.

Maps: A Sequoia and Kings Canyon map is available from Tom Harrison Maps. For topographic maps, go to the USGS website to download Hume and General Grant Grove.

Directions: From Fresno, drive east on Highway 180 for 55 miles to the Big Stump Entrance at Kings Canyon National Park. Continue 1.5 miles and turn left, following signs for Kings Canyon. Drive one mile, passing Grant Grove Village, to the left turnoff for General Grant Tree. Turn left and follow the access road for 0.75 mile to the parking lot.

Contact: Sequoia and Kings Canyon National Parks, Three Rivers, 559/565-3341 or 559/565-4307, www.nps.gov/seki.

26 NORTH GROVE AND DEAD GIANT LOOP

3.0 mi/1.5 hr

in the Grant Grove area of Kings Canyon National Park

Map 11.3, page 545

For people who want a little more hiking than what the General Grant Tree Trail (see listing in this chapter) provides, the combined North Grove and Dead Giant Loop Trails are the answer. The walk begins at the oversized vehicle parking at the General Grant Tree parking lot. Past the gate, follow an old dirt road that leads downhill through a mixed forest of sequoia, sugar pine, white fir, and dogwood. Don't expect to see dense groves of sequoias here; the big trees are few and far between. However, the forest is pleasant, quiet, and shady.

Stay to the right at the first junction to follow the posted North Grove Loop Trail. At the bottom of the hill, you'll pass an obscure junction with an old wagon road that was used to take logged sequoias to the mill. Continue to a more obvious junction at one mile out. Turn right

and walk 0.25 mile downhill to Lion Meadow. Turn right on a single-track trail and circle around the meadow, heading for the Dead Giant. This sequoia, like some others in the park, is a nearly hollow, dead tree that somehow keeps standing. From the Dead Giant, it's a short tromp to the Sequoia Lake Overlook, a tranquil high point where you can have a snack and enjoy the view of the large, private lake in Sequoia National Forest. From the overlook, backtrack a few yards and turn right to finish out the loop, returning uphill on the wide dirt road. There is a 400-foot gain on the return.

User Groups: Hikers only. No dogs, horses, or mountain bikes. No wheelchair facilities.

Permits: No permits are required. There is a $20 entrance fee per vehicle at Sequoia and Kings Canyon National Parks, good for seven days.

Maps: A Sequoia and Kings Canyon map is available from Tom Harrison Maps. For topographic maps, go to the USGS website to download Hume and General Grant Grove.

Directions: From Fresno, drive east on Highway 180 for 55 miles to the Big Stump

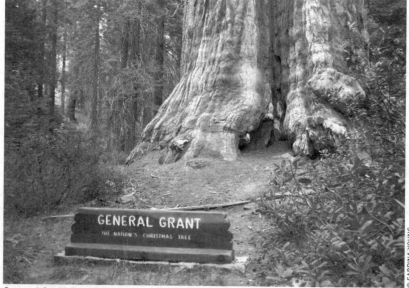

General Grant Tree Trail

© SABRINA YOUNG

Entrance at Kings Canyon National Park. Continue 1.5 miles and turn left, following signs for Kings Canyon. Drive two miles, passing Grant Grove Village, to the left turnoff for General Grant Tree. Turn left and follow the access road for one mile to the parking lot. The North Grove Loop starts from the far end of the lower parking lot.

Contact: Sequoia and Kings Canyon National Parks, Three Rivers, 559/565-3341 or 559/565-4307, www.nps.gov/seki.

27 CHICAGO STUMP TRAIL
0.5 mi/0.5 hr   🚶1 ⛰7

in Giant Sequoia National Monument north of the Grant Grove area of Kings Canyon National Park

Map 11.3, page 545

Note: This trail was in the path of the Rough Fire of August 2015 and is closed at this book's press time. Check with the Hume Lake Ranger District for an update before you visit.

Before the loggers extracted their toll, the Converse Basin once sheltered one of the largest and finest groves of giant sequoias in the world. Where the giants once stood, second-growth sequoias have now taken hold. This short and easy stroll takes you through a re-generated mixed forest to the Chicago Stump, a massive stump that belonged to one of the largest trees in the area. The General Noble tree was cut down in 1893, and the lower portion of the tree was reassembled and exhibited at the Chicago World's Fair. The stump that remains is at least 10 feet high and over 25 feet wide. In addition to its historical interest, this easy trail provides a pleasant, peaceful change from the hustle and bustle of the neighboring national parks.

User Groups: Hikers, horses, and dogs. No mountain bikes. No wheelchair facilities.

Permits: No permits are required. There is a $20 entrance fee per vehicle at Sequoia and Kings Canyon National Parks, good for seven days.

Maps: A Sequoia National Forest map is available from the U.S. Forest Service. A map of Sequoia and Kings Canyon is available from Tom Harrison Maps. For a topographic map, go to the USGS website to download Hume.

Directions: From Fresno, drive east on Highway 180 for 55 miles to the Big Stump Entrance at Kings Canyon National Park. Continue 1.5 miles and turn left, following signs for Kings Canyon. Drive approximately 4.5 miles, passing Grant Grove Village, and turn left at the sign for Forest Road 13S03. Drive two miles, turn right on Road 13S65, and continue 0.1 mile to the Chicago Stump trailhead.

Contact: Giant Sequoia National Monument/ Sequoia National Forest, Hume Lake Ranger District, Dunlap, 559/338-2251, www.fs.usda. gov/sequoia.

28 BOOLE TREE LOOP
2.5 mi/1.0 hr   🚶2 ⛰9

in Giant Sequoia National Monument north of the Grant Grove area of Kings Canyon National Park

Map 11.3, page 545

Note: This trail was in the path of the Rough Fire of August 2015 and is closed at this book's press time. Check with the Hume Lake Ranger District for an update before you visit.

The drive in to the Boole Tree trailhead is worth the trip by itself. You pass through a beautiful, ghostly meadow filled with giant sequoia stumps. It's an otherworldly sight that may stay engrained in your memory for a long time. The Boole Tree hike is a loop, and it's a good idea to take the right side of the loop first, making the ascent more gradual. You climb 500 feet to the top of a ridge, then descend the other side, reaching the Boole Tree in one mile. (It's just off the main loop, accessible via a short, obvious spur.) At 269 feet tall and with a diameter of 35 feet, the Boole Tree is the largest tree in any of the national forests, and it's the sixth largest tree in the world. It is one of a very few giant sequoias left standing in the Converse Basin grove, as the rest were clear-cut in the late 1800s. Although some people go see the Boole Tree and then turn around, it's better to finish out the loop. You'll be rewarded with a stellar view of Spanish Mountain and the Kings River Canyon.

User Groups: Hikers, horses, and dogs. No mountain bikes. No wheelchair facilities.

Permits: No permits are required. There is a $20 entrance fee per vehicle at Sequoia and Kings Canyon National Parks, good for seven days.

Maps: A Sequoia National Forest map is available from the U.S. Forest Service. A map of Sequoia and Kings Canyon is available from Tom Harrison Maps. For a topographic map, go to the USGS website to download Hume.

Directions: From Fresno, drive east on Highway 180 for 55 miles to the Big Stump Entrance at Kings Canyon National Park. Continue 1.5 miles and turn left, following signs for Kings Canyon. Drive approximately six miles, passing Grant Grove Village. Turn left at the sign for Forest Road 13S55, Boole Tree, Converse Basin, and Stump Meadow. Drive 2.6 miles, and park in the wide parking pullout.

Contact: Giant Sequoia National Monument/ Sequoia National Forest, Hume Lake Ranger District, Dunlap, 559/338-2251, www.fs.usda. gov/sequoia.

29 YUCCA POINT

4.0 mi/2.25 hr

in Giant Sequoia National Monument west of the Cedar Grove area of Kings Canyon National Park

Map 11.3, page 545

Note: This trail was in the path of the Rough Fire of August 2015 and is closed at this book's press time. Check with the Hume Lake Ranger District for an update before you visit.

The Yucca Point Trail is an upside-down hike—the kind where you go down on the way in (so easy) and up on the way back (not so easy). The path descends from Highway 180 to the Kings River, dropping 1,200 feet along the way. As long as you don't climb uphill at high noon, the hike back is not as bad as it looks from the top. The trail is well graded; the only hardship is that the terrain is all chaparral, so there's almost no shade, just the occasional tall yucca plant. The path is mostly used by anglers heading down to the wild trout section of the Kings River, but hikers like the excellent views it provides and the access to the river's cool, emerald green pools.

User Groups: Hikers only. No dogs, horses, or mountain bikes. No wheelchair facilities.

Permits: No permits are required. There is a $20 entrance fee per vehicle for access to this section of Sequoia National Forest, payable at any of the entrance stations to Kings Canyon and Sequoia National Parks. The fee is good for seven days in both the national forest and the national parks.

Maps: A Sequoia National Forest map is available from the U.S. Forest Service. A map of Sequoia and Kings Canyon is available from Tom Harrison Maps. For a topographic map, go to the USGS website to download Wren Peak.

Directions: From Fresno, drive east on Highway 180 for 55 miles to the Big Stump Entrance at Kings Canyon National Park. Continue 1.5 miles and turn left, following signs for Kings Canyon. Drive another 16 miles on Highway 180, past Grant Grove and Kings Canyon Lodge, to the Yucca Point trailhead, on the left. Park in the pullouts alongside Highway 180.

Contact: Giant Sequoia National Monument/ Sequoia National Forest, Hume Lake Ranger District, Dunlap, 559/338-2251, www.fs.usda. gov/sequoia.

30 WINDY CLIFFS
3.0 mi/1.5 hr 🥾2 ⛰8

in Giant Sequoia National Monument west of the Cedar Grove area of Kings Canyon National Park

Map 11.3, page 545

Note: This trail was in the path of the Rough Fire of August 2015 and is closed at this book's press time. Check with the Hume Lake Ranger District for an update before you visit.

The Forest Service concessionaire charges a fee for tours of Boyden Cave, one of many limestone caverns in the vicinity of Kings Canyon and Sequoia National Parks, and the parking lot is always busy with carloads and busloads of people waiting to take the tour. The cave is fascinating and worth a visit, but if you're low on cash, you can take this stellar hike instead and get million-dollar views of Kings Canyon for free. From the cave gift shop, walk up the paved path and take the left fork near the entrance to the cave (you'll need to go under the rope that borders the trail to the cave). The trail has a metal bar across it, but the Forest Service says it's perfectly legal to hike it; they just don't want to encourage casual visitors because the trail is unmaintained with very steep drop-offs. Once on the trail, in no time you'll climb a little higher and see a sweeping panorama of Highway 180 and the fast-flowing Kings River below. In one mile, Boulder Creek cascades down the hillside. The path ends when it reaches creekside at 1.5 miles. (A faint path continues, but it's badly overgrown.) Note that poison oak is prolific along this trail, so it might be a good idea to wear long pants and long sleeves.

User Groups: Hikers only. No dogs, horses, or mountain bikes. No wheelchair facilities.

Permits: No permits are required. There is a $20 per vehicle entrance fee for access to this section of Sequoia National Forest, payable at any of the entrance stations to Kings Canyon and Sequoia National Parks. The fee is good for seven days in both the national forest and the national parks.

Maps: A Sequoia National Forest map is available from the U.S. Forest Service. A map of Sequoia and Kings Canyon is available from Tom Harrison Maps. For a topographic map, go to the USGS website to download Wren Peak.

Directions: From Fresno, drive east on Highway 180 for 55 miles to the Big Stump Entrance at Kings Canyon National Park. Continue 1.5 miles and turn left, following signs for Kings Canyon. Drive 22 miles on Highway 180, passing Grant Grove and Kings Canyon Lodge, to the parking area for Boyden Cave, on the right side of the road.

Contact: Giant Sequoia National Monument/ Sequoia National Forest, Hume Lake Ranger District, Dunlap, 559/338-2251, www.fs.usda. gov/sequoia.

31 LEWIS CREEK TRAIL
11.6 mi/6.0 hr or 2 days 🥾4 ⛰9

off Highway 180 in the Cedar Grove area of Kings Canyon National Park

Map 11.3, page 545

Note: This trail was in the path of the Rough Fire of August 2015 and is closed at this book's press time. Check with Kings Canyon National Park for an update before you visit.

Up, up, and up. If you're willing to climb 3,200 feet over the course of 5.5 miles, your reward is pristine Frypan Meadow, at 7,800 feet in elevation. In early summer, the meadow is green and littered with wildflowers, creating a glorious vision after the hot, sunny climb. But there's no way to see it without first putting in some effort on the Lewis Creek Trail. The good news is that if the first mile or so proves to be too demanding, or too hot if you don't start first thing in the morning, you can always take the right fork at 1.6 miles and head back downhill on Hotel Creek Trail, making a seven-mile loop out of the trip. If you push onward on Lewis Creek Trail, you cross lovely Comb Creek (at 3.2 miles), then Lewis Creek one mile farther. Many day hikers make the Lewis Creek crossing their destination; its pools make fine swimming holes. Backpackers continue another 1.5 miles to Frypan Meadow. If you have your wilderness permit, campsites are available there.

User Groups: Hikers and horses. No dogs or mountain bikes. No wheelchair facilities.

Permits: There is a $20 entrance fee per vehicle at Sequoia and Kings Canyon National Parks, good for seven days. Wilderness permits are required for overnight stays. They are available on a first-come, first-served basis at the wilderness permit station at Roads End or the Kings Canyon Visitors Center. For advanced wilderness permits or information on trail conditions, go to www.nps.gov/seki. Trailhead quotas are in effect from May to September.

Maps: A Sequoia and Kings Canyon map is available from Tom Harrison Maps. For a topographic map, go to the USGS website to download Cedar Grove.

Directions: From Fresno, drive east on Highway 180 for 55 miles to the Big Stump Entrance at Kings Canyon National Park. Continue 1.5 miles and turn left, following signs for Kings Canyon and Cedar Grove. Drive 31 miles on Highway 180 to the Lewis Creek Trail parking area, on the north side of the road, before you reach Cedar Grove Village.

Contact: Sequoia and Kings Canyon National Parks, Three Rivers, 559/565-3341 or 559/565-4307, www.nps.gov/seki.

32 HOTEL CREEK TRAIL TO CEDAR GROVE OVERLOOK
5.0 mi/2.5 hr 🏃3 ⛰9

off Highway 180 in the Cedar Grove area of Kings Canyon National Park

Map 11.3, page 545

Note: This trail was in the path of the Rough Fire of August 2015 and is closed at this book's press time. Check with Kings Canyon National Park for an update before you visit.

The destination on this trip is a stunning overlook of Kings Canyon, the deepest canyon in the continental United States with a plunge of 8,200 feet at its deepest point. In truth, the canyon vistas are continual for most of the hike, so if you don't make it to the overlook, you'll still get an eyeful. The Hotel Creek Trail consists of dozens of switchbacks over open, sunny slopes, climbing 1,200 feet over two miles to a trail junction with Overlook Trail. Turn left to head to the overlook, which peers down on Cedar Grove and the length of Kings Canyon. Some of the best views are of Monarch Divide's high peaks to the north. We hope you came with picnic supplies. For a five-mile round-trip, retrace your steps back to Cedar Grove. If you want to walk farther, you can continue from the overlook junction for another 1.5 miles and turn left, hiking downhill on Lewis Creek Trail and making a seven-mile loop out of the trip. This stretch of Lewis Creek Trail is lined with sweet-smelling ceanothus. Unfortunately, the final 1.2 miles of the loop parallels a park road. Along the way, the trail overlooks a level area next to the South Fork Kings River where wildlife can often be spotted among the meadows and shrubs.

User Groups: Hikers and horses. No dogs or mountain bikes. No wheelchair facilities.

Permits: No permits are required. There is a $20 entrance fee per vehicle at Sequoia and Kings Canyon National Parks, good for seven days.

Maps: A Sequoia and Kings Canyon map is available from Tom Harrison Maps. For a topographic map, go to the USGS website to download Cedar Grove.

Directions: From Fresno, drive east on Highway 180 for 55 miles to the Big Stump Entrance at Kings Canyon National Park. Continue 1.5 miles and turn left, following signs for Kings Canyon and Cedar Grove. Drive 31.5 miles on Highway 180 to Cedar Grove Village. Turn left at the sign for the visitors center and Cedar Grove Lodge. Continue on the main road past the lodge for 0.25 mile and turn right. The Hotel Creek trailhead is on the left after a few hundred feet.

Contact: Sequoia and Kings Canyon National

Parks, Three Rivers, 559/565-3341 or 559/565-4307, www.nps.gov/seki.

33 DON CECIL TRAIL TO LOOKOUT PEAK

12.0 mi/7.0 hr   🏃5 ⛰10

off Highway 180 in the Cedar Grove area of
Kings Canyon National Park

Map 11.3, page 545   **BEST (**

Note: This trail was in the path of the Rough Fire of August 2015 and is closed at this book's press time. Check with Kings Canyon National Park for an update before you visit.

Lookout Peak, at 8,531 feet in elevation, is a summit worth ascending, even though it's an all-day trip with a 3,900-foot elevation gain. From the top, you get an unforgettable Sierra view, with Cedar Grove far below you and peaks and ridges all around. In addition, just a few hundred yards from the summit is Summit Meadow, filled with summer wildflowers. The key is to carry plenty of water and plan on an early-morning start to beat the heat. You can filter water from Sheep Creek, one mile in. Luckily, there's a decent amount of shade in the first few miles. Even though this trailhead is located right by the Cedar Grove campgrounds, few people hike all the way to the peak, so you have a chance at peace and quiet along the trail. The only downer on this hike is that when you near the summit, you see that other people have driven their cars on an alternate route to Lookout Peak (from the Big Meadows area of Giant Sequoia National Monument), and they are gaining the summit after only a 0.25-mile hike. Hey, at least you earned it.

User Groups: Hikers and horses. No dogs or mountain bikes. No wheelchair facilities.

Permits: No permits are required. There is a $20 entrance fee per vehicle at Sequoia and Kings Canyon National Parks, good for seven days.

Maps: A Sequoia and Kings Canyon map is available from Tom Harrison Maps. For a topographic map, go to the USGS website to download Cedar Grove.

Directions: From Fresno, drive east on Highway 180 for 55 miles to the Big Stump Entrance at Kings Canyon National Park. Continue 1.5 miles and turn left, following signs for Kings Canyon and Cedar Grove. Drive 31.5 miles on Highway 180 and take the right fork for Cedar Grove. The Don Cecil trailhead is on the right side of the road, just beyond the turnoff for Cedar Grove Village and the visitors center. If you reach Canyon View and Moraine Campgrounds, you've gone too far.

Contact: Sequoia and Kings Canyon National Parks, Three Rivers, 559/565-3341 or 559/565-4307, www.nps.gov/seki.

34 ROARING RIVER FALLS

0.4 mi/0.25 hr   🏃1 ⛰8

off Highway 180 in the Cedar Grove area of
Kings Canyon National Park

Map 11.3, page 545   **BEST (**

Note: This trail was in the path of the Rough Fire of August 2015 and is closed at this book's press time. Check with Kings Canyon National Park for an update before you visit.

It's an easy stroll to Roaring River Falls, a pretty waterfall that drops through a narrow gorge into the South Fork Kings River. It's the only waterfall in Sequoia and Kings Canyon National Parks that is partially accessible via wheelchair. (The trail is paved and accessible for most of its length, but one section may be too steep for some wheelchair users.) If hikers want a longer walk, they can continue downstream on the River Trail to Zumwalt Meadow in 1.6 miles or Road's End in 2.7 miles. What's extraordinary about the waterfall is not the cascade itself, but the giant rocky pool into which it falls; it's at least 50 feet wide. From where the paved trail ends, at the edge of the pool, the waterfall is perfectly framed by two big conifers. Many beautiful photos have been snapped here.

User Groups: Hikers and wheelchairs. No dogs, horses, or mountain bikes.

Permits: No permits are required. There is a $20 entrance fee per vehicle at Sequoia and Kings Canyon National Parks, good for seven days.

Maps: A Sequoia and Kings Canyon map is available from Tom Harrison Maps. For a topographic map, go to the USGS website to download Sphinx.

Directions: From Fresno, drive east on Highway 180 for 55 miles to the Big Stump Entrance at Kings Canyon National Park. Continue 1.5 miles and turn left, following signs for Kings Canyon and Cedar Grove. Continue 35 miles on Highway 180 to the sign for Roaring River Falls and the River Trail, three miles past Cedar Grove Village. The trailhead is on the right side of the road.

Contact: Sequoia and Kings Canyon National Parks, Three Rivers, 559/565-3341 or 559/565-4307, www.nps.gov/seki.

35 ZUMWALT MEADOW LOOP
2.0 mi/1.0 hr 🚶1 ⛺9

off Highway 180 in the Cedar Grove area of Kings Canyon National Park

Map 11.3, page 545   BEST (

Note: This trail was in the path of the Rough Fire of August 2015 and is closed at this book's press time. Check with Kings Canyon National Park for an update before you visit.

What's the prettiest easy hike in Kings Canyon National Park? The Zumwalt Meadow Loop Trail wins hands down. A scenic two-mile walk along the South Fork Kings River, the Zumwalt Meadow Loop is a delight for hikers of all abilities. Many people bring their fishing rods along to try their luck in the river, but for most, the hiking is better than the fishing. From the parking area, walk downstream along the river to an old suspension footbridge, cross it, and walk back upstream. The loop begins at an obvious fork, and you can hike it in either direction. The south side traverses a boulder field of jumbled rocks that have tumbled down from the Grand Sentinel (elevation 8,504 feet).

The north side cuts through a thick, waist-high fern forest and follows a wooden walkway over a marsh. Views of 8,717-foot North Dome are awe inspiring. Trees, meadow, rock, stream, river, canyon walls—Zumwalt Meadow Trail has it all.

User Groups: Hikers only. No dogs, horses, or mountain bikes. No wheelchair facilities.

Permits: No permits are required. There is a $20 entrance fee per vehicle at Sequoia and Kings Canyon National Parks, good for seven days.

Maps: A Sequoia and Kings Canyon map is available from Tom Harrison Maps. For a topographic map, go to the USGS website to download Cedar Grove.

Directions: From Fresno, drive east on Highway 180 for 55 miles to the Big Stump Entrance at Kings Canyon National Park. Continue 1.5 miles and turn left, following signs for Kings Canyon and Cedar Grove. Continue 36 miles on Highway 180 to the parking area for Zumwalt Meadow, on the right side of the road.

Contact: Sequoia and Kings Canyon National Parks, Three Rivers, 559/565-3341 or 559/565-4307, www.nps.gov/seki.

36 MIST FALLS
9.2 mi/5.0 hr 🚶2 ⛺9

off Highway 180 in the Cedar Grove area of Kings Canyon National Park

Map 11.3, page 545

Note: This trail was in the path of the Rough Fire of August 2015 and is closed at this book's press time. Check with Kings Canyon National Park for an update before you visit.

The Mist Falls Trail is probably the most well-used pathway in Kings Canyon National Park, with good reason. It's a stellar 4.6-mile walk to an impressive cascade on the South Fork Kings River, with only a 650-foot gain in elevation along the way. Many backpackers use this trail to access Paradise Valley and points beyond, while most day hikers turn around at

Mist Falls. The first two miles are a flat walk up the Kings River Valley, with canyon walls towering above you on both sides. You spend a lot of time craning your neck, looking up at the high canyon rims, from which springtime waterfalls cascade down. You're in a dry, open forest much of the time.

At two miles, you'll reach a trail junction. Bear left, then start to climb over granite. The farther you go, the more expansive the views become; make sure you keep turning around so you can take in the whole panorama. At four miles, the river starts to look more waterfall-like, with crashing pools and rocky granite slides becoming increasingly vertical. A quarter mile later you reach Mist Falls, which fans out over a 45-foot wide granite ledge and crashes into a boulder-lined pool. It creates a tremendous spray and mist in early summer, and mellows out as the season goes on. Take a look at the falls, then walk back down the trail 0.2 mile to the obvious, immense slab of granite you just passed. This is a favorite spot to have lunch, with its wide-open view of 10,007-foot Avalanche Peak. Look carefully and you can pick out the stone face of The Sphinx.

There are two ways to beat the crowds on this path. First, start early in the morning. Second, hike part of the route on an alternate trail on the river's south side. This trail travels from the Road's End parking lot to the Bailey Bridge at the trail intersection mentioned above. If you get an early start, save this alternate route for the return trip. By then, the day hikers will be out in full force.

User Groups: Hikers and horses. No dogs or mountain bikes. No wheelchair facilities.

Permits: No permits are required. There is a $20 entrance fee per vehicle at Sequoia and Kings Canyon National Parks, good for seven days.

Maps: A Sequoia and Kings Canyon map is available from Tom Harrison Maps. For a topographic map, go to the USGS website to download Sphinx.

Directions: From Fresno, drive east on Highway 180 for 55 miles to the Big Stump Entrance at Kings Canyon National Park. Continue 1.5 miles and turn left, following signs for Kings Canyon and Cedar Grove. Continue 38 miles on Highway 180 to Road's End, six miles past Cedar Grove Village. The trailhead is at the east end of the parking lot, near the wilderness ranger station.

Contact: Sequoia and Kings Canyon National Parks, Three Rivers, 559/565-3341 or 559/565-4307, www.nps.gov/seki.

37 COPPER CREEK TRAIL

21.0 mi/3-4 days

off Highway 180 in the Cedar Grove area of Kings Canyon National Park

Map 11.3, page 545

Note: This trail was in the path of the Rough Fire of August 2015 and is closed at this book's press time. Check with Kings Canyon National Park for an update before you visit.

The Copper Creek trailhead is at 5,000 feet, and Granite Lake is at 9,972 feet, so it's not hard to do the math. If you're up for a backpacking trip with a 5,000-foot elevation gain over 10 miles, the Granite Lake Basin is your ticket to happiness. But keep in mind that the route can be hot and dry as it switchbacks up manzanita-covered slopes; this trail is considered one of the most strenuous in the Cedar Grove area. Your first night's camp is at Lower Tent Meadow, four miles in and at 7,800 feet. After that, things start to get really good. With Mount Hutchings looming over your left shoulder, the second day's six miles will go easier, bringing you to rocky, jewel-like Granite Lake in only a few hours. You must have a backpacking stove for camping by the lake or anywhere above 10,000 feet.

User Groups: Hikers and horses. No dogs or mountain bikes. No wheelchair facilities.

Permits: There is a $20 entrance fee per vehicle at Sequoia and Kings Canyon National Parks, good for seven days. Wilderness permits are required for overnight stays. They are available on a first-come, first-served basis at the wilderness permit station at Roads End or the Kings Canyon Visitors Center. For advanced wilderness permits or information on trail conditions, go to www.nps.gov/seki. Trailhead quotas are in effect from May to September.

Maps: A Sequoia and Kings Canyon map is available from Tom Harrison Maps. For a top-ographic map, go to the USGS website to download Sphinx.

Directions: From Fresno, drive east on Highway 180 for 55 miles to the Big Stump Entrance at Kings Canyon National Park. Continue 1.5 miles and turn left, following signs for Kings Canyon and Cedar Grove. Continue 38 miles on Highway 180 to Road's End, six miles past Cedar Grove Village. The trail begins at the long-term parking area.

Contact: Sequoia and Kings Canyon National Parks, Three Rivers, 559/565-3341 or 559/565-4307, www.nps.gov/seki.

38 REDWOOD CANYON
4.0 mi/2.0 hr ♟2 ⛰10

southeast of the Grant Grove area of Kings Canyon National Park

Map 11.3, page 545   **BEST (**

Several loop trips are possible in the Redwood Mountain area of Kings Canyon National Park, but one of the prettiest and simplest trips is just an out-and-back walk on Redwood Canyon Trail, paralleling Redwood Creek. The beauty begins before you even start walking; on the last mile of the drive to the trailhead, the dirt access road winds through giant sequoias that are so close, you can reach out your car window and touch them. The trail leads downhill from the parking area, and in just over 0.3 mile, you reach a junction and follow Redwood Creek Trail to the right. You'll find that this sequoia grove is far denser than many. Because they are situated by Redwood Creek, the sequoias grow amid a thriving background of dogwoods, firs, ceanothus, and mountain misery. Though the standing sequoias are impressive, some of the fallen ones are really amazing, because you get a close-up look at their immense size. Make sure you hike the full two miles to the stream crossing of Redwood Creek. Some of the best tree specimens are found there, near the junction with Sugar Bowl Loop Trail. The return trip is all uphill but easier than you'd expect.

User Groups: Hikers only. No dogs, horses, or mountain bikes. No wheelchair facilities.

Permits: No permits are required. There is a $20 entrance fee per vehicle at Sequoia and Kings Canyon National Parks, good for seven days.

Maps: A Sequoia and Kings Canyon map is available from Tom Harrison Maps. For a top-ographic map, go to the USGS website to download General Grant Grove.

Directions: From Fresno, drive east on Highway 180 for 55 miles to the Big Stump Entrance at Kings Canyon National Park. Continue 1.5 miles and turn right on the Generals Highway, heading for Sequoia National Park. Drive approximately three miles on the Generals Highway to Quail Flat, signed for Hume Lake to the left, and turn right on the dirt road to Redwood Saddle. Drive 1.5 miles and park in the parking lot. Take the trail signed for the Hart Tree and Redwood Canyon.

Contact: Sequoia and Kings Canyon National Parks, Three Rivers, 559/565-3341 or 559/565-4307, www.nps.gov/seki.

39 REDWOOD MOUNTAIN LOOP
10.0 mi/5.0 hr ♟3 ⛰10

southeast of the Grant Grove area of Kings Canyon National Park

Map 11.3, page 545

If you have most of a day to hike in the Redwood Mountain area of Kings Canyon National Park, you're in luck. This is one of the best day hikes in all of Kings Canyon. The Redwood Mountain Loop combines the best highlights of the area into one long trail, on which you'll wander in near solitude among the giant sequoias. If the paved, crowded trails to the General Grant Tree and the General Sherman Tree turn you off, this trail will turn you on. Start by hiking on the signed Burnt Grove/Sugar Bowl Loop Trail, which leads uphill from the parking lot. It's one mile to Burnt Grove and 2.5 miles to Sugar Bowl Grove; both are very dense stands of sequoias. Beyond the groves you descend for two miles to intersect with Redwood Canyon Trail. Head downhill and cross Redwood Creek, then proceed to the Fallen Goliath, a mammoth downed tree. One mile farther, you reach the Hart Tree, the largest tree in this area and a real show-stopper. In the final three miles, you get to walk through the Tunnel Log, a hollowed sequoia, and pass by pretty Hart Meadow. Note that if you tire out halfway through this loop, you can always follow the Redwood Canyon Trail uphill back to the start, cutting three miles off your round-trip.

User Groups: Hikers only. No dogs, horses, or mountain bikes. No wheelchair facilities.

Permits: No permits are required. There is a $20 entrance fee per vehicle at Sequoia and Kings Canyon National Parks, good for seven days.

Maps: A Sequoia and Kings Canyon map is available from Tom Harrison Maps. For a topographic map, go to the USGS website to download General Grant Grove.

Directions: From Fresno, drive east on Highway 180 for 55 miles to the Big Stump Entrance at Kings Canyon National Park. Continue 1.5 miles and turn right on the Generals Highway, heading for Sequoia National Park. Drive approximately three miles on the Generals Highway to Quail Flat, signed for Hume Lake to the left, and turn right on the dirt road to Redwood Saddle. Drive 1.5 miles and park in the parking lot. Take the trail signed as Burnt Grove/Sugar Bowl Loop.

Contact: Sequoia and Kings Canyon National Parks, Three Rivers, 559/565-3341 or 559/565-4307, www.nps.gov/seki.

40 BUENA VISTA PEAK

2.0 mi/1.0 hr

southeast of the Grant Grove area of Kings Canyon National Park

Map 11.3, page 545

Forget driving to the Kings Canyon Overlook, because just across the road is a trailhead with an easy walk and even better views, plus a chance at a private picnic spot. Buena Vista Peak is not a summit but a rocky dome, peaking at 7,603 feet, and it is one of the highest points west of Generals Highway. It offers far-reaching views of what looks like a million conifers at your feet and the hazy foothills to the southwest. But the best vistas are to the east of the snowcapped peaks of the John Muir and Monarch Wildernesses. An easy half-hour walk takes you up the back side of the dome, passing through pine and fir forest, manzanita, and sage, and walking by some interesting rock formations. Don't miss the giant boulder sculptures in the trail's first 0.25 mile. At the top of Buena Vista Peak, you can wander all around the spacious granite summit, enjoying different perspectives on the vista, before heading back to the parking lot. It's downhill all the way.

User Groups: Hikers only. No dogs, horses, or mountain bikes. No wheelchair facilities.

Permits: No permits are required. There is a $20 entrance fee per vehicle at Sequoia and Kings Canyon National Parks, good for seven days.

Maps: A Sequoia and Kings Canyon map is available from Tom Harrison Maps. For a topographic map, go to the USGS website to download General Grant Grove.

Directions: From Fresno, drive east on Highway 180 for 55 miles to the Big Stump Entrance at Kings Canyon National Park. Continue 1.5 miles and turn right on the Generals Highway, heading for Sequoia National Park. Drive approximately five miles on the Generals Highway to the Buena Vista trailhead on the right, just across the road and slightly beyond the large pullout for the Kings Canyon Overlook, on the left.

Contact: Sequoia and Kings Canyon National Parks, Three Rivers, 559/565-3341 or 559/565-4307, www.nps.gov/seki.

41 WEAVER LAKE

6.2 mi/3.0 hr or 2 days

in the Jennie Lakes Wilderness

Map 11.3, page 545

Note: This trail was in the path of the Rough Fire of August 2015 and is closed at this book's press time. Check with the Hume Lake Ranger District for an update before you visit.

Tucked into a corner just outside the border of Kings Canyon and Sequoia National Parks, the Jennie Lakes Wilderness is a 10,500-acre wilderness area that is often overlooked by park visitors. It offers much of the same scenery as the national parks, with beautiful lakes, meadows, forests, and streams, but without all the fanfare and crowds. Weaver Lake is the easiest-to-reach destination in the wilderness, and it makes a perfect family backpacking trip or an equally nice day hike. The trail is well

signed and passes through a mix of fir forest and meadows. At 1.7 miles, take the left fork for Weaver Lake, climbing uphill to the lake's basin. You'll spy the shelflike slabs of Shell Mountain peeking out above the trees. At just over three miles and at 8,700 feet in elevation, shallow but pretty Weaver Lake is set at the base of Shell Mountain's high, rounded ridge. You can try your luck fishing, or just find a lakeside seat and gaze at the view. On warm days, the brave go swimming.

Note that the road to Big Meadows is usually the last road to open in the area after snowmelt. If you're planning an early season trip, call to check on road and trail conditions.

User Groups: Hikers, dogs, and horses. No mountain bikes. No wheelchair facilities.

Permits: A free campfire permit is required for overnight stays and is available from the Hume Lake Ranger Station. There is a $20 entrance fee per vehicle at Sequoia and Kings Canyon National Parks, good for seven days in both the national forest and the national parks.

Maps: A Jennie Lakes Wilderness map is available from the U.S. Forest Service. A map of

Buena Vista Peak

© ANN MARIE BROWN

Sequoia and Kings Canyon is available from Tom Harrison Maps. For a topographic map, go to the USGS website to download Muir Grove.

Directions: From Fresno, drive east on Highway 180 for 55 miles to the Big Stump Entrance at Kings Canyon National Park. Continue 1.5 miles and turn right on the Generals Highway, heading for Sequoia National Park. Drive seven miles and turn left on Forest Road 14S11, at the sign for Big Meadows and Horse Corral. Drive three miles to the Big Meadows trailhead.

Contact: Giant Sequoia National Monument/Sequoia National Forest, Hume Lake Ranger District, Dunlap, 559/338-2251, www.fs.usda.gov/sequoia.

42 JENNIE ELLIS LAKE
12.0 mi/6.0 hr or 2 days 🥾3 ⛺10

in the Jennie Lakes Wilderness

Map 11.3, page 545

Note: This trail was in the path of the Rough Fire of August 2015 and is closed at this book's press time. Check with the Hume Lake Ranger District for an update before you visit.

This trail into the Jennie Lakes Wilderness offers more of a challenge than the route to Weaver Lake, climbing 1,500 feet over six miles with some short, steep pitches. The rewards are also greater, because Jennie Ellis Lake is a beauty and receives fewer visitors than Weaver Lake. The trail is the same as the Weaver Lake Trail for 1.7 miles, but at the fork, you bear right for Jennie Ellis Lake. The trail climbs and dips through fir, pine, and manzanita forest, then crosses Poop Out Pass at 4.7 miles, the highest point on this trip. At nearly six miles, you reach the outlet stream for Jennie Ellis Lake. Follow the short spur trail to the lake, set at 9,000 feet. With a white granite backdrop and some sparse trees, the shoreline looks austere and barren, but beautiful just the same. Campsites are found around the lake, and catching fish for dinner is a fair possibility. If you only came for

the day, find a comfortable spot to sit and admire the scenery before you head back.

Note that there is a somewhat shorter trail to reach Jennie Ellis Lake from Stony Creek Campground (10 miles round-trip instead of 12), but shorter doesn't necessarily mean easier. The shorter trail requires a 2,500-foot climb over the first 3.5 miles to Poop Out Pass, with several noticeably steep pitches along the way. At the pass, the two trails join and are one and the same on the final stretch to the lake.

User Groups: Hikers, dogs, and horses. No mountain bikes. No wheelchair facilities.

Permits: A free campfire permit is required for overnight stays and is available from the Hume Lake Ranger Station. There is a $20 entrance fee per vehicle at Sequoia and Kings Canyon National Parks, good for seven days in both the national forest and the national parks.

Maps: A Jennie Lakes Wilderness map is available from the U.S. Forest Service. A map of Sequoia and Kings Canyon is available from Tom Harrison Maps. For a topographic map, go to the USGS website to download Muir Grove.

Directions: From Fresno, drive east on Highway 180 for 55 miles to the Big Stump Entrance at Kings Canyon National Park. Continue 1.5 miles and turn right on the Generals Highway, heading for Sequoia National Park. Drive seven miles and turn left on Forest Road 14S11, at the sign for Big Meadows and Horse Corral. Drive three miles to the Big Meadows trailhead.

Contact: Giant Sequoia National Monument/Sequoia National Forest, Hume Lake Ranger District, Dunlap, 559/338-2251, www.fs.usda.gov/sequoia.

43 MITCHELL PEAK
5.2 mi/3.0 hr 🥾4 ⛺9

in the Jennie Lakes Wilderness

Map 11.3, page 545

Note: This trail was in the path of the Rough Fire of August 2015 and is closed at this book's press time. Check with the Hume Lake Ranger District for an update before you visit.

If you have the legs for a 2,000-foot climb over 2.6 miles, you can stand atop the summit of Mitchell Peak, the highest point in the Jennie Lakes Wilderness, at 10,365 feet in elevation. The peak used to have a fire lookout tower on top of it, but the Forest Service stopped using it and burned it down. What remains is the fabulous view, one of the best in this area. It's a one-mile climb from the trailhead to Marvin Pass and the boundary of the Jennie Lakes Wilderness. Bear left (east) and climb some more. At 1.6 miles, you reach the next junction, signed for Mitchell Peak. Head left (north), and in one more mile, you'll make the brief climb to Mitchell's summit, which straddles the border of Kings Canyon National Park. From your rocky perch, you can look out on the Great Western Divide and the Silliman Crest. It's an exemplary spot to catch your breath.

User Groups: Hikers, dogs, and horses. No mountain bikes. No wheelchair facilities.

Permits: A free campfire permit is required for overnight stays and is available from the Hume Lake Ranger Station. There is a $20 entrance fee per vehicle at Sequoia and Kings Canyon National Parks, good for seven days in both the national forest and the national parks.

Maps: A Jennie Lakes Wilderness map is available from the U.S. Forest Service. A map of Sequoia and Kings Canyon is available from Tom Harrison Maps. For a topographic map, go to the USGS website to download Muir Grove.

Directions: From Fresno, drive east on Highway 180 for 55 miles to the Big Stump Entrance at Kings Canyon National Park. Continue 1.5 miles and turn right on the Generals Highway, heading for Sequoia National Park. Drive seven miles and turn left on Forest Road 14S11, at the sign for Big Meadow and Horse Corral. Drive four miles to the Big Meadow Campground and continue six more miles to Horse Corral Meadow. Turn right on Forest Road 13S12 and drive 2.8 miles to the Marvin Pass trailhead.

Contact: Giant Sequoia National Monument/

Sequoia National Forest, Hume Lake Ranger District, Dunlap, 559/338-2251, www.fs.usda.gov/sequoia.

44 BIG BALDY

4.6 mi/2.5 hr

southeast of the Grant Grove area of Kings Canyon National Park

Map 11.3, page 545

The trip to Big Baldy comes with a million views and a little workout besides. Views? We're talking Redwood Canyon, Redwood Mountain, Buena Vista Peak, Little Baldy, Buck Rock, and the Great Western Divide. A little workout? You've got to climb 1,000 feet, but it's nicely spread out over two miles. The trail alternates between thick forest cover and open granite areas as it winds along the rim of Redwood Canyon. In the forested stretches, we were amazed at how many birds were singing in the tall firs and cedars. The trail's initial vistas are to the west, but they keep changing and getting more interesting all the way to Big Baldy's 8,209-foot summit, where your view opens up to 360 degrees. Here you get your first wide-open views of the high Sierra peaks and the Great Western Divide to the east. This trail is so fun and rewarding, with so little suffering involved, that you may feel like you're getting away with something. A bonus: Because the first mile of trail faces to the west, this is a great area for watching the sunset. Big Baldy Trail is also ideal for snowshoeing in the winter.

User Groups: Hikers only. No dogs, horses, or mountain bikes. No wheelchair facilities.

Permits: No permits are required. There is a $20 entrance fee per vehicle at Sequoia and Kings Canyon National Parks, good for seven days.

Maps: A Sequoia and Kings Canyon map is available from Tom Harrison Maps. For a topographic map, go to the USGS website to download Muir Grove.

Directions: From Fresno, drive east on Highway 180 for 55 miles to the Big Stump

Entrance at Kings Canyon National Park. Continue 1.5 miles and turn right on the Generals Highway, heading for Sequoia National Park. Drive approximately 6.5 miles on the Generals Highway to the Big Baldy trailhead, on the right, shortly before the turnoff for Big Meadows, on the left.

Contact: Sequoia and Kings Canyon National Parks, Three Rivers, 559/565-3341 or 559/565-4307, www.nps.gov/seki.

45 MUIR GROVE

4.0 mi/2.0 hr

northwest of the Lodgepole area of Sequoia National Park

Map 11.3, page 545

Few people hike this trail unless they are staying at Dorst Campground, so you have a lot better chance of seeing giant sequoias in solitude in the Muir Grove than at many places in the park. After crossing a wooden footbridge, the trail enters a mixed forest of red fir, white fir, sugar pines, and incense cedars. In early summer, you can count the many varieties of wildflowers along the trail, especially where you cross tiny streams. The trail heads west and curves around a deeply carved canyon at one mile out. Just off the trail to your right is a bare granite slab with an inspiring westward view. The trail undulates, never climbing or dropping much, making this an easy and pleasant stroll. At 1.9 miles, you reach the Muir Grove, a small, pristine grove of huge sequoias. The first one you come to on your left is a doozy. The grove is made even more enchanting by the thick undergrowth of blue and purple lupine blooming amid the trees in early summer.

User Groups: Hikers only. No dogs, horses, or mountain bikes. No wheelchair facilities.

Permits: No permits are required. There is a $20 entrance fee per vehicle at Sequoia and Kings Canyon National Parks, good for seven days.

Maps: A Sequoia and Kings Canyon map is available from Tom Harrison Maps. For a topographic map, go to the USGS website to download Muir Grove.

Directions: From Fresno, drive east on Highway 180 for 55 miles to the Big Stump Entrance at Kings Canyon National Park. Continue 1.5 miles and turn right on the Generals Highway, heading for Sequoia National Park. Drive approximately 17 miles on the Generals Highway to the right turnoff for Dorst Campground. Turn right and drive through the campground to the amphitheater parking lot. Park there; the trail begins at a footbridge between the amphitheater parking lot and the group campground.

Contact: Sequoia and Kings Canyon National Parks, Three Rivers, 559/565-3341 or 559/565-4307, www.nps.gov/seki.

46 LITTLE BALDY

3.5 mi/2.0 hr

northwest of the Lodgepole area of Sequoia National Park

Map 11.3, page 545

Little Baldy, Big Baldy, Buena Vista Peak. Along this stretch of the Generals Highway, there are so many peak trails that offer far-reaching views, it's hard to choose where to start. Start here, on the Little Baldy Trail. It's a little more challenging than the Buena Vista Peak Trail, but it's shorter than Big Baldy Trail, and it offers eye-popping drama for remarkably little effort. Some claim that Little Baldy's view of the Silliman Crest, the Great Western Divide, Castle Rocks, Moro Rock, the Kaweah River Canyon, and the San Joaquin foothills is the best panorama in the park.

To see for yourself, set out from the trailhead, climbing through long, tree-shaded switchbacks, heading first north, then south. Check out the unusual view of Big Baldy off to your left (far across the highway) as you climb. After 1.2 miles, the trail leaves the forest and its many wildflowers, and your views start to open up. Hike along Little Baldy's ridgeline and make the final steep summit ascent. The trail gets a little hard to discern as you near Little Baldy's wide, bare summit, but just wander around until you find the highest spot with the best view. Take a seat—you'll want to stay a while.

Note: Be sure to pick a clear day for this hike. In summer, your best bet is to hike the trail early in the morning, before the Central Valley haze rises to the mountains.

User Groups: Hikers only. No dogs, horses, or mountain bikes. No wheelchair facilities.

Permits: No permits are required. There is a $20 entrance fee per vehicle at Sequoia and Kings Canyon National Parks, good for seven days.

Maps: A Sequoia and Kings Canyon map is available from Tom Harrison Maps. For topographic maps, go to the USGS website to download Muir Grove and Giant Forest.

Directions: From Fresno, drive east on Highway 180 for 55 miles to the Big Stump Entrance at Kings Canyon National Park. Continue 1.5 miles and turn right on the Generals Highway, heading for Sequoia National Park. Drive approximately 18 miles on the Generals Highway to the Little Baldy trailhead, on the left, a mile beyond the turn-off for Dorst Campground.

Contact: Sequoia and Kings Canyon National Parks, Three Rivers, 559/565-3341 or 559/565-4307, www.nps.gov/seki.

47 THE LAKES TRAIL

13.0 mi/2-3 days

off the Generals Highway in the Wolverton area of Sequoia National Park

Map 11.3, page 545

The Wolverton trailhead is at 7,200 feet, which gives you a boost at the start for this trip into the high country. The Lakes Trail is the most popular backpacking trip in Sequoia National Park, and it's easy to see why. Wide-open views and dramatic granite walls are standard fare as you hike. Part of the route is on a loop, with one side of the loop traveling to the Watchtower—a

1,600-foot-tall granite cliff that offers incredible vistas of Tokopah Valley and beyond. The trailside scenery begins in red fir forest, then enters polished granite country, and culminates in a rocky basin with three gemlike lakes—Heather, Emerald, and Pear—as well as many sparkling creeks. The total climb to Pear Lake is a mere 2,300 feet, spread out over 6.5 miles. Backpackers take note: You may camp only at Emerald and Pear Lakes, and no campfires are allowed.

Note: The Watchtower Trail usually isn't open until midsummer. When it is closed, you must take the alternate Hump Trail, which is not as scenic. If you're planning a trip for early in the year, check with the park to be sure Watchtower Trail is open.

User Groups: Hikers only. No dogs, horses, or mountain bikes. No wheelchair facilities.

Permits: There is a $20 entrance fee per vehicle at Sequoia and Kings Canyon National Parks, good for seven days. Wilderness permits are required for overnight stays. They are available on a first-come, first-served basis at the Lodgepole Visitors Center. For advanced wilderness permits or information on trail conditions, go to www.nps.gov/seki. Trailhead quotas are in effect from May to September.

Maps: A Sequoia and Kings Canyon map is available from Tom Harrison Maps. For a topographic map, go to the USGS website to download Lodgepole.

Directions: From Fresno, drive east on Highway 180 for 55 miles to the Big Stump Entrance at Kings Canyon National Park. Continue 1.5 miles and turn right on the Generals Highway, heading for Sequoia National Park. Drive approximately 27 miles on the Generals Highway, past the Lodgepole Village turnoff, to the Wolverton turnoff, on the left (east) side of the road. Turn left and drive to the parking area and trailhead.

Contact: Sequoia and Kings Canyon National Parks, Three Rivers, 559/565-3341 or 559/565-4307, www.nps.gov/seki.

48 HEATHER LAKE AND THE WATCHTOWER
9.0 mi/5.0 hr   🏃3   ⛰10

off the Generals Highway in the Wolverton area of Sequoia National Park

Map 11.3, page 545

There's no reason that day hikers should be denied the incredible joys of hiking Lakes Trail from the Wolverton area of Sequoia National Park. You don't have to carry a backpack, get a wilderness permit, or have two or more free days to hike the first part of Lakes Trail, which ascends to the top of the 1,600-foot Watchtower (a big chunk of granite) and then continues to rocky Heather Lake. If you're hiking in spring or early summer, call the park first to make sure Watchtower Trail is open. Otherwise you'll have to take the alternate Hump Trail, which is steeper and nowhere near as scenic. The route to the Watchtower is a ledge trail, blasted into hard granite, which creeps along the high rim of Tokopah Valley. Your view is 1,500 feet straight down. You can even see tiny people walking on the path to Tokopah Falls. It's incredible, although perhaps not a good idea for people who are afraid of heights. Walking up to the Watchtower is plenty exciting, but it's even more so when you reach the other side, where you can look back and see what you were walking on. Just 0.75 mile farther and you're at Heather Lake, which is designated for day use only, so it has no campsites. It has a steep granite backdrop and a few rocky ledges to sit on. Too many people here when you arrive? No big deal. It's only another 0.5 mile to even prettier Emerald Lake, and the trail is nearly level. After a rest, you get to head back and hike the Watchtower route all over again.

User Groups: Hikers only. No dogs, horses, or mountain bikes. No wheelchair facilities.

Permits: No permits are required. There is a $20 entrance fee per vehicle at Sequoia and Kings Canyon National Parks, good for seven days.

Maps: A Sequoia and Kings Canyon map is available from Tom Harrison Maps. For a topographic map, go to the USGS website to download Lodgepole.

Directions: From Fresno, drive east on Highway 180 for 55 miles to the Big Stump Entrance at Kings Canyon National Park. Continue 1.5 miles and turn right on the Generals Highway, heading for Sequoia National Park. Drive approximately 27 miles on the Generals Highway, past the Lodgepole Village turnoff, to the Wolverton turnoff on the left (east) side of the road. Turn left and drive to the parking area and trailhead.

Contact: Sequoia and Kings Canyon National Parks, Three Rivers, 559/565-3341 or 559/565-4307, www.nps.gov/seki.

49 ALTA PEAK
13.0 mi/1-2 days   🏃5   ⛰10

off the Generals Highway in the Wolverton area of Sequoia National Park

Map 11.3, page 545   **BEST (**

You say you like heights? You like vistas? Here's your trail, a 4,000-foot climb to the top of Alta Peak, an 11,204-foot summit in the Alta Country. Alta Peak and Mount Whitney are the only major summits in Sequoia National Park that have established trails, but both of them are still butt-kickers to reach. The trail to Alta Peak and Alta Meadow starts out the same as the Lakes Trail (from the Wolverton parking area), then it heads south (right) to Panther Gap, at 1.8 miles. After climbing through the forest to Panther Gap (at 8,450 feet), you get your first set of eye-popping views—of the Middle Fork Kaweah River and the Great Western Divide. Continue on the Alta Trail to Mehrten Meadow (at 3.9 miles), a popular camping spot, then reach a junction where you can go left for Alta Peak or right to Alta Meadow. You'll want to take both spurs if you have the time and energy. If you're exhausted, just walk to Alta Meadow, with its flower-filled grasses and exquisite mountain views, a flat one mile away. Alta Peak is two miles away via the left fork, with a 2,000-foot climb. These two miles are considered one of the toughest stretches of trail in Sequoia National Park due to the brutal grade and the 10,000-plus foot elevation here above tree line. The summit is at 11,204 feet, and, of course, it offers a complete panorama. Even Mount Whitney and the Coast Range are visible on a clear day.

User Groups: Hikers only. No dogs, horses, or mountain bikes. No wheelchair facilities.

Permits: There is a $20 entrance fee per vehicle at Sequoia and Kings Canyon National Parks, good for seven days. Wilderness permits are required for overnight stays. They are available on a first-come, first-served basis at the Lodgepole Visitors Center. For advanced wilderness permits or information on trail conditions, go to www.nps.gov/seki. Trailhead quotas are in effect from May to September.

Maps: A Sequoia and Kings Canyon map is available from Tom Harrison Maps. For a topographic map, go to the USGS website to download Lodgepole.

Directions: From Fresno, drive east on Highway 180 for 55 miles to the Big Stump Entrance at Kings Canyon National Park. Continue 1.5 miles and turn right on the Generals Highway, heading for Sequoia National Park. Drive approximately 27 miles on the Generals Highway, past the Lodgepole Village turnoff, to the Wolverton turnoff, on the left (east) side of the road. Turn left and drive to the parking area and trailhead.

Contact: Sequoia and Kings Canyon National Parks, Three Rivers, 559/565-3341 or 559/565-4307, www.nps.gov/seki.

50 PANTHER GAP LOOP
6.0 mi/3.5 hr   🥾3 ⛰8

off the Generals Highway in the Wolverton area of Sequoia National Park

Map 11.3, page 545

If you're not up for the marathon trip to Alta Peak, you can still get a taste of the high country on this loop from the Wolverton trailhead. Start hiking on the Lakes Trail from the east end of the Wolverton parking lot, and at 1.8 miles, bear right on the Alta Trail to parallel Wolverton Creek, following it to Panther Gap. Here, at 8,450 feet, you get an inspiring vista of the Middle Fork Kaweah River and the Great Western Divide. Check out 9,081-foot Castle Rocks, an obvious landmark. From the gap, turn right (west) and follow the Alta Trail to Panther Peak and Panther Meadow, then on to Red Fir Meadow. Finally, at 4.6 miles, bear right and complete the loop by descending to Long Meadow and then edging along its east side to return to the parking lot. By the way, don't get any smart ideas about hiking this loop in the opposite direction—it's a much steeper climb.

User Groups: Hikers and horses. No dogs or mountain bikes. No wheelchair facilities.

Permits: No permits are required. There is a $20 entrance fee per vehicle at Sequoia and Kings Canyon National Parks, good for seven days.

Maps: A Sequoia and Kings Canyon map is available from Tom Harrison Maps. For a topographic map, go to the USGS website to download Lodgepole.

Directions: From Fresno, drive east on Highway 180 for 55 miles to the Big Stump Entrance at Kings Canyon National Park. Continue 1.5 miles and turn right on the Generals Highway, heading for Sequoia National Park. Drive approximately 27 miles on the Generals Highway, past the Lodgepole Village turnoff, to the Wolverton turnoff, on the left (east) side of the road. Turn left and drive to the parking area and trailhead.

Contact: Sequoia and Kings Canyon National Parks, Three Rivers, 559/565-3341 or 559/565-4307, www.nps.gov/seki.

51 TOKOPAH FALLS
3.6 mi/2.0 hr   🥾1 ⛰10

off the Generals Highway in the Giant Forest area of Sequoia National Park

Map 11.3, page 545   **BEST (**

This is unquestionably the best waterfall day

hike in Sequoia and Kings Canyon National Parks, leading to 1,200-foot-high Tokopah Falls. It's also a perfect family hike, easy on the feet and even easier on the eyes. The scenery is spectacular the whole way, from the up-close looks at wildflowers and granite boulders to the more distant views of the Watchtower, a 1,600-foot glacially carved cliff on the south side of Tokopah Valley. Then there's the valley itself, with Tokopah Falls pouring down the smooth back curve of its U shape. Because the trail begins by the three huge Lodgepole Campgrounds, it sees a lot of foot traffic. Your best bet is to start early in the morning. Another unusual feature of the trail? Hikers see more yellow-bellied marmots on the Tokopah Falls route than anywhere else in the two parks. We saw at least 40 of the cute little blond guys sunning themselves on rocks. If you're lucky, one of them will whistle at you as you walk by.

User Groups: Hikers and horses. No dogs or mountain bikes. No wheelchair facilities.

Permits: No permits are required. There is a $20 entrance fee per vehicle at Sequoia and Kings Canyon National Parks, good for seven days.

Maps: A Sequoia and Kings Canyon map is available from Tom Harrison Maps. For a topographic map, go to the USGS website to download Lodgepole.

Directions: From Fresno, drive east on Highway 180 for 55 miles to the Big Stump Entrance at Kings Canyon National Park. Continue 1.5 miles and turn right on the Generals Highway, heading for Sequoia National Park. Drive approximately 25 miles on the Generals Highway to the Lodgepole Campground turnoff, then drive 0.75 mile to the Log Bridge area of Lodgepole Camp. Park in the large lot just before the bridge over the Marble Fork Kaweah River, and walk 150 yards to the trailhead, which is just after you cross the bridge.

Contact: Sequoia and Kings Canyon National Parks, Three Rivers, 559/565-3341 or 559/565-4307, www.nps.gov/seki.

Tokopah Falls

© ANN MARIE BROWN

52 TWIN LAKES
13.6 mi/1-2 days

off the Generals Highway in the Giant Forest area of Sequoia National Park

 Map 11.3, page 545

From the Lodgepole Campground trailhead (at 6,740 feet), the Twin Lakes are a 2,800-foot elevation gain and 6.8 miles away, making this a moderate backpacking trip or a long, strenuous day hike. It's a classic Sequoia National Park trip; one that is heavily traveled each summer. The terrain is an interesting mix of dense conifer forests, glacial moraine, and open meadows. From the trailhead, you climb past Wolverton's Rock to Cahoon Meadow at three miles, 0.5 mile beyond a crossing of Silliman Creek. You then continue to Cahoon Gap at 4.2 miles, cross over Clover Creek at five miles (campsites are found along the creek), bear right at the J. O. Pass Trail junction at 5.5 miles, and reach the Twin Lakes at 6.8 miles. The trail leads you directly to the larger Twin Lake; the smaller one is reached by following a spur. Both are shallow and have forested banks; some hikers try their luck fishing in the larger lake. Backpackers spending the night at Twin Lakes can hike farther the next day—over rocky Silliman Pass (at 10,100 feet) to the less-visited Ranger Lakes, three miles farther. Note that campfires are not allowed at Twin Lakes.

User Groups: Hikers and horses. No dogs or mountain bikes. No wheelchair facilities.

Permits: There is a $20 entrance fee per vehicle at Sequoia and Kings Canyon National Parks, good for seven days. Wilderness permits are required for overnight stays. They are available on a first-come, first-served basis at the Lodgepole Visitors Center. For advanced wilderness permits or information on trail conditions, go to www.nps.gov/seki. Trailhead quotas are in effect from May to September.

Maps: A Sequoia and Kings Canyon map is available from Tom Harrison Maps. For a topographic map, go to the USGS website to download Lodgepole.

Directions: From Fresno, drive east on Highway 180 for 55 miles to the Big Stump Entrance at Kings Canyon National Park. Continue 1.5 miles and turn right on the Generals Highway, heading for Sequoia National Park. Drive approximately 25 miles on the Generals Highway to the Lodgepole Campground turnoff, and then drive 0.75 mile to the Log Bridge area of Lodgepole Camp. The Twin Lakes trailhead is just beyond the Tokopah Falls trailhead and the bridge over the Marble Fork Kaweah River.

Contact: Sequoia and Kings Canyon National Parks, Three Rivers, 559/565-3341 or 559/565-4307, www.nps.gov/seki.

53 CONGRESS TRAIL LOOP
2.9 mi/1.5 hr   🥾1 ⛰9

off the Generals Highway in the Giant Forest area of Sequoia National Park

Map 11.3, page 545   BEST (

The Congress Trail, a two-mile loop that starts (and ends) at the General Sherman Tree, is a much-traveled route through the Giant Forest's prize grove of sequoias. The General Sherman sees the greatest number of visitors, because it is recognized as the largest living thing in the world (not by height, but by volume). After you leave its side and start on the Congress Trail, the crowds lessen substantially. You'll pass by many huge trees with placards displaying their very patriotic names, like the House and Senate clusters, the McKinley Tree, the Lincoln Tree, and... well, you get the idea. Every single giant sequoia is worth stopping to gape at. We rate the Congress Trail as the best level, easy trail for sequoia viewing in the park. Plus, the farther you walk, the more solitude you get. Make sure you pick up an interpretive brochure at the trailhead or at the Lodgepole Visitors Center.

The parking area for the Sherman Tree and the Congress Trail is 0.4 mile from the Sherman Tree for a total mileage of 2.9 miles—two miles for the loop plus the out-and-back to the parking area. (You can't park on the Generals Highway by the Sherman Tree unless your vehicle has a disability license plate. This parking area is now reserved for the Giant Forest shuttle bus and wheelchair users only).

User Groups: Hikers only. No dogs, horses, or mountain bikes. Wheelchair users can access this trail; in some areas they may need assistance.

Permits: No permits are required. There is a $20 entrance fee per vehicle at Sequoia and Kings Canyon National Parks, good for seven days.

Maps: A Sequoia and Kings Canyon map is available from Tom Harrison Maps. For a topographic map, go to the USGS website to download Giant Forest.

Directions: From Fresno, drive east on Highway 180 for 55 miles to the Big Stump Entrance at Kings Canyon National Park. Continue 1.5 miles and turn right on the Generals Highway, heading for Sequoia National Park. Drive approximately 27 miles on the Generals Highway, past Lodgepole Village, to the Wolverton turnoff on the left (east) side of the road. Turn left and drive to the General Sherman Tree parking area. (If you are riding the free Giant Forest shuttle bus, you can disembark right at the Sherman Tree. For details see www.sequoiashuttle.com.)

Contact: Sequoia and Kings Canyon National Parks, Three Rivers, 559/565-3341 or 559/565-4307, www.nps.gov/seki.

54 HAZELWOOD AND HUCKLEBERRY LOOP

4.5 mi/2.0 hr   👣2 ⛰8

off the Generals Highway in the Giant Forest area of Sequoia National Park

Map 11.3, page 545

This hike combines two loop trails in the Giant Forest area for an easy but excellent day hike, passing by many giant sequoias and peaceful grassy meadows. A bonus: These trails are generally less crowded than the other day hikes in the Giant Forest area.

From the Generals Highway, pick up the Hazelwood Nature Trail and take the right side of the loop to join Alta Trail and Huckleberry Meadow Trail Loop. Take Alta Trail for 0.25 mile and bear right on Huckleberry Meadow Trail, climbing a bit for one mile to the site of Squatter's Cabin, one of the oldest structures in Sequoia National Park, dating back to the 1880s. To stay on the loop, turn left by the cabin (don't take the trail signed for The Dead Giant). The trail skirts the edge of Huckleberry Meadow and heads north to Circle Meadow, where giant sequoias line the meadow's edges. There are several junctions, but stay on Huckleberry Meadow Trail. A half mile farther is a short spur trail on the left heading to the Washington Tree. Follow the spur to see the second-largest tree in the world (after General Sherman)—it's 30 feet in diameter and 246.1 feet tall. The trip finishes out on Alta Trail, where you return to Hazelwood Nature Trail and walk the opposite side of its short loop back to the Generals Highway.

User Groups: Hikers only. No dogs, horses, or mountain bikes. No wheelchair facilities.

Permits: No permits are required. There is

a $20 entrance fee per vehicle at Sequoia and Kings Canyon National Parks, good for seven days.

Maps: A Sequoia and Kings Canyon map is available from Tom Harrison Maps. For topographic maps, go to the USGS website to download Giant Forest and Lodgepole.

Directions: From Fresno, drive east on Highway 180 for 55 miles to the Big Stump Entrance at Kings Canyon National Park. Continue 1.5 miles and turn right on the Generals Highway, heading for Sequoia National Park. Drive approximately 30 miles on the Generals Highway, past Lodgepole and Wolverton, to the Giant Forest area of Sequoia National Park. The Hazelwood trailhead is on the south side of the highway, 0.25 mile before you reach the Giant Forest Museum.

Contact: Sequoia and Kings Canyon National Parks, Three Rivers, 559/565-3341 or 559/565-4307, www.nps.gov/seki.

55 HIGH SIERRA TRAIL TO HAMILTON LAKE

30.0 mi/3 days   👣3 ⛰10

off the Generals Highway in the Giant Forest area of Sequoia National Park

Map 11.3, page 545

This is a classic, easy-to-moderate, three-day backpacking trip in the High Sierra, with a two-night stay at Bearpaw Meadow Camp, a shady campground that clings to the edge of a granite gorge. The route follows High Sierra Trail from Crescent Meadow to Eagle View, then continues for 10 nearly level miles along the north rim of the Middle Fork Kaweah River Canyon. It's views, views, views all the way.

After a good night's sleep at Bearpaw Meadow, elevation 7,700 feet (reservations for a wilderness permit are definitely necessary in the summer months), you start out on an eight-mile round-trip day hike to Upper and Lower Hamilton Lake (at 8,300 feet), set in a glacially carved basin at the base of the peaks of the Great Western Divide. On the final day, you hike 11 miles back to Crescent Meadow, once again witnessing 180-degree views from the sunny High Sierra Trail. By the time it's all over and you're back home, your mind is completely blown by all the high-country beauty, and you've shot about a million pictures, none of which can compare to the experience of actually being there.

User Groups: Hikers only. No dogs, horses, or mountain bikes. No wheelchair facilities.

Permits: There is a $20 entrance fee per vehicle at Sequoia and Kings Canyon National Parks, good for seven days. Wilderness permits are required for overnight stays. They are available on a first-come, first-served basis at the Lodgepole Visitors Center. For advanced wilderness permits or information on trail conditions, go to www.nps.gov/seki. Trailhead quotas are in effect from May to September.

Maps: A Sequoia and Kings Canyon map is available from Tom Harrison Maps. For topographic maps, go to the USGS website to download Giant Forest and Lodgepole.

Directions: From Fresno, drive east on Highway 180 for 55 miles to the Big Stump Entrance at Kings Canyon National Park. Continue 1.5 miles and turn right on the Generals Highway, heading for Sequoia National Park. Drive approximately 30 miles on the Generals Highway, past Lodgepole and Wolverton, to the Giant Forest area of Sequoia National Park. Just beyond the museum, turn left on Crescent Meadow Road and drive 3.5 miles to the Crescent Meadow parking area.

Contact: Sequoia and Kings Canyon National Parks, Three Rivers, 559/565-3341 or 559/565-4307, www.nps.gov/seki.

56 HIGH SIERRA TRAIL AND EAGLE VIEW

1.5 mi/1.0 hr   🏃 1 ⛰ 10

off the Generals Highway in the Giant Forest area of Sequoia National Park

Map 11.3, page 545

Are you ready to be wowed? From the lower parking lot at Crescent Meadow, follow the trail that leads to the southern edge of Crescent Meadow, and at 0.1 mile, take the right fork that leads up the ridge on High Sierra Trail toward Eagle View. The High Sierra Trail is a popular trans-Sierra route that eventually leads to Mount Whitney, the highest peak in the contiguous United States. On this trip you won't go quite that far, but you will get a taste of the visual delights of this extraordinary trail. In less than 0.5 mile, you'll gain the ridge and start getting wondrous, edge-of-the-world views. Numerous wildflowers line the path, which hugs the edge of this high ridge. At 0.7 mile, you'll reach Eagle View, an unsigned but obvious lookout from which you get a fascinating look at Moro Rock to your right, Castle Rocks straight ahead, and dozens of peaks and ridges of the Western Divide far across the canyon. The vistas are so fine and the trail is so good that you might just want to keep walking all the way to Mount Whitney.

User Groups: Hikers only. No dogs, horses, or mountain bikes. No wheelchair facilities.

Permits: No permits are required. There is a $20 entrance fee per vehicle at Sequoia and Kings Canyon National Parks, good for seven days.

Maps: A Sequoia and Kings Canyon map is available from Tom Harrison Maps. For topographic maps, go to the USGS website to download Giant Forest and Lodgepole.

Directions: From Fresno, drive east on Highway 180 for 55 miles to the Big Stump Entrance at Kings Canyon National Park. Continue 1.5 miles and turn right on the Generals Highway, heading for Sequoia National Park. Drive approximately 30 miles on the Generals Highway, past Lodgepole and Wolverton, to the Giant Forest area of Sequoia National Park. Just beyond the museum, turn left on Crescent Meadow Road and drive 3.5 miles to the Crescent Meadow parking area.

Contact: Sequoia and Kings Canyon National Parks, Three Rivers, 559/565-3341 or 559/565-4307, www.nps.gov/seki.

57 CRESCENT MEADOW AND THARP'S LOG

1.6 mi/1.0 hr

off the Generals Highway in the Giant Forest area of Sequoia National Park

Map 11.3, page 545

Crescent Meadow is more than 1.5 miles long and is surrounded by giant sequoias. John Muir called it "the gem of the Sierras." We don't know how Muir would feel about the pavement that lines the trail around this precious meadow, but we hope he'd like this loop hike anyhow. Follow the pavement for 200 yards from the eastern side of the parking lot, and just like that, you're at the southern edge of beautiful Crescent Meadow. Take the right fork and head for Log Meadow and Tharp's Log. Log Meadow is as large and beautiful as Crescent Meadow, and Tharp's Log was the homestead of Hale Tharp, the first white man to enter this forest. He grazed cattle and horses here, and built a modest home inside a fallen, fire-hollowed sequoia. You can look inside Tharp's Log and see his bed, fireplace, dining room table, and the door and windows he fashioned into the log. (Children find this incredibly thrilling.) From Tharp's Log, continue your loop back to Crescent Meadow and around its west side, where you return to the north edge of the parking lot.

User Groups: Hikers and wheelchairs (with assistance). No dogs, horses, or mountain bikes.

Permits: No permits are required. There is a $20 entrance fee per vehicle at Sequoia and Kings Canyon National Parks, good for seven days.

Maps: A Sequoia and Kings Canyon map is available from Tom Harrison Maps. For topographic maps, go to the USGS website to download Giant Forest and Lodgepole.

Directions: From Fresno, drive east on Highway 180 for 55 miles to the Big Stump Entrance at Kings Canyon National Park. Continue 1.5 miles and turn right on the Generals Highway, heading for Sequoia National Park. Drive approximately 30 miles on the Generals Highway, past Lodgepole and Wolverton, to the Giant Forest area of Sequoia National Park. Just beyond the museum, turn

High Sierra Trail and Eagle View

left on Crescent Meadow Road and drive 3.5 miles to the Crescent Meadow parking area.
Contact: Sequoia and Kings Canyon National Parks, Three Rivers, 559/565-3341 or 559/565-4307, www.nps.gov/seki.

58 MORO ROCK
0.6 mi/0.5 hr

off the Generals Highway in the Giant Forest area of Sequoia National Park

Map 11.3, page 545   **BEST (**

Just about everybody has heard of Moro Rock, the prominent, pointy granite dome with the top-of-the-world sunset vistas, and if you're visiting the Giant Forest area of Sequoia National Park, well, you just have to hike to the top of it. When you climb those 380 stairs to the dome's summit and check out the view, you realize that unlike many famous attractions, Moro Rock is not overrated. It's as great as everybody says, and maybe even better. If you start your trip from the Moro Rock parking area, it's only 0.3 mile to the top, climbing switchbacks, ramps, and granite stairs the whole way. Railings line the rock-blasted trail to keep you from dropping off the 6,725-foot granite dome. What's the view like? Well, on a clear day, you can see all the way to the Coast Range, 100 miles away. In closer focus is the Middle Fork Kaweah River, the Great Western Divide, Castle Rocks (at 9,180 feet), Triple Divide Peak (at 12,634 feet), Mount Stewart (at 12,205 feet), and on and on. In a word, it's awesome. And even better, you don't get this view just from the top of Moro Rock—you get it all the way up, at every turn in the trail.

If you want the absolute best visibility, show up early in the morning, before the afternoon haze from the Central Valley obscures the view. On the other hand, that same haze creates amazingly colorful sunsets, so early evening is another fine time to be on top of Moro Rock.
User Groups: Hikers only. No dogs, horses, or mountain bikes. No wheelchair facilities.
Permits: No permits are required. There is

a $20 entrance fee per vehicle at Sequoia and Kings Canyon National Parks, good for seven days.

Maps: A Sequoia and Kings Canyon map is available from Tom Harrison Maps. For a topographic map, go to the USGS website to download Giant Forest.

Directions: From Fresno, drive east on Highway 180 for 55 miles to the Big Stump Entrance at Kings Canyon National Park. Continue 1.5 miles and turn right on the Generals Highway, heading for Sequoia National Park. Drive approximately 30 miles on the Generals Highway, past Lodgepole and Wolverton, to the Giant Forest area of Sequoia National Park. Just beyond the museum, turn left on Crescent Meadow Road, drive 1.5 miles, and take the right fork to the Moro Rock parking area.

Contact: Sequoia and Kings Canyon National Parks, Three Rivers, 559/565-3341 or 559/565-4307, www.nps.gov/seki.

59 SUNSET ROCK
2.0 mi/1.0 hr

off the Generals Highway in the Giant Forest area of Sequoia National Park

Map 11.3, page 545

The trail to Sunset Rock is a first-rate easy hike, perfect at sunset or any time. It gets much less traffic than you might expect, considering its proximity to Giant Forest. Leave your car in the lot across from the Giant Forest museum (make sure you stop in before or after your trip), then pick up the trail on the west side of the lot. The level path leads through a mixed forest (with a handful of giant sequoias) and crosses Little Deer Creek on its way to Sunset Rock. The rock is a gargantuan, flat piece of granite—about the size of a football field—set at 6,412 feet in elevation. Standing on it, you get a terrific overlook of Little Baldy to your right and a sea of conifers below, in the Marble Fork Kaweah River Canyon.

User Groups: Hikers only. No dogs, horses, or mountain bikes. No wheelchair facilities.

Permits: No permits are required. There is a $20 entrance fee per vehicle at Sequoia and Kings Canyon National Parks, good for seven days.

Maps: A Sequoia and Kings Canyon map is available from Tom Harrison Maps. For a topographic map, go to the USGS website to download Giant Forest.

Directions: From Fresno, drive east on Highway 180 for 55 miles to the Big Stump Entrance at Kings Canyon National Park. Continue 1.5 miles and turn right on the Generals Highway, heading for Sequoia National Park. Drive approximately 30 miles on the Generals Highway, past Lodgepole and Wolverton, to the Giant Forest area of Sequoia National Park. Park in the lot across from the Giant Forest museum, then pick up the signed trail on the west side of the lot.

Contact: Sequoia and Kings Canyon National Parks, Three Rivers, 559/565-3341 or 559/565-4307, www.nps.gov/seki.

60 PARADISE CREEK TRAIL
1.2 mi/0.75 hr   🥾1 ⛰️8

off Highway 198 in the Foothills region of Sequoia National Park

Map 11.3, page 545	BEST (

From Buckeye Flat Campground, Paradise Creek Trail meanders through oaks and buckeyes, and crosses a long, picturesque footbridge over the Middle Fork Kaweah River. An inviting, Olympic-sized pool is on the right side of the bridge, where campers often go swimming on summer afternoons. Save the pool for after your hike; for now, take the signed Paradise Creek Trail, at the far side of the bridge. You'll briefly visit the creek and then leave it, climbing into oak and grassland terrain. There are some high views of Moro Rock and Hanging Rock, but most of the beauty is right at your feet, in the springtime flowers that grow in the grasses and in the leafy blue oaks that shade them. The

maintained trail ends when it reaches Paradise Creek again, although a faint route continues along its banks.

User Groups: Hikers only. No dogs, horses, or mountain bikes. No wheelchair facilities.

Permits: No permits are required. There is a $20 entrance fee per vehicle at Sequoia and Kings Canyon National Parks, good for seven days.

Maps: A Sequoia and Kings Canyon map is available from Tom Harrison Maps. For a topographic map, go to the USGS website to download Giant Forest.

Directions: From Visalia, drive east on Highway 198 for 47 miles to the turnoff, on the right, for Buckeye Flat Campground, across from Hospital Rock. Turn right and drive 0.6 mile to the campground. Park in any of the dirt pullouts outside of the camp entrance; no day-use parking is allowed in the camp. You can also park at Hospital Rock and walk to the campground. The trailhead is near campsite No. 28.

Contact: Sequoia and Kings Canyon National Parks, Three Rivers, 559/565-3341 or 559/565-3135, www.nps.gov/seki.

61 MIDDLE FORK TRAIL TO PANTHER CREEK
6.0 mi/3.0 hr   🥾2 ⛰️8

off Highway 198 in the Foothills region of Sequoia National Park

Map 11.3, page 545

You want to be alone? You don't want to see anybody else on the trail? Just sign up for this trip any time between June and September, when the foothills have warmed up to their summer extremes. Don't be fooled by this path's name: The Middle Fork Trail is no streamside meander. Rather, it's a shadeless, exposed trail that leads high along the canyon of the Middle Fork Kaweah River—always at least 250 feet above it. In summer, it's hot as Hades, but this trail is perfect in winter and spring. Whereas most other trails in Sequoia and Kings

Canyon are still snowed under, you can take an early-season day hike or backpacking trip along Middle Fork Trail. The main destination is Panther Creek (at three miles), where the trail leads across the brink of Panther Creek's 100-foot dive into the Kaweah River. But you can hike farther if you wish. Although Middle Fork Trail is set in grasslands and chaparral, it offers some stunning views of the area's geology, including Moro Rock, Castle Rocks, and the Great Western Divide. We hiked this trail in August, and despite the fact that we were wilting from the heat, the expansive views kept our spirits up.

User Groups: Hikers only. No dogs, horses, or mountain bikes. No wheelchair facilities.

Permits: No permits are required. There is a $20 entrance fee per vehicle at Sequoia and Kings Canyon National Parks, good for seven days.

Maps: A Sequoia and Kings Canyon map is available from Tom Harrison Maps. For a topographic map, go to the USGS website to download Giant Forest.

Directions: From Visalia, drive east on Highway 198 for 47 miles to the turnoff, on the right, for Buckeye Flat Campground, across from Hospital Rock. Turn right and drive 0.5 mile to a left fork just before the campground. Bear left on the dirt road and drive 1.3 miles to the trailhead and parking area. In the winter, you must park at Hospital Rock and walk in to the trailhead, adding 3.6 miles to your round-trip.

Contact: Sequoia and Kings Canyon National Parks, Three Rivers, 559/565-3341 or 559/565-3135, www.nps.gov/seki.

62 POTWISHA TO HOSPITAL ROCK

5.0 mi/2.5 hr

off Highway 198 in the Foothills region of Sequoia National Park

Map 11.3, page 545

First, some advice: Don't hike this trail on a hot day. If it's summertime and you want to see the Monache Indian historical sites at Potwisha and Hospital Rock, drive to each of them and see them separately. In winter or spring, however, it's far more fun to take this five-mile hike through chaparral and oak woodlands, especially in March, when the wildflowers bloom. In the first 100 yards from the trailhead, you'll see Native American grinding holes and pictographs that look roughly like people and animals. You'll also pass many tempting pools in the Middle Fork Kaweah, which are frequented by swimmers and bathers in the summer. The trail climbs a gradual 2.5 miles from Potwisha to Hospital Rock, crossing the highway after the first mile. When you reach Hospital Rock, which is just a few feet off the road to Buckeye Flat Campground, you see a huge display of pictographs on its side. Across the campground road are more grinding holes in the boulders, and near them, a short paved path leads to deep pools and sandy beaches on the Middle Fork. Another path leads from the camp road to the underside of Hospital Rock, where there's a large, cavelike shelter. This is where a Native American medicine man healed the sick and injured, resulting in a white man naming this place Hospital Rock.

User Groups: Hikers only. No dogs, horses, or mountain bikes. No wheelchair facilities.

Permits: No permits are required. There is a $20 entrance fee per vehicle at Sequoia and Kings Canyon National Parks, good for seven days.

Maps: A Sequoia and Kings Canyon map is available from Tom Harrison Maps. For a topographic map, go to the USGS website to download Giant Forest.

Directions: From Visalia, drive east on Highway 198 for 44 miles to the turnoff, on the left, for Potwisha Campground, 3.8 miles east of the Ash Mountain entrance station to Sequoia National Park. Don't turn left into Potwisha campground; instead, turn right on the paved road opposite the campground. Drive past the RV dumping station to the signed trailhead and parking area.

Contact: Sequoia and Kings Canyon National Parks, Three Rivers, 559/565-3341 or 559/565-3135, www.nps.gov/seki.

63 MARBLE FALLS
7.0 mi/4.0 hr

off Highway 198 in the Foothills region of Sequoia National Park

Map 11.3, page 545

This is the waterfall to see in Sequoia National Park in late winter and spring. March and April are particularly good months to visit because of high flows in the Marble Fork Kaweah River and blooming wildflowers in the grasslands and chaparral that line the trail. From its rather banal start as a dirt road, this trail just keeps getting better as it follows the Marble Fork Kaweah River. There are no trail junctions to worry about; at 3.5 miles, the path simply dead-ends near the lower cascades of Marble Falls. Although much of the falls are hidden in the narrow, rocky river gorge, tucked out of sight, what is visible is an impressive billowing cascade of whitewater. Be very careful on the slippery granite near the river's edges; the current and the cold water are even more dangerous than they look. Aside from the waterfalls and the wildflowers, the other highlights on this trail are the colorful outcroppings of marble, particularly in the last mile as you near the falls. Remember, though, that in summer this area of the park can bake like an oven. If you make the trip to the falls from late May to September, get an early morning start.

User Groups: Hikers only. No dogs, horses, or mountain bikes. No wheelchair facilities.

Permits: No permits are required. There is a $20 entrance fee per vehicle at Sequoia and Kings Canyon National Parks, good for seven days.

Maps: A Sequoia and Kings Canyon map is available from Tom Harrison Maps. For a topographic map, go to the USGS website to download Giant Forest.

Directions: From Visalia, drive east on Highway 198 for 44 miles to the turnoff, on the left, for Potwisha Campground, 3.8 miles east of the Ash Mountain entrance station to Sequoia National Park. The trail begins across from campsite No. 15 in Potwisha Campground; park in the trailhead parking area in the camp.

Contact: Sequoia and Kings Canyon National Parks, Three Rivers, 559/565-3341 or 559/565-3135, www.nps.gov/seki.

64 PARADISE RIDGE
3.2 mi/1.5 hr

off Highway 198 in the Mineral King region of Sequoia National Park

Map 11.3, page 545

OK, you've just driven the 20 twisting miles into Mineral King from Three Rivers. You're tired, dusty, and itching to get out of the car and move your legs. What's the first trail you can reach in Mineral King? The Paradise Ridge Trail, and it climbs right away, getting you huffing and puffing and clearing out the road dust from your lungs. After the initial steepness of the trail, the grade becomes easier as it moves into switchbacks ascending the hill. Although much of this forest has been burned in recent years, the giant sequoia trees are thriving, some in clusters as large as 10 or more. At your feet are tons of ferns. As you climb, the views just keep improving—you see the East Fork Kaweah River Canyon below you, and far off, the Great Western Divide. You can hike all the way to the top of the ridge at three miles, but the views aren't any better there than they are on the way up. Most people just cruise uphill a way, and turn around when they've had enough. Besides the big trees and the big views, our favorite thing about this trail was that we saw more bears than people.

User Groups: Hikers and horses. No dogs or mountain bikes. No wheelchair facilities.

Permits: No permits are required. There is a $20 entrance fee per vehicle at Sequoia and

Kings Canyon National Parks, good for seven days.

Maps: A Mineral King map is available from Tom Harrison Maps. For a topographic map, go to the USGS website to download Silver City.

Directions: From Visalia, drive east on Highway 198 for 38 miles to Mineral King Road, 2.5 miles east of Three Rivers. If you reach the Ash Mountain entrance station, you've gone too far. Turn right on Mineral King Road and drive 20 miles to the Hockett Trail parking area, on the right, 0.25 mile past Atwell Mill Camp. Park there and walk back west on Mineral King Road about 0.3 mile to the trailhead for Paradise Ridge, on the north side of the road.

Contact: Sequoia and Kings Canyon National Parks, Three Rivers, 559/565-3341 or 559/565-3135, www.nps.gov/seki.

65 HOCKETT TRAIL TO EAST FORK BRIDGE

4.0 mi/2.0 hr   🥾1 ⛰️8

off Highway 198 in the Mineral King region of Sequoia National Park

Map 11.3, page 545

The Hockett Trail makes a fine day-hiking path in Mineral King. It's suitable for all kinds of hikers. Families with small children can just walk a mile downhill to the footbridge over the East Fork Kaweah River, where there is a small waterfall and many sculptured granite pools, and then turn around and head back. People looking for a longer trip can continue another mile to the East Fork Grove of sequoias and Deer Creek. Although some of this forest has been burned in recent years, most of the big conifers were spared, and the area is still quite beautiful. The trail starts in an area of sequoia stumps, near where the Atwell Mill cut lumber in the 1880s. Live sequoias still flourish farther down the path, near the river's edge; apparently they were spared because of their distance from the mill. The trail is well graded, and even the uphill return is only a moderate climb.

User Groups: Hikers and horses. No dogs or mountain bikes. No wheelchair facilities.

Permits: No permits are required. There is a $20 entrance fee per vehicle at Sequoia and Kings Canyon National Parks, good for seven days.

Maps: A Mineral King map is available from Tom Harrison Maps. For a topographic map, go to the USGS website to download Mineral King.

Directions: From Visalia, drive east on Highway 198 for 38 miles to Mineral King Road, 2.5 miles east of Three Rivers. If you reach the Ash Mountain entrance station, you've gone too far. Turn right on Mineral King Road and drive 20 miles to the Hockett Trail parking area, on the right, 0.25 mile past Atwell Mill Camp. Park there and walk into the campground to campsite No. 16, where the trail begins.

Contact: Sequoia and Kings Canyon National Parks, Three Rivers, 559/565-3341 or 559/565-3135, www.nps.gov/seki.

66 COLD SPRINGS NATURE TRAIL

2.0 mi/1.0 hr   🥾1 ⛰️8

off Highway 198 in the Mineral King region of Sequoia National Park

Map 11.3, page 545

You may not expect much from a campground nature trail, but Cold Springs Nature Trail is guaranteed to exceed your expectations. Not only is it lined with wildflowers along the East Fork Kaweah River and informative signposts that teach you to identify junipers, red and white firs, cottonwoods, and aspens, but the views of the Sawtooth Ridge are glorious. The loop is less than 0.5 mile, but from the far end of it, the trail continues along the East Fork Kaweah River, heading another mile into Mineral King Valley. Walk to the loop's far end, and then continue at least another 0.25 mile along the trail. It just gets prettier as it goes. You're in for a real treat if you take this walk right before sunset, when the valley's surrounding mountain peaks turn every imaginable shade of pink, orange, and coral, reflecting the sun setting in the west. The vistas are so beautiful that they can practically make you weep.

User Groups: Hikers and horses. No dogs or mountain bikes. No wheelchair facilities.

Permits: No permits are required. There is a $20 entrance fee per vehicle at Sequoia and Kings Canyon National Parks, good for seven days.

Maps: A Mineral King map is available from Tom Harrison Maps. For a topographic map, go to the USGS website to download Mineral King.

Directions: From Visalia, drive east on Highway 198 for 38 miles to Mineral King Road, 2.5 miles east of Three Rivers. If you reach the Ash Mountain entrance station, you've gone too far. Turn right on Mineral King Road and drive 23.5 miles to Cold Springs Campground on the right. The trail begins near site six. If you aren't staying in the camp, you can park by the Mineral King Ranger Station and walk into the campground.

Contact: Sequoia and Kings Canyon National Parks, Three Rivers, 559/565-3341 or 559/565-3135, www.nps.gov/seki.

67 FAREWELL GAP TRAIL TO ASPEN FLAT
2.0 mi/1.0 hr 🚶1 ⛺9

off Highway 198 in the Mineral King region of Sequoia National Park

| Map 11.3, page 545 | BEST (|

If ever there was a perfect family hike, this would have to be it. Actually, if ever there was a perfect hike for every two-legged person on the planet, this would have to be it. The glacial-cut Mineral King Valley—a peaceful paradise of meadows, streams, and 100-year-old cabins—has to be one of the most scenic places in the West, and possibly in the world. An easy stroll along the canyon floor leads you past waterfalls and along the headwaters of the East Fork Kaweah River, in the awesome shelter of thousand-foot cliffs. After walking to the trailhead near the horse corral, you follow Farewell Gap Trail (an old dirt road) for a mile, then cross Crystal Creek and take the right fork off the main trail. This brings you closer to the river, where you follow a narrow use trail to Aspen Flat (a lovely grove of trees), or to Soda Springs, situated right along the river's edge. There you can see mineral springs bubbling up from the ground, turning the earth around them a bright orange color. Bring a fishing rod on this trail if you like, but be absolutely certain to bring your camera.

User Groups: Hikers and horses. No dogs or mountain bikes. No wheelchair facilities.

Permits: No permits are required. There is a $20 entrance fee per vehicle at Sequoia and Kings Canyon National Parks, good for seven days.

Maps: A Mineral King map is available from Tom Harrison Maps. For a topographic map, go to the USGS website to download Mineral King.

Directions: From Visalia, drive east on Highway 198 for 38 miles to Mineral King Road, 2.5 miles east of Three Rivers. If you reach the Ash Mountain entrance station, you've gone too far. Turn right on Mineral King Road and drive 25 miles to the end of the road and the Eagle/Mosquito trailhead. Take the right fork at the end of the road to reach the parking area. Walk back out of the parking lot and follow the road to the horse corral; the Farewell Gap Trail begins just beyond it.

Contact: Sequoia and Kings Canyon National Parks, Three Rivers, 559/565-3341 or 559/565-3135, www.nps.gov/seki.

68 MOSQUITO LAKES
8.0 mi/4.0 hr or 2 days 🚶3 ⛺9

off Highway 198 in the Mineral King region of Sequoia National Park

| Map 11.3, page 545 |

Ah, paradise. You know you're in it as soon as

you park your car at the end of Mineral King Road. The Eagle/Mosquito trailhead is at 7,830 feet, and you set out from the parking lot near one of Mineral King's adorable cabins, left from the early 20th century and privately owned. Feel jealous? Keep walking; you'll get over it. In minutes you cross a footbridge over Spring Creek's cascade, called Tufa Falls because of the calcium carbonate in Spring Creek's water. Don't expect to see much of a waterfall—most of it is hidden by brush. At one mile, you reach the junction for Eagle Lake, the Mosquito Lakes, and White Chief Trails. Take the right fork, climbing steadily. At two miles, you reach the Mosquito Lakes junction and go right, leaving Eagle Lake Trail for another day. Climb up and then down the other side of Miner's Ridge, at 9,300 feet. The final descent covers 0.5 mile; you reach Mosquito Lake number one at 9,040 feet and 3.6 miles. It's considered to be the easiest lake to reach in Mineral King, with a mostly shaded trail and only a 1,500-foot gain on the way in, plus a 250-foot gain on the way out. Still, if you've visited any of the other spectacular Mineral King lakes, this lake will look a little disappointing. It's small, shallow, and greenish. But fear not: This is the first of several Mosquito Lakes, all of which are linked by Mosquito Creek. Hikers with excess energy can follow the stream uphill to four more lakes. There is no maintained trail to the upper lakes, but if you follow the use trail near the stream, the going is easier. The use trail begins on the west side of the stream at the first lake, navigates around the rocky slope behind the lake, and then crosses the stream above it. The climb from lake number one to lake number two is steep, with a 600-foot elevation gain in 0.5 mile, but it's worth it. Lake number two is the usual destination for day hikers; it's a blue, deep, granite-bound beauty and makes for an eight-mile round-trip. Backpackers will find the first campsites at Mosquito Lake number two (no camping is allowed at the first lake). Mosquito Lake number five is five miles from the Eagle/Mosquito trailhead.

User Groups: Hikers and horses. No dogs or mountain bikes. No wheelchair facilities.

Permits: There is a $20 entrance fee per vehicle at Sequoia and Kings Canyon National Parks, good for seven days. Wilderness permits are required for overnight stays. They are available on a first-come, first-served basis at the Mineral King Ranger Station. For advanced wilderness permits or information on trail conditions, go to www.nps.gov/seki. Trailhead quotas are in effect from May to September.

Maps: A Mineral King map is available from Tom Harrison Maps. For a topographic map, go to the USGS website to download Mineral King.

Directions: From Visalia, drive east on Highway 198 for 38 miles to Mineral King Road, 2.5 miles east of Three Rivers. If you reach the Ash Mountain entrance station, you've gone too far. Turn right on Mineral King Road and drive 25 miles to the end of the road and the Eagle/Mosquito trailhead. Take the right fork at the end of the road to reach the parking area. The trail begins at the far end of the parking lot.

Contact: Sequoia and Kings Canyon National Parks, Three Rivers, 559/565-3341 or 559/565-3135, www.nps.gov/seki.

69 EAGLE LAKE TRAIL

6.8 mi/4.0 hr   🏃3 ⛰️10

off Highway 198 in the Mineral King region of Sequoia National Park

Map 11.3, page 545

Eagle Lake has always been the glamour destination in Mineral King; the trail to hike if you can hike only one trail in the area. Why? The blue-green lake is drop-dead gorgeous, that's why, and the trail to reach it is challenging but manageable for most day hikers, with a 2,200-foot elevation gain spread out over 3.4 miles. The Eagle Lake Trail follows the same route as the Mosquito Lakes Trail (see listing in this chapter) until the two-mile point, near the Eagle Sink Holes. These geological oddities are small craters in the ground where Eagle Creek suddenly disappears underground. At the trail junction by the sink holes, go left for Eagle Lake. Enjoy the brief flat stretch here, because shortly, you'll gain another 1,000 feet over 1.4 miles. Much of the climb is in an exposed, rocky area—a large boulder field that gets baked by the sun on warm days. Well-graded switchbacks and beautiful scenery make it easier. Soon you arrive at Eagle Lake's dam, at 10,000 feet. The big lake is surrounded by glacially carved rock and has a few rocky islands. Brook trout swim in its clear waters. The trail continues along the lake's west side to many good picnicking spots and photo opportunities. Campsites are found near the lake; no camping is allowed between the trail and the lake.

User Groups: Hikers and horses. No dogs or mountain bikes. No wheelchair facilities.

Permits: There is a $20 entrance fee per vehicle at Sequoia and Kings Canyon National Parks, good for seven days. Wilderness permits are required for overnight stays. They are available on a first-come, first-served basis at the Mineral King Ranger Station. For advanced wilderness permits or information on trail conditions, go to www.nps.gov/seki. Trailhead quotas are in effect from May to September.

Maps: A Mineral King map is available from Tom Harrison Maps. For a topographic map, go to the USGS website to download Mineral King.

Directions: From Visalia, drive east on Highway 198 for 38 miles to Mineral King Road, 2.5 miles east of Three Rivers. If you reach the Ash Mountain entrance station, you've gone too far. Turn right on Mineral King Road and drive 25 miles to the end of the road and the Eagle/Mosquito trailhead. Take the right fork at the end of the road to reach the parking area. The trail begins at the far end of the parking lot.

Contact: Sequoia and Kings Canyon National Parks, Three Rivers, 559/565-3341 or 559/565-3135, www.nps.gov/seki.

70 FRANKLIN LAKES
10.8 mi/6.0 hr or 2 days 🥾3 ⛰10

off Highway 198 in the Mineral King region of Sequoia National Park

Map 11.3, page 545

Maybe the best thing about hiking to Franklin Lakes is the waterfalls you get to pass along the way—especially our favorite cascades, on Franklin Creek. Or maybe it's the prolific wildflowers along the trail, or the spectacular views over Mineral King Valley that you gain as you climb. Maybe it's the big lake itself, set below Tulare and Florence Peaks, or the fact that the trail to reach it is so well graded, with a 2,500-foot elevation gain spread out over 5.4 miles. What the heck—this trail is about as close to hiking perfection as you get.

The first two miles are nearly flat; the route winds along the bottom of Mineral King's canyon, following Farewell Gap Trail alongside the East Fork Kaweah River. You'll pass Tufa Falls, across the canyon, at 0.25 mile and Crystal Creek's cascades, on your side of the canyon, at one mile. The trail leaves the valley floor and starts to climb moderately, reaching the bottom of Franklin Creek's cascades at 1.7 miles. After crossing Franklin Creek, you continue south along Farewell Canyon, negotiating some switchbacks as you gain elevation. The views get better and better. One mile farther, Franklin Lakes Trail forks left off Farewell Gap Trail and starts climbing in earnest up the Franklin Creek Valley. At nearly 10,000 feet, the trail crosses Franklin Creek again, then parallels the creek for another mile to the largest Franklin Lake. Note that when you see the lake's dam straight ahead and an obvious campsite about 150 yards below it to the right of the trail, you should cut off the main trail. Walk to the camp and follow its use trail to the dam and the lake. The main trail switchbacks up and above the lake but doesn't go directly to its shoreline. Franklin Lake is a dramatic sight, surrounded by steep, snow-covered slopes and a few pines and junipers. Rainbow Mountain is on its northeast side; Tulare Peak is to the southwest.

User Groups: Hikers and horses. No dogs or mountain bikes. No wheelchair facilities.

Permits: There is a $20 entrance fee per vehicle at Sequoia and Kings Canyon National Parks, good for seven days. Wilderness permits are required for overnight stays. They are available on a first-come, first-served basis at the Mineral King Ranger Station. For advanced wilderness permits or information on trail conditions, go to www.nps.gov/seki. Trailhead quotas are in effect from May to September.

Maps: A Mineral King map is available from Tom Harrison Maps. For a topographic map, go to the USGS website to download Mineral King.

Directions: From Visalia, drive east on Highway 198 for 38 miles to Mineral King Road, 2.5 miles east of Three Rivers. If you reach the Ash Mountain entrance station, you've gone too far. Turn right on Mineral King Road and drive 25 miles to the end of the road and the Eagle/Mosquito trailhead. Take the right fork at the end of the road to reach the parking area. Walk back out of the parking lot, and follow the road to the horse corral; Farewell Gap Trail begins just beyond it.

Contact: Sequoia and Kings Canyon National Parks, Three Rivers, 559/565-3341 or 559/565-3135, www.nps.gov/seki.

71 WHITE CHIEF MINE TRAIL
5.8 mi/3.0 hr

off Highway 198 in the Mineral King region of Sequoia National Park

Map 11.3, page 545

If you're one of those liberated hikers who doesn't need to have an alpine lake in your itinerary to be happy, the trail to White Chief Bowl is a scenic route with much to offer, including an exploration of the White Chief Mine tunnel. Until the Park Service purchased it in 1998, the mine was private property within the national park and off-limits to hikers.

The first mile of the trail is the same as the route to Eagle and Mosquito Lakes, but you'll leave most everyone behind when you continue straight at the one-mile junction, while they bear right for Eagle Lake and the Mosquito Lakes. The White Chief Trail continues with a hefty grade—this second mile is the toughest part of the whole trip—until it tops out at the edge of a gorgeous meadow. Just after you cross a seasonal stream (often a dry ravine by late summer), look for the ruins of Crabtree Cabin, to the right of the trail. The cabin ruins are what is left of the oldest remaining structure in Mineral King. It was built by the discoverer of the White Chief Mine in the 1870s. Next comes White Chief Meadows, surrounded by high granite walls and filled with dozens of downed trees, evidence of harsh winter avalanches.

Beyond the meadow, the trail ascends slightly until it nears a waterfall on White Chief Creek. Shortly before the falls, the trail crosses the creek and heads uphill. Look for the opening to White Chief Mine in a layer of white rock just above the trail. Scramble off the trail a few yards to reach it. The mine tunnel is tall enough to walk into and dead-ends in about 150 feet. Beyond the mine the trail continues to Upper White Chief Bowl, passing dozens of limestone caverns along the way. Although tempting, these caverns should only be explored by those who are experienced and well equipped.

User Groups: Hikers and horses. No dogs or mountain bikes. No wheelchair facilities.

Permits: No permits are required. There is a $20 entrance fee per vehicle at Sequoia and Kings Canyon National Parks, good for seven days.

Maps: A Mineral King map is available from Tom Harrison Maps. For a topographic map, go to the USGS website to download Mineral King.

Directions: From Visalia, drive east on Highway 198 for 38 miles to Mineral King Road, 2.5 miles east of Three Rivers. If you reach the Ash Mountain entrance station, you've gone too far. Turn right on Mineral King Road and drive 25 miles to the end of the road and the Eagle/Mosquito trailhead. Take the right fork at the end of the road to reach the parking area. The trail begins from the far end of the parking lot.

Contact: Sequoia and Kings Canyon National Parks, Three Rivers, 559/565-3341 or 559/565-3135, www.nps.gov/seki.

72 TIMBER GAP TRAIL
4.0 mi/2.0 hr   🏃3 ⛰8

off Highway 198 in the Mineral King region of Sequoia National Park

Map 11.3, page 545

On this short but steep trail, you'll stand witness to the mining history of Mineral King. The trail climbs abruptly from the Sawtooth trailhead on an old mining path along Monarch Creek, and forks in 0.25 mile. Take the left fork for Timber Gap, which climbs through a dense fir forest and then opens out to switchbacks in a wide and treeless slope—the result of continual winter avalanches. The exposed slope is home to many mountain wildflowers. The climb ends in two miles at Timber Gap, elevation 9,450 feet, a forested pass. The stumps you see among the red firs remain from early miners who cut down the trees to fuel their fires and support their mining tunnels. A faint path heads east from the pass and leads to the remains of the Empire Mine and its buildings in just over one mile.

User Groups: Hikers and horses. No dogs or mountain bikes. No wheelchair facilities.

Permits: No permits are required. There is a $20 entrance fee per vehicle at Sequoia and Kings Canyon National Parks, good for seven days.

Maps: A Mineral King map is available from Tom Harrison Maps. For a topographic map, go to the USGS website to download Mineral King.

Directions: From Visalia, drive east on Highway 198 for 38 miles to Mineral King Road, 2.5 miles east of Three Rivers. If you reach the Ash Mountain entrance station,

you've gone too far. Turn right on Mineral King Road and drive 24.5 miles to the Sawtooth parking area, 0.5 mile before the end of the road.

Contact: Sequoia and Kings Canyon National Parks, Three Rivers, 559/565-3341 or 559/565-3135, www.nps.gov/seki.

73 MONARCH LAKES
8.4 mi/5.0 hr or 2 days   🏃3 ⛰10

off Highway 198 in the Mineral King region of Sequoia National Park

Map 11.3, page 545

The Monarch Lakes Trail leads from the Sawtooth trailhead at 8,000 feet in elevation and climbs 2,500 feet to the rocky, gemlike Monarch Lakes. The first lake is good, but the second lake is simply awesome, and the scenery along the trail is unforgettable. Walk 0.25 mile from the trailhead and take the right fork for Monarch and Crystal Lakes. After one steep mile, you'll reach Groundhog Meadow, named for the adorable yellow-bellied marmots that inhabit the area. (We like their blond coats and shrill whistles.) Beyond the meadow, the trail starts seriously switchbacking in and out of red fir forest, making a gut-thumping climb to the Crystal Lake trail junction. The trail forks sharply right for Crystal Lake, but you head left for one more mile—a relatively smooth mile, with the easiest grade of the whole route—to Lower Monarch Lake. (This section crosses an incredible talus slope.) Snow can often be found near the lake even in late summer, and the vista is dramatic, with Sawtooth Peak dominating the skyline. If you have a wilderness permit, you can find a campsite near the lake.

While the main trail continues north to Sawtooth Pass, a use trail leads southeast from the lower lake for 0.5 mile to Upper Monarch Lake. Basically you head directly up the cliff that forms the back wall of the lower lake. It's worth the climb. The upper lake is wide, deep blue, and dramatic, set at the base of barren, pointy Monarch Peak. The view from the upper lake's basin, looking back down at the lower lake and various Mineral King peaks, is breathtaking. A big surprise is that the upper lake has been dammed, like many of the high lakes in Mineral King, and is operated by Southern California Edison. Note: If you're backpacking and want to take a first-rate side trip, the trail to Sawtooth Pass is a 1.3-mile, 1,200-foot climb that's not easy, but Sawtooth Pass offers one of the best views in the Southern Sierra.

User Groups: Hikers and horses. No dogs or mountain bikes. No wheelchair facilities.

Permits: There is a $20 entrance fee per vehicle at Sequoia and Kings Canyon National Parks, good for seven days. Wilderness permits are required for overnight stays. They are available on a first-come, first-served basis at the Mineral King Ranger Station. For advanced wilderness permits or information on trail conditions, go to www.nps.gov/seki. Trailhead quotas are in effect from May to September.

Maps: A Mineral King map is available from Tom Harrison Maps. For a topographic map, go to the USGS website to download Mineral King.

Directions: From Visalia, drive east on Highway 198 for 38 miles to Mineral King Road, 2.5 miles east of Three Rivers. If you reach the Ash Mountain entrance station, you've gone too far. Turn right on Mineral King Road and drive 24.5 miles to the Sawtooth parking area, 0.5 mile before the end of the road.

Contact: Sequoia and Kings Canyon National Parks, Three Rivers, 559/565-3341 or 559/565-3135, www.nps.gov/seki.

74 CRYSTAL LAKE TRAIL
9.8 mi/6.0 hr or 2 days 👣4 ⛰10

off Highway 198 in the Mineral King region of Sequoia National Park

Map 11.3, page 545

The long and arduous path to Crystal Lake follows the same route as the trail to Monarch Lakes (see listing in this chapter) for the first 3.2 miles. In Chihuahua Bowl, a sharp right-hand turn puts you on the trail to Crystal Lake. In 0.5 mile, the trail leads past the ruins of the

Monarch Lakes

© ANN MARIE BROWN

Chihuahua Mine (on the right), one of Mineral King's last hopes for silver riches. Like the other mines in the area, it never produced ore to equal the miners' dreams. The trail climbs abruptly over a rocky slope to a ridge of reddish foxtail pines, where your vista opens wide. Far off you can see the Farewell Gap peaks, and down below you see the Cobalt Lakes and Crystal Creek, pouring down to the Mineral King Valley and the East Fork Kaweah River. The trail continues, following more switchbacks, to upper Crystal Creek and Crystal Lake, which has been dammed. Off to the left (north), Mineral Peak stands out at 11,500 feet, and to the right (south), Rainbow Mountain shows off its colorful rock. Views are spectacular in every direction. If you scramble 0.25 mile off-trail toward Mineral Peak, you will reach Little Crystal Lake, where you have a near guarantee of solitude and a vista you won't forget.

User Groups: Hikers and horses. No dogs or mountain bikes. No wheelchair facilities.

Permits: There is a $20 entrance fee per vehicle at Sequoia and Kings Canyon National Parks, good for seven days. Wilderness permits are required for overnight stays. They are available on a first-come, first-served basis at the Mineral King Ranger Station. For advanced wilderness permits or information on trail conditions, go to www.nps.gov/seki. Trailhead quotas are in effect from May to September.

Maps: A Mineral King map is available from Tom Harrison Maps. For a topographic map, go to the USGS website to download Mineral King.

Directions: From Visalia, drive east on Highway 198 for 38 miles to Mineral King Road, 2.5 miles east of Three Rivers. If you reach the Ash Mountain entrance station, you've gone too far. Turn right on Mineral King Road and drive 24.5 miles to the Sawtooth parking area, 0.5 mile before the end of the road.

Contact: Sequoia and Kings Canyon National Parks, Three Rivers, 559/565-3341 or 559/565-3135, www.nps.gov/seki.

7.5 BLACK WOLF FALLS
0.5 mi/0.5 hr

off Highway 198 in the Mineral King region of Sequoia National Park

Map 11.3, page 545

This hike is really just a stroll, and the destination is readily apparent from the Sawtooth trailhead: Black Wolf Falls, tumbling down the canyon wall in Mineral King Valley. But aside from the chance to get close to a pretty waterfall, the hike is interesting because of its historical significance. Black Wolf's name is actually an alteration of its original moniker, which was Black Wall Falls, named for the Black Wall copper mine that was located at the waterfall's base. Back in the 1870s, when miners believed that Mineral King was rich in more than just scenery, they mined the base of Monarch Creek with a modicum of success. Today you can walk right up to the falls and see the mine tunnel on its right side (it looks like a cave, but don't go inside; it's unstable). In summer, rangers lead group hikes to the waterfall and talk about Mineral King's mining history. Although the route to Black Wolf Falls isn't an official trail, the path is well used and clearly visible. If you can find its beginning across the road from the No Parking Any Time sign, the rest of the hike is easy.

User Groups: Hikers only. No dogs, horses, or mountain bikes. No wheelchair facilities.

Permits: No permits are required. There is a $20 entrance fee per vehicle at Sequoia and Kings Canyon National Parks, good for seven days.

Maps: A Mineral King map is available from Tom Harrison Maps. For a topographic map, go to the USGS website to download Mineral King.

Directions: From Visalia, drive east on Highway 198 for 38 miles to Mineral King Road, 2.5 miles east of Three Rivers. If you reach the Ash Mountain entrance station, you've gone too far. Turn right on Mineral King Road and drive 24.5 miles to the Sawtooth parking area, 0.5 mile before the end of the road. Walk up the road toward Black Wolf Falls, then look for a use trail across the road from the No Parking Any Time sign, just beyond where Monarch Creek flows under the road.

Contact: Sequoia and Kings Canyon National Parks, Three Rivers, 559/565-3341 or 559/565-3135, www.nps.gov/seki.

76 LADYBUG TRAIL
3.8 mi/2.0 hr

off Highway 198 in the South Fork region of Sequoia National Park

Map 11.3, page 545   **BEST (**

The South Fork area is the forgotten region of Sequoia National Park. Accessible only by a 13-mile dead-end road out of Three Rivers, South Fork is the place to go when you just want to get away from it all. Solitude in a national park? You can find it here (mostly because it takes about 40 minutes just to drive from Highway 198 in Three Rivers to the trailhead). The elevation is low (only 3,600 feet), so the area is accessible year-round, and there may be no finer winter walk than a hike on Ladybug Trail out of South Fork. The trail leaves the far end of South Fork Campground and heads through an oak and bay forest along the South Fork Kaweah River. At 1.7 miles, you reach Ladybug Camp, a primitive camping area along the river's edge, in the shade of pines and firs. A short scramble downstream of the camp gives you a look at Ladybug Falls, a 25-foot waterfall set in a rocky grotto. If you continue upstream, the trail leads another few hundred yards and then switchbacks uphill, heading for Whiskey Log Camp. A use trail leaves the main trail and continues a short distance upriver, where there are many beautiful rocky pools. And in case you haven't guessed, the trail, camp, and falls are named for the millions of ladybugs that winter near the river, then take flight in the spring to head back to the Central Valley to feed.

User Groups: Hikers and horses. No dogs or mountain bikes. No wheelchair facilities.

Permits: No permits are required. There is

a $20 entrance fee per vehicle at Sequoia and Kings Canyon National Parks, good for seven days.

Maps: A Sequoia and Kings Canyon map is available from Tom Harrison Maps. For a topographic map, go to the USGS website to download Dennison Peak.

Directions: From Visalia, drive east on Highway 198 for 35 miles to one mile west of Three Rivers. Turn right on South Fork Drive and drive 12.8 miles to South Fork Campground. (Nine miles out, the road turns to dirt.) Park at the Ladybug trailhead parking area.

Contact: Sequoia and Kings Canyon National Parks, Three Rivers, 559/565-3341 or 559/565-3135, www.nps.gov/seki.

77 GARFIELD-HOCKETT TRAIL
5.8 mi/3.0 hr

off Highway 198 in the South Fork region of Sequoia National Park

Map 11.3, page 545

The trip to the magnificent Garfield Grove is only 2.9 miles from South Fork Campground, and if you don't mind a steep climb and possibly sharing the trail with horse packers, you should be sure to take this hike. The trail climbs immediately and keeps climbing, but fortunately, it is shaded by oaks most of the way. The ascent rewards you with a continual view of distant Homer's Nose, a granite landmark that, although prominent, looks little like anybody's nose. In just under three miles of nonstop climbing, you reach the first of many sequoias in the Garfield Grove, reported to be one of the largest groves in the national parks. By the time you reach it, you've gained 2,000 feet in elevation, so pick a big tree to lean against, pull out a snack, and take a breather.

User Groups: Hikers and horses. No dogs or mountain bikes. No wheelchair facilities.

Permits: No permits are required. There is a $20 entrance fee per vehicle at Sequoia and

Kings Canyon National Parks, good for seven days.

Maps: A Sequoia and Kings Canyon map is available from Tom Harrison Maps. For topographic maps, go to the USGS website to download Dennison Peak.

Directions: From Visalia, drive east on Highway 198 for 35 miles to one mile west of Three Rivers. Turn right on South Fork Drive and drive 12.8 miles to South Fork Campground. (Nine miles out, the road turns to dirt.) Park at the trailhead at the far end of the campground loop, just before the parking lot for the Ladybug Trailhead.

Contact: Sequoia and Kings Canyon National Parks, Three Rivers, 559/565-3341 or 559/565-3135, www.nps.gov/seki.

78 FORESTRY INFORMATION TRAIL
1.0 mi/0.5 hr 🏃1 ⛰7

in Mountain Home Demonstration State Forest off Highway 190 near Springville

Map 11.3, page 545

Balch Park is the small county-run park within the borders of Mountain Home Demonstration State Forest, and its easy, one-mile nature trail is a great place to take your kids for the afternoon. The trail begins next to the main entrance to Balch Park Camp, across from the kiosk, and your first stop is a visit to the Hollow Log, which was used as a dwelling by various pioneers, Indians, and prospectors. You also get to see the Lady Alice Tree, which was incorrectly billed in the early 20th century as the largest tree in the world. Nonetheless, it's no slacker in the size department. Continuing along the route, you'll see and learn all about the trees and plants that thrive here, plus interesting stuff about forestry management practices. When you're finished hiking the nature trail, you can cross the road and throw a line into one of Balch Park's two small fishing ponds. (Note that the ponds have not been stocked in

2014 and 2015 because of the drought, but may be stocked again in the future.)

User Groups: Hikers, dogs, and horses. No mountain bikes. No wheelchair facilities.

Permits: No permits are required. Balch Park charges a $1 per person day-use fee.

Maps: A free brochure and map of Mountain Home Demonstration State Forest, which includes Balch Park, are available from state forest headquarters. For a topographic map, go to the USGS website to download Camp Wishon.

Directions: From Porterville, drive east on Highway 190 for 18 miles to Springville. At Springville, turn left (north) on Balch Park Road/Road 239, drive 3.5 miles, and turn right on Bear Creek Road/Road 220. Drive 14 miles to Mountain Home Demonstration State Forest Headquarters, pick up a free forest map, and then continue 1.5 miles farther to the entrance to Balch Park.

Contact: Balch Park, 559/539-3896; Mountain Home Demonstration State Forest, Springville, 559/539-2321 (summer) or 559/539-2855 (winter).

79 ADAM AND EVE LOOP TRAIL
2.0 mi/1.0 hr 🏃2 ⛰9

in Mountain Home Demonstration State Forest off Highway 190 near Springville

Map 11.3, page 545

On the Adam and Eve Loop Trail you can see the Adam Tree standing tall and proud, but its companion, the Eve Tree, is no longer thriving. It (she?) was axed during the infamous sequoia logging years, but the tree kept up the good fight until 2001, when a forest fire ended its life. The burnt snag remains. This trail is best accessed at the public corrals, one-quarter mile north of the pack station on Summit Road. Park at the corrals and begin your trip by taking the left side of the loop, heading uphill to the Adam Tree, the second-largest tree in this state forest, at 240 feet tall and 27 feet in diameter. You'll see the Eve Tree snag shortly thereafter. The big draw on the trail is visiting the "Indian bath-tubs" at Tub Flat, halfway around the loop; these are basins, formed in solid granite, that were probably used by Native Americans. No one is sure whether they are natural or hand-made. The basins are much larger than the tra-ditional Indian grinding holes that are found elsewhere in the Sierra. True to their name, they are large enough to bathe in.

User Groups: Hikers, dogs, and horses. No mountain bikes. No wheelchair facilities.

Permits: No permits are required. Parking and access are free.

Maps: A free brochure and map of Mountain Home Demonstration State Forest are available from forest headquarters. For a topographic map, go to the USGS website to download Camp Wishon.

Directions: From Porterville, drive east on Highway 190 for 18 miles to Springville. At Springville, turn left (north) on Balch Park Road/Road 239 and drive 3.5 miles; then turn right on Bear Creek Road/Road 220. Drive 14 miles to Mountain Home Demonstration State Forest Headquarters, pick up a free for-est map, and then continue one mile farther, turning right at the sign for Hidden Falls Recreation Area. Drive 3.5 miles to the pub-lic corrals, which are located one-quarter mile north of the pack station (before Shake Camp Campground). Park at the corrals.

Contact: Mountain Home Demonstration State Forest, Springville, 559/539-2321 (sum-mer) or 559/539-2855 (winter).

80 REDWOOD CROSSING
4.0 mi/2.0 hr

in Mountain Home Demonstration State Forest off Highway 190 near Springville

Map 11.3, page 545

An excellent easy hike for campers and day visi-tors at Mountain Home Demonstration State Forest is on Long Meadow Trail, from Shake Camp Campground to Redwood Crossing, on the Tule River. The trail starts by the public corral (elevation 6,800 feet) and leads through logged sequoia stumps to a thick mixed forest on the slopes high above the Wishon Fork Tule River. When the trail reaches clearings in the trees, the views of the Great Western Divide are excellent. At two miles out, you reach Redwood Crossing, a boulder-lined stretch of the river. Those willing to ford can cross to the other side and head into the Golden Trout Wilderness, but day hikers should pull out a picnic at the river's edge and make an afternoon of it. Backpackers heading for the wilderness need to secure a wilderness permit from the Western Divide Ranger District office.

User Groups: Hikers, dogs, and horses. No mountain bikes. No wheelchair facilities.

Permits: No permits are required. Parking and access are free.

Maps: A free brochure and map of Mountain Home Demonstration State Forest are available from forest headquarters. For a topographic map, go to the USGS website to download Camp Wishon.

Directions: From Porterville, drive east on Highway 190 for 18 miles to Springville. At Springville, turn left (north) on Balch Park Road/Road 239, drive 3.5 miles, and turn right on Bear Creek Road/Road 220. Drive 14 miles to Mountain Home Demonstration State Forest Headquarters, pick up a free forest map, and then continue one mile farther. Turn right at the sign for Hidden Falls Recreation Area. Drive 3.5 miles to Shake Camp Campground. The Long Meadow trailhead is located by the public corral.

Contact: Mountain Home Demonstration State Forest, Springville, 559/539-2321 (sum-mer) or 559/539-2855 (winter); Western Divide Ranger District, Springville, 559/539-2607, www.fs.usda.gov/sequoia.

81 MOSES GULCH TRAIL
4.0 mi/2.0 hr 🥾2 ⛰9

in Mountain Home Demonstration State Forest off Highway 190 near Springville

Map 11.3, page 545

For a less-crowded alternative to the popular Redwood Crossing (see listing in this chapter), you can take the other trail from the public corral at Shake Camp Campground and wind your way through stands of beautiful virgin sequoias to the Wishon Fork Tule River at Moses Gulch Campground. The Moses Gulch Trail crosses forest roads twice—the only downer—but it's an easy walk for families, and it's peaceful besides. Once you reach the river (at two miles), you have the option of hiking alongside it to the north or south, adding some distance to your trip. The northern stretch leads to Hidden Falls Campground (the home of many small falls and pools), and the southern stretch crosses pretty Galena and Silver Creeks, leading past a mining cabin and an old copper mine.

User Groups: Hikers, dogs, and horses. No mountain bikes. No wheelchair facilities.

Permits: No permits are required. Parking and access are free.

Maps: A free brochure and map of Mountain Home Demonstration State Forest are available from forest headquarters. For a topographic map, go to the USGS website to download Camp Wishon.

Directions: From Porterville, drive east on Highway 190 for 18 miles to Springville. At Springville, turn left (north) on Balch Park Road/Road 239, drive 3.5 miles, and then turn right on Bear Creek Road/Road 220. Drive 14 miles to Mountain Home Demonstration State Forest Headquarters and pick up a free forest map, then continue one mile farther and turn right at the sign for Hidden Falls Recreation Area. Drive 3.5 miles to Shake Camp Campground. The Moses Gulch trailhead is behind (south of) the public corral.

Contact: Mountain Home Demonstration State Forest, Springville, 559/539-2321 (summer) or 559/539-2855 (winter).

82 DOYLE TRAIL
6.0 mi/3.0 hr 🥾2 ⛰8

in Giant Sequoia National Monument near Springville

Map 11.3, page 545

The Doyle Trail is a great alternative to the heat of the San Joaquin Valley. It's in the transition zone between foothills and conifers, with plenty of shade from tall manzanita, oaks, madrones, and pines. Squirrels and lizards are your primary companions on the trail, which laterals along the slopes above the Wishon fork of the Tule River. From the gated trailhead, hike up the paved road and bear left to bypass Doyle Springs, a community of private cabins. Follow the trail that is signed Trail to Upstream Fishing. The route climbs gently through the forest for 2.5 miles and then suddenly descends to the same level as the river, where there are some primitive campsites available. Then the trail rises again, climbing for another 0.5 mile to a clearing on the right, where there is an outcrop of jagged green rock alongside the river. Leave the trail and cross over the rock, where you'll find a few picture-perfect swimming holes and small waterfalls.

User Groups: Hikers, dogs, and horses. No mountain bikes. No wheelchair facilities.

Permits: A free wilderness permit is required for overnight stays and is available from the Springville or Kernville Ranger Stations at the addresses below. Parking and access are free.

Maps: A Sequoia National Forest map is available from the U.S. Forest Service. For a topographic map, go to the USGS website to download Camp Wishon.

Directions: From Porterville, drive east on Highway 190 for 18 miles to Springville. From Springville, continue east on Highway 190 for 7.5 miles to Wishon Drive/Road 208, a left fork. Turn left and drive four miles on Wishon Drive, then take the left fork, which is signed for day-use parking (above the campground). Drive 0.25 mile and park off the road, near the gate.

Contact: Giant Sequoia National Monument/ Sequoia National Forest, Western Divide

Ranger District, Springville, 559/539-2607, www.fs.usda.gov/sequoia.

83 JORDAN PEAK LOOKOUT
1.8 mi/1.0 hr 🏃1 ⛰9

in Giant Sequoia National Monument near Quaking Aspen

Map 11.3, page 545

You'll see some logging activity out here by Jordan Peak, but if you can put up with it, you can climb a mere 600 feet over less than a mile to reach the summit of this 9,100-foot mountain. Few summits are so easily attained (it's a well-graded and well-maintained trail), and this one is not lacking in dramatic vistas. You can see the Wishon Fork Canyon of the Tule River, Camp Nelson, the Sequoia Crest, Slate Mountain, Maggie Mountain, and Moses Mountain close up, and the Tehachapis and the Coast Range far, far away. The peak is covered with microwave equipment, but it doesn't mar the stupendous view. Head west from the trailhead on Jordan Lookout Trail, switchbacking up until you reach the catwalked stairs to the lookout, which was built in 1934. All the materials to construct the lookout were hauled in by mules.

User Groups: Hikers, dogs, horses, and mountain bikes. No wheelchair facilities.

Permits: No permits are required. Parking and access are free.

Maps: A Sequoia National Forest map is available from the U.S. Forest Service. For a topographic map, go to the USGS website to download Sentinel Peak.

Directions: From Porterville, drive 45 miles east on Highway 190 to Forest Service Road 21S50, near Quaking Aspen Campground. Turn left on Road 21S50 and drive five miles. Bear left and continue on Road 21S50 for 2.8 miles, bearing left on Road 20S71, signed for Jordan Peak Lookout, and following it one mile to its end, at the trailhead.

Contact: Giant Sequoia National Monument/ Sequoia National Forest, Western Divide

Ranger District, Springville, 559/539-2607, www.fs.usda.gov/sequoia.

84 CLICKS CREEK TRAIL
14.0 mi/2 days 🏃3 ⛰9

in the Golden Trout Wilderness near Quaking Aspen

Map 11.3, page 545

If you like peace and quiet on your backpacking trips, Clicks Creek Trail, in the Golden Trout Wilderness, may suit you just fine. The trail leads northeast from Log Cabin Meadow (elevation 7,800 feet), heading steadily downhill along Clicks Creek to the Little Kern River. The route crosses the creek several times. Shade lovers will thrill at the conifer forests that line the route, interspersed by large and grassy meadows, and anglers can bring along their gear to try their luck with the golden trout in the river. There are many possible campsites along the Little Kern, where the elevation is 6,200 feet.

User Groups: Hikers, dogs, and horses. No mountain bikes. No wheelchair facilities.

Permits: A free wilderness permit is required for overnight stays and is available from the Springville or Kernville Ranger Stations at the addresses below. Parking and access are free.

Maps: A Golden Trout Wilderness map is available from the U.S. Forest Service or Tom Harrison Maps. For a topographic map, go to the USGS website to download Sentinel Peak.

Directions: From Porterville, drive 45 miles east on Highway 190 to Forest Service Road 21S50 near Quaking Aspen Campground. Turn left on Road 21S50 and drive five miles; bear left and continue on Road 21S50 for 1.5 miles to the Clicks Creek trailhead, at Log Cabin Meadow.

Contact: Sequoia National Forest, Western Divide Ranger District, Springville, 559/539-2607, www.fs.usda.gov/sequoia; Sequoia National Forest, Kern River Ranger District, Kernville, 760/376-3781, www.fs.usda.gov/sequoia.

85 JOHN JORDAN/HOSSACK MEADOW TRAIL

5.0-6.0 mi/2.5-3.0 hr 👣2 ⛰8

in Giant Sequoia National Monument near Quaking Aspen

Map 11.3, page 545

Your route on the John Jordan Trail begins with a crossing of McIntyre Creek, then traverses a level mile to an old fence, gate, and McIntyre Rock—a huge pile of granite boulders with an excellent view. Climb on top of the rock's well-graded, cracking-granite back side and peer over its startlingly steep front side. Surprise! It's straight down, about 600 feet. The trail heads downhill through a red fir forest to Nelson Creek, the site of some logging work. Although you can walk another 0.5 mile to the trail's end (at Hossack Meadow), most people turn around at the sight of logged trees, making for a five-mile round-trip with a 1,000-foot elevation gain on the return. So who was John Jordan, anyway? He was a trailblazer in the 1870s who unfortunately was most famous for drowning in the Kern River on his way back to the Central Valley to tell everybody he had completed this trail, a proposed toll road.

User Groups: Hikers, dogs, horses, and mountain bikes. No wheelchair facilities.

Permits: No permits are required. Parking and access are free.

Maps: A Sequoia National Forest map is available from the U.S. Forest Service. For a topographic map, go to the USGS website to download Sentinel Peak.

Directions: From Porterville, drive 45 miles east on Highway 190 to Forest Service Road 21S50, near Quaking Aspen Campground. Turn left on Road 21S50 and drive 6.6 miles, then bear left on Road 20S81. Follow Road 20S81 for 1.4 miles to the signed trailhead.

Contact: Giant Sequoia National Monument/ Sequoia National Forest, Western Divide Ranger District, Springville, 559/539-2607, www.fs.usda.gov/sequoia.

86 FREEMAN CREEK TRAIL

4.0 mi/2.0 hr 👣2 ⛰8

in Giant Sequoia National Monument near Quaking Aspen

Map 11.3, page 545

The easternmost grove of sequoias in the world is your destination on Freeman Creek Trail. Compared to most sequoia groves in the Sierra, the trees of the 1,700-acre Freeman Creek Grove are mere adolescents—probably not more than 1,000 years old. Among them is a tree named for former President George Bush Sr., who visited the grove in 1992. The trail is a pleasant downhill stroll along Freeman Creek, reaching the first sequoias in about one mile, after crossing the creek. In between the big trees are large meadow areas (many of which bloom with spring and summer wildflowers) and forests of red firs. Many campsites are found along the creek. The path finally ends at Lloyd Meadows, three miles from the trailhead, but most people don't travel that far, since it requires too much climbing on the way back. Two miles out and back is just about perfect.

User Groups: Hikers, dogs, horses, and mountain bikes. No wheelchair facilities.

Permits: No permits are required. Parking and access are free.

Maps: A Sequoia National Forest map is available from the U.S. Forest Service. For topographic maps, go to the USGS website to download Sentinel Peak.

Directions: From Porterville, drive 45 miles east on Highway 190 to Forest Service Road 21S50, near Quaking Aspen Campground. Turn left on Road 21S50 and drive 0.5 mile, then turn right at the sign for the Freeman Creek Grove.

Contact: Giant Sequoia National Monument/ Sequoia National Forest, Western Divide Ranger District, Springville, 559/539-2607, www.fs.usda.gov/sequoia.

87 SUMMIT TRAIL TO SLATE MOUNTAIN

8.0 mi/4.0 hr   🏃3 ⛰9

in Giant Sequoia National Monument near
Quaking Aspen

Map 11.3, page 545

If you're staying at Quaking Aspen
Campground, you can set out on Summit
National Recreation Trail from outside your
tent door, but if you're not, drive to the trailhead just south of the camp off Road 21S78.
Few people hike all 12 miles of the trail, but
many take this four-mile jaunt to the summit of 9,302-foot Slate Mountain, the highest
peak in the area. The first two miles of trail
are easy, climbing gently through meadows
and forest (some logging activity can be seen);
then the route climbs more steeply, ascending
first the east side and then the north side of
Slate Mountain. Views of the granite spires of
The Needles and Olancha Peak can be seen. At
3.8 miles you reach a junction with Bear Creek
Trail, and from there, it's a short scramble to
your left to the top of Slate Mountain, which is a
big pile of rocks with a tremendous 360-degree
view. There's no trail, but a couple well-worn
routes are visible.

User Groups: Hikers, dogs, horses, and mountain bikes. No wheelchair facilities.

Permits: No permits are required. Parking and
access are free.

Maps: A Sequoia National Forest map is
available from the U.S. Forest Service. For a
topographic map, go to the USGS website to
download Sentinel Peak.

Directions: From Porterville, drive 46 miles
east on Highway 190 to Forest Service Road
21S78, which is 0.5 mile south of Quaking
Aspen Campground. Turn right on Road 21S78
and drive 0.5 mile to the Summit trailhead.

Contact: Giant Sequoia National Monument/
Sequoia National Forest, Western Divide
Ranger District, Springville, 559/539-2607,
www.fs.usda.gov/sequoia.

88 THE NEEDLES SPIRES

5.0 mi/2.5 hr   🏃2 ⛰10

in Giant Sequoia National Monument near
Quaking Aspen

Map 11.3, page 545   BEST (

Yes, it's sad but true—the historic Needles Fire
Lookout burned down in 2011 after an ember
escaped from its chimney, but you can still take
this wonderful easy day-hike in Giant Sequoia
National Monument and enjoy almost nonstop
views of the Sequoia backcountry. Plans are in
the works to rebuild the lookout tower by 2016,
providing that enough funds are raised (check
with the Western Divide Ranger District for an
update; 559/539-2607). At the trail's start is a
placard with an old black-and-white photo that
shows what the Needles fire lookout looked like
early in the 20th century. Five minutes down
the trail, you leave the forest and come out to
two wooden benches. This is a great spot to
stare out at the magnificent view of the Kern
River Basin before you. Look ahead and you'll
see The Needles' tall granite spires; the highest
spire is at elevation 8,245 feet. The trail goes up,
then down, then up again, through firs, pon-
derosas, sugar pines, granite, and sand. The
only steep section is the final set of switchbacks up The Needles. The fire lookout tower
no longer sits on top of the high spire known as
The Magician by local rock climbers, but hope-
fully it will be there again one day soon. If not,
you can just scramble on top of any boulder
to admire the view of Lloyd Meadow, the Kern
River drainage, Mount Whitney, Olancha Peak,
Farewell Gap, and Dome Rock. This is one of
the most inspiring views in the southern Sierra.

User Groups: Hikers, dogs, horses, and mountain bikes. No wheelchair facilities.

Permits: No permits are required. Parking and
access are free.

Maps: A Sequoia National Forest map is available from the U.S. Forest Service. For topographic maps, go to the USGS website to
download Sentinel Peak and Durrwood Creek.

Directions: From Porterville, drive 46 miles
east on Highway 190 to Forest Service Road

21S05, which is 0.5 mile south of Quaking Aspen Campground. Turn left (east) on Road 21S05 and drive 2.8 miles to the trailhead.

Contact: Giant Sequoia National Monument/ Sequoia National Forest, Western Divide Ranger District, Springville, 559/539-2607, www.fs.usda.gov/sequoia.

89 TRAIL OF 100 GIANTS
0.5 mi/0.5 hr 🥾1 ⛰10

in Giant Sequoia National Monument near Johnsondale

Map 11.3, page 545   BEST (

The Trail of 100 Giants is as good as many of the giant sequoia trails in Sequoia and Kings Canyon National Parks. Trailhead elevation is 6,400 feet, and the trail is an easy and nearly flat loop that is paved and suitable for wheelchairs and baby strollers. Located within the Long Meadow Giant Sequoia Grove, the second-most southern grove where sequoias are found, the big trees on the Trail of 100 Giants are situated amid a mixed forest of cedars and pines. A dozen interpretive signs along the path unlock the secrets of this forest. As you walk in from the parking lot across the road, the first sequoia tree on your right is a doozy—probably the best one on the loop. Of all the sequoia groves we've seen and admired, the Trail of 100 Giants grove stands out because it has an unusual amount of twins—two sequoias growing tightly side by side in order to share resources. In fact, this grove even has one twin that rangers call a "sequedar," a sequoia and a cedar that have grown together. If you're staying at Redwood Meadow Campground, you have your own entrance to this loop, so you don't have to drive down the road to the main trailhead and parking lot.

User Groups: Hikers, wheelchairs, dogs, and horses. No mountain bikes.

Permits: No permits are required. A $5 parking fee is charged per vehicle.

Maps: A Sequoia National Forest map is available from the U.S. Forest Service. For a topographic map, go to the USGS website to download Johnsondale.

Directions: From Kernville on the north end of Isabella Lake, drive north on Sierra Way/ Road 99 for 27 miles to Johnsondale R-Ranch. Continue west (the road becomes Road 50) for 5.5 miles, turn right on the Western Divide Highway, and drive 2.4 miles to the trailhead parking area, on the right, just before Redwood Meadow Campground. Cross the road to begin the trail.

Contact: Giant Sequoia National Monument/ Sequoia National Forest, Western Divide Ranger District, Springville, 559/539-2607, www.fs.usda.gov/sequoia.

90 MULE PEAK LOOKOUT
1.2 mi/1.0 hr 🥾1 ⛰9

in Giant Sequoia National Monument near Johnsondale

Map 11.3, page 545

While rock climbers come to Mule Peak to do their daring work, hikers can take a not-so-daring walk up the back side of Mule Peak; it's attainable for all ages and levels of hikers. The area around the peak has been logged, but much of the forest has grown back. The trail follows a series of easy switchbacks up the hillside, gaining 600 feet to the summit of Mule Peak (elevation 8,142 feet). A lookout tower is positioned there, built in 1936 and still in operation by Sequoia National Forest. The summit view includes Onion Meadow Peak, Table Mountain, the Tule River Valley, and the Tule River Indian Reservation to the west.

User Groups: Hikers, dogs, horses, and mountain bikes. No wheelchair facilities.

Permits: No permits are required. Parking and access are free.

Maps: A Sequoia National Forest map is available from the U.S. Forest Service. For a topographic map, go to the USGS website to download Sentinel Peak.

Directions: From Kernville on the north end of Isabella Lake, drive north on Sierra Way/

Road 99 for 27 miles to Johnsondale R-Ranch. Continue west (the road becomes Road 50), then in 5.5 miles, turn right on the Western Divide Highway. Drive five miles to the left turnoff signed for Mule Peak/Road 22S03. Turn left and follow Road 22S03 for five miles to the Mule Peak trailhead.

Contact: Giant Sequoia National Monument/ Sequoia National Forest, Western Divide Ranger District, Springville, 559/539-2607, www.fs.usda.gov/sequoia.

91 DOME ROCK
0.25 mi/0.5 hr

in Giant Sequoia National Monument near Quaking Aspen

> **Map 11.3, page 545**

Dome Rock wins the prize for "Granite Dome with the Most Pedestrian Name." But never mind. It also wins the prize for "Shortest Walk to an Incredible View." Trailhead elevation is 7,200 feet, and the trail is really just a route leading from the left side of the parking lot. Signs at the parking lot warn you not to drop or throw anything off the top of the dome, because there are rock climbers down below on the dome's steep side. It's a mere five-minute walk to the top of Dome Rock—a huge cap of bare granite—where the views are incredible of Slate Mountain, Isabella Lake, and The Needles. You'll want to hang around here for a while to ooh and aah. If your scrambling skills are good, consider checking out another stunning destination just a few miles from here. Jump back in your car and drive back to the Western Divide Highway, then head south for four miles to an unmarked pullout on the east side of the road, 0.25 mile south of the Crawford Road turnoff. Start hiking on the dirt road that begins at the turnout; bear right where it forks. The path draws near to Nobe Young Creek, and soon you will hear a noisy waterfall. Take one of several spur trails on your left leading down to the base of the 125-foot fall, which drops over three granite ledges. The entire hike is only one

mile round-trip, but because there is no formal trail, it's not for novices. Wear good boots and use caution on the steep and slippery slope.

User Groups: Hikers, dogs, horses, and mountain bikes. No wheelchair facilities.

Permits: No permits are required. Parking and access are free.

Maps: A Sequoia National Forest map is available from the U.S. Forest Service. For a topographic map go to the USGS website to download Sentinel Peak.

Directions: From Kernville on the north end of Isabella Lake, drive north on Sierra Way/ Road 99 for 27 miles to Johnsondale R-Ranch. Continue west (the road becomes Road 50) for 5.5 miles, and turn right on the Western Divide Highway. Drive 12 miles to the Dome Rock/Road 21S69 turnoff, on the right, across from Peppermint Work Center. Turn right and follow the dirt road for a few hundred yards; where it forks, bear left and continue to the trailhead, 0.5 mile from the Western Divide Highway. If you're traveling from the north, the turnoff is two miles south of Ponderosa Lodge.

Contact: Giant Sequoia National Monument/ Sequoia National Forest, Western Divide Ranger District, Springville, 559/539-2607, www.fs.usda.gov/sequoia.

92 ALDER CREEK TRAIL
1.8 mi/1.0 hr

in Giant Sequoia National Monument near Johnsondale

> **Map 11.3, page 545**   **BEST (**

The granite slabs and pools on Alder Creek have gotten so popular with hikers, swimmers, and picnickers that the Forest Service has installed No Parking Any Time signs all over the road near the trailhead. But as long as you park where you're supposed to (off the road, in the day-use parking area), you can still pay a visit to the tons-of-fun pools and slides along Alder Creek. To reach them, walk up the gated dirt road (Road 22S83) and turn right on the single-track trail. The path descends to the confluence of Alder Creek and Dry Meadow Creek, where there is a long length of swimming holes and rocky slides that pour into them. Make sure you wear denim or some other heavy material on your backside so you can while away many happy hours pretending you are a river otter. It's exhilarating, but please use caution as you slip and slide. Slick granite can be very unforgiving.

User Groups: Hikers and dogs. No horses or mountain bikes. No wheelchair facilities.

Permits: No permits are required. Parking and access are free.

Maps: A Sequoia National Forest map is available from the U.S. Forest Service. For a topographic map, go to the USGS website to download Sentinel Peak.

Directions: From Kernville on the north end of Lake Isabella, drive north on Sierra Way/Road 99 for 27 miles to 0.5 mile north of Johnsondale R-Ranch. Turn right on Road 22S82 and drive 5.7 miles to the day-use parking area, on the right side of the road. Walk across Road 22S82 to the gated dirt road and the trailhead.

Contact: Giant Sequoia National Monument/ Sequoia National Forest, Western Divide Ranger District, Springville, 559/539-2607, www.fs.usda.gov/sequoia.

93 KEARSARGE PASS
10.0 mi/6.0 hr or 2 days

in the John Muir Wilderness in Inyo National Forest

Map 11.3, page 545

The trailhead elevation for Kearsarge Pass Trail is 9,200 feet, and the elevation at Kearsarge Pass is 11,823 feet. Five miles and a good amount of climbing lie in between, but the route is well graded, and the scenery is spectacular. The trail, which was once an Indian trading route, leads to the backcountry of Kings Canyon National Park, but most day hikers just make the trip to the pass. Along the way, you are witness to several sparkling lakes and whitewater cascades, and a wealth of high-country

wildflowers. Not surprisingly, this is a very popular trail. Remember to bring sunglasses, sunscreen, and a jacket for the summit, which is windy and exposed.

The trail climbs gradually from the trailhead, often nearing Independence Creek then veering away again as it winds through a multitude of switchbacks. You pass Little Pothole Lake at 1.5 miles, Gilbert Lake at 2.2 miles, and Flower Lake at 2.6 miles. Continue climbing high above tree line to Kearsarge Pass. You'll get a long-distance view of Heart Lake and pass the left spur trail leading to Big Pothole Lake along the way. Finally, just when you think you can climb no farther, you reach the pass, at five miles. A sign announces your arrival in Kings Canyon Park, and extraordinary Sierra views surround you. You'll gaze at Bullfrog and Kearsarge Lakes, University Peak, and Mount Gould.

Note that if you decide to turn this into an overnight trip, food storage regulations are in effect. Bear-resistant canisters are required for all backpackers, and no wood fires are permitted. Good camping and fishing is located 3.5 miles beyond the pass, at Charlotte Lake, but a one-night stay limit is in effect.

User Groups: Hikers, dogs, and horses. Dogs are allowed to Kearsarge Pass, but not beyond it. No mountain bikes. No wheelchair facilities.

Permits: A free wilderness permit is required year-round for overnight stays and is available from the Eastern Sierra Interagency Visitor Center, 1.5 miles south of Lone Pine. Quotas are in effect from May 1 to November 1; permits are available in advance for a $5 reservation fee per person.

Maps: A John Muir Wilderness map is available from the U.S. Forest Service. A Kearsarge Pass map is available from Tom Harrison Maps. For a topographic map, go to the USGS website to download Kearsarge Peak.

Directions: From Lone Pine, drive 15 miles north on U.S. 395 to Independence. Turn west on Market Street, which becomes Onion Valley Road. Drive 14 miles to the end of the road and the trailhead parking area.

Contact: Inyo National Forest, Mount Whitney Ranger Station, Lone Pine, 760/876-6200, www.fs.usda.gov/inyo; Eastern Sierra Interagency Visitor Center, 760/876-6222.

94 FLOWER AND MATLOCK LAKES
6.4 mi/3.5 hr   🚶2 ⛰8

in the John Muir Wilderness in Inyo National Forest

Map 11.3, page 545

If you don't have the time or the energy for Kearsarge Pass (see listing in this chapter), the route to Flower Lake and Matlock Lake is a good second choice. Although it doesn't offer the astounding views that the pass has, it is still a stellar trip into dramatic granite country. Both lakes are deep blue waterways that draw in all the color of the Sierra sky. The trail climbs gradually from the trailhead, switchbacking along Independence Creek. You pass Little Pothole Lake at 1.5 miles and Gilbert Lake at 2.2 miles, reaching a junction for Matlock Lake at 2.5 miles. Continue straight for 0.1 mile to Flower Lake, then retrace your steps to the junction and head south for 0.7 mile to larger Matlock Lake. Pull out your camera and a picnic, and while away some time before returning to the trailhead.

User Groups: Hikers, dogs, and horses. No mountain bikes. No wheelchair facilities.

Permits: No day-hiking permits are required. Parking and access are free.

Maps: A John Muir Wilderness map is available from the U.S. Forest Service. A Kearsarge Pass map is available from Tom Harrison Maps. For a topographic map, go to the USGS website to download Kearsarge Peak.

Directions: From Lone Pine, drive 15 miles north on U.S. 395 to Independence. Turn west on Market Street, which becomes Onion Valley Road. Drive 14 miles to the end of the road and the trailhead parking area.

Contact: Inyo National Forest, Mount Whitney Ranger Station, Lone Pine, 760/876-6200, www.

fs.usda.gov/inyo; Eastern Sierra Interagency Visitor Center, 760/876-6222.

95 ROBINSON LAKE
3.0 mi/2.0 hr   🚶4 ⛰9

in the John Muir Wilderness in Inyo National Forest

Map 11.3, page 545

The Robinson Lake Trail is best described as relentlessly steep but mercifully short. The hike is challenging in places due to the grade, loose surface, and relative obscurity of the trail, but the destination is superlative. In addition to beautiful Robinson Lake (at 10,500 feet), you get a close and personal view of 11,744-foot Independence Peak and an excellent wildflower display along Robinson Creek. Start at the trailhead by campsite No. 7 in Onion Valley Campground. Watch out for the overgrown vegetation that can sometimes hide the trail. Just climb, catch your breath, and climb some more. After a fairly punishing ascent, you'll reach the small, shallow lake in less than an hour. Campsites and picnicking sites are found in the sand on the lake's east side, or in the pine forest on the northwest side. Equally as pretty as the lake are the views from its shores of the valley below. Plan your trip for July to September; the trail is usually free of snow by midsummer. But whenever you go, watch your footing carefully. This trail is not maintained very often.

User Groups: Hikers, dogs, and horses. No mountain bikes. No wheelchair facilities.

Permits: No day-hiking permits are required. Parking and access are free.

Maps: A John Muir Wilderness map is available from the U.S. Forest Service. A Kearsarge Pass map is available from Tom Harrison Maps. For a topographic map, go to the USGS website to download Kearsarge Peak.

Directions: From Lone Pine, drive 15 miles north on U.S. 395 to Independence. Turn west on Market Street, which becomes Onion Valley Road. Drive 14 miles to the end of the road and the hikers' parking area. Walk into Onion Valley Campground to find the trailhead, by site No. 7.

Contact: Inyo National Forest, Mount Whitney Ranger Station, Lone Pine, 760/876-6200, www.fs.usda.gov/inyo; Eastern Sierra Interagency Visitor Center, 760/876-6222.

96 MOUNT WHITNEY TRAIL
22.0 mi/15.0 hr or 2-3 days
👫5 ⚠️10

in the John Muir Wilderness

Map 11.3, page 545   BEST (

Mount Whitney, at 14,505 feet in elevation, is the highest peak in the contiguous United States and is also probably the most frequently climbed. It has become so well traveled that not only are quotas enforced for backpackers, but even day hikers must obtain a wilderness permit to hike the trail. And, yes, many people do hike the entire 22-mile round-trip trail in one single day, ascending and descending more than a vertical mile along the way (6,131 feet in all), but it means a predawn start and a grueling march. Many people who try this suffer from a variety of ailments, including dehydration, hypoglycemia, and even altitude sickness, and never make it to the top. Others make it but realize they would have had a lot more fun if they had divided the trip into two or even three days. So here's the smart way to hike Mount Whitney: Get your wilderness permit way in advance (see the permit information below), and plan your trip for a weekday, not a weekend. If possible, wait to make the climb until September or early October, when the crowds have thinned considerably; August sees the highest trail usage. Spend a couple days at high elevation before you set out on the Mount Whitney Trail, and come prepared with sunglasses, sunscreen, good boots, and warm clothes for the summit. And since all solid human waste must be packed out (not buried, as is permitted in other areas of the Sierra), it's a good idea to obtain a free "human waste pack-out kit" from the Eastern Sierra Interagency Visitor Center before leaving on your trip. Consider this: In a typical summer, visitors to Mount Whitney pack out more than 7,000 pounds of human waste. For more information on the Mount Whitney Trail, see the trail notes for the *Whitney Portal to Lake Thomas Edison (JMT/PCT)* hike in this chapter.

User Groups: Hikers only. No dogs, horses, or mountain bikes. (Dogs are allowed on the first 6.2 miles of trail, but not beyond.) No wheelchair facilities.

Permits: A wilderness permit is required year-round for both day hikers and backpackers and is available from the Eastern Sierra Interagency Visitor Center, 1.5 mile south of Lone Pine. Quotas are in effect from May 1 to November 1 for both day hikers and backpackers. Permit application forms are entered into a lottery during the month of February for all dates in the quota period (May 1 to November 1). Submit a permit application form online, or phone 760/873-2483 for more information. There is a $15 reservation fee per person. Bear canisters are required for overnight stays and no wood fires are permitted.

Note: The reservation system for Mount Whitney hiking permits may change slightly from year to year. Please check the Inyo National Forest website for the most updated information, or contact the Eastern Sierra Interagency Visitor Center (760/876-6222). The visitor center is located 1.5 miles south of Lone Pine at the junction of U.S. 396 and Hwy. 136.

Maps: A Mount Whitney Zone map is available from Tom Harrison Maps. For topographic maps, go to the USGS website to download Mount Whitney and Mount Langley.

Directions: From Lone Pine on U.S. 395, drive west on Whitney Portal Road for 13 miles to the end of the road and the trailhead.

Contact: Inyo National Forest, Mount Whitney Ranger Station, Lone Pine, 760/876-6200, www.fs.usda.gov/inyo; Eastern Sierra Interagency Visitor Center, 760/876-6222.

🔳 WHITNEY PORTAL NATIONAL RECREATION TRAIL

4.0 mi one-way/2.0 hr   🚶1 ⛰9

in Inyo National Forest near Whitney Portal

Map 11.3, page 545

Don't confuse this trail with the Mount Whitney Trail, because except for their nearby trailheads, they have zero in common. Although if you try to hike the Whitney Portal National Recreation Trail in both directions, instead of as a one-way downhill hike, you may find it feels darn near as demanding as the Mount Whitney Trail, which climbs nearly 6,000 feet to the top of Mount Whitney. (Okay, maybe not quite that demanding.) The recreation trail begins at Whitney Portal (elevation 8,360 feet) and heads downhill through conifers and granite to Lone Pine Campground (elevation 5,640). The best thing about the route is that no matter how crowded it is at Whitney Portal, this trail gets surprisingly few hikers, especially after the first 0.5 mile, which skirts Whitney Portal Campground. You get to leave the multitudes behind as you walk downhill along Lone Pine Creek, among the good company of granite formations and big pines. Vistas are excellent along the way, including Mount Whitney to the west and the Alabama Hills and White Mountains to the east.

User Groups: Hikers, dogs, and horses. No mountain bikes. No wheelchair facilities.

Permits: No permits are required. Parking and access are free.

Maps: A Mount Whitney High Country map is available from Tom Harrison Maps. For a topographic map, go to the USGS website to download Mount Langley.

Directions: From Lone Pine on U.S. 395, drive west on Whitney Portal Road for 13 miles to the end of the road and the trailhead, located across from the fishing pond. You will need to leave a shuttle car or arrange a pickup at Lone Pine Campground, four miles downhill on Whitney Portal Road.

Contact: Inyo National Forest, Mount Whitney Ranger Station, Lone Pine, 760/876-6200, www.fs.usda.gov/inyo; Eastern Sierra Interagency Visitor Center, 760/876-6222.

🔳 MEYSAN LAKE

11.0 mi/6.0 hr or 2 days   🚶5 ⛰9

in the John Muir Wilderness near Mount Whitney

Map 11.3, page 545

The Meysan Lake Trail is less popular than the neighboring trail to the top of Mount Whitney, but still, you should get your wilderness permit in advance or plan on day hiking. Better yet, plan your trip for late September and during the week. The trail to Meysan Lake is long, steep, hot, and dry—let's just say it's grueling—but it leads to a beautiful alpine lake basin and provides spectacular views of granite walls. It also gives climbers access to climbing routes on Mount Mallory and Lone Pine Peak. The trail is parallel to Meysan Creek and is not well maintained, which makes it even more demanding. You reach a left fork for Grass Lake at 4.5 miles, where the first water is available. The right fork continues to Camp Lake and its beautiful meadow (at five miles). The elevation here is 11,200 feet. The trail from Camp Lake to Meysan Lake is rather sketchy. Head to the right of Camp Lake, cross the inlet stream, and watch for rock cairns marking the way up the steep, rocky slope. Meysan Lake is often still frozen as late as June, even though the trail can be as hot as an oven. The trailhead elevation is 7,900 feet; Meysan Lake is at 11,460 feet.

User Groups: Hikers and dogs. No horses or mountain bikes. No wheelchair facilities.

Permits: A free wilderness permit is required year-round for overnight stays and is available from the Eastern Sierra Interagency Visitor Center, 1.5 miles south of Lone Pine. Quotas are in effect from May 1 to November 1; permits are available in advance for a $5 reservation fee per person.

Maps: A John Muir Wilderness map is available from the U.S. Forest Service. A Mount

Whitney Zone map is available from Tom Harrison Maps. For topographic maps, go to the USGS website to download Mount Whitney and Mount Langley.

Directions: From Lone Pine on U.S. 395, drive west on Whitney Portal Road for 12 miles to Whitney Portal Campground and the Meysan Lake trailhead. Park on the side of Whitney Portal Road by the camp and walk through the camp to reach the trailhead.

Contact: Inyo National Forest, Mount Whitney Ranger Station, Lone Pine, 760/876-6200, www.fs.usda.gov/inyo; Eastern Sierra Interagency Visitor Center, 760/876-6222.

99 LONE PINE LAKE
5.8 mi/3.0 hr

in the John Muir Wilderness near Whitney Portal

Map 11.3, page 545

The route to the top of Mount Whitney is so popular and so overcrowded that it has permits and quotas and regulations up the wazoo, but guess what? Sweet little Lone Pine Lake is just outside of the regulated Mount Whitney Zone, so you can hike to it anytime without dealing with any bureaucracy. However, you will have to deal with extremely limited parking at the trailhead during the summer months, so plan your trip for September or later if at all possible. Hiking to Lone Pine Lake is a fun trip for people who have always daydreamed of climbing Mount Whitney, because it follows the first three miles of the summit trail. While other people are trudging along carrying heavy backpacks, you're stepping lightly, with only a sandwich and a bottle of water in your day pack. The trail leads through Jeffrey pines and manzanita to the John Muir Wilderness border at one mile, then switchbacks uphill and opens up to views of the Alabama Hills far below. You'll cross Lone Pine Creek at 2.8 miles, then bear left at a junction to leave the main Mount Whitney Trail and head a few hundred yards to Lone Pine Lake. It's a sweet spot, and although

privacy is rare, you have a greater chance of it after Labor Day and on a weekday. Who knows, you might just get so inspired that next time you'll come back and hike all the way to the summit.

User Groups: Hikers and dogs. No horses or mountain bikes. No wheelchair facilities.

Permits: No day-hiking permits are required. A Mount Whitney wilderness permit is required for overnight stays. Parking and access are free.

Maps: A John Muir Wilderness map is available from the U.S. Forest Service. A Mount Whitney Zone map is available from Tom Harrison Maps. For topographic maps, go to the USGS website to download Mount Whitney and Mount Langley.

Directions: From Lone Pine on U.S. 395, drive west on Whitney Portal Road for 13 miles to the end of the road and the Mount Whitney trailhead.

Contact: Inyo National Forest, Mount Whitney Ranger Station, Lone Pine, 760/876-6200, www.fs.usda.gov/inyo; Eastern Sierra Interagency Visitor Center, 760/876-6222.

100 WHITNEY PORTAL TO LAKE THOMAS EDISON (JMT/PCT)
112.0 mi one-way/11 days

from the trailhead parking area at Whitney Portal north to the trailhead parking area at Lake Thomas Edison

Map 11.3, page 545   **BEST (**

You can have a foothold in the sky with every step on the John Muir Trail (JMT). This part of the trail is shared with the Pacific Crest Trail (PCT) and starts at practically the tip-top of North America—Mount Whitney—and takes you northward across a land of 12,000-foot passes and Ansel Adams-style panoramas.

From the trailhead at Whitney Portal, the hike climbs more than 6,100 feet over the course of 11 miles to reach Whitney's summit at 14,505 feet. That includes an ascent more than 100 switchbacks, which are often snow covered even late in summer, to reach Trail Crest (13,560 feet). Here you turn right and take Summit Trail. In the final stretch to the top, the ridge is cut by huge notch windows in the rock; you look through, and the bottom drops out more than 10,000 feet to the town of Lone Pine below, at an elevation of 3,800 feet. Finally you make it to the top and notice how the surrounding giant blocks of rock look as if they were sculpted with a giant hammer and chisel. From here, the entire Western Divide is visible, and to the north, rows of mountain peaks are lined up for miles to the horizon. Be sure to sign your name in the register, kept in a lightning-proof metal box. You may feel a bit dizzy from the altitude, but you'll know you're someplace very special.

The journey farther north is just as captivating. The route drops into Sequoia National Park, then climbs above timberline for almost a day's worth of hiking as it nears Forester Pass (13,180 feet). It's not only the highest point on the PCT; it's the most dangerous section of trail on the entire route as well. The trail is narrow and steep, cut into a high vertical slab of rock, and is typically icy, with an iced-over snowfield near the top that's particularly treacherous. An ice ax is an absolute must. If you slip here, you could fall thousands of feet.

Once through Forester, the trail heads onward into the John Muir Wilderness along Bubbs Creek, with great wildflowers at nearby Vidette Meadow. Then it's up and over Kearsarge Pass (10,710 feet), and after a short drop, you're back climbing again, this time over Glen Pass (11,978 feet)—a spectacular, boulder-strewn ridge with great views to the north looking into Kings Canyon National Park. Just two miles from Glen Pass is Rae Lakes, a fantasy spot for camping (one-night limit), with pristine meadows, shoreline campsites, and lots of eager brook trout.

The JMT then heads through Kings Canyon National Park by following sparkling streams much of the way, finally climbing up and over Pinchot Pass (12,130 feet), then back down

along the upper Kings River for a long, steady ascent over Mather Pass (12,100 feet). The wonders continue as you hike along Palisade Lakes, then down into LeConte Canyon, followed by an endless climb up to Muir Pass (11,965 feet). In early summer, snowfields are common here, and this can be difficult and trying, especially if your boots keep post-holing through the snow. The country near Muir Pass is extremely stark—nothing but sculpted granite, ice, and a few small turquoise lakes—crowned by the stone Muir Hut at the pass, where hikers can duck in and hide for safety from sudden afternoon thunderstorms and lightning bolts.

The views astound many visitors as the trail drops into Evolution Valley. It's like a trip back to the beginning of time, where all is pure and primary, yet incredibly lush and beautiful. You finally leave Kings Canyon National Park, following the headwaters of the San Joaquin River into Sierra National Forest. After bottoming out at 7,890 feet, the trail rises steeply in switchback after switchback as it enters the John Muir Wilderness. Finally you top Selden Pass (10,900 feet), take in an incredible view (where the rows of surrounding mountaintops look like the Great Pyramids), then make the easy one-mile descent to Marie Lakes, a pretty campsite with excellent trout fishing near the lake's outlet.

The final push on this section of the JMT is climbing up Bear Mountain, then down a terrible, toe-jamming stretch to Mono Creek. Here you make a left turn and continue for two more miles until you come to Edison Lake, an excellent place to have a food stash waiting. (To continue north on the JMT/PCT, see the *Lake Thomas Edison to Agnew Meadows* hike in this chapter.)

Note: Crossing Mono Creek at the North Fork can be dangerous during high-runoff conditions.

User Groups: Hikers and horses. No dogs or mountain bikes. No wheelchair facilities.

Permits: A wilderness permit is required for traveling through various wilderness and special-use areas the trail traverses. Contact the

Eastern Sierra Interagency Visitor Center for more information.

Maps: A John Muir Trail Map Pack is available from Tom Harrison Maps. For topographic maps, go to the USGS website to download Mount Whitney, Mount Williamson, Kearsarge Peak, Mount Clarence King, Mount Pinchot, North Palisade, Mount Goddard, Mount Darwin, Mount Henry, Ward Mountain, Florence Lake, and Graveyard Peak.

Directions: To reach the Mount Whitney trailhead from Lone Pine and U.S. 395, head west on Whitney Portal Road for approximately 13 miles to Whitney Portal and the trailhead for the Mount Whitney Trail. To reach the Lake Thomas Edison trailhead from the town of Shaver Lake, drive north on Highway 168 for approximately 21 miles to the town of Lakeshore. Turn northeast onto Kaiser Pass Road/Forest Service 4S01. Kaiser Pass Road becomes Edison Lake Road at Mono Hot Springs. Drive another five miles north past town to the Vermillion Campground and parking area for backcountry hikers. The PCT begins near the east end of the lake.

Contact: Inyo National Forest, Mount Whitney Ranger Station, Lone Pine, 760/876-6200 or 760/873-2400, www.fs.usda.gov/inyo; Sierra National Forest, High Sierra Ranger District, Prather, 559/855-5360, www.fs.usda. gov/sequoia; Sequoia National Forest, Sequoia National Forest, Kern River Ranger District, Kernville, 760/376-3781, www.fs.usda.gov/ sequoia; Eastern Sierra Interagency Visitor Center, 760/876-6222.

101 COTTONWOOD LAKES
10.0-12.5 mi/6.0 hr or 2 days

in the John Muir Wilderness south of Mount Whitney

Map 11.3, page 545

The trailhead elevation is just over 10,000 feet here at Horseshoe Meadow, which makes this a wildly popular trailhead for climbing deeper into the backcountry. With the trailhead situated so high, you get a jump on the ascent; your four wheels do the work, instead of your two feet. An unusual feature of this hike is that it passes through two wilderness areas—first a small portion of the Golden Trout Wilderness and then the John Muir Wilderness. Cottonwood Creek accompanies you for much of the trip. The trail starts out in a sandy pine forest with a mellow grade. At 3.7 miles you reach a junction. Most hikers go left; the trail forms a loop around Cottonwood Lakes numbers one, two, and three. If you just want to see the closest lake and head back without making a loop, Cottonwood Lake number one is to the left, 1.5 miles from the junction. Your round-trip will be an even 10 miles. If you complete the whole loop, passing all three lakes, you'll travel 11.5 miles. But the most beautiful lakes by far are numbers four and five, worth an extra 0.5 mile of hiking beyond the far end of the loop. Total elevation gain is only 1,000 feet. Once at the lakes, remember two points: 1) Because the Cottonwood Lakes are home to golden trout, special fishing regulations are in effect, so get updated on the latest rules. 2) No wood fires are allowed, so bring your backpacking stove.

User Groups: Hikers, dogs, and horses. No mountain bikes. No wheelchair facilities.

Permits: A free wilderness permit is required year-round for overnight stays and is available from the Eastern Sierra Interagency Visitor Center, 1.5 miles south of Lone Pine. Quotas are in effect from May 1 to November 1; permits are available in advance for a $5 reservation fee per person. Bear canisters are required.

Maps: A John Muir Wilderness map is available from the U.S. Forest Service. A Mount Whitney High Country map is available from Tom Harrison Maps. For a topographic map, go to the USGS website to download Cirque Peak.

Directions: From Lone Pine on U.S. 395, drive west on Whitney Portal Road for 3.3 miles and turn left (south) on Horseshoe Meadow Road. Continue 19.5 miles and bear right for the

Cottonwood Lakes trailhead parking area, near the end of Horseshoe Meadow Road.

Contact: Inyo National Forest, Mount Whitney Ranger Station, Lone Pine, 760/876-6200, www.fs.usda.gov/inyo; Eastern Sierra Interagency Visitor Center, 760/876-6222.

102 COTTONWOOD PASS
8.0 mi/5.0 hr or 2 days

in the Golden Trout Wilderness

Map 11.3, page 545

The Cottonwood Pass Trail provides access to the Pacific Crest Trail and the Kern Plateau, a land of stark, sub-alpine meadows. You're entering the Golden Trout Wilderness, home of California's state fish and located at the very south end of the Sierra Nevada. This is where the steep, nearly perpendicular mountains start to mellow out into more gentle terrain—mostly in the form of rolling high-country hills and meadows. Start from wide Horseshoe Meadow and climb gently through forest for the first two miles of trail. Shortly, the switchbacks begin and the ascent becomes serious. After a 1,100-foot climb, you reach the pass (at four miles), where you can gaze out at the Great Western Divide, Big Whitney Meadows, and the Inyo Mountains. Bring a jacket with you for the windy, 11,250-foot summit. Ambitious hikers can continue beyond the pass and take the right fork for Chicken Spring Lake, one mile away on the Pacific Crest Trail (no campfires allowed).

User Groups: Hikers, dogs, and horses. No mountain bikes. No wheelchair facilities.

Permits: A free wilderness permit is required year-round for overnight stays and is available from the Eastern Sierra Interagency Visitor Center, 1.5 miles south of Lone Pine. Quotas are in effect from the last Friday in June to September 15; permits are available in advance for a $5 reservation fee per person.

Maps: A Golden Trout Wilderness map is available from the U.S. Forest Service or Tom Harrison Maps. For a topographic map, go to the USGS website to download Cirque Peak.

Directions: From Lone Pine on U.S. 395, drive west on Whitney Portal Road for 3.3 miles and turn left (south) on Horseshoe Meadow Road. Continue 19.5 miles to the Horseshoe Meadow trailhead, on the left, at the end of Horseshoe Meadow Road.

Contact: Inyo National Forest, Mount Whitney Ranger Station, Lone Pine, 760/876-6200, www.fs.usda.gov/inyo; Eastern Sierra Interagency Visitor Center, 760/876-6222.

103 TRAIL PASS
5.0 mi/3.0 hr

in the Golden Trout Wilderness

Map 11.3, page 545

Trail Pass may not be as spectacular as the other trails at Horseshoe Meadow, but it has two things going for it—far fewer people and an easier grade. It's only five miles round-trip from the trailhead to the pass, with a mere 500-foot elevation gain, unheard of in these parts. The main folks using the trail are backpackers accessing the Pacific Crest Trail and Golden Trout Wilderness, so a lot of the time, you can have this gently rolling, high-country terrain all to yourself. Follow the trail from the parking area to a junction 0.25 mile in, and bear left. In another 0.5 mile, the trail forks, and you bear right for Trail Pass. You'll hike past Horseshoe Meadow and Round Valley, where you'll have the company of many packhorses. Views of Mount Langley and Cirque Peak are sure to inspire you. The pass is situated at 10,500 feet, just below Trail Peak (at 11,600 feet).

User Groups: Hikers, dogs, and horses. No mountain bikes. No wheelchair facilities.

Permits: No day-hiking permits are required. Parking and access are free. A free wilderness permit is required year-round for overnight stays and is available from the Eastern Sierra Interagency Visitor Center, 1.5 miles south of Lone Pine.

Maps: A Golden Trout Wilderness map is available from the U.S. Forest Service or Tom

Harrison Maps. For a topographic map, go to the USGS website to download Cirque Peak.

Directions: From Lone Pine on U.S. 395, drive west on Whitney Portal Road for 3.3 miles and turn left (south) on Horseshoe Meadow Road. Continue 19.5 miles to the Horseshoe Meadow trailhead, on the right, at the end of Horseshoe Meadow Road.

Contact: Inyo National Forest, Mount Whitney Ranger Station, Lone Pine, 760/876-6200, www.fs.usda.gov/inyo; Eastern Sierra Interagency Visitor Center, 760/876-6222.

104 CASA VIEJA MEADOW
4.0 mi/2.0 hr   🥾2 ⛰9

in the Golden Trout Wilderness

Map 11.3, page 545   **BEST (**

The Blackrock Mountain trailhead, at 8,800 feet, is the jump-off point for a variety of backpacking trips into the Golden Trout Wilderness. But day hikers can also sample the delights of this large, waterway-filled land, the home of California's state fish, the golden trout. From the end of Blackrock Road, walk for less than 0.25 mile to the wilderness boundary, then head gently downhill through a red fir forest to the western edge of Casa Vieja Meadow. There you'll find a snow survey cabin and a wide expanse of grass and wildflowers. Hope your day pack is full of picnic supplies. At the far end of the meadow, you must ford Ninemile Creek to continue hiking farther, so make this your turnaround point. Some people try their luck fishing here. You'll have a gradual 800-foot elevation gain on your return trip.

User Groups: Hikers, dogs, and horses. No mountain bikes. No wheelchair facilities.

Permits: No permits are required. Parking and access are free.

Maps: A Golden Trout Wilderness map is available from the U.S. Forest Service or Tom Harrison Maps. For a topographic map, go to the USGS website to download Casa Vieja Meadows.

Directions: From Kernville on the north end of Isabella Lake, drive north on Sierra Way/ Road 99 for 22 miles to the turnoff for Sherman Pass Road/22S05. Turn right and drive approximately 35 miles on Sherman Pass Road to the Blackrock Information Station; continue straight on Road 21S03/Blackrock Road. Follow Road 21S03 north for eight miles to the end of the road and the Blackrock Mountain trailhead.

Contact: Sequoia National Forest, Kern River Ranger District, Kernville, 760/376-3781, www.fs.usda.gov/sequoia; Inyo National Forest, Mount Whitney Ranger Station, Lone Pine, 760/876-6200, www.fs.usda.gov/inyo.

105 JORDAN HOT SPRINGS
12.0 mi/7.0 hr or 2 days   🥾4 ⛰9

in the Golden Trout Wilderness

Map 11.3, page 545

You can do it in a day if you're ambitious, or you can take a more leisurely two-day trip to Jordan Hot Springs. But however you do it, it's critical to remember that almost all the work is on the way home. The trail is a descent (sometimes knee-jarring) to the grounds of an old hot springs resort, which was closed when this area became part of the Golden Trout Wilderness. The original buildings still stand, and the hot springs are still hot, which is the reason that this is one of the most popular trips in the wilderness. From the trailhead, take Blackrock Trail for two miles to Casa Vieja Meadow (see listing in this chapter), then cross Ninemile Creek and turn left (west) on Jordan Hot Springs Trail. Hike another three miles downhill along Ninemile Creek, crossing it a few more times. Once you reach the old resort, have a good soak and pull your energy together, because you've got a 2,600-foot gain on the return trip.

User Groups: Hikers, dogs, and horses. No mountain bikes. No wheelchair facilities.

Permits: A free wilderness permit is required year-round for overnight stays and is available from the Kern River Ranger Station. Parking and access are free.

Maps: A Golden Trout Wilderness map is available from the U.S. Forest Service or Tom Harrison Maps. For a topographic map, go to the USGS website to download Casa Vieja Meadows.

Directions: From Kernville on the north end of Isabella Lake, drive north on Sierra Way/Road 99 for 22 miles to the right turnoff for Sherman Pass Road/22S05. Turn right and drive approximately 35 miles on Sherman Pass Road to the Blackrock Information Station; continue straight on Road 21S03/Blackrock Road. Follow Road 21S03 north for eight miles to the end of the road and the Blackrock Mountain trailhead.

Contact: Sequoia National Forest, Kern River Ranger District, Kernville, 760/376-3781, www.fs.usda.gov/sequoia.

106 NORTH FORK KERN RIVER TRAIL
10.4 mi/5.0 hr or 2 days 🏃2 ⛰8

in Sequoia National Forest north of Kernville

Map 11.4, page 546

Sometimes you just want to walk alongside a beautiful river, and if that's what you're in the mood for, the Wild and Scenic North Fork Kern is a first-rate choice. From the giant parking lot, walk across the hikers' bridge (separate from but next to the highway bridge) to reach the far side of the river, and then descend on stairs to reach the trail. The North Fork Kern River Trail winds along gently, heading deep into the dramatic Kern Canyon, sometimes under the shade of digger pines, live oaks, and incense cedars, and sometimes out in the bright sunshine. Spring wildflowers are stunning, especially in March and April. Spring river rafters are also entertaining to watch. Most people who walk this trail bring a fishing rod with them, and if you do, make sure you're up-to-date on the special fishing regulations. They're in effect for the first four miles of river, which is

a wild trout area. Backpackers will find many campsites along the trail, including some that are under the cavelike canopy of big boulders. This easy, mellow trail offers something for everyone. Note that if you venture out here at the height of spring runoff, parts of the trail may be submerged.

User Groups: Hikers and dogs. No mountain bikes or horses. No wheelchair facilities.

Permits: A free campfire permit is required for overnight stays and is available from the Springville or Kernville Ranger Stations at the addresses below. Parking and access are free.

Maps: A Sequoia National Forest map is available from the U.S. Forest Service. For a topographic map, go to the USGS website to download Fairview.

Directions: From Kernville on the north end of Lake Isabella, drive north on Sierra Way/Road 99 for 22 miles to the Johnsondale highway bridge over the Kern River. Turn right and park in the large paved parking lot by the signboard at the bridge.

Contact: Sequoia National Forest, Kern River Ranger District, Kernville, 760/376-3781, www.fs.usda.gov/sequoia; Western Divide Ranger District, Springville, 559/539-2607, www.fs.usda.gov/sequoia.

107 SHERMAN PEAK TRAIL
4.0 mi/2.0 hr 🏃1 ⛰9

in Sequoia National Forest near Sherman Pass

Map 11.4, page 546

From the Sherman Pass Vista along the highway, you can look to the north to Mount Whitney and the Great Western Divide. After crossing the highway and hiking Sherman Peak Trail to the top of Sherman Peak (at 9,909 feet), you can pivot around and have a panoramic look at an even bigger chunk of the world. The trail is mostly forested with red firs and pines, and is gradual enough for children to climb. If you read the interpretive display at the vista, you'll be able to identify the myriad mountains you're looking at from the peak, including Split

Rock and Dome Rock. It's only a 700-foot climb to the summit, mostly through a series of easy switchbacks. At one time, a fire lookout tower was positioned up here, but modern technology made it obsolete and it was taken down.

User Groups: Hikers, dogs, horses, and mountain bikes. No wheelchair facilities.

Permits: No permits are required. Parking and access are free.

Maps: A Sequoia National Forest map is available from the U.S. Forest Service. For topographic maps, go to the USGS website to download Durrwood Creek and Sirretta Peak.

Directions: From Kernville on the north end of Lake Isabella, drive north on Sierra Way/Road 99 for 22 miles to the right turnoff for Sherman Pass Road/22S05. Turn right and drive approximately 15 miles on Sherman Pass Road to the Sherman Pass Vista. The trailhead is across the road.

Contact: Sequoia National Forest, Kern River Ranger District, Kernville, 760/376-3781, www.fs.usda.gov/sequoia.

108 BALD MOUNTAIN LOOKOUT

0.25 mi/0.25 hr   🥾1 ⛰9

in Sequoia National Forest on the north edge of the Dome Land Wilderness

Map 11.4, page 546

This short hike to the summit of 9,430-foot Bald Mountain is the easiest possible introduction to the Dome Land Wilderness. It's a brief stroll to the lookout, which is perched on the very northern edge of the wilderness. This region is famous for its many granite domes and monolithic rocks, the happy hunting ground of rock climbers from all over Southern California. Of the many big hunks of rock, Church Dome is perhaps the most outstanding, and it can be seen from here directly to the south. White Dome and Black Mountain are also visible (east of Church Dome), as well as a sweeping vista of the Kern Plateau, the Whitney Range, and the Great Western Divide.

Bald Mountain Lookout has the distinction of being the highest fire lookout tower in the southern Sierra Nevada.

User Groups: Hikers, dogs, horses, and mountain bikes. No wheelchair facilities.

Permits: No permits are required. Parking and access are free.

Maps: A Sequoia National Forest or Dome Land Wilderness map is available from the U.S. Forest Service. For a topographic map, go to the USGS website to download Crag Peak.

Directions: From Kernville on the north end of Lake Isabella, drive north on Sierra Way/Road 99 for 22 miles to the right turnoff for Sherman Pass Road/22S05. Turn right and drive approximately 25 miles on Sherman Pass Road to Forest Service Road 22S77, signed for Bald Mountain Lookout. Turn east (right) on Road 22S77 and follow it for one mile to its end.

Contact: Sequoia National Forest, Kern River Ranger District, Kernville, 760/376-3781, www.fs.usda.gov/sequoia.

109 JACKASS CREEK NATIONAL RECREATION TRAIL

5.0 mi/2.5 hr   🥾2 ⛰9

in Sequoia National Forest near the South Sierra Wilderness

Map 11.4, page 546

The Jackass Creek Trail is way out there on the Kern Plateau, at a trailhead elevation of 8,000 feet. The trail climbs 5.5 miles to Jackass Peak (elevation 9,245 feet) on the border of the South Sierra Wilderness. Most people don't bother traveling that far; instead, they follow the trail along Jackass Creek for a couple of miles through red fir forest to the western edge of Jackass Meadow. In addition to the beautiful meadow, the trail offers a look at many handsome old-growth aspens. The trail is an old dirt road, wide enough for holding hands with your hiking partner. Unfortunately, it's also wide enough for motorcycles, which are allowed here. Our recommendation? Hike this trail in late September or early October for the best show of autumn colors, and for the best chance at having the trail to yourself. If you drive all the way out here and see a parking lot full of motorcycle trailers, try hiking the nearby Hooker Meadow Trail instead (the trailhead is at the end of Road 21S29, just east of Fish Creek Campground). The machines aren't allowed there, and this trail also leads to an outstanding grove of quaking aspens.

User Groups: Hikers, dogs, horses, and mountain bikes. No wheelchair facilities.

Permits: No permits are required. Parking and access are free.

Maps: A Sequoia National Forest map is available from the U.S. Forest Service. For a topographic map, go to the USGS website to download Crag Peak.

Directions: From Kernville on the north end of Lake Isabella, drive north on Sierra Way/Road 99 for 22 miles to the right turnoff for Sherman Pass Road/22S05. Turn right and drive approximately 35 miles on Sherman Pass Road to the four-way intersection with Road 21S03, near Blackrock Information Station. Turn right to continue on Road 22S05, and drive five miles to Fish Creek Campground and Road 21S01, where the trail begins.

Contact: Sequoia National Forest, Kern River Ranger District, Kernville, 760/376-3781, www.fs.usda.gov/sequoia.

110 WHISKEY FLAT TRAIL
5.0 mi/2.5 hr   👥2   ⛰8

in Sequoia National Forest near Fairview

Map 11.4, page 546

The Whiskey Flat Trail is a 14.5-mile trail that parallels the Kern River from Fairview Lodge all the way south to Burlando Road in Kernville. Primarily used by anglers working the Kern River, it's also a good springtime stroll for river lovers. If you walk out and back for a few miles on the northern end of the trail by Fairview, you can end the day with a meal at Fairview Lodge's restaurant, where you can

brag about the fish you did or didn't catch, like everybody else there. The Whiskey Flat Trail can be somewhat difficult to follow, especially in springtime, when the numerous creeks you must cross are running full. Early in the year, the creeks can sometimes be impassable. The path begins on a suspension bridge, which is reminiscent of Huck Finn and his friends. You can hike as far as you please; a good distance is 2.5 miles out, or about an hour's walk each way. The terrain is grasslands and chaparral, with occasional digger pines, which means no shade but plenty of spring wildflowers. Although the route is basically level, there are numerous steep stretches where you climb in and out of stream drainages running into the Kern. The trailhead elevation is 2,800 feet.

User Groups: Hikers, dogs, horses, and mountain bikes. No wheelchair facilities.

Permits: No permits are required. Parking and access are free.

Maps: A Sequoia National Forest map is available from the U.S. Forest Service. For a topographic map, go to the USGS website to download Fairview.

Directions: From Kernville on the north end of Lake Isabella, drive north on Sierra Way/Road 99 for 17 miles to Fairview and the Fairview Lodge, on the left side of the road. A large parking area and a trailhead for the Whiskey Flat Trail are to the right of the lodge.

Contact: Sequoia National Forest, Kern River Ranger District, Kernville, 760/376-3781, www.fs.usda.gov/sequoia.

111 PACKSADDLE CAVE TRAIL
4.6 mi/2.3 hr   👥2   ⛰8

in Sequoia National Forest near Fairview

Map 11.4, page 546

Everybody enjoys the trip to Packsaddle Cave, even though the cave was long ago vandalized of its jewel-like stalactites and stalagmites. Nonetheless, the appeal of visiting the limestone cave keeps this trail well used and fairly well maintained. From the parking lot on Sierra Way, cross the highway and hike uphill on the path, huffing and puffing through some steep pitches. This is not a trail for summertime, because there is little shade among the manzanita, sagebrush, and deer brush, and the total climb is about 1,200 feet. At 1.8 miles, you cross Packsaddle Creek and see several campsites near it. Continue a short distance farther; the cave is off to the left, 0.25 mile before this trail's junction with Rincon Trail. Don't forget your flashlight so you can take a peek inside.

User Groups: Hikers, dogs, horses, and mountain bikes. No wheelchair facilities.

Permits: No permits are required. Parking and access are free.

Maps: A Sequoia National Forest map is available from the U.S. Forest Service. For a topographic map, go to the USGS website to download Fairview.

Directions: From Kernville on the north end of Lake Isabella, drive north on Sierra Way/Road 99 for 18 miles to the Packsaddle Cave trailhead, on the right, 0.25 mile beyond Fairview Campground. The parking area is across the road.

Contact: Sequoia National Forest, Kern River Ranger District, Kernville, 760/376-3781, www.fs.usda.gov/sequoia.

112 RINCON TRAIL
4.0 mi/2.0 hr   🥾 2   ⛰️ 7

in Sequoia National Forest near Fairview

Map 11.4, page 546

Let's say right away that this Rincon has absolutely nothing in common with the other Rincon, the classic surfing break on the Ventura coast. For one, there's no water here, and two, there's no cool ocean breeze. That means you should plan your hike for winter or spring, before the Kern Valley heats up. The trail leads first east and then steadily north along the Rincon Fault, heading for Forks of the Kern. It undulates, following the drainages of Salmon and other creeks. The destination on

this trail is the long-distance view of Salmon Creek Falls, about two miles in, and the good fishing and camping prospects on the way along Salmon Creek. The trail crosses Salmon Creek on a bridge 1.7 miles in, but the waterfall view is about 0.25 mile farther. You might want to bring your binoculars to get a good look. If you wish to hike farther on Rincon Trail, it intersects the route to Packsaddle Cave in another two miles, then crosses Sherman Pass Road in another 2.5 miles, and keeps going straight north all the way to Forks of the Kern. The total one-way trail length is a whopping 19.5 miles. Be forewarned that the Rincon Trail is popular with motorcycle enthusiasts, so your peaceful nature experience may be shattered by their noise.

User Groups: Hikers, dogs, and mountain bikes. No horses. No wheelchair facilities.

Permits: No permits are required. Parking and access are free.

Maps: A Sequoia National Forest map is available from the U.S. Forest Service. For a topographic map, go to the USGS website to download Kernville.

Directions: From Kernville on the north end of Isabella Lake, drive north on Sierra Way/Road 99 for 13 miles to the Rincon trailhead, on the right, across from the Ant Canyon dispersed camping area.

Contact: Sequoia National Forest, Kern River Ranger District, Kernville, 760/376-3781, www.fs.usda.gov/sequoia.

113 SUNDAY PEAK TRAIL
3.4 mi/2.0 hr   🥾 2   ⛰️ 9

in Sequoia National Forest near Wofford Heights

Map 11.4, page 546

From the Sunday Peak trailhead, at 7,200 feet in the Greenhorn Mountains, it's a 1,000-foot climb to the top of Sunday Peak, an excellent day hike for families. The grade is moderate and shaded by big conifers, and the destination is perfect on a day when the heat is sweltering down near Isabella Lake. From the top, you can look down at the Kern River Valley and feel sorry for all those people sweating it out down there. The peak's fire lookout tower was abandoned and then destroyed by the Forest Service in the 1950s when it was determined that nearby Tobias Peak was a better spot to have a lookout. However, the wide-angle views of the Kern Valley, Kern Plateau, and far-off high Sierra peaks are still here for the taking. There are many good picnicking spots on the summit.

User Groups: Hikers, dogs, horses, and mountain bikes. No wheelchair facilities.

Permits: No permits are required. Parking and access are free.

Maps: A Sequoia National Forest map is available from the U.S. Forest Service. For a topographic map, go to the USGS website to download Posey.

Directions: From Wofford Heights on the west side of Isabella Lake, turn west on Highway 155 and drive eight miles to Greenhorn Summit. Turn right on Road 24S15/Forest Highway 90, signed for Portuguese Pass, and drive 6.5 miles north to the parking area for Sunday Peak Trail, near the Girl Scout Camp.

Contact: Sequoia National Forest, Kern River Ranger District, Kernville, 760/376-3781, www. fs.usda.gov/sequoia.

114 UNAL TRAIL
3.0 mi/1.5 hr   🏃1 ⛰8

in Sequoia National Forest near Wofford Heights

Map 11.4, page 546   **BEST (**

This is a first-rate trail for families or for anybody who wants a good leg-stretching walk or run around a beautiful mountain. The Unal Trail is a three-mile loop that climbs gently for two miles to Unal Peak, and then descends in one mile of switchbacks back to the trailhead. (After the first 100 yards, where the trail forks, be sure you take the left fork and hike the trail clockwise.) The trail passes a Native American

cultural site on the return of the loop, the homestead of the Tubatulabal Indians. With only a 700-foot climb and an excellent grade, even mountain bikers can manage this trail, although few bother with it. You'll likely see some deer on the hillsides, and the view from the top of Unal Peak makes the whole world seem peaceful and serene. Although most of the trail is lined with conifers, the top of the loop is a little exposed and catches a strong breeze.

User Groups: Hikers, dogs, horses, and mountain bikes. No wheelchair facilities.

Permits: No permits are required. Parking and access are free.

Maps: A Sequoia National Forest map is available from the U.S. Forest Service. For a topographic map, go to the USGS website to download Posey.

Directions: From Wofford Heights on the west side of Lake Isabella, turn west on Highway 155 and drive eight miles to Greenhorn Summit. Turn left at the sign for Shirley Ski Meadows and drive 100 yards to the Greenhorn Fire Station and Unal trailhead, on the right side of the road.

Contact: Sequoia National Forest, Kern River Ranger District, Kernville, 760/376-3781, www. fs.usda.gov/sequoia.

115 CANNELL MEADOW NATIONAL RECREATION TRAIL
24.0 mi/3 days   🏃4 ⛰8

in Sequoia National Forest north of Kernville

Map 11.4, page 546

The Cannell Meadow National Recreation Trail is the first trailhead you reach out of Kernville, and if it's summertime, you should start at the other end of this 12-mile trail. That's because the Kernville end is at 2,800 feet, set in rocky chaparral and digger pine country, and, baby, it's hot out here. Still, if you can time your trip for late winter or spring, hiking this end of Cannell Trail is a great adventure, watching the terrain and environment change as the elevation rises. The shadeless trail climbs right away, through sage and occasional live oaks, affording views of the Kern River Valley. The trail gets more and more steep as you near conifer country at Pine Flat, but then you also get some blessed shade. It crosses Cannell Creek twice and reaches the Cannell Meadow Forest Service Cabin, a log cabin that was built in 1904. Cannell Meadow is a beautiful spot on the western edge of the Kern Plateau, edged by Jeffrey and lodgepole pines. Elevation is 7,500 feet, which means a total climb of 4,700 feet. Spread it out over a few days.

User Groups: Hikers, dogs, horses, and mountain bikes. No wheelchair facilities.

Permits: A free campfire permit is required for overnight stays and is available from the Kernville Ranger Station. Parking and access are free.

Maps: A Sequoia National Forest map is available from the U.S. Forest Service. For a topographic map, go to the USGS website to download Kernville.

Directions: From Kernville on the north end of Isabella Lake, drive north on Sierra Way/Road 99 for 1.4 miles to the Cannell Meadow trailhead, on the right. Parking is available near the horse corrals.

Contact: Sequoia National Forest, Kern River Ranger District, Kernville, 760/376-3781, www.fs.usda.gov/sequoia.

116 SALMON CREEK FALLS
8.0 mi/4.0 hr or 2 days   🥾2   ⛰9

in Sequoia National Forest near Big Meadow

Map 11.4, page 546

The eight-mile round-trip to the brink of Salmon Creek Falls is a stellar walk through lodgepole pines and white fir, with a chance for fishing, skinny-dipping, and admiring a lot of beautiful scenery at 7,600 feet in elevation. Since there are campsites located along the trail, it's easy enough to turn the trip into an overnight excursion, but the trail also makes a good long day hike. The trail is downhill all

the way, dropping 600 feet over 0.5 mile, and follows granite-lined Salmon Creek. After skirting the edge of Horse Meadow, you simply follow the creek's meander. Trails run on both sides of the stream for the first two miles, so you can walk either side, but then they join as one. The path comes to an end above Salmon Creek Falls, where you can swim, fish, and camp, but don't expect to gaze out at the big waterfall. There's no way to get a good look at it from here, since you're perched on top of it.

User Groups: Hikers, dogs, horses, and mountain bikes. No wheelchair facilities.

Permits: A free campfire permit is required for overnight stays and is available from the Springville or Kernville Ranger Stations at the addresses below. Parking and access are free.

Maps: A Sequoia National Forest map is available from the U.S. Forest Service. For topographic maps, go to the USGS website to download Sirretta Peak and Fairview.

Directions: From Kernville on the north end of Isabella Lake, drive north on Sierra Way/Road 99 for 22 miles to the right turnoff for Sherman Pass Road/22S05. Turn right and drive 6.1 miles on Sherman Pass Road, then turn right on Road 22S12, signed for Horse Meadow Campground. Drive 6.3 miles on Road 22S12 until you reach a fork. Stay straight. At eight miles, bear left. At 9.3 miles, turn right at the Horse Meadow Campground sign (Road 23S10). You'll reach the camp at 10.7 miles, but take the right turnoff just before the camp to reach the trailhead.

Contact: Sequoia National Forest, Kern River Ranger District, Kernville, 760/376-3781, www.fs.usda.gov/sequoia; Western Divide Ranger District, Springville, 559/539-2607, www.fs.usda.gov/sequoia.

117 SIRRETTA PEAK
8.0 mi/5.0 hr   🥾4   ⛰10

near the Dome Land Wilderness

Map 11.4, page 546

Hey, what's that big meadow down there? It's

Big Meadow, of course, that huge expanse of green you see from the top of Sirretta Peak. From Sirretta's summit, you get an eyeful of it, as well as long, lingering glances at the many granite domes of the Dome Land Wilderness Area, Sirretta and Deadwood Meadows, and the peaks of the High Sierra. The route to the peak starts at Big Meadow's northern edge, then travels north on Cannell Trail for 0.5 mile. Bear right (northeast) at the fork with Sirretta Peak Trail and climb 2.5 miles to a spur trail that leads to the summit. There are many switchbacks and plenty of fine views along the way. Take the left spur (it's obvious) for 0.5 mile to the rocky summit, and congratulate yourself on your fine mountaineering skills. The trail has an elevation gain of 1,200 feet, and if you decide to make the final summit climb, you'll add on another 700 feet. Sirretta Peak is just shy of 10,000 feet in elevation.

User Groups: Hikers and dogs. No horses or mountain bikes. No wheelchair facilities.

Permits: No day-hiking permits are required. Parking and access are free.

Maps: A Sequoia National Forest map is available from the U.S. Forest Service. For a topographic map, go to the USGS website to download Sirretta Peak.

Directions: From Kernville on the north end of Isabella Lake, drive north on Sierra Way/Road 99 for 22 miles to the right turnoff for Sherman Pass Road/22S05. Turn right and drive 6.1 miles on Sherman Pass Road. Turn right on Road 22S12, signed for Horse Meadow Campground, and drive 6.3 miles on Road 22S12 until you reach a fork. Stay straight. At eight miles, bear left, staying on Road 22S12. Continue four more miles, passing the Horse Meadow Campground turnoff, to Road 23S07, at the northern edge of Big Meadow. Turn left on Road 23S07 and drive 0.5 mile to the Cannell trailhead.

Contact: Sequoia National Forest, Kern River Ranger District, Kernville, 760/376-3781, www.fs.usda.gov/sequoia.

118 MANTER MEADOW LOOP
10.0 mi/6.0 hr   🥾2 ⛰9

in the Dome Land Wilderness

Map 11.4, page 546   **BEST (**

For people who love meadows, granite, and solitude, this loop trip is just about perfect. From the South Manter trailhead at 7,800 feet, the trail goes uphill for four miles to Manter Meadow, so bring your wildflower identification book and a map to identify surrounding peaks and domes. Along the way, several side trails branch off the main trail, leading to some of the granite domes of the Dome Land Wilderness, including spectacular Taylor Dome and Church Dome. A two-mile loop trail encircles the entire perimeter of the meadow, which you can add on to your trip if you wish. At the meadow's western edge, South Manter Trail meets North Manter Trail, and you follow the latter back to Forest Service Road 23S07 (the road you drove in on). Then it's a 1.5-mile walk on the dirt road back to your car. If you want to avoid the road, hike South Manter Trail both ways, and take the loop walk around the meadow. The mileage is about equal to the other trip.

User Groups: Hikers, dogs, and horses. No mountain bikes. No wheelchair facilities.

Permits: No permits are required. Parking and access are free.

Maps: A Sequoia National Forest or Dome Land Wilderness map is available from the U.S. Forest Service. For a topographic map, go to the USGS website to download Sirretta Peak.

Directions: From Kernville on the north end of Isabella Lake, drive north on Sierra Way/Road 99 for 22 miles to the right turnoff for Sherman Pass Road/22S05. Turn right and drive 6.1 miles on Sherman Pass Road. Turn right on Road 22S12, signed for Horse Meadow Campground, and drive 6.3 miles on Road 22S12 until you reach a fork. Stay straight. At eight miles, bear left, staying on Road 22S12. Continue four more miles, passing the Horse Meadow Campground turnoff, to Road 23S07 at the northern edge of Big Meadow. Turn left on Road 23S07 and drive three miles to the southeast edge of Big Meadow and the South Manter trailhead.

Contact: Sequoia National Forest, Kern River Ranger District, Kernville, 760/376-3781, www.fs.usda.gov/sequoia.

119 ROCKHOUSE BASIN

8.6 mi/4.0 hr

on the eastern side of the Dome Land Wilderness

Map 11.4, page 546

You're driving along in no-man's-land on Highway 178 between U.S. 395 and Lake Isabella, staring at thousands of those odd-looking piñon pines. This is the transition zone between the Mojave Desert to the east and the Sierra Nevada to the west, and it doesn't look quite like either one of them. Want to see this strange land up close? This hike to Rockhouse Basin can take you there, and since it requires a long drive on dirt roads to reach the trailhead, you're likely to be free of the Eastern Sierra's hiking masses. The trail heads downhill through a burned area, losing about 1,500 feet in elevation on its way to the Kern River and Rockhouse Basin. A half mile

from the trailhead, turn right and head north to Rockhouse Basin, where the noise of cicadas serenades you almost as loudly as the river. Explore the rocks and cool off in the river. It can be as hot as Hades out here, so plan your trip for early in the year, when you can hike along the Kern River in relative comfort.

User Groups: Hikers, dogs, and horses. No mountain bikes. No wheelchair facilities.

Permits: No permits are required. Parking and access are free.

Maps: A Sequoia National Forest or Dome Land Wilderness map is available from the U.S. Forest Service. For a topographic map, go to the USGS website to download Rockhouse Basin.

Directions: From the junction of Highway 14 and Highway 178 north of Mojave, drive west on Highway 178 for 18 miles to the right turn-off for Chimney Peak National Backcountry Byway, or Canebrake Road. Turn right and drive approximately nine miles. Turn left (west) on Long Valley Loop Road and drive 13 miles to the gate at the start of Rockhouse Basin Trail.

Contact: Bureau of Land Management, Ridgecrest Field Office, Ridgecrest, 760/384-5400, www.ca.blm.gov/ridgecrest; Sequoia National Forest, Kern River Ranger District, Kernville, 760/376-3781, www.fs.usda.gov/sequoia.

RESOURCES

NATIONAL FORESTS

The Forest Service provides many secluded camps and allows camping anywhere except where it is specifically prohibited. If you ever want to clear the cobwebs from your head and get away from it all, this is the way to go.

Many Forest Service campgrounds are quite remote and have no drinking water. You usually don't need to check in or make reservations, and sometimes there is no fee. At many Forest Service campgrounds that provide drinking water, the camping fee is often only a few dollars, with payment made on the honor system. Because most of these camps are in mountain areas, they are subject to winter closure because of snow or mud.

Dogs are permitted in national forests with no extra charge and no hassle. Leashes are required for all dogs in some places. Always carry documentation of current vaccinations.

Interagency Pass

An Interagency Pass (also called the America the Beautiful Pass) is available for $80 annually. The Interagency Pass is honored nationwide at all Forest Service, National Park Service, Bureau of Land Management, Bureau of Reclamation, and U.S. Fish and Wildlife Service sites charging entrance or standard amenity fees. Valid for 12 months from the month of purchase, the pass is available at most national forest or grassland offices or online (http://store.usgs.gov).

National Forest Reservations

Some of the more popular camps (and most group camps), are on a reservation system. Reservations can be made up to 240 days in advance, and up to 360 days in advance for groups. To reserve a site, contact Recreation.gov (877/444-6777, www.recreation.gov, $9-10 reservation fee); major credit cards are accepted. Holders of America the Beautiful (Interagency Pass), Golden Age, or Golden Access Passes receive a 50 percent discount for campground fees, except for group sites.

National Forest Maps

National Forest maps (406/329-3024, www.nationalforeststore.com, $10) are among the best you can get for the price; they detail all backcountry streams, lakes, hiking trails, and logging roads for access. Maps are available online or at forest service offices. Major credit cards are accepted if ordering by telephone.

Forest Service Information

Forest Service personnel are most helpful for obtaining camping or hiking trail information. Unless you are buying a map or Adventure Pass, it is advisable to phone in advance to get the best service. For specific information on a national forest, contact the following offices:

USDA Forest Service
Pacific Southwest Region
1323 Club Drive
Vallejo, CA 94592
707/562-USFS (707/562-8737)
www.fs.usda.gov/r5

Eldorado National Forest
100 Forni Road
Placerville, CA 95667
530/622-5061
www.fs.usda.gov/eldorado

Humboldt-Toiyabe National Forest
1200 Franklin Way
Sparks, NV 89431
775/331-6444
www.fs.usda.gov/htnf

Inyo National Forest
351 Pacu Lane, Suite 200
Bishop, CA 93514
760/873-2400
www.fs.usda.gov/inyo

Klamath National Forest
1312 Fairlane Road
Yreka, CA 96097-9549
530/842-6131
www.fs.usda.gov/klamath

Lake Tahoe Basin Management Unit
35 College Drive
South Lake Tahoe, CA 96150
530/543-2600
www.fs.usda.gov/ltbmu

Lassen National Forest
2550 Riverside Drive
Susanville, CA 96130
530/257-2151
www.fs.usda.gov/lassen

Mendocino National Forest
825 North Humboldt Avenue
Willows, CA 95988
530/934-3316
www.fs.usda.gov/mendocino

Modoc National Forest
800 West 12th Street
Alturas, CA 96101
530/233-5811
www.fs.usda.gov/modoc

Plumas National Forest
P.O. Box 11500
159 Lawrence Street
Quincy, CA 95971
530/283-2050
www.fs.usda.gov/plumas

Sequoia National Forest
Giant Sequoia National Monument
1839 South Newcomb Street
Porterville, CA 93257
559/784-1500
www.fs.usda.gov/sequoia

Shasta-Trinity National Forest
3644 Avtech Parkway
Redding, CA 96002
530/226-2500
www.fs.usda.gov/shastatrinity

Sierra National Forest
1600 Tollhouse Road

Clovis, CA 93611
559/297-0706
www.fs.usda.gov/sierra

Six Rivers National Forest
1330 Bayshore Way
Eureka, CA 95501
707/442-1721
www.fs.usda.gov/sixrivers

Stanislaus National Forest
19777 Greenley Road
Sonora, CA 95370
209/532-3671
www.fs.usda.gov/stanislaus

Tahoe National Forest
631 Coyote Street
Nevada City, CA 95959
530/265-4531
www.fs.usda.gov/tahoe

STATE PARKS

The California State Parks system provides many popular camping spots in spectacular settings. These campgrounds include drive-in numbered sites, tent spaces, and picnic tables, with showers and bathrooms provided nearby. Reservations are often necessary during the summer. Although many parks are well known, there are still some little-known gems in the state parks system where campers can enjoy seclusion, even in the summer.

Though state park fees have increased, camping in a state park is still a good deal. Many of the campgrounds along the California coastline are particularly popular in summer and require planning to secure a campsite.

State Park Reservations

Most of the state park campgrounds are on a reservation system, and campsites can be booked up to seven months in advance. There are also hike-in/bike-in sites at many of the parks available on a first-come, first-served basis. Reservations can be made at ReserveAmerica.com (800/444-7275, www.

reserveamerica.com, $10 reservation fee); major credit cards are accepted online.

Camping discounts of 50 percent are available for holders of the Disabled Discount Pass ($3.50), and free camping is allowed for holders of the Distinguished Veteran Pass.

For general information about California State Parks, contact:

California Department of Parks and Recreation

Public Information Office
P.O. Box 942896
1416 9th Street
Sacramento, CA 94296
800/777-0369
www.parks.ca.gov

NATIONAL PARKS

California's national parks are natural wonders, varying from the spectacular yet crowded Yosemite Valley to the remote and rugged Lava Beds National Monument. Reservations for campsites are available five months in advance for many of the national parks in California. In addition to campground fees, expect to pay a park entrance fee of $20-30 per vehicle (or as low as $5 per person for hike-in/bike-in sites). The entrance fee is valid for seven days. For an additional fee, an America the Beautiful sticker can be added to the National Parks Pass, thereby eliminating entrance fees at sites managed by the U.S. Fish and Wildlife Service, the U.S. Forest Service, and the Bureau of Land Management. Purchasing the annual National Parks Pass will also waive entrance fees. Reservations can be made at Recreation.gov (877/444-6777, www.recreation.gov, $8-9 reservation fee). Major credit cards are accepted.

National Park Service

Pacific West Region
One Jackson Center
1111 Jackson Street, Suite 700
Oakland, CA 94607
510/817-1304

www.nps.gov

Devils Postpile National Monument

P.O. Box 3999
Mammoth Lakes, CA 93546
760/934-2289 (summer only)
www.nps.gov/depo

Golden Gate National Recreation Area

Fort Mason, Building 201
San Francisco, CA 94123-0022
415/561-4700
www.nps.gov/goga

Lassen Volcanic National Park

P.O. Box 100
Mineral, CA 96063-0100
530/595-4444
www.nps.gov/lavo

Lava Beds National Monument

1 Indian Well Headquarters
Tulelake, CA 96134
530/667-2282
www.nps.gov/labe

Pinnacles National Park

5000 Highway 146
Paicines, CA 95043
831/389-4485
www.nps.gov/pinn

Point Reyes National Seashore

Point Reyes Station, CA 94956-9799
415/464-5100
www.nps.gov/pore

Redwood National and State Parks

1111 2nd Street
Crescent City, CA 95531
www.nps.gov/redw

Sequoia and Kings Canyon National Parks

47050 Generals Highway
Three Rivers, CA 93271-9700
559/565-3341
www.nps.gov/seki

Smith River National Recreation Area
P.O. Box 228
Gasquet, CA 95543
707/457-3131
www.fs.usda.gov/srnf

Whiskeytown National Recreation Area
P.O. Box 188
Whiskeytown, CA 96095
530/246-1225 or 530/242-3400
www.nps.gov/whis

Yosemite National Park
P.O. Box 577
Yosemite National Park, CA 95389
209/372-0200
www.nps.gov/yose

U.S. ARMY CORPS OF ENGINEERS

Some of the family camps and most of the group camps operated by the U.S. Army Corps of Engineers (www.spn.usace.army.mil) are on a reservation system. Reservations can be made up to 240 days in advance, and up to 360 days in advance for groups. To reserve a site, call 877/444-6777 or visit the website www.recreation.gov. The reservation fee is usually $10, and major credit cards are accepted. Holders of Golden Age or Golden Access passports receive a 50 percent discount for campground fees, except for group sites.

South Pacific Division
333 Market Street
San Francisco, CA 94105
415/977-8272

Sacramento District
1325 J Street
Sacramento, CA 95814
916/557-5100

BUREAU OF LAND MANAGEMENT

Most of the BLM campgrounds are primitive and in remote areas. Often, there is no fee charged for camping. Holders of Golden Age or Golden Access passports receive a 50 percent discount, except for group camps, at BLM fee campgrounds.

Bureau of Land Management
California State Office
2800 Cottage Way, Suite W-1834
Sacramento, CA 95825-1886
916/978-4400
www.blm.gov/ca

Alturas Field Office
708 West 12th Street
Alturas, CA 96101
530/233-4666
www.blm.gov/ca/alturas

Arcata Field Office
1695 Heindon Road
Arcata, CA 95521-4573
707/825-2300
www.blm.gov/ca/arcata

Bakersfield Field Office
3801 Pegasus Drive
Bakersfield, CA 93308
661/391-6000
www.blm.gov/ca/bakersfield

Bishop Field Office
351 Pacu Lane, Suite 100
Bishop, CA 93514
760/872-5000
www.blm.gov/ca/bishop

Eagle Lake Field Office
2950 Riverside Drive
Susanville, CA 96130
530/257-0456
fax 530/257-4831
www.blm.gov/ca/eaglelake

Folsom Field Office
63 Natoma Street
Folsom, CA 95630
916/985-4474
www.blm.gov/ca/folsom

Hollister Field Office
20 Hamilton Court
Hollister, CA 95023
831/630-5000
www.blm.gov/ca/hollister

Redding Field Office
355 Hemsted Drive
Redding, CA 96002
530/224-2100
www.blm.gov/ca/redding

Ukiah Field Office
2550 North State Street
Ukiah, CA 95482
707/468-4000
www.blm.gov/ca/ukiah

OTHER VALUABLE RESOURCES
State Forests
Jackson Demonstration State Forest
802 North Main Street
Fort Bragg, CA 95437
707/964-5674
http://calfire.ca.gov

Mountain Home Demonstration State Forest
P.O. Box 517
Springville, CA 93265
559/539-2321 (summer)
559/539-2855 (winter)
http://calfire.ca.gov

County/Regional Park Departments
Del Norte County Parks
840 9th Street, Suite 11
Crescent City, CA 95531

707/464-7230
www.co.del-norte.ca.us

East Bay Regional Park District
P.O. Box 5381
Oakland, CA 94605-0381
888/327-2757
www.ebparks.org

Humboldt County Parks
1106 2nd Street
Eureka, CA 95501
707/445-7651
www.co.humboldt.ca.us

Marin Municipal Water District
220 Nellen Avenue
Corte Madera, CA 94925
415/945-1455
www.marinwater.org

Midpeninsula Regional Open Space District
330 Distel Circle
Los Altos, CA 94022-1404
650/691-1200
www.openspace.org

Pacific Gas and Electric Company
Corporate Real Estate/Recreation
5555 Florin-Perkins Road, Room 100
Sacramento, CA 95826
916/386-5164
www.pge.com

Sacramento County Regional Parks
3711 Branch Center Road
Sacramento, CA 95827
916/875-6961
www.regionalparks.saccounty.net

San Mateo County Parks and Recreation Department
455 County Center, 4th floor
Redwood City, CA 94063-1646
650/363-4020
http://parks.smcgov.org

Santa Clara County Parks Department
298 Garden Hill Drive
Los Gatos, CA 95032-7669
408/355-2200
fax 408/355-2290
www.sccgov.org

Sonoma County Regional Parks
2300 County Center Drive, Suite 120-A
Santa Rosa, CA 95403
707/565-2041
www.sonomacounty.com

State and Federal Offices

U.S. Fish and Wildlife Service
1849 C Street NW
Washington, DC 20240
www.fws.gov

U.S. Geological Survey
Branch of Information Services
P.O. Box 25286, Bldg. 810,
MS 306, Federal Center
Denver, CO 80225
888/275-8747 or 303/202-4700
www.usgs.gov

California Department of Fish and Wildlife
1416 9th Street, 12th floor
Sacramento, CA 95814
916/445-0411
www.wildlife.ca.gov

Information Services

Lake County Visitor Information Center
P.O. Box 1025
6110 East Highway 20
Lucerne, CA 95458
707/274-5652 or 800/525-3743
http://lakecounty.com

Mammoth Lakes Visitors Bureau
P.O. Box 48
2520 Main St.
Mammoth Lakes, CA 93546
888/466-2666 or 760/934-2712

www.visitmammoth.com

Mount Shasta Visitors Bureau
300 Pine Street
Mount Shasta, CA 96067
530/926-4865 or 800/926-4865
http://mtshastachamber.com

The Nature Conservancy of California
201 Mission Street, 4th floor
San Francisco, CA 94105-1832
415/777-0487
www.nature.org

Plumas County Visitors Bureau
550 Crescent Street
P.O. Box 4120
Quincy, CA 95971
530/283-6345 or 800/326-2247
http://plumascounty.org

Shasta Cascade Wonderland Association
1699 Highway 273
Anderson, CA 96007
530/365-7500 or 800/474-2782
www.shastacascade.com

Map Companies

Map Link
30 South La Patera Lane, Unit 5
Goleta, CA 93117
805/692-6777 or 800/962-1394
www.maplink.com

Olmsted and Bros. Map Company
P.O. Box 5351
Berkeley, CA 94705
510/658-6534

Tom Harrison Maps
2 Falmouth Cove
San Rafael, CA 94901-4465
415/456-7940
www.tomharrisonmaps.com

U.S. Forest Service
National Forest Store

Attn: Map Sales
P.O. Box 8268
Missoula, MT 59807
406/329-3024
www.nationalforestmapstore.com

U.S. Geological Survey
345 Middlefield Road
Menlo Park, CA 94025
650/329-4390
www.usgs.gov

Index

A

Abbotts Lagoon Trail: 282
Abrigo Falls: 363
Adam and Eve Loop Trail: 597
Agave Trail: 322
Agnew Meadows: 513, 552
Alambique Trail: 344
Alameda: 366
Alameda Creek Regional Trail: 388
Alamere Falls Trail: 297
Alcatraz Island: 322
Alder Creek Falls: 528
Alder Creek Trail: 177, 604
Almaden Quicksilver County Park: 409
Alpine: 298
Alpine Lake Dam: 298, 304
Alpine Meadows: 229
Alpine Pond: 350
Alta Peak: 577
Alturas: 137-141
Alum Rock City Park: 405
Alviso: 394
American River Parkway: 199
Andrew Molera State Park: 442
Angel Island State Park: 320-321
Angora Lakes Trail: 244
Año Nuevo State Reserve: 395-397
Año Nuevo Trail: 354, 396
Ansel Adams Wilderness: 501-504, 510-512, 532-533
Anthony Chabot Regional Park: 369-370, 381
Antioch: 377-378
Aptos: 427-429
Aquinas: 407
Arcata Community Forest: 54
Arcata Marsh and Wildlife Sanctuary: 54
Arcata Marsh Trail: 54
Armstrong Redwoods State Natural Reserve: 182
Arnold: 258
Arrowhead Marsh: 367

Ash Camp: 110, 135
Asilomar Coast Trail: 431
Aspen Flat: 589
Auburn State Recreation Area: 198
Audubon Canyon Ranch Trail: 303
Austin Creek State Recreation Area: 182

B

Bailey Cove Loop Trail: 118
Bakersfield: 464
Balancing Rock: 236
Balconies Cave: 439
Bald Hill: 301
Bald Mountain Loop: 186
Bald Mountain Trail: 408
Baltimore Canyon Open Space Preserve: 309
Barker Pass: 232, 251
Barnabe Peak Loop: 294
Barney Lake Trail: 471
Barrett and TJ Lakes: 506
Barth's Retreat: 306
Bass Lake: 547-548
Battery Godfrey: 323
Battery Spencer: 320
Baxter: 223
Bay Ridge Trail: 338, 420
Bay Trail: 346
Bay View Loop: 355
Bayview Loop: 413
Bayview Trail: 385
Bear Gulch Cave: 437
Bear Lake: 469
Bear Valley Trail: 292
Bear Wallow Trailhead: 176
Belden Trailhead: 161
Ben Lomond: 410-411
Bennettville: 498
Berry Creek Falls: 398
Big Baldy: 574
Big Bar: 113
Big Basin Redwoods State Park: 397-399
Big Bear Lake Trail: 105
Big Hendy Grove: 174
Big Meadow: 619
Big Oak Flat: 175
Big Stump Trail: 559
Big Sur: 442, 444-447
Big Trees Nature Trail: 411

Bishop: 538
Bizz Johnson: 161
Black Butte Reservoir: 175
Black Butte Trail: 87
Black Crater: 130
Black Diamond Mines Regional Preserve: 377
Black Mountain: 349
Black Rock Lake Trail: 114
Black Wolf Falls: 595
Bloody Canyon Trail: 502
Blue Lake: 141, 553
Blue Lake Dam: 263
Blue Lake Loop National Recreation Trail: 141
Blue Lakes: 263
Blue Lakes Road: 265-266
Blue Ridge Trail to Fiske Peak: 181
Boat Taxi to Lake Aloha: 250
Bob Walker Ridge: 378
Bodega Bay: 181
Bodega Head Loop: 181
Bolinas: 297
Bolinas Lagoon: 303
Bolinas Ridge: 293
Boole Tree Loop: 563
Bootjack: 310
Borel Hill Trail: 349
Botanic Garden Loop: 363
Bothe-Napa Valley State Park: 185
Bothin Marsh: 318
Boulder Creek Falls: 119
Boulder Lake: 270
Boy Scout Tree Trail: 42
Brandy Creek Falls: 121
Brentwood: 384
Brewer Creek Trailhead: 92
Bridalveil Creek: 524
Bridalveil Fall: 522
Bridgeport: 471-473
Bridgeville: 56
Briones Peak Loop: 361
Briones Regional Park: 361, 363
Bruhel Point Tidepools: 171
Buck Lake Trailhead: 70
Buckeye Creek Trail: 471
Bucks Lake Wilderness: 193
Bucks Summit Trailhead: 193
Buena Vista Peak: 571
Bull Creek Trail North: 57

Bull Run Lake: 269
Bullards Bar Reservoir: 195
Bullards Bar Trail: 195
Bumpass Hell Trail: 151
Bunchgrass Trailhead: 143
Burney: 134-135, 141
Burney Falls Loop Trail: 134
Burney Mountain Summit: 141
Burnside Lake: 264
Burnt Lava Flow: 133
Burnt Ranch Falls: 112
Burst Rock: 470
Burton Creek Loop: 232
Butano Rim Loop: 353
Butano State Park: 352-354
Butte Lake: 146
Butte Lake Trailhead: 145
Buzzards Roost Overlook: 445
Bypass Trail: 397

C
Calaveras Big Trees State Park: 257
Calero County Park: 410
Calero Reservoir: 410
California Coastal Trail: 44
Calistoga: 183-185
Callahan: 96-98, 105
Camp Lake: 469
Canopy View Trail: 314
Canyon Creek Falls: 155
Canyon Creek Lakes Trailhead: 113
Caples Lake: 254, 259, 261
Caples Lake Trailhead: 254
Captain Jack's Stronghold: 129
Caribou Lake Trailhead: 148
Caribou Lakes Trail: 104
Caribou Wilderness: 147-148, 154
Carlon Falls: 479
Carmel: 432-436
Carmel Valley: 441, 448
Carquinez Strait Regional Shoreline: 357
Carr Lake: 217, 219
Carr/Feely Trailhead to Penner Lake: 217
Carrizo Plain and Painted Rock: 463
Carrizo Plains National Monument: 463
Carson Falls: 299

Carson Falls Loop: 300
Carson Pass: 253, 258-262, 265-266
Carson-Iceberg Wilderness: 256, 268-270
Casa Vieja Meadow: 613
Cascade Falls: 239
Castle Crags State Park: 108-110
Castle Crags to Mumbo Basin: 108
Castle Crags Wilderness: 110
Castle Dome: 109
Castle Lake: 102
Castle Rock State Park: 402-403
Castle Rock Trail: 372
Cataract Falls: 304
Cathedral Lakes: 486
Cecilville: 81
Cecilville Road: 97-98
Cedar Grove: 565-569
Chamberlain Creek Waterfall Trail: 172
Chapman Creek Trail: 214
Charleston Slough: 346
Chester, Sousa, and Winton Marsh Trails: 459
Chicago Stump Trail: 563
Chilnualna Fall: 529
Chimney Rock Trail: 286
China Camp State Park: 302
Chinese Camp: 458
Chowchilla: 547
Cinder Cone Trail: 145
Cisco Grove: 220
Clark Fork: 270
Clark Fork Stanislaus River: 270
Clear Creek Trailhead: 93
Clouds Rest: 484
Clouds Rest Trail: 348
Coal Creek Open Space Preserve: 348
Coalinga: 461
Coalinga Mineral Springs National Recreation Trail: 461
Coast Trail: 290, 310, 323
Coast View Trail: 311
Coastal Trail (Hidden Beach Section): 48
Coastal Trail Loop (Fern Canyon/Ossagon Section): 50
Codfish Creek Trail: 198
Cogswell Marsh Loop: 380

Coit Lake: 417
Cold Springs Nature Trail: 588
Colfax: 225
Columns of the Giants: 271
Condor Gulch and High Peaks Loop: 437
Cone Lake Trailhead: 147
Cone Peak Lookout Trail: 449
Congress Trail Loop: 580
Contra Loma Loop: 378
Contra Loma Regional Park: 378
Convict Canyon to Lake Dorothy: 533
Copper Creek Trail: 569
Cory Peak: 98
Costanoa: 395
Cosumnes River Preserve: 200
Cosumnes River Trail: 200
Cottonwood Lakes: 611
Cottonwood Pass: 612
Cow Mountain Recreation Area: 173
Coyote Hills Regional Park: 385
Coyote Lake-Harvey Bear County Park: 420
Coyote Peak: 185
Coyote Peak Loop: 409
Coyote Point County Park: 336
Coyote Point/Shoreline Trail: 336
Crags Trail: 109
Craig's Creek Trail: 43
Crescent City: 41-48, 69-72
Crescent Meadow: 583
Crest Trail/Vista Grande: 384
Crissy Field: 326
Crockett: 356
Crockett Hills Regional Park: 356
Crown Memorial State Beach: 366
Crystal Bay: 231
Crystal Lake: 506
Crystal Lake Trail: 594
Crystal Springs: 338
Crystal Springs Reservoir: 339
Crystal Springs Trail: 339
Cypress Trailhead: 142

D

D. L. Bliss State Park: 234-236
Danville: 374-376
Dardanelle: 271-272
Dardanelles Lake: 252
Davis Gulch Trail: 119
Dawn Falls: 309
Deadwood to Eldorado Creek: 226
Deer Creek Trail: 157, 159
Deer Lake Trail: 212
Deer Mountain: 85
Deer Park Trail: 301
Del Norte Redwoods State Park: 44
Desolation Wilderness: 234, 238-240, 242-247, 249-250
Devil's Elbow: 375
Devils Kitchen Trail: 153
Devils Postpile and Rainbow Falls: 509
Devils Postpile National Monument: 509
Devils Punchbowl (via Doe Flat/Buck Lake Trail): 71
Diablo Foothills Regional Park: 372
Diana Falls and Pools: 459
Dinkey Lakes: 551
Dinkey Lakes Wilderness: 551
Dipsea Trail: 315
Discovery Stump: 257
Doe Flat: 70
Dog Lake: 493
Dome Land Wilderness: 615, 619-621
Dome Rock: 604
Domingo Spring Campground: 155
Domingo Spring Trailhead: 155
Domingo Springs: 160
Don Castro Lake Loop: 383
Don Castro Regional Recreation Area: 383
Don Cecil Trail to Lookout Peak: 567
Donner Falls: 374
Donner Pass: 232
Donner Pass to the Yuba River: 218
Donner Summit: 222-223
Dowdy Ranch: 419
Doyle Trail: 599
Drake Lake Trail: 152
Drakesbad: 152-153
Dry Creek Community Park: 199
Duck Lake: 256, 508

E

Eagle Creek Trail: 413
Eagle Lake: 237
Eagle Lake Trail: 590
Eagle Peak: 515
Eagle Rock Overlook Loop: 405
Eagle View: 582
Earthquake Trail: 293
East Bay Skyline National Trail: 381
East Carson River Trail: 268
East Creek Loop: 139
East Fork Bridge: 588
East Fork Loop: 112
East Lake: 472
East Ridge Loop: 368
East Ridge Trail: 182
Eastman Lake: 547
Ebbetts Pass: 266-267, 269, 273
Echo and Twin Lakes: 148
Echo Lake: 251, 258
Echo Lakes Resort: 251
Ecology Trail: 324
Ed R. Levin County Park: 395
Ed Z'berg Sugar Pine Point State Park: 233
El Corte de Madera Open Space Preserve: 342
El Sereno Open Space Preserve: 407
Eldorado National Forest: 248
Elizabeth Lake: 489
Elk Camp Ridge Trail: 44
Elkhorn Slough South Marsh Loop: 429
Ellis Peak Trail: 230
Emerald Bay State Park: 237
Emerald Lake and Sky Meadows: 507
Emerson Trailhead: 139
Emigrant Gap: 216-217, 219
Emigrant Lake: 254
Emigrant Wilderness: 271-272, 469-470
Estero Trail: 284
Etna: 80
Etna Summit: 94-95
Eucalyptus Trail: 55
Euchre Bar Trail: 223
Eureka: 53, 55-58
Eureka Peak Loop: 208
Ewoldsen Loop Trail: 447

F

Fairfax: 299-300
Fairview: 616-617
Fallen Leaf Lake: 239-240, 242-243
Fallen Leaf Lake Trail: 243
Falls Loop Trail: 172
False Gun Vista Point: 358
Farewell Gap Trail: 589
Feather Falls Loop: 194
Feather River: 161
Feather River Pacific Crest Trail: 193
Fern Canyon Loop Trail: 51
Fern Canyon Trail: 173
Fern Lake Loop: 511
Ferndale: 55
First and Second Falls: 558
First and Second Lakes: 558
Fisk Mill Cove: 180
Fitzgerald Marine Reserve: 337
Five Allens Trail: 56
Five Lakes: 229
Flag Rock: 390
Flower and Matlock Lakes: 606
Folsom: 199
Foothills: 585-587
Forest of Nisene Marks State Park, The: 427-429
Forest View Loop Trail: 226
Foresthill: 226-227
Forestry Information Trail: 597
Fort Bragg: 171-172
Fort Funston: 328
Fort Point: 326
Founders Grove Nature Trail: 57
Four-Mile Trail: 522
Fourth of July Lake: 261
Fowler Peak: 208
Fowler Peak to Bucks Summit: 208
Fowler's Camp: 103
Franklin Lakes: 591
Franklin Ridge Loop: 357

Frazier Falls Trail: 211
Freeman Creek Trail: 601
Fremont: 385, 389
Fremont Peak State Park: 430
Fremont Peak Trail: 430
French Meadows Reservoir: 227
Fresno: 462
Fresno Dome: 532
Frog Lake: 262
Frog Pond Loop: 415

G

Galt: 200
Garberville: 61-62
Gardisky Lake: 499
Garfield-Hockett Trail: 596
Garin Regional Park: 385
Garland Ranch Regional Park: 435-436
Garrapata State Park: 434-435
General Creek to Lily Pond: 233
General Grant Tree Trail: 561
George Lake: 550
Gertrude Lake: 245
Giacomini Open Space: 297
Giant Forest: 578-584
Giant Sequoia National Monument: 563-564, 599-604
Gibbs Lake: 501
Gilliam Creek Trail: 182
Gilmore Lake: 242
Gilroy: 413
Glacier Lake: 219
Glacier Point Road: 523-527
Glen Aulin and Tuolumne Falls: 491
Glen Eden Trail: 173
Goat Mountain Fire Lookout: 548
Golden Gate Bridge: 319-320, 325
Goose Lake: 136
Graham Trail Loop: 367
Granite Chief Trail to Emigrant Pass: 228
Granite Chief Trail to Tinker Knob: 228
Granite Chief Wilderness: 229
Granite Lake: 115, 263
Grant Grove: 559-562, 570-571, 574

Grant Lake: 503
Grant Lakes: 482
Grass Lake Trail: 209
Grass Valley Loop: 369
Gray Butte: 91
Greeley Hill: 459
Green and Brown Lakes: 556
Green Butte Ridge: 91
Green Hill: 297
Green Lake: 472
Green Valley Trail: 225
Greens Creek Boat-In Trail: 117
Grider Creek: 73, 94
Grizzly Creek Redwoods State Park: 56
Grizzly Lake: 83
Grouse Falls: 227
Grouse Lake: 247
Grouse Ridge to Glacier Lake: 216
Groveland: 458
Grover Hot Springs State Park: 264
Gualala Point Regional Park: 178
Guerneville: 182
Gumboot Overlook Crag: 107
Gumboot Trailhead: 106

H

Half Dome: 520
Half Moon Bay: 337, 340
Halls Valley Loop: 405
Hamilton Lake: 581
Happy Camp: 73
Harden Lake: 481
Harkins Ridge Loop: 340
Hartman Bar National Recreation Trail: 193
Harvey Bear: 420
Haskell Peak Trail: 211
Hat Creek Rim: 143
Hay Meadows Trail: 154
Haypress Creek: 215
Haypress Meadows Trailhead: 74
Hayward: 380, 385
Hayward Regional Shoreline: 380
Hazel-Atlas Mine: 377
Hazelwood and Huckleberry Loop: 581
Headlands Loop: 178
Healdsburg: 178
Heart Lake Trail: 102

Heather Lake: 243
Heather Lake and the Watchtower: 577
Heiser Lake: 269
Hemlock Lake: 247
Hendy Woods State Park: 174
Henry Cowell Redwoods State Park: 412-413
Henry W. Coe State Park: 415-419
Hermit's Hut Trail: 174
Hi Grade National Recreation Trail: 136
Hidden Falls Loop: 198
Hidden Falls Regional Park: 198
High Sierra Trail: 581-582
Hirz Bay Trail: 117
Hite Cove Trail: 514
Hockett Trail: 588
Honeymoon Lake: 553
Hoopa: 81
Hoover Wilderness: 471-474, 499, 505
Horse Trail Ridge National Recreation Trail: 81
Horseshoe Lake: 509
Horsetail Falls Vista: 248
Hospital Rock: 586
Hossack Meadow Trail: 601
Hot Springs Creek Waterfall: 264
Hotel Creek Trail to Cedar Grove Overlook: 566
Hotel Trail: 406
Huckleberry Botanic Regional Preserve: 365
Huckleberry Loop Path: 365
Huddart Park Loop: 341
Humboldt Redwoods State Park: 56-58
Humboldt Summit: 160-161
Humboldt-Toiyabe National Forest: 264, 266-267, 471
Huntington Lake: 549-551

I

Ides Cove National Recreation Trail: 175
Illilouette Fall: 527
Indian Pools: 550
Inspiration and Stanford Points: 521
Inspiration Point: 154, 255, 308, 324

Inyo Craters: 505
Inyo National Forest: 498, 500, 505, 538, 605-606, 608
Iron Horse Regional Trail: 371
Ishi Wilderness: 157, 158, 159
Island Lake: 246
Island Lake Trail: 72
Italian Bar Trail: 224

J
Jackass Creek National Recreation Trail: 615
Jackass Lakes: 533
Jacks Peak County Park: 431
Jackson State Forest: 172
James Irvine Trail: 49
Jamestown: 457
Jedediah Smith Redwoods State Park: 42
Jenner: 179-180
Jennie Ellis Lake: 573
Jennie Lakes Wilderness: 572-573
Jepson: 283
John Jordan: 601
John Muir Trail: 494, 513, 552, 609
John Muir Wilderness: 508-508, 533-537, 553-558, 605-609, 611
Johnsondale: 603-604
Johnstone: 283
Jordan Hot Springs: 613
Jordan Peak Lookout: 600
Joseph D. Grant County Park: 405-406
Julia Pfeiffer Burns State Park: 446-447
Junction City: 83
June Lake: 504-505
Juniper Canyon and High Peaks Loop: 440
Juniper Lake Trailhead: 154

K
Kaiser Peak: 549
Kaiser Wilderness: 549, 550
Kangaroo Lake Trailhead: 98
Kaweah Oaks Preserve: 462
Kearsarge Pass: 605
Kelsey Creek Trail: 76
Kennedy Grove Regional Recreation Area: 360

Kennedy Lake: 271
Kent Dam Trail: 295
Kent Lake Pump Trail: 298
Kernville: 614, 618
Kibbie Lake: 470
King Crest Trail: 59
King Range National Conservation Area: 58-60
Kings Canyon National Park: 559-562, 565-571, 574
Kings Castle Trail: 77
Kinney Lakes: 266
Kirkwood Lake: 253
Klamath: 48-52
Klamath National Forest: 73, 84-85, 98
Klamath River: 84
Klamath Wildlife Refuge: 129

L
La Grange: 458
La Honda: 351
Lace Lichen Trail to Sea Lion Point: 432
Ladybug Trail: 596
Lafayette: 361
Lafayette-Moraga Trail: 365
Laguna Loop Trail: 291
Lagunitas Lake: 300
Lake Almanor: 154-155, 157
Lake Alpine: 255- 256
Lake Berryessa: 181
Lake Britton: 135
Lake Canyon: 474
Lake Cleone Trail: 171
Lake Doris: 244
Lake Eiler: 142
Lake Eleanor: 476
Lake George: 506
Lake Margaret: 253
Lake Mary: 507
Lake Oroville: 193-194
Lake Siskiyou: 101
Lake Sonoma: 178
Lake Sonoma Southlake Trail: 178
Lake Spaulding: 220
Lake Sylvia: 247
Lake Tahoe: 233-237, 252, 258
Lake Thomas Edison: 552, 609
Lakes Basin National Recreation Area: 209-210
Lakes Trail, The: 576

Lakeshore: 549-550
Lakeshore Trail: 255
Lakeview Trail: 547
Lamarck Lakes: 554
Lands End Trail: 326
Larkspur: 309
Las Trampas Regional Wilderness: 370
Lassen National Forest: 141, 155, 157, 160
Lassen Peak Trail: 150
Lassen Volcanic National Park: 142-155
Laurel Dell Loop: 305
Laurel Loop Trail: 360
Lava Beds National Monument: 129-131
Lee Vining: 474, 501-502
Lembert Dome: 492
Lewis Creek National Recreation Trail: 531
Lewis Creek Trail: 565
Lewis S. Eaton Trail: 462
Lexington Dam Trail: 408
Lexington Reservoir County Park: 408
Limekiln Falls: 449
Limekiln State Park Big Sur: 449
Limekiln Trail: 449
Linda Mar: 332
Lindsey Lakes Trail: 216
Little Baldy: 575
Little Giant Loop: 372
Little Glass Mountain: 132
Little Grass Valley Reservoir: 208
Little Jamison Creek: 209
Little Lakes Valley: 536
Little North Fork Trailhead: 80
Little South Fork Lake Trail: 81
Little Yosemite: 389
Livermore: 378
Loch Leven Lakes: 220
Loch Lomond Loop: 410
Loch Lomond Recreation Area: 410-411
Lodgepole: 575
Loma Prieta Earthquake Epicenter: 428
Lone Pine Lake: 609
Long Canyon Trailhead: 115
Long Gulch Lake Loop: 97
Long Lake: 154, 210
Long Ridge Loop: 400

Long Ridge Open Space Preserve: 400-401
Lookout Point Loop Trail: 61
Los Banos: 459
Los Cerritos Trail: 410
Los Gatos: 408
Los Trancos Open Space Preserve: 348
Los Vaqueros Reservoir: 384
Lost Coast Trail: 58, 169
Lost Man Creek Trail: 48
Lower Gaylor Lake: 487
Lower Lola Montez Lake: 221
Lower Mill Creek: 158
Lower Yosemite Fall: 516
Lucia: 449
Lukens Lake: 481
Lundy Canyon Trail: 474
Lupine, Waterfall, and Mesa Loop: 435
Lyell Canyon: 489
Lyons Creek Trail: 247
Lytel Ridge: 55

M
MacDonald Trail: 370
MacKerricher State Park: 171
Mammoth Lakes: 505-512, 533
Manchester State Park: 177
Manter Meadow Loop: 620
Manzanita and Azalea Trails: 560
Manzanita Lake Trail: 145
Manzanita Lake Trailhead: 144
Maple Falls: 427
Marble Falls: 587
Marble Mountain Rim: 78
Marble Mountain Wilderness: 74-80, 94
Marin: 297
Marin Headlands: 316-319
Marin Water District: 306-307
Marin's Hill 88: 317
Marina Green: 326
Mariposa Grove: 530
Markleeville: 264, 268
Marshall Beach Trail: 283
Martin Griffin Preserve: 303
Martin Luther King Regional Shoreline: 367
Martinez: 357-358
Martinez Regional Shoreline: 358

Mary Bowerman Trail: 375
Matt Davis: 310
Mattole Trailhead: 58
Mavericks Beach: 337
May Lake and Mount Hoffman: 483
May Lundy Mine: 474
McArthur-Burney Falls Memorial State Park: 134-135, 143
McClendon Ford Trail: 45
McCloud: 103, 110
McCloud Nature Trail: 110
McClure Trail: 156
McClures Beach Trail: 281
McGee Creek to Steelhead Lake: 534
McGuire Segment: 227
McGurk Meadow and Dewey Point: 523
McNee Ranch: 335
McNee Ranch State Park: 334-335
McWay Falls Overlook: 447
Meadow Loop Trail: 345
Meadowlark Trail: 460
Medicine Lake: 132-133
Medicine Lake Glass Flow: 133
Medicine Lake Shoreline: 131
Meeks Creek Trail: 234
Memorial Trail Loop: 56
Mendocino: 173
Mendocino National Forest: 174, 176-177
Menlo Park: 345
Merced: 460
Merced Grove: 479
Merced National Wildlife Refuge: 460
Meteor Trail: 399
Methuselah Trail: 538
Meysan Lake: 608
Middle and Upper Gaylor Lakes: 496
Middle Falls Trail: 103
Middle Fork Falls Loop: 176
Middle Fork Trail to Panther Creek: 585
Mill Creek: 157
Mill Creek Falls Trailhead: 138
Mill Creek Redwood Preserve: 441
Mill Creek Trail: 441
Mill Ox Loop: 352
Mill Valley: 315, 318

Miller-Knox Regional Shoreline: 358
Millerton Lake: 549
Minaret Lake: 510
Mine Hill Trail Loop: 409
Mineral King: 587-595
Minkalo Trail: 254
Mirror Lake Loop: 519
Mission Peak Regional Preserve: 389
Mission Peak Trail: 389
Mississippi Lake Trail: 416
Mist Falls: 568
Mist Trail and John Muir Loop to Nevada Fall: 518
Mist Trail to Vernal Fall: 517
Mitchell Canyon: 372
Mitchell Peak: 573
Miwok Loop: 317
Moak Trail: 158
Modoc National Forest: 131-133, 136, 141
Mokelumne Wilderness: 254, 256, 260-263
Molera Point Trail: 442
Molera State Park Loop: 442
Monarch Lakes: 593
Mono Lake South Tufa Trail: 501
Mono Lake Tufa State Reserve: 501
Mono Pass: 495, 535
Montara: 334-335
Montara Mountain: 335
Montara Mountain Trail: 333
Monte Bello Open Space Preserve: 349
Monterey: 431
Monument Peak Trail: 395
Moraga: 370
Morgan Hill: 414-417
Morgan Territory Regional Preserve: 378
Mori Point Trail: 332
Morning Sun Trail: 319
Moro Rock: 584
Moses Gulch Trail: 599
Mosquito Lakes: 269, 589
Moss Beach: 337
Moss Landing: 429
Mount Burdell: 296
Mount Dana: 497
Mount Diablo State Park: 372, 374-376
Mount Eddy Trail: 99
Mount El Sombroso: 407
Mount Elwell Trail: 209

Mount Hoffman: 483
Mount Livermore Summit: 321
Mount Madonna County Park: 413
Mount Manuel: 444
Mount Shasta: 85-88, 91-93, 131
Mount Shasta Wilderness: 91
Mount St. Helena Trail: 183
Mount Tallac (Tallac Trailhead): 239
Mount Tallac Loop (Glen Alpine Trailhead): 240
Mount Tamalpais State Park: 298- 301, 304-305, 307-312, 315
Mount Whitney: 608, 611
Mount Whitney Trail: 607
Mount Wittenberg Loop: 292
Mountain Home: 312
Mountain Home Demonstration State Forest: 597-599
Mountain Theater: 307
Mountain View Park: 346
Mud Creek Falls: 93
Muir Beach Overlook and Owl Trail: 313
Muir Grove: 575
Muir Woods National Monument: 313-314
Mule Bridge Trailhead: 80
Mule Peak Lookout: 603
Mumbo Basin: 106
Mumford Bar Trail: 224
Murietta Falls Trail: 392
Myrtle Creek Trail: 41

N

Natural Bridges: 457
Nature Conservancy: 110
Nature Trail: 54
Needles Spires, The: 602
Nevada City: 196, 219
New Melones Reservoir: 457
New River Divide Trail: 113
New River Trailhead: 111
Niche and Cora Lakes, The: 532
Nickel Creek Camp: 44
Niles: 388
Nimitz Way: 362
Noble Lake: 267
Nobles Emigrant Trail: 144
North Arroyo Trail: 386
North Butte: 196

North Chalone Peak: 438
North Dome: 483
North Fork American River: 223-225
North Fork Kern River Trail: 614
North Grove and Dead Giant Loop: 562
North Grove Loop: 257
North Peak: 375
North Sonoma Mountain: 187
North Table Mountain: 194
Novato: 296

O

O'Rourke's Bench: 305
Oakhurst: 531-532, 547-548
Oakland: 367
Ocean Beach Esplanade: 327
Ohlone Ridge Trail: 395
Ohlone Wilderness Trail: 391
Old Landing Cove Trail: 426
Olema: 292-293, 296
Olema Valley: 296
Ollason Peak: 431
Olompali State Historic Park: 296
Omega Overlook: 219
Orestimba Wilderness: 419
Orinda: 363
Orland: 175
Osborne Hill: 255
Ostrander Lake: 524

P

Pacific Crest Trail: 73, 94, 97-98, 106, 108, 110, 135, 143, 153, 155, 160-161, 208, 215, 218, 232, 251, 258, 265-266, 273, 493, 513, 552
Pacific Grove: 431
Pacifica: 332-334
Pacifica State Beach: 332
Packer Lake: 212-213
Palisade Creek Trail to Heath Falls: 221
Palisades Trail: 184
Palo Alto: 346
Palo Alto Baylands Trail: 346
Panorama Trail: 527
Panoramic Point: 560
Panther Gap Loop: 578

Pantoll: 310
Paradise Creek Trail: 585
Paradise Lake Trail: 76
Paradise Ridge: 587
Park Ridge Lookout: 560
Parker Lake Trail: 503
Parks Creek Trailhead: 99
Partington Point and Tanbark Trails: 446
Path of the Padres: 461
Patrick's Point State Park: 53
Patrick's Point: 302
Pebble Beach: 283
Pepperdine Trailhead: 137
Perimeter Trail: 320
Pescadero: 352-354, 396
Pescadero Marsh: 352
Peters Creek Grove: 355
Pfeiffer Big Sur State Park: 444-445
Phoenix Lake Loop: 309
Pine Creek Trailhead: 137
Pine Mountain: 299
Pine Valley: 448
Pinecrest Lake: 270, 469-470
Pinecrest Lake National Recreation Trail: 469
Pinnacles National Park: 437-440
Pioneer Trail: 219
Pioneer Tree Trail: 295
Piute Lake & Piute Pass: 555
Pleasanton: 386
Pleasanton Ridge Regional Park: 386
Plumas National Forest: 161, 193-194, 208
Plumas-Eureka State Park: 208-209
Pohono Trail: 526
Point Arena: 177
Point Isabel Regional Shoreline: 359
Point Lobos: 326
Point Lobos Perimeter: 433
Point Lobos State Reserve: 432-433
Point Pinole Regional Shoreline: 355
Point Reyes Lighthouse: 285
Point Reyes National Seashore: 281-288, 290-293, 296-297
Poore Lake: 273

Portola Redwoods State Park: 355
Potwisha: 586
Powell Lake: 470
Prairie Creek Redwoods State Park: 49-51
Presidio, The: 323-324
Preston Flat Trail: 475
Preston Peak: 69
Princeton: 337
Prospect Peak Trail: 146
Purisima Creek Redwoods Open Space Preserve: 340-341

QR

Quaking Aspen: 600-602, 604
Quincy: 193, 208-209
Rainbow and Lake of the Sky Trails: 240
Rainbow Pool and Confluence Trail: 458
Ralston Peak: 249
Rancheria Falls: 477, 551
Rancheria Trail: 157
Rancho del Oso: 397
Rathert Grove: 56
Ravenswood Open Space Preserve: 345
Raymond Lake: 263
Red Bluff: 114, 122, 144, 148-151, 156-159, 169-170, 175
Red Cones Loop: 509
Red Hills: 458
Redding: 117-118
Redwood Canyon: 570
Redwood Creek Trail: 51, 313
Redwood Crossing: 598
Redwood Grove Loop Trail: 412
Redwood Loop Nature Trail: 397
Redwood Mountain Loop: 570
Redwood National and State Parks: 47-49, 51-52
Redwood Regional Park: 368
Redwood Trail: 341
Redwood Trail Loop: 185
Relief Reservoir: 272
Richardson Grove State Park: 61-62
Richmond: 358
Ridge Trail: 187, 330
Ridge Trail Loop: 351

Ridgeline Trail: 386
Rim Loop Trail: 53
Rim Trail: 135
Rincon Trail: 617
Riverbank Trail: 199
Roaring River Falls: 567
Robert Louis Stevenson State Park: 183
Roberts Regional Recreation Area: 367
Robinson Lake: 606
Rock City: 376
Rock Springs: 305
Rockbound Pass: 244
Rockhouse Basin: 621
Rocky Ridge and Soberanes Canyon Loop: 434
Rocky Ridge Loop: 370
Rohnert Park: 187
Rooster Comb Loop: 418-419
Root Creek Trail: 108
Roseville: 199
Ross: 309
Round Lake: 252
Round Lake Trailhead: 210
Round Top Loop: 261
Round Top Loop Trail: 364
Round Valley Regional Preserve: 379
Rubicon and Lighthouse Loop: 234
Rubicon Trail: 235
Ruby Lake: 537
Rush Creek Trail: 504
Russ City Park: 55
Russian Gulch State Park: 172
Russian Ridge Open Space Preserve: 349
Russian Wilderness: 95-97
Ruth Lake: 114
Ruwau and Chocolate Lakes Loop: 557

S

Sacramento: 199
Saddlebag Lake Loop: 500
Salmon Creek Falls: 619
Salt Point Bluff Trail: 179
Salt Point State Park: 179-180
Sam McDonald County Park: 351
Samuel P. Taylor State Park: 294-295
San Andreas Fault Trail: 348

San Andreas Trail: 331
San Anselmo: 300-301
San Bruno: 330, 332
San Bruno Mountain State and County Park: 329-330
San Francisco: 324-328
San Francisco Bay National Wildlife Refuge: 387, 394
San Geronimo Ridge: 297
San Jose: 409-410
San Juan Bautista: 430
San Leandro Reservoir: 365
San Luis National Wildlife Refuge: 459
San Luis Reservoir State Recreation Area: 461
San Mateo: 332, 336
San Pablo Ridge Loop: 359
San Pedro Mountain: 334
San Pedro Valley County Park: 333-334
San Rafael: 293-295, 302
San Ramon Valley: 371
Sanborn-Skyline County Park: 404
Sand Flat Trailhead: 87
Santa Cruz: 412- 413, 426
Santa Rosa: 185
Santa Teresa County Park: 409
Saratoga Gap Loop: 401
Sardine Falls: 272
Sausalito: 316-317, 319
Sawyer Camp Recreation Trail: 332
Sawyers Bar: 80
Schonchin Butte Trail: 131
Scott Mountain: 98, 106
Scott Mountain Campground: 98
Secret Lake: 273
Seiad Valley: 73
Sentinel Dome: 525
Sentinel Rock: 180, 376
Sequoia National Forest: 614-619
Sequoia National Park: 575-596
Serenity Trail: 407
Shackleford Creek Trail: 79
Shadow Cliffs Regional Recreation Area: 386
Shadow Lake: 512
Shadow Lake Trail: 151
Shadow of the Giants: 531
Shasta Lake: 117-118

Shasta Summit Trail: 88
Shasta-Trinity National
    Forest: 87-88, 99, 101-103,
    106-108,112, 114, 135
Shaver Lake: 551
Sherman Peak Trail: 614
Shingle Falls (Fairy Falls)
    Loop: 197
Shoreline Trail: 302, 366
Showers Lake: 259
Sibley Volcanic Regional
    Preserve: 364
Sierra Azul Open Space
    Preserve: 407-408
Sierra Buttes Trail: 213
Sierra City: 210-211, 214-215
Sierra Discovery Trail: 220
Sierra National Forest: 514,
    531
Silver Lake: 254
Sinkyone Wilderness State
    Park: 169
Sir Francis Drake Trail: 287
Sirretta Peak: 619
Siskiyou Mountains: 73
Siskiyou Wilderness: 69-72
Sisson-Callahan: 101
Six Rivers National Forest:
    81
Ski Bowl: 91
Skinner Ridge Trail to Devil's
    Peak: 441
Skunk Cabbage Trail: 52
Sky High Lakes: 79
Sky Trail Loop: 288
Sky Trail to Palomarin: 287
Skyline Nature and Jacks
    Peak Trails: 431
Skyline Ridge: 350
Skyline Ridge Open Space
    Preserve: 350
Skyline-to-the-Sea Trail: 403
Slate Creek Trail to Green
    Treble Lake: 499
Slate Mountain: 602
Smartville: 197
Smith Lake: 209, 247
Smith Peak: 478
Smith River National
    Recreation Area: 41-46
Snivley's Ridge Trail: 436
Snow Mountain Wilderness:
    176-177
Soaring Eagle Trail: 356
Soberanes Point Trail: 435
Sobrante Ridge Regional
    Preserve: 361

Soda Springs: 221
Soldier Ridge Trail: 169
Soledad: 437-440
Somes Bar: 74-75
Sonoma: 186
Sonoma Mountain Regional
    Park: 187
Sonora: 457
Sonora Pass: 272-273, 493
Soup Spring Trailhead: 138
South Bay Nature Trail: 394
South Beach Trail: 284
South Fork Merced River:
    514
South Fork National
    Recreation Trail: 114
South Grove Loop: 258
South Kelsey Trail: 45
South Lake Tahoe: 237, 239-
    240, 243-244, 248-249
South Sierra Wilderness: 615
South Warner Wilderness:
    137-140
South Yuba Independence
    Trail: 196
Spanish Ridge Trail: 60
Spencer Meadow Trail: 155
Spenceville Wildlife Area:
    197
Spillway and Helen Lakes:
    496
Spirit Lake Trail: 75
Spring Lake Regional Park:
    185
Springville: 597-599
Squaw Leap Loop: 549
Squaw Valley: 228
Stanislaus National Forest:
    270, 458-459, 469, 475,
    479
Stateline Lookout: 231
Statue Lake: 95
Steep Ravine Trail: 311
Stevens Trail: 225
Stillwater Cove Regional
    Park: 180
Stinson Beach: 313, 315
Stockoff Creek Loop: 180
Stony Creek Trail: 43
Stout Grove Trail: 42
Strawberry: 270, 469
Stream Trail Loop: 368
Stuart Fork Trailhead: 116
Sugar Pine Reservoir: 225
Sugarloaf Ridge State Park:
    186
Summit Lake Loop: 149

Summit Lake Trail: 223
Summit Loop: 140
Summit Loop Trail: 329
Summit Rock Loop: 404
Summit Springs Trailhead:
    177
Summit Trail: 602
Summit Valley Trail: 46
Sunday Peak Trail: 617
Sunnyvale Baylands: 394
Sunol Regional Wilderness:
    389-390
Sunol-Ohlone Regional
    Wilderness: 391-392
Sunrise Lakes: 485
Sunset Rock: 584
Sunset Trail: 328, 559
Susanville: 161
Susie Lake: 243
Sutter Buttes: 196
Sweeney Ridge: 330
Swift Creek Trail: 115
Sycamore Nature Trail: 414
Syd Cabin Ridge Trail: 122
Sykes Hot Springs: 445

T
Table Mountain: 457
Tafoni Monolith to Vista
    Point: 342
Taft Point and the Fissures:
    525
Tahoe City: 230, 232
Tahoe National Forest: 195,
    211-224, 226-228, 230,
    244
Tall Trees Trail: 49
Tamarack Lake Trailhead: 107
Tamarack Lakes: 536
Tamarack Trailhead: 142
Taylor Lake Trail: 95
Tehama Wildlife Area: 156
Ten Lakes: 482
Tenaya Lake: 485
Tennessee Valley: 316
Tharp's Log: 583
Thomas Wright Battlefield
    Trail: 130
Thousand Lakes Wilderness:
    142-143
Tidelands Trail: 387
Tilden Regional Park: 362-
    363
Timber Gap Trail: 593
Tioga Pass: 481-485, 487,
    495-500

Toad Lake Trail: 101
Tokopah Falls: 578
Tolowa Dunes State Park: 41
Tomales Bay State Park: 283
Tomales Point Trail: 281
Toro County Park: 431
Toumey Grove Trail: 62
Trail Camp: 353
Trail Camp Loop: 402
Trail Creek Route: 96
Trail Gulch Lake: 97
Trail of Giants: 603
Trail of the Gargoyles: 270
Trail Pass: 612
Tree of Heaven Trail: 84
Trinity Alps Wilderness: 81, 83, 97, 104-105, 111-113, 115-116
Trinity Center: 115
Trinity Lake: 104-105, 115-116
Tsurai Loop: 53
Tule Elk State Natural Reserve: 464
Tulelake Wildlife Refuge: 130-131
Tuolumne Grove: 480
Tuolumne Meadows: 486-494, 513
Twin Lake: 246
Twin Lakes: 550, 579
Two Lakes Trail: 300
Tyee Lakes: 555
Tyler Lake: 245

UV

Ukiah: 173
Unal Trail: 618
Union Lake Trail: 105
Upper Eagle Falls: 237
Upper Yosemite Fall: 515
Uvas Canyon County Park: 414
Uvas Park Waterfall Loop: 414
Valentine Lake Trail: 508
Valley View and Pfeiffer Falls: 444
Van Damme State Park: 173
Velma Lakes: 238
Ventana Wilderness: 441, 444-445, 448-449
Vikingsholm: 237
Virginia Lakes Trail: 473
Visalia: 462
Vista Loop: 385

Vista Point: 320
Vogelsang Loop: 487
Volvon Loop Trail: 378

W

Wapama Fall: 477
Ward Creek Trail: 230
Warner Valley: 155
Warren Lake: 222
Waters Gulch Overlook: 118
Waterwheel Falls: 490
Wawona: 528-530
Wawona Meadow Loop: 529
Way of the Mono: 547
Weaver Lake: 572
Weaverville: 113
Weiler Ranch Road: 334
West Lake: 472
West Point Inn: 307, 310
West Ridge and Aptos Creek Loop: 429
West Snow Mountain Loop: 177
Western States Trail: 226-227
Whaleback, The: 85
Whaler's Knoll and Cypress Grove: 433
Wheeler Lake: 256
Whiskey Flat Trail: 616
Whiskeytown Falls: 120
Whiskeytown Lake National Recreation Area: 119-121
White Chief Mine Trail: 592
White Mountain Peak Trail: 538
Whitney Butte Trail: 129
Whitney Falls Trailhead: 86
Whittemore Gulch Loop: 340
Wild Plum Loop: 215
Wildcat Canyon Regional Park: 359, 381
Wilder Ranch State Park: 426
Wilder Ridge and Zane Grey Trails: 426
Wilderness Falls: 72
Williams Grove Trail: 58
Willow Creek: 111-112, 548
Windy Cliffs: 564
Windy Hill Open Space Preserve: 347
Winnemucca Lake: 260
Wofford Heights: 617-618
Wolf Creek Falls: 268

Wolf Creek Trail: 268
Wolverton: 576-578
Woodchuck Basin: 256
Woodlands Loop Trail: 61
Woods Lake: 260-261
Woodside: 338-339, 341, 344-345
Wrights Valley Trail: 170
Wunderlich County Park: 344-345

XYZ

Yellow Bluff Trail: 319
Yolla Bolly Wilderness: 114, 122, 169-170, 175
Yosemite National Park: 470, 474-497, 523-532
Yosemite Valley: 494, 515-523
Yost Lake: 505
Young Lakes Loop: 490
Youngs Valley Trail: 69
Yreka: 76-79, 84
Yuba City: 196
Yuba River to Fowler Peak: 215
Yucca Point: 564
Yurok Loop: 47
Zumwalt Meadow Loop: 568

Acknowledgments

U.S. Forest Service

Debe Arndt, High Sierra Ranger District, Sierra National Forest

Adam Barnett, High Sierra Ranger District, Sierra National Forest

Susan Burkindine, Sierra National Forest

Mary August, Feather River Ranger District, Plumas National Forest

Paul Bailey, Devil's Garden Ranger District, Modoc National Forest

Cheryl Balle and Ann Wiltshire, Cannell Meadow Ranger District, Sequoia National Forest

Jim Barnhardt, Hat Creek Work Center, Lassen National Forest

Al Buchter, Salmon River Ranger District, Klamath National Forest

Kathy Burnett, Summit Ranger District, Stanislaus National Forest

Joe Chavez, Downieville Ranger District, Tahoe National Forest

Maxine Chittender, Hume Lake Ranger District, Sequoia National Forest

Scott Clemons, Bridgeport Ranger District, Humboldt-Toiyabe National Forest

Pennie Custer, Inyo National Forest

Jim Fedderly, Calaveras Ranger District, Stanislaus National Forest

Dusty Vaughn, Groveland Ranger District, Stanislaus National Forest

Anna Fiorella, Corning Work Center, Mendocino National Forest

Pat Garrahan, Happy Camp Ranger District, Klamath National Forest

Sharon Graham, Covelo Ranger District, Mendocino National Forest

Ken Graves, Hayfork Office, Shasta-Trinity National Forest

Steve Hale, Carson Ranger District, Humboldt-Toiyabe National Forest

Bob Hemus, Orleans Ranger District, Klamath National Forest

Bob Hemus, Six Rivers National Forest

Charlie Kraus, Scott River Ranger District, Klamath National Forest

Don Lee, Mount Shasta Ranger District, Shasta-Trinity National Forest

Mike LeFevre, Bass Lake Ranger Station, Sierra National Forest

John Louth, Ancient Bristlecone Pine Forest, Inyo National Forest

Dean Lutz, Truckee Ranger District, Tahoe National Forest

Patty Mahaffey, Nevada City Ranger District, Tahoe National Forest

Matt Mathes, Pacific Region Headquarters

Geneva May, Sierraville Ranger District, Tahoe National Forest

Marilyn Muse Meyer, Amador Ranger District, Eldorado National Forest

Joe Miranda, Stonyford Ranger Station, Mendocino National Forest

Deborah Nearing, Foresthill Ranger District, Tahoe National Forest

Liz Nelson, Mount Whitney Ranger Station, Inyo National Forest

Barbara Paolinetti, McCloud Ranger District, Shasta-Trinity National Forest

Del Pengilly, Tule River/Hot Springs Ranger District, Sequoia National Forest

Denise Alonzo, Kern River Ranger District, Sequoia National Forest

Joyce Platt, Information Center, Eldorado National Forest

Robin Renteria, Lake Tahoe Basin Management Unit

John Sandstrom, Big Bar Ranger Station, Shasta-Trinity National Forest

Lisa Sedlacek, Almanor Ranger District, Lassen National Forest

Jerry Snyder, Stanislaus National Forest

Cindy Kaplan, Summit Ranger District, Stanislaus National Forest

Cathy Southwick, Shasta Lake Ranger District, Shasta-Trinity National Forest

Jim Stout, Goosenest Ranger District, Klamath National Forest

Dustin Swan, Bridgeport Ranger District, Humboldt-Toiyabe National Forest
Jeffrey Weise, Bridgeport Ranger District, Toiyabe National Forest
Nancy Upham, Inyo National Forest
Debra Schweizer, Inyo National Forest
Pandora Valle, Beckwourth Ranger District, Plumas National Forest
Keith Waterfall, Inyo National Forest
Beverly Way, Warner Mountain Ranger District, Modoc National Forest
Lorraine Worley, Doublehead Ranger District, Modoc National Forest
KC Wylie, Inyo National Forest

National Lands
Nancy Bailey and Karen Haner, Lassen Volcanic National Park
Paul Johnson, Pinnacles National Park
Jan Lemons, Pinnacles National Park
Phil Bono and Don Pass, Smith River National Recreation Area
Cathy Cook, Redwood National and State Parks
Malinee Crapsey, Sequoia and Kings Canyon National Parks
Kris Fister, Sequoia and Kings Canyon National Parks
Trisha Ford, Whiskeytown National Recreation Area
Scott Gediman, Yosemite National Park
Ken Hires, Sequoia and Kings Canyon National Parks
Valerie Pillsbury, Sequoia and Kings Canyon National Parks
Cathy Purchis, Sequoia and Kings Canyon National Parks
Denise Robertson, Sequoia and Kings Canyon National Parks
Barney Stoffel, Lava Beds National Monument
Dave Feliz, Elkhorn Slough National Estuarine Research Reserve
John Fulton, San Luis National Wildlife Refuge Complex

U.S. Army Corps of Engineers
Mary Ann Deeming, Black Butte Lake

Greg Volkman, Eastman Lake
Angie Wulsow, Lake Sonoma

Bureau of Land Management
Larry Ames, Ukiah Field Office
Stan Bell, Eagle Lake Field Office
Jenny Weiss, Arcata Field Office
Zachary Pratt, Barstow Field Office
David Moore, Hollister Field Office

State Parks and Recreation Areas
Garratt Aitchison, Sugar Pine Point State Park
Jill Alford, Mendocino District
John Hiles, Monterey District
Jo Ann Allison, Big Sur Station (Big Sur state parks)
Kim Anbrychowicz, Prairie Creek Redwoods State Park
Jim Baird, Patrick's Point State Park
Katie Bernarding, Tomales Bay State Park
Becky Bradford, Butano State Park
Barry Breckling, Henry W. Coe State Park
Matthew Buonaguidi, Point Lobos State Reserve
Lori Castro, Castle Crags State Park
Sharon Galligan, Henry Cowell Redwoods State Park
Chuck Grennell, Calaveras Big Trees State Park
Bill Grummer, Bothe-Napa Valley State Park
Mike Hanes, Samuel P. Taylor State Park
David Horvitz, Sonoma Coast State Beach
John Kolsrud, Armstrong Redwoods State Reserve
Bill Lindemann, Sierra District
John McGee, Point Lobos State Reserve
Susan McLaughlin, Richardson Grove State Park
Bill Mentzer, Mount Tamalpais State Park
William Moffat, Tule Elk State Reserve
Jennifer Morgan, Pacheco State Park/San Luis Reservoir State Rec. Area
Ken Morse, Jedediah Smith Redwoods State Park
Roger Nelson, Half Moon Bay State Beach
Dean Oertly, Plumas-Eureka State Park

John O'Rourke, Humboldt Redwoods State Park
Derek Davis, Fremont Peak State Park
Paula Pennington, Grover Hot Spring State Park
Richard Ranc, San Luis Reservoir State Recreation Area
Kay Robinson, Henry W. Coe State Park
Kelly Setters, Auburn State Recreation Area
Andrew Urlie, McArthur-Burney Falls State Park
Suzanne Westover, Salt Point State Park
Dan Winkelman, Angel Island State Park
Bill Wisehard, North Coast Redwoods District
Jim Kral, Mountain Home Demonstration State Forest
Matt Gilbert, Jackson Demonstration State Forest

Other Parks and Preserves

Mark Andre, City of Arcata
Edward Arcetta, Santa Clara County Parks Department
David Brooks, Loch Lomond Recreation Area
Linda Chaplin, Sequoya Challenge
Joe DiDonato, East Bay Regional Parks District
Paula Forgi, Pacific Gas & Electric Company
Bill Hogan, Marin Open Space District
Denise Homer, Arcata Marsh Interpretive Center
Ed Hulme, Marin Municipal Water District
Donna LaGraffe, County of Sonoma
Irene Lindsey, Kaweah Oaks Preserve
Dave Lydick, County of Sacramento
Ned MacKay, East Bay Regional Parks District
Nancy McKay, East Bay Regional Parks District
Emily Messenger, TreePeople
Doug Miller, Toro County Park
Frances Scalvini, City of Ferndale
Roger Wilbur, Los Banos Wildlife Area
Jeff Wilson, Tilden Regional Park
Tricia Wilson, Elkhorn Slough National Estuarine Research Reserve
Ann Huber, Kaweah Oaks Preserve/Sequoia Riverlands Trust
Jacob Sanderson, Monterey Peninsula Regional Park District

Annie Ransom, Blue Sky Ecological Reserve

Field Scouts

Lisa Berry, Bob Coomber, David Dayton, Phil Ford, Michael Furniss, John Hamilton, Doug Herbek, Jeremy Keyston, Kris Keyston, John King, Doug McConnell, Jim McDaniel, Paul McHugh, Ethel Mohler, John Reginato, Paul and Patty Sakuma, George Seifert, Peter Shyvers, Bob Simms, Bob and Eleanor Stienstra, Robert Stienstra Jr., John Thomas, Fritz Ward, Larry Yant.